Chambers
School
Dictionary

To Linus,

Good luck with the video-menu,
all the best - Angela.

13th June, 1988.

Chambers
School
Dictionary

Chambers

© 1988 W & R Chambers Ltd Edinburgh

British Library Cataloguing in Publication Data

Chambers school dictionary.
 1. English language. Dictionaries. For
 schools
 423

 ISBN 0-550-10650-2

Printed in Great Britain by Richard Clay Ltd, Bungay, Suffolk

Contents

Preface

Chambers School Dictionary gives clear definitions of 40,000 of the most common English words.

We have compiled the dictionary to meet especially the needs of secondary school students, with appropriate concentration on modern words.

Extra Material

We have included extensive lists of computing and word processing terms, after the dictionary, and you will also find helpful sections on foreign words and phrases, abbreviations, Roman numerals, the Greek alphabet and mathematical symbols.

Chambers is the up-to-date dictionary for school students.

How to use this dictionary

Arrangement of words

Each entry begins with a headword in bold type. Under each of these you will find its part of speech and its meaning(s). After this come the meanings of other parts of speech which have the same form as the headword. Then follows a list of words formed directly from the headword *e.g.* by adding **-ness, -ment, -ly** *etc*. Where these are easily understood from the word from which they are formed, no meanings are given but they are placed as close to that word as possible.

Following these is a list of compounds, also in alphabetical order. These are words consisting of two parts whose first part is the headword, *e.g.* **high-handed**, or a word directly formed from it, *e.g.* **highly-strung**. Sometimes these are written as one word, *e.g.* **hardware**, sometimes with a hyphen, *e.g.* **hard-hearted**, sometimes as two words, *e.g.* **hard labour**.

Next comes a list of phrases in alphabetical order. These are groups of words containing the headword, *e.g.* **hard of hearing**, or a word derived from the headword, *e.g.* **in keeping with**.

Meanings

Where a word has more than one meaning these are separated by a semi-colon (;). In some cases meanings are made clearer by a phrase or sentence in italics showing how the word is used. Sometimes to save space two meanings have been put together in one by the use of brackets, *e.g.* **move** to (cause to) change place or position. The meanings of words which look alike and are pronounced in the same way appear under one headword, *e.g.* **jet, port**, except where this would result in a very complicated entry, *e.g.* **light, mean**.

Separate headwords have been given for words which look alike but are pronounced differently, *e.g.* **bow¹, bow², tear¹, tear²**.

Spelling

Many verbs in English can be spelt with either **-ize** or **-ise** as their ending. Which you use is a matter of choice. This dictionary uses the **-ize** form.

Some words which can be spelt in different ways sometimes appear in the dictionary like this – **acknowledg(e)ment**. This means that this word is correctly spelt with or without the bracketed **e**. Sometimes both spellings have been written out in full, *e.g.* **omelette, omelet**.

Parts of verbs

The past tenses of verbs have been given where these are not formed by simply adding -d or -ed, *e.g.* **referred, flung**. The past participles have been given only where they are different from the past tense, *e.g.* **flown, drunk.**

Adverbs

In general adverbs have not been given unless they are very common.

Plurals

Common plurals have been given where these are not formed by simply adding -s, *e.g.* **bodies, glasses.**

Pronunciation

You will find that the pronunciation of some words has been given in square brackets. The special letters used for this are explained in the table on p. xii. In some cases the special letter has been used in the word itself, *e.g.* **mātron, lēver.**

The pronunciation of words in bold type in an entry follows the pattern of the headword unless a change is shown. This is done either by the use of the special letters or by a new pronunciation in square brackets. Any following words in bold type then follow the new pronunciation pattern.

Labels and abbreviations

Sometimes you will find a word or words in brackets before a meaning or word. The label (*old*) means that the word is no longer commonly used in modern English, *e.g.* **damsel, palfrey**; (*hist*) that the thing referred to is no longer in use, *e.g.* **halberd, musket**; (*myth*) that the thing, person or animal is found only in stories and never existed, *e.g.* **cockatrice, gorgon**; (*US*) that the word or meaning is American, *e.g.* **sidewalk, fender**; (*coll*) or (*slang*) that the word or meaning is common in spoken or informal English but not found in formal written English, *e.g.* **chum, quid.**

Pronunciation key

A stress mark ' comes just before the part of the word which is sounded with greatest emphasis, as in **measure** ['mezhər]; **ex'plain**.

	sound	example	pronunciation
a	as in **hat**	**passion**	['pashən]
ä	as in **path**	**calm**	[käm]
ā	as in **play**	**weigh** **mātron**	[wā] –
e	as in **leg**	**head**	[hed]
ē	as in **clean**	**chief** **lēver**	[chēf] –
i	as in **stick**	**women**	['wimin]
ī	as in **side**	**fight** **title**	[fit] –
o	as in **hot**	**cough**	[kof]
ö	as in **fall**	**caught**	[köt]
ō	as in **toe**	**dough** **mōtor**	[dō] –
o͝o	as in **book**	**sugar**	['sho͝ogər]
o͞o	as in **moon**	**group**	[gro͞op]
oi	as in **boy**	**quoits**	[koits]
ow	as in **shout**	**bough**	[bow]
u	as in **run**	**rough**	[ruf]
ū	as in **tune**	**queue** **fūtile**	[kū] –
ə	as in **infant**	**again**	[ə'gen]
ɜ̄	as in **bird**	**heard**	[hɜ̄rd]
ch	as in **cheese**	**nature**	['nāchər]
j	as in **jam**	**region**	['rējən]
th	as in **thin**	**through**	[thro͞o]
dh	as in **this**	**blithe**	[blīdh]
sh	as in **ship**	**pressure**	['preshər]
zh	as in **pleasure**	**measure**	['mezhər]
ŋ	as in **bring**	**tongue**	[tuŋ]
hh	as in **loch**	**pibroch**	['pēbrohh]

The letter **c** is usually pronounced [s], and **g** is usually pronounced [j], before **e, i** or **y**; elsewhere, **c** is usually pronounced [k] and **g** is usually pronounced [g].

List of abbreviations in the dictionary

adj, adjs   adjective(s)
adv, advs   adverb(s)
cap   capital letter
coll   colloquial
comp   comparative
conj, conjs   conjunction(s)
E.   East
e.g.   for example
etc. (et cetera)   and so on, and
  other things
fem   feminine
Fr   French
Ger   German
Gr   Greek
gram   grammar
hist   historical
i.e.   that is
interj   interjection
It   Italian
L   Latin
masc   masculine
maths   mathematics
myth ·   mythological
N.   North
n, ns   noun(s)

npl   noun plural
n sing   noun singular
orig   originally
pl, pls   plural(s)
pp   past participle
prep, preps   preposition(s)
pres p   present participle
pron, prons   pronoun(s)
pt   past tense
®   registered trade mark
RC   Roman Catholic
relative pron   relative pronoun
S.   South
sing   singular
Sp   Spanish
superl   superlative
TV   television
UK   United Kingdom
US(A)   United States (of
  America)
USSR   Union of Soviet
  Socialist Republics
usu   usually
v, vs   verb(s)
W.   West

Dictionary

A

a, an *adjs* one. *A boy came into the garden*; any. *An ant has six legs*; in, to or for each: *four times a day*. The form *a* is used before words beginning with a consonant, *eg* boy, or consonant sound, *eg* eucalyptus; *an* is used before words beginning with a vowel, *eg* ant, or vowel sound, *eg* honour.

a'back: taken aback surprised.

'abacus *n* a frame with beads on wires for counting: – *pl* **'abacuses**.

a'bandon *v* to leave, without meaning to return to; to give up (an idea *etc*). – *n* **a'bandonment**.

a'base *v* to humble. – *n* **a'basement**.

a'bashed *adj* embarrassed, confused.

a'bate *v* to make or grow less. – *n* **a'batement**.

abattoir ['abɔtwär] *n* a (public) slaughter-house.

'abbess *n* the female head of an abbey or a convent: – *pl* **'abbesses**.

'abbey *n* a monastery or convent ruled by an abbot or an abbess; the church now or formerly attached to it: – *pl* **'abbeys**.

'abbot *n* the male head of an abbey: – *fem* **'abbess**.

ab'brēviate *v* to shorten (a word, phrase *etc*). – *n* **abbrevi'ation** a shortened form of a word *etc* used instead of the whole word (*eg* maths for *mathematics*).

'abdicate *v* to give up (a duty, position, *esp* that of king or queen). – *n* **abdi'cation**.

'abdomen *n* the part of the human body between the chest and the hips. – *adj* **ab'dominal**.

ab'duct *v* to take away by force or fraud. – *n* **ab'duction**.

a'bet *v* to help or encourage (*usu* to do wrong): – *pt* **a'betted**.

abeyance [ə'bāəns]: **in abeyance** undecided, not to be dealt with for the time being.

ab'hor *v* to look on with horror, to hate: – *pt* **ab'horred**. – *n* **ab'horrence**. – *adj* **ab'horrent** hateful.

a'bide *v* to put up with, tolerate. – *adj* **a'biding** lasting. – **abide by** to keep, act according to.

a'bility *n* power or means to do a thing; talent: – *pl* **a'bilities**.

'abject *adj* miserable, degraded.

a'blaze *adj* burning fiercely; gleaming like fire.

'able *adj* having power, means *etc* (to do a thing); clever. – *adv* **'ably**.

ablution [ə'blōōshən] *n* (*usu pl*) washing of the body.

ab'normal *adj* not normal (in behaviour *etc*); unusual. – *n* **abnor'mality**: – *pl* **abnor'malities**.

a'board *adv, prep* on(to) or in(to) (a means of transport).

a'bode *n* a dwelling place.

a'bolish *v* to do away with (*eg* a custom). – *ns* **abo'lition; abo'litionist** one who tries to do away with anything, *esp* slavery.

a'bominate *v* to hate very much. – *adj* **a'bominable** hateful. – *n* **abomi'nation** great hatred; anything hateful. – **the Abominable Snowman** (also **'Yeti**) a large animal which may exist in the Himalayas.

aborigines [abə'rijinēz] *npl* the original or native inhabitants of a country (*esp* Australia). – *adj* **abo'riginal**.

a'bort *v* (of a plan *etc*) to come to nothing; to stay undeveloped; to lose a baby before birth. – *n* **a'bortion** the (deliberate) loss of an unborn child. – *adj* **a'bortive** coming to nothing, useless: *an abortive attempt*.

a'bound *v* to be very plentiful; (with **in**) to have many or much.

a'bout *prep* around. *Look about you*; near (in time, size *etc*): *about ten o'clock*: *about two metres*; here and there in: *scattered about the room.* – *adv* around. *They stood about waiting*; in motion or in action: *running about*; in the opposite direction. *He turned about and walked away.* – **about to** on the point of (doing something).

above [ə'buv] *prep* over, in a higher position than: *above his head*; greater than: *above average*; too good for. *He's above jealousy.* – *adv* overhead, on high; earlier on (in a book *etc*). – *adj, adv* **above board** open(ly).

a'brāsion *n* the act of rubbing off; a graze on the body. – *n* **a'brasive** something used for rubbing or polishing. – *adj* able to wear down; (of persons) able to hurt people's feelings.

abreast [ə'brest] *adv* side by side. – **abreast of** up to date with: *abreast of the times.*

a'bridge *v* to shorten (a book, story *etc*). – *n* **a'bridg(e)ment**.

abroad [ə'bröd] *adv* in another country; outside. *Witches go abroad after dark*; in all directions.

a'brupt *adj* sudden, without warning;

(of speech *etc*) bad-tempered, short, blunt.

abscess ['abses] *n* a boil or similar collection of pus in the body: – *pl* '**abscesses**.

ab'scond *v* to run away secretly.

'**absent** *adj* away, not present. – *v* **ab'sent** (with **oneself**) to keep away. – *ns* '**absence** the state of being away; **absen'tee** one who is absent. – *adj* '**absent-'minded** forgetful.

absolute ['absəlōōt] *adj* complete, not limited by anything: *absolute power*. – *adv* **abso'lutely** completely. – *n* **abso'lution** forgiveness, pardon.

absolve [əb'zolv] *v* to pardon.

absorb [əb'zörb] *v* to soak up; to take up the whole attention of. – *adjs* **ab'sorbed**; **ab'sorbent** able to soak up (liquid). – *n* **ab'sorption** the act of absorbing; complete mental concentration.

ab'stain *v* (with **from**) to hold oneself back. – *ns* **ab'stainer** one who abstains from something, *esp* from alcoholic drink; **ab'stention** a holding back from.

ab'stemious *adj* not greedy, sparing (in food, drink *etc*).

'**abstinence** *n* holding back (from alcoholic drink *etc*).

'**abstract** *adj* existing only as an idea, not as a real thing. – *n* a summary.

abstruse [əb'strōōs] *adj* difficult to understand.

ab'surd *adj* clearly wrong, ridiculous. – *n* **ab'surdity**: – *pl* **ab'surdities**.

a'bundance *n* a plentiful supply. – *adj* **a'bundant** plentiful.

abuse [ə'būz] *v* to use wrongly; to insult, speak unkindly to, treat badly. – *n* **abuse** [ə'būs] wrongful use; insulting language. – *adj* **a'busive**.

abyss [ə'bis] *n* a bottomless depth: – *pl* **a'bysses**. – *adj* **abysmal** [ə'bizməl] bottomless; (*coll*) very bad.

acacia [ə'kāshə] *n* a family of thorny shrubs and trees.

a'cademy *n* a college for special study or training; a society for encouraging science or art; in Scotland, a senior school: – *pl* **a'cademies**. – *adj* **aca'demic** learned; not practical: *purely of academic interest*; of universities *etc*. – *n* a university or college teacher.

accede [ək'sēd] *v* to agree (to).

accelerate [ək'selərāt] *v* to increase in speed. – *ns* **accele'ration**; **ac'celerator** a lever, pedal *etc* by which speed is increased.

accent ['aksənt] *n* (a mark used to show

the) stress on a syllable or word, or in French to show the quality of a vowel; emphasis. *The accent must be on hard work*; a special way of saying words in a particular region *etc*: *a Scottish accent*. – *v* **ac'centūate** to make more obvious, emphasize.

accept [ək'sept] *v* to take something offered; to agree; to submit to. – *adj* **ac'ceptable** satisfactory; pleasing. – *n* **ac'ceptance** the act of accepting.

access ['akses] *n* right or means of approach or entry. – *adj* **ac'cessible** easily approached or reached. – *ns* **accessi'bility**; **ac'cession** a coming to: *the accession of a king to his throne*; **ac'cessory** a (small) additional fitting (to a car *etc*) or article of dress (as a handbag *etc*); a helper (*esp* in crime): – *pl* **ac'cessories**.

accident ['aksidənt] *n* an unexpected event (often unwanted or causing injury *etc*). – *adj* **acci'dental** happening by chance.

ac'claim *v* to welcome enthusiastically. – *n* **accla'mation** noisy sign of approval.

ac'climatize *v* to accustom (*esp* to another climate). – *n* **acclimati'zation**.

ac'commodate *v* to find room for; to make suitable; to oblige; to supply (with). – *adj* **ac'commodating** obliging. – *n* **ac'commo'dation** space; lodgings.

accompany [ə'kumpəni] *v* to go or be with; to play an instrument (*eg* a piano) while a singer sings *etc*: – *pt* **ac'companied**. – *ns* **ac'tompaniment** that which goes along with (something); the music played while a singer sings *etc*; **ac'companist** one who plays an accompaniment.

ac'complice [ə'kumplis] *n* one who helps another (*esp* in crime).

ac'complish [ə'kumplish] *v* to complete; to bring about. – *adj* **ac'complished** completed; skilled (as in music *etc*). – *n* **ac'complishment** completion; something one is good at.

ac'cord *v* to agree (with); to give, grant. – *n* agreement. – *n* **ac'cordance** agreement. – *adv* **ac'cordingly** therefore. – **according to** as told by; in relation to: *paid according to your work*; **of one's own accord** of one's own free will.

ac'cordion *n* a type of small musical wind instrument with a keyboard.

ac'cost *v* to approach and speak to.

ac'count *v* to give a reason (for). – *n* a bill; a reckoning up of money; a description (of events *etc*); an explanation. – *adj* **ac'countable** answerable, responsible. – *n* **ac'countant** a keeper or inspector of accounts. – **on account of** because of.

accoutrements [ə'kōōtrəmənts] *npl* (*esp* military) dress and equipment.

ac'credited *adj* given the official power to act.

ac'crue *v* to be given or added to. *Interest accrues to savings deposited in a bank.* – *adj* **ac'crued**.

ac'cūmulate *v* to collect; to increase. – *ns* **ac'cumu'lation** a collection; a mass or pile; **ac'cumulator** a type of battery (as in a car).

'accūrate *adj* correct, exact. – *n* **'accuracy**.

accursed [ə'kərsid] *adj* under a curse; hateful.

accuse [ə'kūz] *v* to bring a (criminal) charge against. – *ns* **accu'sation** a charge brought against anyone; **ac'cused** one charged with wrongdoing; **ac'cuser**.

ac'customed *adj* used to: *accustomed to travel*; usual.

ace *n* the one on playing cards; a person who is expert in anything.

a'cetylene *n* a kind of gas used for giving light and heat.

ache [āk] *n* a continuous pain. – *v* to be in continuous pain.

achieve [ə'chēv] *v* to get (something) done, accomplish; to win. – *n* **a'chievement**.

'acid *adj* (of taste) sharp; sarcastic. – *n* a substance containing hydrogen which will dissolve metals. – *v* **a'cidifȳ** to make or become acid: – *pt* **a'cidified**. – *n* **acidity** [ə'sidəti] the state of being acid.

acknowledge [ək'nolij] *v* to admit the truth of; to (write to) say one has received something. – *n* **ack'nowledg(e)ment**.

acme ['akmi] *n* the highest point, perfection.

acne ['akni] *n* a common skin disease with pimples.

'ācorn *n* the fruit of the oak tree.

acoustic [ə'kōōstik] *adj* of hearing or sound. – *npl* **a'coustics** the study of sound; the characteristics (of a hall *etc*) which affect the hearing of sound in it.

ac'quaint *v* to make (someone) familiar (with). – *n* **ac'quaintance** knowledge; a person whom one knows slightly.

acquiesce [akwi'es] *v* (*usu* with **in**) to agree (to). – *n* **acqui'escence**.

ac'quire *v* to get (as a possession), gain. – *adj* **ac'quired** gained, not born with.

– *n* **acqui'sition** the act of getting; something got. – *adj* **ac'quisitive** eager to get.

ac'quit *v* to declare (someone) innocent of a crime: – *pt* **ac'quitted**. – *n* **ac'quittal** a legal judgement of 'not guilty'. – **acquit oneself well, badly** to do well, badly; to be successful, unsuccessful.

acre ['ākər] *n* a land measure containing 4840 square yards or about 4000 square metres. – *n* **'acreage** the number of acres in a piece of land.

'acrid *adj* harsh, bitter.

'acrimony *n* bitterness of feeling or speech. – *adj* **acri'mōnious**.

'acrobat *n* one who performs feats of agility, rope-walking *etc*. – *adj* **acro'batic**.

'acronym *n* a word formed from the initial letters of other words (*eg radar* for *ra*dio *d*etecting *a*nd *r*anging).

a'cross *adv*, *prep* to or at the other side (of). *They swam across the river. He saw her across the table.* – **across the board** involving all (things or persons).

a'crostic *n* a poem *etc* in which the first or last letters of each line, taken in order, spell a word or words.

act *v* to do something; to behave: *act foolishly*; to play a part (as in a play). – *n* something done; a government law; a part of a play. – *n* **'action** a deed, an act; a law-case; what happens (in a film, play *etc*). – *adj* **'actionable** likely to cause a law-case: *an actionable statement*. – *v* **'activate** to start (something) working. – *adj* **'active** busy; lively; able to work *etc*; of the form of a verb in which the subject performs the action of the verb as in 'The dog *bit* the man'. – *n* **ac'tivity**: – *pl* **ac'tivities**. – *n* **'actor** one who acts a part in a play or film: – *fem* **'actress**: – *pl* **'actresses**.

actual ['akchōōəl] *adj* real, existing in fact. – *n* **actu'ality**. – *adv* **'actually** really.

'actūary *n* one who works out the price of insurance: – *pl* **'actuaries**. – *adj* **actu'ārial**.

'actūate *v* to put into action; to drive or urge on.

'acūmen *n* quickness of understanding.

'acūpuncture *n* a method of treating illness by piercing the skin with needles.

a'cute *adj* quick at understanding; (of a disease) severe, but not lasting very long; (of an angle) less than a right angle. – *n* **a'cuteness**. – *n* **acute accent** a stroke leaning forwards placed over letters in some languages to show their pronunciation.

ad n short for **advertisement**.

'**adage** n an old saying, a proverb.

'**adamant** adj unwilling to give way.

'**Adam's 'apple** n the natural lump which sticks out from the throat.

a'**dapt** v to make suitable, to alter (so as to fit). – adj a'**daptable** easily altered to suit new conditions. – ns **adap'ta-tion; a'daptor** device which enables an electrical plug to be used in a socket for which it was not designed, or several plugs to be used on the same socket.

add v to make one thing join another to give a sum total or whole; to mix in: add eggs to the flour; to say further. – n ad'**dition** the act of adding; something added. – adj ad'**ditional**.

ad'**dendum** n something added: – pl ad'**denda**.

'**adder** n the common name of the viper, a poisonous snake.

'**addict** n one who is dependent on something (often on a drug or alcohol), either physically or mentally. – **ad-dicted to** dependent on.

ad'**dress** v to speak to; to write the address on (a letter etc). – n the name of the house, street, and town where a person lives etc; a speech: – pl ad'**dresses**.

'**adenoids** npl swellings at the back of the nose which hinder breathing.

a'**dept** adj very skilful.

'**adequate** adj sufficient, enough. – n '**adequacy**.

ad'**here** v to stick (to); to give support (to) or be loyal (to). – n ad'**herence**. – adj ad'**herent** sticking (to). – n a follower, one who supports a cause etc.

ad'**hēsion** n the act of sticking (to). – adj **adhesive** [əd'hēsiv] sticky, gummed. – n something which makes things stick to each other.

ad'**jācent** adj (with **to**) lying next to.

'**adjective** n a word which tells something about a noun (as 'The black dog bites. The work is hard'). – adj **adjec'tival**.

ad'**join** v to be joined to. – adj ad-'**joining**.

ad'**journ** [ə'jörn] v to stop (a meeting etc) with the intention of continuing it at another time or place; to go to another place (eg another room). – n ad'**journ-ment**.

ad'**jūdicate** v to give a judgement on (a dispute etc); to act as a judge at a (musical etc) competition. – ns **adjudi'cation; ad'judicator** one who adjudicates.

'**adjunct** n something joined or added.

ad'**just** v to rearrange or alter to suit the circumstances. – adj ad'**justable**. – n ad'**justment**.

'**adjūtant** n a military officer who assists a commanding officer.

'**ad-'lib** v to speak without plan or preparation. – adj without preparation.

ad'**minister** v to manage or govern; to carry out (the law etc); to give (help, medicine etc). – v ad'**ministrate** to manage or govern. – n adminis'**tra-tion** management; (the body that carries on) the government of a country etc. – adj ad'**ministrative**. – n ad'**ministrator** one involved in the administration of a country etc.

'**admiral** n the commander of a navy. – n '**admiralty** the government office which manages naval affairs.

ad'**mire** v to think very highly of; to look at with pleasure. – adj **admirable** ['admərəbl] worthy of being admired. – adv '**admirably**. – ns **admi'ration; ad'mirer**.

ad'**mit** v to let in; to acknowledge the truth of, confess; (with **of**) to leave room for, allow. This admits of no other explanation: – pt ad'**mitted**. – adj ad'**missible** allowable. – ns ad'**mission** (the price of) being let in; anything admitted; ad'**mittance** the right or permission to enter.

ad'**monish** v to warn; to rebuke, scold. – n admo'**nition** a warning. – adj ad'**monitory**.

ado [ə'dōo] n trouble, fuss.

adolescent [adə'lesnt] n, adj (a person) between childhood and the adult state. – n ado'**lescence**.

a'**dopt** v to take as one's own (esp a child of other parents). – n a'**doption**.

a'**dore** v to love very much; to worship. – adj a'**dorable** worthy of being loved. – adv a'**dorably**. – n ado'**ration** worship; great love.

a'**dorn** v to decorate (with ornaments etc). – n a'**dornment** ornament.

a'**drift** adv drifting, floating.

a'**droit** adj skilful.

adū'**lation** n great flattery. – adj '**adulatory**.

'**adult** adj grown up. – n a grown-up person.

a'**dulterate** v to make impure by adding something else. – n a'**dulte'ration**.

a'**dultery** n breaking of the marriage promise, unfaithfulness to one's wife or husband. – n a'**dulterer**: – fem a'**dulteress**.

ad'**vance** v to go forward; to put forward (a plan etc); to help the progress of; to pay before the usual or agreed time. – n movement forward; improvement; a loan. – *adj* **ad'vanced** well forward in progress. – *n* **ad'vancement** progress. – **in advance** beforehand.

ad'vantage *n* a better position, superiority; gain or benefit. – *v* to help, benefit. – *adj* **advan'tāgeous** profitable; helpful. – **take advantage of** to make use of (a situation, person *etc*) in such a way as to benefit oneself.

'advent *n* coming, arrival: *the advent of television.*

adven'titious *adj* happening by chance.

ad'venture *n* a bold or exciting undertaking or experience. – *n* **ad'venturer** one who takes risks, *esp* in the hope of making a lot of money; a soldier who fights for any side who will pay him.

'adverb *n* a word which gives a more definite meaning to a verb, adjective, or other adverb (as 'He writes *neatly*. The sky is *beautifully* clear. He works *very* slowly'). – *adj* **ad'verbial** of or like an adverb.

'adversary *n* an enemy; an opponent: – *pl* **'adversaries**.

'adverse *adj* unfavourable. – *n* **ad'versity** misfortune: – *pl* **ad'versities**.

'advert *n* short for **advertisement**.

advertise ['advǝrtīz] *v* to make known to the public; to stress the good points of (a product for sale). – *n* **advertisement** [ǝd'vǝrtismǝnt] anything (as a film, picture) which is intended to persuade the public to buy a particular product.

ad'vice *n* something said as a help to someone trying to make a decision *etc*; a formal notice. – *v* **advise** [ǝd'vīz] to give advice to; to recommend (an action *etc*). – *adj* **ad'visable** wise, sensible. – *ns* **advisa'bility; ad'viser**. – *adj* **ad'visory** advice-giving.

'advocate *n* one who pleads for another; (in Scotland) a court lawyer. – *v* to plead or argue for; to recommend.

adze, (*US*) **adz** *n* a kind of axe used by a carpenter.

aeon, eon ['ēon] *n* a very long period of time, an age.

'aerate *v* to put air (or some other gas) into (a liquid).

'aerial *adj* of, in or from the air; placed high up or overhead (as an *aerial* railway). – *n* a wire or rod (or a set of these) by means of which radio or television signals are received or sent.

aerie *see* **eyrie**.

aero'batics *npl* stunts performed by an aircraft.

'aerodrome *n* an aeroplane station.

'aeroplane *n* a flying-machine heavier than air, with wings.

'aerosol *n* a container of liquid and gas under pressure, from which the liquid is squirted in the form of a mist.

aesthetic [is'thetik] *adj* of beauty or its appreciation; artistic, pleasing to the eye.

'affable *adj* pleasant, easy to speak to. – *n* **affa'bility**.

af'fair *n* events *etc* which are connected with one person or thing: *the Suez affair*; (often in *pl*) business, concern; a love affair.

af'fect *v* to act upon; to have an effect on; to move the feelings of; to pretend to feel *etc*. – *n* **affec'tation** pretence. – *adjs* **af'fected** moved in one's feelings; not natural, sham; **af'fecting** moving the feelings.

af'fection *n* a strong liking. – *adj* **af'fectionate** loving. – *adv* **af'fectionately**.

affi'dāvit *n* a written statement made on oath.

af'filiated *adj* (with **with** or **to**) connected, attached. – *n* **affili'ation**.

af'finity *n* a close likeness or agreement: – *pl* **af'finities**.

af'firm *v* to state firmly. – *n* **affir'mation** a firm statement. – *adj* **af'firmative** saying 'yes'.

af'fix *v* to attach to.

af'flict *v* to give continued pain or distress to. – *adj* **af'flicted** suffering. – *n* **af'fliction** great suffering, misery.

affluent ['aflooǝnt] *adj* wealthy. – *n* a stream flowing into a river or lake. – *n* **'affluence** wealth.

af'ford *v* to be able to pay for; to give, yield.

af'forest *v* to cover land with forest. – *n* **affores'tation**.

af'fray *n* a fight, a brawl.

affront [ǝ'frunt] *v* to insult openly. – *n* an insult.

a'float *adv, adj* floating.

a'foot *adv* happening or about to happen.

aforesaid [ǝ'försed] *adj* said or named before.

a'fraid *adj* struck with fear; (*coll*) sorry to have to admit that.

aft *adv* near or towards the stern of a vessel.

'after *prep* later in time than: *after dinner*; following: *one after another: day after day*; in memory or honour of: *named after his father*; in pursuit of: *run after the bus*; about: *ask after someone's health*; despite. *After all his efforts, he still failed*; in the style of: *after (the manner of) Shakespeare*. – *adv* later in time or place. *They arrived soon after.* – *conj* later than the time when. *After she arrived, things improved greatly.* – *adj, prefix* **after(-)** later in time or place: *in after years*: *aftertaste.* – **after all** all things considered. *After all, he's not very well*; despite everything said or done before. *He's coming after all.*

'**aftermath** *n* the bad results of something, *eg* of war *etc.*

after'noon *n* the time between noon and evening.

afterthought ['äftərthöt] *n* a later thought.

'**afterwards** *adv* later.

again [ə'gen] *adv* once more. *Play the tune again*; in(to) the original state, place *etc*: *there and back again*; on the other hand. *Again, I might be wrong*; (*coll*) at another (later) time. *Goodbye, I'll see you again.*

against [ə'genst] *prep* in opposition to: *against the law. He fought against his brother*; in the opposite direction to: *against the wind*; on a background of: *against the sky*; close to, touching: *lean against the wall*; as protection from: *immunized against diphtheria.*

'**agate** *n* a kind of precious stone.

age *n* a long period of time; the time a person or thing has lived or existed. – *v* to grow or make (obviously) older. – *adj* **aged** ['äjid] old; **aged** [äjd] of the age of: *aged five.* – **of age** legally an adult.

a'**genda** *n* a list of things to be done, *esp* at a meeting.

'**agent** *n* a person or thing that acts; one who acts for another; a spy. – *n* '**agency** the office or business of an agent; action, means by which something is done: – *pl* '**agencies**.

ag'grandize *v* to make greater. – *n* **aggrandizement** [ə'grandizmənt].

'**aggravate** *v* to make worse; (*coll*) to annoy. – *adj* '**aggravating**. – *n* **aggra'vation**.

'**aggregate** *n* a total.

ag'gressive *adj* ready to attack first; quarrelsome. – *ns* **ag'gressiveness**; **ag'gression**; **ag'gressor**.

aggrieved [ə'grēvd] *adj* hurt, upset.

aghast [ə'gäst] *adj* struck with horror.

'**agile** *adj* active, nimble. – *n* **agility** [ə'jiləti].

'**agitate** *v* to stir up; to excite, disturb. – *ns* **agi'tation**; '**agitator** one who stirs up (*usu* political) feeling.

ag'nostic *n* one who believes that we cannot know whether God exists or not. – *n* **ag'nosticism**.

a'**go** *adv* in the past. *Two years ago I went*

to *Rome.*

a'**gog** *adj* eager, excited.

'**agony** *n* great pain: – *pl* '**agonies**. – *adjs* '**agonized** showing great pain; '**agonizing** causing great pain.

agora'phōbia *n* great fear of open spaces.

a'**grārian** *adj* of farmland or farming.

a'**gree** *v* to be alike (*esp* in opinions, decisions *etc*); to say that one will do something, consent; (with **with**) to suit. – *adj* a'**greeable** pleasant; ready to agree. – *adv* a'**greeably**. – *n* a'**greement** likeness (*esp* of opinions); a written statement making a bargain.

'**agriculture** *n* the cultivation of the land, farming. – *adj* **agri'cultural**.

a'**ground** *adj, adv* (of boats) stuck on the bottom of the sea or a river. *The ship ran aground.*

ague ['āgū] *n* a fever.

ahead [ə'hed] *adv* in front; in advance: *ahead of time.*

aid *v* to help, assist. – *n* help.

aide-de-camp ['āddə'koŋ] *n* an officer who carries messages to and from a general on the field: – *pl* '**aides-de-camp**.

ail *v* to be ill; to trouble. – *n* '**ailment** a trouble, disease.

'**aileron** *n* a hinged flap on the back edge of an aeroplane's wing, used to control balance.

aim *v* to point at (*esp* with a gun); to intend to do; to have as one's purpose. – *n* the act of, or skill in, aiming; the point aimed at, goal, intention. – *adj* '**aimless** without aim or purpose.

air *n* the mixture of gases (mainly oxygen and nitrogen) which we breathe, the atmosphere; a light breeze; fresh air; space overhead; a tune; the look or manner (of a person). – *v* to expose to the air; to make known (an opinion *etc*). – *n* '**airing** the act of exposing to the air. – *adjs* '**airless**; '**airy** of or like the air; well supplied with fresh air; light-hearted. – *adv* '**airily**. – *n* '**airbed** a mattress which can be blown up. – *adjs* '**airborne** in the air, flying; '**air-con'ditioned** of buildings *etc* in which the air is cleaned and kept to a certain temperature by a special system. – *n(pl)* '**aircraft** flying machine(s). – *ns* **air force** the branch of the armed forces using aircraft; '**air-gun** a gun worked by means of compressed air; **air hostess** a woman whose duty is to serve and look after the passengers on aircraft; '**airlock** a bubble in a pipe obstructing the flow of a liquid; a compartment with two doors for entering and leaving an airtight spaceship *etc*; **'airman** one who pilots an aircraft; **'airport** a place where aircraft land and take off, with buildings for customs, waiting-rooms *etc*; **'air-pump** a pump for forcing air in or out of something; **'air-raid** an attack by aeroplanes; **'airship** a large balloon which can be steered and driven. – *adj* **'airtight** made so that air cannot pass in or out. – **on the air** broadcasting.

aisle [īl] *n* the side part of a church; a passage between seats (*esp* in a church).

a'jar *adv* (of doors *etc*) partly open.

a'kimbo *adv* with hand on hip and elbow bent outward.

a'kin *adj* similar.

a'lacrity *n* briskness, cheerful readiness.

a'larm *n* sudden fear; something which rouses to action or gives warning of danger. – *v* to frighten. – *adj* **a'larming**. – *n* **a'larmist** one who frightens others needlessly.

a'las! a cry showing grief.

'albatross *n* a type of large sea-bird: – *pl* **'albatrosses**.

albino [al'bēnō] *n* a person or animal with no natural colour in their skin and hair (which are white) and eye pupils (which are pink): – *pl* **al'binos**.

'album *n* a book with blank pages for holding photographs, stamps *etc*; a long-playing record.

'albūmen *n* the white of eggs.

alchemy ['alkəmi] *n* (*hist*) the early form of chemistry which aimed to change other metals into gold. – *n* **'alchemist** one who practised alchemy.

'alcohol *n* the pure spirit in strong drinks. – *adj* **alco'holic** of or containing alcohol. – *n* a person suffering from alcoholism. – *n* **'alcoholism** dependence on alcoholic drinks.

'alcove *n* a recess in a room's wall.

alder ['öldər] *n* a type of tree which grows beside ponds and rivers.

alderman ['öldərmən] *n* a councillor next in rank to the mayor of a town *etc*; (*US*) a member of the governing body of a city.

ale *n* a drink made from malt, hops *etc*.

a'lert *n* signal to be ready for action. – *v* to make alert, warn. – *adj* watchful; quick-thinking. – **on the alert** on the watch (for).

al'falfa *n* a kind of grass.

al'fresco *adj, adv* in the open air.

algae ['aljē] *npl* a group of simple plants which includes seaweed.

'algebra *n* a method of counting, using

letters and signs.

'ālias *adv* otherwise known as: *Smith alias Jones*. – *n* a false name: – *pl* **'aliases**.

'alibi *n* the plea that a person charged with a crime was elsewhere when it was done; the state or fact of being elsewhere when a crime was committed.

alien ['ālien] *adj* foreign. – *n* a foreigner. – *v* **'alienate** to make (a person) strange or unfriendly. – **alien to** not in keeping with: *alien to his nature*.

alight [ə'līt] *v* to climb *etc* down; to settle, land. – *adj, adv* on fire, burning.

align [ə'līn] *v* to set in line; to take sides in an argument *etc*. – *n* **a'lignment** arrangement in a line.

a'like *adj* like one another, similar. – *adv* in the same way, similarly.

ali'mentary *adj* of food. – *n* **alimentary canal** the passage through the body which begins at the mouth.

a'live *adj* living; full of activity. – **alive to** aware of.

'alkali *n* a substance such as soda or potash (opposite of **acid**). – *adj* **'alkaline**.

all [öl] *adj, pron* every one (of). *All men are equal. All must go*; the whole (of). *He ate all the cake*. – *adv* wholly, completely. *She was dressed all in red*. – *n* **'all-'rounder** one who shows ability in many kinds of work, sport *etc*. – **all in** with everything included; (*coll*) exhausted; **all-in wrestling** wrestling in which no holds are against the rules; **all over** over the whole of; everywhere; finished, ended.

al'lay *v* to make less, relieve; to calm.

allege [ə'lej] *v* to say without proof. – *n* **alle'gation**.

al'lēgiance *n* loyalty.

'allegory *n* a story or fable which deals with a subject in a way which is meant to suggest a deeper, more serious subject. *'Pilgrim's Progress' is an allegory of the Christian's life*: – *pl* **'allegories**. – *adj* **alle'gorical**.

allergy ['alərji] *n* abnormal sensitiveness (of the body) to something: – *pl* **'allergies**. – *adj* **al'lergic**.

al'lēviate *v* to make lighter, to lessen. – *n* **allevi'ation**.

'alley *n* a narrow passage or lane; an enclosure for bowls or skittles: – *pl* **'alleys**.

alliance *see* **ally**.

'alligātor *n* a kind of large reptile like a crocodile.

alliteration [ə'litə'rāshən] *n* the repetition of the same sound at the beginning of two or more words close together (*eg* 'Sing a Song of Sixpence').

'**allocate** *v* to give to each his share. – *n* **allo'cation**.

al'lot *v* to give to each his share, distribute: – *pt* **al'lotted**. – *n* **al'lotment** the act of distributing; a small plot of ground for growing vegetables *etc*.

allow [ə'low] *v* to let (someone do something); (with **for**) to take into consideration (in sums, plans *etc*); to admit, confess; to give, *esp* at regular intervals. *She allows him £5 a week.* – *adj* **al'lowable**. – *n* **al'lowance** a fixed sum or amount given regularly. – **make allowance(s) for** to treat differently because of taking into consideration special circumstances *etc*.

'**alloy** *n* a mixture of two or more metals.

allude [ə'lōōd] *v* (with **to**) to mention in passing. – *n* **al'lusion**. – *adj* **al'lusive**.

al'lure *v* to tempt, draw on by promises *etc*. – *n* **al'lurement**. – *adj* **al'luring**.

alluvium [ə'lōōviəm] *n* earth, sand *etc* brought down and left by rivers in flood: – *pl* **al'luvia**. – *adj* **al'luvial**.

al'lȳ *v* to join oneself to (by treaty *etc*): – *pt* **al'lied**. – *adj* '**allied**. – *ns* '**ally** a friend, person *etc* in alliance with another: – *pl* '**allies**; **al'liance** a joining together of two people, nations *etc* (*esp* against a enemy of both).

almanac ['ölmənak] *n* a calendar of days, weeks, and months of any year, *usu* with information (about the phases of the moon *etc*).

almighty [öl'mīti] *adj* having much power. – **the Almighty** God.

almond ['ämənd] *n* the kernel of the fruit of the almond-tree.

almost ['ölmōst] *adv* very nearly but not quite: *almost five years old*: *almost at our destination*.

alms [ämz] *npl* gifts to the poor.

a'loft *adv* on high; upward.

a'lone *adj* not accompanied by others, solitary. *He found he was alone again.* – *adv* only, without anything or anyone else. *That alone is bad enough*; not accompanied by others. *He lived alone.*

a'long *prep* over the length of. *He walked along the road.* – *adv* onward. *Hurry along!* – *prep* **a'long'side** beside. – *adv* near a ship's side. – **along with** together with.

a'loof *adj*, *adv* at a distance, apart; showing no interest in others. – *n* **a'loofness**.

a'loud *adv* so as to be heard.

'**alpha** *n* the first letter of the Greek

alphabet.

'**alphabet** *n* letters of a language given in a fixed order. – *adjs* **alpha'betic(al)** in the order of the alphabet.

'**alpine** *adj* of the Alps or other high mountains.

already [öl'redi] *adv* before this or that time. *I've already done that*; now, before the expected time. *You haven't finished already, have you?*

al'sātian *n* a breed of large, wolf-like dog.

also ['ölsō] *adv* in addition, besides, too. *He also must go.* – *n* '**also-ran** a person or thing who competed (as in a race) but was not among the winners.

altar ['öltər] *n* a raised place for offerings to a god; in Christian churches, the communion table.

alter ['öltər] *v* to change. – *n* **alte'ration**.

altercation [öltər'kāshən] *n* an argument or quarrel.

alternate ['öltərnāt] *v* (of two things *etc*) to do or happen in turn. – *adj* **al'ternate** happening *etc* in turns. – *adv* **al'ternately**. – *n* **alter'nation**. – *adj* **al'ternative** offering a second possibility *etc*.

although [öl'dhō] *conj* though, in spite of the fact that.

'**altimeter** *n* an instrument for measuring height above sea level.

'**altitude** *n* height above sea level.

'**alto** *n* the male voice of the highest pitch; the female voice of lowest pitch (also **con'tralto**).

altogether [öltə'gedhər] *adv* considering everything, in all. *Altogether there were 20 of them*; completely. *I am not altogether satisfied.*

altruism ['altrōōizəm] *n* unselfish concern for the good of others. – *adj* **altru'istic**.

alū'minium,   (*US*)   **aluminum** [ə'lōōminəm] *n* an element, a very light metal.

always ['ölwäz] *adv* for ever. *I'll always remember this day*; every time. *He always says the same thing.*

am *see* **be**.

a'malgam *n* a mixture (*esp* of metals). – *v* **a'malgamate** to join together, combine;   to   mix.   –   *n* **a'malga'mation**.

a'mass *v* to collect in large quantity.

amateur ['amətər] *n* one who takes part in a thing for the love of it, not for money (opposite of **professional**). – Also *adj*. – *adj* **ama'teurish** not done properly; not skilful.

a'maze *v* to surprise greatly. –

n a'mazement.

'Amazon *n* (*myth*) ōne of a nation of warrior women; a very strong or manlike woman.

am'bassador *n* a government minister sent to look after the interests of one country in another country; a representative.

'amber *n* a hard yellowish substance like resin used in making jewellery. – *adj* made of amber; of the colour of amber.

ambi'dextrous *adj* able to use both hands with equal skill. – *n* ambidex'terity.

am'bigūous *adj* having two possible meanings; not clear. – *n* ambi'guity: – *pl* ambi'guities.

am'bition *n* the desire for success, power, fame *etc.* – *adj* am'bitious.

'amble *v* to walk without hurrying. – Also *n.*

ambrosia [am'brōziə] *n* (*myth*) the food of the gods, which gave eternal youth and beauty.

'ambūlance *n* a vehicle for carrying the sick or injured.

ambush ['amboōsh] *n* the act of lying hidden in order to make a surprise attack; the people hidden in this way; their place of hiding: – *pl* 'ambushes. – *v* to attack suddenly from a position of hiding.

a'mēnable *adj* open to advice or suggestion.

a'mend *v* to correct, to improve; to alter slightly. – *n* a'mendment a change (*usu* in something written). – make amends to make up for having done wrong.

a'mēnity *n* a pleasant or convenient feature of a place *etc*: – *pl* a'menities.

amethyst ['aməthist] *n* a type of precious stone of a bluish-violet colour.

'āmiable *adj* likeable; friendly. – *n* amia'bility.

'amicable *adj* friendly.

a'mid, a'midst *preps* in the middle of, among. *She seemed very calm amidst all the confusion.*

a'miss *adv* wrong(ly); badly.

'amity *n* friendship.

am'mōnia *n* a strong-smelling gas made of hydrogen and nitrogen.

ammū'nition *n* things with which guns *etc* are charged (such as gunpowder, bullets *etc*).

amnesia [am'nēziə] *n* loss of memory.

'amnesty *n* a general pardon of wrongdoers: – *pl* 'amnesties.

amoeba [ə'mēbə] *n* a very simple form of animal life found in ponds *etc*: – *pls* a'moebas, amoebae [ə'mēbē].

a'mok, a'muck: run amok to become furious or mad and do a lot of damage.

among, amongst [ə'muŋ(st)] *preps* in the midst or in the middle of: *a house among trees: among friends*; in shares, in parts. *Divide the chocolate among all four;* in the group of. *Among all his novels, this is the best.*

a'moral *adj* non-moral, outside the domain of morality.

'amorous *adj* loving; ready or inclined to love.

a'mount *v* to add up (to). – *n* total, sum (*usu* of money).

amp, ampère ['amper] *n* the standard unit of electric current.

am'phibian *n* any animal that lives on land and in water; a vehicle for use on land and in water. – Also *adj.* – *adj* am'phibious.

amphitheatre ['amfithēətər] *n* (*hist*) a theatre with seats surrounding a central arena.

'ample *adj* plenty of; large enough.

'amplifȳ *v* to increase; to make louder: – *pt* 'amplified. – *ns* amplifi'cation; 'amplifier an electrical device for increasing loudness.

'amplitude *n* largeness; size.

'ampūtate *v* to cut off (*esp* a human limb). – *n* ampu'tation.

amuck *see* amok.

amuse [ə'mūz] *v* to make to laugh; to give pleasure to. – *n* a'musement. – *adj* a'musing giving pleasure; funny.

an *see* a.

anachronism [ə'nakrənizəm] *n* the act of mentioning something which did not exist or was not yet invented at the time spoken about.

ana'conda *n* a type.of large S. American water snake.

anaemia, (*US*) anemia [ə'nēmiə] *n* a shortage of red cells in the blood. – *adj* a'naemic suffering from anaemia; pale or ill-looking.

anaesthetic, (*US*) anesthetic [anəs'thetik] *n* a substance which produces lack of feeling for a time in a part of the body, or which makes a person unconscious. – *n* anaesthetist [ə'nēsthətist] a doctor who gives anaesthetics.

'anagram *n* a word or sentence formed by rewriting (in a different order) the letters of another word or sentence (*veil* is an anagram of *evil*).

a'nalogy *n* a likeness, resemblance in certain ways: – *pl* a'nalogies. – *adj* analogous [ə'naləgəs] similar, alike in some way.

a'nalysis *n* a breaking up of a thing into

its parts; a detailed examination (of something): – *pl* **a'nalysēs**. – *v* **'analyse**, (*US*) **'analyze**. – *n* **'analyst** a person who analyses.

anarchy ['anərki] *n* lack or absence of government; disorder or confusion. – *n* **'anarchist** one in favour of anarchy.

a'nathema *n* a curse; a hated person or thing.

a'natomy *n* the study of the parts of the body; the body. – *n* **a'natomist**.

ancestor ['ansistər] *n* one from whom a person is descended by birth, a forefather. – *adj* **an'cestral**. – *n* **'ancestry** line of ancestors.

anchor ['aŋkər] *n* a heavy piece of iron, with hooked ends, for holding a ship fast to the bed of the sea *etc*. – *v* to fix by anchor; to let down the anchor. – *n* **'anchorage** a place where a ship can anchor. – **cast anchor** to let down the anchor; **weigh anchor** to pull up the anchor.

'anchovy *n* a type of small fish of the herring family: – *pl* **'anchovies**.

ancient ['ānshənt] *adj* very old; of times long past.

ancillary [an'siləri] *adj* serving or supporting something more important.

and *conj* joining two statements, pieces of information *etc*. *I opened the door and went inside. The hat was blue and red*; in addition to. *2 and 2 make 4.*

'anecdote *n* a short, interesting or amusing story, *esp* a true one.

anemometer [ani'momitər] *n* an instrument for measuring the speed of the wind.

anemone [ə'neməni] *n* a type of woodland or garden flower.

aneroid barometer ['anəroid] *n* one in which the pressure of the air is measured without the use of mercury.

angel ['ānjəl] *n* a messenger or attendant of God; a very good or beautiful person. – *adj* **angelic** [an'jelik].

angelica [an'jelikə] *n* a plant whose candied leaf-stalks are used as cake decoration.

anger ['aŋgər] *n* a bitter feeling (against someone), annoyance, rage. – *v* to make angry. – *adj* **'angry**. – *adv* **'angrily**.

angina [an'jinə] *n* a type of painful heart disease.

'angle *n* a corner; the V-shape made by two lines meeting at a point; a point of view. – *v* to try to get by hints *etc*: *angling for a job*. – *n* **'angler** one who fishes with rod and line. – *adj* **'angūlar** having angles; thin, bony.

'Anglican *adj* of the Church of England.

'anglicize *v* to turn into the English language; to make English in character.

'Anglo-'Saxon *adj, n* (of) the people of England before the Norman Conquest; (of) their language.

an'gora *n* wool made from the hair of the Angora goat or rabbit. – *ns* **Angora cat, goat, rabbit** a type of cat, goat or rabbit with long silky hair.

angry *see* **anger**.

anguish ['aŋgwish] *n* very great pain or distress.

angular *see* **angle**.

'animal *n* a living being which can feel and move of its own accord; an animal other than man. – *adj* of or like an animal.

'animate *v* to give life to; to make lively. – *adj* living. – *adj* **'animated** lively; (of puppets, cartoon figures *etc*) made to move as if alive. – *n* **ani'mation**.

ani'mosity *n* bitter hatred, enmity.

'aniseed *n* a kind of seed with a flavour like that of liquorice.

'ankle *n* the joint connecting the foot and leg.

'annals *npl* (yearly) historical accounts of events.

an'neal *v* to soften (or toughen) glass or metal by heating strongly and cooling slowly.

an'nex *v* to take possession of; to add, attach. – *n* **'annex(e)** a building added to another. – *n* **annex'ation**.

an'nihilate *v* to destroy completely. – *n* **annihi'lation**.

anni'versary *n* the day of each year when some event is remembered: – *pl* **anni'versaries**.

'annotate *v* to make notes upon; to add notes or explanation to. – *n* **anno'tation**.

an'nounce *v* to make (publicly) known. – *ns* **an'nouncement; an'nouncer** in radio *etc* one who announces programmes or reads the news.

an'noy *v* to make rather angry, irritate. – *n* **an'noyance**.

'annūal *adj* yearly. – *n* a plant that lives only one year; a book published yearly. – *v* **annualize** to convert to a yearly rate, amount *etc*. — *adv* **'annually**.

an'nūity *n* a yearly payment made for a certain time or for life: – *pl* **an'nuities**.

an'nul *v* to put an end to, declare no longer valid: – *pt* **an'nulled**. – *n* **an'nulment**.

'anodȳne *n* something that soothes pain.

a'noint *v* to smear with ointment or oil (as part of a religious ceremony).

a'nomaly *n* something unusual, not according to rule: – *pl* **a'nomalies**. –

adj a'**nomalous**.

a'**non** short for **anonymous**, used when the author of a poem *etc* is not known.

a'**nonymous** *adj* without the name (of the author, giver *etc*) being known or given. – *n* **ano'nymity**.

'**anorak** *n* a hooded waterproof jacket.

another [ə'nudhər] *adj* a different (thing or person). *He moved to another job*; one more of the same kind. *Have another biscuit.* – Also *pron.*

answer ['änsər] *v* to speak, write *etc* in return or reply; to find the result or solution (of a sum, problem *etc*); (with **for**) to be responsible; (with **for**) to suffer, be punished. – *n* something said, written *etc* in return or reply; a solution. – *adj* '**answerable** able to be answered; responsible.

ant *n* a type of small insect, thought to be hard-working.

an'**tagonist** *n* an enemy; an opponent. – *n* an'**tagonism** hostility, opposition, enmity. – *adj* **antago'nistic** opposed (to) unfriendly, hostile. – *v* an'**tagonize** to make an enemy of, cause dislike.

Ant'**arctic** *adj* of the South Pole or regions round it.

ante- [anti] *prefix* before.

ante'cēdent *adj* going before in time. – *n* one who lived at an earlier time, an ancestor; (*pl*) previous conduct, history *etc*.

'**ante'date** *v* to date before the true time; to be earlier in date than.

antediluvian [antidi'lōōviən] *adj* very old or old-fashioned.

'**antelope** *n* a kind of graceful, swift-running, deer-like animal.

ante'nātal *adj* before birth.

an'**tenna** *n* a feeler of an insect; an aerial: – *pls* an'**tennas, antennae** [an'tenē].

'**anteroom** *n* a room leading into a large room.

'**anthem** *n* a piece of music for a church choir; any song of praise.

an'**thology** *n* a collection of specially chosen poems, stories *etc* : – *pl* an'**thologies**.

'**anthracite** *n* a kind of coal that burns with a hot, smokeless flame.

'**anthrax** *n* an infectious disease of cattle, sheep *etc*, sometimes caught by man.

'**anthropoid** *adj* (*esp* of apes) man-like.

anthro'pology *n* the study of mankind. – *n* **anthro'pologist**.

anti- *prefix* against; opposite.

'**antibi'otic** *n* a type of medicine taken to kill disease-causing bacteria.

an'**ticipate** *v* to look forward to, to expect; to see or know in advance; to act before (someone or something). – *n*

an'**tici'pation** expectation; excitement.

'**anti'climax** *n* a dull or disappointing ending.

'**anti'clockwise** *adj, adv* in the opposite direction to the hands of a clock.

'**antics** *npl* tricks, odd or amusing actions.

'**anti'cȳclone** *n* a circling movement of air or wind round an area of high air pressure *usu* causing calm weather.

'**antidote** *n* something given to act against the effect of poison.

antihistamine ['anti'histəmēn] *n* a medicine used to treat an allergy.

an'**tipathy** *n* dislike.

antipodes [an'tipədēz] *npl* places on the earth's surface exactly opposite each other, (*esp* Australia and New Zealand, which are opposite to Europe). – *adj* **antipodean** [an'tipə'dēən].

antique [an'tēk] *adj* old, from earlier times; old-fashioned. – *n* an old, *usu* interesting or valuable object from earlier times. – *adj* **antiquated** ['antikwātid] grown old, or out of fashion. – *n* an'**tiquity** ancient times, *esp* those of the Greeks and Romans; great age; (*pl*) an'**tiquities** objects from earlier times.

anti'septic *adj* germ-destroying. – *n* something which destroys germs.

antisocial ['anti'sōshəl] *adj* not fitting in with, harmful to other people; disliking the company of other people.

an'**tithesis** *n* the direct opposite: – *pl* an'**thesēs**.

'**antler** *n* the horn of a deer.

'**anvil** *n* a metal block on which blacksmiths hammer metal into shape.

anxious ['aŋkshəs] *adj* worried about what may happen. – *n* **anxiety** [aŋ'ziəti]: – *pl* an'**xieties**.

any ['eni] *adj* one: *any book*; some: *any bread*; every, no matter which. *Any time you go, he's always there.* – *pron* some. *There aren't any left.* – *pron* '**anybody** any person. – *adv* '**anyhow** in any case. *Anyhow, I'll go and see him*; carelessly. *The papers were scattered anyhow over his desk.* – *prons* '**anyone** any person; '**anything** a thing of any kind. – *advs* '**anyway** in any case; '**anywhere** in any place. – **at any rate** in any case, whatever happens.

a'**part** *adv* aside; in or into pieces; in opposite directions. – **apart from** separate(ly) from; except for.

apartheid [ə'pärtāt] *n* (the policy of) keeping people of different races apart.

a'**partment** *n* a room in a house; a set of rooms, a flat.

'**apathy** *n* lack of feeling or interest. – *adj* **apa'thetic**.

ape *n* any of a group of animals related to monkeys, but larger, tail-less and walking upright. – *v* to imitate.

'**aperture** *n* an opening, a hole.

'**āpex** *n* the highest point of anything: – *pls* '**apexes**, '**apicēs**.

'**āphid** *n* a type of small insect which feeds on plants.

'**āpiary** *n* a place where bees are kept: – *pl* '**apiaries**. – *n* '**apiarist** one who keeps an apiary or who studies bees.

a'**piece** *adv* to or for each one.

aplomb [ə'plom] *n* self-confidence.

apocryphal [ə'pokrifəl] *adj* unlikely to be true.

a'**pology** *n* an expression of regret that one has done wrong: – *pl* a'**pologies**. – *adj* a'**polo'getic** showing regret about having done wrong. – *v* a'**pologize** to make an apology.

'**apoplexy** *n* sudden loss of ability to feel, move *etc*, a stroke. – *adj* **apo'plectic**.

apostle [ə'posl] *n* one sent to preach the gospel, *esp* one of the twelve disciples of Christ; a leader of a movement or cause (such as for free speech *etc*).

apostrophe [ə'postrəfi] *n* a mark (') to show possession: *John's hat*; or that a letter *etc* has been missed out: *isn't* (for *is not*).

a'**pothecary** *n* (*old*) one who makes and supplies medicines *etc*, a chemist: – *pl* a'**pothecaries**.

appal [ə'pöl] *v* to horrify, shock: – *pt* **ap'palled**. – *adj* **ap'palling** shocking.

appa'rātus *n* an instrument or machine; instruments, tools or material required for a piece of work.

ap'parel *n* clothing.

ap'parent *adj* easily seen, evident. – *adv* **ap'parently**.

appa'rition *n* something strange or remarkable which appears suddenly; a ghost.

ap'peal *v* to ask earnestly (for help *etc*); (in law) to take a case that one has lost to a higher court; to be pleasing (to). – Also *n*. – *adj* **ap'pealing** asking earnestly; arousing liking or sympathy.

ap'pear *v* to come into view; to arrive; to seem. – *n* **ap'pearance**.

appease [ə'pēz] *v* to soothe or satisfy, *esp* by giving what was asked for.

ap'pendix *n* a part added at the end of a book; a small worm-shaped part of the bowels: – *pls* **ap'pendicēs**, **ap'pendixes**. – *n* **ap'pendi'citis** a disease, an inflammation of this part of the body.

apper'tain *v* to belong (to).

'**appetite** *n* desire (for food). – *adj*

'**appetizing** tempting to the appetite.

ap'plaud *v* to praise (by clapping the hands). – *n* **applause** [ə'plöz].

'**apple** *n* a type of round firm fruit, *usu* red or green.

ap'plȳ *v* to put on (an ointment *etc*); to use; to ask formally (for); to be suitable or relevant; (with **to**) to affect: – *pt* **ap'plied**. – *n* **ap'pliance** a tool, instrument *etc*. – *adj* '**applicable** able to be applied; suitable, relevant. – *ns* '**applicant** one who applies or asks; **appli'cation** the act of applying; the thing applied (*eg* an ointment); hard work, close attention; a formal request (*usu* on paper). – **apply oneself** to work hard.

ap'point *v* to fix (a date *etc*); to place in a job. *He was appointed manager*. – *n* **ap'pointment** the act of appointing; a job, a post; an arrangement to meet someone.

apportion [ə'pörshən] *v* to divide in fair shares.

apposite ['apəzit] *adj* suitable, appropriate.

appraise [ə'prāz] *v* to estimate the value or quality of. – *n* **ap'praisal**. – *adj* **ap'praising** (of a glance *etc*) quickly summing up.

appreciate [ə'prēshiāt] *v* to see or understand the good points, beauties *etc* of; to understand; to rise in value. – *n* **appreci'ation**. – *adj* **ap'preciable** noticeable, considerable.

appre'hend *v* to arrest; to understand. – *n* **appre'hension**. – *adj* **appre'hensive** afraid.

ap'prentice *n* one who is learning a trade. – *n* **ap'prenticeship** the time during which one is an apprentice.

ap'proach *v* to come near; to be nearly equal to; to speak to in order to ask for something. – *n* a coming near to; a way leading to a place: – *pl* **ap'proaches**. – *adj* **ap'proachable** able to be reached; (of persons) easy to speak to, friendly.

appro'bation *n* good opinion, approval.

ap'prōpriate *adj* suitable, fitting. – *v* to take possession of; to set (money *etc*) apart for a purpose. – *n* **appropri'ation**.

approve [ə'prōōv] *v* to agree to, permit; (with **of**) to think well of. – *n* **ap'proval**. – **on approval** (of goods) on trial, for return (to shop *etc*) if not bought.

ap'proximate *adj* more or less accurate. – *v* (with **to**) to be or come near (a number *etc*). – *n* **approxi'mation** a rough estimate.

'**āpricot** *n* a type of orange-coloured fruit

like a small peach.

April ['āprəl] *n* the fourth month of the year.

'āpron *n* a garment worn to protect the front of the clothes; a hard surface for aircraft to stand on. – *n* **apron stage** the part of the stage in front of the curtains in a theatre.

apropos [aprə'pō]: **apropos of** in connection with, concerning.

apse *n* a rounded domed section, *esp* at the east end of a church.

apt *adj* (with **to**) likely to; suitable, fitting. – *ns* **'aptitude** talent, ability; **'aptness** suitability.

'aqualung *n* a breathing apparatus worn by divers.

aquamarine [akwəmə'rēn] *n* a type of bluish-green precious stone.

a'quārium *n* a tank or tanks for keeping fish or water animals: – *pl* **a'quaria**.

a'quatic *adj* living, growing or taking place in water.

'aqueduct *n* a bridge for taking water, such as a canal, across a valley.

'aquiline *adj* like an eagle; (of a nose) curved or hooked.

'arable *adj* fit for ploughing; (of land *etc*) growing crops.

'arbitrary *adj* fixed not by rules but by someone's decision or opinion. – *v* **'arbitrate** to act as a judge between people or their claims *etc*. – *ns* **arbi'tration** the act of judging between claims *etc*; **'arbitrator** a judge.

arboreal [är'böriəl] *adj* of trees, living in trees.

arbour ['ärbər] *n* a seat in a garden shaded by tree-branches *etc*.

arc *n* part of the circumference of a circle, a curve. – *ns* **'arc-lamp**, **'arc-light** a bright lamp lit by a special kind of electric current.

ar'cade *n* a covered walk, *esp* one with shops on both sides.

arch *n* the curved part above one's head in a gateway or the curved support for a bridge, roof *etc*: – *pl* **'arches**. – *adj* mischievous, roguish. – *v* to raise or curve in the shape of an arch. – *n* **'archway** a passage or road beneath an arch.

arch- chief (as in **'arch-'enemy**).

archaeology [ärki'oləji] *n* the study of the people of earlier times from the remains of their buildings *etc*. – *adj* **archae'ological**. – *n* **archae'ologist**.

archaic [är'kāik] *adj* (*esp* of words) no longer used, old-fashioned.

archangel ['ärkānjəl] *n* a chief angel.

'arch'bishop *n* a chief bishop.

'arch'deacon *n* a clergyman next in rank below a bishop.

'arch'duke *n* (*hist*) the title of the ruling princes of Austria.

'archer *n* one who shoots arrows from a bow. – *n* **'archery** the art of shooting with a bow and arrows.

archipelago [ärki'peləgō] *n* a group of small islands: – *pls* **archi'pelago(e)s**.

architect ['ärkitekt] *n* one who plans and designs buildings. – *n* **'architecture** the style of a building; the study of building.

archives ['ärkivz] *npl* (a place for keeping) historical papers, written records *etc*.

'Arctic *adj* of the district round the North Pole; **'arctic** very cold.

'ardent *adj* eager, passionate. – *n* **'ardour**.

'ardūous *adj* difficult. – *n* **'arduousness**.

are *see* **be**.

area ['āriə] *n* extent (of a surface) measured in square metres *etc*; a region, a piece of land or ground.

a'rēna *n* any place for a public contest, show *etc*; (*hist*) the centre of an amphitheatre *etc* where gladiators *etc* fought.

'argosy *n* a large trading-ship with a valuable cargo: – *pl* **'argosies**.

argue ['ärgū] *v* to quarrel in words; to (try to) prove by giving reasons (that); to suggest or urge. – *adj* **'arguable** that can be argued as being true. – *n* **'argument** a heated discussion, quarrel; reasoning (for or against something). – *adj* **argu'mentative** fond of arguing.

'aria *n* a song for solo voice in an opera *etc*.

'arid *adj* dry. – *ns* **a'ridity**, **'aridness**.

a'rise *v* to rise up; to come into being: – *pt* **a'rose**, *pp* **arisen** [ə'rizn].

aris'tocracy *n* those of the nobility and upper class. – *n* **'aristocrat** a member of the aristocracy. – *adj* **aristo'cratic** of the aristocracy; having a distinguished appearance.

a'rithmetic *n* a way of counting using numbers. – *adj* **arith'metical**.

ark *n* the covered boat in which Noah lived during the Flood.

arm *n* either of the two upper limbs of the human body; anything jutting out like this; (*pl*) weapons. – *v* to equip with weapons. – *adj* **armed** carrying a weapon, now *esp* a gun. – *ns* **'armchair** a chair with arms at each side; **'arm-pit** the hollow under the arm at the shoulder.

ar'mada *n* a fleet of armed ships.

arma'dillo *n* a type of small American animal whose body is protected by bony plates: – *pl* **arma'dillos**.

'armaments *npl* equipment for war, *esp* the guns of a ship, tank *etc*.

armistice ['ärmistis] *n* in war, a halt in the fighting, a truce.

armorial [är'möriəl] *adj* of a coat-of-arms.

armour ['ärmər] *n* (*hist*) a protective suit of metal worn by knights. – *adj* **'armoured** (of a vehicle) protected by metal plates. – *n* **'armoury** an arms store: – *pl* **'armouries**.

'army *n* a large number of men armed for war; a great number: – *pl* **'armies**.

a'rōma *n* a sweet smell. – *adj* **aro'matic**.

arose *see* **arise**.

a'round *prep* in a circle about; on all sides of, surrounding. *Flowers grew around the tree*; all over, at several places in: *papers scattered around the room*; somewhere near in time, place, amount: *around here: around three o'clock*. – *adv* on every side. – **get around** (of a fact, rumour *etc*) to become known to all; (of a person) to be active.

arouse [ə'rowz] *v* to awaken; to stir, move (a feeling or person).

arraign [ə'rān] *v* to accuse publicly.

arrange [ə'rānj] *v* to put in some order; to plan, to settle. – *n* **ar'rangement**.

'arras *n* a screen of tapestry.

ar'ray *n* order, arrangement; clothing. – *v* to put in order; to dress, to adorn.

ar'rears: in arrears not up to date, behindhand (with payments *etc*).

ar'rest *v* to seize, capture *esp* by power of the law; to stop; to catch (the attention *etc*). – *n* capture by the police; stopping. – *adj* **ar'resting** striking, capturing one's attention.

ar'rive *v* to reach a place. – *n* **ar'rival** the act of arriving; person or thing that arrives. – **arrive at** to reach, come to (a decision *etc*).

'arrogant *adj* proud, haughty, self-important. – *n* **'arrogance**.

arrow ['arō] *n* a straight, pointed weapon made to be shot from a bow; an arrow-shape (on road signs *etc*) showing direction.

'arsenal *n* a factory or store for weapons, ammunition *etc*.

'arsenic *n* an element that, combined with oxygen, makes a strong poison.

'arson *n* the crime of setting fire to a house *etc* on purpose.

art *n* drawing, painting, sculpture *etc*; cleverness, skill; cunning; (*pl*) non-scientific school or university subjects.

– *adjs* **'artful** wily, cunning; **'artless** simple, frank.

'artefact, 'artifact *n* an object made by man.

'artery *n* a tube which carries blood from the heart to pass through the body: – *pl* **'arteries**. – *adj* **ar'tērial** of or like arteries. – *n* **arterial road** a main traffic road.

artesian well [är'tēziən] *n* one in which water rises to the surface by natural pressure.

'artichoke *n* a type of thistle-like plant, part of whose flower-head is eaten. – *n* **Jerusalem artichoke** a type of plant whose roots are used as food.

'article *n* a thing, object; a composition in a newspaper, journal *etc*; (in grammar) the name of the words *the, a, an.*

ar'ticulate *adj* expressing thoughts or words clearly. – *n* **articu'lation**. – *n* **articulated lorry** one with a cab which can turn at an angle to the main part of the lorry, making cornering easier.

artifact *see* **artefact**.

arti'ficial *adj* not natural; made by man. – *n* **artifici'ality**.

ar'tillery *n* big guns; the part of the army that uses these.

artisan [ärti'zan] *n* a skilled workman.

'artist *n* one who paints pictures; one skilled in anything; an artiste. – *adj* **ar'tistic** of artists; having or showing a talent for art. – *n* **'artistry** skill as an artist.

artiste [är'tēst] *n* one who performs in a theatre, circus *etc*.

as *adv, conj* in phrases expressing comparison or similarity: *as good as: the same as.* – *conj* while, when. *He fell as I watched*; because, since. *As it's wet we can't go*; in the same way that. *He thinks as I do.* – *adv* for instance. – **as for** concerning, regarding; **as if, as though** as it would be if; **as to** regarding; **as well (as)** too, in addition (to).

as'bestos [az'bestos] *n* a thread-like mineral which will not burn.

ascend [ə'send] *v* to climb, go up; to rise or slope upwards. – *n* **a'scendancy, a'scendency** control (over). – *adj* **a'scendant, a'scendent** rising. – *n* **a'scent** a going up; a slope upwards. – **ascend the throne** to be crowned king or queen.

ascertain [asər'tān] *v* to find out; to make certain.

ascetic [ə'setik] *n* one who keeps away from all kinds of pleasure. – Also *adj*.

as'cribe *v* to think of as belonging to (a person or thing) or due to (a cause).

ash *n* a type of hard-wood tree with silvery bark; (often in *pl*) what is left after anything is burnt: – *pl* '**ashes**. – *adj* '**ashen** very pale.

a'shamed *adj* feeling shame.

a'shore *adv* on (to the) shore.

a'side *adv* on or to one side; apart. – *n* words spoken (*esp* by an actor) which other persons nearby are supposed not to hear.

'**asinine** *adj* of an ass; stupid.

ask *v* to request information about: *Ask where to go*; to invite.

as'kance : **look askance at** to look at with suspicion.

askew [əs'kū] *adv* off the straight, to one side.

a'sleep *adj* sleeping; (of limbs) numbed.

asp *n* a small poisonous snake.

as'paragus *n* a type of plant whose young shoots are eaten as a vegetable.

'**aspect** *n* look, appearance; view, point of view; side of a building *etc* or the direction it faces in.

'**aspen** *n* a kind of poplar tree.

as'perity *n* harshness, sharpness of temper; bitter coldness.

'**asphalt** *n* a tarry mixture used to make pavements, paths *etc*.

as'phyxia *n* stoppage in breathing, suffocation (as by smoke or other fumes). – *v* **as'phyxiate** to suffocate. – *n* **asphyxi'ation**.

aspi'distra *n* a kind of pot-plant with large leaves.

as'pire *v* (with **to** or **after**) to try to achieve or reach (something difficult, ambitious *etc*). – *n* **aspiration**.

'**aspirin** *n* a pain-killing drug.

ass *n* a horse-like animal with long ears, a donkey; a stupid person: – *pl* '**asses**.

assagai, assegai ['asəgī] *n* a thin wooden spear, with an iron tip.

as'sail *v* to attack. – *n* **as'sailant** one who attacks.

as'sassin *n* one who assassinates, a murderer. – *v* **as'sassinate** to murder (*esp* a politically important person). – *n* **assassi'nation**.

as'sault *n* an attack, *esp* a sudden one. – Also *v*.

as'semble *v* to bring (people) together; to put together (a machine *etc*); to meet together. – *ns* **as'semblage** a collection (of persons or things); **as'sembly** a putting together; a gathering of people, *esp* for a special purpose: – *pl* **as'semblies**. – *n* **assembly line** series of machines and workers necessary for the manufacture of an article.

as'sent *v* to agree. – *n* agreement.

as'sert *v* to state firmly; to insist on (a right *etc*). – *n* **as'sertion**. – *adj* **as'sertive** not shy, inclined to assert onself. – **assert oneself** to make oneself noticed, heard *etc*.

as'sess *v* to fix an amount (to be paid in tax *etc*); to estimate the value, power of *etc*. – *ns* **as'sessment; as'sessor** one who assesses.

'**asset** *n* an advantage, a help; (*pl*) the property of a person, company *etc*.

as'siduous *adj* persevering; hard-working.

assign [ə'sīn] *v* to give to someone as his share or task; to fix (a time or place). – *ns* **assignation** [asig'nāshən] an appointment to meet; **assignment** [ə'sīnmənt] an act of assigning; a task given.

as'similate *v* to take in. – *n* **assimi'lation**.

as'sist *v* to help. – *ns* **as'sistance; as'sistant** a helper, *esp* one who helps a senior worker; one who serves in a shop *etc*.

as'sizes *npl* the name of certain law courts in England.

as'sociate *v* to keep company with; to join (with) in partnership or friendship; to connect in thought. – *adj* joined or connected (with). – *n* a friend, partner, companion. – *n* **associ'ation** a club, society, union *etc*; a partnership, friendship; a connection made in the mind.

as'sorted *adj* various, mixed. – *n* **as'sortment** a variety, mixture.

assuage [ə'swāj] *v* to soothe, ease (pain, hunger *etc*).

as'sume *v* to take upon oneself; to take as true without further proof, take for granted; to put on (a disguise *etc*). – *adj* **as'sumed** taken upon oneself; pretended. – *n* **assumption** [ə'sumpshən] act of assuming; something taken for granted.

assure [ə'shōor] *v* to make (someone) sure; to state positively (that). – *n* **as'surance** a feeling of certainty; confidence; a promise; insurance. – *adj* **as'sured** certain; confident.

'**asterisk** *n* a star(*) used in printing for various purposes, *esp* to point out a note added.

as'tern *adv* (in ships) at or towards the back part.

asthma ['asmə] *n* an illness causing inability to breathe out properly. – *n, adj* **asth'matic** (one) suffering from asthma.

as'tonish *v* to surprise greatly. – *n* **as'tonishment** amazement, wonder.

as'tound *v* to surprise greatly, amaze. –

adj as'tounding.

astra'khan *n* lamb-skin with a curled wool.

'astral *adj* of the stars.

as'tray *adv* out of the right way, straying.

as'tride *adv* with legs apart. – *prep* with legs on each side of.

astringent [əs'trinjənt] *adj, n* (of) a type of lotion *etc* used for closing up the skin's pores. – *adj* (of a manner *etc*) sharp, sarcastic.

as'trology *n* the study of the stars and their supposed power over the lives of humans. – *n* as'trologer.

'astronaut *n* one who travels in space.

as'tronomy *n* the study of the stars and their movements. – *n* as'tronomer. – *adj* astro'nomical of astronomy; (of numbers) very large.

as'tute *adj* cunning, clever.

a'sunder *adv* apart, into pieces.

a'sȳlum *n* a place of refuge or safety; an old name for a home for the mentally ill.

at *prep* showing position, time *etc*: *at home*: *at 3 o'clock*; costing: *bread at 14 pence a loaf*. – at all in any way: *not worried at all*.

ate *see* eat.

atheism ['āthiizəm] *n* belief that there is no God. – *n* 'atheist one who does not believe in a God.

'athlete *n* one good at sport, *esp* running, gymnastics *etc*. – *adj* athletic [əth'letik] of athletics; good at sports, strong, powerful. – *npl* ath'letics running, jumping *etc* or competitions in these.

'atlas *n* a book of maps: – *pl* 'atlases.

'atmosphere *n* the air round the earth; any surrounding feeling: *a friendly atmosphere*. – *adj* atmospheric [atmə's'ferik]. – *npl* atmos'pherics in radio *etc*, air disturbances causing crackling noises. – *n* atmospheric pressure the pressure exerted by the atmosphere at the surface of the earth, due to the weight of the air.

'atoll *n* a coral island or reef.

'atom *n* the smallest part of an element; anything very small. – *n* atomic energy very great force got by breaking up the atoms of some substances as in the atom(ic) bomb.

a'tone *v* to make up for wrong-doing. – *n* a'tonement.

a'trōcious *adj* cruel or wicked; (*coll*) very bad. – *ns* a'trociousness; atrocity [ə'trɒsəti] a terrible crime; (*coll*) something very ugly: – *pl* a'trocities.

at'tach *v* to fasten or join (to); to think of (something) as having: *attach importance to the event*. – *adj* at'tached fastened; fond (of). – *n* at'tachment something attached; a joining by love or friendship.

attaché-case [ə'tashikās] *n* a small case for papers *etc*.

at'tack *v* to fall upon suddenly or violently; to speak or write against. – *n* an act of attacking; a fit (of an illness *etc*).

at'tain *v* to reach; to gain. – *adj* at'tainable able to be attained. – *n* at'tainment act of attaining; the thing attained, an achievement or accomplishment.

at'tempt *v* to try. – *n* a try or effort; an attack (on someone's life *etc*).

at'tend *v* to be present at; to pay attention to; to wait on, look after; to accompany. – *n* at'tendance act of waiting on or of being present; the number of persons present. – *adj* at'tendant going along with. – *n* one who attends; one employed to look after (something): *a cloakroom attendant*. – *n* at'tention careful notice; concentration; care; in (army) drill, a stiffly straight standing position. – *adj* at'tentive giving or showing attention; polite.

'attic *n* a room just under the roof of a house.

at'tire *v* to dress. – *n* clothing.

'attitude *n* way of thinking or feeling; position of the body.

attorney [ə'tõrni] *n* one who has legal power to act for another: – *pl* at'torneys.

at'tract *v* to draw to or towards; to arouse liking or interest. – *n* at'traction act or power of attracting; that which attracts. – *adj* at'tractive pleasing; good-looking, likeable.

at'tribute *v* to think of as belonging to, or due to (a person or cause). – *adj* at'tributable. – *n* 'attribute something that is part of the nature of a person or thing, a quality.

aubergine ['ōbərzhēn] *n* a type of plant whose dark purple fruit is used as a vegetable.

auburn ['ōbərn] *adj* (*esp* of hair) reddish-brown in colour.

'auction *n* a public sale in which articles are sold to the person who offers the highest price. – *v* to sell by auction. – *n* auctio'neer one who sells by auction.

au'dācious *adj* daring, bold. – *n* audacity [ō'dasəti].

'audible *adj* able to be heard. – *n*

audi'bility. – adv 'audibly.

'audience n a number of people gathered to watch or hear (a performance etc); a formal interview with someone important: an audience with the Pope.

'audio-typist n a typist able to type from a recording on a tape-recorder etc.

audio-visual ['ödiō'vizhŏŏəl] adj needing to be heard and seen at the same time.

'audit v to examine accounts officially. – Also n. – n 'auditor one who audits accounts.

'auditory adj of hearing. – ns au'dition a test given to an actor, singer etc; auditorium [ödi'töriəm] the part of a theatre etc where the audience sits: – pls aud'itoria, audi'toriums.

aug'ment v to increase in size, number or amount. – n augmen'tation.

'augur : augur well, augur ill to be a good, bad sign for the future.

'August n the eighth month of the year.

au'gust adj full of dignity, stately.

aunt [änt] n a father's or a mother's sister or an uncle's wife.

'aural adj pertaining to the ear. — adv 'aurally. — adj 'auriform ear-shaped.

auspices ['öspisiz] : under the auspices of under the control or supervision of.

auspicious [ös'pishəs] adj favourable; promising luck.

aus'tere adj severe; without luxury etc, simple. – n austerity [ös'terəti].

au'thentic adj true, real, genuine. – v au'thenticate to show to be true or real. – n authen'ticity.

'author n the writer of a book, poem, play etc.

au'thority n power or right; a person whose opinion is reliable, an expert; a person or body of people having control (over something); (pl) au'thorities persons in power. – adj au'thoritative said etc by an expert or someone in authority.

'authorize v to give (a person) the power or the right to do something; to give permission (for something to be done).

autobi'ography n the story of a person's life written by himself: – pl autobi'ographies. – adj autobio'graphical.

'autocrat n a ruler who has complete power. – n au'tocracy government by such a ruler. – adj auto'cratic of an autocrat; expecting complete obedience.

'autograph n one's own signature; one's own handwriting. – v to write one's own name (on).

auto'matic adj (of a machine etc) self-working; (of an action) unconscious, without thinking. – n something automatic (eg an automatic washing-machine); a kind of self-loading gun. – adv auto'matically. – ns auto'mation the use in factories etc of machines for controlling other machines. – au'tomaton a (human-shaped) machine that can be operated to move by itself; a person who acts like a machine: – pls au'tomatons, au'tomata.

automobile ['ötəməbēl] n (US) a motor car.

au'tonomy n the power or right of a country etc to govern itself. – adj au'tonomous.

'autopsy n an examination of the body after death: – pl 'autopsies.

autumn ['ötəm] n the season of the year when leaves change colour and fruits etc are ripe. – adj autumnal [ö'tumnəl] of or like autumn.

auxiliary [ög'zilyəri] adj helping; additional. – n a helper: – pl au'xiliaries.

a'vail: avail oneself of to make use of; to no avail without any effect, of no use.

a'vailable adj able or ready to be made use of. – n availa'bility.

avalanche ['avəlänsh] n a mass of snow and ice sliding down from a mountain; a great amount: an avalanche of work.

avarice ['avəris] n greed, esp for riches. – adj ava'ricious.

avenge [ə'venj] v to take revenge for (a wrong). – n a'venger.

avenue ['avinū] n a (tree-bordered) street or approach to a house; means, way: avenue of escape.

average ['avərij] n the result got by adding several amounts and dividing the total by the number of amounts (The average of 3, 7, 9, 13 is 8 (32÷4)). – adj obtained by working out an average (of amounts etc): average price; average temperature; ordinary, usual; of medium size etc. – v to form an average; to find the average of.

a'verse adj not fond of, opposed (to). – n a'version dislike; something that is hated.

a'vert v to turn (one's eyes etc) away; to prevent.

'aviary n a place for keeping birds: – pl 'aviaries.

avi'ation n (the science of) flying in aircraft. – n 'aviator an airman.

'avid adj eager, greedy. – n a'vidity.

a'void v to escape, keep clear of. – adj a'voidable. – n a'voidance.

avoirdupois [avwärdŏŏ'pwä] adj, n (of) the system of measuring weights in pounds and ounces.

avow [ə'vow] *v* to declare openly. – *n* **a'vowal**. – *adj* **a'vowed**.

a'wait *v* to wait for.

a'wake *v* to rouse (from sleep); to stop sleeping. – *adj* not asleep; watchful. – *v* **a'waken** to awake; to arouse (interest *etc*). – *ns* **a'wakening, a'waking**.

award [ə'wörd] *v* to give, grant (a prize *etc*); to grant legally. – *n* what is awarded (such as a payment, prize *etc*).

a'ware *adj* having knowledge (of), conscious (of); alert. – *n* **a'wareness**.

a'way *adv* to or at a distance from the person or thing spoken about. *Throw it away. He is away*; in the opposite direction. *He turned away*; into nothing. *The sound died away*; constantly: *working away*. – **do away with** to abolish, get rid of; **get away with** to do (something) without being punished; **make away with** to destroy; to steal and escape with; **right away** immediately.

awe [ö] *n* wonder mixed with fear; dread. – *adjs* **'awesome** causing fear; **'awestruck** full of fear and wonder.

'awful *adj* (*coll*) bad: *an awful headache*; bad; (*coll*) very great: *an awful lot*; terrible. – *adv* **'awfully** (*coll*) very (much): *awfully grateful*. – *n* **'awfulness**.

'awkward *adj* clumsy, not graceful; difficult (to deal with). – *n* **'awkwardness**.

awl *n* a pointed tool for boring small holes.

'awning *n* a covering (of canvas *etc*) to give shelter.

awry [ə'rī] *adj, adv* crooked; not according to plan, wrong.

axe *n* a tool for chopping: – *pl* **'axes**. – *v* to cancel (a plan *etc*); to reduce greatly (costs, services *etc*).

'axis *n* the line, real or imaginary, on which a thing turns (as the axis of the earth, from North to South Pole, around which the earth turns); a fixed line taken as a reference, as in a graph: – *pl* **'axēs**.

axle ['aksl] *n* the rod on which a wheel turns.

azure ['azhər] *adj* sky-coloured, clear blue.

B

'babble *v* to talk indistinctly or foolishly; (of a stream *etc*) to murmur. – Also *n*.

babe *n* a baby.

ba'boon *n* a kind of large monkey with a dog-like snout.

'bāby *n* a very young child, an infant: – *pl* **'babies**. – *ns* **'babyhood** the time when one is a baby; **'babysitter** someone who stays in the house with child(ren) while parents are out.

'bachelor *n* an unmarried man. – *ns* **Bachelor of Arts, Bachelor of Science** *etc* one who has passed examinations at a certain level in subjects at a university *etc*.

ba'cillus *n* a rod-shaped kind of germ: – *pl* **ba'cilli**.

back *n* the part of the body in man from the neck to the base of the spine; the upper part of the body in animals; the part of anything situated behind; one who plays behind the forwards in football, hockey *etc*. – *adj* of or at the back. – *adv* to or in the place from which a person or thing came; to or in a former time or condition *etc*. – *v* to move backwards; to bet on (a horse *etc*); (often with **up**) to help or support. – *ns* **'backer** a supporter;

'backing support; material used on the back of something (*esp* a picture); a musical accompaniment (*esp* on a record). – *n* **'backbone** the spine; the main support of anything; firmness. – *v* **back'fire** (of a motor car *etc*) to make an explosive noise in the exhaust pipe; (of a plan *etc*) to go wrong. – *ns* **'background** the space behind the principal figures *etc* (of a picture); details *etc* that explain something; one's family and upbringing; **'backhand** (in tennis *etc*) a stroke played with the back of the hand facing the ball. – *adj* **'back'handed** (of a compliment *etc*) having a double or unflattering meaning. – *ns* **'backlash** a (violent) reaction (against something); **'backstroke** stroke used in swimming on the back; **'back-wash** a backward current, such as that caused by a wave going out; **'backwater** a river pool not in the main stream; a place not affected by what is happening in the world outside. – **back down** to change one's opinion *etc*; **back out** to move out backwards; to excuse oneself from keeping to an agreement *etc*; **put one's back into** to work hard at; **put**

someone's **back up** to irritate someone; **with one's back to the wall** in desperate difficulties.

'**backgammon** *n* a game rather like draughts, played with dice.

'**backward** *adj* moving towards the back; slow in learning or development. – *adv* '**backward(s)** towards the back; towards the past.

'**bācon** *n* pig's flesh salted and dried, used as food.

bac'tēria *npl* kinds of germs found in the air, water, earth, in living and dead bodies, and *usu* in things going rotten. – *adj* **bac'terial**. – *ns* **bacteri'ology** the study of bacteria; **bacteri'ologist**.

bad *adj* not good; wicked; (*usu* with **for**) hurtful. *Smoking is bad for you*; (of food) rotten; severe, serious: *a bad cut in his foot*; faulty; unwell. – *adv* '**badly** not well; seriously. – *n* '**badness**. – *n* **bad language** swearing *etc*.

badge *n* a mark or sign or brooch-like ornament giving some information about the wearer.

'**badger** *n* a burrowing animal of the weasel family which comes out at night. – *v* to pester or annoy.

'**badminton** *n* a game rather like tennis, played with shuttlecocks.

baffle ['bafl] *v* to prevent (*eg* a plan) from being carried out, to hinder; to be too difficult or too clever for, to puzzle.

bag *n* a holder or container *usu* of a soft material; the quantity of fish or game caught. – *adj* '**baggy** (of clothes) large and loose.

baga'telle *n* a board game, in which balls are struck into numbered holes; something unimportant.

'**baggage** *n* luggage.

'**bagpipes** *npl* musical instrument made up of a bag and several pipes.

bail *v* (with **out**) to get an untried prisoner out of prison for the time being by giving money which will be returned only if he comes back for his trial; *see also* **bale**. – *n* money given to bail out a prisoner; in cricket, one of the crosspieces on the top of the wickets.

bailie ['bāli] *n* (in Scotland) formerly a burgh magistrate.

'**bailiff** *n* an officer who works for a sheriff; a landowner's agent.

bait *n* food put on a hook to make fish bite, or in a trap *etc* to attract animals; anything tempting. – *v* to put bait on a hook or trap; to worry, annoy.

baize *n* a coarse woollen cloth.

bake *v* to cook (in an oven); to dry or harden in the sun or in an oven. – *ns* '**baker** a person who bakes or sells

bread *etc*; '**bakery**, '**bakehouse** a place used for baking in. – *n* **baking powder** a powder added to flour to make cakes *etc* rise.

balalaika [balə'līkə] *n* a type of Russian musical instrument, like a guitar.

'**balance** *n* a weighing machine; the money needed to make the two sides of an account equal; steadiness. – *v* to be the same in weight; to make both sides of an account the same; to make or keep steady.

'**balcony** *n* a platform built out from the wall of a building; an upper floor or gallery in theatres, cinemas *etc*: – *pl* '**balconies**.

bald [böld] *adj* without hair; (of a statement *etc*) plain, bare.

balderdash ['böldərdash] *n* nonsense.

baldric ['böldrik] *n* a cross-belt from shoulder to waist, for carrying sword, bugle etc.

bale *n* a large tight bundle (of cotton, hay *etc*). – **bale out** to escape by parachute from an aircraft in an emergency; to scoop water out of a boat (also **bail out**).

'**baleful** *adj* harmful; full of hate.

balk [bö(l)k] *v* to hinder, to baffle; (with **at**) to refuse (to do something).

ball[1] *n* anything round; the round object used in playing many games. – *npl* '**ball**'**bearings** in machinery *etc*, small steel balls that sit loosely in grooves and ease the revolving of one part over another. – *n* '**ballpoint (pen)** a pen with a tiny ball as the writing point.

ball[2] *n* a formal party at which dancing takes place. – *n* '**ballroom**.

'**ballad** *n* a simple poem telling a story *usu* in verses of four lines; a simple song.

'**ballast** *n* heavy material (such as sand, gravel *etc*) put into a ship *etc* to steady it.

ballerina [balə'rēnə] *n* a female ballet dancer.

ballet ['balā] *n* a kind of graceful dancing which tells a story by mime.

bal'listic missile *n* one which moves under power and is guided on its way, but simply falls on to its target.

bal'loon *n* an airtight ball of thin rubber *etc*, which floats in the air when filled with light gas.

'**ballot** *n* a way of voting in secret by marking a paper and putting it into a special box.

balm [bäm] *n* anything that soothes; a sweet-smelling healing ointment. – *adj* '**balmy** mild, soothing; sweet-smelling. – *n* '**balminess**.

balsa ['bölsə] *n* a type of tropical American tree giving a very light wood (**'balsawood**).

balsam ['bölsəm] *n* a kind of flowering plant; an oily sweet-smelling substance obtained from certain trees.

balus'trade *n* a row of pillars (on a balcony *etc*) joined by a rail.

bam'boo *n* the hard, woody, jointed stem of a type of very tall Indian grass.

bam'boozle *v* to trick, puzzle.

ban *n* an order forbidding something. – *v* to forbid officially (the publication of a book *etc*): – *pt* **banned**.

ba'nal *adj* lacking originality or wit, commonplace. – *n* **ba'nality**.

ba'nana *n* the long yellow fruit of a type of tropical tree.

band *n* a group of people; a group of musicians playing together; a strip of some material to put round something; a stripe (of colour *etc*); (in radio) a group of wavelengths. – *v* to join together.

'bandage *n* a strip of cloth *etc* or special dressing for a wound *etc*.

bandeau ['bandō] *n* hairband: – *pl* **'bandeaux**.

'bandit *n* an outlaw, robber, *esp* a member of a gang of robbers.

bandolier, bandoleer [bandə'lēr] *n* a belt across the body for carrying cartridges.

'bandy *adj* (of legs) bent outward at the knee. – **bandy words** to argue.

bane *n* (a cause of) ruin or trouble.

bang *n* a sudden, loud noise; a heavy blow. – *v* to close with a bang, slam; to hit, strike. *He banged his head on the door.*

bangle ['baŋgl] *n* a large ring worn on arms (or legs).

'banish *v* to order to leave (a country); to drive away (doubts, fear *etc*). – *n* **'banishment**.

'banister *n* the posts and handrail of a staircase.

'banjo *n* a type of musical stringed instrument like a guitar, having a long neck and a round body: – *pls* **'banjo(e)s**.

bank *n* a mound or ridge of earth *etc*; the edge of a river *etc*; a place where money is put for safety; a place where blood *etc* is stored till needed. – *n* **'banker** one who manages a bank. – *ns* **bank holiday** a day on which all banks (and most other shops *etc*) are closed; **'banknote** a piece of paper money issued by a bank; **'bankrupt** one who has no money to pay his debts. – *adj* unable to pay one's debts; utterly lacking (in ideas *etc*). – *n* **'bankruptcy**. – **bank on** to depend on, count on.

'banner *n* a kind of flag carried in processions *etc*, *usu* hung between two poles; any flag.

banns *npl* a public announcement that a marriage is to take place.

banquet ['baŋkwit] *n* a feast or ceremonial dinner.

'bantam *n* a small kind of hen.

'banter *v* to tease in fun. – Also *n*.

bap'tize *v* to sprinkle with water as a sign of being taken into the Christian church; to christen, give a name to. – *n* **'baptism**. – *adj* **bap'tismal**.

bar *n* a rod of anything solid; a broad line or band; a cake (of soap, chocolate *etc*); something standing in the way, a hindrance; a bank of sand *etc*, lying at the mouth of a river; the counter across which drinks are served in a public house; the rail at which prisoners stand for trial; the lawyers in a court; a division in music. – *prep* except: *the best runner bar none.* – *v* to fasten with a bar; to hinder or shut out: – *pt* **barred**. – *prep* **'barring** except for, but for. *They have all gone, barring you and me. Barring accidents he will be there.*

barb *n* the backward-pointing spike on an arrow, fish-hook *etc*. – *adj* **barbed** having a barb or barbs. – *n* **barbed wire** wire with clusters of sharp points placed regularly along it, used for fencing *etc*.

bar'bārian *adj, n* (of) an uncivilized person. – *adj* **barbaric** [bär'barik] uncivilized; cruel. – *n* **bar'barity**.

barbecue ['bärbikū] *n* a frame on which to grill meat *etc*, *esp* outdoors; a party at which a barbecue is used. – *v* to cook (meat *etc*) on a barbecue.

'barber *n* one who shaves beards and cuts hair, a men's hairdresser.

bard *n* a poet.

bare *adj* uncovered, naked; plain, simple; empty. – *v* to uncover or expose. – *adv* **'barely** hardly, scarcely. – *adj* **'barefaced** impudent.

bargain ['bärgin] *n* an agreement (about buying or selling something); something bought cheaply. – *v* to argue about a price *etc*. – **bargain for** to expect: *more than he bargained for*; **into the bargain** in addition, besides.

barge [bärj] *n* a flat-bottomed boat used on rivers and canals. – *v* to move or rush clumsily; to push or bump (into); to push one's way into rudely.

'baritone *n* (a male singer with) a voice between high (tenor) and low (bass).

bark *n* the sharp cry made by a dog *etc*; the rough outer covering of a tree's trunk and branches. – *v* to utter a bark; to speak sharply or angrily; to injure by scraping the skin.

'**barley** *n* a type of grain used for food.

barn *n* a building in which grain, hay *etc* are stored.

'**barnacle** *n* a type of shellfish which sticks to rocks, ships' hulls *etc*.

ba'rometer *n* an instrument which measures the weight or pressure of the air and shows changes in the weather.

'**baron** *n* a nobleman, the lowest in the British peerage; (*hist*) a powerful nobleman. – *n* '**baroness** a baron's wife or a female baron: – *pl* '**baronesses**. – *adj* **ba'rōnial**.

'**baronet** *n* the lowest title that can be passed on to an heir. – *n* '**baronetcy** the rank of baronet.

'**barracks** *npl* a place for housing soldiers.

barrage ['baräzh] *n* something that hinders an enemy, *esp* heavy gunfire; an overwhelming number (of questions *etc*); a bar across a river to make the water deeper.

'**barrel** *n* a wooden cask or vessel with curved sides; the metal tube of a gun through which the shot is fired.

'**barren** *adj* not able to produce (fruit, crops, children *etc*), infertile. – *n* '**barrenness**.

barri'cāde *n* a barrier put up to block a street *etc*. – *v* to block (a street *etc*) in this way; to make (doors *etc*) strong against attack; to shut behind a barrier.

'**barrier** *n* something (*eg* a strong fence *etc*) standing in the way; any obstacle.

barring see **bar**.

'**barrister** *n* a lawyer who pleads cases in court.

barrow ['barō] *n* a small hand-cart; (*hist*) a mound raised over a grave.

'**barter** *v* to give one thing in exchange for another. – *n* trading by exchanging goods without using money.

basalt ['basōlt] *n* a hard, dark-coloured rock thrown up as lava from volcanoes.

base *n* that on which a thing stands or rests; the lowest part; a place from which a military or other action is carried on. – *v* to use as a foundation. *I base my opinion on what I have heard.* – *adj* worthless, cowardly. – *adj* '**base-less** without a foundation; untrue. – *n* '**basement** a storey below ground level in a building. – *n* '**baseball** an American ball game, rather like rounders.

bash *v* to hit hard. – Also *n*.

'**bashful** *adj* shy.

'**bāsic** *adj* of, forming a base; necessary, fundamental.

basil ['bazl] *n* a herb used as flavouring.

basilisk ['bazilisk] *n* (*myth*) a reptile whose look or breath killed; a type of American lizard.

'**bāsin** *n* a wide, open dish; any large hollow holding water (*eg* a dock); the land drained by a river and its tributaries.

'**bāsis** *n* that on which a thing rests, the foundation. *Mutual trust was the basis of their friendship*; the main ingredient: – *pl* '**bāsēs**.

bask *v* to lie in warmth; to enjoy, feel great pleasure (in).

'**basket** *n* a container made of strips of wood, rushes *etc* woven together; anything resembling a basket in shape. – *n* '**basket-ball** a team game like netball.

bass[1] [bās] *n* the low part in music; (a male singer with) a deep voice: – *pl* '**basses**. – *adj* low or deep in tone.

bass[2] [bas] *n* a kind of fish of the perch family: – *pls* **bass**, '**basses**.

bas'soon *n* a kind of musical wind instrument with low notes.

bāste *v* to spoon fat over (meat) while roasting to keep (it) from burning; to sew loosely together with big stitches, to tack.

'**bastion** *n* a defence (against something); a kind of tower on a castle *etc*.

bat *n* a shaped piece of wood *etc* for striking a ball in some games; a kind of mouse-like flying animal. – *v* to use the bat in cricket *etc*; to flutter (one's eyelids *etc*): – *pt* '**batted**. – *n* '**batsman** one who bats in cricket *etc*.

batch *n* a quantity of things made, sent off *etc* at one time: – *pl* '**batches**.

'**bāted: with bated breath** anxiously.

bath *n* a vessel which holds water in which to wash the body; a washing or soaking of the body in water *etc*. – *v* to wash (oneself or another) in a bath. – *n* '**bath'chair** an invalid's wheeled chair.

bathe [bādh] *v* to swim in water; to wash gently; to take a bath. – Also *n*. – **bathed in** covered with.

'**bathyscāphe**, '**bathysphere** *ns* deep-sea observation chambers.

'**batik** *n* a method of dyeing patterns on cloth by waxing certain areas so that they remain uncoloured.

'**batman** *n* an army officer's servant.

'**baton** *n* a small wooden stick; a light stick used by a conductor of music.

bat'talion *n* a part of a regiment of foot soldiers.

'**batten** *n* a piece of sawn timber; in ships, a strip of wood used to fasten down the hatches.

'**batter** *v* to hit repeatedly. – *n* a beaten mixture *usu* of flour, milk and eggs, for cooking. – *adj* '**battered** beaten, ill-treated; worn out by use *etc*. – *n* '**battering-ram** (*hist*) in warfare, a machine with a heavy beam for breaking through walls *etc*.

'**battery** *n* in an army, a number of large guns; a device for storing and transmitting electricity; a series of cages *etc* in which farm animals or birds are reared or fattened, or kept for egg-laying: – *pl* '**batteries**.

'**battle** *n* a fight, *esp* between armies. – Also *v*. – *ns* '**battleaxe** (*hist*) a kind of axe used in fighting; (*coll*) a fierce, domineering woman; '**battlefield**; '**battleship** a heavily armed and armoured warship.

'**battlement** *n* a wall on the top of a building, with openings or notches for firing guns *etc* from.

'**bauble** *n* a brightly-coloured ornament of little value.

bawl *v* to shout or cry out loudly. – Also *n*.

bay *n* a wide inlet of the sea in a coastline; a space in a room *etc* set back, a recess; a compartment in an aircraft; the laurel tree. – *v* (of dogs) to bark. – *n* **bay window** a window that forms a recess. – **hold at bay** to fight off; **stand at bay** to stand and face attackers *etc*.

'**bayonet** *n* a steel stabbing blade that can be fixed to the muzzle of a rifle. – *v* to stab with this.

ba'zaar, ba'zar *n* a sale of goods for charity *etc*; an Eastern market-place; a shop.

be *v* to live, exist. *There may be a few sweets left*; to have a position, quality *etc*. *He wants to be a dentist. He will be angry*. – Also used to form tenses of other verbs. – *pres tense* **am, are, is**, *pt* **was, were**, *pp* **been**. – *n* '**being** existence; any living person (or thing).

beach *n* the shore of the sea *etc*, *esp* when sandy or pebbly: – *pl* '**beaches**. – *v* to drive or haul a boat up on the beach. – *n* '**beachcomber** a person who searches beaches for useful or saleable articles.

'**beacon** *n* a (flashing) light or other warning signal; (*hist*) a fire on a hill used as a signal of danger.

bead *n* a small pierced ball of glass or other hard material (for threading along with others to form a necklace *etc*); a drop of liquid.

'**beadle** *n* an officer of a church or college.

'**beagle** *n* a small hound used in hunting hares.

beak *n* the hard, horny part of a bird's mouth with which it gathers food; anything pointed or projecting.

'**beaker** *n* a tall cup or glass, *usu* without a handle.

beam *n* a long, straight piece of wood or metal; a shaft of light; a radio signal; the greatest breadth of a ship. – *v* to shine; to smile broadly; to divert by radio wave.

bean *n* a kind of pod-bearing plant; the seed of this used as food.

bear [bār] *n* a heavy animal with shaggy fur and hooked claws. – *v* to carry; to endure, put up with; to produce (fruit, children *etc*): – *pt* **bore**, *pp* **borne** (but *usu* **born** of children, ideas *etc*. *The baby was born last year*). – *adj* '**bearable** able to be borne or endured. – *ns* '**bearer** a carrier or messenger; '**bearing** behaviour; direction; connection; part of a machine supporting a moving part. – *n* '**bearskin** the high fur cap worn by the Guards in the British Army. – **bear in mind** to remember, to take into account; **bear out** to confirm. *What has happened bears out what you said yesterday*; **bear with** to be patient with; **bring to bear** to bring into use.

beard *n* the hair that grows on a man's chin and cheeks. – *v* to face up to, defy.

beast *n* a four-footed animal; a brutal person. – *adj* '**beastly** like a beast in actions or behaviour; horrible; (*coll*) unpleasant. – *n* '**beastliness**.

beat *v* to hit (repeatedly); to overcome or defeat; (of a heart or pulse) to move or throb in the normal way; to mark (time) in music *etc*; to stir (a mixture *etc*) with quick movements; to strike bushes *etc* to rouse birds: – *pp* '**beaten**. *pt* **beat**. – *n* a stroke; a round or course which one (*eg* a policeman) follows regularly. – *adj* '**beaten** (of metal) shaped; (of earth) worn smooth by treading; defeated. – **beat up** to injure by repeated hitting, kicking *etc*.

beatific [bēə'tifik] *adj* of, or showing, great happiness.

beauty ['būti] *n* (of a person or thing) very pleasing appearance; (of music, poetry, voices *etc*) pleasing sound; a very attractive woman *etc*: – *pl* '**beauties**. – *adjs* '**beautiful**, *esp* in poetry *etc* '**beauteous**. – *v* '**beautify** to make beautiful: – *pt* '**beautified**.

'**beaver** *n* a type of gnawing animal that can dam streams; its fur.

becalmed [bi'kämd] *adj* (of a sailing

ship) unable to move for lack of wind.

because [bi'koz] *for the reason that. He didn't go because it was raining. – adv* (with **of**) *on account of. Because of his interference, I shall not succeed.*

beck: at one's beck and call obeying all one's orders or requests.

'**beckon** *v* to make a sign (with the finger) to summon someone.

become [bi'kum] *v* to come to be. *He became angry*; to suit. *That dress becomes you. – adj* be'**coming** (of clothes *etc*) suiting well; (of behaviour) suitable.

bed *n* a place on which to rest or sleep; a plot (for flowers *etc*) in a garden; the bottom of a river *etc. – v* to plant in soil *etc*; to provide a bed for: – *pt* '**bedded**. – *n* '**bedding** mattress, bedcovers *etc*; straw *etc* for cattle to lie on. – *npl* '**bedclothes** bedcovers. – *adj* '**bedridden** kept in bed by weakness, illness *etc. – ns* '**bedrock** the solid rock under the soil; '**bedroom** a room for sleeping; **bedspread** ['bedspred] a top cover for a bed; **bedstead** ['bedsted] a frame for supporting a bed.

'**bedlam** *n* a place of uproar, confusion.

be'**draggled** *adj* (wet and) untidy.

bee *n* a type of winged insect that makes honey in wax cells; a gathering for combined work *etc. – n* '**beehive** a (dome-shaped) case or box in which bees are kept. – **make a beeline for** to go directly towards.

beech *n* a type of forest tree with grey smooth bark: – *pl* '**beeches**.

beef *n* the flesh of an ox or cow, used as food. – *adj* '**beefy** stout, muscular. – *n* '**beefeater** a guardian of the Tower of London; a member (Yeoman) of the (Queen's or King's) Guard.

been *see* **be**.

beer *n* an alcoholic drink flavoured with hops.

beet *n* a kind of plant with a carrot-like root, one type (**sugar beet**) used as a source of sugar, the other with a root ('**beetroot**) used as a vegetable.

'**beetle** *n* a kind of insect with four wings, the front pair forming hard covers for the back pair; a kind of hammer.

'**beetling** *adj* (of cliffs *etc*) overhanging; (of eyebrows) heavy, frowning.

befall [bi'föl] *v* to happen (to). *A disaster befell him.*

be'**fit** *v* to be suitable or right for.

before [bi'för] *prep* in front of. *He stood before the entrance to the cave*; earlier than: *before three o'clock*; rather than, in preference to. *He would die before he would give in. – adv* in front; earlier. –

conj earlier than the time that. – *adv* be'**forehand** previously, before the time when something else is done.

befriend [bi'frend] *v* to act as a friend to, to help.

beg *v* to ask for money *etc*; to ask earnestly: – *pt* **begged**. – *n* '**beggar** one who begs; a very poor person. – *v* to make poor. – *adj* '**beggarly** poor; worthless. – **beggar description** to be greater than the speaker *etc* can find words to describe; **beg the question** to take as being proved the very point that needs to be proved.

began *see* **begin**.

be'**get** *v* to be the father of; to cause: – *pres p* be'**getting**, *pt* be'**gat**, *pp* be'**gotten**.

be'**gin** *v* to make a start on: – *pres p* be'**ginning**, *pt* be'**gan**, *pp* be'**gun**. – *n* be'**ginning**.

begone [bi'gon] *interj* be off, go away!

be'**grudge** *v* to grudge, envy. *He begrudged Jane her success.*

beguile [bi'gīl] *v* to cheat; to pass (time) pleasantly; to amuse, entertain.

begun *see* **begin**.

behalf [bi'häf]: **on behalf of** as the representative of; in aid of: *collecting on behalf of the blind.*

be'**have** *v* to conduct oneself (well); to act (in a certain way). – *n* be'**haviour**. – *adj* **well- (badly-)behaved** having good (bad) manners.

behead [bi'hed] *v* to cut off the head of.

be'**hest** *n* command.

be'**hind** *prep* at or towards the back of: *behind the door*; after; in support of, encouraging. *His friends were behind him in his struggle. – adv* at the back; not up to date: *behind with his work.*

be'**hōld** *v* to look (at), see.

be'**hōlden** *adj* grateful because of a good turn done. *I felt beholden to them.*

be'**hove: it behoves one to** it is right for one to.

belabour [bi'lābər] *v* to beat, thrash. – **belabour the point** to discuss a subject at too great length.

be'**lated** *adj* arriving late.

be'**lay** *v* on ships, to fasten a rope round a peg.

belch *v* to bring up wind (noisily) from the stomach through the mouth; (of a fire *etc*) to send up (smoke *etc*) violently.

beleaguer [bi'lēgər] *v* to besiege.

belfry ['belfri] *n* the part of a steeple or tower in which the bells are hung: – *pl* '**belfries**.

be'**lie** *v* to prove false: – *pres p* be'**lying**, *pt* be'**lied**.

believe [bi'lēv] *v* to think of as true or as existing; to trust (in); to think or suppose. – *n* **be'lief** what we think to be true; faith. – **make believe** to pretend.

be'little *v* to make to seem small or unimportant.

bell *n* a hollow object *usu* of metal which gives a ringing sound when struck by the tongue or clapper inside.

bellicose ['belikōs] *adj* inclined to fight, quarrelsome.

belligerent [bi'lijərənt] *adj* carrying on war; quarrelsome, aggressive.

bellow ['belō] *v* to roar like a bull. – Also *n*.

bellows ['belōz] *npl* an instrument for making a blast of air.

'**belly** *n* the abdomen; the underpart of an animal's body; the bulging part of anything: – *pl* '**bellies**. – *v* to swell or bulge out: – *pt* '**bellied**.

be'long *v* to be one's property. *That book belongs to me*; to be a member of (a club *etc*); to be born in or live in. *I belong to Glasgow*; (of an object) to have its place in. *Those knives belong in the kitchen drawer.* – *npl* **be'longings** what one possesses.

beloved [bi'luvid] *adj* much loved, very dear. – Also *n*.

below [bə'lō] *prep* lower in position, rank *etc* than. *Her skirt reached below her knees. A captain ranks below a major.* – *adv* in a lower position. *We looked down at the river below.*

belt *n* a band or strip of leather, cloth *etc* worn around the waist; a continuous band of tough material used in machines or for conveying objects in a factory *etc*; a broad strip of anything (such as land). – *v* to put a belt round, to thrash with a belt; (*coll*) to beat, hit. – *adj* '**belted** wearing or having a belt.

be'moan *v* to weep about, mourn.

bench *n* a long seat; a work-table; the judges of a court: – *pl* '**benches**.

bend *v* to curve; (of persons) to stoop: – *pt, adj* **bent**. – *n* a turn (in a road *etc*).

be'neath *prep* under, in a lower position than. *A toad sat beneath the dripping tap*; covered by. *Beneath her coat she wore a black dress*; (felt to be) too low a task *etc* for. *Sweeping floors was beneath him.* – *adv* below.

benediction [benə'dikshən] *n* a blessing.

benefactor ['benəfaktər] *n* one who does good to another.

beneficial [benə'fishəl] *adj* bringing gain or advantage (to). – *n* **bene'ficiary** a person who receives a gift, a legacy, an advantage *etc*: – *pl* **bene'ficiaries**.

benefit ['benəfit] *n* something good to receive or have done to one; money received under an insurance plan *etc*: *unemployment benefit*. – *v* to do good to; to gain advantage.

be'nevolence *n* wish to do good; a kind act. – *adj* **be'nevolent** kindly.

benign [bi'nin] *adj* gentle, kindly; (of disease) not causing death (opposite of **malignant**).

bent *n* a natural liking. – *adj* see **bend**.

bequeath [bi'kwēdh] *v* to leave by will. – *n* **be'quest** money *etc* left by will.

be'rate *v* to scold.

be'reaved *adj* deprived by death of a relative *etc*. – *n* **be'reavement**.

be'reft *adj* lacking, deprived (of).

beret ['berā] *n* a flat, round hat.

'**berry** *n* a (*usu* juicy) fruit enclosing seeds: – *pl* '**berries**.

ber'serk *adv* in a frenzy, mad.

berth *n* a room or sleeping place in a ship *etc*; the place where a ship is tied up in a dock. – *v* to moor (a ship). – **give a wide berth to** to keep well away from.

'**beryl** *n* a type of precious stone such as an emerald or aquamarine.

be'seech *v* to ask earnestly.

be'set *v* to attack from all sides; to surround.

be'side *prep* by the side of, near: *the house beside the river*; compared with. *Beside her sister she seems plain*; away from, wide of: *beside the point*. – **be beside oneself** to lose self-control.

be'sides *prep* in addition to. *Besides me, there are plenty others*; other than, except: *nothing at all besides water*. – *adv* also, moreover. *Besides, you can't go*; in addition: *plenty more besides*.

besiege [bi'sēj] *v* to surround (a town *etc*) with an army; to crowd round.

be'smirch *v* to stain (a person's name *etc*).

be'sotted: besotted with foolishly fond of.

be'spoke *adj* (of clothes) ordered to be made.

best *adj* good in the most excellent way. – *adv* in the most excellent way. – *v* to defeat. – *ns* **best man** one who attends a man who is being married; **best part** the largest or greatest part; '**best-'seller** a book *etc* which sells exceedingly well. – **at best** under the most favourable circumstances; **do one's best** to try as hard as one can; **make the best of** do as well as possible with.

'**bestial** *adj* like a beast, beastly.

be'stir *v* to waken up, make lively.

bestow [bi'stō] *v* to give.

bet *n* money put down to be lost or kept depending on the outcome of a race *etc*. – *v* to place a bet: – *pt* **bet** or **'betted**.

be'take: betake oneself to go.

be'tray *v* to give up (secrets, one's friends *etc*) to an enemy; to show signs of. *His face betrayed no emotion.* – *n* **be'trayal**.

betroth [bi'trōdh] *v* to promise in marriage. – *n* **be'trothal**. – **betrothed to** engaged to be married to.

'better *adj* good to a greater degree, of a more excellent kind; (of persons) healthier; completely recovered (from an illness). – *adj* in a more excellent way. – *v* to improve. – **better off** in a better position, wealthier; **get the better of** to defeat, to overcome; **had better** would be wise to; ought to; **think better of** to change one's mind about.

be'tween *prep* in or through the space dividing (two persons, places, times *etc*): *between 3 o'clock and 6 o'clock*; in parts, in shares to (two people). *Divide the chocolate between you*; from one (thing) to another: *the road between the cities*; one or the other of. *Choose between the boys*.

'bevel *n* a slanting edge. – *v* to give a slanting edge to: – *pt, adj* **'bevelled**.

beverage ['bevərij] *n* a liquid for drinking.

'bevy *n* a group of women or girls; a flock of birds (*eg* quails): – *pl* **'bevies**.

be'wail *v* to mourn loudly over.

be'ware *v* to be watchful for (something dangerous).

be'wilder *v* to puzzle, confuse. – *n* **be'wilderment** confusion.

be'witch *v* to put under a spell; to charm. – *adj* **be'witching** charming; very beautiful.

be'yond *prep* on the far side of: *beyond the post office*; later than: *beyond three o'clock*; more than: *beyond what was required*; too far gone for: *beyond repair*; too difficult for. *The problem was beyond him.* – *adv* on or to the far side, further away.

bi- *prefix* twice; having two; occurring *etc* twice (in a period of time) or once in every two (periods of time).

'bias *n* a favouring of one person, one side of an argument *etc* rather than another; a tendency to move *etc* in a particular direction; a weight on or in an object making it move in a particular direction. – *v* to give a bias to: – *pt* **'bias(s)ed**. – *n* **bias binding** a piece of material cut on the slant and used for finishing hems *etc*.

bib *n* a piece of cloth *etc* put under a child's chin to prevent his clothes being stained by food *etc*; the part (of an apron, overalls *etc*) covering the front, upper part of the body.

'Bible *n* the holy book of the Christian Church. – *adj* **Biblical** ['biblikəl].

bibli'ography *n* a list of books (about a subject): – *pl* **bibli'ographies**. – *n* **bibli'ographer** one who puts together a bibliography.

'bibliophile *n* a lover of books.

bicen'tenary *n* the two-hundredth year after an event *eg* someone's birth: – *pl* **bicen'tenaries**.

biceps ['biseps] *n* the muscle in front of the upper part of the arm.

'bicker *v* to quarrel (*usu* over small matters).

'bicycle *n* a cycle with two wheels and driven by foot-pedals.

bid *v* to offer a price (for); to tell, say: *I bid you farewell*; to command; to invite. – *n* an offer of a price; a bold attempt: *a bid for freedom*.

bi'ennial *adj* lasting two years; happening once every two years. – *n* a plant that flowers only in its second year.

bier [bēr] *n* a carriage or frame for carrying a dead body.

big *adj* large, great in size, amount, extent *etc*; important; boastful: – *comp* **'bigger**, *superl* **'biggest**.

'bigamy *n* the crime of or state of having two wives or two husbands at once. – *n* **'bigamist**. – *adj* **'bigamous**.

bight [bīt] *n* a small bay.

'bigot *n* one who too strongly believes or supports anything. – *n* **'bigotry**.

bike *n* short for **bicycle**.

bikini [bi'kēni] *n* a woman's brief two-piece bathing suit: – *pl* **bi'kinis**.

bi'lateral [bī'latərəl] *adj* having two sides; affecting two sides, parties *etc*: *a bilateral agreement*.

'bilberry *n* a type of plant with an edible dark-blue berry.

bile *n* a fluid coming from the liver. – *adj* **bilious** ['bilyəs] ill with too much bile; sick; greenish-yellow in colour. – *n* **'biliousness**.

bilge [bilj] *n* the broadest part of a ship's bottom; bilgewater; (*slang*) nonsense. – *n* **'bilgewater** water which lies in the ship's bottom.

bilingual [bī'liŋgwəl] *adj* speaking two languages (well).

bill *n* the beak of a bird; an account for money; an early version of a law before it has been passed by parliament; a printed sheet of information.

'**billet** *n* a lodging, *esp* for soldiers. – *v* to lodge (soldiers) in private houses.

'**billiards** *n* a game played with a **cue** and balls on a table.

'**billion** *n* a million millions (1,000,000,000,000); (*US*, now often in Britain) a thousand millions (1,000,000,000).

billow ['bilō] *n* a great wave. – *v* to rise in billows. – *adj* '**billowy**.

'**billy**, '**billycan** *n* a container for cooking, making tea *etc*, *esp* outdoors. – *n* '**billy-goat** a male goat.

bin *n* a container for storing corn, wine *etc* or for holding dust and ashes.

'**binary** *adj* made up of two. – *n* **binary system** a mathematical system in which numbers are expressed by two digits only, 1 and 0.

bind *v* to tie with a band; to fasten together; to make to promise: – *pt* **bound**. – *n* '**binding** anything that binds; the cover, stitching *etc* which holds a book together.

bingo ['biŋgō] *n* a popular gambling game using numbers.

bi'noculars *npl* a device with lenses and two eyepieces for seeing distant things more closely.

bi'ography *n* a written account of the life of a person: – *pl* **bi'ographies**. – *n* **bi'ographer** one who writes a biography. – *adj* **bio'graphical**.

bi'ology *n* the study of living things. – *adj* **bio'logical**.

biped ['biped] *n* an animal with two feet (*eg* a bird).

birch *n* a type of hardwood tree; a bundle of birch twigs, used for beating people: – *pl* '**birches**. – *v* to beat with a birch.

bird *n* a feathered, egg-laying creature. – *n* '**birdwatching** the study of birds in their natural surroundings. – **bird of prey** a bird (*eg* a hawk) which kills and eats animals (*esp* mammals) or birds; **bird's-eye view** a wide view, as would be seen from above.

'**Birō**® *n* a type of ballpoint pen.

birth *n* the very beginning of a person's (or animal's) life in the world. – *ns* '**birthday** the day on which one is born; the day of the same date each year; '**birthmark** a mark on the body from birth; '**birthright** the right which one may claim because of one's parentage.

biscuit ['biskit] *n* dough baked hard in small cakes.

bi'sect *v* to cut in two equal parts.

'**bishop** *n* a clergyman of high rank (next to an archbishop) in the Roman Catholic church and the Church of England. – *n* '**bishopric** the district ruled by a bishop.

'**bison** *n* a large wild ox of which there two types, the American one, commonly called **buffalo**, and the European one, which is almost extinct: – *pl* '**bison**.

bit *n* a small piece; a small tool for boring; the part of the bridle which the horse holds in its mouth.

bit *see* **bite**.

bitch *n* a female dog, wolf *etc*; (*coll*) an unpleasant, ill-tempered woman: – *pl* '**bitches**.

bite *v* to grip, cut or tear with the teeth: – *pt* **bit**, *pp* '**bitten**. – *n* a grip with the teeth; the part bitten off; (in fishing) a nibble at the bait; a wound on the body caused by an animal's or insect's bite.

'**bitter** *adj* unpleasant to the taste; harsh: *bitter cold*; resentful, angry through disappointment.

'**bittern** *n* a type of bird like a heron.

bivouac ['bivooak] *n* a rest for the night in the open air without tents. – Also *v*: – *pt* '**bivouacked**.

'**bi-'weekly** *adj* happening twice a week or once every two weeks.

bi'zarre *adj* odd, strange.

blab *v* to talk much; to let out a secret: – *pt* **blabbed**.

black *adj* dark and colourless. – *n* black colour. – *v* '**blacken** to make black or dark; to make to appear wicked. – *adj* '**black-and-'blue** badly bruised. – *ns* **black belt** an award for skill in judo; '**blackberry** a type of black-coloured soft fruit growing on a prickly stem; '**blackbird** a type of black, thrush-like bird; '**blackboard** a dark-coloured board for writing on in chalk; '**blackcock** a kind of grouse; **black eye** a bruised area round the eye *usu* as result of a blow; **blackguard** ['blagärd] a wicked person; '**blackleg** one who works when other workers are on strike; '**blackmail** the crime of threatening to reveal a person's secrets unless he pays money; '**blackmailer**; **black market** illegal or dishonest buying and selling. – Also *adj*. – *n* '**blackout** (a period of) total darkness caused by putting out or obscuring all lights; a faint, loss of consciousness. – *v* **black out** to become unconscious. – *ns* **black sheep** a person who is less successful, or less righteous than others in his group (*usu* a family); '**blacksmith** a man who makes or repairs articles of iron; **black widow** a type of very poisonous American spider.

'**bladder** *n* a thin bag of skin *etc, esp* that in which urine collects in the body.

blade *n* the cutting part of a knife, sword *etc*; a leaf of grass or corn.

blame *v* to find fault with; to consider responsible for. – *n* fault; responsibility (for something bad). – *adjs* '**blameless**; '**blameworthy** deserving blame.

blancmange [blə'monzh] *n* a type of jelly-like pudding made with milk.

bland *adj* polite, gentle; mild, not irritating; dull, not exciting.

'**blandishments** *npl* acts or words meant to flatter.

blank *adj* (of paper *etc*) without writing or marks; expressionless: *a blank look*. – *n* an empty space; a cartridge without a bullet. – *n* **blank verse** poetry without rhyme.

'**blanket** *n* a bed-covering of wool *etc*; a covering. – *adj* covering a group of things: *a blanket agreement*. – *v* to cover (with something thick).

blare *v* to sound loudly. – Also *n*.

'**blarney** *n* flattery or coaxing talk.

blas'pheme *v* to speak lightly or wickedly of God; to curse and swear. – *ns* **blas'phemer**; **blasphemy** ['blasfəmi]: – *pl* '**blasphemies**. – *adj* '**blasphemous**.

blast *n* a blowing or gust of wind; a loud note (as on a trumpet); an explosion. – *v* to break (stones, a bridge *etc*) by explosion; to wither, destroy; to produce a loud noise. *Music blasted from the radio*. – *ns* **blast furnace** a furnace (such as is used in iron-smelting) into which hot air is blown; '**blast-off** the moment of the launching of a rocket. – Also *v*. – **at full blast** as quickly, strongly *etc* as possible.

'**blatant** *adj* very obvious; shameless. – *adv* '**blatantly**.

blaze *n* a rush of light or flame. – *v* to burn with a strong flame; to throw out a strong light. – *n* '**blazer** a kind of jacket worn by schoolchildren, sportsmen *etc*.

'**blāzon** *v* to make known publicly; to display very obviously.

bleach *v* to whiten, remove the colour from. – *n* a substance which bleaches, used for cleaning, whitening clothes *etc*: – *pl* '**bleaches**.

bleak *adj* dull and cheerless; cold, unsheltered. – *n* '**bleakness**.

'**bleary** *adj* (of eyes) tired and inflamed.

bleat *v* to cry like a sheep; to complain in an irritating or whining way. – Also *n*.

bleed *v* to lose blood; to draw blood from: – *pt* **bled**. – *n* '**bleeding** a flow of blood.

bleep *v* to give out a high-pitched intermittent sound. – Also *n*.

'**blemish** *n* a stain; a fault or flaw: – *pl* '**blemishes**. – *v* to stain or spoil.

blend *v* to mix together. – Also *n*. – *n* '**blender** an electric machine which mixes thoroughly and liquidizes.

bless *v* to wish happiness to; to make happy; to make holy. – *adjs* **blessed** [blest, 'blesid], (in poetry *etc*) **blest** happy; fortunate; made holy, consecrated. – *n* '**blessing** a wish or prayer for happiness or success; any means or cause of happiness. *The children were a blessing to them*.

blight [blīt] *n* a disease in plants which withers them; anything that destroys. – *v* to destroy.

blind *adj* unable to see. – *n* a window screen; something which deceives. – *v* to make blind; to dazzle. – *n* '**blindness**. – *n* **blind alley** a street open only at one end; anything which leads nowhere. – *adj* '**blindfold** having the eyes bandaged, so as not to see. – *n* **blindman's buff** a game in which a blindfold person tries to catch others.

blink *v* to close the eyes for a moment; to shine unsteadily. – *npl* '**blinkers** pieces of leather over a horse's eyes to prevent it seeing in any direction except in front.

bliss *n* very great happiness. – *adj* '**blissful**.

'**blister** *n* a thin bubble on the skin full of watery matter. – *v* to rise up in a blister.

blithe [blīdh] *adj* happy, gay.

blitz *n* a sudden violent attack (*esp* from the air).

'**blizzard** *n* a fierce storm of wind and snow.

'**bloated** *adj* swollen, puffed out. – *n* '**bloater** a type of smoked herring.

blob *n* a drop of liquid; a round spot.

block *n* a lump (of wood, stone *etc*); a connected group (of buildings *etc*); something which hinders or obstructs: *a road block*; an engraved piece of wood or metal for printing; (*hist*) the wood on which people were beheaded. – *v* to hinder, prevent from going on. – *n* '**blockhead** a stupid person. – *npl* **block letters** capital letters written in imitation of printing type (*eg* NAME).

bloc'kade *v* to surround a fort or country so that food *etc* cannot reach it. – Also *n*.

blonde *adj, n* (of) a woman of fair skin and light-coloured hair. – *adj* **blond** light-coloured; fair-haired.

blood [blud] *n* the red liquid which flows in the bodies of men and animals; one's descent or parentage: *royal blood.* – *adjs* '**bloodless**; '**bloody**. – *ns* **blood donor** one who gives blood which is stored and given to ill people; **blood group** any one of the types into which human blood is divided; '**bloodhound** a breed of large dog with a good sense of smell; '**bloodshed** the shedding of blood, slaughter. – *adjs* '**bloodshot** (of eyes) inflamed with blood; '**bloodthirsty** cruel, eager to kill. – *n* '**blood-vessel** a vein or artery (of the body) in which the blood circulates.

bloom *v* (of plants) to flower; to be in good health. – *n* a blossom or flower; rosy colour; freshness, perfection; a powder on the skin of fresh fruits.

'**blossom** *n* a flower; the flowers on a fruit tree. – *v* to put forth flowers; to open out, develop, flourish.

blot *n* a spot or stain (of ink *etc*). – *v* to spot or stain; to dry writing with **blotting paper**: – *pt* '**blotted**. – **blot out** to remove or conceal from sight or memory.

blotch *n* a spot or patch of colour *etc*: – *pl* '**blotches**. – *v* to mark with blotches. – *adjs* **blotched**; '**blotchy**.

blouse [blowz] *n* a loose piece of clothing for the upper body.

blow [blō] *n* a hard stroke or knock (*eg* with the fist); (*coll*) a sudden piece of bad luck. – *v* (of air or wind) to move; to drive air upon or into; to sound (a wind instrument); to breathe hard or with difficulty: – *pt* **blew** [blōō], *pp* **blown**. – *adj* '**blowy** windy. – *ns* '**blowfly** a fly which lays its eggs in dead flesh *etc*, a bluebottle; '**blowlamp**, '**blowtorch** a lamp for aiming a very hot flame at a particular spot. – **blow over** to pass and be forgotten; **blow up** to destroy by explosion.

'**blubber** *n* the fat of whales and other sea animals.

'**bludgeon** *n* a short stick with a heavy end.

blue [blōō] *adj*, *n* (of) the colour of a clear sky; (*coll*) unhappy, depressed. – *ns* '**bluebell** the wild hyacinth; (in Scotland) the harebell; '**bluebottle** a large fly with a blue abdomen; **Blue Peter** a blue flag with white centre, raised when a ship is about to sail; '**blueprint** a sketch-plan of work to be done; '**bluestocking** a learned lady. – **out of the blue** unexpectedly.

bluff *adj* rough and jolly in manners, outspoken. – *v* to (try to) deceive (by a display of self-confidence). – *n* a high steep bank overlooking the sea or a river; deception, trickery.

'**blunder** *v* to make a bad mistake. – Also *n*.

'**blunderbuss** *n* a short hand gun with a wide mouth: – *pl* '**blunderbusses**.

blunt *adj* having an edge or point that is not sharp; rough in manner. – *v* to make less sharp or less painful. – *adv* '**bluntly**.

blur *n* a spot, thing *etc* that cannot be seen clearly; a smudge, a smear. – Also *v*. – *adj* **blurred**.

blurt *v* (*usu* with **out**) to speak suddenly and without thinking.

blush *n* a red glow on the face caused by shame *etc*; a reddish glow: – *pl* '**blushes**. – *v* to go red in the face.

'**bluster** *v* to blow strongly; to boast noisily (but without good reason). – *n* a blast or roaring as of the wind; words of noisy, empty boasting.

boa ['bōə] *n* a long scarf of fur or feathers. – *n* **boa (con'strictor)** a type of large snake which kills its prey by winding itself round it and crushing it.

boar *n* the male pig; a wild pig.

board *n* a sheet of wood; a group of people who run a business *etc*: *board of directors*; stiff card used in the binding of books; food. – *v* to cover with boards; to supply with food at fixed terms; to enter (a ship *etc*). – *n* '**boarder** one who receives food and lodging. – *ns* '**boarding-house** a house where paying guests receive meals at a fixed price; '**boarding-school** a school in which food and lodging is given.

boast *v* to brag, to speak proudly and exaggeratedly, *esp* about oneself and one's actions. – *n* something said in a bragging or boasting manner. – *adj* '**boastful** fond of boasting.

boat *n* a vessel for sailing or rowing; a ship; a boat-shaped dish: *a sauceboat.* – *v* to sail about in a boat. – *n* '**boater** a straw hat with a brim.

boatswain, bosun ['bōsn] *n* an officer who looks after a ship's boats, rigging *etc*.

bob *v* to move up and down; to cut (hair) to about neck level: – *pt* **bobbed**.

'**bobbin** *n* a small cylindrical piece of wood *etc* on which thread is wound.

bobsleigh ['bobslā] *n* a long sledge or two short sledges joined together with one long seat.

bode : **bode well, ill** to be a good, bad sign.

bodice ['bodis] *n* the (close-fitting) part of a woman's or a child's dress above the waist.

'**bodkin** *n* a large blunt needle.

'**body** *n* the whole or main part of a man

or animal; a corpse; the main part of anything; a mass (*esp* of persons): – *pl* **'bodies**. – *adj* **'bodily** of the body. – *adv* all in one piece, as one whole. – *n* **'bodyguard** a person or group of people whose job is to protect another person from harm or attack.

'boffin *n* (*coll*) a (research) scientist.

bog *n* a marsh. – *adj* **'boggy**. – **bog down** to hinder, prevent from making progress.

bogey ['bōgi] *n* something greatly feared.

'boggle *v* to be astonished at, refuse to believe.

'bōgus *adj* false.

boil *v* (of a liquid) to reach the temperature at which it turns to vapour; to bubble up owing to heat; (*coll*) to be hot; (*coll*) to be angry. – *n* a kind of inflamed swelling. – *n* **'boiler** a container in which water is heated or steam is produced.

'boisterous *adj* wild, noisy; (of weather) stormy.

bōld *adj* daring, full of courage; cheeky; striking, well-marked: *a picture in bold colours*; (of printing type) thick and clear.

'bollard *n* on ships or quays, a post for fastening ropes to; in a street, a short post used in controlling traffic.

'bōlster *n* a long pillow or cushion. – *v* (with **up**) to support.

bōlt *n* a (small) metal sliding bar used to fasten a door *etc*; a large screw or pin; a roll of cloth. – *v* to fasten with a bolt; to swallow (food) hurriedly; to rush away, escape. – **bolt upright** (sitting) with a very straight back.

bomb [bom] *n* a case containing explosive or other harmful material, thrown, dropped, timed to go off automatically *etc*. – *v* to drop bombs on. – *ns* **'bomber** an aeroplane built for bombing; a person who throws, plants *etc* bombs; **'bombshell** formerly, a bomb; a startling piece of news.

bom'bard [bom'bard] *v* to attack with artillery; to batter or pelt. – *n* **bom'bardment**.

'bombast *n* high-sounding language. – *adj* **bom'bastic**.

bond *n* (often *pl*) that which binds (*eg* chains, ropes *etc*); that which brings people together. *Their interest in ballet was a bond between them*; a (written) promise to pay or do something. – *n* **'bondage** slavery. – **bonded store, bonded warehouse** one where goods are kept until taxes have been paid on them; **in bond** in a bonded warehouse.

bone *n* a hard material forming the skeleton of animals; one of the connected pieces of a skeleton: *the hip bone*. – *v* to take the bones out of (meat *etc*). – *adj* **'bony** (of food) full of bones; not fleshy, thin; made of bone or bone-like substance.

'bonfire *n* a large fire in the open air.

'bonnet *n* a type of hat for women, *usu* fastened by ribbons *etc*; the covering over a motor-car engine.

'bonny *adj* good-looking; healthy-looking.

'bōnus *n* an extra payment in addition to wages *etc*; something extra: – *pl* **'bonuses**.

boo *v* make a sound of disapproval. – Also *n*.

'booby *n* a silly or stupid person. – *ns* **booby prize** a prize for the person who is last in a competition; **booby trap** an explosive or other harmful device hidden or disguised as something harmless, intended to injure the first person to come near it.

book *n* (printed) pages bound together; a written work which has appeared, or is intended to appear, in the form of a book. *I read your book and enjoyed it.* – *v* to order (places *etc*) beforehand. – *ns* **'book-keeping** the keeping of accounts; **'booklet** a small (paper-covered) book; **'book-maker** (also (*coll*) **'bookie**) one who takes bets and pays winnings; **'bookworm** a person who is very fond of reading; a grub that eats holes in books.

boom *v* to make a hollow sound or roar; to increase in prosperity, success *etc*. – *n* a loud, hollow sound; a rush or increase of trade, prosperity *etc*: *the oil boom*; a pole by which a sail is stretched.

'boomerang *n* a curved piece of wood which when thrown returns to the thrower, used as a hunting weapon by Australian aborigines.

boon *n* a blessing or favour to be grateful for. – *n* **boon companion** a close friend with whom one makes merry.

boor *n* a rough or rude person. – *adj* **'boorish**.

boost *v* to push up, raise, increase: *boost the sales of shampoo*: *boost resistance to polio*. – Also *n*. – *n* **'booster** that which boosts; a device for increasing the power of a machine *etc*; the first of several stages of a rocket.

boot *n* a covering (of leather *etc*) for the foot and lower part of the leg; a place for stowing luggage in a car. – *v* to kick. – *n* **'boo'tee** a (knitted) boot for a baby.

– **to boot** in addition, as well.

booth [boodh] *n* a covered stall (at a fair or market); a small (enclosed) compartment (for telephoning, voting etc).

'bootlegger *n* one who deals illegally in alcoholic drink.

'booty *n* plunder or gains *usu* taken in war *etc*.

'border *n* the edge or side of anything; the boundary of a country; a flowerbed in a garden. – *v* (*usu* with **on, upon**) to be near to. *His behaviour borders on madness.* – *adj* **'bordered** edged.

bore[1] [bör] *v* to make a hole by piercing; to weary, seem tiresome or dull to. – *n* a hole made by boring; the size across the tube of a gun; a tiresome person or thing; a flood or wave that rushes up some river mouths at high tide. – *n* **'boredom** lack of interest, weariness.

bore[2] *see* **bear**.

born *adj* by birth, natural: *a born athlete.* Also *see* **bear**. – **be born** (of a baby) to come out of the mother's womb; to come into existence.

borne *see* **bear**.

borough ['burə] *n* (*hist*) a town with special privileges granted by royal charter; a town that elects Members of Parliament.

borrow ['borō] *v* to get (from another) on loan.

'borzoi *n* a breed of long-haired dog.

bosh *n* nonsense.

bosom ['boozəm] *n* the breast; midst, centre: *the bosom of his family.* – *adj* (of friends *etc*) close.

boss *n* a leader or master: – *pl* **'bosses**. – *v* to manage, order about in a high-handed way. – *adj* **'bossy** tending to boss others too much, domineering.

bosun *see* **boatswain**.

'botany *n* the study of plants. – *adjs* **bo'tanic(al)**. – *n* **'botanist** one who studies or is an expert in botany. – *n* **botanic garden** a large public garden where plants and trees of different countries are grown.

botch *v* to mend clumsily; to do badly. – *n* a badly done piece of work.

bōth *adj, pron* the two, the one and the other. *We both went. Both of us went. Both* (*the*) *men are dead. The men are both dead. Both are dead.* – *adv* equally, together. *He is both dishonest and cunning.*

bother ['bodhər] *v* to be a nuisance to; to trouble (oneself or others). – *n* trouble, inconvenience.

'bothy *n* (in Scotland) a hut to give shelter to climbers *etc*; a simply furnished hut for farm labourers: –

pl **'bothies**.

'bottle *n* a hollow narrow-necked vessel for holding liquids. – *v* to put in a bottle. – *n* **'bottleneck** a narrow part of a road likely to become crowded with traffic; any stage in a process where progress is held up. – **bottle up** to keep in, hold in (one's feelings).

'bottom *n* the lowest part or underside of anything; the sitting part of the body, the buttocks. – *adj* **'bottomless** extremely deep.

boudoir ['boodwär] *n* a lady's private room.

bough [bow] *n* a branch of a tree.

bought *see* **buy**.

boulder ['bōldər] *n* a large stone.

bounce *v* to (cause to) jump or spring up after striking the ground *etc*; to move about noisily. – Also *n.* – *n* **'bouncer** a person whose job it is to force troublemakers (at a club *etc*) to leave. – *adj* **'bouncing** (large and) lively.

bound *n* a leap, a jump; (*usu pl*) borders, limits. – *v* to jump, leap; to limit; to surround; *see also* **bind**. – *n* **'boundary** (line *etc* marking) the edge or limit: – *pl* **'boundaries**. – *adj* **'boundless** having no limit, vast. – **bound for** ready to go to, on the way to; **bound to** certain to. *He is bound to notice it*; **out of bounds** beyond the permitted limits.

'bounty *n* a gift; generosity; money given as a help: – *pl* **'bounties**. – *adjs* **bounteous** ['bowntiəs], **'bountiful** generous; plentiful.

bouquet [boo'kā] *n* a bunch of flowers; a scent (of wine).

bourgeois ['boorzhwä] *n, adj* (a person) of the middle class.

bout *n* a (round in a) fight or contest; a period, spell, fit (of illness *etc*).

boutique [boo'tēk] *n* a small shop *usu* selling goods (*esp* clothes) of the latest fashion.

'bōvine *adj* of or like cattle; stupid.

bow[1] [bow] *v* to bend; to nod the head or bend the body in greeting; to give in; to weigh down, crush. – *n* a bending of the head or body; (*usu pl*) the front part of a ship.

bow[2] [bō] *n* anything in the shape of a curve or arch; a weapon for shooting arrows, made of a stick of springy wood bent by a string; a looped knot; a wooden rod with horsehair stretched along it, by which the strings of a violin *etc* are played. – *adj* **'bow-'legged** having legs curving outwards. – *ns* **'bowman** a soldier *etc* who uses a bow; **bow window** a window built in a curve.

bowels ['bowəlz] *npl* in the body, the large and small intestines; the innermost parts of anything: *in the bowels of the earth.*

bower ['bowər] *n* a shady spot in a garden.

bowl [bōl] *n* a basin for holding liquids *etc*; a basin-shaped hollow in anything; a heavy wooden ball for rolling along the ground, as in the game skittles; (*pl*) a game played on a green with specially weighted bowls. – *v* to play at bowls; to move speedily like a bowl; (in cricket) to send the ball at the wicket; to put out a batsman by knocking his wicket with the ball. – *n* **'bowler** one who bowls in cricket; a (black) hat with a rounded top. – **bowl over** to knock down; to surprise greatly.

box *n* a case for holding anything; a hardwood tree; an evergreen shrub; (in a theatre) private closed-in seats: – *pl* **'boxes**. – *v* to enclose, confine in a box or any small space; to strike with the hand or fist; to fight with the fists, wearing padded gloves, as a sport. – *ns* **'boxing** the name of this sport; **'boxer** one who boxes as a sport; a breed of large smooth-haired dog with a head like a bulldog's. – *ns* **Boxing Day** December 26, the day after Christmas Day; **box office** an office where theatre tickets *etc* may be bought.

boy *n* a male child; a male servant. – *adj* **'boyish**. – *ns* **'boyhood** the time of being a boy; **Boy Scout** *see* **Scout**.

'boycott *v* to refuse to do business or trade with. – Also *n*.

bra short for **brassière**.

brace *n* anything that draws together and holds tightly; a pair or couple (*esp* of pheasant, grouse *etc* when shot); a carpenter's tool used in boring; (*pl*) shoulder-straps for holding up trousers. – *v* to tighten or strengthen; to give firmness to. – *adj* **'bracing** giving strength.

'bracelet *n* an ornament for the wrist.

'bracken *n* a coarse kind of fern.

'bracket *n* a support for something fastened to a wall; in printing *etc* a mark (*eg* ( ), [ ]) used to group together several words *etc*. – *v* to enclose in brackets; to group together.

'brackish *adj* (of water) rather salty.

'bradawl *n* a tool to pierce holes.

brag *v* to boast. – Also *n*.

braid *v* to plait (the hair). – *n* decorative ribbon used as trimming; a plait of hair.

braille [brāl] *n* a system of raised marks

on paper which blind people can read by feeling.

brain *n* the part of the body inside the skull, the centre of feeling and thinking. – *v* to knock out the brains of; to hit on the head. – *adj* **'brainy** (*coll*) clever. – *ns* **'brainwashing** forcing (a person) to change his views; **'brainwave** a good idea.

braise [brāz] *v* to stew (meat) in little liquid.

brake *n* a part of a vehicle, used for stopping or slowing down. – *v* to slow down by using the brake(s).

'bramble *n* the blackberry bush; (in Scotland) its fruit.

bran *n* the inner husks of wheat *etc*, *usu* separated from flour after grinding.

branch *n* a shoot or arm-like limb of a tree; a small shop, bank, library *etc* belonging to a bigger one: – *pl* **'branches**. – *v* to divide or spread out like branches.

brand *n* a make of goods (having a special trademark); a burning piece of wood; a permanent mark *esp* one made by a red-hot iron. – *v* to mark with a brand; to put a permanent mark on, impress deeply; to mark with disgrace: *branded as a thief.* – *adj* **'brand-'new** absolutely new.

'brandish *v* to wave (a weapon *etc*) about.

'brandy *n* a strong drink, a spirit made from wine: – *pl* **'brandies**.

brass *n* metal made by mixing copper and zinc; (in music) brass wind instruments: – *pl* **'brasses**. – *adj* of, made of brass; playing brass musical instruments. – *adj* **'brassy** like brass; showily dressed or harsh-voiced. – *n* **brass plate** a nameplate on a door *etc*.

brassière ['brasiər] *n* an article of women's underwear for supporting the breasts.

brat *n* a disapproving name for a child.

bra'vado *n* a show of bravery, bold pretence.

brave *adj* ready to meet danger, pain *etc* without showing fear, courageous; noble. – *v* to face or meet boldly and without fear. – *n* a Red Indian warrior. – *n* **bravery** ['brāvəri].

'bra'vo *interj* well done!

brawl *n* a noisy quarrel; a fight. – Also *v*.

brawn *n* muscle power. – *adj* **'brawny** big and strong.

bray *n* a cry (like that) of an ass. – Also *v*.

'brāzen *adj* of or like brass; impudent, shameless. – **brazen (it) out** to face (a difficult situation) with bold impudence.

'**brāzier** *n* a kind of iron basket for holding burning coals.

bra'zil-nut *n* the three-sided nut from a type of tree found in Brazil.

breach *n* a break or gap; a breaking of a law, of a promise *etc*; a quarrel: – *pl* '**breaches**. – *v* to make a breach or opening in. – **breach of the peace** a breaking of the law by noisy, offensive behaviour.

bread [bred] *n* food made of flour or meal and baked; necessary food, means of living. – *n* '**breadwinner** one who earns a living for a family.

breadth [bredth] *n* distance from side to side, width; extent.

break [brāk] *v* to (cause to) fall to pieces or apart; to act against (a law, promise *etc*); to interrupt (a silence *etc*); to tell (news); to check, soften the effect of (a fall); to cure (of a habit); (of a teenage boy's voice) to drop to a deep male tone; (often with **in**) to tame or train (a horse): – *pt* **broke**, *pp* '**broken**. – *n* an opening; a pause; (*coll*) a lucky chance. – *adj* '**breakable**. – *ns* '**breakage** the act of breaking; the thing broken; '**breaker** a large wave. – *ns* '**break-in** illegal entry (by force) of a house *etc* with intent to steal; '**break-through** a sudden success after effort; '**breakwater** a barrier to break the force of the waves. – **break down** (*n* '**breakdown**) to divide into parts; (of engines *etc*) to fail; to be overcome with weeping or (nervous) exhaustion; **break into** to get into by force; **break out** to appear suddenly; to escape; (with **in**) to become covered (with a rash *etc*); **break up** to (cause to) fall to pieces or apart; to separate, depart. *The meeting broke up.*

breakfast ['brekfəst] *n* the first meal of the day. – Also *v*.

bream *n* a type of small fish.

breast [brest] *n* the front part of a human or animal body between neck and belly; either of the milk-producing parts of the body of a woman. – *n* '**breastplate** a piece of armour for the breast.

breath [breth] *n* the air drawn into and then sent out from the lungs; one act of breathing; a very slight breeze. – *adj* '**breathless** breathing very fast, panting; excited. – *n* '**breathalȳser** a device into which one breathes to indicate the amount of alcohol in the blood.

breathe [brēdh] *v* to draw in and send out air from the lungs; to whisper: – *pres p* '**breathing**. – *n* '**breather** a rest or pause.

bred *see* **breed**.

breech *n* the back part, *esp* of a gun; (*pl*) **breeches** ['brichiz] trousers (*esp* those coming just below the knee).

breed *v* to produce (children, a family); to mate and rear (animals); to cause. *Dirt breeds disease*: – *pt* **bred** [bred]. – *n* a group (of animals or people) alike in looks *etc*, being descended from the same ancestor, race, type; kind, sort: *a new breed of salesmen*. – *n* '**breeding** act of producing or rearing; good manners; education and training.

breeze *n* a gentle wind. – *adj* '**breezy** windy; bright, lively.

brethren ['bredhrən] *n* old *pl* of **brother**.

'**brevity** *n* shortness.

brew [broo] *v* to make beer; to make (tea *etc*); (of a storm, trouble *etc*) to be gathering or forming; to plot, plan: *brewing mischief*. – *n* '**brewery** a place where beer is made: – *pl* '**breweries**.

'**briar**, '**brier** *n* the wild rose; a type of heather plant whose wood is used for making tobacco pipes.

bribe *n* a gift (*usu* money) given to persuade a person to do something *usu* dishonest. – *v* to win over with a bribe. – *n* **bribery** ['bribəri].

'**bric-à-brac** *n* small odds and ends.

brick *n* an (oblong) block of baked clay for building; a toy building-block of wood *etc*.

bride *n* a woman about to be married, or newly married. – *adj* '**bridal** of a bride or a wedding. – *ns* '**bridegroom** a man about to be married, or newly married; '**bridesmaid** an unmarried woman who attends the bride at a wedding.

bridge *n* something built to carry a track or road across a river *etc*; the captain's platform on a ship; a card game; the bony part of the nose; a thin piece of wood holding up the strings of a violin *etc*. – *v* to be or build a bridge over; to get over (a difficulty).

'**bridle** *n* the harness on a horse's head to which the reins are attached. – *v* to put on a bridle; to toss the head indignantly. – *n* '**bridle-path** a path for horseriders.

brief [brēf] *adj* short; taking a short time. – *n* (a set of notes giving) information or instructions, *esp* to a lawyer about a law case; (*pl*) women's short-legged knickers; short underpants. – *v* to instruct or inform. – **in brief** in a few words.

brier *see* **briar**.

brig *n* a sailing vessel with two masts and square-cut sails.

bri'gade *n* a body (*usu* two battalions) of soldiers. – *n* **brigadier** [briga'dēr] a senior army officer.

'**brigand** *n* a robber, bandit.

bright [brīt] *adj* shining; full of light; clever; cheerful. – *v* '**brighten** to make or grow bright.

'**brilliant** *adj* very clever; sparkling; splendid. – *n* '**brilliance**.

brim *n* the edge (of a cup *etc*); the outer edge of a hat which sticks out. – *v* to be full: – *pt* **brimmed**. – *adj* '**brim'ful** full to the brim.

'**brimstone** *n* sulphur.

brine *n* salt water. – *adj* '**briny**.

bring *v* to fetch, lead or carry (to a place); to cause to come. *The medicine brings him relief*: – *pt* **brought** [bröt]. – **bring about** to cause; **bring home to** to make (someone) realize (something); **bring off** to do (something) successfully; **bring to** to revive; **bring up** to rear, to feed and educate; to mention. *He brought up that point in his speech.*

brink *n* the edge (of a cliff, *etc*). – **on the brink of** almost at the point of, on the verge of: *on the brink of war*.

brisk *adj* moving quickly; lively and efficient: *a brisk manner*. – *n* '**briskness**.

bristle ['brisl] *n* a short, stiff hair (as of a pig). – *v* (of hair *etc*) to stand on end; to show anger and indignation. – *adj* '**bristly** having bristles; rough.

'**brittle** *adj* hard but easily broken.

broach *v* to begin to talk about (a subject *etc*); to open, begin using (*eg* a cask of wine).

broad [bröd] *adj* wide, extensive; (of an accent *etc*) strong, obvious. – *v* '**broaden** to make or grow broader. – *n* '**broadness**. – *v* '**broadcast** to send out by radio *etc*. – Also *n*. – *n* '**broadside** a shot by all the guns on one side of a ship; a strong attack (in an argument *etc*).

bro'cade *n* a silk cloth on which fine patterns are sewn.

'**broccoli** *n* a type of green vegetable.

brochure ['brōshōor] *n* a booklet: *a holiday brochure*.

brogue [brōg] *n* a strong shoe; a broad accent (*esp* Irish) in speaking.

broil *v* to grill; to make or be very hot.

broke *adj* (*coll*) without money. – *v see* **break**.

broken *see* **break**.

'**brōker** *n* one who buys and sells (stocks and shares *etc*) for others.

bronchitis [bron'kitis] *n* an illness (affecting the windpipe) in which breathing is difficult. – *adj* **bronchial** ['broŋkiəl] having to do with the windpipe.

'**bronco** *n* (*US*) a half-tamed horse.

bronto'saurus *n* a type of large extinct dinosaur.

bronze *n* a golden-brown mixture of copper and tin. – Also *adj*. – *adj* **bronzed** sunburnt (to a colour like that of bronze).

brooch [brōch] *n* an ornament pinned to the clothing: – *pl* '**brooches**.

brood *v* (of a hen *etc*) to sit on eggs; to think (anxiously) for some time. – *n* a number of young birds hatched at one time; young animals or children of the same family.

brook *n* a small stream. – *v* to put up with, endure.

broom *n* a type of shrub with yellow flowers; a brush for sweeping. – *n* '**broomstick** the handle of a broom.

broth *n* soup, *esp* one made with vegetables.

brother ['brudhər] *n* a male born of the same parents as oneself; a companion, a fellow-worker *etc*. – *adj* '**brotherly** of or like a brother; affectionate. – *ns* '**brotherhood** an association of men; '**brother-in-law** the brother of one's husband or of one's wife; the husband of one's sister or of one's sister-in-law.

brought *see* **bring**.

brow [brow] *n* the forehead; an eyebrow; the edge of a hill. – *v* '**browbeat** to bully.

brown [brown] *adj* of a dark colour made by mixing red, yellow, black *etc*; suntanned. – Also *n*.

brownie ['browni] *n* (*myth*) a helpful fairy or goblin; a Brownie Guide. – *n* **Brownie Guide** a junior Girl Guide.

browse [browz] *v* to feed (on the shoots or leaves of plants); to glance through (books), reading here and there.

bruise [brōōz] *n* a mark, a discoloured area (*eg* on the body) where it has been struck *etc*. – *v* to cause bruises (to).

brunette [brōō'net] *n* a woman with dark hair.

brunt: bear, take the brunt to take the chief strain.

brush *n* an instrument with tufts of bristles, hair, wire *etc* for smoothing the hair, cleaning, painting *etc*; a disagreement, a brief quarrel or fight; the tail of a fox; undergrowth: – *pl* '**brushes**. – *v* to pass a brush over; to remove by sweeping; to touch lightly in passing. – *n* '**brushwood** broken branches, twigs *etc*; undergrowth.

brusque ['brōōsk] *adj* sharp and short in

manner, rude. – n '**brusqueness**.

Brussels sprouts npl a type of vegetable with sprouts like small cabbages on the stem.

brute [broot] n an animal; a cruel person. – adj '**brutal** like a brute, cruel. – n **bru'tality**. – adj '**brutish** like a brute, savage, coarse. – n **brute strength** pure physical strength.

'**bubble** n a thin ball of liquid blown out with air. – v to rise in bubbles. – adj '**bubbly**.

bucca'neer n (hist) pirate. – adj **bucca'neering** like a pirate.

buck n the male of the deer, goat, hare and rabbit; (US coll) a dollar. – v (of a horse etc) to attempt to throw a rider by rapid jumps into the air.

'**bucket** n a container for water etc.

'**buckle** n a clip (of metal etc) for fastening straps or belts. – v to fasten with a buckle. – n '**buckler** a small shield.

'**buckshot** n large lead shot fired from a shotgun.

bud n the first shoot of a tree or plant. – v to produce buds. – adj '**budding** showing signs of becoming: a budding author.

Buddhism ['boodizəm] n a religion whose followers worship Buddha. – n, adj '**Buddhist**.

budge v to move slightly, stir.

'**budgerigar** n a kind of small parrot often kept as a pet.

'**budget** n the plan for a government's spending made each year by parliament; anyone's plan of their future spending. – v to allow for in a budget.

'**budgie** n short for **budgerigar**.

buff n a light yellowish brown colour. – v to polish.

'**buffalo** n a large kind of ox, esp one used in Asia to draw loads; (US) the American bison: – pl '**buffaloes**.

'**buffer** n something which lessens the force of a blow or collision.

'**buffet**[1] n a slap or a blow. – v to strike, knock about.

buffet[2] ['boofā] n a counter or café where food and drink may be bought; a (cold) meal set out on tables for people to serve themselves.

buf'foon n a clown, fool. – n **buf'-foonery**.

bug n a name for any small insect, esp one which is disliked; a tiny device which may be concealed in a room to record conversations. – v to put such a device in (a room etc): – pt **bugged**. – n '**bugbear** a thing that frightens or annoys.

'**bugle** n a type of small trumpet. – n '**bugler** one who plays the bugle.

build [bild] v to put together the parts of anything: – pt **built**. – n (of persons) physical type: a heavy build. – ns '**builder**; '**building** the act or trade of building (houses etc); a house or other built dwelling etc. – n **building society** a kind of bank which lends people money to buy a house. – adj '**built-'up** (of an area etc) containing houses and other buildings.

bulb n the rounded part of the stem of certain plants (eg hyacinth, onion) which store their food; a pear-shaped glass globe surrounding the element of an electric light. – adj '**bulbous** bulb-shaped.

bulge [bulj] n a swelling; a (temporary) noticeable increase. – v to swell out.

bulk n (large) size; the greater part. – adj '**bulky** taking up much room. – n '**bulkhead** a wall in the inside of a ship, meant to keep out water in a collision.

bull [bool] n the male of animals of the ox family, also of the whale, elephant etc. – n '**bulldog** a breed of strong, fierce-looking dog. – v '**bulldoze** to use a bulldozer on; to force. – ns '**bulldozer** a machine for levelling land and clearing away obstacles; '**bullfight** (in Spain etc) a public entertainment in which a bull is angered and usu finally killed; '**bullfinch** a small pink-breasted bird; '**bullfrog** a type of large frog; '**bullring** the arena in which bullfights take place; '**bull's-eye** the mark in the middle of a target; a striped sweet.

bullet ['boolit] n the piece of metal fired from a gun. – adj '**bullet-proof** not able to be pierced by bullets.

bulletin ['boolətin] n a report (as of a person's health, of news etc).

bullion ['boolion] n gold and silver in the form of bars etc.

bullock ['boolək] n a young bull.

bully ['booli] n one who unfairly uses his size and strength to hurt or frighten weaker persons: – pl '**bullies**. – v to act like a bully. – v '**bully-'off** (in hockey etc) to put the ball in play.

bulrush ['boolrush] n a type of large strong reed which grows on wet land or in water: – pl '**bulrushes**.

bulwark ['boolwərk] n anything strong for defence (such as a wall).

'**bumble-bee** n a type of large bee.

bump v to strike heavily; to knock by accident. – n the sound of a heavy blow; the act of striking (by accident); a raised lump. – n '**bumper** a bar round the front and back of a car's body to protect it from damage. – *adj* large: *a bumper crop.*

'**bumpkin** *n* a clumsy, awkward, country person, often used insultingly.

bumptious ['bumpshəs] *adj* self-important.

bun *n* a kind of cake; hair wound into a rounded mass.

bunch *n* a number of things tied together or growing together: – *pl* '**bunches**. – *v* to crowd together.

'**bundle** *n* a number of things loosely bound together. – *v* to tie in a bundle; to push roughly. *He bundled the children into the car.*

bung *n* the stopper of the hole in a barrel, bottle *etc*. – *v* to stop up with a bung. – *n* '**bung-hole**.

bungalow ['buŋgəlō] *n* a house of one storey, *usu* standing by itself.

bungle ['buŋgl] *v* to do a thing badly or clumsily. – Also *n*.

'**bunion** *n* a lump or swelling on the joint of the big toe.

bunk *n* a narrow bed *esp* in a ship's cabin. – *n* '**bunker** a large box for keeping coal; a sandpit on a golf course; an underground shelter. – *n* '**bunk-'bed** one of a pair of narrow beds one above the other.

'**bunkum** *n* nonsense.

'**bunny** *n* a child's name for a rabbit: – *pl* '**bunnies**.

'**bunting** *n* a thin cloth used for making flags; flags; a type of bird of the finch family.

buoy [boi] *n* a floating mark which acts as a guide or as a warning for ships; something which acts as a float (*eg* a lifebuoy). – *n* '**buoyancy** ability to float, lightness; ability to recover quickly. – *adj* '**buoyant** light; cheerful.

bur(r) *n* the prickly seedcase or head of certain plants.

'**burden** *n* a load; something difficult to bear (*eg* poverty, sorrow); (*old*) the chorus of a song. – *adj* '**burdensome**.

bureau ['būrō] *n* a writing table; an office: – *pls* **bureaux, bureaus** ['būrōz].

bureaucracy [bū'rokrəsi] *n* government by officials: – *pl* **bu'reaucracies**. – *n* '**bureaucrat** an administrative official. – *adj* **bureau'cratic**.

burgh ['burə] *n* (in Scotland) a borough.

'**burglar** *n* one who breaks into a house to steal. – *n* '**burglary**: – *pl* '**burglaries**.

burial *see* **bury**.

burlesque [bər'lesk] *n* a piece of writing, acting *etc*, making fun of somebody.

'**burly** *adj* broad and strong.

burn *v* to set fire to; to be on fire, or scorching; to injure by burning: – *pt* **burnt, burned**. – *n* a hurt or mark caused by fire; (in Scotland) a small stream. – *n* '**burner** the part of a lamp or gas-jet from which the flame rises.

'**burnish** *v* to polish. – Also *n*.

burnt *see* **burn**.

burrow ['burō] *n* a hole or passage in the ground dug by certain animals for shelter. – *v* to make a passage beneath the ground.

burst *v* to break suddenly (after increased pressure); to move, speak *etc* suddenly or violently. – Also *n*.

bury ['beri] *v* to put beneath the earth (*esp* a dead body); to cover, hide: – *pt* '**buried**. – *n* '**burial**.

bus *n* a (public) road vehicle for carrying passengers: – *pl* '**buses**. – *n* **bus stop** an official stopping place for buses.

busby ['buzbi] *n* a tall, fur hat worn by certain soldiers: – *pl* '**busbies**.

bush [boosh] *n* a growing thing between a plant and a tree in size; wild, unfarmed country (*esp* in Africa *etc*): – *pl* '**bushes**. – *adj* '**bushy** full of bushes; like a bush. – *ns* '**bush-baby** a type of small lemur; '**bush-ranger** in Australia, an outlaw living in the wilds; **bush telegraph** the quick passing-on of news from person to person.

business ['biznis] *n* one's work or job; trade. *Business is good just now;* something that concerns a person. *This is my business:* – *pl* '**businesses**.

busk *v* to play or sing in the street *etc* for money. – *n* '**busker**.

bust *n* a work of art (*usu* a sculpture) showing only the head and shoulders of the person; a woman's breasts.

'**bustard** *n* a kind of large, swift-running bird similar to a turkey.

bustle ['busl] *v* to busy oneself noisily. – *n* noisy activity, fuss; a stuffed pad once worn by ladies under the skirt of their dress.

busy ['bizi] *adj* having a lot to do: – *comp* '**busier**, *superl* '**busiest**. – *adv* '**busily**. – *n* '**busybody** one too concerned with others' affairs. – **busy oneself with** to occupy oneself.

but *conj* showing a contrast between two ideas *etc*. *John was there but Peter was not: not brown but blue;* except that, without that. *It never rains but it pours.* – *prep* except, with the exception of. *No one but John had any money: the next road but one* (*ie* the second road). – *adv* only. *She's but a girl. We can but hope.* –

but for were it not for. *But for your help we would have been late.*

butcher ['boŏchər] *n* one whose work is to (kill animals for food and) sell meat. – *v* to kill cruelly. – *n* '**butchery** great or cruel slaughter.

'**butler** *n* the chief manservant in a household who looks after the wines *etc*, and who serves them.

butt *n* a large cask, a barrel; one of whom others make fun; the thick heavy end of a rifle *etc*; the end of a finished cigarette or cigar; a push with the head. – *v* to strike with the head. – **butt in** to interrupt or interfere.

'**butter** *n* a fatty food made by churning cream. – *v* to spread over with butter. – *ns* '**buttercup** a plant with a cup-like yellow flower; '**buttermilk** the milk that is left after butter has been made; '**butterscotch** a kind of hard toffee made with butter.

'**butterflȳ** *n* a kind of insect with large (*usu* coloured) wings: – *pl* '**butterflies**.

'**buttocks** *see* **bottom**.

'**button** *n* a knob of metal, plastic *etc* used to fasten clothing; a knob pressed to work an electrical device (*eg* a doorbell). – *v* to fasten by means of buttons. – *n* '**buttonhole** a hole through which a button is passed. – *v* to catch the attention of (someone) and force (him) to listen.

'**buttress** *n* a support (as on the outside of a wall): – *pl* '**buttresses**. – *v* to support, as by a buttress.

'**buxom** *adj* plump and pretty.

buy [bī] *v* to get by giving money for: – *pt* **bought** [böt]. – *n* '**buyer**.

buzz *v* to make a humming noise like bees; (of aircraft) to fly close to. – Also *n*. – *n* '**buzzer** a device which makes a buzzing noise as a signal.

'**buzzard** *n* a type of large bird of prey.

by [bī] *adv* near. *A crowd stood by, watching*; past. *A dog trotted by*; aside: *money put by for an emergency*. – *prep* next to, near: *standing by the door*; past: *passing by the house*; through, along, across. *We came by the main road*; showing person *etc* who does something: *written by him*; (of time) not after. *Do it by four o'clock*; during the (time of): *by day: by moonlight*; by means of: *by train*; to the extent of: *taller by a head*; used to express measurements, compass directions *etc*: *a room 6 metres by 4 metres: North by East*; in the quantity of. *We sell potatoes by the pound. They're paid by the week.* – *n* '**by-election** an election for parliament during a parliamentary session. – *adj* '**by-gone** past. – *npl* '**by-gones** old grievances or events that are or should be forgotten. – *ns* '**by-law**, '**bye-law** a local (not a national) law; '**by-pass** a road built round a town *etc* so that traffic need not pass through it; '**bypath**, '**byroad**, '**byway** a side road; '**by-product** something useful obtained during the manufacture of something else; '**bystander** one who stands watching something; '**byword** a common saying; someone or something well-known for some special quality.

bye [bī] *n* in cricket, a ball bowled past the wicket; a run made from this.

C

cab *n* a taxi; (*hist*) a hired carriage.

cabaret ['kabərā] *n* an entertainment with dancing, singing *etc*.

'**cabbage** *n* a type of vegetable, the leaves of which are eaten.

'**cabin** *n* a hut; a small room, *esp* in a ship.

'**cabinet** *n* a cupboard with shelves and doors; a similar container for storage *etc*; a wooden case with drawers; a number of government ministers who decide on policy. – *n* '**cabinet-maker** a maker of fine furniture.

'**cāble** *n* a strong rope or thick metal line; a line of covered telegraph wires laid under the sea or underground; a telegram sent by such a line; an under-ground wire. – *v* to telegraph by cable. – *n* '**cable television** the transmission of television programmes to people's houses by cable.

cacao [kə'kāō] *n* a tree from whose seeds cocoa and chocolate are made.

cache [kash] *n* a store or hiding place of treasure, arms *etc*; things hidden.

'**cackle** *n* the sound made by a hen or goose; a laugh which sounds like this.

ca'cophony *n* an unpleasant noise. – *adj* **ca'cophonous**.

'**cactus** *n* a type of prickly plant: – *pls* '**cactuses**, '**cacti**.

cad *n* a low, despicable person.

cadaverous [kə'davərəs] *adj* corpse-like; very pale and thin.

'**caddie** *n* a golfer's assistant (and adviser) who carries his clubs.

'**caddy** *n* a box in which tea is kept.

'**cādence** *n* the fall of the voice (as at the end of a sentence); a group of chords which ends a piece of music.

ca'det *n* a youth training to be an officer in the armed forces or to be a police officer; a schoolboy who takes military training.

cadge *v* to get by begging; to beg. – *n* '**cadger**.

café ['kafə] *n* a small restaurant where coffee, tea, snacks *etc* are served.

cafeteria [kafə'tēriə] *n* a self-service restaurant.

caffeine ['kafēn] *n* a drug found in coffee and tea *etc*.

'**caftan** *n* a kind of long-sleeved garment reaching to the ankles.

cage [kāj] *n* a box made of metal *etc* rods in which birds or animals are enclosed; in a mine, a lift used by the miners. – *v* to close up in a cage.

cagey, cagy ['kāji] *adj* unwilling to speak freely, wary. – *n* '**caginess**.

cairn *n* a heap of stones, *esp* one set up over a grave, or as a mark on a mountain-top; a breed of small terrier. – *n* '**cairn'gorm** a brown or yellow variety of quartz, used for brooches *etc*.

ca'jole *v* to coax by flattery. – *n* **cajolery** [kə'jōləri].

cake *n* a baked piece of dough *etc, usu* sweetened; anything pressed into a lump: *a cake of soap*. – *v* to form into a mass, harden. – **have one's cake and eat it** to enjoy both of two alternative things.

'**calamine** *n* a pink powder containing a zinc salt, used in lotion or ointment to soothe skin.

ca'lamity *n* a great disaster, a misfortune: – *pl* **ca'lamities**. – *adj* **ca'lamitous**.

calcium ['kalsiəm] *n* an element, a metal which forms the chief part of lime.

'**calcūlate** *v* to count, work out by mathematics; to think out in an exact way. – *adjs* '**calculable** able to be counted or measured; '**calculating** thinking selfishly. – *ns* **calcu'lation** a mathematical reckoning, a sum; '**calculator** a machine which makes mathematical calculations; '**calculus** a mathematical system of calculation.

'**calendar** *n* a table or list showing the year divided into months, weeks and days.

calf [käf] *n* the young of cattle *etc*; its skin cured as leather; the back of the lower part of a person's leg:

– *pl* **calves**.

'**calibrate** *v* to mark the scale on (a measuring instrument); to check or adjust the scale of (a measuring instrument).

'**calibre**, (*US*) '**caliber** *n* measurement across the opening of a tube or gun; (of a person) quality of character, ability.

'**calico** *n* a kind of cotton cloth. – *Also adj*.

'**cal(l)ipers** *npl* an instrument like compasses, used for measuring thicknesses of tubes *etc*; (*sing*) a splint to support the leg, made of two metal rods.

call [köl] *v* to cry aloud; to name; to summon; to make a short visit; (*US*) to telephone. – *Also n.* – *n* '**calling** one's trade or job.

cal'ligraphy *n* (beautiful) handwriting. – *n* **cal'ligrapher**. – *adj* **calli'graphic**.

cal'losity *n* a hard thickening of the skin.

'**callous** *adj* cruel, hardhearted. – *n* a callosity. – *n* '**callousness**.

callow ['kalō] *adj* not mature, inexperienced.

'**callus** *n* a callosity: – *pl* '**calluses**.

calm [käm] *adj* still or quiet; not anxious or flustered. – *n* absence of wind; quietness, peacefulness. – *v* to make peaceful. – *n* '**calmness**.

calorie ['kaləri] *n* a measure of heat; a measure of the energy-giving value of food. – *n* **calo'rimeter** an instrument for measuring heat.

'**calumny** *n* a false accusation or lie about a person: – *pl* '**calumnies**.

calve [käv] *v* to give birth to a calf.

ca'lypso *n* a West Indian folksong made up as the singer goes along: – *pl* **ca'lypsos**.

'**cālyx** *n* the outer covering or cup of a flower: – *pls* **calyces** ['kālisēz], '**calyxes**.

'**camber** *n* a slight curve or bulge on a road *etc*, making the middle higher than the sides.

came *see* **come**.

'**camel** *n* a type of animal of Asia and Africa with a humped back, used for both carrying and riding.

camelopard ['kaniləpärd] *n* the giraffe.

cameo ['kamiō] *n* a gem or other stone on which a carved figure or design stands out: – *pl* '**cameos**.

'**camera** *n* an instrument for taking photographs. – **in camera** in private.

'**camomile** *n* a type of plant, or its dried flowers, used in medicine.

camouflage ['kaməfläzh] *n* the disguising of the appearance of (something) so that it is not easily seen against its background; such an appearance occurring naturally (in animals *etc*), protective colouring. – Also *v*.

camp *n* a group of tents, huts *etc* in which people (holidaymakers, explorers *etc*) live for a short time; fixed military quarters or settlement. – *v* to pitch tents; to set up a temporary home. – *ns* **camp bed** a small portable folding bed; **'campsite** (official) place for pitching tents.

campaign [kam'pān] *n* organized action in support of a cause or movement; a war or part of a war. – *v* to organize support; to serve in a military campaign.

campa'nology *n* the study or art of bell-ringing.

'campus *n* the grounds of a university, college *etc*: – *pl* **'campuses**.

can[1] *v usu* used with another verb to express the ability to do something. *He can play the guitar*; used to express permission given. *You can go swimming tomorrow*: – *pt* **could** [kŏŏd].

can[2] *n* a tin container for liquids, preserved food *etc*. – *v* to put (food) into a closed tin to keep it from going bad. – *n* **'cannery** a place where food is canned.

ca'nal *n* a waterway for boats, made by man.

ca'nāry *n* a type of yellow-feathered songbird kept as a pet: – *pl* **ca'naries**.

ca'nasta *n* a kind of card-game.

'cancan *n* a high-kicking dance.

'cancel *v* to put off permanently, call off: *cancel one's holiday plans*; to cross out by crossing with lines. – **cancel out** to make ineffective by balancing each other. *His sins and good deeds cancel one another out.*

'cancer *n* a disease which eats away part of the body. – *adj* **'cancerous**.

'candid *adj* saying just what one thinks, frank. – *n* **'candour** ['kandər].

'candidate *n* one who enters for an examination or competition for a job, prize *etc*. – *n* **'candidature**.

candied *see* **candy**.

'candle *n* a stick of wax, containing a wick, used for giving light. – *ns* **'candle-power** the amount of light given by one candle; **'candlestick** a holder for a candle; **'candlewick** a cotton tufted material, used for bedspreads *etc*.

candour *see* **candid**.

'candy *n* sugar crystallized by boiling; (*US*) a sweet. – *v* to preserve in sugar, to coat with sugar. – *adj* **'candied**.

cane *n* the stem of certain kinds of plant (such as bamboo and sugar cane); a walking stick. – *v* to beat with a cane. – *n* **'caning** a thrashing with a cane. – *n* **cane sugar** sugar got from the sugar cane.

'cānine *adj* of dogs. – *n* **canine** (**tooth**) any of the four sharp-pointed teeth, one on each side of the upper and lower jaw.

'canister *n* a box or case, *usu* of tin, for holding tea *etc*.

'canker *n* a spreading sore; a disease in trees, plants *etc*.

'cannabis *n* a preparation made from hemp, used as a drug.

'cannibal *n* a person who eats human flesh; an animal that eats its own kind. – *n* **'cannibalism**.

'cannon *n* a large, *usu* mounted gun. – *v* to run into, collide with. – *n* **'cannonball** a solid metal ball to be shot from a cannon.

'cannot *v usu* used with another verb to express the inability to do something. *I cannot understand this*; used to refuse permission. *I've told him he cannot go today*. – **cannot but** can only, cannot avoid (doing something). *We cannot but wait.*

'canny *adj* wise, shrewd, cautious. – *n* **'canniness**.

canoe [kə'nōō] *n* a light narrow boat driven by paddles.

'canon *n* a law or rule; a standard to judge by; a clergyman connected with a cathedral; a list of saints. – *v* **'canonize** to put someone on the list of saints.

cañon *see* **canyon**.

'canopy *n* a covering over a throne, bed, pulpit *etc*: – *pl* **'canopies**.

cant *n* words understood by people in a particular occupation *etc* only; talk which is not sincere; a slope; a tilted position. – *v* to tilt something from a level position.

can't short for **cannot**.

can'tankerous *adj* bad-tempered, quarrelsome.

can'tata *n* a short piece of music for a choir of singers.

can'teen *n* a place where drink and food may be bought and eaten (*usu* in some place of work); a water-flask; a case containing cutlery.

'canter *v* to move at an easy gallop. – Also *n*.

'cantilēver *n* a large projecting bracket used in building for holding up heavy parts like balconies and stairs. – *n* **cantilever bridge** a bridge made of a row of upright piers with cantilevers extending to meet one another.

'**canton** *n* one of the Swiss federal states.

'**canvas** *n* a coarse, strong cloth used for sails, tents *etc* and for painting on: – *pl* '**canvases.**

'**canvass** *v* to go round asking for votes, money *etc.*

canyon, cañon ['kanyən] *n* a deep, steep-sided valley containing a river or stream.

cap *n* a soft hat *usu* with a peak; a cover or top (as of a bottle, pen *etc*). – *v* to put a cap on; to give a university degree to; to choose (a player) for a national sports team (*esp* football or cricket); to do better than, improve on. *He capped my story with a better one*: – *pt* **capped.**

'**capable** *adj* able to cope with difficulties without help; (often with **of**) able or likely (to): *capable of doing great things.* – *n* capa'**bility**: – *pl* capa'**bilities.**

ca'**pacious** *adj* roomy, wide.

ca'**pacitor** *n* an apparatus for collecting and storing electricity.

ca'**pacity** *n* power of understanding; ability to do a thing; the amount that something can hold; position: *in his capacity as leader*: – *pl* ca'**pacities.** – **to capacity** to the greatest extent possible: *filled to capacity*: *working to capacity.*

cape *n* a covering for the shoulders; a point of land running into the sea.

'**caper** *v* to leap, dance about. – *n* a leap; (*coll*) a prank or adventure; the flower-bud of a shrub which, when pickled, is used in sauces.

capercaillie,   capercailzie [kapər'kāl(y)i] *n* a kind of large grouse.

ca'**pillary** *adj* very fine, like a hair. – *n* a very fine tube; a tiny blood vessel: – *pl* ca'**pillaries.**

'**capital** *adj* chief, most important; involving death; excellent. – *n* the chief city (of a country); a large letter (as that which begins a sentence); money for carrying on a business; money invested, accumulated wealth. – *ns* '**capitalism** a system in which the country's wealth is owned by individuals, not by the State; '**capitalist** one who supports or practises capitalism. – *v* '**capitalize** to write in capitals; to turn to one's advantage. – *n* **capital punishment** punishment by death. – **make capital out of** to turn to one's advantage.

ca'**pitulate** *v* to give in (*eg* to an enemy). – *n* ca'**pitu'lation.**

'**capon** *n* a young fattened cock.

caprice [kə'prēs] *n* a sudden, impulsive change of mind or mood. – *adj* **capricious** [kə'prishəs] full of caprice,

apt to change one's mind often.

cap'**size** *v* to upset, to overturn.

'**capstan** *n* on a ship or quay, a machine turned by spokes or by a steam engine, used for winding or hauling.

'**capsule** *n* the case containing the seeds of a plant; a small gelatine case for powdered medicine; the part of a space rocket which contains the crew.

'**captain** *n* the commander of a company of soldiers, a ship or an aircraft; the leader of a team, club *etc.* – *v* to lead. – *n* '**captaincy** the rank of a captain.

'**caption** *n* a heading (for a newspaper article, photograph *etc*).

'**captious** *adj* ready to find fault.

'**captivate** *v* to charm, fascinate.

'**captive** *n* a prisoner. – *adj* taken or kept as a prisoner; not able to get away: *a captive audience.* – *ns* cap'**tivity** the state of being a prisoner; '**captor** one who takes a prisoner. – *v* '**capture** to take by force; to get hold of, seize: *capture the imagination.* – *n* the act of capturing; the thing captured.

car *n* a motor-car; (*esp US*) a carriage of a train. – *n* **car park** a place where motor-cars *etc* may be left for a time.

carafe [kə'raf] *n* a bottle for serving wine, water *etc.*

'**caramel** *n* sugar melted and browned; a kind of sweet, made of sugar and butter.

'**carat** *n* a measure of the purity of gold; a measure of the weight of gems.

'**caravan** *n* a house on wheels drawn originally by horse, now *usu* by car; a number of travellers *etc* crossing the desert together. – *n* **caravanserai** [karə'vansəri] an inn where desert caravans stop.

'**caraway** *n* a type of plant whose spicy seeds are used to flavour cakes *etc.*

'**carbine** *n* a short light musket.

'**carbo'hydrate** *n* one of a group of substances containing carbon, hydrogen and oxygen, such as sugar, starch *etc.*

car'**bolic acid** *n* an acid used to kill germs.

'**carbon** *n* an element of which charcoal is one form. – *adjs* **car'bonic** (made) of carbon; **carboniferous** [kärbə'nifərəs] producing or containing coal or carbon. – *ns* **carbon copy** a copy of a piece of typing *etc* made by using carbon paper; an exact copy; **carbon dioxide** a gas present in the air and breathed out by men and animals; **carbon monoxide** a poisonous gas with no smell; **carbon paper** a paper coated with black ink for making copies

39

in typing *etc.*

'**carbuncle** *n* a type of fiery-red precious stone; an inflamed swelling under the skin.

'**carbūrettor**, '**carbūretter**, (*US*) '**carbūretor** *n* the part of a motor-car engine which changes the petrol into vapour.

carcass, carcase ['kärkəs] *n* the dead body (of an animal).

card *n* (a piece of) pasteboard or very thick paper; a tool for combing wool *etc*; (*pl*) any of the many types of games played with a pack of special cards. – *v* to comb wool *etc.* – *n* '**cardboard** stiff pasteboard.

'**cardiac** *adj* of the heart: *cardiac failure*.

'**cardigan** *n* a knitted woollen jacket.

'**cardinal** *adj* principal, important. – *n* a person of high rank in the Roman Catholic Church. – *npl* **cardinal numbers** numbers telling how many (1, 2, 3 *etc*).

care *n* close attention; worry, anxiety; protection, keeping: *in my care.* – *v* to be concerned or worried; (with **for**) to look after; to feel affection or liking (for). – *adjs* '**carefree** having no worries; '**careful** attentive, taking care; '**careless** paying little attention, not taking care. – *n* '**carelessness**. – *n* '**caretaker** one who looks after a building. – *adj* in temporary charge: *a caretaker government.* – *adj* '**careworn** looking very worried, worn out by anxiety. – **care of, c/o** at the house of.

ca'**reer** *n* one's life's work, trade, profession; course, progress through life, headlong rush. – *v* to move or run rapidly and wildly.

ca'**ress** *v* to touch gently and lovingly. – Also *n*: – *pl* ca'**resses**.

'**cargo** *n* a ship's load: – *pl* '**cargoes**.

caribou ['kariboo] *n* the N. American reindeer.

'**caricature** *n* a picture of someone which exaggerates certain of their features. – *v* to draw a caricature of. – *n* '**caricaturist**.

caries ['kariēz] *n* rottenness, *esp* of the teeth. – *adj* '**carious**.

'**carillon** *n* a set of bells on which tunes can be played; the tune played on these.

'**carmine** *adj, n* (of) a bright red colour.

'**carnage** *n* slaughter, killing.

car'**nātion** *n* a type of garden flower, often pink, red or white.

'**carnival** *n* a celebration with merriment, feasting *etc.*

'**carnivore** *n* a flesh-eating animal: – *pl* car'**nivora**. – *adj* car'**nivorous**.

'**carol** *n* a song of joy or praise (*esp* one sung at Christmas).

carouse [kə'rowz] *v* to take part in a drinking bout.

carp *n* a freshwater fish found in ponds. – *v* to find fault with small errors, complain about nothing.

'**carpenter** *n* a worker in wood, *esp* as used in buildings *etc.* – *n* '**carpentry** the trade of a carpenter.

'**carpet** *n* the woven covering of floors, stairs *etc.* – *v* to cover with a carpet.

'**carriage** ['karij] *n* the act or cost of carrying; a vehicle for carrying people; way of walking. *She has a dignified carriage.*

'**carrion** *n* rotting animal flesh.

'**carrot** *n* a type of vegetable whose long orange-coloured root is eaten.

'**carry** *v* to pick up and take to another place; to contain and take to a destination: *cables carrying electricity*; to bear, have as a mark: *carry a scar*; (of a voice *etc*) to be able to be heard at a distance; to win, succeed: *carry the day*; to keep for sale: *carry cigarettes*: – *pt* '**carried**. – *n* '**carrier** one who carries goods; a machine or container for carrying; one who passes on a disease. – *n* **carrier pigeon** a pigeon which carries letters. – **carried away** overcome by one's feelings; **carry on** to continue (doing); **carry out** to bring to a successful finish.

cart *n* a vehicle (drawn by a horse) used on farms; a small wheeled vehicle pushed by hand. – *v* to carry (in a cart); to drag (off). – *n* '**carter** one who drives a cart. – *ns* '**cart-horse** a large, heavy horse, used for working; '**cartwheel** the wheel of a cart; a sideways somersault with hands touching the ground; '**cartwright** a maker of carts.

'**cartilage** *n* gristle, a strong elastic material in the bodies of men and animals.

car'**tography** *n* the science of mapmaking.

'**carton** *n* a container made of cardboard, plastic *etc.*

car'**toon** *n* a comic drawing with a comic caption; a (*usu* amusing) film made of a series of drawings of animals *etc* which gives an impression of their movement; a large drawing on paper, later to be copied in its final form. – *n* car'**toonist**.

'**cartridge** *n* a case holding the powder and bullet fired by a gun; a spool of film or tape enclosed in a case; a tube of ink for loading a pen; the part of a record-player which holds the stylus.

carve *v* to make or shape by cutting; to cut up (meat) into slices.

cas'cade *n* a waterfall. – *v* to fall like or in a waterfall.

case *n* a container or outer covering; that which happens, an occurrence; statement of facts, argument; state of affairs, what is true; a trial in a law-court: *a murder case.*

'casement *n* a window-frame; a window that swings on hinges.

cash *n* money in the form of coins and notes. – *v* to turn into, or change for, money. – *n* **cashier** [ka'shēr] one who looks after the receiving and paying of money. – *v* to dismiss (*esp* from the army or navy) in disgrace. – *n* **cash register** a machine for holding money that records the amount put in. – **cash in on** to profit from (in terms of money or advantage).

cashew ['kashoo] *n* a type of kidney-shaped nut, or the large tropical tree that bears it.

'cashmere *n* fine soft goats' wool.

casino [kə'sēnō] *n* a building in which gambling takes place: – *pl* **ca'sinos**.

cask *n* a barrel (*usu* containing wine *etc*).

'casket *n* a small box (for holding jewels *etc*); (*US*) a coffin.

cas'sava *n* a kind of tropical plant from whose roots tapioca is obtained.

'casserole *n* a covered dish in which food can be cooked and served; the food cooked in it.

cas'sette *n* a holder for film, magnetic tape for recording sound *etc*; the magnetic tape itself.

'cassock *n* a long robe worn by priests.

cassowary ['kasəwəri] *n* a type of large, flightless bird of Australia and New Guinea.

cast *v* to throw or fling (objects, light *etc*); to throw off, drop, shed; to shape (*esp* metal) in a mould; to choose (actors *etc*) for a play or film; to give a part to (an actor *etc*): – *pt* **cast**. – *n* something shaped in a mould; the actors in a play; a small heap of earth thrown up by a worm; a type: *cast of mind*; a squint (in the eye). – *ns* **'castaway** a deserted or shipwrecked person; **cast iron** unpurified iron melted and moulded into shape. – *adjs* **cast down** depressed; **'cast-off** used by someone else, second-hand.

casta'nets *npl* hollow shells of ivory or hard wood, which are clicked together to accompany a dance.

caste [käst] *n* a class or rank of people (*esp* in India).

castellated *see* **castle**.

caster *see* **castor**.

'castigate *v* to scold; to punish. – *n* **casti'gation**.

castle ['käsl] *n* a fortified house or fortress. – *adj* **castellated** ['kastəlātid] having walls, towers *etc* like those of a castle.

'castor *n* a small wheel (as on the legs of furniture). – Also **'caster**. – *ns* **'castor-'oil** an oil made from a kind of palm, used as a medicine; **castor sugar, caster sugar** very fine granulated sugar.

cas'trate *v* to remove the testicles (of a male animal) and deprive of the ability to reproduce.

casual ['kazhōoəl] *adj* happening by chance; not regular, temporary: *casual labour*; (of clothes) informal. *She wears casual clothes at the weekend*; not careful, unconcerned: *a casual attitude to work.* – *n* **'casualty** a person who is killed or wounded. – *n* **casualty department** a hospital department for treating accidental injuries *etc*.

cat *n* a sharp-clawed furry animal kept as a pet; one of the cat family which includes, lions, tigers *etc*. – *ns* **'cat-burglar** a burglar who breaks into houses by climbing walls *etc*; **'catgut** cord made from the stomachs of sheep, used as strings for violins *etc*; **'cat-o'-'nine-tails** a whip with nine tails or lashes; **cat's cradle** a children's game with string; **'cat's-eye®** a small mirror fixed in the surface of a road to reflect light and so guide drivers at night.

cataclysm ['katəklizəm] *n* a great flood of water; a violent change.

catacomb ['katəkōom] *n* an underground burial place.

catalogue ['katəlog] *n* a list of names, books, objects for sale *etc* set out in some order. – *v* to list in order.

'catalyst *n* any substance which helps or prevents a chemical reaction without itself changing; anything that brings about a change.

catama'ran *n* a boat with two parallel hulls.

'catapult *n* a small forked stick with a length of elastic fixed to the two prongs, used for firing small stones *etc*; (*hist*) a weapon for throwing heavy stones in warfare.

'cataract *n* a waterfall; a disease of the outer eye.

catarrh [kə'tär] *n* inflammation of the lining of the nose and throat causing a discharge; the discharge caused.

catastrophe [kə'tastrəfi] *n* a sudden

disaster. – *adj* **catas'trophic**.

catch *v* to take hold of, capture; to take (a disease): *catch a cold*; to be in time for: *catch the train*; to surprise (in an act): *catch him stealing*: – *pt* **caught** [kōt]. – *n* a haul (of fish); something one is lucky to have got or won; a hidden flaw or disadvantage; something which fastens: *a window-catch*. – *adjs* **'catching** infectious, liable to be caught; **'catchy** (of a tune) not easily forgotten. – *ns* **catchment area** an area from which a river or a reservoir draws its water supply; an area from which the pupils in a school are drawn; **'catch-phrase**, **'catchword** phrase or word which is popular for a while. – **catch on** to become popular; **catch up on** to draw level with, overtake; to get up-to-date with (work *etc*).

catechize ['katikiz] *v* to ask many questions. – *n* **catechism** ['katikizəm] a book (*esp* a religious one) which teaches by asking questions and giving the answers; a series of searching questions.

category ['katəgəri] *n* a class or division of things (or people) of the same kind: – *pl* **'categories**. – *adj* **cate'gorical** allowing of no doubt or argument. – *adv* **cate'gorically**.

'cāter *v* to provide food; to supply what is required: *cater for all tastes*. – *ns* **'caterer; 'catering**.

'caterpillar *n* the larva of an insect that feeds upon the leaves of plants. – *adj* moving on endless metal belts: *a caterpillar tractor*.

'caterwaul *v* to howl or yell like a cat. – *n* **'caterwauling**.

catgut *see* **cat**.

ca'thēdral *n* the church of a bishop; the chief church in the district ruled by a bishop.

catherine-wheel ['kathərinwēl] *n* a firework which turns like a wheel when burning.

'cathode ray tube *n* a device in which a narrow beam of electrons strikes against a screen, as in a television set.

'catholic *adj* wide, comprehensive: *catholic taste in books*; **'Catholic** (short for **Roman Catholic**) of the Roman Catholic Church.

'catkin *n* a tuft or spike of small flowers on certain trees, *esp* the willow and hazel.

'cattle *npl* animals that eat grass, *esp* oxen, bulls and cows.

caught *see* **catch**.

'cauldron *n* a large pan.

cauliflower ['koliflowər] *n* a kind of cabbage, of which one eats the white flower-head.

cause [köz] *n* that which makes something happen; a reason (for action): *cause for complaint*; an aim for which a group or person works: *the cause of peace*. – *v* to make happen.

causeway ['kōzwā] *n* a raised road over wet ground or shallow water.

'caustic *adj* burning, corroding; bitter, severe: *caustic wit*.

'cauterize *v* to burn away flesh with a caustic substance or a hot iron in order to make a sore heal cleanly.

'caution *n* a warning; carefulness (owing to presence of some danger). – *v* to warn. – *adjs* **'cautionary** giving a warning; **'cautious** careful, showing caution.

caval'cade *n* a procession on horseback, in cars *etc*.

cavalier [kavə'lēr] *n* (*hist*) a supporter of the king in the Civil War of the 17th century. – *adj* offhand: *in a cavalier fashion*.

'cavalry *n* horse soldiers.

cave *n* a hollow place in the earth or in rock. – *n* **'caveman** prehistoric man who lived in caves. – **cave in** (to cause) to fall or collapse inwards.

'cavern *n* a deep hollow place in the earth. – *adj* **'cavernous** huge and hollow; full of caverns.

caviare, caviar ['kaviär] *n* the pickled eggs of the sturgeon.

'cavil *v* to make objections over small, unimportant details: – *pt* **'cavilled**.

'cavity *n* hollow place, a hole: – *pl* **'cavities**.

ca'vort *v* to dance or leap around.

caw *v* to call like a crow. – Also *n*.

cayenne [kā'en] *n* a type of very hot red pepper.

'cayman *n* any of various kinds of alligator, *esp* those of S. America.

cease *v* to come or bring to an end. – *adj* **'ceaseless** without stopping.

'cēdar *n* a type of large evergreen tree with a hard sweet-smelling wood.

cede *v* to yield or give up (to another).

ceiling ['sēliŋ] *n* the inner roof of a room; the upper limit.

'celandine *n* a type of small yellow wild flower.

celebrate ['seləbrāt] *v* to feast and make merry in honour of a marriage, birthday or other happy event. – *adj* **'celebrated** famous. – *ns* **cele'bration**; **ce'lebrity** a famous person; fame: – *pl* **ce'lebrities**.

celery ['seləri] *n* a type of vegetable the stalks of which are eaten.

ce'lestial *adj* of the sky. *Stars are celestial bodies*; heavenly.

'celibacy *n* the state of not being married. – *adj* 'celibate.

cell *n* a small room in a prison, monastery *etc*; the smallest, fundamental part of living things; the part of an electric battery containing electrodes. – *adj* 'cellular made of or having cells or small hollow spaces.

'cellar *n* an underground room, *esp* one for storing coal, wine *etc*.

cello ['chelō] *n* (short for **violoncello**) a type of large musical, stringed instrument similar in shape to a violin. – *n* 'cellist one who plays the cello.

'cellophane® *n* a kind of transparent wrapping material.

cellular *see* cell.

'celluloid *n* a very hard elastic substance used for making film *etc*.

'cellulose *n* a substance found in plants and wood used to make paper, textiles *etc*.

ce'ment *n* the mixture of clay and lime used to stick bricks together in buildings; anything that makes two things stick together. – *v* to put together with cement; to join firmly.

cemetery ['semətri] *n* a place where the dead are buried: – *pl* 'cemeteries.

'cenotaph *n* a monument to a person or persons buried elsewhere.

'censor *n* one whose job is to remove from books, films *etc* anything which might be found offensive. – *adj* censorious [sen'sōriəs] fault-finding.

censure ['senshər] *n* blame, expression of disapproval. – *v* to blame, criticize.

'census *n* a counting of the people in a country: – *pl* 'censuses.

cent *n* a coin which is the hundredth part of a larger coin (*eg* of a dollar).

'centaur *n* (*myth*) a monster, half man and half horse.

cen'tenary *n* a hundredth birthday; the hundredth year since an event took place: – *pl* cen'tenaries. – *n* cente'narian a person a hundred or more years old. – *adj* centennial [sən'teniəl] having lasted a hundred years; happening every hundred years.

'centigrade *adj* having a hundred degrees; as measured on a centigrade thermometer: *5 degrees centigrade*. – centigrade thermometer a thermometer which shows the temperature at which water freezes as 0 degrees, and that at which it boils as 100 degrees.

'centigramme *n* a hundredth part of a gramme.

centilitre ['sentilētər] *n* a hundredth

part of a litre.

'centimētre *n* a hundredth part of a metre.

'centipede *n* a small crawling creature with many legs.

'centre, (*US*) 'center *n* the middle point or part; a place built or used for some special activity or service: *sports centre*. – *adj* 'central belonging to the centre; chief. – *v* 'centralize to group in a single place: to bring (government authority) under one central control. – *n* central heating heating of a building by water, steam or air from a central point.

cen'trifūgal *adj* moving away from the centre.

centripetal [sen'tripitl] *adj* moving towards the centre.

cen'tūrion *n* (*hist*) a commander of 100 Roman soldiers.

century ['senchoŏri] *n* a hundred years; a hundred in number (such as runs in cricket): – *pl* 'centuries.

ce'ramic *adj* of (the making of) pottery. – *n* something made of pottery; (*pl*) the art of pottery.

cereal ['sēriəl] *n* grain used as food; a (breakfast) food prepared from grain.

cerebral ['serəbrəl] *adj* of the brain.

ceremony ['serəməni] *n* the formal acts and solemn show or display that goes with an important event: *the marriage ceremony*: – *pl* 'ceremonies. – *n* cere'mōnial *adj* with or of ceremony. – *adj* cere'monious full of ceremony.

cerise [sə'rēs] *adj, n* (of) the colour of cherries, red.

'certain *adj* sure; not to be doubted; fixed, settled; some or one, not definitely named: *certain places*: *a certain shop*. – *adv* 'certainly. – *n* 'certainty.

cer'tificate *n* a written or printed statement that something has happened or been done: *birth certificate*. – *v* 'certify to put down in writing as an official promise, statement *etc*: – *pt* 'certified.

ces'sation *n* a ceasing or stopping.

'cesspool *n* a pool or tank in which liquid waste or sewage is collected.

chafe *v* to make hot or sore by rubbing; to wear away by rubbing; to become annoyed.

chaff *n* the husks of corn after threshing; anything of no great value; good-natured teasing. – *v* to tease jokingly.

'chaffinch *n* a type of small bird: – *pl* 'chaffinches.

chagrin ['shagrin] *n* annoyance.

chain *n* a number of links or rings (*esp* of

metal) passing through one another; (*pl*) these used to tie prisoners' limbs, fetters; a number of connected things: *a mountain chain*; a group of things owned by one person or firm: *a chain of shops*; a number of atoms of an element joined together; a measure of distance (22 yards, 20·1 metres). – *v* to fasten or imprison with a chain. – *ns* **chain reaction** a (chemical) process in which each reaction in turn causes a similar reaction; **'chain-store** one of several shops under the same ownership.

chair *n* a seat for one person with a back to it; an official position (as of the person in charge of a meeting or of a university professor). – *ns* **'chairlift** a row of chairs on an endless cable for carrying people up mountains *etc*; **'chairman** one who presides at or is in charge of a meeting.

chalcedony [kal'sedəni] *n* a type of precious or semi-precious stone.

chalet ['shalā] *n* a small wooden house often used by holidaymakers; a summer hut used by Swiss herdsmen in the Alps.

chalice ['chalis] *n* a cup for wine, *esp* that used in church services.

chalk [chök] *n* a type of limestone; a similar substance used for writing, drawing. – *v* to mark with chalk. – *adj* **'chalky** of chalk; white, pale.

'challenge *v* to question another's right to do a thing *etc*; to ask (someone) to take part in a contest of some kind *eg* to settle a quarrel. – *n* a call to a contest of any kind, *esp* to a duel. – *n* **'challenger**. – *adj* **'challenging** (of a problem *etc*) interesting but difficult.

'chāmber *n* a room; the place where an assembly (such as parliament) meets, or where legal cases are heard by a judge; an enclosed space or cavity; the part of a gun that holds the cartridges. – *n* **chamber music** music for a small group of players, suitable for performance in a room rather than in a large hall.

'chāmberlain *n* one appointed by a king or local authority to carry out certain duties.

chameleon [kə'mēliən] *n* a type of small lizard able to change its colour to match its surroundings.

chamois ['shamwä] *n* a type of goat-like deer living in mountainous country; (also **shammy** ['shami]) a soft kind of leather made from its skin.

champ *v* to chew noisily. – **champing at the bit** impatient to act.

champagne [sham'pān] *n* a type of white sparkling wine.

'champion *n* a person, animal *etc* who has beaten all others in a competition; one who strongly supports a cause (such as freedom of speech *etc*). – *v* to support the cause of (a person, freedom *etc*). – *n* **'championship** the act of championing; a contest to find a champion; the title of champion.

chance *n* a risk, possibility; something unexpected, not planned; an opportunity. – *v* to risk; to happen by accident. – *adj* happening by accident. – *adj* **'chancy** risky. – **by chance** not arranged, unexpectedly; **chance upon** to meet or find unexpectedly.

'chancel *n* the part of a church near the altar.

'chancellor *n* a high government minister (*eg Chancellor of the Exchequer* who is in charge of government spending, *Lord Chancellor* the head of the English legal system); the head of a university.

chancery ['chansəri] *n* (in England) the Lord Chancellor's court.

chandelier [shandə'lēr] *n* a fixture hanging from the ceiling with branches for holding lights.

change [chānj] *v* to make or become different; to give up or leave one thing for another (*eg* one's job, house); to put on different clothes; to give or get (money of one kind) in exchange for (money of another kind). – *n* the act of making or becoming something different; another set of clothing; money in the form of coins; money given back by a shopkeeper when a buyer gives more than the price of an article. – *adj* **'changeable** likely to change; often changing. – *n* **'changeling** a child secretly taken or left in place of another.

'channel *n* the bed of a stream; a passage for ships; a narrow sea; a groove; a gutter; a band of frequencies for radio or television signals. – *v* to direct into a particular course.

chant *v* to sing; to recite in a singing manner. – Also *n*.

chanty *see* **shanty**.

chaos ['kāos] *n* disorder, confusion. – *adj* **cha'otic**.

chap *n* (*coll*) a man. – *adj* **chapped** (of skin) cracked by cold or wet weather.

'chapel *n* a small part of a larger church; a small church for (private) worship.

chaperone ['shapərōn] *n* an older lady who attends a younger one when she goes out in public. – *v* to act as a chaperone to.

chaplain ['chaplin] *n* a clergyman with the army, navy, or air force or on a ship *etc.*

'**chapter** *n* a division of a book; (a meeting of) the clergy of a cathedral. – **chapter of accidents** a series of accidents.

char *v* to burn until black; to do odd jobs of housework, cleaning *etc*: – *pt* **charred**. – *n* '**charwoman** a woman hired to do housework for other people.

charabanc ['sharəbaŋ] *n* a long motor-coach with rows of seats.

character ['karəktər] *n* the nature and qualities of a person *etc*; the good points and bad points which make up a person's nature; self-control, firmness; a person noted for odd or strange ways; reputation; a person in a play, story, film *etc*. – *n* **characte'ristic** a point or feature which is typical of a person *etc* and easily noticed. – *adj* typical. – *v* '**characterize** to be typical of; to describe (as).

charade [shə'räd] *n* a word-guessing game, in which the syllables of a word and then the whole word are acted.

'**charcoal** *n* wood burnt black.

charge [chärj] *v* to accuse. *He was charged with murder*; to ask (a price); to attack; to load (a gun *etc*); to fill (with); to lay a task upon a person. – *n* blame, accusation (for a crime); price, fee; an attack; the gunpowder in a shell or bullet; care. *The money was given into my charge*; someone looked after by another person. – *n* '**charger** a horse used in battle. – **in charge** in command or control; **take charge of** to take command of.

'**chariot** *n* (*hist*) (two-wheeled) carriage used in battle. – *n* **chario'teer** chariot-driver.

'**charity** *n* giving of money to the poor *etc*; an organization which collects money and gives it to those in need; love for all people; kindness: – *pl* '**charities**. – *adj* '**charitable** giving to the poor; kindly; of a charity.

charlatan ['shärlətən] *n* one who claims greater powers, abilities *etc* than he really has.

charm *n* something thought to have magical powers; a spell; power to attract (by appearance, manner *etc*). – *v* to please greatly, delight; to put under a spell.

'**charnel-house** *n* a place where the bones of the dead are put.

chart *n* a table or diagram giving some form of information (*eg* a temperature chart); a map, *esp* one of seas or lakes, showing rocks, islands, currents, depth *etc*; a rough map. – *v* to make a chart of; to plan.

'**charter** *n* a written paper showing the granting of rights, favours, lands *etc*, *esp* by a king or a government. – *v* to hire (a boat, aeroplane *etc*). – *adj* '**chartered** having a charter; (of an aeroplane *etc*) hired for a special purpose.

charwoman *see* **char**.

'**chāry** *adj* cautious, careful (of).

chase *v* to run after, pursue; to hunt. – *n* a pursuit; a hunt.

chasm ['kazəm] *n* a deep hole or drop between high rocks *etc*; a wide difference.

chassis ['shasi] *n* the frame, wheels, and machinery of a motor-car; an aeroplane's landing carriage: – *pl* **chassis** ['shasiz].

chāste *adj* pure, virtuous. – *n* **chastity** ['chastəti].

chasten ['chāsn] *v* to make humble; to punish, *usu* by scolding. – *adj* '**chastened**.

chas'tise *v* to punish, *usu* by whipping or beating. – *n* **chastisement** ['chastizmənt].

chat *v* to talk in an easy, friendly way (about unimportant things): – *pt* '**chatted**. – Also *n*. – *adj* '**chatty** willing to talk, talkative.

chateau ['shatō] *n* a French castle or country house: – *pl* **chateaux** ['shatōz].

'**chattels** *npl* movable possessions. – **goods and chattels** personal possessions.

'**chatter** *v* to talk idly, rapidly or indiscreetly; (of teeth) to rattle together through cold *etc*. – Also *n*. – *n* '**chatterbox** one who chatters a great deal.

chauffeur ['shōfər] *n* a person employed to drive a motor-car.

cheap *adj* low in price, inexpensive; of little value, worthless. – *v* '**cheapen** to make cheap.

cheat *v* to deceive; to act dishonestly to gain an advantage. – *n* one who cheats; a dishonest trick.

check *v* to bring to a stop; to hinder or hold back; to see if something (*eg* a sum) is correct or accurate; to see if something (*eg* a machine) is in good condition or working properly. – *n* a sudden stop; something that hinders; a test of the correctness or accuracy of; a square (*eg* on a draughtboard); (a fabric with) a pattern of squares. – *adj* **checked**. – *ns* '**checkmate** in chess, a position from which the king cannot escape; **'checkout** a place where payment is made in a supermarket. – **check in, check out** to record one's arrival at or departure from (*eg* work, an airport *etc*).

checkers *see* **chequers**.

cheek *n* the side of the face below the eye; insolence, disrespectful speech or behaviour. – *adj* **'cheeky** impudent, insolent. – *n* **'cheekiness**.

cheep *v* to make a faint sound like a small bird. – Also *n*.

cheer *n* a shout of approval or welcome. – *v* to shout approval; to encourage, urge on; to comfort, gladden. – *adjs* **'cheerful** happy, in good spirits; **'cheerless** sad, gloomy; **'cheery** lively and merry. – **cheer up** to make or become less gloomy.

'cheeri'o *interj* goodbye!

cheese [chēz] *n* a solid food made from milk. – *adj* **'cheeseparing** mean.

'cheetah *n* a type of swift-running animal like the leopard.

chef [shef] *n* a male head cook.

chemistry ['kemistri] *n* the study of the elements and the ways they combine or react with each other. – *adj* **'chemical** of chemistry or reactions between elements *etc*. – *n* a substance which is formed by or used in a chemical process. – *n* **'chemist** one who studies chemistry; one who makes up and sells medicines.

cheque, (*US*) **check** [chek] *n* a written order to a banker telling him to pay money from one's bank account to another person. – *n* **cheque book** a book containing cheques.

chequers, checkers ['chekərz] *n* a pattern of squares, as on a chessboard; the game of draughts. – *adj* **'chequered, 'checkered** marked like a chessboard; partly good, partly bad: *a chequered life*.

'cherish *v* to protect and treat with fondness or kindness; to keep in one's mind or heart: *cherish a hope*.

cheroot [shə'rōōt] *n* a small cigar.

'cherry *n* a type of small bright-red fruit with a stone, or the tree that bears it: – *pl* **'cherries**.

'cherub *n* an angel having wings and the plump face and body of a child; a beautiful child: – *pls* **'cherubs, 'cherubim**.

chess *n* a game for two persons, played with pieces (**'chessmen**) which are moved on a board marked off into alternate black and white squares (**'chessboard**).

chest *n* a large strong box; the part of the body between the neck and the stomach. – **chest of drawers** a piece of furniture fitted with a set of drawers.

chesterfield ['chestərfēld] *n* a kind of sofa.

chestnut ['chesnut] *n* a type of reddish-brown nut, or the tree that bears it; a reddish-brown horse; an old joke.

'cheviot *n* a kind of sheep.

chevron ['shevrən] *n* a V-shape (*esp* on a badge, road-sign *etc*).

chew *v* to break up (food) with the teeth before swallowing.

chic [shēk] *adj* smart and fashionable. – *n* style, fashionable elegance.

chicanery [shi'kānəri] *n* dishonest cleverness.

chick, 'chicken *ns* the young of (domestic) fowls, *esp* of the hen. – *adj* **'chicken-'hearted** cowardly. – *n* **'chickenpox** an infectious disease which causes red, itchy spots.

'chicory *n* a type of plant whose root is ground to mix with coffee and whose leaves are used as a vegetable.

chide *v* to scold by words.

chief [chēf] *adj* head; main, most important; largest. – *n* a leader or ruler; the head (of a department, organization *etc*). – *adv* **'chiefly** mainly, for the most part. – *n* **'chieftain** the head of a clan or tribe.

chiffon ['shifon] *n* a thin flimsy material.

'chilblain *n* a painful swelling which occurs in cold weather on hands and feet.

child *n* a young human being; a son or daughter (of any age): – *pl* **children** ['children]. – *n* **'childhood** the time of being a child. – *adjs* **'childish** of or like a child; silly; **'childlike** innocent.

chill *n* coldness; an illness that causes shivering, a feverish cold; (of manner *etc*) lack of warmth or enthusiasm. – *adj* cold. – *v* to make cold (without freezing). – *adj* **'chilly** cold.

'chilli, 'chili *n* the dried, hot-tasting pod of a kind of pepper; a sauce made with this.

chime *n* the sound of bells ringing; (*pl*) a set of bells (as in a clock). – *v* to ring; (of clocks) to strike.

'chimney *n* a passage for the escape of smoke or heated air from a fire: – *pl* **'chimneys**. – *ns* **'chimneypot** a pipe of earthenware, iron *etc* placed at the top of a chimney; **'chimneystack** a number of chimneys built up together; **'chimneysweep(er)** one who sweeps or cleans chimneys.

chimpan'zee n a type of African ape.

chin n the part of the face below the mouth.

'china n fine kind of earthenware, porcelain; articles make of this.

chin'chilla n a type of small S. American animal, valued for its soft grey fur.

chink n a narrow opening; a sound like that of coins striking together.

chintz n a cotton cloth with brightly coloured patterns.

chip v to break or cut small pieces (from or off): – pt **chipped**. – n a small piece chipped off; a part damaged by chipping; a long thin piece of potato fried; (US) a (potato) crisp.

'chipmunk n a kind of N. American squirrel.

chipo'lata n a type of small sausage.

chiropodist [ki'ropədist] n one who treats minor disorders and diseases of the feet (eg corns). – n **chi'ropody** the treatment of these.

chirp, **'chirrup** n the sharp, shrill sound (of birds etc). – Also v. – adj **'chirpy** merry, cheerful.

chisel ['chizl] n an iron or steel tool to cut or hollow out wood, stone etc. – v to cut with a chisel: – pt **'chiselled**.

chit n a short note; a child, a young woman: chit of a girl. – n **'chit-chat** gossip, talk.

chivalry ['shivəlri] n kindness, esp towards women or the weak; (hist) the standard of behaviour expected of knights in medieval times. – adj **'chivalrous**.

chive n a herb like the leek and onion, used as flavouring.

chlorine ['klörēn] n an element, a yellowish-green gas with a sharp, distinctive smell, used as a bleach and disinfectant. – v **chlorinate** ['klorināt] to add chlorine, or a substance containing it, to (eg water).

chloroform ['klorəförm] n a liquid, the vapour of which when breathed in, causes unconsciousness.

'chock-a-'block, **'chock'full** adjs completely full.

'chocolate n a paste got from the seeds of the cacao-tree, used in sweet-making; a sweet made from this paste when hardened; a drink made from it. – adj dark brown in colour, like chocolate.

choice n the act or power of choosing; something chosen. – adj of a high quality: choice vegetables.

choir ['kwir] n a group or society of singers; the part of a church where the choir sits. – adj **choral** ['körəl] of or for a choir.

choke v to stop or partly stop the breathing of; to block or clog (a pipe etc); to have one's breathing stopped or interrupted (eg by smoke or chemicals). – n a valve in a petrol engine which controls the flowing-in of air.

cholera ['kolərə] n a deadly disease commonest in hot countries.

choose [chōōz] v to pick out and take (one) from two or several things, to select; to decide, prefer to. We chose to go: – pt **chose** [chōz], pp **'chosen**.

chop v to cut into small pieces; to cut with a sudden blow: – pt **chopped**. – n a chopping blow; a slice of mutton, pork etc, containing a bone. – n **'chopper** a knife or axe for chopping; (coll) a helicopter. – adj **'choppy** (of the sea) not calm, having small waves. – **chop and change** to keep changing.

'chopsticks npl two small sticks of wood, ivory etc used by the Chinese etc instead of a knife and fork.

choral see **choir**.

chord [körd] n a musical sound made by the playing of several notes together; a straight line joining any two points on a curve.

chore [chör] n dull, boring job; (pl) housework.

choreography [kori'ogrəfi] n the arrangement of dancing and dance steps (in a ballet etc). – n **chore'ographer**.

chorister ['koristər] n a member of a choir.

'chortle v to laugh, chuckle.

chorus ['körəs] n a band of singers and dancers; a choir or choral group; the repeated part of a song: – pl **'choruses**.

chose, **chosen** see **choose**.

chow [chow] n a breed of dog from China with a bushy coat and a blue-black tongue.

christen ['krisn] v to baptize and give a name to. – n **'christening**.

Christian ['krischən] .n a follower of Christ. – Also adj. – n **Christianity** [kristi'anəti] the religion having Christ as its centre. – n **Christian name(s)** one's first name (or names): John William Smith.

Christmas ['krisməs] n a yearly holiday or festival, in memory of the birth of Christ, held on December 25. – ns **Christmas Eve** December 24; **Christmas tree** an evergreen tree hung with lights, decorations and gifts at Christmas.

chromatic [krə'matik] adj of colours; coloured. – n **chromatic scale** a series of musical notes, each separated from the next by a semitone.

chromium ['krōmiəm] *n* an element, a metal which does not rust.

chronic ['kronik] *adj* (*esp* of a disease) lasting a long time.

chronicle ['kronikl] *n* a record of events in order of time. – *v* to write down events in order. – *n* '**chronicler**.

chronological [kronə'lojikəl] *adj* arranged in the order of the time of happening.

chronometer [krə'nomitər] *n* an instrument for measuring time.

chrysalis ['krisəlis] *n* an insect (*esp* a butterfly or moth) at an early part of its life when it is without wings and shut up in a soft covering (**cocoon**).

chrysanthemum [kri'santhəməm] *n* a type of garden flower with a large, bushy head.

'**chubby** *adj* plump: – *comp* '**chubbier**, *superl* '**chubbiest**. – *n* '**chubbiness**.

chuck *v* to throw, toss; to pat gently (under the chin).

'**chuckle** *n* a quiet laugh. – *v* to laugh quietly.

chum *n* (*coll*) a close friend.

chunk *n* a thick piece.

church *n* a building used for public, *esp* Christian, worship; any group of people of the same beliefs who meet together for worship: – *pl* '**churches**. – *n* '**churchyard** the burial ground round a church.

'**churlish** *adj* rude, bad-mannered.

churn *n* a machine used for making butter. – *v* to make (butter) in a churn; to shake or stir about violently.

chute [shoot] *n* a sloping trough for sending things down to a lower level (*eg* water, logs, parcels); a similar structure with steps in a playground, for children to slide down.

'**chutney** *n* any of various sauces made from vegetables, fruits, vinegar: – *pl* '**chutneys**.

'**cider** *n* an alcoholic drink made from the juice of apples.

ci'**gar** *n* a roll of tobacco leaves for smoking. – *n* **ciga'rette** a tube of fine tobacco enclosed in thin paper.

'**cinder** *n* a burnt-out piece of coal.

cinema ['sinəmə] *n* a place where films are shown; (with **the**) films generally, or films regarded as a form of art.

'**cinnamon** *n* a yellowish-brown spice got from the bark of a tree.

'**cipher** *n* a secret writing, code; nought, 0; a person of no importance.

'**circa** *prep* about: *circa 5,000 men*.

'**circle** *n* a figure formed from an endless curved line, ○; something in the form

of a circle, a ring; any society or group of people; a balcony or tier of seats in a theatre *etc*. – *v* to enclose in a circle; to move round (something). – *n* '**circlet** a little circle, *esp* one used as an ornamental headband.

circuit ['sərkit] *n* a movement in a circle; a connected group of places, sporting events *etc*: *the American tennis circuit*; the path of an electric current. – *adj* **circuitous** [sər'kūitəs] (of a route *etc*) not direct, roundabout.

'**circular** *adj* round, like a circle. – *n* a letter sent round to a number of persons. – *v* '**circularize** to send a circular to.

'**circulate** *v* to move round (as the blood moves in the body); to send round. – *n* **circu'lation** the act of circulating; the movement of the blood; the total sales of a newspaper, magazine *etc*.

cir'cumference *n* (the length of) the outside line of a circle.

circumlo'cution *n* a roundabout way of saying something.

circum'navigate *v* to sail round (*eg* the world). – *n* **circum'navigator**.

'**circumscribe** *v* to draw a line round; to lay down limits (*eg* for a person's actions), restrict. – *n* **circum'scription**.

'**circumspect** *adj* wary, looking carefully at circumstances, cautious. – *n* **circum'spection** caution.

'**circumstance** *n* a condition (of time, place, manner *etc*) which affects a person, an action or an event; (*pl*) the state of a person's (financial) affairs. – *v* **circum'stantiate** to prove by giving details. – *n* **circumstantial evidence** evidence which points to a conclusion but does not give proof of it.

circum'vent *v* to get round (a difficulty); to outwit. – *n* **circum'vention**.

'**circus** *n* a travelling company of performing animals, acrobats, clowns *etc*; a large arena for sports events.

'**cirrus** *n* a fleecy kind of cloud.

'**cistern** *n* a tank for holding or storing water.

'**citadel** *n* fortress, *esp* one in a city.

cite *v* to quote as an example or as proof; to summon a person to appear in court. – *n* **ci'tation** something quoted; a summons to appear in court; official recognition of an achievement, a brave act *etc*.

'**citizen** *n* one who lives in a city, town or state. – *n* '**citizenship** the rights of or state of being a citizen.

'**citric acid** *n* a type of sharp-tasting acid

found in citrus fruits.

'**citron** *n* a type of fruit similar to a lemon.

'**citrus fruit** *n* any one of certain fruits including the orange, lemon and lime.

'**city** *n* a large town; a town with a cathedral: – *pl* '**cities**. – **the City** that part of London regarded as the centre of business.

'**civic** *adj* having to do with a city or a citizen. – *npl* '**civics** the study of one's duties as a citizen.

'**civil** *adj* of the ordinary people of a country, not its armed forces; polite. – *ns* **ci'vilian** one who is not in the armed forces; **ci'vility** politeness, good manners. – *ns* **civil engineer** an engineer who plans bridges, roads *etc*; **civil law** law concerned with the rights of a citizen, not concerned with criminal acts; **civil list** the expenses of the king's or queen's household; **civil marriage** a marriage which does not take place in church; **civil rights** the rights of a citizen; **civil service** the paid administrative officials of the country who are not in the armed forces; **civil war** war between citizens of a country.

'**civilize** *v* to bring (a people) under a regular system of laws, education *etc* from a primitive state. – *adj* '**civilized** living under such a system; not savage. – *n* **civili'zation** making or becoming civilized; life under a civilized system; the civilized nations as a whole.

clad *adj* clothed (in).

claim *v* to demand as a right; to state as a truth, assert (that). – Also *n*. – *n* '**claimant** one who makes a claim.

clairvoyance [klār'voiəns] *n* the supposed power to see into the future or into the world of spirits. – *n, adj* **clair'voyant**.

clam *n* a type of large shellfish with two shells hinged together.

'**clamber** *v* to climb awkwardly or with difficulty.

'**clammy** *adj* moist and sticky.

clamour ['klamər] *n* a loud, continuous noise or outcry. – *v* to cry aloud; to make a loud demand (for). – *adj* '**clamorous** noisy.

clamp *n* a piece of timber, iron *etc* used to fasten things together. – *v* to bind with a clamp. – **clamp down on** to stop (something, *eg* vandalism) by forceful action.

clan *n* (in Scotland) a tribe, or a number of families, under a chieftain *usu* having the same surname. – *adj* '**clannish** loyal to one another, like the members of a clan. – *n* '**clansman** a

member of a clan.

clandestine [klan'destin] *adj* hidden, secret, underhand.

clang *v* to make a loud, deep, ringing sound. – Also *n*.

clank *n* a sound like that made by metal hitting metal. – Also *v*.

clap *n* the noise made by the sudden striking together of two things (*esp* the hands); a burst of sound, *esp* thunder. – *v* to strike noisily together (*esp* the hands to show pleasure); to put or place suddenly. *Clap him in jail*: – *pt* **clapped**. – *n* '**clapper** the tongue of a bell. – *n* '**claptrap** meaningless words, nonsense.

'**claret** *n* a type of red wine.

'**clarify** *v* to make clear and understandable; to make (*eg* a liquid) clear and pure: – *pt* '**clarified**.

clari'net *n* a type of musical wind instrument, *usu* of wood. – *n* **clari'nettist** one who plays the clarinet.

'**clarion** *n* (*old*) a kind of trumpet; a shrill, rousing noise. – *n* **clarion call** a loud, clear call to action.

'**clarity** *n* clearness.

clash *n* a loud noise, as of the striking together of weapons; a disagreement or fight: – *pl* '**clashes**. – *v* to bang noisily together; to disagree; (of events) to take place at the same time; (*usu* with **with**) not to look well together. *The two shades of red clashed with each other*.

clasp *n* a hook *etc* for fastening; a fastening for the hair; a handshake; an embrace. – *v* to hold closely; to grasp; to fasten.

class *n* a rank or order of persons or things; a number of schoolchildren or students who are taught together; (of animals, plants *etc*) a group of different kinds, all of which have something in common: – *pl* '**classes**. – *v* to place in a class; to arrange in some order. – *v* '**classify** to arrange in classes; to put into a class or category: – *pt* '**classified**. – *n* **classifi'cation**.

'**classic** *n* any great writer, book or other work of art; (*pl*) (the study of) ancient Greek and Latin writers' works. – *adjs* '**classic** excellent; standard: *the classic example*; simple and elegant in style; '**classical** of a classic or the classics; (of music) serious, not light.

'**clatter** *n* noise as of plates *etc* banged together.

clause [klöz] *n* a part of a sentence containing a finite verb; a part of a will, act of parliament *etc*.

claustrophobia [klöstrə'föbiə] *n* an abnormal fear of enclosed spaces. –

adj **claustro'phobic**.

claw *n* one of the hooked nails of an animal or bird; the foot of an animal or bird with hooked nails. – *v* to scratch or tear.

clay *n* soft, sticky earth, different kinds of which are used in making pottery, bricks *etc*. – *adj* **'clayey**.

'claymore *n* (*hist*) a a kind of large sword once used by the Scottish Highlanders.

clean *adj* free from dirt; pure; neat; complete: *a clean break*. – *adv* completely. *He got clean away*. – *v* to make clean, or free from dirt. – *n* **'cleaner** one whose job is to clean; something which cleans. – *adv* **'cleanly**. – *ns* **cleanliness** ['klenlinəs]; **cleanness** ['klennis].

cleanse [klenz] *v* to make clean.

clear *adj* bright, undimmed; free from mist or cloud; transparent; free from difficulty or hindrance; easy to see or hear or understand; after deductions and charges have been made: *clear profit*; without a stain; without touching, without being caught by: *clear of the rocks*: *clear of the enemy*. – *v* to make clear; to empty: *clear the streets of snow*; to free from blame; to leap over (without touching); (of the sky, weather) to become bright. – *ns* **'clearance** act of clearing; **'clearing** land free of trees; **'clearness**. – *adj* **'clear-'cut** distinct, obvious. – **clear out, clear off** to go away.

cleave *v* to divide, split; to crack; to stick (to): – *pt* **clove, cleft**, *pp* **'cloven, cleft**. – *ns* **'cleavage** the act of splitting; the way in which two things are split or divided; **'cleaver** that which cleaves, a chopper.

clef *n* a musical sign fixing the pitch of the notes.

cleft *n* an opening made by splitting; a crack. – *v* see **cleave**.

cleg *n* a type of horsefly.

'clematis *n* a flowering, climbing shrub.

'clement *adj* mild; merciful. – *n* **'clemency** readiness to forgive; mercy.

clench *v* to press firmly together. *He clenched his teeth.*

'clergy *n* the ministers of the Christian religion. – *ns* **'clergyman, 'cleric** one of the clergy, a minister.

clerk [klärk, (*US*) klərk] *n* one who works in an office, writing letters, keeping accounts *etc*. – *v* to act as clerk. – *adj* **clerical** ['klerikəl] of office work; of the clergy.

'clever *adj* quick in learning and understanding; skilful. –

n **'cleverness**.

cliché ['klēshā] *n* something (*esp* an idea, phrase *etc*) that has been used too much and has little meaning.

click *n* a short, sharp sound. – Also *v*.

client ['klɪənt] *n* a customer of a shopkeeper *etc*; one who goes to a lawyer *etc* for advice. – *n* **clientele** [klēon'tel] the customers of a lawyer, shopkeeper *etc*.

cliff *n* a very steep, rocky slope, *esp* one by the sea.

'climate *n* the weather conditions (heat, cold, rain, wind *etc*) of a place or country; the conditions (*eg* economic) in a country *etc*. – *adj* **cli'matic**.

'climax *n* (of events *etc*) the point of greatest interest, feeling or importance: – *pl* **'climaxes**.

climb [klim] *v* to go to the top of; to go up using the hands or feet or both; to slope upward. – *n* an act of climbing; a place for climbing. – *n* **'climber** one who climbs; a plant which climbs up other plants, walls *etc*.

clinch *v* to grasp tightly; to settle (an argument, bargain *etc*). – *n* (in boxing) a position in which the boxers hold each other with their arms; a passionate embrace: – *pl* **'clinches**.

cling *v* to stick or hang on (to): – *pt* **clung**.

'clinic *n* a place or part of a hospital where a particular kind of medical advice or treatment is given. – *adj* **'clinical** of a clinic; based on observation: *clinical medicine*; objective, cool and unemotional: *a clinical view of the situation*.

clink *n* a ringing sound. – Also *v*.

'clinker *n* the waste stuff when iron is smelted or coal burnt.

clip *v* to cut (off); to fasten with a clip. – *n* the thing clipped off; a small fastener (*eg* for paper); (*coll*) a smart blow. – *n* **'clipper** a fast-sailing vessel; (*pl*) tool for clipping.

clique [klēk] *n* a small group of people who help each other but keep others at a distance.

cloak *n* a loose outer garment; something which hides: *cloak of darkness*. – *v* to cover as with a cloak; to hide. – *n* **'cloakroom** a place where coats, hats *etc* may be left for a time.

cloche [klosh] *n* a transparent frame for protecting plants: – *pl* **'cloches**.

clock *n* a machine for measuring time. – *adj* **'clockwise** turning or moving in the same direction as the hands of a clock. – *adj, n* **'clockwork** (worked by) machinery such as that of a clock. –

clock in, clock out (or **on, off**) to record one's time of arrival or departure (*usu* at one's place of work). – **like clockwork** smoothly, without difficulties.

clod *n* a thick lump, *esp* of turf; a stupid man. – *n* **'clodhopper** a stupid clumsy person. – *n* **'clodhopping**.

clog *n* a shoe with a wooden sole. – *v* to block (pipes *etc*): – *pt* **clogged**.

'cloister *n* a covered-in walk in a monastery or convent; a monastery or convent. – *adj* **'cloistered** shut up in a monastery *etc*; sheltered.

close[1] *adj* near in time, place *etc*; shut up, with no opening; without fresh air, stuffy; narrow, confined; mean; secretive; beloved, very dear: *a close friend*; decided, won by a small amount: *a close contest*. – *n* a narrow passage off a street; the gardens, walks *etc* near a cathedral. – *n* **'closeness**. – *n* **'close-up** a film or photograph taken very near the subject.

close[2] [klōz] *v* to shut; to finish; to come closer to and fight (with). – *n* the end. – *n* **closure** ['klōzhər] the act of closing. – *ns* **closed-circuit television** a system of television cameras and receivers for private use (as in shops *etc*); **closed shop** a place of work where only members of a (particular) trade union are employed.

closet ['klozit] *n* (*US*) a cupboard. – *v* to take into a room *etc* for a private conference. – **closeted with** in private conference with.

closure *see* **close**[2].

clot *n* a lump or thickening that forms in some liquids (*eg* blood, cream). – *v* to form into clots: – *pt* **'clotted**.

cloth *n* woven material of cotton, wool, linen, silk *etc*; a piece of this; a table-cover.

clothes [klōdhz] *npl* things worn to cover the body and limbs (as shirt, trousers, skirt *etc*); bedclothes. – *v* **clothe** to put clothes on; to provide with clothes. *He has barely enough money to clothe the children*; to cover. – *n* **'clothing** clothes.

cloud *n* a mass of tiny drops of water or ice floating in the sky; a great number or quantity of anything small in the air (*eg* locusts, dust). – *v* to blot out, hide or become dark, as with a cloud. – *adjs* **'clouded; 'cloudless; 'cloudy** darkened with clouds; not clear or transparent. – *n* **'cloudburst** a sudden heavy fall of rain.

clout *n* (*coll*) a blow. – *v* (*coll*) to hit.

clove *n* a flower bud of the clove tree, used as a spice; a small section of a bulb of garlic *etc*. – *v* *see* **cleave**.

'cloven-'hoofed *adj* having the hoof divided, as the ox, sheep *etc*.

'clover *n* a type of field plant with leaves *usu* in three parts, common in pastures. – **in clover** in luxury.

clown [klown] *n* a comedian with a painted face and comical clothes in a circus; a fool. – *n* **'clowning** silly or comical behaviour. – *adj* **'clownish** like a clown; awkward.

cloy *v* (of *eg* something sweet) to become unpleasant when too much is taken. – *adj* **'cloying**.

club *n* a heavy stick; a bat or stick used in certain games, *esp* golf; a group of people who meet for study, games, entertainment *etc*; the place where these people meet sometimes provided with refreshments, entertainment *etc*; (*pl*) one of the four suits in playing-cards. – *v* to beat with a club: – *pt* **clubbed**. – **club together** (of a group of people) to put money into a joint fund for some purpose.

cluck *n* a sound like that made by a hen. – Also *v*.

clue [klōō] *n* any sign or piece of evidence that helps to solve a mystery, problem *etc*.

clump *n* a cluster of trees or shrubs. – *v* to walk heavily.

clumsy ['klumzi] *adj* awkward in movement or actions; tactless, not skilfully carried out: *a clumsy apology*: – *comp* **'clumsier**, *superl* **'clumsiest**. – *n* **'clumsiness**.

clung *see* **cling**.

'cluster *n* a bunch; a crowd. – *v* to group together in clusters.

clutch *v* to hold firmly; to seize or grasp. – *n* a grasp; part of a motor-car engine used in changing the gears: – *pl* **'clutches**.

'clutter *n* a collection (of objects) in a crowded or confused state; disorder, confusion, untidiness. – *v* to crowd together untidily; (with **up**) to fill or cover in an untidy, disordered way.

cō- *prefix* joint, working *etc* with as in **'co-'author, 'co-'driver**.

coach *n* a bus for long-distance travel; a large, closed, four-wheeled horse carriage; a railway carriage; a private teacher, *esp* one who trains sportsmen: – *pl* **'coaches**. – *v* to prepare (someone) for an examination, sports contest *etc*.

coagulate [kō'agūlāt] *v* to (cause to) become a thickened mass (as when milk goes sour or blood clots).

coal *n* a black substance (the wood of prehistoric trees *etc*) dug out of the earth and used for burning, making gas *etc*. – *ns* '**coalfield** a district where there is coal to be mined; **coal gas** the mixture of gases, obtained from coal, used for lighting and heating; '**coalmine** a mine from which coal is dug.

coalesce [kōə'les] *v* to come together and unite.

coalition [kōə'lishən] *n* a joining together of different parts or parties.

coarse *adj* not fine in texture *etc*, rough; harsh; vulgar. – *v* '**coarsen** to make coarse. – *n* '**coarseness**.

coast *n* the side or border of land next to the sea. – *v* to sail along or near a coast; to move without the use of any power (as downhill on a bike, car *etc*). – *adj* '**coastal**. – *n* '**coastguard** one who acts as a guard along the coast to prevent smuggling and help those in danger in boats.

coat *n* an outer garment with sleeves; hair or wool (of an animal); a covering (*eg* paint). – *v* to cover with a coat or layer. – *n* '**coating** a covering. – **coat of arms** the badge or crest of a family.

coax *v* to get (someone) to do what is wanted without using force.

cob *n* a head of corn, wheat *etc*; a male swan.

cobalt ['kōbölt] *n* an element, a silvery metal; a blue colouring got from it.

'**cobble** *n* a rounded stone once used in paving roads. – Also '**cobblestone**. – *v* to mend (shoes); to repair, patch roughly or hurriedly. – *n* '**cobbler** one who mends shoes.

'**cobra** *n* a type of poisonous snake, found in India and Africa.

'**cobweb** *n* a spider's web.

co'caine *n* a type of drug used to deaden pain.

'**cochineal** *n* a scarlet dye, used to colour food, made from the dried bodies of certain insects.

cock *n* the male of most kinds of bird, *esp* the male of the farmyard hen; a tap or valve for controlling the flow of a liquid *etc*; a hammer-like part of a gun which, when the trigger is pulled, fires the shot; a small heap (of hay). – *v* to draw back the cock of a gun; to set upright (ears *etc*); to tilt to one side (*eg* one's head). – *adj* '**cocky** conceited, self-confident. – *ns* '**cockerel** a young cock; '**cocker spaniel** a breed of small spaniel; '**cockpit** the space for the pilot or driver in an aeroplane, small boat or racing car; a pit or enclosed space where game cocks fight; '**cockroach** a

type of crawling insect: – *pl* '**cockroaches**; '**cockscomb** the comb or crest on a cock's head; a fop, a conceited person. – *adj* '**cock'sure** quite sure, often without cause. – *n* '**cocktail** a mixed alcoholic drink.

coc'kade *n* a knot of ribbons or something similar worn on the hat.

cocka'too *n* a kind of parrot.

'**cockatrice** *n* (*myth*) a monster like a cock with a dragon's tail.

cockerel *see* **cock**.

'**cockle** *n* a type of shellfish. – *n* '**cockleshell** the shell of a cockle.

'**cockney** *n* one born in the East End of London, *esp* one born within the sound of Bow Bells; the way of speaking in this area: – *pl* '**cockneys**. – Also *adj*.

'**cocoa** *n* a drink made from the ground seeds of the cacao tree.

'**coconut** *n* the large, hard-shelled nut of a type of palm tree.

co'coon *n* a covering or case of silk spun by the larva (grub) of certain insects to protect it while it turns into a butterfly, moth *etc*.

cod *n* a fish much used as food, found in the northern seas.

'**coddle** *v* to treat as an invalid, pamper, over-protect.

code *n* a way of signalling or sending secret messages, using words, letters *etc* agreed on beforehand; a book or collection of laws, rules *etc*. – *v* '**codify** to arrange in an orderly way, classify: – *pt* '**codified**.

'**codicil** *n* a note added to a will or treaty.

coeducation ['kōedū'kāshən] *n* the education of boys and girls together. – *adj* '**coedu'cational**.

coelacanth ['sēləkanth] *n* a type of primitive fish.

co'erce *v* to make (to do), to compel. – *n* **coercion** [kō'ərshən]. – *adj* **co'ercive** using force.

co'ēval *adj* of the same age or time.

coexist ['kōig'zist] *v* to exist at the same time. – *n* '**coex'istence**. – *adj* '**coex'istent**.

'**coffee** *n* a drink made from the ground beans or seeds of the coffee shrub; a pale brown colour.

'**coffer** *n* a chest for holding money, gold *etc*. – *n* '**coffer-dam** a watertight dam placed in a river inside which the foundations of a bridge are built.

'**coffin** *n* the box in which a dead body is buried or cremated.

cog *n* a tooth on a wheel. – *n* '**cogwheel** a toothed wheel.

'**cōgent** *adj* (of speaking or writing) convincing, having the power to make people believe what is said. – *n* '**cogency**.

'**cogitate** *v* to think carefully. – *n* **cogi'tation**.

cognac ['konyak] *n* a kind of French brandy.

'**cognizance** *n* awareness, notice. – **take cognizance of** to take notice of, take into consideration.

co'here *v* to stick together. – *n* **co'herence** connection (between thoughts, ideas *etc*). – *adj* **co'herent** sticking together; clear and logical in thought or speech. – *n* **co'hesion** the act of sticking together. – *adj* **co'hesive**.

'**cohort** *n* (*hist*) a tenth part of a Roman legion.

coiffure [kwa'fūr] *n* a style of hairdressing.

coil *v* to wind in rings, to twist. – *n* a coiled arrangement (of rope *etc*).

coin *n* a piece of stamped metal used as money. – *v* to make metal into money; to make up (a new word *etc*). – *n* '**coinage** the act of coining; coins; the system of coins used in a country; a newly-made word.

coincide [kōin'sīd] *v* (sometimes with **with**) to be like or the same as. *Their interests coincide. His story coincides with hers*; (sometimes with **with**) to happen at the same time as. *Her arrival coincided with his departure.* – *n* **coincidence** [kō'insidəns] the happening of one thing at the same time as another, by chance or without planning. – *adj* **coinci'dental**.

coir *n* outside fibre of the coconut.

coke *n* a type of fuel made by heating coal till the gas is driven out.

colander ['kuləndər] *n* a kind of bowl with small holes in it for straining vegetables *etc*.

cōld *adj* low in temperature; lower in temperature than is comfortable; causing shivering; unfriendly. – *n* the state of being cold or of feeling the coldness of one's surroundings; a disease, due to germs, causing shivering, running nose *etc*. – *n* '**coldness**. – *adj* '**cold-'blooded** (of fishes *etc*) having cold blood; cruel; lacking in feelings. – *ns* **cold feet** lack of courage; **cold war** a struggle between nations for power without the use of open warfare.

'**cole-slaw** *n* a salad made from raw cabbage.

'**colic** *n* a severe stomach pain.

col'laborate *v* to work together (with); to work with (an enemy) to betray one's country *etc*. – *ns* **col'labo'ration**; **col'laborator**.

collage [ko'läzh] *n* a design made of scraps of paper and other odds and ends pasted on paper *etc*.

col'lapse *v* to fall or break down; to cave or fall in; to become unable to continue. – Also *n.* – *adj* **col'lapsible** (of a chair *etc*) able to be folded up.

'**collar** *n* a band, strip *etc* worn round the neck by man or animals; the part of an article of clothing at the neck. – *v* (*coll*) to seize. – *n* '**collarbone** either of two bones joining the breast bone and shoulderblade.

col'late *v* to examine and compare. – *n* **col'lation** a light (often cold) meal; a comparison.

collateral [kə'latərəl] *adj* side by side; parallel.

colleague ['kolēg] *n* a person who does the same kind of work as another or who works in the same firm *etc* as another.

col'lect *v* to bring together; to gather together. – *adj* **col'lected** gathered together; (of persons) calm. – *n* **col'lection** the act of collecting; a number of objects or people; money gathered at a meeting, *esp* a church service. – *adj* **col'lective** acting together; of several things or persons, not of one. – *n* **col'lector** one who collects (tickets, money, stamps *etc*).

college ['kolij] *n* (a building used by) a group of people gathered together to learn and study; a building which is part of a university *etc*. – *adj* **col'lēgiate**.

col'lide *v* (of moving things *etc*) to come together with great force. – *n* **col'lision** a violent meeting of two moving things, *esp* vehicles; a disagreement, clash (of interests *etc*).

'**collie** *n* a breed of long-haired dog with a pointed nose, a sheepdog.

collier ['koliər] *n* one who works in a coalmine; a coal ship. – *n* '**colliery** a coalmine: – *pl* '**collieries**.

col'lōquial *adj* used in everyday talk but not in very correct writing or speaking. – *n* **col'loquialism** an example of colloquial speech.

collusion [kə'lōōzhən] *n* a secret agreement (*usu* for some dishonest purpose).

'**cōlon** *n* in punctuation, the mark (:), used to show a break in a sentence; a part of the bowel.

colonel ['kərnl] *n* an officer next below brigadier who has command of a regiment.

colon'nade n a row of columns or pillars.

'colony n a group of settlers or the settlement they make in another country; any group of people, animals *etc* of the same type living together: – *pl* **'colonies**. – *adj* **co'lōnial** of colonies abroad. – n **'colonist** a settler. – *v* **'colonize** to set up a colony in.

co'lossal *adj* huge, enormous. – n **co'lossus** anything enormous (*eg* a huge statue).

colour, (*US*) **color** ['kulər] n a quality that an object shows in the light, as redness, blueness *etc*; any shade or tint; vividness, brightness; (*pl*) a flag or standard. – *v* to put colour on; to blush; to influence. *Unemployment coloured his attitude to life.* – *adjs* **'coloured** having colour; not white-skinned; **'colourful** brightly coloured; vivid, interesting. – n **'colouring** the putting on of colours; the effect of combining colours; complexion. – *adj* **'colourless** without colour; dull. – *adj* **'colour-blind** unable to distinguish certain colours (*eg* red and green). – **off colour** unwell.

cōlt n a young horse.

column ['koləm] n a stone (or wooden) pillar standing upright; anything of a long or tall, narrow shape; a line of print, figures *etc* stretching from top to bottom of a page; an arrangement (of troops, ships *etc*) one behind the other.

'cōma n unconsciousness lasting a long time. – *adj* **'comatose** in or of a coma; drowsy, sluggish.

comb [kōm] n a toothed instrument for separating, smoothing or cleaning hair, wool, flax *etc*; the crest of certain birds; a collection of cells for honey. – *v* to arrange, smoothe or clean with a comb; to search (a place) thoroughly.

'combat v to fight or struggle against. – n a fight or struggle. – n, *adj* **'combatant** (one who is) fighting. – *adj* **'combative** quarrelsome.

com'bine v to join together. – n **'combine** a number of traders *etc* who join together. – n **combi'nation** a joining together of things or people; a set of things or people combined; the series of letters or figures dialled to open a safe; (*pl*) an article of underwear for the body and legs. – n **'combine 'harvester** a machine that both cuts and threshes crops.

com'bustible *adj* liable to catch fire and burn. – n anything that will catch fire. – n **com'bustion** burning.

come [kum] v to move towards this place (opposite of **go**). *Come here!*; to draw near. *Christmas is coming*; to arrive. *We'll have tea when you come*; to happen, occur. *The index comes at the end of the book*: – *pt* **came**, *pp* **come**. – **come about** to happen; **come across**, **come upon** to meet, find accidentally; **come by** to obtain; **come into** to get (by inheriting); **come of age** to reach the age at which one becomes an adult for legal purposes; **come round**, **come to** to recover (from a faint *etc*); **come upon** *see* **come across**; **to come** in the future.

comedy ['komədi] n a play of light-hearted or amusing kind (opposite of **tragedy**): – *pl* **'comedies**. – n **co'mēdian** a performer who tells jokes, acts in comedy *etc*.

comely ['kumli] *adj* pleasing, good-looking. – n **'comeliness**.

'comet n a kind of star which has a tail of light.

comfort ['kumfərt] v to help, soothe (someone in pain or distress). – n ease, quiet enjoyment; state of being comfortable; anything that makes one happier or more at ease. – *adj* **'comfortable** at ease, free from trouble, pain, hardship *etc*; giving comfort.

'comic *adj* of comedy; funny. – n someone amusing, *esp* a professional comedian; a (comic) picture paper. – *adj* **'comical** funny, amusing. – n **comic strip** a strip of small pictures showing stages in an adventure.

'comma n in punctuation, the mark (,).

com'mand v to give an order; to be in charge of; to look over or down upon (a view *etc*). – n an order; control. – *ns* **comman'dant** an officer who has command of a place or of troops; **com'mander** one who commands; in the navy, an officer next in rank below captain. – *adj* **com'manding** powerful; having a wide view. – n **com'mandment** an order or command.

comman'deer v to seize (something) *esp* for the use of an army.

com'mando n (a soldier serving in) a unit of the army trained for hard or dangerous tasks: – *pl* **com'mandoes**.

com'memorate v to bring to memory by some solemn act; to serve as a memorial of. – n **commemo'ration**.

com'mence v to begin. – n **com'mencement**.

com'mend v to praise; to give into the care of. – *adj* **com'mendable** praiseworthy. – n **commen'dation** praise. – *adj* **com'mendatory**

praising.

commensurate [kə'menshərət] *adj* (with **with**) equal in size, importance *etc*, in proportion to.

'**comment** *n* a remark or series of remarks; a criticism. – Also *v*. – *ns* '**commentary** a description of an event *etc* (by one who is watching it) (also **running commentary**); a set of explanatory notes for a book *etc*: – *pl* '**commentaries**; '**commentator** one who gives or writes a commentary.

'**commerce** *n* the buying and selling of goods between people or nations; trade, dealings. – *adj* **com'mercial** of commerce; (of radio, TV *etc*) paid for by advertisements.

commiserate [kə'mizərāt] *v* to sympathize (with). – *n* **commise'ration** pity.

commis'sar *n* (in USSR) the head of a government department.

commis'sariat *n* that part of an army or other organization that looks after the food supply.

com'mission *n* the act of committing; a warrant or document giving authority to an officer in the armed forces; an order *esp* for a work of art; a fee for doing business *etc* on another's behalf; a body of persons appointed to investigate something. – *v* to give a commission or power to. – *ns* **commissio'naire** a uniformed doorkeeper; **com'missioner** one who represents high authority in a district *etc*; a member of a commission. – **in** (**out of**) **commission** in (not in) use.

com'mit *v* to give or hand over, to entrust; (with **oneself** *etc*) to promise; to do (something *usu* wrong): *commit a crime*: – *pt* **com'mitted**. – *ns* **com'mitment** a promise; a task that must be done; **com'mittal** the act of committing. – *adj* **com'mitted** pledged to support (something): *a committed Communist*. – *n* **com'mittee** a number of people chosen from a larger body to attend to some special business.

com'modious *adj* roomy, spacious.

com'modity *n* an article to be bought or sold; (*pl*) **com'modities** goods, produce.

'**commodore** *n* an officer next above a captain in the navy.

'**common** *adj* shared by all or by many; seen or happening often; ordinary; without special rank. – *n* land belonging to the people of a town, parish *etc*. – *n* '**commoner** one who is not a noble. – *n* '**Commons** (**House of Commons**) the lower House of Parliament. – *ns* **common law** unwritten law based on custom; **Common Market** an association of certain European countries to establish free trade (without duty, tariffs *etc*) among them; **common noun** a name for any one of a class of things (opposite of **proper noun**). – *adj* '**commonplace** ordinary. – *ns* '**common-room** in a school *etc*, a sitting-room for the use of a group; **common sense** practical good sense; '**commonwealth** an association of self-governing states.

com'motion *n* a disturbance *esp* among people.

'**commune** *n* a group of people living together, sharing work *etc*. – *v* **com'mune** to talk together. – *adj* '**communal** common, shared.

com'municate *v* to make known, tell; to give, pass on. *He communicated his fear to the rest*; to get in touch (with); to have a connecting door. – *adj* **com'municable** able to be passed on to others: *a communicable disease*. – *n* **communi'cation** an act or means of conveying information; a message; a way of passing from place to place. – *adj* **com'municative** willing to give information, talkative.

communiqué [kə'mūnikā] *n* an official announcement.

Com'mūnion *n* in the Christian Church, the celebration of the Lord's supper; **com'munion** the act of sharing (thoughts, feelings *etc*), fellowship.

'**communism** *n* the kind of socialism developed in Russia or China where industry is controlled by the state. – *n* '**communist** of communism; one who believes in communism.

com'mūnity *n* a group of people living in one place; the public in general: – *pl* **com'munities**.

com'mute *v* to travel regularly between two places *esp* to work (in a city *etc*) from one's home; to change (a punishment) for one less severe. – *n* **com'muter** one who travels regularly to work from his home in a different place.

com'pact *adj* fitted or packed closely, neatly together. – *n* '**compact** a bargain or agreement.

com'panion *n* someone or something that accompanies; a friend. – *adj* **com'panionable** friendly. – *n* **com'panionship** friendship; the act of accompanying. – *n* **com'panionway**

on a ship, a staircase from deck to cabin.

company ['kumpəni] *n* a gathering of persons; a number of persons who have joined together for trade *etc*, a business firm; part of a regiment; a ship's crew; companionship: – *pl* '**companies**.

com'pare *v* to set things together to see how far they are or are not alike; to liken. – *adjs* '**comparable; comparative** [kəm'parətiv] judged by comparing with something else: *a comparative improvement*; (*gram*) the degree of adjective or adverb between positive and superlative (*eg* blacker, better, more courageous). – *n* **com'parison** the act of comparing. – **beyond compare** much better than all rivals.

com'partment *n* a separate part or division (*eg* of a railway carriage).

compass ['kumpəs] *n* an instrument with a magnetized needle for showing direction; (*usu pl*) '**compasses** an instrument (made up of a fixed leg and a movable leg) for drawing circles.

compassion [kəm'pashən] *n* pity for another's suffering; mercy. – *adj* **com'passionate** pitying, merciful.

com'patible *adj* able to live with, agree with *etc*. – *n* **com'pati'bility**.

com'patriot *n* a fellow-countryman.

com'pel *v* to force (someone to do something): – *pt* **com'pelled**.

'**compensate** *v* to make up for wrong or damage done, *esp* by giving money. – *n* **compen'sation** something (*usu* money) given to make up for wrong or damage.

compère ['kompȧr] *n* one who introduces different acts of an entertainment. – Also *v*.

com'pete *v* to try to beat others (in a race *etc*). – *ns* **compe'tition; competitor** [kəm'petitər] one who competes; a rival. – *adj* **com'petitive** (of sport *etc*) based on competitions; (of a person) fond of competing.

'**competent** *adj* capable, efficient; skilled; properly trained or qualified. – *n* '**competence**.

com'pile *v* to make (a book *etc*) from information that one has collected. – *ns* **compi'lation; com'piler**.

com'plăcent *adj* satisfied (with oneself). – *ns* **com'placence; com'placency**.

com'plain *v* to express dissatisfaction (about something); to grumble. – *n* **com'plaint** a statement of one's dissatisfaction, sorrow *etc*; an illness. *The common cold is not a serious complaint.*

'**complement** *n* that which completes or

fills up; the full number or quantity needed to fill (something); the angle that must be added to a given angle to make up a right angle. – *adj* **comple'mentary** completing; together making up a whole; (of an angle) making up a right angle.

com'plete *adj* having nothing missing; finished; whole. – *v* to finish; to make perfect. – *ns* **com'pleteness; com'pletion** the act of completing.

'**complex** *adj* made up of many parts; complicated, difficult. – *n* a set of repressed emotions and ideas which affect a person's behaviour; an exaggerated reaction (to something), an obsession: *a complex about her weight*; a group of related buildings *etc*: *a shopping complex* : – *pl* '**complexes**. – *n* **com'plexity**: – *pl* **com'plexities**

com'plexion *n* the colour or look of the skin of the face; appearance.

compliance *see* **comply**.

'**complicate** *v* to make difficult. – *adj* '**complicated** difficult to understand; detailed. – *n* **compli'cation** a (new) difficulty; a development (in an illness *etc*) which makes things worse.

com'plicity *n* a share in a crime or other misdeed.

'**compliment** *n* an expression of praise or flattery; (*pl*) good wishes. – *v* **compli'ment** to praise, to congratulate (on). – *adj* **compli'mentary** flattering, praising; given free: *a complimentary ticket*.

com'plȳ *v* (to agree) to do something that someone else orders or wishes: – *pt* **com'plied**. – *n* **com'pliance**. – *adj* **com'pliant** yielding, giving agreement.

com'pōnent *adj* forming one of the parts of a whole. – *n* a part (of a machine *etc*).

compose [kəm'pōz] *v* to put together or in order, to arrange, form; to create (a piece of music, a poem *etc*). – *adjs* **com'posed** quiet, calm; **composite** ['kompəzit] made up of parts. – *ns* **compo'sition** the act of composing; the thing composed, *esp* a piece of writing or music; a mixture of substances; **com'positor** a person who puts together the types for printing; **com'posure** calmness.

'**compost** *n* a gardener's mixture of natural manures.

'**compound** *adj* made up of a number of different parts; not simple. – *n* (in chemistry) a substance formed from two or more elements; an enclosure (round a building).

compre'hend *v* to understand; to

include. – *adj* **compre'hensible** able to be understood. – *n* **compre'hension** the act or power of understanding. – *adj* **compre'hensive** taking in or including much or all. – *n* **comprehensive school** a school providing all types of secondary education.

com'press *v* to press together; to force into a narrower or smaller space. – *n* **'compress** a folded cloth or pad used to create pressure on a part of the body or to reduce inflammation. – *n* **com'pression**.

comprise [kəm'priz] *v* to include, contain; to consist of.

'compromise ['komprəmiz] *n* a settlement, an agreement reached by both sides giving up something. – *v* to make a compromise; to put in a difficult or embarrassing position.

com'pulsion *n* a force driving a person to do a thing. – *adj* **com'pulsory** requiring to be done; forced upon one.

com'punction *n* regret.

com'pute *v* to count, calculate. – *n* **compu'tation** – *n* **com'puter** an electronic machine that carries out many stages of calculations and stores and sorts information of various kinds.

comrade ['komrid] *n* a companion, a friend.

con *v* to trick, play a confidence trick on. – *ns* **'con-man** one who (regularly) cons people; **'con-trick** a confidence trick.

'concave *adj* hollow or curved inwards (opposite of **convex**). – *n* **concavity** [kon'kavəti] a hollow.

con'ceal *v* to hide, keep secret. – *n* **con'cealment** the act of hiding; a hiding-place.

con'cede *v* to give (up), yield; to admit (the truth of something). *I concede that you may be right.*

conceit [kən'sēt] *n* a too high opinion of oneself or of one's abilities. – *adj* **con'ceited** having a very good opinion of oneself, vain. – *n* **con'ceitedness**.

conceive [kən'sēv] *v* to form in the mind, to imagine; to become pregnant. – *adj* **con'ceivable** able to be imagined.

'concentrate *v* to direct all one's attention or effort towards (something); to bring together to one place. – *adj* **'concentrated** (of an acid *etc*) made stronger or less dilute. – *n* **concen'tration**.

con'centric *adj* (*esp* of circles placed one inside the other) having the same point for centre.

'concept *n* a general idea about something. – *n* **con'ception** the act of conceiving; an idea.

con'cern *v* to have to do with; to make uneasy; to interest, to affect; (with **oneself** *etc*) to be interested or anxious. – *n* that which concerns; anxiety; a business. – *prep* **con'cerning** about: *concerning your inquiry.*

'concert *n* a musical entertainment, performance or show. – *adj* **con'certed** planned or practised together. – **in concert** together.

concertina [konsər'tēnə] *n* a type of musical wind instrument, with bellows and keys.

concerto [kən'chərtō] *n* a long piece of music for solo instrument with an accompaniment from an orchestra: – *pl* **con'certos**.

con'cession *n* a granting or allowing of something; that which is granted, allowed.

conch *n* a kind of sea-shell: – *pl* **'conches**.

con'ciliate *v* to win over (someone previously unfriendly or angry). – *n* **con'cili'ation**. – *adj* **con'ciliatory**.

concise [kən'sīs] *adj* brief, in a few words. – *n* **con'ciseness**.

conclude [kən'klōōd] *v* to end; to reach a decision or a judgement; to settle. – *adj* **con'cluding** last, final. – *n* **con'clusion** end; decision, judgement. – *adj* **con'clusive** settling, deciding: *conclusive proof.*

con'coct *v* to mix (a food or drink); to make up, invent: *concoct a story.* – *n* **con'coction**.

'concord *n* agreement.

concourse ['koŋkörs] *n* a crowd; a crowding together; a large open space in a building *etc*.

'concrete *adj* solid, real; made of concrete. – *n* a mixture of gravel, cement *etc* used in building.

con'cur *v* to agree: – *pt* **con'curred**. – *n* **con'currence**. – *adj* **con'current** happening *etc* together; agreeing.

con'cussion *n* temporary harm done to the brain when one receives a knock on the head.

condemn [kən'dem] *v* to blame; to give judgement against or to sentence to a certain punishment; to declare (houses *etc*) unfit for use. – *n* **condem'nation**. – *n* **condemned cell** a cell for a prisoner condemned to death.

con'dense *v* to make to go into a smaller space; (of steam, vapour) to turn to liquid. – *n* **conden'sation** the act of condensing; drops of liquid formed from vapour.

condescend [kondi'send] *v* to act towards someone as if one is better than he is; to make oneself humble. – *adj* **conde'scending**. – *n* **conde'scension**.

'**condiment** *n* something that seasons or flavours food, *esp* salt or pepper.

con'dition *n* the state in which anything is; something that must happen or be done before some other thing happens or is done; a term of or a point in a bargain, treaty *etc*. – *adj* **con'ditional** depending on certain things happening.

con'dole *v* to share another's sorrow, to sympathize. – *n* **con'dolence**.

con'done *v* to forgive, allow (an offence) to pass unchecked.

con'dūcive *adj* helping, favourable (to): *conducive to peace.*

con'duct *v* to lead, guide; to control, be in charge of, organize; to direct (an orchestra *etc*); to pass on, transmit (electricity *etc*); (with **oneself**) to behave. – *ns* '**conduct** act or method of controlling or organizing; behaviour; **con'duction** a passing on, transmission of heat, electricity *etc*; **con'ductor** one who directs an orchestra *etc*; one in charge of a bus *etc*: – *fem* **con'ductress**; something that transmits (heat, electricity *etc*).

conduit ['kondit] *n* a channel or pipe to carry water, electric wires *etc*.

cone *n* a shape or figure, round at the bottom and coming to a point; anything cone-shaped (*eg* a fir-cone). – *adj* **conical** ['konikəl] cone-shaped.

coney *see* **cony**.

con'fectioner *n* one who makes or sells sweets, cakes *etc*. – *n* **con'fectionery** sweets, cakes *etc*; the shop or business of a confectioner.

confederate [kən'fedərət] *adj* joined together by treaty. – *n* a person who has agreed to act with others (often for an evil purpose). – *ns* **con'federacy** a league, alliance: – *pl* **con'federacies**; **con'fede'ration** a union, a league (of states *etc*).

con'fer *v* to talk together; to give, grant: – *pt* **con'ferred**. – *n* '**conference** a meeting for discussion.

con'fess *v* to own up, to admit (*eg* that one has done wrong). – *adj* **con'fessed** admitted, not secret. – *n* **con'fession** owning up to (a crime or fault).

con'fetti *n* small pieces of coloured paper thrown at weddings or other celebrations.

con'fide *v* (with **in**) to tell (secrets *etc*) to; to hand over to someone's care. – *ns* **confidant** [konfi'dant] one trusted with a secret: – *fem* **confi'dante**; '**confidence** trust or belief; self-reliance; boldness; something told privately. – *adjs* '**confident** very sure; bold; **confi'dential** to be kept as a secret: *confidential information*; having to keep secrets: *confidential secretary*; **con'fiding** trusting. – *n* **confidence trick** a trick to get money *etc* from someone by first gaining his trust.

con'fine *v* to shut up, imprison; to keep within limits. – *npl* '**confines** limits. – *n* **con'finement** the state of being confined; imprisonment; (the time of) giving birth to a child.

con'firm *v* to make firm, strengthen; to make sure; to show to be true; to take into the Church. – *n* **confir'mation** a making sure; proof; the ceremony in which a person is made a full member of the Church. – *adj* **con'firmed** settled in a habit *etc*: *a confirmed bachelor.*

'**confiscate** *v* to take away, as a punishment. – *n* **confis'cation**.

confla'gration *n* a big fire.

'**conflict** *n* a struggle or contest; a battle. – *v* **con'flict** (of statements *etc*) to contradict each other. – *adj* **con'flicting**.

confluence ['konfloo͞ons] *n* a place where rivers join.

con'form *v* to follow the example of most other people (in behaviour, dress, religion *etc*). – *ns* **confor'mation** form, shape or structure; **con'formity** likeness; the act of conforming.

con'found *v* to puzzle, confuse.

confront [kən'frunt] *v* to face, meet (*eg* an enemy, a difficulty); to bring face to face (with). *He was confronted with the evidence.* – *n* **confron'tation**.

confuse [kən'fūz] *v* to mix up, to put in disorder; to mix up in the mind; to puzzle; to embarrass. – *n* **con'fusion**.

con'geal *v* to become solid *esp* by cooling; to freeze.

con'gēnial *adj* agreeable, pleasant.

con'genital *adj* (of a disease *etc*) present in a person from birth.

conger ['kongər] *n* a kind of large sea-eel.

con'gested *adj* overcrowded; clogged; (of a part of the body) too full of blood. – *n* **con'gestion** (of traffic *etc*) overcrowded condition; a gathering of too much blood in one part of the body.

conglomeration [kənglomə'rāshən] *n* a heap or collection.

con'gratūlate *v* to express one's joy (to a

person) at his success. – *n* **congratu-**
'lation (often in *pl*). – *adj* **con-**
'gratulatory.
congregate ['koŋgrigāt] *v* to come
together in a crowd. – *n* **congre'gation**
a gathering *esp* of people in a church.
congress ['koŋgres] *n* a large meeting of
persons from different places for
discussion: – *pl* **'congresses**; **'Con-**
gress the name given to the parliament
of the United States.
congruent ['koŋgrōōənt] *adj* (of triangles *etc*) exactly matching.
congruous ['koŋgrōōəs] *adj* suitable,
appropriate. – *n* **con'gruity**.
conical *see* **cone**.
'conifer *n* a cone-bearing tree. – *adj*
co'niferous.
con'jecture *n* a guess. – *v* to guess. – *adj*
con'jectural.
conjugal ['konjōōgəl] *adj* of marriage.
conjugate ['konjōōgāt] *v* to give the
different parts of a verb. – *n*
conju'gation.
con'junction *n* a word that joins
sentences, phrases *etc* (*eg* and, but); a
union, combination with. – **in con-**
junction with together with, acting
with.
conjuncti'vitis *n* a kind of inflammation
of the inside of the eyelid and surface of
the eye.
conjure ['kunjər] *v* to do tricks that seem
magical. – *n* **'conjuror** one who does
conjuring tricks.
'conker *n* a horse-chestnut, *esp* one used
in a game (**'conkers**) in which one tries
to hit one's opponent's chestnut.
con'nect *v* to join or fasten together. – *n*
con'nection something that connects;
a state of being connected; a train,
aeroplane *etc* which takes one on the
next part of one's journey; a friend,
relation *etc*. – **in connection with**
concerning.
'conning-tower *n* the place on a warship
or submarine from which orders for
steering are given.
con'nive *v* (with **at**) to take no notice of,
disregard (a misdeed *etc*). – *n*
con'nivance.
connoisseur [konə'sör] *n* one who has an
expert knowledge (of pictures, music,
wines *etc*).
conno'tation *n* a meaning; what is
suggested by a word in addition to its
simple meaning.
con'nubial *adj* of marriage.
conquer ['koŋkər] *v* to gain by force; to
overcome. – *ns* **'conqueror** one who
conquers; **conquest** ['koŋkwest] something won by force or effort; an act of

conquering.
conscience ['konshəns] *n* one's inward
sense of what is right and wrong. – *adj*
consci'entious careful and earnest in
one's   work   *etc*.   –   *n*
consci'entiousness.
conscious ['konshəs] *adj* aware of
oneself and one's surroundings, awake
(after being unconscious); aware,
knowing; deliberate, intentional. – *n*
'consciousness.
'conscript *n* a person who is obliged by
law to serve in the armed forces. – *v*
con'script to compel to serve (in the
armed forces). – *n* **con'scription**.
'consecrate *v* to set apart for a holy use. –
n **conse'cration**.
con'secutive *adj* coming in order, one
after the other.
con'sensus *n* an agreement (of opinion).
con'sent *v* to agree (to). – *n* agreement;
permission.
'consequence *n* that which comes after,
result; importance. – *adjs* **'consequent**
following as a result; **conse'quential**
following as a result; important.
con'serve *v* to keep from being wasted,
spoilt or lost. – *ns* **conser'vation** the
act of conserving (old buildings,
countryside, wild animals and flowers
etc); **conser'vationist** one who encourages and practises conservation. –
adj **con'servative** not liking changes;
(of a guess or estimate) moderate, not
exaggerated. – *n*, *adj* **Con'servative** (a
supporter) of the Conservative Party. –
n **con'servatory** a glass-house for
plants: – *pl* **con'servatories**. – *n*
Conservative Party one of the main
political parties of the UK.
con'sider *v* to think; to think about
(carefully); to think of as, regard as; to
pay attention to the wishes *etc* of
(someone). – *adjs* **con'siderable**
(fairly) large; important; **con'siderate**
thoughtful about others' wishes *etc*,
kind. – *n* **conside'ration** serious
thinking; thoughtfulness for others; a
small payment. – *prep* **con'sidering**
taking into account: *considering his age*.
consign [kən'sin] *v* to give into the care
of. – *n* **con'signment** a load (*eg* of
goods).
con'sist *v* to be made up (of). – *n*
con'sistency thickness or firmness;
the quality of (always) being the same:
– *pl* **con'sistencies**. – *adj* **con'sistent**
not changing, regular; (of statements
etc) not contradicting each other.
con'sole *v* to comfort, cheer up. – *n*
conso'lation something that makes
trouble *etc* more easy to bear.

con'solidate v to make or become solid or strong; to unite. – n **consoli'dation**.

'consonant n a letter of the alphabet that is not a vowel (eg b, c).

'consort n a husband or wife; a companion. – v **con'sort** to keep company (with).

con'spicūous adj clearly seen, noticeable.

con'spire v to plan or plot together. – ns **conspiracy** [kən'spirəsi] a plot by a group of people: – pl **con'spiracies**; **con'spirator** one who takes part in a conspiracy.

constable ['kunstəbl] n a policeman; (hist) a high officer of state or the keeper of a castle. – n **con'stabūlary** the police force.

'constant adj never stopping; never changing; faithful. – n **'constancy**. – adv **'constantly** always; often.

constel'lation n a group of stars.

conster'nation n dismay, astonishment.

consti'pation n too slow working of the bowels. – v **'constipate** to cause constipation.

'constitute v to set up, establish; to form or make up. – n **con'stituency** (the voters in) a district which has a member of parliament: – pl **con'stituencies**. – adj **con'stituent** making or forming. – n a necessary part; a voter in a constituency. – n **consti'tution** the way in which a thing is made up; the natural condition of a body with regard to strength, health etc; a set of rules, laws etc by which a country or body of people is governed. – adj **consti'tutional** of a constitution. – n a short walk for the sake of one's health.

con'strain v to force (a person) to act in a certain way. – n **con'straint** compulsion, force; embarrassment.

con'strict v to press together tightly, to cramp; to surround and squeeze.

con'struct v to build, make. – n **con'struction** the act of constructing; anything built; the arrangement of words in a sentence; meaning. – adj **con'structive** of construction; helping to improve: constructive criticism.

'consul n a person who looks after his country's affairs in a foreign country; in ancient Rome, a chief ruler. – adj **'consūlar**. – n **'consulate** the official residence of a consul; the duties and authority of a consul.

con'sult v to seek advice or information from. – n **con'sultant** one (esp a doctor) who gives professional or expert advice. – Also adj. – n **consul'tation** the act of consulting (for

expert advice). – n **consulting room** a room where a doctor etc sees his patients.

con'sume v to eat up; to use (up); to destroy. – n **con'sumer** one who buys, eats or uses (goods etc).

'consummate v to complete. – adj complete, perfect.

con'sumption n the act of consuming; the amount consumed; (old) tuberculosis.

'contact n touch; meeting; communication; an acquaintance, esp one who can be of help; a person who has been with someone suffering from an infectious disease. – v to get into contact with.

con'tāgious adj (of disease etc) spreading from person to person (esp by touch).

con'tain v to hold or have inside; to hold back: contain her anger. – n **con'tainer** a box, tin, jar etc for holding anything.

con'taminate v to make impure or dirty. – n **contami'nation**.

'contemplate v to look at or think about attentively; to intend. – n **contem'plation**.

con'temporary adj, n (of) a person living at or belonging to the same time.

con'tempt n complete lack of respect, scorn. – adjs **con'temptible** deserving scorn, worthless; **con'temptūous** scornful. – **contempt of court** deliberate disobedience to and disrespect for the law and those who carry it out.

con'tend v to struggle against; to hold firmly to a belief, maintain (that). – n **con'tention** an opinion strongly held; a quarrel, dispute. – adj **con'tentious** quarrelsome.

con'tent adj happy, satisfied. – n happiness, satisfaction. – v to make happy or to satisfy. – n **'content** (often pl) that which is contained in anything. – adj **con'tented** happy, content. – n **con'tentment** happiness, content.

contention, contentious see **contend**.

con'test v to fight for, argue against. – n **'contest** a fight, a competition. – n **con'testant** one who contests.

'context n the place in a book, speech etc to which a certain part belongs; the setting, background of an event etc.

con'tiguous adj touching, close. – n **conti'guity**.

'continent n one of the five great divisions of the earth's land surface (Europe, Asia, Africa, Australia, America). – adj **conti'nental** of or like a continent; European. – **the Continent** the mainland of Europe.

con'tingent adj depending (on something else). – *n* a batch, a group (*esp* of soldiers). – *n* **con'tingency** a chance happening: – *pl* **con'tingencies**.

continue [kən'tinū] *v* to keep on, go on (doing something). – *adj* **con'tinual** going on without stop. – *ns* **con'tinuance** the state of going on without interruption; **continu'ation** the act of carrying something farther or continuing; a part that continues, an extension; **conti'nuity** the state of having no gaps or breaks. – *adj* **con'tinuous** coming one after the other (without a gap or break).

con'tort *v* to twist or turn violently. – *ns* **con'tortion** a violent twisting; **con'tortionist** one who can twist his body violently.

contour ['kontoor] *n* (often *pl*) outline, shape. – *n* **contour line** a line drawn on a map through points all at the same height above sea-level.

'contraband *n* goods, legally forbidden to be brought into a country; smuggled goods. – Also *adj*.

contra'ception *n* the prevention of conceiving children. – *adj*, *n* **contra'ceptive** (of) a drug or device which prevents the conceiving of children.

con'tract *v* to become or make smaller; to bargain for; to promise in writing. – *ns* **'contract** a (written) agreement; **con'traction** a shortening; a shortened form (*esp* of a word); **con'tractor** one who promises to do work, or supply goods, at an arranged price.

contra'dict *v* to say the opposite of; to deny. – *n* **contra'diction**. – *adj* **contra'dictory**.

con'tralto *n* the deepest or lowest singing voice in women: – *pl* **con'traltos**.

con'traption *n* a machine, a device.

contrapuntal *see* **counterpoint**.

'contrary[1] *adj* opposite. – *n* the opposite. – **on the contrary** just the opposite.

con'trary[2] *adj* always doing or saying the opposite, perverse. – *n* **con'trariness**.

con'trast *v* to compare so as to show differences; to show a marked difference from. – *n* **'contrast** a difference between (two) things.

contra'vene *v* to break (a law *etc*). – *n* **contravention** [kontrə'venshən].

contretemps ['kontrətöŋ] *n* a mishap at an awkward moment.

con'tribute *v* to give (money, help *etc*) along with others; to supply, give (written articles to a magazine *etc*); to help to cause (something). – *ns* **contri'bution; con'tributor**.

'contrite *adj* very sorry for having done

wrong. – *n* **contrition** [kən'trishən].

con'trive *v* to plan; to bring about (with difficulty), manage. – *n* **con'trivance** an act of contriving; an invention.

con'trol *n* power or authority to guide, rule, manage, restrain *etc*; (often *pl*) means by which a driver keeps a machine under his power or guidance. – *v* to exercise control over; to have power over. – *adj* **con'trolled**. – *n* **con'troller**. – *n* **control tower** an airport building from which landing and take-off instructions are given.

con'troversy *n* an argument, a disagreement: – *pl* **con'troversies**. – *adj* **contro'versial** likely to cause argument.

co'nundrum *n* a riddle, a question.

conur'bation *n* a group of towns forming a single built-up area.

convalesce [konvə'les] *v* to recover health gradually after being ill. – *n* **conva'lescence** a gradual return to health and strength. – *adj*, *n* **conva'lescent** (of) a person convalescing.

con'vection *n* the spreading of heat by movement of heated air or water. – *n* **con'vector** a heater which works by convection.

con'vene *v* to call or come together. – *n* **con'vener** one who calls a meeting.

con'vēnient *adj* suitable; easy to reach or use, handy. – *n* **con'venience** suitableness, handiness; any means of giving ease or comfort; (*coll*) a (public) lavatory. – **at your convenience** when it suits you best.

'convent *n* a dwelling for nuns (or monks).

con'venticle *n* (*hist*) a secret meeting (for worship).

con'vention *n* a way of behaving that has become usual, a custom; a large meeting or assembly; a treaty or agreement. – *adj* **con'ventional** done by habit or custom.

converge [kən'vörj] *v* to come together, meet at a point. – *n* **con'vergence**. – *adj* **con'vergent**.

con'verse *v* to talk. – *n* **'converse** talk; the opposite. – *adj* opposite. – *n* **conver'sation** talk, exchange of ideas, news *etc*. – *adj* **conver'sational** of or used in conversation; talkative.

con'vert *v* to change (from one thing into another); to turn from one religion to another, or from an evil to a religious life. – *ns* **con'version** the act of converting; something converted to another use; **'convert** one who has been converted. – *adj* **con'vertible** able to be changed (from one thing to another). – *n* a car with a folding roof.

'**convex** *adj* curved on the outside (opposite of **concave**). – *n* **con'vexity**.

convey [kən'vā] *v* to carry, transport; to send; (in law) to hand over: *convey property*. – *n* **con'veyance** the act of conveying; a vehicle of any kind. – *n* **conveyor belt** an endless moving band for conveying articles, *esp* in a factory.

con'vict *v* to declare or to prove that a person is guilty. – *ns* '**convict** one found guilty of a crime (and sent to prison); **con'viction** (in a law court) the passing of a sentence upon a guilty person; a strong belief.

con'vince *v* to make (someone) believe that something is true; to persuade (someone) by showing.

con'vivial *adj* jolly, festive. – *n* **convivi-'ality**.

convo'cation *n* a meeting *esp* of bishops, or of heads of a university.

con'volvūlus *n* a kind of twining plant with trumpet-shaped flowers.

'**convoy** *v* to go along with and protect. – *n* merchant ships protected by warships; a line of army lorries with armed guard.

con'vulse *v* to cause to shake violently: *convulsed with laughter*. – *n* **con'vulsion** a sudden stiffening or jerking of the muscles; a violent disturbance. – *adj* **con'vulsive**.

'**cōny**, '**coney** *n* a rabbit or its fur.

coo *v* to make a sound like that of a dove. – Also *n*.

cook *v* to prepare (food) by heating; (*coll*) to alter (accounts *etc*) dishonestly. – *n* one who cooks and prepares food ready for table. – *ns* '**cooker** a stove for cooking; an apple *etc* used in cooking, not for eating raw; '**cookery** the art of cooking.

cool *adj* slightly cold; calm, not excited; rather cheeky. – *v* to make or grow cool; to calm. – *adv* '**coolly**. – *n* '**coolness**.

coop *n* a box or cage for hens *etc*. – *v* to shut (up) as in a coop. – *n* '**cooper** one who makes barrels.

cō-'operate *v* to work or act together. – *n* **co-ope'ration** a working together; willingness to act together. – *n* **co-operative society** a trading organization in which the profits are shared among members.

cō-'opt *v* to choose (someone) to join a committee or other body.

cō-'ordinate *v* to make things fit in or work smoothly together. – *n* **co-ordi'nation**.

coot *n* a type of water-bird with a white spot on the forehead.

cope *v* to struggle or deal successfully (with), manage.

'**cōping** *n* the top layer of stone in a wall. – *n* '**coping-stone** the top stone of a wall.

'**cōpious** *adj* plentiful.

'**copper** *n* an element, a hard reddish-brown metal; a coin made from (metal containing) copper; a large vessel made of copper, *usu* to boil water in. – *n* '**copperplate** very fine and regular handwriting.

'**copra** *n* the dried kernel of the coconut, yielding coconut oil.

copse, **coppice** [kops], ['kopis] *n* a wood of low-growing trees.

'**copy** *n* an imitation; a print or reproduction (of a picture *etc*); an individual example of a certain book *etc*: – *pl* '**copies**. – *v* to make a copy of; to imitate. – *n* '**copyright** the right of one person or body to publish a book, perform a play, print music *etc*. – *adj* of or protected by the law of copyright.

coquette [ko'ket] *n* a woman who flirts.

'**coral** *n* a hard substance made up of the skeletons of a kind of tiny animal, gradually building up from the sea-bottom to form a rock-like mass (**coral reef**).

cord *n* thin rope or strong string; anything of cord-like appearance:

'**cordial** *adj* cheery, friendly. – *n* a refreshing drink. – *n* **cordi'ality** friendliness.

'**cordite** *n* a kind of explosive.

'**cordon** *n* a line of guards, police *etc* to keep people back. – *adj*, *n* **cordon bleu** ['kördoŋ'blö] (of) a first class cook.

cordu'roy *n* a ribbed cloth (*usu* cotton) looking like velvet.

core [kör] *n* the inner part of anything, *esp* of fruit. – *v* to take out the core of fruit.

co-respondent [ko-rə'spond-ənt] *n* a man or woman charged with adultery, and proceeded against along with the wife or husband who is the **respondent**.

'**corgi** *n* a breed of short-legged dog.

cork *n* the outer bark of the cork-tree (an oak found in southern Europe *etc*); a stopper for a bottle *etc* made of cork. – *adj* made of cork. – *v* to plug, to stop up (with a cork). – *n* '**corkscrew** a tool with a screw-like spike for taking out corks. – *adj* shaped like a cork-screw.

corm *n* the bulb-like underground stem of certain plants.

'**cormorant** *n* a type of big sea-bird.

corn *n* (a grain or seed of) wheat, oats or

maize; a little lump of hard skin *usu* on a toe. – *ns* **'corncrake** a kind of bird with a harsh croaking cry; **corned beef** salted (tinned) beef; **'cornflour** finely ground (maize) flour; **'cornflower** a type of plant, with a blue flower.

cornea ['körniə] *n* the transparent covering of the eyeball.

'corner *n* the point where two lines, walls, roads *etc* meet; a small (quiet) place; (*coll*) a difficult situation. – *v* to drive into a place from which there is no escape. – *n* **'corner-stone** the stone at the corner of (the foundation of) a building; something upon which much depends.

'cornet *n* a type of musical instrument like a trumpet; an ice-cream in a cone-shaped wafer.

cornice ['körnis] *n* an ornamental border round a ceiling.

co'rolla *n* the petals of a flower.

co'rollary *n* something which may be taken for granted when something else has been proved; a natural result: – *pl* **co'rollaries**.

'coronary *n* (short for **coronary thrombosis**) a heart disease caused by blockage of one of the arteries supplying the heart: – *pl* **'coronaries**.

coro'nation *n* the crowning of a king or queen.

'coroner *n* a government officer who holds inquiries into the causes of sudden or accidental deaths.

'coronet *n* a small crown; a crown-like head-dress.

'corporal *n* in the British Army, the rank next below sergeant. – *adj* of the body. – *n* **corporal punishment** beating, caning *etc*.

'corporate *adj* of or forming a whole, united. – *n* **corpo'ration** a body of people acting as one, *eg* for administrative or business purposes.

corps [kör] *n* a division of an army; an organized group: – *pl* **corps** [körz].

corpse *n* a dead body.

'corpulence *n* fatness of body. – *adj* **'corpulent**.

corpuscle ['körpusl] *n* a very small particle or cell in a fluid (*esp* blood).

cor'ral *n* (*US*) a fenced space for (captured) animals; (*US*) a circle of wagons formed for defence.

cor'rect *v* to remove faults and errors from; to set right; to punish. – *adj* having no errors; true. – *n* **cor'rection** the putting right of a mistake; punishment. – *adj* **cor'rective**.

corres'pond *v* to write letters to; to be similar (to), to match. – *ns*

corres'pondence letters; likeness to; **corres'pondent** one who writes letters; one who contributes reports to a newspaper *etc*.

'corridor *n* a passage-way.

corrigendum [kori'jendəm] *n* a correction to a book *etc*: – *pl* **corri'genda**.

cor'roborate *v* to give evidence which strengthens evidence already given. – *n* **corrobo'ration**. – *adj* **cor'roborative**.

cor'rode *v* to rust; to eat away, as acid eats into metal. – *n* **cor'rosion**. – *adj* **cor'rosive**.

'corrugated *adj* folded or shaped into ridges: *corrugated iron*.

cor'rupt *v* to make evil or rotten; to bribe. – *adj* dishonest, taking bribes; bad, rotten. – *adj* **cor'ruptible** able to be corrupted or bribed. – *n* **cor'ruption** evil, sin; bribery.

'corsair *n* a pirate; a pirate-ship.

'corset *n* a tight-fitting under-garment to support the body.

cortège [kör'tezh] *n* a (funeral) procession.

cor'vette *n* a type of small swift warship, used against submarines.

cosh *n* a short heavy stick: – *pl* **'coshes**. – *v* to hit with a cosh.

cosmetic [koz'metik] *n* something designed to improve the appearance, *esp* of the face. – *adj* improving the appearance of.

cosmic ['kozmik] *adj* of the universe or outer space. – *n* **'cosmonaut** an astronaut.

cosmopolitan [kozmə'politən] *adj* belonging to all parts of the world; made up of people of many races; used to, feeling at home in, many different parts of the world.

'cosset *v* to treat with too much kindness, pamper.

cost *v* to be priced at; to cause loss (of something) as though in payment. *War costs lives*: – *pt, pp* **cost**. – *n* what must be spent or suffered in order to get something. – *adj* **'costly** high-priced, valuable. – *n* **'costliness**.

'coster(monger) *n* a street-seller of fruit *etc*.

'costume *n* (a set of) clothes. – *n* **costume jewellery** inexpensive, imitation jewellery.

cosy ['közi] *adj* warm and comfortable. – *n* a covering used for a teapot *etc* to keep it warm.

cot *n* a small bed with high sides for children; (*US*) a small bed which can be folded away, a camp bed; (in poetry *etc*) a cottage.

coterie ['kōtəri] *n* a number of persons interested in the same things who tend to exclude other people.

'**cottage** *n* a small house, *usu* in the countryside or a village. – *n* '**cottager** one who lives in a cottage.

'**cotton** *n* a soft fluffy substance got from the seeds of the cotton plant; cloth made of cotton. – Also *adj*. – *n* '**cotton'wool** cotton in a fluffy state, used for wiping, absorbing.

couch *n* a sofa: – *pl* '**couches**. – *v* to express (in words). *The letter was couched in old-fashioned English.* – *n* **couch grass** a kind of grass, a troublesome weed.

'**couchant** *adj* (in heraldry) lying down: *lion couchant*.

cougar ['kōōgər] *n* (*esp US*) the puma.

cough [kof] *n* a noisy effort of the lungs to throw out air and harmful matter from the throat. – *v* to make this effort.

could [kōōd] *v* the form of the verb **can** used to express a condition. *He could do it if he tried. I could understand a small mistake, but this is ridiculous*; *see* also **can**[1].

coulomb ['kōōlom] *n* a unit of electric charge.

'**council** *n* a group of (elected) persons who meet to discuss or give advice about policy, government *etc*. – *n* '**councillor** a member of a council.

'**counsel** *n* advice; one who advises in matters of law, a lawyer. – *v* to give advice to. – *n* '**counsellor** one who gives advice.

count *v* to find the total number of, add up; to say numbers in order (1, 2, 3, *etc*); to think, consider. *Count yourself lucky!* – *n* the act of counting; the number counted; a charge, accusation; a point being considered; a nobleman in certain countries: – *fem* '**countess**. – *n* '**counter** a person who or a thing which counts; a token used in counting; a small plastic disc used in ludo *etc*; a table on which money is counted or goods are laid for show. – *adj* '**countless** too many to be counted, very many. – **count on** to rely on, depend on.

'**countenance** *n* the face; the look on a person's face. – *v* to allow, encourage.

'**counter** *v* to answer or oppose (a move, act *etc*) by another. – *adv* in the opposite direction. – *adj* opposed; opposite. – *n see* **count**.

counter- *prefix* against, opposing; opposite.

counte'ract *v* to block or defeat (an action) by doing the opposite.

'**counterattack** *n* an attack made by the defenders upon an attacking enemy. – Also *v*.

'**counterattraction** *n* something which draws away the attention from something else.

'**countercharge** *v* to bring a charge against someone who has accused one. – Also *n*.

counterfeit ['kowntərfit] *adj* not genuine, not real; made in imitation *esp* with a dishonest purpose: *counterfeit money*. – Also *n*. – *v* to make a copy of for dishonest purposes.

'**counterfoil** *n* a part of a cheque, postal order *etc* kept by the payer or sender.

counter'mand *v* to give an order which goes against one already given.

'**counterpane** *n* a top cover for a bed.

'**counterpart** *n* something which is just like or which corresponds to something or someone.

'**counterpoint** *n* the combining of two or more melodies to make a piece of music. – *adj* **contra'puntal**.

'**counterpoise** *n* a weight which balances another weight.

countersign ['kowntərsin] *v* to sign one's name after another has done so to show that a document is genuine.

countess *see* **count** and **earl**.

country ['kuntri] *n* a nation; a land under one government; the land in which one lives; a district which is not in a town or city; an area or stretch of land: – *pl* '**countries**. – *adj* belonging to the country. – *n* '**countryside** the parts of the country other than towns and cities.

'**county** *n* a division of a country: – *pl* '**counties**.

coup [kōō] *n* any sudden outstandingly successful move or act; a sudden and violent change in government. *The president was killed during the coup.*

couple ['kupl] *n* a pair, two of a kind together; husband and wife. – *v* to join together. – *ns* **couplet** ['kuplit] two lines of rhyming verse; '**coupling** a kind of link for joining parts of machinery, railway carriages *etc*.

coupon ['kōōpon] *n* a part of a ticket *etc* that can be torn off *esp* a piece cut from an advertisement *etc* which may be exchanged for goods or money; (**football coupon**) a form in which one tries to forecast the result of football matches in the hope of winning money.

courage ['kurij] *n* bravery, lack of fear. – *adj* **cou'rāgeous**.

courgette [kōōr'zhet] *n* a type of vegetable, a small marrow.

courier ['kooriər] *n* one who acts as guide for tourists; a messenger.

course [körs] *n* a path in which anything moves; the act of moving from point to point; the road or ground on which one runs, travels, plays games *etc*; the direction to be followed. *The ship held its course*; line of action (what one should do); a part of a meal; a number of things following each other: *a course of twelve lectures*; one of the rows of bricks in a wall. – *v* to move quickly; to hunt. – *ns* **'courser** a swift horse; **'coursing** the hunting of hares with greyhounds. – **in due course** after a while, when it's the proper time; **in the course of** during.

court [kört] *n* a shut-in space (*eg* one surrounded by houses, or one used for certain sports such as tennis); the persons who attend a king, queen *etc*; any place where a king, queen *etc* lives; the place where legal cases are heard or tried. – *v* to try to persuade (a woman) to marry one, to woo; to try to gain (*eg* admiration) or seem to be trying to gain (danger *etc*). – *adj* **courteous** ['körtiəs] polite; obliging. – *n* **courtier** ['körtiər] a member of a royal court. – *adj* **'courtly** having fine manners. – *ns* **'court-'martial** a court held by navy or army officers to try those who break navy or army laws: – *pl* **'courts-'martial; 'courtship** the act or time of courting or wooing; **'courtyard** a court or enclosed space beside a house.

courtesy ['körtəsi] *n* politeness.

courtier *see* **court**.

cousin ['kuzn] *n* the son or daughter of an uncle or aunt.

cove *n* a small inlet on the sea coast; a bay.

coven ['kuvən] *n* a gathering of witches.

covenant ['kuvənənt] *n* an important agreement or promise between people to do or not to do something.

cover ['kuvər] *v* to put or spread something on, over or about; to hide; to stretch over (an area or a length of time). *Trees covered the land. His diary covered three years*; to include; to be enough for. *Five pounds should cover the cost*; to travel over. *He covers 3 kilometres a day*; to point a weapon at. *He had the gangster covered*. – *n* something that covers, hides or protects. – *ns* **'coverage** the area covered; the amount or extent of news covered by a newspaper *etc*; the amount of protection given by an insurance policy; **'covering** something which covers; **'coverlet** a bed cover. – **cover up** to

cover completely; to conceal deliberately (a wrong, an illegal or dishonest deed *etc*) (*n* **'cover-up**).

covert ['kuvərt] *adj* secret, not done openly. – *n* a hiding place (trees, bushes *etc*) for animals or birds when hunted.

covet ['kuvit] *v* to desire eagerly, *esp* something belonging to another person. – *adj* **'covetous**. – *n* **'covetousness**.

covey ['kuvi] *n* a flock of birds, *esp* partridges.

cow [kow] *n* the female animal of the ox kind used for giving milk; the female of certain other animals (*eg* elephant, whale). – *v* to frighten. – *adj* **cowed**. – *ns* **'cowboy** a man who has the charge of cattle on a ranch in America; **'cowherd** one who looks after cows.

coward ['kowərd] *n* person who has no courage and shows fear easily. – *adj* **'cowardly**. – *n* **cowardice** ['kowərdis] lack of courage.

cowed *see* **cow**.

cower ['kowər] *v* to crouch down or shrink back, through fear.

cowl [kowl] *n* a cap or hood, *esp* that of a monk; a cover for a chimney.

cowslip ['kowslip] *n* a type of yellow wild flower.

cox short for **coxswain**.

coxcomb ['kokskōm] *n* (*hist*) a strip of red cloth notched like a cock's comb, which court jesters used to wear; a person who is conceited *esp* about his dress.

coxswain ['koksn] *n* one who steers a boat; an officer in charge of a boat and crew.

coy *adj* too modest or shy.

coyote [koi'ōti] *n* a type of small wolf of N. America: – *pls* **coy'ote, coy'otes**.

coypu ['koipoo] *n* a type of large, beaver-like animal living in rivers and marshes.

crab *n* a kind of sea animal with a shell and five pairs of legs, the first pair of which have large claws. – *adj* **crabbed** ['krabid] bad-tempered. – *n* **crab apple** a type of small, bitter apple. – *adj, adv* **'crabwise** (moving) sideways like a crab.

crack *v* to (cause to) make a sharp sudden sound; to break partly without falling to pieces; to break into (a safe); to solve, decipher (a code); to break open (a nut); to make (a joke). – *n* a sharp sound; a break; a narrow opening; (*coll*) a sharp, witty remark. – *adj* excellent: *a crack tennis player*. – *adj* **cracked** split, damaged, crazy. – *n* **'cracker** a hollow tube of paper, often containing a small gift, which breaks with a bang when the ends are pulled; a thin, crisp biscuit. – **crack up** to fail suddenly, go to pieces, collapse.

'**crackle** to make a continuous cracking noise. – n '**crackling** a cracking sound; the rind or outer skin of roast pork.

'**cradle** n a baby's bed *esp* one in which it can be rocked; anything shaped like a cradle in which something is laid (*eg* a frame under a ship that is being built).

craft n a trade or skill; a boat or small ship; slyness. – n '**craftsman** one who works at a trade. – *adj* '**crafty** cunning, sly.

crag n a rough steep rock. – *adj* '**craggy** rocky; (*usu* of faces) with strong or rough features.

cram v to fill full, stuff; to learn up in a short time facts for an examination: – *pt* **crammed**.

cramp n a painful stiffening of the muscles. – v to put into too narrow or small a space; to hinder, restrict. – *adj* **cramped** without enough room; (of handwriting) small and closely-written.

'**crampon** n a metal plate with spikes, fixed to the boots when climbing on ice *etc*.

'**cranberry** n a type of red, sour berry.

crane n a kind of large wading bird with long legs, neck and bill; a machine for lifting heavy weights. – v to stretch out the neck (to see round or over something).

'**cranium** n the skull: – *pls* '**crania**, '**craniums**.

crank n a handle with which something (*eg* an axle) can be made to turn; a lever or arm which turns movement to and fro into movement round and round; a person with unusual or odd ideas. – v to start (an engine) with a crank. – *adj* '**cranky** odd, with unusual ideas *etc*; cross, irritable.

'**cranny** n a small opening or crack: – *pl* '**crannies**.

crape *see* **crêpe**.

crash n a noise of heavy things breaking or banging together; a collision, a violent meeting together of a vehicle (*eg* car, train, aeroplane) with another vehicle or another object (*eg* a tree, the ground) *usu* resulting in damage; the failure of a business: – *pl* '**crashes**. – v (of a car *etc*) to be involved in a crash; (of a business) to fail; to force one's way noisily through; (*coll*) to attend a party) uninvited (also '**gatecrash**). – n '**crash-helmet** a covering for the head worn for protection by motor-cyclists

etc. – v '**crash-'land** to land (an aircraft), *usu* in an emergency, in a way which damages it. – n '**crash-'landing**.

crass *adj* stupid.

crate n an openwork container, *usu* made of wooden slats, for carrying goods, sometimes with compartments for bottles.

'**crater** n the bowl-shaped mouth of a volcano; a hole in the earth made by an explosion.

cra'vat n a scarf worn in place of a tie.

crave v to long for. – n '**craving**.

'**craven** *adj* cowardly.

crawfish *see* **crayfish**.

crawl v to move on hands and knees; to move slowly; to be covered (with): *crawling with wasps*; to behave in too humble a manner. – n the act of crawling; a kind of swimming stroke.

'**crayfish**, '**crawfish** n a kind of shellfish, something like a small lobster.

'**crayon** n a coloured pencil or stick used for drawing.

craze n a temporary fashion or enthusiasm. – *adj* '**crazy** mad, unreasonable. – n **crazy paving** paving made with stones of irregular shape.

creak v to make a sharp, grating sound like the sound of a hinge in need of oiling.

cream n the fatty substance which forms on milk and gives butter when churned; anything like cream: *cold cream*: *ice cream*; the best part of anything: *cream of society*. – v to take off the cream; to take away the best part of anything. *The school creamed off the best pupils and put them in one class.* – *adj* '**creamy** full of or like cream.

crease n a mark made by folding or doubling anything; (in cricket) a line showing the position of a batsman and bowler. – v to make creases in; to become creased.

create [kri'āt] v to bring into being; to make; (*coll*) to make a fuss. – n **cre'ation** the act of creating; that which is created. – *adj* **cre'ative** having the ability to create, artistic. – n **cre'ator** one who creates. – **the Creator** God.

creature ['krēchər] n an animal or person.

crèche [kresh] n a (public) nursery for children.

cre'dentials *npl* evidence, *esp* letters which a person carries to show people that they may trust him.

'**credible** *adj* able to be believed. – n **credi'bility**.

credit *n* recognition of good qualities, achievements *etc*. *Give him credit for some common sense*; good qualities, honour; source of honour: *a credit to the school*; trustworthiness regarding ability to pay for goods *etc*; time allowed for payment of goods *etc*; the sale of goods to be paid for at a later time; the side of an account on which payments received are entered; a sum of money which one has in an account at a bank; belief, trust; (*pl*) (the giving of) the names of people who have helped in a film *etc*. – *v* to believe; to enter on the credit side of an account; (with **with**) to give credit for; to think (someone) has. *I credited him with more sense*. – *adj* **'creditable** bringing honour or good reputation to. – *n* **'creditor** one to whom money is due.

'credulous *adj* believing too easily. – *n* **cre'dulity**.

creed *n* what is believed, *esp* in one's religion.

creek *n* a small inlet or bay on the sea coast; a short river.

creep *v* to move slowly or secretly and silently; to move on hands and knees or with the body close to the ground; to shiver with fear or disgust. *It makes your flesh creep*; (of a plant *etc*) to grow along the ground or a wall *etc*: – *pt* **crept** [krept]. – *n* a moving in a creeping way; (*coll*) a person one dislikes; (*pl*) great fear or disgust. *Spiders give me the creeps.* – *n* **'creeper** a plant growing along the ground, or up a wall. – **creep up on** to approach (*usu* from behind) unseen.

cre'mate *v* to burn (a dead body). – *ns* **cre'mation**; **crematorium** [kremə'töriəm] a place where dead bodies are burnt.

crenellated ['krenəlātid] *adj* having battlements.

'creosote *n* an oily liquid made from wood tar, used to keep wood from rotting.

crêpe, crape [krāp] *n* a type of fine, crinkly material. – *n* **crêpe paper** paper with a crinkled appearance.

crept *see* **creep**.

crescent ['kresnt] *adj* curve-shaped, like the new or old moon, not the full moon. – *n* anything shaped in a curve; a name for a curved road or street.

cress *n* a type of plant with leaves of a slightly bitter taste, used in salads.

crest *n* the tuft on the head of a cock or other bird; the top of a hill, wave *etc*; feathers on the top of a helmet; a badge. – *adj* **'crestfallen** down-hearted, dis-couraged.

cre'vasse *n* a deep crack or split in snow or ice.

crevice ['krevis] *n* a crack or narrow opening.

crew [krōō] *n* the people who man a ship, aircraft, bus *etc*; a gang or mob. – *v* to act as a member of a crew; *see* **crow**. – *n* **'crewcut** a hairstyle in which the hair is very, very short.

crib *n* a manger; a child's bed; a ready-made translation *etc* used by school-children to avoid preparing their own. – *v* to copy the work of another: – *pt* **cribbed**.

'cribbage *n* a type of card game.

crick *n* a sharp pain (in the neck). – *v* to produce a crick in.

'cricket *n* an outdoor game played with bats, a ball and wickets, between two sides of 11 each; a kind of insect similar to a grasshopper. – *n* **'cricketer** one who plays cricket. – *n* **cricket match** a game of cricket.

cried *see* **cry**.

crier ['kriər] *n* short for **town-crier**.

crime *n* an act or deed which is against the law. – *adj* **criminal** ['kriminl] forbidden by law; very wrong. – *n* one guilty of a crime.

crimson ['krimzn] *adj*, *n* (of) a deep red colour.

cringe [krinj] *v* to crouch or shrink back in fear *etc*; to behave in too humble a way.

'crinkle *v* to wrinkle, crease; to make a crackling sound. – *adj* **'crinkly** having a wrinkled appearance.

crinoline ['krinəlēn] *n* a petticoat or skirt made to stick out all round by means of hoops.

'cripple *n* a lame or disabled person. – *v* to make lame; to make less strong, less efficient *etc*, throw out of action. *The strike crippled the country.* – *adj* **'crippled**.

'crisis *n* a deciding moment or turning point; a time of great danger or suspense: – *pl* **'crises**.

crisp *adj* stiff and so dry as to be crumbled easily, brittle; cool and fresh: *crisp air*; curly, wavy; firm and fresh: *a crisp lettuce*; sharp, clearly defined. – *v* to make crisp. – *n* a thin crisp piece of fried potato eaten cold. – *n* **'crispness**. – *adj* **'crispy**.

'criss-cross *adj*, *n* (having) a pattern of crossing lines. – Also *adv*.

cri'tērion *n* a means or rule by which something can be judged, a test, a standard: – *pl* **cri'teria**.

'critic *n* one who judges the good points

or faults in a thing (such as a picture, play, book *etc*); one who finds faults in a thing or person. – *adj* '**critical** fault-finding; of criticism; of or at a crisis; very ill; serious; very important. – *n* '**criticism** a judgement or opinion on (something) *esp* one showing up faults; the act of criticizing. – *v* '**criticize** to find fault with; to give an opinion or judgement on.

croak *v* to make a low, hoarse sound. – Also *n*. – *adj* '**croaky**.

crochet ['krōshā] *n* a kind of knitting done with one hooked needle.

crock *n* an earthenware pot or jar; a worthless, old and decrepit person or thing. – *n* '**crockery** china or earthenware dishes.

'**crocodile** *n* a type of large reptile found in rivers in Asia, Africa *etc*; a procession (*usu* of children) walking two by two. – *npl* **crocodile tears** pretended tears.

'**crōcus** *n* a type of yellow, purple or white flower which grows from a bulb: – *pl* '**crocuses**.

croft *n* a small farm with a cottage *esp* in the Scottish Highlands. – *n* '**crofter**.

crone *n* an ugly old woman.

'**crōny** *n* (*coll*) a close friend: – *pl* '**cronies**.

crook *n* anything bent (such as a shepherd's or bishop's stick bent at the end); a criminal; a cheat. – *v* to bend or form into a hook. – *adj* '**crooked** ['krookid] bent like a crook; not straight; not honest. – *n* '**crookedness**.

croon *v* to sing or hum in a low voice. – *ns* '**crooner**; '**crooning**.

crop *n* that which is gathered for food from fields, trees or bushes; a part of a bird's stomach; a kind of riding whip; the hair on the head; a short haircut. – *v* to cut short; to gather a crop (of wheat *etc*): – *pt* **cropped**. – **come a cropper** to fail badly; to have a fall; **crop up** to happen unexpectedly.

croquet ['krōkā] *n* a game in which the players, using long-handled wooden hammers, try to drive wooden balls through hoops in the ground.

cross *n* anything shaped like this: + or ×; a frame consisting of two bars of wood *etc* placed across each other, of the type on which Christ and criminals were nailed; a monument in a street, often but not always cross-shaped, where proclamations used to be made and markets held; the result of breeding an animal or plant with one of another kind: *a cross between a horse and*

a donkey; a trouble or grief that one must bear. – *v* to mark with a cross; to go to the other side of (a room, road *etc*); to lie or pass across; to meet and pass; to go against the wishes of, annoy; to draw two lines across (cheques); to breed (one kind) with (another). – *adj* ill-tempered, angry. – *ns* '**crossing** a place where a street, river *etc* may be crossed; a journey over the sea; '**crossness** bad temper, sulkiness. – *n* '**crossbow** (*hist*) a bow fixed to a wooden stand with a device for pulling back the bowstring. – *n*, *adj* '**cross-'country** (a race) across fields *etc*, not on roads. – *vs* '**cross-ex'amine**, '**cross-'question** to test the truth of someone's words (in a court) by close questioning. – *adj* '**cross-'eyed** having a squint. – *ns* '**cross-'reference** in a book such as a dictionary, a statement that what is looked for will be found in another place; '**crossroads** a place where roads each other; '**cross-'section** a section made by cutting across (something); a sample, a part or quantity taken as being representative of the whole: *a cross-section of voters*; '**crossword** a form of word puzzle.

'**crotchet** *n* a note of a certain length in music. – *adj* '**crotchety** bad-tempered.

crouch *v* to stand with the knees well bent; (of an animal) to lie close to the ground.

croup [kroop] *n* a disease of children causing difficulty in breathing and a harsh cough; the hindquarters of a horse.

croupier ['kroopiā] *n* a person who collects the money and pays the winners at gambling.

crow [krō] *n* a type of large bird, generally black; the cry of a cock; the happy sounds made by a baby. – *v* to cry like a cock: – *pt* **crew** [kroo], **crowed**; to boast: – *pt* **crowed**; (of a baby *etc*) to make happy noises: – *pt* **crowed**. – *ns* '**crowbar** a large iron bar used as a lever; '**crow's foot** one of the wrinkles near the eye, produced by ageing; '**crow's-'nest** a sheltered and enclosed platform near the mast-head of a ship for a man to keep a lookout. – **as the crow flies** in a straight line.

crowd [krowd] *n* a number of persons or things together (without order or arrangement). – *v* to gather into a crowd; to fill (a room *etc*) too full; to give too little space to, to hinder by being too close.

crown [krown] *n* the jewelled head-dress

worn by kings or queens on great occasions; the best or most magnificent part of anything; the highest part or top of anything (*eg* of the road, the head); an old coin which was worth five shillings. – *v* to set a crown on; to make king; (*coll*) to hit on the head; to reward, finish happily. *Her efforts were crowned with success.*

crucial ['krōōshəl] *adj* testing, involving making a decision: *the crucial moment*; of great and far-reaching importance. *The crucial question is whether he will succeed.*

crucible ['krōōsibl] *n* a small container for melting metals *etc.*

crucify ['krōōsifi] *v* to put to death by fixing the hands and feet to a cross: – *pt* 'crucified. – *ns* 'crucifix a figure or picture of Christ fixed to the cross: – *pl* 'crucifixes; cruci'fixion the act of crucifying; death on the cross, *esp* that of Christ.

crude [krōōd] *adj* raw, not purified or refined: *crude oil*; roughly made or done; rude, blunt, tactless. – *ns* 'crudeness, 'crudity.

cruel ['krōōəl] *adj* causing pain or distress; having no pity for others' sufferings. – *n* 'cruelty: – *pl* 'cruelties.

cruet ['krōōit] *n* a small jar for salt, pepper, sauces *etc*; two or more such jars on a stand.

cruise [krōōz] *v* to travel (by car, ship *etc*) at a steady speed. – *n* a journey by ship made for pleasure and relaxation. – *n* 'cruiser a middle-sized warship.

crumb [krum] *n* a small bit of anything, *esp* bread. – *v* **crumble** ['krumbl] to break into crumbs or small pieces; to fall to pieces. – *adj* 'crumbly.

'crumpet *n* a kind of soft cake, baked on a griddle and eaten with butter.

'crumple *v* to crush into creases or wrinkles; to become creased; to collapse.

crunch *v* to chew anything hard, and so make a noise; to crush. – *n* a noise as of crunching; (*coll*) a testing moment or turning-point.

crusade [krōō'sād] *n* any movement undertaken for some good cause; (*hist*) an expedition of Christians to win back the Holy Land from the Turks. – *n* cru'sader one who goes on a crusade.

crush *v* to squeeze together; to beat down or overcome; to crease or crumple (a dress *etc*). – *n* a violent squeezing; a vast crowd of persons or things; a drink made by squeezing fruit. – *adj* **crushed** squeezed, squashed; completely defeated or miserable.

crust *n* the hard outside coating of anything (such as bread, a pie, the earth *etc*). – *adj* 'crusty having a crust; (of people) cross.

crustacean [krus'tāshən] *n* any of a large group of animals, often having a hard shell, including crabs, lobsters, shrimps *etc.*

crutch *n* a stick with a bar across the top for lame people; any support: – *pl* 'crutches.

crux *n* the difficult or most important part of a problem.

cry *v* to make a loud sound, as in pain or sorrow; to weep; to call loudly: – *pt* **cried**. – Also *n*: – *pl* **cries**. – *adj* 'crying weeping; calling loudly; calling for, requiring notice or attention: *a crying need.* – **cry off** cancel: *cry off a match*; **cry over spilt milk** to be worried about a misfortune that is past and cannot be helped.

crypt *n* an underground cell or chapel, *esp* one used for burial. – *adj* 'cryptic full of mystery, secret; difficult to understand: *a cryptic remark.*

'crystal *n* a special kind of very clear glass often used for cut-glass ornaments *etc*; the regular shape taken by each small part of certain substances (*eg* salt, sugar). – *adj* 'crystalline made up of (or like) crystals. – *v* 'crystallize to form into the shape of a crystal; to take a form or shape, become clear. – *n* crystalli'zation.

cub *n* the young of certain animals (such as foxes); a Cub Scout. – *n* **Cub Scout** a junior Scout.

cube *n* a solid body having six equal square sides; the answer to a sum in which a number is multiplied by itself twice (8 is the cube of 2). – *adj* 'cubic of cubes; having the shape of a cube.

'cubicle *n* a small room closed off in some way from a larger one.

'cubit *n* (*hist*) the distance from elbow to middle-finger tip, once used as a means of measurement.

cuckoo ['kōōkōō] *n* a type of bird, named after its call, which visits Britain in summer and lays its eggs in the nests of other birds.

'cucumber *n* a creeping plant with a long green fruit used in salads.

cud *n* food brought back from the stomach and chewed a second time by certain animals (*eg* the sheep, cow).

'cuddle *v* to put one's arms round, hug. – Also *n.*

'cudgel *n* a heavy stick, a club. – *v* to beat with a cudgel.

cue [kū] *n* a hint or sign (telling a person

69

when to speak, or what to say next); the stick used in billiards and snooker.

cuff *n* the end of a sleeve (of a shirt, coat *etc*) near the wrist; the turned back hem of a trouser leg; a blow with the open hand. – *v* to hit with the hand. – *n* 'cufflinks two ornamental buttons *etc* joined by a small bar, chain *etc* used to fasten a shirt cuff. – **off the cuff** without planning or rehearsal.

cuisine [kwi'zēn] *n* (the art of) cookery.

'cul-de-sac *n* a street closed at one end.

'culinary *adj* of kitchen or cookery.

cull *v* to gather; to choose from a group; to pick out (seals, deer *etc*) from a herd and kill for the good of the herd. – *n* such a killing.

'culminate *v* to reach the highest point; to reach the most important or greatest point, to end (in). – *n* culmi'nation.

'culpable *adj* guilty, blameworthy.

'culprit *n* a person who is to blame for something; (in English and US law) a prisoner accused but not yet tried.

cult *n* worship or religious belief; a strong devotion to or enthusiasm for a person, thing or idea: *the cult of physical fitness.*

'cultivate *v* to grow (vegetables *etc*); to plough, sow *etc* (land); to try to develop and improve. *He cultivated their friendship.* – *adj* 'cultivated having been cultivated; educated, informed. – *n* culti'vation ploughing *etc*; education and refinement.

'culture *n* a form or type of civilization of a certain race or nation and the customs associated with it: *Jewish culture*; improvement or development of the mind *etc* by education, training *etc*; educated tastes in art, music, literature; cultivation (of plants *etc*). – *adj* 'cultured well-educated *esp* in literature, art *etc*.

'culvert *n* an arched drain for carrying water under a road, railway *etc*.

cumbersome ['kumbərsəm] *adj* heavy, difficult to manage, handle *etc*.

'cummerbund *n* a sash worn around the waist.

'cumulative *adj* increasing as parts *etc* are added on.

'cumulus *n* a kind of cloud common in summer, made up of rounded heaps.

'cunning *adj* sly, clever in a deceitful way; skilful, clever. – *n* slyness; skill, knowledge.

cup *n* a hollow container to hold liquid for drinking; an ornamental vessel *usu* of metal, given as a prize in sports events *etc*. – *v* to make or put in the shape of a cup. *She cupped her hands*: – *pt* **cupped**. – *n* 'cupful as much as fills

a cup: – *pl* 'cupfuls. – *n* 'cup-tie (in football *etc*) one of a series of games *eg* in a competition for which the prize is a cup.

cupboard ['kubərd] *n* a recess in a room with a door and shelves or a box with doors, often hung on walls, used for storing things.

cu'pidity *n* greed.

'cupola *n* a curved ceiling or dome on the top of a building.

cur *n* a dog of mixed breed; a cowardly person.

curare [kū'räri] *n* a kind of poison used by some S. American Indians on the tips of their arrows.

'curate *n* a Church of England clergyman assisting a rector or a vicar.

cu'rator *n* one who has charge of a museum, art gallery *etc*.

curb *v* to hold back, try to prevent from going on. – Also *n*.

curd *n* milk thickened by acid; the cheese part of milk, as opposed to the **whey**. – *v* 'curdle to turn into curd. – **curdle someone's blood** to shock or terrify someone.

cure *n* the act of freeing from disease, healing; that which heals. – *v* to heal; to get rid of (a bad habit *etc*); to preserve, *eg* by drying, salting *etc*. – *adjs* 'curable; 'curative likely to cure.

curfew ['kərfū] *n* an order forbidding people to be in the streets after a certain hour; (*hist*) the ringing of an evening bell, as a signal to put out all fires and lights.

'curio *n* an article valued for its oddness or rareness: – *pl* 'curios.

'curious *adj* anxious to find out; unusual, odd. – *n* curi'osity strong desire to find out; anything unusual: – *pl* curi'osities.

curl *v* to twist (hair) into small coils or rolls; (of hair) to grow naturally in small coils; (of smoke *etc*) to move in a spiral; to twist out of shape, form a curved shape; to play at the game of curling. – *n* a small coil or roll as of hair. – *n* 'curling a game played by throwing round, flat stones along a sheet of ice. – *adj* 'curly having curls.

curlew ['kərlū] *n* a type of wading bird with very long slender bill and legs.

'currant *n* a kind of small black raisin; any of various kinds of small, soft, round fruit: *redcurrant*.

'current *adj* belonging to the present time: *the current year*; passing from person to person, generally accepted. *That story is current.* – *n* a stream of water, air or electrical power moving in a certain direction. – n **'currency** the money (notes and coins) of a country; state or time of being current or well-known. *The story gained currency*: – *pl* **'currencies**. – n **current account** a bank account from which money may be withdrawn by cheque.

cur'**rīcūlum** n the course of study at a university, school *etc*. – n **curriculum vitae** ['vētī] a brief account of the main events of a person's life.

'**curry** n a kind of food (meat, vegetables *etc*) containing a mixture of spices which gives a strong, peppery flavour: – *pl* **'curries**. – v to cook (meat *etc*) using the spices necessary for a curry; to rub down (a horse): – *pt* **'curried**. – n **curry powder** a selection of spices ground together used in making a curry. – **curry favour** to try hard to be someone's favourite.

curse v to use swear words; to wish evil on (someone). – n a wish for evil or a magic spell. *The witch put a curse on him*; an evil or a great misfortune or the cause of this. – *adjs* **cursed** under a curse; **cursed** ['kərsid] hateful.

'**cursory** adj hurried.

curt adj impolitely short, abrupt. – n **'curtness**.

cur'**tail** v to make less, reduce. – n cur'**tailment**.

'**curtain** n a piece of material hung to cover a window, stage *etc*.

'**curtsy**, '**curtsey** n a bow made by women by bending the knees: – *pl* **'curtsies**.

curve n a rounded line, like part of the edge of a circle: anything shaped like this: *curve in the road*. – v to bend; to form into a curve. – n **'curvature** a curving or bending; a curved piece (of something); an abnormal curving, as of the spine.

cushion ['kŏoshən] n a casing of some soft material filled with stuffing (rags, foam rubber *etc*) for resting on; any soft pad.

cushy ['kŏoshi] adj (*coll*) easy and comfortable: *a cushy job*.

'**custard** n a dish consisting of milk, eggs *etc* flavoured, and cooked together.

'**custody** n care, guardianship; imprisonment. – n **cus'tōdian** a keeper; a caretaker (*eg* of a museum).

'**custom** n something done by habit or because it is usual; the regular or frequent doing of something; habit; the regular buying of goods at the same shop *etc*; (*pl*) taxes on goods coming into a country; (*pl*) the department of the government that collects these or

the place where they are collected. – *adj* '**customary** usual. – n '**customer** one who buys (regularly) from a shop; (*coll*) a person: *an awkward customer*. – *adj* '**custom-'built** built to suit a particular demand or purpose.

cut v to make a slit or opening in, or divide, with something sharp (*eg* scissors, a knife): *cut a hole in*: *cut a slice of bread*; to wound; to remove with something sharp (*eg* scissors, lawnmower): *cut hair*: *cut the grass*; to reduce in amount; to shorten (a play, book *etc*) by removing parts (of it); to ignore (a person one knows); to divide in two (a pack of cards); to stop filming; (*coll*) to stay away from: *cut school for the day*: – *pres p* '**cutting**, *pt* **cut**. – n a slit or opening made by cutting; a wound made with something sharp; a stroke or blow; a thrust with a sword; the way a thing is cut; the shape and style (of clothes); a piece (of meat). – n '**cutting** a piece cut from a newspaper; a trench or passage, cut in the earth or rock for a railway or road; a twig or shoot of a tree or plant. – *adj* '**cut-and-'dried** (of plans *etc*) arranged carefully and exactly. – n **cut glass** glass with ornamental patterns cut on the surface, used for vases, drinking-glasses *etc*. – *adj* '**cut-'price** sold at a price lower than usual. – n '**cut-throat** a wicked dangerous person. – *adj* '**cut-'up** distressed. – **cut down** to take down by cutting; to reduce (supply, amount taken *etc*); **cut in** to interrupt; **cut off** to separate. *They were cut off from the mainland by the tide*; to stop: *cut off supplies*; **cut out** to shape (a dress *etc*) by cutting; (*coll*) to stop; of an engine, to fail.

cute adj smart, clever; pretty and pleasing.

'**cūticle** n the skin at the bottom and edges of finger and toe nails.

'**cutlass** n a short broad sword: – *pl* '**cutlasses**.

'**cutlery** n knives, forks, spoons *etc*.

'**cutlet** n a slice of meat *usu* with the bone attached.

'**cuttlefish** n a type of sea creature like a squid.

'**cyanide** n a kind of poison.

'**cycle** n short for **bicycle**; a number or round of events coming one after the other, over and over again: *the cycle of the seasons*; a period of time in which events happen in this way; a number of poems, songs, stories, written about one main person or event. – v to ride a bicycle. – n '**cyclist** one who rides a bicycle.

'**cȳclone** *n* a whirling windstorm; a system of winds blowing in a spiral. – *adj* **cyclonic** [si'klonik].

'**cygnet** *n* a young swan.

'**cylinder** *n* a solid or hollow tube-shaped object; in machines, motor-car engines *etc*, the hollow tube in which a piston works. – *adj* **cy'lindrical** shaped like a cylinder.

'**cymbals** *npl* brass, plate-like musical instruments, beaten together in pairs.

'**cynic** *n* one who believes the worst about people. – *n* '**cynicism**. – *adj* '**cynical** sneering; believing the worst of people.

cynosure ['sinəzūr] *n* centre of attraction.

'**cȳpress** *n* a type of evergreen tree.

cyst *n* a kind of liquid-filled blister on an internal part of the body or just under the skin.

cys'titis *n* inflammation of the bladder.

czar *see* **tsar**.

D

dab *v* to touch gently with a pad, cloth *etc*, *eg* to soak up moisture: – *pt* **dabbed**. – *n* the act of dabbing; a small lump of anything soft or moist; a gentle blow, pat; a small kind of flounder. – *n*, *adj* **dab-'hand** (*coll*) expert.

'**dabble** *v* to play in water with hands or feet; to do (something) in a half-serious way or as a hobby. *He dabbles in witchcraft.* – *n* '**dabbler**.

dace *n* a type of small river fish.

dachshund ['daks-hoŏnd] *n* a breed of dog with short legs and a long body.

dad, '**daddy** *ns coll* or child's names for **father**.

'**dādo** *n* the lower part of an inside wall when decorated in a different way from the rest: – *pl* '**dado(e)s**.

'**daffodil** *n* a type of yellow flower which grows from a bulb.

daft *adj* silly.

'**dagger** *n* a short sword for stabbing.

dahlia ['dālyə] *n* a type of garden plant with large flowers.

'**daily** *adj, adv* every day. – *n* a paper published every day; a person who is paid to clean a house regularly (also **daily help**): – *pl* '**dailies**.

'**dainty** *adj* small and neat; pleasant-tasting. – *n* anything pleasant (*esp* tasty food): – *pl* '**dainties**. – *n* '**daintiness**.

'**dairy** *n* the place where milk is kept, and butter and cheese are made; a shop which sells milk *etc*: – *pl* '**dairies**. – *ns* **dairy cattle** cows kept for their milk, not their meat; **dairy farm** a farm mainly concerned with the production of milk, butter *etc*; '**dairymaid**, '**dairyman** woman, man working in a dairy.

dais ['dāis] *n* a raised floor 'at the upper end of a hall *etc*: – *pl* **daises** ['dāisiz].

daisy ['dāzi] *n* a type of small common flower with white petals: – *pl* '**daisies**.

dale *n* low ground between hills.

'**dally** *v* to waste time by idleness or play; to play (with): – *pt* '**dallied**. – *n* '**dalliance**.

Dal'matian *n* a breed of large spotted dog.

dam *n* a bank or wall of earth, concrete *etc* to keep back water; the water kept in like this; a mother, *esp* of animals. – *v* to keep back by a dam; to hold back, control (tears *etc*): – *pt* **dammed**.

'**damage** *n* hurt or injury *esp* to a thing; (*pl*) money paid, by order of a law court, by one person to another to make up for injury, insults *etc*. – *v* to spoil, make less effective or unusable.

'**damask** *n* silk, linen or cotton cloth, with figures and designs.

dame *n* a comic woman in a pantomime, *usu* played by a man dressed up as a woman; **Dame** the title of a woman of the same rank as a knight.

damn [dam] *v* to sentence to unending punishment (in hell); to condemn as wrong, bad *etc*. – *adj* **damnable** ['damnəbl] deserving to be condemned; hateful. – *n* **dam'nation** unending punishment; condemnation.

damp *n* moist air; wetness. – *v* to wet slightly; to make less fierce or intense (*eg* a fire). – *adj* moist, slightly wet. – *n* '**dampness**. – *v* '**dampen** to make or become damp or moist; to lessen (enthusiasm *etc*). – *n* '**damper** that which damps or dampens.

damsel ['damzəl] *n* (*old*) an unmarried girl.

damson ['damzən] *n* a type of small dark-red plum.

dance *v* to move in time to music. – Also *n*. – *n* '**dancer**.

'**dandelion** *n* a type of common plant with a yellow flower.

'**dandruff** *n* dead skin which collects under the hair and falls off in small pieces.

'dandy *n* a man who pays great attention to his dress and looks: – *pl* **'dandies**.

danger ['dānjər] *n* something which may harm. *The canal is a danger to children*; a state in which one may be harmed. *He is in danger.* – *adj* **'dangerous** unsafe, likely to cause harm; full of risks.

dangle ['daŋgl] *v* to hang loosely.

dank *adj* moist, wet.

'dapper *adj* small and neat.

'dappled *adj* marked with spots or splashes of colour.

dare *v* to be brave or bold enough (to); to lay oneself open to, to risk: *dare his anger*; to challenge. *He dared him to cross the railway line.* – *adj* **'daring** bold, fearless. – *n* boldness. – *n* **'dare-devil** a rash person fond of taking risks. – Also *adj.* – **I dare say** I suppose. *I dare say you're right.*

dark *adj* without light; black or of a colour near to black; gloomy; evil: *dark deeds.* – *ns* **dark, 'darkness.** – *v* **'darken** to make or grow dark or darker. – *adj* **'dark-'haired** having dark-brown or black hair. – **a dark horse** a person about whom little is known; **in the dark** knowing nothing (about something); **keep dark** to keep (something) secret.

'darling *n* a word showing affection; one dearly loved; a favourite.

darn *v* to mend (clothes) with crossing rows of stitches. – *n* the place so mended.

dart *n* a pointed, arrow-like weapon for throwing or shooting; something which pierces; (*pl*) a game in which small darts are aimed at a board (**'dartboard**) marked off in circles and numbered sections. – *v* to move quickly and suddenly.

dash *v* to throw, knock *etc* violently, *esp* so as to break; to ruin (*esp* hopes); to depress, sadden (spirits *etc*); to rush with speed or violence. – *n* a rush; a short race; a small amount (as of soda water *etc*); liveliness; in writing, a short line (–) to show a break in a sentence *etc*: – *pl* **'dashes.** – *adj* **'dashing** hasty; spirited, smart.

'dastardly *adj* cowardly.

'dāta *npl* available facts (from which conclusions may be drawn): – *sing* **'datum**.

date[1] *n* a statement of time expressed in terms of the day, month and year (*eg* 23 December 1946); the time at which an event occurs or occurred; the period of time to which something belongs; an appointment. *I have a date with her next Wednesday.* – *v* to give a date to; to belong to a certain time. *This castle dates from the 12th century*; to become old-fashioned. *That dress will date quickly.* – **out of date** old-fashioned; no longer used; no longer valid; **up to date** in fashion, modern; including, or knowledgeable about, the latest information; at the point (in work *etc*) that one should be.

date[2] *n* a type of palm-tree, or its fruit.

datum *see* **data**.

daub *v* to smear; to paint roughly or without skill.

daughter ['dötər] *n* a female child (when spoken of in relation to her parents). – *n* **'daughter-in-law** a son's wife.

daunt *v* to frighten; to be discouraging. – *adj* **'dauntless** unable to be frightened.

'Dāvy-lamp *n* a kind of safety lamp for coalminers.

daw short for **jackdaw**.

'dawdle *v* to move slowly. – *n* **'dawdler**.

dawn *n* beginning (*esp* of a day). – *v* to become day; to begin to appear. – *n* **'dawning** dawn. – **dawn on** to become suddenly clear to (someone).

day *n* the time of light, from sunrise to sunset; twenty-four hours, from one midnight to the next; the time or hours *usu* spent at work; (sometimes *pl*) a particular time or period: *in the days of steam.* – *n* **'daydream** a dreaming or imagining of pleasant events while awake. – Also *v.* – *ns* **'daylight** the light of day, of the sun; **'day-re'lease** time off from work for education. – **day in, day out** on and on, continuously; **the other day** recently.

daze *v* to make to feel confused *eg* by a blow, to stun; to bewilder.

'dazzle *v* (of a strong light) to prevent one from seeing clearly; to shine brilliantly; to fascinate, impress deeply.

'deacon *n* the lowest rank of clergyman in the Church of England; a church official in other churches: – *fem* **'deaconess**.

dead [ded] *adj* without life; cold and cheerless; numb; (of an engine *etc*) not working; no longer in use; complete: *dead silence*; exact: *dead centre*; certain: *a dead shot.* – *adv* completely: *dead certain*; suddenly and completely: *stop dead.* – *n* those who have died. *Speak well of the dead*; the time of greatest stillness, coldness, darkness *etc*: *the dead of night.* – *n* **'deadness.** – *v* **'deaden** to lessen pain *etc*. – *adj* **'deadly** likely to cause death, fatal; intense, very great. – *adv* intensely, extremely. – *n* **'deadliness.** – *adjs* '**dead-and-a'live** dull, having little life; '**dead-'beat** having no strength left; '**dead-'end** of a road *etc* closed at one end; of a job *etc* not leading to promotion. – *ns* **dead heat** a race in which two or more runners are equal; '**deadline** a date by which something must be done; '**deadlock** a standstill resulting from a complete failure to agree. – *adj* '**deadpan** without expression on the face.

deaf [def] *adj* unable to hear; refusing to listen. – *v* '**deafen** to make deaf; to have an unpleasant effect on the hearing; to make (walls *etc*) soundproof. – *n* '**deafness**. – *n* '**deaf-'mute** one who is both deaf and dumb.

deal *n* a (business) agreement or arrangement; an amount or quantity: *a good deal of paper*; the dividing out of playing cards in a game; a kind of softwood. – *v* to divide, give out; to trade (in); to do business (with); (with **with**) to take action concerning, cope with. *He deals with all the problems.* – *n* '**dealer** one who deals; a trader.

dean *n* the chief clergyman in a cathedral church; an important official of a university.

dear *adj* high in price; highly valued; much loved. – *n* one who is loved; one who is lovable or charming. – *adv* at a high price. – *adv* '**dearly**. – *n* '**dearness**.

dearth [dȫrth] *n* a scarcity, shortage.

death [deth] *n* the state of being dead, the end of life; the end (of something): *the death of music halls.* – *adj, adv* '**deathly** like death; very pale or ill-looking. – *ns* '**death-blow** a blow that causes death; an event *etc* that causes the end of something; '**death-mask** a plastercast taken of a dead person's face; **death rattle** a rattling in the throat which is sometimes heard before a person's death; **death roll** a list of the dead; **deathwatch beetle** a kind of insect that makes a ticking noise and whose larva destroys wood.

de'bar *v* to keep from, prevent: – *pt* **de'barred**.

de'base *v* to lessen in value; to make bad, wicked *etc*. – *adj* **de'based**. – *n* **de-'basement**.

de'bate *n* a discussion, *esp* a formal one before an audience; an argument. – Also *v*. – *adj* **de'batable** able to be argued about, doubtful: *a debatable point*.

debauchery [di'bȫchəri] *n* excessive indulgence in drunkenness and other (immoral) pleasures. – *adj*

de'bauched given to, inclined to debauchery.

de'bilitate *v* to make weak. – *n* **de'bility** weakness of the body.

'**debit** *n* a debt. – *v* to mark something down as a debt.

debo'nair *adj* of pleasant and cheerful appearance and manners.

de'bouch *v* to come out from a narrow or confined place.

de'brief ['dē'brēf] *v* to gather information (from an astronaut, spy *etc*) after a mission.

débris ['dābrē] *n* the remains of something broken, destroyed *etc*; rubbish.

debt [det] *n* what one owes to another. – *n* '**debtor** one who owes a debt. – **in debt** owing money; **in someone's debt** under an obligation to someone, owing someone a favour *etc*.

début ['dābū] *n* the first public appearance (*eg* of an actor). – *n* **debutante** ['debūtänt] a young woman making her first appearance in upper-class society.

'**decade** *n* a period of ten years; a set or series of ten.

'**decadence** *n* a falling (from high) to low standards in morals, the arts *etc*. – *adj* '**decadent**.

de'camp *v* to run away.

de'cant *v* to pour (wine) from a bottle into a decanter. – *n* **de'canter** a bottle (*usu* ornamental) with a glass stopper for wine, whisky *etc*.

de'capitate *v* to cut the head from. – *n* **decapi'tation**.

de'cathlon *n* a contest consisting of ten events in the Olympic Games *etc*.

de'cay *v* to become bad, worse or rotten. – Also *n*. – *adj* **de'cayed**.

de'cease *n* death. – *adj* **de'ceased** dead. – *n* (with **the**) a dead person.

deceit [di'sēt] *n* the act of deceiving. – *adj* **de'ceitful**.

deceive [di'sēv] *v* to tell untruths so as to mislead; to cheat. – *n* **de'ceiver**.

decelerate [dē'selərāt] *v* to slow down.

De'cember *n* the twelfth month of the year.

'**decent** *adj* respectable; good enough, adequate: *a decent salary*; kind. *It's decent of you to help.* – *n* '**decency**.

de'ception *n* the act of deceiving, cheating; something that deceives or is intended to deceive. – *adj* **de'ceptive** different from what it seems or looks, misleading. *Appearances may be deceptive.* – *adv* **de'ceptively**.

'**decibel** *n* a unit of loudness of sound.

de'cide *v* to make up one's mind (to do something); to settle (an argument *etc*). – *adj* **de'cided** clear: *a decided difference*; with one's mind made up. – *adv* **de'cidedly** definitely.

de'cidūous *adj* (of trees) having leaves that fall in autumn.

'decimal *adj* numbered by tens; of ten parts or the number 10. – *n* a decimal fraction. – *v* **'decimalize** to convert (figures or a country's currency) to decimal form. – *n* **decimali'zation**. – *ns* **decimal currency** a system of money in which each coin or note is either a tenth of another or ten times another in value; **decimal fraction** a fraction expressed as so many tenths, hundredths, thousandths *etc* and written using a **decimal point** like this $0.1=\frac{1}{10}$, $2.33=2\frac{33}{100}$.

'decimate *v* to make much smaller in numbers, *esp* by destruction.

de'cipher *v* to translate (writing in code) into ordinary, understandable language; to make out the meaning of (something difficult to read).

decision [di'sizhən] *n* the act of deciding; the ability to decide; judgement; firmness. *He acted with decision.* – *adj* **de'cisive** final, putting an end to a contest *etc*: *a decisive defeat*; showing decision and firmness: *a decisive manner*.

deck *v* to put ornaments *etc* on, adorn. – *n* a platform extending from one side of a ship *etc* to the other and forming the floor; a floor on a bus *etc*; a pack (of playing cards). – *n* **'deck-chair** a collapsible chair of wood and canvas *etc*.

de'claim *v* to make a speech in impressive dramatic language; to speak violently (against someone). – *n* **decla'mation**. – *adj* **declamatory** [di'klamətəri].

de'clare *v* to make known (*eg* goods on which duty is payable, income on which tax is payable); to announce *esp* formally or publicly: *declare war*; to say firmly; (in cricket) to end an innings before ten wickets have fallen. – *n* **decla'ration**.

declension [di'klen·shən] *n* a system of cases and case-endings (*gram*); a class of words similarly declined; decay, descent.

de'cline *v* to say 'no' (to an invitation, offer *etc*), refuse; to become less strong, less good *etc*; to slope down. – *n* a downward slope; a gradual worsening (of health *etc*).

de'clivity *n* a downward slope: – *pl* **de'clivities**.

dē'code *v* to translate (a coded message)

into ordinary, understandable language.

decompose [dēkəm'pōz] *v* to rot, decay; to separate in parts or elements. – *n* **decompo'sition**.

décor ['dākör] *n* the decoration of a room *etc* and the arrangement of objects in it.

'decorate *v* to add some form of ornament to (someone or something); to make more beautiful, impressive *etc*; to paint, paper the walls of (a room *etc*); to pin a badge or medal on (someone) as a mark of honour. – *n* **deco'ration**. – *adj* **'decorative** ornamental; pretty. – *n* **'decorator** one who decorates houses, rooms *etc*.

'decorous *adj* behaving in an acceptable or dignified way. – *n* **de'corum** good behaviour.

de'coy *v* to lead into a trap or into evil. – *n* ['dēkoi] anything intended to lead another into a trap.

de'crease *v* to make or become less in number. – *n* **'dēcrease** a growing less.

de'cree *n* an order or law; a judge's decision. – *v* to give an order: – *pt* **de'creed**.

de'crepit *adj* weak and infirm because of old age; in ruins or disrepair. – *n* **de'crepitude**.

de'crȳ *v* to make (something) seem worthless, belittle; to express disapproval of: – *pt* **de'cried**.

'dedicate *v* to give up wholly to, devote to: *dedicated to teaching*: *dedicated to football*; to set apart *esp* for a holy or sacred purpose; to name a person in the front page of a book. *I dedicate this book to my father.* – *n* **dedi'cation**.

de'duce *v* to find out something by putting together all that is known. – *n* **deduction** [di'dukshən].

de'duct *v* to subtract, take away (from). – *n* **de'duction** a subtraction; an amount subtracted.

deed *n* something done, an act; (in law) a signed statement or bargain.

deep *adj* being or going far down; hard to understand; cunning; occupied or involved to a great extent: *deep in debt*; intense, strong: *of a deep red colour*; heartfelt: *deep love*; low in pitch. — *n* (with **the**) the sea. — *v* **'deepen** to make deep. — *adj* **'deep-seated** firmly fixed, not easily removed. — **in deep water** in difficulties or trouble.

deer *n* a kind of animal with antlers (*usu* in the male only), such as the reindeer: – *pl* **deer**.

de'face *v* to spoil the appearance of, disfigure. – *n* **de'facement**.

de'fame *v* to (try to) harm the reputation

of. – *n* **defamation** [defə'māshən]. – *adj* **defamatory** [di'famətəri].

de'fault *v* to fail to do something one ought to do, *eg* to pay a debt. – Also *n*. – *n* **de'faulter**.

de'feat *v* to beat, win a victory over (in a fight, competition *etc*). – Also *n*.

'dēfect *n* a lack of something necessary for completeness or perfection, a flaw. – *v* **de'fect** to desert a country, political party *etc* to join or go to another: *defect to the West*. – *n* **de'fection** failure in duty; desertion. – *adj* **de'fective** faulty; incomplete; (of a person) not having normal mental or physical ability.

de'fence, (*US*) **de'fense** *n* the act or action of defending against attack; a means or method of protection; a person's answer to a charge made against him, *esp* in a law-court. – *adj* **de'fenceless** without defence.

de'fend *v* to guard or protect against attack; to conduct the defence of in a law-court. – *n* **de'fendant** one who resists attack; the accused person in a law case. – *adjs* **de'fensible** able to be defended; **de'fensive** defending or protecting. – **on the defensive** prepared to defend oneself against attack or criticism.

de'fer *v* to put off to another time; to give way (to the wishes *etc* of another): – *pt* **de'ferred**. – *n* **'deference** respect, willingness to consider the wishes *etc* of others; the act of giving way to another. – *adj* **defe'rential** showing deference or respect.

de'fiance *n* open disobedience or opposition. – *adj* **de'fiant**.

de'ficient *adj* lacking in what is needed. – *n* **de'ficiency** lack, want; the amount lacking: – *pl* **de'ficiencies**.

'deficit *n* amount by which something (*eg* a sum of money) is too little.

de'file *v* to make dirty, to soil; to corrupt, make bad or evil. – *n* **de'filement**.

de'fine *v* to fix the bounds or limits of; to outline or show clearly; to state the exact meaning of. – *adj* **definite** ['definit] having clear limits, fixed; exact; certain; clear. – *ns* **'definiteness, defi'nition** an explanation of the exact meaning of a word or phrase; sharpness or clearness of outline. – *adj* **de'finitive** quite fixed, final, settling once and for all. – *n* **definite article** the name given to the adjective *the*.

de'flate *v* to let the air or gas out of (a tyre *etc*); to reduce (a person's) self-importance or self-confidence.

– *n* **de'flation**.

de'flect *v* to turn aside (from a fixed course or direction). – *n* **de'flection**.

de'form *v* to spoil the shape of; to make ugly. – *adj* **de'formed** badly or abnormally formed. – *n* **de'formity** a part abnormal in shape; state of being badly shaped: – *pl* **de'formities**.

de'fraud *v* to cheat; (with **of**) to take by cheating or fraud.

de'fray *v* to pay for (the expenses of anything).

'dē'frost *v* to remove frost or ice (from a refrigerator), thaw.

deft *adj* clever (*esp* with the fingers). – *n* **'deftness**.

de'funct *adj* no longer active or in use.

de'fȳ *v* to dare someone (to do something), to challenge; to resist boldly or openly; to make impossible. *Her beauty defies description*: – *pt* **de'fied**.

degenerate [di'jenərət] *adj* having become immoral or very bad. – *v* to become or grow bad or worse. – *n* **degene'ration**.

de'grade *v* to lower in grade, rank *etc*; to disgrace. – *adj* **de'grading**. – *n* **degradation** [degrə'dāshən].

de'gree *n* a step or stage in a process *etc*; rank or grade; amount, extent: *a degree of certainty*; a unit of temperature; a unit by which angles are measured, one 360th part of the circumference of a circle; a title or certificate given by a university (gained by examination or as an honour).

'dēhȳ'drate *v* to remove water from (*esp* food), dry out. – *n* **'dehy'dration**.

deify ['dāifi] *v* to worship as a god: – *pt* **'deified**.

deign [dān] *v* to do as a favour, or act as if one is doing a favour. *She deigned to answer us*.

deity ['dāəti] *n* a god or goddess: – *pl* **'deities**.

de'jected *adj* gloomy, dispirited. – *n* **de'jection**.

de'lay *v* to put off to a later time; to keep back, hinder. – Also *n*.

de'lectable *adj* delightful, pleasing.

delegate ['deligāt] *v* to give (a task) to someone else to do. – *n* ['deligət] someone acting on behalf of another or others, a representative. – *n* **dele'gation** a group of delegates.

de'lete *v* to rub or strike out (*eg* a piece of writing). – *n* **de'letion**.

deleterious [deli'tēriəs] *adj* harmful.

deliberate [di'libərāt] *v* to think carefully or seriously (about). – *adj* [di'libərət] intentional, not by accident; slow in deciding; not hurried. – *adv* **de'liberately**. – *n* **delibe'ration** careful thought; calmness, coolness; (*pl*) formal discussions.

'**delicate** *adj* not strong, frail; easily damaged; of fine texture; dainty, done by fine work; pleasing to the senses, *esp* the taste; tactful; requiring careful handling. – *n* '**delicacy** the state of being delicate; tact; something delicious to eat: – *pl* '**delicacies**.

delica'tessen *n* a shop selling food cooked or prepared ready for serving.

delicious [di'lishəs] *adj* pleasant to the taste; giving pleasure. – *n* **de'liciousness**.

delight [di'lït] *v* to please highly; to take great pleasure (in). – Also *n*. – *adjs* **de'lighted; de'lightful**.

delinquent [di'liŋkwənt] *adj* guilty of an offence or misdeed; not carrying out one's duties. – *n* a person who is guilty of an offence; a person who fails in his duty. – *n* **de'linquency** wrongdoing, misdeeds; failure in duty.

de'lirious *adj* raving, wandering in the mind (*usu* as a result of fever); wildly excited. – *n* **de'lirium** state of being delirious; wild excitement. — *n* **delirium tremens** a delirious disorder of the brain produced by over-absorption of alcohol.

de'liver *v* to hand over; to give out (*eg* a speech, blow); to set free; to rescue; to assist at the birth of (a child). – *ns* **de'liverance** a freeing; **de'livery** a handing over (as of letters, parcels *etc*); the birth of a child; way of speaking: – *pl* **de'liveries**.

del'phinium *n* a kind of branching garden plant, *usu* with blue flowers.

'**delta** *n* the triangular stretch of land at the mouth of a river which reaches the sea in two or more branches.

delude [di'lood] *v* to deceive. – *n* **de'lusion** the act of deluding; a false belief, *esp* as a symptom of mental illness.

deluge ['delūj] *n* a great flow of anything, *esp* water (also work to be done, letters to be answered *etc*). – *v* to flood (with water, work *etc*).

delve *v* to dig; to search deeply and carefully.

de'mand *v* to ask, or ask for, firmly or sharply; to insist; to require, call for. *This demands instant attention.* – *n* a request which seems like a command; urgent claim: *demands on my time*; a wish or willingness to buy or a need for (certain goods *etc*).

de'mean *v* to lower, degrade (*esp*

oneself).

de'meanour *n* behaviour, conduct.

de'mented *adj* out of one's mind, insane.

de'mise *n* death.

'**dē'mob** short for **demobilize** or **demobilization**.

dē'mōbilize *v* to break up an army after a war is over; to free (a soldier) from army service. – *n* **demobili'zation**.

de'mocracy *n* government of the people by the people through their elected parliament. – *n* '**democrat** one who believes in this kind of government; (*US*) '**Democrat** a member of the American Democratic Party. – *adj* **demo'cratic**. – *adj*, *n* (*US*) **Demo'cratic** (of, belonging to) one of the two chief political parties in the USA.

de'molish *v* to lay in ruins, pull or tear down (a building *etc*). – *n* **demo-'lition**.

'**dēmon** *n* an evil spirit, a devil.

'**demonstrate** *v* to show clearly; to prove; to show (a machine *etc*) in action; to express a (*usu* political) opinion by marching, showing placards *etc* in public. – *adj* '**demonstrable** able to be shown clearly. – *n* **demon'stration** a show; a display; proof; a public expression of opinion by processions, mass-meetings *etc*. – *adj* **de'monstrative** pointing out; proving; (in the habit of) showing one's feelings openly. – *n* '**demonstrator** one who shows (*eg* the working of a machine); a person who takes part in a public demonstration.

de'moralize *v* to take away the confidence of.

de'mote *v* to reduce to a lower rank or grade. – *n* **de'motion**.

de'mur *v* to object, say 'no': – *pt* **de'murred**.

de'mure *adj* shy and modest. – *n* **de'mureness**.

den *n* the lair or cave of a wild animal; a small private room for working *etc*.

denier ['deniər] *n* a unit of weight of nylon, silk, rayon yarn.

'**denigrate** *v* to attack the reputation of, defame.

'**denim** *n* a type of cotton cloth used for jeans, overalls *etc*.

'**denizen** *n* a dweller, an inhabitant.

denomi'nation *n* name or title; a value (as of a coin, stamp *etc*); a group of people of the same religious beliefs. – *adj* **denomi'national**. – *n* **de'nominator** the lower number in a vulgar fraction by which the upper number is divided (as the 3 in $^2/_3$).

de'note v to mean, be a sign of.

dénouement [dā'nōōmöṅ] n the most important part of a story (eg where a mystery is solved).

de'nounce v to accuse (of a crime etc) publicly; to inform against. He denounced him to the enemy. – n **denunciation** [dinunsi'āshɔn].

dense adj closely packed together; thick; very stupid. – ns **'denseness; 'density** the state of being dense; the weight of a standard volume of something (eg water): – pl **'densities**.

dent n a hollow made by a blow or pressure. – v to make a dent in.

'dental adj of a tooth or teeth.

'dentist n one who cures tooth troubles (by filling, taking teeth out etc). – ns **'dentistry** the work of a dentist; **'denture** (often pl) a set of false teeth.

de'nūde v to make bare, strip (something) of a covering of any kind. The wind denuded the trees of leaves. – n **dēnu'dation**.

denunciation see denounce.

de'nȳ v to declare to be untrue. I deny that I did it; to refuse, forbid. I deny you the right to leave : – pt **de'nied**. – n **de'nial**. – **deny oneself** to do without (things that one desires or needs).

dē'ōdorant n something that removes or hides unpleasant smells.

de'part v to go away; to turn aside from : depart from one's plans. – n **de'parture**. – **a new departure** a new course of action of some kind.

de'partment n a separate part or branch (of a shop, university, government etc).

de'pend v (with **on** or **upon**) to rely on; (with **on**) to receive necessary support (esp financial) from; (with **on** or **upon**) to be controlled or decided by. It all depends on the weather. – adj **de'pendable** to be trusted. – ns **de'pendant** one who is kept or supported by another; **de'pendence** the state of being dependent. – adj **de'pendent** depending; relying on another for (esp financial) support.

de'pict v to draw, paint etc; to describe.

de'plete v to make smaller in amount, number etc. – n **de'pletion**.

de'plore v to feel or express disapproval or regret about (something). – adj **de'plorable** regrettable; very bad.

de'ploy v to place in position ready for action.

dē'popūlate v to reduce greatly the number of people in (an area etc). – adj **de'populated** empty of people; reduced in population.

deport v to send (a person) out of a country. – n **depor'tation**. – n **de'portment** way of carrying or holding oneself; behaviour.

de'pose v to remove from a high position (esp a king from his throne). – n **depo'sition** the act of deposing; see also **deposit**.

deposit [di'pozit] v to place; to put or set down; to put in for safe keeping (eg money in a bank). – n money paid in part payment of something which one means to buy; money put in a bank; a solid that has settled at the bottom of a liquid; a layer (of coal, iron etc) occurring naturally in rock etc. – ns **depo'sition** a written piece of evidence; **de'pository** a place where anything is deposited : – pl **de'positories**. – n **deposit account** a bank account from which money must be withdrawn in person, not by cheque.

depot ['depō] n a storehouse; a military station where stores are kept; the place where railway engines, buses etc are kept and repaired.

de'prave v to make wicked. – adj **de'praved** wicked. – n **depravity** [di'pravɔti].

'deprecate v to show disapproval of, condemn as bad. – n **depre'cation**.

depreciate [di'prēshiāt] v to lessen the value of; to fall in value. – n **depreci'ation**.

depre'dation n (often pl) plundering.

de'press v to make gloomy, unhappy or of low spirits; to press down; to lower in value, amount etc. – n **de'pression** low spirits, gloominess; a hollow; a lowering in value etc; a period in which the economic situation of a country is bad with unemployment, lack of trade etc; a region of low atmospheric pressure.

de'prive v to take away. They deprived the king of his power. – n **deprivation** [depri'vāshɔn] the act of depriving; the state of being deprived. – adj **de'prived** suffering from hardship etc, disadvantaged.

depth n deepness; a deep place; the deepest part; the middle : depth of winter; intensity, strength. – **in depth** thorough(ly), careful(ly); **out of one's depth** in water deeper than one can stand up in; concerned in problems too difficult to understand.

depū'tation n persons chosen (and sent) to speak or act for others. – n **'deputy** one acting in place of another; a delegate, representative : – pl **'deputies**. – v **'deputize** to take another's place for a time, act as substitute.

de'rail *v* to cause to leave the rails. – *n* **de'railment**.

de'range *v* to put out of place or out of working order. – *adj* **de'ranged** out of one's mind, insane; out of order. – *n* **de'rangement**.

derelict ['derilikt] *adj* broken-down, abandoned (*esp* buildings, ships *etc*). – *n* **dere'liction** the neglecting of what should be attended to: *dereliction of duty*.

de'ride *v* to laugh at, mock. – *n* **derision** [di'rizhən] act of deriding; mockery. – *adj* **de'risive**.

de'rive *v* to be descended or formed (from); to trace (a word) back to the beginning of its existence; to receive, obtain: *derive satisfaction*. – *n* **derivation** [deri'vāshən]. – *n, adj* **de'rivative** (something) derived from something else, not original; a word made from another word (*eg fabulous* from *fable*).

derma'titis *n* inflammation of the skin.

derma'tology *n* the study and treatment of skin diseases. – *n* **derma'tologist**.

de'rogatory *adj* harmful to one's reputation, dignity *etc*; scornful, belittling, disparaging.

'derrick *n* a kind of crane for lifting weights; a framework over an oil well that holds the drilling machinery.

'descant *n* (in music) a tune played or sung above the main tune.

descend [di'send] *v* to go or climb down; to slope downwards; to be passed down from parent to child; to have as one's ancestor. *I'm descended from Napoleon*; to go from a greater to a lesser or worse state. – *ns* **de'scendant** a person descended from another; **de'scent** the act or state of descending; a downward slope; the way down.

des'cribe *v* to give an account of in words; to draw the outline of, trace. – *n* **description** [dis'kripshən] the act of describing; an account in words; sort, kind: *people of all descriptions*. – *adj* **des'criptive**.

des'crȳ *v* to notice, see: – *pt* **des'cried**.

desecrate ['desikrāt] *v* to spoil (something sacred); to treat without respect. – *n* **dese'cration**.

desert[1] [di'zɜrt] *v* to run away (from) (*eg* the army), to leave, abandon. *He deserted his family. His courage deserted him.* – *ns* **de'serter** one who deserts *esp* from the army *etc*; **de'sertion** the act of deserting (*esp* from the army *etc*).

desert[2] ['dezərt] *n* a stretch of barren country, *usu* hot, dry and sandy with very little water. – *n* **desert island** an

uninhabited island in a tropical area.

deserve [di'zɜrv] *v* to have earned as a right by one's actions *etc*, be worthy of. – *adj* **de'serving**. – *adv* **deservedly** [di'zɜrvidli] justly.

'desiccate *v* to dry up; to preserve by drying: *desiccated coconut*.

design [di'zīn] *v* to make a plan or a sketch of something (*eg* a building) before it is made; to intend. – *n* a plan or sketch; a painted picture, pattern *etc*; an intention or plan. – *adj* **de'signing** crafty, cunning. – **have designs on** to plan to get (someone or something) for oneself.

designate ['dezignāt] *v* to point out, indicate; to name; to appoint, select (for a duty *etc*). – *adj* appointed to a post but not yet occupying it: *director designate*. – *n* **desig'nation** a name, title.

desire [di'zīr] *v* to wish for (greatly). – *n* a longing for; a wish. – *adj* **de'sirable** pleasing; worth having. – *n* **desira'bility**. – **desirous of** wishing for, wanting something.

desist [di'zist] *v* to stop (doing something).

desk *n* a table for writing, reading *etc*.

'desolate *adj* lonely; sorrowful, unhappy; empty of people, deserted; barren. – *adj* **'desolated** overcome by grief; made desolate. – *n* **deso'lation** the state of being desolated; loneliness; deep sorrow; barren land; ruin.

des'pair *v* to give up hope. – *n* lack of hope; that which causes despair. *He was the despair of his parents*. – *adj* **des'pairing** having no hope.

despatch *see* **dispatch**.

despe'rado *n* a bold or violent criminal, a gangster: – *pls* **despe'rado(e)s**.

'desperate *adj* having lost all hope, despairing; very bad; reckless; violent. – *n* **despe'ration**.

des'picable *adj* contemptible, worthless and hateful.

des'pise *v* to look upon with contempt, regard as worthless or hateful.

des'pite *prep* in spite of. *Despite the rain they went to the seaside.*

des'poil *v* to rob, plunder. – *n* **despoli'ation**.

des'pondent *adj* downhearted, dejected. – *n* **des'pondency**.

'despot *n* one (*usu* king or ruler of a country) with unlimited power, a tyrant. – *adj* **des'potic**. – *n* **'despotism**.

dessert [di'zɜrt] *n* fruits, sweets *etc* served at the end of a meal; pudding, the sweet course in a meal.

destine ['destin] *v* to set apart for a

certain use *etc.* – *adj* **'destined** bound (for a place); intended (as if by fate): *destined to succeed.* – *ns* **desti'nation** the place to which someone or something is going; **'destiny** what is destined to happen; fate: – *pl* **'destinies**.

'destitute *adj* in need of food, shelter *etc*; (with **of**) completely lacking in: *destitute of kindness.* – *n* **desti'tution**.

des'troy *v* to pull down, knock to pieces; to ruin; to kill. – *n* **des'troyer** one who destroys; a type of fast warship.

des'truction *n* the act of destroying or being destroyed; ruin; death. – *adjs* **des'tructible** able to be destroyed; **des'tructive** causing destruction; doing great damage; (of criticism *etc*) pointing out faults without suggesting improvements.

'desultory *adj* moving from one thing to another without a fixed plan; (of conversation *etc*) changing from subject to subject, rambling.

de'tach *v* to unfasten, remove (from). – *adjs* **de'tachable** able to be taken off: *a detachable lining*; **de'tached** standing apart, by itself: *a detached house*; separated; not personally involved, showing no emotion or prejudice. – *n* **de'tachment** state of being detached; the act of detaching; a body or group (*eg* of troops on special service).

'detail *n* a small part, fact, item *etc*. – *v* to describe fully, give particulars of; to set (a person) to do a special job or task. *The airman was detailed for night-flying.* – *adj* **'detailed** with nothing left out. – **in detail** giving attention to details, item by item.

de'tain *v* to hold back; to keep late; to keep under guard. – *n* **de'tention** imprisonment; a forced stay (as a punishment at school at the end of the day).

de'tect *v* to discover; to notice. – *ns* **de'tection; de'tective** one who tries to find criminals or watches suspected persons.

détente [dā'tönt] *n* a lessening of hostility between nations.

detention *see* detain.

de'ter *v* to discourage or prevent from (by frightening): – *pt* **de'terred**. – *adj, n* **de'terrent** (of) something (*esp* a weapon) which deters.

de'tergent *n* a (soapless) substance used with water for washing dishes *etc*.

de'teriorate *v* to grow worse. *His health is deteriorating rapidly.* – *n* **deterio'ration**.

determine [di'tȝrmin] *v* to decide; to fix or settle. *He determined his course of action.* – *n* **determi'nation** the state of being determined; the act of determining; stubbornness, firmness of character and purpose. – *adj* **de'termined** having one's mind made up, decided: *determined to succeed*; stubborn; fixed, settled.

deterrent *see* deter.

de'test *v* to hate greatly. – *adj* **de'testable** very hateful. – *n* **dētes'tation** great hatred.

dē'throne *v* to remove from a throne. – *n* **de'thronement**.

'detonate *v* to (cause to) explode. – *ns* **deto'nation** an explosion; **'detonator** something which sets off an explosive.

detour ['dētoōr] *n* a wandering from the main route.

de'tract *v* to take away (from), lessen (an achievement, value *etc*). – *n* **de'traction**.

'detriment *n* harm, damage, disadvantage. – *adj* **detri'mental** disadvantageous, causing harm or damage.

deuce [dūs] *n* a playing card with two pips; (in tennis scoring) having forty points each.

'devastate *v* to lay waste, leave in ruins; to overcome (a person) with grief *etc*. – *n* **devas'tation**.

de'velop *v* to (make to) grow bigger or to a more advanced state; to acquire gradually (an interest *etc*); to become active, visible *etc*. *Spots developed on her face*; to unfold gradually; to use chemicals (called **de'veloper**) to make a photograph appear. – *n* **de'velopment**.

'dēviate *v* to turn aside, *esp* from the right, normal or standard course. – *n* **devi'ation**.

de'vice *n* something made for a purpose *eg* a tool or an instrument; a plan; a picture or design on a coat of arms.

'devil *n* the spirit of evil, Satan; any evil spirit or person. – *adj* **'devilish** of or like a devil; very wicked. – *ns* **'devilment, 'devilry** mischief. – *adj* **'devil-may-'care** not caring what happens.

'dēvious *adj* not direct, roundabout; not straightforward.

de'vise *v* to make up, put (quickly) together; to plan or plot.

de'void *adj* (with **of**) empty of, free from: *devoid of generosity*.

de'volve *v* to fall as a duty (upon someone).

de'vote *v* to give up wholly (to). – *adj* **de'voted** loving and loyal; given up (to): *devoted to his work*. – *ns* **devo'tee** a keen follower; **de'votion** great love.

de'vour *v* to eat up greedily; to destroy.

de'vout *adj* earnest, sincere; religious. – *n* **de'voutness**.

dew [dū] *n* tiny drops of water coming from the air as it cools at night. – *adj* **'dewy**.

dex'terity *n* skill, quickness. – *adj* **'dext(e)rous**.

diabetes [dīə'bētēz] *n* a disease in which there is too much sugar in the blood. – *adj, n* **diabetic** [dīə'betik].

dia'bolic(al) *adj* devilish, very wicked.

'diadem *n* a kind of crown.

diagnose [dīəg'nōz] *v* to say what is wrong (with a sick person) after making an examination. – *n* **diag'nosis**: – *pl* **diag'nosēs**. – *adj* **diagnostic** [dīəg'nostik].

di'agonal *n, adj* (a line) going from one corner to the opposite corner.

'diagram *n* a drawing to explain something.

'dial *n* the face of a clock or watch; the turning disc over the numbers on a telephone; any disc *etc* containing numbers and a pointer. – *v* to turn a telephone dial to get a number: – *pt* **'dialled**.

'dialect *n* a way of speaking found only in a certain district or among a certain class or group of people.

dialogue ['dīəlog] *n* a talk between two (or more) people.

diameter [dī'amitər] *n* the line (drawn) across a circle, passing through its centre.

'diamond *n* a very hard, precious stone; a kind of four-cornered shape: ◇; a playing card bearing red marks of this shape.

'diaper *n* (*US*) a baby's nappy.

diaphragm ['dīəfram] *n* a layer of muscle separating the lower part of the body from the chest; any thin dividing layer.

diarrhoea [dīə'rēə] *n* looseness of bowel movements.

'diary *n* a (small book containing a) record of daily happenings: – *pl* **'diaries**.

'diatribe *n* an angry attack in words or writing.

dice *n* a small cube *usu* with numbered sides or faces, used in certain games (also **die**): – *pl* **dice**.

Dictaphone® ['diktəfōn] *n* a type of machine which records what is spoken into it.

dic'tate *v* to read out (something) so that another may write (it) down; to give firm commands. – *n* **'dictate** an order, command. – *ns* **dic'tation**; **dic'tator**

an all-powerful ruler. – *adj* **dictatorial** [diktə'töriəl] of or like a dictator; domineering, in the habit of giving orders.

'diction *n* manner of speaking; choice of words.

'dictionary *n* a book having the words of a language in (alphabetical) order, along with their meanings; a book containing other information alphabetically arranged: – *pl* **'dictionaries**.

did *see* **do**.

die *v* to lose life; to wither: – *pres p* **'dying**, *pt* **died**. – *n* a stamp or punch for making raised designs on money *etc*; *see* also **dice**.

diesel engine ['dēzəl] *n* an internal combustion engine in which heavy oil is ignited by heat generated by compression.

diet ['dīət] *n* food; a course of recommended foods *eg* for the purpose of losing weight; a meeting of a court *etc*. – *v* to eat certain kinds of food only, *esp* to lose weight. – *adj* **die'tetic** of a diet or diets.

'differ *v* (with **from**) to be unlike; to disagree: – *pt* **'differed**. – *n* **'difference** a point in which things are unlike; the amount by which one number is greater than another; a disagreement. – *adj* **'different** unlike. – *v* **differentiate** [difə'renshiāt] to make a difference or distinction between.

'difficult *adj* not easy, hard to do, understand or deal with; hard to please. – *n* **'difficulty** lack of easiness, hardness; anything difficult; anything which makes something difficult, an obstacle, hindrance *etc*; (*pl*) **'difficulties** troubles.

'diffident *adj* shy, not confident. – *n* **'diffidence**.

diffuse [di'fūz] *v* to spread in all directions. – *adj* **diffuse** [di'fūs] widely spread.

dig *v* to turn up (earth) with a spade *etc*; to make (a hole) by this means; to poke or push (something) into: – *pres p* **'digging**, *pt* **dug**. – *n* a poke or thrust; a digging up (or the place dug) to find archaeological remains. – *n* **'digger** a machine for digging.

di'gest *v* to break up food (in the stomach) and turn it into a form in which the body can make use of it; to think over. – *n* **'digest** a summing-up; a collection of written material. – *adjs* **di'gestible** able to be digested; **di'gestive** making digestion easy. – *n* **di'gestion** the act or power of digesting.

'**digit** *n* a finger or toe; any of the numbers 0–9. – *adj* '**digital** (of an electronic calculator, clock *etc*) using the numbers 0–9.

digi'tālis *n* a family of plants, including the foxglove, from which a medicine used in heart disease is obtained.

'**dignified** *adj* stately, serious. – *ns* '**dignity** a stately or serious manner; manner showing a sense of one's own worth or of the seriousness of the occasion; high rank; '**dignitary** a person of high rank or office: – *pl* '**dignitaries**.

di'gress *v* to wander from the point in speaking or writing. – *n* **di'gression**.

dike, dyke *n* a wall; an embankment; a ditch.

di'lapidāted *adj* falling to pieces, needing repair.

di'late *v* to make or grow larger, swell out. – *ns* **dila'tation, di'lation**.

dilatory ['dilətəri] *adj* slow (in doing things), inclined to delay.

di'lemma *n* a position or situation giving a choice of two things, neither of which is pleasant.

dilettante [dili'tanti] *n* one who has a slight but not serious interest in several subjects.

'**diligent** *adj* hard-working, industrious. – *n* '**diligence**.

'**dilly-'dally** *v* to loiter, waste time.

di'lūte *v* to lessen the strength of a liquid *etc*, *esp* by adding water. – Also *adj*. – *adj* **di'luted**. – *n* **di'lution**.

dim *adj* not bright or clear; not seeing or understanding clearly. – *v* to make or become dim: – *pt* **dimmed**. – *n* '**dimness**.

dime *n* the tenth part of an American dollar, ten cents.

di'mension *n* a measurement (of length, width or thickness); (*pl*) size, measurements.

di'minish *v* to make or grow less. – *n* **dimi'nūtion** a lessening. – *adj* **di'minutive** very small.

'**dimple** *n* a small hollow, *esp* on the cheek or chin.

din *n* a loud, lasting noise. – *v* (with **into**) to put (information *etc*) into someone's mind by constant repetition: – *pt* **dinned**.

dine *v* to take dinner.

dinghy ['diŋgi] *n* a small rowing boat, *esp* one carried on board a bigger boat: – *pl* '**dinghies**.

dingy ['dinji] *adj* dull, faded, dirty-looking. – *n* '**dinginess**.

'**dinner** *n* the main meal of the day.

'**dinosaur** *n* any of various types of extinct (giant) reptile.

dint *n* a hollow made by a blow, a dent. – **by dint of** by means of.

diocese ['diəsis] *n* a bishop's district.

dip *v* to plunge into any liquid for a moment; to lower (*eg* a flag) and raise again; to slope down; to look briefly into (a book *etc*): – *pt* **dipped**. – *n* a liquid substance in which anything is dipped; a downward slope; a hollow; a short bathe.

diphtheria [dif'thēriə] *n* an infectious throat disease.

diphthong ['difthoŋ] *n* two vowel-sounds pronounced as one syllable (as in *out*).

di'plōma *n* a written statement giving an honour, or saying that one has passed a certain examination.

di'plōmacy *n* the business of making agreements, treaties *etc* between countries; cleverness in making people agree, tact. – *n* '**diplomat** one engaged in diplomacy. – *adj* **diplo'matic** of diplomacy; tactful.

'**dire** *adj* dreadful: *in dire need*.

di'rect *adj* straight, not roundabout; (of a person's manner) straightforward, outspoken. – *v* to point or aim at; to show the way; to order, instruct; to control, organize; to put a name and address on (a letter). – *ns* **di'rection** the act of directing; the place or point to which one moves, looks *etc*; an order; guidance; (*pl*) instructions; **di'rectness; di'rector** one who directs, *esp* one who guides or manages (a business *etc*); **di'rectory** a book of names and addresses *etc*: – *pl* **di'rectories**. – *ns* **direct speech** speech reported in the speaker's exact words; **direct tax** a tax on income or property.

dirge [dörj] *n* a lament; a funeral hymn.

dirk *n* a kind of dagger.

dirt *n* any unclean substance, such as mud, dust, dung *etc*. – *adj* '**dirty** not clean, soiled; bad, evil. – *v* to soil with dirt: – *pt* '**dirtied**. – *adv* '**dirtily**. – *n* '**dirtiness**. – *n* **dirt track** an earth track for motor-cycle racing.

dis'āble *v* to take away (wholly or partly) the power or strength from, cripple. – *ns* **disability** [disə'biləti] something which disables: – *pl* **dis'abilities; dis'ablement** the act of disabling; state of being disabled.

disabuse [disə'būz] *v* to set right (someone) about a wrong belief or opinion. *You must disabuse him of that idea.*

disad'vantage *n* an unfavourable circumstance, a drawback. – Also *v*. – *adjs* **disad'vantaged** having a disadvantage

of some kind *esp* poverty, homelessness;
disadvantageous ['dısadvən'tājəs].

disaf'fected *adj* discontented, rebellious. – *n* **disaf'fection**.

disa'gree *v* (sometimes with **with**) to hold different opinions *etc* (from another); to quarrel; (of food) to be unsuitable (to someone) and cause pain. – *adj* **disa'greeable** unpleasant. – *n* **disa'greement**.

disallow [dısə'low] *v* not to allow.

disap'pear *v* to go out of sight, vanish. – *n* **disap'pearance**.

disap'point *v* to fail to come up to the hopes or expectations (of); to fail to fulfil. – *adj* **disap'pointed**. – *n* **disap'pointment**.

disapprove [dısə'prōōv] *v* to have an unfavourable opinion (of). – *n* **disap'proval**.

dis'arm *v* to take weapons away from; to get rid of war weapons; to make less angry *etc*, to charm. – *n* **dis'armament** the act of doing away with war weapons. – *adj* **dis'arming** gaining friendliness, charming: *a disarming smile*.

disarrange [dısə'rānj] *v* to throw out of order, make untidy. – *n* **disar'rangement**.

disar'ray *n* disorder.

disaster [di'zästər] *n* an extremely unfortunate happening, *esp* one that causes great damage, loss *etc*. – *adj* **di'sastrous**.

dis'band *v* to (cause to) break up. *The gang disbanded.* – *n* **dis'bandment**.

disbelieve [dısbi'lēv] *v* not to believe. – *ns* **disbe'lief; disbe'liever**.

dis'burse *v* to pay out. – *n* **dis'bursement**.

disc, disk *n* a flat, round shape; a gramophone record. – *n* **disc jockey** one who introduces and plays recorded music (for radio programmes *etc*).

dis'card *v* to throw away as useless.

discern [di'sɔrn] *v* to see, realize. – *adjs* **di'scernible** able to be seen (or understood; **di'scerning** quick or clever at noticing or understanding. – *n* **di'scernment** the state of quality of being discerning.

discharge [dis'chärj] *v* to unload (cargo); to set free; to dismiss; to fire (a gun); to perform (duties); to pay (a debt); to give off (*eg* smoke), let out (*eg* pus). – *n* **'discharge** unloading; setting free; firing (of a gun); dismissal; something discharged (*eg* pus); the performance (of duties); payment.

disciple [di'sipl] *n* one who believes in another's teaching, *esp* one of the followers of Christ.

discipline ['disiplin] *n* training in an orderly way of life; order kept by means of control. – *v* to bring to order; to punish. – *n* **discipli'narian** one who insists on strict discipline. – *adj* **disci'plinary** of or enforcing discipline (by punishment).

dis'claim *v* to refuse to have anything to do with, deny. – *n* **dis'claimer** a denial.

disclose [dis'klōz] *v* to uncover, reveal, make known. – *n* **disclosure** [dis'klōzhər] the act of disclosing; something disclosed.

'disco short for **discothèque**.

discolour, (*US*) **discolor** [dis'kulər] *v* to change or spoil the colour of; to stain. – *n* **discolo'ration**.

discomfiture [dis'kumfichər] *n* embarrassment; defeat.

discomfort [dis'kumfərt] *n* want of comfort, uneasiness.

discon'cert *v* to upset, embarrass.

discon'nect *v* to separate, break the connection between. – *adj* **discon'nected** separated, no longer connected; (of speech *etc*) not well joined together, rambling.

dis'consolate *adj* sad, disappointed.

discon'tent *n* dissatisfaction. – *adj* **discon'tented** dissatisfied, cross. – *n* **discon'tentment**.

discon'tinue *v* to stop, cease to continue.

'discord *n* disagreement, quarrelling; (in music) a jarring of notes. – *adj* **dis'cordant**.

discothèque ['diskətek] *n* a club, hall *etc* at which recorded music is played for dancing.

'discount *n* a small sum taken off the price of something. *He received a 10% discount on his order.* – *v* **dis'count** to leave out, not to consider; to allow for exaggeration in (*eg* a story).

discourage [dis'kurij] *v* to take away the confidence, hope *etc* of. *His low marks discouraged him*; to try to prevent (by showing disapproval of). *She discouraged his attempts.* – *n* **dis'couragement**. – *adj* **dis'couraging** giving little hope or encouragement.

discourse ['diskōrs] *n* a speech, sermon, lecture; an essay; a conversation. – *v* **dis'course** to talk.

discourteous [dis'kɔrtiəs] *adj* not polite, rude. – *n* **discourtesy** [dis'kɔrtəsi].

discover [dis'kuvər] *v* to find out; to find by chance, *esp* for the first time. – *ns* **dis'coverer; dis'covery** the act of finding or finding out; the thing discovered: – *pl* **dis'coveries**.

dis'credit *n* loss of good reputation, disgrace; disbelief. – *v* to refuse to believe; to cause disbelief in; to disgrace. – *adj* **dis'creditable** disgraceful.

dis'creet *adj* wise, cautious, tactful. – *n* **discretion** [dis'kreshən].

dis'crepancy *n* a difference, disagreement (between two stories, amounts of money *etc*): – *pl* **dis'crepancies**.

discretion *see* **discreet**.

dis'criminate *v* to make differences (between), to distinguish; to treat (people) differently. – *adj* **dis'criminating** showing good sense in judging things *etc*. – *n* **discrimi'nation** the act of or ability in discriminating.

'discus *n* a heavy disc thrown in a kind of athletic competition.

dis'cuss *v* to talk about. – *n* **dis'cussion**.

dis'dain *v* to look down on, scorn (something); to be too proud (to do something). – *n* scorn. – *adj* **dis'dainful**.

disease [di'zēz] *n* illness. – *adj* **di'seased**.

disem'bark *v* to put or go ashore. – *n* **'disembar'kation**.

disembodied [disim'bodid] *adj* (of a spirit, soul *etc*) separated from the body.

disen'gage *v* to separate, free. – *adj* **disen'gaged** separated, freed; not busy; vacant, not engaged.

disentangle [disin'taŋgl] *v* to free from entanglement, to unravel.

disfavour [dis'fāvər] *n* the state of being out of favour; dislike.

disfigure [dis'figər] *v* to spoil the beauty or appearance of. – *n* **dis'figurement**.

dis'franchise *v* to take away the right to vote.

dis'gorge *v* to vomit; to throw out; to give up (what has been taken).

dis'grace *n* the state of being out of favour; shame. – *v* to bring shame upon. – *adj* **dis'graceful** shameful; very bad.

disgruntled [dis'gruntld] *adj* sulky, discontented.

disguise [dis'gīz] *v* to change the appearance of, by a change of dress *etc*; to hide (feelings *etc*). – *n* a disguised state; that which disguises.

dis'gust *n* strong dislike, loathing; indignation. – *v* to arouse dislike, loathing or indignation. – *adj* **dis'gusting** sickening; causing disgust.

dish *n* a plate, bowl *etc* for food; food prepared for table: – *pl* **'dishes**. – *v* to

put into a dish, serve out.

dishearten [dis'härtn] *v* to take away courage or hope from. – *adjs* **dis'heartened; dis'heartening**.

dishevelled [di'shevəld] *adj* untidy, with hair *etc* disordered.

dishonest [dis'onist] *adj* not honest, deceitful. – *n* **dis'honesty**.

dishonour [dis'onər] *n* disgrace, shame. – *v* to cause shame to. – *adj* **dis'honourable** having no sense of honour; disgraceful.

disillusion [disi'lōozhən] *v* to take away a false belief from. – Also *n*. – *adj* **disil'lusioned**. – *n* **disil'lusionment**.

disin'clined *adj* unwilling.

disin'fect *v* to destroy disease-causing germs in. – *n* **disin'fectant** a substance that kills germs.

disin'herit *v* to take away the rights of an heir.

dis'integrate *v* to fall into pieces; to break up into parts. – *n* **disinte'gration**.

disinterested [dis'intristid] *adj* unselfish, not influenced by private feelings or interests.

dis'jointed *adj* (*esp* of speech *etc*) not well connected together.

disk *see* **disc**.

dis'like *v* not to like, to disapprove of. – Also *n*.

'dislocate *v* to put (a bone) out of joint; to upset, to put out of order. – *n* **dislo'cation**.

dis'lodge *v* to drive from a place of rest, hiding or defence; to knock out of place accidentally.

dis'loyal *adj* not loyal, unfaithful. – *n* **dis'loyalty**.

dismal ['dizməl] *adj* gloomy; sorrowful, sad.

dis'mantle *v* to strip off or take down fittings, furniture *etc*; to take to pieces.

dis'may *v* to surprise and upset. – Also *n*.

dis'member *v* to tear to pieces; to cut the limbs from. – *n* **dis'memberment**.

dis'miss *v* to send or to put away; to send (a person) from a job, sack; to stop, close (a law-case *etc*). – *n* **dis'missal**.

dis'mount *v* to come down off a horse, bicycle *etc*.

disobey [disə'bā] *v* to fail or refuse to do what is commanded. – *adj* **disobedient** [disə'bēdyənt] refusing or failing to obey. – *n* **diso'bedience**.

diso'bliging *adj* not willing to carry out the wishes of others.

dis'order *n* lack of order, confusion; disturbance; disease. – *v* to throw out of order. – *adj* **dis'orderly** out of order; behaving in a lawless (noisy) manner. – *n* **dis'orderliness**.

disown [dis'ōn] *v* to refuse or cease to recognize as one's own.

dis'parage *v* to speak of as being of little worth or importance, belittle. – *n* **dis'paragement**. – *adj* **dis'paraging**.

dis'parity *n* great difference, inequality: – *pl* **dis'parities**.

dispassionate [dis'pashənət] *adj* favouring no one, unbiassed; judging calmly, cool.

dis'patch, des'patch *v* to send off (a letter *etc*); to kill, finish off; to do or deal with quickly. – *n* the act of sending off; a report (*eg* to a newspaper); speed in doing something; killing; (*pl*) **dis'patches** official papers (*esp* military or diplomatic). – *n* **dispatch rider** a carrier of military dispatches by motor cycle.

dis'pel *v* to drive away, make to disappear: – *pt* **dis'pelled**.

dis'pense *v* to give or deal out; to prepare (medicines, prescriptions) for giving out. – *adj* **dis'pensable** able to be done without. – *ns* **dis'pensary** a place where medicines are given out; **dispen'sation** special leave to break a rule *etc*; **dis'penser** one who dispenses; a machine which dispenses. – **dispense with** to do without.

dis'perse *v* to scatter; to spread; to (cause to) vanish. – *ns* **dis'persal**, **dis'persion** a scattering.

dis'pirited *adj* sad, discouraged.

dis'place *v* to put out of place; to disarrange; to put (a person) out of office. – *n* **dis'placement** a movement out of place; the quantity of water moved out of place by a ship *etc* when floating. – *n* **displaced person** a person forced to leave his own country because of war, political opinions *etc*.

dis'play *v* to set out for show. – *n* a show, exhibition.

displease [dis'plēz] *v* not to please; to offend, annoy. – *n* **displeasure** [dis'plezhər] annoyance, disapproval.

dispose [dis'pōz] *v* to arrange, settle; to get rid (of); to make inclined. – *adj* **dis'posable** intended to be thrown away. – *n* **dis'posal** the act of disposing. – *adj* **dis'posed** inclined, willing. – **at one's disposal** available for one's use.

disposition [dispə'zishən] *n* arrangement; nature, personality; (in law) a giving over of (property *etc*) to another.

dispossess [dispə'zes] *v* to take away from, deprive (someone) of ownership (of).

disproportionate [disprə'pörshənət] *adj* too big or too little, not in proportion.

disprove [dis'prōōv] *v* to prove to be false.

dis'pūte *v* to argue (about). – *n* an argument, quarrel. – *adj* **dis'putable** not certain, able to be argued about. – *n* **dispu'tation** an argument.

disqualify [dis'kwolifi] *v* to put out of a competition *etc* for breaking rules; to take away a qualification or right: – *pt* **dis'qualified**. – *n* **disqualifi'cation**.

dis'quiet [dis'kwīət] *n* uneasiness, anxiety. – Also *v*.

disre'gard *v* to pay no attention to, ignore. – *n* want of attention, neglect.

disre'pair *n* the state of being out of repair.

disre'pūte *n* bad reputation. – *adj* **dis'reputable** having a bad reputation, not respectable.

disres'pect *n* rudeness, lack of politeness. – *adj* **disres'pectful**.

dis'rupt *v* to break up; to throw (a meeting *etc*) into disorder. – *n* **dis'ruption**. – *adj* **dis'ruptive** breaking up or causing disorder.

dis'satisfȳ *v* not to satisfy, to displease. – *adj* **dis'satisfied**. – *n* **dissatis'faction**.

dis'sect *v* to cut into parts in order to examine; to study and criticize. – *n* **dis'section**.

dis'semble *v* to hide, disguise (one's true intentions *etc*).

dis'seminate *v* to scatter, spread. – *n* **dissemi'nation**.

dis'sent *v* to have a different opinion; to refuse to agree. – *n* disagreement. – *ns* **dis'sension** disagreement, quarrelling; **dis'senter** a member of a church that has broken away from the officially established church.

disser'tation *n* a long piece of writing or talk on a particular (often scholarly) subject.

disservice [dis'sȫrvis] *n* harm, an ill turn.

dis'similar *adj* not the same. – *n* **dissimi'larity**: – *pl* **dissimi'larities**.

dis'simūlate *v* to pretend; to disguise, hide (one's true intentions *etc*).

'dissipate *v* to (cause to) disappear; to waste. – *adj* **'dissipated** having wasted one's energies *etc* on too many pleasures. – *n* **dissi'pation**.

dissociate [di'sōshiāt] *v* to separate. – **dissociate oneself from** to refuse to be associated with or to give one's support to.

dissolve [di'zolv] *v* to melt; to break up;

to put an end to. – *n* **dissolution** [disə'looshən].

dissolute ['disəloot] *adj* having bad habits, wicked.

'**dissonance** *n* discord, *esp* when deliberately used in music; disagreement. – *adj* '**dissonant**.

dissuade [di'swād] *v* to stop (from doing something) by advice or persuasion. – *n* **dis'suasion**.

'**distaff** *n* the stick which holds the bunch of flax or wool in spinning. – *adj* of women, female: *on the distaff side*.

'**distance** *n* the space between things *etc*; a far-off place or point: *in the distance*; coldness of manner. – *adj* '**distant** far off or far apart in place or time; not close: *a distant cousin*; cold in manner.

dis'tāste *n* dislike. – *adj* **dis'tasteful** disagreeable, unpleasant.

dis'temper *n* a kind of paint used chiefly for walls; a disease of dogs. – *v* to paint with distemper.

dis'tend *v* to swell; to stretch outwards. – *n* **dis'tension**.

dis'til *v* to get (a liquid) in a pure state by heating to a steam or vapour and cooling; to extract the spirit or essence from something by this method; to (cause to) fall in drops: – *pt* **dis'tilled**. – *ns* **distil'lation** the act of distilling; **dis'tillery** a place where distilling (of whisky, brandy *etc*) is done: – *pl* **dis'tilleries**.

dis'tinct *adj* clear; easily seen or made out; different. – *adj* **dis'tinctive** different, special. – *ns* **dis'tinctiveness**; **dis'tinction** a difference; outstanding worth or merit; a mark of honour.

distinguish [dis'tingwish] *v* to recognize a difference (between); to mark off as different; to make out, recognize; to give distinction to. – *adj* **dis'tinguished** outstanding, famous.

dis'tort *v* to twist out of shape; to turn or twist (a statement *etc*) from the true meaning; to cause (a sound) to be unclear and harsh. – *n* **dis'tortion**.

dis'tract *v* to draw aside (the attention); to trouble, confuse; to make mad. – *adj* **dis'tracted** mad (with pain, grief *etc*). – *n* **dis'traction** something which draws away attention; anxiety, confusion; amusement; madness.

distraught [dis'tröt] *adj* extremely agitated or anxious.

dis'tress *n* pain, trouble, sorrow; a cause of suffering. – *v* to cause pain or sorrow to. – *adjs* **dis'tressed; dis'tressing**.

dis'tribute *v* to divide among several, deal out; to spread out widely. – *n* **distri'bution**.

'**district** *n* a region of a country or town.

dis'trust *n* lack of trust or faith; suspicion. – *v* to have no trust in – *adj* **dis'trustful**.

dis'turb *v* to throw into confusion; to worry, make anxious; to interrupt. – *n* **dis'turbance** an act of disturbing; a noisy or disorderly happening; an interruption.

disuse [dis'ūs] *n* the state of being no longer used. – *adj* **disused** [dis'ūzd] no longer used.

ditch *n* a long narrow hollow trench dug in the ground, *esp* one for water: – *pl* '**ditches**.

dither ['didhər] *v* to hesitate, be undecided; to act in a nervous, uncertain manner. – *n* a state of indecision or nervousness.

'**ditto** often written **do.**, the same as already written or said.

'**ditty** *n* a simple, little song: – *pl* '**ditties**.

di'van *n* a long, low couch without a back; a kind of bed without a headboard.

dive *v* to plunge headfirst into water; to swoop through the air; to go down steeply and quickly. – Also *n*. – *n* '**diver** one who dives; one who works under water using special breathing equipment *etc*; any of several types of diving bird.

di'verge *v* to separate and go in different directions; to differ. – *n* **di'vergence**. – *adj* **di'vergent**.

di'verse *adj* different, various. – *v* **di'versifȳ** to make or become different or varied: – *pt* **di'versified**.

di'version *n* a turning aside; an alteration to a traffic route; (an) amusement.

di'versity *n* difference; variety.

di'vert *v* to turn aside, change the direction of; to amuse. – *adj* **di'verting** amusing.

di'vest *v* to strip or deprive of. *They divested him of his authority.*

di'vide *v* to separate into parts; to share (among); to (cause to) go into separate groups; in arithmetic, to find out how many times one number contains another. – *npl* **di'viders** measuring compasses used in geometry.

'**dividend** *n* that which is to be divided (see **divisor**); a share of profit (of a business *etc*).

di'vine *adj* of God; holy. – *v* to guess; to foretell, predict. – *ns* **divination** [divi'nāshən] (the art of) foretelling; **di'viner** one who claims a special ability in finding hidden water or metals; **divinity** [di'vinəti] a god; the nature of a god; religious studies: – *pl* di'vinities; Di'vinity God. – *n* di'vining rod a (hazel) stick, used by water diviners.

di'vision *n* the act of dividing; a barrier, something which divides or separates; a part or section (of an army *etc*); separation; disagreement. – *adjs* di'visional of a division; divisible [di'vizəbl] able to be divided. – *ns* divisi'bility; divisor [di'vizər] the number by which another number (the 'dividend) is divided.

di'vorce *n* the legal ending of a marriage; a complete separation. – *v* to end one's marriage with; to separate (from).

di'vulge *v* to let out, make known (a secret *etc*).

'dizzy *adj* giddy, confused; causing giddiness: *dizzy heights*. – *n* 'dizziness.

do [dōō] *v* to carry out, perform (a job *etc*); to carry out some action on, *eg* to wash or clean (dishes *etc*), to cook or make (a meal *etc*), to comb *etc* (hair); (*slang*) to swindle; to act. *Do as you please*; to get on. *He is doing well*; to be enough. *A penny will do*; used to avoid repeating a verb. *I sometimes see her, but when I do, she runs away*; used with a more important verb (1) in questions. *Do you see*? (2) in sentences with not. *I do not know*; (3) to emphasize. *I do hope*: – *pres t* do, does [duz], *pt* did, *pp* done [dun]. – *n* (*coll*) an affair; a festivity, party. – *n* doer ['dōōər]. – *npl* doings ['dōōiŋz] actions. – *adj* done [dun] finished. – do away with to put an end to, destroy.

do. *see* ditto.

'docile *adj* (of a person or animal) easy to manage. – *n* docility [də'siləti].

dock *n* (often *pl*) a deepened part of a harbour *etc* where ships go for loading, unloading, repair *etc*; the box in a law court where the accused person stands; a kind of weed with large leaves. – *v* to put in or enter a dock; to clip or cut short. – *n* 'docker one who works in the docks. – *n* 'dockyard a naval harbour with docks, stores *etc*.

'docket *n* a label or note giving the contents of something.

'doctor *n* one who is trained to treat ill people; one who has the highest university degree in any subject. – *v* to treat, as a doctor does a patient; to tamper with, add something harmful to.

doctrine ['doktrin] *n* a belief that is taught.

'document *n* a written statement, giving proof, evidence, information *etc*. – *adj* docu'mentary of or found in documents; of a documentary. – *n* a film,

programme *etc* giving information about a certain subject: – *pl* docu'mentaries.

'dodder *v* to shake, tremble, *esp* as a result of old age.

dodge *v* to avoid (by a sudden or clever movement). – *n* a trick.

'dōdō *n* a type of large extinct bird: – *pls* 'dodo(e)s.

doe *n* the female of certain animals (as deer, rabbit, hare).

doer, does *see* do.

doff *n* to take off (one's hat *etc*).

dog *n* a type of animal often kept as a pet; one of the dog family which includes wolves, foxes *etc*; the male of this animal. – *adj* (of animal) male. – *v* to follow and watch constantly. – *n* 'dog-collar a collar for dogs; a clergyman's collar. – *adj* 'dog-eared (of the pages of a book) turned down at the corner. – *ns* 'dogfish a kind of small shark; 'dog-rose the wild rose; 'dogsbody (*coll*) a person who is given odd jobs, *esp* unpleasant ones; dog's life a life of misery. – *adj* 'dog-'tired completely worn out. – *n* 'dog-watch on a ship, the period of lookout from 4 to 6 a.m. or 6 to 8 p.m.

dogged ['dogid] *adj* refusing to give in, determined. – *n* 'doggedness.

'doggerel *n* bad poetry.

'dogma *n* an opinion accepted or fixed by an authority (such as the Church); opinion that is not to be contradicted. – *adj* dog'matic of dogma; forcing one's opinions on others.

'doily, 'doyley *n* a fancy napkin (as on plates in a cakestand).

'doldrums *npl* those parts of the ocean about the equator where calms and variable winds are common; low spirits.

dole *v* to deal (out) in small pieces. – *n* money given by a country to unemployed people. – *adj* 'doleful sad, unhappy. – *n* 'dolefulness.

doll *n* a toy in the shape of a small human being.

'dollar *n* the main unit of money in some countries, *esp* that of N. America.

'dolmen *n* an ancient tomb in the shape of a stone table.

'dolphin *n* a type of sea animal like a porpoise.

dolt *n* a stupid person. – *adj* 'doltish.

do'main *n* kingdom; land in the country, an estate; area of interest or knowledge.

dome *n* anything shaped like a half-ball (*esp* a roof). – *adj* domed.

do'mestic *adj* of the home or household;

(of animals) tame, sharing man's life or used by man; not foreign, of one's own country: *domestic products.* – *n* a servant in a house. – *adj* do'mesticated (of an animal) accustomed to live near man; (of a person) fond of doing jobs associated with running a house. – *n* domes'ticity fondness for home. – *ns* domestic help (a person paid to give) assistance with housework; domestic science the study of subjects associated with running a house (*eg* cookery, sewing).

'domicile *n* the country, place *etc* in which a person lives permanently.

'dominant *adj* ruling; most powerful, most important. – *n* 'dominance.

'dominate *v* to have command or influence over; to be most strong, or most noticeable *etc*; to tower above, overlook. – *n* domi'nation.

domi'neering *adj* overbearing, like a tyrant.

do'minion *n* lordship, rule; an area with one ruler, owner, or government.

'domino *n* a hooded cloak with a mask for the face; one of the pieces used in dominoes; (*pl*) 'dominoes a game played with wooden or ivory pieces marked with dots.

don *n* a college or university lecturer *etc*. – *v* to put on (a coat *etc*): – *pt* donned.

do'nation *n* a gift of money or goods. – *v* do'nate to present a gift.

done *see* do.

'donkey *n* an ass, a type of animal with long ears, related to the horse: – *pl* 'donkeys.

donor ['dōnər] *n* a giver of a gift or of a part of the body to replace a diseased part of someone else's body.

don't [dōnt] short for do not.

doom *n* judgement; fate; ruin. – *adj* doomed condemned; destined, certain (to fail, be destroyed *etc*).

door [dōr] *n* the hinged barrier, *usu* of wood, which closes the entrance to a room, house *etc*; the entrance itself. – *ns* 'doorstep the step in front of the door of a house; 'doorway the space *usu* filled by a door, entrance.

dope *v* to drug. – *n* (*coll*) any drug or drugs; a kind of quick-drying paint or varnish used *eg* in making models of aeroplanes.

'dormant *adj* sleeping; not active: *a dormant volcano.*

'dormer *n* (also dormer window) a small window jutting out from a sloping roof.

'dormitory *n* a room with beds for several people: – *pl* 'dormitories.

'dormouse *n* a type of small animal which hibernates: – *pl* 'dormice.

'dorsal *adj* of the back: *dorsal fin.*

dose *n* the quantity of medicine to be taken at one time; any unpleasant thing (*eg* an illness, punishment) that must be endured. – *v* to give medicine to.

doss *v* (*coll*) to lie down to sleep in a makeshift or temporary place. – *n* 'doss-house (*coll*) a cheap lodging-house.

dossier ['dosiā] *n* a set of papers containing information about a person or subject.

dot *n* a small, round mark. – *v* to mark with a dot; to scatter: – *pt* 'dotted.

'dotage *n* the foolishness and childishness of old age.

dote: dote on to be foolishly fond of.

double ['dubl] *v* to multiply by two; to fold. – *n* twice as much. *He ate double the amount*; a person so like another as to be mistaken for him. – *adj* containing *etc* twice as much: *a double dose*; made up of two of the same sort together; folded over; deceitful: *a double game.* – *adv* 'doubly. – *ns* double agent a spy paid by each of two countries hostile to each other, but who is loyal to only one of them; double bass a type of large stringed musical instrument. – *adj* 'double-'breasted (of a suit or coat) having one half of the front overlapping the other and a double row of buttons but a single row of bottonholes. – *v* 'double'cross to cheat. – Also *n.* – *ns* 'double-'dealer a deceitful, cheating person; 'double-'dealing; 'double-'decker a vehicle (*usu* a bus) with two floors; double glazing two sheets of glass in a window to keep in the heat or keep out noise. – at the double very quickly; double back to turn sharply and go back the way one has come.

doublet ['dublit] *n* (*hist*) a close-fitting jacket, once worn by men.

doubloon [dub'lōon] *n* (*hist*) an old Spanish gold coin.

doubt [dowt] *v* to be unsure or undecided about; not to trust. – *n* a feeling of not being sure; suspicion, a thing doubted. – *adj* 'doubtful. – *adv* 'doubtless.

dough [dō] *n* a mass of flour, moistened and kneaded. – *n* 'doughnut a ring-shaped cake with a hole in the middle fried in fat.

doughty ['dowti] *adj* strong; brave.

dove [duv] *n* a pigeon. – *n* dovecote ['duvkot] a pigeon house. – *v* 'dovetail to fit one thing exactly into another.

dowdy ['dowdi] *adj* not smart, badly dressed.

down [down] *adv* towards or in a lower place or position; to a smaller size *etc*: *to grind down*; from an earlier to a later time: *handed down from father to son*; on the spot, in cash: *£2 down*. – *prep* towards or in the lower part of; along: *down the road*. – *adj* descending, going, *etc* downwards. – *n* light, soft feathers; (*pl*) low, grassy hills. – *adj* '**downy** soft like feathers. – *adjs* '**down-at-'heel** (of shoes) worn down at the heel; shabby; '**downcast** sad. – *n* '**downfall** (of a person) ruin, defeat. – *adj* **down'hearted** discouraged. – *n* '**downpour** a heavy fall of rain. – *adj, adv* '**down'stairs** on or to a lower floor (of a house *etc*). – *adv* '**down'stream** further down a river or stream (in the direction of its flow). – *adj* '**downtrodden** kept in a humble, inferior position. – *adv* '**downwards** moving, leading *etc* down. – **go, be down with** to become or be ill with. *He has gone down with flu.*

dowry ['dowri] *n* money and property brought by a woman to her husband on their marriage: – *pl* '**dowries**.

doyley *see* **doily**.

doze *v* to sleep lightly. – Also *n*.

dozen ['duzn] *adj, n* twelve.

drab *adj* of dull colour.

draft *n* a rough sketch or outline of something; a group (*eg* of soldiers) picked out for a special purpose; (*US*) conscription into the army *etc*; an order for payment of money. – *v* to make a rough plan; to pick out (*esp* soldiers) for some special purpose; (*US*) to conscript into the army *etc*. – *n* '**draftsman** (also '**draughtsman**) one who draws plans.

drag *v* to pull *esp* roughly or by force; to move slowly and heavily; (to cause) to trail along the ground *etc*; to search (the bed of a lake *etc*) by means of a net or hook.

'**dragon** *n* (*myth*) a winged, fire-breathing serpent; a fierce or rather frightening person. – *n* '**dragonfly** a kind of winged insect with a long body and double wings.

dra'goon *n* a heavily-armed horse soldier. – *v* to force or bully (a person into doing something).

drain *v* to clear (land) of water by trenches or pipes; to drink everything in (a cup *etc*); to use up completely (money, strength *etc*). – *n* anything (such as a ditch, waterpipe, trench) in which liquids may flow away. – *n*

'**drainage** the drawing-off of water by rivers, pipes etc. – *adj* **drained** emptied of liquid; with no strength left.

drake *n* the male of the duck.

'**drama** *n* a play for acting on the stage; an exciting or tense happening. – *adj* **dra'matic** having to do with plays; exciting, thrilling; unexpected, sudden. – *n* '**dramatist** a writer of plays. – *v* '**dramatize** to turn (a story) into a play for acting; to make real events seem like scenes from a play; to make vivid, striking or sensational. – *n* **dramati'zation**.

drank *see* **drink**.

'**drāper** *n* a dealer in cloth and cloth goods. – *v* **drape** to arrange (cloth coverings) to hang gracefully. – *n* '**drapery** cloth goods; a draper's shop. – *npl* **drapes** (*US*) curtains.

'**drastic** *adj* severe; thorough.

draught [drȧft] *n* the act of drawing or pulling; something drawn out; an amount of liquid drunk at once, without stopping; a current or rush of air; *see* also **draft**; (*pl*) a game for two, played by moving pieces on a squared board. – *adj* '**draughty** full of air currents, cold. – *n* '**draughtsman** same as **draftsman**.

draw *v* to make a picture (*esp* with pencil, crayons *etc*); to pull after or along; to attract (a crowd, attention *etc*); to obtain money from a fund *etc*: *to draw a pension*; to require depth for floating. *This ship draws 20 feet*; to move or come (near *etc*). *Night draws near*; to score equal points in a game. *Their team might draw with ours*: – *pt* **drew** [drōō], *pp* **drawn**. – *ns* '**drawer** one who draws; a sliding box for clothes *etc* which fits into a chest, cabinet, table *etc*; '**drawing** a picture made by pencil, crayon *etc*. – *ns* '**drawback** a disadvantage; '**drawbridge** a bridge (at the entrance to a castle) which can be drawn up or let down; '**drawing-pin** a pin with a large flat head for fastening paper on a board *etc*; '**drawing-room** a sitting-room. – **draw a conclusion** to form an opinion from evidence heard; **drawn and quartered** (*hist*) having the body cut in pieces after being hanged; **draw up** (of a car *etc*) to stop; to move closer; to plan, write out (a contract *etc*).

drawl *v* to speak in a slow, lazy manner. – Also *n*.

drawn *see* **draw**.

dread [dred] *n* great fear. – *adj* terrifying. – *v* to be greatly afraid of. – *adj* '**dreadful** terrible; (*coll*) very bad. – *n*

dreadnought ['drednöt] (*hist*) a kind of battleship.

dream *n* thoughts, pictures in the mind that come mostly during sleep; something imagined, not real; something very beautiful; a hope or ambition. – *v* to see visions and pictures in the mind while asleep: – *pt, pp* **dreamed** or **dreamt** [dremt]. – *adj* 'dreamy looking as if not quite awake; vague, dim; beautiful. – **dream up** to invent.

'**dreary** *adj* gloomy, cheerless.

dredge *v* to drag a net, bucket *etc* along the bed of a river or sea in order to bring up fish, mud *etc*; to sprinkle with (*eg* sugar). – *n* an instrument for dredging a river *etc*. – *n* '**dredger** a ship which deepens a channel *etc* by lifting mud from the bottom; a box or jar with a sprinkler top (*eg* a sugar dredger).

dregs *npl* sediment, the solid part that falls to the bottom of a liquid: *dregs of wine*; the least useful part of anything; the last remaining part.

drench *v* to soak.

dress *v* to put on clothes or a covering; to prepare (food *etc*) for use *etc*; to arrange (hair); to treat and bandage (wounds). – *n* covering for the body; a lady's gown, frock *etc*; style of clothing: – *pl* '**dresses**. – *adj* (of clothes *etc*) for wearing on formal occasions. – *ns* '**dresser** a kitchen sideboard for dishes *etc*; '**dressing** something put on as a covering; a seasoned sauce added to salads *etc*; a bandage *etc* to cover a wound. – *adj* '**dressy** fond of stylish clothes; stylish, smart. – *ns* '**dress-'coat** a black tailcoat; '**dressing-gown** a loose, light coat worn indoors over pyjamas *etc*; **dress rehearsal** the final rehearsal of a play, in which the actors wear their costumes.

drew *see* **draw**.

drey [drā] *n* a squirrel's nest: – *pl* **dreys**.

'**dribble** *v* to (cause to) fall in small drops; to let saliva run down the chin; (in football) to kick the ball on, little by little. – Also *n*.

dried *see* **dry**.

drift *n* something driven by wind (such as ice, snow, sand); the direction in which a thing is driven; (of words spoken or written) the general meaning. – *v* to go with the tide or current; (of snow *etc*) to be driven into heaps by the wind; to wander or live aimlessly. – *n* '**drifter** one who drifts; a fishing boat which uses nets ('**drift-nets**) which remain near the surface of the water. – *n* '**driftwood** wood driven on to the seashore by winds or tides.

drill *v* to make a hole in; to make with a drill; to exercise soldiers *etc*; to sow (seeds) in rows. – *n* a tool for making holes in wood *etc*; exercise, practice *esp* of soldiers; a row of seeds or plants.

drink *v* to swallow (a liquid); to take alcoholic drink, *esp* to too great an extent: – *pt* **drank**, *pp* **drunk**. – *n* something to be drunk; alcoholic liquids. – **drink in** to take eagerly into the mind, listen eagerly; **drink to** to wish (someone) well while drinking, to toast; **drink up** drink (a liquid) to the last drop.

drip *v* to fall in drops; to let (water *etc*) fall in drops: – *pt* **dripped**. – *n* a drop; a continual dropping (*eg* of water); liquid that drips; a device for adding liquid slowly to a vein *etc*. – *n* '**dripping** fat from meat in roasting *etc*. – *v* '**drip-'dry** to dry (a garment) by hanging it up to dry without squeezing moisture out of it in any way; (of a garment) to dry in this way. – *adj* able to be dried in this way.

drive *v* to control or guide (*eg* a car *etc*); to go in a vehicle; to force or urge along; to hurry on; to hit hard (a ball, nail *etc*); to bring about: *drive a bargain*: – *pt* **drove**, *pp* **driven** ['drivn]. – *n* a journey in a car; a private road to a house; an avenue or road; energy, enthusiasm; a campaign: *a drive to put an end to racialism*; a hard stroke with a club or bat (in golf, cricket, tennis *etc*). – *n* '**driver** one who drives; a wooden-headed golf club. – *n* '**drive-in** (*US*) a cinema, restaurant where people are catered for while remaining in their cars. – **what are you driving at?** what are you suggesting or implying?

drivel ['drivl] *n* (*coll*) nonsense. – *v* (*coll*) to talk nonsense: – *pt* '**drivelled**.

driven *see* **drive**.

'**drizzle** *n* rain in small drops. – Also *v*. – *adj* '**drizzly**.

dröll *adj* funny, amusing; odd.

dromedary ['dromədəri] *n* a type of Arabian camel with one hump: – *pl* '**dromedaries**.

drone *v* to make a low humming sound; to speak in a dull boring voice. – *n* a low humming sound; a dull boring voice; the low-sounding pipe of a bagpipe; the male of the honey-bee; a lazy, idle person.

drool *v* to let saliva flow in anticipation of food; to anticipate (something) in a very obvious way.

droop *v* to hang down. *The hem of her dress is drooping*; to grow weak, faint or discouraged.

drop n a small round or pear-shaped particle of liquid, usu falling: raindrop: teardrop; a small quantity (of liquid); a fall or descent from a height: a drop of six feet; a small sweet: acid drop. – v to fall suddenly; to let fall; to fall in drops; to set down from a car etc; to give up, abandon (a friend, habit etc): – pt **dropped**. – n '**droplet** a tiny drop. – npl '**droppings** dung (of animals or birds). – **drop off** to fall asleep; **drop out** to withdraw (eg from a university course).

dross n the scum which metals throw off when melting; waste matter, impurities; anything worthless.

drought [drowt] n a period of time when no rain falls, esp when this causes hardship.

drove n a number of moving cattle or other animals; a crowd (of people). – v see **drive**. – n '**drover** one who drives cattle.

drown [drown] v to sink in water and so die; to kill (a person or animal) in this way; to flood or soak completely; to cause (a sound) not to be heard by making a louder sound.

drowsy ['drowzi] adj sleepy.

drub v to beat or thrash: – pt **drubbed**. – n '**drubbing** a thrashing.

drudge v to do very humble or boring work. – n one who does such work. – n '**drudgery** hard, uninteresting work.

drug n a substance used in medicine (eg to kill pain); a substance taken habitually by people to achieve a certain effect eg great happiness or excitement. – v to give a drug or drugs to; to make to lose consciousness by a drug: – pt **drugged**. – n '**druggist** one who deals in drugs; a chemist. – n '**drugstore** (US) a shop which sells various articles (eg cosmetics, newspapers, soft drinks) as well as medicines.

drum n a musical instrument of skin etc stretched on a round frame of wood or metal, and beaten with sticks; anything shaped like a drum (eg a container for oil). – v to beat a drum; to tap continuously (with the fingers): – pt **drummed**. – ns '**drummer**; '**drumstick** a stick for beating a drum; the lower part of the leg of a cooked chicken etc.

drunk adj suffering from or showing the effects (giddiness, unsteadiness etc) of taking too much alcoholic drink. – n one who is drunk; one who is often drunk. – v see **drink**. – n '**drunkard** one who is in the habit of drinking too much alcohol. – adj '**drunken** drunk; in the habit of being drunk. – n '**drunkenness**.

dry adj not moist or wet; thirsty; uninteresting; (of manner) reserved, matter-of-fact; (of wine) not sweet. – v to make or become dry: – pt **dried**. – adv '**dryly**, '**drily**. – v '**dry-'clean** to clean (clothes etc) with chemicals, not with water. – n '**dry-'rot** a disease of wood, in which it becomes dry and crumbly. – adj '**dry-'stone** (of walls) built of stone without cement or mortar.

'**dryad** n (myth) a nymph of the woods.

'**dual** adj double; made up of two. – n **dual carriageway** a road divided by a central barrier or boundary, with each side used by traffic moving in one direction. – adj '**dual-'purpose** able to be used for more than one purpose.

dub v to declare (someone) a knight by touching each shoulder with a sword; to name or nickname; to add sound-effects to a film etc; to provide (a film) with a new sound-track (eg in a different language): – pt **dubbed**.

'**dubbin**, '**dubbing** n a grease for softening leather or making it waterproof.

'**dubious** adj doubtful, uncertain; probably not honest: dubious dealings. – n **du'biety**.

'**ducal** adj of a duke.

'**ducat** n (hist) an old European gold coin.

'**duchess** n the wife, or widow, of a duke; a woman of the same rank as a duke in her own right: – pl '**duchesses**.

'**duchy** n the land owned, or ruled over, by a duke: – pl '**duchies**.

duck n a kind of web-footed bird, with a broad flat beak; (in cricket) a score of no runs. – v to push (someone's head) under water; to lower the head quickly as if to avoid a blow. – n '**duckling** a baby duck.

duck-billed platypus see **platypus**.

duct n a tube or pipe for carrying liquids (eg in the human body), electric cables etc.

dudgeon ['dujən]: **in high dudgeon** very angry, indignant.

due adj owed, that ought to be paid etc; expected to be ready, to arrive etc; proper: due care. – adv directly: due south. – n that which is owed; what one has a right to; (pl) the amount of money charged for some service or for belonging to a club etc. – **due to** brought about by, caused by. His success was due to hard work; because of. The game was cancelled due to rain.

duel ['dūəl] n (hist) a fight (with pistols or swords) between two people. – Also *v. – n* **'duellist** one who fights in a duel.

dū'et *n* musical piece for two singers *etc*.

'duffel-coat, 'duffle-coat *n* a coat of coarse woollen cloth, *usu* with toggles instead of buttons.

dug *see* **dig**.

'dugout *n* a boat made by hollowing out the trunk of a tree; a rough shelter dug out of a slope or bank or in a trench.

duke *n* a nobleman next in rank below a prince. – *n* **'dukedom** the title, rank, or lands of a duke.

'dulcet *adj* sweet to the ear; melodious.

'dulcimer *n* a type of musical instrument with stretched wires which are struck with small hammers.

dull *adj* not lively; (of persons) slow to understand or learn; not exciting or interesting; (of weather) cloudy, not bright or clear; not bright in colour; (of sounds) not clear or ringing; blunt, not sharp. – Also *v*. – *adv* **'dully**. – *n* **'dullness** the state of being dull.

dulse *n* a type of eatable seaweed.

'dūly *adv* at the proper or expected time; as expected. *He duly handed it over.*

dumb [dum] *adj* without the power of speech; silent; (*coll*) stupid. – *adv* **'dumbly** in silence. – *n* **'dumbness**. – *v* **dumb'found** to astonish. – *n* **dumb show** acting without words.

'dummy *n* one who is dumb; something which seems real but is not (*eg* an empty package for shop-window display) , a model of a human used for displaying clothes *etc*; an artificial teat put in a baby's mouth to comfort it.

dump *v* to throw down heavily; to unload and leave (rubbish *etc*); to sell at a low price. – *n* a place for leaving rubbish; (*pl*) depression, low spirits. *He's in the dumps today.*

'dumpling *n* a ball of cooked dough.

'dumpy *adj* short and thick or fat.

dun *adj* greyish-brown, mouse-coloured. – *v* to demand payment: – *pt* **dunned**.

dunce *n* one slow at learning; a stupid person.

dune *n* a low hill of sand.

dung *n* the waste matter passed out of an animal's body, manure. – *n* **'dunghill** a heap of dung in a farmyard.

dungarees [duŋgə'rēz] *npl* trousers made of coarse, hard-wearing material with a bib.

dungeon ['dunjən] *n* a dark underground prison.

dūpe *n* one easily cheated. – *v* to deceive; to trick.

'dūplicate *adj* exactly the same. – *n* another of exactly the same kind; an

exact copy. – *v* to make a copy or copies of. – *n* **dupli'cation**.

dū'plicity *n* deceit, double-dealing.

'dūrable *adj* lasting, able to last; wearing well.

dū'ration *n* the time a thing lasts.

dū'ress *n* illegal force used to make someone do something. – **under duress** under the influence of force, threats *etc*.

'dūring *prep* throughout all or part of. *We lived here during the war*; at a particular point within (a period of time). *He died during the war.*

dusk *n* twilight, partial dark. – *adj* **'dusky** dark-coloured. – *n* **'duskiness**.

dust *n* fine grains or specks of earth, sand *etc*; anything in the form of fine powder. – *v* to free from dust. *She dusted the table*; to sprinkle lightly with powder. – *n* **'duster** a cloth for removing dust. – *adj* **'dusty** covered with dust. – *ns* **'dustbin** a container for household rubbish; **'dust-bowl** an area with little rain in which the wind raises storms of dust; **dust jacket** a paper cover on a book; **'dustman** one whose job it is to collect household rubbish.

'dūty *n* something one ought to do; an action or task required to be done; a tax; (*pl*) **'duties** the various tasks involved in a job. – *adjs* **'dutiable** (of goods) on which tax is to be paid; **'dutiful** obedient; careful to do what one should. – *adj* **'duty-'free** not taxed.

duvet ['dōōvā] *n* a kind of quilt stuffed with feathers, down *etc*, used instead of blankets.

dux *n* (in Scotland) the top boy or girl in a school or class.

dwarf [dwörf] *n* an under-sized person, animal or plant. – *v* to make to appear small. *A seven-foot man dwarfs one of ordinary height.* – *adj* not growing to full or usual height.

dwell *v* to live or stay (somewhere); (with **on**) to think or speak for a long time (about something). *Don't dwell on the past.*

'dwindle *v* to grow less, waste away.

dye [dī] *v* to give a colour to clothes, cloth *etc*. – *n* a powder or liquid for colouring. – *n* **'dyeing** the putting of colour into cloth.

dying *see* **die**.

dyke *see* **dike**.

dȳ'namic *adj* of force; (of a person) forceful, energetic. – *n* **dy'namics** the scientific study of movement and force.

'dȳnamite *n* a type of powerful explosive.

'dȳnamo *n* a machine for turning the

energy produced by movement into electricity: – *pl* '**dynamos**.

'**dynasty** *n* a succession of kings *etc* of the same family: – *pl* '**dynasties**. – *adj* **dy'nastic**.

'**dysentery** *n* an infectious disease caus-ing fever, pain and diarrhoea.

dyslexia [dɪs'leksɪə] *n* great difficulty in learning to read and in spelling.

dys'pepsia *n* indigestion. – *n, adj* **dys-'peptic** (a person) suffering from indi-gestion.

E

each *adj* (of two or more things *etc*) every one taken individually: *on each side of the fence*: *on each occasion*. – *pron* every one individually. *Each of them received a prize.* – **each other** used when an action takes place between two (loosely, between more than two) people. *He and I don't see each other often.*

'**eager** *adj* keen, anxious to do or get (something). – *n* '**eagerness**.

'**eagle** *n* a kind of large bird of prey. – *n* '**eaglet** a young eagle.

'**eagre** *n* the rise of the tide in a river.

ear *n* the part of the body through which one hears sounds; the ability to tell one sound from another: *a good ear* (*for music*); a spike or head (of corn *etc*). – *n* '**eardrum** the middle part of the ear. – *v* '**earmark** to mark or set aside for a special purpose. – *adj* '**ear-piercing** very loud or shrill. – *ns* '**earshot** the distance at which a sound can be heard; '**earwig** a type of insect with pincers at its tail. – **lend an ear** to listen.

earl [ɜrl] *n* a British nobleman ranking between a marquis and a viscount: – *fem* '**countess**. – *n* '**earldom** the lands or title of an earl.

early ['ɜrli] *adj* in good time; at or near the beginning (of a period of time, an event, a book *etc*); sooner than ex-pected; soon: – *comp* '**earlier**, *superl* '**earliest**. – Also *adv*. – *n* '**earliness**. – *n* **early bird** an early riser; one who gains an advantage by acting more quickly than his rivals.

earn [ɜrn] *v* to get (money) by work; to deserve. – *npl* '**earnings** pay for work done.

earnest ['ɜrnɪst] *adj* serious, serious-minded. – *n* seriousness; something (*usu* money) given to make sure that a bargain will be kept. – *n* '**earnestness**. – **in earnest** meaning what one says or does.

earth [ɜrth] *n* the planet on which we live; its surface; soil; the hole of a fox, badger *etc*; an electrical connection (*usu* a wire) with the ground. – *v* to connect electrically with the ground. – *adjs* '**earthen** made of earth or clay; '**earthly** of the earth as opposed to heaven; '**earthy** like soil; covered in soil; (of persons *etc*) coarse, not re-fined. – *ns* '**earthenware** pottery, dis-hes made of clay; '**earthquake** a shak-ing of the earth's crust; '**earth-tremor** a slight earthquake; '**earthwork** a man-made fortification (*usu* a bank) of earth; '**earthworm** the common worm.

ease [ēz] *n* freedom from difficulty; freedom from pain, worry or embar-rassment; rest from work. – *v* to make or become less painful, strong, difficult *etc*; to put carefully and gradually (into or out of a position). – *adj* '**easy** not hard to do; free from pain, worry or discomfort: – *comp* '**easier**, *superl* '**easiest**. – *adv* '**easily**. – *n* '**easiness**. – **stand at ease** to stand with the legs apart and arms behind one's back.

easel ['ēzl] *n* a stand for an artist's picture, a blackboard *etc*.

east *n* one of the four chief directions, that in which the sun rises. – Also *adj*. – *adjs* '**easterly** coming from or facing the east; '**eastern** of the east; '**eastward(s)** towards the east. – Also *adv*.

'**Easter** *n* the time when Christ's rising from the dead is celebrated.

eat *v* to chew and swallow (food); to destroy gradually, waste away: – *pt* **ate**, *pp* '**eaten**. – *adj* '**eatable** fit to eat, edible.

eaves *npl* the edge of a roof overhanging the walls. – *v* '**eavesdrop** to listen secretly to a private conversation. – *n* '**eavesdropper**.

ebb *n* the flowing away of the tide after high tide; a lessening, a worsening. – *v* to flow away; to grow less or worse.

'**ebony** *n* a type of black, hard wood. – *adj* made of ebony; black as ebony.

ebullient [i'bulyənt] *adj* lively and en-thusiastic. – *n* e'**bullience**.

eccentric [ik'sentrik] *adj* odd, acting strangely; (of circles) not having the same centre. – *n* **eccentricity** [eksen'trɪsəti] oddness of manner or conduct: – *pl* **eccen'tricities**.

ecclesiastic(al) [iklēzi'astik(əl)] *adj* of the church or clergy.

echo ['ekō] *n* the repeating of a sound caused by its striking a surface and coming back: – *pl* **'echoes**. – *v* to send back sound; to repeat (a thing said); to imitate.

e'clipse *n* the disappearance of the whole or part of a heavenly body, as of the sun when the moon comes between it and the earth; loss of glory or brilliance. – *v* to throw into the shade; to blot out (a person's success *etc*) by doing better.

e'cology *n* the study of plants, animals *etc* in relation to their natural surroundings. – *adj* **eco'logical**. – *n* **e'cologist**.

e'conomy *n* the management of the money affairs of a country *etc*; the careful use of something *esp* money: – *pl* **e'conomies**. – *adjs* **eco'nomic** concerning economy or economies; making a profit; **eco'nomical** careful in spending or using *esp* money, not wasteful. – *ns* **eco'nomics** the study of the manner in which men and nations make and spend money; **e'conomist** one who studies or is an expert on economics. – *v* **e'conomize** to be careful in spending or using.

'ecstasy *n* very great joy or pleasure: – *pl* **'ecstasies**. – *adj* **ec'static**.

eczema ['eksimə] *n* a type of skin disease.

'eddy *n* a current of water, air *etc* running against the main stream, causing a circular movement: – *pl* **'eddies**. – Also *v*.

edelweiss ['ādlvīs] *n* a kind of Alpine plant with white flowers.

edge *n* the border of anything, the part farthest from the middle; the cutting side of a knife, weapon *etc*; sharpness, as of appetite, mind *etc*; advantage. – *v* to put an edge or border on; to move little by little: *edge forward*. – *n* **'edging** a border or fringe. – *adj* **'edgy** on edge, unable to relax, irritable. – *adv* **'edgeways** sideways.

'edible *adj* fit to be eaten.

'ēdict *n* an order, command.

edifice ['edifis] *n* a large building.

'edifȳ *v* to improve the mind: – *pt* **'edified**. – *adj* **'edifying**. – *n* **edifi'cation** progress in knowledge.

'edit *v* to prepare matter for printing, broadcasting *etc*. – *ns* **e'dition** the form in which a book *etc* is published after being edited; the number of copies of a book, newspaper *etc* printed at one time; an issue of a newspaper altered in some way for a particular area (*eg* with

local news added); **'editor** one who edits a book *etc*. – *adj* **edi'torial** of an editor. – *n* the part of a newspaper *etc* written by its editor.

'edūcate *v* to teach (persons), *esp* in a school, college *etc*. – *n* **edu'cation**. – *adj* **edu'cational** of education.

eel *n* a kind of long ribbon-shaped fish.

'eerie *adj* causing fear of the unknown.

ef'face *v* to rub out; (with **oneself**) to keep from being noticed.

ef'fect *n* the result of an action; strength, power (of a drug *etc*); an impression produced: *the effect of the lighting*; general meaning; use, operation. *That law is not yet in effect*; (*pl*) goods, property. – *v* to bring about. – *adjs* **ef'fective** producing the desired effect; actual; **ef'fectūal** able to do what is required.

ef'feminate *adj* unmanly, womanish.

effervesce [efər'ves] *v* to froth up; to be very lively, excited *etc*. – *n* **effer-'vescence**. – *adj* **effer'vescent**.

effi'cācious *adj* effective. – *n* **'efficacy**.

ef'ficient *adj* able to do things well, fit, capable. – *n* **ef'ficiency**.

'effigy *n* a likeness of a person, *esp* made of stone, wood *etc*: – *pl* **'effigies**.

effluent ['eflŏŏənt] *n* a stream flowing from another stream or lake; sewage.

'effort *n* a try, *esp* one using all one's strength, ability *etc*; hard work.

effrontery [i'fruntəri] *n* impudence.

ef'fūsive *adj* pouring forth words.

egg *n* an almost round object, laid by birds, insects *etc* from which their young are produced. – **egg on** to urge.

'egōism *n* the habit of considering only one's own interests, selfishness; egotism. – *n* **'egoist**. – *adj* **ego'istic**. – *ns* **'egotism** the habit of speaking much of oneself, boastfulness; **'egotist**.

eider(-duck) ['īdər(duk)] *n* a northern sea duck. – *n* **'eiderdown** soft feathers from the eider; a quilt.

eight [āt] *n* the number 8. – *adj* 8 in number. – *adj* **eighth** [ātth] the last of eight. – *n* one of eight equal parts.

eighteen ['ā'tēn] *n* the number 18. – *adj* 18 in number. – *adj* **'eigh'teenth** the last of eighteen (things *etc*). – *n* one of eighteen equal parts.

eighty ['āti] *n* the number 80. – *adj* 80 in number. – *adj* **'eightieth** the last of eighty. – *n* one of eighty equal parts.

either ['īdhər] *adj*, *pron* one or other of two. *Either bus will take you there. Either of the boys can play*; each of two, both. *Trees grow on either side of the river*. – *conj* used with **or** to show alternatives. *Either you go or he does*. – *adv* any more than another. *I cannot go either. That doesn't work either.*

e'jacūlate *v* to shout out, exclaim. – *n* **ejacu'lation**.

e'ject *v* to throw out; to make (someone) leave a house, job *etc*. – *n* **e'jection**.

eke: eke out to make enough (by adding to in some way). *She eked out the stew by adding vegetables.*

e'laborate *v* to work out in detail. *You must elaborate your escape plan*; (often with **on**) to explain (too) fully. – *adj* done with fullness and exactness, often too much so; having much ornament or decoration. – *n* **elabo'ration**.

élan [ā'lan] *n* enthusiasm, dash.

'ēland *n* a type of African deer.

e'lapse *v* (of time) to pass.

e'lastic *adj* able to stretch and spring back again, springy. – *n* a piece of cotton *etc* made springy by having rubber, woven into it. – *n* **ēlas'ticity**.

e'lated *adj* in high spirits, very pleased. – *n* **e'lation**.

elbow ['elbō] *n* the joint where the arm bends. – *v* to push with the elbow, jostle. – *ns* **elbow grease** hard rubbing; **'elbow-room** plenty of room to move.

'elder *adj* older; having lived a longer time. – *n* one who is older; an office-bearer in certain churches; a type of tree with purple-black berries (**'elderberries**). – *adjs* **'elderly** nearing old age; **'eldest** oldest.

e'lect *v* to choose (someone) by voting; to choose (to). – *adj* chosen; chosen for a post but not yet in it: *president elect*. – *n* **e'lection** the choosing, *usu* by voting (of people to sit in parliament *etc*). – *v* **e'lectio'neer** to try to get votes in an election. – *n* **e'lectorate** all those who have the right to vote.

elec'tricity *n* a form of energy used to give light, heat and power. – *adjs* **e'lectric, e'lectrical** [ə'lektrik(əl)] of, produced by, worked by *etc* electricity. – *n* **electrician** [elek'trishən] one skilled in working with electricity. – *vs* **e'lectrifȳ** to supply with electricity; to excite or surprise greatly: – *pt* **e'lectrified**; **e'lectrocute** to kill by an electric current. – *n* **electric charge** a quantity of electricity *eg* that stored in a battery.

e'lectrode *n* a conductor through which an electric current enters or leaves a battery *etc*.

e'lectron *n* a very light particle within an atom, having the smallest possible charge of electricity. – *adj* **elec'tronic** of or using electrons or electronics. – *n*

elec'tronics a branch of physics dealing with the movement and effects of electrons, and with their application to machines *etc*.

'elegant *adj* graceful, well-dressed, fashionable; (of clothes *etc*) well-made and tasteful. – *n* **'elegance**.

elegy ['eliji] *n* a poem about sad things, such as the death of a friend: – *pl* **'elegies**.

'element *n* a part of anything; a substance that cannot be split into simpler substances by chemical means, as oxygen, iron *etc*; surroundings necessary for life or those which suit one best; the heating wire carrying the current in an electric heater *etc*; (*pl*) first steps in learning; (*pl*) the powers of nature, the weather. – *adjs* **ele'mental** of the elements; **ele'mentary** at the first stage; simple.

'elephant *n* a type of very large animal, with a thick skin, a trunk and two ivory tusks. – *adj* **ele'phantine** big and clumsy.

'elevate *v* to raise to a higher position; to make cheerful; to improve (the mind). – *ns* **ele'vation** the act of raising up; rising ground; height; a drawing of a building as seen from the side; an angle measuring height: *the sun's elevation*; **'elevator** (*US*) a lift in a building.

eleven [i'levn] *n* the number 11. – *adj* 11 in number. – *adj* **e'leventh** the last of eleven (things *etc*). – *n* one of eleven equal parts; a team (for cricket *etc*) of eleven people. – *n* **e'levenses** coffee, biscuits *etc* taken around eleven o'clock in the morning.

elf *n* (*myth*) a mischief-working fairy: – *pl* **elves**. – *adjs* **'elfin, 'elfish, 'elvish**.

e'licit *v* to draw out (information *etc*).

'eligible *adj* fit or worthy to be chosen. – *n* **eligi'bility**.

e'liminate *v* to get rid of; to exclude, omit. *He was eliminated at the first interview.* – *n* **e'limi'nation**.

élite [ā'lēt] *n* those thought to be the best people, as the richest, best educated *etc*.

e'lixir *n* a liquid which people once thought would make them live for ever or would turn iron *etc* into gold.

elk *n* a very large kind of deer.

ell *n* an old measure of length.

el'lipse *n* an oval shape: – *pl* **el'lipses**. – *adjs* **el'liptic, el'liptical** oval; having part of the words or meaning left out.

elm *n* a type of tree with a rough bark and leaves with saw-like edges.

elo'cūtion *n* the art of what is thought to be correct speech; style of speaking.

'**ēlongate** v to stretch out lengthwise, make longer. – n elon'gation.

e'**lope** v to run away from home to get married. – n e'lopement.

'**eloquent** adj good at putting one's thoughts etc into spoken words (to influence others). – n 'eloquence.

else adv otherwise. Eat or else you will starve; apart from the person or thing mentioned. Someone else has taken her place. – adv 'else'where in or to another place.

elucidate [i'lōōsidāt] v to make (something) easy to understand.

elude [i'lōōd] v to escape (by a trick); to be too difficult to remember or understand. – adj **elusive** [i'lōōsiv] hard to catch.

'**elver** n a young eel.

elves, elvish see elf.

e'**māciated** adj very thin, like a skeleton.

'**emanate** v to flow, come out from. – n **ema'nation** something given out by a substance, as gas, rays etc.

e'**mancipate** v to set free, as from slavery or strict or unfair social conditions. – n **emanci'pation**.

embalm [im'bäm] v to preserve (a dead body) from decay by treating it with spices or drugs.

em'bankment n a bank of earth or stone to keep water back, to carry a railway etc over low-lying places etc.

em'bargo n an official order forbidding something, esp trade with another country: – pl em'bargoes.

em'bark v to put or go on board ship; (with on) to start (a new career etc). – n **embar'kation**.

em'barrass v to make to feel uncomfortable and self-conscious; to put difficulties (sometimes lack of money) in the way of. – n **em'barrassment**.

'**embassy** n the offices etc of an ambassador in a foreign country: – pl 'embassies.

em'bellish v to make beautiful, to decorate; to add details to (a story etc). – n **em'bellishment**.

'**ember** n a piece of wood or coal glowing in a fire.

em'bezzle v to use for oneself money given to one to look after. – n **em'bezzlement**.

em'blāzon v to set out in bright colours or in some very noticeable way.

'**emblem** n an object, picture etc which represents something. The dove is the emblem of peace. The leek is the emblem of Wales; a badge.

em'body v to include; to give form or expression (to an idea etc). His first novel embodies the hopes of youth: – pt em'bodied. – n em'bodiment.

em'boss v to make a pattern which stands out from a flat surface (of leather, metal etc). – adj em'bossed.

em'brace v to throw the arms round in affection; to include; to accept, adopt eagerly (a political party etc). – Also n.

embro'cation n an ointment for rubbing on the body (for stiffness etc).

em'broider v to ornament with designs in needlework; to add (untrue) details to (a story etc). – n em'broidery.

em'broil v to get (a person) into a quarrel, or into a difficult situation etc; to throw into confusion.

embryo ['embriō] n the young of an animal or plant in its earliest stages in the womb, egg or seed; the beginning of anything: – pl 'embryos. – adj **embryonic** [embri'onik] in an early stage of development.

ē'**mend** v to remove faults or errors from. – n emen'dation.

emerald ['emərəld] n a type of gem of a bright green colour.

e'**merge** v to come out; to become known or clear. – ns e'mergence; e'mergency an unexpected happening, usu dangerous or worrying, requiring very quick action: – pl e'mergencies. – adj e'mergent arising; newly formed or newly independent: emergent nation. – n emergency exit a way out of a building if anything goes wrong.

emery ['eməri] n a very hard mineral, for smoothing and polishing, used in emery paper, emery board etc.

e'**metic** adj causing vomiting. – Also n.

'**emigrate** v to leave one's country to settle in another. – ns emi'gration; 'emigrant one who emigrates.

'**eminent** adj famous, notable. – n 'eminence distinction, fame; a title of honour; a rising ground, hill. – adv 'eminently very, obviously: eminently suitable.

'**emissary** n one sent on private (often secret) business: – pl 'emissaries.

e'**mit** v to send, give out (light, sound etc): – pt e'mitted. – n e'mission the act of emitting.

e'**mollient** adj, n softening and smoothing (substance).

e'**molūment** n wages, salary.

e'**mōtion** n any feeling that disturbs or excites the mind (fear, love, hatred etc). – adj e'motional moving the feelings; (of persons) having feelings easily excited. – adj e'motive causing emotion (rather than thought).

'**empathy** n the ability to share another

96

person's feelings *etc.* – *v* '**empathize**.

'**emperor** *n* the ruler of an empire: – *fem* '**empress**.

'**emphasis** *n* greater force of voice used on some words or parts of words to make them more noticeable; greater attention or importance. *The emphasis is on freedom.* – *v* '**emphasize** to put emphasis on; to call attention to. – *adj* **em'phatic** spoken strongly.

'**empire** *n* a large and powerful nation or group of nations (*usu* ruled by an emperor); area of power or control.

em'pirical *adj* based on experiment and experience, not on theory alone. – *n* **em'piricism**.

em'ploy *v* to give work to; to use; to occupy the time of. – *ns* **em'ploy** employment; **employ'ee** one who works for an **em'ployer; em'ployment** work, trade, occupation.

em'porium *n* a market; a shop, *esp* a big shop: – *pls* **em'poria, em'poriums**.

empress *see* **emperor**.

'**empty** *adj* having nothing (or no one) in it; unlikely to result in anything: *empty threats*. – *v* to make or become empty: – *pt* '**emptied**. – *n* an empty bottle *etc.*: – *pl* '**empties**. – *n* '**emptiness**.

'**ēmū** *n* a type of Australian bird which cannot fly.

'**emulate** *v* to try to do as well as, or better than. – *n* **emu'lation**.

e'mulsion *n* a milky liquid, *esp* that made by mixing oil and water.

e'nāble *v* to make it possible for, allow. *The money enabled him to retire.*

e'nact *v* to act, perform; to make a law.

e'namel *n* any thin, hard, glossy coating, as paint on metal; the smooth white coating of the teeth *etc.* – *v* to coat or paint with enamel: – *pt* **e'namelled**. – *n* **e'namelling**.

enamoured [i'namərd]: **enamoured of** fond of.

en'campment *n* a camp for troops *etc.*

en'chant *v* to delight, please greatly; to put a spell or charm on. – *ns* **en'chanter**: – *fem* **en'chantress; en'chantment** state of being enchanted; act of enchanting.

enclose [in'klōz] *v* to put inside an envelope *etc* with a letter *etc*; to put (*eg* a wall) around. – *n* **enclosure** [in'klōzhər] the act of enclosing; something enclosed.

encompass [in'kumpəs] *v* to surround; to include.

encore ['oŋkör] *n* an extra performance of a song *etc* given in reply to a call from an audience; this call.

en'counter *v* to meet, *esp* unexpectedly;

to come up against (a difficulty, enemy *etc*). – *n* a meeting, a fight.

encourage [in'kurij] *v* to give hope or confidence to; to urge (to do). – *n* **en'couragement**.

en'croach *v* to go beyond one's rights or land and interfere with another's. – *n* **en'croachment**.

en'cumbrance *n* something which hinders or weighs heavily on (someone).

encyclop(a)edia [insiklə'pēdiə] *n* a book or books containing much information, either on all subjects or on one particular subject. – *adj* **encyclo'p(a)edic** giving complete information.

end *n* the last point or part; death; the farthest point of the length of something, as of a table *etc*; purpose or object aimed at, the result; a small piece left over. – *v* to bring or come to an end. – *n* '**ending** the last part. – **on end** standing *etc* on one end; in a row or series, without a stop. *He fasted for days on end.*

endanger [in'dānjər] *v* to put in danger or at risk.

en'dear *v* to make dear or more dear. – *n* **en'dearment** a word of love.

endeavour [in'devər] *v* to try hard (to). – *n* a determined attempt.

en'demic *adj* of a disease *etc* found regularly in a certain area.

endive ['endiv] *n* a type of plant whose curly leaves are eaten as a salad.

en'dorse *v* to give one's support to something said or written; to write on the back of a cheque to show that money has been received for it; to indicate on a motor licence that the owner has broken a driving law. – *n* **en'dorsement**.

endow [in'dow] *v* to give money for the buying and upkeep of. *He endowed a bed in the hospital*; to give a talent, quality *etc* to. *Nature endowed her with a good brain.* – *n* **en'dowment**.

en'dūre *v* to bear without giving way; to last. – *adj* **en'durable** bearable. – *n* **en'durance** the power of enduring.

enemy ['enəmi] *n* a person who wishes to harm one; a person, army *etc* armed to fight against one; one who is against (something): *an enemy of Communism*: – *pl* '**enemies**. – *n* '**enmity**.

'**energy** *n* strength to work; vigour; ability to work, play *etc* very actively; power (such as electricity, heat *etc*): – *pl* '**energies**. – *adj* **ener'getic** active, lively.

'**enervate** *v* to take strength out of.

en'force *v* to cause (a law *etc*) to be

carried out.

en'gage *v* to begin to employ (workmen *etc*); to book in advance; to take or keep hold of (one's attention *etc*); to be busy with, occupied in; (of machine parts) to fit together; to begin fighting. – *adj* **en'gaged** bound by a promise *esp* of marriage; busy (on something); in use. – *n* **en'gagement** a promise of marriage; an appointment (to meet someone); a fight: *naval engagement*. – *adj* **en'gaging** pleasant, charming.

engine ['enjin] *n* a machine in which heat or other energy is used to produce motion; the part of a train which pulls the coaches *etc*. – *n* **engi'neer** one who makes or works with any kind of engine or machine; one who designs machines, engines *etc*; one who designs or makes bridges, roads, canals *etc*. – *v* to bring about by clever or cunning planning. – *n* **engi'neering** the science of machines, roadmaking *etc*.

en'grave *v* to write or draw with a special tool on wood, steel *etc*; to make a deep impression on. *The event was engraved on his memory*. – *n* **en'graving** (a print made from) a cut-out drawing *etc* in metal or wood.

en'gross *v* to take up the whole interest or attention.

en'gulf *v* to swallow up wholly.

en'hance *v* to make to appear greater or better. *Candlelight enhances her beauty.*

e'nigma *n* anything or anyone difficult to understand, a mystery. – *adj* **enig'matic**.

en'joy *v* to find or take pleasure in; to be in the habit of having, *esp* something of advantage. *He enjoys good health*. – *adj* **en'joyable**. – *n* **en'joyment**. – **enjoy oneself** to have a pleasant time.

en'large *v* to make larger; (with **on**) to say much or more about something. – *n* **en'largement** an increase in the size of anything; a larger photograph made from a smaller one.

enlighten [in'litn] *v* to give more knowledge or information to. – *n* **en'lightenment**.

en'list *v* to join an army *etc*; to obtain the support and help of.

en'liven *v* to make more active or cheerful.

enmity *see* **enemy**.

enormous [i'normɔs] *adj* very large. – *n* **e'normity** hugeness; great wickedness; ability to shock. *The enormity of his remarks silenced all.*

enough [i'nuf] *adj, pron* (in) the number or amount wanted or needed: *enough pages*: *enough money*. *He has quite*

enough now. – *adv* as much as is wanted or necessary. *She's been there often enough to know her way.*

enquire *see* **inquire**.

en'rage *v* to make angry.

en'rol, en'roll *v* to enter (a name) in a register or list: – *pt* **en'rolled**. – *n* **en'rolment**.

en'sconce: ensconce oneself to settle comfortably.

ensemble [ön'sömbl] *n* all the parts of a thing taken together; an outfit of clothes; (a performance given by) a group of musicians *etc*.

ensign ['ensin] *n* the flag of a nation, regiment *etc*: *the White Ensign of the Royal Navy*; (*hist*) a young officer who carried the flag.

ensue [in'sū] *v* to follow, come after; to result (from).

ensure [in'shoor] *v* to make sure

en'tail *v* to leave land so that the heir cannot sell any part of it; to bring as a result, involve. *The exam entailed extra work.*

entangle [in'tangl] *v* to make tangled or complicated; to involve (in difficulties).

'enter *v* to go or come in or into; to put (a name *etc*) into a list; to take part (in); to begin (on, upon).

'enterprise *n* anything new (*esp* if risky or difficult) undertaken; a spirit of boldness in trying new things; a business concern. – *adj* **'enterprising** showing boldness *esp* in attempting new things.

enter'tain *v* to amuse; to receive as a guest; to give a party; to consider (*eg* a suggestion); to hold in the mind. *He entertained the belief that he was Napoleon*. – *n* **enter'tainer** one who entertains, *esp* one paid to amuse people. – *adj* **enter'taining** amusing. – *n*. **enter'tainment** something that entertains, as a theatrical show, a party *etc*.

enthral [in'throl] *v* to give great delight to: – *pt* **en'thralled**.

en'thusiasm *n* great interest and keenness. – *n* **en'thusiast**. – *adj* **en'thusi'astic** acting with all one's powers; greatly interested, keen. – *adv* **enthusi'astically**. – *v* **en'thuse** to be enthusiastic (over).

en'tice *v* to draw on by promises, rewards *etc*. – *n* **en'ticement** a bribe, promise or reward. – *adj* **en'ticing**.

en'tire *adj* whole, complete. – *n* **entirety** [in'tirɔti].

en'title *v* to give a name to a book *etc*; to give (a person) a right to.

'**entity** *n* something which exists: – *pl* '**entities**.

ento'**mology** *n* the study of insects. – *n* ento'**mologist**.

'**entrails** *npl* the inner parts of an animal's body, the bowels.

'**entrance**[1] *n* a place for entering (*eg* a door); the act of coming in; the right to enter. – *n* '**entrant** one who comes in; one who goes in for a race, competition *etc*.

en'**trance**[2] *v* to fill with great delight; to bewitch. – *adj* en'**trancing** charming.

en'**treat** *v* to ask earnestly. – *n* en'**treaty**: – *pl* en'**treaties**.

en'**trenched** *adj* firmly established, difficult to move or change.

en'**trust**, in'**trust** *v* to trust (something) to the care of (someone else).

'**entry** *n* the act of entering; a place for entering; something written in a book, as a name *etc*: – *pl* '**entries**.

e'**nūmerate** *v* to count; to mention individually. – *n* **enume'ration**.

e'**nunciate** *v* to pronounce distinctly; to state formally. – *n* **enunci'ation**.

en'**velop** *v* to cover by wrapping; to surround entirely: *enveloped in mist*. – *n* '**envelope** a wrapping or cover, *esp* for a letter.

en'**vironment** *n* surroundings, circumstances in which a person or animal lives.

en'**visage** [in'vizij] *v* to picture in one's mind and consider.

'**envoy** *n* a messenger, *esp* one sent to deal with a foreign government.

'**envy** *v* to look greedily at someone and wish that one had what he has: – *pt* '**envied**. – Also *n*. – *adjs* '**enviable** worth envying, worth having; '**envious** feeling envy.

'**enzyme** *n* a substance produced in a living body which affects the speed of chemical changes without itself changing.

eon *see* **aeon**.

'**epaulet**, '**epaulette** *n* a shoulder ornament on a uniform.

ephemeral [i'femərəl] *adj* lasting a very short time.

'**epic** *n* a long poem, story, film *etc* about great deeds. – *adj* of or like an epic; heroic; greater than usual.

'**epicūre** *n* one who is fond of eating and drinking good things. – *adj* **epicu'rēan**.

epi'demic *n* an outbreak (*eg* of disease or crime) which affects many people.

epi'dermis *n* the top covering of the skin.

epi'glottis *n* a piece of skin at the back of the tongue which closes the windpipe during swallowing.

epigram *n* any short, neat, witty saying in prose or verse. – *adj* **epigram'matic**.

'**epilepsy** *n* an illness causing attacks of unconsciousness and (*usu*) fits. – *adj* **epi'leptic** suffering from epilepsy; of epilepsy: *an epileptic fit*. – *n* one suffering from epilepsy.

epilogue, (*US*) **epilog** ['epilog] *n* the very end part of a book, programme *etc*; a speech at the end of a play *etc*.

e'**piscopal** *adj* of or ruled by bishops. – *adj* e'**pisco'pālian** believing in e'**piscopacy**, the ruling of the Church by bishops.

'**episode** *n* one of several parts of a story *etc*; an interesting event or happening. – *adj* **episodic** [epi'sodik] of episodes; happening at irregular intervals.

epistle [i'pisl] *n* a (formal) letter *esp* one from an apostle of Christ in the Bible.

'**epitaph** *n* words about a dead person put on a gravestone.

'**epithet** *n* a describing word, an adjective.

epitome [i'pitəmi] *n* something or someone that represents something on a small scale. *He is the epitome of politeness*; a summary (of a book, story). – *v* e'**pitomize** to make or be the epitome (of something).

epoch ['ēpok] *n* an event or time marking the beginning of a new period in history, development *etc*; an extended period of time, *usu* marked by an important series of events. – *adj* '**epochmaking** marking an important point in history.

'**equable** *adj* of calm temper; (of climate) neither very hot nor very cold.

'**ēqual** *adj* of the same size, value, quantity *etc*; evenly balanced; (with **to**) able, fit for: *equal to the job*. – *n* a person of the same rank, cleverness *etc* (as another). – *v* to be or make equal to; to be the same as: – *pt* '**equalled**. – *n* **equality** [i'kwoləti] the state of being equal. – *v* '**equalize** to make equal.

equa'nimity *n* evenness of temper, calmness.

e'**quate** *v* to regard or treat as being in some way the same; to state the equality of. – *n* **equation** [i'kwāzhən] a statement, *esp* in mathematics, that two things are equal.

e'**quātor** *n* an imaginary line around the earth, halfway between the North Pole and South Pole. – *adj* **equa'torial** of, situated on or near, the equator.

'**equerry** *n* an official who attends a king

or prince *etc*: – *pl* **'equerries**.

e'questrian *adj* of horse-riding; on horseback. – *n* a horseman.

ēqui- *prefix* equal. – *adjs* **'equi'distant** equally distant; **'equi'lateral** having all sides equal.

ēqui'librium *n* a state of equal balance between weights, forces *etc*; a balanced state of mind or feelings.

'equine *adj* of or like a horse or horses.

'equinox *n* either of the times (about 21st March and 23rd September) when the sun crosses the equator, making night and day equal in length. – *adj* **equi'noctial**.

e'quip *v* to supply with everything needed (for a task): – *pt* **e'quipped**. – *ns* **'equipage** carriages, attendants *etc* for a rich or important person; **e'quipment** a set of articles needed to equip (a person or thing).

'equity *n* fairness, just dealing. – *adj* **'equitable** fair, just.

e'quivalent *adj* equal in value, power, meaning *etc*. – Also *n*.

e'quivocal *adj* having more than one meaning; uncertain, doubtful. – *v* **e'quivocate** to use words with more than one meaning in order to mislead; to tell lies cleverly.

'ēra *n* a number of years counting from an important point in history: *the Elizabethan era*; a period of time marked by an important event or events: *the era of steam*.

e'radicate *v* to get rid of completely. – *n* **eradi'cation**.

erase [i'rāz] *v* to rub out; to remove. – *ns* **e'raser** something which erases, a rubber; **erasure** [i'rāzhǝr] the act of erasing; something erased.

ere [ār] *prep, conj* before: *ere long*.

e'rect *v* to build; to set upright. – *adj* standing straight up. – *n* **e'rection** the act of erecting; anything erected.

ermine ['ɜrmin] *n* a stoat; its white fur.

e'rode *v* to wear away, destroy gradually. – *n* **e'rosion**.

e'rotic *adj* of or arousing sexual desire.

err *v* to make a mistake; to sin. – *adj* **er'ratic** irregular, wandering, not following a fixed course; not steady or reliable in behaviour. – *n* **er'ratum** an error in a book: – *pl* **er'rata**.

'errand *n* a (*usu* short) journey on which a person is sent to say or do something for someone else; the purpose of this journey.

'errant *adj* doing wrong; straying; wandering in search of adventure: *a knight errant*.

erratic, erratum *see* **err**.

'error *n* a mistake; wrongdoing. – *adj* **er'rōneous** wrong.

erudite ['erŏŏdīt] *adj* clever, having learned much from books. – *n* **eru'dition**.

e'rupt *v* to break out or through. – *n* **e'ruption** a breaking or bursting forth, as a volcano, a rash on the body *etc*.

'escalate *v* to increase in amount, intensity *etc*. – *ns* **esca'lation**; **'escalator** a moving stairway.

es'cape to get away safe or free; (of gas *etc*) to leak; to slip from (the memory *etc*). – *n* the act of escaping. – *ns* **esca'pade** a mischievous adventure; **es'capement** something which controls the movement of a watch *etc*; **es'capism** the (habit of) trying to escape from reality into daydreaming *etc*.

es'carpment *n* the steep, cliff-like side of a hill *etc*.

'escort *n* person(s), ship(s) *etc* accompanying others for protection, courtesy *etc*. – *v* **es'cort** to act as escort to.

es'cutcheon *n* a shield on which a coat of arms is shown.

'Eskimo *n* one of a people inhabiting the Arctic regions: – *pl* **Eskimos**.

eso'teric *adj* of or understood by a small number of people.

es'parto *n* a type of strong grass grown in Spain and N. Africa, used for making paper, ropes *etc*.

especial [is'peshǝl] *adj* more than ordinary; particular. – *adv* **es'pecially**.

espionage ['espiǝnäzh] *n* spying; the use of spies, *esp* by one country to find out the secrets of another.

espla'nade *n* a level roadway, *esp* one along a seafront.

Esq *see* **Esquire**.

Es'quire *n* (*usu* written **Esq**) a title of politeness after a man's name: *John Brown, Esq*.

'essay *n* a written composition; an attempt. – *v* **es'say** to try. – *n* **'essayist** a writer of essays.

'essence *n* the most important part or quality; substance got from a plant *etc* in concentrated form: *vanilla essence*.

es'sential *adj* absolutely necessary. – Also *n*. – *adv* **es'sentially** basically; necessarily.

es'tablish *v* to settle in position; to found, set up; to show to be true, prove (that). – *adj* **es'tablished** firmly set up; accepted, recognized; (of a church) officially recognized as national. – *n* **es'tablishment** anything established, *esp* a place of business, residence *etc*. – **The Establishment** the people holding important, influential positions in a community.

es'tate *n* a large piece of land owned by a person or group of people; a person's total possessions; land developed for houses, factories *etc.* – *ns* **estate agent** one whose job it is to sell houses; **estate car** a car with a large inside luggage compartment and an additional door at the back.

es'teem *v* to think highly of, to value. – Also *n*. – *adj* **es'teemed**.

'estimate *v* to judge the size, amount, value of something *esp* roughly, without measuring. – Also *n*. – *n* **esti'mation** opinion, judgement.

estranged [is'trānjd] *adj* no longer friendly.

'estūary *n* the wide lower part of a river, up which the tide travels: – *pl* **'estuaries**.

etc *see* **et cetera**.

et cetera [it'setrə] (written **etc**) and other things of the same sort.

etch *v* to make drawings on metal, glass *etc* by eating out the lines with acid. – *n* **'etching** the picture from the etched plate.

e'ternal *adj* lasting for ever; seemingly endless. – *n* **e'ternity** time without end; the time or state after death.

'ēther *n* a colourless liquid used to dissolve fats, to deaden feeling *etc*. – *adj* **ethereal** [i'thēriəl] delicate, fairy-like.

'ethical *adj* having to do with right behaviour, justice, duty; right, just, honourable. – *n* **'ethics** the study of right and wrong; (belief in) standards leading to right, ethical behaviour.

'ethnic *adj* of race; of the customs, dress, food of a particular race or group.

eth'nology *n* the study of the different races of mankind.

etiquette ['etiket] *n* (rules setting out) polite or correct behaviour.

ety'mology *n* the study of the history of words; a (short) description of the history of a word: – *pl* **ety'mologies**. – *adj* **etymo'logical**. – *n* **ety'mologist**.

euca'lyptus *n* a type of large Australian evergreen tree giving timber, oils, gum: – *pls* **euca'lyptuses, euca'lypti**.

'eulogize *v* to praise greatly. – *n* **'eulogy** great praise, written or spoken: – *pl* **'eulogies**.

'euphemism *n* a pleasant name for something unpleasant (*eg* 'passed on' for 'died'). – *adj* **euphe'mistic**.

eu'phōnious *adj* pleasant in sound. – *n* **'euphony**. – *n* **eu'phonium** a brass musical instrument with a low tone.

eu'phoria *n* a feeling of great happiness,

joy. – *adj* **euphoric** [ū'forik].

eurhythmics [ū'ridhmiks] *n* the art of graceful movement of the body, *esp* to music.

eutha'nāsia *n* the killing of someone painlessly, *esp* to end suffering.

e'vacūate *v* to (cause to) leave *esp* because of danger; to make empty. – *ns* **evacu'ation; evacu'ee** a person who has been evacuated (from danger).

e'vade *v* to avoid or escape *esp* by cleverness or trickery. – *n* **e'vasion**. – *adj* **e'vasive** with the purpose of evading; not straightforward: *an evasive answer*.

e'valūate *v* to find or state the value of.

evanescent [evə'nesnt] *adj* passing away quickly.

ēvan'gelical *adj* spreading Christ's teaching. – *n* **e'vangelist**.

e'vaporate *v* to (cause to) change into vapour. *Heat evaporates water*; to vanish. – *n* **evapo'ration**.

evasion *see* **evade**.

eve *n* the evening or day before a festival: *Christmas Eve*; the time just before an event: *on the eve of the battle*.

'ēven *adj* level, smooth; (of numbers) able to be divided by 2 without a remainder; calm. – *adv* used to emphasize a word or words. *The job was even harder than before. Even young children could understand that*; exactly, just. – *v* to make even or smooth. – *n* **'evenness**. – **get even with** to harm (someone) who has harmed one.

'ēvening *n* the last part of the day and early part of the night.

e'vent *n* something (*esp* something important) that happens; an item in a sports programme *etc*. – *adjs* **e'ventful** exciting; **e'ventūal** final; happening as a result. – *n* **e'ventu'ality** a possible happening: – *pl* **e'ventu'alities**. – *adv* **e'ventually** at last, finally.

'ever *adv* always; at any time. – *n* **'evergreen** a kind of tree *etc* with green leaves all the year round. – *adv* **'evermore** for ever.

'every *adj* each (of several things *etc*) without exception. – *prons* **'everybody, 'everyone** every person. – *adj* **'everyday** daily; common, usual. – *pron* **'everything** all things. – *adv* **'everywhere** in every place. – **every other** one out of every two, alternate.

e'vict *v* to put (someone) out of house and home *esp* by force of law. – *n* **e'viction**.

'evident *adj* easily seen or understood. – *adv* **'evidently**. – *n* **'evidence** a clear sign; proof; information given in a law case.

'**ēvil** *adj* wicked; harmful; unpleasant. – *n* wickedness.

e'**vince** *v* to show. *The men evinced surprise at these words.*

e'**voke** *v* to draw out, produce. *The house evoked memories of their childhood.* – *adj* **evocative** [i'vokətiv] evoking, *eg* memories, a certain atmosphere.

e'**volve** *v* (to cause) to develop; to work out (a plan *etc*). – *n* **evolution** [ēvə'lōōshən] gradual development; the teaching or belief that the higher forms of life have gradually developed out of the lower. – *adj* **evo'lutionary**.

ewe [ū] *n* a female sheep.

ewer ['ūər] *n* a large jug with a wide spout.

ex- *prefix* no longer, former: *the ex-president*; outside, not in: *an ex-directory (telephone) number.*

ex'**act** *adj* accurate; punctual; careful. – *v* to compel to pay, give *etc*. – *adj* **ex'acting** asking too much; tiring. – *n* **ex'actness** accuracy, correctness.

exaggerate [ig'zajərāt] *v* to make (something) seem larger, greater *etc* than it is. – *n* **exagge'ration**.

exalt [ig'zölt] *v* to raise in rank; to praise; to make joyful. – *n* **exal'tation**.

examine [ig'zamin] *v* to put questions to (pupils *etc*) to test knowledge; to question (a witness); to look at closely, inquire into; (of a doctor) to look at (one's body) to check for illness or disease. – *ns* **exami'nation** a test of knowledge (also **ex'am**); a close inspection or inquiry; formal questioning; **ex'aminer**.

ex'**ample** *n* one case given to show what other things of the same kind are like; a warning. *Let this be an example to you.*

ex'**asperate** *v* to make very angry. – *n* **exaspe'ration**.

'**excavate** *v* to dig, scoop out; to uncover by digging. – *ns* **exca'vation** the act of digging out; a hollow made by digging; '**excavator** a machine used for excavating.

exceed [ik'sēd] *v* to go beyond, be greater than. – *adv* **ex'ceedingly** very.

excel [ik'sel] *v* to do very well; to be better than: – *pt* **ex'celled**. – *ns* '**excellence** the state of being excellent, very high quality; '**Excellency** a title of ambassadors *etc*: – *pl* '**Excellencies**. – *adj* '**excellent** unusually or extremely good.

except [ik'sept] *prep* leaving out, not counting. – *conj* with the exception (that). – *v* to leave out, not to count. – *prep* **ex'cepting** except. – *n*

ex'**ception** something left out; something that is unlike the rest: *an exception to the rule.* – *adj* **ex'ceptional** standing out from the rest. – *adv* **ex'ceptionally** very. – **except for** with the exception of; **take exception to** to object to, be offended by.

excerpt ['eksörpt] *n* a part chosen from a whole work: *an excerpt from a play.*

excess [ik'ses] *n* a going beyond what is usual or proper; the amount by which one thing is greater than another; (*pl*) **ex'cesses** very bad behaviour. – *adj* beyond the amount allowed. – *adj* **ex'cessive** too much, too great *etc*. – *adv* **ex'cessively**.

exchange [iks'chānj] *v* to give one thing and get another in return. – *n* the act of exchanging; exchanging money of one country for that of another; the difference between the value of money in different places; a central office or building (*eg* where telephone lines are connected); a place where business shares are bought and sold.

exchequer [iks'chekər] *n* the part of government that has to do with the money affairs of a country. – **Chancellor of Exchequer** *see* **chancellor**.

excise[1] [ik'sīz] *v* to cut off or out. – *n* **excision** [ik'sizhən].

excise[2] ['eksīz] *n* tax on goods *etc* made and sold within a country and on certain licences *etc*.

excite [ik'sīt] *v* to rouse the feelings of; to move to action. – *adjs* **ex'citable** easily excited; **ex'citing**. – *n* **ex'citement**.

ex'**claim** *v* to cry or shout out. – *n* **excla'mation** a sudden shout. – *adj* **ex'clamatory**. – *n* **exclamation mark** in punctuation, a mark (!) to show that an exclamation has been made.

ex'**clude** *v* to shut out; to prevent from sharing; to leave out (of consideration). – *n* **ex'clusion**. – *adj* **ex'clusive** shutting out unwanted persons, select: *an exclusive club*; not obtainable elsewhere: *an exclusive offer.* – **exclusive of** not including.

excom'**mūnicate** *v* to expel from membership of a church, to forbid to take part in church sacraments. – *n* **excommuni'cation**.

excrescence [iks'kresns] *n* something unwanted which grows outwards (such as a wart).

ex'**crete** *v* to cast out, discharge waste matter from the body. – *n* '**excrement** the waste matter cast out by humans or animals.

excruciating [iks'krōōshiātiŋ] *adj* (of pain *etc*) very severe.

ex'cursion *n* an outing, *usu* for pleasure (such as a picnic).

excuse [iks'kūz] *v* to forgive, pardon; to set free from a duty or task. – *n* **excuse** [iks'kūs] one's reason or explanation for having done something wrong. – *adj* **excusable** [iks'kūzəbl] pardonable.

'**execrable** *adj* very bad.

'**execute** *v* to perform: *execute a dance step*; to carry out: *execute commands*; to put to death legally. – *ns* **exe'cution** a doing or performing; killing by order of the law; **exe'cutioner** one whose duty it is to put to death condemned persons. – *adj* **ex'ecutive** having power to act, carry out laws. – *n* the part of a government (or society) having such power; a person in a business organization who has the power to act on important decisions. – *n* **ex'ecutor** a person who sees to the carrying out of what is stated in a will.

ex'emplary *adj* worth following as an example: *exemplary conduct*; acting as a warning: *exemplary punishment*.

ex'emplify *v* to be an example of; to show by giving example: – *pt* **ex'emplified**.

ex'empt *v* to grant freedom from some duty, task, payment, *etc*. – *adj* free (from), not liable (to do something that others have to do). – *n* **ex'emption**.

'**exercise** *n* a task for practice; training for body, mind *etc*. – *v* to give exercise to; to use. *Exercise great care!*

ex'ert *v* bring into action, use. *He exerts great influence on her*. – *n* **ex'ertion** effort; hard work. – **exert oneself** to make a great effort.

ex'hale *v* to breathe out. – *n* **exha'lation**.

exhaust [ig'zöst] *v* to tire out; to use up completely: *exhaust our supplies*; to say all that can be said about (a subject *etc*). – *n* the way out for the waste products of fuel-using engines (steam, fumes *etc*). – *adj* **ex'hausted** tired out; emptied; used up. – *n* **ex'haustion** great tiredness, weariness; the act of exhausting. – *adj* **ex'haustive** saying all that can be said.

exhibit [ig'zibit] *v* to show (in public). – *n* anything shown (*eg* a picture in a picture gallery). – *ns* **exhibition** [eksi'bishən] a public show, an open display; **exhi'bitionism** a tendency to try to attract people's attention; **exhi'bitionist; exhibitor** [ig'zibitər].

exhilarate [ig'zilərāt] *v* to make joyful or lively, refresh. – *adj* **ex'hilarating**.

exhort [ig'zört] *v* to urge (to do). – *n* **exhor'tation**.

ex'hume *v* to dig out (*esp* a body from a grave). – *n* **exhu'mation**.

'**exigent** *adj* demanding immediate attention, urgent. – *n* **ex'igency** an urgent need or demand. *He was forced by the exigencies of the situation to sell his house*: – *pl* **ex'igencies**.

'**exile** *n* a person who lives outside his own country, either by choice or unwillingly; a (*usu* long) stay in a foreign land. – *v* to drive (a person) away from his own country, to banish.

exist [ig'zist] *v* to be, have life; to live; to live in poor circumstances. – *n* **ex'istence**. – *adj* **ex'istent**.

'**exit** *n* a way out; the act of going out.

'**exodus** *n* a going away of many people (*esp* those leaving a country for ever).

exonerate [ig'zonərāt] *v* to free from blame. – *n* **exone'ration**.

exorbitant [ig'zörbitənt] *adj* going beyond what is usual or reasonable: *an exorbitant price*. – *n* **ex'orbitance**.

'**exorcize** *v* to drive out (an evil spirit or spell); to free (someone or something) from an evil spirit dwelling in them. – *ns* '**exorcism** the act of driving away evil spirits or spells; '**exorcist**.

exotic [ig'zotik] *adj* coming from a foreign country; unusual, colourful.

ex'pand *v* to grow wider or bigger; to open out. – *ns* **ex'panse** a wide stretch (as of land *etc*); **ex'pansion** a growing, stretching or spreading. – *adj* **ex'pansive** spreading out; (of persons) talkative, telling much.

expatiate [iks'pāshiāt] *v* to talk a great deal (about something).

ex'patriate *adj* living outside one's native country. – Also *n*.

ex'pect *v* to think of as likely to happen, come *etc* soon; to think, assume. *I expect he's too busy*. – *adj* **ex'pectant** hopeful, expecting; expecting to become (*esp* a mother). – *ns* **ex'pectancy** state of expecting; hope; **expec'tation** state of expecting; what is expected. – *adj* **ex'pecting** (*coll*) pregnant.

ex'pedient *adj* suited to the time and to the occasion but sometimes not just or fair. – *n* something done to get round a difficulty. – *ns* **ex'pedience, ex'pediency**.

ex'pedite *v* to hasten, hurry on. – *adj* **expe'ditious** swift, speedy.

expe'dition *n* a journey with a purpose (often exploration); people making such a journey.

ex'pel *v* to drive or force out; to send away in disgrace (*esp* from a school): –

pt ex'**pelled**. – *n* ex'**pulsion**.

ex'**pend** *v* to spend, use up. – *n* ex'**penditure** amount spent or used up, *esp* money.

ex'**pense** *n* cost; cause of spending. *The house was a continual expense*; (*pl*) money spent in carrying out a job *etc*. – *adj* ex'**pensive** costing much money.

experience [iks'pēriəns] *n* any event in which one is involved: *a horrible experience*; wisdom, knowledge gained from events, practice *etc*. – *v* to go through, undergo. – *adj* ex'**perienced** skilled, knowledgeable.

ex'**periment** *n* a trial, test (of an idea, machine *etc*). – *v* to carry out experiments. – *adj* experi'**mental**.

'**expert** *adj* highly skilful or knowledgeable (in a particular subject). – *n* one who is highly skilled or knowledgeable. – *n* **expertise** [ekspər'tēz] skill.

'**expiate** *v* to make up for (a crime *etc*). – *n* expi'**ation**.

ex'**pire** *v* to die; to come to an end. – *n* ex'**piry** the end or finish.

ex'**plain** *v* to make clear; to give reasons for. – *n* expla'**nation** a statement which makes clear something difficult or puzzling; a reason (*eg* for one's behaviour). – *adj* ex'**planatory** meant to make clear.

ex'**plētive** *n* an exclamation, *esp* a swear word.

ex'**plicable** *adj* able to be explained.

ex'**plicit** *adj* plainly stated; outspoken.

ex'**plode** *v* to blow up like a bomb with loud noise; to prove (a theory *etc*) to be wrong. – *n* ex'**plosion** a sudden burst or blow-up, with a loud noise. – *adj* ex'**plosive** liable to explode; hot-tempered. – *n* anything (such as gunpowder) that will explode.

'**exploit** *n* a daring deed; a feat. – *v* ex'**ploit** to make use of selfishly; to make good use of (resources *etc*). – *n* exploi'**tation**.

ex'**plore** *v* to make a journey of discovery. – *ns* explo'**ration**; ex'**plorer**.

explosion *see* explode.

ex'**pōnent** *n* one who shows skill in a particular art or craft: *an exponent of karate.* — *adj* expon'**ential**.

ex'**port** *v* to sell goods *etc* in a foreign country. – *ns* '**export** act of exporting; something exported; expor'**tation**.

ex'**pose** *v* to place (something) where all can see it; to show up (a hidden evil, crime *etc*); to lay open to sun, wind, cold *etc*; to allow light to reach and act on (a film). – *ns* ex'**posure**; expo'**sition** a public show; a statement which makes clear a writer's meaning.

ex'**postulate** *v* to protest. – *n* expostu-'**lation**.

ex'**pound** *v* to explain fully.

ex'**press** *v* to show by action; to put into words; to press or squeeze out. – *adj* clearly stated: *express instructions*; sent in haste: *express messenger*. – *n* a fast train. – *n* ex'**pression** the look on one's face; showing meaning, feeling by means of language, art *etc*; a show of feeling in a performance of music *etc*; a word or phrase: *a slang expression*; pressing or squeezing out. – *adj* ex'**pressive** expressing; expressing meaning or feeling clearly.

ex'**prōpriate** *v* to take (property *etc*) away from its owner.

expulsion *see* expel.

ex'**punge** *v* to rub out, remove.

exquisite ['ekskwizit] *adj* of great beauty; excellent; (of pleasure *etc*) very great; keen, sharp.

ex'**tant** *adj* still existing.

extempore [iks'tempəri] *adv, adj* at a moment's notice, without preparation. – *v* ex'**temporize** to make up (music, a speech *etc*) as one plays, speaks *etc*.

ex'**tend** *v* to stretch, make longer; to hold out: *he extended his hand*; to last. *This holiday extends into next week*. – *n* ex'**tension** a part added (to a building, a holiday *etc*); a telephone connected with a main one. – *adj* ex'**tensive** wide; covering a large space; happening or being in many places. – *n* ex'**tent** the space something covers; degree: *to a great extent*.

ex'**tenūate** *v* to lessen; to make to seem less bad. – *n* extenu'**ation**.

ex'**tērior** *adj* lying *etc* on the outside, outer: *an exterior wall*. – *n* the outside (of something).

ex'**terminate** *v* to destroy completely, kill off (a race, a type of animal *etc*). – *n* extermi'**nation**.

ex'**ternal** *adj* outside; on the outside.

ex'**tinct** *adj* no longer active: *an extinct volcano*; of a kind no longer found alive. *The dodo is extinct.* – *n* ex'**tinction** making or becoming extinct.

extinguish [iks'tiŋgwish] *v* to put out (fire *etc*); to put an end to. – *n* ex'**tinguisher** a spray containing chemicals for putting out fires.

ex'**tōl** *v* to praise greatly: – *pt* ex'**tolled**.

ex'**tort** *v* to take by force or threats. – *n* ex'**tortion**. – *adj* ex'**tortionate** (of a price) much too high.

'**extra** *adj* more than is usual or necessary; additional. – *adv* unusually. – *n* anything extra; a person employed to be one of a crowd in a film.

extra- *prefix* outside, beyond, as in **'extra-ter'restrial** outside, or from outside the earth.

ex'tract *v* to draw or pull out *esp* by force; to choose and take out parts of a book *etc*; to take out (a substance forming part of something else) by pressure *etc* or by chemical means. – *ns* **'extract** a part chosen (from a book *etc*); a substance obtained by extraction; **ex'traction** act of extracting; one's descent. *He was of English extraction.*

'extradite *v* to hand over to the police of another country (someone wanted by them). – *n* **extra'dition**.

ex'trāneous *adj* having nothing to do with the subject: *extraneous information.*

extraordinary [iks'trördənəri] *adj* not usual, exceptional; very surprising; specially employed: *ambassador extraordinary.*

extra'sensory *adj* beyond the range of the ordinary senses.

ex'travagant *adj* spending too freely; wasteful; too great: *extravagant praise.* – *n* **ex'travagance**.

'extravert, 'extrovert *n* one who is chiefly interested in matters outside of himself.

ex'treme *adj* far from the centre; far from the ordinary or usual; very great. – *n* an extreme point. – *ns* **ex'trēmist** one who carries ideas foolishly far;

extremity [iks'treməti] the farthest-off part or place; great distress or pain; (*pl*) **ex'tremities** farthest-off parts of the body, as hands, feet.

'extricate *v* to set free (from difficulties *etc*).

extrovert *see* **extravert**.

exuberant [ig'zūbərənt] *adj* in very high spirits. – *n* **ex'uberance**.

exude [ig'zūd] *v* to give off (in great amounts): *exude sweat: exude happiness.*

exult [ig'zult] *v* to be very glad, rejoice greatly. *They exulted in their victory.* – *adj* **ex'ultant**. – *n* **exul'tation**.

eye [i] *n* the part of the body with which one sees; the ability to notice: *an eye for detail*; sight; anything like an eye (*eg* the hole in a needle *etc*). – *v* to look at. – *ns* **'eyeball** the round part of the eye; the eye itself (the part between the eyelids); **'eyebrow** the hairy ridge above the eye; **'eyeglass** a lens to correct faulty eyesight; **'eyelash** one of the hairs on the edge of the eyelid; **'eyelet** a small hole for a lace *etc*; **'eyelid** the skin cover of the eye; **'eye-opener** that which shows up something unexpected; **'eyesore** anything that is ugly (*esp* a building); **'eyewitness** one who sees a thing done (*eg* a crime committed).

eyrie, eyry, aerie ['iri] *n* the nesting place of eagles or other birds of prey.

F

'fāble *n* a story (about animals *etc*) that has a lesson or moral. – *adj* **fabulous** ['fabūləs] existing (only) in fable. *The griffin is a fabulous creature*; (*coll*) very good.

'fabric *n* cloth; the outside parts (walls *etc*) of a building.

'fabricate *v* to make up (lies). – *n* **fabri'cation**.

façade [fə'säd] *n* the front of a building; a deceptive appearance.

face *n* the front part of the head; the front of anything; appearance. – *v* to turn, stand *etc* in the direction of; to stand opposite to; to put an additional surface (**'facing**) on. – *n* **'facepowder** powder put on the face to improve the appearance. – **face up to** to meet or accept boldly. *He faced up to his responsibilities.*

'facet *n* a side of a many-sided object, *esp* a cut gem.

fa'cētious *adj* funny, joking. – *n* **fa'cetiousness**.

facial ['fāshəl] *adj* of the face.

'facile *adj* not deep or thorough, superficial; easily persuaded; (too) fluent. – *n* **facility** [fə'siləti] ease; skill in doing a thing; (*pl*) **fa'cilities** the means for doing a thing (easily). – *v* **fa'cilitate** to make easy.

facsimile [fak'siməli] *n* an exact copy.

fact *n* something known or held to be true; reality; (in law) a deed. – **in fact** actually, really.

'faction *n* a group of people (part of a larger group) acting together. *The rival factions hated each other.* – *adj* **'factious** trouble-making, riotous.

'factor *n* something which affects the

course of events; one who does business for another; a number which exactly divides into another (*eg* 3 is a factor of 6). – *v* '**factorize** to find factors of.

'**factory** *n* a workshop where goods are made in large quantities: – *pl* '**factories**.

fac'tōtum *n* a person employed to do all kinds of work.

'**faculty** *n* power of the mind, *eg* reason *etc*; a natural power of the body, as hearing *etc*; ability, aptitude; a department of study in a university *etc*: *Faculty of Science*: – *pl* '**faculties**.

fad *n* an odd like or dislike. – *adj* '**faddy**.

fade *v* to (make to) lose colour, strength *etc*; to go from sight, hearing *etc*.

faeces ['fēsēz] *n* solid waste material excreted from the body.

fag *v* to work hard; to weary; (*coll*) to work as a school fag: – *pt* **fagged**. – *n* any tiresome bit of work; (*coll*) a young schoolboy forced to do jobs for an older one; (*slang*) a cigarette.

'**faggot**, '**fagot** *n* a bundle of sticks.

Fahrenheit ['farənhīt] *adj* as measured on a Fahrenheit thermometer: *50 degrees Fahrenheit*. – **Fahrenheit thermometer** a thermometer which shows the temperature at which water freezes as 32 degrees, and that at which it boils as 212 degrees.

fail *v* to (declare to) be unsuccessful; to break down, stop; to lose strength; to be lacking, not to be enough; to disappoint. – *ns* '**failing** a fault; a weakness; '**failūre** the act of failing; someone or something which fails. – **without fail** certainly. *Do it without fail by tomorrow*.

fain *adv* (in poetry *etc*) willingly.

faint *adj* lacking in strength, brightness, courage *etc*; about to lose consciousness. – *v* to become faint; to fall down unconscious. – *n* a loss of consciousness. – *adv* '**faintly** dimly, not clearly. – *n* '**faintness**.

fair[1] *adj* of a light colour *esp* of hair; free from rain; not favouring one side, just; good enough but not excellent; beautiful. – *n* '**fairness**. – *adj* '**fair-'haired** having light-coloured hair, blond. – *n* '**fairway** the deep-water part of a channel, river *etc*; the mown part on a golf course, between the tee and the green.

fair[2] *n* a large market held at fixed times; an exhibition of goods from different countries, firms *etc*; a sale of goods for charities; a collection of entertainments (merry-go-rounds *etc*) which moves

from place to place.

'**fairy** *n* (*myth*) a (small) being like a man or woman with magical powers: – *pl* '**fairies**. – *ns* **fairy light** a small coloured light for decoration (of Christmas trees *etc*); **fairy story**, **fairy tale** an old story of fairies, giants *etc*; (*coll*) a lie.

faith *n* trust, belief (*eg* in God); loyalty to a promise. *He kept faith with them*. – *adjs* '**faithful** loyal; keeping one's promises; true, accurate: *a faithful account of events*; believing (in God); '**faithless**.

fake *v* to make an imitation of (*esp* in order to deceive). – *adj* not genuine, forged. – *n* one who pretends to be something he is not; a forgery.

falcon ['fölkən] *n* a kind of bird of prey. – *n* '**falconry** the training of falcons for hunting.

fall [föl] *v* to drop down; to become less; (of a fortress *etc*) to be captured; to die in battle; to happen, occur. *Christmas falls on Tuesday this year*: – *pt* **fell**, *pp* '**fallen**. – *n* a dropping down; something that falls: *a fall of snow*; lowering (in value *etc*); (*US*) autumn; an accident in which one falls (as from a horse, when running *etc*); ruin, downfall, surrender; (*pl*) a waterfall. – *n* '**fallout** radioactive dust resulting from the explosion of an atomic bomb *etc*. – **fall flat** to fail to have the intended effect; **fall in love** to begin to be in love; **fall out with** to quarrel with; **fall through** (of plans *etc*) to fail, come to nothing.

'**fallacy** *n* a wrong idea or belief; something which is thought to be true but is really false; unsound argument or reasoning: – *pl* '**fallacies**. – *adj* **fal'lācious** misleading, false; not showing sound reasoning.

'**fallible** *adj* liable to make a mistake or to be wrong. – *n* **falli'bility**.

fallow ['falō] *adj* (of land) left unsown for a time after being ploughed; of a yellowish-brown colour. – *n* **fallow deer** a type of yellowish-brown deer.

false [föls] *adj* untrue; not real, fake; not natural: *false teeth*. – *ns* '**falsehood** a lie, an untruth; '**falseness**, '**falsity** quality of being false. – *v* '**falsify** to make false, alter for a dishonest purpose. *He falsified the firm's accounts*: – *pt* '**falsified**.

falter ['föltər] *v* to stumble or hesitate.

fame *n* the quality of being well-known or much talked about, renown. – *adjs* **famed**, '**famous** well-known, having fame. – *adv* '**famously** (*coll*) very well.

fa'miliar *adj* well-known; seen, known

etc before; well-acquainted (with); too friendly, cheeky. – *n* famili'arity. – *v* fa'miliarize to make quite accustomed or acquainted (with).

'family *n* a man, his wife and their children; the children alone; a group of people related to one another; a group (such as plants, animals, languages) having some likeness: – *pl* 'families.

famine ['famin] *n* great shortage *esp* of food or water.

'famished *adj* very hungry.

famous *see* fame.

fan *n* an instrument or device for making a rush of air; a small hand-held device, *usu* shaped like part of a circle, for cooling the face; an admirer (of an actor, singer *etc*). – *v* to cause a rush of air with a fan; to increase the strength of: *fan his anger*: – *pt* fanned. – *n* 'fanlight a window above a door, *esp* one shaped like a half circle. – fan out to spread out in the shape of a fan.

fa'natic *n* a person who is over-enthusiastic or eager about something (*esp* religion). – *adj* fa'natic(al) wildly or excessively enthusiastic.

'fancy *n* a sudden liking or desire; the power of the mind to imagine things *esp* things unlike reality; something imagined: – *pl* 'fancies. – *adj* not plain; ornamented. – *v* to picture, imagine; to have a sudden wish for; to think without being sure: – *pt* 'fancied. – *n* 'fancier one whose hobby is to keep prize animals, birds *etc*. – *adj* 'fanciful inclined to have fancies; imaginary, not real.

'fanfare *n* a great blowing of trumpets or bugles.

fang *n* a tooth of a wild animal (*esp* a fierce one); the poison-tooth of a snake.

'fantasy *n* an imaginary (*esp* unreal) scene, story *etc*; an idea not based on reality: – *pl* 'fantasies. – *adj* fan'tastic very unusual, strange; (*coll*) very great; (*coll*) excellent.

far *adv* at or to a long way: *far off*; very much: *far better*. – *adj* a long way off, distant: *a far country*; more distant: *the far side*. – *adjs, advs* 'farther, 'farthest. – *adjs* 'far-'fetched very unlikely: *a far-fetched story*; 'far-'flung extending over a great distance; 'far-'sighted foreseeing what is likely to happen and preparing for it.

farce *n* a play with unlikely and ridiculous characters and plot; anything silly and useless. – *adj* 'farcical absurd, ridiculous.

fare *v* to get on (well, badly). *He fared well in the competition.* – *n* the price of a

journey; a person who pays to be carried on a journey; food. – *interj, n* fare'well goodbye.

farm *n* an area of land used for growing crops, breeding and feeding cows, sheep *etc*; a place where certain animals, fish *etc* are reared: *an oyster farm*. – *v* to work the lands *etc* of a farm. – *n* 'farmer the owner or tenant of a farm who works the land *etc*. – *ns* 'farmhouse the house where a farmer lives; farmstead ['färmsted] a farm and farmhouse; 'farmyard the yard surrounded by farm buildings. – farm out to give (work) to others to do for payment.

farrow ['farō] *n* a family of baby pigs. – *v* to give birth to a family of pigs.

farthing ['färdhiŋ] *n* an old coin, ¼ of an old penny.

fascinate ['fasināt] *v* to charm, attract or interest irresistibly; to make (a victim) still and powerless. *The snake fascinated the rabbit.* – *adj* 'fascinating. – *n* fasci'nation.

fashion ['fashən] *n* the make or cut of a thing (*esp* clothes); a way of behaving, dressing *etc* which is popular for a time; a way of doing a thing: *acting in a strange fashion*. – *v* to shape (according to a pattern). – *adj* 'fashionable agreeing with the latest style of dress, way of living *etc*. – in fashion fashionable.

fast *adj* quick-moving; (of a clock *etc*) showing a time in advance of the correct time; of colour (in clothes *etc*) fixed, not likely to be removed by washing. – *adv* quickly; firmly: *stand fast*. – *v* to go without food (of one's own free will). – Also *n*. – *n* 'fastness quickness, speed; a stronghold, fortress, castle.

fasten ['fäsn] *v* to fix: *fasten it to the wall*; to make firm (by tying, nailing *etc*).

fas'tidious *adj* difficult to please.

fat *n* an oily substance made by the bodies of animals and by plants. – *adj* having much fat; plump; thick, wide. – *v* 'fatten to make or become fat.

'fātal *adj* causing death or disaster. – *n* fatality [fə'taləti] (an accident causing) death: – *pl* fa'talities.

fate *n* what the future holds for one, fortune, luck; end or death. *He met his fate bravely.* – *adjs* 'fated controlled by fate; doomed; 'fateful having important results.

father ['fädhər] *n* a male parent; a priest; a person who first makes, invents *etc* something. *Jules Verne is the father of science fiction.* – *ns* 'father-in-law the

father of one's husband or wife;
'fatherland one's native land.
fathom ['faðəm] *n* a measure of depth
(6 feet, 1·83 metres). – *v* to understand, get to the bottom of (a mystery
etc).
fatigue [fə'tēg] *n* great tiredness; weakness or strain (of metals *etc*) caused by
use. – *v* to tire out.
'fatūous *adj* very foolish.
'faucet *n* (*US*) a tap.
fault *n* a mistake; a flaw, something bad
or wrong (*eg* with a machine). – *adjs*
'faultless; **'faulty** having a fault or
faults.
faun *n* (*myth*) an imaginary creature,
half man, half animal.
'fauna *n* the animals of a district or
country as a whole.
favour ['fāvər] *n* a kind action; goodwill,
kindness, approval; gift, token, badge
etc. *The knight wore his lady's favour*. –
v to show preference for; to be an
advantage to. *The darkness favoured his
escape*. – *adj* **'favourable** friendly;
showing approval; advantageous, helpful (to). – *n* **favourite** ['fāvərit] a liked
or best-loved person or thing; one, *esp*
a horse, likely to win. – Also *adj*. – *n*
'favouritism showing favour toward
one person *etc* more than another. – **in
favour of** in support of; for the benefit
of.
fawn *n* a young deer; its colour, a light
yellowish-brown. – *adj* of this colour. –
v to show affection as a dog does; (with
upon) to flatter in too humble a way.
fear *n* a feeling caused by danger, evil *etc*.
– *adj* **'fearful** timid; afraid; terrible;
(*coll*) very bad: *a fearful headache*;
'fearless brave, daring.
feasible ['fēzəbl] *adj* able to be done,
likely. – *n* **feasi'bility**.
feast *n* a rich and plentiful meal; a
festival day on which some event is
remembered. – *v* to hold or eat a feast.
feat *n* a deed difficult to do.
feather ['feðər] *n* one of the growths
which form the outer covering of a
bird. – *adj* **'feathery** having or covered
in feathers; soft; light.
feature ['fēchər] *n* a mark by which
anything is known, a characteristic; an
important or special article in a newspaper *etc*; the main film *etc* in a
programme; a special attraction; (*pl*)
the various parts of a person's face
(eyes, nose *etc*). – *v* to show or exhibit
as a feature; to take part (in).
February ['febrōoəri] *n* the second
month of the year.
'fēcund *adj* fertile. – *n* **fe'cundity**.

fed *see* **feed**.
federal ['fedərəl] *adj* joined by treaty or
bargain. – *adj* **'federated** joined after
an agreement is made. – *n* **fede'ration**
those joined together for a common
purpose, a league.
fee *n* a price paid for work done, or for
some special service or right.
'feeble *adj* weak. – *n* **'feebleness**. – *adv*
'feebly.
feed *v* to give food to; to eat food; tò
supply with necessary materials: – *pt*
fed [fed]. – *n* food for animals: *cattle
feed*. – **fed up** tired, bored and disgusted.
feel *v* to explore by touch; to experience,
be aware of (pain, pleasure *etc*); to
believe, consider; to think (oneself) to
be. *I feel ill*; to be sorry (for). *I feel for
you in your sorrow*: – *pt* **felt** [felt]. – *ns*
'feeler one of two thread-like parts of
an insect's body (on the head) by which
it senses danger *etc*; **'feeling** sense of
touch; emotion. *He spoke with great
feeling*; affection; an impression, belief; (*pl*) what one feels inside one such
as love, anger. – **feel like** to want, have
an inclination to or for. *He feels like
going out. He feels like an apple*.
feet *see* **foot**.
feign [fān] *v* pretend to feel or be. *He
feigned illness*.
feint [fānt] *n* a pretence; a move to put
an enemy off his guard. – Also *v*.
fe'licity *n* happiness. – *npl* **felici'tations**
good wishes, congratulations. – *adj*
fe'licitous lucky; well-chosen, suiting
well.
'fēline *adj* cat-like; of the cat family.
fell *n* a barren hill. – *v* to bring to the
ground; to cut down; *see* also **fall**. –
adj cruel, fierce.
fellow ['felō] *n* an equal; one of a pair; a
member of a learned society, college
etc; a man, boy. – *n* **'fellowship** state
of being on equal terms; friendship; an
award to a university graduate.
'felon *n* one who has committed a serious
crime. – *n* **'felony** serious crime: – *pl*
'felonies.
felt *n* a type of rough cloth made of rolled
and pressed wool. – *v see* **feel**.
'fēmale *n, adj* (one) of the sex which
produces young.
feminine ['feminin] *adj* womanly; having to do with women. – *ns*
femi'ninity; **'feminism** the movement which aims to win rights for
women equal to those of men; **'femin-
ist** a supporter of this movement.
'fēmur *n* the thigh bone.
fen *n* low marshy land, often covered

with water.

fence *n* a railing, hedge *etc* for closing in animals or land; (*slang*) a receiver of stolen goods. – *v* to close in with a fence; to fight with swords; to give answers that tell nothing. – *n* '**fencing** fences; material for fences; the sport of fighting with swords, using blunted weapons.

fend: fend for oneself to look after, provide for oneself.

'**fender** *n* a low guard round a fireplace to keep in coals *etc*; something (a piece of matting *etc*) lowered over a ship's side to act as a buffer against the quay; (*US*) the bumper of a car *etc*.

fermen'tation *n* the change which takes place when certain substances are brought together (as when yeast is added to the dough in the making of bread); a state of great excitement. – *v* **fer'ment** (of a mixture) to change by fermentation; to stir up trouble *etc*. – *n* '**ferment**.

fern *n* a kind of plant with no flowers and feather-like leaves.

fe'rōcious *adj* fierce, savage. – *n* **ferocity** [fə'rosəti].

'**ferret** *n* a type of small weasel-like animal used to chase rabbits out of their warrens. – *v* to search busily and persistently.

ferrule ['ferōōl] *n* a metal ring or cap on the tip of a walking stick or umbrella.

'**ferry** *v* to carry (people, cars *etc*) over water by boat or overland by aeroplane *etc*. – *n* a crossing place for boats; the boat which crosses: – *pl* '**ferries**.

'**fertile** *adj* fruitful, producing much; full of ideas. – *v* **fertilize** ['fɔrtiliz] to make (soil *etc*) fertile or more fertile. – *n* **fer'tility** fruitfulness, ability of land to produce crops *etc*, ability of a woman or female animal to produce children; **fertili'zation**; '**fertilizer** a substance (*eg* manure, chemicals) for making fields (more) fertile.

'**fervent** *adjs* very eager; intense. – *n* **fervour** ['fɔrvər].

'**fester** *v* (of a cut, sore) to have pus in it because of infection.

festive ['festiv] *adj* of a feast; in a happy, celebrating mood, joyful. – *ns* '**festival** a celebration; a feast; a season of musical, theatrical or other performances; **fes'tivity** joyfulness, merrymaking: – *pl* **fes'tivities**.

fes'toon *v* to decorate with chains of ribbons, flowers *etc*.

fetch *v* to go and get; to bring in (a price). *The vase fetched £100 at the auction.*

fête [fāt] *n* an occasion with stalls, competitions, displays *etc* to raise money (often for charity). – *v* to entertain lavishly, make much of (a person).

fetid, foetid ['fētid] *adj* having a rotten smell, stinking.

'**fetish** *n* something of which a person is excessively (and unnaturally) fond: – *pl* '**fetishes**.

'**fetlock** *n* the part of a horse's leg just above the foot.

'**fetters** *npl* chains, bonds (for imprisonment).

'**fettle: in fine fettle** in good health or condition.

feud [fūd] *n* a private, drawn-out war *esp* between families, clans, tribes *etc*.

feudal ['fūdl] *adj* (*hist*) of the system by which, in earlier times, certain services were given to the overlord by the tenants, as a return for their lands. – *n* '**feudalism**.

'**fēver** *n* (any illness causing) high body temperature and quickened pulse. – *adjs* '**feverish**; '**fevered** having a fever; very excited.

few *adj, n* not many: *a few* (*pounds*) *left: the few* (*pounds*) *which were left.* – *n* '**fewness** the state of being few. – **a good few, quite a few** several, a considerable number.

fez *n* a close-fitting red hat (shaped like a flowerpot) with a tassel and formerly the national head-dress of the Turks: – *pl* '**fezzes**.

fiancé [fi'önsā] *n* a person to whom one is engaged to be married: *her fiancé*: – *fem* **fi'ancée**: *his fiancée*.

fi'asco *n* a complete failure: – *pl* **fi'ascos**.

fib *v* to lie about something unimportant: – *pt* **fibbed**. – Also *n*.

'**fibre** *n* any fine thread or threadlike stuff. – *adj* '**fibrous**. – *n* '**fibreglass** a material made of very fine threadlike pieces of glass used for many purposes *eg* building boats.

'**fickle** *adj* changeable, not constant or loyal.

'**fiction** *n* stories *etc* which tell of imagined characters and events; an untruth, a lie. – *adjs* '**fictional** (of novels, stories *etc*) about imagined characters and events; **fic'titious** not real, imaginary; untrue.

'**fiddle** *n* a violin. – *v* to play the violin; to make restless, aimless movements (with); to interfere, tamper (with); (*coll*) to falsify (accounts *etc*) with the intention of cheating.

fi'delity *n* faithfulness; truth; accuracy.

'**fidget** *v* to move (the hands, feet *etc*) restlessly.

field [fēld] *n* a piece of ground enclosed for pasture, crops, sports *etc*; an area of land which contains a natural resource (*eg* coal, gold); an area or branch of interest, knowledge *etc*; those taking part in a race, competition *etc*. – *v* (in cricket *etc*) to catch the ball and return it. – *n* '**field-day** a day of unusual activity or success. – *npl* '**fieldglasses** a small double telescope. – *ns* '**field-gun** a light, mobile cannon; '**field-'marshal** an officer of the highest rank in the army.

fiend [fēnd] *n* an evil spirit; a wicked person. – *adj* '**fiendish**.

fierce [fērs] *adj* very angry-looking, hostile, likely to attack; intense, strong: *fierce competition*. – *n* '**fierceness**.

fiery ['fīri] *adj* like fire; easily made angry; high-spirited.

fife *n* a type of small flute.

'**fif'teen** *n* the number 15. – *adj* 15 in number. – *adj* '**fif'teenth** the last of fifteen (things *etc*). – *n* one of fifteen equal parts.

fifth *see* **five**.

'**fifty** *n* the number 50. – *adj* 50 in number. – *adj* '**fiftieth** the last of fifty (things *etc*). – *n* one of fifty equal parts.

fig *n* a soft, pear-shaped fruit containing many seeds and often eaten dried; the tree which bears it.

fight [fīt] *v* to struggle (with) with fists, weapons *etc*; to quarrel; to go to war with: – *pt* **fought** [föt]. – *n* a struggle; a battle. – *n* '**fighter** one who fights; a fast military aircraft armed with guns.

'**figment** *n* a made-up story or an idea which has no real existence.

figure ['figər] *n* outward form or shape; a number; a geometrical shape; a person. *A mysterious figure approached*; (in a book *etc*) a diagram or drawing; a set of movements (as in skating *etc*). – *v* to appear. *He figures in the story*; (*usu* with **out**) to work out, understand. – *adjs* '**figurative** (of words) used not in the ordinary meaning but to show likenesses (*eg* in 'He was a lion in battle' for 'He was as brave as or like a lion in battle.'); '**figured** marked with a design: *figured silk*. – *n* '**figurehead** a person who does little but who serves as a leader.

'**filament** *n* a slender threadlike object (*eg* the thin wire in an electric-light bulb).

filch *v* to steal.

file *n* a folder, loose-leaf book *etc* to hold papers; a line of soldiers *etc* walking one behind another; a steel tool with a roughened surface for smoothing or wearing away wood, metal *etc*. – *v* to put (papers *etc*) in a file; to rub with a file; to walk in a file.

'**filial** *adj* of or natural to a son or daughter.

'**filibuster** *n* a very long speech made to delay the passing of a law. – Also *v*.

'**filigree** *n* very fine gold or silver thread lace-work.

fill *v* to put (something) into (until there is no room for more). *He fills the bucket with water*; to become full. *Her eyes filled with tears*; to satisfy, fulfil (a requirement *etc*); to occupy: *fill a post*: *fill time*; to appoint a person to (a job *etc*). *Have you filled the vacancy?*; to put something in a hole (in a tooth *etc*) to stop it up. – *n* as is needed to fill. *He ate his fill*. – *ns* '**filler**; '**filling** anything used to fill a hole or gap. – *n* '**filling-station** a garage where petrol is sold. – **fill in** to fill (*esp* a hole); to complete (a form *etc*); to do another person's job while they are absent. *I'm filling in for George*; **fill up** to fill completely.

'**fillet** *n* a piece of meat or fish without bones. – *v* to remove the bones from.

'**fillip** *n* an encouragement.

'**filly** *n* a young female horse: – *pl* '**fillies**.

film *n* a thin skin or coating; a thin celluloid strip with a chemical coating on which photographs are taken; a story, play *etc* photographed on film and shown in a cinema, on television *etc*. – *v* to photograph on a film. – *n* '**filmstar** a famous actor or actress in films.

'**filter** *n* a strainer or other device for removing solid material from liquids; a green arrow on a traffic light which allows one lane of traffic to move while the main stream is held up. – *v* to purify by a filter; to come in drops or gradually; (of cars *etc*) to join gradually a stream of traffic; (of a lane of traffic) to move in the direction shown by the filter.

filth *n* dirt. – *adj* '**filthy** foul, very dirty.

fin *n* a part of a fish's body with which it balances itself and swims.

'**final** *adj* last; allowing of no argument. *The judge's decision is final*. – *n* the last contest in a competition. – *n* fi'**nality** the quality of being final and decisive. – *v* '**finalize** to get or put (*eg* plans) in a final or finished form.

finale [fi'näli] *n* the last part of anything (*eg* a concert).

fi'nance *n* money affairs; the study or management of these; (*pl*) the money one has to spend. – *v* to supply with sums of money. – *adj* **fi'nancial**. – *n* **fi'nancier** one who manages (public) money.

finch *n* a kind of small bird: – *pl* **'finches**.

find *v* to come upon or meet with either accidentally (*I found this ring in the street*) or after searching (*After looking everywhere I found my book under the bed*); to discover; to judge to be. *I find it difficult*: – *pt* **found**. – *n* something found *esp* something of interest or value. – **find out** to discover; detect.

fine *n* money to be paid as a punishment. – Also *v*. – *adj* made up of very small pieces, drops *etc*; not coarse: *fine linen*; thin, delicate; slight: *a fine distinction*; beautiful, handsome; of good quality; pure; bright, not rainy; well, healthy. – *n* **'finery** splendid clothes *etc*. – *n* **fine arts** painting, sculpture, music.

fi'nesse *n* cleverness and subtlety (in handling situations *etc*).

finger ['fiŋgər] *n* one of the five branching parts of the hand. – *v* to touch with the fingers. – *n* **'fingering** (in music) the positioning of the fingers in playing an instrument; the showing of this by numbers. – *n* **'fingerprint** the mark made by the tip of a finger, used by the police as a means of identification.

'finish *v* to end or complete the making *etc* of; to stop: *finish work for the day*. – *n* the end (*eg* of a race); the last touch (of paint, polish *etc*) that makes a perfect job. – *adj* **'finished** ended; complete; perfect; (of a person) ruined, not likely to achieve further success *etc*.

'finite *adj* having an end or limit.

fiord, fjord [fyörd] *n* a long narrow inlet between steep hills (*esp* in Norway).

fir *n* a kind of cone-bearing tree. – *n* **'fir-cone**.

'fire *n* the heat and light given off by something burning; a mass of burning material, objects *etc*; a heating device: *electric fire*; eagerness, keenness. – *v* to set on fire; to make eager: *fired by his enthusiasm*; to make (a gun) explode, to shoot. – *ns* **fire alarm** a device (*eg* a system of bells) to give warning of a fire; **fire brigade** a company of firemen; **'fire-damp** a dangerous gas found in coal mines; **fire engine** a vehicle carrying firemen and their equipment; **fire escape** a means of escape (*esp* an outside metal staircase) from a building in case of fire; **'firefly** a

type of insect which glows in the dark; **'fire-guard** a framework of iron placed in front of a fireplace for safety; **'fireman** one whose job it is to put out fires; **'fireplace** a recess in a room below a chimney for a fire; **'firewood** wood for burning on a fire. – *npl* **'fireworks** squibs, rockets *etc* sent up at night for show; (*coll*) angry behaviour.

'firkin *n* a small barrel.

firm *adj* not easily moved or shaken; with mind made up. – *n* a business company. – *n* **'firmness**.

'firmament *n* the heavens, sky.

first *adj, adv* before all others in place, time or rank. – *adv* before doing anything else. – *ns* **'first-'aid** treatment of a wounded or sick person before the doctor's arrival; **'first-born** the eldest child. – *adjs* **'first-'class** of the highest standard, best kind *etc*; **'first-'hand** direct; **'first-'rate** first class.

firth *n* a narrow arm of the sea, *esp* at a river mouth.

'fiscal *adj* of the public revenue; of financial matters.

fish *n* a kind of animal that lives in water, and breathes through gills: – *pl* **fish** or **'fishes**. – *v* to (try to) catch fish with rod, nets *etc*; to search (for). *She fished for a handkerchief in her bag*; to try cunningly to obtain: *fish for compliments*. – *adj* **'fishy** like a fish; doubtful, arousing suspicion. – *ns* **'fisherman** one who fishes (*esp* for a living); **'fishmonger** one who sells fish.

fission ['fishən] *n* splitting.

fissure ['fishər] *n* a crack.

fist *n* a tightly-shut hand. – *npl* **'fisticuffs** a fight with the fists.

fit *adj* suited to a purpose; proper; in good training or health. – *n* a sudden attack or spasm of laughter, illness *etc*. – *v* to be of the right size or shape; to be suitable: – *pt* **'fitted**. – *adj* **'fitful** coming or doing in bursts or spasms. – *n* **'fitness**. – *adj* **'fitting** suitable. – *n* something fixed or fitted *esp* in a room, house *etc*.

five *n* the number 5. – *adj* 5 in number. – *adj* **fifth** the last of five (things *etc*). – *n* one of five equal parts.

fives *npl* a handball game played in a walled court.

fix *v* to make firm; to fasten; to mend, repair. – *adj* **fixed** settled; set in position. – *adv* **fixedly** ['fiksidli] steadily, intently. *He stared fixedly at me*. – *n* **'fixture** anything fixed (such as a shelf); a match or race that has been arranged.

fizz *v* to make a hissing sound. – *n* a
hissing sound. – *adj* '**fizzy** of a drink in
which tiny bubbles form on the
surface.
'**fizzle: fizzle out** to fail, coming to
nothing.
fjord *see* **fiord**.
'**flabbergasted** *adj* very surprised.
'**flabby** *adj* not firm, soft, limp; weak,
feeble. – *n* '**flabbiness**.
flaccid ['flaksid] *adj* hanging in loose
folds, not firm, limp.
flag *n* a banner, standard, or ensign; a
flat paving-stone; a type of water-plant,
esp an iris. – *v* to become tired or weak:
– *pt* **flagged**.
flagellation [flajə'lāshən] *n* whipping.
'**flagon** *n* a large container for liquid.
'**flagrant** *adj* conspicuous; openly
wicked. – *n* '**flagrancy**.
flail *v* to wave or swing in the air. – *n* a
tool for threshing corn made of a
wooden bar (the **swingle**) tied to a
handle.
flair *n* talent, skill: *a flair for organizing*.
flak *n* anti-aircraft fire; strong criticism.
flake *n* a thin slice or chip of anything; a
very small piece (as of snow *etc*). – *v* to
form into flakes. – **flake off** to break off
in flakes.
flam'boyant *adj* splendidly coloured;
too showy, intended to attract notice.
flame *n* the bright leaping light of a fire.
– *v* to burn brightly. – *adj* '**flaming**
burning; red; violent: *a flaming temper*.
flamingo [flə'miŋgō] *n* a type of long-
legged bird of pink or bright-red colour: – *pl* **fla'mingo(e)s**.
'**flammable** *adj* easily set on fire.
flan *n* a flat, open tart.
flange *n* a raised edge on the rim of a
wheel.
flank *n* the side of anything (as of a
person's or animal's body, of an army
etc). – *v* to go by the side of; to be
situated at the side of.
flannel *n* loosely woven woollen cloth; a
small piece of material used *esp* for
washing the face; (*pl*) trousers of this
or similar material. – *n* **flanne'lette**
cotton cloth made in imitation of
flannel.
flap *n* anything broad and loose-
hanging: *the flap of a tent*; the sound
made when such a thing moves; a time
of feverish activity; a panic. – *v* to hang
down loosely; to (cause to) move with a
flapping noise; to get into a panic: – *pt*
flapped.
flare *v* to blaze up. – *n* a bright light, *esp*
one used at night as a signal, to light up
an enemy country *etc*.

flash *n* a quick burst of light; a moment,
instant; a distinctive mark on a uniform: – *pl* '**flashes**. – *v* to shine out
suddenly; to pass quickly. – *adj* '**flashy**
dazzling for a moment; showy, gaudy;
cheaply smart. – *n* '**flashlight** a burst
of light in which a photograph is taken;
an electric torch. – **in a flash** suddenly.
flask *n* a narrow-necked bottle.
flat *adj* level: *a flat surface*; (of drinks)
not fizzy; leaving no doubt, downright:
a flat denial; below the right musical
pitch; (of a tyre) punctured; dull,
uninteresting. – *adv* stretched out:
lying flat on her back. – *n* an apartment
which lies on one storey of a building; a
sign (♭) in music which lowers a note; a
punctured tyre. – *n* '**flatness**. – *v*
'**flatten** to make or become flat. – *ns*
'**flatfish** a sea fish with a flat body (*eg* a
sole); **flat race** a race over level ground
without hurdles; **flat rate** a rate which
is the same in all cases. – **flat out** as fast
as possible, with as much effort as
possible.
'**flatter** *v* to praise insincerely; to make
out (a person or thing) to be better than
he (or it) really is. – *n* '**flattery**.
'**flatulence** *n* wind in the stomach. – *adj*
'**flatulent**.
flaunt *v* to display in an obvious way.
'**flautist** *n* a flute-player.
flavour ['flāvər] *n* taste: *the flavour of
lemons*; quality or atmosphere. *The
celebrations had an Eastern flavour*. – *v*
to give a taste to. – *n* '**flavouring**
anything used to give a special taste.
flaw *n* a fault, an imperfection, a defect.
– *adj* '**flawless** without fault or
blemish.
flax *n* a type of plant whose fibres are
woven into linen cloth. – *adj* '**flaxen**
made of or looking like flax; (of hair)
fair.
flay *v* to strip the skin off.
flea *n* a type of small, wingless, blood-
sucking insect having great jumping
power.
fleck *n* a spot, a speck. – *adj* **flecked**
marked with spots or patches.
fled *see* **flee**.
fledgling ['flejliŋ] *n* a young bird with
fully-grown feathers.
flee *v* to run away (from danger *etc*): – *pt*
fled [fled].
fleece *n* a sheep's coat of wool. – *v* to clip
wool from; (*coll*) to rob by cheating. –
adj '**fleecy** soft and fluffy like wool.
fleet *n* a number of ships; a number of
vehicles (taxis *etc*). – *adj* swift; nimble,
quick in movement. – *adj* '**fleeting**
passing quickly. – *n* '**fleetness**

swiftness.

flesh *n* the soft substance (muscle *etc*) which covers the bones of animals; meat; the body; the soft eatable part of fruit. – *adj* '**fleshy** fat, plump. – **flesh and blood** relations, family; human nature.

flew *see* **fly**.

flex *v* to bend. – *n* a length of covered wire attached to electrical devices. – *adj* '**flexible** easily bent; (of persons) willing or able to adapt to new or different conditions. – *n* **flexi'bility** ease in bending; willingness *etc* to adapt. – *n* '**flexitime** a system in which a worker does an agreed number of hours' work at times partly chosen by himself.

flick *v* to strike lightly with a quick, sharp movement; to remove (dust *etc*) with a movement of this kind. –*n* a quick, sharp movement: *a flick of the wrist.*

'**flicker** *v* to burn unsteadily. – Also *n*.

flight [flīt] *n* the act of flying; a journey by plane; the act of fleeing or escaping; a flock (of birds); a number (of steps). – *adj* '**flighty** changeable, impulsive.

flimsy ['flimzi] *adj* thin; easily torn or broken *etc*; weak: *a flimsy excuse.*

flinch *v* to move or shrink back in fear, pain *etc*.

fling *v* to throw: – *pt* **flung**. – *n* a throw; a casual attempt; a period of time devoted to pleasure.

flint *n* a kind of hard stone. – *adj* made of flint. – *n* '**flintlock** a gun fired by sparks from a flint.

flip *v* to toss lightly: – *pt* **flipped**. – *n* a light toss or stroke. – *n* '**flipper** a limb of a seal, walrus *etc*.

'**flippant** *adj* joking, not serious. – *n* '**flippancy**.

flirt *v* to play at courtship without any serious intentions. – *n* one who flirts. – *n* **flir'tation**. – *adj* **flir'tatious** fond of flirting.

flit *v* to move quickly and lightly from place to place: – *pt* '**flitted**.

float *v* to keep on the surface of a liquid; to set going: *float a fund.* – *n* a cork *etc* on a fishing line; a raft; a van (for milk *etc*); a large lorry for transporting cattle *etc*; a platform on wheels, used in processions *etc*; a sum of money set aside for giving change *etc*.

flock *n* a number of animals or birds together; a large number of people; the congregation of a church; a shred or tuft of wool; wool or cotton waste. – *v* (*usu* with **together**) to gather in a crowd; to go in a crowd.

floe *n* a sheet of floating ice.

flog *v* to beat, lash: – *pt* **flogged**. – *n* '**flogging**.

flood [flud] *n* a great flow (*esp* of water); the rise or flow of the tide; a great quantity: *a flood of letters.* – *v* to (cause to) overflow; to cover or fill with water. – *n* '**floodlighting** strong lighting from many sources.

floor [flör] *n* the part of a room on which one walks; a storey of a building. – *v* to make a floor; (*coll*) to knock flat; (*coll*) to puzzle.

flop *v* to sway or swing about loosely; to fall or sit down suddenly and heavily; to move about in a heavy, clumsy way; to fail badly: – *pt* **flopped**. – Also *n*. – *adj* '**floppy** flopping, soft and flexible.

'**flora** *n* the plants of a district or country as a whole. – *adj* **floral** ['flörəl] (made) of flowers. – *n* **florist** ['florist] a seller or grower of flowers.

'**florid** *adj* (of persons) high-coloured, flushed; too ornate.

floss *n* fine silk thread.

flo'tilla *n* a fleet of small ships.

'**flotsam** *n* floating objects washed from a ship or wreck.

flounce *v* to walk (away) suddenly and impatiently (*eg* in anger). – *n* a plaited decorative strip on the hem of a dress.

'**flounder** *v* to struggle to move one's legs and arms (in water, mud *etc*); to have difficulty in speaking or thinking clearly or in acting efficiently. – *n* a small flatfish.

'**flour** *n* finely-ground wheat; anything crushed to powder. – *adj* '**floury**.

flourish ['flurish] *v* be successful, *esp* financially; (of flowers *etc*) to grow well, thrive; to be healthy; to wave (something) as a show or threat. – *n* fancy strokes in writing; a sweeping movement (with the hand, sword *etc*); showy splendour; an ornamental passage in music: – *pl* '**flourishes**.

flout *v* to treat with contempt, defy openly.

flow [flō] *v* to run, as water; to move smoothly; (of the tide) to rise. – Also *n*.

flower ['flowər] *n* the part of a plant or tree from which fruit or seed grow; the best of anything. – *v* (of plants *etc*) to produce a flower; to be at one's best, flourish. – *adj* '**flowery** full of, decorated with flowers; of a piece of writing, using fine-sounding, fancy language.

flown *see* **fly**.

flu [flōō] short for **influenza**.

'**fluctuate** *v* to vary (in number, price *etc*); to be always changing. – *n* **fluctu'ation**.

flue [flōō] *n* a passage for air and smoke

113

in a stove or chimney.

fluent ['flōōənt] *adj* finding words easily in speaking or writing without any awkward pauses. – *n* **'fluency**.

fluff *n* any soft, downy stuff. – *adj* **'fluffy**.

fluid ['flōōid] *n* a substance whose particles can move about freely – a liquid or gas; a liquid. – *adj* flowing; not settled.

fluke [flōōk] *n* a type of small worm which harms sheep; the part of an anchor which holds fast in sand; a success due to chance.

flung *see* **fling**.

fluoride ['flōōərid] *n* a substance containing the element **fluorine** ['flōōərēn] which prevents tooth decay. – *vs* **'fluoridize, 'fluoridate** to add fluoride to drinking water. – *n* **fluori-'dation**.

'flurry *n* a sudden rush (of wind *etc*) : – *pl* **'flurries**. – *v* to excite : – *pt* **'flurried**.

flush *n* a reddening of the face; freshness, glow : – *pl* **'flushes**. – *v* to become red in the face; to clean by a rush of water. – *adj* (with **with**) having the surface level (with the surface around); (*coll*) well supplied with money.

'fluster *n* excitement caused by hurry. – Also *v*.

flute [flōōt] *n* a type of high-pitched musical wind instrument. – *adj* **'fluted** decorated with grooves.

'flutter *v* to move (*esp* wings) quickly. – *n* a quick beating (of pulse *etc*); nervous excitement.

flux *n* an ever-changing flow. *Events are in a state of flux*.

fly *n* a type of small winged insect; a fish-hook made to look like a fly; a flap of material with buttons or a zip *esp* at the front of trousers : – *pl* **flies**. – *v* to move through the air on wings or in an aeroplane; to run away : – *pt* **flew** [flōō], *pp* **flown** [flōn]. – *ns* **flying squad** a branch of the police using fast cars; **'flyover** a road *etc* built on pillars to cross over another; **'flysheet** the outer covering of a tent; **'flywheel** a heavy wheel which enables a machine to run at a steady speed.

foal *n* a young horse. – *v* to give birth to a foal.

foam *n* a mass of small bubbles on liquids. – *v* to produce foam. – *n* **foam rubber** sponge-like form of rubber for stuffing chairs, mattresses *etc*.

fob *n* a small watch pocket; a fancy chain hanging from the watch pocket. – *v* to make (someone) accept (something worthless *etc*). *I was fobbed off with a silly excuse* : – *pt* **fobbed**.

fo'c'sle *see* **forecastle**.

'focus *n* meeting point for rays of light; point to which light, a look, attention, is directed : – *pls* **'focuses, foci** ['fōsi]. – *v* to get the right length of ray of light for a clear picture; to direct (one's attention *etc*) to one point. – *adj* **'focal** of or at a focus.

'fodder *n* dried food (hay, oats *etc*) for farm animals.

foe *n* an enemy.

foetid *see* **fetid**.

fog *n* thick mist. – *v* to cover in fog; to bewilder, confuse. – *adj* **'foggy**. – *n* **'foghorn** a horn used as a warning to or by ships in fog.

foil *v* to defeat, disappoint. – *n* metal in the form of paper-thin sheets; a dull person or thing against which someone or something else seems brighter; a blunt sword with a button at the end, used in fencing practice.

foist *v* to pass off as genuine.

fold *n* a part laid on top of another; an enclosure for sheep *etc*. – *v* to lay one part on top of another. – *n* **'folder** a cover to hold papers.

'foliage *n* leaves.

folk [fōk] *n* people; a nation, race; (*pl*) one's family or relations. – *ns* **'folklore** the study of the customs, beliefs, fairy tales *etc* of a people; **'folksong** a song passed on from person to person over a period of time.

follow ['folō] *v* to go or come after; to happen as a result; to act according to; to understand; to work at (a trade). – *ns* **'follower; 'following** supporters. – *prep* **'following** after, as a result of. *Following the fire, the house collapsed*.

'folly *n* foolishness : – *pl* **'follies**.

fo'ment *v* to stir up, encourage growth of (a rebellion *etc*).

fond *adj* loving; tender. – *n* **'fondness**. – **fond of** having a liking for.

'fondle *v* to caress.

font *n* the basin holding water for baptism.

food *n* that which living beings eat. – *n* **'foodstuff** something used for food. – *n* **food processor** electrical appliance for chopping, blending *etc* food.

fool *n* a silly person; (*hist*) a court jester; a pudding made of fruit, sugar and cream. – *v* to deceive; to play the fool. – *adj* **'foolish**. – *ns* **'foolishness, 'foolery** foolish behaviour. – *adjs* **'foolhardy** rash, taking foolish risks; **'foolproof** (of engines, plans *etc*) unable to go wrong. – **fool about** to behave in a playful or silly manner.

'foolscap *n* a large size of paper for

writing or printing.

foot *n* the part of the leg below the ankle; the lower part of anything; twelve inches, 30 centimetres: – *pl* **feet**. – *v* to pay (a bill *etc*). – *n* **'footing** balance; degree of friendship, seniority *etc*. – *ns* **'football** (a game played by kicking) a large ball; **'foothill** a smaller hill at the foot of a mountain; **'foothold** a place to put the foot in climbing; a firm position from which one can begin to do something; **'footlight** a light at the front of a stage, which shines on the actors; **'footnote** a note at the bottom of a page; **'footpad** (*hist*) a highway robber; **'footplate** a driver's platform on a railway engine; **'footprint** a mark of a foot; **'footstep** the sound of a person's foot when walking; **'footwear** shoes *etc*.

fop *n* a person who is vain about dress. – *adj* **'foppish**.

for *prep* sent to or to be given to: *a letter for you*; towards. *They headed for home*; during (a period). *They waited for three hours*; on behalf of. *Do it for me*; because of: *for good reason*; as the price of: *£1 for a saucepan*; (in order) to have. *He did it for the money.*

'forage *n* food for horses and cattle. – *v* to search for food, fuel *etc*.

'foray *n* a sudden raid for plunder.

forbade *see* **forbid**.

forbearance [för'bārǝns] *n* control of temper. – *adj* **for'bearing** patient.

for'bid *v* to order not to: – *pt* **forbade** [fǝr'bad]. – *adjs* **for'bidden; for'bidding** rather frightening.

force *n* strength; violence; the police; a group of workers, soldiers *etc*; (*pl*) soldiers, sailors, airmen. – *v* to make, compel. *They forced him to go*; to get by violence: *force an entry*; to break open; to hurry on; to make vegetables *etc* grow more quickly. – *adjs* **forced** done unwillingly, with effort: *a forced laugh*; **'forceful** acting with power; **'forcible** done by force.

'forceps *n* a tool with two arms for gripping.

ford *n* a shallow crossing place in a river. – *v* to cross (water) on foot.

fore- *prefix* before; beforehand; in front.

forearm[1] ['förärm] *n* the lower part of the arm.

fore'arm[2] *v* to prepare beforehand.

fore'boding *n* a feeling of coming evil.

'forecast *v* to tell (about) beforehand, to predict. – Also *n*.

forecastle, fo'c'sle ['fōksl] *n* a raised deck at the front of a ship; the part of ship under the deck where the crew live.

'forefather ['förfädhǝr] *n* an ancestor.

'forefinger ['förfiŋgǝr] *n* the finger next to the thumb.

forefront ['förfrunt] *n* the very front.

foregone ['förgon]: **a foregone conclusion** a result that can be guessed rightly in advance.

'foreground *n* the part of a view (or picture of one) nearest the front or nearest the person looking at it.

forehead ['forid] *n* the part of the face above the eyebrows.

foreign ['forǝn] *adj* belonging to another country; not belonging naturally in a place *etc*: *a foreign body in an eye*; not familiar. – *n* **'foreigner** a person from another country; somebody unfamiliar.

'foreleg *n* a front leg (of an animal).

'forelock *n* the lock of hair next to the forehead.

'foreman *n* an overseer or leader of a group (such as workmen, jury): – *pl* **'foremen**.

'foremast *n* ship's mast nearest the bow.

'foremost *adj* the most famous or important.

fo'rensic *adj* having to do with courts of law: *forensic medicine*.

'forerunner *n* a person or thing which is a sign of what is to follow.

fore'see *v* to see or know beforehand: – *pt* **fore'saw**, *pp* **fore'seen**. – *n* **'foresight** ability to see what will happen later; a fitting on the front of the barrel of a rifle to make correct aiming possible.

'foreshore *n* the part of the shore between high and low tidemarks.

foresight *see* **foresee**.

forest ['forist] *n* a large piece of land covered with trees; a stretch of country kept for game (such as deer). – *ns* **'forester** a worker in a forest; **'forestry** (the science of) forest-growing.

forestall [för'stöl] *v* to upset someone's plan by acting earlier than he expects. *He forestalled him.*

'foretaste *n* a sample of what is to come.

fore'tell *v* to tell before, to prophesy: – *pt* **fore'töld**.

forethought ['förthöt] *n* thought or care for the future.

foretold *see* **foretell**.

forewarn [för'wörn] *v* to warn beforehand. – *n* **fore'warning**.

forewoman ['förwŏŏmǝn] *n* a woman overseer; a head woman in a shop or factory.

foreword ['förwŭrd] *n* a piece of writing at the beginning of a book.

forfeit ['förfit] v to lose (a right) as a result of doing something. – n that which must be given up for some (criminal) action; a fine. – n 'forfeiture the loss of something as a punishment.

forge n a blacksmith's workshop; a furnace in which metal is heated. – v to hammer (metal) into shape; to imitate for criminal purposes; to move steadily on. *He forged ahead with his plans.* – n 'forgery something imitated for criminal purposes; the act of criminal forging: – pl 'forgeries.

for'get v to lose or put away from the memory: – pt **forgot**, pp **for'gotten**. – adj **for'getful** likely to forget. – n **for'getfulness**.

forgive [far'giv] v to be no longer angry with (someone); to overlook (a fault, debt etc). – n **for'giveness** pardon; readiness to pardon. – adj **for'giving**.

for'go v to give up, do without.

forgot, forgotten see **forget**.

fork n a pronged tool for piercing and lifting things; anything divided like a fork (eg a road, tree branch). – v to divide into two branches etc.

for'lorn adj pitiful, unhappy. – n **forlorn hope** a wish which seems to have no chance of being granted.

form n shape or appearance; kind, type; a paper with printed questions and space for the answers; a long seat; a school class; the nest of a hare. – v to give shape to; to make. – adj 'formal (of a person's manner) cold, business-like; done according to established rule, custom or convention. – ns for'mality something which must be done but has little meaning. *The chairman's speech was only a formality*; cold correctness of manner: – pl for'malities; for'mation the act of forming; arrangement (as of aeroplanes when flying). – n **formal dress** the kind of clothes required to be worn on certain social (ceremonial) occasions eg balls, banquets etc.

'format n (of books) the size, shape, kind of print etc; the design or arrangement of an event etc (such as a television programme).

'former adj of an earlier time; of the first-mentioned of two (opposite of **latter**). – Also n. – adv 'formerly in earlier times.

'formidable adj causing fear; difficult to overcome.

'formula n a set of rules to be followed; an arrangement of signs or letters used in chemistry, arithmetic etc to express an idea briefly (such as H_2O = water): – pls **formulae** ['förmülē], 'formulas. – v 'formulate to set down clearly; to make into a formula.

for'sake v to desert: – pt **for'sook**. – adj **for'saken** left alone; miserable.

forswear [för'swär] v to give up (something).

fort n a place of defence against an enemy.

forte ['förtä] n that at which one is very good.

forth adv forward; onward. – adjs **forth'coming** happening or appearing soon; (of person) willing to tell what he knows; friendly and open; **'forthright** outspoken, straightforward. – adv **forth'with** immediately.

'fortify v to strengthen (against attack): – pt 'fortified. – npl **fortifi'cations** walls etc built to strengthen a position.

'fortitude n courage in meeting danger or bearing pain.

fortnight ['förtnīt] n two weeks. – adj, adv 'fortnightly once a fortnight.

'fortress n a fortified place: – pl 'fortresses.

for'tuitous adj happening by chance.

'fortune n luck (good or bad); large sum of money. – adj 'fortunate lucky.

'forty n the number 40. – adj 40 in number. – adj 'fortieth the last of forty (things etc). – n one of forty equal parts.

'forum n (hist) market-place in ancient Rome; any public place where speeches are made; a meeting to talk about a particular subject.

'forward adj advancing: *a forward movement*; near or at the front; (of fruit etc) ripe earlier than usual; too ready in word or action. – v to help (toward success): *forward one's plans*; to send on (eg letters). – advs 'forward, 'forwards onward; towards the front.

foss, fosse n a ditch round an ancient fort or castle.

'fossil n the hardened remains of the shape of a plant or animal found in rock. – v 'fossilize to change into a fossil.

'foster v to bring up or nurse (esp a child not one's own); to help on, encourage (something). – ns 'foster-child (-brother, -sister) a boy or girl fostered by a family; 'foster-mother (-father) mother (father) who brings up a fostered child.

fought see **fight**.

foul adj very dirty; smelling or tasting bad; (of weather, temper) stormy. – v to become entangled with; to dirty; to play unfairly. – *n* a breaking of the rules of a game. – *n* **foul play** a criminal act.

found *v* to establish, set up; to shape by pouring melted metal into a mould; *see* also **find**. – *ns* **foun'dation** that on which anything rests; a sum of money left or set aside for a special purpose *eg* to support an organization *etc*; an organization *etc* supported in this way; **'founder** one who founds; **'foundry** workshop where metal founding is done: – *pl* **'foundries**.

'founder *v* (of a ship) to sink; (of a horse) to stumble or go lame. – *n see* **found**.

'foundling *n* a child abandoned by its parents.

'fountain *n* a jet of water rising up; the pipe or structure from which it comes; the beginning of anything.

four [för] *n* the number 4. – *adj* 4 in number. – *adj* **fourth** the last of four (things *etc*). – *n* one of four equal parts.

'four'teen *n* the number 14. – *adj* 14 in number. – *adj* **'four'teenth** the last of fourteen (things *etc*). – *n* one of fourteen equal parts.

fowl [fowl] *n* a bird, *esp* of the farmyard or poultry kind.

fox *n* a type of dog-like reddish-brown animal of sly cunning: – *pl* **'foxes**. – *v* to trick by cleverness or cunning; to puzzle, baffle. – *adj* **'foxy** cunning. – *ns* **'foxglove** a tall wild flower; **'foxhound** a breed of dog trained to chase foxes; **fox terrier** a breed of dog trained to drive foxes from their earths; **'foxtrot** a dance made up of walking steps and turns.

foyer ['foiä] *n* an entrance hall to a theatre, hotel *etc*.

fracas ['fraká] *n* uproar; a noisy quarrel.

'fraction *n* a part, not a whole number (such as ¹/₂, ²/₅, ⁷/₈ *etc*); a small part.

'fractious *adj* cross, quarrelsome.

'fracture *n* a break in something hard, *esp* in a bone of the body.

'fragile *adj* easily broken.

'fragment *n* a part broken off; something not complete. – *v* **frag'ment** to break into pieces. – *adj* **'fragmentary** broken.

'frāgrant *adj* sweet-smelling. – *n* **'fragrance** sweet scent.

'frail *adj* weak; easily tempted to do wrong. – *n* **'frailty** weakness: – *pl* **'frailties**.

frame *v* to put a frame round; to put together, to construct; (*slang*) to make (someone) appear to be guilty of a crime. – *n* a case or border round anything; build of human body; state (of mind). – *n* **'framework** the out-

line, shape, or skeleton of anything.

franc *n* the standard unit of French, Belgian and Swiss money.

'franchise *n* the right to vote (*esp* in a general election).

frank *adj* open, speaking one's mind. – *v* to mark a letter by machine to show that postage has been paid.

'frankfurter *n* kind of smoked sausage.

'frankincense *n* a sweet-smelling resin used as incense.

'frantic *adj* wildly excited or anxious.

fra'ternal *adj* brotherly; of a brother. – *n* **fra'ternity** a company of persons who regard each other as equals: – *pl* **fra'ternities**. – *v* **'fraternize** to make friends with.

'fratricide *n* the murder or murderer of a brother.

fraud *n* deceit, dishonest dealing; one who pretends to be other than he is; a fake. – *adj* **'fraudūlent**.

fraught [fröt] *adj* anxious, tense; (with **with**) filled.

fray *n* a fight, a brawl. – *v* to wear away.

freak *n* an unusual event; an odd or unconventional person or thing.

'freckle *n* a brown spot on the skin.

free *adj* not bound or shut in; generous; frank (in manner); costing nothing. – *v* to make or set free; (with **from** or **of**) to get rid. – *n* **'freedom** liberty. – *adj* **'freehand** (of drawing) done without the help of rulers, tracing *etc*. – *ns* **'freelance** a person working on his own (such as a writer who is not employed by any one newspaper); **'Freemason** a member of a certain men's society, sworn to secrecy. – *adj* **'free-'range** (of poultry) allowed to move about freely and feed out of doors; (of eggs) laid by poultry of this kind. – *n* **free speech** the right to express opinions of any kind. – *adj* **'freestyle** (of swimming race *etc*) in which any style may be used.

freeze *v* to turn into ice; to make (food) very cold in order to preserve; to go stiff (as with cold, fear); to fix (prices, wages *etc*) at a certain level: – *pt* **froze**, *pp* **'frozen**. – *n* **'freezer** a type of cabinet in which food is made, or kept, frozen.

freight [frāt] *n* load, cargo; charge for carrying a load. – *v* to load with goods. – *n* **'freighter** a ship or aircraft that carries cargo. – *n* **freight train** a goods train.

French: *ns* **French polish** a kind of varnish for furniture; **French window** a long window also used as a door. – **take French leave** to go or remain absent without permission.

fre'netic *adj* frantic.

'frenzy *n* a fit of madness; wild excitement. – *adj* **'frenzied** mad.

'frēquent *adj* happening often. – *v* **fre-'quent** to visit often. – *n* **'frequency** the rate at which something happens; the number per second of vibrations, waves *etc*: – *pl* **'frequencies**.

'fresco *n* a picture painted on a wall while the plaster is still damp: – *pl* **'fresco(e)s**.

fresh *adj* new, unused; (of food) newly made, gathered *etc*, not preserved; (of weather) cool, refreshing; (of persons) not tired; cheeky. – *adv* newly: *fresh-laid eggs.* – *v* **'freshen** to make fresh; to grow strong. – *ns* **'freshman, 'fresher** a first-year university student. – *adj* **'freshwater** of inland rivers, lakes *etc*, not of the sea.

fret *v* to worry or show discontent: – *pt* **'fretted**. – *n* one of the ridges on the fingerboard of a guitar. – *adj* **'fretful**.

'fretwork *n* decorated cut-out work in wood. – *n* **'fretsaw** a narrow-bladed, fine-toothed saw for fretwork.

'friar *n* a member of one of the brotherhoods of the Church, *esp* one who has vowed to live in poverty. – *n* **'friary** the friars' house: – *pl* **'friaries**.

'friction *n* rubbing of two things together; the wear caused by rubbing; bad feeling, quarrelling.

'Friday *n* sixth day of the week.

fridge *n* (*coll*) refrigerator.

fried *see* **fry**.

friend [frend] *n* one who likes and knows well another person. *He is my friend. We are good friends*; sympathizer, helper. – *adj* **'friendly** kind; (with **with**) on good terms. – *ns* **'friendliness; 'friendship**.

frieze [frēz] *n* a part of a wall below the ceiling, often ornamented with designs; a picture on a long strip of paper *etc*, often displayed on a wall.

'frigate *n* a small warship.

fright [frit] *n* sudden fear. *It gave me a fright. He took fright and ran away.* – *v* **'frighten** to make afraid. – *adj* **'frightful** causing terror; (*coll*) very bad.

'frigid *adj* frozen, cold; cold in manner. – *n* **fri'gidity** coldness.

frill *n* an ornamental edging (of linen, lace *etc*); something unnecessary added on (to thing, action *etc*).

fringe *n* a border of loose threads; hair cut to hang over the forehead; a border (*esp* of soft material, paper etc). – *v* to edge round.

Frisbee® ['frizbi] *n* a plastic plate-like

object skimmed through the air as a game.

frisk *v* to skip about playfully; (*coll*) to search (person) for weapons *etc*. – *adj* **'frisky**.

'fritter *n* a piece of fried batter containing fruit *etc*. – *v* (with **away**) to waste time *etc*.

'frivolous *adj* playful, not serious. – *n* **fri'volity**: – *pl* **fri'volities**.

'frizzy *adj* (of hair) massed in small curls.

fro: to and fro forwards and backwards.

frock *n* a woman's or girl's dress; a monk's wide-sleeved garment. – *n* **'frock-coat** a man's long coat.

frog *n* a small greenish jumping animal living on land and in water. – *n* **'frogman** an underwater swimmer wearing flippers and breathing apparatus.

'frolic *n* merrymaking or an outburst of gaiety. – *v* to play gaily: – *pt* **'frolicked**. – *adj* **'frolicsome**.

from *prep* used before the place, thing, person *etc* that is the starting point of an action, period of time *etc*: *from England to France*: *from Friday to Monday*: *from the first of March* (*onwards*): *made from fruit and sugar*; used to show separation: *to keep away from there*: *take it from him.*

frond *n* a leaf-like growth *esp* a branch of a fern or palm.

front [frunt] *n* the part of anything nearest the person who sees it; the part which faces the direction in which the thing moves; (in war) the fighting line. – Also *adj*. – *n* **'frontage** front part of a building. – **in front of** at the head of, before.

frontier ['fruntēr] *n* a boundary between countries. – Also *adj*.

frontispiece ['fruntispēs] *n* a picture at the very beginning of a book.

frost *n* frozen dew; the coldness of weather needed to form ice. – *v* to cover with frost or anything sparkling like it. – *adjs* **'frosted; 'frosty**.

froth *n* foam on liquids. – *v* to throw up foam. – *adj* **'frothy**.

frown [frown] *v* to wrinkle the brows (in deep thought, disapproval *etc*). – Also *n*. – **frown on** to look upon with disapproval.

frowzy ['frowzi] *adj* rough and tangled.

froze, frozen *see* **freeze**.

frugal ['frōōgəl] *adj* careful in spending, thrifty; costing little, small: *a frugal meal.* – *n* **fru'gality**.

fruit [frōōt] *n* the part of a plant containing the seed; result. *Their hard work* *bore fruit. – n* **'fruiterer** one who sells fruit. – *adj* **'fruitful** producing (much) fruit; producing good results. – *n* **fruition** [froo'ishən] ripeness; a good result. – *adj* **'fruitless** useless, done in vain. – *n* **fruit machine** a gambling machine into which coins are put.

frump *n* a plain badly or unfashionably dressed woman. – *adj* **'frumpish**.

frus'trate *v* to make (someone feel) powerless; to bring to nothing. *They frustrated his wishes. – n* **frus'tration**.

frȳ *v* to cook in hot fat: – *pt* **fried**. – *n* anything fried; young fishes. – **small fry** people or things of little importance.

fuchsia ['fūshə] *n* a type of shrub with long hanging flowers.

'fuddle *v* to make stupid (with drink).

fudge *n* a soft, sugary sweet.

fuel ['fūəl] *n* any substance (*eg* coal, oil, petrol, gas) by which a fire, engine *etc* is kept going.

'fūgitive *adj* running away (from police *etc*). – *n* one who is running away (from someone or something): *a fugitive from justice.*

fugue [fūg] *n* a piece of music with several interwoven tunes.

fulcrum ['foolkrəm] *n* the point on which a lever turns, or a balanced object rests.

fulfil [fool'fil] *v* to carry out (a task, promise *etc*): – *pt* **ful'filled**. – *n* **ful'filment**.

full [fool] *adj* holding as much as can be held; (with **of**) having plenty; plump: *full face. – adv* (used with *adjs*) fully: *full-grown. – n* **'fullness**. – *adv* **'fully**. – *ns* **full moon** the moon when it appears at its largest; **full stop** point placed at the end of a sentence *etc*.

fulmar ['foolmər] *n* a type of white seabird.

'fulminate *v* to flash like lightning; (with **against**) to speak fiercely. – *n* **fulmi-'nation**.

fulsome ['foolsəm] *adj* overdone: *fulsome praise*.

'fumble *v* to use the hands awkwardly; to drop (something thrown, as a ball).

fūme *n* (*usu pl*) smoke or vapour. – *v* to give off smoke or vapour; to be (quietly) in a rage.

'fūmigate *v* to kill germs by means of strong fumes. – *n* **fumi'gation**.

fun *n* enjoyment, a good time: *to have fun. – adj* **'funny** amusing; odd. – *adv* **'funnily**. – *ns* **'funfair** amusement park; **funny bone** part of the elbow. – **make fun of** to tease, make others laugh at.

'function *n* a special job, use or duty (of a machine, person, part of the body *etc*); (large) arranged gathering of people. – *v* (of a machine *etc*) to work, operate; to carry out usual duties. – *n* **'functionary** one holding an office, an official: – *pl* **'functionaries**.

fund *n* a sum of money for a special purpose; a store or supply.

funda'mental *adj* of great or far-reaching importance; going to the very bottom of the matter. – *n* a necessary part; (*pl*) the groundwork or first stages.

'fūneral *n* the ceremony of burial or cremation. – *adj* **funereal** [fū'nēriəl] mournful.

fungus ['fuŋgəs] *n* a soft, spongy plant growth (*eg* toadstool, mushroom); disease-growth on animals and plants: – *pl* **'fungi**.

fū'nicular railway *n* a kind of railway in which carriages are pulled uphill by a cable.

'funnel *n* a wide-mouthed filler by which liquids are poured into bottles; a tube or passage for escape of smoke, air *etc*.

fur *n* the short fine hair of certain animals; their skins covered with fur (used for clothing); a coating on the tongue, on the inside of kettles, boilers *etc*. – *v* to line or cover with fur: – *pt* **furred**. – *adj* **'furry**. – *n* **'furrier** one who buys, sells, or works with furs.

'furbish *v* to rub up until bright.

furious *see* **fury**.

'furlong *n* one-eighth of a mile (220 yards, 201·17 metres).

'furnace *n* a very hot oven or closed-in fireplace for melting iron ore, making steam for heating *etc*.

'furnish *v* to fit up (a room or house) completely; to supply. *He was furnished with enough food for a week. – ns* **'furnishings** (*pl*) fittings of any kind; **'furniture** movable articles in a house *etc* (as tables, chairs).

furore [fū'rōr] *n* uproar; excitement.

furrow ['furō] *n* the groove made by a plough; any groove; a deep wrinkle. – *v* to cut deep grooves in; to wrinkle.

further ['fərdhər] *adv, adj* to a greater distance or degree; in addition. – *v* to help on or forward. – *adv* **'further'more** in addition to what has been said. – *adj* **'furthest** to the greatest distance or degree.

'furtive *adj* stealthy, sly; done slyly.

'fūry *n* violent anger. – *adj* **'furious**.

furze another name for **gorse**.

fuse [fūz] *v* to melt; to join together; to put a fuse in (a plug *etc*); (of a circuit *etc*) to stop working because of the melting of a fuse. – *n* easily-melted wire put in an electric circuit for safety; any device for causing an explosion to take place automatically. – *n* '**fusion** a melting; close union of things, as if melting into one another.

fuselage ['fūzəläzh] *n* the body of an aeroplane.

fuss *n* unnecessary activity, excitement or attention, often about something unimportant; strong complaint. – *v* to be unnecessarily concerned about details; to worry overmuch. – *adj* '**fussy**.

'**fusty** *adj* mouldy; stale-smelling.

'**fūtile** *adj* useless; having no effect. – *n* **futility** [fū'tilət] uselessness.

future ['fūchər] *adj* happening *etc* later in time. – *n* (with **the**) the time to come; (in grammar) the future tense.

fuzz *n* fine, light hair, feathers *etc*; (*slang*) the police. – *adj* '**fuzzy** covered with fuzz, fluffy; curly.

G

'**gabble** *v* to talk fast, chatter. – Also *n*.

gaberdine [gabər'dēn] *n* a kind of cloth; a kind of coat.

'**gāble** *n* the triangular area of wall at the end of a building with a ridged roof.

'**gadabout** *n* a person who loves travelling about.

'**gadfly** *n* a fly which bites cattle.

'**gadget** *n* a (small) simple machine or tool.

Gaelic ['gālik] *n* the language of the Scottish Highlanders and the Irish.

gaff *n* a large hook used for landing fish, such as salmon; a spar made from a mast, for raising the top of a sail. – **blow the gaff** (*coll*) to let out a secret.

gag *v* to silence by stopping the mouth: – *pt* **gagged**. – *n* something put in a person's mouth to silence him; (*coll*) a joke or funny story.

'**gaggle** *n* a flock (of geese).

gaiety, gaily *see* **gay**.

gain *v* to win; to earn; to reach; to get closer, *esp* in a race; (of clocks, watches) to go ahead (of correct time); to take on (*eg* weight). – *n* something gained; profit.

gait *n* way or manner of walking.

'**gaiter** *n* a cloth ankle-covering, fitting over the shoe, sometimes reaching to the knee.

'**gala** *n* a time of rejoicing and merrymaking; a sports meeting: *swimming gala*.

'**galaxy** *n* a system of stars; a splendid gathering (*eg* of women, famous people): – *pl* '**galaxies**. – *n* '**Galaxy** the Milky Way.

gale *n* a strong wind.

gall [göl] *n* bile (a bitter fluid coming from the liver and stored in the '**gallbladder**); bitterness of feeling; a growth (caused by insects) on oaks and other trees and plants. – *v* to annoy. – *adj* '**galling**.

'**gallant** *adj* brave; noble; paying great attention to ladies. – *n* a man who is a favourite with ladies because of his fine manners. – *n* '**gallantry** bravery; politeness to ladies.

galleon ['galiən] *n* (*hist*) a large Spanish sailing ship.

'**gallery** *n* a long passage; the top floor of seats in a theatre; a room for showing paintings *etc* (also **art gallery**): – *pl* '**galleries**.

'**galley** *n* (*hist*) a long, low-built ship driven by oars; a place where cooking is done on board ship: – *pl* '**galleys**. – *n* '**galley-slave** a prisoner condemned to work at the oars of a galley.

'**gallon** *n* a measure for liquids (8 pints, 3·636 litres).

'**gallop** *v* to move by leaps; to (cause to) move very fast. – *n* a fast pace.

gallows ['galōz] *n* wooden framework on which criminals were hanged.

ga'lore *adv* in great plenty: *whisky galore*.

ga'losh, go'losh *n* a rubber shoe worn over ordinary shoes in wet weather: – *pl* **ga'loshes**.

'**galvanism** *n* electricity got by action of chemicals (*usu* acids) on metal. – *adj* **gal'vanic**. – *v* '**galvanize** to stir into activity; to stimulate by electricity; to coat (iron *etc*) with zinc. – *n* **galva'nometer** an instrument for measuring electric currents.

'**gambit** *n* a first move (as in chess) in which something is lost in order to make one's position stronger; an opening move in a transaction or an opening remark in a conversation.

'**gamble** *v* to play games for money; to risk money on the result of a game, race *etc*; to take a wild chance. – Also *n*.

'**gambol** *v* to leap playfully. – Also *n*.

game *n* a contest played according to

rules; (*pl*) athletic competition: *Olympic Games*; wild animals and birds hunted for sport. – *adj* plucky; (of limbs *etc*) lame. – *n, adj* '**gaming** gambling. – *n* '**gamekeeper** one who looks after game birds, animals, fish *etc*. – **big game** large hunted animals (*eg* lions).

'**gammon** *n* leg of a pig, salted and smoked.

'**gamut** *n* the whole range of notes which a voice or instrument can produce; the whole extent of anything.

'**gander** *n* a male goose.

gang *n* any group of people who meet regularly; a team of criminals; a number of labourers. – *ns* '**ganger** foreman of a company of workmen (*eg* labourers); '**gangster** one of a gang of criminals.

gangrene ['gaŋgrēn] *n* the rotting of some part of the body. – *adj* **gangrenous** ['gaŋgrənəs].

gangster *see* **gang**.

'**gangway** *n* a passage between rows of seats; a movable bridge leading from a quay to a ship.

'**gannet** *n* a type of large white sea bird.

'**gantry** *n* a platform or structure for supporting (a travelling crane *etc*).

gaol, gaoler *see* **jail, jailer**.

gap *n* an opening or space between things.

gape *v* to open the mouth wide (as in surprise); to be wide open.

garage ['garäj] *n* a building for storing a car (or cars); a shop where car repairs are done, and petrol, oil *etc* sold.

garb (*old*) *n* dress. – *v* to clothe.

'**garbage** *n* rubbish.

'**garble** *v* to mix up, muddle: *a garbled account of what happened*.

'**garden** *n* a piece of ground on which flowers or vegetables are grown. – *v* to work in a garden; to take care of a garden. – *n* '**gardener**. – *n* **garden party** a large tea party, held out of doors.

gar'gantuan *adj* very large, huge.

'**gargle** *v* to wash the throat with (but without swallowing) a soothing or germ-killing liquid.

'**gargoyle** *n* a jutting-out roof-spout, carved in the shape of a human or animal head.

'**gārish** *adj* over-bright.

'**garland** *n* flowers or leaves tied or woven into a circle.

'**garlic** *n* an onion-like plant with a strong smell and taste, used in cooking.

'**garment** *n* any article of clothing.

'**garnet** *n* a semi-precious stone *usu* red in colour.

'**garnish** *v* to decorate (a dish of food). – Also *n*: – *pl* '**garnishes**. – *n* '**garnishing**.

'**garret** *n* a room next to the roof of a house.

'**garrison** *n* a body of troops for guarding a fortress.

gar'rotte *v* to strangle (by tightening a noose of rope *etc* round someone's neck, *orig* by tightening an iron collar).

'**garrulous** *adj* fond of talking. – *ns* **garrulity** [gə'rōōləti], '**garrulousness**.

'**garter** *n* a broad elastic band to keep a stocking up.

gas *n* a substance like air (though some gases may be smelled); natural or manufactured form of this which will burn and is used as a fuel; (*US*) petrol: – *pl* '**gases**. – *v* to poison with gas: – *pt* **gassed**. – *adj* **gaseous** ['gasiəs]. – *ns* **gas mask** a covering for the face to prevent breathing in of poisonous gas; **gasoline, gasolene** ['gasəlēn] (*US*) petrol; **ga'someter** a tank for storing gas; '**gasworks** place where gas is made.

gash *n* a deep, open wound: – *pl* '**gashes**. – Also *v*.

gasp *n* sound made by a sudden intake of the breath. – *v* to breathe with difficulty; to say breathlessly; (*coll*) to want badly: *gasping for a drink*.

'**gastric** *adj* of the stomach.

gate *n* (that which closes) the opening in a wall, fence *etc*; the number of people at a (football) match; the total sum they pay to get in. – *n* '**gatecrasher** one who comes to a party uninvited. – *v* '**gatecrash**. – *n* '**gateway** an opening containing a gate; an entrance.

gâteau ['gatō] *n* a fancy cake.

gather ['gadhər] *v* to bring together, or to meet, in one place; to pick (flowers *etc*); to increase in. *The car gathered speed*; to learn, come to the conclusion (that). *I gather that you have finished*. – *n* '**gathering** a crowd.

gauche [gōsh] *adj* awkward and clumsy in people's company.

gaucho ['gowchō] *n* a cowboy of the S. American plains, noted for horse-riding.

'**gaudy** *adj* showy; vulgarly bright in colour. – *n* '**gaudiness**.

gauge [gāj] *v* to measure; to make a guess. – *n* a measuring device. – *ns* '**broad-**, '**narrow-gauge** railways having the distance between rails greater or less than the *standard gauge* (4 ft 8½ in, 1·435 metre).

gaunt

gaunt *adj* thin, haggard.

'gauntlet *n* a long glove (often of leather) with a guard for the wrist used by motor cyclists *etc*; (*hist*) the iron glove of armour.

gauze *n* thin cloth that can be seen through.

ga'votte *n* (music for) a type of lively dance.

'gawky *adj* awkward.

gay *adj* lively; merry, full of fun; brightly coloured. – *n* **gaiety** ['gāəti]. – *adv* **'gaily**.

gaze *v* to look steadily. – *n* a fixed look.

ga'zelle *n* a type of small deer.

ga'zette *n* a newspaper, *esp* one having lists of government notices. – *n* **gazetteer** [gazə'tēr] a geographical dictionary.

gear [gēr] *n* anything needed for a particular job, sport (*eg* harness, tools, clothes); (in cars *etc*) a connection by means of a set of toothed wheels between the engine or source of power and the wheels. – *v* (with **to**) to adapt to, design for what is needed.

geese *see* **goose**.

geisha ['gāshə] *n* a Japanese girl trained to entertain.

gelatine ['jelətēn] *n* a jelly-like substance made from hooves, animal bones *etc*, and used in food. – *adj* **gelatinous** [jə'latənəs] jelly-like.

gelding ['geldiŋ] *n* a castrated horse.

gem *n* any precious stone, *esp* when cut to shape; anything greatly valued.

'gender *n* (in grammar, *esp* in languages other than English) any of three types of noun – masculine, feminine or neuter.

gene *n* the basic unit of heredity responsible for passing on specific characteristics from parents to offspring. – *adj* **genetic** [jə'netik].

genealogy [jēni'alǝji] *n* history of families from generation to generation; the ancestors of a person or family shown as a plan: – *pl* **gene'alogies**. – *adj* **genea'logical**. – *n* **gene'alogist** one who studies or makes genealogies.

general ['jenərəl] *adj* not detailed, broad: *a general idea of the person's interests*; involving everyone: *a general election*; to do with several different things: *general knowledge*; of most people: *the general opinion*. – *n* a high-ranking army officer. – *n* **generali'zation** a (too) general view, statement *etc*. – *v* **'generalize** to make a broad general statement (meant to cover all individual cases). – *adv* **'generally, in general** usually; in

most cases; by most people. – *n* **general practitioner** a doctor who treats most ordinary illnesses.

generate ['jenərāt] *v* to produce, bring into being: *generate electricity*: *generate hatred*. – *ns* **gene'ration** act of creating or making; a step in family descent; people born at about the same time; **'generator** a machine for making electricity *etc*.

generic *see* **genus**.

generous ['jenərəs] *adj* giving plentifully; kind. – *n* **gene'rosity**.

genesis ['jenəsis] *n* beginning.

genetic *see* **gene**.

'gēnial *adj* good-natured.

genie ['jēni] *n* a guardian spirit: – *pl* **genii** ['jēnii].

'gēnius *n* unusual cleverness; a person who is unusually clever: – *pl* **'geniuses**.

gen'teel *adj* (too) good-mannered.

'gentile *n* (in the Bible) anyone not a Jew.

gen'tility *n* noble birth, aristocracy; good manners, refinement often to too great an extent.

'gentle *adj* (of persons) soft in manner, not brutal; (of things) mild, not extreme: *gentle breeze*. – *n* **'gentleness**.

'gentleman *n* a man (opposite of **lady**), *esp* one of noble birth; a well-mannered man. – *adj* **'gentlemanly** behaving in a polite manner.

'gentry *n* a wealthy, land-owning class of people.

genuine ['jenūin] *adj* real, not fake; (of persons) honest and straightforward. – *n* **'genuineness**.

'gēnus *n* a group (*usu* of living things) made up of a number of kinds: – *pl* **genera** ['jenərə]. — *adj* **generic** general, applicable to any member of a group or class.

ge'ography *n* the study of the surface of the earth and its inhabitants. – *n* **ge'ographer** one who studies geography. – *adjs* **geo'graphic(al)**.

ge'ology *n* the study of the earth's history as shown in its rocks and soils. – *adj* **geo'logical**. – *n* **ge'ologist**.

ge'ometry *n* the branch of mathematics which deals with the study of lines, angles, and figures. – *adjs* **geo'metric(al)** having regular shape; (of patterns *etc*) made up of angles and straight lines.

ge'rānium *n* a kind of plant, often with bright red flowers.

gerbil ['jörbl] *n* a type of small, rat-like desert animal, often kept as a pet.

germ *n* a very small living thing which may cause a disease; the smallest form of what will become a living thing (as a fertilized egg, a flower bud); that from which anything grows: *germ of an idea*. – *n* **'germicide** a germ-killer. – *v* **'germinate** to begin to grow, to sprout. – *n* **germi'nation**.

ger'mane *adj* closely related.

ges'ticūlate *v* to wave hands and arms about in excitement *etc*. – *n* **gesticu'lation**.

'gesture *n* a movement of the hands, head *etc*; an action made to show one's feelings: *a gesture of friendship*.

get [get] *v* to obtain; to go or move; to cause to be done: *get your hair cut*; to receive: *get a letter*; to cause to be in some condition: *get the car going*; to arrive: *get home*; to catch, or have (a disease); to become: *get old*: – *pt, pp* **got**, (*US*) *pp* **'gotten**. – **get at** to reach; to hint at; to criticize continually; (*slang*) to try to influence by bribes or threats; **get away with** to do and escape punishment for; **get on with** to be on friendly terms with; **get over** to recover from; **get up** to stand up; to get out of bed.

geyser ['gēzər] *n* a hot spring which spouts water into the air; a gas or electric water heater.

ghastly ['gästli] *adj* very pale, death-like; ill: *feeling ghastly*; horrible, ugly; (*coll*) very bad. – *n* **'ghastliness**.

gherkin ['gərkin] *n* a small pickled cucumber.

ghetto ['getō] *n* a (poor) part of a city *etc* in which a certain group (*esp* of immigrants) lives: – *pl* **'ghettos**.

ghost [gōst] *n* a spirit, *usu* of a dead person. – *adj* **'ghostly** like a ghost. – *n* **'ghostliness**.

ghoul [gōōl] *n* an evil spirit which plunders dead bodies; a person un-naturally interested in death and disaster. – *adj* **'ghoulish**.

'giant *n* (in old stories) a huge, man-like being; a person of great height or size: – *fem* **'giantess**. – *adj* huge.

'gibber *v* to speak nonsense; to make meaningless noises. – *n* **'gibberish** words without meaning.

'gibbet *n* (*hist*) a gallows on which criminals used to be executed or hung up after execution.

gibbon ['gibən] *n* a large, tail-less ape.

gibe *see* **jibe**.

'giblets *npl* eatable parts from the inside of a fowl *etc*.

giddy ['gidi] *adj* unsteady, dizzy; causing dizziness: *from a giddy height*. – *n* **'giddiness**.

gift [gift] *n* something freely given (*eg* a present); a natural talent: *a gift for music*; (*coll*) something easily done *etc*. *The examination paper was a gift*. – *adj* **'gifted** having special natural power or ability. – **look a gift horse in the mouth** to find fault with a gift.

gi'gantic *adj* huge, of giant size.

giggle ['gigl] *v* to laugh in a nervous or silly manner. – Also *n*.

gila ['hēlə] *n* (also **gila monster**) a type of poisonous lizard.

gild [gild] *v* to cover with gold; to make bright. – *n* **gilt** the gold covering used in gilding. – *adj* covered with thin gold; coloured like gold. – *adj* **'gilt-'edged** not risky, safe to invest in: *gilt-edged stocks*. – **gild the lily** to try to improve something already beautiful enough.

gill[1] [jil] *n* a measure (¼ pint, 11·36 cubic centimetres) for liquids.

gill[2] [gil] *n* one of the openings on the side of a fish's head through which it breathes.

gillie ['gili] *n* a man who helps and guides a sportsman while fishing or shooting (*esp* in Scotland).

gilt *see* **gild**.

'gimcrack *adj* cheap and badly-made.

gimlet ['gimlit] *n* a small tool for boring holes by hand.

gimmick ['gimik] *n* something meant to attract attention.

gin *n* an alcoholic drink made from grain, and flavoured with juniper berries; a trap or snare.

ginger ['jinjər] *n* a hot-tasting root, used as a seasoning in food. – *adj* flavoured with ginger; reddish-brown in colour (*esp* hair). – *adv* **'gingerly** very carefully. – *n* **'gingerbread** cake flavoured with ginger.

gingham ['giŋəm] *n* a striped or checked cotton cloth.

gipsy *see* **gypsy**.

gi'raffe *n* a type of African animal with very long legs and neck.

gird [gərd] *v* to bind round. – *ns* **'girder** a beam of iron, steel, or wood used in building; **'girdle** belt, cord *etc* which goes round something (*usu* the waist).

girl [gərl] *n* a female child or young woman. – *n* **'girlhood** the state or time of being a girl. – *adj* **'girlish** like a girl. – *n* **Girl Guide** *see* **Guide**.

giro ['jīrō] *n* a system by which payment may be made through banks, post offices *etc*; (also **'girocheque**) a form like a cheque by which such payment is made.

girth [gərth] *n* measurement round the middle; a strap that keeps a saddle on a horse *etc*.

gist *n* the main points or ideas (of a story, argument *etc*).

give [giv] *v* to hand over freely or in exchange; to utter (a shout, cry); to break or crack. *The bridge gave under the weight of the train*; to produce. *This lamp gives a good light*: – *pt* **gave**, *pp* **'given**. – *n* **'giver**. – **give away** to hand over (something) to someone without payment; to betray; **give in** to yield; **give over** (*coll*) to stop (doing something); **give rise to** to cause; **give up** to hand over; to yield; to stop, abandon (a habit *etc*); **give way** to yield; to collapse; to let traffic crossing one's path go before one.

glacé ['glasā] *adj* iced or sugared.

glacier ['glasiǝr] *n* a slowly-moving river of ice in valleys between high mountains. – *adj* **'glācial** of ice or glaciers.

glad *adj* pleased; giving pleasure: *the glad news*. – *v* **'gladden** to make glad. – *n* **'gladness**.

glade *n* an open space in a wood.

'gladiātor *n* (*hist*) in ancient Rome, a man trained to fight with other men or with animals for the amusement of spectators.

glamour ['glamǝr] *n* fascination, charm, beauty, *esp* artificial. – *adj* **'glamorous**.

glance *n* a quick look. – *v* to take a quick look at; (with **off**) to hit and fly off sideways.

gland *n* a part of the body which takes substances from the blood and stores them either for use or so that the body may get rid of them. – *adj* **'glandular**.

glare *n* an unpleasantly bright light; an angry or fierce look. – *v* to shine with an unpleasantly bright light; to look angrily. – *adj* **'glaring** dazzling; very clear, obvious: *a glaring mistake*.

glass *n* a hard transparent substance made from certain metal oxides and other oxides; anything made of glass *esp* a glass drinking vessel or a mirror; (*pl*) **'glasses** a pair of lenses set in a frame used to correct bad eyesight, spectacles. – *adjs* **glass** made of glass; **'glassy** (of eyes) without expression. – *n* **'glasshouse** a greenhouse.

glaze *v* to cover with a thin coating of glass or other shiny stuff; to make shiny; to put panes of glass in a window; (of eyes) to become glassy. – *n* a shiny surface; a sugar-coating. – *n* **glazier** ['glāziǝr] one who sets glass in window-frames.

gleam *v* to glow; to flash. – *n* a beam of light; brightness.

glean *v* to collect (*esp* things overlooked

before); (*old*) to gather corn in handfuls after the reapers.

glee *n* joy; a song in parts. – *adj* **'gleeful** merry.

glen *n* in Scotland, a long narrow valley.

glib *adj* speaking smoothly and fluently (often insincerely and superficially); (of a reply *etc*) quick and ready, but showing little thought. – *n* **'glibness**.

glide *v* to move smoothly and easily; to travel by glider. – *n* the act of gliding. – *n* **'glider** an aeroplane without an engine.

'glimmer *v* to burn or shine faintly. – *n* a faint light; a faint appearance (of): *a glimmer of hope*.

glimpse *n* a brief view. – *v* to get a brief look at.

glint *v* to sparkle, gleam. – Also *n*.

glisten ['glisn] *v* to sparkle.

'glitter *v* to sparkle. – Also *n*.

'gloaming *n* twilight, dusk.

gloat *v* to look at or think about with wicked joy. *She gloated over his defeat*.

globe *n* a ball; the earth; a ball with a map of the world drawn on it; a glass covering for a lamp. – *adjs* **'global** of, or affecting, the whole world; applying generally: *global increase in earnings*; **globular** ['globūlǝr] ball-shaped. – *n* **'globule** a drop; a small ball-shaped piece.

gloom *n* dullness, darkness; sadness. – *adj* **'gloomy** dimly lighted; sad, depressed.

'glory *n* fame, honour; great show, splendour: – *pl* **'glories**. – *v* to rejoice, take great pleasure (in). – *v* **'glorify** to make glorious; to praise highly: – *pt* **'glorified**. – *adj* **'glorious** splendid; deserving great praise; delightful.

gloss *n* brightness on the surface. – *v* to make bright; to explain; (with **over**) to try to hide (a fault *etc*) by treating (it) rapidly or superficially or by giving (it) a false appearance. – *n* **'glossary** a list of words with their meanings: – *pl* **'glossaries**. – *adj* **'glossy** shiny, highly polished.

glove [gluv] *n* a covering for the hand with a separate covering for each finger; a boxing glove.

glow [glō] *v* to burn without flame; to give out a steady light; to be flushed (from heat, cold *etc*); to tingle (with an emotion): *glowed with pride*. – *n* a glowing state; great heat; bright light. – *adj* **'glowing** giving out a steady light; tingling; flushed; full of praise. *I hear glowing accounts of his bravery*. – *n* **'glow-worm** a kind of beetle which glows in the dark.

glower ['glowər] *v* to stare (at) with a frown. – *adj* '**glowering** scowling; threatening.

glucose ['glōokōs] *n* a kind of sugar found in the juice of fruits.

glue [glōō] *n* a substance for sticking things together. – *v* to join with glue. – *adj* '**gluey** sticky.

glum *adj* sad, gloomy.

glut *v* to take one's fill greedily; to supply too much to (a market): – *pt* '**glutted**. – *n* an over-supply (of something): *a glut of fish on the market.*

'**glutton** *n* one who eats too much; one eager (for anything): *a glutton for punishment.* – *adj* '**gluttonous** fond of overeating; eating greedily. – *n* '**gluttony** greediness in eating.

glycerine ['glisərēn] *n* a colourless, sticky, sweet-tasting liquid.

gnarled [närld] *adj* knotty, twisted.

gnash [nash] *v* to grind (the teeth).

gnat [nat] *n* a small (blood-sucking) fly, a midge.

gnaw [nö] *v* to bite at with a scraping action.

gnome [nōm] *n* (*myth*) a goblin who lives underground, often guarding treasure.

gnu [nōō] *n* a type of African antelope.

go *v* to move: *go home*: *go to London*; to leave: *time to go*; to lead. *The road goes north*; to become: *go mad*; to work. *The machine is going at last*; to intend (to do). *I'm going to eat an apple*; to be removed, taken away *etc. The food's all gone*; to be given, awarded *etc. The prize has gone to John*: – *pt* **went**, *pp* **gone** [gon]. – *n* the act or process of going; energy, spirit; (*coll*) attempt, try; (*coll*) fashion, style. – *adj* '**go-ahead** eager to succeed. – *n* permission to act. – *n* '**go-between** one who helps two people to communicate with each other. – *adj* '**go-go** energetic. – *n* '**go-kart** a small low-powered racing car. – **from the word go** from the start; **go about** to try, set about; **go ahead** to proceed, to begin on an action *etc*; **go along with** to agree with; **go back on** to fail to keep (a promise *etc*); **go for** to aim to get; to attack; **go off** to explode; to become rotten; to come to dislike (a person *etc*); **go on** to continue; to talk too much; **go round** to be enough for everyone. *Will the food go round?*; **go steady (with)** to court (a person); **go the whole hog** to do (something) thoroughly; **go under** to be ruined; **on the go** very active.

goad *n* a sharp-pointed stick for driving oxen *etc*; anything that urges on. – *v* to urge on by annoying.

goal *n* the upright posts between which the ball is to be driven in football and other games; a score in football; anything aimed at or wished for.

goat *n* a type of animal of the sheep family with horns and a long-haired coat.

'**gobble** *v* to swallow quickly; to make a noise like a turkey.

'**goblet** *n* (*hist*) a large cup without handles; a drinking glass with a stem.

'**goblin** *n* (*myth*) a mischievous and ugly spirit.

god *n* a being who is worshipped, an idol: – *fem* '**goddess**; **God** the creator and ruler of the world in the Christian, Jewish *etc* religions. – *adj* '**godly** holy, good living. – *ns* '**godfather** a man who says that he will see that a child is brought up according to the beliefs of the Christian Church: – *fem* '**godmother**; '**godsend** a very welcome piece of unexpected good fortune; '**godspeed** a wish for success or for a safe journey.

'**goggle-eyed** *adj* with staring eyes.

'**goggles** *npl* spectacles for protecting the eyes from dust, glare, water *etc*.

go-go *see* **go**.

goitre ['goitər] *n* a swelling in the neck.

gōld *n* an element, a precious yellow metal; riches. – *adj* of, or like, gold. – *adj* '**golden** of, or like, gold; very fine. – *ns* '**gold-digger** a woman who views men merely as a source of wealth; **golden wedding** *see* **wedding**; '**goldfield** a place where gold is found; '**goldfinch** a type of small many-coloured bird; '**goldfish** a kind of golden-yellow Chinese carp, often kept as a pet; '**gold-'leaf** gold beaten to a thin sheet; '**goldsmith** a maker of gold articles.

golf *n* a game in which a ball is struck with various clubs. – *n* '**golfer** one who plays golf. – *n* **golf club** a club used in golf; a society of players of golf; the place where they meet.

'**gollywog** *n* a doll with a black face and bristling hair.

golosh *see* **galosh**.

'**gondola** *n* a boat used on Venice canals; the car suspended from an airship, cable railway *etc*. – *n* **gondolier** [gondə'lēr] a boatman who rows a gondola.

gone *see* **go**.

gong *n* a metal plate which, when struck, gives a booming sound, used *eg* to call people to meals.

good *adj* having the qualities which the

speaker wants in the thing or person spoken of: *a good fire, hammer, engineer, butcher etc*; virtuous: *a good person*; kind. *She was good to me*; pleasant, enjoyable: *a good time*; large: *a good income*. – *npl* **goods** one's belongings; things to be bought and sold. – *n* **goodness** the quality of being good. – *adj* '**good-for-**'**nothing** useless, lazy. – *n* **good name** (good) reputation. – *adj* '**good-**'**natured** kind, cheerful. – *ns* **good morning, good-**'**day, good afternoon, good evening, good night, good**'**bye** words used as greeting when meeting or leaving someone; **good**'**will** kind wishes; a good reputation in business.

goose *n* a web-footed bird larger than a duck: – *pl* **geese**. – *npl* '**goosepimples** small bumps on the skin caused by cold or fear.

gooseberry ['goōzbəri] *n* an eatable *usu* green berry.

gore *n* (a thick mass of) blood; a triangular-shaped piece of cloth in a garment *etc*. – *v* to pierce with horns, tusks *etc*. – *adj* '**gory** covered with blood; of blood or bloodshed.

gorge *n* the throat; a narrow valley between hills. – *v* to swallow greedily till one is full.

gorgeous ['görjəs] *adj* showy, splendid; beautiful, very attractive; (*coll*) excellent, enjoyable, very fine *etc*.

'**gorgon** *n* (*myth*) a monster whose glance turned people to stone; any very stern-looking person.

gorgon'**zola** *n* a kind of strong cheese.

go'**rilla** *n* the largest kind of ape.

gorse *n* a kind of prickly bush with yellow flowers.

goshawk ['gos-hök] *n* a short-winged hawk.

gosling ['gozliŋ] *n* a young goose.

'**gospel** *n* the teaching of Christ; the absolute truth.

'**gossamer** *n* fine spider-threads floating in the air or lying on bushes; any very thin material.

'**gossip** *n* (one who listens to and passes on) talk, not necessarily true, about someone's personal affairs *etc*. – *v* to pass on gossip; to chatter.

got *see* **get**.

gouache [goō'äsh] *n* a kind of paint containing water, gum and honey; a painting done with this paint.

gouge [gowj] *n* a chisel with a hollow blade for cutting grooves. – *v* to scoop (out).

goulash ['goōlash] *n* a stew of meat and vegetables, highly seasoned: – *pl* '**goulashes**.

gourd [goōrd] *n* a large fleshy fruit; the skin of a gourd used as a bottle, cup *etc*.

gourmand ['goōrmöŋ] *n* a glutton.

gourmet ['goōrmā] *n* one with a taste for good wines or food.

gout *n* a painful swelling of the smaller joints, *esp* of the big toe. – *adj* '**gouty**.

govern ['guvərn] *v* to rule, control; to put into action the laws *etc* of a country. – *ns* '**governess** a woman who teaches young children at their home; '**government** rule; control; the persons who rule and administer the laws of a country; '**governor** one who rules.

gown [gown] *n* a woman's dress; a loose robe worn by clergymen, lawyers, teachers *etc*.

grab *v* to seize or grasp suddenly; to lay hands on, *esp* by rough or unjust means: – *pt* **grabbed**. – *n* a sudden grasp or catch.

grace *n* beauty of form or movement; a short prayer at a meal; the title of a duke or archbishop; favour or mercy: *God's grace*. – *adjs* '**graceful** beautiful in appearance; done in a neat way; **gracious** ['grāshəs] kind, polite. – **with good** (or **bad**) **grace** willingly (or unwillingly).

grade *n* a step or placing according to quality or rank; class. – *v* to arrange in order (*eg* from easy to difficult). – *ns* **gra**'**dation** arrangement in order (of rank, difficulty *etc*); **gradient** ['grādiənt] a slope (on a road, railway *etc*). – *adj* **gradual** ['gradūəl] step by step; going slowly but steadily. – *adv* '**gradually**. – **make the grade** to do as well as is necessary (in a job, examination *etc*).

'**graduate** *v* to divide into regular spaces; to pass university examinations and receive a degree. – *n* one who has done so. – *n* **gradu**'**ation** the act of getting a degree from a university.

graffiti [grə'fētē] *npl* words or drawings scratched or painted on a wall *etc*.

graft *v* to fix a shoot or twig of one plant upon another, so that it may grow there; to fix (skin) from one part of the body upon another part; to transfer (a part of the body) from one person to another; to get illegal profit by graft. – *n* living tissue (*eg* skin) which is grafted; a shoot *etc* grafted; hard work; profit gained by illegal or unfair means.

Grail *n* the plate said to be used by Christ at the Last Supper.

grain *n* a seed (*eg* of wheat, oats); corn in general; a very small quantity; a very small measure of weight; the run of the lines of fibre in wood, leather *etc.* – **against the grain** against (a person's) natural feelings.

gram *see* **gramme**.

'**grammar** *n* (the study of) the correct use of words in speaking or writing. *His grammar is bad.* – *n* **gram'mārian** an expert on grammar. – *adj* **grammatical** [grə'matikəl] correct according to rules of grammar. – *n* **grammar school** a kind of secondary school.

gramme, gram *n* the basic unit of weight in the metric system.

'**gramophone** *n* an older name for a record-player.

'**granary** *n* a storehouse for grain: – *pl* '**granaries**.

grand *adj* great; noble; fine. – *ns* '**grandchild**, '**grand-daughter**, '**grandson** one's son's or daughter's child; **grand duke** in some countries a duke of specially high rank; '**grandfather** one's father's or mother's father; **grand master** a chess-player of the greatest ability; '**grandmother** one's father's or mother's mother; **grand opera** opera without spoken dialogue; **grand piano** a piano with a large flat top; '**grandstand** rows of raised seats at a sports ground giving a good view.

gran'dee *n* a man of high rank.

grandeur ['granjər] *n* greatness.

gran'diloquent *adj* speaking in a high-sounding language.

'**grandiose** *adj* planned on a large scale.

granite ['granit] *n* a hard rock of greyish or reddish colour.

'**granny** *n* (*coll*) a grandmother: – *pl* '**grannies**.

grant *v* to give; to allow (something asked for); to admit as true. – *n* something given (normally money) for a special purpose. – *conjs* '**granted**, '**granting** (often with **that**) (even) if, assuming: *granted that you are right.* – **take for granted**, to assume (that something will happen) without checking; to treat (a person) casually, without respect or kindness.

'**granule** *n* a tiny grain or part. – *adjs* '**granular** made up of grains; '**granulated** broken into grains.

grape *n* the green or black smooth-skinned berry from which wine is made. – *ns* '**grapefruit** a fruit like a large yellow orange; '**grapeshot** shot which scatters when fired.

graph *n* line (or lines) drawn on squared paper to show changes in quantity (*eg* in temperature, money spent). – *adj* '**graphic** vivid, well told.

'**graphite** *n* a form of carbon used in making pencils.

'**grapple** *v* to struggle (with); to try to deal (with a problem *etc*).

grasp *v* to clasp and grip with the fingers or arms; to understand. – *n* a grip with one's hand *etc*; one's power of understanding. – *adj* '**grasping** greedy, mean.

grass *n* the plant covering fields of pasture; a kind of plant with long narrow leaves (*eg* wheat, reeds, bamboo): – *pl* '**grasses**. – *adj* '**grassy** covered with grass. – *ns* '**grasshopper** a type of jumping insect; '**grass-snake** a type of green harmless snake; '**grass-'widow** a woman whose husband is away.

grate *n* a framework of iron bars for holding a fire. – *v* to rub down into small pieces; to make a harsh, grinding sound; to irritate. – *ns* '**grater** an instrument with a rough surface for rubbing cheese *etc* into small pieces; '**grating** a frame of iron bars.

'**grateful** *adj* feeling thankful; showing or giving thanks. – *n* **gratification** [gratifi'kāshən] pleasure; satisfaction. – *v* '**gratify** to please; to satisfy: – *pt* '**gratified**. – *n* '**gratitude** thankfulness; desire to repay kindness shown.

gratis ['gratis] *adv* for nothing, without payment.

gra'tuity *n* a money gift in return for something done, a tip: – *pl* **gra'tuities**. – *adj* **gra'tuitous** uncalled-for, done without good reason or excuse: *a gratuitous insult.*

grave *n* a pit in which a dead person is buried. – *adj* serious, important: *grave problems*; not gay, dignified, solemn. – *adv* '**gravely**. – *ns* '**graveness, gravity** ['gravəti]. – *ns* '**gravestone** a stone placed to mark a grave; '**graveyard** a place where the dead are buried, a cemetery.

'**gravel** *n* small stones or pebbles.

'**grāven** *adj* (*old*) carved: *graven images.*

'**gravity** *n* seriousness, importance: *the gravity of the situation*; seriousness, lack of gaiety, solemnity; weight; the force which attracts things towards earth and causes them to fall to the ground. – *v* '**gravitate** to move towards as if strongly attracted (to). – *n* **gravi'tation**.

'**grāvy** *n* the juices from meat that is cooking; a sauce made from these.

gray *see* **grey**.

graze *v* to feed on (growing grass); to scrape the skin of; to touch lightly in passing. – *n* a scraping of the skin; a light touch. – *n* '**grazing** grass land for animals to graze in.

grease *n* thick animal fat; oily substance of any kind. – *v* to smear with grease, apply grease to. – *adj* 'greasy. – *n* 'greasepaint a kind of make-up used by actors *etc*.

great [grāt] *adj* very large; powerful; very important, distinguished; very talented: *a great singer*; of high rank, noble. – *n* 'greatness. – *ns* 'great-'grandchild the son or daughter of a grandson or granddaughter; 'great-'grandparents the father and mother of a grandfather or grandmother.

grebe *n* a fresh-water diving bird.

greed *n* great and selfish desire (for food, money *etc*). – *adj* 'greedy. – *n* 'greediness.

green *adj* of the colour of growing grass *etc*; without experience; easily fooled. – *n* the colour of growing grass; a piece of ground covered with grass; (*pl*) green vegetables for food. – *ns* 'greenery green plants; 'greenness. – *ns* green belt open land surrounding a city *etc*; 'greenfly the aphid; 'greengage a kind of plum, green but sweet; 'greengrocer one who sells fresh vegetables; 'greenhouse a building, *usu* of glass, in which plants are grown. – the green light permission to begin (anything).

greet *v* to meet a person with kind words; to say 'Hullo,' 'Good-day,' *etc*; to react to, respond to. *They greeted his speech with approval*; to meet (the eyes *etc*). – *n* 'greeting words of welcome or kindness; reaction, response.

gre'gārious *adj* living in flocks and herds; liking the company of others.

gre'nade *n* a small bomb thrown by hand.

grew *see* **grow**.

grey, gray *adj, n* (of) a colour between black and white; grey-haired, old. – *n* grey colour; a grey horse. – *ns* 'greybeard an old man; 'greyhound a breed of fast-running dog; grey matter (*coll*) brains.

grid *n* a grating of bars; a network of lines, *eg* for helping to find a place on a map; a network of wires carrying electricity through the country. – *n* 'gridiron a frame of iron bars for cooking food over a fire.

grief [grēf] *n* deep sorrow. – come to grief to meet with misfortune or ruin.

grieve [grēv] *v* to feel sorrow; to make sorrowful. – *n* 'grievance a cause for complaining. – *adj* 'grievous painful; serious; causing grief.

'griffin, 'griffon *n* (*myth*) an animal with the body and legs of a lion and the beak and wings of an eagle.

grill *v* to cook directly under heat (provided by an electric or gas cooker); to cook on a gridiron over a fire; to question (someone) closely. – *n* a frame of bars for grilling food on; grilled food; the part of a cooker used for grilling; a restaurant serving grilled food.

grille [gril] *n* a metal grating over a door, window *etc*.

grim *adj* stern, fierce-looking; terrible; very unpleasant: *a grim sight*; unyielding, stubborn: *grim determination*. – *n* 'grimness.

gri'mace *n* a twisting of the face in fun or pain. – Also *v*.

grime *n* dirt. – *adj* 'grimy.

grin *v* to smile broadly: – *pt* grinned. – Also *n*. – grin and bear it to suffer something without complaining.

grind *v* to crush to powder; to sharpen by rubbing; to rub together (*eg* the teeth): – *pt* ground. – *n* hard or unpleasant work. – *n* 'grinder a person or thing that grinds. – *n* 'grindstone a revolving stone for grinding or sharpening tools. – back to the grindstone back to work; keep one's nose to the grindstone to work, or make someone work, without stopping.

grip *n* a firm hold, grasp; a way of holding or grasping; control; the handle or part by which anything is held; a travelling bag, a holdall. – *v* to take a firm hold of: – *pt* gripped.

gripe *n* a sharp pain in the stomach; a complaint. – *v* to complain.

grisly ['grizli] *adj* frightful, hideous.

grist *n* corn for grinding. – grist to the mill something which brings profit or advantage.

gristle ['grisl] *n* a tough elastic substance in meat. – *adj* 'gristly.

grit *n* tiny pieces of stone; courage. – *v* to apply grit to (*eg* icy roads); to clench (one's teeth): – *pt* 'gritted. – *adj* 'gritty.

grizzled ['grizld] *adj* grey, or mixed with grey. – *adj* 'grizzly of a grey colour. – *n* 'grizzly (bear) a type of large bear of N. America: – *pl* 'grizzlies.

groan *v* to utter a moaning sound (in pain, disapproval *etc*); to be loaded: *a table groaning with food*.

groats *npl* oat grains without the husks.

'grōcer *n* a dealer in certain kinds of food and household supplies. – *npl* 'groceries food (sold by grocers).

'groggy *adj* weak and staggering (from blows or illness).

groin *n* the part of the body where the inner part of the thigh joins the rest of the body.

groom *n* one who has charge of horses; a man who is being married (*usu* '**bridegroom**). – *v* to look after (*esp* a horse); to make smart and tidy.

groove *n* a furrow, a long hollow. – *v* to cut a groove.

grope *v* to search (for) by feeling as if blind.

grōss *adj* coarse; very fat; great, obvious: *gross error*; (of sums of money) total, before any deductions (*eg* income tax) are made: *gross profit*. – *n* the whole taken together; twelve dozen. – *n* '**grossness** coarseness.

grotesque [grǝ'tesk] *adj* very odd or strange looking.

'**grotto** *n* a cave: – *pl* '**grotto(e)s**.

ground *n* the surface of the earth; a good reason: *ground(s) for complaint*; (*pl*) lands surrounding a castle, large house *etc*; (*pl*) dregs: *coffee grounds*. – *v* (of ships) to strike the sea-bed *etc* and remain stuck; to prevent (aeroplanes) from flying; *see* also **grind**. – *adj* '**grounded** (of aeroplanes) unable to fly. – *n* '**grounding** the first steps in learning something.– *adj* '**groundless** without reason. – *ns* **ground floor** the storey of a building at street level; '**groundhog** same as **marmot**; '**ground-swell** broad ocean waves; '**groundwork** the first stages of a task.

groundsel ['grownsl] *n* a type of common wild plant with small yellow flowers.

group [groōp] *n* a number of persons or things together. – *v* to form or gather into a group; to classify.

grouse *n* a kind of game bird hunted on moors and hills (*pl* **grouse**); a grumble, complaint (*pl* '**grouses**). – *v* to grumble, complain.

grove *n* a small group of trees.

'**grovel** *v* to crawl or lie on the ground; to make oneself too humble: – *pt* '**grovelled**.

grow [grō] *v* to become bigger or stronger; to become: *grow old*; to rear, cause to grow (plants, trees *etc*): – *pt* **grew** [groō], *pp* **grown**. – *n* **growth** growing; increase; something that grows; something abnormal that grows on the body.

growl [growl] *v* to utter a deep sound like a dog. – Also *n*.

grown *see* **grow**.

grub *n* the form of an insect after being hatched from the egg (*eg* a caterpillar); (*coll*) food. – *v* to dig. – *adj* '**grubby**

dirty. – *n* '**grubbiness**.

grudge *v* to be unwilling to give, grant, allow *etc*. *I grudge him his success*; to give *etc* unwillingly, with reluctance. – *n* feeling of resentment. *I bear a grudge against him.*

gruel ['groōǝl] *n* a thin mixture of oatmeal boiled in water. – *adj* '**gruelling** very tiring.

gruesome ['groōsǝm] *adj* horrible.

gruff *adj* rough in manner; (of voice *etc*) deep and harsh.

'**grumble** *v* to complain in a badtempered, discontented way. – Also *n*.

'**grumpy** *adj* cross, badtempered.

grunt *v* to make a sound like that of a pig. – Also *n*.

guarantee [garǝn'tē] *n* a (written) promise (to do something); a statement by the maker that something will work well; money put down which will be given up if a promise is broken. – *v* to give a guarantee. – *n* **guaran'tor** one who promises to pay if another person fails to keep an agreement to pay.

guard [gärd] *v* to keep safe from danger or attack. – *n* a man or group of men whose duty it is to protect; something (*eg* a fireguard) which protects from danger; one in charge of railway train or coach; a position of defence (in boxing, cricket, fencing *etc*). – *adj* '**guarded** careful. – *n* '**guardian** one who has the legal right to take care of an orphan; one who protects or guards.

guava ['gwävǝ] *n* a type of yellow pear-shaped fruit, or the tree that bears it.

gudgeon ['gujǝn] *n* a type of small freshwater fish.

guerrilla [gǝ'rilǝ] *n* a member of a small band which makes sudden attacks on a larger army but does not fight openly. – *adj* of a method of fighting in which many small bands acting independently make sudden raids on an enemy.

guess [ges] *v* to say without sure knowledge; to say what is likely to be the case. – Also *n*: – *pl* '**guesses**. – *n* '**guesswork** guessing.

guest [gest] *n* a visitor received and entertained in another's house or in a hotel *etc*.

guf'faw *v* to laugh loudly. – Also *n*.

guide [gīd] *v* to show the way to, lead, direct; to influence. – *n* one who shows the way (to travellers *etc*); one who points out interesting things about a place; a book ('**guidebook**) telling about a place; **Guide** a girl belonging to the Girl Guides organization. – *n* '**guidance** help or advice towards doing something *etc.* – *n* **guided missile** an explosive rocket which after being fired can be guided to its target by radio waves.

guild [gild] *n* a company or association of persons working in the same trade or profession or sharing the same interests; a name used by some societies or clubs.

guile [gil] *n* cunning, deceit.

guillemot ['gilimot] *n* a type of diving sea-bird.

guillotine ['gilətēn] *n* (*hist*) an instrument for beheading (formerly used in France); a machine for cutting paper. – *v* to behead with the guillotine; to cut (paper) with a guillotine.

guilt [gilt] *n* a sense of shame; blame for wrongdoing (*eg* breaking the law). – *adj* **'guilty**.

guinea ['gini] *n* (*hist*) a British gold coin; now a word for £1·05, sometimes used in expressing prices, fees *etc*. – *ns* **'guinea-fowl** a bird, something like a pheasant, having white-spotted feathers; **'guinea-pig** a gnawing animal about the size of a rabbit; a person used as the subject of an experiment.

guise [gīz] *n* appearance, dress *esp* a disguised or false appearance: *in the guise of a priest*.

guitar [gi'tär] *n* a type of stringed musical instrument.

gulch *n* a narrow rocky valley.

gulf *n* a large inlet of the sea.

gull *see* **seagull**.

'gullet *n* a passage by which food goes down into the stomach.

'gullible *adj* easily tricked.

'gully *n* a channel worn by water: – *pl* **'gullies**.

gulp *v* to swallow eagerly or in large mouthfuls. – Also *n*.

gum *n* the firm flesh in which the teeth grow; sticky juice got from some trees and plants; a kind of sweet. – *v* to stick with gum. – *adj* **'gummy** sticky.

'gumption *n* good sense.

gun *n* any weapon firing bullets or shells. – *ns* **'gunboat** a small warship with heavy guns; **'gun-carriage** a wheeled support for a field-gun; **gun dog** a dog trained to fetch birds *etc* after they have been shot; **'gunfire** the firing of guns; **'gun-metal** a mixture of copper and tin; **'gunpowder** an explosive in pow-

der form; **'gun-running** bringing guns into a country illegally. – **stick to one's guns** to keep determinedly to one's opinion.

gunwale, gunnel ['gunl] *n* the upper edge of a boat's side.

'gurgle *v* to flow making a bubbling sound; to make such a sound. – Also *n*.

gush *v* to flow out in a strong stream; to talk at great length, exaggerating one's emotions, enthusiasms *etc. She would gush about her daughter's wedding for hours.* – *n* a strong or sudden flow: – *pl* **'gushes**.

'gusset *n* a cornered piece of cloth put into a garment to strengthen part of it.

gust *n* a sudden blast (such as wind). – *adj* **'gusty** windy.

'gusto *n* enthusiasm.

gut *n* a narrow passage in the lower part of the body; animal intestines made for use as violin-strings *etc*. – *v* to take out the inner parts of: *gut a fish*; to destroy completely (often by fire): *a gutted building*: – *pt* **'gutted**.

'gutter *n* a water channel (on the roof, at the edge of a roadside *etc*). – *n* **'guttersnipe** a poor child who spends most of his time in the streets.

'guttural *adj* harsh in sound, as if formed in the throat.

guy [gī] *n* a steadying rope for a tent *etc*; an image of Guy Fawkes made of old clothes *etc*, burned in Britain on 5th November; (*coll*) a man.

'guzzle *v* to eat or drink greedily.

gym [jim] *n* short for **gymnasium** or **gymnastics**.

gymkhana [jim'känə] *n* a meeting for competitions (often between horse-riders).

gymnasium [jim'nāziəm] *n* a building or room fitted out for physical exercises: – *pls* **gym'nasiums**, **gym'nasia**. – *n* **'gymnast** one who does gymnastics. – *adj* **gym'nastic**. – *npl* **gymnastics** [jim'nastiks] exercises to strengthen the body.

gypsum ['jipsəm] *n* a softish chalk-like mineral.

gypsy, gipsy ['jipsi] *n* a member of a wandering people; a Romany: – *pl* **'gypsies**.

gyrate [jī'rāt] *v* to whirl round. – *n* **gy'ration**. – *adj* **gyratory** ['jīrətəri].

H

'haberdashery *n* materials for sewing, mending *etc*. – *n* **'haberdasher** a person who sells haberdashery.

'habit *n* something one is used to doing; one's ordinary behaviour; dress: *a monk's habit*. – *adj* **ha'bitūal** usual, formed by habit. – *v* **ha'bituate** to make accustomed.

'habitable *adj* that may be lived in. – *ns* **'habitat** the natural home of an animal or plant; **habi'tation** a dwelling place.

hack *v* to cut or chop up roughly; to ride on horseback *esp* along ordinary roads. – *n* a rough cut, gash; person who does hard work for low pay, *esp* a writer; an ordinary riding horse (kept for hire). – *n* **'hacksaw** a saw for cutting metal.

'hackles *npl* the feathers on the neck of a farmyard cock; the hair on a dog's neck. – **make someone's hackles rise** to make someone angry.

hackneyed ['haknid] *adj* (*esp* of sayings *etc*) too much used, not fresh or original. – *n* **hackney carriage, hackney cab** a carriage or taxi let out for hire.

'haddock *n* a kind of small eatable sea-fish: – *pls* **'haddock, 'haddocks**.

Hades ['hādēz] *n* (*myth*) the dwelling place of the dead, hell.

haemoglobin, (*US*) **hemoglobin** [hēmə'glōbin] *n* the oxygen-carrying substance in the red blood cells.

haemorrhage, (*US*) **hemorrhage** ['hemərij] *n* bleeding, *esp* in great quantity.

haft *n* a handle (of a knife *etc*).

hag *n* an ugly old woman; a witch.

'haggard *adj* thin-faced, hollow-eyed *etc*, with tiredness.

'haggis *n* a Scottish food made from the chopped-up heart, lungs and liver of a sheep and cooked in a sheep's stomach: – *pl* **'haggises**.

'haggle *v* to argue in a determined way (*esp* over a price).

'ha-ha *n* a sunken fence round a garden or park.

hail *v* to greet, welcome; to call to. – *n* a call from a distance; greeting; welcome; frozen raindrops; a shower (*eg* of bullets, things thrown *etc*). – *v* to shower with hail. *It's hailing*; to pour down. *Arrows hailed down*. – *n* **'hailstone** a piece of hail. – **hail from** to come from, belong to (a place).

hair *n* a thread-like growth on the skin of an animal; the whole mass of these (as on the head). – *adj* **'hairy** covered with hair. – *ns* **'hair-breadth, 'hair's-breadth** a very small distance; **'hairdresser** one who cuts, washes and sets hair. – *adj* **'hair-raising** causing great fear. – *n* **'hairspring** a very fine spring in a watch *etc*. – **split hairs** to be very particular over unimportant details.

hake *n* a kind of eatable sea-fish something like a cod.

'halberd *n* (*hist*) a battle-axe fixed on a long pole. – *n* **halberdier** [halbər'dēr] a soldier armed with a halberd.

halcyon ['halsiən]: **halcyon days** a time of peace and happiness.

hale: hale and hearty healthy.

half [häf] *n* one of two equal parts: – *pl* **halves** [hävz]. – *adj* being one of two equal parts; not full or complete: *half measures*: *a half smile*. – *adv* partly, to some extent. – *v* **halve** to cut, divide in two. – *ns* **'half-breed, 'half-caste** a person having father and mother of different races, *esp* white and black; **'half-brothers, 'half-sisters** brothers or sisters sharing only one parent; **'half-'crown** a coin in old British money of the value of two shillings and sixpence (12½ pence). – *adj* **'half-'hearted** not eager. – *adv* **'half-'mast** (of flags) hoisted half-way up the mast to show that some well-known person has died. – *ns* **'halfpenny** the lowest value British coin; **'half-'time** ['häf'tim] in sport, a short rest half-way through a game. – *adv, adj* **'half-'way** at or of a point equally far from the beginning and the end (of a distance, journey, period of time, task *etc*). – *adj* **'half-'witted** weak in the mind.

'halibut *n* a kind of large eatable flatfish.

hali'tōsis *n* bad breath.

hall [höl] *n* a passage or large room at the entrance to a house; a large public room; a large country house, the home of a squire or landowner. – *n* **'hallmark** a mark put on gold and silver articles to show the quality of the gold or silver; any mark which shows that a thing is good.

hallo *see* **hello**.

hallow ['halō] *v* to make holy; to set apart for holy use. – *n* **Hallowe'en** ['halō'ēn] the evening of October 31st, when witches and spirits are supposed to be around.

hallucination [həloōsi'nāshən] *n* the seeing of something that is not really there. *He had hallucinations after he took* *the drugs. – adj* **hal'lucinatory** causing hallucinations.

'**hālo** *n* a circle of light round the sun or moon or around a person's head (as in the pictures of a saint): – *pl* '**halo(e)s**.

halt [hōlt] *v* to come or bring to a stop; to be lame, limp; to hesitate, be uncertain. – *adj* lame. – *n* a stop, standstill; stopping place. – *adv* '**haltingly** hesitantly.

halter ['hōltər] *n* a head-rope for holding and leading a horse.

halve *see* **half**.

'**halyard** *n* a rope for raising or lowering a sail or flag.

ham *n* the thigh of a pig salted and dried; the back of the thigh; (*coll*) an amateur radio operator. – *n* '**hamburger** a round cake of minced beef, usually fried. – *adj* '**ham-'fisted** clumsy.

'**hamlet** *n* a small village.

'**hammer** *n* a tool for beating or breaking hard substances or driving nails; a striking piece in a clock, piano, pistol *etc*. – *v* to drive or shape with a hammer; to defeat overwhelmingly. – **hammer and tongs** violently.

'**hammock** *n* a length of netting, canvas *etc* hung up by the corners, and used as a bed.

'**hamper** *v* to hinder. – *n* a large basket with a lid.

'**hamster** *n* a kind of animal, similar to a rat, with large cheek pouches.

'**hamstring** *n* a tendon at the back of the knee. – *v* to lame by cutting this; to make ineffective or powerless.

hand *n* the part of the human body at the end of the arm; a pointer (*eg* of a clock); help: *lend a hand*; a measure (four inches, 10·16 centimetres) used for measuring the height of horses; a workman; one's style of handwriting; side or direction: *left-hand side*; a set of playing cards dealt to a person; clapping, applause: *a big hand*. – *v* to pass (something) with the hand; (with **over**) to give. – *ns* '**handbag** a small bag carried by women for personal belongings; '**handbill** a small printed notice; '**handbook** a small book giving information or directions (a guidebook); '**handcuffs** steel bands, joined by a short chain, put round the wrists of prisoners; '**handful** as much as can be held in one hand; a small amount; '**handhold** something which the hand can grip (*eg* in climbing). – *adj* '**hand-'picked** chosen carefully. – *n* '**handwriting** writing with pen or pencil. – **at hand** near by; **hand-to-hand fighting** fighting in which those

involved are in close contact with each other; '**hand-to-'mouth** (of an existence *etc*) with barely enough to live on and nothing to spare; **in hand** in one's possession: *cash in hand*; in preparation; under control; **out of hand** out of control; at once.

'**handicap** *n* something that makes doing something more difficult; (in a race, competition *etc*) a disadvantage (*eg* having to run a greater distance in a race) given to the best competitors so that others have a better chance of winning; the race, competition *etc*; a physical or mental disability. – Also *v*. – *adj* '**handicapped** having or given a handicap; physically or mentally disabled.

'**handicraft** *n* skilled work done by hand, not machine.

handiwork ['handiwərk] *n* thing(s) made by hand; work done by, or a result of the action of a particular person *etc*. *This is the handiwork of a vandal*.

handkerchief ['haŋkərchif] *n* a cloth for wiping the nose *etc*.

'**handle** *v* to touch, hold or use with the hand; to manage, cope with. – *n* that part of anything meant to be held in the hand. – *npl* '**handlebars** (on a bicycle) a bar at the front with a handle at each end, used for steering.

handsome ['hansəm] *adj* good-looking; generous: *a handsome gift*.

'**handy** *adj* useful or convenient to use; easily reached, near; clever with the hands. – *ns* '**handiness**; '**handyman** a man who does odd jobs.

hang *v* to fix or be fixed to some point off the ground *esp* with string *etc*; to remain more or less still in the air (*eg* of a hawk, a cloud); (with **down**) to droop, fall or incline downwards; to depend (on); to attach wall-paper to a wall: – *pt* **hung**; to put a criminal to death by putting a rope round his neck and letting him fall: – *pt* **hanged**. – *ns* '**hanger** that on which a coat *etc* is hung; '**hanging** the killing of a criminal by hanging. – *adj* '**hangdog** guilty-looking. – *ns* '**hanger-'on** one who stays near someone in the hope of gaining some advantage: – *pl* '**hangers-'on**; '**hangman** the man who hangs criminals; '**hangover** uncomfortable after-effects of being drunk; something remaining (from). – **get the hang of** to understand, learn how to use; **hang about, around** to remain near, loiter; **hang back** to hesitate; **hang fire** to delay.

'**hangar** *n* a shed for aeroplanes.

hank *n* a coil or loop of string, rope, wool *etc*.

'**hanker** *v* to long for.

'**hankie,** '**hanky** short for **handkerchief**.

'**hansom-cab** *n* a light two-wheeled cab with the driver's seat raised behind.

'**hap'hazard** *adj* depending on chance, without planning or system. – Also *adv*.

'**hapless** *adj* unlucky.

'**happen** *v* to take place; to occur by chance; to chance to do. *I happened to find him.* – *n* '**happening** an event.

'**happy** *adj* joyful; contented; lucky: *a happy chance*; willing: *happy to help*: – *comp* '**happier**, *superl* '**happiest**. – *adv* '**happily**. – *n* '**happiness**. – *adj* '**happy-go-'lucky** easy-going, taking things as they come.

hara-kiri ['harə'kērē] *n* suicide as practised in Japan in earlier times.

harangue [hə'raŋ] *n* an intense, rousing speech (to a crowd). – Also *v*.

'**harass** *v* to annoy (often); to make sudden attacks on. – *n* '**harassment**.

harbinger ['härbinjər] *n* a sign of something to come: *harbinger of spring*.

harbour ['härbər] *n* a place of shelter for ships; any place of shelter or safety. – *v* to give shelter or refuge; to store (*eg* unkind thoughts) in the mind.

hard *adj* solid, firm; not easily broken or put out of shape; not easy to do, understand *etc*; not easy to please; not easy to bear; having no kind or gentle feelings; (of water) containing many minerals and so not lathering well when soap is added; (of drugs) habit-forming. – *adv* strongly, violently. – *v* '**harden** to make hard. – *adv* '**hardly** scarcely; only just; with difficulty. – *n* '**hardness** the state of being hard. – *adjs* '**hard-'headed** clever, shrewd; '**hard-'hearted** having no kind feelings. – *ns* **hard labour** tiring work given to prisoners as part of their punishment; '**hardship** something not easy to bear (*eg* cold, lack of money); '**hardware** goods such as pots and pans; equipment (machinery, weapons *etc*); part or parts of a computer (*see* **software**); '**hardwood** the wood of certain trees (as oak, ash, elm *etc*). – **hard and fast** (*esp* of rules) strict; **hard hit** hurt, badly affected (as by a loss of money); **hard of hearing** rather deaf; **hard up** short of money.

'**hardy** *adj* daring, brave; strong, tough. – *n* '**hardiness**.

hare *n* a type of fast-running animal, like a large rabbit. – *n* '**harebell** a plant with blue, bell-shaped flowers. – *adj* '**hare-brained** careless about what one does; mad, foolish. – *n* '**hare-'lip** a split in the upper lip at birth, like that of a hare.

harem ['hārəm] *n* the women's rooms in a Muslim house; the women who occupy these.

haricot ['harikō] *n* a type of bean.

hark *interj* listen! – **hark back** to refer back to what was being spoken of earlier.

harlequin ['härlikwin] *n* a comic character in a dress of several colours, in a pantomime or comedy.

harm *n* hurt; damage. – *v* to cause damage; to do a wrong to. – *adjs* '**harmful**; '**harmless**.

'**harmony** *n* agreement of one part, colour or sound with another; agreement between people: *living in harmony*: – *pl* '**harmonies**. – *adj* **har'monic** having to do with harmony. – *n* **har'monica** a mouth organ. – *adj* **har'mōnious** pleasant-sounding; peaceful, without disagreement. – *n* **har'mōnium** a type of musical wind instrument like a small organ. – *v* **harmonize** ['härmənīz] to be in, or bring into, harmony; to agree, go well (with); (in music) to add the different parts to a melody.

'**harness** *n* the leather and other fittings for a horse at work. – *v* to put harness on a horse; to use (a source of power *etc*) for a special purpose. – **in harness** working, not on holiday or retired.

harp *n* a musical instrument played by plucking the strings with the fingers. – *n* '**harpist**. – **harp on** to talk too much about.

har'poon *n* a spear tied to rope, used for killing whales. – *v* to strike with a harpoon.

harpsichord ['härpsikörd] *n* a kind of musical instrument something like a piano.

'**harpy** *n* (*myth*) a monster with the body of a woman, and the wings, feet and claws of a bird of prey; a cruel woman: – *pl* '**harpies**.

'**harrier** *n* a breed of small dog for hunting hares; a kind of bird of prey; a cross-country runner.

harrow ['harō] *n* a frame with iron spikes for breaking up lumps of earth in ploughed land. – *v* to drag a harrow over; to distress greatly. – *adj* '**harrowing** very distressing.

'**harry** *v* to plunder, lay waste (an area, country *etc*); to harass, worry (a person): – *pt* '**harried**.

harsh *adj* rough, bitter; cruel. – *n* '**harshness**.

hart *n* the stag or male deer, *esp* from the age of six years.

'**hart(e)beest** *n* a type of S. African antelope.

'**harvest** *n* the time of the year when the ripened crops are gathered in; the crops gathered at this time. – *v* to gather in (a crop). – *n* '**harvester** a person or machine that harvests; a kind of creature like a spider. – *n* **harvest home** the feast held when the harvest is gathered in.

hash *n* a dish of chopped meat *etc*. – **make a hash of** to spoil completely.

hasp *n* a clasp (of a padlock *etc*).

'**hassock** *n* a thick cushion used as a footstool or for kneeling on.

hāste *n* speed, hurry. – *v* **hasten** ['hāsn] to hurry (on); to drive forward. – *adj* **hasty** ['hāsti] hurried; done without thinking. – *adv* '**hastily**. – **make haste** to hurry.

hat *n* a kind of covering for the head. – *n* '**hatter** one who makes or sells hats. – *n* '**hat-trick** (in cricket) the putting out of three batsmen by three balls in a row; (in football *etc*) three goals scored by the same player; any action performed three times in a row. – **keep (something) under one's hat** to keep secret.

hatch *n* (the door or cover of) an opening in a floor, wall *etc*: – *pl* '**hatches**. – *v* to produce young from eggs; to form and set working a plan (*usu* evil); to shade (part of a picture *etc*) with fine lines. – *ns* '**hatchery** a place for hatching eggs (*esp* of fish): – *pl* '**hatcheries**; '**hatchway** an opening in a floor or ship's deck.

'**hatchet** *n* a small axe. – *adj* '**hatchet-**'**faced** thin-faced, with sharp features. – **bury the hatchet** to put an end to a quarrel.

hate *v* to dislike very much. – *n* great dislike. – *adj* '**hateful** causing hatred. – *n* **hatred** ['hātrid] extreme dislike.

haughty ['höti] *adj* proud, looking on others with scorn. – *n* '**haughtiness**.

haul *v* to drag, pull with force. – *n* a strong pull; (*coll*) a difficult or tiring job: *a long haul*; that which is caught at one pull: *a haul of fish*; a rich find, booty. – *n* '**haulage** (money charged for) the carrying of goods.

haunch *n* the fleshy part of the hip; a leg and loin of meat (*esp* venison): – *pl* '**haunches**.

haunt *v* to visit often; (of a ghost) to stay about a place. *A ghost haunts this house*. – *n* a place often visited. – *adj* '**haunted** inhabited by ghosts.

have [hav] *v* used with another verb to show that an action is in the past and completed. *I have bought a shirt*; to own or possess. *I have a fur coat*; to hold, contain. *This house has three bedrooms*; to give birth to: *to have a baby*; to suffer from: *to have a cold*; to cause (to be done): *have your hair cut*; to put up with. *I won't have her being so rude*: – *pt* **had**. – **have done with** to finish; **have it out** to settle (as an argument).

'**hāven** *n* a safe harbour; a place of safety.

'**haversack** *n* a bag made of canvas *etc* with shoulder-strap, for carrying food *etc*.

'**havoc** *n* great destruction.

haw *see* **hawthorn**.

hawk *n* a bird of prey of the falcon kind. – *v* to hunt birds with trained hawks; to carry goods about for sale. – *n* '**hawker** a door-to-door salesman.

'**hawthorn** *n* a type of prickly tree, with white flowers and small red berries (**haws**).

hay *n* grass, cut and dried, used as cattle food. – *ns* '**hay-cock** a pile of hay in a field; '**hay-**'**fever** an illness like a bad cold caused by pollen *etc*; '**hay-fork** a long-handled fork used in turning and lifting hay; '**hayrick, -stack** hay built up into a house-like block. – *adj* '**haywire** tangled, in a state of disorder.

'**hazard** *n* chance; risk of harm or danger. – *v* to risk; to put forward (a guess *etc*) at the risk of being wrong. – *adj* '**hazardous** dangerous, risky.

haze *n* a thin mist. – *adj* '**hazy** misty; not clear, vague. – *n* '**haziness**.

'**hāzel** *n* a type of light-brown nut, or the tree that bears it.

he [hē] *pron* some male person or animal already spoken about (used only as the subject of a verb). *He ate a banana*.

head [hed] *n* the uppermost part of the body, containing the brain, jaw *etc*; the chief part, place or person. – *v* to lead; to go in front of; to go in the direction of. *They headed for home*; to hit (a ball) with the head; (with **off**) to turn aside: *head off an attack*. – *ns* '**header** a dive, head first; '**heading** that which stands at the head (such as the title of a book or chapter). – *adj* '**heady** exciting. – *ns* '**headache** a pain in the head; a worrying problem; '**headband** a band worn round the head; '**headboard** a board across the top end of a bed; '**head-dress** a covering for the head. – *adv* '**head**'**first** with the head first; rashly, without thinking. – *ns* '**headland** a point of land running out into the sea, a cape; '**headlight** a strong light on the front of a motor car *etc*; '**headline** a line in large letters at the top of a page in a newspaper *etc*. – *adj, adv* '**headlong** with the head first; without stopping; without thought. – *n* '**head**'**master** the principal master of a school: – *fem* '**head**'**mistress**. – *adj, adv* '**head**-'**on** with the head or front first. – *ns* '**head**'**quarters** place from which the chief officers of an army *etc* control their operations; the chief office (of a business *etc*); '**headstone** a gravestone. – *adj* '**headstrong** determined to do as one likes. – *ns* '**headway** forward movement; '**headwind** a wind blowing straight in one's face. – **head over heels** in a somersault; completely, thoroughly.

heal *v* to make or become healthy or sound, cure. – *n* **health** [helth] the state of one's body *etc*; soundness of body *etc*; a wish (said while drinking) that someone may have good health. – *adj* '**healthy** in good health or condition; encouraging good health.

heap *n* a pile of things thrown one on top of another; a great many (of). – *v* to throw in a pile.

hear *v* to receive (sounds, news, music) by the ear; to listen to: – *pt* **heard** [hẽrd]. – *n* '**hearing** ['hēriŋ] the act or power of listening; a court case. – *n* '**hearsay** what one hears people say, rumour. – **Hear! Hear!** a cry to show agreement with a speaker; **will not hear of** will not allow. *He would not hear of her going home alone.*

hearse [hẽrs] *n* a car for carrying a dead body to the grave.

heart [härt] *n* the part of the body which acts as a blood pump; the inner or chief part of anything; courage; eagerness; one of the signs on playing cards. – *v* '**hearten** to cheer on, encourage. – *adjs* '**heartless** cruel; '**hearty** strong, healthy; (of a meal) large; done eagerly, over-cheerful. – *adv* '**heartily**. – *n* '**heartache** sorrow. – *adj* '**heartbroken** very upset, very sad. – *ns* '**heartburn** a burning feeling in the chest after eating, indigestion; '**heartfailure** (death caused by) the sudden stopping of the heart's beating. – *adj* '**heartfelt** felt deeply, sincere.

hearth [härth] *n* (the floor of) the fireplace.

heat *n* (high) temperature; anger; a division or round in a competition, race

etc. – *v* to make or become hot. – *n* **heat wave** a period of hot weather. – **in heat** (of female animals) sexually excited in the breeding season.

heath *n* barren, open country; heather.

heathen ['hēdhən] *n* one who does not believe in God, *esp* one who worships idols. – Also *adj*.

heather ['hedhər] *n* a plant with small purple or white flowers growing on moorland. – *adj* of the colour of purple heather.

heave *v* to lift by force; to throw; to rise and fall; to produce, let out (*esp* a sigh). – Also *n*.

heaven ['hevn] *n* the sky (often in *pl*); the dwelling place of (the Christian) God; the place of reward of the good after death; any place of great happiness. – *adj* '**heavenly** dwelling in heaven; (*coll*) delightful. – **heavenly bodies** the sun, moon and stars.

heavy ['hevi] *adj* of great weight; great in amount, force *etc*: *heavy rainfall*; not easy to bear; slow; sleepy: – *comp* '**heavier**, *superl* '**heaviest**. – *adv* '**heavily**. – *n* '**heaviness**.

'**heckle** *v* (in an election) to ask awkward questions of a public speaker. – *n* '**heckler** one who heckles.

'**hectare** ['hektär] *n* 10,000 square metres.

'**hectic** *adj* rushed; feverish.

'**hector** *v* to bully.

hedge *n* a fence of bushes, shrubs *etc*. – *v* to make a hedge; to shut in with a hedge; to avoid giving a straight answer. – *ns* '**hedgehog** a small pricklybacked animal; '**hedgerow** a row of bushes forming a hedge.

heed *v* to give attention to, listen to. – *adj* '**heedless** careless. – **pay heed to** to take notice of.

heel *n* the back part of the foot. – *v* to hit (*esp* a ball) with the heel; to put a heel on (a shoe); (of ships) to lean over. – **take to one's heels, show a clean pair of heels** to run away.

'**hefty** *adj* (of persons) powerful, muscular; heavy.

heifer ['hefər] *n* a young cow.

height [hit] *n* the state of being high; distance from bottom to top; the highest point; (often *pl*) a high place. – *v* '**heighten** to make higher.

heinous ['hānəs] *adj* very wicked.

heir [är] *n* one who by law receives a title or property on the death of the owner: – *fem* '**heiress**. – *ns* '**heir**-**ap**'**parent** one who is expected to receive a title or property when the present holder dies; '**heirloom** something valuable that has been handed down in the family from generation to generation.

held *see* **hold**.

'**helicopter** *n* a flying machine kept in the air by propellers rotating on a vertical axis.

'**hēliograph** *n* a means of signalling, using the sun's rays.

'**hēliotrope** *n* a plant with small, sweet-smelling, lilac-blue flowers; a light purple colour.

'**hēlium** *n* an element, a very light gas.

hell *n* in some religions, the place of punishment of the wicked after death; the dwelling place of the Devil; any place of great misery or pain. – *adj* '**hellish**. – **hellbent on** determined to.

hel'lo, hal'lo, hul'lo *n* a greeting used between people. *I said hello to him. Hello! How are you?*

helm *n* the wheel or handle by which a ship is steered. – *n* '**helmsman** the one who steers.

'**helmet** *n* an armoured covering for the head.

help *v* to aid, do something necessary or useful for; to give the means for doing something to; to stop oneself from (doing). *I cannot help liking him.* – *n* aid, assistance; one who assists. – *adj* '**helpful** useful, able to help. – *n* '**helping** a share (of food). – *adj* '**helpless** useless; powerless. – *n* '**helpmate** a partner. – **help oneself** serve oneself (with food).

'**helter-'skelter** *adv* in a great hurry, in confusion. – *n* a spiral slide in a fairground *etc*.

hem *n* the border of a garment doubled down and stitched. – *v* to put or form a hem on; (with **in**) to surround: – *pt* '**hemmed**.

'**hemisphere** *n* a half of the earth or a map of it: *western, eastern, northern* or *southern hemisphere.* – *adj* **hemi'spherical** like half a ball in shape.

'**hemlock** *n* a type of poisonous plant.

hemoglobin *see* **haemoglobin**.

hemorrhage *see* **haemorrhage**.

hemp *n* a type of plant used for making ropes, bags, sails *etc* and which supplies a drug. – *adj* '**hempen**.

hen *n* a female bird; a female domestic fowl. – *v* '**henpeck** (of a wife) to worry (a husband) into always giving way.

hence *adv* from this place or time: *ten years hence*; for this reason. *Hence, I shall have to stay.* – *advs* '**hence'forth**, '**hence'forward** from now on.

'**henchman** *n* a follower; a servant.

'**henna** *n* a reddish dye taken from a plant for colouring the hair *etc*.

'**heptagon** *n* a seven-sided figure. – *adj* **hep'tagonal**.

her *pron* a female person already spoken about (used only as the object in a sentence). *He helps her.* – *adj* belonging to such a person: *her house.* – *pron* **hers**. *This house is hers.* – *pron* **her'self** used reflexively. *She washed herself*; used for emphasis. *She herself won't be there but her brother will.*

'**herald** *n* something that is a sign of future things; (*hist*) a person who carries and reads important notices. – *v* to announce loudly; to be a sign of. – *adj* **he'raldic** of heraldry. – *n* '**heraldry** the study of coats of arms, badges, crests *etc*.

herb *n* a plant the stem of which dies every year; a plant used in the making of medicines or in cooking. – *adjs* **herbaceous** [hɜr'bāshəs] of herbs: *herbaceous border*; '**herbal** of or using herbs: *herbal remedy.* – *n* '**herbalist** one who sells herbs used in cooking or medicine. – *adj* **her'bivorous** eating or living on grass *etc*.

Herculean [hɜrkū'lēən] *adj* needing or showing great strength *etc*; very strong.

herd *n* a group of animals of one kind; (with **the**) most people. – *v* to treat or group together like a herd of animals.

here *adv* at, in or to this place. *He's here already. Come here!* – *advs* **here-a'bouts** approximately in this place; **here'after** after this. – *n* (with **the**) life after death. – *adv* **here'by** by this means.

he'redity *n* the passing on of qualities (appearance, intelligence *etc*) from parents to children. – *adj* **he'reditary** passed on in this way.

heresy ['herəsi] *n* an opinion which goes against the official (*esp* religious) view: – *pl* '**heresies**. – *n* '**heretic** one who holds or teaches such an opinion. – *adj* **he'retical**.

'**heritage** *n* something passed on by or inherited from an earlier generation, a parent *etc*.

her'maphrodite *n* an animal which has the qualities of both male and female sexes.

her'metically: hermetically sealed closed completely and airtight.

'**hermit** *n* one who lives alone (*esp* for religious reasons). – *n* '**hermitage** the dwelling of a hermit. – *n* **hermit crab** a kind of crab which lives in the abandoned shell of a shellfish.

'**hēro** *n* one admired (by many) for his brave deeds; the chief male person in a story *etc*: – *pl* **'heroes**, *fem* **heroine** ['herōin]. – *adj* **he'roic** brave as a hero; of heroes. – *n* **'heroism** bravery.

'heron *n* a type of large water bird, with long legs and neck.

'herring *n* an eatable sea fish: – *pls* **'herring, 'herrings**.

hers, herself *see* **her**.

hertz *n* a unit of frequency, used of radio waves *etc*.

hesitate ['hezitāt] *v* to pause because of uncertainty; to be unwilling (to do something). – *ns* **'hesitancy, hesi'tation**. – *adj* **'hesitant**.

'hessian *n* a type of coarse cloth.

het: het up (*coll*) excited.

hew *v* to cut with blows; to shape with blows: – *pt* **hewed**, *pp* **hewed, hewn**.

'hexagon *n* a six-sided figure. – *adj* **hex'agonal**.

heyday ['hādā] *n* the time of greatest strength, the prime.

'hibernate *v* to pass the winter in rest, as some animals do. – *ns* **hiber'nation, 'hibernator**.

hiccup, hiccough ['hikup] *n* a sharp gasp, caused by laughing, eating, drinking; (*pl*) a fit of such gasping. – Also *v*.

'hickory *n* a N. American tree.

hide *v* to put or keep out of sight: – *pt* **hid** [hid], *pp* **'hidden**. – *n* a place of hiding from which birds *etc* are watched; the skin of an animal. – *adj* **'hidden** out of sight; unknown. – *n* **'hiding** a thrashing. – *adj* **'hidebound** (of persons *etc*) not open to new ideas.

hideous ['hidiəs] *adj* frightful; very ugly.

hierarchy ['hirärki] *n* a number of things or persons arranged in order of rank.

hieroglyphics [hirə'glifiks] *npl* ancient Egyptian writing, in which pictures are used as letters; writing difficult to read.

'hi-fi short for **high fidelity**.

higgledy-piggledy ['higldi'pigldi] *adv, adj* in great disorder.

high [hī] *adj* raised far above; of (great) extent upward, tall; well up on any scale of measurement, judgement, rank *etc*; great, large: *high hopes: high prices*; (of sound) shrill, acute in pitch; (of food, *esp* meat) beginning to go bad. – *adv* far above in the air; well up on any scale; to a high degree. – *adv* **'highly** very: *highly delighted*; in a high position or degree. – *n* **'highness** height; **'Highness** a title of a king *etc*. – *adj* **'high-born** of noble birth. – *ns* **'highbrow** a person of intellectual tastes; **High Court** a supreme court. –

adjs **'high-ex'plosive** (of shells, bombs) causing great damage; **high fidelity** reproducing sound very clearly; **high-'flown** (of language, style) using words that sound too grand or pompous; **'high-'handed** (of actions) done without thought for others. – *ns* **'Highlands** a mountainous region, *esp* the north of Scotland; **'Highlander** one who comes from the Highlands; **'highlight** a bright spot or area in a picture; a colour (in hair *etc*) made obvious by bright light; (most) memorable event or experience. – *adj* **'highly-'strung** nervous, easily excited. – *n* **'highroad** a main road. – *adj* **'high-'spirited** bold, lively. – *ns* **high tea** a cooked meal in the late afternoon; **high tide, high water** the time when the tide is farthest up the shore; **high treason** the crime of acting against the safety of one's own country; **'highway** the public road; **'highwayman** (*hist*) a robber who attacks people on the public road. – **Highway Code** a set of official rules for road users in Britain; **the high seas** the open seas.

'hijack *v* to steal (a car, aeroplane *etc*) while it is moving; to force the driver or pilot (of a vehicle) to head for a place chosen by the **'hijacker**. – Also *n*.

hike *v* to travel on foot. – Also *n*. – *n* **'hiker**.

hi'lārious *adj* very funny; very merry. – *n* **hi'larity** [hi'larəti].

hill *n* a mound of high land, less high than a mountain. – *adj* **'hilly**. – *n* **'hillock** a small hill.

hilt *n* the handle, *esp* of a sword. – **up to the hilt** thoroughly, completely.

him *pron* a male person already spoken about (used only as the object in a sentence): *help him: say to him.* – *pron* **him'self** used reflexively. *He has cut himself*; used for emphasis. *He himself could not do the job but his friend could.*

hind *n* a female deer. – *adj* placed behind. – *adj* **'hindmost** farthest behind. – *n* **'hindsight** wisdom or knowledge got only after something has happened.

'hinder *v* to keep back, delay, prevent. – *n* **'hindrance** something that hinders.

hinge *n* a joint on which a door, lid *etc* turns. – *v* to move on a hinge; to depend (on). *Everything hinges on the weather.*

hint *n* a mention which suggests one meaning without stating it clearly; a slight impression, or one not clearly stated: *a hint of fear in his words.* – Also *v*. *He hinted that he might go.*

'**hinterland** *n* the district lying inland from the coast.

hip *n* the part of the side of the body just below the waist; the fruit of the (wild) rose.

hippo'potamus *n* a large African animal living in and near rivers: – *pls* **hippo-'potamuses, hippo'potami**.

'**hire** *n* money paid for work done, or for the use of something belonging to another person. – *v* to give or get the use of something by paying money. – *n* '**hire-'purchase** a way of buying an article by paying for it in weekly or monthly parts or instalments.

'**hirsute** *adj* hairy, shaggy.

his [hiz] *adj* belonging to him: *his book*. – *pron. This book is his.*

hiss *v* to make a sound like a snake. – *n* such a sound, made to show anger or displeasure: – *pl* '**hisses**.

'**history** *n* the study of the past; a description in speech or (*esp*) writing of past events, ways of living *etc*: – *pl* '**histories**. – *n* **historian** [his'tōriən] one who writes history. – *adjs* **his'toric** [his'torik] important, likely to be remembered; **his'torical** of history; true of something in the past.

histri'onic *adj* having to do with stage-acting or actors. – *npl* **histri'onics** a dramatically exaggerated display of strong feeling.

hit *v* to strike with a blow *etc*; (with **upon**) to come upon, discover: – *pres p* '**hitting**, *pt* **hit**. – *n* a blow; a stroke; a shot which hits a target; a success (*esp* a successful song, recording, play *etc*). – *n* **hit parade** (weekly) list of best-selling records.

hitch *v* to fasten (by a hook *etc*); to lift with a jerk; to hitch-hike. – *n* a jerk; an unexpected stop or delay; one of several kinds of knot: – *pl* '**hitches**. – *v* '**hitch-hike** to travel by relying on lifts in other people's vehicles. – *n* '**hitch-hiker**.

hither ['hidhər] *adv* to this place. – *adv* '**hither'to** up till now. – **hither and thither** back and forward.

hive *n* a place where bees live; a busy place: *hive of industry*.

hoard *n* a (hidden) store (of treasure, food *etc*). – *v* to store up (in secret).

'**hoarding** *n* a fence of boards.

hoarse *adj* having a harsh voice, as from a cold or cough.

'**hoary** *adj* white with age; of great age. – *n* '**hoar-frost** white frost.

hoax *n* a trick played to deceive people: – *pl* '**hoaxes**. – *v* to play a hoax on.

hob *n* a small shelf next to a fireplace on which pans *etc* may be kept hot; the top of an electric *etc* stove.

'**hobble** *v* to walk with difficulty with short steps. – Also *n*.

'**hobby** *n* a favourite way of passing one's spare time: – *pl* '**hobbies**. – *n* '**hobby-horse** a wooden horse on rockers or in a merry-go-round; a favourite subject, which one continually talks about.

'**hobgoblin** *n* (*myth*) a mischievous fairy.

'**hobnail** *n* a big-headed nail used for horseshoes and in the soles of heavy boots.

'**hobnob** *v* to be on very friendly terms (with): – *pt* '**hobnobbed**.

hock *n* a kind of white wine; a joint on the hind leg of an animal, below the knee.

'**hockey** *n* an eleven-a-side ball game played with clubs curved at one end.

'**hōcus-'pōcus** *n* a juggler's trick; deception, trickery.

hod *n* a wooden trough on a pole, for carrying bricks and mortar; a container for coal.

hoe *n* a tool used for weeding, loosening earth *etc*. – *v* to use a hoe.

hog *n* a pig. – *v* (*coll*) to take or use selfishly: – *pt* **hogged**.

'**Hogmanay** *n* (in Scotland) the last day of the year (December 31) when many parties are held and people visit each other.

hoist *v* to lift, to raise. – *n* a lift, an elevator for goods.

hōld *v* to keep in one's hand or power; to have; to contain; to think, believe; to cause to take place: *hold a meeting*; to apply (still). *That rule doesn't hold any longer*; celebrate: *not to hold Christmas*: – *pt* **held**. – *n* grip, grasp; influence. *He has a hold over the others*; (in ships) a large space where cargo is carried. – *ns* '**holder** something made to hold something else; one who holds; '**holding** the amount held (*eg* land, shares in a company). – *ns* '**holdall** a (large) bag with a zip; '**holdup** an attack with intent to rob. – **hold forth** to speak at length; **hold good** to be true; **hold out** to continue to fight; **hold over** to keep till later; **hold up** to support; to hinder; to attack and demand money from.

hole *n* an opening in something solid; a pit or burrow; a miserable place; (*coll*) a difficulty.

'**holiday** *n* a day (or longer time) of rest and amusement.

hollow ['holō] *adj* having empty space inside, not solid; fake, unreal: *a hollow victory*. – *n* a sunken place; a dip in the land. – *v* to scoop (out).

'**holly** *n* a type of evergreen shrub with scarlet berries and prickly leaves.

'**hollyhock** *n* a type of tall garden plant.

'**holocaust** *n* a great destruction (by fire).

'**holster** *n* the (leather) case for a pistol.

holt *n* an otter's den.

'**holy** *adj* of or like God; religious; set apart for use in worshipping God. – *n* '**holiness** the state of being holy. – *n* **Holy Writ** the Bible.

'**homage** *n* a sign of respect: *to pay homage to the king.*

home *n* the place where one *usu* lives or where one's family lives; the place from which anything comes originally. *America is the home of jazz*; a place where children or elderly or sick people live and are looked after. – *adj* of one's dwelling place or one's country. – *adv* to one's home; to the full length. *He drove the nail home.* – *adjs* '**homely** plain but pleasant; (*US*) plain, not attractive; '**homing** (*esp* of pigeons) having the habit of making for home. – *npl* **home economics** the study of how to run a home. – *adj* '**home-'made** made at home. – *n* **Home Secretary** (in Britain) the government minister who looks after matters relating to law and order, immigration *etc*. – *adj* '**homesick** longing for home. – *ns* **homestead** ['hōmsted] farmhouse; **home truth** a plain statement of something true but unpleasant made to a person's face. – *adv* '**homewards** towards home. – *n* '**homework** work (*usu* for school) done at home. – **bring home** to make (someone) realize (something).

'**homicide** *n* the killing of a human being; one who kills a human being. – *adj* **homi'cidal**.

ho'mogenize *v* to treat (milk) so that the cream does not separate itself and rise to the surface. – *n* **ho'mogeni'zation**.

'**homonyms** *npl* words having the same sound but a different meaning (*eg there, their*).

hone *v* to sharpen (a knife *etc*).

honest ['onist] *adj* truthful; not inclined to steal, cheat *etc*. – *n* '**honesty**.

honey ['huni] *n* a sweet, thick fluid made by bees from the nectar of flowers. – *n* '**honeycomb** a network of wax cells in which bees store honey. – *adj* '**honeycombed** having holes like the cells in an empty honeycomb. – *ns* '**honeymoon** a holiday spent immediately after marriage; '**honeysuckle** a climbing shrub with sweet-smelling flowers.

honk *n* a noise like the cry of the wild goose or the sound of a motor horn. – Also *v*.

honorary ['onərəri] *adj* done to give honour; acting without payment. – *n* **hono'rārium** a gift or fee for services not paid for by wages.

honour, (*US*) **honor** ['onər] *n* respect for truth, honesty *etc*; fame, glory; reputation, good name; a title which shows respect: *Your Honour*; a privilege; (often *pl*) recognition given for exceptional achievements *etc*. – *v* to give respect to (what is good); to give high rank to; to pay money when due: *honour a debt.* – *adj* '**honourable** worthy of honour.

hood *n* a covering for the head; anything which covers or protects like a hood; a folding cover over seats in a carriage, car *etc*; (*US*) the bonnet of a car.

'**hoodwink** *v* to deceive.

hoof *n* the horny part on the feet of certain animals (*eg* horses): – *pls* **hooves, hoofs**.

hook *n* a bent piece of metal *etc* for hanging things on (*eg* coats) or for catching things (*eg* fish). – *v* to catch, hold or drag with (anything like) a hook. – *adj* **hooked** curved like a hook; caught (by a hook); (*slang*) addicted to, fascinated by. – **by hook or by crook** by one means or another, whatever the cost.

'**hookah**, '**hooka** *n* a tobacco pipe through which smoke is drawn through water, used by Turks and Arabs.

'**hooligan** *n* a wild, unruly person. – *n* '**hooliganism** unruly behaviour.

hoop *n* a thin ring of wood or metal.

hoopoe ['hōōpōō] *n* a kind of bird with a large crest.

hooray *see* **hurrah**.

hoot *v* to sound a motor horn *etc*; (of an owl) to call, cry; (of persons) to make a similar sound, *esp* in laughter. – *n* the sound made by a motor horn, siren or owl; a shout of scorn *etc*. – *n* '**hooter** a device which makes a hooting sound (*eg* a motor horn).

'**Hoover**® *n* a kind of vacuum cleaner. – *v* '**hoover** to use a vacuum cleaner on (a floor *etc*).

hop *v* to leap on one leg: – *pt* **hopped**. – *n* a short jump on one leg; a climbing plant, the bitter fruits of which are used in brewing beer. – *n* '**hopper** a box or funnel for shaking down corn *etc* to the grinding (or other) machinery. – *n* '**hopscotch** a hopping game over lines drawn on the ground (scotches).

hope *n* a state of mind in which one

expects or wishes good to come; something desired. – v to expect or wish good to happen. – adjs '**hopeful**; '**hopeless** without hope; very bad.

horde [hörd] n a large crowd or group.

ho'rizon n the line which seems to be formed by the meeting of the earth and sky; the limit of what a person can see or understand. – adj **hori'zontal** lying level or flat.

horn n a hard growth on the heads of certain animals (eg oxen, sheep, deer); something made of horn or curved or sticking out like an animal's horn; part of a motor car which gives a warning sound; a kind of wind instrument, once made of horn, now of brass. – adjs **horned** having horns or something like horns; '**horny** hard like horn.

'**hornet** n a kind of large wasp.

'**hornpipe** n a lively sailor's dance.

'**horoscope** n the telling of a person's fortune by studying the position of the stars at his birth.

'**horror** n great fear, terror; something which causes fear; someone who causes great dislike (esp a child). – adjs '**horrible** causing horror; very unpleasant or bad; '**horrid** hateful; very unpleasant. – v '**horrify** to frighten greatly; to shock. I was horrified by the child's behaviour: – pt '**horrified**.

horse n a type of four-footed animal with hooves and a mane; a wooden frame for hanging clothes to dry; an apparatus for vaulting etc in a gymnasium. – ns '**horse-'chestnut** a type of tree or its brown, shiny nut; '**horsefly** a large fly which bites; **horse laugh** a loud, harsh laugh; '**horseplay** rough play, fooling around; '**horsepower** a unit of mechanical power used in giving power of cars etc (usu shortened to **h.p.**); '**horse-radish** a type of plant, the root of which has a sharp taste, used in sauces; '**horseshoe** a shoe for horses, made of a curved piece of iron; a horseshoe-shaped thing.

'**horticulture** n the study and art of gardening. – adj **horti'cultural** having to do with gardening. – n **horti'culturist** one skilled in gardening.

hosanna [hə'zanə] n an exclamation of praise to God.

hose [hōz] n a covering for the legs or feet: – pl **hose**; a tubing of rubber etc for carrying water: – pl '**hoses**. – n **hosiery** ['hōziəri] knitted goods (such as tights).

hospice ['hospis] n a home which provides special nursing care for incurable invalids.

hos'pitable adj showing kindness to guests or strangers. – n **hospi'tality** a friendly welcome often including food, drink etc for guests or strangers.

'**hospital** n a building for the treatment of the ill and injured.

hōst n one who welcomes and entertains guests; an innkeeper or hotelkeeper: – fem '**hostess**; a very large number.

'**hostage** n a person held prisoner by an enemy or opponent to make sure that an agreement will be kept to or a condition fulfilled.

'**hostel** n a building providing rooms for students etc. – ns '**hostelry** an inn: – pl '**hostelries**; **hostler, ostler** ['oslər] (hist) the servant who looks after the horses at an inn.

'**hostile** adj of an enemy; not friendly; showing dislike or opposition (to). – n **hostility** [hos'tiləti] unfriendliness; opposition; the state of being an enemy; (pl) **hos'tilities** acts of warfare.

hot adj very warm; (of food) having much spice; passionate; radioactive; (slang) stolen; (slang) not safe: – comp '**hotter**, superl '**hottest**. – n '**hotbed** a place where there is much disease, wickedness etc: a hotbed of rebellion. – adj '**hot-'blooded** passionate, easily roused to anger etc. – n '**hot-'dog** a hot sausage in a roll. – adv '**hot-foot** in great haste. – adj '**hot-'headed** inclined to act rashly without thinking. – ns '**hothouse** a heated glasshouse for plants; **hot line** a direct telephone line between heads of government. – **in(to) hot water** in(to) trouble.

'**hotchpotch** n a confused mixture.

ho'tel n a building where travellers etc may stay for payment.

hound n a dog used in hunting. – v to hunt, pursue.

hour [owr] n sixty minutes, the 24th part of a day; a time or occasion: the hour of reckoning. – adj '**hourly** happening or done every hour. – Also adv. – n '**hour-glass** an instrument for measuring the hours by the running of sand from one glass into another.

house n a building in which people (often a single family) live; a family household; a business firm; a building where school boarders stay. – v **house** [howz] to provide a house for; to shelter. – n '**housing** accommodation eg houses, flats etc; a casing or covering for machines etc. – ns **houseboat** ['howsbōt] a river barge with a cabin for living in; '**housebreaker** a person who breaks into a house to steal;

'**household** the people who live together in a house; a family; '**householder** one who owns or pays the rent of a house; the chief person in a family; '**housekeeper** one paid to look after the running of a house; '**housewarming** a party held when someone moves into a new house; '**housewife** a woman who looks after a house and her husband and family. – **a household word** something which everyone is talking about.

'**hovel** n a small dirty dwelling.

'**hover** v (of birds etc) to remain in the air in the same spot; to stay near, linger (about); to be undecided or uncertain. – n '**hovercraft** a craft able to travel over land or sea supported on a cushion of air.

how [how] adv in what manner. How is she dressed?; to what extent. How old are you?; to a great extent. How beautifully she sings; by what means. How do you do it?; in what state of health, condition etc. How are you? – adv **how'ever** no matter how; in spite of that.

howdah ['howdə] n a seat fixed on an elephant's back.

howitzer ['howɪtsər] n a short cannon used to attack a besieged town or trench.

howl [howl] v to make a long, loud sound like that of a dog or wolf; to yell (as in pain, anger, joy). – Also n. – n '**howler** (coll) a very silly mistake.

hub n the centre part of a wheel through which the axle passes; the centre of much traffic, business etc.

'**hubbub** n a confused sound of many voices.

'**huddle** v to crowd together. – n a close group.

hue n colour. – **hue and cry** an alarm and general chase.

huff n a fit of bad temper and sulking. – adj '**huffy**.

hug v to hold tightly with the arms; to keep close to. The ships hug the shore: – pt **hugged**.

huge [hūj] adj of great size. – n '**hugeness**.

hula-hoop ['hōōləhōōp] n a light hoop for spinning round the waist.

hulk n an old ship unfit for use; anything big and clumsy. – adj '**hulking** big and clumsy.

hull n the body or framework of a ship.

hullaba'loo n noisy disturbance.

hullo see **hello**.

hum v to make a buzzing sound like that of bees; to sing with the lips shut; (of a place etc) to be noisily busy: – pt **hummed**. – ns **hum,** '**humming** the noise of bees; any buzzing, droning sound. – n '**humming-bird** a type of small brightly-coloured bird whose rapidly moving wings make a humming noise.

'**hūman** adj having to do with mankind as opposed to God or animals; (of persons) having the qualities, feelings etc natural to mankind. – n a man, woman or child. – adj **humane** [hū'mān] kind, showing mercy, gentle. – ns **humanism** ['hūmənizəm] a set of ideas about or interest in ethics and mankind, not including religious belief; '**humanist**. – adj **hu'mani'tārian** kind to one's fellowmen. – n **hu'mani-ty** men and women in general; kindness, gentleness.

'**humble** adj modest, meek; not of high rank, unimportant. – v to make to feel low and unimportant. – **eat humble pie** to acknowledge openly that one has made a mistake.

'**humbug** n a fraud; nonsense; a kind of hard sweet.

'**humdrum** adj dull, not exciting.

'**hūmid** adj (of air, climate) moist, damp. – n **hu'midity** moisture; amount of wetness.

hū'mility n humble state of mind, meekness. – v **hu'miliate** to make to feel humble or ashamed, hurt someone's pride. – adj **hu'miliating**. – n **humili'ation** something which humiliates; shame.

humour, (US) **humor** ['hūmər] n the ability to see things as amusing or ridiculous (also **sense of humour**); funniness; the amusing side of anything; one's state of mind, temper, mood. – v to do as another wishes. – n '**humorist** one who can bring out the amusing side of things. – adj '**humorous** funny, causing laughter.

hump n a lump (eg on the back). – n '**humpback** a back with a hump; a person with a hump on his back. – adj '**humpbacked** having a hump on the back; (of a bridge etc) rising and falling so as to form a hump shape.

'**hūmus** n soil made of rotted leaves etc.

hunch n a hump; a suspicion that something is untrue or is going to happen etc: – pl '**hunches**. – n '**hunchback** humpback. – adj '**hunchbacked** humpbacked.

hundred ['hundrəd] n the number 100. – adj 100 in number. – adj '**hundredth** the last of a hundred (things etc). – n one of a hundred equal parts.

hundredweight ['hundrədwāt] *n* 112 lb, 50·8 kilogrammes (*usu* written **cwt**).

hunger ['hungər] *n* desire for food; a strong desire for anything. – *v* to go without food; to long (for). – *adj* '**hungry** wanting or needing food. – *n* '**hunger-strike** a refusal to eat (*eg* by prisoners) as a protest.

hunt *v* to chase animals or birds for food or for sport; to search (for). – *n* chasing wild animals; a search. – *n* '**hunter** one who hunts: – *fem* '**huntress**; a horse trained for hunting. – *n* '**huntsman** one who hunts.

'**hurdle** *n* a frame to be jumped over in a race; any difficulty which must be overcome.

'**hurdy'gurdy** *n* a musical instrument played by turning a handle, a hand-organ, a barrel organ.

hurl *v* to throw with force.

'**hurly'burly** *n* a great stir, uproar.

hur'rah, hur'ray, hoo'ray *interj* a shout of joy, approval *etc*.

'**hurricane** *n* a violent storm of wind blowing at a speed of over 75 miles (120 kilometres) per hour. – *n* **hurricane lamp** a lamp specially made to keep alight in strong wind.

'**hurry** *v* to act or move quickly; to make (someone) act *etc* quickly: – *pt* '**hurried**. – *n* eagerness to act or move quickly, haste. – *adj* '**hurried** done in a hurry.

hurt *v* to cause pain or distress; to wound; to damage. – *n* a wound; damage. – *adj* '**hurtful** causing pain, distress or damage.

'**hurtle** *v* to (cause to) move at great speed.

husband ['huzbənd] *n* a married man (the partner of a **wife**). – *v* to spend or use (*eg* one's money, strength) carefully. – *n* '**husbandry** farming; care with one's money, thrift.

hush *inter* be quiet! – *n* (*coll*) silence. – *v* to make quiet. – *adj* '**hush-'hush** (*coll*) top secret. – **hush up** to stop (a scandal *etc*) becoming public.

husk *n* the dry thin covering of certain fruits and seeds.

'**husky** *adj* (of the voice) hoarse, rough in sound; big and strong. – *n* a Canadian sledge dog: – *pl* '**huskies**.

hussar [hə'zär] *n* a light-armed horse soldier.

'**hussy** *n* a forward, cheeky girl: – *pl* '**hussies**.

'**hustings** *npl* speeches, campaigning *etc* which take place just before an election.

hustle ['husl] *v* to push rudely; to hurry. – Also *n*.

hut *n* a small wooden building; a simple dwelling place.

hutch *n* a box in which pet rabbits are housed: – *pl* '**hutches**.

'**hyacinth** *n* a type of sweet-smelling flower which grows from a bulb.

hyaena *see* **hyena**.

'**hybrid** *n* something (*usu* an animal or plant) made or bred from two different kinds (*eg* a mule, which is a hybrid from a horse and an ass); a word formed of parts from different languages. – Also *adj*.

'**hydra** *n* (*myth*) a many-headed water serpent that grew two heads for each one cut off; a water creature that can divide and redivide itself.

'**hydrant** *n* a connection to which a hose can be attached to draw water off the main water supply.

hy'draulic *adj* carrying water; worked by water or other fluid.

hydro- *prefix* water. – *n* '**hydro** (short for **hydro'pathic**) a type of hotel (originally with special swimming baths *etc* for health improvements); **hydroelec'tricity** electricity got from water-power. – *adj* **hydroe'lectric**.

'**hydrogen** *n* an element, the lightest gas, which with oxygen makes up water. – *n* **hydrogen bomb** an exceedingly powerful bomb using hydrogen.

hydro'phobia *n* fear of water, a symptom of rabies; rabies.

hyena, hyaena [hī'ēnə] *n* a dog-like wild animal with a howl sounding like laughter.

hygiene ['hījēn] *n* (the study of) cleanliness as a means to health. – *adj* **hy'gienic**.

hymn [him] *n* a song of praise, *esp* one sung to God. – *ns* **hymnal** ['himnəl], '**hymnary** a book of hymns: – *pl* '**hymnaries**.

hyper- *prefix* to a greater extent than usual, excessive as in **hyper'active**.

hyperbole [hī'pərbəli] *n* exaggeration. – *adj* **hyper'bolical**.

'**hypermarket** *n* a very large supermarket.

'**hyphen** *n* a short stroke (-) used to link or separate parts of a word or phrase: *sweet-and-sour: re-create*.

'**hypnotize** *v* to put a person into a sleep-like state in which he obeys suggestions. – *n* **hyp'nosis** a hypnotized state; hypnotism. – *adj* **hypnotic** [hip'notik] of hypnosis or hypnotism; causing hypnosis or a sleep-like state. – *ns* '**hypnotism** the production of a hypnotized state; hypnosis; '**hyp-notist**.

hȳpō- *prefix* below, under.

hypochondria [hipɔ'kondriə] *n* over-anxiety about one's own health. – *n, adj* **hypo'chondriac**.

hypocrite ['hipɔkrit] *n* a person who pretends to be good but is not. – *n* **hy'pocrisy** false pretence of goodness. – *adj* **hypo'critical**.

hȳpo'dermic *n* a hypodermic syringe. – *n* **hypodermic syringe** an instrument with a fine, hollow needle

(hypodermic needle) for giving an injection of a drug just below the skin.

hȳ'potenūse *n* the longest side of a right-angled triangle.

hȳ'pothesis *n* something taken as true (for the sake of argument): – *pl* **hy'pothesēs**. – *adj* **hypo'thetical** supposed.

hys'tēria *n* nervous excitement causing uncontrollable laughter, crying *etc*; a nervous illness. – *npl* **hysterics** [his'teriks] a fit of hysteria. – *adj* **hys'terical**.

I

I [i] *pron* the word used by a speaker or writer in mentioning himself (as the subject of a verb). *He and I went together.*

'**ibex** *n* a wild mountain goat: – *pl* '**ibexes**.

ice *n* frozen water; ice cream. – *v* to cover with icing; to freeze. – *n* '**icing** melted sugar, flavoured and allowed to set. – *adj* '**icy** covered with ice; very cold. – *adv* '**icily**. – *ns* **ice age** an age when the earth was mostly covered with ice; '**iceberg** a huge mass of floating ice; '**icebox** (*US*) refrigerator; **ice cream** a sweet creamy mixture, flavoured and frozen; **ice floe** a piece of floating ice; **ice hockey** hockey played with a rubber disc (**puck**) on an ice rink. – **dry ice** solid carbon dioxide.

ichthyology [ikthi'olɔji] *n* the study of fishes.

'**icicle** *n* a hanging, pointed piece of ice formed by the freezing of dropping water.

'**icon**, '**ikon** *n* a painted or mosaic image (*eg* of Christ or of a saint).

i'conoclasm *n* the act of breaking images; the attacking of long established beliefs.

I'd [id] short for **I would, I should, I had**. *I'd sooner go than stay.*

idea [i'dēə] *n* a thought, notion; mental picture; plan.

ideal [i'dēəl] *adj* perfect; existing in imagination only (opposite of **real**). – *n* that which is highest and best; a standard of perfection. – *ns* **i'dealism; i'dealist** one who thinks that perfection can be reached. – *v* **i'dealize** to think of as perfect. – *n* **ideali'zation**. – *adv* **i'deally** in ideal circumstances. *Ideally all under-fives should attend a play group.*

i'dentifȳ *v* to (claim to) recognize, prove to be the same. *He identified the man as his attacker*; to think of as the same. *He identifies money with happiness*: – *pt* **i'dentified**. – *n* **identifi'cation**. – *adj* **i'dentical** the same in all details. – **identify (oneself) with** to feel close to or involved with.

i'dentikit picture *n* a rough picture of a wanted person which police put together from descriptions.

i'dentity *n* who or what a person or thing is; the state of being the same: – *pl* **i'dentities**.

idē'ology *n* a set of (usually political) ideas: – *pl* **ide'ologies**. – *adj* **ideo'logical**.

idiocy *see* '**idiot**.

'**idiom** *n* a common form of expression whose meaning cannot be guessed from the actual words. 'The boy *turned up* unexpectedly one day'. – *adj* **idio'matic**.

idio'syncrasy *n* a personal oddness of behaviour: – *pl* **idio'syncrasies**. – *adj* **idiosyn'cratic**.

'**idiot** *n* a feeble-minded person; a fool. – *n* '**idiocy** feeble-mindedness, foolishness. – *adj* **idi'otic**.

'**idle** *adj* without work to do; lazy; meaningless: *idle chatter*. – *v* to spend (time) in doing nothing; (of an engine) to run without doing any work. – *ns* '**idler; 'idleness**. – *adv* '**idly**.

'**idol** *n* an image worshipped as a god; a person or thing loved or honoured too much. – *v* '**idolize** to love (too) greatly.

idyllic [i'dilik] *adj* very happy in a simple way.

if *conj* on condition that, supposing that. *If you go, he will go*; whether. *I don't know if he's going.*

'**igloo** *n* an Eskimo's snow hut.

igneous ['igniəs] *adj* having to do with fire; (of rock) formed by the action of great heat within the earth.

ig'nite *v* to set on fire; to catch fire. – *n* **ig'nition** the act of setting on fire or catching fire; the sparking part of a motor engine.

ig'nōble *adj* dishonourable; of low birth.

'**ignominy** *n* (public) disgrace. – *adj* **igno'minious** dishonourable, disgraceful.

igno'rāmus *n* an ignorant person.

ig'nore *v* to take no notice of. – *adj* '**ignorant** knowing very little; (with **of**) not knowing, not aware. – *n* '**ignorance**.

iguana [i'gwänə] *n* a type of tree lizard.

ikon *see* **icon**.

I'll [il] short for **I shall, I will**. *I'll be there soon.*

ill *adj* unwell; evil, bad; unlucky. – *adv* badly. – *n* evil; (*pl*) misfortunes. – *n* '**illness** disease, sickness. – *adjs* '**ill-at-'ease** uncomfortable; '**ill-'gotten** (of profits *etc*) obtained in a wrongful way; '**ill-'humoured**, '**ill-'natured** bad-tempered; '**ill-'starred** unlucky. – *ns* '**ill-'will**, '**ill-'feeling** dislike, resentment. – *vs* '**ill-'treat**, '**ill-'use** to treat badly.

il'lēgal *adj* against the law. – *n* **ille'gality**: – *pl* **ille'galities**.

il'legible *adj* (almost) impossible to read, indistinct.

ille'gitimate *adj* born of parents not married to each other.

il'licit *adj* unlawful, forbidden.

il'literate *adj* not able to read or write. – *n* **il'literacy**.

il'logical *adj* not logical, not showing sound reasoning.

il'lūminate *v* to light up; to make (more) clear. – *adj* **il'luminated** (of a document *etc*) decorated with (coloured) lettering *etc*. – *n* **illumi'nation**; (*pl*) a decorative display of lights.

illusion [i'loozhən] *n* something which deceives the mind or eye; a mistaken belief. – *adjs* **il'lusive**; **il'lusory**.

'**illustrate** *v* to draw pictures for (a book *etc*); to explain, show (through examples, diagrams, slides *etc*). – *n* **illus-'tration** a picture in a book *etc*; an example which illustrates. – *adj* '**illus-trative**. – *n* '**illustrator** one who illustrates.

il'lustrious *adj* famous, distinguished.

I'm [im] short for **I am**. *I'm older now.*

'**image** *n* a likeness made of someone or something; a striking likeness; a picture in the mind; public reputation. – *n* '**imagery** pictures suggested by words that help to make a piece of writing more vivid.

i'magine *v* to form a picture in the mind often of something that is not present or does not exist; to think, suppose. – *adj* **i'maginary** existing only in the imagination, not real. – *n* **i'magi'nation** the power of forming pictures in the mind (of things not present); the creative ability of an artist *etc*. – *adj* **i'maginative** having a lively imagination; done with imagination: *an imaginative piece of writing.*

imago *see* **pupa**.

imbecile ['imbəsēl] *n* a feeble-minded person; a fool. – *n* **imbecility** [imbə'siləti] feeble-mindedness, stupidity.

im'bibe *v* to drink (in).

im'būe *v* to fill the mind (with). *The general's actions imbued his troops with feelings of patriotism.*

'**imitate** *v* to try to be the same as, to copy. – *n* **imi'tation** a copy. – *adj* made to look like: *imitation leather*. – *n* '**imitator**.

im'maculate *adj* spotless; very clean and neat.

imma'tērial *adj* of little importance.

imma'tūre *adj* not mature.

im'mēdiate *adj* happening straight away: *immediate reaction*; close: *immediate family*; direct: *his immediate successor*. – *adv* **im'mediately** without delay. – *n* **im'mediacy**.

imme'morial *adj* going further back in time than can be remembered.

im'mense *adj* very large. – *n* **im'mensity**.

im'merse *v* to plunge into liquid. – *n* **im'mersion**. – *n* **immersion heater** an electric water-heating instrument (inside the hot water tank). – **immerse oneself in** to give one's whole attention to.

'**immigrate** *v* to come into a country and settle there. – *n* **immi'gration**. – *adj, n* '**immigrant** (of) one who immigrates.

'**imminent** *adj* about to happen: *imminent danger*.

im'mōbile *adj* without moving; not easily moved. – *n* **immo'bility**. – *v* **im'mobilize** put out of action.

immoderate [i'modərət] *adj* going beyond reasonable limits.

im'moral *adj* wrong, evil; indecent: *immoral suggestions*. – *n* **immo'rality**.

im'mortal *adj* living for ever; famous for ever. – *n* **immor'tality** unending life or fame. – *v* **im'mortalize** to make

immovable

immortal or famous for ever.

immovable [i'mōōvəbl] *adj* not able to be moved or changed.

im'mūne *adj* not likely to catch (a disease) or be affected by: *immune to measles*: *immune to his charm.* – *n* **im'munity.** – *v* **'immunize** to make a person immune from (a disease) (*esp* by an injection of something to fight the disease).

imp *n* a mischievous child or fairy. – *adj* **'impish.**

'impact *n* the blow of one thing striking another; a collision; strong effect. *Her appearance made an impact on the audience.* – *v* **im'pact** to press firmly together.

im'pair *v* to damage, weaken. – *n* **im'pairment.**

im'pala *n* a large African antelope.

im'pale *v* to pierce through (with a spear *etc*).

im'part *v* to tell to others (what one knows).

im'partial *adj* not favouring one side more than another; just. – *n* **imparti'ality.**

im'passable *adj* (of roads *etc*) not able to be passed.

impasse [am'päs] *n* a situation from which there seems to be no way out.

im'passioned *adj* moved by strong feeling.

im'passive *adj* not easily moved either by pleasure or pain.

impatient [im'pāshənt] *adj* restlessly eager; short-tempered. – *n* **im'patience.**

im'peach *v* to accuse publicly (*esp* a high official) of misconduct. – *n* **im'peachment.**

im'peccable *adj* faultless. – *adv* **im'peccably**: *impeccably dressed.*

impe'cūnious *adj* having no money.

im'pede *v* to hinder, keep back. – *n* **impediment** [im'pedimənt] a hindrance; a defect in a person's speech *eg* a stutter or stammer.

im'pel *v* to urge; to drive on: – *pt* **im'pelled.**

im'pending *adj* about to happen: *an impending storm.*

im'perative *adj* necessary, urgent; (*gram*) expressing command.

imper'ceptible *adj* so small as not to be noticed.

im'perfect *adj* having a fault or flaw, not perfect. – *n* **imper'fection** a fault or a flaw.

im'pērial *adj* of an emperor or empire. – *ns* **im'perialism** the policy of gaining the territory of, and ruling other

impose

people; **im'perialist.**

im'peril *v* to put in danger: – *pt* **im'perilled.**

im'pērious *adj* having an air of authority, haughty.

impermeable [im'pərmiəbl] *adj* not able to be passed through. *Clay is impermeable by water.*

im'personal *adj* not showing or influenced by personal feelings; not connected with any person.

im'personate *v* to dress up as, or act the part of, someone. – *ns* **imperso'nation; im'personator.**

im'pertinent *adj* cheeky, bad-mannered; not pertinent. – *n* **im'pertinence.**

imper'turbable *adj* not easily worried, calm.

im'pervious *adj* (with **to**) able to remain unaffected by. *He is impervious to hints.*

impe'tigo *n* a kind of skin disease.

im'petūous *adj* rushing into action, rash. – *n* **impetu'osity.**

'impetus *n* moving force. *The impetus of the blow sent him flying*; impulse.

im'piety *n* lack of respect for holy things. – *adj* **impious** ['impiəs] wicked.

im'pinge *v* (with **on, upon**) come in contact with; trespass (on) (*eg* another person's rights or privacy).

im'placable *adj* not able to be soothed or calmed.

im'plant *v* to fix in, plant firmly. – Also *n.*

'implement *n* a tool (*eg* a spade, a painter's brush). – *v* to carry out, to fulfil (*eg* a promise).

'implicate *v* to bring in, involve (a person). *The statements of other gang members implicate you in the crime.* – *n* **impli'cation** the act of implicating; something meant though not actually said.

im'plicit *adj* understood, meant though not actually said; unquestioning: *implicit obedience.*

im'plȳ *v* to suggest. *His silence implied disapproval*: – *pt* **im'plied.**

impo'lite *adj* not polite, rude.

im'port *v* to bring in (goods) from abroad (for sale). – *ns* **'import** act of importing; something imported; meaning; importance; **impor'tation** act of importing.

im'portant *adj* worth taking notice of; special. – *n* **im'portance.**

impor'tūne *v* to keep asking for something. – *adj* **im'portunate** repeatedly asking. – *n* **impor'tunity.**

im'pose *v* to place something (as a tax burden *etc*) on (someone or

145

something); (with **on**) to take advantage (of a person), to deceive. – *adj* im'**posing** impressive, making much show. – *n* impo'**sition** a burden; an exercise given as a punishment.

im'**possible** *adj* not able to be done or to happen; (of a person *etc*) not able to be dealt with, intolerable. – *n* impossi-'**bility**.

im'**postor** *n* one who pretends to be someone else in order to deceive. – *n* im'**postūre** (the act of) deceiving in this way.

'**impotent** *adj* without power, strength or effectiveness; (of males) without sexual power. – *n* '**impotence**.

im'**pound** *v* to take possession of (something) by law (*eg* furniture in payment of the rent).

im**poverish** [im'povərish] *v* to make (a person *etc*) poor; to make poor in quality. – *n* im'**poverishment**.

im'**practicable** *adj* not able to be done. – *n* im'**practica'bility**.

im'**practical** *adj* lacking common sense. – *n* im**practi'cality**.

im'**pregnable** *adj* too strong to be taken by, or overthrown by, attack.

impre'**sario** *n* the organizer of a (musical) entertainment: – *pl* impre-'**sarios**.

im'**press** *v* to arouse (someone's) interest or admiration; to mark by pressing upon; to fix deeply in the mind. – *n* im'**pression** what a person thinks or feels about something. *The play left a lasting impression on me. My impression is that it's likely to rain*; a mark made by impressing; a quantity of copies of a book printed at one time. – *adj* im'**pressionable** easily influenced or affected. – *n* im'**pressionism** the attempt, in painting, writing, *etc* to reproduce the actual effect of something. – *adj* im'**pressive** having a great effect on the mind.

im'**print** *v* to print; to mark; to set a permanent mark on (the mind *etc*). – *n* '**imprint** that which is imprinted; the printer's name on a book.

imprison [im'prizn] *v* to shut up as in a prison. – *n* im'**prisonment**.

im'**probable** *adj* not likely to happen. – *n* improba'**bility**.

im'**promptū** *adj*, *adv* without preparation or rehearsal.

im'**proper** *adj* not suitable; wrong; indecent. – *n* impro'**priety** something improper: – *pl* impro'**prieties**. – *n* im'**proper fraction** a fraction greater than 1 (as $^5/_4$, $^{21}/_8$).

improve [im'proōv] *v* to make or become better. – *n* im'**provement**.

im'**provident** *adj* taking no thought for future needs. – *n* im'**providence**.

'**improvise** *v* to put together, produce from available materials or on the spur of the moment: *improvised stretcher*: *an improvised tune*. – *n* improvi'**sation**.

'**impūdent** *adj* cheeky, insolent. – *n* '**impudence**.

'**impulse** *n* sudden force such as a push; a sudden urge resulting in sudden action. – *adj* im'**pulsive** acting on impulse, without time to consider. – *n* im'**pulsiveness**.

im'**pūnity** *n* freedom from punishment, injury or loss.

im'**pūre** *adj* mixed with other substances; not clean. – *n* im'**purity**: – *pl* im'**purities**.

im'**pūte** *v* to think of (something blameworthy) as being caused, done *etc* (by someone). – *n* impu'**tation** suggestion of fault, blame.

in *prep* showing position in space or time: *in the garden*: *in the year 1921*; showing state, condition, manner *etc*: *in part*: *in a high voice*. – **be in for** to be trying to get; to be about to receive (something unpleasant).

in- *prefix* into, on, towards as in **in-shore**; not, as in **inaccurate**.

ina'**bility** *n* lack of power, means *etc* (to do something): – *pl* ina'**bilities**.

inaccessible [inək'sesəbl] *adj* not able to be (easily) reached, approached or obtained.

in'**accurate** *adj* not correct; not exact. – *n* in'**accuracy**: – *pl* in'**accuracies**.

in'**active** *adj* not active; not working, doing nothing. – *ns* in'**action** lack of action; inac'**tivity** idleness; rest.

in'**adequate** *adj* not enough; unable to cope (in an emergency *etc*).

inad'**missible** *adj* not allowable.

inad'**vertent** *adj* unintentional. – *adv* inad'**vertently**.

i'**nane** *adj* silly, foolish. – *n* inanity [i'nanəti].

in'**animate** *adj* without life.

in'**applicable** *adj* not applicable.

inap'**prōpriate** *adj* not suitable.

in'**apt** *adj* not apt; unfit or unqualified. — *ns* in'**aptitude**, in'**aptness** unfitness, awkwardness. — *adv* in'**aptly**.

inar'**ticulate** *adj* unable to express oneself (clearly); uttered indistinctly.

inasmuch [inəz'much]: **inasmuch as** *conj* because, since.

inat'**tentive** *adj* not paying attention. – *n* inat'**tention**.

in'**audible** *adj* not loud enough to be heard.

inaugurate

i'naugūrate *v* to make a start on, *usu* with show or ceremony. – *adj* **i'naugural**. – *n* **inaugu'ration**.

inaus'picious *adj* unlucky, unlikely to end in success.

'in'bred *adj* natural; resulting from **'in-'breeding** repeated mating within the family.

in'calcŭlable *adj* not able to be counted or estimated.

incandescent [inkan'desnt] *adj* white-hot.

incan'tation *n* (words sung or said as) a spell.

in'cāpable *adj* unable (to do what is expected); helpless (through drink *etc*).

inca'pacitate *v* to take away power, strength or rights; to disable. – *n* **inca'pacity** inability; disability.

incarcerate [in'kärsərāt] *v* to imprison.

in'carnate *adj* having human form. – *n* **incar'nation** appearance in the form of a human body.

in'cendiary *adj* meant for setting (buildings *etc*) on fire: *an incendiary bomb.*

in'cense *v* to make angry. – *n* **'incense** spices *etc* burned (*esp* in religious ceremonies) to give off a pleasant smell.

in'centive *n* that which encourages one to do something.

in'ception *n* beginning.

in'cessant *adj* going on without pause.

inch *n* one twelfth of a foot (about 2·5 centimetres): – *pl* **'inches**. – *v* to move very gradually.

'incident *n* a happening. – *n* **'incidence** how often or in what quantity a thing occurs; a falling (of a ray of light *etc*). – *adj* **inci'dental** happening in connection with something: *an incidental expense*; casual. – *adv* **inci'dentally** by the way.

incinerate [in'sinərāt] *v* to burn to ashes. – *ns* **incine'ration**; **in'cinerator** an apparatus for burning rubbish *etc*.

in'cipient *adj* beginning to exist: *an incipient dislike.*

in'cision *n* the act of cutting into something; a cut, a gash. – *adj* **in'cisive** (of words, manner *etc*) sharp, clear, firm. – *ns* **in'cisiveness**; **in'cisor** a front tooth.

in'cite *v* to move to action; to urge on. – *n* **in'citement**.

inci'vility *n* impoliteness: – *pl* **inci'vilities**.

in'clement *adj* (of weather) stormy. – *n* **in'clemency**.

in'cline *v* to lean or slope (towards); to

incontinent

bend, bow; to (cause to) have a liking, tendency, (slight) desire for. – *n* **'incline** a slope. – *adj* **in'clined**. – *n* **inclination** [inklə'nāshən] liking, tendency; slope; bending.

include [in'klood] *v* to count in, along with others. – *n* **in'clusion**. – *adj* **in'clusive** including everything mentioned *etc*. *From Tuesday to Thursday inclusive is 3 days.*

incognito [iŋkog'nētō] *adj, adv* with one's identity concealed (by use of a disguise, false name *etc*). – *n* a disguise: – *pl* **incog'nitos**.

inco'hērent *adj* (of a speech *etc*) not coherent, unconnected, rambling; (of a person) speaking in this way. – *n* **inco'herence**.

incom'bustible *adj* not able to be burned by fire.

income ['iŋkəm] *n* a person's earnings; gain or profit.

incoming ['inkumiŋ] *adj* approaching; new, next.

incom'mode *v* to cause bother or trouble to.

incommūni'cado *adj, adv* without means of communicating with others.

in'comparable *adj* without equal. – *adv* **in'comparably**.

incom'patible *adj* (of statements *etc*) contradicting each other; (of persons) bound to disagree. – *n* **incompati-'bility**.

in'competent *adj* not good enough at doing a job. – *n* **in'competence**.

incom'plete *adj* not finished.

incompre'hensible *adj* not able to be understood, puzzling. – *n* **incompre hension**.

incon'ceivable *adj* not able to be imagined or believed.

inconclusive [iŋkən'kloosiv] *adj* not leading to a definite decision or conclusion.

incongruous [iŋ'koŋgroōəs] *adj* not matching well; out of place, unsuitable. – *n* **incon'gruity**: – *pl* **incon-'gruities**.

inconse'quential *adj* unimportant.

inconsiderable [inkən'sidərəbl] *adj* slight, unimportant.

inconsiderate [inkən'sidərət] *adj* not thinking of others.

incon'sistent *adj* not consistent, contradicting.

incon'sōlable *adj* not able to be comforted.

incon'spicūous *adj* not noticeable.

in'constant *adj* often changing. – *n* **in'constancy**.

in'continent *adj* unable to control one's

147

bladder and bowels; uncontrolled.

incon'vēnient *adj* causing awkwardness or difficulty. – *n* **incon'venience**. – *v* to cause inconvenience, trouble to.

incontro'vertible *adj* not to be doubted.

in'corporate *v* to contain as part of a whole. *The new sports complex will incorporate a gymnasium, swimming pool etc*; to include within a group *etc*. – *adj* **in'corporated** (shortened to **inc**) formed into a company or society.

incor'rect *adj* wrong.

in'corrigible *adj* too bad to be put right or reformed.

incor'ruptible *adj* not able to be bribed; that can never decay.

in'crease *v* to grow, to make greater or more numerous. – *n* **'increase** growth; the amount added by growth. – *adv* **in'creasingly** more and more.

in'credible *adj* impossible to believe. – *adv* **in'credibly**. – *n* **incredi'bility**.

in'credulous *adj* not believing (what is said). – *n* **incre'dulity**.

'increment *n* an increase, *esp* one added annually to a salary.

in'criminate *v* to show that a person has taken part in a crime or misdeed.

'incūbātor *n* a large heated box for hatching eggs or one for rearing premature babies. – *v* **'incubate**. – *n* **incuba-tion period** the time (between being infected and the appearance of the symptoms) that it takes for a disease to develop.

'inculcate *v* to impress something on (a person's mind) by much repeating.

in'cumbent *adj* resting on (someone) as a duty. *It is incumbent upon me to warn you*. – *n* one who holds an office, *esp* in the church.

in'cur *v* to bring something (as blame, debt *etc*) upon oneself: – *pt* **in'curred**.

in'cūrable *adj* unable to be cured.

in'cursion *n* an invasion, raid.

indebted [in'detid] *adj* having cause to be grateful (to someone for something received). – *n* **in'debtedness**.

in'dēcent *adj* offending (often in a sexual sense) against normal or usual standards of behaviour. – *n* **in'decency**.

inde'cision *n* slowness in making up one's mind, hesitation. – *adj* **inde'cisive** not coming to a definite result; unable to make up one's mind.

in'deed *adv* in fact; (used for emphasis) really. – *interj* expressing surprise *etc*.

inde'fatigable *adj* untiring.

inde'fensible *adj* unable to be defended; (of behaviour *etc*) inexcusable.

inde'finable *adj* not able to be stated or described clearly.

in'definite *adj* not fixed, uncertain; without definite limits. – *adv* **in'definitely** for an indefinite period of time. – *n* **indefinite article** the name given to the adjectives *a, an*.

in'delible *adj* unable to be rubbed out or removed.

in'delicate *adj* impolite, rude. – *n* **in'delicacy**.

in'demnity *n* money paid to make up for (possible) damage or loss.

in'dent *v* to begin a new paragraph by going in from the margin; (with **for**) to apply for (stores, equipment *etc*). – *ns* **inden'tation** a hollow, dent; a notch or inward curve in an outline, coastline *etc*; **in'denture** a written agreement or contract.

inde'pendent *adj* free to think or act for oneself; not relying on someone (or something) else for support, guidance *etc*. – *n* **inde'pendence**.

indes'cribable *adj* not able to be described.

indes'tructible *adj* not able to be destroyed.

inde'terminate *adj* not fixed, indefinite.

'index *n* an alphabetical list giving the page number of subjects dealt with in a book; an indication: – *pl* **'indexes**; (in mathematics) an upper number which shows how many times a number is multiplied by itself (*eg* 4^3 means $4 \times 4 \times 4$): – *pl* **'indicēs**.

'Indian: *ns* **Indian corn** maize; **Indian ink** a very black ink used by artists; **Indian summer** a period of summer warmth in autumn.

'india'rubber *n* rubber, *esp* a piece for rubbing out pencil *etc*.

'indicate *v* to point out, show. – *n* **indi'cation** a sign. – *adj* **in'dicative** pointing out, being a sign of: *indicative of his attitude*. – *n* **'indicator** that which indicates; a pointer; a name given to many instruments *etc* that give information (*esp* by means of a pointer or the like, as the left and right flashing lights on a vehicle).

indict [in'dīt] *v* to accuse of a crime *esp* formally or in writing. – *n* **in'dict-ment**.

in'different *adj* neither very good nor very bad; (with **to**) showing no interest in. – *n* **in'difference**.

indigenous [in'dijinəs] *adj* native to a country or area.

'indigent *adj* living in want, poor. – *n* **'indigence**.

indi'gestion *n* discomfort or pain experienced in digesting food. – *adj* **indi'gestible** difficult to digest.

in'dignant *adj* angry (*usu* because of wrong done to oneself or others). – *ns* indig'nation; in'dignity loss of dignity; insult: – *pl* in'dignities.

'indigo *adj, n* (of) a purplish-blue colour.

indi'rect *adj* not straight or direct; not affecting or affected directly. – *ns* indirect speech speech reported not in the speaker's actual words; indirect tax a tax on particular goods, paid by the customer in the form of a higher price.

indis'creet *adj* rash, not cautious; giving away too much information. – *n* indiscretion [indis'kreshən] a rash or unwise saying or act.

indis'criminate *adj* making no (careful) distinction between one thing (or person) and another: *indiscriminate killing*: *indiscriminate buying*.

indis'pensable *adj* not able to be done without, necessary.

indis'posed *adj* unwell. – *n* indispo'sition.

indis'pūtable *adj* not able to be denied.

indis'tinct *adj* not clear.

indis'tinguishable *adj* difficult to make out; too alike to tell apart.

indi'vidūal *adj* of a person or thing (out of a group) taken singly; distinctive; unusual. – *n* a single person, animal or thing. – *ns* indi'vidualist one who believes in independent actions *etc*; individu'ality separate existence; quality of standing out from others.

indivisible [indi'vizəbl] *adj* not able to be divided.

in'doctrinate *v* to fill with a certain teaching or set of ideas.

'indolent *adj* lazy. – *n* 'indolence.

in'domitable *adj* unconquerable, unyielding.

indoor ['indör] *adj* done *etc* inside a building. – *edv* 'in'doors in or into a building *etc*.

in'dūbitable *adj* not to be doubted. – *adv* in'dubitably.

in'dūce *v* to persuade; to bring on, cause. – *n* in'ducement something which encourages or persuades. *Money is an inducement to work.*

in'duction *n* the formal installing (of someone, *esp* a clergyman) in a new post; the production of electricity in something by placing it near something else containing electricity; the process of drawing a conclusion from particular cases. – *adj* in'ductive.

in'dulge *v* to be in the habit of giving in to the wishes of (someone). *She indulges that child too much*; to give way to, not to restrain. *He indulged in grief in*

private. – *n* in'dulgence the act of indulging; a pardon for a sin. – *adj* in'dulgent not strict, kind.

'industry *n* (any branch of) trade or manufacture: *steel industry*: *clothing industry*; steady attention to work: – *pl* 'industries. – *adj* in'dustrial. – *n* in'dustrialist someone involved in organizing an industry. – *adj* in'dustrious hard-working.

i'nēbriated *adj* drunk.

in'edible *adj* not eatable.

in'effable *adj* not able to be described.

inef'fective *adj* useless, having no effect. – *n* inef'fectiveness.

ineffectual [ini'fekchōoəl] *adj* achieving nothing.

inefficient [ini'fishənt] *adj* not efficient, not capable; wasting time, energy *etc*. – *n* inef'ficiency: – *pl* inef'ficiencies.

inelegant [in'eligənt] *adj* not graceful. – *n* in'elegance.

in'eligible *adj* not qualified, not suitable (to be chosen).

i'nept *adj* clumsy; foolish. – *n* i'neptitūde.

inequality [ini'kwoləti] *n* lack of equality, unfairness; unevenness: – *pl* ine'qualities.

i'nert *adj* without the power of moving; disinclined to move or act; not lively; chemically inactive. – *ns* i'nertness; inertia [i'nərshiə].

ines'cāpable *adj* unable to be avoided.

in'estimable *adj* too good *etc* to be estimated.

in'evitable *adj* not able to be avoided. – *n* inevita'bility. – *adv* in'evitably.

inex'cūsable *adj* not to be excused.

inexhaustible [inig'zöstəbl] *adj* very plentiful; not likely to become used up.

in'exorable *adj* not able to be persuaded or moved by pleading, relentless.

inex'pensive *adj* cheap in price.

inex'pērience *n* lack of (skilled) knowledge or experience. – *adj* inex'perienced.

inex'plicable *adj* not able to be explained.

inex'pressible *adj* not able to be told or described in words.

inex'tricable *adj* not able to be disentangled. – *adv* inex'tricably.

in'fallible *adj* never making an error; certain to produce the desired result expected: *an infallible remedy*. – *n* infalli'bility.

'infamous *adj* having a very bad reputation; disgraceful. – *n* 'infamy (public) disgrace.

'infant *n* a baby. – *n* 'infancy the state or time of being an infant; the beginning of anything. *Civilization was still in its infancy.* – *n* **in'fanticide** the murder of a child; one who murders a child. – *adj* **'infantile** of babies; childish.

'infantry *n* foot-soldiers.

in'fatuated *adj* filled with foolish love. – *n* **infatu'ation**.

in'fect *v* to fill with disease-causing germs; to pass on disease to; to pass on, spread (*eg* enthusiasm). – *n* **in'fection** the means (*usu* germs) by which disease is spread; a disease; anything that spreads widely and affects many people. – *adj* **in'fectious** likely to spread from person to person.

in'fer *v* to reach a conclusion (from facts or reasoning); to hint: – *pt* **in'ferred**. – *n* **'inference**.

in'ferior *adj* lower in any way; not of best quality. – *n* one lower in rank *etc.* – *n* **inferi'ority**. – *n* **inferiority complex** a constant feeling that one is less good in some way than others.

in'fernal *adj* of hell; (*coll*) annoying. – *n* **in'ferno** hell; any place of horror or fire.

in'fertile *adj* (of soil *etc*) not producing much; (of persons or animals) not able to bear young. – *n* **infer'tility**.

in'fest *v* to swarm over. *The dog is infested with lice.*

'infidel *adj* one who does not believe in religion (*esp* Christianity). – *n* **infi'delity** unfaithfulness, disloyalty.

'in-fighting *n* rivalry or quarrelling between members of the same group.

'infiltrate *v* to pass into in small amounts. *Enemy soldiers infiltrated our lines.* – *n* **infil'tration**.

infinite ['infinit] *adj* without end or limit. – *adj* **infini'tesimal** very small. – *ns* **in'finitive** part of the verb that expresses the action but has no subject (*eg* I hate *to lose*); **in'finity** space or time stretching so far as to be beyond our power of thinking.

in'firm *adj* feeble, weak. – *ns* **in'firmary** a name given to some hospitals: – *pl* **in'firmaries**; **in'firmity** a weakness of the body or of the character: – *pl* **in'firmities**.

in'flame *v* to make hot or red; to cause violent feelings *esp* anger. – *adjs* **in'flamed**; **inflammable** [in'flaməbl] easily set on fire; easily excited. – *n* **inflammation** [inflə'māshən] heat in a part of the body, with pain, redness and swelling. – *adj* **in'flammatory** rousing to anger or excitement.

in'flate *v* to blow up (a balloon, tyre *etc*); to puff up (with pride), exaggerate. *She has an inflated sense of her own impor-*

tance; to increase to a great extent. – *n* **in'flation** the act of inflating; the state of a country's economy in which prices and wages keep forcing each other to increase.

in'flexible *adj* not yielding, unbending.

in'flexion, in'flection *n* a change of tone in the voice.

in'flict *v* to bring down (something unpleasant *eg* blows, punishment) on. – *n* **in'fliction**.

influence ['inflŏŏəns] *n* the power to affect other persons or things. – *v* to have power over. – *adj* **influ'ential**.

influenza [inflŏŏ'enzə] *n* an infectious illness with fever, headache, a cold *etc*.

'influx *n* a flowing in; (of people *etc*) a coming in in large numbers.

in'form *v* to give knowledge to; (with **on**) to tell (something) against (someone), betray. – *ns* **in'formant** one who informs; **infor'mation** knowledge, news. – *adj* **in'formative** giving information. – *n* **in'former** one who gives information (to the police, authorities *etc*).

in'formal *adj* not formal; relaxed, friendly. – *n* **infor'mality**.

infra- *prefix* below, beneath.

'infra-'red *adj* of rays of heat with wavelengths longer than visible light.

in'fringe *v* to break (a rule or law). – *n* **in'fringement**.

in'furiate *v* to drive into a rage.

in'fuse *v* to pour upon or over; to fill the mind (with a desire *etc*). – *n* **in'fusion** the act of infusing; liquid (such as tea) formed by pouring water on something.

ingenious [in'jēniəs] *adj* skilful in inventing; cleverly thought out. – *n* **ingenuity** [injə'nūəti] cleverness; quickness of ideas.

ingenuous [in'jenūəs] *adj* open, frank; without cunning. – *n* **in'genuousness**.

'inglenook *n* a fireside corner.

ingot ['iŋgət] *n* a lump (*usu* cast in oblong shape) of unworked metal, *esp* of gold or silver.

'in'grained *adj* deeply fixed: *ingrained laziness.*

ingratiate [in'grāshiāt] *v* to get oneself into the favour of someone. – *adj* **in'gratiating**.

in'gratitude *n* lack of gratitude or thankfulness.

in'gredient *n* one of the things of which a mixture is made.

in'habit *v* to live in. – *n* **in'habitant** someone who lives permanently in a place.

in'hale *v* to breathe in. – *ns* **in'halant** a

medicine which is inhaled; **inhalation** [in(h)ə'lāshən] the act of inhaling; a medicine which is inhaled.

in'**hērent** *adj* inborn, belonging naturally.

in'**herit** *v* to receive property *etc* as an heir; to possess the qualities of one's parents *etc*. *She inherits her quick temper from her mother.* – *ns* in'**heritance** that which one gets (by will) when a relative dies; in'**heritor** an heir.

in'**hibit** *v* to hold back, prevent. – *adj* in'**hibited** unable to let oneself go. – *n* inhi'**bition** a holding back (of natural impulses *etc*), restraint.

inhos'**pitable** *adj* unwelcoming, unfriendly.

in'**hūman** *adj* not human; brutal. – *n* inhu'**manity**.

inhū'**mane** *adj* cruel.

i'**nimical** *adj* unfriendly, hostile.

i'**nimitable** *adj* impossible to imitate.

i'**niquity** *n* wickedness; a sin: – *pl* i'**niquities**. – *adj* i'**niquitous** unjust; wicked.

initial [i'nishəl] *adj* of or at a beginning. *There were initial problems in running the new school.* – *n* the letter beginning a word *esp* a name. – *v* to put the initials of one's name to: – *pt* i'**nitialled**.

initiate [i'nishiāt] *v* to begin, start. *It was he who initiated the reforms*; to give first lessons to; to admit (*esp* with secret ceremonies) to a society *etc*. – *ns* initi'**ation**; i'**nitiative** (the right to take) the first step; readiness to take a lead.

in'**ject** *v* to force (a fluid *etc*) into the veins or muscles by means of a needle and syringe; to put (*eg* enthusiasm) into. – *n* in'**jection**.

injudicious [injoo'dishəs] *adj* unwise.

in'**junction** *n* an order or command.

injure ['injər] *v* to harm, damage; to wrong. – *adj* '**injured** hurt; offended. – *n* '**injury** hurt, damage, harm; a wrong: – *pl* '**injuries**.

in'**justice** *n* unfairness; a wrong.

ink *n* a coloured (often dark blue or black) liquid used in writing, printing *etc.* – *v* to mark with ink. – *adj* '**inky** of or covered in ink; very dark.

'**inkling** *n* a hint or slight sign.

inlaid *see* inlay.

'**inland** *adj* not beside the sea; carried on *etc* inside a country (as **inland revenue** taxes *etc* collected within the country). – *adv* in'**land** toward the inner part of a country.

'**inlay** *n* a kind of decoration done by fitting pieces of different shapes and colours into a background. – *v* to do

this kind of work. – *adj* '**in'laid**.

'**inlet** *n* a small bay.

'**inmate** *n* a resident or occupant (*esp* of an institution): *the inmates of the mental hospital.*

'**inmōst** *adj* the most inward, the farthest in.

inn *n* a house for the lodging of travellers, a small country hotel. – *n* '**innkeeper** one who keeps an inn.

in'**nate** *adj* inborn, natural.

'**inner** *adj* farther in; (of feelings *etc*) hidden. – *adj* '**innermost** farthest in; most secret.

'**innings** *n* a team's turn for batting in cricket; a turn or a go (at something).

'**innocent** *adj* not guilty, blameless; harmless; (with **of**) lacking, without: *innocent of make-up.* – *n* '**innocence**.

in'**nocuous** *adj* not harmful.

inno'**vation** *n* something new.

innū'**endo** *n* (a remark containing) a disagreeable hint: – *pl* innu'**endoes**.

in'**nūmerable** *adj* too many to be counted.

in'**nūmerate** *adj* having no understanding of arithmetic or mathematics. – *n* in'**numeracy**.

i'**noculate** *v* to give (a person *etc*) a mild form of a disease (by injecting germs in his blood) so that he may not easily catch it. – *n* i'**nocu'lation**.

inof'**fensive** *adj* harmless, giving no offence.

in'**opportūne** *adj* at a bad or inconvenient time.

i'**nordinate** *adj* going beyond the limit, unreasonably great.

inor'**ganic** *adj* not having the characteristics of living bodies.

in-patient ['inpāshənt] *n* a patient who lives in, as well as being treated in a hospital.

input ['inpŏot] *n* an amount (of energy, labour *etc*) that is put into something; information fed into a computer.

inquest *n* a legal inquiry into a case of sudden death.

in'**quire**, en'**quire** *v* to ask. – *adj* in'**quiring**, en'**quiring** questioning; eager to find out. – *ns* in'**quirer**, en'**quirer**; in'**quiry**, en'**quiry** a question; a search for information; an investigation: – *pl* in'**quiries**, en'**quiries**.

inqui'**sition** *n* a careful questioning or investigation. – *n* in'**quisitor** an official investigator.

in'**quisitive** *adj* eager to find out; fond of prying into the affairs of others.

'**inroad** *n* a raid, an advance (into). – **make inroads into** to use up large amounts of. *While unemployed he made inroads into his savings.*

in'sane *adj* mad, not sane. – *n* **insanity** [in'sanəti].

in'sanitary *adj* not sanitary, likely to help the spread of disease.

insatiable [in'sāshiəbl] *adj* not able to be satisfied.

in'scribe *v* to write or engrave on (*eg* a name on the first page of a book, or on a monument). – *n* **in'scription** the writing on a book, monument *etc*.

inscrutable [in'skrōōtəbl] *adj* not able to be searched into and understood, mysterious.

'insect *n* any small six-legged creature with wings and a body divided into sections. – *n* **in'secticide** powder or liquid for killing insects. – *adj* **insec-'tivorous** (of plants and animals) feeding on insects.

inse'cūre *adj* not safe; not firm; not feeling secure or settled. – *n* **inse-'curity**.

in'sensible *adj* unconscious, unaware (of); not having feeling.

in'sensitive *adj* (with **to**) not feeling: *insensitive to cold*; unsympathetic (to): *insensitive to her grief*; unappreciative of (*eg* beauty).

in'separable *adj* not able to be separated or kept apart.

in'sert *v* to put in or among. – *ns* **'insert**; **in'sertion** the act of putting in; something put in.

'inset *n* something set in (*eg* a small picture, map *etc* in a corner of a larger one).

'in'shore *adj* (of fishing *etc*) carried on near the shore. – *adv* to or near the shore.

'in'side *n* the side, space or part within; indoors. – *adj* being on or in the inside; indoor; coming from or done by someone within an organization *etc*: *inside information.* – *adv* to, in or on the inside. – *prep* to the inside of; within.

in'sidious *adj* likely to trap those who are not careful, treacherous; (of a disease *etc*) coming on gradually and unnoticed.

insight ['insīt] *n* power of looking into a matter and understanding clearly.

in'signia *npl* signs or badges showing that one holds an office, award *etc*.

insig'nificant *adj* of little importance. – *n* **insig'nificance**.

insin'cere *adj* not sincere. – *n* **insincerity** [insin'serəti].

in'sinūate *v* to hint (at a fault); to put in (something) gradually (and secretly); to work oneself into (favour). – *n*

insinu'ation a sly hint.

in'sipid *adj* dull, without liveliness; tasteless.

in'sist *v* to urge something strongly: *insist on punctuality*; to refuse to give way, to hold firmly to one's intentions *etc*. *He insists on walking there*; to go on saying (that). *He insists that he saw a ghost.* – *adj* **in'sistent** holding fast to what one claims; compelling attention. – *n* **in'sistence**.

'insolent *adj* rude, impertinent, insulting. – *n* **'insolence**.

in'solūble *adj* not able to be dissolved; (of a problem *etc*) not able to be solved.

in'solvent *adj* not able to pay one's debts. – *n* **in'solvency**.

in'somnia *n* sleeplessness. – *adj*, *n* **in'somniac** (of) one who suffers from insomnia.

in'spect *v* to look carefully into, to examine; to look over (troops *etc*) ceremonially. – *ns* **in'spection** careful examination; **in'spector** an official who inspects; a police officer below a superintendent and above a sergeant in rank.

in'spire *v* to encourage, rouse; to be the source of (poetic) ideas; to breathe in. – *n* **inspiration** [inspə'rāshən] something or someone that influences or encourages; a very good idea; breathing in. – *adj* **in'spired** [in'spird] seeming to be aided by higher powers; brilliantly good.

insta'bility *n* lack of steadiness or stability (*esp* in the personality).

install, instal [in'stöl] *v* to place in position, or put in ready for use (as electricity into a house); to introduce formally to a new job *etc* : – *pt* **in'stalled**. – *n* **instal'lation** the act of installing; something installed.

instalment [in'stölmənt] *n* a part of a sum of money paid at fixed times until the whole amount is paid; one part of a serial story.

'instance *n* an example, a particular case. – *v* to mention as an example. – **at the instance of** at the request of.

'instant *adj* immediate, urgent; able to be prepared *etc* almost immediately: *instant coffee.* – *n* a very short time, a moment; a point or moment of time. – *adj* **instan'tāneous** done, happening very quickly. – *adv* **'instantly** immediately.

instead [in'sted] *adv* in place of someone or something. *He will go instead.* – **instead of** in place of. *Walk instead of running.*

'instep *n* the arching, upper part of the

foot.

'**instigate** *v* to stir up, encourage. – *n* **insti'gation**.

in'stil *v* to put in little by little (*esp* ideas into the mind): – *pt* **in'stilled**.

'**instinct** *n* a natural feeling or knowledge, which living things seem to have without thinking and without being taught. – *adj* **in'stinctive** due to instinct.

'**institute** *v* to set up, establish, start. – *n* a society, organization *etc* or the building it uses. – *n* **insti'tution** a society, organization, building *etc* established for a particular purpose (*esp* care or education); an established custom. – *adj* **insti'tutional**.

in'struct *v* to teach; to direct or command. – *n* **in'struction** teaching; a command; (*pl*) rules showing how something is to be used. – *adj* **in'structive** containing or giving information or knowledge. – *n* **in'structor**.

'**instrument** *n* a thing used in doing something, a tool; something for producing musical sounds (such as a piano, trumpet). – *adj* **instru'mental** helpful in bringing (something) about; belonging to or produced by musical instruments. – *n* **instru'mentalist** one who plays on a musical instrument.

insu'bordinate *adj* rebellious, disobedient. – *n* **insubordi'nation**.

in'sufferable *adj* not able to be endured.

insuf'ficient *adj* not enough. – *n* **insuf'ficiency**.

'**insular** *adj* of an island or islands; (of opinions) narrow, prejudiced.

'**insulate** *v* to cover (something) with a material that will not let through electrical currents, or heat, or sound; to cut off, isolate. – *n* **insu'lation**.

'**insulin** *n* a substance used in the treatment of diabetes.

in'sult *v* to treat with scorn or rudeness. – *n* '**insult**. – *adj* **in'sulting** scornful, rude.

in'superable *adj* that cannot be overcome.

insure [in'shoor] *v* to arrange for payment of a sum of money on (something) if it should be lost, damaged, stolen *etc*. – *n* **in'surance**.

in'surgent *adj* rising up in rebellion. – *n* a rebel.

insur'mountable *adj* not able to be got over.

insur'rection *n* a rising up in rebellion.

in'tact *adj* whole, unbroken.

'**intake** *n* a thing or quantity taken in.

in'tangible *adj* not able to be felt by touch; difficult to define or describe,

not clear.

integer ['intijər] *n* a whole number, not a fraction. – *adj* **integral** ['intigrəl] of or essential to a whole: *an integral part of the machine*; made up of parts forming a whole. – *v* '**integrate** to fit parts together to form a whole; to enable (racial) groups to mix freely with each other and live on equal terms. – *ns* **inte'gration; in'tegrity** honesty; state of being whole.

'**intellect** *n* the thinking power of the mind. – *adj* **intel'lectual** showing or requiring intellect. – *n* a person of natural ability or with academic interests.

in'telligent *adj* clever, quick at understanding. – *n* **in'telligence** mental ability; information sent, news. – *adj* **in'telligible** able to be understood.

in'temperate *adj* going beyond reasonable limits, uncontrolled; having the habit of drinking too much. – *n* **in'temperance**.

in'tend *v* to mean or plan to (do something). – *n* **in'tent** purpose. – *adj* with all one's mind (on), attentive; determined (on). – *n* **in'tention** what one means to do; meaning. – *adj* **in'tentional** done on purpose. – *adv* **in'tentionally**.

in'tense *adj* very great; (of a person) over-serious, inclined to feel strongly. – *n* **in'tensity**. – *v* **in'tensify** to increase: – *pt* **in'tensified**. – *adj* **in'tensive** very thorough, concentrated.

inter- *prefix* between, among, together as in **intertwine**.

in'ter *v* to bury: – *pt* **in'terred**. – *n* **in'terment**.

inter'act *v* to act on one another.

inter'cede *v* to act as peacemaker between two persons, nations *etc*. – *ns* **inter'cession; inter'cessor**.

inter'cept *v* to stop or seize on the way; to cut off, interrupt (a view, the light *etc*).

inter'change *v* to put each in the place of the other; to (cause to) alternate. – *n* '**interchange** the act of interchanging; a junction of two or more major roads on separate levels to allow cars *etc* to transfer from one to another without lines of traffic crossing each other. – *adj* **inter'changeable** able to be used one for the other.

'**intercom** *n* a telephone system within a building, aeroplane *etc*.

intercourse ['intərkörs] *n* communication; dealings between people *etc*; sexual intercourse.

'**interdict** *n* an order forbidding something.

'**interest** *n* special attention, curiosity; a thing with which one concerns oneself; advantage, benefit; a sum paid for the loan of money. – *v* to catch or hold the attention of. – *adjs* '**interested** having or taking an interest; '**interesting** holding the attention.

inter'**fere** *v* (with **in**) to take part in what is not one's business, meddle; (with **with**) to get in the way of, hinder: *interfere with the progress of the plan.* – *n* inter'**ference** the act of interfering; the spoiling of radio or television reception by another station or local disturbance (lightning, traffic *etc*).

'**interim** *n* time between; the meantime. – *adj* temporary.

in'**tērior** *adj* inner; inside a building; inland. – *n* the inside of anything; the inland part of a country.

inter'**ject** *v* to throw a remark in (to a conversation); to exclaim. – *n* inter'**jection** word or words of exclamation (*eg* Ah! Oh dear!).

inter'**lock** *v* to lock or clasp together; to fit into each other.

'**interlōper** *n* one who goes in where he has no right, an intruder. – *v* inter'**lope**.

interlude ['intərlōōd] *n* an interval, or what happens in it; a short piece of music played between the parts of a play, film *etc*.

'**inter'marry** *v* (of a race or group) to marry with members of another race *etc*; to marry with members of the same group, race *etc*.

inter'**mēdiary** *n* one who acts between two persons (*eg* in trying to settle a quarrel): – *pl* inter'**mediaries**.

inter'**mēdiate** *adj* in the middle; coming between.

interment *see* **inter**.

in'**terminable** *adj* never ending, boringly long.

inter'**mission** *n* an interval, a pause.

inter'**mittent** *adj* ceasing every now and then and starting again.

in'**tern** *v* to keep someone from the enemy side prisoner in a country while a war is going on. – *ns* inter'**nee** someone who is confined in this way; in'**ternment**.

in'**ternal** *adj* of the inner part *esp* of the body; inside, within (a country, organization *etc*).

inter'**national** *adj* happening between nations; world-wide. – *n* a match between teams of two countries.

inter'**nēcine** *adj* (of feuds *etc* within a group) causing deaths on both sides.

interplanetary [intər'planətəri] *adj* between the planets.

'**interplay** *n* the action of one thing on another.

inter'**pose** *v* to place or come between, to put in (a remark *etc*) by way of interruption.

in'**terpret** *v* to explain the meaning of something; to translate; to bring out the meaning of something (as music, a part in a play *etc*) in one's performance; to take the meaning of something to be. – *ns* in'**terpre'tation**; in'**terpreter** one who translates (on the spot) the words of a speaker into the language of his hearers.

inter'**regnum** *n* the time between the end of one reign and the beginning of the next.

in'**terrogate** *v* to examine by asking questions, to question. – *ns* in'**terro'gation**; inter'**rogative** a word used in asking a question (*eg* Why? Who?). – *adj* questioning. – *n* in'**terrogator**.

inter'**rupt** *v* to stop (a person) while he is saying or doing something; to stop (something that one is doing); to get in the way of, cut off (a view *etc*). – *n* inter'**ruption**.

inter'**sect** *v* (of lines *etc*) to meet and cross. – *n* inter'**section** the point where two lines cross; a crossroads.

inter'**sperse** *v* to scatter here and there in. – *n* inter'**spersion**.

interstice [in'tərstis] *n* a small space between things placed close together, a chink.

inter'**twine** *v* to twine or twist together.

'**interval** *n* a time or space between; a short pause in a programme *etc*.

inter'**vene** *v* to come or be between, or in the way; to join in (in order to stop) a fight or quarrel between other persons or nations. – *n* **intervention** [intər'venshən].

interview ['intərvū] *n* a formal meeting of one person with one or more others for purposes of business (*eg* an appointment to a job) or of broadcasting information. – Also *v*.

in'**testate** *adj* without having made a will. *He died intestate.*

intestines [in'testinz] *npl* the inside parts of the body, *usu* the bowels and passages leading to them. – *adj* in'**testinal**.

'**intimate** *adj* knowing much about, familiar (with); (of friends) close; private, personal. – *n* a close friend. – *v* to hint; to announce. – *ns* '**intimacy** close friendship; familiarity; **inti'mation** a hint; an announcement.

in'timidate v to frighten (esp by threatening violence). – adj **in'timidating**. – n **intimi'dation**.

into ['intoŏ] prep to the inside: into the room; to a different state. A tadpole changes into a frog; (maths) expressing the idea of division. 2 into 4 goes twice.

intolerable [in'tolərəbl] adj not able to be endured. – adj **in'tolerant** not willing to put up with (people of different ideas, race, religion etc). – n **in'tolerance**.

in'tone v to speak in a singing manner, to chant. – n **into'nation** the rise and fall of the voice.

in'toxicate v to make drunk; to excite. – ns **in'toxicant** a strong drink; **intoxi'cation** drunkenness.

intra- prefix within.

in'tractable adj difficult, stubborn.

in'transigent adj refusing to come to an agreement. – n **in'transigence**.

in'transitive adj (of verbs) not of the kind that can take an object (as to go, to fall).

in'trepid adj without fear, brave. – n **intre'pidity**.

'intricate adj complicated, having many twists and turns. – n **'intricacy** the state of being intricate; something intricate: – pl **'intricacies**.

intrigue [in'trēg] n a secret plot or scheming; a secret love affair. – v to plot; to rouse the curiosity of, fascinate. – adj **in'triguing**.

in'trinsic adj belonging to a thing as part of its nature.

intro'duce v to bring in or put in; to make (a person) known (to another). – n **introduction** [intrə'dukshən] the introducing of a person or thing; something written (or said) at the beginning of a book (or speech etc) briefly explaining its contents etc. – adj **intro'ductory** coming at the beginning.

intro'spective adj inward-looking, fond of examining one's thoughts, feelings etc. – n **intro'spection**.

intrude [in'trood] v to thrust (oneself) in uninvited or unwanted. – ns **in'truder** someone who breaks in or intrudes; **in'trusion**. – adj **in'trusive**.

intu'ition n the power of grasping a fact or idea without thinking it out; an idea so grasped.

'inundate v to flood; to overwhelm. I'm inundated with work. – n **inun'dation**.

i'nure v to make accustomed (to pain etc).

in'vade v to enter (a country etc) as an enemy intending to take possession; to interfere with (someone's rights, priv-

acy etc). – ns **in'vader**; **invasion**.

in'valid[1] adj (of a passport etc) not valid, not legally effective. – v **in'validate** to make invalid. – n **inva'lidity**.

'invalid[2] n a person who is ill or disabled. – Also adj. – v to cause to be an invalid; (with **out**) to discharge as an invalid (esp out of the army).

in'valuable adj too precious to have its value estimated, priceless.

in'variable adj unchanging. – adv **in'variably** always.

invasion see **invade**.

in'vective n words of scorn or hate, violent abuse.

inveigle [in'vēgl] v to coax, entice. – n **in'veiglement**.

in'vent v to make or think up (a machine, scheme etc) for the first time; to make up (a story, an excuse). – ns **in'vention** something invented; **in'ventor**. – adj **in'ventive** good at inventing, resourceful.

'inventory n a detailed list of articles (as the contents of a house etc): – pl **'inventories**.

in'vert v to turn upside down; to reverse the order of. – adj **'in'verse** opposite, reverse. – n the opposite. – adv **in'versely**. – n **in'version** a turning upside-down; a reversal. – npl **inverted commas** commas upside down ("—", '—') or similar marks used in writing to show where direct speech begins and ends.

in'vertebrate adj (of animals) having no backbone (eg worms, insects). – Also n.

in'vest v to put money in a firm etc (usu in the form of shares) to make a profit; to clothe, surround something with a quality; to surround, lay siege to (a stronghold etc). – ns **in'vestiture** a ceremony of giving (the robes etc of) high office to someone; **in'vestment** something (esp money) invested; something in which money is invested; a siege; **in'vestor** one who invests.

in'vestigate v to search into with care. – ns **investi'gation** a careful search; **in'vestigator**.

inveterate [in'vetərət] adj firmly fixed in a habit by long practice: an inveterate gambler; (of a quality, habit etc) deep-rooted. – n **in'veteracy**.

in'vidious adj likely to cause ill-will or envy.

in'vigilate v to supervise (an examination etc). – n **in'vigilator**.

in'vigorate v to strengthen, refresh. – adj **in'vigorating**.

in'vincible adj not able to be defeated or surmounted. – n **invinci'bility**.

in'violable *adj* (of an oath, a right, a person) to be treated as sacred, not to be broken or disregarded or harmed. – *n* **inviola'bility**. – *adj* **in'violate** not violated, free from harm *etc*.

invisible [in'vizəbl] *adj* not able to be seen. – *n* **invisi'bility**.

in'vite *v* to ask a person politely to do something, *esp* to come (to one's house, to a meal *etc*); to ask for or to seem by one's behaviour to be asking for. *His behaviour invites punishment.* – *n* **invitation** [invi'tāshən] a (written) request (to come). – *adj* **in'viting** tempting, attractive.

invocation *see* **invoke**.

'invoice *n* a letter sent with goods with details of price and quantity. – *v* to make such a list.

in'voke to call upon (in prayer); to ask for (*eg* help); to call forth (a spirit). – *n* **invo'cation**.

in'voluntary *adj* not done willingly or intentionally. – *adv* **in'voluntarily**.

in'volve *v* to have as a consequence, to require; to (cause a person to) take part (in) or be concerned (in): *involved in social work*: *involved in the disgrace.* – *adj* **in'volved** complicated. – *n* **in'volvement**.

'inward *adj* placed within; situated in the mind or soul. – *advs* **'inward, 'inwards** towards the inside; **'inwardly** within; in the heart, privately.

iodine ['īədēn] *n* an element, used in liquid form to kill germs.

'ion *n* an electrically-charged atom or group of atoms.

i'ota *n* a little bit.

IOU ['īō'ū] *n* short for *I owe you*, a note given as a receipt for money borrowed.

irascible [i'rasibl] *adj* easily made angry. – *n* **irasci'bility**.

'ire *n* anger. – *adj* **i'rate** angry.

iridescent [iri'desnt] *adj* coloured like a rainbow; shimmering with changing colours. – *n* **iri'descence**.

'iris *n* the coloured part of the eye round the pupil; a type of lily-like flower which grows from a bulb: – *pl* **'irises**.

irk *v* to weary, annoy. – *adj* **'irksome** tiresome.

iron ['īərn] *n* an element, the most common metal, widely used to make tools *etc*; an instrument of iron (such as one for smoothing clothes, a golf club *etc*); (*pl*) a prisoner's chains. – *adj* made of iron; like iron; stern; (of a rule *etc*) not to be broken. – *v* to smooth with an iron; (with **out**) to smooth out (difficulties). – *n* **ironmonger** ['īərnmuŋgər] a dealer in articles made

of iron (**'ironmongery**).

'irony *n* a form of deliberate mockery in which one says the opposite of what is obviously true; apparent mockery in a situation, words *etc*. *The irony of it was that she would have given him the money if he hadn't stolen it*: – *pl* **'ironies**. – *adjs* **i'ronic; i'ronical**.

irrational [i'rashənl] *adj* against (the rules of) common-sense.

ir'regular *adj* not regular; uneven, variable; against the rules. – *n* **irregu'larity**: – *pl* **irregu'larities**.

irrelevant [i'relivənt] *adj* not having to do with what is being spoken about. – *n* **ir'relevancy**.

ir'reparable *adj* not able to be repaired.

irre'placeable *adj* too good, precious, rare *etc* to be replaced.

irre'pressible *adj* (of high spirits *etc*) not able to be kept in check.

irre'proachable *adj* not able to be found fault with.

irresistible [iri'zistəbl] *adj* too strong or too charming to be resisted.

irresolute [i'rezəlōōt] *adj* not able to make up one's mind or keep to one's decision.

irres'pective *adj* taking no account of. *He went every day irrespective of the weather.*

irres'ponsible *adj* having no sense of responsibility, thoughtless.

irreverent [i'revərənt] *adj* having no respect (*eg* for holy things). – *n* **ir'reverence**.

ir'revocable *adj* not to be changed.

'irrigate *v* to supply (land) with water (by canals *etc*). – *n* **irri'gation**.

'irritate *v* to annoy; to cause discomfort, inflammation (to the skin, eyes *etc*). – *adj* **'irritable** cross, easily annoyed. – *n* **irri'tation** annoyance; discomfort *etc* of the skin *etc*.

island ['īlənd] *n* land surrounded with water; anything resembling this, as a **traffic island**, built in the middle of a street for pedestrians to stand on. – *n* **'islander** an inhabitant of an island.

isle [il] *n* an island.

'isobar *n* a line on the map connecting places where atmospheric pressure is the same.

'isolate *v* to place a person by himself; to consider a thing by itself. – *n* **iso'lation**.

isosceles [i'sosəlēz] *adj* (of a triangle) having two sides equal.

'isotherm *n* a line on the map connecting places which have the same temperature.

issue ['ishōō] *v* to go, flow, or come out;

to give out (orders *etc*); to publish. – *n* a flow; children: *he died without issue*; publication; the copies of a book published at one time; one number in the series (of a magazine *etc*); result, consequence; the actual question which is being argued about or discussed. – **to take issue** to disagree (with).

isthmus ['isməs] *n* a narrow neck of land connecting two larger portions: – *pl* **'isthmuses**.

it *pron* the thing spoken of. *My hat disappeared but I found it again*; used in sentences that have no real subject. *It snowed today. It is too late*; used in phrases as a kind of object. *Go it alone. Brave it out.* – *adj* **its** belonging to it. – *pron* **it'self** used reflexively. *The cat licked itself*; used for emphasis. *When we've seen the garden we'll see the house itself.*

i'talics *npl* a kind of type which *slopes to the right.* – *v* **i'talicize** to print in italics.

itch *n* an irritating feeling in the skin which is made better by scratching; a strong desire. – *v* to have an itch; to long (to). – *adj* **'itchy**.

'item *n* a separate article or detail (in a list).

itinerant [i'tinərənt] *adj* making journeys from place to place (on business *etc*), travelling. – *n* one who travels around, *esp* a tramp, gypsy, pedlar *etc*.

itinerary [i'tinərəri] *n* a route or plan of a journey: – *pl* **i'tineraries**.

its, itself *see* **it**.

it's [its] short for **it is**.

'ivory *n* the hard white substance which forms the tusks of the elephant, walrus *etc*.

'ivy *n* a creeping evergreen plant.

J

jab *v* to poke, stab: – *pt* **jabbed**. – Also *n*.

'jabber *v* to talk rapidly (and indistinctly). – Also *n*.

jack *n* an instrument for raising heavy weights such as motor cars; the playing card between ten and queen, the knave. – *v* (*usu* with **up**) to raise with a jack. – *ns* **'jackboots** large boots reaching above the knee; **'jack-in-the-box** a figure that is fixed to a spring inside a box and leaps out when the lid is opened; **'jack-knife** a large folding knife; a dive resembling a jack-knife's action. – *v* (of a vehicle and its trailer) to swing together to form a sharp angle.

jackal ['jakōl] *n* a dog-like wild animal.

'jackass *n* a male ass; a stupid person. – *n* **laughing jackass** the Australian giant kingfisher or kookaburra.

'jackdaw *n* a type of small crow.

'jacket *n* a short coat; a covering, *esp* a loose paper cover for a book.

'jackpot *n* a fund of prize money which has mounted up because of being so far unwon.

jade *n* hard green mineral substance, used for ornaments. – *adj* **'jaded** tired.

jagged ['jagid] *adj* rough-edged, uneven.

'jaguar *n* a type of South American animal like a leopard.

jail, gaol [jāl] *n* a prison. – *n* **'jailer,**

'gaoler one who has charge of a jail or of prisoners. – *n* **'jailbird, gaolbird** a person who has been in jail.

jam *n* fruit boiled with sugar till it is set; a crush; a stopping or blockage caused by crowding together; (*coll*) a difficult situation. – *v* to press or squeeze tight; to crowd full; to stick and so be unable to move. *This wheel has jammed*; to cause interference with another radio station's broadcast: – *pt* **jammed**.

jamb [jam] *n* the side post of a door.

jambo'ree *n* a large, lively gathering; a rally of Boy Scouts.

jangle ['jaŋgl] *v* to sound harshly with a ringing noise; to irritate.

'janitor *n* a caretaker; a doorkeeper.

'January *n* the first month of the year.

jar *n* a glass or earthenware bottle with a wide mouth. – *v* to have a harsh, startling effect; to hurt by a sudden (violent) movement: – *pt* **jarred**. – *adj* **'jarring** harsh, startling.

'jargon *n* special words used within a particular trade, profession *etc*; grand-sounding but meaningless talk.

jasmine ['jazmin] *n* a shrub with white or yellow sweet-smelling flowers.

'jaundice *n* a disease which causes yellowness of the skin *etc*. – *adj* **'jaundiced** having jaundice; discontented, bitter.

jaunt *n* a journey, *esp* one for pleasure. –

javelin

adj **'jaunty** cheerful, gay.

javelin ['javəlin] *n* a long spear for throwing.

jaw *n* the mouth, chin *etc*, the lower part of the face; (*pl*) mouth (*esp* of an animal).

jay *n* a brightly-coloured bird of the crow kind. – *n* **'jaywalker** one who walks carelessly among traffic.

jazz *n* popular music of American Negro origin.

jealous ['jeləs] *adj* wanting to have what someone else has, envious; carefully looking after what one thinks much of. – *n* **'jealousy**.

jeans *npl* denim trousers.

jeep *n* a small army motor vehicle.

jeer *v* to make fun of, scoff. – Also *n*.

'jelly *n* the juice of fruit boiled with sugar till it becomes firm; a transparent wobbly food *usu* fruit-flavoured; anything in a jelly-like state: – *pl* **'jellies**. – *n* **'jellyfish** a sea animal with a jelly-like body.

'jemmy *n* a burglar's iron tool: – *pl* **'jemmies**.

'jenny wren *n* a female wren.

jeopardy ['jepərdi] *n* danger. – *v* **'jeopardize** to put in danger or at risk.

jer'bōa *n* a small rat-like desert animal with very long hindlegs.

jerk *v* to give a sudden sharp movement. – Also *n*. – *adj* **'jerky** moving or coming in jerks.

'jerkin *n* a type of short coat.

jersey ['jörzi] *n* a sweater, pullover: – *pl* **'jerseys**.

jest *n* a joke. – *v* to joke. – *n* **'jester** (*hist*) a court fool, once employed by kings, nobles *etc* to amuse them. – **in jest** jokingly, for a joke.

jet *n* a hard black mineral substance, used for ornaments *etc*; a spout of flame, air or liquid; a jet plane. – *adj* **'jet-'black** very black. – *ns* **jet plane** one driven by jet propulsion; **jet propulsion** high speed forward motion produced by sucking in air, liquid *etc* and forcing it out from behind.

'jetsam *n* goods thrown overboard and washed ashore.

'jettison *v* to throw overboard; to abandon.

'jetty *n* a small pier: – *pl* **'jetties**.

Jew *n* one who is of the race or religion of the Israelites. – *adj* **'Jewish** of the Jews. – *n* **Jew's harp** a small harp-shaped musical instrument played between the teeth.

'jewel *n* a precious stone; anything or anyone highly valued. – *adj* **'jewelled**,

(*usu US*) **'jeweled** set with jewels. – *ns* **'jeweller**, (*usu US*) **'jeweler** one who makes or deals in articles made of precious jewels and metals; **'jewellery**, (*usu US*) **'jewelry** articles made or sold by a jeweller.

jib *n* a three-cornered sail in front of a ship's foremast; the jutting-out arm of a crane. – *v* (with **at**) to refuse to (do something), object to: – *pt* **jibbed**.

jibe, gibe *v* to jeer, scoff. – Also *n*.

jig *n* a lively dance. – *v* to jump about: – *pt* **jigged**.

'jigsaw (puzzle) *n* a puzzle consisting of many differently shaped pieces that fit together to form a picture.

jilt *v* to cast aside (someone with whom one has been in love).

jingle ['jiŋgl] *n* a clinking sound (as of coins); a simple rhyme. – Also *v*.

job *n* a person's daily work; any piece of work. – *adj* **'jobbing** doing odd jobs of work for payment: *jobbing gardener*. – *n* **'job-'lot** a collection of odds and ends. – **it is a good job (that)** it is fortunate that.

'jockey *n* one who rides horses in a race: – *pl* **'jockeys**. – *v* to push one's way (into a good position).

'jocular *adj* joking, merry. – *n* **jocu'larity**.

jodhpurs ['jodpərz] *npl* riding breeches, fitting tightly from knee to ankle.

jog *v* to nudge, push slightly; to travel slowly; to run at a gentle pace: – *pt* **jogged**. – *n* **'jogging**.

'joggle *v* to shake slightly. – Also *n*.

join *v* to put or come together; to connect, fasten; to become a member of; to come and meet. – *n* the place where two or more things join. – *ns* **'joiner** one who joins; a worker in wood; **joint** the place where two or more things join; the place where two bones are joined (*eg* elbow, knee); meat containing a (joint) bone. – *adj* united; shared among more than one. – *adv* **'jointly** together. – **join battle** to begin fighting in battle.

joist *n* the beam to which the boards of a floor or the laths of a ceiling are nailed.

joke *n* anything said or done to cause laughter. – Also *v*. – *n* **'joker** one who jokes; an extra card in a pack.

'jolly *adj* merry. – *ns* **jollifi'cation** noisy (feasting and) merriment; **'jolliness**, **'jollity** merriment.

'jollyboat *n* a small boat belonging to a ship.

jōlt *v* to shake suddenly; to go forward with sudden jerks. – *n* a sudden jerk.

'joss-stick *n* a stick of gum which gives

158

off a sweet smell when burned.

jostle ['josl] v to push or knock against.

jot n a very small part. – v to write down hurriedly or briefly: – pt '**jotted**. – n '**jotter** a book for note-taking.

joule [jōol] n a unit of energy.

journal ['jɔ̄rnl] n an account kept of each day's doings, a diary; a newspaper, a magazine. – ns '**journalism** the business of running, or writing for, papers and magazines; '**journalist** one who writes for newspapers etc.

journey ['jɔ̄rni] n a distance travelled: – pl '**journeys**. – v to travel. – n '**journeyman** one whose apprenticeship is finished.

joust n (hist) the armed contest between two knights on horseback at a tournament. – v to fight on horseback at a tournament.

'**jōvial** adj cheerful, good-humoured. – n **jovi'ality**.

jowl [jowl] n the lower part of the jaw or cheek.

joy n gladness. – adjs '**joyful**, '**joyous** full of joy; '**joyless** dismal.

jubilant ['jōobilənt] adj full of rejoicing, triumphant. – n **jubi'lation**.

jubilee ['jōobilē] n celebrations arranged in memory of some event (such as a wedding, coronation etc).

judge v to hear the evidence etc in a question of law and make a decision on it; to form an opinion; to decide which is best in a competition etc. – n (in the courts of law) one who hears cases and decides on them according to the country's laws; one skilled in finding out good and bad points (esp of those in a competition). – n '**judg(e)ment** a decision (in a court of law etc); an opinion; good sense in forming opinions.

judicial [jōo'dishəl] adj of a judge or court of justice.

judiciary [jōo'dishiəri] n the judges of a country taken as a whole.

judicious [jōo'dishəs] adj wise.

judo ['jōodō] n a Japanese form of wrestling.

jug n a dish for liquids usu with a handle and a shaped lip for pouring.

'**juggernaut** n a vast and dangerous force; a large (articulated) lorry.

'**juggle** v to toss a number of things (balls, clubs etc) into the air and catch them; to handle or present in a deceitful way. – n '**juggler**.

'**jugūlar vein** n the large vein at the side of the neck.

juice [jōos] n the liquid in vegetables, fruits etc. – adj '**juicy**.

ju-jitsu [jōo'jitsōo] n an earlier form of **judo**.

jukebox ['jōokboks] n a coin-operated machine which plays selected records automatically.

July [jōo'lī] the seventh month of the year.

'**jumble** v to throw together without order, muddle. – n a confused mixture. – n '**jumble-sale** a sale of odds and ends, cast-off clothing etc.

'**jumbo** n a child's name for an elephant: – pl '**jumbos**. – adj very large: jumbo-jet.

jump v to leap; to make a sudden (startled) movement (upwards). – Also n. – adj '**jumpy** easily startled.

'**jumper** n a sweater or jersey.

'**junction** n a place or point of joining (eg of roads or railway lines).

'**junctūre** n point. At this juncture he collapsed.

June [jōon] n the sixth month of the year.

jungle ['juŋgl] n a dense growth of trees and plants in tropical areas.

junior ['jōonyər] adj younger; in a lower class or rank. – Also n.

juniper ['jōonipər] n a type of evergreen shrub with berries and prickly leaves.

junk n a Chinese flat-bottomed sailing ship, high in the bow and stern; worthless articles, rubbish.

'**junket** n a dish made of curdled milk sweetened and flavoured. – n '**junketing** feasting, merriment.

jurisdiction [jōoris'dikshən] n legal authority or power; the district over which a judge, court etc has power.

jurisprudence ['jōorisprōodəns] n the study or knowledge of law.

jury ['jōori] n a group of men or women selected to reach a decision on whether an accused prisoner is guilty or not; a group of judges for a competition etc: – pl '**juries**. – ns '**juror**, '**juryman** one who serves on a jury.

just adj not favouring one more than another, fair; in keeping with one's rights; correct. – adv exactly; not long since; merely, only; really: just longing to see you.

'**justice** n fairness in making judgements; what is right or rightly deserved; a judge. – **Justice of the Peace** (shortened to **JP**) a citizen who acts as a judge for certain matters.

'**justify** v to prove or show to be just, right or desirable: – pt '**justified**. – adj '**justifiable** able to be justified or defended. – n **justifi'cation** good reason.

jut v to stand or stick out: – pt '**jutted**.

jute [jōōt] *n* the fibre from certain plants for making sacking, canvas *etc.*

juvenile ['jōōvənīl] *adj* young, of young people; childish. – *n* a young person.

juxta'pose *v* to place side by side. – *n* **juxtapo'sition**.

K

kale *n* a cabbage with open curled leaves.

kaleidoscope [kə'līdəskōp] *n* a tube-shaped toy in which loose, coloured shapes reflected in two mirrors can be seen changing patterns. – *adj* **kaleidoscopic** [kəlīdə'skopik] with changing colours; changing quickly.

kangaroo [kaŋgə'rōō] *n* a large Australian animal with long hindlegs and great power of leaping. The female carries its young in a pouch on the front of its body.

'kāpok *n* light waterproof fibre fluff got from the seeds of a tropical tree, used for stuffing pillows *etc.*

karate [kə'räti] *n* a Japanese form of unarmed fighting using blows and kicks.

kart *see* **go-kart**.

kayak ['kīak] *n* a canoe *esp* an Eskimo canoe made of sealskins stretched on a frame.

ke'bab *n* small pieces of meat *etc usu* cooked on a skewer.

kedgeree [kejə'rē] *n* a dish made with rice, fish and other ingredients.

keel *n* the long supporting piece of a ship's frame that lies lengthways along the bottom. – *v* (with **over**) to overturn; to fall (over). – *v* **'keelhaul** (*hist*) to punish by hauling under the keel of a ship by ropes.

keen *adj* eager, enthusiastic; very sharp; biting cold. – *n* **'keenness**.

keep *v* to hold on to, not to give or throw away; to look after; to feed and clothe; to have or use; to fulfil (one's promise); to stay, (cause to) remain in any position or state; (sometimes with **on**) to continue (doing something); (of food) to remain in good condition; to celebrate: *keep Christmas*: – *pt* **kept** [kept]. – *n* food and other necessities; a castle stronghold. – *ns* **'keeper** one who looks after something; **'keeping** care; charge. – *n* **'keepsake** a gift in memory of the giver or an occasion *etc.* – **in keeping with** suited to; **keep out** to exclude; to stay outside; **keep up** to go on with, to continue (something); **keep up with** to go as fast *etc* as.

keg *n* a small cask or barrel.

kelp *n* a type of large brown seaweed.

'kelvin *n* a measure of temperature.

ken *n* the amount or extent of one's knowledge or understanding: *beyond the ken of the average person.*

'kennel *n* a hut for a dog; (*pl*) a place where dogs can be looked after.

kept *see* **keep**.

kerb *n* the edge of something, *esp* a pavement.

kerchief ['körchif] *n* a square of cloth used in dress to cover the head *etc.*

'kernel *n* the softer substance in the shell of a nut or inside the stone of a pulpy fruit; the important part of anything.

'kerosene *n* paraffin oil.

'kestrel *n* a type of small falcon which hovers.

ketch *n* a two-masted sailing vessel: – *pl* **'ketches**.

'ketchup *n* a flavouring sauce made from tomatoes *etc.*

'kettle *n* a metal pot *usu* with a spout for heating liquids. – *n* **'kettledrum** a drum made of a metal bowl covered with stretched skin *etc.*

key [kē] *n* that by which something (*eg* a door lock, a nut) is turned or screwed; in musical instruments, one of the small parts for sounding the notes; in a typewriter, one of the parts which one presses to type a word; the chief note of a piece of music; that which explains a mystery, code *etc*; a book containing answers to exercises *etc.* – *adj* important, essential. – *ns* **'keyboard** the keys in a piano or organ arranged along a flat board; **'keyhole** the hole in which a key of a door *etc* is placed; **'keynote** the chief note of a piece of music; the chief point about anything; **'keystone** the stone at the highest point of an arch holding the rest in position. – *adj* **'keyed-'up** excited.

khaki ['käki] *adj, n* (of) greenish-brown. – *n* cloth of this colour used for soldiers' uniforms.

kibbutz [ki'boots] *n* a (farming) settlement in modern Israel in which all share the work: – *pl* **kibbutzim** [ki'bootsēm].

kick *v* to hit or strike out with the foot;

(of a gun) to spring back violently when fired. – *n* a blow with the foot; the springing-back of a gun when fired. – *n* '**kick-off** the start (of a football game). – **for kicks** for fun.

kid *n* a young goat; goatskin; (*coll*) a child. – *adj* made of kid leather.

'**kidnap** *v* to carry off (a person or child) by force, often demanding money in exchange for them: – *pt* '**kidnapped**. – *n* '**kidnapper**.

'**kidney** *n* one of a pair of urine-controlling organs placed in the lower part of the back, one on each side. Some animals' kidneys are used as meat: – *pl* '**kidneys**.

kill *v* to put to death; to put an end to. – *n* the act of killing; the animals killed by a hunter. – *n* '**killer**. – **be at the kill** to be there at the most exciting moment.

kiln *n* a large oven or furnace for baking pottery, bricks *etc* or for drying grain, hops *etc*.

'**kilogramme** *n* a measure of weight – 1000 grammes (about 2⅕ lb).

'**kilomètre** *n* a measure of length – 1000 metres (about ⅝ of a mile).

kilowatt ['kiləwot] *n* a measure of electrical power.

kilt *n* (in Scotland) a pleated tartan skirt reaching to the knee, traditionally worn by men.

ki'mōno *n* a loose Japanese robe, fastened with a sash: – *pl* **ki'monos**.

kin *n* persons of the same family, relations. – **kith and kin** *see* **kith; next of kin** one's nearest relative.

kind *n* a sort, type; goods, not money: *paid in kind*. – *adj* having good feelings towards others; generous; gentle. – *adv* '**kindly**. – *adj* kind: *a kindly old man*. – *ns* '**kindness;** '**kindliness**. – *adj* '**kind'hearted** kind.

'**kindergarten** *n* a school for very young children.

'**kindle** *v* to light a fire; to catch fire; to stir up (feelings). – *n* '**kindling** material for starting a fire.

kindred ['kindrid] *n* one's relatives. – *adj* of the same sort; related.

ki'netic *adj* of motion.

king *n* the male ruler of a nation, inheriting his position by right of birth; the playing card with a picture of a king; the most important chess piece. – *adj* '**kingly** like a king; royal. – *ns* '**kingcup** marsh marigold; '**kingdom** the area ruled by a king; any of the three great divisions of natural objects – animal, vegetable or mineral; '**kingfisher** a type of fish-eating bird

with brightly-coloured feathers; '**kingpin** the most important person in an organization.

kink *n* a bend or curl in a rope, hair *etc*; a peculiarity of the mind.

kinsman ['kinzmən] *n* a man of the same family as oneself: – *fem* '**kinswoman**. – *npl* '**kinsfolk** one's own people, relations.

kiosk ['kēosk] *n* a small stall for the sale of papers, sweets *etc*; a telephone box.

'**kipper** *n* a smoked and dried herring.

kirk *n* (in Scotland) a church.

kiss *v* to touch lovingly with one's lips; to touch gently. – Also *n*: – *pl* '**kisses**. – **kiss of life** a mouth-to-mouth method of restoring breathing.

kit *n* an outfit of clothes, tools *etc* (necessary for a particular job *etc*).

'**kitchen** *n* a room where food is cooked. – *n* **kitche'nette** a small kitchen. – *n* '**kitchen-'garden** a vegetable garden.

kite *n* a light frame, covered with paper or other material, for flying in the air; a kind of hawk.

kith: kith and kin friends and relatives.

'**kitten** *n* a young cat.

'**kittiwake** *n* a type of gull.

'**kitty** *n* a sum of money set aside for a purpose.

kiwi ['kēwē] *n* a swift-running almost wingless bird of New Zealand.

klepto'mānia *n* an uncontrollable desire to steal. – *n, adj* **klepto'maniac**.

knack [nak] *n* a special clever ability.

knacker ['nakər] *n* a buyer of old horses for slaughter.

knapsack ['napsak] *n* a bag for food, clothes *etc* slung on the back.

knave [nāv] *n* a cheating rogue; (in cards) the jack. – *n* '**knavery** dishonesty. – *adj* '**knavish** cheating, wicked.

knead [nēd] *v* to work (dough *etc*) by pressing with the fingers; to massage.

knee [nē] *n* the joint at the bend of the leg. – *n* '**kneecap** the flat round bone on the front of the knee joint.

kneel [nēl] *v* to go down on one or both knees: – *pt* **knelt** [nelt].

knell [nel] *n* the tolling of a bell for a death or funeral; a warning of a sad end or failure.

knickerbockers ['nikərbokərz] *npl* loose breeches tucked in at the knee.

knickers ['nikərz] *npl* women's and girls' underwear for the lower part of the body; knickerbockers.

knick-knack ['niknak] *n* a small, ornamental article.

knife [nīf] *n* a tool for cutting: – *pl* **knives** [nīvz]. – *v* to stab.

knight [nīt] *n* (*hist*) one of noble birth,

trained to use arms; a rank, with the title *Sir*, which does not go down from father to son; a piece used in chess. – *v* to raise to the rank of knight. – *adj* **'knightly** of knights; gallant, courageous. – *ns* **'knight-'errant** (*hist*) a knight who travelled in search of adventures; **'knighthood** the rank of a knight.

knit [nit] *v* to form a garment or fabric from yarn or thread (by means of knitting needles); to join closely: – *pt* **'knitted**. – *n* **'knitting** work done by knitting. – *npl* **knitting needles** (a pair of) thin pointed rods used in knitting.

knob [nob] *n* a hard rounded part standing out from the main part; a (door-)handle.

knock [nok] *v* to strike, hit; to drive or be driven against; to tap on a door to have it opened. – *n* a sudden stroke; a tap (on a door). – *n* **'knocker** a hinged weight on a door for knocking with. – *adj* **'knock-'kneed** having knees that touch in walking. – **knock out** to hit (someone) hard enough to make him unconscious.

knoll [nōl] *n* a small rounded hill.

knot [not] *n* a hard lump, *esp* one made by tying string *etc*, or one in wood at the join between trunk and branch; a tangle; a small gathering, cluster (*eg* of people); a measure of speed for ships (about 1·85 kilometre per hour). – *v* to tie in a knot: – *pt* **'knotted**. – *adjs* **'knotted** full of knots; **'knotty** having knots; difficult.

know [nō] *v* to be aware or sure of; to recognize: – *pt* **knew**. – *adj* **'knowing** clever; cunning. – *adv* **'knowingly** intentionally. – *n* **knowledge** ['nolij] that which is known; information; ability, skill. – *adj* **'knowledgeable** showing or having knowledge.

knuckle ['nukl] *n* a joint of the fingers. – *v* (with **under**) to give in, yield.

kō'ala bear *n* an Australian tree-climbing animal that looks like a small bear.

kookaburra *see* **jackass**.

Ko'ran *n* the holy book of the Mohammedans.

'kōsher *adj* pure and clean according to Jewish law.

kowtow ['kow'tow] *v* (with **to**) to treat with too much respect.

kung-fu ['kuŋ'fōō] *n* a form of self-defence, developed in China.

kraal [kräl] *n* a South African village.

'kūdos *n* fame, glory.

L

lab short for **laboratory**.

'lābel *n* a small written note fixed on to something (to tell its contents, owner *etc*). – *v* to fix a label to; to call something by a certain name: – *pt* **'labelled**.

'lābial *adj* of the lips.

la'boratory *n* a scientist's workroom: – *pl* **la'boratories**.

labour, (*US*) **labor** ['lābər] *n* (hard) work; workmen on a job; (in a pregnant female) the process of childbirth. – *v* to work hard; to move slowly or with difficulty; emphasize (a point) too greatly. – *adjs* **laborious** [lə'bōriəs] requiring hard work; wearisome; **'laboured** showing signs of effort. – *n* **'labourer** one who does heavy unskilled work. – *n* **Labour Party** one of the chief political parties of Great Britain.

la'burnum *n* a kind of tree with large hanging clusters of yellow flowers and poisonous seeds.

labyrinth ['labərinth] *n* a place full of puzzling windings, a maze.

lace *n* a string or cord, for fastening shoes *etc*; decorative openwork fabric made with fine thread. – *v* to fasten with a lace.

lacerate ['lasərāt] *v* to tear, wound. – *n* **lace'ration**.

lack *v* to be in want; to be without. – *n* want, need.

lacka'daisical *adj* bored, half-hearted.

'lackey *n* a manservant; one who acts like a slave: – *pl* **'lackeys**.

la'conic *adj* using few words to express one's meaning. – *adv* **la'conically**.

lacquer ['lakər] *n* a varnish. – Also *v*.

la'crosse *n* a twelve-a-side ball game played with sticks having a shallow net at the end.

'lactic *adj* of milk.

lad *n* a boy, a youth.

'ladder *n* a set of rungs or steps between two supports, for climbing up or down; a run from a broken stitch, in a stocking *etc*.

lade *n* a channel for leading water to a millwheel.

'lāden *adj* loaded, burdened. – *n* **'lading** that which is loaded; cargo.

'**lādle** *n* a large spoon for lifting out liquid. – *v* to lift with a ladle.

'**lády** *n* a woman (of good manners); a title of the wives of knights, lords and baronets, and of the daughters of noblemen: – *pl* '**ladies**. – *n* '**ladybird** a small beetle, usually red with black spots. – **Her Ladyship** the title of a lady.

lag *v* to move slowly and fall behind; to cover (a boiler or pipes) with a warm covering: – *pt* **lagged**. – *n* a delay. – *n* '**lagging** material for covering pipes *etc.*

lager ['lägər] *n* a light beer.

la'goon *n* a shallow stretch of water separated from the sea by low sandbanks, rocks *etc.*

laid *see* **lay**[1].

lain *see* **lie**.

lair *n* the den of a wild beast.

laird *n* (in Scotland) a land-owner, squire.

laity *see* **lay**[2].

lake *n* a large stretch of water surrounded by land.

'**lama** *n* a Buddhist priest of Tibet.

lamb [lam] *n* a young sheep; the meat of this animal; one gentle as a lamb.

lame *adj* unable to walk, crippled; not good enough: *a lame excuse.* – *v* to make lame. – *n* '**lameness**.

la'ment *v* to mourn, feel or express grief for; to regret. – *n* a show of grief (also **lamen'tation**); a mournful poem or piece of music. – *adj* '**lamentable** pitiful; very bad.

lamp *n* a (glass-covered) light.

lam'poon *n* a violent criticism (in writing) of a person.

'**lamprey** *n* a type of fish like an eel: – *pl* '**lampreys**.

lance *n* a long shaft of wood, with a spearhead. – *v* to cut open (a boil *etc*) with a knife. – *n* '**lancer** a light cavalry soldier. – *n* '**lance-'corporal** a soldier with rank just below a corporal.

land *n* the solid portion of the earth's surface; ground, soil; a (part of a) country. – *v* to set or come on land or on shore. – *adj* '**landed** consisting of or owning lands and estates: *landed property: landed gentry.* – *n* '**landing** a coming ashore or to ground; a place for getting on shore; the level part of a staircase between the flights of steps. – *n* '**landfall** an approach to land after a voyage; the land approached. – *adj* '**landlocked** almost shut in by land. – *ns* '**landlord** the owner of land or houses; the master of an inn: – *fem* '**landlady**; '**landlubber** one who

lives, works *etc* on land and knows little about the sea; '**landmark** any object on land that serves as a guide; an important event; '**landscape** (picture of a) view of inland scenery; '**landslide** a mass of land that slips down from the side of a hill; **landslide victory** (in elections *etc*) one in which a great mass of votes goes to one side.

landau ['landö] *n* a kind of carriage with a removable top.

lane *n* a narrow road, street or passage; a course or part of the road, sea *etc* to which cars, ships, aircraft *etc* must keep.

language ['langwij] *n* human speech; the speech of a particular people or nation.

languid ['langwid] *adj* lacking liveliness and spirit. – *v* **languish** ['langwish] to grow weak, to droop; to long (for). – *adj* '**languishing**. – *n* **languor** ['langər] state of being languid.

lank *adj* tall and thin; (of hair) straight and limp. – *adj* '**lanky** tall and thin.

'**lantern** *n* a case for holding or carrying a light. – *adj* '**lantern-'jawed** hollow-cheeked, long-jawed.

'**lanyard, 'laniard** *n* (on a ship) a short rope used for fastening; a cord for hanging a whistle *etc* round the neck.

lap *v* to lick up with the tongue; to wash or flow against; (with **up**) to accept (praise *etc*) greedily; to wrap round, surround; to make (something) lie partly (over); in a race, to get a lap ahead of other competitors: – *pt* **lapped**. – *n* the front part (from waist to knees) of a person seated; the clothes covering that part; a fold; one round of a racetrack or other competition course. – *n* '**lapdog** a small pet dog.

la'pel *n* the part of a coat joined to the collar and folded back on the chest.

'**lapidary** *n* one who cuts, polishes and shapes (precious) stones: – *pl* '**lapidaries**. – *adj* engraved on stone.

lapse *v* to fall (into evil ways or careless habits); to cease. – *n* a mistake, a failure; a passing away (of time).

'**lapwing** *n* a type of bird of the plover family (also '**peewit**).

'**larboard** *n* the left side of a ship looking from the stern, now called **port**.

'**larceny** *n* stealing, theft.

larch *n* a kind of cone-bearing deciduous tree: – *pl* '**larches**.

lard *n* the melted fat of the pig. – *v* to put strips of bacon *etc* in meat before cooking; to smear, lay on thickly.

'**larder** *n* a room or place where food is kept; stock of food.

large *adj* great in size, amount *etc.* – *adv* **'largely** mainly, to a great extent. – *n* **'largeness.** – **at large** at liberty, free; in general: *the public at large*.

largesse [lär'jes] *n* a generous giving away of money *etc.*

'lariat *n* a rope for fastening horses while they are grazing; a lasso.

lark *n* a general name for several kinds of singing bird; a piece of fun or mischief. – *v* to fool about, behave mischievously.

'larkspur *n* a tall plant with blue, white or pink spurred flowers, a kind of delphinium.

'larva *n* an insect in its first stage after coming out of the egg, a grub: – *pl* **larvae** ['lärvē].

larynx ['lariŋks] *n* the upper part of the windpipe containing the cords that produce the voice. – *n* **laryngitis** [larin'jitis] a disease of the larynx.

lascivious [lǝ'siviǝs] *adj* full of indecent desires, lustful.

laser ['lāzǝr] *n* (an instrument that concentrates light into) a very narrow powerful beam.

lash *n* a thong or cord of a whip; a stroke with a whip: – *pl* **'lashes.** – *v* to strike with a whip; to fasten with a rope *etc*; to attack with bitter words.

lass *n* a girl: – *pl* **'lasses.**

'lassitūde *n* lack of energy, weariness.

lasso [la'sōō] *n* a long rope with a loop that tightens when the rope is pulled, used for catching wild horses *etc*: – *pl* **las'so(e)s.** – *v* to catch with a lasso.

last *adj* coming after all the others. *He was the last person to arrive. The audience left before the last act*; most recent, next before the present. *His last job was boring.* – Also *adv.* – *v* to continue, go on; to remain in good condition. – *n* a foot-like shape on which shoes are made or repaired. – *adv* **'lastly** finally. – **at last** in the end; **on one's last legs** completely worn out, about to collapse; **to the last** to the end.

latch *n* a catch of wood or metal used to fasten a door: – *pl* **'latches.** – *v* to fasten with a latch. – *n* **'latchkey** a door-key (to raise the latch of a door).

late *adj* coming after the expected time. *The train was late*; far on (in time). *It's getting late*; recent: *our late disagreement*; recently dead: *the late king*; recently, but no longer, holding an office or position: *the late chairman*. – Also *adv.* – *adv* **'lately** recently. – *n* **'lateness.** – **of late** recently.

'lātent *adj* hidden, undeveloped but capable of becoming developed or active:

latent ability: latent hostility.

'lateral *adj* of, at, to, or from the side.

'lātex *n* the milky juice of plants *esp* of the rubber tree.

lath *n* a thin narrow strip of wood.

lathe [lādh] *n* a machine for turning and shaping articles of wood, metal *etc.*

lather ['lädhǝr] *n* a foam or froth (*eg* from soap and water). – *v* to cover with lather.

'Latin *n* the language of ancient Rome.

'latitude *n* the distance, measured in degrees on the map, of a place north or south from the equator; freedom of action or choice. *His new job allows him far more latitude than his previous one.*

'latter *adj* the last of two mentioned; recent. – *adv* **'latterly** recently. – *adj* **'latter-day** of recent times.

lattice ['latis] *n* a network of crossed wooden *etc* strips (also **'lattice-work**); a window having this.

'laudable *adj* worthy of being praised. – *adj* **'laudatory** expressing praise.

laugh [läf] *v* to make sounds with the voice in showing amusement, happiness, scorn *etc.* – *n* the sound of laughing. – *adj* **'laughable** comical, ridiculous. – *n* **'laughter** the act or noise of laughing. – *n* **laughing stock** an object of scornful laughter.

launch *v* to cause a boat, ship, to slide into the water; to start (someone or something) off on a course; to throw or hurl. – *n* the act of launching; a large motor boat: – *pl* **'launches.**

'launder *v* to wash and iron clothes. – *ns* **launderette** [lön'dret] a shop where customers may wash clothes in washing machines; **'laundry** a place where clothes are washed (*pl* **'laundries**); clothes to be washed.

'laurel *n* the bay tree, from which wreaths were made for crowning victors *etc*; (*pl*) honours or victories gained.

'lava *n* molten rock *etc* thrown out by a volcano, becoming solid as it cools.

'lavatory *n* a toilet: – *pl* **'lavatories.**

'lavender *n* a plant with small pale-purple, sweet-smelling flowers; a pale-purple colour.

'lavish *v* to spend or give very freely. – *adj* too free in giving or spending, very generous.

law *n* the collection of rules according to which a country is governed; any one of such rules; (in science) a rule that says that in certain conditions certain things always happen. – *adjs* **'lawful** allowed by law; **'lawless** paying no attention to, and not observing the laws. – *n*

'lawyer one whose work it is to give advice in matters of law. – *adj* **'law-abiding** obeying the law. – *ns* **law court** a place where people accused of crimes are tried; **'lawsuit** a quarrel or dispute to be settled by a court of law.

lawn *n* an area of smooth grass *eg* as part of a garden; a kind of fine linen. – *ns* **'lawnmower** a machine for cutting grass; **lawn tennis** tennis played on a grass court.

lax *adj* not strict; careless, negligent. – *ns* **'laxity; 'laxness; 'laxative** a medicine which loosens the bowels.

lay[1] *v* to place or set down; to put (*eg* a burden, duty) on (someone); to beat down; to cause to disappear or subside: *lay a ghost*; to set in order, arrange; (of hens) to produce eggs; to bet, wager: – *pt* **laid**. – *adj* **'laid-'up** ill in bed. – *ns* **'layabout** a lazy idle person; **'layby** a parking area at the side of a road. – **lay about someone** to deal blows on all sides; **lay off** to dismiss (workers) temporarily; (*coll*) to stop: *lay off arguing*; to talk at great length; **lay up** to store for future use; **lay waste** to ruin, destroy.

lay[2] *adj* not of the clergy; without special training in or special knowledge of a particular subject. – *ns* **laity** ['läəti] ordinary people, not clergymen; **'layman** one of the laity; someone without special training in a subject.

lay[3] *n* (*hist*) a short poem; a song.

'layer *n* a thickness or covering.

lay'ette *n* a baby's complete outfit.

'lazy *adj* not caring for work; idle: – *comp* **'lazier**, *superl* **'laziest**. – *v* **laze** to be lazy. – *n* **'laziness**.

lea *n* (*old*) a meadow.

lead[1] *v* to show the way by going first; to direct; to guide; to persuade; to live (a busy *etc* life); (of a road) to form a way (to), go (to): – *pt* **led**. – *n* the first or front place; guidance, direction; a leash for a dog *etc*. – *ns* **'leader** one who leads or goes first; a chief; a column in a newspaper expressing the editor's opinions; **'leadership** the state of being a leader; the ability to lead. – *n* **leading question** a question asked in such a way as to suggest the desired answer.

lead[2] [led] *n* an element, a soft bluish-grey metal; the part of a pencil that writes, really made of graphite; a weight used for sounding depths at sea *etc*. – *adj* **'leaden** made of lead; lead-coloured; dull, heavy.

leaf *n* a part of a plant growing from the side of a stem, *usu* green, flat and thin but of various shapes according to the plant; anything thin like a leaf; a page of a book; a hinged flap or movable extra part of a table *etc*: – *pl* **leaves** [lēvz]. – *adj* **'leafy**. – *n* **'leaflet** a small printed sheet. – **turn over a new leaf** to begin again and do better.

league [lēg] *n* a union of persons, nations *etc* for the benefit of each other; an association of clubs for games; an old measure of distance, *usu* 3 miles (about 4·8 kilometres). – **in league with** allied with.

leak *n* a hole through which liquid passes; an escape of gas *etc* or of secret information. – Also *v*. – *n* **'leakage** that which enters or escapes by leaking.

lean *v* to slope over to one side, not to be upright; to rest (against); to rely (on): – *pt* **leant** [lent]. – *adj* thin; poor, scanty; (of meat) not fat. – *ns* **'leaning** a liking (for something); **'leanness** thinness; poorness. – *n* **'lean-to** a shed *etc* built against another building or wall.

leap *v* to move with jumps; to jump (over): – *pt* **leapt** [lept]. – *n* a jump. – *ns* **'leapfrog** a game in which one player leaps over another's bent back; **leap year** a year which has 366 days (February having 29), occurring every fourth year.

learn [lėrn] *v* to get to know (something); to gain skill: – *pp* and *pt* **learned, learnt**. – *adj* **learned** ['lėrnid] having or showing great knowledge. – *ns* **'learner; 'learning** knowledge.

lease *n* (the period of) an agreement giving the use of a house *etc* on payment of rent. – *v* to let or rent. – *n* **'leasehold** property, or land, held by lease.

leash *n* a lead by which a dog *etc* is held: – *pl* **'leashes**. – *v* to put (a dog *etc*) on a leash.

least *adj*, *n* the smallest (of), amount (of): *least money. He has least*. – *adv* (often with **the**) the smallest or lowest degree. *I like her least*. – **at least** at any rate, anyway; **not in the least** not at all.

leather ['ledhər] *n* the skin of an animal, prepared (by tanning) for use. – *v* to beat. – *n* **'leathering** a thrashing. – *adj* **'leathery** like leather; tough.

leave *n* permission to do something (*eg* to be absent); (*esp* of soldiers, sailors) a holiday. – *v* to allow to remain; to abandon, forsake; to depart (from); to make a gift to a person by one's will; to give to a person's charge, care *etc*. *Leave the decision to him*: – *pt* **left**. – *npl* **'leavings** things left over. – **take one's**

leave (of) to part from; to say goodbye to.

'**lecherous** *adj* lustful in a sexual way. – *n* '**lechery**.

'**lectern** *n* a stand for a book to be read from.

lecture ['lekchər] *n* something written or read to an audience, on a certain subject; a scolding. – *v* to deliver a lecture; to scold. – *n* '**lecturer** one who lectures, *esp* to students.

led *see* **lead**¹.

ledge *n* a shelf or an object that sticks out like a shelf: *a window-ledge*; an underwater ridge.

'**ledger** *n* the book of accounts of an office or shop.

lee *n* the side away from the wind, the sheltered side. – *adj, adv* '**leeward** in the direction towards which the wind blows. – *n* '**leeway** a drift (of a ship) off course; lost time, lost ground *etc. He has a lot of leeway to make up since he has been off ill.*

leech *n* a kind of blood-sucking worm: – *pl* '**leeches**.

leek *n* a long green and white vegetable of the onion family.

leer *n* a sly, sidelong or lustful look. – Also *v.*

lees *npl* dregs that settle at the bottom of liquid.

left¹ *adj* on, for, or belonging to the side of the body that in most people has the less skilful hand (opposite to **right**). – Also *adv.* – *n* the left side; a group with left-wing ideas *etc.* – *adjs* '**left-'handed** using the left hand rather than the right; awkward; '**left-'wing** extremely socialist or radical in political views, ideas *etc.*

left² *see* **leave**.

leg *n* one of the limbs by which animals (including man) walk; a long slender support of anything (as of a table); one stage in a journey, contest *etc.* – *npl* '**leggings** outer coverings for the lower legs. – *adj* '**leggy** having long legs.

'**legacy** *n* something which is left by will; something left behind by someone who had one's job, house *etc* previously: – *pl* '**legacies**. – *n* **lega'tee** one to whom a legacy is left.

'**legal** *adj* allowed by law, lawful; of law. – *n* **le'gality** the state of being legal: – *pl* **le'galities**. – *v* '**legalize** to make lawful.

le'gation *n* (the headquarters of) an official body of people acting on behalf of the government of their own country *etc* in another country, an embassy.

'**legend** *n* a story handed down from long

ago, a myth; the words accompanying a picture, a caption. – *adj* '**legendary** of legend; famous; not to be believed.

legerdemain ['lejərdəmān] *n* conjuring by quickness of the hand.

'**legible** *adj* (of writing) that can be read (easily). – *n* **legi'bility**.

'**legion** *n* (*hist*) a body of Roman soldiers of from three to six thousand; a great many, a very large number. – *n* '**legionary** a soldier of a legion.

'**legislate** *v* to make laws. – *n* **legis'lation**. – *adj* '**legislative** law-making. – *ns* '**legislator** one who makes laws; '**legislature** the part of the government which has the powers of making laws.

le'gitimate *adj* lawful; (of a child) born of parents married to each other; correct, reasonable. – *n* **le'gitimacy**.

leisure ['lezhər] *n* time free from work, spare time. – *adj* '**leisured** not occupied with business. – *adj, adv* '**leisurely** taking plenty of time.

'**lemming** *n* a kind of small rat-like animal of the arctic regions.

'**lemon** *n* an oval fruit with pale yellow rind and very sour juice, or the tree that bears it. – *n* **lemo'nade** a (fizzy) drink flavoured with lemons.

'**lemur** *n* a kind of animal related to the monkey but with a pointed nose.

lend *v* to give use of (something) for a time; to give, add (a quality) to someone or something. *His presence lent an air of respectability to the occasion:* – *pt* **lent**. – **lend itself to** to be suitable for, adapt easily to.

length *n* the extent from end to end in space or time; the quality of being long; a great extent; a piece (of cloth *etc*). – *v* '**lengthen** to make or grow longer. – *advs* '**lengthways, 'lengthwise** in the direction of the length. – *adj* '**lengthy** long; tiresomely long. – **at length** in detail; at last.

'**lēnient** *adj* merciful, punishing only lightly. – *ns* '**lenience**; '**leniency**.

lens [lenz] *n* a piece of glass *etc* curved on one or both sides, used in spectacles, contact lenses, cameras *etc*; a part of the eye: – *pl* '**lenses**.

Lent *n* (in the Christian church) a period of fasting before Easter lasting forty days.

lent *see* **lend**.

'**lentil** *n* the seed of a pod-bearing plant, used in soups *etc.*

'**lēonine** *adj* like a lion.

leopard ['lepərd] *n* a type of animal of the cat family with a spotted skin.

'**lēotard** *n* a kind of tight-fitting garment worn for dancing, gymnastics *etc.*

'**leper** *n* a person with leprosy; an out-cast. – *n* '**leprosy** a contagious skin disease.

leprechaun ['leprəkön] *n* (*myth*) a kind of Irish fairy.

less *adj* not as much: *less time*; smaller. *Think of a number less than 40.* – *adv* not as much, to a smaller extent. *He goes less (often) than he should.* – *n* a smaller portion, amount. *He has less than I have.* – *prep* minus: *5 less 2 equals 3.* – *v* '**lessen** to make smaller. – *adj* '**lesser** smaller.

'**lesson** *n* that which is learned or taught; a part of the Bible read in church; a period of teaching.

lest *conj* for fear that, in case.

let *v* to allow; to grant use of (*eg* a house, shop, farm) in return for payment: – *pres p* '**letting**, *pt, pp* **let**. – **let down** to fail to help *etc*, disappoint; **let off** to excuse, not to punish *etc*; **let up** to become less.

'**lethal** *adj* causing death.

'**lethargy** *n* lack of energy or interest; sleepiness. – *adj* **le'thargic**.

'**letter** *n* a mark expressing a sound; a written message; (*pl*) learning: *a man of letters.* – *n* '**lettering** the way in which letters are formed; the letters formed. – (**to**) **the letter** (according to) the exact meaning of the words. *He followed his father's instructions to the letter.*

lettuce ['letis] *n* a kind of green plant whose leaves are used in a salad.

leukaemia [loo'kēmiə] *n* a disease of the white blood cells in the body.

levee ['levi] *n* a reception, meeting *etc* held by a king or queen.

'**level** *n* a flat, smooth surface; a height, position, strength *etc* in comparison with some standard: *water level*; a kind of instrument for showing whether a surface is level: *spirit level*; suitable or appropriate position or rank. – *adj* flat, even, smooth or horizontal. – *v* to make flat, smooth or horizontal; to make equal; to aim (a gun *etc*); to pull down (a building *etc*): – *pt* '**levelled**. – *adj* '**level-'headed** having good sense. – *n* **level crossing** a place where a road crosses a railway track.

'**lever** *n* a bar of metal, wood *etc* used to raise up or shift something heavy; a bar or handle for operating a machine *etc*; any method of gaining advantage. *He used the information as a lever to get a better job.*

leveret ['levərit] *n* a young hare.

le'viathan *n* a kind of huge (sea) monster; anything huge or powerful.

levi'tation *n* (the illusion of) raising a heavy body in the air without support. – *v* '**levitate** to (cause to) float in the air.

'**levity** *n* lack of seriousness, frivolity.

'**levy** *v* to collect by order (*eg* a tax, men for an army): – *pt* '**levied**. – *n* money, troops *etc* collected by order: – *pl* '**levies**.

lewd *adj* taking delight in indecent thoughts or acts. – *n* '**lewdness**.

lexi'cographer *n* a maker of a dictionary.

'**liable** *adj* legally responsible (for) or bound to do something; likely or apt (to do something or happen); (with **to**) likely to have, get, suffer from: *liable to colds.* – *n* **lia'bility** (legal) responsibility; a debt; a disadvantage: – *pl* **lia'bilities**.

liaison [lē'āzon] *n* contact, communication.

liar *see* **lie**.

'**libel** *n* anything written with the purpose of hurting a person's reputation. – Also *v*: – *pt* '**libelled**. – *adj* '**libellous**.

liberal ['libərəl] *adj* generous; broad-minded, tolerant. – *ns* '**Liberal** a member of the Liberal Party; **libe'rality**. – *n* **Liberal Party** one of the chief political parties of Great Britain.

liberate ['libərət] *v* to set free. – *n* **libe'ration**.

libertine ['libərtēn] *n* one who lives a wicked, immoral life.

'**liberty** *n* freedom; too great freedom of speech or action; (*pl*) '**liberties** rights, privileges. – **take liberties** to behave rudely or impertinently.

'**library** *n* (a building or room containing) a collection of books or some other collection (*eg* gramophone records): – *pl* '**libraries**. – *n* **li'brārian** the keeper of a library.

li'bretto *n* (a book of) the words of an opera, musical show *etc*: – *pl* **libretti** [li'bretē] or **li'brettos**.

lice *see* **louse**.

'**licence** *n* a (printed) form giving permission to do something (*eg* to keep a dog, television set *etc*, to drive a car *etc*); too great freedom of action *etc*. – *v* '**license** to permit. – *n* **licen'see** one to whom a licence (*esp* one to keep a hotel or public house) is given. – *adj* **li'centious** given to behaving immorally or improperly. – *n* **li'centiousness**.

lichen ['likən] *n* a large group of moss-like plants that grow on rocks *etc*.

lick *v* to pass the tongue over; (of flames) to reach up, to touch. – *n* the act of licking; a tiny amount. – **lick into**

shape to make vigorous improvements on.

lid *n* a cover for a box, pot *etc*; the cover of the eye.

lie *n* a false statement meant to deceive. – *v* to tell a lie: – *pres p* '**lying**, *pt* **lied**; to rest in a flat position: – *pt* **lay**, *pp* **lain**; to be or to remain in a state or position: – *pt* **lay**, *pp* **lain**. – *n* the position or situation in which something lies. – *n* '**liar** one who tells lies. – *adj*, *n* '**lying**. – **lie in wait (for)** to keep hidden in order to surprise someone (with an attack); **lie low** to keep quiet or hidden; **the lie of the land** the state of affairs.

liege [lēj] *n* a loyal subject; a lord or superior. – *n* '**liege-lord** (*hist*) an overlord.

lieu [lōō]: **in lieu (of)** instead of.

lieutenant [ləf'tenənt]   *n* in the army, an officer next below captain, in the navy, an officer below a lieutenant-commander; a rank below a higher officer, as **lieu'tenant-'colonel**.

life *n* the period between birth and death; the state of being alive; liveliness; manner of living; the story of a person's life; living things: *animal life*: – *pl* **lives**. – *adj* '**lifeless** dead; not lively. – *ns* '**lifebelt** a ring or belt made of cork or filled with air for keeping a person afloat; '**lifeboat** a boat for saving shipwrecked persons; **life cycle** the various stages through which a living thing passes. – *adjs* '**life-like** like a living person; '**lifelong** lasting the length of a life; '**life-size** (of a portrait *etc*) full size.

lift *v* to bring to a higher position, raise; to take up; (*coll*) to steal; (of fog *etc*) to disappear. – *n* a platform *etc* that moves up and down (between floors) carrying goods or people; a ride in someone's car *etc*; a raising (of spirits *etc*), a boost. – *n* '**lift-off** the take-off of a rocket *etc*.

'**ligament** *n* a tough substance that connects the bones of the body.

'**ligature** *n* something which binds.

light [līt] *n* the brightness given by the sun, moon, lamps *etc* that makes things able to be seen; a source of light (*eg* a lamp); a flame (of a match *etc*); knowledge. – *adj* bright; (of a colour) pale; having light, not dark. – *v* to give light to; to set fire to: – *pt* **lit** or '**lighted**. – *v* '**lighten** to make or become brighter; (of lightning) to flash. — *ns* '**lightening** a making or becoming lighter or brighter; '**lighter** something used for lighting (a cigarette *etc*); '**lighting** a means of providing

light. — *ns* '**lighthouse** a tower-like building with a flashing light to warn or guide ships; '**lightship** a ship anchored in a fixed position to serve as a lighthouse; '**light-year** the distance light travels in a year (6 billion miles). — **bring to light** to reveal, cause to be noticed; **come to light** to be revealed or discovered; **in the light of** taking into consideration (information acquired *etc*).

light² [līt] *adj* not heavy; easy to bear or to do; easy to digest; nimble, lively; not grave, gay; not serious: *light music*; (of rain *etc*) little in quantity. – *v* '**lighten** to make less heavy. – *n* '**lighter** a large open boat used in unloading and loading ships. – *adv* '**lightly**. – *adjs* '**light-'fingered** apt to steal; '**light-'headed** dizzy; '**light-'hearted** cheerful.

light³ [līt] *v* (with **on, upon**) to land, settle on; to come upon by chance: – *pt* '**lighted** or **lit**.

lightning ['lītniŋ] *n* an electric flash in the clouds. – *n* **lightning conductor** a metal rod that protects buildings *etc* from the electricity of lightning by conducting it down to earth.

'**lignite** *n* brown, woody coal.

like¹ *adj* the same as or similar to. – *adv* in the same way as. *He runs like a hare.* – *n* something or someone that is the equal of another. *You won't see his like again*; the same thing: *do the like.* – *v* '**liken** to think of as similar, to compare. – *adj* '**likely** probable; promising; liable (to do something). – *adv* probably. – *ns* '**likelihood** probability; '**likeness** a similarity, a resemblance; a portrait, photograph *etc* of someone. – *adv* '**likewise** in the same way; also.

like² *v* to be pleased with; to be fond of. – *adj* '**lik(e)able** attractive, lovable. – *n* '**liking** a fondness; satisfaction: *to my liking.*

'**lilac** *n* a small tree with hanging clusters of pale purple or white flowers. – *adj* of pale purple colour.

lilt *n* (a tune *etc* with) a striking rhythm or swing. – Also *v*.

'**lily** *n* a tall plant grown from a bulb with large white or coloured flowers: – *pl* '**lilies**. – *n* '**lily-of-the-'valley** a plant with small white bell-shaped flowers.

limb [lim] *n* a leg or arm; a branch.

'**limber** *adj* easily bent, supple. – **limber up** to exercise so as to become supple.

'**limbo**: **in limbo** forgotten, neglected.

lime *n* the white substance, quicklime, left after heating limestone, used in making cement; a type of tree related to the lemon or its greenish-yellow fruit;

another name for the **linden** tree. – **in the limelight** attracting publicity or attention.

'**limit** *n* the farthest point or place; a boundary; largest (or smallest) extent, degree *etc*; restriction. – *v* to set or keep to a limit. – *n* **limi'tation** that which limits; the act of limiting; a weak point about a person or thing.

limousine ['liməzēn] *n* a kind of large motor car, *esp* one with a separate compartment for the driver.

limp *adj* lacking stiffness; weak. – *v* to walk lamely; of a damaged ship *etc* to move with difficulty. – *n* the act of limping; a limping walk.

'**limpet** *n* a small cone-shaped shellfish that clings to rocks; a person who is difficult to get rid of.

'**limpid** *adj* clear, transparent.

'**linchpin** *n* a pin-shaped rod used to keep a wheel on an axle.

'**linden** *n* (also called **lime**) a tree with small flowers and heart-shaped leaves.

line *n* a cord, rope *etc*; a long thin stroke or mark; a wrinkle; a row (of printed words, ships, soldiers *etc*); a service of ships or aircraft; a railway; a telephone wire *etc*, or any connected system; a short letter; a family from generation to generation; course, direction; a kind or sort (of thing, activity *etc*); (*pl*) army trenches; (*pl*) a written school punishment exercise. – *v* to mark out with lines; (*esp* with **up**) to place in a row or alongside of; to form lines along (a street); to cover on the inside: *line a dress*. – *n* **lineage** ['liniij] one's descent, traced back to one's ancestors. – *adj* **lineal** ['liniəl] directly descended through the father, grandfather *etc*. – *n* '**lineament** a feature, *esp* of the face. – *adj* '**linear** made of lines; (of measurement) in one dimension (length, breadth or height) only. – *ns* '**liner** a ship or aeroplane working on a regular service; '**lining** a covering on the inside. – *n* '**linesman** (in sport) an umpire at a boundary line. – (**ship, regiment**) **of the line** (a ship or regiment) belonging to the regular fighting forces.

'**linen** *n* cloth made of flax; articles made of linen (*eg* tablelinen, bedlinen).

ling *n* a type of long slender fish like the cod; heather.

linger ['lingər] *v* to remain for a long time or for longer than the expected time; to loiter, delay.

lingerie ['lōnzhəri] *n* women's underwear.

lingua franca ['lingwə'frankə] *n* any (often simplified) language used amongst people from different nations *etc* so that they can talk together.

linguist ['lingwist] *n* one skilled in languages; one who studies language. – *adj* **lin'guistic**. – *n* **lin'guistics** the scientific study of languages and of language in general.

'**liniment** *n* an oil or ointment rubbed into the skin to cure stiffness in the muscles, joints *etc*.

'**lining** *n* the cover of the inside of anything.

link *n* a ring of a chain; a single part of a series; anything connecting two things. – *v* to connect as by a link; to join closely; to be connected.

links *npl* a stretch of flat or slightly hilly ground near the seashore; a golfcourse.

'**linnet** *n* a type of small songbird of the finch family.

'**lino** *n* short for **linoleum**. – *n* '**linocut** a design for printing cut into a block of linoleum.

linoleum [li'nōliəm] *n* a type of smooth, hard-wearing covering for floors.

'**linseed** *n* flax seed. – *n* **linseed oil** oil from flax seed.

lint *n* linen scraped into a soft woolly material for putting over wounds; fine pieces of fluff.

'**lintel** *n* a timber or stone over a doorway or window.

'**lion** *n* a type of powerful animal of the cat family, the male of which has a shaggy mane: – *fem* '**lioness**. – *v* '**lionize** to treat (someone) as a celebrity. – **the lion's share** the largest share.

lip *n* the fleshy rim of the mouth; the edge of an opening, container *etc*. – *ns* '**lip-reading** reading what a person says from the movement of the lips; '**lip-service** saying one thing but believing another. *He pays lip-service to the rules*; '**lipstick** a stick of red, pink *etc* colouring for the lips.

'**liquefy** *v* to make or become liquid: – *pt* '**liquefied**. – *n* **lique'faction**.

liqueur [li'kūr] *n* a strong alcoholic drink, strongly flavoured and *usu* sweet.

'**liquid** *n* a flowing, water-like substance. – *adj* flowing; looking like water; soft and clear. – *v* '**liquidate** to close down, wind up the affairs of (a bankrupt business company); to get rid of by violence. – *ns* **liqui'dation**; '**liquidator**.

liquor ['likər] *n* any alcoholic drink, *esp* a strong kind (*eg* whisky).

liquorice, licorice ['likəris] *n* a plant with a sweet root; a black, sticky sweet made from this root.

lira ['lērə] *n* the standard unit of Italian money.

lisp *v* to say *th* for *s* or *z* because of being unable to pronounce these letters correctly; to speak imperfectly, like a child. – Also *n*.

'lissom(e) *adj* nimble, bending easily.

list[1] *n* a series *eg* of names, numbers, prices *etc* written down one after the other. – *v* to write (something) down in this way. – *n* **listed building** one protected from being knocked down because it is of architectural or historical interest.

list[2] *v* (of a ship) to lean over to one side. – *n* a slope to one side.

listen ['lisn] *v* to give attention to so as to hear or to pay attention to the advice of. – *n* **'listener**.

'listless *adj* weary, without energy or interest. – *n* **'listlessness**.

lists *npl* (*hist*) the ground enclosed for a battle between knights on horseback.

lit *see* **light**[1] and **light**[3].

'litany *n* a set form of prayer: – *pl* **'litanies**.

literal ['litərəl] *adj* following the exact or most obvious meaning word for word with no exaggeration and nothing added by the imagination. – *adv* **'literally** exactly as stated. *He was literally blinded by the flash* means he actually lost the power of sight.

literary ['litərəri] *adj* of writing, books, authors *etc*; knowledgeable about books. – *n* **'literacy** ability to read and write. – *adj* **'literate** able to read and write.

literature ['litərəchər] *n* the books *etc* that are written in any language, *esp* novels, poetry *etc*; anything in written form on a subject.

lithe [lidh] *adj* (of a person or body) bending easily, supple, flexible.

'lithograph *n* a picture made from a drawing done on stone or metal. – *ns* **li'thographer; li'thography** printing done by this method.

liti'gation *n* a law case. – *adj* **li'tigious** fond of taking one's troubles to court.

litre ['lētər] *n* a metric measure of liquids (1·76 pint).

'litter *n* an untidy mess of paper, rubbish *etc*; a heap of straw as bedding for animals *etc*; a number of animals born at one birth; (*hist*) a kind of bed for carrying the sick and injured. – *v* to scatter carelessly about, *esp* rubbish *etc*; to produce a litter of young.

'little *adj* small in quantity or size. – *adv* in a small quantity or degree; not

much; not at all. *Little does he know.* – *pron* a small quantity, amount, distance *etc*. *Have a little more. Move a little to the right.*

'liturgy *n* the form of service of a church: – *pl* **'liturgies**. – *adj* **li'turgical**.

live[1] [liv] *v* to have life; to dwell; to pass one's life; to continue to be alive; to survive; (with **on**) to keep oneself alive; (with **on**) to be supported by; to be lifelike or vivid. – *n* **livelihood** ['livlihood] one's means of living (as one's daily work). – **live and let live** to allow others to live as they please; **live down** (*eg* one's past) to live until one's past acts are forgotten; **live up to** to be as good as expected.

live[2] [liv] *adj* having life, not dead; full of energy; (of a television broadcast *etc*) seen as the event takes place, not recorded; apt to burn, explode, or give an electric shock. – *adj* **'lively** full of life, high spirits, movement. – *n* **'liveliness**. – *v* **'liven** to make lively. – *ns* **'livestock** farm animals; **'livewire** a very lively, energetic person.

liveiong ['livloŋ] *adj* whole: *the livelong day.*

liver ['livər] *n* a large gland in the body that carries out several important functions including purifying the blood. The liver of some animals is used as meat.

livery ['livəri] *n* the uniform of a manservant *etc*: – *pl* **'liveries**.

'livid *adj* of a bluish lead-like colour; (of a person) very angry.

'living *adj* having life; active, lively; (of a likeness) exact. – *n* means of living. – *ns* **'living-room** a sitting-room; **living wage** a wage on which it is possible to live comfortably.

'lizard *n* a kind of four-footed reptile.

llama ['lämə] *n* a type of S. American animal of the camel family without a hump.

lo! *interj* look!

loach *n* a type of small river fish: – *pl* **'loaches**.

load *v* to put on what is to be carried; to put the ammunition in (a gun); to put a film in (a camera); to weight for some purpose: *loaded dice.* – *n* as much as can be carried at once; cargo; a heavy weight or task; the power carried by an electric circuit. – *ns* **loaded question** one meant to trap a person into making an admission which is harmful to him; **'loadline** a line along a ship's side to mark the waterline when fully loaded.

loaf *n* a shaped mass of bread: – *pl* **loaves** [lōvz]. – *v* to pass time idly or lazily. – *n* '**loafer**.

loam *n* a rich soil. – *adj* '**loamy**.

loan *n* anything lent *esp* money. – *v* to lend.

loath, lōth *adj* unwilling (to).

loathe [lōdh] *v* to dislike greatly. – *n* '**loathing** great hate or disgust. – *adj* '**loathsome** causing loathing or disgust, horrible.

loaves *see* **loaf**.

lob *n* (in cricket) a slow, high ball bowled underhand; (in tennis) a ball high overhead dropping near the back of the court. – *v* to send such a ball; (*coll*) to throw: – *pt* **lobbed**.

'**lobby** *n* a small entrance hall; a passage off which rooms open; group of people who try to influence the government or other authority in a particular way: – *pl* '**lobbies**.

lobe *n* the hanging-down part of an ear; a division of the brain, lungs *etc*.

'**lobster** *n* a kind of shellfish with large claws, used for food. – *n* **lobster pot** a basket in which lobsters are caught.

lobworm ['lobwɜrm] *n* a kind of sea worm.

'**lōcal** *adj* of or confined to a certain place. – *n* (*coll*) one's nearest public house; (*usu pl*) the people living in a particular place or area. – *n* **locale** [lɔ'käl] the scene (of an) event. – *n* **locality** [lɔ'kalɔti] a particular place and the area round about. – *vs* **localize** ['lōkɔliz] to keep (something) to one area, keep from spreading; **lo'cate** to find; to set in a particular place: *house located in north London*. – *n* **lo'cation** the act of locating; situation. – *ns* **local colour** details in a story which make it more interesting and realistic; **local government** administration of the local affairs of a district *etc* by elected inhabitants. – **on location** (of filming) in natural surroundings, not in a studio.

loch [lohh] *n* (in Scotland) a lake; an arm of the sea.

lock *n* a fastening for doors *etc* (needing a key to open it); a part of a canal for raising or lowering boats; the part of a gun by which it is fired; a tight hold; a section of hair; (*pl*) hair. – *v* to fasten with a lock; to become fastened; (with **up**) to shut in (with a lock). – *ns* '**locker** a small cupboard; '**locket** a little ornamental case hung round the neck. – *ns* '**lockjaw** a form of the disease tetanus which stiffens the jaw muscles; '**lockout** the act of locking out (*esp* of factory workers *etc* by their employer during wages disputes);

'**locksmith** a smith who makes locks. – **lock, stock and barrel** completely.

locomotive [lōkɔ'mōtiv] *n* a railway engine. – *adj* of or capable of locomotion. – *n* **loco'motion** movement from place to place.

locum ['lōkɔm] *n* one taking another's place (*esp* a doctor, dentist *etc*) for a time: – *pl* '**locums**.

'**lōcust** *n* a type of large insect of the grasshopper family which destroys growing crops.

lodge *n* a small house (*esp* one at the entrance to a larger building); a beaver's dwelling; a house occupied during the shooting or hunting season; (the meeting place of) a branch of some societies. – *v* to live in rented rooms; to become fixed (in); to put in a safe place; to make (a complaint, appeal *etc*) officially. – *ns* '**lodger** one who stays in rented rooms; '**lodging** a place to stay, sleep *etc*; (*pl*) a room or rooms rented in another's house.

loft *n* a room or space just under a roof; a gallery in a hall, church *etc*. – *adj* '**lofty** high up; noble, proud. – *n* '**loftiness**.

log *n* a thick, rough piece of wood, part of a felled tree; a device for measuring a ship's speed; a logbook. – *v* to write down (events) in a logbook: – *pt* **logged**. – *n* '**logbook** a daily record of (a ship's or aeroplane's) progress.

'**lōganberry** *n* a kind of fruit like a large raspberry: – *pl* '**loganberries**.

loggerhead ['logɔrhed]: **at loggerheads** quarrelling.

'**logic** *n* the study of reasoning correctly; correctness of reasoning. – *adj* '**logical** according to the rules of logic or sound reasoning. – *adv* '**logically**.

loin *n* the back of an animal cut for food; (*pl*) the lower part of the back. – *n* '**loincloth** a piece of cloth worn round the hips, *esp* in India and south-east Asia.

'**loiter** *v* to proceed, move slowly; to linger; to stand around.

loll *v* to lie lazily about; (of the tongue) to hang down or out.

lone *adj* alone; standing by itself. – *adj* '**lonely** lone; lacking or wanting companionship; (of a place) having few people. – *n* '**loneliness**. – *adj* '**lonesome** lone; feeling lonely.

long *adj* not short, measuring much from end to end; measuring a certain amount in distance or time: *2 cm long: 2 minutes long*; far-reaching; slow to do something. – *adv* for a great time; through the whole time: *all day long*. – *v* to wish (for) very much. – *n* '**longing**

an eager desire. – *ns* **'longboat** the largest and strongest boat of a ship; **'longbow** a large bow bent by the hand in shooting; **'longhand** ordinary writing, not shorthand. – *adjs* **'long-'playing** (of a record) playing for a long time because of very fine grooves; **'long-'range** able to reach a great distance; (of a forecast) looking a long way into the future; **'long-'sighted** able to see things at a distance but not those close at hand; **'long-'suffering** putting up with troubles without complaining; **'long-'term** taking the future, not just the present, into account; **'long-'winded** using too many words. – **before long** soon; **in the long run** in the end.

lon'gevity [lon'jevəti] *n* great length of life.

longitude ['loŋgitūd] *n* the distance, measured in degrees on the map, of a place east or west of the Greenwich meridian.

loo *n* (*coll*) toilet.

look *v* to turn the eye towards so as to see; to seem; to face. *This room looks south.* – *n* the act of looking; the expression on one's face; appearance; (*pl*) personal appearance. – *ns* **'looking-glass** a mirror; **'lookout** (one who keeps) a careful watch; a high place for watching from; concern, responsibility. – **look down on** to despise, think of as being inferior; **look for** to search for; **look into** to investigate; **look on** to stand by and watch; to think of (as). *He looks on you as his mother*; **look out!** be careful! **look over** to examine briefly.

loom *n* machine for weaving cloth. – *v* to appear indistinctly, often threateningly.

loop *n* a doubled-over part in a piece of rope, string *etc*; a U-shaped bend (as in a river). – *n* **'loophole** a narrow slit in a wall; means of escaping or avoiding. – **loop the loop** to fly (an aircraft) upwards, backwards and down.

loose *adj* not tight, slack; not tied; free; not closely packed; vague, not exact; careless. – *adv* **'loosely**. – *vs* **loose**, **'loosen** to make loose, to slacken; to untie. – **break loose** to escape; **on the loose** free.

loot *n* goods stolen or plundered. – *v* to plunder, ransack.

lop *v* to cut off the top or ends of (*esp* a tree): – *pt* **lopped**. – *adjs* **'lop-'eared** having ears hanging down; **'lop-'sided** leaning to one side, not having the sides the same.

lope *v* to run with a long stride.

loquacious [lə'kwāshəs] *adj* talkative. – *ns* **lo'quaciousness**, **loquacity** [lə'kwasəti].

lord *n* the owner of an estate; a title given to noblemen, bishops and judges and used in other titles (as **Lord Mayor**); (*mainly hist*) a master, a ruler; **Lord** (with **the**) God. – *adj* **'lordly** like or belonging to a lord; noble, proud. – *ns* **Lord's day** Sunday; **'lordship** power, rule; used to or of a lord: *his lordship*. – **(House of) Lords** the upper (non-elected) house of the British parliament; **lord it over (someone)** to act like a lord, domineer.

lore *n* knowledge, beliefs *etc* handed down.

lorgnette [lör'nyet] *n* eyeglasses with a handle.

'lorry *n* a motor vehicle for carrying heavy loads: – *pl* **'lorries**.

lose [lōōz] *v* to cease to have, have no longer; to have (something) taken away from; to put (something) where it cannot be found; to waste (time); to miss (the train, a chance *etc*); not to win (a game *etc*): – *pt* **lost** [lost]. – *ns* **loser** ['lōōzər] one who loses; **loss** [los] the act of losing; that which is lost; waste, harm, destruction: – *pl* **'losses**. – *adj* **lost** not able to be found; no longer possessed; not won; thrown away; ruined; (with **in**) with attention totally taken up (by): *lost in thought*. – **at a loss** uncertain what to do.

loss, lost *see* **lose**.

lot *n* a large number or quantity; one's fortune or fate; a separate portion. – **cast** (or **draw**) **lots** to decide who is to do something by drawing names out of a box *etc*.

loth *see* **loath**.

'lotion *n* a liquid for soothing or cleaning the skin.

'lottery *n* the sharing-out of money or of prizes won by chance, through drawing lots: – *pl* **'lotteries**.

'lotus *n* kind of water-lily; (*myth*) a tree whose fruit was said to cause forgetfulness: – *pl* **'lotuses**.

loud *adj* making a great sound; noisy; showy, over-bright. – *advs* **loud**, **'loudly**. – *n* **'loud'speaker** an instrument for increasing the loudness of the voice *etc* to make it more widely heard.

lounge [lownj] *v* to lie back at one's ease; to move about lazily. – *n* a sitting room. – *n* **'lounger** a lazy person. – *n* **lounge suit** a man's suit for ordinary everyday (but not casual) wear.

lour *see* **lower**.

louse *n* a small blood-sucking insect sometimes found on the bodies of animals and people: – *pt* **lice**.

lout *n* a clumsy, awkward fellow.

love [luv] *n* great fondness, liking, affection; a loved person; (in tennis *etc*) no score, nothing. – *v* to be very fond of, to like very much. – *adjs* **'lovable** worthy of love; **'lovely** beautiful; delightful. – *n* **'lover** one who loves (someone); an admirer (of something); a person who is having a love affair with someone. – *adj* **'loving** full of love. – *n* **love affair** a (temporary) relationship between people in love but not married. – **in love (with)** feeling love and desire (for); having a great liking (for).

low [lō] *adj* not high, not lying or reaching far up; (of a voice) not loud; cheap; feeling sad; humble; mean, unworthy. – *v* to make the noise of cattle, to bellow or moo. – *adv* in or to a low position; not loudly; cheaply. – *n* **'lowness**. – *adj* **'lower** less high. – *v* to make less high; to let or come down. – *n* **'lowing** bellowing, mooing. – *adj* **'lowly** low in rank, humble. – *ns* **'lowliness**; **'lowland** low or level country, without hills.

lower[1] *see* **low**.

lower[2], **lour** ['lowər] *v* (of the sky) to become dark and cloudy; to frown. – *adj* **'lowering**.

'loyal *adj* faithful, true. – *ns* **'loyalty**: – *pl* **'loyalties**; **'loyalist** one who is true to his king and country.

'lozenge *n* a diamond-shaped figure; a small sweet for sucking.

lubricate ['lōōbrikāt] *v* to oil (a machine *etc*) to make it move more easily and smoothly. – *ns* **lubri'cation**; **'lubricant** something which lubricates, oil.

lucerne [lōō'sɜrn] *n* a type of plant used for feeding cattle, alfalfa.

lucid ['lōōsid] *adj* easily understood; (of a mind) clear, not confused. – *n* **lu'cidity**.

luck *n* fortune, whether good or bad; chance; good fortune. – *adjs* **'luckless** unfortunate, unhappy; **'lucky** fortunate, having good luck; bringing good luck: – *comp* **'luckier**, *superl* **'luckiest**.

lucrative ['lōōkrətiv] *adj* giving gain or profit.

lucre ['lōōkər] *n* gain; money.

ludicrous ['lōōdikrəs] *adj* ridiculous.

ludo ['lōōdō] *n* a game played with counters on a board.

lug *v* to pull or drag with effort: – *pt* **lugged**. – *n* **'lugger** a type of small sailing vessel.

'luggage *n* suitcases and other baggage of a traveller.

lugubrious [lə'gōōbriəs] *adj* mournful, dismal.

lugworm ['lugwɜrm] *n* a kind of large worm found on the seashore, used for bait by fishermen.

lukewarm ['lōōkwörm] *adj* neither hot nor cold; not very eager, not enthusiastic.

lull *v* to soothe or calm. – *n* a period of calm. – *n* **'lullaby** a song to lull children to sleep: – *pl* **'lullabies**.

lum'bāgo *n* a pain in the lower part of the back.

'lumbar *adj* of or in the lower part of the back.

'lumber *n* useless old furniture *etc*; timber sawn up. – *v* to move about clumsily, heavily. – *n* **'lumberjack** one who fells, saws and shifts trees.

luminous ['lōōminəs] *adj* giving light; shining; clear. – *n* **lumi'nosity**.

lump *n* a small, solid mass of no particular shape; a swelling; the whole taken together: *considered in a lump*; a heavy, dull person. – *v* to form into lumps; to treat as being alike, class (together). – *adjs* **'lumpish** heavy; dull; **'lumpy** full of lumps. – *n* **lump sum** an amount of money given all at once, not in instalments.

lunacy *see* **lunatic**.

lunar ['lōōnər] *adj* of the moon.

lunatic ['lōōnətik] *n, adj* (one who is) insane or crazy. – *n* **'lunacy**.

lunch *n* a midday meal: – *pl* **'lunches**. – *v* to eat lunch. – *n* **luncheon** ['lunchən] lunch.

lung *n* one of two bag-like parts of the body which fill and empty with air in the course of breathing.

lunge [lunj] *n* a sudden thrust or push. – Also *v*.

lupin ['lōōpin] *n* a type of plant with flowers on long spikes.

lurch *v* to roll or pitch suddenly to one side, stagger. – Also *n*. – **leave in the lurch** to leave in a difficult position without help.

lure [lōōr] *n* that which attracts or leads on, bait. – *v* to attract, entice away.

lurid ['lōōrid] *adj* (of colour *etc*) glaring; horrifying, sensational; pale, like a ghost.

lurk *v* to keep out of sight; to be hidden; to move or act secretly and slyly. – *adj* **'lurking** (of a feeling) vague, hidden.

luscious ['lushəs] *adj* sweet, delicious, juicy.

lush *adj* (of grass *etc*) green, thick and plentiful.

lust *n* greedy desire (for power, riches *etc*); a strong sexual desire. – Also *v*. – *adj* **'lustful**.

lustre ['lustər] *n* brightness, splendour; gloss. – *adj* **'lustrous** bright, shining.

'lusty *adj* lively, strong.

lute [lōot] *n* an old type of stringed musical instrument.

luxury ['lukshəri] *n* something pleasant (and expensive) but not necessary; the use or enjoyment of things of this sort: – *pl* **'luxuries**. – *adj* **luxuriant** [lug'zūriənt] having very great growth of leaves, branches *etc*; richly ornamented. – *v* **lu'xuriate** to be luxuriant; to enjoy, take delight (in). – *adj* **lu'xurious** supplied with luxuries; very comfortable.

'lychgate *n* a churchyard gate with a porch.

lying *see* **lie**.

lymph *n* a colourless fluid in the body. – *n* **lymph gland** one of the glands carrying lymph.

lynch *v* to condemn and put to death without legal trial.

lynx *n* a kind of wild animal of the cat family, noted for its keen sight: – *pl* **'lynxes**.

'lȳre *n* an old kind of musical instrument like the harp. – *n* **'lyrebird** a type of Australian bird with a lyre-shaped tail.

'lyric *n* a short poem (expressing the poet's feelings); (*pl*) the words of a song. – *adjs* **'lyric** of a lyric; full of (joyful) feeling; **'lyrical** lyric; song-like; full of enthusiastic praise.

M

macabre [mə'käbr] *adj* gruesome, horrible.

ma'cadamize *v* to surface (a road) with small broken stones.

maca'rōni *n* dried wheat paste made into long tubes and cooked.

maca'roon *n* a sweet cake or biscuit made mainly of almonds and sugar.

ma'caw *n* a kind of long-tailed brightly-coloured parrot.

mace *n* a heavy staff with an ornamental head (carried as a sign of office); (*hist*) a heavy stick; a spice made from the covering of a nutmeg.

Mach number [mähh] *n* the ratio of the speed of an aircraft to the velocity of sound (*eg* Mach 5 means 5 times the speed of sound).

machete [mə'cheti] *n* a kind of heavy knife used as a weapon *etc*.

machination [maki'näshən] *n* (often *pl*) a crafty scheme, plot.

machine [mə'shēn] *n* a working arrangement of wheels, levers, or other parts; a (motor) bicycle. – *v* to sew (or do other jobs) with a machine. – *ns* **machinery** [mə'shēnəri] machines; the working parts of a machine; organization: *machinery of local government*; **ma'chinist** one who makes or works machinery. – *n* **ma'chine-gun** a gun which fires bullets very quickly one after the other.

'mackerel *n* a type of eatable seafish with wavy markings.

'mackintosh *n* a kind of waterproof overcoat: – *pl* **'mackintoshes**.

mad *adj* out of one's mind, insane; wildly foolish; furious with anger. – *n* **'madness**. – *v* **'madden** to make angry or mad. – *ns* **'madcap** a rash, hot-headed person; **'madhouse** any place of confusion and noise; (*hist*) a house for mad people; **'madman** one who is mad. – **like mad** very quickly, very energetically *etc*.

'madam *n* a polite form of address used to a woman.

made *see* **make**.

madeira [mə'dērə] *n* a kind of wine; a kind of sponge cake.

Ma'donna *n* the mother of Jesus, *esp* as shown in statues, pictures *etc*.

'madrigal *n* a part-song for several voices.

maelstrom ['mälstrəm] *n* a whirlpool; any place of great confusion.

maestro ['mistrō] *n* one highly skilled in some art, *esp* a conductor or composer of music: – *pl* **'maestros**.

magazine [magə'zēn] *n* a paper published weekly, monthly *etc*, containing articles, stories, pictures *etc*; a storage place for military equipment, gunpowder *etc*; in a rifle, a place for extra cartridges.

ma'genta *adj, n* (of) a reddish-purple colour.

'maggot *n* a small worm-like creature, the grub of a blue-bottle *etc*. – *adj* **'maggoty** full of maggots.

'magic *n* any influence which produces results which cannot be explained or which are remarkable; conjuring tricks. – *adj* using magic; used in magic; magical. – *adj* 'magical of, produced by magic; very mysterious and beautiful; very wonderful or mysterious. – *n* magician [mə'jishən] one skilled in magic. – *n* magic lantern a device which throws pictures on a screen. – black magic magic which is done for an evil purpose, witchcraft.

'magistrate *n* one who has the power of putting the law into force in a police court, or as a Justice of the Peace. – *adj* magis'tērial of magistrates; having an air of authority.

magna'nimity *n* generosity. – *adj* mag'nanimous very generous.

'magnate *n* a person of great power or wealth.

magnesium [məg'nēziəm] *n* an element, a white metal which burns with a dazzling white light. – *n* mag'nesia a white powder formed from magnesium.

'magnet *n* a piece of iron, steel *etc* which has the power to attract other pieces of iron *etc*; a person or thing that attracts strongly. – *adj* mag'netic having the powers of a magnet; (of a person) strongly attractive. – *n* 'magnetism the power of a magnet; the science which deals with magnets; attraction, great charm. – *v* 'magnetize to make magnetic; to attract, influence. – *ns* magnetic north the direction in which the magnetized needle of a compass points; magnetic tape tape on which sound, pictures, computer material *etc* can be recorded.

mag'nēto *n* a device producing electric sparks, *esp* one for lighting the fuel in a motor-car engine: – *pl* mag'netos.

magnification *see* magnify.

mag'nificent *adj* splendid in appearance; great or noble in deeds; excellent, very fine. – *n* mag'nificence.

'magnify *v* to make something appear larger (by using a magnifying glass); to exaggerate: – *pt* 'magnified. – *n* 'magnitude *n* greatness; size.

mag'nōlia *n* a type of tree with large white or purplish sweet-scented flowers.

'magpie *n* a black-and-white chattering bird of the crow family, known for its habit of collecting objects.

Maha'rajah *n* the title given to a great Indian prince: – *fem* Maha'rani, Maha'ranee.

ma'hogany *n* a type of tropical American tree or its hard reddish-brown wood, much used for furniture.

maid *n* a female servant; an unmarried woman, a young girl. – *n* 'maiden an unmarried girl. – *adj* of a maiden, unmarried; first: *maiden speech*: *maiden voyage*. – *ns* maiden name the surname of a married woman before her marriage; maiden over (in cricket) an over in which no runs are made.

mail *n* letters, parcels *etc* carried by post; body armour of steel rings or plates; armour. – *v* to post.

maim *v* to cripple, disable.

main *adj* chief, most important. – *n* the ocean; (often *pl*) a chief pipe, wire *etc* supplying gas, water or electricity. – *adv* 'mainly chiefly, mostly. — *n* 'mainframe the central processing unit and storage unit of a computer. — *adj* (of a computer) of the large, powerful type rather than the small-scale kind. — *ns* 'mainland a large piece of land off whose coast smaller islands lie; 'mainsail the principal sail of a ship or boat; 'mainspring the chief spring, *esp* one which causes the wheels to move in a watch or clock; the chief cause of action; 'mainstay the chief support. — in the main for the most part.

main'tain *v* to keep (something) as it is; to continue to keep in good working order; to support (a family *etc*); to state (an opinion) firmly. – *n* 'maintenance the act of maintaining; upkeep, repair; means of support, *esp* money for food, clothing *etc*.

maize *n* a type of cereal crop grown widely in America.

'majesty *n* greatness of rank or manner; a title used to or of a king or queen (*eg* Your Majesty): – *pl* 'majesties. – *adj* ma'jestic stately.

'mājor *adj* greater or great in size, importance *etc*; opposite of minor. – *n* a senior army officer. – *n* majority [mə'jorəti] the greater number or quantity; the difference in amount between the greater and the lesser number; the age when one becomes legally an adult, in UK 18: – *pl* ma'jorities.

make *v* to form, construct; to cause to be. *You make me angry*; to bring about: *make trouble*; to amount to. *2 and 2 make 4*; to earn. *He makes £5 a day*; to force. *I made him do it*; to perform (a journey, an attempt *etc*); to prepare (*eg* a meal): – *pt* made. – *n* kind; shape, form; brand. – *n* 'maker. – *n*, *adj* 'makeshift (a thing) used for a time for want of something better. – *n* 'make-up cosmetics for a woman, or for an actor or actress. – make believe to pretend (*n* '**make-believe**); **make good** to do well; to carry out (a promise); to make up for (a loss); **make light of** to treat as unimportant; **make much of** to fuss over, treat as important; **make nothing of** not to be able to understand, do *etc*; make light of; **make off** to run away; **make out** to see (in the distance or indistinctly); to declare, prove; to write out (a bill *etc*) formally; **make up** to form a whole. *Eleven players make up the side*; to put together, invent (a false story); to put make-up on the face; to be friendly again after a quarrel; **make up for** to give or do something in return for damage *etc* that one has done.

maladjusted [malə'justid] *adj* unable to fit in happily in one's work, way of life *etc*.

'**maladminis'tration** *n* bad management, *esp* of public affairs.

'**malady** *n* illness, disease: – *pl* '**maladies**.

malaise [mə'lāz] *n* a feeling of discomfort.

'**malapropism** *n* the use of a wrong word which sounds something like the one intended *eg* contemptuous for contemporary.

ma'lāria *n* a fever caused by the bite of a certain type of mosquito.

male *adj* of the sex that is able to father children or young, masculine. – Also *n*.

malefactor ['malifaktər] *n* an evildoer.

malevolent [mə'levələnt] *adj* wishing ill to others, spiteful. – *n* **ma'levolence**.

malfor'mation *n* faulty or wrong shape.

malice ['malis] *n* ill will, spite. – *adj* **malicious** [mə'lishəs].

malign [mə'līn] *v* to speak evil of, *esp* falsely.

ma'lignant *adj* wishing to do great harm, spiteful; (of a disease *etc*) likely to cause death.

malinger [mə'liŋgər] *v* to pretend to be ill (to avoid work *etc*). – *n* **ma'lingerer**.

'**mallard** *n* the (male of the) common wild duck.

malleable ['maliəbl] *adj* (of metal *etc*) able to be beaten out by hammering; (of people) easy to influence.

'**mallet** *n* a kind of wooden hammer.

malnū'trition *n* underfeeding or poor feeding.

ma'lōdorous *adj* having a bad smell.

malpractice ['mal'praktis] *n* wrongdoing; failure to practise one's profession in a correct or proper way.

malt [mölt] *n* barley or other grain prepared for making beer or whisky.

mal'treat *v* to treat roughly or unkindly. – *n* **mal'treatment**.

ma'm(m)a *n* a name sometimes used for mother.

'**mammal** *n* any of the kinds of animals of which the female feeds her young with her own milk.

'**mammoth** *n* a type of very large elephant, now extinct. – *adj* huge.

man *n* a human being; the human race; a grown-up human male; a husband; a piece in chess or draughts: – *pl* **men**. – *v* to supply with men: *man the boats*: – *pt* **manned**. – *adj* '**manful** courageous. – *adv* '**manfully**. – *adjs* '**manly** brave, strong; '**mannish** (of a woman) behaving, looking like a man. – *n* '**man-at-'arms** a soldier. – *v* '**manhandle** to handle roughly. – *ns* '**manhole** a hole (into a drain, sewer *etc*) large enough to let a man through; '**manhood** the state of being a man; manly quality; **man'kind** the human race; '**man-of-'war** a warship; '**manpower** the number of people available for work; '**manslaughter** the unintentional but blameworthy killing of a man. – Also *v*. – **the man in the street** the ordinary person; **to a man** every single one.

'**manacle** *n* a handcuff. – Also *v*.

'**manage** *v* to have control or have charge of; to deal with; to cope; to succeed. – *adj* '**manageable** easily managed or controlled. – *ns* '**management** the people in charge of organizing a business *etc*; the art of managing a business *etc*; '**manager** a person who looks after a business *etc*: – *fem* '**manage'ress**.

'**mandarin** *n* a type of fruit like a small orange; (*hist*) a senior Chinese official.

'**mandate** *n* a command; power given to person or nation to act in the name of another. – *adj* '**mandatory** compulsory.

'**mandible** *n* the jaw or lower jawbone.

'**mandolin(e)** *n* a kind of round-backed stringed musical instrument like a guitar.

mane *n* long hair on the head and neck *eg* on the horse and the male of the lion.

maneuver *see* **manoeuvre**.

manganese [maŋgə'nēz] *n* an element, a hard easily-broken metal of a greyish-white colour.

mange [mānj] *n* a skin disease of dogs, cats *etc*. – *adj* '**mangy**.

'**mangel-wurzel** *n* a kind of beetroot, grown as food for cattle.

manger ['mānjər] *n* a box or trough holding dry food for horses and cattle.

mangle ['maŋgl] *n* a machine for squeezing water out of clothes or for smoothing them. – v to squeeze (clothes) through a mangle; to smooth (clothes) by means of a mangle; to crush, tear, damage badly.

mango ['maŋgō] n a type of tree found in India or its reddish, juicy fruit: – pl '**mangoes**.

mangrove ['maŋgrōv] n a type of tree which grows on swamps in hot countries.

'**mānia** n a form of mental illness in which the sufferer is over-active, over-excited and unreasonably happy; (too) great fondness or enthusiasm (for something): a mania for collecting records. – n '**maniac** a madman; a very rash or over-enthusiastic person. – adj **manic** ['manik] suffering from mania; very energetic, very active, very excited.

'**manicure** n the care of hands and nails. – Also v. – n '**manicurist** one who cares for and treats hands and nails.

'**manifest** adj easily seen or understood. – v to show plainly. – ns **manifes'tation**; **mani'festo** a public announcement of intentions (esp by a political party): – pl **mani'festo(e)s**.

'**manifold** adj many and various.

ma'nipulate v to handle or manage skilfully, cunningly or dishonestly.

mankind, manly see **man**.

'**manna** n in the Bible, the food provided miraculously for the Israelites in the wilderness; any unexpected or delicious treat.

mannequin ['manikin] n a person, usu a woman, who wears clothes to show intending buyers how they look, a model.

'**manner** n the way (in which anything is done); the way in which a person behaves; (pl) (polite) behaviour usu towards others. – n '**mannerism** an odd and obvious habit in someone's behaviour etc. – adj '**mannerly** polite. – **all manner of** all kinds of.

manoeuvre,   (US)   **maneuver** [mə'nōōvər] n a planned movement of troops, ships or aircraft; a trick, a cunning plan. – v to perform a manoeuvre; to move or manage cunningly.

'**manor** n (hist) the land belonging to a lord or squire; a large house usu attached to a country estate. – adj **ma'norial**.

manse n (in Scotland) the house of a clergyman.

mansion ['manshən] n a large house.

mantelpiece ['mantlpēs] n a shelf over a fireplace.

mantilla [man'tilə] n a kind of veil covering the head and shoulders sometimes worn by Spanish women.

'**mantle** n a cloak or loose outer garment; a covering: a mantle of snow; a piece of thin, transparent, material round the light in gas or some paraffin lamps.

'**manūal** adj of the hand or hands; worked by hand; working with the hands: manual worker. – n a handbook used eg to give instructions as to how to use something: a car manual; the keyboard of an organ etc.

manū'facture v to make (articles, materials etc), formerly by hand, now usu by machinery, and in large quantities. – n the process of manufacturing; anything manufactured. – n **manu'facturer**.

ma'nure n a substance, esp animal dung, used to make soil more fertile. – v to treat (soil, plants) with manure.

'**manūscript** n the prepared material for a book etc before it is printed; a book or paper written by hand.

Manx cat [maŋks] n a type of cat that has no tail.

many ['meni] adj a large number of: many people were present. – pron a large number. Many survived. – **many a** (followed by a sing noun) a large number of. Many a man had to die before the war ended.

map n a flat drawing of (part of) the earth's surface, showing various details eg rivers, mountains etc. – v to make a map of; (with **out**) to plan: – pt **mapped**.

'**māple** n any of several kinds of tree of the same type as the sycamore, one of which produces sugar; its hard light-coloured wood used for furniture etc.

mar v to spoil eg the appearance of someone. The scar marred her beauty: – pt **marred**.

ma'raud v to plunder, raid. – n **ma'rauder** a plundering robber. – adj **ma'rauding**.

'**marble** n any kind of limestone that takes a high polish, used for sculpture, decorating buildings etc; a little ball, now usu of glass, used in a children's game.

'**marcasite** n crystals formed from iron and used in jewellery.

March n the third month of the year.

march v (to cause) to walk in time with regular step; to go on steadily. – n a marching movement; a piece of music for marching to; the distance covered by marching; a steady going forward (of events etc): the march of time; a boundary: – *pl* 'marches.

marchioness *see* **marquess.**

mare *n* the female of the horse.

margarine ['märjərēn] *n* a substance like butter, made mainly of vegetable fats.

'**margin** *n* an edge, border; the blank edge on the page of a book; something extra (*eg* time, money *etc*) beyond what seems to be needed. – *adj* 'marginal placed in the margin; of or in a margin; borderline, close to a limit; (of a political constituency *etc*) without a clear majority for any one candidate or party; of little effect or importance: *a marginal improvement.*

marguerite [märgə'rēt] *n* a kind of large daisy.

'**marigōld** *n* a kind of plant with a yellow flower.

marijuana [mari'wänə] *n* a drug made from the plant hemp.

marina [mə'rēnə] *n* a place with moorings for yachts, sailing dinghies *etc.*

marine [mə'rēn] *adj* of the sea. – *n* a soldier serving on board a ship; shipping in general. – *n* **mariner** ['marinər] a sailor.

mario'nette *n* a puppet moved by strings.

'**marital** *adj* of marriage.

'**maritime** *adj* of the sea or ships; lying near the sea.

'**marjoram** *n* a type of sweet-smelling herb used as a flavouring.

mark *n* a sign that can be seen; a stain, spot *etc*; a target, a thing aimed at; trace; a point or unit used in establishing how good a piece of work is (*esp* in schools); the starting-line in a race: *on your marks*; the standard unit of German money. – *v* to make a mark on; to observe, watch; to stay close to (an opponent in football *etc*); to award marks to (a piece of schoolwork *etc*); (with **off**) to separate, distinguish. – *adj* **marked** easily noticed: *a marked improvement.* – *adv* **markedly** ['märkidli] noticeably. – *n* '**marker** one who marks the score at games; any object (as a counter *etc*) used to mark the score. – *n* '**marksman** one who shoots well. – **mark time** to move the feet up and down, as if marching, but without going forward; **up to the mark** coming up to the required standard.

'**market** *n* a public place for buying and selling; (a country, place *etc* where there is) a need or demand (for certain types of goods); sale. *His house is on the market.* – *v* to put on sale. – *n*

'**market-'garden** a garden in which fruit and vegetables are grown to be sold.

marlinspike ['märlinspik] *n* a spike for separating the strands of a rope *etc.*

'**marmalade** *n* a jam made from oranges, grapefruit or lemons.

marmoset ['märməzet] *n* a type of small monkey found in America.

'**marmot** *n* a kind of burrowing animal of the squirrel family (also **woodchuck** or **groundhog**).

ma'roon *adj, n* (of) a brownish-red colour. – *n* a firework used as a distress signal *etc.* – *v* to leave on an island without means of escape; to leave in a helpless or uncomfortable position.

marquee [mär'kē] *n* a large tent used for large gatherings (*eg* a wedding reception) or public entertainment (*eg* a circus).

'**marquess, 'marquis** *n* a nobleman below a duke in rank: – *pl* '**marquesses, 'marquises** – *fem* **marchioness** ['märshənis]: – *pl* **marchio'nesses.**

marriage *see* **marry.**

marrow ['marō] *n* the soft substance in the hollow parts of bones; a type of long thick-skinned vegetable.

'**marry** *v* to join (or be joined) together as husband and wife: – *pt* 'married. – *n* **marriage** ['marij] the ceremony by which a man and woman become husband and wife; a joining together. – *adj* '**marriageable** suitable or old enough for marriage.

marsh *n* a piece of low-lying wet ground: – *pl* 'marshes. – *adj* 'marshy. – *ns* **marsh'mallow** a type of marsh plant with pink flowers; a foam-like sweet sticky substance; **marsh marigold** a type of marsh plant with yellow flowers (also **kingcup**).

'**marshal** *n* a high-ranking officer in the army or air force; one who directs processions *etc*; (*US*) a kind of law-court official; (*US*) a head of a police force. – *v* to arrange (troops, facts, arguments *etc*) in order; to show the way, conduct, lead: – *pt* 'marshalled. – *n* **marshalling yard** a place where railway wagons are shunted about to make up trains.

mar'sūpial *n* any animal which carries its young in a pouch (*eg* the kangaroo, opossum).

mar'tello tower *n* a round coastal fort.

'**marten** *n* a kind of animal related to the weasel, with valuable fur.

martial ['märshəl] *adj* warlike; of, or suitable for war. – *n* **martial law** the government of a country by army rules and rulers.

'**martin** *n* a kind of bird of the swallow family.

marti'net *n* one who keeps strict order.

'**martyr** *n* one who suffers death or hardship for what he believes. – *v* to put a person to death or make him suffer for his beliefs. – *n* '**martyrdom** the death or suffering of a martyr.

'**marvel** *n* anything astonishing or wonderful. – *v* to feel amazement (at): – *pt* '**marvelled**. – *adj* '**marvellous** astonishing, extraordinary; (*coll*) excellent, very good.

marzi'pan *n* a mixture of ground almonds, sugar *etc*, used in the making of sweets and cakes.

'**mascot** *n* a person, animal or thing that is supposed to bring good luck. *The football team's mascot was a teddy bear.*

masculine ['maskūlin] *adj* of the male sex; manly. – *n* **mascu'linity**.

mash *v* to beat or crush into a pulp-like mixture. – *n* mashed potato; a mixture, *esp* one of bran, meal *etc*, used as food for animals.

mask *n* a cover for the face (for disguise or protection); something pretended, disguise. – *v* to cover the face with a mask; to hide.

masochism ['masəkizm] *n* unnatural pleasure taken in being dominated or cruelly treated. – *n* '**masochist** one who takes such pleasure.

'**māson** *n* a worker in stone; a Freemason. – *adj* **ma'sonic**. – *n* '**masonry** stonework.

masque [mäsk] *n* an old type of theatre show in which the actors wore masks.

masquerade [maskə'rād] *n* a dance at which masks are worn; pretence. – *v* to pretend to be someone else. *He masqueraded as a butler.*

mass *n* a lump or quantity gathered together; a large quantity; the main part or body: – *pl* '**masses; Mass** (in some Christian Churches) the celebration of Christ's last supper with his disciples; music for this celebration. – *adj* of a mass; of or consisting of large numbers or quantities. – *v* to form into a mass. – *adj* '**massive** bulky, heavy, huge. – *ns* **mass media** means of communicating information to a large number of people *eg* television; **mass production** production in large quantities of articles all exactly the same.

massacre ['masəkər] *n* the cruel killing of great numbers of people. – *v* to kill (large numbers) in a cruel way.

massage ['masäzh] *n* the rubbing of parts of the body (muscles, knees *etc*)

esp to remove pain or stiffness. – Also *v*. – *n* **masseur** [ma'sör] one who massages: – *fem* **masseuse** [ma'söz].

mast *n* a long upright pole, *esp* one holding up the sails *etc* in a ship or one holding an aerial, flag *etc*.

'**master** *n* one who controls or commands; an owner (of a dog *etc*); an employer; a male teacher; the commander of a merchant ship: one very skilled in something, an expert; a degree awarded by universities, as **Master of Arts, Science** *etc*. – *adj* chief; controlling: *master switch*. – *v* to overcome, defeat; to become able to do (a thing) thoroughly. – *adjs* '**masterful** strong-willed; '**masterly** showing the skill of an expert or master, clever. – *n* '**mastery** victory (over); control (of); great skill (in). – *n* '**master-key** a key which is so made that it opens a number of different locks. – *v* '**mastermind** to plan, work out the details of (a scheme *etc*). – Also *n*. – *ns* '**masterpiece** the best example of someone's work, *esp* a very fine picture, book, piece of music *etc*; '**masterstroke** a clever act or move.

'**masticate** *v* to chew. – *n* **masti'cation**.

'**mastiff** *n* a breed of large, powerful dog.

mat *n* a piece of material (coarse plaited plant fibre, carpet *etc*) for wiping shoes on, covering the floor *etc*; a piece of material, wood *etc* put below dishes at table. – *adj see* **matt**. – *adj* '**matted** thickly tangled. – *n* '**matting** material from which mats are made.

'**matador** *n* the man who kills the bull in bullfights.

match *n* a small stick of wood or other material ('**matchstick**) tipped with a substance which easily catches fire when rubbed against something hard; a person or thing similar to or the same as another; a person or thing agreeing with or suiting another; an equal; a (person suitable for) marriage; a contest or game: – *pl* '**matches**. – *v* to be of the same make, size, colour *etc*; to set (two things, teams *etc*) against each other; to hold one's own with, be equal to. – *adj* '**matchless** having no equal. – *ns* '**matchbox** a box for holding matches; '**matchwood** wood broken into small pieces.

mate *n* a companion or fellow-worker; a husband or wife; either the male or female of a pair of animals, birds *etc*; a merchant ship's officer, next in rank to the captain. – *v* to marry; (of animals or birds) to bring or come together for breeding purposes.

ma'tērial *adj* made of matter, able to be seen and felt; not spiritual, concerned with physical comfort, money *etc*: *a material outlook on life*; important, essential: *a material difference*. – *n* something out of which anything is, or may be, made; cloth. – *adv* **ma'terially** to a large extent, greatly. – *ns* **ma'terialism** a tendency to attach too much importance to material things (*eg* physical comfort, money); the belief that only things we can see or feel really exist or are important. – *n* **ma'terialist**. – *adj* **materia'listic**. – *v* **ma'terialize** to appear in bodily form; to happen, come about.

ma'ternal *adj* of a mother; like a mother, motherly; related through one's mother: *maternal grandmother*. – *n* **ma'ternity** the state of being a mother, motherhood. – *adj* of or for a woman having or about to have a baby: *maternity clothes*.

mathematics [mathə'matiks] *n* the study of measurements, numbers and quantities. – *adj* **mathe'matical** of or done by mathematics; very exact. – *n* **mathema'tician** one good at mathematics; one whose job is concerned with mathematics.

matinée ['matinā] *n* an afternoon performance in a theatre *etc*. – *n* **matinée coat** a baby's short jacket.

'matins *npl* the morning service in certain churches.

'matricide *n* the killing of one's own mother; one who kills his own mother.

ma'triculate *v* to admit, or be admitted to a university.

'matrimony *n* marriage. – *adj* **matri'mōnial**.

'mātrix *n* a mould in which metals, *etc* are shaped; a mass of rock in which gems *etc* are found: – *pl* **matrices** ['mātrisēz].

'mātron *n* a married woman; a senior nurse in charge of a hospital; a woman in charge of housekeeping or nursing in a school, hostel *etc*. – *adj* **'matronly** (of a woman) dignified, staid; plump.

matt, mat *adj* having a dull surface, not shiny or glossy.

'matter *n* anything that takes up space, can be seen, felt *etc*; material, substance; a subject written or spoken about; (sometimes *pl*) affair, business; trouble, difficulty. *What is the matter?*; importance. *It is of no great matter*; pus. – *v* to be of importance. *It does not matter*; to give out pus. *His wound is mattering*. – *adj* **'matter-of-'fact** keeping to the actual facts, not imaginative;

uninteresting. – **a matter of course** something that is to be expected. *His promotion came as a matter of course*; **a matter of opinion** a subject on which different opinions are held; **as a matter of fact** in fact.

'mattock *n* a kind of tool like a pickaxe.

'mattress *n* a thick firm layer of padding covered in cloth *etc*, for lying on, *usu* as part of a bed: – *pl* **'mattresses**.

ma'ture *adj* fully grown or developed; ripe, ready for use. – *v* to (cause to) become mature; of an insurance policy *etc* to be due to be paid out. – *n* **ma'turity** ripeness.

'maudlin *adj* silly, sentimental.

maul *v* to hurt badly by rough or savage treatment.

mauso'lēum *n* a very fine tomb.

mauve [mōv] *adj, n* (of) a purple colour.

'mawkish *adj* weak and sentimental.

'maxim *n* a general truth or rule showing how one should behave *etc*.

'maximum *adj* greatest, most. – *n* the greatest number or quantity; the highest point or degree: – *pl* **'maxima**.

May *n* the fifth month of the year. – *ns* **'Mayday** the first day of May; **'mayday** an international distress signal; **'maypole** a decorated pole for dancing round on Mayday.

may *v usu* used with another verb to express permission, possibility *etc*. *Yes, you may watch the film. I may find him there*; used to express a wish. *May you always be happy!*: – *pt* **might** [mīt].

'maybē *adv* perhaps.

mayonnaise [māə'nāz] *n* a sauce made of eggs, oil, vinegar or lemon juice *etc*.

mayor [mār] *n* the chief public official of a city or town. – *n* **'mayoress** a mayor's wife; a mayor who is a woman.

maze *n* a series of winding paths in a park *etc* deliberately laid out in such a way that it is difficult to find the way out; something complicated and confusing: *a maze of regulations*.

ma'zurka *n* (the music for) a kind of lively Polish dance.

mē *pron* the word used by a speaker or writer in mentioning himself (as the object in a sentence). *He hit me. Give it to me*.

mead *n* an alcoholic drink made with honey.

meadow ['medō] *n* a field of grass. – *n* **'meadowsweet** a type of wild flower with sweet-smelling cream-coloured flowers.

'meagre, (*US*) **'meager** *adj* thin; poor in quality; scanty, not enough. – *n* **'meagreness**.

meal *n* the food taken at one time (*eg* breakfast, dinner, supper); grain ground to a coarse powder. – *adj* '**mealy-'mouthed** not frank and straightforward in speech.

mean[1] *adj* not generous with money *etc*; unkind, selfish; lowly, humble. – *n* '**meanness**.

mean[2] *adj* middle, coming midway between two other things, points, quantities *etc*; average. – *n* something lying midway between two other things *etc*; (*pl*) a method, instrument, action *etc* by which anything is brought about; money, property *etc*: *a man of means*. – **by all means** certainly, of course; in any or every way possibly; **by no means** certainly not; not at all; (**in the**) '**meantime, 'meanwhile** in the time between two happenings.

mean[3] *v* (to intend) to express, indicate. *'Halt' means 'stop'. By 'several' I mean three or more*; to intend: – *pt, pp* **meant** [ment]. – *n* '**meaning** what is (intended to be) expressed or conveyed; purpose, intention. – *adj* (of a look, glance *etc*) full of a certain meaning indicating a certain feeling. – *adjs* '**meaningful; 'meaningless**. – **mean well (ill)** to have good (bad) intentions.

mē'ander *v* (of a river) to flow in a winding course; to wander about slowly and aimlessly.

measles ['mēzlz] *n sing* a kind of infectious disease, with red spots. – *adj* '**measly** (*coll*) ungenerous, mean.

measure ['mezhər] *n* size or amount (found by measuring); an instrument, container *etc* for measuring; musical time; (often *pl*) a plan of action. *They took measures to prevent their house from being burgled*; a law brought before parliament to be considered. – *v* to find out the size, quantity *etc* by using some form of measure; to be of a certain length, amount *etc*. *This wall measures 2 metres across*; to indicate the measurement of (something). *A thermometer measures temperature*; to mark (off), weigh (out) *etc* in portions. – *adj* '**measured** steady, unhurried. – *n* '**measurement** the act of measuring; the size, amount *etc* found by measuring.

meat *n* flesh of animals used as food. – *adj* '**meaty** full of meat; tasting of meat; (of a book *etc*) full of information.

mechanic [mi'kanik] *n* a skilled worker with tools or machines. – *adj* **me'chanical** of machinery: *mechanical engineer-*

ing; worked by machinery; done without thinking. – *adv* **me'chanically**. – *n* **me'chanics** the study of forces and motion; the study and art of constructing machinery; the actual details of how something works. *The mechanics of his plan are beyond me*. – *n* '**mechanism** a piece of machinery; the way a piece of machinery works; an action by which a result is produced – *v* '**mechanize** to equip (a factory *etc*) with machinery; to supply (troops) with armoured vehicles. – *n* **mechani'zation**.

'**medal** *n* a piece of metal *etc* in the form of a coin or a coin-like object, with a design, inscription *etc* stamped on it, made in memory of an event or given as a reward for merit. – *ns* **me'dallion** a large medal; '**medallist** one who has gained a medal.

'**meddle** *v* to concern oneself with things that are not one's business, to interfere or tamper (with). – *n* '**meddler**. – *adj* '**meddlesome** fond of meddling.

media *see* **medium**.

mediaeval *see* **medieval**.

'**mēdiate** *v* to act as a peacemaker (between). – *ns* **medi'ation**; '**mediator** one who tries to make peace between people who are quarrelling.

medicine ['medsin] *n* something given to a sick person in order to make him better; the science of the treatment of illnesses. – *adj* **medical** ['medikəl] of doctors or their work. – *n* **me'dicament** a medicine. – *adj* **medicated** ['medikātid] mixed with a healing or disinfecting substance. – *n* **medi'cation** medical treatment; a medicine. – *adj* **medicinal** [mə'disinl] used in medicine; used as a medicine; having the power to cure. – *n* **medicine man** a witch doctor.

medieval mediaeval [medi'ēvəl] *adj* of the Middle Ages.

mēdi'ōcre *adj* not very good, ordinary. – *n* **mediocrity** [mēdi'okrəti].

'**meditate** *v* to think deeply and in quietness; to consider, think about. – *n* **medi'tation** deep, quiet thought. – *adj* '**meditative** thoughtful.

'**mēdium** *n* something (a means, a substance, a material *etc*) through which an effect is produced: – *pl* '**media** or '**mediums**; a means (*esp* television, radio or newspapers) by which news *etc* is made public: – *pl* '**media**; a person through whom spirits (of dead people) are said to speak: – *pl* '**mediums**. – *adj* middle or average in size, quality *etc*.

'**medley** *n* a mixture; a piece of music put

together from a number of other pieces: – pl 'medleys.

meek adj gentle, uncomplaining. – n 'meekness.

meerschaum ['mērshəm] n a fine white clay used to make tobacco pipes; a pipe made of this.

meet v to come face to face (with); to come together, join; to make the acquaintance of; to pay (bills etc) fully; to be suitable for, satisfy (requirements, a demand etc): – pt met. – n a meeting of huntsmen or other sportsmen. – adj proper, suitable. – n 'meeting a coming together, esp of people; an assembly, gathering.

mega- prefix great, huge.

'megalith n a huge stone set up in prehistoric times.

megalo'mania n an exaggerated idea of one's own importance or abilities.

'megaphone n a large trumpet-like device for making louder the sound of the voice.

megaton ['megətun] adj of a bomb with an explosive force equalling a million tons of TNT.

melancholy ['melənkəli] n lowness of spirits, sadness. – adj sad, depressed.

mêlée ['melā] n a confused fight between two groups of people.

mellifluous [mə'liflōoəs] adj sweetsounding.

mellow ['melō] adj (of fruit) ripe, juicy, sweet; having become pleasant or agreeable with age; (of light, colour etc) soft, not harsh. – v to make or become mellow. – n 'mellowness.

'melodrama n a type of play, intended to arouse great sympathy, horror etc. – adj melodra'matic of or like a melodrama, sensational, over-dramatic.

'melody n a tune; sweet music: – pl 'melodies. – adjs me'lodic of melody; me'lodious pleasing to the ear; tuneful.

'melon n a type of large juicy fruit or the plant that bears it.

melt v to make or become liquid, esp by heat; to soften; to disappear. The crowd melted away; to become tender in feeling. His heart melted at the sight of the orphan.

'member n one who belongs to any group, society etc; a limb of the body. – n 'membership the members of a club etc; the state of being a member. – n Member of Parliament (shortened to MP) a person elected to the House of Commons.

'membrane n a thin skin which covers or lines parts of a human or animal body, plants etc.

me'mento n something by which an event is remembered: – pl me'mentos.

'memo short for memorandum: – pl 'memos.

memoir ['memwär] n a written statement of what has happened; (pl) a person's account of his own life, an autobiography.

memo'randum n a note which helps one to remember; a written statement of a matter being discussed; a brief note sent round colleagues in an office etc: – pl memo'randa.

'memory n the power to remember; the mind's store of remembered things; something remembered; what is remembered about a person, his reputation: – pl 'memories. – adj 'memorable worthy of being remembered, famous. – n me'morial something (eg a monument) which helps us to remember persons or events of the past. – adj commemorating, honouring the memory of a person etc. – v memorize ['meməriz] to learn by heart. – in memory of in remembrance of or as a memorial of.

menace ['menəs] n harm or danger that may happen; a threat. – v to be a danger to; to threaten. – adj 'menacing evil-looking; threatening.

ménage [mā'näzh] n household.

menagerie [mi'najəri] n (a place for keeping) a collection of wild animals.

mend v to put right something broken, torn etc, to repair; to make or grow better. – n a part which has been mended. – on the mend getting better.

mendacious [men'dāshəs] adj untruthful. – n mendacity [men'dasəti].

'mendicant n a beggar. – Also adj.

menhir ['menhēr] n a tall upright prehistoric stone.

'menial adj (of work) humble, uninteresting, not requiring skill.

menin'gitis n an illness caused by inflammation of the covering of the brain.

menstruation [menstrōo'āshən] v (in women) the monthly discharge of blood from the womb. – adj 'menstrual of menstruation. – v 'menstruate.

mensū'ration n the act or art of measuring length, height etc.

'mental adj of the mind; done, made, happening etc in the mind; (of illness) affecting the mind. – n men'tality mental power; personality: – pl men'talities. – n mental hospital a hospital for people suffering from mental illness.

'**menthol** *n* a sharp-smelling substance got from peppermint oil.
'**mention** *v* to speak of briefly; to remark (that). – *n* (act of) mentioning or remarking.
'**mentor** *n* a (wise) giver of advice.
'**menū** *n* (a card with) a list of dishes to be served at a meal: – *pl* '**menus**.
'**mercantile** *adj* of buying and selling, trading.
mercenary ['mɔrsinɔri] *adj* working for money; influenced by the desire for money. – *n* a soldier who is paid by a foreign country to fight in its army: – *pl* '**mercenaries**.
'**merchant** *n* one who carries on a business in the buying and selling of goods, a trader. – *adj* of trade. – *n* '**merchandise** goods to be bought and sold. – *ns* '**merchantman** a trading ship; **merchant navy** ships and crews employed in trading.
'**mercūry** *n* an element, a heavy, silvery liquid metal (also **quicksilver**). – *adj* **mer'curial** lively, often changing.
'**mercy** *n* kindness, forgiveness towards an enemy, wrongdoer *etc*; pity; (*coll*) a bit of good luck. – *adjs* '**merciful** willing to forgive or to punish only lightly; '**merciless** cruel. – **at one's mercy** in one's power.
mere *n* a pool or a lake. – *adj* nothing more than, no more than: *mere nonsense*. – *adv* '**merely** only, simply.
merge *v* to (cause to) combine or join together; to blend, come together gradually. – *n* '**merger** a joining together *esp* of business firms *etc*.
me'ridian *n* a (semi-)circle drawn round the globe passing through the north and south poles; the highest point of the sun's course; the highest point of success *etc*.
meringue [mɔ'raŋ] *n* a cake made of sugar and white of egg.
merino [mɔ'rēnō] *n* a kind of sheep which has very fine wool; soft cloth made from its wool: – *pl* **me'rinos**.
'**merit** *n* that which deserves praise or reward; worth, value; (*pl*) the rights and wrongs (of a case, affair *etc*). – *v* to deserve. – *adj* **meri'torious** deserving honour or reward.
'**mermaid** *n* an imaginary sea creature with a woman's body down to the waist, and a fish's tail: – *masc* '**merman**.
'**merry** *adj* full of fun, cheerful and lively; slightly drunk. – *n* '**merriment** fun; laughter. – *ns* '**merry-go-round** a kind of roundabout with wooden horses, seats *etc* for riding on; '**merrymaking** cheerful celebrating,

festivity.
mesh *n* the opening between the threads of a net; network: – *pl* '**meshes**.
mesmerize ['mezmɔriz] *v* to hypnotize; to hold the attention of completely, fascinate. – *n* '**mesmerism**.
mess *n* an untidy or disgusting sight; disorder, confusion; (in the army, navy *etc*) a number of persons who take their meals together; the place where they eat: – *pl* '**messes**. – *v* (*usu* with **up**) to make untidy, dirty, muddled. – *npl* '**messmates** those who eat together.
'**message** *n* a piece of news or information sent from one person to another; a lesson, moral. – *n* '**messenger** a person who carries a message.
'**metal** *n* any of a group of substances (*eg* gold, silver, iron *etc*) *usu* shiny and able to conduct heat and electricity. – *adj* **me'tallic** made of metal; like metal. – *n* **me'tallurgy** the study of metals. – *adj* **metal'lurgic(al)**.
metamorphosis [metɔ'mörfɔsis] *n* a change in appearance, form, character *etc*, a transformation; a change that takes place in some creature during growth (*eg* a tadpole into a frog): – *pl* **metamorphoses** [metɔ'mörfɔsēz].
'**metaphor** *n* a way of describing something by suggesting that it is, or has the qualities of, something else. *The camel is the ship of the desert*. – *adj* **meta'phorical**.
mete *v* (with **out**) to deal out (punishment *etc*).
meteor ['mētiɔ] *n* a small mass, body *etc*, moving rapidly through space, becoming bright as it enters the earth's atmosphere, a shooting star. – *adj* **mete'oric** of, like a meteor; rapid; rapidly and brilliantly successful. – *ns* '**meteorite** a meteor which falls to the earth in the form of a piece of rock; **meteo'rologist** one who studies or makes forecasts about the weather. – *adj* **meteoro'logical. meteo'rology** the study of weather and climate.
'**mēter** *n* an instrument for measuring the amount of gas, electricity, water *etc* used; *see also* **metre**.
'**method** *n* a (planned or orderly) way of doing something; orderly arrangement. – *adj* **me'thodical** orderly, done or acting according to some plan.
'**methylāted 'spirit(s)** *n* a type of alcohol used as fuel in lamps, stoves *etc*.
me'ticulous *adj* (too) careful and accurate about small details.
'**mētre**, (*US*) '**mēter** *n* the chief unit of length in the metric system (about 1·1 yard); (in poetry, music) the arrange-

ment of syllables or notes in a regular rhythm. – *adjs* **metric** ['metrik] of the metric system; metrical; '**metrical** (in poetry) of, in metre; arranged in the form of verse. – *n* **metri'cation** the change-over of a country's units of measurements to the metric system. – *v* '**metricate**. – *n* **metric system** the system of weights and measures based on tens (1 metre=10 decimetres=100 centimetres *etc*).

'**metronome** *n* an instrument that keeps a regular beat, used for music practice.

me'**tropolis** *n* the capital city of a country; a chief centre: – *pl* **me'-tropolises**. – *adj* **metro'politan**.

'**mettle** *n* courage, pluck. – **on one's mettle** out to do one's best.

mew *n* the cry of a cat; *see* **sea-mew**; (*pl*) stables (now often used as flats) built round a yard or in a lane. – *v* to make the cry of a cat.

mezzo-soprano ['metsōsə'pranō] *n* (a person with) a singing voice between alto and soprano: – *pl* '**mezzo-so'pranos**.

miaow [mi'ow] *n* the sound made by a cat. – Also *v*.

'**mica** *n* a type of mineral which glitters and divides easily into thin transparent layers.

mice *see* **mouse**.

Michaelmas daisy ['miklməs] *n* a kind of large daisy, a kind of aster.

micro- *prefix* very small.

'**microbe** *n* a kind of very tiny living thing; a germ.

'**microchip** *n* a tiny piece of silicon *etc* designed to act as a complex electronic circuit.

microcom'puter *n* a very small computer containing a microprocessor.

microcosm ['mikrəkozəm] *n* a version on a small scale. *The misery in the household was a microcosm of the misery to be found throughout the whole country.*

'**microfilm** *n* a very narrow photographic film on which whole books, documents *etc* can be reproduced on a tiny scale.

mi'crometer *n* an instrument used for measuring tiny distances or angles.

'**microphone** *n* an instrument for picking up sound waves to be broadcast, recorded or amplified.

micro'processor *n* a microcomputer (or part of one) consisting of one or more microchips.

'**microscope** *n* an instrument (containing magnifying glass) which makes small objects easily seen. – *adj* **microscopic** [mikrə'skopik] very tiny.

microwave oven *n* an oven in which food is cooked by the heat produced by the passage of '**microwaves** (very short waves).

mid- *adj, prefix* placed or coming in the middle. – *n* '**mid'day** noon. – *adj* '**midland** in the middle of a country, away from the coast. – *ns* '**midnight** twelve o'clock at night; '**midshipman** formerly a junior naval officer, below sub-lieutenant; '**mid'summer** the time about June 21 which is the longest day of the year. – *adj, adv* '**mid'way** half-way. – *n* '**mid'winter** the time about December 21 which is the shortest day of the year.

'**midden** *n* a rubbish or dung heap.

'**middle** *adj* equally distant from the ends or edges; coming between. – *n* the middle point or part, centre; the course (of an action, job *etc*). – *adj* '**middling** of middle size, quality *etc*; not very good or bad. – *adj* '**middle-'aged** between youth and old age. – *ns* **Middle Ages** the time roughly between the years AD 500 and AD 1500; '**middle-'class** the class of people between the working and upper classes.

midge *n* any of several kinds of small fly.

'**midget** *n* a person who has not grown up to the normal size. – *adj* very small.

'**midriff** *n* the middle of the body, just below the ribs.

midst *n* the middle (*eg* of a job). – **in our midst** among us.

'**midwife** *n* a woman who helps at the birth of babies: – *pl* '**midwives**. – *n* **midwifery** [mid'wifəri] the art of assisting at the birth of babies.

mien [mēn] *n* look or appearance.

might [mit] *n* power, strength. – *v see* **may**. – *adj* '**mighty** having great power; very great: – *comp* '**mightier**, *superl* '**mightiest**. – *adv* (*coll*) very. – *n* '**mightiness** greatness. – **with might and main** with all possible effort.

migraine ['mēgrān] *n* a very severe type of headache.

mi'grate *v* to change one's home to another region or country; to pass regularly from one region to another, as certain birds *etc* do. – *n* **mi'gration**. – *adj, n* '**migrant** (of) a person, bird *etc* that migrates. – *adj* '**migratory** migrating; wandering.

mike short for **microphone**.

mild *adj* gentle; (of a taste) not sharp or bitter; not harsh or severe; (of weather) not cold. – *n* '**mildness**.

'**mildew** *n* a mark on plants, cloth, leather *etc* caused by tiny fungi.

mile *n* a measure of length (1·61 kilometre or 1760 yards). – *ns* '**mileage**

distance in miles; travel expenses (counted by the mile); '**milestone** a stone beside the road showing the number of miles to a certain place; something which marks an important event.

milieu ['mēlyə] *n* surroundings.

'**military** *adj* of, for soldiers or warfare. – *n* the army. – *adj* '**militant** fighting, warlike; aggressive, favouring or taking part in forceful action. – *n* a person who is militant. – *v* '**militate** to fight, work (against); to work (against), act to one's disadvantage. – *n* **militia** [mi'lishə] a body of men (not regular soldiers) trained to fight in emergencies.

milk *n* a white liquid produced by female animals as food for their young. – *v* to draw milk from; to force, take (money *etc*) from. – *adj* '**milky** of, like milk. – *ns* '**milkmaid** (*old*) woman who milks cows; '**milkman** a man who sells or delivers milk; '**milksop** a weak, unmanly man; **Milky Way** bright band of stars stretching across the sky.

mill *n* a machine for grinding or crushing grain, coffee *etc*; a building where grain is ground; a factory where things are made. – *v* to grind; to put grooves round the edge of (a coin); to move round and round in a crowd. – *n* '**miller** a person who grinds grain. – *ns* '**millrace** the stream of water which turns a millwheel and so drives the machinery of a mill; '**millstone** one of two heavy stones between which grain was ground; a great trouble or difficulty which keeps one from making progress; '**millwheel** a wheel, *esp* a waterwheel, used for driving a mill.

mil'lennium *n* a period of a thousand years; a period of great happiness hoped for on earth: – *pl* **mil'lennia**.

'**millet** *n* a type of grain used for food.

milli- *prefix* thousand; a thousandth part of.

'**milligramme** *n* a thousandth of a gramme.

millilitre ['mililētər] *n* a thousandth of a litre.

'**millimetre** *n* a thousandth of a metre.

milliner ['milinər] *n* one who makes and sells women's hats. – *n* '**millinery** the goods sold by a milliner.

'**million** *n* a thousand thousands (1,000,000). – *n* **millio'naire** a person who has a million pounds (or dollars) or more.

'**millipede** *n* a type of small crawling creature with a long body and very many legs.

mime *n* the use of, or the art of using actions, movements of the arms *etc* in place of speech; a play performed through mime; an action in such a play. – *v* to act using actions and movements but no words. – *v* **mimic** ['mimik] to imitate *esp* in a mocking way: – *pt* '**mimicked**. – *n* one who mimics. – *n* '**mimicry** the act of mimicking; (in an animal) a likeness to its surroundings or to another animal.

mimosa [mi'mōzə] *n* a type of tree with bunches of yellow, scented flowers.

mina'ret *n* a slender tower on a Mohammedan mosque.

mince *v* to cut or chop into small pieces; to walk in a prim way with short steps. – *n* meat chopped finely. – *n* '**mincer** a machine for mincing. – *ns* '**mincemeat** a chopped-up mixture of dried fruit, suet *etc*; '**mince-'pie** a pie filled with mincemeat. – **not to mince matters** not to try to soften an unpleasant statement by using tactful words.

mind *n* the power by which we think *etc*; intelligence, understanding; intention. *I have a (good) mind to tell him so.* – *v* to see to, look after. *Mind the baby*; to watch out for, be careful of. *Mind the step*; to object to. *I don't mind your saying so.* – *adjs* '**mindful** paying attention (to); '**mindless** foolish; without reason or thought. – **change one's mind** to change one's opinion or intention; **in two minds** undecided; **make up one's mind** to decide; **out of one's mind** mad; **presence of mind** ability to act calmly and sensibly; **speak one's mind** to speak frankly.

mine *pron* a thing or things belonging to me. *That book is mine.* – *n* a place (*usu* a pit or system of underground tunnels) from which metals, coal *etc* are dug; a heavy charge of explosive material for blowing up (a vehicle, ship *etc*). – *v* to dig or work a mine; to lay explosive mines in. – *n* '**miner** one who works in a (coal) mine. – *ns* '**minefield** an area covered with explosive mines; '**minelayer**, '**minesweeper** a ship which places mines in, or removes them from, the sea.

mineral ['minərəl] *adj*, *n* (of) any of the substances (coal, metals, gems *etc*) that are found in the earth and mined. – *ns* **mine'ralogy** the study of minerals; **mine'ralogist**. – *n* **mineral water** water containing small amounts of minerals; a fizzy type of soft drink.

mingle ['miŋgl] *v* to mix.

mini- *prefix* small (as in **minibus** *etc*). – *n* '**Mini** ® a type of small car.

miniature ['minichər] *n* a painting (or

something else) made on a small scale.
– *adj* on a small scale.

'**minibus** *n* a type of small bus: – *pl*
'**minibuses**.

'**minim** *n* (in music) a note equal to two
crotchets in length.

'**minimize** *v* to make to seem small or
unimportant. *He minimized the help he
received*; to make as little as possible. –
n '**minimum** the smallest possible
quantity: – *pl* '**minima**. – *adj* the least
possible.

'**minion** *n* a slave-like follower.

'**minister** *n* the head of one of the
divisions or departments of the government; a clergyman; a representative of
a government in a foreign country. – *v*
(with **to**) to help, supply the needs of. –
adj **minis'terial** of a minister. – *n*
'**ministry** a department of government
or its headquarters; the work of a
clergyman: – *pl* '**ministries**.

mink *n* a small weasel-like kind of animal
or its fur.

minnow ['minō] *n* a type of very small
river or pond fish.

'**minor** *adj* of less importance, size *etc*;
small, unimportant; opposite of
major. – *n* a person who has not come
of age legally, in UK a person under 18
years old. – *n* **mi'nority** the smaller
number or part; the state of being a
minor: – *pl* **mi'norities**.

'**minster** *n* a large church or cathedral.

'**minstrel** *n* (*hist*) a (travelling) musician;
a singer, entertainer. – *n* '**minstrelsy** a
collection of songs.

mint *n* a type of plant with strong-
smelling leaves, used as flavouring; a
place where coins are made; (*coll*) a
large sum (of money). – *v* to make
coins. – **in mint condition** in perfect
condition, as good as new.

minū'et *n* (the music for) an earlier kind
of slow, graceful dance.

'**minus** *prep* used to show subtraction
and represented by the sign (−). *Five
minus two equals three, or* $5 - 2 = 3$;
(*coll*) without. *I'm minus my car today.*
– *adj, n* (of) a quantity less than zero.

minute[1] ['minit] *n* the sixtieth part of an
hour; in measuring an angle, the sixtieth part of a degree; a very short time;
(*pl*) the notes taken of what is said at a
meeting.

mi'nūte[2] *adj* very small; very exact.

minx *n* a cheeky young girl: – *pl*
'**minxes**.

'**miracle** *n* a wonderful act beyond the
power of men; a fortunate happening
that has no natural cause or explanation. – *adj* **mi'raculous**.

mirage ['miräzh] *n* something not really
there that one imagines one sees, *esp* an
expanse of water imagined by travellers
in the desert.

'**mire** *n* deep mud. – *adj* '**miry**.

'**mirror** *n* a surface that reflects light, *esp*
a piece of glass which shows the image
of the person looking into it. – *v* to
reflect as a mirror does.

'**mirth** *n* merriment, laughter. – *adjs*
'**mirthful**; '**mirthless**.

mis- *prefix* wrong(ly), bad(ly).

misad'venture *n* an unlucky happening.

misanthropist [mi'zanthrəpist] *n* one
who hates mankind. – *adj* **mis-
an'thropic**. – *n* **mi'santhropy**.

misap'propriate *v* to put to a wrong use
esp to use (someone else's money) for
oneself.

misbe'have *v* to behave badly. – *n*
misbe'haviour.

mis'carry *v* to go wrong or astray; to be
unsuccessful; in pregnancy, to have a
miscarriage: – *pt* **mis'carried**. – *n*
mis'carriage a going wrong, failure;
in pregnancy, the loss of the baby from
the womb before it is able to survive.

miscellaneous [misə'lāniəs] *adj* as-
sorted, made up of several kinds. – *n*
mis'cellany a mixture or collection of
things (*esp* writings) of different kinds:
– *pl* **mis'cellanies**.

mis'chance *n* an unlucky accident.

mischief ['mischif] *n* naughtiness; evil,
harm, damage. – *adj* '**mischievous**
naughty; teasing; causing trouble.

miscon'ception *n* a wrong idea, a mis-
understanding.

mis'conduct *n* bad or immoral behaviour.

misconstrue [miskən'strōō] *v* to take a
wrong meaning from, misunderstand.

miscreant ['miskriənt] *n* a wicked
person.

mis'deed *n* a bad deed; a crime.

misde'meanour *n* a misdeed or offence
(*esp* against the law).

miser ['mizər] *n* one who hoards his
money and spends very little on himself
or others; a mean person. – *adj*
'**miserly** very mean.

misery ['mizəri] *n* great unhappiness,
pain, poverty *etc*: – *pl* '**miseries**. – *adj*
'**miserable** very unhappy; very poor,
worthless or wretched.

mis'fire *v* (of guns *etc*) to fail to go off;
(of a plan *etc*) to go wrong.

'**misfit** *n* a person who cannot fit in
happily at home, work *etc*; a thing that
fits badly.

misfortune [mis'förchən] *n* bad luck; an
unlucky accident.

misgiving [mis'givɪŋ] *n* a feeling of fear or doubt (*eg* about the result of an action).

misguided [mis'gīdid] *adj* led astray, mistaken.

mis'handle *v* to treat badly or roughly.

mishap ['mis-hap] *n* an unlucky accident.

mis'lay *v* to put (a thing) aside and forget where it is, to lose: – *pt* **mis'laid**.

mis'lead *v* to give a false idea (to), to deceive: – *pt* **mis'led**. – *adj* **mis-'leading**.

mis'nōmer *n* a wrong or unsuitable name.

misogynist [mi'sojənist] *n* one who hates women.

'misprint *n* a mistake in printing.

mis'quote *v* to make a mistake in repeating what someone has written or said.

misrepresent [misrepri'zent] *v* to give a wrong idea (of someone's words, actions *etc*).

miss *n* a form of address used before the name of an unmarried woman; a young woman or girl: – *pl* **'misses**. – *v* to fail to hit, reach, catch, find, see, hear, take (an opportunity), understand; to discover the loss or absence of; to feel the lack of. *He misses his old friends*; (with **out**) to leave out. – *n* the act of missing; a failure to hit the target; a loss. – *adj* **'missing** lost.

'missal *n* the Mass book of the Roman Catholic Church.

'mis'shāpen *adj* badly, abnormally shaped.

'missile *n* a weapon or other object that is thrown or fired.

'mission *n* a task, duty *etc* that a person or group is sent to do; a group of representatives sent (to another country) for negotiations *etc*, or one sent to spread a religion; the headquarters of such groups; one's chosen task or purpose. *His mission in life is to make people happy*. – *n* **'missionary** one who is sent to spread a religion: – *pl* **'missionaries**.

missive ['misiv] *n* something sent, *esp* a letter.

'mis'spell *n* to spell wrongly. – *n* **'mis'spelling**.

'mis'spent *adj* spent in the wrong way, wasted: *misspent youth*.

mist *n* a cloud of moisture seen in the air, thin fog or drizzle; anything that blurs one's sight, judgement *etc*. – *v* (with **up** or **over**) to cover or become covered with mist. – *adj* **'misty**.

mis'take *v* to misunderstand, be wrong or make an error about; to take (one thing or person) for another: – *pt* **mis'took**, *pp* **mis'taken**. – *n* a wrong action, statement *etc*, an error. – *adj* **mis'taken** making an error, unwise: *mistaken belief*.

mister *see* **Mr.**

mistletoe ['misltō] *n* a type of plant with white berries, used as a Christmas decoration.

'mistress *n* a female employer; a female teacher; a female owner (of a dog); a woman skilled in an art *etc*: *a mistress of sculpture*; a woman who is the lover though not the legal wife of a man; *see* **Mrs**: – *pl* **'mistresses**.

mis'trust *n* lack of trust or confidence in. – *v* not to trust, not to have confidence in.

misunder'stand *v* to take a wrong meaning from what is said or done. – *n* **misunder'standing** a mistake about a meaning; a slight disagreement.

'mis'ūse *n* bad or wrong use. – *v* **misuse** ['mis'ūz] to use wrongly; to treat badly.

mite *n* anything very small (*eg* a little child); a kind of very tiny spider; (*hist*) a very small coin.

'mitigate *v* to make (trouble, punishment, anger *etc*) less great or severe. – *n* **miti'gation**.

'mitre *n* the pointed head-dress worn by archbishops and bishops; a slanting joint between two pieces of wood.

'mitt(en) *n* a kind of glove without separate divisions for the four fingers.

mix *v* to unite or blend two or more things together to form one mass; (often with **up**) to confuse, muddle; to go into the company of others, associate (with). *He does not mix with his neighbours.* – Also *n.* – *adj* **mixed** jumbled together; confused, muddled; made up of, including different kinds (or sexes). – *ns* **'mixer** a machine (or person) that mixes; **mixture** ['mikschər] the act of mixing; the state of being mixed; a number of things mixed together; a medicine. – **mixed up** confused; bewildered.

'mizzen-mast *n* the mast nearest the stern of the ship.

mnemonic [ni'monik] *n* something (*eg* a rhyme *etc*) which helps one to remember (something).

moan *v* to make a low sound of grief or pain. – Also *n.*

moat *n* a deep trench round a castle *etc*, *usu* filled with water.

mob *n* a noisy crowd. – *v* to crowd round, or attack, in a disorderly way: – *pt* **mobbed**.

'**mōbile** *adj* able to move; moving or moved easily; changing quickly. – *n* a decorative object hung so that it moves slightly in the air. – *n* **mobility** [mə'biləti].

'**mōbilize** *v* to gather (troops *etc*) together ready for active service. – *n* **mobili'zation**.

'**moc(c)asin** *n* a soft leather shoe of the type worn by the N. American Indians.

mock *v* to laugh at, make fun of. – *adj* false, pretended, imitation: *a mock battle*. – *n* '**mockery** the act of mocking; a ridiculous imitation.

mode *n* manner (of doing or acting); kind, sort; fashion. – *adj* '**modish** fashionable, smart.

'**model** *n* a design, pattern *etc* to be copied; a copy of something made in a small size: *model railway*; a living person who poses for an artist; someone who is employed to wear and show off new clothes. – *adj* acting as a model; fit to be copied, perfect: *model behaviour*. – *v* to make a model of; to shape; to form according to a particular pattern; to wear and show off (clothes): – *pt* '**modelled**.

moderate ['modəreit] *v* to make or become less great or severe. – *adj* ['modərət] keeping within reasonable limits, not going to extremes; of medium or average quality, ability *etc*. – *adv* '**moderately**. – *ns* mode'ration a lessening or calming down; the practice of not going to extremes; '**moderator** the chairman at a meeting (*esp* of clergymen).

'**modern** *adj* belonging to the present or to a time not long past, not old. – *n* mo'**dernity**. – *v* '**modernize** to bring up to date.

'**modest** *adj* not exaggerating one's achievements *etc*, not boastful; not very large: *a modest salary*; behaving in a decent way, not shocking. – *n* '**modesty**.

'**modicum** *n* a small quantity or amount: *a modicum of kindness*: – *pl* '**modicums**.

'**modifȳ** *v* to make a change in. *He modified the design*; to make less extreme. *He modified his demands*: – *pt* '**modified**. – *n* modifi'**cation**.

'**modūlate** *v* to vary or soften the tone or pitch of (the voice *etc*). – *n* modu'**lation**.

'**module** *n* (in architecture) a standard unit of size; a separate, self-contained section of a spacecraft.

'**mōhair** *n* (fabric made from) the long silky hair of an Angora goat.

Mo'**hammedan** *n* one who follows the religion founded by Mohammed. – Also *adj*. – *n* Mo'**hammedanism**.

moist *adj* damp, very slightly wet. – *v* **moisten** ['moisn] to make slightly wet or damp. – *n* **moisture** ['moischər] slight wetness; water or other liquid in tiny drops in the atmosphere or on a surface. – *v* '**moisturize** to add moisture to. – *n* '**moisturizer**.

'**mōlar** *n* a back tooth which grinds one's food.

mo'**lasses** *n sing* a type of thick syrup left when sugar is made, treacle.

mole *n* a kind of small burrowing animal, with very small eyes and soft fur; a small (often dark brown) spot on the skin; a stone jetty or pier. – *n* '**molehill** a little heap of earth cast up by a burrowing mole.

molecule ['molikūl] *n* the smallest part of a substance that has the same qualities as the substance itself.

mo'**lest** *v* to annoy or torment.

'**mollifȳ** *v* to calm down, soothe, or lessen the anger of: – *pt* '**mollified**.

'**mollusc** *n* the name of a group of boneless animals *usu* with hard shells (*eg* shellfish, snails).

'**mollycoddle** *v* to pamper, over-protect.

'**mōlten** *adj* (of metal, lava *etc*) melted.

'**mōment** *n* a very short space of time, an instant; importance. – *adjs* '**momentary** lasting for a moment; mo'**mentous** of great importance. – *n* mo'**mentum** the force of a moving body: – *pl* mo'**menta**.

monarch ['monərk] *n* a king, queen, emperor or empress. – *n* '**monarchy** government by a monarch; an area governed by a monarch: – *pl* '**monarchies**.

'**monastery** *n* a house where a group of monks live: – *pl* '**monasteries**. – *adj* mo'**nastic** of or like monasteries or monks. – *n* mo'**nasticism** the way of life in a monastery.

Monday ['mundi] *n* the second day of the week.

monetary ['munitəri] *adj* of money or coinage.

money ['muni] *n* the coins and banknotes which are used for payment; wealth: – *pls* '**moneys**, '**monies**. – *adj* '**moneyed**, '**monied** wealthy.

mongoose ['mongōos] *n* a type of small weasel-like animal which kills snakes: – *pl* '**mongooses**.

mongrel ['mungrəl] *adj*, *n* (of) an animal, *esp* a dog, of mixed breed.

'**monitor** *n* any of several kinds of instruments used for checking if some system, apparatus *etc* is working correctly; a pupil who helps in the running of a school; a screen in a television studio showing the picture being transmitted; a kind of large lizard. – *v* to use, or to be, a monitor; to check, keep a check on something; to listen to and report on foreign broadcasts *etc*.

monk [muŋk] *n* one of a male religious group that lives apart from the world in a monastery.

monkey ['muŋki] *n* the type of animal most like man, *usu* the small long-tailed kind walking on four legs (unlike the apes); a mischievous child: – *pl* '**monkeys**. – *v* to meddle, tamper with something. – *ns* '**monkey-nut** a peanut, groundnut; '**monkey-'puzzle** a kind of pine tree with prickly spines along its branches.

mono- *prefix* one, single.

'**monocle** *n* a single eyeglass.

mo'nogamy *n* marriage to one wife or husband only at a time. – *adj* **mo'nogamous**.

'**monogram** *n* two or more letters (often a person's initials) made into a single design. *He wore his monogram on his shirt.*

monologue ['monəlog] *n* a long speech by one person.

'**monoplane** *n* an aeroplane having one pair of wings.

mo'nopoly *n* the right, not shared by others, of doing, making or selling something; complete unshared possession, control *etc*: – *pl* **mo'nopolies**. – *v* **mo'nopolize** to have the full, unshared rights in anything; to take up the whole of (*eg* someone's attention, a conversation *etc*).

'**monorail** *n* a railway on which the trains run along a single rail.

'**monosyllable** *n* a word of one syllable. – *adj* **monosyl'labic**.

'**monotone** *n* a single, unchanging tone; dull. – *n* **mo'notony** lack of variety.

mon'soon *n* a wind that blows in the Indian Ocean; the rainy season caused by the south-west monsoon in summer.

'**monster** *n* anything of unusual size or appearance; a huge creature, causing fear; a very wicked person. – *adj* huge. – *n* **mons'trosity** something not natural; something very ugly: – *pl* **mons'trosities**. – *adj* '**monstrous** huge; horrible.

month [munth] *n* a twelfth part of a year, about four weeks. – *adj, adv* '**monthly** happening once a month. – *n* a paper published once a month: – *pl* '**monthlies**.

'**monument** *n* a building, pillar, tomb *etc* built in memory of a person or an event. – *adj* **monu'mental** of or acting as a monument; very great in size, quantity *etc*. – *n* **ancient monument** any structure (such as a dwelling-place, grave *etc*) remaining from ancient times.

moo *n* the sound made by a cow. – Also *v*.

mood *n* the state of a person's feelings or temper. – *adj* '**moody** often changing one's mood; ill-tempered, cross.

moon *n* the heavenly body which travels round the earth once each month and reflects light from the sun. – *v* to wander (about); to gaze dreamily (at). – *ns* '**moonbeam** a beam of light from the moon; '**moonlight** the light of the moon; '**moonshine** the shining of the moon; rubbish, foolish ideas or talk; '**moonstone** a precious stone with a pearly shine.

moor *n* a large stretch of open ground, often covered with heather. – *v* to tie up or anchor (a ship *etc*). – *npl* '**moorings** the place where a ship is moored; the anchor, rope *etc* holding it. – *ns* '**moorhen** a kind of water bird, a female coot; '**moorland** a stretch of moor.

moose *n* a large kind of deer-like animal, found in N. America: – *pl* **moose**.

moot point a debatable point, a question with no obvious solution.

mop *n* a pad of sponge or a bunch of short pieces of coarse yarn *etc* on a handle for washing or cleaning; a thick head of hair. – *v* to clean with a mop; to clean or wipe. *He mopped his brow*: – *pt* **mopped**. – **mop up** clean or wipe up.

mope *v* to be unhappy and gloomy.

'**moped** *n* a pedal bicycle with a motor.

mo'raine *n* a line of rocks and gravel left by a glacier.

'**moral** *adj* having to do with right and wrong behaviour and character; having to do with right behaviour or character. – *n* the lesson of a fable or story; (*pl*) one's character and behaviour. – *n* **mo'rality** (the right) moral standards. – *v* '**moralize** to draw a lesson from a story or happening. – *ns* **moral support** encouragement without active help; **moral victory** a failure that can really be seen as a success.

morale [mə'räl] *n* spirit and confidence.

mo'rass *n* a marsh or bog; something that bewilders (someone) or is difficult to cope with: *involved in a morass of government regulations*: – *pl* **mo'rasses**.

'**morbid** *adj* (of a person, thoughts *etc*)

too concerned with gloomy, unpleasant things; diseased, unhealthy.

more *adj* a greater number, amount of: *more cakes: more money.* – *adv* to a greater extent: *more beautiful. I love you more than I can say.* – *n* a great proportion, amount; a further or additional number, amount. *There's more where this came from.* – *adv* **more'over** besides.

morgue [mörg] *n* a place where dead bodies are laid, awaiting identification *etc*.

'moribund *adj* in a dying state.

morn *n* (in poetry *etc*) morning.

'morning *n* the first part of the day. – *adj* taking place in the morning. – *n* **morning star** Venus or another planet, when it rises before the sun.

mo'rocco *n* a fine goat-skin leather first brought from Morocco.

'moron *n* a person of low mental ability, an idiot. – *adj* **mo'ronic**.

mo'rose *adj* gloomy, bad-tempered.

'morphia *n* a kind of drug which causes sleep or deadens pain (also **morphine** ['mörfēn]).

'morris-dance *n* a kind of country dance in which dancers wear traditional clothes, decorated with bells.

morrow ['morō] *n* (in poetry *etc*) the next day, the day after.

morse *n* a code of signals (made up of dots and dashes) used in signalling and telegraphy.

'morsel *n* a small piece, *esp* of food.

'mortal *adj* liable to die; causing death, deadly. – *n* a human being. – *n* **mor'tality** the state of being mortal; the number of deaths; deaths in proportion to the population, death-rate: – *pl* **mor'talities**. – *adv* **'mortally** fatally: *mortally wounded*.

'mortar *n* a kind of bowl in which substances are crushed and ground *usu* by a **pestle**; a short gun for throwing shells; a mixture of lime, sand and water, used for fixing stones in a building *etc*. – *n* **'mortarboard** a university or college cap with a square flat top.

mortgage ['mörgij] *n* a sum of money lent through a legal agreement for buying buildings, land *etc* (which the borrower must give up if he fails to repay the loan). – *v* to offer buildings *etc* as security for money borrowed.

mortice *see* **mortise**.

'mortifȳ *v* to make to feel ashamed or humble; (of a part of the flesh) to die: – *pt* **'mortified**. – *n* **mortifi'cation**.

mortise ['mörtis] *n* a hole made in a

piece of wood to receive the shaped end (**tenon**) of another piece.

mortuary ['mörchŏŏəri] *n* a place where dead bodies are kept before burial or cremation: – *pl* **'mortuaries**.

mosaic [mə'zāik] *n* a picture or design made up of many small pieces of coloured glass, stone *etc*.

Moslem, Muslim ['mozləm] *adj, n* Mohammedan.

mosque [mosk] *n* a Mohammedan place of worship.

mosquito [məs'kētō] *n* any of several types of biting or blood-sucking insects, some carrying disease: – *pl* **mos'quito(e)s**.

moss *n* any of several kinds of very small flowerless plant, found in moist places; a bog: – *pl* **'mosses**. – *adjs* **'mossy**; **'moss-grown**.

mōst *adj* the greatest number of, amount of: *most boys: most food.* – *adv* very, extremely. *I'm most grateful*; (often with **the**) to the greatest extent. *He was the most ill of the family.* – *n* the greatest number, amount. *He got most.* – *adv* **'mostly** mainly, chiefly. – **at most** not more than; **for the most part** mostly.

moth *n* the name of a family of insects like butterflies, seen mostly at night; the cloth-eating grub of the **clothes moth**. – *n* **'mothball** a small ball of a chemical used to protect clothes from moths. – *adj* **'moth-eaten** (of cloth) full of holes made by moths; old, shabby.

mother ['mudhər] *n* a female parent; the female head of a convent. – *v* to give birth to, be the mother of; to care for as a mother does. – *adj* **'motherly** of, like a mother. – *ns* **'mother-country, -land** the country of one's birth; **'motherhood** the state of being a mother; **'mother-in-law** the mother of one's husband or wife; **'mother-of-'pearl** the shining, hard, smooth substance which forms inside certain shells; **'mother-'tongue** a person's native language.

motif [mō'tēf] *n* a distinctive, important feature or idea in a piece of music, a play, a design *etc*.

'motion *n* the act, state or power of moving; a single movement; a suggestion put before a meeting for discussion. – *v* to make a signal or sign by a movement or gesture; to direct (a person) in this way. *The policeman motioned him forward.* – *adj* **'motionless** without movement.

'mōtive *n* that which causes a person to

act or to do something, a reason. – v 'motivate to cause (someone) to act in a certain way.

'motley adj made up of different colours or kinds.

'mōtor n a machine (usu an engine worked by petrol) which brings about motion or does work; a motor-car. – Also adj. – v to go by motor vehicle. – n 'motorist one who drives a motor-car. – v 'motorize to supply with an engine. He motorized his bicycle. – ns 'motor-bicycle (-bike, -cycle, -boat, -bus, -car) a bicycle (boat etc) driven by an engine worked by petrol; 'motor-way a special kind of dual carriageway on which traffic is allowed to drive faster than on other roads.

'mottled adj marked with spots of many colours or shades.

'motto n a short sentence or phrase, which acts as a guiding principle or rule of behaviour. 'Death before defeat' was the family motto: – pl 'mottoes.

mould [mōld] n a shape into which a substance in liquid form is poured so that it may take on that shape when it cools or sets: a jelly mould; soil (containing rotted leaves etc); a fluffy growth found on stale food etc. – v to form in a mould; to shape. – v 'moulder to crumble away to dust. – n 'moulding a decorated border (usu of moulded plaster) round a ceiling, picture frame etc. – adj 'mouldy affected by mould.

moult [mōlt] v (of birds) to shed the feathers.

mound n a bank of earth or stones; a hill; a heap.

mount v to go up; to get up, or place, on a horse, bicycle etc; to fix (a jewel etc) in a holder, or (a picture etc) on to a backing, for display; to fix anything on to a support; to prepare, organize (an exhibition). – n a mountain; a support or backing on which something is displayed; a horse, bicycle etc to ride on. – The Mounties ['mowntiz] the Canadian mounted police.

'mountain n a large hill; a large heap or quantity. – n mountai'neer a climber of mountains. – adj 'mountainous having many mountains; huge. – n 'mountain-'ash the rowan tree.

mountebank ['mowntibaŋk] n one who makes untrue claims about himself, his abilities etc.

mourn [mörn] v to grieve for (a person, loss etc); to be sorrowful. – n 'mourner. – adj 'mournful sad. – n 'mourning the showing of grief; the

dark-coloured clothes traditionally worn by mourners; a period of time during which signs of grief (eg dark-coloured clothes) are shown.

mouse n a type of little gnawing animal (often greyish-brown) found in houses and in the fields; a shy, timid, uninteresting person: – pl mice. – adj 'mousy of a light-brown colour; (of a person) shy, timid, uninteresting.

mousse [mōōs] n a mixture, often containing cream, that has been whipped up and set.

moustache [məs'täsh] n the hair upon the upper lip of men.

mouth n the opening in the head by which an animal or person eats and utters sounds; that part of a river where it flows into the sea; an opening or entrance (of a bottle, a cave etc). – v mouth [mowdh] to speak; to shape words in an exaggerated way. – ns mouthful ['mowthfōol] as much as fills the mouth: – pl 'mouthfuls; 'mouth-organ a kind of small musical instrument played by the mouth; 'mouthpiece the part of a musical instrument, tobacco-pipe etc held in the mouth; one who speaks for others.

move [mōōv] v to (cause to) change place or position; to change one's house; to rouse or affect the feelings of. He was moved by the beautiful music; to rouse into action; to propose, suggest. – n an act of moving; a step or action; a shifting of pieces in a game (of chess etc). – adj 'movable able to be moved, lifted, changed etc. – n 'movement the act or manner of moving; a change of position; a division of a piece of music; a group of people united to achieve some aim: the Communist movement; an organized attempt to achieve an aim. He took part in the movement to reform the divorce laws. – n 'movie a cinema film. – adj 'moving in motion; causing emotion (eg pity).

mow [mō] v to cut grass, hay etc with a scythe or machine; to destroy in great numbers. – n 'mower machine for mowing.

Mr ['mistər] (short for mister) the form of address used before the surname of men.

Mrs ['misiz] (short for mistress) the form of address used before the surname of married women.

Ms [miz] a form of address sometimes used before the surnames of married or unmarried women.

much adj a great amount of. – adv to, by a great extent: much loved: much faster.

– *pron* a great amount; something important. *He made much of it.* – **much the same** nearly the same.

muck *n* dung, dirt, filth.

'**mūcus** *n* the slimy fluid from the nose *etc*. – *adj* '**mucous** like or covered by mucus.

mud *n* wet, soft earth. – *adj* '**muddy** covered with or containing mud. – *n* '**mudguard** a shield or guard over wheels to catch mudsplashes.

'**muddle** *v* to confuse, bewilder; to mix up; to make a mess of. – *n* a mess; a (state of) confusion.

muezzin [mōō'ezin] *n* a Mohammedan priest who calls out the hour of prayer from a mosque.

muff *n* a tube-shaped (often furry) cover to keep the hands warm. – *v* to fail in trying to do something (*eg* catch a ball *etc*).

'**muffin** *n* a round, flat spongy cake to be toasted and eaten hot with butter; (*US*) a small, round cake made of flour, bran *etc* eaten with butter.

'**muffle** *v* to wrap up for warmth *etc*; to deaden (a sound). – *n* '**muffler** a scarf; (*US*) a silencer for a car *etc*.

'**mufti** *n* clothes worn when he is off duty by someone normally in uniform.

mug *n* a straight-sided cup. – *v* to attack and rob (someone) in the street: – *pt* **mugged**. – *n* '**mugger**.

'**muggy** *adj* (of the weather) close and damp.

mū'latto *n* a person one of whose parents was coloured, the other white: – *pl* **mu'lattoes**.

'**mulberry** *n* a kind of tree on whose leaves silkworms are fed; its purple berry: – *pl* '**mulberries**.

mulch *n* loose straw *etc* laid down to protect the roots of plants. – *v* to cover with mulch.

mule *n* an animal whose parents are a horse and an ass; a backless kind of slipper. – *adj* '**mulish** stubborn.

mull *v* to think or ponder (òver). – *adj* **mulled** (of wine *etc*) sweetened, spiced and warmed.

'**mullet** *n* a type of eatable small sea fish.

'**mullion** *n* an upright (often stone) division in a window.

multi- *prefix* many.

multi-coloured ['multikulərd] *adj* many-coloured.

multi'fārious *adj* of many kinds.

multimillionaire ['multimiljə'nār] *n* one who has property worth several million pounds.

multi'national *adj*, *n* (of) a company which has branches in several different countries.

'**multiple** *adj* having or affecting many parts: *multiple injuries*; involving many things of the same sort, as vehicles in a *multiple crash*. – *n* a number or quantity which contains another an exact number of times.

'**multiplȳ** *v* to increase; to increase a number by adding it to itself a certain number of times, as 2 multiplied by 3 (or 2 × 3) = 2 + 2 + 2 = 6: – *pt* '**multiplied**. – *ns* **multipli'cation** the act of multiplying; **multi'plicity** a great number; the state of being many or varied; '**multiplier** the number by which another is to be multiplied.

'**multitude** *n* a great number; a crowd. – *adj* **multi'tudinous** very many.

mum *n coll* for **mother**. – *adj* silent.

'**mumble** *v* to speak indistinctly.

'**mummy** *n coll* or child's name for **mother**; a dead body kept whole for a very long time by wrapping in bandages and treating with wax, spices *etc*: – *pl* '**mummies**. – *v* '**mummifȳ** to make into a mummy: – *pt* '**mummified**.

mumps *n sing* an infectious disease affecting certain glands at the side of the neck, causing swelling.

munch *v* to chew (with the mouth shut).

mun'dane *adj* dull, ordinary.

mū'nicipal *adj* of, belonging to, owned by a city or town.

mū'nificent *adj* very generous. – *n* **mu'nificence**.

mū'nitions *npl* weapons, ammunition *etc* used in war.

'**mūral** *adj* of or on a wall. – *n* a painting, design *etc* made on a wall.

'**murder** *v* to kill a person unlawfully and on purpose. – *n* the act of murdering. – *n* '**murderer**: – *fem* '**murderess**. – *adj* '**murderous** capable of, guilty of murder; wicked.

'**murky** *adj* dark, gloomy.

'**murmur** *n* a low, indistinct, continuous sound; a low muttering or grumbling; hushed speech or tone. – *v* to make a murmur; to complain, grumble.

muscle ['musl] *n* fleshy, bundle-like parts of the body which, by drawing together or stretching out, cause the movements of the body. – *adj* **muscular** ['muskūlər] of muscles; strong.

muse [mūz] *v* to think (over) in a quiet, leisurely way. – *n* (*myth*) one of the nine goddesses of poetry, music, dancing *etc*.

museum [mū'zēəm] *n* a building in which objects of artistic, scientific or historic interest are kept and displayed:

– *pl* **mu'seums**.

mush *n* anything soft and pulpy; anything (*eg* a film, song) oversentimental. – *adj* **'mushy**.

'mushroom *n* a kind of (eatable) fungus, *usu* umbrella-shaped. – *adj* growing or springing up very quickly. – *v* to grow very quickly. *New buildings mushroomed all over the town.*

music ['mūzik] *n* the art of arranging, combining *etc* certain sounds able to be produced by the voice, or by instruments; an arrangement of such sounds or its written form; any sweet or pleasant sound. – *adj* **'musical** of music; sounding sweet, pleasant; having a talent for music. – *n* **musician** [mū'zishən] someone skilled in music; someone who plays a musical instrument. – *n* **music centre** apparatus consisting of a record-player, tape-recorder, and radio, with loudspeakers.

musk *n* a strong perfume, obtained from the male **'musk-deer** (a small hornless deer found in Central Asia). – *n* **'musk-rat** same as **musquash**.

'musket *n* (*hist*) a kind of gun once used by soldiers. – *n* (*hist*) **muske'teer** a soldier armed with a musket.

Muslim ['mŏŏzlim] same as **Moslem**.

muslin ['muzlin] *n* a kind of fine, soft, cotton cloth.

musquash ['muskwosh] *n* a type of large N. American water-rat or its fur (also **musk-rat**): – *pl* **'musquashes**.

'mussel *n* a kind of shellfish, used as food and having two separate halves to its shell.

must *v usu* used with another verb to express necessity. *You must learn to cross the road safely*; to express compulsion. *You must do as you're told*; to express certainty or probability. *This sum must be right.* – *n* something that must be done, a necessity.

'mustang *n* a kind of wild horse found in America.

'mustard *n* a type of plant with a sharp taste; a hot, dark yellow-coloured seasoning (for meat, *etc*) made from its seeds.

'muster *v* to gather up or together (*eg* troops, courage). – **pass muster** to be accepted as satisfactory.

'musty *adj* smelling old and stale.

mute *adj* dumb; silent; (of a letter in a word) not sounded. – *n* a dumb person. – *adj* **'muted** (of sounds) made quieter, hushed; (of colours) not bright.

'mūtilate *v* to cut off (a limb *etc*) from; to damage greatly. – *n* **muti'lation**.

'mūtiny *v* to rise against those in power; to refuse to obey the commands of officers in the army, navy or air force: – *pt* **'mutinied**. – *n* refusal to obey commands, *esp* in the armed forces: – *pl* **'mutinies**. – *n* **muti'neer** one who takes part in a mutiny. – *adj* **'mutinous** rebellious; refusing to obey orders.

'mutter *v* to speak words in a low voice; to grumble.

'mutton *n* the flesh of the sheep used as food.

mutual ['mūchŏŏəl] *adj* given by each to the other(s): *mutual trust*: *mutual help*; common to two or more, shared by two or more: *mutual friend*.

'muzzle *n* the nose and mouth of an animal; a fastening placed over the mouth of an animal to prevent biting; the open end of a gun. – *v* to put a muzzle on (a dog *etc*); to prevent from speaking (freely). *The president muzzled the press.*

'muzzy *adj* cloudy, confused.

mȳ *adj* belonging to me. *This is my book.* – *pron* **my'self** used reflexively. *I hurt myself*; used for emphasis. *I myself can't go, but my brother can.*

mȳ'ōpia *n* short-sightedness. – *n, adj* **myopic** [mi'opik].

'myriad *n* a very great number. – *adj* very many, countless.

myrrh [mər] *n* a kind of resin with a bitter taste, used in medicines, perfumes *etc*.

'myrtle *n* a type of evergreen shrub.

myself *see* **my**.

'mystery *n* something that cannot be or has not been explained, something puzzling; a deep secret: – *pl* **'mysteries**. – *adjs* **mys'tērious** puzzling, difficult to understand; secret, hidden; **'mystic(al)** having a secret or sacred meaning beyond ordinary human understanding. – *n* **'mystic** a person who tries to commune with God or obtain knowledge of sacred or mystical things *esp* by going into a state of spiritual ecstasy. – *v* **'mystifȳ** to puzzle greatly; to confuse, bewilder: – *pt* **'mystified**. – *n* **mystique** [mis'tēk] an atmosphere of mystery about someone or something.

myth *n* a story about gods, heroes *etc* of ancient times; a fable; something imagined or untrue. – *adjs* **'mythical** of a myth; invented, imagined, never having existed; **mytho'logical** of myth or mythology; mythical. – *ns* **my'thology** a collection of myths; the study of myths; **my'thologist**.

myxoma'tōsis *n* a contagious disease of rabbits.

N

'**nābob** *n* a title given to certain Indian princes.

nadir ['nādẽr] *n* the point of the heavens opposite the **zenith**; the lowest point of anything.

nag *v* to find fault with constantly: – *pt* **nagged**. – *n* a (small) horse.

naiad ['niad] *n* (*myth*) a goddess of rivers.

nail *n* a horny covering, protecting the tips of the fingers and toes; a thin pointed piece of metal for fastening wood *etc*. – *v* to fasten with nails; to fasten (something up) in this way (*eg* in a box); (*coll*) to catch, trap.

naive [nī'ēv] *adj* simple in thought, manner or speech; inexperienced and lacking knowledge of the world. – *n* **naiveté** [nī'ēvtā].

'**nāked** *adj* without clothes; having no covering. – *n* '**nakedness**.

'**namby'pamby** *adj* childish, insipid, lacking liveliness.

name *n* a word by which a person, place or thing is known or called; fame, reputation. *He has made a name for himself*; authority. *I arrest you in the name of the king.* – *v* to give a name to; to speak of by name, mention; to appoint. – *adj* '**nameless** without a name, not named. – *adv* '**namely** that is to say. – *ns* '**nameplate** a piece of metal or other material, having on it the name of a person, house *etc*; '**namesake** one having the same name as another.

'**nanny** *n* a children's nurse: – *pl* '**nannies**.

'**nanny-goat** *n* a female goat.

nap *n* a short sleep; a woolly or fluffy surface on cloth; a kind of card game. – *v* to take a short sleep: – *pt* **napped**. – **caught napping** taken unawares.

napalm ['nāpām] *n* petrol in a jelly-like form, used in bombs.

nape *n* the back of the neck.

naphtha ['nafthə] *n* a kind of clear liquid which readily catches fire, obtained from coal and other substances.

'**napkin** *n* a small piece of cloth or paper for wiping the lips at meals; *see also* **nappy**.

'**nappy** *n* a piece of cloth folded and put between a baby's legs to absorb urine *etc*; a thick piece of absorbent paper for the same purpose.

nar'cissus *n* a type of plant like a daffodil with a white, star-shaped flower: – *pls* **nar'cissi, nar'cissuses**.

nar'cotic *n* a type of drug that brings on sleep or stops pain.

nar'rate *v* to tell a story. – *ns* **nar'ration** the telling of a story; **narrative** ['narətiv] a story. – *adj* telling a story. – *n* **nar'rātor** one who tells a story.

narrow ['narō] *adj* of small extent from side to side, not wide: *a narrow road*; with little to spare: *a narrow escape*; lacking wide interests or experience: *narrow views*. – *v* to make or become narrow. – *adv* '**narrowly** closely; barely. – *npl* '**narrows** a narrow sea passage, a strait. – *adj* '**narrow-'minded** unwilling to accept ideas different from one's own.

narw(h)al ['närwəl] *n* a kind of whale with a large tusk.

nasal ['nāzəl] *adj* of the nose; sounded through the nose.

nasturtium [nəs'tẽrshəm] *n* a climbing plant with brightly-coloured flowers.

'**nasty** *adj* dirty; very disagreeable or unpleasant; (of a problem *etc*) difficult to deal with. – *n* '**nastiness**.

'**nātal** *adj* of birth.

'**nātion** *n* the people living in the same country, or under the same government; a race of people: *the Jewish nation.* – *adj* **national** ['nashənəl] of or belonging to a nation or race. – *n* a person belonging to a nation: *a British national.* – *ns* '**nationalism** the desire to bring the people of a nation together under their own government; '**nationalist; natio'nality** state of being a member of a particular nation. – *v* '**nationalize** to make (something *esp* industries) the property of the nation. – *n* **nationali'zation**. – *n* **national anthem** any nation's official song or hymn.

native ['nātiv] *adj* born in a person: *native intelligence*; of one's birth: *my native land*. – *n* a person born in a certain place: *a native of Scotland*; one of those inhabiting a country from earliest times before the discovery by explorers, settlers *etc*. – **The Nativity** the birth of Christ.

'**natty** *adj* trim, tidy, smart.

nature ['nāchər] *n* the world around us (animals, trees, grass, streams, mountains *etc*); the qualities which make a thing, person, animal what it or he is. *She has a kindly nature.* – **-natured** (used with another word) having a certain temper or personality: *good-natured*: *ill-natured etc.* – *adj* **natural** ['nachərəl] of nature; produced by nature, not artificial; (of a quality, ability *etc*) in one at birth, not learned afterwards; (of manner, personality) unaffected, simple; (of a result *etc*) expected, normal. – *n* an idiot; one having a natural ability; (in music) a note which is neither a sharp nor a flat (shown by the sign ♮). – *adv* **naturally** by nature; simply; of course. – *n* **naturalist** one who studies animal and plant life. – *v* **naturalize** to give the rights of a citizen to (one born in another country). – *ns* **natural gas** gas suitable for burning found in the earth or under the sea; **natural history** the study of animals and plants; **natural resources** the natural wealth of a country (as forests, minerals, water for power *etc*).

naught [nöt] *n* nothing; *see* also **nought**.

naughty ['nöti] *adj* bad, misbehaving. – *n* **naughtiness**.

nausea ['nöziə] *n* a feeling of sickness. – *v* **nauseate** to make sick, to fill with disgust. – *adj* **nauseous** sickening; disgusting.

nautical *adj* of ships or sailors. – *n* **nautical mile** 1·85 kilometre (6080 ft).

nautilus *n* a small type of sea creature related to the octopus.

naval *see* **navy**.

nave *n* the middle or main part of a church.-

navel *n* the small hollow in the centre of the front of the stomach.

navigate *v* to direct, steer or pilot a ship, aircraft *etc* on its course; to sail on, over or through. – *adj* **navigable** able to be used by ships. – *ns* **navigation** the art of navigating; **navigator** one who steers or sails a ship *etc*.

navvy *n* a labourer working on roads *etc*: – *pl* **navvies**.

navy *n* a nation's fighting ships; the men serving on these: – *pl* **navies**. – *adj* **naval** of the navy. – *adj* **navy-'blue** dark blue.

nay (*old*) no.

neap *adj* (of the tide) having the smallest extent between its low and high level.

near *adj* not far away in place or time; close in relationship, friendship, *etc*; nearside; barely avoiding or almost reaching (something): *a near disaster*. – *adv* to, at a little distance (also **near'by** *He lives quite near*(*by*). – *prep* close to. – *v* to approach. – *adv* **nearly** almost:

nearly four o'clock; closely: *nearly related*. – *n* **nearness**. – *adjs* **near'side** (of the side of a vehicle *etc*) furthest from the centre of the road; **near-'sighted** short-sighted.

neat *adj* trim, tidy; skilfully done; (of liquor *esp* alcoholic) not diluted with water *etc*.

nebula *n* shining cloud-like appearance in the night sky, produced by very distant stars or by a mass of gas and dust: – *pl* **nebulae** ['nebūlē]. – *adj* **nebulous** hazy, vague.

necessary ['nesisəri] *adj* not able to be done without. – *n* something that cannot be done without, as food, clothing *etc*: – *pl* **necessaries**. – *v* **ne'cessitate** to make necessary; to force. – *n* **ne'cessity** that which cannot be done without; great need; want, poverty: – *pl* **ne'cessities**.

neck *n* the part between the head and body; anything like the neck: *the neck of a bottle*: *a neck of land*. – *ns* **necklace** a string of beads or precious stones *etc* worn round the neck; **necktie** (*US*) a man's tie. – **neck and neck** (in a race *etc*) running side by side, staying exactly equal.

necromancer *n* one who deals in magic. – *n* **necromancy**.

necropolis *n* a cemetery. – *pl* **ne'cropolises**.

nectar *n* the sweet liquid collected from flowers by bees to make honey; (*myth*) the drink of the ancient Greek gods; a delicious drink.

nectarine ['nektərēn] *n* a kind of peach.

née [nā] *adj* born, used in stating a woman's surname before her marriage: *Mrs Jane Brown, née Black*.

need *v* to be without, to be in want of; to require. – *n* state of needing; necessity; difficulty, want, poverty. – *adjs* **needful** necessary; **needless** unnecessary; **needy** poor.

needle *n* a small, sharp piece of steel, with a small hole (**eye**) at the top for thread, used in sewing; a similar, longer object with no hole, used for various purposes, *eg* in knitting, hypodermic syringes *etc*; (in a compass) the moving pointer; the long, sharp-pointed leaf of a pine, fir *etc*.

ne'er [nār] *adj* (in poetry *etc*) never. – *adj*, *n* **ne'er-do-well** (of) a lazy, worthless person who makes no effort.

nefarious *adj* very wicked.

negative ['negətiv] meaning or saying 'no', as an answer; (of a person, attitude *etc*) timid, lacking spirit or ideas. – *n* a word or statement by which something

neglect

is denied; the photographic film, from which prints are made, in which light objects appear dark and dark objects appear light. – *v* to prove the opposite; to refuse to accept, to reject (a proposal made at a meeting *etc*).

ne'glect *v* to treat carelessly; to fail to give proper attention to; to fail to do. – *n* lack of care and attention. – *adj* **ne'glectful**.

negligée ['neglizhā] *n* a type of loose dressing gown *usu* made of thin material, worn by women.

'negligence *n* lack of proper care. – *adjs* **'negligent** careless; **'negligible** not worth thinking about, very small: *negligible amount*.

ne'gotiate *v* to bargain (with), discuss a subject (with), in order to reach agreement; to arrange (a treaty, a payment *etc*); to get past (an obstacle or difficulty). – *ns* **negoti'ation**; **ne'gotiator**. – *adj* **ne'gotiable** able to be negotiated.

'Negro *n* a member of an African race with black skin and tightly curling hair: – *pl* **'Negroes**. – *adj* **'negroid** of, like a Negro.

neigh [nā] *v* to cry like a horse. – Also *n*.

neighbour, (*US*) **neighbor** ['nābər] *n* one who lives near another. – *n* **'neighbourhood** (surrounding) district or area: *in the neighbourhood of Paris: a poor neighbourhood*. – *adjs* **'neighbouring** near or next in position; **'neighbourly** friendly. – **in the neighbourhood of** approximately, nearly.

neither ['nīdhər] *adj, pron* not either. *Neither bus goes that way. Neither of us feels well.* – *conj* used (often with **nor**) to show alternatives in the negative. *Neither John nor David is tall. He neither talks nor laughs.*

nemesis ['nemisis] *n* fate, punishment that is bound to follow wrongdoing.

neo- [nēō] *prefix* new as in **neo'natal** of newborn babies.

ne'ologism *n* a new word or expression.

'neon lighting *n* a form of lighting in which an electric current is passed through a small quantity of gas, used in advertising signs *etc*.

'nephew *n* the son of a brother or sister, or of a brother-in-law or sister-in-law.

nerve *n* one of the fibres which carry feeling from all parts of the body to the brain; courage, coolness; (*coll*) impudence. – *v* to strengthen the nerve or will of. – *adjs* **'nervous** of the nerves; easily excited or frightened; timid; **'nervy** excitable, jumpy. – *n* **nervous system** the brain, spinal cord and

never

nerves of an animal or human being.

nest *n* structure or place in which birds (and some animals and insects) live and rear their young; a shelter or den. – *v* to build a nest and live in it. – *v* **nestle** ['nesl] to lie close together as in a nest; to settle comfortably. – *n* **nestling** ['nestliŋ] a young newly hatched bird.

net *n* cord, string or finer material knotted so as to form a loose arrangement of crossing lines and spaces, used for catching birds, fish *etc* or for wearing over the hair *etc*; fine material made like a net, with meshes. – *adj* (also **nett**) (of a profit *etc*) remaining after expenses *etc* have been paid; (of the weight of something) not including packaging. – *v* to catch or cover with a net; to put (a ball) into a net; to make by way of profit: – *pt* **'netted**. – *n* **'netting** fabric of netted string, wire *etc*. – *ns* **'netball** a type of game in which a ball is thrown into a high net; **'network** an arrangement of lines crossing one another; a widespread organization; a system of linked radio stations *etc*.

nether ['nedhər] *adj* lower. – *adj* **'nethermost** lowest.

nett *see* **net**.

'nettle *n* a type of plant covered with hairs which sting sharply. – *v* to make angry, provoke. – *n* **'nettlerash** a skin rash, like that caused by a sting from a nettle.

neur(o)- [nūr(ō)] *prefix* of the nerves.

neuralgia [nū'raljə] *n* a pain in the nerves, *esp* in those of the head and face.

neurosis [nū'rōsis] *n* a type of mental illness in which the patient suffers from extreme anxiety.

neurotic [nū'rotik] *adj* suffering from neurosis; in a bad nervous state. – Also *n*.

neuter ['nūtər] *adj* (in grammar) neither masculine nor feminine; (of animals) neither male nor female; unable to bear or father young. – *v* to make (a horse *etc*) unable to bear or father young.

neutral ['nūtrəl] *adj* taking no side (in a quarrel or war); (of a colour) not strong or definite. – *n* a person or nation that takes no side in a war *etc*; the gear position *usu* used when a vehicle is remaining still. – *n* **neu'trality**. – *v* **'neutralize** to make neutral; to make useless or harmless.

neutron ['nūtron] *n* one of the particles (without electrical charge) which with protons make up the nucleus of an atom.

'never *adv* not ever; at no time; under no

circumstances. – *adv* neverthe'less in spite of that. *I feel ill. Nevertheless I shall come with you.*

new *adj* recent; not before seen or known; different; not used or worn; fresh. – *adv* 'newly. – *n* 'newness. – *n* 'newcomer one who has lately arrived. – *adj* newfangled ['nūfaŋgld] (of things, ideas *etc*) new and not thought very good.

news *n sing* report of a recent event; new information. – *ns* 'newsagent a shopkeeper who sells newspapers; 'newspaper a paper printed daily or weekly containing news.

newt *n* a small lizard-like kind of animal, living on land and in water.

next *adj* nearest, closest in place, time *etc*: *the next page.* – *adv* in the nearest place or at the nearest time. *She led and I came next. Do that sum next.*

nib *n* a pen point.

'nibble *v* to take little bites (of). – *n* a little bite.

nice *adj* agreeable, pleasant; careful, precise, exact. – *adv* 'nicely pleasantly; very well. – *n* nicety ['nisəti] a small fine detail; – *pl* 'niceties. – to a nicety with great exactness.

niche [nich] also [nēsh] *n* a hollow in a wall for a statue, vase *etc*; a suitable place in life.

nick *n* a little cut, notch; (*slang*) prison, jail. – *v* to cut notches in; (*slang*) to steal.

'nickel *n* an element, a greyish-white metal used *esp* for mixing with other metals and for plating: *nickel-plating*; (in *US*) a 5-cent coin.

'nickname *n* a name used instead of a person or thing's real name, *usu* in fun or scorn.

nicotine ['nikətēn] *n* a substance contained in tobacco.

niece [nēs] *n* the daughter of a brother or sister, or of a brother-in-law or sister-in-law.

'niggardly *adj* mean, ungenerous.

'niggling *adj* unimportant, trivial, fussy; (of a worry, fear, *etc*) small but always present.

nigh [nī] *adj* (*old*) near.

night [nīt] *n* the period of darkness between sunset and sunrise; darkness. – *adj* of, for night; happening, active *etc* at night: *nightshift: a night worker.* – *adj, adv* 'nightly by night; every night. – *ns* 'nightdress, -gown a kind of garment worn in bed; 'nightfall the beginning of night; 'nightjar a kind of bird like a swallow which is active at night; 'nightmare a frightening

dream; 'nightshade a family of plants some of which have poisonous berries, *eg* deadly nightshade; 'night-'watchman one who looks after a building during the night.

nightingale ['nitiŋgāl] *n* a type of small bird, the male of which sings beautifully by night and day.

nil *n* nothing.

'nimble *adj* quick and neat (in action or thought). – *n* 'nimbleness.

'nimbus *n* a rain cloud.

'nincompoop *n* a weak, foolish person.

nine *n* the number 9. – *adj* 9 in number. – *adj* ninth the last of nine (things *etc*). – *n* one of nine equal parts.

'ninepins *n* a game in which nine bottle-shaped objects, *usu* wooden, are set up and knocked down by a ball.

'nine'teen *n* the number 19. – *adj* 19 in number. – *adj* 'nine'teenth the last of nineteen (things *etc*). – *n* one of nineteen equal parts.

'ninety *n* the number 90. – *adj* 90 in number. – *adj* 'ninetieth the last of ninety (things *etc*). – *n* one of ninety equal parts.

'ninny *n* a fool.

nip *v* to pinch, squeeze tightly (*eg* the skin); to be stingingly painful; to bite, cut (off); to check the growth of, to damage (plants *etc*); (*coll*) to go nimbly or quickly: – *pt* nipped. – *n* a pinch; a sharp coldness in the weather; a small quantity: *a nip of whisky.*

'nipple *n* the pointed part of the breast from which a baby sucks milk.

nit *n* the egg of a louse or other small insect; (*coll*) a nitwit.

'nitwit *n* a very stupid person.

'nitric acid *n* a kind of strong acid containing nitrogen. – *n* 'nitrate any of several substances formed from nitric acid, often used as soil fertilizers.

'nitrogen *n* an element, a type of gas forming nearly four-fifths of the air we breathe. – *n* 'nitro-'glycerine a powerful kind of explosive.

no *adj* not any. *We have no food*; not a. *She is no beauty.* – *adv* not at all. *The patient is no better.* – *interj* expressing a negative. *Are you feeling better today? No.* – *n* a refusal; a vote against: – *pl* noes. – *prons* 'nobody not any person; a person of no importance. *He is a nobody in politics*; 'no-one not any person, nobody.

'noble *adj* great and good, fine; brave; of high birth or rank. – *n* a person of high rank or birth (also 'nobleman). – *adv* 'nobly. – *n* no'bility the nobles of a country; goodness, greatness of mind or character.

nobody *see* **no**.

noc'turnal *adj* happening or active (as certain kinds of animals) at night. – *n* 'nocturne** a piece of music intended to give a feeling of night-time.

nod *v* to bend the head forward quickly (often as a sign of agreement); to let the head drop in weariness: – *pt* **'nodded**. – *n* an action of nodding. – **nod off** to fall asleep.

node *n* the swollen part of a branch or twig where leaf-stalks join it; a swelling. – *n* **nodule** ['nodūl] a small rounded lump.

Noël, Nowell [nō'el] *n* Christmas.

noise [noiz] *n* a sound, often one which is loud or harsh. – *v* to spread (a rumour *etc*). – *adjs* **'noiseless**; **'noisy** making a loud sound.

'nōmad *n* one of a group of people without a fixed home who wander about with flocks of sheep *etc* in search of pasture; someone who wanders from place to place. – *adj* **no'madic**.

'no-man's-land *n* land owned by no-one, *esp* that lying between two opposing armies.

nom de plume ['nomdə'plōom] *n* a name used by an author instead of his own name, a pen-name: – *pl* **'noms de 'plume**.

nomenclature [nə'menkləchər] *n* (system of) naming; names.

'nominal *adj* in name only; very small: *a nominal fee*.

'nominate *v* to propose (someone) for a post or for election; to appoint. – *ns* **nomi'nation; nomi'nee** one whose name is put forward for a post.

non- *prefix* not – used with a great many words to change their meaning to the opposite.

nonagenarian [nonəji'nāriən] *n* a person between ninety and ninety-nine years old.

nonchalant ['nonshələnt] *adj* not easily roused or upset, cool. – *n* **'nonchalance**.

non-commissioned ['nonkə'mishənd] *adj* belonging to the lower ranks of army officers, below second-lieutenant.

'non-com'mittal *adj* unwilling to express, or not expressing, an opinion.

noncon'formist *n* one who does not agree with those in authority, *esp* in church matters. – Also *adj*.

'nondescript *adj* not easily described, lacking anything noticeable or interesting.

none [nun] *adv* not at all: *none the worse*. – *pron* not one, not any.

no'nentity *n* a person of no importance: – *pl* **no'nentities**.

'non-ex'istent *adj* not existing, not real.

'non'plussed *adj* taken aback, confused.

'nonsense *n* words that have no sense or meaning; foolishness. – *adj* **non'sensical**.

'non-'stop *adj* going on without a stop.

'noodle *n* (*usu pl*) a strip of dough, eaten in soup *etc* or served with a sauce.

nook *n* a corner; a small recess.

noon *n* twelve o'clock midday.

no-one *see* **no**.

noose *n* a kind of loop in a rope *etc* that tightens when pulled.

nor *conj* used (often with **neither**) to show alternatives in the negative. *Neither Mary nor Susan has been here.*

norm *n* a pattern or standard to judge other things from. – *adj* **'normal** ordinary, usual according to a standard.

north *n* one of the four chief directions, that to the left of someone facing the rising sun (opposite to **south**). – Also *adj, adv*. – *adjs* **northerly** ['nördhərli] of, from or towards the north; **'northern** of the north; **northward(s)** ['nörthwərd(z)] towards the north. – Also *adv*. – *ns* **north-'east (-'west)** the point of the compass midway between north and east (or west); **north pole** *see* **pole**.

nose *n* the part of the face by which people and animals smell and breathe; a jutting-out part of anything (*eg* the front of an aeroplane). – *v* to track by smelling; (*coll*) to interfere in others' affairs, to pry (into); to push a way through. *The ship nosed through the ice.* – *adj* **'nos(e)y** inquisitive, fond of prying. – *n* **'nosedive** a headfirst dive (by an aeroplane). – Also *v*. – *n* **'nosegay** a bunch of flowers.

nos'talgia *n* a longing for past times; a longing for home. – *adj* **nos'talgic**.

'nostril *n* one of the openings of the nose.

not *adv* expressing negative, refusal or denial. *I am not going. Give it to me, not to him. I did not break the window.*

'nōtable *adj* worth taking notice of; important, remarkable. – *n* an important person. – *n* **nota'bility** a well-known person: – *pl* **nota'bilities**. – *adv* **'notably** in a notable or noticeable way; particularly.

'nōtary (public) *n* an official whose job is to see that written documents or statements are drawn up in a way required by law: – *pl* **'notaries (public)**.

no'tation *n* the showing of numbers, musical sounds *etc* by signs: *sol-fa* *notation*; a set of such signs.

notch *n* a small V-shaped cut: – *pl* **'notches**. – *v* to make a notch. – *adj* **notched**.

note *n* a sign or piece of writing to draw someone's attention; (*pl*) ideas, details (for a speech, from a talk *etc*) set down in a short form; a short explanation; a short letter; a piece of paper used as money (*eg* a £1 note); a single sound or the sign standing for it in music; a key on the piano *etc*. – *v* to make a note of; to notice. – *adjs* **'noted** well-known; **'noteworthy** notable, remarkable. – *ns* **'notebook** a small book in which to make notes; **'notepaper** writing paper. – **of note** well-known, distinguished; **take note (of)** to notice particularly.

nothing [ˈnuthiŋ] *n* no thing, not anything; (in arithmetic) nought; something of no importance. – *adv* not at all. *He's nothing like his father.* – *n* **'nothingness** state of being nothing or of not existing; space, emptiness.

notice [ˈnōtis] *n* an announcement, made or shown publicly; attention. *The bright colour attracted my notice*; a warning given *eg* before leaving or before dismissing someone from a job, house *etc*. – *v* to see, observe, take note of. – *adj* **'noticeable** (likely to be) easily noticed.

'notify *v* to inform; to give notice of: – *pt* **'notified**. – *adj* **'notifiable** that must be reported: *a notifiable disease.* – *n* **notification** [nōtifiˈkāshən].

'notion *n* an idea; a vague belief or opinion.

no'torious *adj* well known because of badness. *He is a notorious thief.* – *n* **notoriety** [nōtəˈriəti].

notwith'standing *prep* in spite of. *Notwithstanding his poverty, he refused all help.*

nougat [ˈnoogä] *n* a sticky kind of sweet (containing nuts *etc*).

nought [nöt] *n* nothing; naught; the figure 0.

noun *n* (in grammar) the word used as the name of any person or thing (as *John* and *box* in the sentence *John opened the box*).

nourish [ˈnurish] *v* to feed; to encourage the growth of. – *adj* **'nourishing** giving the body what is necessary for health and growth. – *n* **'nourishment** food; an act of nourishing.

'novel *adj* new and strange. – *n* a book telling a long story. – *ns* **'novelist** a writer of novels; **'novelty** something new and strange; newness; a small, *usu* cheap, manufactured article, *orig* of

unusual design, sold as a souvenir or toy. *These crackers have novelties inside them*: – *pl* **'novelties**.

No'vember *n* the eleventh month of the year.

novice [ˈnovis] *n* a beginner.

now [now] *adv* at the present time. *I can see him now*; immediately before the present time. *I thought of her just now*; in the present circumstances. *I can't go now because my mother is ill.* – *conj* (*usu* **now that**) because, since. *I can go out now that it's fine.* – *adv* **'nowadays** in present times. – **now and then, now and again** sometimes, from time to time. *I see him now and again.*

nowhere [ˈnōwār] *adv* not in, or to, any place.

noxious [ˈnokshəs] *adj* harmful: *noxious fumes.*

'nozzle *n* a spout fitted to the end of a pipe, tube *etc.*

nuance [ˈnūöns] *n* a slight difference in meaning or colour *etc.*

nucleus [ˈnūkliəs] *n* the central part of an atom; the central part round which something collects or from which something grows: *the nucleus of his collection of books*; the part of a plant or animal cell that controls its development: – *pl* **'nuclei**. – *adj* **nuclear** [ˈnūklēr] of a nucleus, *esp* that of an atom; produced by the splitting of the nuclei of atoms. – *ns* **nuclear energy** atomic energy; **nuclear missile** a missile whose warhead is an atomic bomb; **nuclear reactor** apparatus for producing nuclear energy.

nude *adj* without clothes, naked. – *n* an unclothed human figure; a painting or statue of such a figure. – *ns* **'nudism; 'nudist** one who approves of going without clothes; **'nudity** the state of being nude. – **in the nude** naked.

nudge *n* a gentle push, *usu* with the elbow. – Also *v.*

'nugget *n* a lump, *esp* of gold.

nuisance [ˈnūsns] *n* a person or thing that is annoying or troublesome.

null: null and void having no legal force.

'nullify *v* to make useless or of no effect; to declare to be null and void: – *pt* **'nullified**.

numb [num] *adj* having lost the power to feel or move. – *v* to make numb.

'number *n* a word or figure showing how many, or showing a position in a series (as house numbers in a street); a collection of things or persons; one issue of a newspaper or a magazine; a popular song or piece of music. – *v* to count; to give numbers to; to amount to in number. – *adj* **'numberless** more than can be counted.

numeral ['nūmərəl] *n* a figure (*eg* 1, 2 *etc*) used to express a number. – *n* **'numerator** (in vulgar fractions) the number above the line (as 2 in ²/₃). – *adjs* **nu'merical** of, in, using or consisting of numbers; **'numerous** many.

numerate ['nūmərət] *adj* having some understanding of mathematics and science.

numismatist [nū'mizmətist] *n* one who collects and studies coins. – *n* **numis'matics** the study of coins.

'numskull *n* a stupid person.

nun *n* a member of a female religious group living in a convent. – *n* **'nunnery** a house where a group of nuns live: – *pl* **'nunneries**.

nuptial ['nupshəl] *adj* of marriage. – *npl* **'nuptials** a wedding ceremony.

nurse *n* a person who looks after sick or injured people, or small children. – *v* to look after sick people *etc*, *esp* in hospital; to give (a baby) milk from the breast; to hold or look after with care. *He nurses his tomato plants*; to encourage (feelings, as anger, hope *etc*) in oneself. *He nurses a grudge against her.* – *n* **nursery** ['nörsəri] a room for young children; a place where young plants

are reared: – *pl* **'nurseries.** – *ns* **nursery school** a school for very young children; **nursing home** a small private hospital.

nurture ['nörchər] *v* to bring up, rear; to nourish: *nurture resentment.* – *n* care, upbringing; food, nourishment.

nut *n* a fruit having a hard shell and, in it, a kernel; a small block *usu* of metal with a hole in it for screwing on the end of a bolt. – *adj* **'nutty** containing, or having the flavour of nuts; (*coll*) mad. – *n* (*pl*) **'nutcracker(s)** any of several types of instruments for cracking nuts open. – *n* **'nuthatch** a small kind of bird living on nuts and insects: – *pl* **'nuthatches. – in a nutshell** expressed very briefly.

'nutmeg *n* a hard kind of seed used as a spice in cooking.

'nūtrient *adj, n* (of) a substance giving nourishment. – *n* **'nutriment** nourishment, food. – *adjs* **nu'tritious, 'nutritive** valuable as food, nourishing.

'nuzzle *v* to press, rub or caress with the nose; to lie close to, snuggle, nestle.

'nȳlon *n* a type of material made from chemicals; (*pl*) stockings made of nylon.

nymph *n* (*myth*) a goddess of the rivers, trees *etc*; a beautiful girl; an insect not yet fully developed.

O

O!, Oh! [ō] *interj* expressing surprise, admiration, pain *etc*.

oaf *n* a stupid or clumsy person: – *pl* **oafs**.

oak *n* a type of tree having acorns as fruit; its hard wood. – *adjs* **oak, 'oaken** made of oak. – *n* **oak apple** a kind of growth on the leaves and twigs of oaks, caused by insects.

oar *n* a pole for rowing, with a flat, blade-like end. – *v* to row. – *n* **'oarsman** one who rows. – **put one's oar in** to interfere in.

oasis [ō'āsis] *n* in a desert, a place where water is found and trees *etc* grow: – *pl* **oases** [ō'āsēz].

oast *n* a large oven to dry hops. – *n* **'oast-house**.

oath *n* a solemn promise to speak the truth, to keep one's word, to be loyal *etc*; a swear word: – *pl* **oaths** [ōdhz].

oats *npl* a type of grassy plant or its grain, used as food. – *ns* **'oatcake** a thin flat cake made of oatmeal; **'oatmeal** meal made by grinding down oat grains.

'obdūrate *adj* stubborn, firm, unyielding.

obedience, obedient *see* **obey.**

obeisance [ə'bāsəns] *n* a bow or curtsy showing respect.

obelisk ['obəlisk] *n* a tall four-sided pillar with a pointed top.

o'bese [ə'bēs] *adj* very fat. – *n* **o'besity.**

obey [ə'bā] *v* to do what one is told to do: *obey one's father: obey an order.* – *n* **o'bēdience** the act of obeying; willingness to obey. – *adj* **o'bedient.**

o'bitūary *n* a notice (*usu* in a newspaper) of a person's death, sometimes with an account of his career: – *pl* **o'bituaries.**

'object *n* anything that can be seen or felt; an aim or purpose. *His main object was to make money*; (in grammar) the word in a sentence which stands for the person or thing on which the action of the verb is done (as *me* in the sentences *He hit me. He likes me.*). – *v* **ob'ject** (often with **to**) to feel or show disapproval of. – *n* **ob'jection** the act of objecting; a reason for objecting. – *adjs*

ob'jectionable nasty, disagreeable;
ob'jective not influenced by personal
interests, fair. – *n* aim, purpose, goal.

o'blige *v* to force or compel. *I was obliged
to go home*; to do a favour or service to.
Oblige me by shutting the door. – *n*
obligation [obli'gāshɔn] a promise or
duty by which one is bound. *I am under
an obligation to help him*; a debt of
gratitude for a favour received. – *adjs*
o'bligatory compulsory; required as a
duty; **obliged** [ɔ'blijd] owing or feeling gratitude; **'obliging** ready to help
others.

oblique [ɔ'blēk] *adj* slanting; not
straight or direct; not straightforward:
an oblique reference.

obliterate [ɔ'blitɔrāt] *v* to blot out; to
destroy completely. – *n* **oblite'ration.**

o'blivion *n* forgetfulness; state of being
forgotten. – *adj* **o'blivious** (with **of** or
to) unaware, not paying attention;
forgetful.

'oblong *n* a figure of this shape: ☐ . –
Also *adj.*

obnoxious [ɔb'nokshɔs] *adj* offensive,
causing dislike.

'ōboe *n* a type of high-pitched woodwind
instrument: – *pl* **'oboes.** – *n* **oboist**
['ōbōist] one who plays the oboe.

obscene [ɔb'sēn] *adj* (sexually) indecent; disgusting. – *n* **obscenity**
[ɔb'senɔti]: – *pl* **ob'scenities.**

ob'scure *adj* dark; not clear or easily
understood; unknown, humble: *an obs-
cure painter.* – *v* to darken; to make less
clear. – *n* **ob'scurity.**

ob'sēquious *adj* trying to win favour by
being too humble or too ready to agree,
flatter *etc.*

observe [ɔb'zɔrv] *v* to notice; to watch
with attention; to remark; to obey (a
law *etc*); to keep, preserve: *observe a
tradition.* – *n* **ob'servance** the act of
keeping (a law, a tradition *etc*). – *adj*
ob'servant good at noticing. – *ns*
obser'vation the act or habit of seeing
and noting; attention; a remark;
ob'servatory a place for making obser-
vations of the stars, weather *etc*: – *pl*
ob'servatories; ob'server one' who
sees or observes; one who is sent to
listen to, but not take part in, a
discussion *etc.*

ob'sess *v* to fill the mind completely. – *n*
ob'session a feeling or idea from which
the mind cannot get away; the state of
being obsessed. – *adj* **ob'sessive** of
obsession; having or liable to have an
obsession.

'obsolete *adj* gone out of use. – *adj*
obsolescent [obsɔ'lesnt] going out of-

date. – *n* **obso'lescence.**

'obstacle *n* something which stands in
the way and hinders. – *n* **obstacle race**
a race in which obstacles are laid across
the course.

ob'stetrics *npl* the study and act of
helping women before, during and
after the birth of babies. – *adjs*
ob'stetric, ob'stetrical of obstetrics. –
n **obste'trician** a doctor trained in this.

'obstinate *adj* stubborn; not yielding. –
n **'obstinacy** stubbornness.

obstreperous [ɔb'strepɔrɔs] *adj* noisy,
unruly.

ob'struct *v* to block up, keep from
passing; to hold back. – *n* **ob'struction**
something which hinders; something
which blocks up.

ob'tain *v* to get, gain; to be in use. *This
rule still obtains.* – *adj* **ob'tainable** able
to be got.

obtrude [ɔb'trōōd] *v* to thrust
(something unwanted on someone); to
thrust (oneself) forward when not
wanted. – *n* **ob'trusion.** – *adj*
ob'trusive too noticeable; pushing,
impudent.

ob'tuse *adj* (of an angle) greater than a
right angle; blunt, not pointed; stupid,
not quick to understand.

'obverse *n* the side of a coin on which is
the head or main design.

'obviate *v* to remove, prevent or get
round (a difficulty *etc*).

'obvious *adj* easily seen or understood,
plain, evident.

occasion [ɔ'kāzhɔn] *n* a particular time:
on that occasion; a special event: *a great
occasion*; a cause or reason; opportunity. – *v* to cause. – *adj* **oc'casional**
happening (or used) now and then. –
adv **oc'casionally.**

Occident ['oksidɔnt] *n* the West. – adj
occi'dental.

oc'cult *adj* secret, mysterious; supernatural. – Also *n.*

'occūpy *v* to dwell in; to keep busy; to
take up, fill (space, time, a place *etc*); to
seize, capture (a town, fort *etc*): – *pt*
'occupied. – *ns* **'occupancy** the act,
fact, or period of occupying; **'occupant; occu'pation** state of being occupied; that which occupies one; one's
trade or job; possession (of a house
etc); **'occupier** one who has possession
(of a house *etc*).

oc'cur *v* to happen; to appear or to be
found; (with **to**) to come into the mind
of. *That never occurred to me*: – *pt*
oc'curred. – *n* **oc'currence** a happening or event; the act or fact of occurring.

ocean ['ōshən] *n* the stretch of salt water surrounding the land of the earth; one of its five great divisions (Atlantic, Pacific, Indian, Arctic, Antarctic).

ochre ['ōkər] *n* a type of fine pale-yellow or red clay, used for colouring.

octa- octo- oct- *prefix* eight.

'**octagon** *n* an eight-sided figure. – *adj* **oc'tagonal**.

'**octave** *n* (in music) a series or stretch of eight notes (as from one C to the C next above it).

oc'tet *n* a group of eight (lines of poetry, singers *etc*).

Oc'tōber *n* the tenth month of the year.

octogenarian [oktəji'nāriən] *n* a person between eighty and eighty-nine years old.

'**octopus** *n* a type of sea creature with eight arms: – *pl* '**octopuses**.

'**ocūlar** *adj* of the eye.

'**ocūlist** *n* one who specializes in diseases and defects of the eye.

odd *adj* (of a number) not even, leaving a remainder of one when divided by two (*eg* the numbers 1, 17, 315); unusual, strange; not one of a matching pair, set or group *etc*, something left out or left over: *an odd glove*: *odd screw*: *odd minute*; (*pl*) chances or probability. *The odds are that he will win*; (*pl*) difference. *It makes no odds*. – *n* '**oddity** queerness, strangeness; a queer person or thing: – *pl* '**oddities**. – *npl* '**oddments** scraps. – **at odds** quarrelling; **odd jobs** jobs of different kinds, not part of regular employment; **odds and ends** objects, scraps *etc* of different kinds.

ode *n* a type of poem, *usu* written to a person or thing.

'**ōdious** *adj* hateful. – *n* '**odium** dislike, hatred.

odour ['ōdər] *n* smell (pleasant or unpleasant). – *adj* '**odourless** without smell.

of [ov] *prep* belonging to: *the house of my parents*; from (a place, person *etc*): *within two miles of his home*; from among: *one of my pupils*; made from, made up of: *a house of bricks*; indicating an amount, measurement *etc*: *a gallon of petrol*; about, concerning: *talk of old friends*; with, containing: *a cup of water*; as a result of: *die of hunger*; indicating removal or taking away. *He robbed her of her jewels*; indicating a connection between an action and its object: *the joining of the pieces*; indicating character, qualities *etc*. *He is a man of judgement. It was good of you to come*;

(*US*) (in telling the time) before, to: *ten (minutes) of eight.*

off *adv* away (from a place, from a particular state, standard, position *etc*). *He walked off rudely. Your work has gone off. The light was switched off*; entirely, completely. *Finish off your work.* – *adj* cancelled. *The expedition is off*; not up to the required or normal standard or condition. *The meat is off*; not working, not on. *The control is in the off position*; not quite pure in colour: *off-white*. – *prep* not on, away from. *It fell off the table*; taken away: *10% off the usual price*; below the normal standard: *off his game*. – **badly off, well off** poor, rich; **off and on** occasionally.

'**offal** *n* the parts of an animal unfit for use as food; certain internal organs of an animal (heart, liver *etc*) that are eaten.

'**off-'chance** *n* a slight chance.

off-colour ['of'kulər] *adj*, *adv* not feeling well.

of'fend *v* to make angry or hurt the feelings of; to displease; to do wrong. – *ns* **of'fence** (any cause of) anger, displeasure, hurt feelings; a crime, a sin; **of'fender**; **of'fensive** the position of one who attacks; an attack. – *adj* annoying; insulting, disgusting; used in attacking or assaulting: *an offensive weapon*. – **take offence at** to be angry or feel hurt at.

'**offer** *v* to put forward (a gift, payment *etc*) for acceptance or refusal; to lay (a choice, chance *etc*) before; to say that one is willing to do something. – *n* an act of offering; a bid of money; something proposed. – *n* '**offering** a gift; collection of money in church.

'**off'hand** *adj* said or done without thinking or preparation; lacking politeness. – *adv* without previous preparation.

office ['ofis] *n* a place where business is carried on; the people working in such a place; a duty, a job; a position of authority, *esp* in the government; (*pl*) services, helpful acts. – *n* '**officer** a person who carries out a public duty; a person holding a commission in the army, navy or air force. – *adj* **official** [ə'fishəl] done, given out by those in power: *official announcement*: *official action*; forming part of one's task when holding a job or office: *official duties*; having full and proper authority. – *n* one who holds an office in the service of the government *etc*. – *adv* **of'ficially** as an official, formally; as announced or said in public (though not necessarily truthfully). – *v* **officiate** [ə'fishiāt] to perform a duty or service, *esp* as a clergyman at a wedding *etc.* – *adj* **of'ficious** fond of interfering *esp* in a pompous way.

'**offing: in the offing** at a place or time not far off.

'**off-licence** *n* a shop selling alcohol which must not be drunk on the premises.

'**off'set** *v* to weigh against, to make up for. *The high cost of the project was partly offset by a government grant.*

'**offshoot** *n* a shoot growing out of the main stem; anything (of lesser importance) growing out of or starting from something else. *That firm is an offshoot of an international firm.*

'**off'side** *adj, adv* (in football) in a position between the ball and the opponent's goal; (of the side of a vehicle *etc*) nearest to the centre of the road.

'**offspring** *n* one's child or children; the young (of animals *etc*).

oft *adv* (in poetry *etc*) often.

often ['ofn] *adv* many times.

'**ōgle** *v* to eye (someone) impudently in order to show admiration.

ogre ['ōgər] *n* (*myth*) a (man-eating) giant; someone or something that frightens or threatens.

oil *n* a greasy liquid, got from plants (*eg* olive oil), from animals (*eg* whale oil), and from minerals (*eg* petroleum); (*pl*) oil colours for painting. – *v* to smear with oil, put oil on or in. – *adj* '**oily** of or like oil; (of person, manner *etc*) trying to be too friendly or flattering. – *ns* **oil colour** paint made by mixing a colouring substance with oil; '**oilfield** an area where mineral oil is found; **oil painting** a picture painted in oil colours; '**oilrig** a structure set up for drilling an oil-well; '**oilskin** cloth made waterproof by means of oil; a garment of this; '**oil-well** a hole drilled into the earth's surface or into the sea bed to obtain petroleum.

'**ointment** *n* any of many greasy substances rubbed on the skin to soothe, heal *etc.*

OK, okay ['ō'kā] *interj, adv* all right. – *v* '**o'kay** to mark or pass as being all right: – *pt* '**o'kayed**.

ōld *adj* advanced in age, aged; having a certain age: *ten years old*; not new, having existed a long time; belonging to far-off times; worn, worn-out; out-of-date, old-fashioned. – *n* **old age** the later part of life. – *adj* '**old-'fashioned** in a style common in the past, out-of-date. – **of old** long ago.

olive ['oliv] *n* a type of fruit which gives an oil used for cooking; the tree that

bears it. – *adj* of a yellowish-green colour. – *n* **olive branch** a sign of a wish for peace.

Ombudsman ['ombo͞odzmən] *n* an official appointed to look into complaints against the government.

omega ['ōmigə] *n* the last letter of the Greek alphabet.

omelette, omelet ['omlit] *n* beaten eggs fried (and *usu* folded over) in a pan.

omen ['ōmən] *n* a sign of future events. – *adj* **ominous** ['ominəs] suggesting future trouble.

o'mit *v* to leave out; to fail to do: – *pt* **o'mitted**. – *n* **o'mission** something omitted; the act of omitting.

'**omnibus** *n* a large public motor vehicle for passengers (*usu* shortened to **bus**): – *pl* '**omnibuses**.

om'nipotent *adj* having absolute, unlimited, power: *the omnipotent ruler.* – *n* **om'nipotence**.

omniscient [om'nisiənt] *adj* knowing everything. – *n* **om'niscience**.

omnivorous [om'nivərəs] *adj* feeding on all kinds of food.

on *prep* touching, fixed *etc* to the outer or upper side *etc* of a thing or person: *on the table*; supported by: *standing on one foot*; receiving, taking *etc*: *on half-pay*: *on drugs*; occurring in the course of a specified time *etc*: *on the following day*; about: *a book on churches*; with. *He had his wallet on him*; next to, near: *a city on the Thames*; indicating membership of. *He is on the committee*; in the condition, process or state of: *on sale*: *on show*; by means of. *He played the tune on the piano*; followed by: *disaster on disaster.* – *adv* so as to be touching, or fixed to the outer or upper side *etc* of a thing. *Put your coat on*; onwards, further. *They carried on towards London: from now on*; at a further point: *later on.* – *adj* working, performing. *The television is on*; arranged, planned. *Do you have anything on this afternoon?*

once [wuns] *adv* at an earlier time in the past. *Men once lived in caves*; for one time only. *I've read this book only once.* – *n* one time only. *Do it just this once.* – *conj* when. *Once you've finished, go!* – **all at once** suddenly. *All at once he appeared from nowhere; see* also **at once; at once** without delay. *Come here at once!*; (sometimes with **all**) at the same time, together. *She did several things (all) at once; once (and) for all* for the last time; **once upon a time** at some time in the past, often used at the beginning of stories.

oncoming ['onkumiŋ] *adj* approaching

from the front: *oncoming traffic*.

one [wun] *n* the number 1; a particular member of a group. *She's the one I hate most.* – *pron* a single particular person or thing: *one of my cats*; in formal or pompous English used instead of **you**, meaning anyone. *One must beware of thieves.* – *adj* 1 in number; a single. *Only one man survived*; identical, the same. *We're all of one mind*; some (unnamed time): *one day soon.* – *pron* **one'self** used reflexively: *wash oneself*; used for emphasis. *One always has to go oneself, because nobody else will.* – *adjs* **'one-'sided** (of a contest *etc*) with one person, side *etc* having a great advantage over the other; **'one-'way** (of a road, street) meant for traffic moving in one direction only. – **one another** used when an action takes place between more than two (loosely, between two) people. *They hit one another.*

onerous ['ōnərəs] *adj* heavy, hard to bear or do: *an onerous task*.

'ongōing *adj* continuing: *an ongoing task*.

onion ['unyən] *n* a type of vegetable with a strong taste and smell.

'onlooker *n* one who watches (an event).

'ōnly *adv* not more than: *only two matches left*; alone, solely. *Only you went*; not longer ago than. *I saw him only yesterday*; indicating the unavoidable result (of an action). *He'll only be offended if you mention it*; (with **too**) extremely. *I'll be only too pleased to come.* – *adj* single, solitary: *an only child.* – *conj* (*coll*) but, except that. *I'd like to go, only I have to work.*

'onrush *n* a rush forward.

'onset *n* beginning; a fierce attack.

onslaught ['onslöt] *n* a fierce attack.

'ōnus *n* burden; responsibility.

'onward *adj* going forward in place or time. – *advs* **'onward, 'onwards**.

onyx ['oniks] *n* a type of precious stone with layers of different colours.

ooze *v* to flow gently or slowly. – *n* soft mud; a gentle flow.

opacity *see* **opaque**.

'ōpal *n* a type of bluish-white precious stone, with flecks of various colours.

opaque [ə'pāk] *adj* not able to be seen through. – *n* **opacity** [ə'pasəti].

'ōpen *adj* not shut, allowing entry or exit; not enclosed or fenced; showing the inside or inner part; uncovered; not blocked; free for all to enter; honest, frank; (of land) without many trees. – *v* to make open; to unlock; to begin. – *ns* **'opener** something that opens (something): *a tin opener*; **'opening** a hole or gap; an opportunity; a vacant

job. – *adv* **'openly** without trying to hide or conceal anything. – *n* **open air** any place not indoors or underground *etc*. – *adjs* **'open-'air; 'open-'minded** ready to take up new ideas. – **in the open** out-of-doors, in the open air; **open to** likely or willing to receive *etc*: *open to attack*: *open to criticism*.

opera ['opərə] *n* a play in which music by voices and orchestra is of the greatest importance. – *adj* **ope'ratic**.

operate ['opərāt] *v* to act, work; to bring about an effect; to perform an operation. – *adj* **'operating** of or for an operation on a person's body. – *n* **ope'ration** action; method or way of working; the cutting of a part of the human body in order to cure disease; (*pl*) movements of armies, troops. – *adj* **'operative** working, in action; (of a rule *etc*) in force, having effect. – *n* a workman in a factory *etc*. – *n* **'operator** one who works a machine; one who connects telephone calls.

operetta [opə'retə] *n* a play with music and singing.

ophthalmic [of'thalmik] *adj* of the eye: *an ophthalmic surgeon.* – *n* **ophthal'mologist** a doctor who specializes in diseases of and injuries to the eye.

opiate ['ōpiət] *n* a drug containing opium used to make a person sleep; anything that calms or dulls the mind or feelings.

o'pinion *n* what one thinks or believes; (professional) judgement, point of view. *He wanted another opinion on his son's case*; what one thinks of the worth or value of someone or something. *I have a very low opinion of his work.* – *adj* **o'pinionated** having strong opinions which one is confident are right.

'ōpium *n* a drug made from the dried juice of a type of poppy.

o'possum *n* a type of small American animal that carries its young in a pouch.

opponent *see* **oppose**.

'opportune *adj* coming at the right or convenient time. – *ns* **oppor'tunism** the state of being an opportunist; **oppor'tunist** a person who takes advantage of any opportunity or circumstance which will be to his advantage; **oppor'tunity** a chance (to do something).

oppose [ə'pōz] *v* to struggle against, resist; to stand against, compete against. – *n* **opponent** [ə'pōnənt] one who opposes; an enemy; a rival. – *adj* **opposite** ['opəzit] facing, across from; lying on the other side (of); as different as possible. – *prep* facing, across from. *He lives opposite the post office*; acting a role (in a play, opera *etc*) corresponding in importance to. *She played Ophelia opposite his Hamlet.* – *n* something as different as possible (from something else). *Black is the opposite of white.* – *n* **opposition** [opə'zishən] resistance; those who resist; (in parliament) the party which is against the governing party.

op'press *v* to govern harshly like a tyrant; to treat cruelly; to distress or worry greatly. – *adj* **op'pressive** oppressing; cruel, harsh; (of weather) close, tiring. – *n* **op'pression**.

op'prōbrium *n* great or public disgrace; something that brings great disgrace. – *adj* **op'probrious** disgraceful; scornful.

opt *v* (with **for**) to choose; to decide (to do). – **opt out** to decide not to (do something).

'optic, 'optical *adjs* having to do with the eye or sight. – *ns* **optician** [op'tishən] one who makes and sells spectacles; **'optics** the science of light. – *n* **optical illusion** an impression that something seen is different from what it is.

'optimism *n* the habit of taking a bright, hopeful view of things (opposite of **pessimism**). – *n* **'optimist** one who is in the habit of taking such a view. – *adj* **opti'mistic**.

'optimum *adj* best, most favourable: *optimum conditions*.

'option *n* choice; the right or power to choose; the thing chosen. – *adj* **'optional** left to one's choice.

'opūlent *adj* wealthy; luxurious. – *n* **'opulence** riches.

'ōpus *n* a work, *esp* a musical composition: – *pl* **opera** ['opərə].

or *conj* used (often with **either**) to show alternatives. *You can either go out or stay in: tea or coffee*; because if not. *You'd better go or you'll miss your bus.*

'oracle *n* a person thought to be very wise or knowledgeable; (*hist*) a holy place where a god was thought to give answers to difficult questions; an answer of this kind; a person through whom such answers were made known.

oral ['örəl] *adj* spoken, not written; having to do with the mouth. – *adv* **'orally**. – *n* an oral examination or test.

orange ['orinj] *n* a type of juicy citrus fruit, with a thick reddish-yellow skin.

orang-utan ['öraŋ'ōōtan] *n* a type of large, man-like ape.

o'rātion *n* a public speech *esp* one in fine, formal language. – *ns* **orator** ['orətər] a

public speaker, *esp* a very eloquent one; **'oratory** the art of speaking well in public.

oratorio [orə'töriō] *n* a sacred story set to music, performed by soloists, choir and *usu* orchestra: – *pl* **ora'torios**.

orb *n* anything in the shape of a ball, a sphere.

'orbit *n* the path of a planet *etc* round another heavenly body, of a space capsule round the earth *etc*; range or area of influence: *within his orbit.* – *v* to go round the earth *etc* in space. *The spacecraft orbited the earth.*

'orchard *n* a large garden of fruit trees.

orchestra ['örkəstrə] *n* a group of musicians playing together under a conductor. – *v* **'orchestrate** to arrange (a piece of music) for an orchestra.

orchid ['örkid] *n* a kind of plant *usu* with brightly coloured or unusually shaped flowers.

or'dain *v* to declare something to be law; to receive (a clergyman) into the Church. – *ns* **ordinance** ['ördinəns] a command; a law; **ordi'nation** the receiving of a clergyman into the church.

or'deal *n* a hard trial or test; suffering, painful experience.

'order *n* an instruction to act (made from a position of authority). *The captain gave his orders to his lieutenants*; a request, list of requests. *He left his order with the grocer*; an arrangement according to a system; an accepted way of doing things; a tidy or efficient state; peaceful conditions: *law and order*; rank, position, class; a society or brotherhood (*eg* of monks). – *v* to tell (to do something) from a position of authority; to give an order for; to arrange. – *adj* **'orderly** in proper order; well-behaved, quiet. – *n* a soldier who carries the orders and messages of an officer; a hospital attendant who does routine jobs: – *pl* **'orderlies**. – **in order** correct according to what is regularly done; in a tidy arrangement; **in order to** for the purpose of. *In order to live you must eat*; **out of order** not working; not the correct way of doing things; not in a tidy arrangement.

'ordinal numbers *npl* those showing order (as first, second, third *etc*).

'ordinary *adj* common, usual; normal; not unusually good *etc*. – **out of the ordinary** unusual.

'Ordnance 'Survey *n* a government office which produces official detailed maps.

ore [ör] *n* a mineral from which a metal is obtained (*eg* iron ore).

'organ n a part of the body (eg the liver); a large musical wind instrument with a keyboard; a means of spreading information, eg a newspaper: *an organ of Communism*. – *adj* **or'ganic** of or produced by the bodily organs; of living things; made up of parts all having their own work to do; (of food) grown without the use of artificial fertilizers *etc.* – *ns* **'organism** any living thing; **'organist** one who plays the organ.

organdie ['örgəndi] n a fine thin stiff muslin.

'organize v to arrange, set up (an event *etc*); to form into a whole. – n **organi'zation** the act of organizing; a body of people working together for a purpose.

orgy ['örji] n a drunken or other unrestrained celebration: – *pl* **'orgies**.

Orient ['öriənt] n the East. – *adj* **ori'ental**.

orientate ['öriəntāt] v to find one's position and sense of direction; to set or put facing a particular direction. – *ns* **orien'tation; orien'teering** the sport of finding one's way across country with the help of map and compass.

orifice ['orifis] n an opening.

'origin n the starting point; the place from which a person or thing comes; cause. – *adj* **o'riginal** first in time; not copied; able to think or do something new. – n the earliest version; a model from which other things are made. – v **o'riginate** to bring or come into being; to produce.

'ornament n anything that adds, or is supposed to add, beauty. – v to adorn, decorate. – *adj* **orna'mental** used for ornament; beautiful. – n **ornamen'tation**.

or'nate *adj* richly decorated.

orni'thologist n one who studies or is an expert on birds. – n **orni'thology**.

'orphan n a child who has lost one or both parents (*usu* both). – n **'orphanage** a home for orphans.

'orthodox *adj* holding (*esp* religious) views that are held generally in one's country, religion *etc.* – n **'orthodoxy**.

or'thography n correct or usual spelling.

orthopaedics, (*US*) **orthopedics** [örthə'pēdiks] n the branch of medicine which deals with bone diseases and injuries. – *adj* **ortho'paedic**.

oscillate ['osilāt] v to swing to and fro like the pendulum of a clock; to keep changing one's mind. – n **oscil'lation**.

osier ['ōziər] n a type of willow tree, the twigs of which are used in making baskets *etc*; one of the twigs.

osprey ['ospri] n a type of hawk which eats fish: – *pl* **'ospreys**.

os'tensible *adj* (of reasons *etc*) outwardly shown, apparent, but not always real or true.

osten'tātious *adj* showy, meant to catch the eye. – n **osten'tation**.

osteopath ['ostiəpath] n a person who treats injuries to bones, muscles *etc* by manipulating the patient's body, not by drugs or surgery.

ostler *see* **hostler**.

'ostracize v to banish (someone) from the company of a group of people. – n **'ostracism**.

'ostrich n a type of large bird which cannot fly: – *pl* **'ostriches**.

other ['udhər] *adj* second of two: *the other shoe*; remaining, not previously mentioned: *the other men*; different, additional: *some other reason*; (with **every**) second: *every other day*; recently past: *the other day*. – *pron* the second of two; those remaining, those not previously mentioned. *The others went home later*; the previous one: *one after the other*. – **other than** except: *no hope other than to retreat*; **someone, something or other** a person, thing not named or specified. *There's always someone or other here*.

'otter n a type of river animal living on fish.

'ottoman n a kind of low, cushioned seat without a back.

ought [öt] v used with other verbs to indicate duty or need. *He ought to set an example. You ought to keep yourself tidy*; or to indicate what can be reasonably expected. *The weather ought to be fine.*

ounce n a unit of weight, one-sixteenth of a pound, 28·35 grammes.

our *adj* belonging to us: *our house*. – *pron* **ours**. *The green car is ours*. – *pron* **our'selves** used reflexively. *We exhausted ourselves playing football*; used for emphasis. *We ourselves don't like it, but other people may.*

oust v to drive out (from position or possessions); to take the place of. *He ousted him as leader of the party.*

out *adv* into, towards the open air. *Go out for a walk*; from within. *Take out a pencil*; not inside. *He's out of prison now*; far from here: *out at sea*; not at home, not in the office *etc.* *He's out at the moment*; aloud: *shouted out*; to or at an end. *Hear me out*; inaccurate. *The calculation was two miles out*; (*coll*) on strike; published. *The book isn't out yet*; no longer hidden or secret; dismissed

from a game (of cricket, baseball *etc*);
finished, having won (at cards *etc*); no
longer in power or office; determined:
out to win. – *adjs* **'outer** nearer the edge,
surface *etc*; further away; **'outermost**
nearest the edge *etc*; furthest. – *n*
'outing a trip, excursion. – *adj* **'out-
and-'out** complete, thorough: *an out-
and-out villain.*
'outback *n* (in Australia) wild inland
areas.
out'bid *v* to offer a higher price than
(somebody else): – *pres p* **out'bidding**,
pt **out'bid.**
'outboard *adj* outside of a ship or boat:
an outboard motor.
outbreak ['owtbrāk] *n* beginning (of a
war, of disease *etc*).
outbuilding ['owtbildiŋ] *n* a shed or
building separate from the main buildings.
'outburst *n* a bursting out, *esp* of angry
feelings.
'outcast *adj, n* (of) a person driven away
from friends and home.
outcome ['owtkum] *n* result.
'outcrop *n* the part of a rock formation
that can be seen at the surface of the
ground.
'outcrȳ *n* a show of anger, disapproval *etc*
(*esp* by the general public): – *pl*
'outcries.
outdo [owt'dōō] *v* to do better than: – *pt*
out'did, *pp* **out'done.**
outdoor ['owtdör] *adj* of or in the open
air. – *adv* **'out'doors.**
'outfit *n* a set of clothes worn together
(sometimes for a special occasion *etc*):
her wedding outfit. – *n* **'outfitter** a seller
of outfits, *esp* men's clothes.
'outgōings *npl* money spent or being
spent.
outgrow [owt'grō] *v* to get too big or old
for (clothes, toys *etc*).
'out-house *n* a shed.
out'landish *adj* looking or sounding
very strange.
'outlaw *n* someone put outside the protection of the law; a robber or bandit. –
v to place someone beyond the protection of the law; to ban, forbid.
'outlay *n* money paid out.
'outlet *n* a passage outwards *eg* for a
water-pipe; a means of letting something out (*esp* a feeling, energy *etc*).
Football was an outlet for his high spirits;
a market for goods.
'outline *n* the outer line (as of a figure in a
drawing); a sketch showing only the
main lines; a rough sketch; a brief
description. – *v* to draw or describe an
outline of.

outlive [owt'liv] *v* to live longer than.
'outlook *n* a view (from a window *etc*);
what is thought likely to happen: *the
weather outlook.*
'outlȳing *adj* far from the centre, distant.
out'number *v* to be greater in number
than. *Their team outnumbered ours.*
out-patient ['owtpāshənt] *n* a patient
who does not live in a hospital while
receiving treatment.
'outpōst *n* a military station in front of or
far from the main army; an outlying
settlement.
output ['owtpŏŏt] *n* the goods produced
by a machine, factory *etc*; the amount
of work done by a person.
'outrage *n* a wicked act of great violence;
an act which hurts the feelings or that
causes offence. – *v* to injure, hurt by
violence; to insult, shock. – *adj*
out'rageous violent, very wrong; not
moderate.
outright [owt'rit] *adv* completely. – *adj*
'outright complete, thorough.
'outset *n* start, beginning.
'out'side *n* the outer surface or place: *the
outside of the box.* – *adj* in, on, or of the
outer surface or place: *the outside seat*;
connected with leisure *etc* rather than
one's full-time job: *outside interests*;
slight: *an outside chance of winning.* –
adv beyond the limits (of): *outside the
walls: outside working hours*; out-of-
doors, in(to) the open air. – *prep*
beyond the borders *etc* of, not within. –
n **'out'sider** a stranger; a person who is
not included in a particular social group
etc; a runner *etc* whom no-one expects
to win. – **at the outside** at the most: *ten
miles at the outside.*
'outsize *adj* of a very large size. – Also *n.*
'outskirts *npl* the outer borders of a city
etc.
out'spōken *adj* bold and frank in speech.
out'standing *adj* well-known; very
good; (of accounts, debts) unpaid.
'outstretched *adj* (*esp* of one's hand)
reaching out.
out'vote *v* to defeat (*eg* in an election *etc*)
by a greater number of votes.
'outward *adj* toward or on the outside;
(of a journey) away from home, not
towards it. – *advs* **'outwardly, 'outwards.**
outweigh [owt'wā] *v* to be more important than. *The advantages outweigh the
disadvantages.*
out'wit *v* to defeat by cunning: – *pt*
out'witted.
'ōval *adj* having the shape of an egg. –
Also *n.*
'ōvary *n* the part of the female body in

which eggs are formed: – *pl* **'ovaries.**

o'vātion *n* an outburst of cheering, hand-clapping *etc*.

oven ['uvn] *n* a covered place for baking; a small furnace.

'ōver *prep* higher than, above in position, number, rank *etc*: *over the door*: *over £10*: *ruling over the people*; across: *going over the bridge*; on the other side of: *the house over the road*; on top of. *He threw his coat over the body*; here and there on: *paper scattered over the carpet*; about. *They quarrelled over their money*; by means of: *over the telephone*; during, throughout: *over the years*; while doing, having *etc*. *He fell asleep over his dinner*. – *adv* above, higher in position or movement. *Two birds flew over*; across (a distance). *He walked over and spoke*; downwards. *I fell over*; above in number *etc*: *anyone aged four and over*; as a remainder: *three left over*; through: *read the passage over*. – *adj* finished. *The war is over*. – *n* (in cricket) a fixed number of balls bowled from one end of the wicket. – **over again** once more.

ōver- *prefix* often meaning too much, to too great an extent: *overcook*: *over-excited*: *over-payment*.

overall ['ōvəröl] *n* a garment worn over ordinary clothes to protect them against dirt; trousers with a bib made of hard-wearing material worn by workmen *etc*. – *adj* from one end to the other: *overall length*; including everything: *overall cost*.

ōver'awe *v* to make silent by fear or astonishment.

ōver'balance *v* to (make to) lose one's balance and fall.

overbearing [ōvər'bāriŋ] *adj* too sure that one is right, domineering.

'ōverboard *adv* out of a ship into the water. *Man overboard!*

'ōver'cast *adj* (of the sky) cloudy.

'over'charge *v* to charge too great a price; to fill or load too heavily.

'overcoat *n* an outdoor coat worn over all other clothes.

overcome [ōvər'kum] *v* to get the better of, conquer: – *pt* **over'came.** – *adj* helpless (from exhaustion, emotion *etc*).

overdo [ōvər'dōō] *v* to do too much; to exaggerate. *They rather overdid the sympathy*; to cook (food) too long: – *pt* **overdone** [ōvər'dun].

'overdose *n* too great an amount (of medicine *etc*).

'ōver'draw *v* to draw more money from the bank than one has in it. – *n* **'overdraft** the amount of money over-

drawn from a bank, sometimes by official arrangement.

'over'due *adj* later than the stated time. *The train is overdue*; (of a bill *etc*) still unpaid although the time for payment has passed.

overflow [ōvər'flō] *v* to flow over the edge or limits of. *The river overflowed its banks. The crowd overflowed into the next room*; to be so full as to flow over. – *n* **'overflow** a running-over of liquid; a pipe or channel for getting rid of extra or waste water *etc*.

overgrown ['ōvər'grōn] *adj* covered (with wild growth of plants); grown too large.

'over'hang *v* to jut out over.

ōver'haul *v* to examine carefully and carry out repairs. – *n* **'overhaul.**

overhead [ōvər'hed] *adv* above, over one's head. – *adj* **'overhead.** – *npl* the general expenses of a business *etc*.

ōver'hear *v* to hear what one was not meant to hear.

ōver'joyed *adj* filled with great joy.

ōver'land *adv* on or by land, not sea. – *adj* **'overland.**

ōver'lap *v* to extend over and cover a part of. *The two pieces of cloth overlapped*; (of work *etc*) to cover a part of the same area or subject (as another), partly to coincide. – *n* **'overlap** the amount by which something overlaps.

'over'load *v* to load or fill too much.

ōver'look *v* to look down upon from a higher point, to have or give a view of. *The hill overlooked the town*; to fail to see, to miss; to pardon, not to punish.

'ōverlord *n* (*hist*) a lord, *esp* one who may command other lords.

'over'much *adv* too much.

overnight ['ōver'nīt] *adv* during the night. *He stayed overnight with a friend*; in a very short time. *He changed completely overnight*. – *adj* for the night: *an overnight bag*; got or *made in a very short time: *an overnight success*.

'ōverpass *n* a road going over above another road, railway, canal *etc*.

overpower [ōvər'powər] *v* to defeat by a greater strength; to overwhelm, make helpless. – *adj* **over'powering** unable to be resisted; overwhelming, very strong *etc*: *an overpowering smell*.

'ōver'rate *v* to value more highly than one ought.

ōver'reach: overreach oneself to try to do or get more than one can and so fail.

ōver'ride *v* to ignore, set aside. *He overrode the teacher's authority*.

overrule [ōvə'rōōl] *v* to go against or cancel an earlier judgement or request.

ōver'run *v* to grow or spread over. *The garden is overrun with weeds and the house with mice*; to take possession of (a country).

'ōver'seas *adj, adv* abroad; beyond the sea.

'ōver'see *v* to watch over, supervise. – *n* **'overseer**.

overshadow [ōvər'shadō] *v* to lessen the importance of by doing better than.

oversight ['ōvərsit] *n* a mistake (*eg* when something has been left out); failure to notice.

'ōver'step *v* to go further than (a set limit, rules *etc*).

o'vert *adj* not hidden or secret; openly done.

'ōver'take *v* to catch up with and pass.

overthrow [ōvər'thrō] *v* to defeat.

'ōvertime *n* time spent in working beyond one's set hours; payment, *usu* at a special rate, for this.

'ōverture *n* a proposal or offer often intended to open discussions: *overtures of peace*; a piece of music played as an introduction to an opera *etc*.

ōver'whelm *v* to defeat completely; to load, cover *etc* with too great an amount: *overwhelmed with work*; (of emotion *etc*) to overcome, make helpless: *overwhelmed with grief.*

– *adj* **over'whelming**.

overwork ['ōvər'wörk] *v* to work more than is good for one. – *adj* **'over'worked**.

overwrought [ōvə'röt] *adj* excessively nervous or excited, agitated.

'ōvum *n* the egg from which the young of animals and people develop: – *pl* **'ova**.

owe [ō] *v* to be in debt to. *He owes John ten pence*; to have (a person or thing) to thank for. *I owe my success to my family.* – **owing to** because of.

owl [owl] *n* a kind of bird of prey which comes out at night. – *n* **'owlet** a young owl.

own [ōn] *v* to have as a possession; to admit, confess to be true. – *adj* belonging to the person mentioned. *Is that your own penknife?* – *ns* **'owner** one who possesses; **'ownership** possession. – **on one's own** by one's own efforts; alone.

ox *n* the male of the cow (*usu* castrated) used for drawing loads *etc*: – *pl* **'oxen** used for both male and female cattle.

'oxygen *n* an element, a gas without taste, colour or smell, forming part of the air and of water.

'oyster *n* a type of eatable shellfish.

'ōzone *n* a form of oxygen.

P

pace *n* a step; rate (of walking *etc*). – *v* to measure by steps; to walk backwards and forwards.

pachyderm ['pakidörm] *n* a thick-skinned animal such as an elephant.

'pacifȳ *v* to make peaceful; to calm, soothe. – *pres p* **'pacifying**, *pt* **'pacified**. – *n* **'pacifist** one who is against war and works for peace.

pack *n* a bundle, *esp* one carried on one's back; a set of playing cards; a number of animals (*esp* dogs, wolves *etc*). – *v* to place (clothes *etc*) in a case or trunk for a journey; to press or crowd together closely. – *n* **'package** a bundle or parcel. – *v* to put into a container; to wrap. – *ns* **'packet** a small parcel; a container made of paper, cardboard *etc*; **'packing** the act of putting things in cases, parcels *etc*; material for wrapping goods to pack; something used to fill an empty space. – *ns* **package holiday, package tour** a holiday or tour arranged by an organizer before it is advertised; **'pack-ice** a mass of large

pieces of floating ice driven together by wind, currents. *etc*; **packing case** a wooden box in which goods are transported. – **send packing** to send (a person) away roughly.

pact *n* an agreement; a bargain or contract.

pad *n* a soft cushion-like object to prevent jarring or rubbing *etc*; sheets of paper fixed together; the paw of certain animals; a rocket-launching platform. – *v* to stuff or protect with anything soft; (often with **out**) to fill up (*eg* a book) with unnecessary material; to walk making a dull, soft, noise: – *pt* **'padded**. – *n* **'padding** stuffing material; (in writing or speech) words, sentences put in just to fill space or time.

'paddle *v* to move forward by the use of paddles; to row; to wade in shallow water. – *n* a short, broad spoon-shaped oar. – *n* **'paddle-steamer** a steamer driven by two large wheels made up of paddles.

'paddock *n* a small closed-in field *usu*

near a house or stable, used for pasture.

paddy-field ['padifēld] *n* a muddy field in which rice is grown.

'**padlock** *n* a removable lock with hinged hook.

'**pāgan** *n* a person who does not believe in any religion; a heathen. – Also *adj*. – *n* '**paganism**.

page [pāj] *n* one side of a blank, written or printed sheet of paper; a boy servant; a boy who carries the train of the bride's dress in a marriage service.

pageant ['pajənt] *n* a show or procession made up of scenes from history; any fine show. – *n* '**pageantry** splendid show or display.

pa'gōda *n* an Eastern temple, *esp* in China and India.

paid *see* **pay**.

pail *n* an open vessel of tin, zinc, plastic *etc* for carrying liquids, a bucket.

pain *n* feeling caused by hurt to mind or body; threat of punishment: *under pain of death*; (*pl*) care. *He takes great pains with his work*. – *v* to cause suffering to, distress. – *adjs* **pained** showing pain or distress; '**painful**; '**painless**. – *adj* '**painstaking** very careful.

paint *v* to put colour on in the form of liquid or paste; to describe in words. – *n* something in liquid form used for colouring and put on with a brush, a spray *etc*. – *ns* '**painter** one whose trade is painting; an artist; a rope used to fasten a boat; '**painting** the act or art of covering with colour or making a picture; a painted picture.

pair *n* two of the same kind; a set of two. – *v* to join to form a pair; to go two and two; to mate.

pal *n* (*coll*) a friend.

palace ['paləs] *n* the house of a king, queen, archbishop or nobleman.

pal(a)eolithic [paliə'lithik] *adj* of the early Stone Age when man used stone tools.

'**palate** *n* the roof of the mouth; taste. – *adj* '**palatable** pleasant to the taste; acceptable, pleasing. *He does not find the truth palatable*.

palatial [pə'lāshəl] *adj* like a palace, magnificent.

pa'laver *n* light, idle talk; (*hist*) a conference, *esp* with African chiefs.

pale[1] *n* a piece of wood, a stake, used in making a fence to enclose ground. – *n* '**paling** a row of stakes of wood *etc* in the form of a fence; a pale.

pale[2] *adj* light or whitish in colour; not bright. – *v* to make or turn pale.

'**palette** *n* a little oval board on which an artist mixes his paints.

palfrey ['pölfri] *n* (*old*) a horse for riding (not a warhorse).

'**palindrome** *n* a word *etc* that reads the same backwards as forwards (*eg* level).

paling *see* **pale**.

pali'sade *n* a fence of pointed (wooden) stakes.

pall [pöl] *n* the cloth over a coffin at a funeral; a dark covering or cloud: *a pall of smoke*. – *v* to become dull or uninteresting.

'**pallet** *n* a straw bed or mattress.

palliative ['paliətiv] *adj* making less severe or harsh. – *n* something which lessens pain, *eg* a drug.

'**pallid** *adj* pale. – *n* '**pallor** paleness.

palm [päm] *n* a kind of tall tree, with broad, spreading fan-shaped leaves, which grows in hot countries; the inner surface of the hand between the wrist and the start of the fingers. – *ns* '**palmist** someone who claims to tell fortunes by the lines and markings of the hand; '**palmistry** the telling of fortunes in this way. – **palm off** to give with the intention of cheating. *That shopkeeper palmed off a foreign coin on me*.

'**palpable** *adj* able to be touched or felt; easily noticed, obvious.

'**palpitate** *v* (of the heart) to beat rapidly, to throb. – *n* **palpi'tation** uncomfortable rapid beating of the heart.

palsy ['pölzi] *n* a loss of power and feeling in the muscles. – *adj* '**palsied**.

paltry ['pöltri] *adj* of little value.

'**pampas** *npl* the vast treeless plains of S. America.

'**pamper** *v* to spoil (a child *etc*) by giving too much attention to.

'**pamphlet** *n* a small book not bound in a cover.

pan *n* a broad shallow pot used in cooking; a saucepan; a shallow dent in the ground. – *v* to move a television or film camera so as to follow an object or give a wide view: – *pt* **panned**. – *n* '**pancake** a thin cake of eggs, sugar and milk, fried in a pan. – **pan out** to turn out (well or badly).

pan- *prefix* all, whole, as in '**Pan-A'merican** including all America or Americans, North and South.

panacea [panə'sēə] *n* a cure for all things.

panache [pə'nash] *n* a sense of style, swagger. *He always does things with great panache*.

pancake *see* **pan**.

'**panda** *n* a large black-and-white bear-like animal found in Tibet *etc*; a raccoon-like animal found in the

Himalayas.

pan'demic adj (of a disease etc) occurring over a wide area and affecting a large number of people.

pande'mōnium n a state of confusion and uproar.

'pander v (with **to**) to be over-anxious to give way (to other people or their wishes).

pane n a sheet of glass.

panegyric [panə'jirik] n a speech praising highly (a person, achievement etc).

'panel n a flat rectangular piece of wood such as is set into a door or wall; a group of people chosen for a particular purpose eg to judge a contest, take part in a television quiz etc. – adj **'panelled**.

pang n a sudden sharp pain.

'panic n a sudden and great fright; fear that spreads from person to person. – v to throw into panic; to act wildly through fear: – pt **'panicked**.

'pannier n a basket, esp one slung on a horse's back.

'panoply n all the splendid and magnificent dress, equipment etc associated with a particular event etc: the panoply of a military funeral; (hist) a full suit of armour: – pl **'panoplies**.

pano'rama n a wide view of a landscape, scene etc.

pansy ['panzi] n a kind of flower like the violet but larger: – pl **'pansies**.

pant v to gasp for breath; to say breathlessly; to wish eagerly (for). – npl **pants** underpants; women's short-legged knickers; trousers.

pantechnicon [pan'teknikən] n a large van for transporting furniture.

'panther n a large leopard; (US) a puma.

'pantomime n a Christmas play, with songs, jokes and dancing, based on a popular fairy tale eg Cinderella.

'pantry n a room for storing food: – pl **'pantries**.

pa'pa n a name sometimes used for father.

'pāpacy n the position or the power of the Pope. – adj **'papal**.

'pāper n a material made from rags, grass, wood etc used for writing, wrapping etc; a single sheet of this; a newspaper; an essay on a learned subject; a set of examination questions; (pl) documents proving one's identity, nationality etc. – v to cover (esp walls) with paper. – ns **'paperback** a book bound in a paper cover; **'paper-chase** a game in which one runner leaves a trail of paper so that others may track him; **'paperweight** a heavy glass, metal etc object used to keep a pile of

papers in place.

papier-mâché ['papiā'mashā] n a substance consisting of paper pulp and some sticky liquid or glue, shaped (by moulding) into models, bowls, boxes etc.

pa'poose n a N. American Indian baby.

'paprika n a type of red pepper powder.

pa'pȳrus n a type of reed from which people used to make paper.

par n an accepted standard, value, level etc; (in golf) the number of strokes allowed for each hole if the play is perfect. – **below par** not up to standard; not feeling very well; **on a par with** equal to or comparable with.

'parable n a story (esp in the Bible) which teaches a moral lesson.

parachute ['parəshōōt] n an umbrella-shaped arrangement made of a light material and rope with which a person may drop slowly and safely to the ground from an aeroplane. – v to drop by parachute. – n **'parachutist** a person dropped by parachute from an aeroplane.

pa'rade n an orderly arrangement of troops for inspection or exercise; a procession of people, vehicles etc often in celebration of some event. – v to arrange (troops) in order; to march in a procession; to display in an obvious way.

paradigm ['parədīm] n an example showing a certain pattern.

'paradise n any place or state of great happiness; **'Paradise** heaven.

'paradox n a saying which seems to contradict itself but which may be true: – pl **'paradoxes**. – adj **para'doxical**. – adv **para'doxically**.

'paraffin n an oil which burns and is used as a fuel (for heaters, lamps, etc).

'paragon n a model of perfection or excellence. This boy is a paragon of good manners.

'paragraph n a division of a piece of writing shown by beginning the first sentence on a new line, usu leaving a short space at the beginning of the line; a short item in a newspaper.

'parakeet n a type of small parrot.

'parallel adj (of lines) going in the same direction and never meeting, always remaining the same distance apart; similar or alike in some way. The judge treats all parallel cases in the same way. – n a parallel line; something comparable in some way with something else; a line drawn east and west across a map or round a globe at a set distance from the equator to mark latitude. – n

paral'lelogram a four-sided figure, the opposite sides of which are parallel and equal in length.

'paralȳse v to affect with paralysis; to make helpless or ineffective; to bring to a halt. *The strike paralysed production at the factory.* – n **paralȳsis** [pə'raləsis] loss of the power to move and feel in one or more parts of the body. – adj **para'lytic** suffering from paralysis. – n a paralysed person.

'paramount adj above all others in rank or power; the very greatest: *of paramount importance.*

paramour ['parəmoͦor] n (old) a lover esp of a married person.

parapet ['parəpit] n a low wall on a bridge or balcony to prevent persons from falling off.

parapher'nālia npl one's belongings, equipment etc.

paraphrase ['parəfrāz] v to express (a piece of writing) in other words. – Also n.

paraplegia [parə'plējə] n paralysis of the lower part of the body and legs. – adj, n **para'plegic** (of) one who suffers from this.

'parasite n an animal, plant or person which lives on another without being any use in return. – adj **parasitic** [parə'sitik].

'parasol n a light umbrella used as a sunshade.

'paratroops npl soldiers carried by air to be dropped by parachute into enemy country. – n **'paratrooper**.

'parboil v to boil (food) slightly.

'parcel n thing(s) wrapped and tied, usu to be sent by post. – v (usu with **out**) to divide into portions: – pt **'parcelled**. – **part and parcel** an absolutely necessary part.

parch v to make hot and very dry; to make thirsty. – adj **parched**.

'parchment n the dried skin of a goat or sheep used for writing on; paper resembling this.

'pardon v to forgive; to free from punishment; to allow to go unpunished. – n forgiveness; the act of pardoning. – adj **'pardonable** able to be forgiven.

pare v to peel or cut off the edge, outer surface or skin of; to make smaller little by little. – npl **'parings** small pieces cut away or peeled off.

'pārent n a father or mother. – n **'parentage** descent from parents or ancestors: *of noble parentage.* – adj **parental** [pə'rentl] of parents; with the manner or attitude of a parent.

pa'renthesis n a word or group of words inserted in a sentence as an explanation, comment etc, usu separated from the rest of the sentence by brackets, dashes etc. *His father (so he said) was dead;* (pl) **parentheses** [pə'renthəsēz] brackets. – adj **paren'thetical**.

pa'riah n one driven out from a community or group, an outcast.

'parish n a district having its own church and minister: – pl **'parishes**. – n **pa'rishioner** a member of a parish.

'parity n the state of being equal.

park n a public place for walking with grass and trees; an enclosed piece of land surrounding a country house. – v to stop and leave (a car etc) in a place for a time.

'parka n a type of thick jacket with a hood.

'parley v to hold a conference, esp with an enemy: – pt **'parleyed**. – n a meeting between enemies to settle terms of peace etc: – pl **'parleys**.

parliament ['pärləmənt] n the chief law-making council of a nation – in Britain, the House of Commons and the House of Lords. – adj **parlia'mentary**.

parlour ['pärlər] n a sitting room in a house. – n **'parlourmaid** a woman or girl whose job is to wait at table.

parochial [pə'rōkiəl] adj having to do with a parish; interested only in local affairs; narrow-minded.

'parody n an amusing imitation of a serious author's subject and style: – pl **'parodies**. – v to make a parody of: – pt **'parodied**.

pa'role n the release of a prisoner before the end of his sentence on condition that he will have to return if he breaks the law.

paroxysm ['parəksizəm] n a fit of pain, rage, laughter etc.

parquet ['pärkā] n a type of flooring of wooden blocks arranged in a pattern.

parr n a young salmon before it leaves a river for the sea.

'parricide n the murder of a parent or a close relative; a person who commits such a crime.

'parrot n a kind of bird found in warm countries with a hooked bill and usu brightly coloured feathers, a good imitator of human speech.

'parry v to keep off, turn aside (a blow, question etc): – pt **'parried**.

parse [pärz] v to name the parts of speech of (words in a sentence) and say how the words are connected with each other.

'parsimony n great care in spending

one's money, meanness.

'parsley *n* a type of bright green leafy herb, used in cookery.

'parsnip *n* a type of plant with an eatable, yellowish root shaped like a carrot.

'parson *n* a clergyman, *esp* one in charge of a parish. – *n* **'parsonage** a parson's house.

part *n* a portion or share; a piece, something which, together with other things, makes up a whole: *the various parts of a car engine*; character taken by an actor in a play; a role in an action, campaign *etc*: *the part he played in the war*; (in music) the notes to be played or sung by a particular instrument or voice; (*pl*) talents: *a man of many parts*. – *v* to divide; to separate, to send or go in different ways; to put or keep apart. – *n* **'parting** the act of separating or dividing; a place of separation; a going away (from each other), a leave-taking; a line dividing hair on the head brushed in opposite directions. – *adv* **'partly** not wholly or completely. – *n* **'part-song** a song in which singers sing different parts in harmony. – **in good part** without being hurt or taking offence; **part of speech** one of the grammatical groups into which words are divided, *eg* noun, verb, adjective, preposition; **part with** to let go, be separated from. *He refused to part with his stick*; **take someone's part** to support someone in an argument *etc*.

par'take *v* (*usu* with **of**) to eat or drink some of something; to take a part (in): – *pt* **par'took**, *pp* **par'taken**.

partial ['pärshəl] *adj* in part only, not total or complete: *partial payment*; having a liking for (a person or thing): *partial to cheese*. – *n* **partiality** [pärshi'aləti] the favouring of one side *etc* more than another, bias; a particular liking for.

par'ticipate *v* to take part (in); to have a share in. – *ns* **par'ticipant, par'ticipator** one who takes part in; **partic'ipation** the act of taking part.

'participle *n* a form of a verb which can be used with other verbs to form tenses. *'He was eating. He had turned'*; used as an adjective: *'stolen jewels'*; used as a noun. *'Running makes me tired'*.

'particle *n* a very small piece: *a particle of sand*.

par'ticular *adj* of, relating to *etc* a single definite person, thing *etc* considered separately from others: *this particular waiter: this particular question*; special: *particular friend: particular care*; very exact, difficult to please: *particular*

about his food. – *npl* the facts or details about any thing or person.

partisan [pärti'zan] *adj* giving strong and enthusiastic support or loyalty to a particular cause, theory *etc, esp* without considering other points of view. – Also *n*.

partition [pər'tishən] *n* a division; something which divides, as a wall between rooms. – *v* to divide into parts; to divide by making a wall *etc*.

'partner *n* one who shares the ownership of a business *etc* with another or others; one of a pair *esp* in games, dancing *etc*; a husband or wife. – *v* to act as someone's partner. – *n* **'partnership** state of being partners: *business partnership: dancing partnership*; a joining of people as partners.

partridge ['pärtrij] *n* a type of bird which is shot as game.

'party *n* a gathering of guests: *a birthday party*; a group of people travelling *etc* together: *a party of tourists*; a number of people having the same plans or ideas: *a political party*; a person taking part in, knowing of, or approving an action: – *pl* **'parties**. – *n* **party line** a shared telephone line; policy laid down by the leaders of a political party.

pass *v* to go, move, travel *etc*. *He passed out of sight over the hill*; to cause to go or move (to another person or place): *pass the salt*; to go by. *I saw the bus pass our house*; to overtake. *He passed me because I slowed down*; (of parliament *etc*) to put (a law) into force; to be (declared) successful in an examination *etc*; to be declared healthy or in good condition (in an inspection); to come to an end. *The feeling of sickness soon passed*; to hand on, give. *He passed the story on to his son*; to spend (time). *He passed a pleasant hour by the river*; to make, utter (*eg* a remark): – *pt* **passed**. – *n* a narrow passage, *esp* over or through a range of mountains; a ticket or card allowing one to go somewhere; success in an examination. – *adjs* **'passable** fairly good; (of a river, ford *etc*) able to be crossed; **'passing** going by: *a passing car*; not lasting long: *a passing interest*; casual: *a passing remark*. – *n* the act of someone or something which passes; a going away, coming to an end; death. – *ns* **'passer-'by** one who happens to pass by when something happens: – *pl* **'passers-'by; 'passport** a card or booklet which gives the name and description of a person, and which is needed to travel in another country; **'password** a secret word which allows those who know it to pass.

'**passage** *n* the act of passing: *passage of time*; a journey (*esp* in a ship); a long narrow way, a corridor; a way through; a part of what is written in a book.

passenger ['pasinjər] *n* a traveller, not a member of the crew, in a train, ship, aeroplane *etc*.

passion ['pashən] *n* strong feeling, *esp* anger or love; '**Passion** the sufferings (*esp* the death) of Christ. – *adj* '**passionate** easily moved to passion; full of passion.

passive ['pasiv] *adj* making no resistance; acted upon, not acting. – *ns* '**passiveness, pas'sivity**.

past *n* (with **the**) the time gone by; a person's previous life or career; (in grammar) the past tense. – *adj* of an earlier time. *He thanked me for past kindnesses*; just over, recently ended: *the past year*; gone, finished. *The time for argument is past*. – *prep* after. *It's past midday*; up to and beyond, further than. *Go past the church*. – *adv* by. *He marches past, looking at no-one*.

'**pasta** *n* a dough used in making spaghetti, macaroni *etc*.

pāste *n* a mixture of flour, water *etc* used for pies, pastry *etc*; a sticky liquid for sticking paper *etc* together; any soft mixture: *almond paste*; a kind of fine glass used in making imitation gems. – *n* '**pasteboard** cardboard.

'**pastel** *adj* (of colours) soft, pale. – *n* a chalk-like crayon used in drawing; a drawing made with this.

pasteurize ['paschəriz] *v* to heat food (*esp* milk) in order to kill harmful germs in it.

pastille ['pastəl] *n* a small sweet sucked as a medicine *etc*.

'**pastime** *n* a hobby, a spare-time interest.

'**pastor** *n* a clergyman. – *adj* '**pastoral** having to do with country life; of a clergyman or his work.

pāstry *n* flour paste used in the making of pies, tarts *etc*: – *pl* '**pastries**.

'**pasture** *n* ground covered with grass on which cattle graze. – *n* '**pasturage** grazing land.

pasty[1] ['pāsti] *adj* like paste; pale.

pasty[2] ['pasti] *n* a pie containing meat and vegetables in a covering of pastry.

pat *n* a light, quick blow or tap, *usu* with the hand; a small lump (*esp* of butter). – *v* to strike gently: – *pt* '**patted**. – **off pat** memorized thoroughly, ready to be said when necessary.

patch *v* to mend (clothes) by putting in a new piece of material to cover a hole; (with **up**) to mend, *esp* hastily or clumsily: *patch up the roof*; (with **up**) to settle (a quarrel). – *n* a piece of material sewn on to mend a hole; a small piece of ground: – *pl* '**patches**. – *adj* '**patchy** uneven, mixed in quality. *Her work is very patchy*. – *n* '**patchwork** a piece of material formed of small patches or pieces of material sewn together.

pate *n* the head: *a bald pate*.

pâté ['patā] *n* a paste made of finely minced meat or fish, flavoured with herbs, spices *etc*.

'**pātent** *n* an official written statement which gives to one person or business for a stated number of years the sole right to make or sell something that they have invented. – *adj* protected from copying by a patent; open, easily seen. – *v* to obtain a patent for. – *adv* '**patently** openly, clearly: *patently obvious*. – *n* **patent (leather)** leather with a very glossy surface.

pa'ternal *adj* of a father; like a father, fatherly; on one's father's side of the family: *my paternal grandfather*. – *n* **pa'ternity** the state or fact of being a father.

path *n* a way made by people or animals walking on it, a track: *a hill-path*; the route to be taken (by a person or vehicle): *in the lorry's path*; a course of action, way of life. – *n* '**pathway** a path.

pa'thology *n* the study of diseases. – *n* **pa'thologist** a doctor who studies the causes and effects of disease; a doctor who makes post-mortem examinations.

'**pāthos** *n* the quality (of something) that causes one to feel pity. *The pathos of the situation made me weep*. – *adj* **pathetic** [pə'thetik] causing pity; causing contempt, totally useless or inadequate: *a pathetic attempt*.

patient ['pāshənt] *adj* suffering delay, pain, discomfort *etc* without complaint or anger. – *n* a person under the care of a doctor *etc*. – *n* '**patience** the ability or willingness to be patient; a card game played *usu* by one person.

patio ['patiō] *n* a paved open yard attached to a house: – *pl* '**patios**.

patois ['patwä] *n* a dialect of language spoken by the ordinary people of a certain area.

patriarch ['pātriärk] *n* the male head of a family or tribe; the head of the Greek Orthodox Church *etc*. – *adj* **patri'archal**.

patrician [pə'trishən] *adj* aristocratic.

'**patricide** *n* the murder of one's own father; one who commits such a murder.

'patrimony *n* property handed down from one's father or ancestors.

'pātriot *n* one who loves (and serves) his country. – *n* **'patriotism** love of and loyalty to one's country. – *adj* **patri'otic**.

pa'trōl *v* to keep guard or watch by moving (on foot or in a vehicle) to and fro: – *pt* **pa'trolled**. – *n* the act of keeping guard in this way; the people *etc* keeping watch; a small group of Scouts or Girl Guides. – Also *adj*: *the patrol van*.

'pātron *n* one who protects or supports (a person, an artist, a form of art *etc*); a customer of a shop *etc*. – *n* **patronage** ['patrənij] the support given by a patron. – *v* **'patronize** to act as a patron toward. *He patronizes his local shop*; to treat a person as if one is superior to him. *He patronizes his brother-in-law*. – *n* **patron saint** a saint chosen as a protector. *St Patrick is the patron saint of Ireland*.

'patter *v* (of falling rain, footsteps *etc*) to make a quick tapping sound. – *n* the sound of falling rain, of footsteps *etc*; chatter, rapid talk, *esp* that used by salesmen to encourage people to buy their goods.

'pattern *n* an example suitable to be copied; a model or guide for making something; a decorative design; a sample: *a book of tweed patterns*. – *adj* **'patterned** having a design, not self-coloured.

'patty *n* a small flat cake of chopped meat *etc*: – *pl* **'patties**.

'paucity *n* smallness of number or quantity. *There's a paucity of good builders*.

paunch *n* a fat stomach: – *pl* **'paunches**.

'pauper *n* a very poor person.

pause [pöz] *n* a short stop, an interval; a break or hesitation in speaking or writing; (in music) (a mark showing) the holding of a note or rest. – *v* to stop for a short time.

pave *v* to lay (a street or pathway) with stone or concrete pieces to form a level surface for walking on. – *n* **'pavement** a paved surface *esp* a paved footway at the side of a road for pedestrians. – **pave the way for** to prepare or make the way easy for.

pa'vilion *n* a building in a sports ground in which sportsmen change their clothes; a large ornamental building; a large tent.

paw *n* the foot of an animal. – *v* to scrape with the forefoot; to handle or touch roughly, clumsily or rudely; to strike

out wildly with the hand: *paw the air*.

pawn *v* to put (an article of some value) in someone's keeping in exchange for a sum of money which, when repaid, buys back the article. – *n* (in chess) a small piece of the lowest rank; a person who lets himself be used by another for some purpose: the state of having been pawned. *My watch is in pawn*. – *ns* **'pawnbroker** one who lends money in exchange for pawned articles; **'pawnshop** a pawnbroker's place of business.

pay *v* to give (money) in exchange for (goods *etc*). *He paid £10 for it*; to suffer the punishment (for); to be advantageous or profitable. *It pays to be careful*; to give (*eg* attention): – *pt* **paid**. – *n* money given or received for work *etc*, wages. – *adj* **'payable** requiring to be paid. – *ns* **pay'ee** one to whom money is paid; **'payment** the act of paying; money paid (or its value in goods *etc*). – *adj* **'pay-as-you-'earn** of a system of collecting income tax by deducting it from the pay or salary before this is given to the worker. – **pay off** to pay in full and discharge (workers) owing to lack of work *etc*; to have good results. *His hard work paid off*; **pay out** to spend; to give out (a length of rope *etc*).

pea *n* a kind of climbing plant, having round green seeds in pods; the seed itself, eaten as a vegetable.

peace *n* quietness; freedom from war or disturbance; a treaty bringing this about. – *adjs* **'peaceable** of a quiet nature, fond of peace; **'peaceful** quiet; calm. – *n* **'peace-offering** something offered to bring about peace.

peach *n* a type of juicy, velvet-skinned fruit, orangey-pink in colour; the tree that bears it: – *pl* **'peaches**.

'peacock *n* a type of large bird, noted for its splendid feathers, *esp* in its tail: – *fem* **'peahen**.

peak *n* the pointed top of a mountain or hill; the highest point; the jutting-out part of the brim of a cap. – *v* to rise to a peak; to reach the highest point. *Prices peaked in July and then fell steadily*. – *adjs* **peaked** pointed; (of a hat, cap) having a peak; **'peaky** looking pale and unhealthy.

peal *n* a set of bells tuned to each other; the changes rung on such bells; a loud sound or succession of loud sounds: *peals of laughter*. – *v* to sound loudly.

'peanut *n* a type of nut similar to a pea in shape (also **'groundnut, 'monkeynut**). – *n* **peanut butter** a paste of ground roasted peanuts, spread on bread *etc.*

pear [pār] *n* a type of fruit narrowing towards the stem and bulging at the end; the tree that bears it. – *adj* 'pear-shaped: *a pear-shaped woman.*

pearl [pərl] *n* a gem formed in the shell of the oyster and several other shellfish; something resembling a pearl in shape, size, colour or value: *pearls of wisdom.*

peasant ['peznt] *n* one who works and lives on the land, *esp* in a primitive or underdeveloped area.

peat *n* a kind of turf, cut out of boggy places, dried and used as fuel.

'**pebble** *n* a small, roundish stone. – *adj* '**pebbly** full of pebbles. – *n* **pebble dash** a kind of coating for outside walls.

pe'can *n* a kind of oblong, thin-shelled nut, common in N. America; the tree bearing it.

pecca'dillo *n* a wrong or sin felt to be unimportant: – *pl* **pecca'dillo(e)s.**

peck *v* to strike with the beak; to pick up with the beak; to eat little, nibble (at); to kiss quickly and briefly. – *n* a sharp blow with the beak; a brief kiss. – *adj* '**peckish** slightly hungry.

'**pectoral** *adj* of or on the breast or chest.

pe'cūliar *adj* belonging to one person or thing in particular and to no other: *a custom peculiar to France*; strange, odd. *He is a very peculiar person.* – *n* **peculi'arity** that which marks a person or thing off from others in some way; something odd: – *pl* **peculi'arities.** – *adv* **pe'culiarly.**

pe'cūniary *adj* of money.

pedagogue ['pedəgog] *n* a teacher. – *adj* **pedagogic** [pedə'gojik] of a teacher or of education.

'**pedal** *n* a lever worked by the foot, as on a bicycle, piano *etc*; (on an organ) a key worked by the foot. – *v* to work the pedals of; to ride on a bicycle: – *pt* '**pedalled.**

'**pedant** *n* one who makes a great show of his knowledge; one who considers minor details to be of great importance. – *adj* **pe'dantic.** – *n* '**pedantry** too great a concern with unimportant details; a display of knowledge.

'**peddle** *v* to travel from door to door selling small objects. – *n* '**pedlar** one who peddles, a hawker.

pedestal ['pedistl] *n* the foot or support of a pillar, statue *etc.*

pe'destrian *adj* going on foot; for those on foot; unexciting, dull: *a pedestrian account of his adventures.* – *n* one who goes or travels on foot. – *n* **pedestrian crossing** a place where pedestrians

may cross the road when the traffic stops.

'**pedigree** *n* a list of the ancestors from whom a person or animal is descended; (distinguished) descent or ancestry. – *adj* of an animal, pure-bred, from a long line of ancestors of the same breed.

pedlar *see* **peddle.**

pe'dometer *n* an instrument for measuring the distance covered by a walker.

peek *v* to peep, glance *esp* secretively. – Also *n.*

peel *v* to strip off the outer covering or skin of: *peel an apple*; (of skin, paint, bark *etc*) to come off in small pieces; to lose skin in small flakes (as a result of sunburn *etc*). – *n* skin, rind.

peep *v* to look through a narrow opening, round a corner *etc*; to look slyly or quickly (at); to begin to appear. *The sun peeped out*; to make a high, small sound. – *n* a quick look, a glimpse (*usu* from a hidden position); a high, small sound.

peer *v* to look at with half-closed eyes, (as if) with difficulty. – *n* one's equal in rank, merit or age; a nobleman of the rank of baron upwards; a member of the House of Lords. – *n* '**peerage** a peer's title; the peers as a group. – *adj* '**peerless** without any equal, better than all others.

'**peevish** *adj* ill-natured, cross, fretful.

'**peewit** *n* the lapwing.

peg *n* a pin or stake of wood, metal *etc*; a hook fixed to a wall for hanging clothes *etc.* – *v* to fasten with a peg; to fix (prices *etc*) at a certain level: – *pt* **pegged.**

pejorative [pə'jorətiv] *adj* showing disapproval, dislike, scorn *etc*: *a pejorative remark.*

Pekin(g)ese [pēki'nēz] *n* a breed of small dog with long coat and flat face.

'**pelican** *n* a type of large waterbird with a pouched bill for storing fish.

'**pellet** *n* a little ball (of shot *etc*); a small pill.

pell-'mell *adv* in great confusion; headlong.

'**pelmet** *n* a strip or band (of wood *etc*) hiding a curtain rail.

pelt *n* the (untreated) skin of an animal. – *v* to throw (things) at; to run fast; (of rain, sometimes with **down**) to fall heavily. – **at full pelt** at top speed.

'**pelvis** *n* the frame of bone which circles the body below the waist.

'**pemmican** *n* dried meat, pressed hard into cakes.

pen *n* an instrument for writing in ink: a small enclosure, for sheep, cattle *etc*; a female swan. – *v* to shut up, enclose in a pen; to write (*eg* a letter): – *pt* **penned**. – *adj* **pent** (also **'pent-'up**) shut up, not allowed to go free; (of emotions *etc*) not freely expressed. – *ns* **'pen-friend** a person one has never seen (*usu* living abroad) with whom one exchanges letters; **'penknife** a pocket knife with folding blades; **'pen-name** a name adopted by a writer instead of his own name.

'pēnal *adj* of, or as, punishment. – *v* **'penalize** to punish; to put under a disadvantage. – *n* **penalty** [ˈpenlti] punishment; a disadvantage put on a player or team which breaks a rule of a game. – *n* **penal servitude** imprisonment with hard labour as an added punishment.

'penance *n* punishment willingly suffered by a person to make up for a wrong.

pence *see* **penny**.

'pencil *n* an instrument containing a length of graphite or other substance for writing, drawing *etc*. – *v* to draw, mark *etc* with a pencil: – *pt* **'pencilled**.

'pendant *n* an ornament hung from a necklace *etc*.

'pendent *adj* hanging.

'pending *adj* awaiting a decision or attention. *This matter is pending.* – *prep* awaiting, until the coming of: *in jail pending further evidence.*

'pendūlum *n* a swinging weight which drives the mechanism of a clock.

penetrate [ˈpenitrāt] *v* to pierce or pass into or through; to enter (*usu* by force). – *adj* **'penetrating** (of a sound) piercing; keen, probing: *a penetrating look.* – *n* **pene'tration** the act of breaking through or into; cleverness in understanding.

penguin [ˈpeŋgwin] *n* a kind of large sea bird of Antarctic regions, which cannot fly.

penicillin [peniˈsilin] *n* a medicine got from mould, which kills many germs.

pe'ninsūla *n* a piece of land almost surrounded by water. – *adj* **pe'ninsular**.

'pēnis *n* the part of the body of a male human or animal used in sexual intercourse and for urinating.

'penitent *adj* sorry for one's sins. – *n* a penitent person. – *n* **penitentiary** [peniˈtenshəri] (*US*) a prison.

'pennant *n* a long flag coming to a point at the end.

'penny *n* a coin worth ¹⁄₁₀₀ of £1: – *pls* **'pennies** used for a number of coins. *I need three pennies for the coffee machine;*

pence used to show an amount in pennies. *A ticket costs ten pence.* – *adj* **'penniless** having no money.

pension [ˈpenshən] *n* a sum of money paid regularly to a retired person, a widow, one wounded in a war *etc*. – *adj* **'pensionable** having or giving the right to a pension: *pensionable age: pensionable post.* – *n* **'pensioner** one who receives a pension. – **pension off** to dismiss or allow to retire with a pension.

pensive [ˈpensiv] *adj* thoughtful.

pent, pent-up *see* **pen**.

'pentagon *n* a five-sided figure. – *adj* **pen'tagonal**.

pen'tathlon *n* a five-event contest in the Olympic Games *etc*.

penthouse [ˈpent-hows] *n* a (luxurious) flat at the top of a building.

pe'nultimate *adj* last but one.

'penūry *n* poverty, want.

'pēony *n* a type of garden plant with large red, white or pink flowers: – *pl* **'peonies**.

people [ˈpēpl] *n* the men, women and children of a country or nation; persons generally. – *v* to fill with living beings, *esp* people; to inhabit, make up the population of.

'pepper *n* a type of plant whose berries are dried, powdered and used as seasoning; the powder so used; any of several hollow fruits containing many seeds, used as a food either raw, cooked or pickled. – *v* to sprinkle with pepper; (with **with**) to throw at or hit. *He peppered him with bullets.* – *adj* **'peppery** containing much pepper; inclined to be hot-tempered. – *adj* **'pepper-and-'salt** mixed black and white: *pepper-and-salt hair.* – *ns* **'peppercorn** the dried berry of the pepper plant; **pepper mill** a small device for grinding peppercorns for flavouring food; **'peppermint** a type of plant with a powerful taste and smell; a flavouring taken from this and used in sweets *etc*.

pep-talk [ˈpeptök] *n* a talk meant to encourage or arouse enthusiasm.

per *prep* in, out of: *five per cent* (often written as *5%*) *ie* five out of every hundred; for each: *£1 per dozen*; in each: *six times per week.* – **per annum** in each year; **per head** for each person.

peradventure [pərədˈvenchər] *adv* (*old*) by chance.

perambulator *see* **pram**.

perceive [pərˈsēv] *v* to become aware of through the senses; to see; to understand. – *adj* **perceptible** [pərˈseptəbl] able to be seen *etc* or understood. – *n*

per'ception the act of perceiving; the ability to perceive; understanding. – *adj* **per'ceptive** able or quick to perceive or understand.

per'centage *n* the rate per hundred.

perch *n* a type of freshwater fish; a rod on which birds roost; any high seat or position: – *pl* **'perches**. – *v* to roost.

per'chance *adv* (*old*) by chance; perhaps.

'percolate *v* (of a liquid) to drip or drain through small holes; to cause (a liquid) to do this; (of news *etc*) to pass slowly down or through. – *n* **'percolator** a device for percolating: *a coffee percolator.*

percussion [pər'kushən] *n* a striking of one object against another; musical instruments played by striking, *eg* drums, cymbals *etc.*

per'dition *n* utter loss or ruin; everlasting punishment.

peregrine ['perigrin] *n* a type of falcon used in hawking.

pe'remptory *adj* urgent; (of a command *etc*) to be obeyed at once; (of a manner) commanding in an arrogant way, dictatorial.

pe'rennial *adj* lasting through the year; everlasting, perpetual; (of plants) growing from year to year without replanting or sowing. – *n* a perennial plant.

'perfect *adj* complete; finished; faultless; exact. – *v* **per'fect** to make perfect; to finish. – *ns* **per'fection** the state of being perfect; complete freedom from flaws; the highest state or degree; **per'fectionist** one who is satisfied only by perfection.

per'fidious *adj* treacherous, unfaithful. – *ns* **per'fidiousness; 'perfidy**.

'perforate *v* to make a hole or holes through. – *adj* **'perforated** pierced with holes.

perforce [pər'förs] *adv* (*old*) of necessity, unavoidably.

per'form *v* to do or act; to act (a part), as on the stage; to provide any kind of entertainment for an audience; to play (a piece of music). – *ns* **per'formance** an entertainment (in a theatre *etc*); the act of doing something; the level of success of a machine, a car *etc*; **per'former** one who acts or performs.

'perfume *n* sweet smell, fragrance; a liquid which gives off a sweet smell when put on the skin, scent. – *v* **per'fume** to put scent on or in; to give a sweet smell to. – *n* **per'fumery** the shop or factory where perfume is sold or made.

per'functory *adj* done carelessly or half-heartedly. – *adv* **per'functorily**.

per'haps *adv* it may be (that), possibly. *Perhaps I'll forget to do it.*

peri- *prefix* around.

'peril *n* great danger. – *adj* **'perilous** very dangerous. – **at one's peril** at one's own risk.

perimeter [pə'rimitər] *n* the outside line enclosing a figure or shape: *perimeter of a circle*; the outer edge of any area. *He went outside the perimeters of the city.*

'period *n* any stretch of time; the time during which something (*eg* a revolution of the earth round the sun) takes place; a stage in the earth's development or in history; a full stop, as after a sentence; a sentence; an occurrence of menstruation. – *adjs* **peri'odic** of a period; happening at regular intervals (*eg* every month, year); happening every now and then: *a periodic clearing out of rubbish*; **peri'odical** issued, done *etc*, at regular intervals; periodic. – *n* a magazine which appears at regular intervals.

peripa'tetic *adj* moving from place to place: *a peripatetic salesman.*

pe'riphery *n* the line surrounding something; the outer boundary or edge (of something): – *pl* **pe'ripheries**. – *adj* **pe'ripheral** of or on a periphery; away from the centre; not essential, of little importance.

'periscope *n* a tube with mirrors by which an observer in a trench or submarine is able to see objects on the surface.

'perish *v* to be destroyed or pass away completely; to die; to decay, rot. – *adj* **'perishable** liable to go bad quickly.

'periwig *n* (*hist*) a wig.

'periwinkle *n* a type of small shellfish, shaped like a small snail, eaten as food when boiled; a type of creeping evergreen plant, with a small blue flower.

perjure ['pərjər] *v* (with **oneself** *etc*) to tell a lie when one has sworn to tell the truth, *esp* in a court of law. – *ns* **'perjurer; 'perjury**.

perk *n* short for **perquisite**. – *adj* **'perky** jaunty, in good spirits. – **perk up** to recover one's energy or spirits.

perm *n* short for **permanent wave**. – *v* to give a permanent wave to (hair).

'permanent *adj* lasting, not temporary. – *ns* **'permanence; 'permanency** the state of being permanent; person or thing that is permanent. – *n* **permanent wave** a wave or curl put into the hair by a special process and *usu* lasting for some months.

permeate ['pɔ̄rmiāt] *v* to pass into through small holes, to soak into; to fill every part of. – *adj* '**permeable**.

per'mit *v* to agree to another's action, to allow; to make possible: – *pt* **per'mit-ted**. – *n* '**permit** a written order, allowing a person to do something. – *adj* **permissible** [pɔr'misɔbl] allowable. – *n* **permission** [pɔr'mishɔn] freedom given to do something. – *adj* **per'missive** allowing something to be done; (too) tolerant.

permū'tation *n* the arrangement of things, numbers, letters *etc* in a certain order; the act of changing the order of things.

pernicious [pɔr'nishɔs] *adj* destructive.

per'nickety *adj* fussy about small details.

pero'ration *n* the closing part of a speech; a speech.

pe'roxide *n* a chemical (hydrogen peroxide) used for bleaching hair *etc*.

perpen'dicūlar *adj* standing upright, vertical; at right angles (to). – *n* a line at right angles to another.

'**perpetrate** *v* to do or commit (a sin, error *etc*). – *ns* **perpe'tration**; '**perpetrator**.

perpetual [pɔr'pechooɔl] *adj* everlasting, unending. – *adv* **per'petually**. – *v* **per'petuate** to cause to last for ever or for a long time. – *n* **perpetuity** [pɔ̄rpɔ'chooɔti]. – **in perpetuity** for ever; for the length of one's life.

per'plex *v* to puzzle, bewilder; to make more complicated. – *n* **per'plexity** a puzzled state of mind; something which puzzles.

perquisite ['pɔ̄rkwizit] *n* something of value one is allowed in addition to one's pay.

persecute ['pɔ̄rsikūt] *v* to harass, worry, *usu* over a period of time; to kill, make to suffer, *esp* because of religious beliefs. – *ns* **perse'cution**; '**persecutor**.

persevere [pɔ̄rsi'vēr] *v* to keep trying to do a thing (in spite of difficulties). – *n* **perse'verance** the act of persevering.

per'sist *v* to hold fast to something (*eg* an idea); to continue to do something in spite of difficulties; to survive, last. *The idea that snakes are slimy still persists.* – *adj* **per'sistent** (of persons) obstinate, refusing to be discouraged; lasting, not dying out. – *n* **per'sistence**.

'**person** *n* a human being; one's body. *He had jewels hidden on his person*; form, shape. *Trouble arrived in the person of Jeremy.* – *adj* '**personable** goodlooking. – *n* '**personage** a (well-known) person. – *adj* '**personal** one's own; private; (of remarks) insulting, offensive to the person they are aimed at. – *n* **perso'nality** all of a person's characteristics (of feeling, mind, body *etc*) as seen by others; a well-known person. – *adv* '**personally** speaking from one's own point of view; by one's own act, not using an agent or representative. *He thanked me personally.* – *v* **per'sonifȳ** to talk about things, ideas *etc* as if they were living persons (as in 'Time marches on.'); to be typical or a perfect example of: – *pt* **per'sonified**. – *n* **per'sonifi'cation**. – **in person** personally, not represented by someone else.

person'nel *n* the people employed in a firm *etc*.

perspective [pɔr'spektiv] *n* a point of view; in painting *etc*, (the art of giving) a sense of depth, distance *etc* like that in real life. – **in perspective** (of an object *etc* in a photograph *etc*) having the size *etc* in relation to other things that it would have in real life; (of an event *etc*) in its true degree of importance *etc* when considered in relation with other events *etc*. *You must learn to see things in perspective.*

'**Perspex**® *n* a transparent plastic which looks like glass.

perspicacious [pɔ̄rspi'kāshɔs] *adj* of clear or sharp understanding. – *n* **perspicacity** [pɔ̄rspi'kasɔti] keenness of understanding.

perspi'cūity *n* clearness in expressing one's thoughts.

per'spire *v* to sweat. – *n* **perspi'ration** sweat.

persuade [pɔr'swād] *v* to bring a person to do or think something, by arguing with him or advising him. – *n* **persuasion** [pɔr'swāzhɔn] act of persuading; a firm belief *esp* a religious belief. – *adj* **persuasive** [pɔr'swāsiv] having the power to convince. – *n* **per'suasiveness**.

pert *adj* saucy, cheeky.

per'tain *v* (with **to**) to belong, have to do with: *duties pertaining to the job.*

pertinacious [pɔ̄rti'nāshɔs] *adj* holding strongly to an idea, obstinate. – *n* **pertinacity** [pɔ̄rti'nasɔti].

'**pertinent** *adj* connected with the subject spoken about, to the point.

per'turb *v* to disturb greatly; to make anxious or uneasy. – *n* **pertur'bation** great worry, anxiety.

peruse [pɔ'rooz] *v* to read (with care). – *n* **pe'rusal**.

per'vade *v* to spread through. *Silence pervaded the room.*

per'verse *adj* obstinate in holding to the wrong point of view; unreasonable. – *ns* **per'verseness, per'versity** stubbornness; wickedness.

per'vert *v* to turn away from what is normal or right: *pervert the course of justice*; to turn (a person) to crime or evil. – *n* **'pervert** one who commits unnatural or perverted acts. – *n* **per'version** the act of perverting; an unnatural or perverted act.

peseta [pə'sātə] *n* the standard unit of Spanish currency.

'pessimism *n* the habit of thinking that things will always turn out badly (opposite of **optimism**). – *n* **'pessimist** a person who tends to think in this way. – *adj* **pessi'mistic**.

pest *n* a troublesome person or thing; a creature that is harmful or destructive, *eg* a mosquito. – *ns* **'pesticide** any substance which' kills animal pests; **'pestilence** a deadly, spreading disease. – *adj* **'pestilent** very unhealthy; troublesome.

'pester *v* to annoy continually.

pestle ['pesl] *n* a tool for pounding things to powder.

pet *n* a tame animal *usu* kept in the home (such as a cat *etc*); a favourite (child); a fit of sulks. – *adj* kept as a pet; favourite; chief: *my pet hate*. – *v* to fondle: – *pt* **'petted**. – *adj* **'pettish** sulky. – *n* **pet name** one used to express affection or love.

'petal *n* one of the leaf-like parts of a flower.

'pēter: peter out to fade or dwindle away to nothing.

petite [pə'tēt] *adj* small and neat in appearance.

pe'tition *n* a request, *esp* one signed by many people and sent to a government or authority. – Also *v*. – *n* **pe'titioner**.

'petrel *n* a kind of small, long-winged sea-bird.

'petrifỹ *v* to turn into stone; to turn (someone) stiff, *esp* with fear: – *pt* **'petrified**. – *n* **petri'faction**.

pe'trōleum *n* oil in its raw, unrefined form, extracted from natural wells below the earth's surface. – *n* **'petrol** petroleum when refined as fuel for use in motor-cars *etc*.

petticoat *n* an underskirt worn by women.

'petty *adj* of little importance, trivial. – *n* **'pettiness**. – *ns* **petty cash** money paid or received in small sums; **petty officer** a rank of officer in the navy (equal to a non-commissioned officer in the army).

'petūlant *adj* cross, irritable; unreasonably impatient. – *n* **'petulance**.

pew [pū] *n* a seat or bench in a church.

pewter ['pūtər] *n* a mixture of tin and lead.

'phalanx *n* a company of foot soldiers,` drawn up for battle in an oblong-shaped body; a group of supporters: – *pl* **'phalanxes**.

phantasy *see* **fantasy**.

'phantom *n* a ghost.

Pharaoh ['fārō] *n* (*hist*) a ruler of Egypt in ancient times.

pharmaceutical [färmə'sūtikəl] *adj* having to do with the making up of medicines and drugs. – *ns* **'pharmacist** one who prepares and sells medicines; **'pharmacy** the art of preparing medicines; a chemist's shop.

pharmacology [färmə'koləji] *n* the scientific study of drugs and their effects. – *n* **pharma'cologist**.

'pharynx *n* the back part of the throat behind the tonsils. – *n* **pharyn'gitis** an illness in which the pharynx becomes inflamed.

phase [fāz] *n* one in a series of changes in the shape, appearance *etc* of something (*eg* the moon); a period, stage in the development of something (*eg* a war, a scheme *etc*).

pheasant ['feznt] *n* a type of bird with brightly-coloured feathers which is shot as game.

phenomenon [fə'nomənən] *n* any happening or fact (*esp* in nature) that is observed by the senses: *the phenomenon of lightning*; anything remarkable or very unusual, a wonder: – *pl* **phe'nomena**. – *adj* **phe'nomenal** very unusual, remarkable.

'phial *n* a small glass bottle.

phi'lander *v* to make love, to flirt. – *n* **phi'landerer**.

phi'lanthropy *n* the love of mankind, *usu* as shown by money given or work done for the benefit of others. – *adj* **philan'thropic** doing good to one's fellow men. – *n* **phi'lanthropist** one who does good to others.

philately [fi'latəli] *n* the study and collecting of stamps. – *n* **phi'latelist**.

philharmonic [filər'monik] *adj* (*usu* in names of orchestras *etc*) music-loving.

phi'lology *n* the study of words and their history. – *n* **phi'lologist**.

phi'losopher *n* one who studies philosophy. – *adjs* **philo'sophic, philo'sophical** of philosophy; calm, not easily upset. – *n* **phi'losophy** the study of the nature of the universe, or of man and his behaviour; a person's view of life.

phlegm [flem] *n* the thick slimy matter brought up from the throat by coughing; coolness of temper, calmness. – *adj* **phlegmatic** [fleg'matik] not easily aroused.

phlox *n* a type of garden plant with flat white or purplish flowers.

'**phōbia** *n* an intense (*usu* irrational) fear, dislike or hatred.

phoenix ['fēniks] *n* (*myth*) a bird which was said to burn itself and to rise again from its ashes.

phone short for **telephone**.

phonetic [fə'netik] *adj* of the sounds of language; spelt according to sound (as *feeniks* for **phoenix**). – *n* **pho'netics** the study of the sounds of language; a system of writing according to sound.

'**phōn(e)y** *adj* (*coll*) fake, not genuine.

'**phosphorus** *n* an element, a wax-like, poisonous substance that gives out light in the dark. – *ns* '**phosphate** a kind of soil fertilizer containing phosphorus; **phosphorescence** [fosfə'resns] faint glow of light in the dark. – *adj* **phospho'rescent**.

'**phōtocopy** *n* a copy of a document *etc* made by a device which photographs and develops images of the document. – Also *v*.

phōto'genic *adj* being a good or striking subject for a photograph.

pho'tography *n* the art of taking pictures by means of a camera, making use of the action of light on special films or plates. – *n* '**phōtograph** (*coll* '**phōtō**) a picture so made. – *v* to take a picture with a camera. – *ns* **photographer** [fə'togrəfər]; '**Phōtostat** ® a type of special camera for making photographic copies of documents, pages of books *etc*; a photographic copy so made.

phrase [frāz] *n* a small group of words expressing a single idea: *after dinner*: *on the water*; a short saying or expression; (in music) a short group of bars forming a distinct unit. – *v* to express in words. *You could have phrased your excuse more tactfully.* – *n* **phraseology** [frāzi'oləji] one's choice of words and phrases used in expressing oneself.

physical ['fizikəl] *adj* of the body: *physical strength*: *physical exercises*; of things that can be seen or felt. – *adv* '**physically**. – *ns* **physician** [fi'zishən] a doctor (specializing in medical rather than surgical treatment); **physicist** ['fizisist] one who specializes in physics; **physics** ['fiziks] the science which includes the

study of heat, light, sound, electricity, magnetism *etc*.

physiognomy [fizi'onəmi] *n* (the features or expression of) the face.

physiology [fizi'oləji] *n* the study of the way in which living bodies work (including blood circulation, food digestion, breathing *etc*). – *n* **physi'ologist**.

physiotherapy [fiziə'therəpi] *n* the treatment of disease by bodily exercise, massage *etc* rather than by drugs. – *n* **physio'therapist**.

physique [fi'zēk] *n* the build of one's body; bodily strength.

pi'ano *n* a type of large musical instrument played by striking keys: – *pl* **pi'anos**. – *n* **pianist** ['pēənist] one who plays the piano.

piazza [pi'atsə] *n* a market-place, square in a town *etc* surrounded by buildings.

pibroch ['pēbrohh] *n* a kind of bagpipe music.

'**picador** *n* a bullfighter armed with a lance and mounted on a horse.

'**piccolo** *n* a kind of small, high-pitched flute: – *pl* '**piccolos**.

pick *v* to choose; to pluck, gather (flowers, fruit *etc*); to peck, bite, nibble (at); to poke, probe (teeth *etc*); to open (a lock) with a tool other than a key. – *n* choice; the best or best part; a kind of heavy tool for breaking ground *etc* pointed at one end or both ends; any instrument for picking (*eg* a toothpick). – *ns* '**pickaxe** a pick; '**pickpocket** one who robs people's pockets. – **pick a quarrel** to start a quarrel deliberately; **pick on** to single out *usu* for something unpleasant; to nag at; **pick up** to lift up; to learn (a language, habit *etc*); to take into a vehicle, give someone a lift; to find or get by chance; to improve, gain strength.

'**picket** *n* a pointed stake; a small sentry-post or guard; a number of men on strike who prevent others from working or from going into work. – *v* to fasten (a horse *etc*) to a stake; to place a guard of soldiers or a group of strikers at (a place).

'**pickle** *n* a liquid in which food is preserved; vegetables preserved in vinegar; (*coll*) an awkward, unpleasant situation. – *v* to preserve with salt, vinegar *etc*.

'**picnic** *n* a meal eaten out-of-doors, *usu* during an outing *etc*. – Also *v*: – *pt* '**picnicked**.

pictorial *see* **picture**.

picture ['pikchor] *n* a painting or

drawing; a portrait; a photograph; a film; (*pl*) the cinema; a vivid description; representation. – *v* to make a picture of; to form a likeness of in the mind, to imagine. – *adjs* **pictorial** [pik'tōriəl] having pictures; consisting of pictures; calling up pictures in the mind; **picturesque** [pikchə'resk] such as would make a good or striking picture, pretty, colourful.

pie *n* meat, fruit or other food baked in a casing or covering of pastry.

piebald ['pībōld] *adj* (*esp* of horses) white and black in patches; spotted.

piece [pēs] *n* a part or portion of anything; a single article or example: *a piece of paper*; a composition in music, writing, painting or other form of art: *a piece of popular music*; a coin; a man in chess, draughts *etc*. – *v* to put (together). – *adv* **'piece'meal** by pieces, little by little. – *n* **'piecework** work paid for according to how much work is done, not according to the time spent on it.

pied *adj* with two or more colours in patches.

pier [pēr] *n* a platform of stone, wood *etc* stretching from the shore into the sea *etc* as a landing place for ships; a pillar (supporting an arch, bridge *etc*).

pierce [pērs] *v* to make a hole through; to force a way into; to move (the feelings) deeply. – *adj* **'piercing** shrill, loud; sharp.

pierrot ['perō] *n* a comic entertainer with a white face and loose white clothes.

piety *see* **pious**.

'piffle *n* nonsense.

pig *n* a type of farm animal, from whose flesh ham and bacon are made; an oblong moulded piece of metal (*eg* pig-iron). – *ns* **'piggery, 'pigsty** a place where pigs are kept. – *adj* **'pig-'headed** stubborn. – *ns* **'pigskin** a kind of leather made from a pig's skin; **'pigtail** the hair of the head formed into a plait.

pigeon ['pijən] *n* a kind of bird of the dove family. – *n* **'pigeon-hole** a small division in a case or desk for papers *etc*. – *v* lay aside; to classify, put into a category.

'pigment *n* paint or other substance used for colouring; a substance in animals and plants that gives colour to the skin *etc*. – *n* **pigmen'tation** colouring (of skin *etc*).

pigmy *see* **pygmy**.

pike *n* a type of freshwater fish; a weapon like a spear, with a long shaft and a sharp head.

'pilchard *n* a small type of herring-like sea fish used as food.

pile *n* a number of things lying one on top of another, a heap; a great quantity; a large building; a large stake or pillar driven into the earth as a foundation for a building, bridge *etc*; the thick, soft surface on carpets *etc* and on certain kinds of cloth, *eg* velvet. – *v* (often with **up**) to make or form a pile or heap.

'pilfer *v* to steal small things. – *n* **'pilfering**.

'pilgrim *n* a traveller to a holy place. – *n* **'pilgrimage** a journey to a holy place.

pill *n* a little tablet, ball *etc* of medicine; (sometimes with **the**) a contraceptive in the form of a small tablet.

'pillage *v* to seize goods, money *etc esp* as loot in war. – *n* the act of plundering in this way.

'pillar *n* an upright support for roofs, arches *etc*; an upright post or column as a monument *etc*; anything or anyone that supports. *He is a pillar of the church*. – *n* **'pillarbox** a pillar-shaped box with a slot through which letters *etc* are posted.

'pillion *n* a seat for a passenger on a motor-cycle; (*old*) a light saddle for a passenger on horseback, behind the main saddle.

'pillory *n* (*hist*) a wooden frame (with holes for the head and hands) in which wrongdoers were placed in a standing position: – *pl* **'pillories**. – *v* to mock in public: – *pres p* **'pillorying**, *pt* **'pilloried**.

pillow ['pilō] *n* a kind of cushion for the head. – *v* to rest or support on, or as if on, a pillow. – *ns* **'pillowcase, 'pillowslip** a cover for a pillow.

'pilot *n* one who steers a ship in or out of a harbour; the person flying an aeroplane; a guide, leader. – *v* to steer or guide. – *ns* **'pilot-light** a small gas-light from which larger jets are lit; an electric light showing that a current is switched on; **pilot scheme** a scheme introduced on a small scale to act as a guide to a full-scale one.

'pimpernel *n* a kind of plant of the primrose family, with small pink or scarlet flowers.

'pimple *n* a small round swelling on the skin. – *adjs* **'pimpled, 'pimply** having pimples.

pin *n* a short pointed piece of metal with a small round head, used for fastening, *esp* in dressmaking; a wooden or metal peg or nail; a skittle. – *v* to fasten with a pin; to hold fast, pressed against something. *The fallen branch pinned him to the ground*: – *pres p* '**pinning**, *pt* **pinned**.

'**pinafore** *n* a covering to protect the front of a dress, a kind of apron; (also **pinafore dress**) a sleeveless dress worn over a jersey, blouse *etc*.

pince-nez ['pans'nā] *n* a pair of eyeglasses with a spring for gripping the nose.

'**pincers** *npl* a kind of tool like pliers, but with sharp points for gripping, pulling out nails *etc*; the claw of a crab or lobster.

pinch *v* to squeeze (*esp* flesh) between the thumb and forefinger, to nip; to grip tightly, hurt by tightness; (*coll*) to steal. – *n* a squeeze, a nip; a small amount (*eg* of salt *etc*): – *pl* '**pinches**. – *adj* **pinched** (of a face) looking cold, pale or thin. – **at a pinch** if really necessary or urgent; **feel the pinch** to suffer from the lack of something (*usu* money).

pine *n* any of several kinds of evergreen, cone-bearing trees with needle-like leaves; the soft wood of such a tree used for furniture *etc*. – *v* to waste away, lose strength (with pain, grief *etc*); to long (for something). – *n* '**pineapple** a type of large fruit shaped like a pine-cone.

ping *n* a whistling sound such as that of a bullet. – Also *v*. – *n* '**ping-pong** ® table-tennis.

'**pinion** *n* a bird's wing; a small toothed wheel. – *v* to hold (someone) fast by binding or holding their arms; to cut or fasten the wings (of a bird).

pink *n* a pale red colour; a type of sweet-scented garden flower like a carnation; very good state: *in the pink of health*. – *v* (*esp* of an engine) to make a faint clinking noise; to cut (cloth *etc*) leaving a zig-zag edge with **pinking scissors** or **pinking shears**.

'**pinnacle** *n* a slender spire or turret; a high pointed rock or mountain; the highest point.

pint *n* a liquid measure equal to just over $\frac{1}{2}$ litre.

pio'neer *n* one who goes before to clear the way for others; an explorer; one who is the first to do, study *etc* something. – *v* to act as a pioneer (in).

'**pious** *adj* respectful in religious matters. – *n* **piety** ['piəti].

pip *n* a seed (of fruit); a spot or symbol on dice, cards *etc*; a star on an army officer's tunic; a short high-pitched note given on the radio or telephone as a time signal *etc*.

pipe *n* any tube, *esp* one of earthenware, metal *etc* for carrying water, gas *etc*; a kind of tube with a bowl at the end, for tobacco smoking; a kind of musical instrument in which the sound is made by blowing in a tube; (*pl*) a type of musical instrument made of several small pipes joined together; (*pl*) bagpipes. – *v* to play (notes, a tune) on a pipe or pipes; to whistle, chirp; to speak in a shrill high voice; to convey (*eg* water) by pipe. – *n* '**piper** one who plays a pipe, *esp* the bagpipes. – *adj* '**piping** high-pitched, shrill; piping hot. – *n* a length of tubing; a system of pipes; a narrow kind of cord for trimming clothes *etc*; a strip of decorative icing round a cake. – *ns* **pipe clay** a kind of fine white clay used to whiten leather *etc* and in making clay pipes; '**pipeline** a long line of pipes such as carry oil from an oil-field. – **in the pipeline** in preparation, soon to become available; **pipe down** to become silent, stop talking; **piping hot** very hot.

pi'pette *n* a kind of small glass tube used *esp* in laboratories.

'**pippin** *n* a kind of apple.

piquant ['pēkənt] *adj* sharp; appetizing; arousing interest.

pique [pēk] *n* anger caused by wounded pride, spite, resentment. – *v* to wound the pride of; to arouse (curiosity).

'**pirate** *n* one who robs ships at sea; his ship; one who, without permission, prints or broadcasts what another has written *etc*. – *n* '**piracy**. – *adj* **pi'ratical**.

pirou'ette *n* a rapid whirling on the toes in dancing. – Also *v*.

pistachio [pis'tāshiō] *n* a kind of greenish seed or nut, used as a flavouring: – *pl* **pis'tachios**.

'**pistil** *n* the seed-bearing part of a flower.

'**pistol** *n* a small gun held in the hand.

'**piston** *n* a round piece of metal that moves up and down inside a cylinder (in engines, pumps *etc*). – *n* '**piston-rod** the rod to which the piston is fitted.

pit *n* a hole in the ground; a place from which minerals (*eg* coal) are dug; the ground floor of a theatre behind the stalls; (often *pl*) a place beside the racecourse for repairing and refuelling racing cars *etc*. – *v* to set one thing or person against another. *I had to pit my wits against his*: – *pt* '**pitted**. – *adj* '**pitted** (of a surface) marked with small holes.

pitch *v* to fix a tent *etc* in the ground; to throw; to fall heavily. *He suddenly pitched forward*; (of a ship) to lurch; to set the level or key of a tune. – *n* a thick dark substance obtained by boiling down tar; a throw; the height or depth of a note; a peak, an extreme point, intensity. *His anger reached such a pitch that he hit her*; the field, ground for certain games; (in cricket) the ground between wickets; the slope (of a roof *etc*); the part of a street *etc* where a street seller or street-entertainer is stationed: – *pl* **'pitches**. – *adj* **'pitch-'dark** very dark. – *n* **'pitchfork** a fork for lifting and throwing hay. – *v* to throw (someone) suddenly into (a position or state). – *n* **pitched battle** a battle on chosen ground between sides that have been arranged in position beforehand.

'pitcher *n* a kind of large jug.

piteous *see* **pity**.

pitfall ['pitföl] *n* a trap, a possible danger.

pith *n* the soft substance in the centre of the stems of plants; the white substance under the rind of an orange *etc*; the important part of anything. – *adj* **'pithy** full of pith; very full of meaning, to the point: *a pithy saying*.

'pittance *n* a very small wage or allowance.

'pity *n* a feeling for the sufferings of others, sympathy; a cause of grief; a regrettable fact. – *v* to feel sorry for: – *pl* **'pitied**. – *adjs* **piteous** ['pitiəs], **'pitiable** deserving pity; wretched; **'pitiful** sad; poor, wretched.

'pivot *n* the pin or centre on which anything turns; that on which something or someone depends to a great extent. *He is the pivot of the firm*. – *v* to turn on a pivot; to depend (on). – *adj* **'pivotal**.

'pixy, 'pixie *n* (*myth*) a kind of fairy: – *pl* **'pixies**.

pizza ['pētsə] *n* a flat piece of dough spread with tomato, cheese *etc* and baked.

'placard *n* a printed notice (as an advertisement *etc*) placed on a wall *etc*.

pla'cate *v* to calm, soothe, make less angry *etc*.

place *n* a city, town, village; a dwelling or home; a building, room, area *etc*; a particular spot; an open space in a town: *a market place*; a seat in a theatre, train, at table *etc*; a position (as in football *etc*); job or position (often one won by competing against others); rank. – *v* to put in a particular place; to find a place for; to give (an order for goods *etc*); to remember who a person is. *I can't place him*: – *pres p* **'placing**. –

adj **placed** having a place; among the first three in a race *etc*. – *n* **in place** in the proper position; suitable; **in place of** instead of; **out of place** not in the proper position; unsuitable.

'placid *adj* calm, not easily disturbed.

plagiarize ['plājərīz] *v* to steal or borrow from the writings or ideas of another. – *ns* **'plagiarism, 'plagiarist**.

plague [plāg] *n* a fatal infectious disease *esp* a fever caused by rat fleas; a great and troublesome quantity: *a plague of flies*. – *v* to pester or annoy.

plaice *n* a type of eatable flatfish.

plaid [plad] *n* a long piece of (tartan) cloth worn over the shoulder.

plain *adj* flat, level; simple, ordinary; without ornament or decoration; without luxury; clear, easy to see or understand; not good-looking, not attractive. – *n* a level stretch of land. – *adjs* **'plain-'clothes** (of a police detective *etc*) wearing ordinary clothes, not uniform; **'plain-'spoken** speaking one's thoughts frankly.

'plaintiff *n* a person who takes action against another in the law courts.

plaintive ['plāntiv] *adj* sad, sorrowful.

plait [plat] *n* a length of hair arranged by intertwining three (or more) separate pieces; any material so intertwined. – *v* to form into a plait.

plan *n* a diagram of a building, town *etc* as if seen from above; a scheme or arrangement to do something. – *v* to make a sketch or plan of; to decide or arrange to do, or how to do (something): – *pt* **planned**.

plane *n* short for **aeroplane**; any level surface; a kind of carpentry tool for smoothing wood; a level or standard (of achievement *etc*); a type of tree with broad leaves. – *adj* flat, level. – *v* to smooth with a plane; to glide (over water *etc*).

'planet *n* any of the bodies (such as the earth) which move round the sun or round another fixed star. – *adj* **'planetary**.

plank *n* a long, flat piece of timber.

'plankton *n* very tiny living creatures floating in seas, lakes *etc*.

plant *n* anything growing from the ground, having stem, root and leaves; a factory or machinery. – *v* to put (something) into the ground so that it will grow; to put (an idea *etc*) into the mind; to set down firmly; (*coll*) to place (something) as false evidence. – *ns* **plan'tation** a place planted *esp* with trees; a colony; an estate for growing cotton, sugar, rubber, tobacco *etc*; **'planter** the owner of a plantation.

'plantain *n* a type of plant with broad leaves spreading out flat over the ground; a kind of banana.

plaque [pläk] *n* a plate of metal, china *etc* (for fixing to a wall) as a decoration or as a memorial; a film or deposit of saliva and bacteria which forms on the teeth.

plasma ['plazmə] *n* the liquid part of blood and of certain other fluids.

'plaster *n* a mixture of lime, water and sand which sets hard, for covering walls *etc*; a finer mixture (**plaster of Paris**) containing gypsum used for making moulds, supporting broken limbs *etc*; a piece of sticky tape to hold a dressing on a wound *etc*; a small dressing which can be stuck over a wound. – *adj* made of plaster. – *v* to apply plaster to; to cover too thickly (with). – *n* **'plasterer** one who plasters (walls). – *n* **plaster cast** a mould made of plaster of Paris; a mould made of plaster of Paris and gauze put round an injured limb *etc*.

'plastic *adj* easily moulded or shaped; made of plastic. – *n* any of many chemically manufactured substances that can be moulded when soft, formed into fibres *etc*. – *n* **plas'ticity** the state or quality of being plastic or easily moulded. – *n* **plastic surgery** operation(s) to repair or replace damaged areas of skin or to improve the appearance of a facial feature *eg* a nose.

Plasticine ® ['plastisēn] *n* a soft clay-like substance used for modelling.

plate *n* a shallow dish for holding food; a flat piece of metal, glass, china *etc*; gold and silver articles; a sheet of metal used in printing; a book illustration *usu* on glossy paper; the part of false teeth that fits to the mouth. – *v* to cover with a coating of metal. – *n* **'plating** a thin covering of metal. – *n* **'plate-'glass** a kind of glass, in thick sheets, used for shop windows, mirrors *etc*.

plateau ['platō] *n* a broad level stretch of high land; a steady, unchanging state or condition. *Prices have now reached a plateau*: – *pls* **plateaus, plateaux** ['platōz].

'platform *n* a raised level surface, such as that for passengers at a railway station; a raised floor, *esp* one for speakers, entertainers *etc*.

'platinum *n* an element, a kind of heavy and very valuable steel-grey metal.

'platitude *n* a dull, ordinary remark made as if it were important.

pla'tonic *adj* (of a relationship *etc*) not involving sexual love.

pla'toon *n* (in the army) a section of a company of soldiers.

'platter *n* a kind of large, flat plate.

'platypus *n* a small type of water animal of Australia that has webbed feet and lays eggs (also **duck-billed platypus**): – *pl* **'platypuses**.

'plaudit *n* (*usu pl*) applause, praise.

plausible ['plözəbl] *adj* seeming (often misleadingly) to be truthful or honest; seeming probable or reasonable. – *n* **plausi'bility**.

play *v* to amuse oneself; to take part in a game; to gamble; to act (on a stage *etc*); to perform (on a musical instrument); to carry out (a trick); to trifle or fiddle (with). *The child is playing with his food*; to (cause to) flicker over. *The firelight played on his face*; to (cause to) splash over. *The firemen played their hoses over the house.* – *n* amusement, recreation; gambling; a story for acting, a drama; a way of acting or behaving: *foul play*; (of machinery *etc*) freedom of movement. – *n* **'player** an actor; one who plays a game, musical instrument *etc*. – *adj* **'playful** wanting to play: *a playful kitten*; fond of joking *etc*, not serious. – *ns* **'playfellow, 'playmate** a friend with whom one plays; **'playground** a place for playing in at school, in a park *etc*; **'playgroup** a group of children (*usu* aged less than five) who play together supervised by adults; **playing card** one of a pack of cards used in playing card games. **'playschool** a nursery school or playgroup; **'plaything** a toy; **'playwright** a writer of plays. – **play at** to treat or act towards in a light-hearted, not serious way. *He only plays at being a business man*; **play off** to set off (one person) against another to gain some advantage for oneself; **play on** to make use of (someone's feelings *etc*) to turn to one's own advantage; **a play on words** a pun *etc*; **play the game** to act fairly and honestly.

plea *n* an excuse; a prisoner's answer to a charge in a law-court; an urgent request.

plead *v* to state one's case, *esp* in a law-court; (with **with**) to beg earnestly; to give as an excuse. – **plead guilty** or **not guilty** (in a law-court) to admit or deny one's guilt.

please [plēz] *v* to give pleasure or delight (to); to satisfy; to choose, like (to do). *Do as you please.* – **please, if you please** if you are willing (added for politeness to a command or request).

Pass me the sugar, please. Please keep off the grass. – *adj* **pleasant** ['pleznt] giving pleasure; agreeable. – *ns* **'pleasantness; 'pleasantry** good-humoured joking. – *adj* **pleasurable** ['plezhərəbl] delightful, pleasant. – *n* **'pleasure** enjoyment, joy, delight; what one wishes. *What is your pleasure?* – **at pleasure** when or if one pleases.

pleat *n* a fold in cloth, which has been pressed or stitched down. – *v* to put pleats in. – *adj* **'pleated**.

plebeian [plə'bēən] *adj* of the ordinary or common people. – Also *n* (*hist*). – *n* **plebiscite** ['plebisit] a system of deciding a matter by asking everybody to give his vote, for or against.

'plectrum *n* a small piece of horn, metal *etc* used for plucking the strings of a guitar *etc*.

pledge *n* something handed over by a person who borrows money *etc* which will not be given back if he does not repay the loan *etc*; a solemn promise. – *v* to give as security, to pawn; to promise solemnly to do something. *He pledged himself to carry out the plan*; to drink to the health of, to toast.

'plēnary *adj* full, complete.

'plenty *n* a full supply, as much as is needed; a large number or quantity (of). – *adjs* **plenteous** ['plentiəs], **'plentiful** not scarce; abundant.

'plethora *n* too large a quantity of anything: *a plethora of politicians.*

pleurisy ['ploorəsi] *n* an illness in which the covering of the lungs becomes inflamed.

'pliable *adj* easily bent or folded; easily persuaded. – *adj* **'pliant** pliable.

pliers ['plīərz] *npl* a kind of tool used for gripping tightly, bending and cutting (wire) *etc*.

plight [plīt] *v* to promise solemnly. – *n* situation, state (*usu* bad).

'plimsoll *n* a light rubber-soled canvas shoe, used for sports *etc*. – *n* **Plimsoll line, mark** loadline.

plinth *n* the square slab at the foot of a column; the base or pedestal of a statue, vase *etc*.

plod *v* to travel slowly and steadily; to work on steadily: – *pt* **'plodded**. – *n* **'plodder** a dull or slow but hard-working person.

plop *n* the sound like that of a small object falling into water. – Also *v*: – *pt* **plopped**.

plot *n* a small piece of ground; a plan, *esp* for doing evil; the story of a play, novel *etc*. – *v* to plan secretly; to make a chart, plan, graph *etc* of; to mark points on

one of these: – *pt* **'plotted**. – *n* **'plotter**.

plough [plow] *n* a type of farm tool for turning up the soil; **Plough** (with **the**) a group of seven stars forming a shape like a plough. – *v* to turn up the ground in furrows; to work one's way through slowly. *He is ploughing through his homework*. – *n* **'ploughshare** the blade of the plough.

plover ['pluvər] *n* any of several kinds of birds that nest on the ground in open country.

pluck *v* to pull, pull out or off; to pick (flowers, fruit *etc*); to strip off the feathers of (a bird which is to be eaten). – *n* courage, spirit. – *adj* **'plucky** brave, determined. – **pluck up courage** to prepare oneself (to face a danger, difficulty *etc*).

plug *n* an object which can be fitted into a hole to stop it up; a fitting put into a socket to connect an appliance to an electric current. – *v* to stop up with a plug; (*coll*) to advertise, publicize *etc* by mentioning repeatedly: – *pt* **plugged**.

plum *n* a kind of fruit, *usu* dark red or purple with a stone in the centre; the tree that bears it. – *adj* very good, very profitable *etc*: *a plum job*. – *ns* **plum cake, pudding**, a rich cake, pudding containing raisins, currants *etc*.

plumage *see* **plume**.

plumb [plum] *n* a lead weight hung on a string (**'plumbline**), used *eg* to test if a wall has been built straight up. – *adj*, *adv* standing straight up, vertical. – *v* to test the depth of (the sea *etc*).

plumber ['plumər] *n* one who fits and mends water, gas and sewage pipes. – *n* **'plumbing** the work of a plumber; the drainage and water systems of a building *etc*.

plume [ploom] *n* a feather, *esp* a large showy one, or one worn as an ornament on a hat *etc*; something looking like a feather: *a plume of smoke*; a crest. – *n* **'plumage** the feathers of a bird.

'plummet *n* a weight of lead hung on a line, for taking depths at sea. – *v* to plunge.

plump *adj* fat, rounded, well-filled out. – *v* to (cause to) grow fat, swell; to beat or shake cushions (*etc*) back into shape; to sit or sink down heavily; (with **for**) to choose, give one's vote for.

'plunder *v* to carry off (another's) goods by force, to loot, rob. – *n* goods seized by force.

plunge [plunj] *v* to throw oneself (into water *etc*), to dive; to rush or lurch forward; to put or thrust suddenly into water or other material *etc*. *He plunged the knife into its neck.* – *n* an act of plunging; a dive.

plural ['plooərəl] *adj* more than one. – *n* (in grammar) the form which shows more than one (*eg* mice is the plural of *mouse*).

plus *prep* used to show addition and represented by the sign (+). *Five plus two equals seven, or* 5+2=7. – *adj*, *n* (of) a quantity more than zero. – *adv* (*coll*) and a bit extra. *He earns £3000 plus.*

plush *n* a type of cloth with a soft velvety surface on one side. – *adj* luxurious.

plutocrat ['plootəkrat] *n* a wealthy person or one who is powerful because of his money. – *adj* pluto'cratic.

plȳ *v* to work at steadily; to make regular journeys. *This ferry plies between Dover and Calais*; to use (energetically), *eg* a tool *etc*; to keep supplying someone with something (*eg* food, questions to answer *etc*): – *pt* **plied.** – *ns* 'plier one who plies; (*see* also **pliers**); 'plywood a board made up of thin sheets of wood glued together. – *adj* 'two- ('three- *etc*) **ply** having two (three *etc*) layers, thicknesses, single strands *etc*.

pneumatic [nū'matik] *adj* filled with air; worked by air: *pneumatic drill.*

pneumonia [nū'mōniə] *n* a type of disease in which the lungs become inflamed.

poach *v* to cook something (as eggs without their shells) in boiling water, or other liquid; (to trespass in order) to catch fish or hunt game illegally. – *n* 'poacher one who steals game.

'pocket *n* a small pouch or bag (as in a garment, suit, billiard table); one's supply of money; a small isolated area or group: *a pocket of unemployment.* – *v* to put in the pocket; to steal. – *ns* 'pocket-book a wallet for holding papers or money carried in the pocket; **pocket money** (an allowance of) money for personal spending. – **in, out of, pocket** having gained, having lost money on a deal *etc*.

'pockmark *n* a scar or small hole in the skin left by smallpox *etc*.

pod *n* the long seed-case of the pea, bean *etc*. – *v* to remove from the pod; to form pods: – *pt* 'podded.

podgy ['poji] *adj* (short and) fat.

poem ['pōim] *n* a piece of writing (of a striking or imaginative kind) set out in lines which *usu* have a regular rhythm and often rhyme. – *n* 'poet one who writes poetry. – *adj* pō'etic of or like poetry. – *n* poetry ['pōitri] the art of writing poems.

'pogrom *n* an organized killing or massacre of certain people (*esp* the Jews).

poignant ['poinyənt] *adj* sharp, keen; very painful, sad or moving.

point *n* a sharp end of anything; a headland; a dot: *a decimal point*; (in punctuation) a full stop; an exact place or spot; an exact moment of time; the chief matter or a detail of an argument; the meaning of a joke *etc*; a mark (*eg* in a competition); a purpose, advantage. *There is no point in going*; a movable rail to direct a railway engine from one line to another; an electrical wall socket into which plugs are inserted; a mark of character. *He has many good points.* – *v* to make pointed. *Point your toes*; to direct, aim; to call attention to. *He pointed to the building*; to fill the joints (of a wall) with mortar. – *adj* 'pointed having a (sharp) point; sharp; (of a remark *etc*) obviously aimed at someone. – *n* 'pointer a rod for pointing; a type of dog that can show a huntsman *etc* where game is. – *adj* 'pointless having no meaning or purpose. – *adj* 'point-'blank (of a shot) fired from very close range; (of a question *etc*) direct.

poise [poiz] *v* to balance, keep (something) in a steady position; to hover in the air. – *n* state of balance; dignity, self-confidence. – *adj* poised balanced; having poise; (with **for**) prepared or ready for action.

poison ['poizn] *n* any substance which, when taken into the body, kills or harms; anything harmful. – *v* to kill or harm with poison; to make harmful by adding poison to; to make bitter or bad (*eg* someone's mind). – *adj* 'poisonous harmful because of having poison in it; causing evil.

poke *v* to push (something *eg* a finger, stick into something) prod, thrust at; to search about, *esp* inquisitively. – *n* a nudge or a prod; a prying search. – *n* 'poker a kind of rod for stirring up a fire; a kind of card game. – *adj* 'poky small, cramped, shabby.

polar *see* **pole.**

'pōlder *n* land below the level of the sea reclaimed for use.

pole *n* a long rounded rod or post; formerly, a measure of length (about 5 metres) or area (about 27·6 square metres; the north or south end of the earth's axis (**the north, south, pole**); (*pl*) the points in the heavens opposite to the north and south poles; (*pl*) the opposite points of a magnet or electric battery. – *adj* **'polar** of the regions round the north or south poles. – *n* **'pole-star** the star nearest to the north pole of the heavens.

polecat ['pōlkat] *n* a large kind of weasel; (*US*) a skunk.

police [pə'lēs] *n* the body of men and women whose work it is to keep order, see that the laws are obeyed *etc*. – *v* to keep law and order (in a place) by use of police. – *ns* **po'liceman, po'licewoman; police station** the headquarters of the police in a district.

'policy *n* a (planned or agreed) course of action; a written agreement with an insurance company: – *pl* **'policies**.

'pōlio short for **poliomyelitis**.

poliomyelitis ['pōliōmiə'lītis] *n* a kind of disease of the spinal cord, causing weakness or paralysis of the muscles.

'polish *v* to make smooth and shiny by rubbing; to improve (a piece of writing *etc*); to make polite or refined (a person's manner *etc*). – *n* a gloss on a surface; a substance used for polishing; fine manners, style *etc*.

po'lite *adj* having good manners, courteous. – *n* **po'liteness**.

'politic *adj* wise, cautious. – *adj* **po'litical** of government, politicians, or politics. – *ns* **poli'tician** someone (*eg* a member of parliament) whose business is politics; **'politics** the art or study of government.

'polka *n* a kind of lively dance or the music for it.

pōll *n* a counting of voters at an election; total number of votes; the testing of public opinion by means of questioning (also **opinion poll**). – *v* to cut or clip off (hair, horns, branches *etc*); to receive a certain number of votes. *He polled 5000 votes.* – *n* **polling station** a place where voting is done.

'pollard *n* a tree having the whole top cut off, so that new branches grow from the top of the stem. – *v* to cut the top off (a tree).

'pollen *n* the fertilizing powder of flowers. – *v* **'pollinate** to fertilize with pollen. – *n* **polli'nation**.

pollute [pə'lōōt] *v* to make dirty or impure. – *n* **pol'lution** the act of polluting; dirt.

'pōlo *n* a kind of game like hockey played on horseback. – *n* **polo neck** on a garment, a close fitting neck with a part turned over at the top; a garment with a neck like this.

poltergeist ['poltərgīst] *n* a kind of ghost said to move furniture and throw objects around a room.

poly- *prefix* many, much.

po'lygamy *n* the custom or state of having more than one wife (or husband) at the same time. – *n* **po'lygamist**. – *adj* **po'lygamous**.

'polyglot *adj* speaking (or written in) many languages.

'polygon *n* a figure of many angles and sides. – *adj* **po'lygonal**.

'polysyllable *n* a word of three or more syllables. – *adj* **polysyl'labic**.

polytechnic [poli'teknik] *n* a kind of college in which technical subjects such as engineering, building *etc* are taught.

polythene ['polithēn] *n* the name of several types of plastic that can be moulded when hot.

pomegranate ['pomigranət] *n* a type of fruit with a thick skin and many seeds.

pommel ['puml] *n* the knob on the hilt of a sword; the high part of a saddle.

pomp *n* solemn and splendid ceremony, magnificence. – *adj* **'pompous** self-important in manner or speech, excessively dignified.

'poncho *n* a type of S. American cloak made of, or made like, a blanket with a hole for the head: – *pl* **'ponchos**.

pond *n* a small lake or pool.

'ponder *v* to think over, consider. – *adj* **'ponderous** weighty; clumsy; sounding very important.

poniard ['ponyərd] *n* a kind of small dagger.

'pontiff *n* (in the Roman Catholic Church) a bishop, *esp* the pope. – *adj* **pon'tifical** of, belonging to a pontiff; pompous in speech. – *v* **pon'tificate** to speak in a pompous manner.

pon'toon *n* a kind of flat-bottomed boat used with others to support a temporary platform or roadway (a **pontoon bridge**); a kind of card-game.

'pōny *n* a small horse: – *pl* **'ponies**. – *n* **'pony-trekking** riding cross-country in small parties.

'poodle *n* a breed of dog, with curly hair often clipped in a fancy way.

pool *n* a small area of still water; a deep part of a stream or river; a (joint) fund, stock or supply (*eg* of money, typists *etc*); the money played for in certain games, gambles *etc*. – *v* to put money *etc* into a joint fund. – *n* (**football**) **pools** organized betting on football match results.

poop *n* the back part (or stern) of a ship; a high deck in the stern.

poor *adj* having little money or property; not good. *Your work is poor*; lacking (in): *poor in sports facilities*; deserving pity. *Poor Tom has broken his leg.* – *n* (with **the**) those with little money. – *adj* **'poorly** in bad health, ill.

pop *n* a sharp quick kind of noise, like that made by a cork as it comes out of a bottle; a kind of fizzy drink; popular music. – *v* to (cause to) make a pop; to move quickly: *pop in*: – *pt* **popped**. – *adj* (of music *etc*) short for **popular**. – *n* **'popcorn** a kind of maize that bursts open when heated.

pope *n* the bishop of Rome, head of the Roman Catholic Church.

'popinjay *n* a person who is conceited, *esp* about his dress.

'poplar *n* a type of tall, narrow quick-growing tree.

'poplin *n* a strong kind of (cotton) cloth.

'poppy *n* a type of plant with large *usu* red flowers: – *pl* **'poppies**.

'populace *n* the common people.

'popular *adj* of the people: *popular vote*; liked by most people; widely held or believed: *popular belief*. – *n* **popu'larity** the state of being generally liked. – *v* **'popularize** to make popular or widely known.

popu'lation *n* the (number of) people living in a place. – *v* **'populate** to fill (an area *etc*) with people. – *adj* **'populous** full of people.

porcelain ['pörsəlin] *n* a kind of fine china.

porch [pörch] *n* a covered entrance to a building: – *pl* **'porches**.

porcupine ['pörküpin] *n* one of the largest kinds of gnawing animals, covered with sharp quills.

pore *n* a tiny hole *esp* that of a sweat gland in the skin. – *v* (with **over**) to study closely or eagerly. – *adj* **'porous** having pores; (of a material *etc*) allowing fluid to pass through.

pork [pörk] *n* the flesh of the pig.

por'nography *n* literature or art that is indecent in a sexual way. – *adj* **porno'graphic**.

porous *see* **pore**.

porpoise ['pörpəs] *n* a type of blunt-nosed sea animal of the dolphin family, about 1½ metres (5 feet) long.

'porridge *n* a food made from oatmeal boiled in water (or milk).

port [pört] *n* a harbour, or a town with a harbour; the left side of a ship as one faces the front; a strong, dark-red kind of sweet wine. – *n* **'porter** one who carries luggage *etc*; a doorkeeper; a kind of dark brown beer.

portable ['pörtəbl] *adj* able to be lifted and carried.

portal ['pörtl] *n* an entrance or doorway, *usu* of a grand kind.

portcullis [pört'kulis] *n* a grating of crossed woodwork or ironwork which can be let down quickly to close a gateway (as in old castles): – *pl* **port'cullises**.

portend [pör'tend] *v* to give warning of, foretell. – *n* **'portent** a warning sign. – *adj* **por'tentous** like a warning; strange or wonderful; important, solemn.

porter *see* **port**.

portfolio [pört'föliö] *n* a case for carrying papers, drawings *etc*; the post or job of a government minister: – *pl* **port'folios**.

port-hole ['pört-höl] *n* a small (*usu* round) window in a ship's side.

portico ['pörtikö] *n* a row of columns in front of a building forming a porch or covered walk: – *pl* **'portico(e)s**.

portion ['pörshən] *n* a part; a share, a helping (of food *etc*). – *v* to divide into parts.

portly ['pörtli] *adj* stout (and dignified).

portmanteau [pört'mantö] *n* a kind of large leather travelling bag.

portrait ['pörtrət] *n* a drawing, painting, or photograph of a person; a description (of a person, place *etc*). – *v* **por'tray** to paint or draw (someone or something); to describe in words; to act the part of: – *pt* **por'trayed**. – *n* **por'trayal** an act of portraying; a description or portrait.

pose [pöz] *n* a position or attitude of the body: *a relaxed pose*; a manner or some kind of behaviour put on to impress others, a pretence. – *v* to place or position oneself (for a photograph, for a good effect *etc*); (with **as**) to pretend or claim to be what one is not. *He posed as a doctor*; to put forward or set (a problem, question *etc*). – *ns* **'poser** one who poses; a difficult question; **poseur** [pö'zör] one who puts on poses.

posh *adj* (*coll*) high-class; smart.

position [pə'zishən] *n* place, situation: *the position of the house*; manner of standing, sitting *etc*, posture: *in a crouching position*; a rank or job: *a high position in a bank*. – *v* to place.

positive ['pozətiv] *adj* meaning or saying 'yes': *a positive answer*; not able to be doubted: *positive proof*; certain, convinced. *I am positive that she did it*; definite: *a positive improvement*; (of a quantity) greater than zero; (in grammar) of the first degree of comparison of adjectives or adverbs *eg big* in 'He is big but she is bigger'.

posse ['posi] *n* a force or body (of police *etc*).

possess [pə'zes] *v* to own or to have; to

take hold of one's mind: *anger possesses me*. – *adj* **pos'sessed** in the power of a driving (and evil) force or spirit; self-possessed, calm. – *n* **pos'session** the state of possessing; the state of being possessed; something owned. – *adj* **pos'sessive** showing possession *esp* in grammar, as the adjectives *my*, *your*, *his* *etc*; regarding or treating (a person *eg* one's child) as a possession. – *n* **pos'sessor** the owner.

'possible *adj* able to happen or to be done; able to be true, not unlikely (as a reason, explanation *etc*). – *n* **possi'bility** the state of being possible; something that may happen or that may be done: – *pl* **possi'bilities**. – *adv* **'possibly** perhaps.

pōst *n* a pole or stake (of wood, iron *etc*) *usu* fixed upright in the ground; (the system of carrying) letters and other mail; a job: *a teaching post*; a place of duty. *The soldier remained at his post*; a settlement, camp *etc* often in a remote area: *a military post: trading post*. – *v* to put (a letter in on a postbox for collection; to send or to station somewhere. *His army unit was posted abroad*; to put up, stick up (*a notice etc*). – *n* **'postage** money paid for sending a letter *etc* by post. – *adj* **'postal** of or by post. – *n* **'poster** a large notice or placard. – *ns* **postage stamp** a small printed label to show that postage has been paid; **postal order** a paper form bought at a post office which can be exchanged for the amount of money printed on it; **'postbox** a box with an opening in which to post letters *etc*; **'postcard** a card on which a message may be sent by post, often sent by people on holiday. – *adv* **post-'free** without charge for postage. – *adv* **post-'haste** with great speed. – *ns* **'postman** one who delivers letters; **'postmark** a mark showing the date, put on a letter at a post office; **'postmaster** an official in charge of a post office; **post office** an office for receiving and sending off letters by post *etc*.

pōst- *prefix* after.

pos'tērior *adj* situated behind, coming after. – *n* the buttocks.

pos'terity *n* all future generations; a person's descendants.

'pōstern *n* a back door or gate (to a castle *etc*).

pōst'gradūate *adj* (of studies, degree *etc*) following on from a first university degree. – *n* a person continuing his studies after he has gained his first degree.

posthumous ['postūməs] *adj* (of a book) published after the author's death; (of a child) born after the father's death.

pos'til(l)ion *n* (*old*) one who guides the horses of a carriage, and rides on one of them.

pōst'mortem *n* an examination of a dead body (to find out the cause of death).

postpone [pəs'pōn] *v* to put off to a future time, to delay. – *n* **post'ponement**.

'postscript *n* a part added as an afterthought at the end of a letter, after the sender's name.

'postūlate *v* to assume or take for granted (that).

'posture ['poschər] *n* the manner in which one holds oneself in standing, walking *etc*; a position or pose.

postwar ['pōst'wör] *adj* of, belonging to the time after a war.

posy ['pōzi] *n* a small bunch of flowers: – *pl* **'posies**.

pot *n* any one of many kinds of deep vessels, containers, jars *etc* used in cooking, for holding foods, liquids *etc*, or for growing plants; (*slang*) marijuana; (*pl*) (*coll*) a great deal of: *pots of money*. – *v* to plant in a pot; to make articles of baked clay: – *pt* **'potted**. – *adj* **'potted** (of meat *etc*) pressed down and preserved in a pot or jar; (of a book *etc*) made shorter and easier to understand. – *n* **'pothole** a hole made in a rock by swirling water, a deep cave (sometimes explored by **'potholers**); a hole worn in a road surface. – **take pot-luck** to have a meal with someone as a guest without any special preparations being made.

'potash *n* potassium carbonate, a substance obtained from the ashes of wood.

po'tassium *n* an element, a type of silvery-white metal.

po'tāto *n* a type of plant with round underground stems (**tubers**) which are used as a vegetable; the vegetable itself: – *pl* **po'tatoes**.

'pōtent *adj* powerful, strong. – *ns* **'potency**; **'potentate** one with power, a prince, a ruler. – *adj* **potential** [pə'tenshəl] that may develop, possible. – *n* the possibility or promise of further development. – *n* **potentiality** [pətenshi'aləti] a possibility; something that may develop.

potion ['pōshən] *n* a drink (often one containing medicine or poison).

pot-pourri [pōpoo'rē] *n* a scented mixture of dried petals *etc*; a mixture or medley.

'potter *n* one who makes articles of baked clay. – *v* to do small odd jobs; to dawdle. – *n* **'pottery** articles made of baked clay; a place where such things are made; the art of making them.

pouch *n* a kind of pocket or small bag; a bag-like formation, *esp* that on the front of a kangaroo, for carrying its young: – *pl* **'pouches**.

pouffe [pōof] *n* a kind of low, stuffed seat.

poultice ['pōltis] *n* a (hot) wet and sticky type of dressing spread on a bandage and put on inflamed areas of skin. – *v* to put a poultice on.

poultry ['pōltri] *n* farmyard fowls, *eg* hens, ducks, geese, turkeys. – *n* **'poulterer** one who sells poultry and game for food.

pounce *v* (with **on**) to fall upon, swoop down on, and seize or attack. – *n* the claw of a bird; a sudden swoop.

pound *n* the standard unit of money in Britain, shown by the sign (£), 100 new pence (in old money, 20 shillings); a measure of weight, written lb (about $\frac{1}{2}$ kilogramme, 16 ounces); a pen or enclosure (*esp* one for animals). – *v* to beat into small pieces or powder; to beat or bruise; to walk or run with heavy steps.

pour [pōr] *v* to (cause to) flow in a stream. *The blood poured out. She poured the tea*; to rain heavily. *It is pouring.*

pout *v* to push out the lips sulkily to show displeasure. – Also *n*.

'poverty *n* the state of being poor; want or need: *poverty of ideas.*

powder ['powdər] *n* any substance made up of very fine particles, fine dust; gunpowder; face powder. – *v* to sprinkle with powder, put powder on; to grind down to powder. – *adjs* **'powdered** in the form of a fine dust; covered with powder; **'powdery** covered with powder; like powder: *powdery snow.*

power ['powər] *n* strength; force; ability to do things; authority or legal right; a strong nation; a person or persons in authority; rule; the force used for driving machines: *electric power: steam power*; (in physics *etc*) the rate of doing work; (in mathematics) the product obtained by multiplying a number by itself a given number of times (*eg* $2 \times 2 \times 2$ or 2^3 is the third power of 2). – *adjs* **'powered** supplied with mechanical power; **'powerful; 'powerless** without power or ability. – *adj* **'power-'driven** worked by electricity *etc*, not

by hand. – *n* **power station** a building where electricity is produced.

pow-wow ['pow-wow] *n* (*hist*) a discussion with, or held by, N. American Indians; (*coll*) any conference.

'practicable *adj* able to be used or done.

'practical *adj* liking action (rather than thought *etc*); efficient; learned by practice, rather than from books. *He has practical knowledge of carpentry.* – *adv* **'practically** in a practical way; in effect or reality; (*coll*) almost: *practically no money.* – *n* **practical joke** a joke consisting of action, not words, *usu* causing annoyance to the person it is played on.

practice ['praktis] *n* habit. *It is my practice to get up early*; the actual doing (of something). *I always intend to get up early but in practice I stay in bed late*; exercise by means of repeated performance to gain skill (in playing a musical instrument, in preparation for a race, match *etc*); the business of a doctor, lawyer, dentist *etc*.

practise, (*US*) **practice** ['praktis] *v* to do exercises in, train in, take lessons in so as to get and keep a skill. *He practises judo nightly*; to put into action or practice, make a habit of: *to practise self-control*; to follow (one's profession). *He used to practise as a surgeon.* – *n* **prac'titioner** one engaged in a profession: *a medical practitioner.*

prag'matic(al) *adj* concerned with matters of fact, rather than ideas and theories, practical.

prairie ['prāri] *n* (in N. America) a stretch of level land, without trees and covered with grass.

praise [prāz] *v* to speak highly of (a person or thing); to glorify (God) by singing hymns *etc*. – *n* an expression of approval or honour. – *adj* **'praiseworthy** deserving to be praised.

pram *n* a kind of small four-wheeled carriage for pushing a baby in (short for **perambulator**).

prance *v* to strut or swagger about; to dance or jump about; (of a horse) to spring from the hind legs.

prank *n* a trick played for mischief.

prate *v* to talk foolishly.

'prattle *v* to talk or chatter meaninglessly or in a childish way. – Also *n*.

prawn *n* a type of shellfish like the shrimp.

pray *v* to ask earnestly, beg; to speak to God in prayer. – *n* **prayer** an act of praying; an earnest request for something; (often *pl*) that part of worship in which requests are made, and thanks given to God.

prē- *prefix* before.

preach *v* to give a sermon; to teach, speak in favour of. *He preaches caution.* – *n* **'preacher**.

prē'amble *n* something said as an introduction.

prearrange [prēə'rānj] *v* to arrange beforehand.

pre'cārious *adj* uncertain, risky, dangerous.

pre'caution *n* care taken beforehand (to avoid an accident, a disease *etc*). – *adj* **pre'cautionary**.

pre'cede *v* to go before in time, rank or importance. – *n* **precedence** ['presidəns] the act or right of going before; **'precedent** a past action which may serve as an example or rule in the future. – *adj* **pre'cēding** going before; previous.

'precept *n* a rule to guide one's action; a commandment.

'precinct *n* the ground enclosed by the boundary walls of a building *esp* a cathedral; (*pl*) the area closely surrounding any place; (*esp US*) an administrative district. – *n* **shopping precinct** a shopping centre *esp* when closed to cars *etc*.

precious ['preshəs] *adj* of great price or worth; highly valued.

precipice ['presipis] *n* a steep cliff. – *adj* **pre'cipitous** very steep.

pre'cipitate *v* to throw head foremost; to force into (hasty action *etc*); to bring on suddenly, to hasten (death, illness *etc*). – *adj* headlong; hasty, rash. – *n* the substance which settles at the bottom of a liquid. – *n* **precipi'tation** an act of precipitating; great hurry; rash haste; (the amount of) rainfall.

precipitous *see* **precipice**.

précis ['prāsē] *n* a summary of a piece of writing: – *pl* **précis** ['prāsēz].

pre'cise *adj* definite; exact, accurate. – *n* **precision** [prə'sizhən] preciseness; exactness, accuracy.

preclude [pri'kloōd] *v* to prevent; to make impossible.

precocious [prə'kōshəs] *adj* (often of children, their speech or knowledge) unexpectedly advanced or well-developed. – *n* **precocity** [prə'kosəti].

preconceive [prēkən'sēv] *v* to form (ideas *etc*) before having actual knowledge or experience. – *n* **preconception** [prēkən'sepshən] an act of preconceiving; an idea formed without actual knowledge.

pre'cursor *n* a person or thing which goes before, *esp* as a sign of something to come: *the precursor of jazz.*

'predator *n* a bird or animal that attacks and kills others for food; a creature that plunders (crops *etc*). – *adj* **'predatory** of a predator; (of a person) in the habit of using others for one's own gain, *esp* financial.

predecease ['prēdi'sēs] *v* to die before (someone).

predecessor ['prēdisesər] *n* a person who has held an office or position before another.

predetermine [prēdi'tərmin] *v* to settle beforehand.

pre'dicament *n* an unfortunate or difficult situation.

'predicate *n* (in grammar) what is said about the subject of a sentence (as *is sad* in the sentence *Jack is sad*).

pre'dict *v* to foretell, forecast. – *adj* **pre'dictable** able to be foretold, forecast. – *n* **pre'diction** an act of predicting; something predicted.

prēdi'lection *n* a preference, a liking for something.

prēdis'pose *v* to turn a person in favour of (something) beforehand. *We were predisposed to believe him*; to make liable or subject (to). *His weak chest predisposes him to colds.* – *n* **predispo'sition**.

pre'dominate *v* to be the stronger or the greater in number; to have control (over). – *n* **pre'dominance**. – *adj* **pre'dominant** ruling; most or more noticeable or outstanding.

prē-'eminent *adj* outstanding, excelling all others. – *n* **pre-'eminence**.

preen *v* to arrange feathers, as birds do; to smarten one's appearance *esp* in a conceited way. – **preen oneself** to take or show obvious pride in one's achievements *etc*.

prē'fabricated *adj* (of a building *etc*) made of parts manufactured beforehand, ready to be fitted together.

preface ['prefəs] *n* an introduction (to a book *etc*). – *v* to start or introduce with a preface. *He prefaced his rebuke with a smile.*

'prēfect *n* one set in authority over others; (in schools) a senior pupil having certain powers.

pre'fer *v* to like better, choose one thing rather than another. *I prefer tea to coffee. I prefer to walk rather than go by bus*; to put forward (a claim or request): – *pt* **pre'ferred**. – *adj* **'preferable** more desirable. – *n* **'preference** greater liking, the choice of one thing rather than another; the thing that is preferred. – *adj* **prefe'rential** showing, giving preference.

– *n* **pre'ferment** promotion.

'**prefix** *n* a syllable or word put at the beginning of a word to alter its meaning (as *dis-*, *un-*, *re-*, in *dis*like, *un*happy, *re*gain): – *pl* '**prefixes**.

'**pregnant** *adj* carrying an unborn baby (or young) in the womb; (of words, a pause *etc*) full of meaning. – *n* '**pregnancy** the state of being pregnant.

pre'hensile *adj* able to grasp or hold on to something: *a prehensile tail.*

prehistoric [prēis'torik] *adj* belonging to the time before history was written down. – *n* **prehistory** ['prē'histəri].

'**prē'judge** *v* to judge or decide (something) before hearing the facts of a case.

prejudice ['prejədis] *n* an unreasonable or unfair feeling (for or against anything); an opinion formed without careful thought; harm, injury: *to the prejudice of your chances.* – *v* to fill with prejudice; to do harm to, damage. *His late arrival prejudiced his chances of success in the examination.* – *adjs* '**prejudiced** having, showing prejudice; **prejudicial** [prejə'dishəl] damaging, harmful.

prelate ['prelət] *n* a bishop, archbishop or other clergyman of high rank. – *n* '**prelacy** the office of a prelate: – *pl* '**prelacies**.

pre'liminary *adj* going before, preparing the way: *a preliminary investigation.* – *n* something that goes before: – *pl* **pre'liminaries**.

'**prelude** *n* a piece of music played as an introduction to the main piece; an event *etc* that goes before and acts as an introduction. *That first success was a prelude to a brilliant career.*

premature ['premәchoor] *adj* coming, born *etc* before the right, proper or expected time.

pre'meditate *v* to think out beforehand, plan, intend: *premeditated murder.* – *n* **premedi'tation**.

premier ['premiər] *adj* first, leading, foremost. – *n* a prime minister. – *n* **première** ['premiər] a first performance (of a play *etc*).

premise, premiss ['premis] *n* something assumed from which a conclusion is drawn: – *pls* '**premises, 'premisses**.

premises ['premisiz] *npl* a building (or part of a building) and its grounds. *These premises are used by the local football team.*

'**premium** *n* a reward; (yearly) payment on an insurance policy: – *pl* '**premiums**. – **at a premium** much

valued or desired and so difficult to obtain. *Tickets for the cup final were at a premium.*

prēmo'nition *n* feeling that something is going to happen; a warning.

pre'occupy *v* to take up completely the attention of (someone). – *n* **preoccu- 'pation** the act of preoccupying; the state of being preoccupied; that which preoccupies. – *adj* **pre'occupied** deep in thought.

prepaid *see* **prepay**.

pre'pare *v* to make or get ready; to train or equip. – *n* **preparation** [prepə'rāshən] an act of preparing; (shortened to **prep**) study for a lesson in class; something prepared, made ready (*eg* a medicine, face-cream *etc*). – *adjs* **preparatory** [prə'parətəri] acting as an introduction or first step; **pre'pared** ready; willing. – *n* **pre- paratory school** a private school educating children in preparation for a public or other senior school. – **pre- paratory to** before, in preparation for.

'**prē'pay** *v* to pay beforehand: – *pt* '**prē'paid**. – *n* '**pre'payment**.

pre'ponderate *v* to be greater in weight, power, or number. – *n* **pre'ponder- ance** greater weight, power, or number. *There was a preponderance of young people in the audience.*

prepo'sition *n* (in grammar) a word placed before a noun or pronoun to show how it is related to another word, as '*through* the door', '*in* the town', 'written *by* me'.

prepossessing [prēpə'zesiŋ] *adj* pleasant, attractive, making a good impression.

pre'posterous *adj* very foolish, absurd.

prerequisite [prē'rekwizit] *n* something necessary before a thing can be done or can happen.

prerogative [prə'rogətiv] *n* a privilege or right enjoyed by a person because of his rank or position.

presage ['presij] *v* to foretell, warn of.

Presbyterian [prezbi'tēriən] *adj* (of a church) having business and other affairs managed by **presbyters** ['prezbitərz] (ministers and elders). – *n* '**presbytery** a body of presbyters; (in the Roman Catholic Church) a priest's house.

pres'cribe *v* to lay down as a rule; to order the use of (a medicine). – *n* **prescription** [prəs'kripshən] a doc- tor's (*usu* written) instructions for the preparing of a medicine; something prescribed; the act of prescribing. – *adj* **prescriptive** [prəs'kriptiv] laying down rules; (of rights *etc*) based on custom or habit.

presence ['prezns] *n* the state of being present (opposite of **absence**); one's personal appearance, manner *etc*. – *adj* '**present** being here or in the place spoken of, thought of *etc*; belonging to the time in which we are: *the present prime minister*: *the present situation*. – *n* the time we are now at; a gift; (in grammar) the present tense. – *v* **pre'sent** to hand over (a gift) *esp* formally; to offer; to set forth, put forward; to introduce (a person) to another. – *adj* **pre'sentable** fit to be seen (or given). – *n* **presen'tation** the act of handing over a present; the present itself; a setting forth (of a statement, ideas *etc*); a showing (of a play *etc*); — *adv* **presently** soon. **presence of mind** calmness, ability to act sensibly in an emergency, difficulty *etc*.

presentiment [pri'zentimənt] *n* a feeling that something unpleasant is about to happen, a foreboding.

preserve [pri'zɜrv] *v* to keep safe from harm; to keep in existence, to maintain; to treat (food) in such a way that it will not go bad or rotten. – *n* private ground; a place where game animals, birds *etc* are protected; jam. – *ns* **preser'vation** the act of preserving; the state of being preserved; **pre'servative** something that preserves, *esp* something that helps to prevent food from going bad.

preside [pri'zid] *v* to be chairman or to be in charge at a meeting *etc*. – *ns* **presidency** ['prezidənsi] the office or rank of a president; '**president** the leading member of a club, institution *etc*; the head of a republic.

press *v* to push on, against or down; to squeeze; to urge, force; to smooth out, iron (clothes *etc*). – *n* an act of pressing; a crowd; a printing machine; newspapers and magazines as a whole; those involved in writing and producing newspapers *etc*. – *adj* '**pressing** requiring action at once, insistent. – *n* **pressure** ['preshər] the act of pressing; the state of being pressed; force on or against a surface; strong persuasion, compulsion; stress, strain; urgency. – *v* '**pressurize** to fit (an aeroplane *etc*) with a device that maintains normal air pressure; to force (someone to do something). – *ns* **pressure cooker** a type of pan in which food is cooked quickly by steam under great pressure; **pressure group** a group of people who

try to persuade the authorities *etc* to take a particular course of action.

'**pressgang** *n* (*hist*) a body of men once employed to carry off men by force into the army or navy. – Also *v*.

prestige [pres'tēzh] *n* reputation, influence due to rank, success *etc*.

presume [prə'zūm] *v* to take for granted; to act impertinently, take the liberty of (doing something); (with **on**) to take advantage of (someone's kindness *etc*). – *adv* **pre'sumably** probably. – *n* **presumption** [pri'zumpshən] something supposed; a strong likelihood; impertinent behaviour. – *adj* **presumptuous** [pri'zumpshəs] unsuitably bold.

presuppose [presə'pōz] *v* to take for granted.

pre'tend *v* to make believe. *Pretend you are a witch*; to put on a false show or make a false claim. *He pretended to be ill.* – *ns* **pre'tence** the act of pretending; make-believe; a (false) claim; **pre'tender** one who lays claim to something (*esp* to the title of king); **pre'tension** a claim (whether true or not); self-importance. – *adj* **pretentious** [pri'tenshəs] claiming more than is deserved or justified; self-important; showy, ostentatious.

preterite, preterit ['pretə-rit] *adj* past. — *n* (a word in) the past tense.

preternatural [prētər'nachərəl] *adj* beyond what is natural, abnormal.

'**prētext** *n* an excuse.

pretty ['priti] *adj* pleasing or attractive to see, listen to *etc*. – *adv* fairly, quite: *pretty good*. – *n* '**prettiness**.

pre'vail *v* (with **against** or **over**) to gain control or victory over; to win, succeed; (with **on**, **upon**) to persuade. *He prevailed upon me to stay*; to be (most) usual or common. – *adj* **pre'vailing** controlling; most common. – *adj* **prevalent** ['prevələnt] common, widespread. – *n* '**prevalence**.

pre'varicate *v* to avoid telling the truth. – *n* **prevari'cation**.

pre'vent *v* to hinder; to prevent from happening. – *n* the act of preventing. – *n, adj* **pre'ventive** (something) that helps to prevent (illness *etc*).

preview ['prēvū] *n* a viewing of a performance, exhibition *etc* before it is open to the public.

'**prēvious** *adj* going before in time; former. – *adv* '**previously**.

prey [prā] *n* animals (that may be) killed by others for food; a victim. – *v* (with **on** or **upon**) to seize and eat. *The hawk preys upon smaller birds.*

price *n* the money for which a thing is bought or sold, the cost; something that one must give up or suffer in order to gain something. *The price of victory was the lives of many.* – *adj* '**priceless** of very great value; (*coll*) very funny.

prick *v* to pierce slightly; to give a sharp pain to; to stick up (the ears). – *n* an act of piercing; a feeling of being pierced with a small sharp point. – *n* '**prickle** a sharp point growing on a plant or animal. – *v* to be prickly; to feel prickly. – *adj* '**prickly** full of prickles; stinging, pricking.

pride *n* the state of feeling proud; too great an opinion of oneself; a feeling of pleasure in having done something well; dignity; a group of lions. – **pride oneself on** to allow oneself to feel or show pride (about some achievement). *I pride myself on my writing.*

priest [prēst] *n* a clergyman in some Christian religions; an official in a non-Christian religion. – *n* '**priesthood** the office, position of a priest; those who are priests.

prig *n* a smug, self-righteous person. – *adj* '**priggish**.

prim *adj* (of a person, manner *etc*) unnecessarily formal and correct.

prima ballerina ['prēməbalə'rēnə] *n* the leading female dancer of a ballet company. – *n* '**prima** '**donna** a leading female opera singer; an over-sensitive, temperamental woman.

'**primary** *adj* first; chief. – *ns* **primary colours** those from which all others can be made *eg* red, blue and yellow; **primary school** a school for the early stages of education.

primate ['primāt] *n* a member of the highest order of mammals (man, monkeys, apes, lemurs); **primate** ['primət] an archbishop.

prime *adj* first in time, rank or importance; of highest quality, excellent. – *n* the time of greatest health and strength: *the prime of life.* – *v* to prepare by putting something in or on. *He primed the wood before painting it. He primed the pump;* to supply with detailed information. *She was well primed before the meeting.* – *n* '**primer** a simple introductory book in any subject; something that primes (a surface to be painted *etc*). – *n* **prime minister** the head of a government.

pri'mēval *adj* of, belonging to the first ages of the world.

'**primitive** *adj* belonging to very early times; old-fashioned; not skilfully made, rough, clumsy.

primrose ['primrōz] *n* a kind of pale-yellow spring flower common in woods and hedges.

prince *n* a male member of a royal family, *esp* the son of a king or queen; a title given to the ruler of some states or countries: – *fem* **prin'cess**: – *pl* **prin'cesses**. – *adj* '**princely** fit for a prince; splendid.

'**principal** *adj* highest in rank or importance; chief. – *n* the head of a school, college or university; someone who takes a leading part (in a show *etc*); money in a bank *etc* on which interest is paid. – *n* **princi'pality** a country ruled by a prince: – *pl* **princi'palities**. – *adv* '**principally** chiefly, mostly.

'**principle** *n* a general truth, rule or law; the theory on which the working of a machine *etc* is based: *the principle of the combustion engine;* (*pl*) one's own rules of behaviour, sense of right and wrong.

print *v* to mark letters on paper with type (*eg* by using a printing press); to write in capital letters or unjoined small letters; to publish (a book *etc*) in printed form; to stamp patterns on (cloth *etc*); to make a finished photograph. – *n* a mark made by pressure: *footprint*: *fingerprint;* printed lettering; a photograph made from a negative; a printed state. *The book is in print;* a printed reproduction of a painting or drawing; cloth printed with a design. – *n* '**printer** one who prints books, newspapers *etc*.

'**prior** *adj* earlier; previous (to). – *n* the head of a priory: – *fem* '**prioress**. – *ns* **pri'ority** the state of being first in time or position; the right to be first. *An ambulance must have priority in traffic;* something that must be considered or done first. *Our priority is to get him into hospital*: – *pl* **pri'orities**; '**priory** a building where a community of monks or nuns live: – *pl* '**priories**.

prise *v* to force open or off with a kind of lever. *He prised open the safe. He prised off the lid.*

prism ['prizm] *n* a solid body with parallel sides whose two ends are the same shape and size; a glass prism (often with triangular ends).

prison ['prizn] *n* a building for holding criminals, a jail; any place where someone is shut up against his will. – *n* '**prisoner** someone under arrest or locked up in jail; a captured enemy soldier or anyone held in captivity.

pristine ['pristēn] *adj* in the original or unspoilt state.

'**privacy** *n* the state of being away from

company or from observation; secrecy.

'**private** *adj* of, belonging to a person (or a group of people), not to the general public; hidden from view; secret, not made generally known; personal. – *n* the lowest rank of ordinary soldier (not an officer).

priva'teer *n* an armed private vessel with orders from a government to seize and plunder enemy ships.

pri'vation *n* want, poverty, hardship; the act of taking away, loss.

'**privet** *n* a type of shrub used for hedges.

privilege ['privəlij] *n* a favour or right granted to or available to one person or to only a few people. – *adj* '**privileged** having privileges.

'**privy: privy council** *n* a body of statesmen appointed as advisers to a king or queen. – **privy to** knowing about (something secret).

prize *n* reward for good work *etc*; something won in a competition; something captured, *esp* an enemy ship; something highly valued. – *adj* very fine, worthy of a prize. – *v* to value highly. – *n* **prize fight** a boxing match fought for money.

prō- *prefix* before, forward, front; in favour of: *pro-British.* – **pros and cons** the arguments for and against (a plan *etc*).

'**probable** *adj* likely; that may happen; that is likely to be true. – *n* **proba'bility** likelihood; something that is probable: – *pl* **proba'bilities**. – *adv* '**probably** very likely.

pro'bation *n* the testing of a person's conduct, powers, or character; a system of letting law-breakers go without punishment on condition that they commit no more offences and report to social workers (**probation officers**) regularly. – *n* **pro'bationer** one who is training to be a member of a profession.

probe *n* a long, thin instrument used by doctors to examine a wound; a thorough investigation. – *v* to examine very carefully; to investigate thoroughly to try to find out information.

'**prōbity** *n* honesty, goodness of character.

'**problem** *n* a question to be solved; a matter which is difficult to deal with. – *adjs* **proble'matic, proble'matical** doubtful, uncertain.

proboscis [prə'bosis] *n* the nose of an animal or mouth of an insect; the trunk of an elephant: – *pl* **pro'boscises**.

pro'ceed *v* to go on; to begin (to do something); to go on with, continue; to take legal action (against). – *ns* **proce-dure** [prə'sējər] the order or method of doing business; a course of action, or a particular action; **pro'ceeding** a step, a going forward; an action; (*pl*) a record of matters dealt with at the meetings of a society *etc*; (*pl*) a law action. – *npl* '**proceeds** money, profit made from a sale *etc*.

'**prōcess** *n* a method or series of operations used in manufacturing goods; a series of events, actions *etc* producing change or development; course; a law-court case: – *pl* '**processes**. – **in the process of** in the course of. *He lost his watch in the process of moving house.*

pro'cession *n* a line of persons or vehicles moving forward in order.

pro'claim *v* to announce publicly, declare openly. – *n* **proclamation** [proklə'māshən] an official announcement made to the public.

pro'crastinate *v* to put off, delay doing something till a later time. – *n* **procrasti'nation**.

pro'cure *v* to obtain; to bring about. – *n* **procurator-fiscal** ['prokūrātər'fiskəl] (in Scotland) the law officer of a district.

prod *v* to poke; to urge on: – *pt* '**prodded**.

'**prodigal** *adj* spending one's money *etc* without care or thought, wasteful. – *n* **prodi'gality**.

'**prodigy** *n* something astonishing or strange; a person of amazing cleverness: *a child prodigy*: – *pl* '**prodigies**. – *adj* **pro'digious** strange, astonishing; enormous.

pro'duce *v* to bring forth, bring out; to bring into being, to yield; to bring about, cause; to prepare (a programme, play *etc*) for the stage, television *etc*; to make, manufacture. – *ns* '**produce** something that is produced, *esp* on a farm or in a garden, as crops, eggs, milk *etc*; **pro'ducer** one who produces anything, *esp* a play, film *etc*; **product** ['prodəkt] a thing produced; a result; (*pl*) the goods which a country produces; (in mathematics) the number that results from the multiplication of two or more numbers; **pro'duction** the act or process of producing; that which is produced. – *adj* **pro'ductive** fruitful, producing much; bringing results. – *n* **produc'tivity** the rate or efficiency of work done *esp* in industrial production.

pro'fane *adj* not sacred; treating holy things without respect. – *n* **profanity** [prə'fanəti] swearing; lack of respect for sacred things: – *pl* **pro'fanities**.

profess / prompt

pro'fess *v* to declare (a belief *etc*) openly; to pretend or to claim. *He professed to be an expert on Shakespeare.* – *adj* **pro'fessed** declared; pretended. – *n* **pro'fession** an occupation (of a non-mechanical kind) requiring special knowledge (as the work of a doctor, lawyer *etc*); an open declaration. – *adj* **pro'fessional** of a profession; earning (one's living) from a game or an art (opposite of **amateur**): *a professional footballer: a professional singer*; showing the skill *etc* of one who is trained. – Also *n*. – *n* **pro'fessor** a teacher of the highest rank in a university; (*US*) a university teacher.

'proffer *v* to offer. – *n* an offer.

proficiency [prə'fishənsi] *n* skill. – *adj* **pro'ficient** skilled, expert.

'profile *n* an outline; a side view of a face, head *etc*; a short description of someone's life, achievements *etc*.

'profit *n* gain, benefit; the money got by selling an article for a higher price than was paid for it. – *v* to gain or receive benefit (from); to bring gain or benefit to. – *adj* **'profitable** bringing profit or gain. – *n* **profi'teer** one who makes large profits unfairly. – Also *v*.

'profligate *adj* living an immoral life; very extravagant. – Also *n*. – *n* **'profligacy**.

pro'found *adj* very deep; (of a feeling) deeply felt; showing great knowledge or understanding: *a profound comment.* – *n* **pro'fundity** depth; the state or quality of being profound.

pro'fuse *adj* abundant, lavish, extravagant. *He was profuse in his thanks.* – *n* **profusion** [prə'fūzhən] great abundance.

pro'genitor *n* an ancestor. – *n* **'progeny** children.

prog'nosticate *v* to foretell. – *n* **prognosti'cation**.

'programme, (*US*) **'program** *n* (a booklet or sheet giving details of) the items in an entertainment, ceremony *etc*; a scheme or plan; **program** a set of instructions given to a computer to carry out certain actions. – *v* to prepare the series of operations to be carried out by (a machine, *esp* a computer).

'progress *n* advance, forward movement; improvement. – *v* **pro'gress** to go forward; to improve. – *n* **pro'gression** onward movement; advance. – *adj* **pro'gressive** going forward; advancing by stages; favouring reforms.

pro'hibit *v* to forbid; to prevent. – *n* **prohibition** [prōi'bishən] an act of forbidding; the forbidding by law of making and selling alcoholic drinks. – *adj* **prohibitive** [prə'hibitiv] prohibiting; (of prices) so high as to make buying almost impossible.

'project *n* a plan, scheme; a task; a piece of study or research. – *v* **pro'ject** to throw out, forward or up; to jut out; to cast (an image, a light *etc*) on to a surface *etc*; to plan or propose. – *ns* **pro'jectile** a missile; **pro'jection** an act of projecting; something projected; something which juts out; **pro'jector** a machine for projecting pictures on a screen.

proletariat [prōlə'tāriət] *n* the ordinary working people.

proliferate [prə'lifərāt] *v* to grow or increase rapidly. – *adj* **pro'lific** producing much, fruitful; abundant.

'prōlix *adj* using too many words, tiresomely long. – *n* **pro'lixity**.

prologue ['prōlog] *n* a preface or introduction (*esp* to a play *etc*).

pro'long *v* to make longer.

promenade [promə'näd] *n* a level roadway or walk for the public (*esp* alongside the sea); a walk or a stroll. – *v* to walk for pleasure. – *n* **promenade concert** a concert at which a large part of the audience stands instead of being seated (also **prom**).

'prominent *adj* standing out; easily seen; famous, distinguished. – *n* **'prominence**.

pro'miscuous *adj* having many sexual relationships; mixed in kind; not making distinctions between one thing or person and another. – *n* **promis'cuity**.

promise ['promis] *v* to say, give one's word (that one will do or will not do something); to say that one will give (a gift, help *etc*); to show signs for the future. *The weather promises to improve.* – *n* (a statement of) something promised; a sign (of something to come); a sign of future success. *His essay showed great promise.* – *adj* **'promising** showing signs of turning out well or being successful.

'promontory *n* a headland jutting out into the sea: – *pl* **'promontories**.

pro'mote *v* to raise to a higher rank or position; to help onwards, encourage (a scheme, a charity *etc*); to advertise, encourage the buying of (goods). – *n* **pro'motion**.

prompt *adj* acting without delay, quick, immediate; punctual. – *v* to move to action. *She prompted him to demand higher wages*; to supply words to a

237

speaker (*esp* an actor) when he has forgotten what to say. – *ns* '**promptitude**, '**promptness** quickness, readiness; punctuality.

'**promulgate** *v* to make widely known. – *n* **promul'gation**.

prone *adj* lying face downward; inclined (to): *prone to laziness*.

prong *n* the spike of a fork. – *adj* **pronged** having prongs.

'**pronoun** *n* a word used instead of a noun (*eg* I, you, who).

pro'nounce *v* to speak (words, sounds); to announce (one's opinion), declare. – *adj* **pro'nounced** noticeable, marked. – *ns* **pro'nouncement** a statement, announcement; **pronunciation** [prə'nunsiāshən] the way a word is said; the act of saying something.

proof *n* evidence that makes something clear beyond doubt; the standard of strength of whisky *etc*; a copy of a printed sheet for correction before the final printing and publication. – *adj* able to keep out or withstand: *proof against attack*; (also used as part of a word: *waterproof, bulletproof*).

prop *n* something that holds up, a support; short for **propeller**: *turbo-prop aeroplane*; (*pl*) short for stage **properties**. – *v* to hold up by placing something under or against: – *pt* **propped**.

'**propagate** *v* to spread; to (cause plants or animals to) produce seedlings or young *etc.* – *ns* **propa'ganda** organized activity for the spreading of particular ideas, opinions *etc*; (misleading) ideas spread by such means; **propa'gandist** one who sees to the spreading of such ideas.

pro'pel *v* to drive forward: – *pt* **pro'pelled**. – *n* **pro'peller** a shaft with blades which revolves to drive forward ships, aircraft *etc.* – *n* **propulsion** [prə'pulshən] an act of driving forward.

pro'pensity *n* a natural inclination: *a propensity to criticize*: *propensity for bumping into things*: – *pl* **pro'pensities**.

'**proper** *adj* right, correct: *the proper way to fire a gun*; full, thorough: *a proper search*; prim, well-behaved: *a very proper young lady*. – *adv* '**properly** in the right way; (*coll*) thoroughly. – *ns* **proper noun, name** (in grammar) a noun, name, naming a particular person, thing, place: *John: New York*.

'**property** *n* that which one owns; land or buildings; a quality. *Hardness is a property of the diamond*; (*pl*) the furniture *etc* required by actors in a play: –

pl '**properties**.

'**prophesy** *v* to (try to) tell what will happen in the future, predict: – *pt* '**prophesied**. – *ns* **prophecy** ['profəsi] foretelling the future; something prophesied: – *pl* '**prophecies**; '**prophet** one who claims to be able to foretell events *etc* to come; one who tells what he believes to be the will of God.

propinquity [prə'piŋkwəti] *n* nearness.

propitiate [prə'pishiāt] *v* to calm the anger of. – *adj* **pro'pitious** favourable: *propitious circumstances*.

proportion [prə'pörshən] *n* a part of a total amount. *A large proportion of income is taxed*; the relation in size, number, amount, degree of a thing or part as compared with other things or parts. *The proportion of girls to boys is small*. – *adjs* **pro'portional**, **pro'portionate** in proportion. – **in (out of) proportion** suitable or appropriate (unsuitable or not appropriate) in size, quantity or degree when compared with other parts or things. *An elephant's tail seems out of proportion to the rest of its body*.

propose [prə'pōz] *v* to put forward (a plan, someone's name for a job *etc*) for consideration, to suggest. *He proposed his cousin for president*; to intend; to make an offer *esp* of marriage. – *ns* **pro'posal** an act of proposing; anything proposed; an offer of marriage. – **propo'sition** a proposal, suggestion; a statement; a situation, thing *etc* that must be dealt with: *a tough proposition*.

pro'pound *v* to state, put forward for consideration.

proprietor [prə'priətər] *n* an owner: *the proprietor of the hotel*: – *fem* **pro'prietress** or **pro'prietrix**.

propriety [prə'priəti] *n* rightness, fitness, suitability; right behaviour, decency. *She always behaves with propriety*: – *pl* **pro'prieties**.

propulsion *see* propel.

prosaic [prə'zāik] *adj* dull, not interesting.

prose [prōz] *n* writing which is not in verse; ordinary written or spoken language.

prosecute ['prosikūt] *v* to bring a law-court action against; to carry on (one's studies, an investigation *etc*). – *ns* **prose'cution** an act of prosecuting; those bringing the case in a law court.

'**prospect** *n* a view, a scene; what one may expect to happen, one's outlook for the future: *the prospect of starvation*: *a job with good prospects*. – *v* **pros'pect** to make a search (*esp* for gold or other minerals). – *adj* **pros'pective** likely to be or to happen: *the prospective headmaster*. – *n* **pros'pector** one who prospects, *esp* for minerals. – *n* **pros'pectus** a booklet giving information about a school, organization *etc*: – *pl* **pros'pectuses**.

'**prosper** *v* to get on well or succeed. – *n* **pros'perity** success, good fortune, wealth. – *adj* '**prosperous**.

'**prostitute** *n* a woman who offers herself for sexual intercourse for payment.

'**prostrate** *adj* lying flat, *esp* face downwards; worn out, exhausted, in a state of collapse. – *v* **pros'trate** to throw forwards to the ground. *They prostrated themselves before the king*; to exhaust, tire out completely. – *adj* **pros'trated** worn out (by grief, tiredness *etc*). – *n* **pros'tration**.

pro'tagonist *n* a chief character (in a play *etc*).

pro'tect *v* to shield or defend from danger, keep safe. – *n* **pro'tection** the act of protecting; safety, shelter. – *adj* **pro'tective** giving protection; intended to protect. – *ns* **pro'tector** a guardian, defender; **pro'tectorate** a country which is partly governed and defended by another country.

protégé ['protəzhā] *n* a person who is guided and helped in his career by someone important or powerful: – *fem* '**protégée**.

protein ['prōtēn] *n* any of a large number of substances (present in milk, eggs, meat *etc*) necessary as part of the food of human beings and animals.

pro'test *v* to express a strong objection (against); to declare solemnly: *to protest one's innocence*. – *ns* '**protest** a strong statement or demonstration of disapproval or objection; **protes'tation** a solemn declaration; a protest.

Protestant ['protəstənt] *n* a member of one of the Christian churches that broke away from the Roman Catholic Church at the time of the Reformation.

'**protocol** *n* correct (diplomatic) procedure.

'**proton** *n* a particle with a positive electrical charge, forming part of the nucleus of an atom or the whole of the nucleus of a hydrogen atom.

'**protoplasm** *n* the half-liquid substance which is the chief material found in all living cells.

'**prototype** *n* the first or original model from which anything is copied.

pro'tract *v* to draw out or lengthen in time. – *n* **pro'tractor** an instrument for drawing and measuring angles on paper.

protrude [prə'trōod] *v* to stick out, or thrust forward. *His front teeth protrude.* – *n* **pro'trusion** the act of sticking or thrusting out; something that sticks out.

protuberance [prə'tūbərəns] *n* a swelling, a bulge. – *adj* **pro'tuberant**.

proud *adj* thinking too highly of oneself, haughty; having a feeling of pleasure, satisfaction at an achievement *etc*; showing a spirit of independence. *He was too proud to accept the offer of help.*

prove [prōov] *v* to show to be true or correct; to try out, test; to turn out (to be). *His remarks proved correct.*

provender ['provəndər] *n* food, *esp* for horses and cattle.

'**proverb** *n* a well-known wise saying (*eg* 'Nothing venture, nothing gain'). – *adj* **pro'verbial** like a proverb; widely known, spoken about by everybody. *His kindness is proverbial.*

pro'vide *v* to supply. – *conjs* **pro'vided (that), pro'viding** on condition (that).

'**providence** *n* foresight; thrift; the care of God for all creatures; '**Providence** God. – *adjs* '**provident** showing thought for and making plans for the future; thrifty; **provi'dential** fortunate, coming as if by divine help.

'**province** *n* a division of a country; the extent or scope of one's duties or knowledge. *Mending fuses is not my province*; (*pl*) all parts of a country outside the capital. – *adj* **provincial** [prə'vinshəl] of a province; of the provinces; rough in manners, narrow in one's views, interests *etc*.

provision [prə'vizhən] *n* an act of providing; an agreed arrangement; a rule or condition; a supply or store; (*pl*) (a supply of) food. – *adj* **pro'visional** temporary, arranged for the time being.

proviso [prə'vizō] *n* a condition laid down beforehand: – *pl* **pro'visos**.

pro'voke *v* to cause, result in (laughter, trouble *etc*); to rouse to anger or action. *Don't let him provoke you.* – *n* **provo'cation** an act of provoking; an act which arouses anger. – *adjs* **provocative** [prə'vokətiv] tending to cause anger; intended to or likely to arouse interest *etc*: *a provocative neckline*; **pro'voking** annoying.

prow [prow] *n* the front part of a ship.

prowess ['prowis] *n* skill, ability.

prowl [prowl] *v* to go about stealthily in search of prey or plunder.

prox'imity *n* nearness.

'**proxy** *n* one who acts or votes on behalf of another; a document giving someone the authority to act on behalf of another; such authority: – *pl* '**proxies**.

prude [prŏod] *n* an over-modest, priggish person. – *n* '**prudery** the attitude of such a person. – *adj* '**prudish**.

prudent ['prŏodənt] *adj* wise and cautious. – *n* '**prudence**.

prune [prŏon] *n* a dried plum. – *v* to trim (a tree *etc*) by cutting off unneeded twigs *etc*; to shorten, reduce (*eg* a story, expenditure *etc*).

prȳ *v* to look or inquire closely into things that are not one's business: – *pt* **pried**. – *adj* '**prying**.

psalm [säm] *n* a sacred song, *esp* one in the Book of Psalms. – *n* '**psalmist** a writer of psalms.

psalter ['söltər] *n* a book of psalms.

pseud(o)- [sūd(ō)] *prefix* false.

pseudo ['sūdō] *adj* false, fake, pretended. *His Spanish accent is pseudo.*

pseudonym ['sūdənim] *n* a false name used by an author.

psych(o)- [sik(ō)] *prefix* mind.

psychiatry [si'kiətri] *n* the treatment of mental diseases. – *adj* **psychiatric** [siki'atrik] of, or needing, such treatment. – *n* **psy'chiatrist** one who treats diseases of the mind.

psychic(al) ['sikik(əl)] *adj* of the mind or soul; of mysterious forces and influences on the mind and senses; sensitive to feeling such forces. *She thinks she is psychic because she guessed his thoughts.*

psychoanalysis ['sikōə'naləsis] *n* a method of treating a mental illness by discussing with the patient its possible causes in his past.

psychology [si'koləji] *n* the science which studies the human mind. – *adj* **psycho'logical** of psychology or the mind. – *n* **psy'chologist**.

ptarmigan ['tärmigən] *n* a type of mountain-dwelling bird of the grouse family, which turns white in winter.

pterodactyl [terə'daktil] *n* a kind of extinct flying reptile.

pub short for **public house**.

'**puberty** *n* the time during youth when the body becomes sexually mature.

'**public** *adj* of, concerning, open to, shared by the people (of a community or nation) in general: *public opinion*: *public announcement*: *public library*; generally or widely known: *a public figure*. – *n* people in general. – *ns* '**publican** the keeper of an inn or public house; **publi'cation** the act of making (news *etc*) public; the act of publishing (a book, newspaper *etc*);

something published (*eg* a book, magazine *etc*); **publicity** [pəb'lisəti] the act of bringing something to the notice of the public, often through advertising; public notice or attention. – *n* **public house** a house where alcoholic drinks are sold to the public. – **in public** in front of, among other people.

'**publish** *v* to make generally known; to prepare, and put out a book *etc* for sale. – *n* '**publisher** one who publishes books.

puce *adj* of a brownish-purple colour.

'**pucker** *v* to wrinkle. – *n* a wrinkle or fold.

pudding ['pŏodiŋ] *n* the sweet course of a meal; any of several types of soft foods made with eggs, flour, milk *etc*; any of several types of sausages.

'**puddle** *n* a small (muddy) pool.

puerile ['pūəril] *adj* childish, silly.

puff *v* to blow out in small gusts; to breathe heavily (as after running); to blow up, inflate; to swell (up, out). – *n* a short, sudden gust of wind, breath *etc*; a powder puff; a piece of advertising. – *adj* '**puffy** swollen, flabby; breathing heavily. – *n* **puff pastry** a light, flaky kind of pastry.

'**puffin** *n* a type of sea bird, with a short, thick beak.

pug *n* a breed of small dog with a snub nose.

'**pūgilist** *n* a boxer. – *n* '**pugilism** boxing.

pugnacious [pug'nāshəs] *adj* quarrelsome, fond of fighting. – *n* **pugnacity** [pug'nasəti].

pull [pŏol] *v* to move or try to move (something) towards oneself *esp* by using force; to drag, tug; to stretch or strain: *to pull a muscle*; to tear: *to pull to pieces*. – *n* the act of pulling; a pulling force (*eg* of a magnet *etc*); a handle for pulling; (*coll*) advantage, influence. – **pull oneself together** to regain one's self-control or self-possession; **pull through** to get safely to the end of a difficult or dangerous experience; **pull up** to stop, halt.

pullet ['pŏolit] *n* a young hen.

pulley ['pŏoli] *n* a grooved wheel fitted with a cord and set in a block, used for lifting weights *etc*: – *pl* '**pulleys**.

pullover ['pŏolōvər] *n* a knitted garment for the top half of the body, a jersey.

'**pulmonary** *adj* of, affecting, the lungs.

pulp *n* the soft fleshy part of a fruit; a soft mass (made of wood *etc*) which is made into paper; any soft mass. – *v* to reduce to pulp.

pulpit ['poolpit] *n* an enclosed platform in a church, for the preacher.

pulse *n* the beating or throbbing of the heart and blood vessels of the body as blood flows through them; beans, peas, lentils and other similar edible seeds. – *v* to beat or throb (also **pul'sate**).

pulverize ['pulvəriz] *v* to make or crush into powder.

'**pūma** *n* a type of American wild animal like a large cat.

pumice (stone) ['pumis(stōn)] *n* (a piece of) a light kind of solidified lava used for smoothing skin *etc* and for rubbing away stains.

'**pummel** *v* to beat with the fists: – *pt* '**pummelled**.

pump *n* a machine used for making water *etc* rise to the surface; a machine for drawing out or forcing in air, gas *etc*: *a bicycle pump*; any of several kinds of thin- or soft-soled shoes for dancing, gymnastics *etc*. – *v* to raise or force with a pump; (*coll*) to draw out information from (a person) by cunning questions.

'**pumpkin** *n* a kind of large roundish, thick-skinned, yellow fruit, used for food.

pun *n* a play upon words alike in sound but different in meaning, as 'They went and *told* the sexton, and the sexton *tolled* the bell'. – *v* to make a pun: – *pt* **punned**.

punch *v* to beat with the fist; to make a hole in with a tool or machine. *The conductor punched the ticket.* – *n* a blow with the fist; a tool used for punching holes; a kind of drink made of spirits or wine, water, sugar *etc*: – *pl* '**punches**. – *n* '**punch-bowl** a bowl for mixing punch. – *adj* '**punchdrunk** (of a boxer) dizzy from blows. – *n* **punch line** the sentence or phrase that gives the main meaning or point to a story (*esp* a joke).

punc'tilious *adj* paying great care to small points, *esp* in one's behaviour.

punctual ['puŋkchooəl] *adj* up to time, not late; strict in keeping time of appointments. – *n* **punctu'ality**.

punctuate ['puŋkchooāt] *v* to divide up sentences by commas, full stops *etc*; to interrupt at intervals. *The silence was punctuated by occasional coughing.* – *n* **punctu'ation** the act of punctuating; the use of punctuation marks. – *npl* **punctuation marks** the symbols used in punctuating sentences, as full stop, comma, colon, question mark *etc*.

puncture ['puŋkchər] *n* an act of pricking or piercing; a small hole made with a sharp point; a hole in a tyre.

'**pundit** *n* a learned man, an expert. *The pundits disagree about the state of the economy.*

pungent ['punjənt] *adj* sharp-tasting or sharp-smelling; (of remarks *etc*) strongly sarcastic.

'**punish** *v* to cause (a person) to suffer for a fault or crime; to inflict suffering on; to treat roughly or harshly. – *adj* '**punishable** (of crimes *etc*) likely to or liable to be punished. – *n* '**punishment** pain or unpleasantness inflicted (for a fault or crime). – *adj* **punitive** ['pūnətiv] inflicting punishment or suffering.

'**punnet** *n* a small basket made of strips of wood *etc* for holding fruit.

punt *n* a type of flat-bottomed boat with square ends. – *v* to move (a punt) by pushing a pole against the bottom of a river *etc*.

'**pūny** *adj* little and weak.

pup *n* a young dog (also '**puppy**); one of the young of certain other animals, *eg* the seal *etc*.

'**pūpa** *n* the stage (often passed inside a cocoon) in the growth of an insect in which it changes from a larva (*eg* a caterpillar) to its perfect form or **imago** (*eg* a butterfly): – *pl* **pupae**.

'**pūpil** *n* one who is being taught by a teacher; the round opening in the middle of the eye through which the light passes.

'**puppet** *n* a doll which is moved by strings or wires; a kind of doll that fits over the hand and is moved by the fingers; one who acts just as another tells him.

puppy *see* **pup**.

purchase ['pərchəs] *v* to buy. – *n* the act of buying; that which is bought; the power to lift or shift got by using a lever *etc*; firm grip or hold. – *n* '**purchaser** one who buys.

pure *adj* clean, spotless; free from dust, dirt, infection *etc*; not mixed with other (polluting or adulterating) substances; free from faults or sin, innocent: *a pure young girl*; utter, absolute, nothing but: *pure nonsense.* – *adv* '**purely** in a pure way; wholly, entirely: *purely on merit*; merely, only: *purely for the sake of appearance.* – *v* '**purify** to make pure: – *pt* '**purified**. – *ns* **purifi'cation**; '**purist** one who insists on correctness; '**purity** the state of being pure.

purée ['pūrā] *n* food made into a pulp by putting it through a sieve or liquidizing machine.

purge [pərj] *v* to make clean, purify; to

clear (something) of anything unwanted. *He purged his party of those who disagreed with him.* – *ns* **purgative** ['pɔ̄rgətiv] a medicine which clears waste matter out of the body; **'purgatory** in the Roman Catholic church, a place where a soul is made pure before entering heaven; any state of suffering for a time.

purification, purify *see* **pure**.

'pūritan *n* a strict, *usu* narrow-minded person; **'Puritan** (*hist*) one of a group believing in strict simplicity in religious worship and daily life. – *adj* **puri'tanical**.

purity *see* **pure**.

purl *v* to knit in stitches made with the wool *etc* in front of the work.

pur'loin *v* to steal.

'purple *n* a dark colour formed by the mixture of blue and red.

purport ['pɔ̄rpört] *n* meaning. – *v* **pur'port** to mean; to seem or appear (to be, to do). *He purports to be an expert on the theatre.*

purpose ['pɔ̄rpəs] *n* the aim towards which an effort or action is directed; intention; use, function (of a tool *etc*). – *v* to intend. – *adv* **'purposely** intentionally. – **on purpose** intentionally; **to the purpose** to the point.

purr *n* the low, murmuring sound a cat makes when pleased. – Also *v*.

purse *n* a small bag for carrying money; (*US*) a handbag. – *v* to close (the lips) tightly. – *n* **'purser** the officer who looks after a ship's money.

pur'sūe *v* to follow after (in order to overtake or capture), chase; to be engaged in, carry on (studies, an enquiry *etc*); to follow (a route, path *etc*). – *ns* **pur'suer** one who pursues; **pursuit** [pər'sūt] the act of pursuing; an occupation or hobby.

purvey [pər'vā] *v* to provide, supply (food, *etc*) *usu* as a business. – *n* **pur'veyor**.

pus *n* a thick yellowish liquid produced from infected wounds *etc*.

push [poŏsh] *v* to press hard against; to move or thrust (something) away with force, to shove; to urge on; to make a thrust or an effort. – *n* a thrust; effort; (*coll*) energy and determination. – *adj* **'pushing** determined to get what one wants, aggressive.

pūsil'lanimous *adj* cowardly.

'pustule *n* a small pimple containing pus.

put [poŏt] *v* to place; to lay or set. *Put the book on the table*; to bring to a certain position or state. *Put the light on. He put it out of his mind*; to express. *You did not*

put your question very politely: – *pres p* **'putting**, *pt* **put**. – **put about** to change course at sea; to spread (news); **put by** to set aside, save up; **put down** to defeat; **put in for** to make a claim for, apply for; **put off** to delay or end (an arrangement *etc*); to turn (a person) away from an intention or purpose; **put out** to extinguish (a fire *etc*); to annoy or embarrass; **put up** to build; to propose, suggest (a plan, candidate *etc*); to let someone stay in one's house *etc*; to stay as a guest in someone's house; **put-up job** (*coll*) a dishonest scheme; **put up with** to bear patiently, tolerate.

'pūtative *adj* supposed, commonly accepted.

'pūtrefȳ *v* to go bad, to rot: – *pt* **'putrefied**. – *n* **putre'faction**. – *adj* **'putrid** rotten; stinking.

putt *v* (in golf) to send a ball gently forward. – *n* **'putter** a golf club used for this.

'putty *n* a type of cement made from ground chalk, used in putting glass in windows *etc*.

'puzzle *v* to present with a problem which is difficult to solve or with a situation *etc* which is difficult to understand; to be difficult (for someone) to understand. *Her attitude puzzled him*; (with **out**) to think long and carefully (about) and *usu* solve a problem. – *n* a difficulty which causes much thought; a problem, a kind of toy or riddle to test one's thinking, knowledge or skill: *a crossword puzzle: a jigsaw puzzle.*

'pygmy, 'pigmy *n* one of a race of very small human beings: – *pls* **'pygmies, 'pigmies**.

py'jamas *npl* a sleeping suit consisting of trousers and a jacket.

'pȳlon *n* a high, tower-like steel construction for supporting electric power cables; a guiding mark at an airfield.

'pyramid *n* a solid shape having flat sides which come to a point at the top; something built in this shape, *esp* one of these used as tombs in ancient Egypt.

'pyre *n* a pile of wood on which a dead body is burned.

'Pȳrex ® *n* a type of glassware for cooking that will withstand heat.

pyrotechnics [pirə'tekniks] *n* (a display of) fireworks.

Pyrrhic ['pirik]: **Pyrrhic victory** *n* a victory gained at so great a cost that it is equal to a defeat.

'pȳthon *n* a type of large, non-poisonous snake which crushes its victims.

quack *n* the cry of a duck; a person who claims to have skill and knowledge (*esp* in medicine) that he does not possess. – *v* to make the noise of a duck:

quad [kwod] *n* short for **quadruplet**; short for **quadrangle**.

quadr(i)- [kwodr(i)] *prefix* four.

quadrangle ['kwodraŋgl] *n* (in mathematics) a figure having four equal sides and angles; a four-sided courtyard surrounded by buildings, *esp* in a school, college *etc*. – *adj* **qua'drangular**.

quadrant ['kwodrənt] *n* one quarter of the circumference or area of a circle; an instrument used in astronomy, navigation *etc* for measuring heights.

quadrennial [kwə'dreniəl] *adj* happening *etc* every four years.

quadrilateral [kwodri'latərəl] *n* a four-sided figure or area.

quadrille [kwə'dril] *n* a dance for four couples arranged to form a square.

quadruped ['kwodrōoped] *n* any four-footed animal.

quadruple [kwod'rōopl] *adj* four times as much or many; made up of four parts. – *v* to make or become four times greater. *He quadrupled the price.* – *n* **quad'ruplet** one of four children born of one mother at one birth.

quaff [kwof] *v* to drink up eagerly.

quagmire ['kwogmīr] *n* wet, boggy ground.

quail *v* to shrink back in fear. – *n* a type of small bird like a partridge.

quaint *adj* pleasantly odd, unusual, *esp* because of being old-fashioned.

quake *v* to shake, tremble, *esp* with fear: – *pres p* **'quaking**.

qualify ['kwolifi] *v* to (cause to) become fit or suitable to follow a profession or trade *etc*, or to hold a position; to prove oneself fit for this, *esp* by passing a test; to reach a certain standard of knowledge or ability; to lessen the force of a statement by adding something that makes it less strong. *That's good – no, I'd better qualify that – quite good.* – *n* **qualifi'cation** the act of qualifying; something which qualifies (*eg* a statement); a skill or achievement that makes a person suitable or fit for a job *etc*. – *adj* **'qualified** having the necessary qualification for a job *etc*.

quality ['kwoləti] *n* an outstanding feature of a person or thing. *Kindness is a quality admired by all*; degree of worth:

cloth of poor quality: – *pl* **'qualities**. – *adj* **'qualitative** having to do with quality rather than quantity.

qualm [kwäm] *n* doubt about whether one is doing right.

quandary ['kwondəri] *n* a state of uncertainty; a situation in which it is difficult to decide what to do.

quantity ['kwontəti] *n* amount: *a large quantity of paper*; a symbol which represents an amount. *x is the unknown quantity*: – *pl* **'quantities**. – *adj* **'quantitative** having to do with quantity, not quality.

quarantine ['kworəntēn] *n* the (period of) keeping apart of people or animals who might be carrying an infectious disease. *My dog was in quarantine for six months*; the state of being kept apart for this reason. – *v* to put in quarantine.

quarrel ['kworəl] *n* an angry disagreement or argument. – *v* to disagree violently or argue angrily (with); to find fault (with a person or action): – *pt* **'quarrelled**. – *adj* **'quarrelsome** fond of quarrelling, inclined to quarrel.

quarry ['kwori] *n* a pit or other place from which stone is taken for building *etc*; a hunted animal; an intended victim; anything eagerly looked for, chased *etc*: – *pl* **'quarries**. – *v* to dig (stone *etc*) from a quarry: – *pt* **'quarried**.

quart [kwört] *n* a measure of liquids, 1·136 litre (2 pints).

quarter ['kwörtər] *n* any one of four equal parts (of a thing); a fourth part of a year (three months); a measure of weight, 12·7 kilogrammes (28 lb); direction. *No help came from any quarter*; a district: *in a poor quarter of the city*; mercy shown to an enemy. *No quarter was given by either side*; (*pl*) lodgings (*esp* for soldiers). – *v* to divide into four equal parts; to place (*esp* soldiers) in lodgings. – *adj*, *adv* **'quarterly** (happening *etc*) every three months. – *n* a magazine *etc* published every three months. – *ns* **'quarter-deck** the part of the upper deck of a ship between the stern and the mast nearest it; **'quartermaster** an officer who looks after the lodging of soldiers and their supplies.

quartet [kwör'tet] *n* a group of four players or singers; a piece of music written for such a group.

quartz [kwörts] *n* a kind of hard substance, often in crystal form, found in rocks.

'**quāsar** *n* a star-like object (not really a star) which gives out light and radar waves.

quash [kwosh] *n* to crush, put down (*eg* a rebellion); to wipe out, annul (*eg* a judge's decision).

quasi- ['kwāsī] *prefix* apparently or to some extent, but not completely: *quasi-historical*.

'**quāver** *v* to shake, tremble; to speak or sing in a shaking voice. – *n* a trembling of the voice; (in music) a note equal to half a crotchet in length.

quay [kē] *n* a solid landing place, built for the loading and unloading of boats.

queasy ['kwēzi] *adj* as if about to vomit, sick; easily shocked or disgusted. – *n* '**queasiness**.

queen *n* a female ruler; the wife of a king; the most powerful piece in chess; a high value of playing card with a picture of a queen; the egg-laying female of certain kinds of insect (*esp* bees, ants and wasps). – *adj* '**queenly** of or like a queen. – *n* **queen mother** the mother of the reigning king or queen who was once herself queen.

queer *adj* odd, strange.

quell *v* to crush (a rebellion *etc*); to remove (fears, suspicions *etc*).

quench *v* to drink and so satisfy (one's thirst); to put out (*eg* a fire).

querulous ['kwerələs] *adj* complaining.

'**quēry** *n* a question; a question mark (?): – *pl* '**queries**. – *v* to question (*eg* a statement): – *pt* '**queried**.

quest *n* a search.

question ['kweschən] *n* something requiring an answer (*eg* 'Where are you going?'); a subject, matter *etc*: *the energy question*: *a question of ability*; a matter for dispute or doubt. *There's no question of him leaving.* – *v* to ask questions of (a person); to express doubt about. – *adj* '**questionable** doubtful. – *n* **question'naire** a written list of questions to be answered by a series of people to provide information for a (statistical) report or survey. – *n* **question mark** in writing, a mark (?) put after a question. – **out of the question** not even to be considered, unthinkable.

queue [kū] *n* a line of people waiting (*eg* for a bus). – *v* to stand in, or form, a queue.

'**quibble** *v* to avoid an important part of an argument *eg* by quarrelling over details. – Also *n*.

quiche [kēsh] *n* an open pastry case

filled with beaten eggs, cheese *etc* and baked.

quick *adj* done or happening in a short time; acting without delay, fast-moving: *a quick brain*. – *adv* without delay, rapidly. – *n* a very tender part of the body, *esp* under the nails; (*old*) (with **the**) the living. – *v* '**quicken** to speed up, become or make faster. – *adv* '**quickly**. – *ns* '**quicklime** lime which has not been mixed with water; '**quicksand** sand that sucks in anyone who stands in it; '**quicksilver** mercury. – *adj* '**quick-'tempered** easily made angry.

quid *n* a lump of tobacco for chewing; (*slang*) a pound (£1).

quiescent [kwi'esnt] *adj* not active.

quiet ['kwiət] *adj* making little or no noise; calm: *a quiet life*. – *n* the state of being quiet; lack of noise, peace. – *v* to make or become quiet. – *n* '**quietness**. – *v* '**quieten** to make or become quiet.

quill *n* a large feather, *esp* the feather of a goose or other bird made into a pen; one of the sharp spines of certain animals (*eg* the porcupine).

quilt *n* a bedcover filled with down, feathers *etc*. – *adj* '**quilted** (of clothes) made of two layers of material with padding or stuffing between them.

quin short for **quintuplet**.

quince *n* a type of pear-like fruit with a sharp taste, used in jams *etc*.

quinine ['kwinēn] *n* a bitter drug taken from the bark of a type of tree, used as a medicine, *esp* for malaria.

quin'quennial *adj* happening once every five years; lasting five years.

quin'tessence *n* the most important part of anything; the purest part or form of something. – *adj* **quintes'sential**.

quin'tet *n* a group of five players or singers; a piece of music written for such a group.

quin'tūplet *n* one of five children born to a mother at the same time.

quip *n* a witty remark or reply. – Also *v*: – *pt* **quipped**.

'**quire** *n* a set of 24 sheets of paper.

quirk *n* an odd feature of (a person's) behaviour; a trick or sudden turn (*esp* of fate). – *adj* '**quirky**.

quit *v* to give up, stop. *I'm going to quit smoking*; (*coll*) to leave, resign from (a job): – *pt* '**quitted, quit**. – **be quits** to be even with each other.

quite *adv* completely, entirely: *quite empty*; fairly, moderately: *quite warm*.

'**quiver** *n* a case for arrows; a tremble, shake. – *v* to tremble, shake.

quix'otic *adj* having noble but foolish

and unrealistic aims which cannot be carried out.

quiz *v* to question: – *pt* **quizzed**. – *n* a competition to test knowledge: – *pl* '**quizzes**. – *adj* '**quizzical** (of a look *etc*) as if asking a question, *esp* humorously or mockingly.

quoits [koits] *n* a game in which heavy flat rings (**quoits**) are thrown on to small rods.

quorum ['kwörəm] *n* the least number of people who must be present at a meeting before any business can be done.

'**quota** *n* a part or share to be given or received by each member of a group.

quote *v* to repeat the words of (anyone) exactly as they were said or written; to state (a price for something). – *n* a quotation; a quotation mark. – *n* **quo-'tation** the act of repeating something said or written; the words repeated; a price stated. – *npl* **quotation marks** marks used in writing to show that someone's words are being repeated exactly (*eg* He said 'I'm going out.').

quoth *v* (*old*) said. 'The stagecoach awaits,' quoth he.

quotient ['kwōshənt] *n* the result obtained by dividing one number by another. *4 is the quotient when 12 is divided by 3.*

R

rabbi ['rabi] *n* a Jewish priest or teacher of the law: – *pl* '**rabbis**.

'**rabbit** *n* a type of small, burrowing, long-eared animal.

'**rabble** *n* a disorderly, noisy crowd.

'**rabid** *adj* (of dogs) suffering from **rabies** ['rābēz], a disease which causes madness; violently enthusiastic or extreme: *a rabid nationalist.*

rac'coon, ra'coon *n* a type of small furry animal of N. America.

race[1] *n* a group of living beings with the same ancestors and physical characteristics; the state of belonging to a particular one of these groups; descent: *of noble race.* – *adj* **racial** ['rāshəl] of or according to race. – *ns* '**racialism** the belief that some races of men are better than others; prejudice on the grounds of race; '**racialist** one who believes in, or practises, racialism. – Also *adj*. – *n* **racism** ['rāsizəm] racialism; the (political) belief that ability *etc* is determined by one's race; '**racist** one who believes in or practises racism. – Also *adj*.

race[2] *n* a competition to find the fastest (person, animal, vehicle *etc*). – *v* to run fast; to take part in a race. – *adj* '**racy** (of stories) full of action. – *ns* '**racecourse, 'racetrack** a course over which races are run; '**racehorse** a horse bred and used for racing.

rack *n* a framework for holding objects (*eg* letters, plates, hats *etc*); (*hist*) an instrument for torturing victims by stretching the joints; a bar with teeth which fits into and moves a toothed wheel *etc*. – **rack and ruin** a state of

neglect and decay; **rack one's brains** to think hard (about something).

racket[1], **racquet** ['rakit] *n* a kind of bat made up of a strong frame strung with nylon *etc* for playing tennis, badminton *etc*; (*pl*) a form of tennis played against a wall.

'**racket**[2] *n* great noise; a dishonest way of making a profit. – *n* **racke'teer** one who makes money dishonestly.

raconteur [rakon'tər] *n* one who tells stories (*esp* in an entertaining way).

racoon *see* **raccoon**.

racquet *see* **racket**.

'**radar** *n* a method of detecting solid objects using radio waves which bounce back off the object and form a picture of it on a screen.

'**radiant** *adj* sending out rays of light, heat *etc*; showing joy and happiness: *a radiant smile.* – *n* '**radiance** brightness; splendour.

'**radiate** *v* to send out rays of light, heat *etc*; to spread out or send out from a centre. – *ns* **radi'ation** the act of radiating; the giving off of rays of light, heat *etc* or of those from radioactive substances; '**radiator** any of various devices (*esp* a series of connected hot-water pipes) which send out heat; the part of a motor car which cools the engine.

'**radical** *adj* thorough: *a radical change*; basic, deep-seated: *radical differences*; (in politics) wishing for, involving *etc* great changes in the method of government. – *n* one who has radical political views.

'**radio** *n* (an apparatus for) the sending

and receiving of signals by means of electromagnetic waves: – *pl* 'radios. – *v* to send a message to (a person) in this way: – *pt* 'radioed. – *adj* radio'active (of some metals *etc*) giving off rays which are often dangerous but which can be used in medicine. – *ns* radioac'tivity; radiology [rādi'oləji] the science of radioactive substances and radiation; (the branch of medicine involving) the use of these (*eg* X-rays and radium); radiō'therapy the treatment of certain diseases by X-rays or radioactive substances.

'radish *n* a type of plant with a sharp-tasting root, eaten raw in salads: – *pl* 'radishes.

'rādium *n* an element, a radioactive metal used in radiotherapy.

'rādius *n* a straight line from the centre to the circumference of a circle; an area within a certain distance from a central point: – *pl* radii ['rādii].

'raffia *n* strips of fibre from the leaves of a type of palm tree, used in weaving mats *etc*.

'raffle *n* a way of raising money by selling numbered tickets, one or more of which wins a prize. – *v* to give as a prize in a raffle.

raft *n* a number of logs *etc* fastened together and used as a boat.

'rafter *n* one of the sloping beams supporting a roof.

rag *n* a torn or worn piece of cloth; (*pl*) worn-out, shabby clothes. – *adj* made of rags: *rag doll*. – *v* to tease or play tricks on (someone). – *adj* ragged ['ragid] in ragged clothes; torn and tattered.

ragamuffin ['ragəmufin] *n* a ragged, dirty person.

rage [rāj] *n* great anger, fury. – *v* to be violently angry; to be violent (of a storm, wind *etc*); (*eg* of an argument, a battle). – all the rage very fashionable or popular.

'ragwort *n* a large coarse weed with a yellow flower.

raid *n* a short, sudden, *usu* unexpected attack; an unexpected visit by the police (to catch a criminal, recover stolen goods *etc*). – Also *v*. – *n* 'raider.

rail *n* a bar of metal used in fences *etc*; (*pl*) strips of steel which form the track on which trains run; the railway. *I came here by rail.* – *v* (with against, at) to speak angrily or bitterly. – *ns* 'railing a fence or barrier of rails; 'railway, (*US*) 'railroad a track laid with steel rails on which trains run.

'raiment *n* (*old*) clothing. –

rain *n* water falling from the clouds in drops; a great number (of things) falling. – *v* to pour or fall in drops. *It's raining today.* – *adj* 'rainy full of rain: *rainy skies*; showery, wet: *a rainy day.* – *ns* rainbow ['rānbō] the brilliant coloured bow or arch sometimes to be seen in the sky opposite the sun when rain is falling; 'raincoat a waterproof coat to keep out the rain; 'rainfall the amount of rain that falls in a certain time.

raise [rāz] *v* to lift up: *raise the flag*; to cause to rise, make higher: *raise the price*; to bring up (a subject) for consideration; to bring up (a child, family *etc*); to breed or grow (*eg* pigs, crops); to collect, get together (a sum of money).

raisin ['rāzin] *n* a dried grape.

'rajah *n* an Indian prince.

rake *n* a tool, like a large comb with a long handle, for smoothing earth, gathering hay *etc*; (*usu old*) a person who lives an immoral life. – *v* to draw a rake over; to scrape (together); to aim gunfire at (*eg* a ship) from one end to the other. – *adj* 'rakish at a slanting, jaunty angle.

'rally *v* to gather again. *The general rallied his troops after the defeat*; to come together for a joint action or effort. *The club's supporters rallied to save it*; to recover from an illness: – *pt* 'rallied. – *n* the act of rallying; a gathering; an improvement in health after an illness; (in tennis *etc*) a long series of shots before the point is won or lost: – *pl* 'rallies.

ram *n* a male sheep; something heavy, *esp* as part of a machine, for ramming. – *v* to press or push down hard; (of ships, cars *etc*) to run into and cause damage to. *The destroyer rammed the submarine*: – *pt* rammed.

'ramble *v* to walk about for pleasure, *esp* in the countryside; to speak in an aimless or confused way. – *n* a walk (*esp* in the countryside) for pleasure. – *n* 'rambler one who rambles; a climbing rose or other plant.

ramifi'cation *n* a branch or part of a subject, plot (of a play, book) *etc*; a consequence (*esp* indirect and one of several).

ramp *n* a sloping surface (*eg* of a road).

'rampage *v* to rush about angrily or violently. – on the rampage rampaging.

'rampant *adj* widespread and uncontrolled. *Vandalism is rampant in the city*; (in heraldry) standing on the left hind leg:

lion rampant.

'**rampart** *n* a mound or wall built as a defence.

'**ramshackle** *adj* badly made, falling to pieces.

ran *see* **run**.

ranch *n* (*esp* in America) a farm for rearing cattle or horses: – *pl* '**ranches**.

'**rancid** *adj* (*esp* of butter) smelling or tasting stale.

rancour ['raŋkər] *n* ill will, hatred. – *adj* '**rancorous**.

rand *n* the standard unit of S. African money.

'**random** *adj* done *etc* without any aim or plan in mind, chance: *a random sample*. – **at random** without any plan or purpose.

range [rānj] *n* a line or row: *a range of mountains*; extent, number: *a wide range of goods*; a piece of ground with targets where shooting, archery *etc* is practised; the distance which an object can be thrown, sound can be heard *etc*; the distance between the top and bottom notes of a voice *etc*; a large kitchen stove with a flat top. – *v* to set in a row or in order; to wander (over); to stretch, extend. *His kingdom ranged from the Trent to the Humber.* – *n* '**ranger** a keeper who looks after a forest or park. – *n* **Ranger Guide** an older member of the Girl Guide movement.

rank *n* a row or line (*esp* of soldiers); class or order: *the upper ranks of society*: *the rank of captain*; (*pl*) private soldiers (not officers). – *v* to place in order (of importance, merit *etc*); to have a place in an order. *Apes rank above dogs in intelligence.* – *adj* (of plants *etc*) growing too plentifully; having a strong, unpleasant taste or smell; absolute: *rank nonsense*. – **rank and file** soldiers of the rank of private; ordinary people, the majority.

'**rankle** *v* to cause lasting annoyance, bitterness *etc*.

'**ransack** *v* to search thoroughly; to plunder.

'**ransom** *n* price paid for the freeing of a captive. – *v* to pay money to free (a captive).

rant *v* to talk foolishly and angrily for a long time. – *n* '**ranting**.

rap *n* a sharp blow or knock. – *v* (often with **on**) to strike with a quick, sharp blow; (with **out**) to speak hastily: – *pt* **rapped**.

rapacious [rə'pāshəs] *adj* greedy, eager to seize as much as possible.

rape *v* to assault sexually. – *n* the act of raping; the act of seizing and carrying off by force; a type of plant like the turnip whose seeds give oil.

'**rapid** *adj* quick, fast: *a rapid rise to fame*. – *npl* a part in a river where the current flows swiftly. – *n* ra'**pidity** swiftness.

rapier ['rāpiər] *n* a type of light sword with a narrow blade.

rapt *adj* having the mind *etc* fully occupied: *rapt attention*.

rapture ['rapchər] *n* great delight. – *adj* '**rapturous**.

rare *adj* seldom found, uncommon; (of meat) lightly cooked. – *v* **rarefy**, **rarify** ['rārəfi] to make thin, less dense: – *pt* '**rarefied**. – *n* '**rarity** something uncommon; uncommonness: – *pl* '**rarities**.

'**rāring**: **raring to go** very keen to go, start *etc*.

'**rascal** *n* a naughty or wicked person.

rash *adj* acting, or done, without thought. – *n* redness or outbreak of spots on the skin. – *n* '**rashness** the state of being rash.

'**rasher** *n* a thin slice (of bacon or ham).

rasp *n* a coarse file; a rough, grating sound. – *v* to rub with a file; to make a rough, grating noise; to say in a rough voice. – *adj* '**rasping** (of a sound, voice) rough and unpleasant.

raspberry ['räzbəri] *n* a type of red berry similar to a blackberry, or the bush which bears it: – *pl* '**raspberries**.

rat *n* a kind of gnawing animal, larger than the mouse. – *v* to hunt or kill rats: – *pt* '**ratted**. – *n* '**rat-race** a fierce, unending competition for success, wealth *etc*.

'**ratchet** *n* (a wheel with a toothed edge and) a catch allowing winding in one direction only (*eg* in a watch); a toothed wheel (also '**ratchet-wheel**).

rate *n* the frequency with which something happens or is done: *a high rate of road accidents*; speed: *speak at a tremendous rate*; level of cost, price *etc*: *paid at a higher rate*; (*usu pl*) the sum of money to be paid by the owner of a house, shop *etc* to pay for local public services. – *v* to work out the value of (for taxation *etc*); to value. *I don't rate his work very highly.* – *n* **rat(e)able value** a value of a house *etc* used to work out the rates to be paid on it.

rather ['rädhər] *adv* somewhat, fairly. *It's rather cold today*; more willingly. *I'd rather talk about it now than later*; more correctly speaking. *He agreed, or rather he didn't say no.*

'**ratify** *v* to approve officially and formally. *Parliament ratified the treaty*:

– *pt* 'ratified. – *n* ratifi'cation.

'rating *n* in the navy, a sailor below the rank of an officer.

ratio ['rāshiō] *n* the proportion of one thing to another: *a ratio of two girls to one boy in the class*: – *pl* 'ratios.

ration ['rashən] *n* a measured amount of food given out at intervals to a person or animal; an allowance. – *v* to deal out (*eg* food) in measured amounts; to allow only a certain amount (*eg* of food) to (a person *etc*).

rational ['rashənl] *adj* able to reason; sensible; based on reason: *rational arguments*. – *v* 'rationalize *v* to think up a good reason for (an action or feeling) so as not to feel guilty about it. – *n* rationali'zation.

'rattle *v* to (make to) give out short, sharp, repeated sounds. *The coins rattled in the tin when he shook it*; (*usu* with off) to speak quickly. – *n* a sharp noise, quickly repeated; a toy or instrument which makes such a sound. – *ns* 'rattlesnake, 'rattler a type of poisonous snake having bony rings on its tail which rattle when shaken.

ratty *see* rat.

raucous ['rökəs] *adj* hoarse, harsh.

'ravage *v* to cause destruction or damage in, plunder. – *npl* damaging effects. *The ravages of time had affected her beauty.*

rave *v* to talk wildly, as if mad; (*coll*) to talk very enthusiastically (about). – *n*, *adj* 'raving.

'rāven *n* a type of large black bird of the crow family. – *adj* (of hair) black and glossy.

ravenous ['ravənəs] *adj* very hungry.

ravine [rə'vēn] *n* a deep, narrow valley between hills.

'ravish *v* to plunder; to rape; to fill with delight. – *adj* 'ravishing filling with delight.

raw *adj* not cooked: *raw onions*; not prepared, not refined *etc*, in its natural state: *raw cotton*; (of weather) cold; sore. – a raw deal unjust treatment.

ray *n* a line of light, heat *etc*; a small degree or amount: *a ray of hope*; one of several lines going outwards from a centre; a kind of flat-bodied fish.

'rayon *n* a type of artificial silk.

raze *v* to destroy, knock flat (a town, house *etc*).

'rāzor *n* a sharp-edged instrument for shaving. – *ns* 'razorbill a type of seabird of the auk family; 'razorfish a type of long narrow shellfish.

rē *prep* concerning, about.

rē- *prefix* again, once more as in re-

create; back as in reclaim.

reach *v* to arrive at. *We reached the summit of the hill. Your message never reached me*; to stretch out (the hand) so as to touch *etc*. *I couldn't reach the top shelf*; to extend. *His influence reached as far as the next town*. – *n* a distance that can be travelled easily: *within reach of home*; the distance one can stretch one's arm; a straight part of a stream or river between bends.

re'act *v* to act or behave in response to something done or said; to undergo a chemical change. *Metals react with sulphuric acid*. – *n* re'action behaviour as a result of action; a chemical change; a (movement for a) return to things as they were: *a reaction against Victorian morality*. – *adj* re'actionary favouring a return to old ways, laws *etc*. – Also *n*.

read *v* to look at and understand, or say aloud (written or printed words); to study a subject (*esp* in a university or college or for a profession). *He is reading law*: – *pt* read [red]. – *adj* readable ['rēdəbl] quite interesting. – *n* 'reader a person who reads (books *etc*); a person who reads manuscripts of books *etc* for a publisher; a senior university lecturer; a reading book (*esp* for children).

ready ['redi] *adj* prepared: *packed and ready to go*; willing: *always ready to help*; quick: *too ready to find fault*; available (for use *etc*). *Your coat is ready for collection*. – *adv* 'readily easily; willingly. – *n* 'readiness. – *adj* 'ready-'made (*esp* of clothes) made for sale to anyone whom they will fit or suit, not made specially for one person.

real [rēəl] *adj* actually existing, not imagined; not imitation, genuine: *real leather*; sincere: *a real love of art*. – *ns* 'realism the showing or viewing of things as they really are; 'realist one who claims to see life as it really is. – *adj* rea'listic life-like; viewing things as they really are. – *n* re'ality that which is real and not imaginary; truth: – *pl* re'alities. – *adv* 'really in fact; very: *really dark hair*.

realize ['rēəliz] *v* to come to understand, know. *I never realized you were here*; to make real, accomplish, fulfil. *The soldier realized his ambition when he became a general*; get (money) for. *He realized £16,000 on the sale of his house*. – *n* reali'zation.

realm [relm] *n* a kingdom, a country; an area of activity, interest *etc*: *the realm of sport*.

ream *n* a measure for paper, 20 quires;

(*pl*) a large quantity (*esp* of paper). *He wrote reams in his English exam.*

reap *v* to cut and gather (corn *etc*); to gain. *He reaped the benefit of his hard work.* – *n* **'reaper** one who reaps; a machine for reaping.

rear *n* the back part (of anything); the last part of an army or fleet. – *v* to bring up (children); to breed (animals); (of animals) to stand on the hindlegs. – *ns* **'rear-'admiral** an officer who commands the rear division of the fleet; **'rearguard** troops which protect the rear of an army. – **bring up the rear** to come or be last (*eg* in a line of walkers).

reason ['rēzn] *n* cause, excuse. *What is the reason for this noise?*; purpose. *What is your reason for going to London?*; the power of the mind to form opinions, judge right and truth *etc*; common sense. – *v* to think out (opinions *etc*); (with **with**) to try to persuade (a person) by arguing. – *adj* **'reasonable** sensible; fair.

reassure [rēə'shoor] *v* to take away (a person's) doubts or fears. – *n* **reas'surance**.

'rēbate *n* a part of a payment or tax which is given back to the payer.

'rebel *n* one who opposes or fights against those in power. – *v* **re'bel** to take up arms against or oppose those in power: – *pt* **re'belled**. – *n* **re'bellion** an open or armed fight against those in power; a refusal to obey. – *adj* **re'bellious**.

re'bound *v* to bounce back. *The ball rebounded off the wall.* – *n* **'rēbound** the act of rebounding; a reaction following an emotional situation or crisis.

re'buff *n* a blunt refusal or rejection. – Also *v*.

re'buke *v* to scold, blame. – *n* a scolding.

re'but *v* to deny (what has been said): – *pt* **re'butted**. – *n* **re'buttal**.

recalcitrant [rə'kalsitrənt] *adj* stubborn; disobedient. – *n* **re'calcitrance**.

recall [rə'köl] *v* to call back. *The soldier was recalled to headquarters*; to remember. – *n* a signal or message to return; the act of recalling.

recant [ri'kant] *v* to take back what one has said; to reject publicly one's beliefs. – *n* **rēcan'tation**.

'rēcap short for **recapitulation** or **recapitulate**: – *pt* **'recapped**.

rēca'pitūlate *v* to go over again quickly the chief points of anything (*eg* a discussion). – *n* **recapitu'lation**.

recapture [ri'kapchər] *v* to capture (what has escaped or been lost).

'rē'cast *v* to fashion or shape in a new form: – *pt* **'re'cast**.

re'cede *v* to go back; to become more distant; to slope backwards. – *adj* **re'ceding** going or sloping backwards; becoming more distant.

receipt [rə'sēt] *n* the act of receiving (*esp* money or goods); a written note saying that money has been received.

receive [rə'sēv] *v* to have something given or brought to one: *receive a gift*: *receive a letter*; to meet and welcome; to take goods, knowing them to be stolen. – *n* **re'ceiver** one who receives stolen goods; the part of a telephone through which words are heard and into which they are spoken; an apparatus through which television or radio broadcasts are received.

'rēcent *adj* happening, done or made only a short time ago. – *adv* **'recently**.

re'ceptacle *n* an object to receive or hold things, a container.

re'ception *n* a welcome. *The new boy had a good reception*; a large meeting to welcome guests; the quality of radio or television signals. – *n* **re'ceptionist** a person employed (*eg* in an office, hotel) to receive callers, answer the telephone *etc*. – *adj* **re'ceptive** quick to take in or accept ideas *etc*.

re'cess *n* part of a room set back from the rest, an alcove; the time during which parliament or the law-courts do not work; (*pl*) **re'cesses** remote parts: *in the recesses of my memory*.

recession [rə'seshən] *n* the act of moving back; a temporary fall in (a country's or world) business activities: *a trade recession*.

recipe ['resipi] *n* instructions on how to prepare or cook a certain kind of food.

re'cipient *n* one who receives.

re'ciprocal *adj* both given and received: *their reciprocal affection.* – *v* **re'ciprocate** to feel or do the same in return. *I reciprocate his dislike of me.*

re'cite *v* to repeat aloud from memory. – *ns* **re'cital** the act of reciting; a musical performance; the facts of a story told one after the other; **recitation** [resi'tāshən] a poem *etc* recited.

'reckless *adj* rash, careless. – *n* **'recklessness**.

'reckon *v* to count; to consider; to believe. – *n* **'reckoning** the settling of debts, grievances *etc*; payment for one's sins: *day of reckoning*; a bill; a sum, calculation.

re'claim *v* to claim back; to win back (land from the sea) by draining, building banks *etc*; to make waste land fit for use. – *n* **recla'mation**.

re'cline *v* to lean or lie on one's back or

side. – *adj* **re'clining**.

recluse [rə'kloōs] *n* one who lives alone and avoids other people.

recognize ['rekəgniz] *v* to know from a previous meeting *etc*; to admit, acknowledge. *Everyone recognized his skill*; to show appreciation of. *They recognized his courage by giving him a medal*. – *adj* **recog'nizable**. – *n* **recog'nition** act of recognizing.

re'coil *v* to shrink back (in horror or fear); (of guns) to jump back after a shot is fired. – Also *n*.

recol'lect *v* to remember. – *n* **recol'lection** the act or power of remembering; something remembered.

recom'mend *v* to urge, advise. *I recommend a long holiday*; to speak highly of. – *n* **recommen'dation** the act of recommending; a point in favour of a person or thing.

'recompense *v* to pay money to or reward (a person) to make up for loss, inconvenience *etc*. – Also *n*.

'reconcile *v* to bring together in friendship, after a quarrel; to show that two statements, facts *etc* do not contradict each other; (with **to**) to make to accept patiently. *I became reconciled to her absence*. – *n* **reconciliation** [rekənsili'āshən].

'recondite *adj* secret, little-known.

reconnaissance [rə'konəsəns] *n* a survey to obtain information (*esp* before a battle).

reconnoitre [rekə'noitər] *v* to make a reconnaissance of.

'rē'constitute *v* to put back into its original form. *The dried milk must be reconstituted before use*; to make up, form in a different way.

re'cord *v* to write something down for future reference; to put (the sound of music, speech *etc*) on tape or disc so that it can be listened to later; to show, *esp* in writing (*eg* one's vote); (of an instrument) to show, register. *The thermometer recorded 30° C yesterday*. – *n* **'record** a written report of any fact or facts; a round, flat piece of plastic on which sounds are recorded for playing on a record-player; (in races, games *etc*) the best known performance. *John holds the school record for the mile*. – *ns* **re'corder** one who records; a type of simple musical wind instrument; a judge in certain courts; **re'cording** the act of recording; recorded music, speech *etc*. – *n* **'record-player** a machine for playing records. – **break** or **beat the record** to do better than any previous performance (in a sport-

ing event); **off the record** (of a comment, remark *etc*) not to be made public.

'rē'count *v* to count again; **re'count** to tell (the story of). – *n* **'recount** a second count (*eg* of votes).

recoup [ri'koōp] *v* to make good, recover (expenses, losses *etc*).

recourse [rə'kōrs]: **have recourse to** to make use of in an emergency.

recover [rə'kuvər] *v* to get possession of again; to become well again after an illness – *adj* **re'coverable** able to be recovered. – *n* **re'covery** a return to health; the act of getting back (something lost *etc*).

re-cover ['rē-kuvər] *v* to cover again.

re-create ['rēkri'āt] *v* to describe or create again (something past). – *n* **'re-cre'ation**.

recreation [rekri'āshən] *n* a pleasurable or refreshing activity (*eg* a sport, hobby) done in one's spare time.

re'criminate *v* to accuse one's accuser in return. – *n* **re'crimi'nation** (often *pl*) accusation made by one who is himself accused. – *adj* **re'criminatory**.

recruit [rə'kroōt] *n* a newly-enlisted soldier, member *etc*. – *v* to enlist (someone in an army, political party *etc*). – *n* **re'cruitment**.

'rectangle *n* a four-sided figure with all its angles right angles and its opposite sides equal in length, an oblong. – *adj* **rec'tangular**.

'rectifȳ *v* to put right: – *pt* **'rectified**. – *adj* **'rectifiable**.

'rectitude *n* honesty; correctness of behaviour.

'rector *n* in the Church of England, a clergyman in charge of a parish; (in Scotland) the headmaster of some secondary schools; (in Scotland) a university official elected by the students. – *n* **'rectory** the house of a Church of England rector: – *pl* **'rectories**.

'rectum *n* the lower part of the alimentary canal.

re'cumbent *adj* lying down.

recuperate [rə'kūpərāt] *v* to recover strength or health. – *n* **recupe'ration**.

re'cur *v* to happen again: – *pt* **re'curred**. – *n* **recurrence** [ri'kurəns] the act of happening again: *a recurrence of his illness*. – *adj* **re'current** happening every so often.

red *adj, n* (of) the colour of blood. – *v* **'redden** to make or grow red. – *n* **'redness**. – *ns* **'redbreast** the robin; **red deer** a type of reddish-brown deer. – *adv* **'red-'handed** in the act of doing wrong. *The police caught the thief red-*

handed. – *ns* **red herring** something mentioned to lead a discussion away from the main subject; a false clue; **Red Indian** a member of the N. American red-skinned race. – *adj* 'red-'letter (of a particular day) especially important or happy for some reason. – *ns* **red light** a danger signal; a signal to stop; 'redskin a Red Indian; **red tape** unnecessary and troublesome rules about how things are to be done; 'redwood a type of American tree which grows to a great height. – **see red** to become very angry.

re'deem *v* to buy back (*eg* articles from a pawnbroker); to save from sin or condemnation; to make amends for. – *n* **Re'deemer** Jesus Christ. – *adj* re'deeming making up for other faults. *Good spelling was the redeeming feature of his composition.* – *n* **redemption** [rə'dempshən] the act of redeeming; the state of being redeemed.

'rēde'ploy *v* to move (*eg* soldiers, workers) to a different place where they will be more useful.

'redolent *adj* sweet-smelling; smelling (of); suggestive, making one think (of): *a city redolent of earlier times.*

redouble [ri'dubl] *v* to make twice as great: *redouble your efforts.*

redoubtable [rə'dowtəbl] *adj* brave, bold.

re'dress *v* to set right, to make up for (a wrong *etc*). – *n* something done or given to make up for a loss or wrong, compensation.

re'duce *v* to make smaller; to lessen; to bring to the point of by force of circumstances. *He was reduced to begging in the streets*; to bring (to a lower rank or state); to change into other terms: *reduce pounds to pence.* – *adj* re'ducible. – *n* **reduction** [rə'dukshən].

re'dundant *adj* more than what is needed; (of a worker) no longer needed because of a lack of a suitable job. – *ns* re'dundance; re'dundancy: – *pl* re'dundancies.

reed *n* a kind of tall stiff grass growing in moist or marshy places; a part, originally made of reed, in certain wind instruments (*eg* the oboe) which vibrates when the instrument is played. – *adj* 'reedy full of reeds; like a reed; sounding like a reed instrument: *a reedy voice.*

reef *n* a chain of rocks lying at or near the surface of the sea. – *n* **reef knot** a square, very secure knot.

'reefer *n* a short coat, as worn by sailors;

(*slang*) a marijuana cigarette.

reek *n* a strong (*usu* unpleasant) smell; smoke. – *v* to send out smoke; to smell strongly.

reel *n* a bobbin (for cotton, fishing lines *etc*); a length of cinema film; a lively Scottish or Irish dance. – *v* to wind on a reel; (with **in**) to draw, pull in (a fish on a line); to stagger. – **reel off** to repeat or recite quickly, without pausing.

re'fectory *n* a dining hall, for monks, students *etc.*

re'fer *v* (with **to**) to mention; to turn (to) for information; to relate, apply (to); to direct (to) for information, consideration *etc. I refer you to the managing director*: – *pt* re'ferred. – *ns* refe'ree one to whom a matter is taken for settlement; (in games) a judge; a person willing to provide a note about one's character *etc*; 'reference the act of referring; a mention; a note about a person's character, work *etc.* – *ns* **reference book** a book to be consulted for information, *eg* an encyclopaedia; **reference library** a library of books to be looked at for information but not taken away.

referendum [refə'rendəm] *n* a vote given by the people of a country about some important matter: – *pls* refe'renda, refe'rendums.

re'fine *v* to purify; to improve, make more exact, elegant *etc.* – *adj* re'fined purified; polite in one's manners, free of vulgarity. – *ns* re'finement good manners, taste, learning; an improvement; refinery [rə'finəri] a place where sugar, oil *etc* are refined: – *pl* re'fineries.

'rē'fit *v* to repair damages (*esp* to a ship): – *pt* 're'fitted.

re'flect *v* to throw back (light or heat). *The white sand reflected the sun's heat*; to give an image of: *reflected in the mirror*; (with **on**) to throw blame. *Her behaviour reflects on her mother*; (with **on**) to think over something carefully. – *n* re'flection the act of throwing back (*eg* a ray of light, an image of a person *etc* in a mirror); the image of a person *etc* reflected in a mirror; blame, unfavourable criticism. – *adj* re'flective thoughtful. – *n* re'flector something (*eg* a piece of shiny metal or a piece of glass) which throws back light.

'rēflex *n* an action which is automatic, not intended (*eg* jerking the leg when the kneecap is struck). – Also *adj.*

re'flexive *adj* in grammar, showing that the object (**reflexive pronoun**) of the verb (**reflexive verb**) is the same as its subject (*eg* in '*He cut himself*', *himself* is a *reflexive pronoun* and *cut* a *reflexive verb*).

re'form *v* to improve, remove faults from (a person, one's conduct, an organization *etc*); to give up bad habits, evil *etc*. – *n* an improvement. – *ns* **refor'mation** a change for the better; **Refor'mation** the great religious movement in the Christian Church in the 16th century from which the Protestant Church arose; **re'former** one who wishes to bring about improvements.

'rē-'form *v* to form again (*eg* a society).

re'fract *v* to change the direction of (a ray of light). – *n* **re'fraction**.

re'fractory *adj* (of persons) unruly, not easily controlled.

re'frain *n* a chorus coming at the end of each verse of a song. – *v* to keep oneself back (from doing something). *Please refrain from smoking.*

re'fresh *v* to give new strength, power, or life to. – *adj* **re'freshing** bringing back strength; cooling. – *n* **re'freshment** that which refreshes (*eg* food and drink). – *n* **refresher course** a course of study intended to keep up or increase skill or knowledge that one already has. – **refresh one's memory** to go over facts again so that they are clear in one's mind.

refrigerator [rəˈfrijərātər] *n* a machine which keeps food cold and so prevents it from going bad. – *v* **re'frigerate**. – *n* **refrige'ration**.

refuel ['rēˈfūəl] *v* to supply with, or take in, fresh fuel: – *pt* **'re'fuelled**.

refuge ['refūj] *n* a place of safety (from attack, danger *etc*). – *n* **refu'gee** one who seeks shelter (from persecution *etc*) in another country.

re'fund *v* tō pay back. – *n* **'rēfund**.

refuse[1] [rəˈfūz] *v* to say that one will not (do something). *He refused to leave the room*; to withhold, not to give (*eg* permission). – *n* **re'fusal**.

refuse[2] ['refūs] *n* that which is thrown aside as worthless, rubbish.

re'fute *v* to prove wrong (something that has been said or written). – *n* **refu'tation**.

re'gain *v* to win back again; to get back to. *He jumped from the boat and regained the shore in ten minutes.*

'rēgal *adj* kingly, royal. – *npl* **re'gālia** certain marks or signs of royalty (*eg* crown and sceptre).

re'gale *v* to entertain in a splendid way.

re'gard *v* to look upon, consider. *I regard you as a nuisance*; to look at

carefully; to pay attention to. – *n* concern; affection; respect; (*pl*) good wishes. – *prep* **re'garding** concerning, to do with. *He received a reply regarding his application for a job.* – **re'gardless of** paying no care or attention to; **with** (or **in**) **regard to** concerning.

re'gatta *n* a meeting for yacht or boat races.

regency *see* regent.

regenerate [rəˈjenərāt] *v* to make new and good again. – *n* **regene'ration**.

'rēgent *n* one who governs in place of a king or queen. – *n* **'regency** (a time of) rule by a regent.

'regicide *n* the killing of a king; one who kills a king.

régime [rāˈzhēm] *n* method or system of government or administration.

regimen ['rejimən] *n* diet and habits to be followed.

'regiment *n* a body of soldiers, commanded by a colonel. – *v* **regi'ment** to organize or control too strictly. – *adj* **regi'mental** of a regiment. – *n* **regimen'tation** too strict control *etc*.

region ['rējən] *n* a stretch of land; an area or district. – *adj* **'regional**. – **in the region of** somewhere' near (in position or amount): *in the region of the stomach.*

'register *n* a written list (*eg* of attendances at school, of people who have votes *etc*); the distance between the highest and lowest notes of a voice or instrument. – *v* to write down, or have one's name put, in a register; to record, make (one's vote *etc*); to show, record. *A thermometer registers temperature.* – *ns* **regis'trar** one whose duty it is to keep a register of births, deaths, marriages; **'registry** an office where a register is kept: – *pl* **'registries**. – *ns* **registered letter** one insured against loss by the post office; **registry office** one where records of births, marriages and deaths are kept and where marriages may be performed.

re'gret *v* to be sorry about. *I regret any inconvenience you have suffered. I regret that I missed him*; to be sorry (to have to say something): – *pt* **re'gretted**. – *n* sorrow for anything. – *adjs* **re'gretful**; **re'grettable** to be regretted, unwelcome.

'regular *adj* done according to rule or habit; usual; arranged in order; even: *regular teeth*; happening at certain fixed times. – *n* a soldier of the regular army. – *n* **regu'larity**. – *v* **'regulate** to control by rules; to adjust to a certain order or rate. – *ns* **regu'lation** a rule or order; **'regulator** a person or thing that regulates. – *n* **regular army** the part of the army which is kept always in training, even in peacetime.

regurgitate [ri'gȯrjitāt] *v* to bring back into the mouth after swallowing. – *n* **regurgi'tation**.

rēha'bilitate *v* to give back rights, powers or health to; to train or accustom (a disabled person *etc*) to live a normal life. – *n* **rehabili'tation**.

rehearsal [rə'hȯrsəl] *n* a private practice of a play, concert *etc* before performance in public; any practice for a future event or action. – *v* **re'hearse** to practise beforehand; to tell (facts, events *etc*) in order.

reign [rān] *n* rule; the time during which a king or queen rules. – *v* to rule; to prevail: *silence reigned at last.*

rēim'burse *v* to pay (a person an amount) to cover expenses. – *n* **reim'bursement**.

rein [rān] *n* one of two straps attached to a bridle for guiding a horse; (*pl*) a simple device for controlling a child when walking. – *v* to control (with reins).

reincarnation [rēinkär'nāshən] *n* the rebirth of the soul in another body after death.

reindeer ['rāndēr] *n* a type of deer found in the far North: – *pl* **'reindeer**.

reinforce [rēin'fȯrs] *v* to strengthen (*eg* an army with men, concrete with iron). – *n* **rein'forcement** the act of reinforcing; anything which strengthens.

reinstate [rēin'stāt] *v* to put back in a former position. – *n* **rein'statement**.

reiterate [rē'itərāt] *v* to repeat, *esp* several times. – *n* **reite'ration**.

re'ject *v* to throw away, cast aside; to refuse to take. *He rejected his offer of help*; to turn down (*eg* an application, request). – *ns* **'reject, re'jection**.

re'joice *v* to feel or show joy. – *n* **re'joicing**.

re'joinder *n* an answer to a reply.

rejuvenate [rə'jōōvənāt] *v* to make young again. – *n* **rejuve'nation**.

re'lapse *v* to fall back (*eg* into ill health, bad habits). – Also *n*.

re'late *v* to show a connection between (two or more things); to tell (a story). – *adj* **re'lated** (often with **to**) of the same family (as). *I'm related to him*; connected. – *ns* **re'lation** one who is of the same family, either by birth or marriage; a connection between two or more things; **re'lationship** connection; **relative** ['relətiv] one who is of

the same family *etc*. – *adj* comparative: *the relative speed of a car and a train.*

re'lax *v* to become or make less tense; to slacken (*eg* one's grip or control); to make (laws, rules) less severe. – *n* **relax'ation** a slackening; rest from work. *He played tennis for relaxation.*

'relay *v* to receive and pass on (*eg* news, a message, a television programme): – *pt* **'relayed**. – *n* the sending out of a radio or television broadcast received from another station; a fresh set of people *etc* to replace others at some job, task *etc*. – *n* **relay race** a race in which members of each team take over from each other, each member running *etc* an arranged distance. – **in relays** in groups which take over from one another in doing something.

re'lease *v* to set free; to let go; to allow (news *etc*) to be made public. – Also *n*.

relegate ['religāt] *v* to put down (to a lower position, group *etc*); to leave (a task *etc* to someone else). – *n* **rele'gation**.

re'lent *v* to become less severe (with a person). – *adj* **re'lentless** without pity; refusing to be turned from one's purpose.

relevant ['reləvənt] *adj* having to do with what is being spoken about. – *n* **'relevance**.

reliable, reliance *see* **rely**.

'relic *n* something left over from a past time.

relief [rə'lēf] *n* a lessening of pain or anxiety; release from a post or duty; person(s) taking over one's duty *etc*; help given to those in need: *famine relief*; the act of freeing (a town *etc*) from a siege; a way of carving or moulding in which the design stands out from its background. – *v* **relieve** [rə'lēv] to lessen (pain or anxiety); to take over a duty from (someone else); to come to the help of (a town *etc* under attack).

religion [rə'lijən] *n* belief in, or worship of, a god. – *adj* **re'ligious**.

re'linquish *v* to give up, abandon: *relinquish control.*

'relish *v* to enjoy; to like the taste of. – *n* enjoyment; flavour; something which gives flavour: – *pl* **'relishes**.

re'luctant *adj* unwilling. – *n* **re'luctance**.

re'lȳ *v* to have full trust in, depend (on): – *pt* **re'lied**. – *adj* **re'liable** able to be trusted or counted on. – *ns* **relia'bility; re'liance** trust. – *adj* **re'liant**.

re'main *v* to stay, not to leave; to be left. *Only two tins of soup remained*; to be still (the same). *The problem remains unsolved.* – *n* re'mainder that which is left behind after removal of the rest; (in arithmetic) the number left after subtraction or division. – *npl* re'mains that which is left; a dead body.

re'mand *v* to put a person back in prison until more evidence is found. – **on remand** having been remanded.

re'mark *v* to say; to comment (on); to notice. – *n* something said. – *adj* re'markable deserving notice, unusual.

remedy ['remədi] *n* a cure for an illness, evil *etc*. – *pl* 'remedies. – *v* to cure; to put right.

re'member *v* to keep in mind; to recall to the mind after having forgotten; to send one's best wishes (to). *Remember me to your mother*; to reward, give a present to. *He remembered her in his will.* – *n* re'membrance the act of remembering; memory; something given *etc* to remind someone of a person or an event, a keepsake, a souvenir; (*pl*) a friendly greeting.

re'mind *v* to bring (something) back to a person's mind. *Remind me to post that letter*; to cause (someone) to think about (a person or thing) by resembling (the person or thing) in some way. *She reminds me of her sister. Her nose reminds me of a pig's snout.* – *n* re'minder one who or that which reminds.

reminiscence [remi'nisns] *n* something (*eg* an event) remembered from the past; (*pl*) memories (*esp* when told or written). – *adj* remi'niscent reminding one of: *reminiscent of Paris*; in a mood to think about past events *etc*. – *v* remi'nisce to think and talk about things remembered from the past.

re'miss *adj* careless. *It was remiss of me to forget your birthday.*

remission [rə'mishən] *n* the act of remitting; a shortening (of a person's prison sentence); (of a disease *etc*) a lessening in force or effect.

re'mit *v* to pardon, excuse (a crime *etc*); to wipe out, cancel (a debt *etc*); to lessen, (cause to) become less intense; to send (money); to hand over (*eg* a prisoner to a higher court): – *pt* re'mit-ted. – *n* re'mittance the sending of money *etc esp* to a distance; the money sent.

'remnant *n* a small piece or small number of things left over from a larger piece or number.

'remonstrate *v* to make a protest. *He remonstrated with me about my extravagance.* – *n* re'monstrance.

re'morse *n* regret about something bad or wrong which one has done. – *adjs* re'morseful; re'morseless having no remorse; cruel.

re'mote *adj* far away in time or place; far from any (other) village, town *etc*; slight: *a remote chance.*

remove [rə'mōōv] *v* to take (something) from its place; to dismiss (a person from a post); to take off (clothes *etc*); to get rid of. *I can't remove this stain from my skirt.* – *n* a stage or degree away (from): *one remove from tyranny.* – *n* re'moval the act of removing, *esp* of furniture *etc* to a new home. – *adj* re'moved separated or distant (from); (of cousins) separated by a generation: *first cousin once removed* (*eg* a cousin's child).

remunerate [rə'mūnərāt] *v* to pay (someone) for something done. – *n* remune'ration pay, salary. – *adj* re'munerative profitable.

'rēnal *adj* of the kidneys.

rend *v* to tear (apart), divide: – *pt* rent.

render *v* to give back (*eg* property); to give (*eg* thanks): to translate into another language; to perform (music *etc*); to cause to be. *His words rendered me speechless.* – *n* 'rendering a translation; a performance.

rendezvous ['rondivōō] *n* a meeting place fixed beforehand; the meeting itself: – *pl* 'rendezvous.

renegade ['renigād] *adj, n* (of) one who deserts his side, religion or beliefs.

renew [rə'nū] *v* to make as if new again; to begin again: *renew one's efforts*; to make usable for a further period of time (*eg* a driving licence); to replace: *renew the water in the tank.* – *n* re'newal.

'rennet *n* a substance used in curdling milk for making junket *etc.*

re'nounce *v* to give up, *esp* publicly or formally. *He renounced his claim to the title.* – *n* renunci'ation.

'renovate *v* to make (something) like new again, to mend. – *n* reno'vation.

renown [rə'nown] *n* fame. – *adj* re'nowned famous.

rent *n* a tear, a split; a payment made for the use of a house, shop, land *etc.* – *v* see rend; to pay or receive rent for a house *etc.* – *n* 'rental money paid as rent. – rent out to give for use in return for money.

renunciation *see* renounce.

rē'organize *v* to put in a different order. – *n* reorgani'zation.

rep short for representative (salesman) or repertory.

re'pair *v* to mend; to make up for (a

wrong); (*old*) to go. *He repaired once more to his house.* – *n* the condition in which a thing is. *The house is in bad repair;* the act or process of mending: *in need of repair;* a mended place. – *n* **repa'ration** something which makes up for a wrong.

repar'tee *n* a quick, witty reply; an exchange of witty remarks between people; skill in witty conversation.

re'past *n* (*old*) a meal.

rē'patriate *v* to send (someone) back to his own country. – *n* **repatri'ation**.

rē'pay *v* to pay back; to give or do something in return. *He repaid her kindness with a gift:* – *pt* **re'paid**. – *n* **re'payment** the act of repaying; that which is paid back.

re'peal *v* to do away with, cancel (*esp* a law). – Also *n*.

re'peat *v* to say or do over again; to say from memory; to tell, pass on (someone's words), sometimes when one ought not to. – *n* something repeated (*eg* a television programme, a passage of music). – *adv* **re'peatedly** again and again. – *ns* **re'peater** a gun which fires several shots; **repetition** [repə'tishən] the act of repeating; something repeated. – *adj* **re'petitive** repeating (something) too often.

re'pel *v* to drive back or away; to disgust: – *pt* **re'pelled**. – *adj* **re'pellent** disgusting. – *n* something that drives away (something): *an insect repellent*.

re'pent *v* to be sorry (for what one has done); (with **of**) to regret. – *n* **re'pent-ance**. – *adj* **re'pentant** repenting.

repercussion [rēpər'kushən] *n* an indirect or resultant effect of something which has happened. *The event, though itself minor, had wide repercussions.*

repertoire ['repərtwär] *n* the range of works that a performer, singer, theatre company *etc* is able or ready to perform.

'repertory *n* repertoire. – *n* **repertory theatre** a theatre with a more or less permanent company which performs a series of plays.

repetition see **repeat**.

re'place *v* to put (something) back where it was; to put (something or someone) in place of another.' *He replaced the cup he broke with the new one.*

re'plenish *v* to fill up one's supply (of something) again.

re'plete *adj* full.

'replica *n* an exact copy (of a picture, a piece of furniture *etc*).

re'plȳ *v* to speak or act in answer to something: – *pt* **re'plied**. – *n* an

answer: – *pl* **re'plies**.

report [rə'pört] *v* to pass on news; to give a description (of an event *etc*); to tell about; to write down and take notes of (a speech, meeting *etc*) *esp* for a newspaper; to make a complaint against (*esp* to the police or the authorities). – *n* a statement of facts; an account, description, *esp* in a newspaper; a rumour; a written description of a pupil's work; a loud noise, *esp* the sound made by the firing of a gun. – *n* **re'porter** one who reports, *esp* one who writes articles for a newspaper.

repose [rə'pōz] *n* sleep, rest. – *v* to rest; to place (*eg* trust in a person). – *n* **repository** [rə'pozitəri] a place where things are stored,*esp* for safe keeping: – *pl* **re'positories**.

repre'hensible *adj* deserving blame.

represent [reprə'zent] *v* to speak or act on behalf of a person or a group of people. *He represents the tenants' association;* to stand for, to be a sign or symbol of. *Each letter represents a sound;* to claim to be. *He represents himself as an expert;* to explain, point out. – *n* **represen'tation** the act of representing or being represented; an image, picture; (often *pl*) a strong claim or appeal. – *adj* **repre'sentative** typical, having the characteristics of all its kind: *a representative specimen;* standing or acting for another or others. – *n* one who acts or speaks on behalf of a group of people (*eg* in parliament, at a conference); a travelling salesman for a firm.

re'press *v* to keep down by force; to keep under control. – *n* **re'pression**.

reprieve [rə'prēv] *v* to pardon (a criminal); to give a period of freedom (from trouble, difficulty) to. – Also *n*.

repri'mand *v* to scold severely. – *n* **'reprimand**.

'rē'print *v* to print again; to print more copies of (a book *etc*). – *n* **'reprint** another printing of a book.

reprisal [rə'prīzəl] *n* the act of paying back wrong for wrong. *The attack was a reprisal for an earlier one by the other side.*

re'proach *v* to express disappointment or displeasure; to scold; to blame. – *n* the act of reproaching; blame, discredit; something that brings blame or discredit. *This pile of rubbish is a reproach to the council.* – *adj* **re'proachful** showing that one blames: *a reproachful glance.*

'reprobate *n* a person of evil or immoral habits. – Also *adj*.

rēpro'duce v to produce a copy of; (of humans, animals and plants) to produce (young, seeds etc). – n **reproduction** [rēprə'dukshən] the act or process of reproducing; something reproduced, a copy.

re'proof n a scolding, criticism for a fault or wrong. – v **reprove** [rə'proōv] to scold, blame. – adj **re'proving**.

'reptile n any of the group of creeping, cold-blooded animals which includes snakes, lizards etc. – adj **reptilian** [rep'tiliən].

re'public n a form of government in which power is in the hands of the people's elected representatives with a president instead of a king etc. – adj **re'publican**. – adj, n (US) **Re'publican** (of, belonging to) one of the two chief political parties in the United States.

re'pūdiate v to refuse to acknowledge as one's own; to refuse to recognize or accept. He repudiated the committee's suggestion. – n **repudi'ation**.

re'pugnant adj hateful, distasteful. – n **re'pugnance**.

re'pulse v to drive back (an enemy etc); to reject, snub (a person). – Also n. – n **re'pulsion** disgust. – adj **re'pulsive** causing disgust, loathsome.

repū'tation n the opinion held by people in general of a particular person; good name. – adj **'reputable** having a good reputation, well thought of. – n **re'pute** reputation. – adj **re'puted** considered, thought (to be something): reputed to be dangerous; supposed: the reputed author of the book. – adv **re'putedly** in the opinion of most people.

re'quest v to ask for. – n the act of asking for (something); something asked for.

'requiem n a hymn or mass sung for the dead; the music for this.

re'quire v to need; to demand, order. – n **re'quirement** something needed; a demand.

requisite ['rekwizit] adj required, necessary. – n something needed or necessary. – n **requi'sition** a (formal) demand or request for supplies (eg for a school or an army). – Also v.

re'quite v to repay, give back in return; to repay or avenge (one action) by another. – n **re'quital** payment in return.

rescind [rə'sind] v to do away with, cancel (an order or law).

rescue ['reskū] v to save from a dangerous situation; to free from capture. – n an act which saves (someone or something) from danger or capture.

research [rə'sərch] n a close and careful (scientific) study or investigation to try to find out new facts (about something): cancer research: – pl re-'searches. – v to study carefully; (with **into**) to take part in such a study or investigation. – n **re'searcher** one who researches.

resemble [rə'zembl] v to look like or be like. He doesn't resemble either of his parents. – n **re'semblance** likeness.

resent [ri'zent] v to feel injured, annoyed or insulted by. – adj **re'sentful**. – n **re'sentment** ill will, bitterness, annoyance.

reserve [rə'zərv] v to set aside (for future or special use); to book, have kept for one (eg a seat, a table, a library book). – n something reserved; (esp pl) troops or forces outside the regular army kept ready to help those already fighting; a piece of land set apart for some reason: nature reserve; the habit of not speaking or acting in an open friendly manner, shyness. – n **reser'vation** the act of reserving, booking; an exception or condition. He agreed to the plan, but with certain reservations; doubt, objection. I had reservations about his appointment. – adj **re'served** unwilling to speak one's thoughts openly or to behave in a friendly way; kept back for a particular person or purpose.

reservoir ['rezərvwär] n a place (usu a manmade lake) where water is kept in store.

reside [rə'zīd] v to live, have one's home (in); (of power, authority etc) to be present in, be placed (in). – ns **residence** ['rezidəns] a house or other place (esp an impressive or large building) where one lives; the act of living in a place; the period of time one lives in a place; **'resident** one who has his home in a particular place or area: a resident of Blackpool. – adj living in (a place); living in, or having to live in, the place where one works: resident caretaker. – adj **resi'dential** (of an area) containing houses rather than shops, factories etc; providing living accommodation. The university runs a residential course.

residue ['rezidū] n what is left over. – adj **re'sidual**.

resign [rə'zin] v to give up (one's job, position etc). – n **resignation** [rezig'nāshən] the act of resigning; a letter to say one is resigning; patient, calm acceptance of a situation. – adj **resigned** [rə'zind] patient, not actively complaining. – **resign oneself to** to accept (a situation *etc*) with patience and calmness.

resilient [rə'ziliənt] *adj* (of a person) readily recovering from misfortune, hurt *etc*; (of an object) readily recovering its original shape after being bent, twisted *etc*. – *n* **re'silience**.

resin ['rezin] *n* a sticky substance produced by certain plants (*eg* firs, pines). – *adj* **'resinous**.

resist [rə'zist] *v* to struggle against, oppose (*esp* successfully); to stop oneself from (doing something). – *n* **re'sistance** the act of resisting; any organized opposition to something (*esp* a force occupying a country); the ability of a substance to turn an electric current passing through it into heat.

resolute ['rezəlōōt] *adj* determined, with mind made up. – *n* **reso'lution** firmness or determination of mind or purpose; a firm decision (to do something); a proposal put before a meeting; an opinion or decision formally expressed by a group of people *eg* a public meeting.

resolve [rə'zolv] *v* to decide firmly (to do something); to solve (a difficulty); to break up into parts. – *n* a firm purpose.

resonate ['rezənāt] *v* to echo. – *n* **'resonance** a deep, echoing tone. – *adj* **'resonant** echoing, resounding.

resort [rə'zört] *v* to begin to use *etc*, turn (to) *esp* in a difficulty. *Finally he had to resort to violence*. – *n* a frequently visited place (*esp* for holidays). – **in the last resort** when all else fails.

resound [rə'zownd] *v* to sound loudly; to echo. – *adj* **re'sounding** echoing; thorough: *a resounding victory*.

resource [rə'zörs] *n* (*usu pl*) a source or means of supplying what is required; (*usu pl*) a natural source of wealth in a country *etc*; (*pl*) money or other property; an ability to handle situations skilfully and cleverly. – *adj* **re'sourceful** good at finding ways out of difficulties.

res'pect *v* to show or feel a high regard or admiration for; to treat with care or consideration: *respect his wishes*. – *n* high regard, esteem, admiration; consideration; a detail, way: *alike in some respects*; (*pl*) good wishes. – *adj* **res'pectable** worthy of respect; having a good reputation; considerable, large, fairly good: *a respectable score*. – *n* **respecta'bility** the state of being respectable. – *adjs* **res'pectful** showing respect; **res'pective** belonging to each (person or thing mentioned) separately. *Peter and George went to their*

respective homes (*eg* each went to his own home). – *adv* **res'pectively** in the order given. *Peter, James and John were first, second and third respectively.* – **in respect of** concerning, as regards; **with respect to** with reference to.

res'pire *v* to breathe. – *ns* **respiration** [respə'rāshən] breathing; **'respirator** a mask worn over the mouth and nose to purify the air breathed in *eg* in the presence of gas; a device used to help very ill or injured people breathe, when they are unable to do so naturally.

'respite *n* a pause, rest: *no respite from work*.

res'plendent *adj* very bright or splendid in appearance.

res'pond *v* to answer; to act or react in response to (something or an action). *The baby responded to her new toy with a smile. I smiled but she did not respond*; to show a reaction to *esp* as a sign of improvement. *He responded to treatment*. – *n* **res'ponse** a reply; an action, feeling *etc* in return for or in answer to another action *etc*; the answer made to the priest during church services. – *adj* **res'ponsible** (sometimes with **for**) being the cause of: *responsible for this mess*; liable to be called to account for or blamed for (actions, standard of work *etc*) to (someone in authority). *He is responsible to the manager for the conduct of his staff*; involving the making of important decisions *etc*: *a responsible post*; trustworthy. – *n* **responsi'bility**: – *pl* **responsi'bilities**. – *adj* **res'ponsive** quick to react *eg* to show interest, sympathy *etc*.

rest *n* a pause or break in work; a sleep; a support or prop for something: *a book rest*; (with **the**) what is left, the remainder: *the rest of the meat*; all the other people not mentioned. *Jack went home but the rest went to the cinema*. – *v* to stop working *etc* for a time; to be still; to sleep; to depend (on), be based on. *The case rests on your evidence*, to stop, develop no further. *I can't let the matter rest there*; to lean, lie or place on a support. – *adjs* **'restful** relaxing; relaxed; **restive** ['restiv] restless, impatient; not easily managed or controlled; **'restless** unable to keep or lie still; getting no rest; agitated. – **rest with** to be the duty, right or responsibility of. *The choice rests with you.*

restaurant ['restəront] *n* a place where meals may be bought and eaten. – *n* **restaurateur** [restərə'tör] the owner or manager of a restaurant.

resti'tution *n* the act of giving back what

has been lost or taken away; compensation for harm or injury done.

restive see **rest**.

res'tore v to put or give back; to repair (a building, a painting *etc*) so that it looks as it used to; to cure (a person). – n **resto'ration**.

res'train v to hold back (from); to keep under control. – n **res'traint** the act of restraining; the state of being restrained; self-control.

res'trict v to limit, keep within the bounds of space, time, quantity *etc*: *a restricted space*; (of an area *etc*) to make open only to certain people: *restricted area: restricted zone*. – n **res'triction** the act of restricting; something (*esp* a rule, law *etc*) which restricts. – *adj* **res'trictive** having the effect or aim of restricting.

result [rə'zult] n anything which is due to something already done, said *etc*; a consequence; the answer to a sum; (in games) the score. – v (with **from**) to be the result or effect (of something done, said *etc*); (with **in**) to have as a result. *The match resulted in a draw.* – *adj* **re'sultant**.

resume [rə'zūm] v to begin again after a pause or interruption: *resume a discussion*; to take again. *He resumed his seat by the fire.* – n **resumption** [rə'zumpshən].

résumé ['rāzōōmā] n a summary.

re'surgent *adj* rising again. – n **re'surgence** a rising again into activity or prominence.

resurrection [rezə'rekshən] n a rising from the dead, *esp* of Christ; the act of bringing back into use. – v **resur'rect** to bring back to life; to bring back into use.

resuscitate [rə'susətāt] v to bring back to consciousness, revive. – n **resusci'tation**.

'rētail v to sell goods to the person who is going to use them (not to someone who is going to sell them to someone else); to tell (*eg* a story) fully and in detail. – n the sale of goods to the actual user not to another seller. – n **'retailer** one who retails (goods); a shopkeeper.

re'tain v to keep possession of, continue to have; to keep (something) in mind; to reserve (a person's services) by paying a fee beforehand; to hold back, keep in place. – n **re'tainer** a fee for services paid beforehand; (*old*) a servant (to a family).

'rē'take v to take or capture again. – n **'retake** the filming of part of a film again.

re'taliate v to return like for like, to hit back. *If you insult him he will retaliate.* – n **retali'ation**.

re'tard v to keep back, hinder; to make slow or late. – n **retar'dation**. – *adj* **re'tarded** slow in mental or physical growth.

retch v to make the muscular actions and sound of vomiting, *usu* without actually vomiting.

re'tention n the act of holding in; the act of keeping possession of; the act of retaining the services of (*eg* a lawyer). – *adj* **re'tentive** able to hold or retain: *a retentive memory*.

'reticent *adj* unwilling to, or not in the habit of speaking openly and freely, reserved. – n **'reticence**.

'retina n the part of the back of the eye that receives the image of what is seen: – *pls* **'retinas, retinae** ['retinē].

retinue ['retinū] n the attendants who follow a person of rank or importance.

re'tire v to give up work permanently *usu* because of age; to go to bed; to draw back, retreat. – n **re'tiral** retirement. – *adj* **re'tired** having given up work; (of a place) out-of-the-way, quiet. – n **re'tirement** the act of retiring from work; one's life after one has given up work. – *adj* **re'tiring** shy, liking to avoid being noticed.

re'tort v to make a quick and sharp or witty reply. – n a ready and sharp reply; a bottle of thin glass, (*esp* one with its neck pointing downwards and used for distilling liquids).

re'trace v to go over again. *He retraced his steps to the place he started from.*

re'tract v to take back (what one has said or given); to draw back. *The cat retracted its claws.* – *adj* **re'tractable** able to be retracted. – n **re'traction**.

re'treat v to draw back, withdraw; to go away. – n the act of moving backwards before the advance of an enemy or opponent, or from danger *etc*; a withdrawal; a quiet, peaceful place.

retri'bution n punishment.

retrieve [rə'trēv] v to get back, recover (*eg* something lost); to search for and fetch. *The dog retrieved the pheasant.* – n **re'triever** a breed of dog trained to find and fetch birds which have been shot.

'retrograde *adj* going backward; going from a better to a worse stage.

'retrospect: in retrospect in considering or looking back on the past. – *adj* **retro'spective** looking back on past events; (of a law *etc*) applying to the past as well as the present and the future. *The new tax laws were* *made retrospective.*

re'turn *v* to go or come back; to give, send, pay *etc* back; to elect (a person to parliament *etc*). – *n* the act of returning; a profit: *a return on your investment*; a statement of income *etc* (for calculating one's income tax). – *adj* re'turnable able to be returned; that must be returned. – *ns* return match a second match played between the same team or players; return ticket a ticket which covers a journey both to and from a place. – by return (of a letter *etc*) sent by the first post back.

rē'ūnion *n* a meeting of people who have been apart for some time. – *v* reu'nite to join after having been separated.

re'veal *v* to make known; to show. – *n* revelation [revə'lāshən] the act of revealing; that which is made known, *esp* something unexpected.

reveille [rə'vali] *n* a bugle call at daybreak to waken soldiers.

'revel *v* to take great delight (in); to make merry: – *pt* 'revelled. – *n* (*usu pl*) merrymaking. – *ns* 'reveller; 'revelry noisy merrymaking.

revelation *see* reveal.

revenge [rə'venj] *n* harm done to another person in return for harm which he has done; the desire to do such harm. – *v* to inflict punishment, injury *etc* in return for harm or injury done. *He revenged his father's murder*; (with oneself) to take revenge. *He revenged himself on his enemies.*

revenue ['revənū] *n* money received as payment, income (*esp* that of a country) from all sources.

re'verberate *v* to echo and re-echo, resound. – *n* reverbe'ration.

re'vere *v* to look upon with great respect. – *n* reverence ['revərəns] great respect; expression of this. – *adjs* 'reverend worthy of respect; 'Reverend (*usu* written Rev) a title given to a clergyman; 'reverent, reve'rential showing respect.

reverie ['revəri] *n* a daydream.

re'verse *v* to turn upside down or the other way round; to (cause to) move backwards; to undo (a decision, policy *etc*). – *n* the opposite (of); the other side (of a coin *etc*); a defeat. – *n* re'versal the act of reversing or being reversed. – *adj* re'versible (of clothes *etc*) able to be worn with either side out.

re'vert *v* to come or go back to an earlier subject; (of an object, title *etc*) to return or be returned to its previous owner or members of his family. –

n re'version.

review [rə'vū] *v* to give a written opinion or criticism of (*eg* a new book); to look at or consider again. *He reviewed the facts*; to inspect (*eg* troops). – *n* a written critical opinion and account (of a book, play *etc*); a magazine consisting of such accounts; a second look at or consideration of; an inspection of troops *etc*. – *n* re'viewer one who reviews, a critic.

re'vile *v* to say harsh things about.

revise [rə'vīz] *v* (to examine in order) to correct faults and make improvements; to study one's previous work, one's notes *etc* as preparation for an examination; to change (*eg* one's opinion). – *n* revision [rə'vizhən] the act of revising; a revised form (of something *esp* a book).

re'vive *v* to bring or come back to life, use, strength, or fame. – *ns* re'vival a return to life, use *etc*; (a time of) a fresh show of interest: *a religious revival*; re'vivalist a person who helps to create a religious revival.

re'voke *v* to do away with, cancel (a decision *etc*); (in card games) to fail to follow suit.

re'volt *v* to rise up (against), to rebel; to feel disgust (at); to disgust. – *n* a rising against those in power, a rebellion. – *adj* re'volting causing disgust.

revolution [revə'lōōshən] *n* a full turn round a centre, as that made by a record on a record-player; the act of turning round a centre; a rising of a people or party against those in power; a complete change (as in ideas, way of doing things). – *adj* revo'lutionary (aimed at) bringing about great changes (as in government, ideas); tending to do this; turning. – *n* a person who is involved in or who is in favour of revolution: – *pl* revo'lutionaries. – *v* revo'lutionize to bring about a complete change in.

re'volve *v* to roll or turn round. – *n* re'volver a kind of pistol.

revue [rə'vū] *n* a light theatre show, *usu* with short plays or sketches, often based on recent events.

revulsion [rə'vulshən] *n* disgust; a sudden change of feeling (*esp* from love to hate).

reward [rə'wörd] *n* something given in return for service or work done or for good behaviour *etc*; a sum of money offered for finding or helping to find a criminal, lost property *etc*. – *v* to give a reward to (a person); to give a reward for (a service). – *adj* re'warding giving pleasure, satisfaction, profit *etc*.

rhapsody ['rapsədi] *n* music, poetry, or speech which shows strong feeling or excitement. – *v* '**rhapsodize** to talk or write wildly and enthusiastically (about). – **go into rhapsodies over** to show wild enthusiasm for.

rhetoric ['retərik] *n* the art of good speaking or writing; language which is too showy, consisting of unnecessarily long or difficult words *etc*. – *adj* **rhe-'torical**. – *n* **rhetorical question** one which the asker answers himself, or which does not need an answer.

rheumatism ['rōōmətizəm] *n* a disease which causes stiffness and pain in one's joints. – *adj* **rheu'matic**.

rhinoceros [ri'nosərəs] *n* a type of large, thick-skinned animal, with one horn (or two) on the nose: – *pl* **rhi'noceros(es)**.

rhododendron [rōdə'dendrən] *n* a type of flowering shrub with thick evergreen leaves and large flowers.

rhubarb ['rōōbärb] *n* a plant, the stalks of which are used in cooking.

rhyme [rīm] *n* in poetry, a likeness between the sounds of words or of their endings (such as *humble* and *crumble* or *convention* and *prevention*); a word which is like another word in this way; a short poem. – *v* (sometimes with **with**) to sound like, to be rhymes. 'Star' rhymes with 'car'.

rhythm ['ridhəm] *n* a regular repeated pattern of sounds, beats or stresses in music, speech (*esp* poetry) *etc*; a regularly repeated pattern of movements. – *adjs* '**rhythmic**, '**rhythmical**.

rib *n* any one of the bones which curve round and forward from the backbone, enclosing the heart and lungs; one of the spars of wood which form the framework of a boat, curving up from the keel. – *adj* **ribbed** arranged in ridges and furrows.

'**ribald** *adj* (of jokes, songs *etc*) coarse, vulgar.

'**ribbon** *n* a narrow strip or band of silk or other material, used in decorating clothes, tying hair *etc*.

rice *n* the seeds of a plant, grown in well-watered ground in tropical countries, used as a food.

rich *adj* possessing much money or much of value, wealthy; valuable: *a rich reward*; (with **in**) having much of: *a country rich in natural resources*; (of food) containing much fat, eggs, sugar *etc*; (of material, clothes *etc*) splendid; (of a colour) deep in tone; (*pl*) '**riches** wealth. – *adv* '**richly**. – *n* '**richness**.

'**rickets** *n* a disease of children, causing

softening and bending of the bones. *Rickets is caused by lack of calcium.* – *adj* '**rickety** suffering from rickets; unsteady: *a rickety table*.

'**rickshaw** *n* a two-wheeled carriage pulled by a man.

ricochet ['rikəshā] *v* (of a bullet *etc*) to rebound at an angle from a surface. – Also *n*: – *pt* **ricochet(t)ed** ['rikəshād].

rid *v* to free from, clear of: *to rid the city of rats*: – *pt*, *pp* **rid**. – **get rid of** to free oneself of; **good riddance to** I am happy to have got rid of.

'**riddle** *n* a puzzle in the form of a question *etc* which describes an object or person in a misleading or mysterious way; anything difficult to understand, a mystery; a tray with holes for separating large objects from smaller ones, or solid objects from something in a powder-like form (*eg* stones from soil).

ride *v* to travel, be carried on a horse, bicycle *etc*, or in car, train *etc*; to travel on and control (a horse); (of a ship) to float at anchor: – *pt* **rode**, *pp* **ridden** ['ridn]. – *n* a journey on horseback, bicycle *etc*; a path *esp* through a wood, for riding horses. – *n* '**rider** one who rides; something added to what has already been said. – **ride up** to work itself up out of position. *Her skirt is riding up*.

ridge [rij] *n* a raised part between furrows or anything resembling this; a long crest on high ground.

'**ridicule** *v* to laugh at, mock. – Also *n*. – *adj* **ri'diculous** deserving to be laughed at, very silly.

rife *adj* very common. *Disease was rife in the country*.

'**riff-raff** *n* used insultingly, worthless people.

'**rifle** *n* a gun fired from the shoulder. – *v* to search through and rob; to steal.

rift *n* a crack; a disagreement between friends. – *n* **rift valley** a long valley formed by the fall of part of the earth's crust between faults in the rock.

rig *v* (with **out**) to clothe, to dress; (with **up**) to fit (a ship) with sails and ropes; to manage or control (a ballot, an election result) illegally or dishonestly: – *pt* **rigged**. – *n* '**rigging** ship's spars, ropes *etc*. – **rig up** to make or build (*esp* hastily).

right [rīt] *adj* on, for, or belonging to the side of the body which in most people has the more skilful hand (opposite to **left**); correct, true; just, good; straight. – *adv* to or on the right side; correctly; straight; all the way: *right along the pier and back*. – *n* that which is correct or good, and which ought to be done; something one is entitled to: *a right to a fair trial*; the right-hand side, direction, part *etc*; a group holding the more traditional conservative beliefs. – *v* to mend, set in order; to put back in the proper position. – *adj* **righteous** ['richəs] living a good life; just. – *n* **'righteousness**. – *adj* **'rightful** by right, proper: *the rightful king*. – *n* **right angle** an angle like one of those in a square, an angle of 90°. – *adjs* **'right-'handed** using the right hand more easily than the left; **Right Honourable** used before the names of cabinet ministers in the British government. – *n* **'right-of-'way** a road or path over private land along which people may go as a right. – *adj* **'right-'wing** in politics, of conservative political beliefs. – **by right** because one has the right; **in one's own right** not because of anyone else, independently: *a peeress in her own right*.

'rigid *adj* not easily bent; stiff; strict.

'rigmarole *n* a long, rambling speech.

rigour ['rigər] *n* strictness; harshness. – *adj* **'rigorous** very strict.

rill *n* a small stream.

rim *n* an edge or border, *esp* the outer ring of a wheel or the top edge of a cup *etc*.

rime *n* thick white frost; old form of **rhyme**.

rind *n* a thick firm covering, *esp* the peel of fruit, the skin of bacon, the outer covering of cheese.

ring *n* a small hoop, *esp* of metal, worn on the finger, in or on the ear *etc*; a hollow circle; anything in the shape of a ring; an enclosed space, as for boxing, circus performances *etc*; the sound of a bell or a similar sound; a small group of people *esp* one formed for business or criminal purposes: *a drug ring*. – *v* to encircle, go round; to mark (a bird *etc*) by putting on a ring: – *pt* **ringed**; to make the sound of a bell, or a strong clear sound; to cause (a bell *etc*) to sound; to telephone: – *pt* **rang**, *pp* **rung**. – *ns* **'ringleader** one who takes the lead in mischief *etc*; **'ringlet** a long curl of hair; **'ringmaster** a person who is in charge of the performance in a circus ring; **ring road** a road that circles a town *etc* avoiding the centre; **'ringworm** a skin disease causing circular red patches.

rink *n* a sheet of ice, often artificially made, for skating or curling.

rinse *v* to wash lightly to remove soap *etc*; to clean (a cup, one's mouth *etc*) by putting in and emptying out water. – *n* the act of rinsing; a liquid for rinsing, *esp* one for tinting the hair.

'riot *n* a noisy disturbance, disorder among a group of people; a striking display (of colour). – *v* to take part in a riot. – *adj* **'riotous** noisy, uncontrolled.

rip *v* to tear apart or off; to come apart: – *pt* **ripped**. – *n* a tear.

ripe *adj* (of fruit, grain *etc*) ready to be gathered in or eaten; fully developed, mature. – *v* **'ripen** to make or become ripe or riper. – *n* **'ripeness**.

'ripple *n* a little wave or movement on the surface of water; a soft sound *etc* that rises and falls quickly and gently: *a ripple of laughter*.

rise [rīz] *v* to get up from bed; to stand up; to move upwards, go up, become higher; (of a river *etc*) to have its source (in), to start (in). *The Rhone rises in the Alps*; to rebel. *The people rose against the tyrant*: – *pt* **rose** [rōz], *pp* **risen** ['rizn]. – *n* a slope upwards; an increase in wages, prices *etc*. – *n* **'rising** an act of rising; rebellion. – **give rise to** to cause.

risk *n* a chance of loss or injury; a danger. – *v* to take the chance of: *to risk death*; to take the chance of losing: *to risk one's life, health etc.* – *adj* **'risky** possibly resulting in loss or injury.

risotto [rə'zotō] *n* a dish made with rice.

'rissole *n* a fried cake or ball of minced meat, fish *etc*.

rite *n* a solemn ceremony, *esp* a religious one. – *n* **ritual** ['richōōəl] a traditional or set way of carrying out religious worship *etc*. – *adj* of or forming a rite or ceremony.

'rival *n* one who tries to equal or beat (another). – *v* to (try to) equal: – *pt* **'rivalled**. – *n* **'rivalry**: – *pl* **'rivalries**.

'riven *adj* (*old*) split.

'river *n* a large stream of water flowing across land.

'rivet *n* a bolt for fastening plates of metal together. – *v* to fasten with a rivet; to fix firmly (someone's attention *etc*): *riveted by the play*: *riveted to the spot*.

'rivulet *n* a small stream.

roach *n* a type of freshwater fish: – *pl* **'roaches**.

road *n* a way (*usu* with a hard, level surface) for vehicles and people; a way of getting to (somewhere), a route; (*pl*) a place where ships may lie at anchor (also **'roadstead**). – *n* **'roadway** the part of a road used by cars *etc*. – *adj* **'roadworthy** (of a vehicle) fit to be used on the road.

roam *v* to wander about.

roan *n* a horse with a dark-brown coat spotted with grey or white.

roar *v* to give a loud, deep sound; to laugh loudly; to say (something) loudly. – Also *n*.

roast *v* to cook or be cooked in an oven or over or in front of a fire. – *adj* roasted: *roast beef*. – *n* meat roasted; meat for roasting.

rob *v* to steal from (a person or place): – *pt* **robbed**. – *ns* **'robber; 'robbery** the act of stealing: – *pl* **'robberies**.

robe *n* a long loose garment; (*US*) a dressing gown; (*pl*) the dress (as of a judge *etc*) showing rank or position. – *v* to dress.

'robin *n* a type of small bird, known by its red breast.

'rōbot *n* a mechanical man or woman.

ro'bust *adj* strong, healthy.

rock *n* a large lump or mass of stone; a hard sweet made in sticks; music or songs with a heavy beat and *usu* with a simple melody (also **rock music**). – *v* to sway backwards and forwards or from side to side. – *ns* **'rocker** a curved support on which anything (*eg* a cradle *etc*) rocks; **'rockery** a collection of stones amongst which small plants are grown: – *pl* **'rockeries**. – *adj* **'rocky** full of rocks; inclined to rock, shaky, unsteady. – *ns* **'rock-and-'roll** a simpler, earlier form of rock music (also **rock 'n' roll**); **'rocking-chair, -horse** a chair, a toy horse which rocks backwards and forwards on rockers.

'rocket *n* a tube containing materials which, when set on fire, give off a jet of gas driving the tube forward, used for launching a spacecraft, for signalling, and as a firework; a spacecraft so launched. – *v* to move, *esp* upwards, very rapidly. *House prices are rocketing*.

rod *n* a long thin stick or bar; a fishing rod; an old measure of distance, about 5 metres.

rode *see* **ride**.

'rōdent *n* any gnawing animal (as the rat, beaver *etc*).

rodeo ['rōdiō] *n* a roundup of cattle for marking; a show of riding by cowboys.

roe *n* the eggs of fishes; (also **roe deer**) a small kind of deer; a female red deer. – *n* **'roebuck** the male roe deer.

rogue [rōg] *n* a dishonest person; a mischievous person, a rascal. – *n* **roguery** ['rōgəri] dishonesty; mischief. – *adj* **'roguish** mischievous; wicked.

rôle [rōl] *n* a part played, *esp* by an actor.

rōll *v* to move along by turning over like a wheel or ball; (of a ship *etc*) to rock or move from side to side; (of thunder, drums *etc*) to rumble; to wrap round and round: *to roll up a carpet*; to flatten with roller(s): *to roll the lawn*. – *n* anything *eg* a sheet of paper, length of cloth *etc* rolled or formed into the shape of a tube or cylinder; a very small loaf of bread; a rocking or turning over movement; a list of names; a long, rumbling sound. – *n* **'roller** something cylinder-shaped, often for flattening, as a roller of a mangle; a tube-shaped object on which something (*eg* hair) is rolled up; a small solid wheel; a long heavy wave on the sea. – *ns* **'rollcall** the calling of names from a list; **'rollerskate** a skate with wheels instead of a blade; **rolling pin** a roller of wood *etc* for flattening dough; **rolling stock** the stock of engines, carriages, wagons *etc* that run on a railway.

'rollicking *adj* noisy and full of fun.

'Rōman *adj* (of a number, numerals) written in letters, as I, II, III, IV *etc* for 1, 2, 3, 4 *etc*. – **Roman Catholic Church** the Church whose head is the Pope, the Bishop of Rome.

ro'mance *n* a tale about heroic, adventurous *etc* events not likely to happen in real life nowadays; a love story; a love affair. – *v* to write or tell tales rich in imagination. – *adj* **ro'mantic** of romance; full of feeling and imagination; dealing with love.

romp *v* to play in a lively way; to move quickly and easily. – *n* a lively game. – *npl* **'rompers** a short suit for a baby.

rood *n* (*old*) a measure of area (a quarter of an acre); a cross carrying an image of Christ.

roof *n* the top covering of a building, car *etc*; the upper part of the mouth: – *pl* **roofs**. – *v* to cover with a roof.

rook *n* a kind of crow; (in chess) the castle. – *n* **'rookery** a nesting place of rooks in a group of trees; a breeding place of penguins or seals: – *pl* **'rookeries**.

room *n* an inside division or compartment in a house; space: *room for everybody*; (*pl*) lodgings. – *adv* **'roomy** having plenty of space.

roost *n* a perch on which a bird rests at night. – *v* to sit or sleep on a roost. – *n* **'rooster** a farmyard cock.

root *n* the underground part of a plant; the base of anything, as a tooth *etc*; a cause, a source; a word from which other words have developed. – *v* to form roots and begin to grow; to be fixed; (of an animal) to turn up ground *etc* in a search for food; to search (about). – *adj* **'rooted** firmly planted. – **root out, root up,** to tear up by the roots; to get rid of completely; **take root** to form roots and grow firmly; to become firmly fixed.

rope *n* a thick cord, made by twisting strands of hemp, nylon *etc*; anything resembling a thick cord. – *v* to fasten or catch with a rope; to enclose, mark off with a rope. – *adj* **'ropy** like ropes, stringy; (*coll*) bad, not well.

rosary ['rōzəri] *n* a set of prayers; a string of beads used in saying prayers; a rose garden: – *pl* **'rosaries**.

rose [rōz] *v see* **rise.** – *n* a type of flower, often scented, growing on a *usu* prickly bush; a deep pink colour. – *adj* **'rosy** red, pink; (of the future *etc*) bright, hopeful.

rosemary ['rōzməri] *n* a kind of evergreen sweet-smelling shrub, used as a flavouring herb in cooking.

rosette [rə'zet] *n* a kind of badge shaped like a rose, made of ribbons.

'roster *n* a list showing a repeated order of duties *etc*.

'rostrum *n* a platform for public speaking: – *pls* **'rostrums, 'rostra.**

rot *v* to go bad or cause to go bad, to decay: – *pt* **'rotted.** – *n* decay; (*coll*) nonsense. – *adj* **'rotten** (of meat, fruit *etc*) having gone bad, decayed; worthless, disgraceful. – *n* **'rotter** (*coll*) a very bad, worthless person.

'rōta *n* a list of duties *etc* to be repeated in a set order.

'rōtary *adj* turning round like a wheel.

ro'tate *v* to turn round like a wheel; to (cause to) go through a repeating series of changes. – *n* **ro'tation.**

rote: by rote off by heart, automatically.

rotten, rotter *see* **rot.**

ro'tund *adj* round; plump.

rouge [rōozh] *n* a powder or cream used to give colour to the cheeks.

rough [ruf] *adj* not smooth; uneven; coarse, harsh; boisterous, wild; not exact: *a rough guess*; stormy. – *n* a hooligan or bully; rough ground. – *n* **'roughage** bran or fibre in food. – *v* **'roughen** to make rough. – *n* **'roughcast** plaster mixed with fine gravel, used to coat outside walls. – **rough and ready** not fine or carefully made, but effective; **rough out** to sketch or shape roughly.

roulette [rōo'let] *n* a game of chance, played with a ball which is placed on a wheel.

round *adj* shaped like a ring or circle; plump; even, exact: *a round dozen.* –

adv, prep on all sides (of); around: *look round the room*; in a circle (about). *The earth moves round the sun*; from one (person, thing, place *etc*) to another. *The news went round.* – *n* a circle or something round in shape; a single bullet or shell; a burst of firing, cheering *etc*; a song in which the singers take up the tune in turn; a usual route: *a postman's round*; set of tasks *etc*: *a round of duties*; each stage of a boxing match or other contest *etc*. – *v* to make or become round; (of a ship) to go round (*eg* a headland). – *n* **'rounders** a type of ball game played with a bat. – *adv* **'roundly** boldly, plainly. – *n* **'roundabout** a revolving machine for riding on, a merry-go-round; a meeting place of roads, where traffic must move in a circle. – *adj* not straight or direct. – *n* **round trip** a journey to a place and back. – **round on** to make a sudden attack on; **round up** to gather or drive together.

rouse [rowz] *v* to awaken; to stir up, excite. – *adj* **'rousing** stirring, exciting.

rout *n* a disorderly flight (of an army *etc*); a complete defeat. – *v* to defeat utterly.

route [rōot] *n* the course to be followed, a way of getting to somewhere. – *v* to fix the route of.

routine [rōo'tēn] *n* a fixed, unchanging order of doing things. – *adj* regular, ordinary, usual: *routine enquiries.*

rove *v* to wander or roam. – *n* **'rover** wanderer; an unsettled person; (*hist*) a pirate. – *n* **Rover Scout** an older member of the Boy Scout movement.

row¹ [rō] *n* a line of persons or things; an act of rowing; a trip in a rowing boat. – *v* to drive (a boat) by oars. – *n* **'rower** one who rows. – *n* **rowing boat** a boat rowed by oars.

row² [row] *n* a noisy quarrel; a noise; (*coll*) a scolding.

rowan ['rowən] *n* a type of tree with clusters of bright red berries, the mountain ash.

rowdy ['rowdi] *adj* noisy, disorderly. – *n* **'rowdyism.**

rowlock ['rolək] *n* a place to rest an oar on the side of a rowing boat.

'royal *adj* of, or given by, a king or queen; splendid, magnificent: *royal feast.* – *ns* **'royalist** one who supports a king or queen; **'royalty** the state of being royal; a royal person, or royal persons as a whole; a sum paid to the author of a book *etc* for each copy sold: – *pl* **'royalties.** – *n* **royal blue** a deep, bright blue.

rub *v* to move one thing against the surface of another; to wipe, clean, polish (something); (with **out, away**) to remove (a mark): – *pt* **rubbed**. – *n* the act of rubbing; a wipe. – **rub in** to work into (a surface) by rubbing; to keep reminding (someone of something unpleasant).

'**rubber** *n* a tough elastic substance made from the juice of certain plants (or an artificial substitute for this), used in tyres *etc*; (also '**indiarubber**) a piece of rubber used for rubbing out pencil *etc* marks; an odd number (three or five) of games in cards, cricket *etc*. – *n* **rubber stamp** an instrument with rubber figures or letters for stamping names, dates *etc* on books or papers.

'**rubbish** *n* waste material, litter; nonsense.

'**rubble** *n* small rough stones, bricks *etc* used in building, or remaining from a ruined building.

rubicund ['rōōbikənd] *adj* red or rosy-faced.

ruby ['rōōbi] *n* a type of red, precious stone: – *pl* '**rubies**.

ruck *n* a wrinkle or crease.

'**rucksack** *n* a type of bag carried on the back by walkers, climbers *etc*.

'**rudder** *n* the flat piece of wood or metal fixed by a hinge to the stern of a boat for steering; a similar object fixed to the tail of an aeroplane.

'**ruddy** *adj* red; (of the face, complexion *etc*) rosy, as in good health.

rude [rōōd] *adj* showing bad manners, not polite; roughly made: *a rude shelter*; rough, not refined; startling and sudden: *a rude awakening*; coarse, vulgar, indecent.

rudiments ['rōōdimənts] *npl* the first simple rules or facts of anything. – *adj* **rudi'mentary** in an early stage of development.

rue [rōō] *n* a type of shrub with bitter leaves. – *v* to be sorry for (having done something), regret. – *adj* '**rueful** sorrowful, regretful.

ruff *n* (*hist*) a pleated frill worn round the neck; a frill-like band of feathers or hair on a bird or animal's neck.

'**ruffian** *n* a rough, brutal person. – *adj* '**ruffianly**.

'**ruffle** *v* to disturb the smoothness of anything (*eg* hair, a bird's feathers *etc*); to annoy, offend.

rug *n* a mat for the floor; a thick covering or blanket (also **travelling rug**).

'**Rugby,** '**rugby** *n* a form of football using an oval ball which may be carried.

rugged ['rugid] *adj* of rough, uneven surface or appearance; strong; stern, harsh.

ruin ['rōōin] *n* complete loss of money *etc*; (a cause of) downfall; a wrecked or decayed state; (*pl*) broken-down remains of buildings *etc*. – *v* to destroy; cause to decay; to spoil completely: *ruin his chances*; to make very poor. – *n* **rui'nation** the act of ruining; the state of being ruined; something which ruins. – *adjs* '**ruined** in ruins; destroyed, in ruins; '**ruinous** ruined; likely to bring ruin.

rule [rōōl] *n* government: *a country under military rule*; an order or regulation: *school rules*; what usually happens, is done *etc*; a general idea guiding one's actions. *My rule is never to lend books*; a marked strip of wood, metal *etc* for measuring length. – *v* to govern (as king *etc*), be in power; to decide (that); to draw (a line); to mark with lines. – *n* '**ruler** one who rules; an instrument for drawing straight lines. – *adj* '**ruling** governing; most important. – *n* a decision or rule. – **as a rule** usually; **rule out** to leave out, not to consider.

rum *n* a type of alcoholic drink, a spirit made from sugarcane.

'**rumble** *v* to make a low rolling noise like that of thunder *etc*. – Also *n*.

ruminant ['rōōminənt] *adj, n* (of) an animal, such as a cow, that chews the cud. – *v* '**ruminate** to chew the cud; to be deep in thought. – *n* **rumi'nation** deep thought.

'**rummage** *v* to turn things over in search. – Also *n*.

'**rummy** *n* a kind of card game.

rumour ['rōōmər] *n* general talk; a story *etc* passed from person to person which may not be true. – *v* to spread a rumour of; to tell widely.

rump *n* the hind part of an animal; the meat from this part.

'**rumple** *v* to make untidy; to crease.

'**rumpus** *n* uproar, a noisy disturbance.

run *v* to move swiftly, hurry; to race; (of trains) to travel; (of water) to flow; (of machines) to work; to spread (rapidly). *This colour runs*; to go on, continue, extend. *The programme runs for two hours*; to cause (vehicles, machinery *etc*) to run or work; to organize, conduct (a business *etc*): – *pres p* '**running**, *pt* **ran**, *pp* **run**. – *n* an act of running; a trip; a distance run; a time or spell of running; a period, continuous stretch: *a run of good luck*; a ladder (in a stocking *etc*); free use of: *the run of the house*; a single score in cricket; an

enclosure for hens *etc*. – *ns* '**runner** one
who runs; a messenger; a rooting stem
of a plant; a blade of a skate or sledge;
'**running** the act of moving fast, flowing *etc*; management, control. – *adj* for
use in running: *running shoes*; giving
out fluid: *a running sore*; carried on
continuously: *a running commentary*. –
adv one after another: *three days running*. – *n* '**runaway** a person, animal or
vehicle *etc* that runs away. – Also *adj*. –
adj '**run-**'**down** in poor health or
condition. – *n* '**runner-**'**up** one who
comes second in a race or competition.
– *adj* '**run-of-the-**'**mill** ordinary. – *n*
'**runway** a path for aircraft to take off
from or land on. – **in (out of) the
running** having (or not having) a
chance of success; **run a risk** to take a
chance of harm, loss, failure *etc*; **run
down** (of a vehicle or driver) to knock
(someone) down; to speak ill of; **run
into** to bump into, collide with; to meet
(someone) accidentally; **run out of** to
become short of; **run over** to knock
down or pass over with a car *etc*.
rune [rōōn] *n* one of the letters of an
early kind of alphabet used in some
ancient writings. – *adj* '**runic**.
rung *n* a step of a ladder. – *v see* **ring**.
'**runnel** *n* a little stream or river.
runner *see* **run**.
rupee [rōō'pē] *n* the standard coin of
India, Pakistan, Ceylon.
rupture ['rupchər] *n* a breaking (*eg* of
friendship, peace *etc*); a tear or burst
(often in a part of the body). – *v* to

break or burst.
rural ['rōōrəl] *adj* of the country.
ruse [rōōz] *n* a trick or cunning plan.
rush *v* to move quickly, hurry; to make
(someone) hurry; to take (a fort *etc*) by
a quick, sudden attack. – *n* a quick,
forward movement; a hurry; a kind of
tall grasslike plant growing near water:
– *pl* '**rushes**.
rusk *n* a kind of hard biscuit like toast.
'**russet** *adj* reddish-brown. – *n* a type of
apple of russet colour.
rust *n* the reddish-brown coating (caused
by air and moisture) which forms
on iron and steel. – *v* to form rust. –
adjs '**rustless**, '**rustproof** not rusting;
'**rusty** covered with rust; ´(*coll*)
showing lack of practice. *My French
is rusty*.
'**rustic** *adj* of the country; roughly made;
simple, unsophisticated. – *n* a country-
man; a peasant.
rustle ['rusl] *v* (of silk, straw *etc*) to make
a soft, whispering sound; to steal
(cattle); (*coll*) (with **up**) to get, prepare
quickly: *rustle up a meal*. – Also *n*. – *n*
'**rustler** a person who steals (cattle).
rut *n* a deep track made by a wheel *etc*. –
adj '**rutted** full of ruts. – **in a rut**
having a fixed, rather dull, routine or
way of life.
ruthless ['rōōthlis] *adj* without pity,
cruel.
rye [ri] *n* a kind of grain. – *ns* '**rye-**
'**bread** a bread made with flour from
this grain; '**rye-grass** a kind of grass
grown for cattle-feeding.

S

'**Sabbath** *n* the day of the week regularly
set aside for religious services and rest
(among the Jews, Saturday, and among
Christians, Sunday).
'**sable** *n* a small type of animal like the
weasel, or its dark brown or blackish
fur. – *adj* black, dark.
sabot ['sabō] *n* a kind of wooden shoe.
sabotage ['sabətäzh] *n* deliberate destruction of machinery *etc* by enemies,
dissatisfied workers *etc*. – *v* to destroy,
damage or cause to fail.
'**sabre** *n* (*hist*) a curved sword used by
cavalry. – *n* '**sabre-rattling** an obvious
display of force or military power to
frighten the enemy.
sac *n* (in plants and in animal's bodies) a
bag often containing a liquid.
saccharine ['sakərin] *n* a very sweet

substance used as a substitute for
sugar.
sachet ['sashā] *n* a small bag (to hold
handkerchiefs *etc*); a (small) sealed
packet containing something in a liquid
or powder form, *eg* shampoo.
sack *n* a large bag of coarse cloth for
holding grain, flour *etc*; dismissal from
one's job; a plundering (of a captured
town). – *v* to dismiss (someone) from a
job; to plunder (a captured town). – *n*
'**sacking** a coarse cloth or canvas used
for sacks *etc*. – *n* '**sackcloth** coarse
cloth for making sacks; a garment made
of this worn as a sign of repentance. –
get the sack to be dismissed from one's
job.
'**sacrament** *n* a religious ceremony such
as baptism.

sacred ['sākrid] *adj* holy; devoted to or dedicated to some purpose or person: *sacred to her memory*; connected with religion: *sacred music*: *sacred art*.

'**sacrifice** *n* the act of offering something (as an animal that has been specially killed) to a god; the thing offered; something given up in order to benefit another person or to gain something more important. *He became successful because of the sacrifices his mother made*; the giving up of something for this purpose. – *v* to offer (an animal *etc*) as a sacrifice to God in worship; to give up something for someone or something else. – *adj* **sacri'ficial** of sacrifice.

sacrilege ['sakrəlij] *n* the using of a holy thing or place in a wicked way. – *adj* **sacri'legious**.

'**sacrosanct** *adj* very sacred; not to be harmed.

sad *adj* sorrowful, unhappy; showing sorrow; causing sorrow. – *v* '**sadden** to make or become sad.

'**saddle** *n* a seat for a rider used on the back of a horse or on a bicycle *etc*; a certain cut or joint of meat (from the back of an animal). – *v* to put a saddle on; (with **with**) to put a load or burden on (a person). *His son saddled him with debts*. – *n* '**saddler** a maker of saddles and harness.

'**sadism** *n* taking pleasure in, enjoyment of, cruelty to others. – *n* '**sadist**. – *adj* **sadistic** [sə'distik].

sa'fari *n* an expedition, *esp* for observing or hunting wild animals.

safe *adj* unharmed; free or secure from harm or danger; reliable, trustworthy. – *n* a heavy metal chest or box in which money and jewels may be locked away; a kind of cupboard for meat *etc*. – *n* '**safety** freedom from harm or danger. – *adj* giving protection or safety: *safety belt*. – *n* '**safeguard** anything that gives protection or security. – *v* to protect. – *ns* **safety belt** a belt fixed to a seat in a car or aircraft to prevent a passenger from being jolted out of his seat; '**safety-pin** a curved pin in the shape of a clasp, with a guard covering its point. – **safe and sound** unharmed.

'**saffron** *n* a type of crocus from which is obtained a yellow food dye and flavouring agent.

sag *v* to droop or sink *esp* in the middle: – *pt* **sagged**.

'**saga** *n* an ancient story about the deeds of heroes *etc*; a novel or series of novels about several generations of a family; a long detailed story.

sagacious [sə'gāshəs] *adj* very wise,

quick at understanding. – *n* **sagacity** [sə'gasəti].

sage [sāj] *n* a type of herb with grey-green leaves which are used for flavouring; a wise man. – *adj* wise.

'**sago** *n* a white starchy substance (got from certain Eastern palms) often used in puddings.

sahib [säb] *n* a term of respect given in India to persons of rank *etc*.

said [sed] *adj* mentioned before: *the said shopkeeper*. – *v see* **say**.

sail *n* a sheet of canvas *etc* spread out to catch the wind by which a ship or boat may be driven forward; a journey in a ship or boat; an arm of a windmill. – *v* to go by water in a ship or boat (with or without sails); to navigate or steer a ship or boat; to begin a (sea) voyage; to glide along easily. – *n* '**sailor** one who sails; a member of a ship's crew, a seaman. – **set sail** to set out on a (sea) voyage.

saint *n* a very good or holy person; a title given by the Roman Catholic Church or other church after death to very holy persons (often shortened to **St** *esp* if used in names of places *etc*: *St John's Road*). – *adjs* '**sainted**, '**saintly** very holy or very good.

sake *n* cause, purpose. *He did it for the sake of making money*; benefit, advantage: *for my sake*.

sa'laam *n* an Eastern greeting; a deep bow. – Also *v*.

'**salad** *n* a dish of vegetables, *eg* lettuce, cucumber *etc* cut up and served raw. – *ns* **salad cream**, **salad dressing** kinds of sauce for putting on salad.

'**salamander** *n* a kind of small lizard-like animal.

sa'lami *n* a type of highly seasoned sausage.

'**salary** *n* fixed wages regularly paid for work (*esp* to someone in a profession): – *pl* '**salaries**.

sale *n* the exchange of anything for money; a selling of goods at reduced prices; an auction. – *ns* '**saleroom** an auction room; '**salesman**, '**saleswoman** a person who sells or shows goods to customers.

'**salient** *adj* (of an angle *etc*) pointing outwards; standing out, chief: *the salient points of a speech*.

'**saline** *adj* containing salt, salty: *saline solution*.

sa'liva *n* the liquid that forms in the mouth to help digestion, spittle. – *adj* **salivary** ['salivəri] of saliva. – *v* '**salivate** to form saliva.

sallow ['salō] *adj* (of a face, complexion)

pale, yellowish. – *n* a type of willow tree.

'sally *n* a sudden rushing forth; a trip, an excursion; a witty remark, a joke: – *pl* 'sallies. – *v* to rush out suddenly; (with **forth**) to go out *eg* for a walk: – *pt* 'sallied.

salmon ['saman] *n* a large type of fish with yellowish-pink flesh.

'salon *n* a place, shop, in which hair-dressing *etc* is done; a large room for receiving or entertaining notable people; a gathering of such people.

sa'loon *n* a passengers' dining-room or sitting-room in a ship; a covered-in motor car; a public-house, bar.

salt [sölt] *n* a substance used for seasoning, either mined from the earth or obtained from sea water; any other substance formed (as salt is) from a metal and an acid; (*coll*) a sailor? – *adj* containing salt; tasting of salt; preserved in salt. – *v* to sprinkle with salt; to preserve with salt. – *adj* 'salty. – *ns* salt cellar a small table dish or container for salt; 'salt-pan a dried-up hollow near the sea where salt can be found.

salubrious [sə'loōbriəs] *adj* (of a place, climate *etc*) healthy.

'salūtary *adj* giving health or safety; having a good effect: *a salutary lesson*.

salute [sə'loōt] *v* to greet (a person) with words, a kiss or other gesture; (in the armed forces *etc*) to raise the hand to the forehead to show respect (to); to honour a person by a firing of guns *etc*. – *n* an act or way of saluting. – *n* salū'tation an act of greeting.

'salvage *n* goods saved from destruction or waste; the act of saving a ship or cargo, or of saving goods from a fire *etc*; payment made for this act. – *v* to save from loss or ruin.

sal'vation *n* the act, means, or cause of saving. *The arrival of the police was his salvation*; the saving of man from sin.

salve *n* an ointment for healing or soothing. – *v* to soothe (pride, conscience *etc*).

'salver *n* a small tray often of silver *etc*.

'salvo *n* a great burst of gunfire, of bombs, or of clapping: – *pl* 'salvo(e)s.

same *adj* exactly alike, identical. *They both had the same feeling*; not different; unchanged. *He still looks the same*; mentioned before. *The same person came again*. – *pron* the thing just mentioned. – *n* 'sameness lack of change or variety. – **all the same, just the same** in spite of that; **at the same time** still, nevertheless.

'sampan *n* a kind of small boat used in Far Eastern countries.

'sample *n* a small part taken from something to show what the whole is like. – *v* to test a sample of: *sample a cake*. – *n* 'sampler one who samples; a piece of embroidery *etc* to show one's skill.

sana'torium *n* a hospital, *esp* for people suffering from a disease of the lungs; a place set aside for those who are ill, in a school, college *etc*.

sancti'mōnious *adj* trying to appear full of holiness and goodness, priggish.

'sanction *n* permission, approval; a penalty for not keeping a law, rule of conduct *etc*; (often in *pl*) a measure applied, *eg* to a nation, to force it to stop a course of action. *Britain enforced sanctions against Rhodesia*.

'sanctity *n* holiness; sacredness. – *v* 'sanctifȳ to make holy, sacred or free of sin: – *pt* 'sanctified. – *n* sancti'cation.

sanctūary *n* a sacred place; (the most sacred part of) a temple or church; a place where one can be safe from arrest or violence; an area within which birds, animals *etc* are protected, a nature reserve: – *pl* 'sanctuaries.

sand *n* a mass of tiny particles of crushed or worn rocks *etc*; (*pl*) stretch of sand (on the seashore). – *v* to sprinkle with sand; to add sand to; to smooth or polish (with sandpaper). – *adj* 'sandy having much sand; like sand; (of hair) yellowish-red in colour. – *ns* 'sandbag a bag filled with sand, used as a protective barrier or covering; **sand dune** a ridge of sand blown up by the wind; **sand martin** a type of small bird which nests in sandy banks; 'sandpaper paper with a layer of sand glued to it for smoothing and polishing; 'sandpiper a type of wading bird; 'sandshoe a light shoe, *usu* with a rubber sole; 'sandstone a kind of soft rock made of layers of sand pressed together.

'sandal *n* a shoe in which the sole is held on to the foot by straps.

sandwich ['sanwij] *n* two slices of bread with any kind of food between: – *pl* 'sandwiches. – *v* to place, fit something between two other objects.

sane *adj* of sound mind, not mad; sensible. – *n* 'saneness; sanity ['sanəti] soundness of mind; mental health; good sense or judgement.

sanguine ['saŋgwin] *adj* hopeful, cheerful; (of a complexion) red. – *adj* 'sanguinary bloodthirsty, bloody.

'sanitary *adj* of conditions or arrangements that encourage good health, *eg* good drainage; free from dirt, infection *etc*. – *n* **sani'tation** arrangements for protecting health, *esp* drainage, sewage disposal *etc*.

sanity *see* **sane**.

sank *see* **sink**.

sap *n* the juice in plants, trees *etc*. – *v* to weaken (a person's strength *etc*): – *pt* **sapped**. – *n* **'sapling** a young tree.

sapphire ['safīr] *n* a kind of precious stone of a deep blue colour.

sarcasm ['särkazəm] *n* a hurtful remark made in scorn; the use of such remarks. – *adj* **sarcastic** [sär'kastik] containing sarcasm; often using sarcasm, scornful.

sar'cophagus *n* a stone coffin.

sardine [sär'dēn] *n* a type of small fish of the herring kind often tinned in oil.

sar'donic *adj* bitter, mocking, scornful.

'sari *n* a long piece of cloth worn by Indian women, wrapped round the waist and hanging loose over the shoulder.

sa'rong *n* kind of skirt worn by men and women in Malaya.

sartorial [sär'törīəl] *adj* having to do with dress, or with tailor-made clothes: *sartorial elegance*.

sash *n* a band, ribbon or scarf worn round the waist or over the shoulder; a frame (*usu* one that slides up and down) for panes of glass: *window sash*: – *pl* **'sashes**.

sat *see* **sit**.

'Sātan *n* the Devil. – *adj* **Satanic** [sə'tanik] of Satan, devilish.

'satchel *n* a small bag for carrying schoolbooks *etc*.

sate *v* (*old*) to satisfy fully or give more than enough to. – *adj* **'sated**.

'satellite *n* a smaller body moving round a larger – as the moon round the earth; a man-made object fired into space to travel round a planet; a state *etc* controlled by a more powerful neighbouring one.

satiate ['sāshiāt] *v* to satisfy fully; to give more than enough to. – *n* **satiety** [sə'tiəti] state of being satiated.

'satin *n* a closely woven silk with a glossy surface. – *n* **'satinwood** a smooth kind of wood.

'satire *n* a piece of writing *etc* which makes fun of certain people or their ways; ridicule, scorn. – *adj* **satirical** [sə'tirikəl]. – *n* **'satirist** a writer of satire.

'satisfȳ *v* to give enough (of something) to (a person); to please, make content; to give enough to quieten or get rid of (hunger, curiosity *etc*); to convince. *I*

was satisfied that he was innocent; to fulfil (conditions, requirements for a job *etc*): – *pt* **'satisfied**. – *n* **satis'faction** the act of satisfying or state of being satisfied; a feeling of pleasure or comfort; something that satisfies; a making up for (damage *etc*), compensation. – *adj* **satis'factory** satisfying; fulfilling the necessary requirements.

saturate ['sachərāt] *v* to soak or fill completely (with water *etc*); to cover (an area) completely *eg* with bombs. – *n* **satu'ration**.

'Saturday *n* the seventh day of the week.

'saturnine *adj* gloomy, sullen.

'satyr *n* (*myth*) a god of the woods who was half man, half goat.

sauce *n* a liquid seasoning added to food to improve flavour; (*coll*) cheek, impudence. – *adj* **'saucy** cheeky. – *n* **'saucepan** a rather deep pan, often with a long handle, for boiling, stewing food *etc*.

'saucer *n* a small, shallow dish for placing under a cup.

sauerkraut ['sowərkrowt] *n* a dish of cabbage cut up fine and pickled in salt *etc*.

'saunter *v* to stroll about without hurry. – Also *n*.

'sausage *n* minced meat seasoned and stuffed into a tube of animal gut *etc*.

'savage *adj* wild; fierce and cruel; uncivilized; very angry. – *n* a human being in an uncivilized state; a fierce or cruel person. – *v* to attack very fiercely. – *n* **savagery** ['savijəri] cruelty.

sa'vanna(h) *n* a grassy, treeless plain.

save *v* to bring out of danger, rescue; to protect from harm, damage, loss; to keep from spending or using (money, time, energy *etc*); to put money aside for the future. – *prep* except (for). *All were broken save one*. – *ns* **'savings** money put aside for the future; **saviour** ['sāvyər] one who saves from harm or evil; **'Saviour** Jesus Christ. – *n* **saving grace** a good quality that makes up for faults. – **save up** to put money aside for future use.

savour ['sāvər] *n* characteristic taste or flavour; an interesting quality. – *v* to taste or smell of; to taste (with enjoyment); to have a trace or suggestion (of). *Her reaction savours of jealousy*; to experience. – *adj* **'savoury** having a pleasant taste or smell; salt or sharp in flavour, not sweet. – *n* a savoury dish, *esp* one eaten at the end of dinner: – *pl* **'savouries**.

sa'voy *n* a type of winter cabbage.

saw *n* a tool with a toothed edge for

cutting wood *etc*; (*old*) a wise saying. –
v to cut with a saw: – *pt* **sawed**, *pp*
sawn or **sawed**; *see* also **see**. – *ns*
'**sawdust** a dust of fine fragments of
wood, made in sawing; '**sawmill** a mill
where wood is sawn up.

'**saxifrage** *n* a type of rock plant.

'**saxophone** *n* a kind of wind instrument,
with a curved metal tube and keys for
the fingers.

say *v* to speak, utter a (word *etc*): *to say
'Yes'*; to express in words, to state or
tell. *They say they are going*: – *pt* **said**
[sed]. – *n* the right to speak. *I have no
say in the matter*; the opportunity to
speak. *I have had my say*. – *n* '**saying**
something often said, *esp* a proverb. – **I
say!** an exclamation expressing surprise or protest or trying to attract
someone's attention; **that is to say** in
other words.

scab *n* a crust formed over a sore; any of
several diseases of animals or plants. –
adj '**scabby**.

'**scabbard** *n* the sheath in which the
blade of a sword is kept.

scabies ['skābēz] *n* a kind of itchy skin
disease.

'**scaffold** *n* a platform on which people
are put to death. – *n* '**scaffolding** the
poles and wooden platforms used by
men at work on a building.

scald [sköld] *v* to burn with hot liquid or
steam; to cook or heat (milk *etc*) just
short of boiling point. – *n* a burn caused
by hot liquid or steam.

scale *n* a set of regularly spaced marks
made on something (*eg* a thermometer
etc) for use as a measure; a series or
system of increasing values: *salary
scale*; (in music) a group of notes going
up or down in order; the measurements
of a map, model, plan *etc* compared
with the actual size of country, object,
area *etc* that is shown by them: *a map
drawn to the scale 1 : 50,000*; the size of
an activity, business *etc*: *manufacture on
a small (or large) scale*; a small thin
flake or layer on the skin of a fish, snake
etc, or on a leaf bud; (*pl*) a weighing
machine. – *v* to climb up; to clear of
scales; to remove in thin layers. – *adj*
'**scaly** having flakes or scales.

scallop ['skoləp] *n* a type of shellfish
with a pair of hinged fan-shaped shells.
– *adj* '**scalloped** (of a hem or edge of a
garment *etc*) cut into curves or notches,
wavy.

'**scallywag** *n* a rogue.

scalp *n* the outer covering of the skull;
the skin and hair of the top of the head.
– *v* to cut the scalp from.

'**scalpel** *n* a doctor's small, thin-bladed
knife.

scamp *n* a rascal.

'**scamper** *v* to run about gaily; to run off
in haste.

'**scampi** *npl* Norway lobsters cooked and
used as food.

scan *v* to count the beats in a line of
verse; (of verse) to have the correct
number of beats; to examine carefully;
(*coll*) to glance hastily at (a newspaper
etc); (in television *etc*) to pass a beam of
light over every part of: – *pt* **scanned**.
– *n* **scansion** ['skanshən] scanning of
verse.

'**scandal** *n* something disgraceful or
shocking, arousing general disapproval; talk or gossip about people's
(supposed) misdeeds. – *v* '**scandalize**
to shock, horrify. – *adj* '**scandalous**
shameful, disgraceful; containing scandal. – *n* '**scandalmonger** one who
spreads gossip or scandal.

scant *adj* not plentiful, hardly enough: *to
pay scant attention*. – *adj* '**scanty** little
or not enough in amount: *scanty
clothing*.

'**scapegoat** *n* one who bears the blame for
the wrongdoing of others.

'**scapula** *n* the shoulderblade.

scar *n* the mark left by a wound, a sore
etc; any mark or blemish. – *v* to mark
with a scar: – *pt* **scarred**.

scarce *adj* not plentiful, not enough;
rare, seldom found. – *adv* '**scarcely**
only just, barely. *I could scarcely hear*;
probably, or definitely, not. *You can
scarcely expect me to work when I'm ill*. –
n '**scarcity** want, shortage: – *pl* '**scar-
cities**. – **make oneself scarce** to go,
run away.

scare *v* to drive away by frightening; to
startle, frighten. – *n* a sudden fright or
alarm. – *n* '**scarecrow** a figure (dressed
in old clothes) set up to scare birds
away from crops.

scarf *n* a piece or a strip of material worn
round the neck, shoulders or head: –
pls **scarves, scarfs**.

scarlatina [skärlə'tēnə] *n* scarlet fever,
esp in a mild form.

'**scarlet** *n* a bright red colour. – Also *adj*.
– *n* **scarlet fever** a type of infectious
illness, causing a rash.

scathing ['skādhiŋ] *adj* (of something
said, written *etc*) cruel, bitter, hurtful.

'**scatter** *v* to throw loosely about, sprinkle; to spread widely, send in all directions; to go away or flee in all directions. – *adj* '**scattered** thrown, sent or
placed widely here and there. – *n*
'**scattering** an act of spreading, or

being spread, widely; a small number or amount thinly spread or scattered. – n **'scatterbrain** a thoughtless person.

'scavenger n a person who cleans streets or picks up rubbish; an animal which feeds on dead flesh.

scene [sēn] n the place where something, real or imaginary, happens; a view, landscape; a division of a play or opera; a particular area of activity: *the business scene*; a show of bad temper, a violent quarrel. – n **scenery** ['sēnəri] the painted background on a theatre stage; the general appearance of a stretch of country. – adj **'scenic** of scenery; picturesque.

scent [sent] v to discover by the smell; to have a suspicion of, to sense: *scent danger*; to cause to smell pleasantly. *The roses scented the air.* – n perfume; an odour, smell; the trail of smell by which an animal or person may be tracked.

'sceptic n a person who is always inclined to doubt what he is told. – adj **'sceptical** unwilling to believe, doubtful. – n **'scepticism** a doubting or questioning attitude.

sceptre ['septər] n the ornamental rod carried by a monarch on ceremonial occasions as a symbol of his power.

schedule ['shedūl, (*US*) 'skedūl] n the time set or fixed for doing something *etc*, a timetable. *The plane is 2 hours behind schedule*; a written statement of details; a form for filling in information. – v to form into, put into a schedule or list; to plan, arrange.

scheme [skēm] n a plan or systematic arrangement; a dishonest or crafty plan. – v to make (crafty) plans, to plot. – adj **'scheming** crafty, cunning.

schism ['skizəm] n a breaking away of some persons from the main group (*esp* in the Church).

schist [shist] n a type of rock that splits easily into layers.

schizophrenia [skitsə'frēniə] n a form of mental illness in which the patient's personality and behaviour undergo a complete change. – adj **schizophrenic** [skitsə'frenik].

scholar ['skolər] n a man of great learning; one who has been awarded a scholarship; a pupil, student. – adj **'scholarly** showing or having knowledge, high intelligence and love of accuracy. – ns **'scholarliness**, **'scholarship** learning; a sum of money given to help a clever student to carry on further studies. – adj **scho'lastic** of schools or scholars.

school [skool] n a place for teaching *esp* children; a group of thinkers, artists *etc* who have the same ideas; a large number of fish, whales *etc*. – v to send to, or educate in, a school; to train by practice. – n **'schooling** education (in a school); training. – ns **'schoolfellow**, **'schoolmate** a person taught at the same school as oneself; **'schoolmaster, 'schoolmistress** a teacher at a school.

schooner ['skoonər] n a type of sailing ship with two masts.

sciatica [sī'atikə] n severe pain in the upper part of the leg.

science ['sīəns] n knowledge obtained by observation and experiment; any branch of such knowledge *eg*, chemistry, physics, biology *etc*; such sciences as a whole. – adj **scien'tific**. – n **'scientist** one who studies one or more branches of science.

scimitar ['simitər] n a type of sword with a short curved blade.

scintillate ['sintilāt] v to sparkle; to show brilliance in wit *etc*.

scion ['sīən] n a young member of a family; a descendant; a cutting or twig for grafting on another plant.

scissors ['sizərz] npl a type of cutting instrument with two blades.

scoff v to express scorn; (with **at**) to make fun of, mock.

scold v to find fault with, blame, rebuke, with angry words. – n a bad-tempered person *esp* a woman. – n **'scolding**.

scone [skon] n a kind of small plain cake.

scoop n any of several kinds of instruments of a hollow shape, as a ladle, shovel *etc*, used for lifting up or digging out (loose material, water *etc*); a piece of news which one newspaper prints before others. – v to lift up or dig out, as with a scoop.

'scooter n a kind of two-wheeled toy vehicle pushed along by the foot; a type of small motor cycle.

scope n opportunity or room (for something, to do something): *scope for improvement*; extent, range or area dealt with: *outside the scope of this dictionary*.

scorch v to burn slightly, singe; to dry up with heat. – adj **'scorching** burning, singeing; very hot; harsh, severe: *scorching criticism*.

score [skōr] n a gash, notch or line; an account, a debt: *settle old scores*; the total number of points gained in a game, test *etc*; a written piece of music showing separately all the parts for voices and instruments; a set of twenty:

a score of soldiers; (*pl*) a great many: *scores of people*; a reason, account. *Don't worry on that score*. – *v* tó mark with lines, notches *etc*, to scratch; to gain points; to keep a note of points gained, in a game *etc*. – *n* 'scorer. – **score out** to cross out.

scorn *v* to look down on, despise; to refuse (help *etc*) *esp* because of pride. – Also *n*. – *adj* 'scornful full of scorn.

'scorpion *n* a type of spider-like creature with a poisonous sting in its tail.

scotch *v* to cut or wound slightly; to stamp out (a rumour *etc*).

Scotch *n* (*coll*) whisky. – *ns* **Scotch tape** ® (*US*) a kind of (transparent) adhesive tape; **Scotch terrier** a breed of small rough-coated, short-legged dog.

'scot-'free *adj* unhurt; unpunished.

'scoundrel *n* a rascal, a worthless person.

scour *v* to clean (a pan *etc*) by hard rubbing, to scrub; to move swiftly over or along, *esp* in search of something or someone.

scourge [skörj] *n* a cause of suffering, *esp* widespread (as an infectious disease *etc*); a whip made of leather thongs. – *v* to cause great suffering; to whip.

scout *n* someone sent out to spy and bring in information; **Scout** a member of the Boy Scouts' Association.

scowl [skowl] *v* to wrinkle the brows in displeasure or anger. – Also *n*.

'scrabble *v* to scratch, scrape, or grope (about). – *n* 'Scrabble ® a kind of word-building game.

'scraggy *adj* long and thin; uneven, rugged.

'scramble *v* to struggle to seize something before others; to wriggle along on hands and knees; to mix or toss together: *scrambled eggs*; to jumble up (a message *etc*) so that it must be decoded before it can be understood. – *n* an act of scrambling; a rush and struggle to get something; a motor-cycle race over rough country.

scrap *n* a small piece, a fragment; a picture *etc* for pasting in a scrapbook; (*coll*) a fight; articles or parts (*eg* of a car) no longer required for the original purpose: *sold as scrap*; (*pl*) small pieces, odds and ends. – *v* to throw away, to abandon as useless; (*coll*) to fight, quarrel: – *pt* **scrapped**. – *adj* 'scrappy made up of odd scraps, not well put together. – *ns* 'scrapbook a blank book in which to stick pictures *etc*; 'scrap-heap a heap of old metal *etc*, a rubbish heap; **scrap metal** metal for melting and re-using.

scrape *v* to rub and (*usu*) mark with something sharp; to drag or rub (something) against or across (a surface) with a harsh grating sound; (with **up** or **together**) to collect (money *etc*) with difficulty. – *n* an act of scraping; a mark or sound made by scraping; (*coll*) a difficult, troublesome situation. – **scrape through** only just to avoid failure.

scratch *v* draw a sharp point across the surface of; to mark by doing this; to tear or to dig with claws, nails *etc*; to rub with the nails to relieve or stop itching; to (cause to) withdraw from a competition. – *n* a mark or sound made by a scratching; a slight wound: – *pl* 'scratches. – *adj* (in golf) too good to be allowed a handicap; (of a team) made up of players hastily got together. – **come up to scratch** to be satisfactory; **start from scratch** to start from nothing, right at the beginning.

scrawl *v* to write or draw untidily or hastily. – *n* untidy, hasty or bad writing; something scrawled.

'scrawny *adj* thin, skinny.

scream *v* to utter a shrill, piercing cry as in pain, fear *etc*, to shriek. – Also *n*.

scree *n* loose stones covering a steep mountain side.

screech *v* to utter a harsh, shrill and sudden cry. – Also *n*.

screed *n* a long (tiresome) speech or letter.

screen *n* any of several kinds of movable pieces of furniture (*usu* a flat, (folding) covered framework) to shelter from view or protect from heat, cold *etc*; something that shelters from wind, danger, difficulties *etc*; the surface on which films *etc* are shown; the surface on which television pictures appear. – *v* to shelter, hide; to make a film of; to show on a screen; to sift or sieve; to sort out (*eg* the good from the bad) by testing *etc*; to conduct (a series of) examinations on a person or group of people to test for disease.

screw *n* a kind of nail with a slotted head and a winding groove or ridge (called the **thread**) on its surface; a kind of propeller (a 'screw-propeller) with spiral blades, used in ships and aircraft; a turn or twist (of a screw *etc*). – *v* to fasten or tighten with a screw; to fix (*eg* a stopper) in place with a twisting movement; to twist, turn round (one's head *etc*); to twist up, crumple, pucker. – *n* 'screwdriver a kind of tool for turning screws.

'scribble *v* to write carelessly; to make untidy or meaningless marks with a pencil *etc*. *The child loved to scribble.* – *n* careless writing; meaningless marks (*eg* written by a child).

scribe *n* (*hist*) a clerk or secretary, or one who copied out manuscripts; (among the Jews) a teacher of law.

scrimp *v* to be sparing or stingy (*usu* with money). *He scrimps and saves for his holiday.*

script *n* the text of a play, talk *etc*; handwriting like print.

scripture ['skripchər] *n* sacred writings; (often *pl*) 'Scripture the Bible.

scroll *n* a piece of paper rolled up; an ornament shaped like this.

scrub *v* to rub hard in order to clean: – *pt* **scrubbed.** – *n* (country covered with) low bushes.

scruff *n* the back of the neck. – *adj* '**scruffy** untidy.

scrum *n* (in rugby) a struggle for the ball by the forwards of the opposing sides bunched together.

scruple ['skroōpl] *n* hesitation or doubt over what is right or wrong that keeps one from acting or doing something. – *v* to hesitate because of a scruple. – *adj* '**scrupulous** careful over the smallest details.

scrutiny ['skroōtəni] *n* careful examination, a close look: – *pl* '**scrutinies.** – *v* '**scrutinize** to examine very closely.

scud *v* to move or sweep along quickly: *scudding waves*: – *pt* '**scudded.**

'**scuffle** *n* a confused fight.

scull *n* a short oar. – *v* to move (a boat) with a pair of these or with one oar worked at the back of the boat.

'**scullery** *n* a room for rough kitchen work.

'**sculptor** *n* an artist who carves or models figures, designs *etc* in wood, stone, clay *etc*: – *fem* '**sculptress.** – *n* **sculpture** ['skulpchər] the art of the sculptor; (a piece of) his work.

scum *n* foam or skin that rises to the surface of liquids; the most worthless part of anything: *the scum of the earth.*

'**scupper** *n* (*usu pl*) a hole in the side of a ship to drain water from the deck. – *v* to put an end to, ruin: *scupper his chances.*

scurf *n* small flakes of dead skin (*esp* on the scalp).

'**scurrilous** *adj* insulting, abusive: *a scurrilous attack on his rival's work.*

'**scurry** *v* to hurry along, scamper: – *pt* '**scurried.** – Also *n*.

'**scurvy** *n* a type of disease caused by a lack of fresh fruit and vegetables.

'**scuttle** *n* a wooden or metal fireside container for coal; an opening with a lid in a ship's deck or side. – *v* to make a

hole in (a ship) in order to sink it; to hurry along, scamper.

scythe [sīdh] *n* a large curved blade, on a long handle, for cutting grass *etc* by hand. – *v* to cut with a scythe.

sea *n* the mass of salt water covering most of the earth's surface; a great stretch of water of less size than an ocean; a great expanse or number: *a sea of faces*. – *adj*, *adv* '**seaward** towards the sea. – *ns* **sea anemone** a type of small plant-like animal found on rocks at the seashore; '**seaboard** land along the edge of the sea; **sea dog** an old sailor; a pirate; '**seafarer** a traveller by sea, a sailor. – *adj* '**seafaring.** – *n* '**seafront** a promenade with its buildings facing the sea. – *adj* '**seagoing** (of a ship) sailing on the ocean. – *ns* '**seagull** a type of web-footed sea bird; '**sea-horse** a type of small fish looking a little like a horse; **sea level** the level of the surface of the sea; '**sea-lion** a large kind of seal the male of which has a mane; '**seaman** a sailor, *esp* a member of a ship's crew who is not an officer: – *pl* '**seamen;** '**seamanship** the art of steering and looking after ships at sea; '**sea-mew** the seagull; '**seaplane** an aeroplane which can take off from and land on the water; '**seascape** a picture of a scene at sea; '**seashore** the land next to the sea. – *adj* '**seasick** made ill by the rocking movement of a ship. – *ns* '**seaside** the land beside the sea; '**sea-trout** a type of large trout living in the sea but spawning in rivers; **sea urchin** a type of small sea creature with a spiny shell; '**seaweed** any of many kinds of plants growing in the sea. – *adj* '**seaworthy** (of ships) in a good enough condition to go to sea. – **at sea** on the sea; completely puzzled.

seal *n* a type of furry sea animal living partly on the land; a piece of wax *etc* having a design pressed into it, attached to a document to show that it is legal or official; a piece of wax used to keep (a parcel *etc*) closed; anything that joins tightly or closes up completely; a piece of sticky paper with a design or picture on it: *a Christmas seal*. – *v* to mark or fasten with a seal; to close up completely; to make (legally) binding and definite: *to seal a bargain*. – *n* **sealing wax** a hard kind of wax for sealing letters *etc*.

seam *n* the line formed by the sewing together of two pieces of cloth *etc*; a line or layer of metal, ore, coal *etc* in the earth. – *n* '**seamstress** a woman who sews *esp* for a living. – **the seamy side**

the more unpleasant side (of life *etc*).

séance ['saōns] *n* a meeting of people who believe that it is possible to receive messages from the spirits of dead people.

sear *v* to scorch, burn, dry up; to hurt severely.

search [sэrch] *v* to look over, examine (a place, a person) in order to find something; (with **for**) to look for, seek. – *n* an act of searching; an attempt to find: – *pl* **'searches**. – *adj* **'searching** examining closely and carefully: *a searching question*. – *ns* **'searchlight** a strong beam of light used for picking out objects at night; **'search-warrant** permission given to the police to search a house *etc* for stolen goods *etc*.

season ['sēzn] *n* one of the four divisions of the year (spring, summer, autumn, winter); the usual or proper time for anything; a time associated with a particular activity: *football season*. – *v* to add (salt *etc*) to improve the flavour of (food); to dry (wood) till it is ready for use. – *adjs* **'seasonable** happening at the proper time; (often of weather) suitable for the season; **'seasonal** of the seasons or a season; (of work, sports *etc*) taking place in one particular season only. *Hotel work is often seasonal*; **'seasoned** (of food) flavoured; (of wood) ready to be used; trained, experienced: *a seasoned traveller*. – *n* **'seasoning** something (as salt, pepper *etc*) added to food to give it more taste. – *n* **season ticket** a ticket that can be used over and over again for a certain period of time.

seat *n* a piece of furniture (as a chair, bench *etc*) for sitting on; the part of a chair *etc* on which one sits; the part of the body or a garment on which a person sits; a (country) mansion; a place in parliament, on a council *etc*; the place from which something is carried on *etc*: *the seat of government: the seat of the trouble*. – *v* to cause to sit down; to have seats for (a certain number). *The room seats forty people*.

secateurs [sekэ'tȯrz] *npl* a type of tool like scissors, for trimming bushes *etc*.

se'cede *v* to break away from a group, society *etc*. – *n* **se'cession**.

seclude [si'klōōd] *v* to keep apart or away (from people's notice or company). – *n* **se'clusion**.

'second *adj* next after, or following the first in time, place *etc*; other, alternate: *every second week*; another of the same kind as. *They thought him a second Mozart*. – *n* a person or thing that is

second; one who acts as attendant to a person who boxes or fights a duel; the 60th part of a minute of time, or of a degree (in measuring angles); an article not quite perfectly made. *These tights are seconds*. – *v* to support, back up. *He seconded his friend's appointment as chairman*; **se'cond** to transfer temporarily to a special job. – *adj* **'secondary** second in position or importance. – *adv* **'secondly** in the second place. – *adjs* **'second-'best** next to the best, not the best; **'second-'hand** not new; having been used by another: *second-hand clothes*; (of a shop *etc*) dealing in second-hand goods; **'second-'rate** not of the best quality, inferior. – *ns* **second nature** a firmly fixed habit. *Organizing people is second nature to her*; **secondary school, education** a school, education, between primary school and university *etc*.

'secret *adj* hidden from, not known to, or told to, others; secretive. – *n* a fact, purpose, method *etc* that is not told or is not known. *He intends to keep his secret*. – *n* **'secrecy** state of being secret, mystery. – *adj* **'secretive** inclined to hide or conceal one's feelings, activities *etc*. – *n* **secret service** a government department dealing with spying *etc*.

'secretary *n* a person employed to write letters, keep records and carry out routine business arrangements; a person elected or employed to deal with the written business of a club *etc*: – *pl* **'secretaries**. – *adj* **secre'tārial** of a secretary or his or her work. – **Secretary of State** a government minister in charge of an administrative department: *Secretary of State for Industry*; (*US*) the person in charge of foreign affairs.

se'crete *v* to hide, conceal in a secret place; (of a part of the body, *eg* the liver *etc*) to store up and give out (a fluid). – *n* **se'crētion** an act of secreting; fluid secreted.

sect *n* a group of people who hold certain views *esp* in religious matters. – *adj* **sec'tārian** of a sect; loyal, or devoted to, a sect; (of opinions, attitudes *etc*) narrow-minded.

'section *n* a part or division: *a section of the community*: a thin slice (of something) for examination under a microscope; the view of the inside of anything when it is cut right through or across: *a section of a plant*.

'sector *n* a three-sided part of a circle whose sides are two radii and a part of the circumference; a part or section: *the Communist sector of Germany.*

'secular *adj* of worldly, not spiritual or religious things; (of music *etc*) not sacred or religious.

se'cure *adj* safe, free from danger or from fear; confident, without doubts or fears: *secure in the knowledge that he had no rivals*; firmly fixed or fastened. *The lock is secure. – v* to make safe, firm or established: *secure his position*; to seize, get hold of: *secure the diamonds*; to fasten: *secure the lock. – n* **se'curity** safety; property or goods which a lender of money may keep until his loan is paid back.

se'dan *n* an enclosed chair for one person, carried on two poles by two bearers (also **sedan chair**); (*US*) a saloon car.

se'date *adj* calm, serious, dignified. – *n* **se'dateness.** – *n* **se'dation** use of sedatives to calm a patient. – *n, adj* **'sedative** (a medicine that is) calming, soothing.

'sedentary *adj* (of a job *etc*) requiring much sitting.

sedge [sej] *n* a type of coarse grass growing in swamps and rivers.

'sediment *n* the grains or solid parts which settle at the bottom of a liquid.

se'dition *n* (the stirring up of) rebellion against the government. – *adj* **se'ditious** encouraging rebellion, rebellious.

se'duce *v* to succeed in tempting (someone) away from right or moral behaviour, *esp* to persuade (someone) to have sexual intercourse; to attract. – *ns* **se'ducer; seduction** [si'dukshən]. – *adj* **se'ductive** attractive, tempting.

see *v* to have sight. *After years of blindness he found he could see*; to be aware of, notice by means of the eye. *He sees her coming*; to form a picture of in the mind; to understand. *I see what you mean*; to find out. *I'll see what is happening*; to make sure. *See that he finishes his homework*; to accompany. *I'll see you home*; to meet. *I'll see you at the usual time: – pt* **saw,** *pp* **seen.** – *n* the district over which a bishop or archbishop has authority. – *conj* **seeing that** since, because. – **see through** to take part in, or support, to the end; not to be deceived by (a person, trick *etc*); **see to** to attend to (the preparation of): *to see to a meal.*

seed *n* the part of a tree, plant *etc* from which a new plant may be grown; a seed-like part of a plant (as a grain or a nut); the beginning from which any-

thing grows: *the seeds of rebellion*; (in a tournament) a ·seeded player; (*old*) children, descendants. – *v* (of a plant) to produce seed; to sow; to remove the seeds from (*eg* a fruit); to arrange (good players) in a tournament (of golf, tennis *etc*) so that they do not compete against each other till the later rounds. – *n* **'seedling** a young plant just sprung from a seed. – *adj* **'seedy** full of seeds; shabby; sickly, not very well. – **go to seed, run to seed** (of plants) to develop seeds; (of a person, area *etc*) to deteriorate, to become much worse in condition *etc*.

seek *v* to look or search for. *He is seeking evidence of an old civilization*; to try (to do something): *seek to establish proof*; to try to get (advice *etc*): – *pt* **sought** [söt]. – **sought after** popular, much in demand.

seem *v* to appear to be. *He seems kind*; to appear. *She seems to like it. – adjs* **'seeming** apparent but not actual or real: *a seeming success*; **'seemly** suitable; decent.

seen *see* **see.**

seep *v* to flow slowly through a small opening, leak. *Water seeped from the crack in the rock.*

seer *n* one who sees; a prophet.

'seesaw *n* a plank balanced across a stand so that one end of it goes up when the other goes down, used as a plaything by children; an up-and-down movement like that of a seesaw. – *v* to go up and down on a seesaw; to move with a seesaw-like movement.

seethe [sēdh] *v* to boil; to be very angry. – *adj* **'seething.**

'segment *n* a part cut off; a part of a circle cut off by a straight line.

'segregate *v* to separate (a person or group) from others. – *n* **segre'gation.**

seine [sān] *n* a large type of fishing net.

seismic ['sizmik] *adj* of earthquakes. – *n* **'seismograph** an instrument that records earthquake shocks and measures their force.

seize [sēz] *v* to take suddenly, *esp* by force; to overcome. *He was seized with fury*; (of machinery *etc*, *usu* with **up**) to become stuck, to break down. – *n* **seizure** ['sēzhər] the act of seizing; capture; a sudden attack (of illness, rage *etc*).

'seldom *adv* not often, rarely. *You seldom see an owl during the day.*

se'lect *v* to pick out from a number according to one's preference, to choose. – *adj* picked out, chosen; very good; (of a club *etc*) allowing only certain people in. – *n* **se'lection** the act of choosing; thing(s) *etc* chosen; number of things from which to choose. – *adj* **se'lective** having or using the power of choice; selecting carefully. – *n* **se'lector** one who chooses.

self *n* one's own person; one's personality, character: – *pl* **selves** [selvz]. – *adj* **'selfish** caring only for one's own pleasure or advantage. – *n* **'selfishness**. – *adj* **'selfless** thinking of others before oneself, unselfish. – *adjs* **'self-as'sured** trusting in one's own power or ability, confident; **'self-'centred** concerned with one's own affairs, selfish; **'self-'confident** believing, trusting in one's own powers or abilities; **'self-'conscious** too aware of oneself, one's faults, blemishes *etc*, and therefore embarrassed in the company of others; **'self-con'tained** (of a house) complete in itself, not sharing any part with other houses. – *ns* **'self-con'trol** control over oneself, one's feelings *etc*; **'self-de'fence** (the act of) defending one's own person, property *etc*; **'self-de'nial** doing without something (*esp* in order to give to others). – *adj* **'self-ef'facing** keeping oneself from being noticed, modest. – *n* **'self-es'teem** respect for oneself; conceit. – *adj* **'self-'evident** clear enough to need no proof. – *n* **'self-ex'pression** expressing one's own personality in one's activities, *esp* art, writing *etc*. – *adj* **'self-im'portant** having a mistakenly high sense of one's importance; **'self-in'dulgent** too ready to satisfy one's own inclinations and desires. – *n* **'self-'interest** a selfish desire to consider only one's own interests or advantage. – *adj* **'self-'made** owing one's success *etc* to one's own efforts: *a self-made man*. – *n* **'self-'portrait** an artist's portrait of himself. – *adjs* **'self-pos'sessed** calm in mind or manner, quietly confident; **'self-re'liant** trusting in one's own abilities *etc*. – *n* **'self-res'pect** respect for oneself and concern for one's own character and reputation. – *adj* **'self-'righteous** thinking (too) highly of one's own goodness and virtue. – *n* **'self-'sacrifice** the act of giving up one's own life, possessions, advantages *etc* in order to do good to others. – *adjs* **'selfsame** the very same; **'self-'satisfied** pleased, smug, satisfied with oneself. – *n* **'self-'service** helping or serving oneself (as in a restaurant, petrol station *etc*). – Also *adj*. – *adjs* **'self-suf'ficient** needing no help or support from anyone else; **'self-**

'willed determined to have one's own way, obstinate. – **self-raising flour** flour already containing an ingredient to make it rise.

sell *v* to give or hand over for money; to have or keep for sale. *He sells newspapers*; to be sold for, cost. *This book sells for £5*: – *pt* **sōld**. – *n* **'seller** one who sells.

'Sellotape ® *n* a kind of transparent adhesive tape, used *eg* for sticking pieces of paper together.

'selvage *n* the firm edge of a piece of cloth, that does not fray.

'semaphore *n* a form of signalling by means of two arms which form different positions for each letter.

'semblance *n* an outward, often false, appearance. *She gave a semblance of listening.*

semi- *prefix* half; (*coll*) partly. – *ns* **'semibreve** (in music) a note equal to four crotchets in length; **'semicircle** half of a circle; **'semi'colon** the punctuation mark (;). – *adj* **'semi-de'tached** (of a house) joined to another house on one side but not on the other. – *n* **'semi-'final** the stage or match of a contest immediately before the final. – *adj* **'semi-'precious** (of a stone) having some value, but not considered a gem.

'seminar *n* a group of students *etc* working on, or meeting to discuss, a particular subject.

'seminary *n* a school or college: – *pl* **'seminaries**.

semolina [semə'lēnə] *n* the hard particles of wheat sifted from flour, used for puddings *etc*.

'senate *n* the upper house of parliament in some countries, as USA, Australia; the governing council of some universities; (*hist*) the law-making body in ancient Rome. – *n* **'senator** a member of a senate.

send *v* to cause (a person) to go; to cause (a thing) to be carried (to a place): – *pt, pp* **sent**. – *n* **'sender**. – *n* **'send-off** a start; a friendly farewell (or party) for someone departing on a journey *etc*. – **send for** to order (a person or thing) to be brought.

'sēnile *adj* of old age; showing the (mental) feebleness of old age. – *n* **senility** [sə'niləti].

'sēnior *adj* older in age or higher in rank. – Also *n*. – *n* **seni'ority** state of being senior.

'senna *n* the dried leaves of certain plants, used as a laxative.

sen'sation *n* a feeling through any of the

five senses; a feeling, a vague effect: *a floating sensation*; a great stir, a state of excitement. – *adj* **sen'sational** (aimed at) causing great excitement, horror *etc.*

sense *n* one of the five powers by which we feel or notice (hearing, taste, sight, smell, touch); a feeling: *a sense of loss*; an ability to understand or appreciate: *a sense of humour*; (*pl*) one's right mind: *to take leave of one's senses*; wisdom, ability to act in a reasonable or sensible way; that which can be understood or be meaningful. *Your sentence does not make sense*; meaning. *To what sense of this word are you referring?* – *v* to feel, realize: *to sense someone's disapproval.* – *adjs* **'senseless** stunned, unconscious; foolish; **'sensible** wise; able to be felt or noticed; (with **of**) aware of. – *n* **sensi'bility** ability to feel, sensitivity. – *adj* **'sensitive** feeling, *esp* easily, strongly or painfully; strongly affected by light, small changes, movements *etc.* – *v* **'sensitize** to make sensitive (*esp* to light). – *adjs* **'sensory** of the senses; **'sensual** of the senses rather than the mind; inclined to indulge too much in bodily pleasures; **'sensuous** affecting the senses in a pleasant way; easily affected through the senses.

sent *see* **send.**

'sentence *n* a number of words which together make a complete statement; a judgement or punishment announced by a judge or a court. – *v* to condemn (a person) to a particular punishment.

'sentiment *n* a thought, opinion (expressed in words); (a show of) feeling or emotion, often excessive. – *adj* **senti'mental** having or showing too much feeling or emotion.

'sentinel *n* a soldier on guard.

'sepal *n* one of the green leaves beneath the petals of a flower.

'separate *v* to set or keep apart; to divide (something) into parts; to disconnect; to go different ways; to live apart by choice. – *adj* placed, kept *etc* apart; divided; not connected; different. – *n* **sepa'ration** a dividing or putting apart.

'sēpia *n* a brown colour.

sept- *prefix* seven.

Sep'tember *n* the ninth month of the year.

'septic *adj* (of a wound *etc*) full of germs that are poisoning the blood. – *n* **septic tank** a tank in which sewage is partially purified.

septūage'nārian *n* a person between seventy and seventy-nine years old.

sepulchre ['sepəlkər] *n* a tomb. – *adj* **se'pulchral** of sepulchres; dismal, gloomy; (of a voice) deep, hollow in tone.

'sēquel *n* a result, consequence; a story that is a continuation of an earlier story.

'sēquence *n* the order (of events) in time; a number of things following in order, a connected series.

se'questered *adj* (of a place) lonely, quiet.

'sēquin *n* a small round sparkling ornament sewn on a dress *etc.*

'seraph *n* an angel of the highest rank: – *pls* **'seraphs, 'seraphim.** – *adj* **se'raphic** like an angel.

sere *adj* (in poetry *etc*) dry, withered.

serenade [serə'nād] *n* music (suitable to be) played or sung in the open air at night, *esp* under a lady's window. – *v* to sing or play a serenade (to).

se'rene *adj* calm; not worried, happy, peaceful. – *n* **serenity** [sə'renəti] calmness, peacefulness.

serf *n* (*hist*) a slave bought and sold with the land on which he worked. – *n* **'serfdom** slavery.

serge [sərj] *n* a strong type of cloth.

sergeant ['särjənt] *n* an army rank above corporal; a rank in the police force above a constable. – *n* **'sergeant-'major** an army rank above sergeant.

series ['sērēz] *n* a number of things following each other in order; a set of things of the same kind. *He wrote a series of books on sport*: – *pl* **'series.** – *n* **'serial** a story which is published or broadcast in instalments.

'sērious *adj* grave, thoughtful: *a serious expression on her face*; not joking, in earnest: *a serious remark*; important, needing careful thought: *a serious matter*; causing worry, likely to have dangerous results: *serious injury.*

'sermon *n* a serious talk, *esp* one given in church.

'serpent *n* a snake. – *adj* **'serpentine** like a serpent; winding, full of twists.

ser'rāted *adj* (of the edge of a blade *etc*) having notches or teeth like a saw.

serried ['serid] *adj* crowded together: *serried ranks.*

'sērum *n* a clear watery fluid in the blood that helps fight disease; any of several fluids injected into the body to help fight disease.

serve *v* to work for and obey; to attend or wait upon at table *etc*; to give out food, goods *etc*; to be able to be used (as). *The cave will serve as a shelter*; to do what is required for, be suitable for: *serve a purpose*; to carry out duties (as a

serviette

member of the armed forces *etc*); to undergo, be subjected to (a sentence in prison *etc*); in starting the play in tennis, to throw up the ball and hit it with the racket. – *ns* **'servant** one who is paid to work for another, *esp* in helping to run a house; one employed by the government or administration of a country: *public servant: civil servant*; **service** ['sɜrvis] an act of serving; the duty required of a servant or other employee; a performance of (public) worship or other religious ceremony; use. *It is time to bring the new machine into service*; time spent in the army, navy, air force *etc*; (*pl*) the armed forces; (often *pl*) help. *He was thanked for his services to refugees*; a regular supply (of something, *eg* transport): *bus service*; (*pl*) public supply of water, gas, electricity to houses *etc*; a set of dishes: *dinner service*. – *v* to keep (a car, machine *etc*) in good working order by regular repairs. – *adj* **'serviceable** useful; lasting a long time: *serviceable clothes*. – **active service** service in battle; **at one's service** ready to help or be of use; **serve someone right** to be deserved by someone.

servi'ette *n* a table napkin.

servile ['sɜrvil] *adj* slave-like; showing lack of spirit: *a servile attitude to his employer*. – *ns* **servility** [sɜr'viliti]; **'servitude** slavery; the state of being under strict control.

session ['seshən] *n* a meeting or series of meetings of a court, council *etc*; the period of the year when classes are held in a school *etc*; a period of time spent on a particular activity. *We'll have a session on that particular problem this afternoon.*

set *v* to place or put; to fix in the proper place (*eg* broken bones); to arrange (a table for a meal, jewels in a necklace *etc*); to fix (a date, a price *etc*); to fix hair (in waves or curls); to adjust (a clock *etc*, or a machine *etc* so that it is ready to work or perform some function); to give (a task *etc*): *set him three problems*; to put in a certain state or condition: *set free*; (with **off, out, forth**) to start (on a journey *etc*); (of a jelly *etc*) to become firm or solid; to compose music for. *He set the poem to music*; (of the sun) to go out of sight below the horizon: – *pt, pp* **set**, *pres p* **'setting**. – *adj* fixed or arranged beforehand; ready: *all set*; fixed, stiff: *a set expression on his face*. – *n* a group of people; a number of things of a similar kind, or used together: *set of carving tools*; an apparatus: *a television set*;

sew

scenery made ready for a play *etc*; pose, position: *the set of his head*; a series of six or more games in tennis; a fixing of hair in waves or curls; a badger's burrow (also **sett**); a street paving-block (also **sett**). – *n* **'setting** act of someone who or something that sets; an arrangement; a background: *against a setting of hills and lochs*. – *ns* **'setback** a movement in the wrong direction, a failure; **'set-square** a triangular draw-ing instrument, with one right angle. – **set about** to begin (doing something); to attack; **set in** to begin: *winter has set in*; **set on, upon** to (cause to) attack.

sett *see* **set**.

set'tee *n* a kind of sofa.

'setter *n* a dog of certain breeds that can be trained to point out game in hunting.

'settle *v* to place in a position or at rest; to come to rest; to agree over (a matter): *settle the price*; (sometimes with **down**) to (come to) be calm or quiet; (sometimes with **down**) to make one's home in a place; to pay (a bill); to fix, decide (**on**); to bring (a quarrel *etc*) to an end; to sink to the bottom. – *n* a long high-backed bench. – *n* **'settlement** the act of settling; a decision, arrange-ment, agreement; payment for a bill; money given to a woman on her mar-riage; a number of people who have come to live in a country. – *n* **'settler** one who, or that which, settles; some-one who goes to live in a new country.

'seven *n* the number 7. – *adj* 7 in number. – *adj* **'seventh** the last of seven (things *etc*). – *n* one of seven equal parts.

'seven'teen *n* the number 17. – *adj* 17 in number. – *adj* **'seven'teenth** the last of seventeen (things *etc*). – *n* one of seventeen equal parts.

'seventy *n* the number 70. – *adj* 70 in number. – *adj* **'seventieth** the last of seventy (things *etc*). – *n* one of seventy equal parts.

'sever *v* to cut apart or away, to break off; to separate, part. – *n* **'severance**.

several ['sevrəl] *adj* more than one or two, but not a great many; various; different. *The boys went their several ways.* – *pron* more than one or two people, things *etc*, but not a great many.

se'vere *adj* serious: *a severe illness*; harsh; strict; very plain and simple, not fancy. – *n* **severity** [sə'veriti].

sew [sō] *v* to join together with a needle and thread; to make or mend in this way: – *pt* **sewed**, *pp* **sewn**.

sewer ['sūər] *n* an underground drain for carrying off water and waste matter. – *n* **'sewage** water and waste matter.

sex *n* either of the two classes (male, female) into which animals are divided according to the part they play in producing children or young; sexual intercourse. – *adj* **sexual** ['sekshōōəl] of sex; involving sex or sexual intercourse. – *n* **sexual intercourse** a relationship between a man and a woman involving the union of the parts of the body involved in reproducing young.

sex- *prefix* six.

sexagenarian [seksəji'nāriən] *n* a person from sixty to sixty-nine years old.

'sextant *n* an instrument used for calculating distances by means of measuring angles *eg* the distance between two stars.

'sexton *n* a man who has various responsibilities in a church, as bellringing, gravedigging *etc*.

'shabby *adj* worn-looking; poorly dressed; (of behaviour *etc*) mean, unfair.

shack *n* a roughly-built hut.

'shackle *v* to fasten with a chain; to hold back, prevent, hinder. – *npl* **'shackles** chains fastening the legs or arms of prisoners.

shade *n* slight darkness caused by cutting off some light; a place not in full sunlight; anything that screens or shelters from the heat or light; the deepness or a variation of a colour; the dark parts in a picture; a very small amount or difference: *a shade larger*; a ghost. – *v* to shelter from the sun or light; to make parts of a picture darker; to change gradually (*eg* from one colour into another *etc*). – *n* **'shading** the act of making shade; the marking of the darker places in a picture. – *adj* **'shady** sheltered from light or heat; (*coll*) dishonest, underhand: *a shady character*.

shadow ['shadō] *n* darkness, shade caused by some object coming in the way of a light; the dark shape of that object on the ground *etc*; a dark part, in *eg* a picture; a very small amount: *a shadow of doubt*. – *v* to shade, darken; to follow a person about and watch him closely. – *n* **shadow cabinet** leading members of the opposition in parliament.

shaft *n* anything long and straight; the long rod on which the head of an axe, spear, arrow *etc* is fixed; an arrow; a revolving rod which turns a machine or engine; the pole of a cart *etc* to which

the horses are tied; the deep, narrow passageway leading to a mine; a deep vertical hole, as that for a lift; a ray (of light).

'shaggy *adj* rough, hairy, or woolly.

shake *v* to (cause to) move backwards and forwards, up and down, or from side to side with quick, jerky movements; to make or be made unsteady; to shock, disturb. *His parting words shook me*: – *pt* **shook**, *pp* **'shaken**. – *n* the act of shaking or trembling; a shock; a drink mixed by shaking or stirring quickly: *milk shake*. – *adj* **'shaky** unsteady; trembling.

shale *n* a kind of rock from which oil can be obtained.

shall *v* used to form future tenses of other verbs when the subject is **I** or **we**. *I shall tell you later*; used for emphasis, or to mean 'must', or to express a promise, when the subject is **you, he, she, it** or **they**. *You shall go if I say you must. You shall go if you want to; see* also **should**.

shal'lot *n* a kind of onion.

shallow ['shalō] *adj* not deep; (of a person, his mind *etc*) not capable of thinking or feeling deeply. – *n* (often *pl*) a place where the water is not deep.

sham *n* something which is not what it appears to be, a pretence, a deception. – *adj* false, imitation, pretended: *a sham fight*. – *v* to pretend. *He's shamming sleep. I think he's shamming*: – *pt* **shammed**.

'shamble *v* to walk in a shuffling or awkward manner. – *npl* **'shambles** (*coll*) a mess, confused disorder; a slaughterhouse.

shame *n* an uncomfortable feeling caused by awareness or realization of guilt, fault or failure; disgrace, dishonour. *He brought shame on his family*; (*coll*) bad luck, a pity. *It's a shame that you can't go*. – *v* to make to feel shame or ashamed; (with **into**) to cause (someone to do something) by making him ashamed. *They shamed him into paying his share*. – *adjs* **'shameful** disgraceful; **'shameless** feeling, showing no shame. – *adj* **'shame'faced** showing shame or embarrassment. – **put to shame** to cause to feel ashamed.

shammy *see* **chamois**.

sham'poo *v* to wash (the hair and scalp). – *n* an act of shampooing; a soapy preparation (*usu* a liquid) used for this; a similar substance for cleaning carpets or upholstery.

'shamrock *n* a type of plant like clover with leaves divided in three.

shank *n* the part of the leg between the knee and the foot; a long straight part (of a tool *etc*); a shaft.

shan't short for **shall not.**

'shanty *n* a roughly-made hut *etc*; a sailors' song: – *pl* **'shanties.**

shape *n* the form or outline of anything; a mould (for a jelly *etc*); a jelly *etc*, turned out of a mould; condition: *in good shape.* – *v* to make in or into a certain form or shape; to model, mould; to (cause to) develop (in a particular way). *Our plans are shaping well.* – *adjs* **'shapeless** having no shape or regular form; **'shapely** having an attractive shape.

share *n* one of the parts of something that is divided among several people *etc*; one of the parts into which the money of a business firm is divided. – *v* to divide out among a number of people; to allow others to use (one's toys *etc*); to have, use, own in common with someone else or some others. *We share a liking for music.* – *n* **'shareholder** a person who owns shares in a business company.

shark *n* a type of large, very fierce, flesh-eating fish; (*coll*) a wicked and greedy person, a swindler.

sharp *adj* cutting, piercing; having a thin edge or fine point; hurting, stinging, biting: *sharp wind*: *sharp words*; alert, quick-witted; severe, inclined to scold; (of a note in music) raised half a tone, or too high in pitch; (of a voice) shrill; (of an outline *etc*) clear. – *adv* punctually. *Come at ten o'clock sharp.* – *n* a sign (♯) used in music to show that a note is to be raised half a tone. – *v* **'sharpen** to make or grow sharp. – *ns* **'sharpener** an instrument for sharpening: *a pencil sharpener*; **'sharper** a cheat (*esp* at cards). – *n* **sharp practice** cheating. – *adjs* **'sharp-'sighted** having keen sight; **'sharp-'witted** quick thinking. – **look sharp** to hurry.

'shatter *v* to break in pieces; to upset, ruin (hopes, health *etc*).

shave *v* to cut away hair with a razor; to scrape or cut away the surface of (wood *etc*); to touch lightly, or just avoid touching, in passing. – *n* the act of shaving; a narrow escape: *a close shave.* – *adj* **'shaven** shaved. – *npl* **'shavings** very thin slices *esp* of wood.

shawl *n* a loose covering for the shoulders.

shē *pron* some female person, animal, or thing (as a ship) thought of as female, already spoken about (used only as the subject of a verb). *When the girl saw us, she asked the time.*

sheaf *n* a bundle (*eg* of corn, papers) tied together: – *pl* **sheaves** [shēvz].

shear *v* to clip, cut (*esp* wool from a sheep); to cut through, cut off: – *pt* **sheared**, *pp* **shorn**. – *npl* **shears** large scissors; a large type of cutting tool like scissors.

sheath *n* a case for a sword or dagger; a long close-fitting covering. – *v* **sheathe** [shēdh] to put into a sheath.

shed *n* a building for storage or shelter: *a coalshed*: *a bicycle shed*; an out-house. – *v* to throw or cast off (leaves, a skin, clothing); to (let) pour out (tears, blood); to give out (light *etc*).

sheen *n* brightness, gloss.

sheep *n* a type of animal whose flesh is used as food and from whose wool clothing is made; a very meek person, afraid to think for himself. – *adj* **'sheepish** shy; embarrassed, shamefaced. – *ns* **'sheep-dip** a liquid for disinfecting sheep; **'sheepdog** a dog trained to look after sheep or of a breed used for this work; **'sheepshank** a kind of knot, used for shortening a rope; **'sheepskin** the skin of a sheep; a kind of leather made from it.

sheer *adj* very steep: *a sheer drop from the cliff*; pure, not mixed: *sheer delight*: *sheer nonsense*; (of cloth) very thin or fine. – *adv* straight up and down, very steeply. – *v* to (cause to) turn aside from a straight line, swerve.

sheet *n* a large piece of linen, cotton, nylon *etc* for a bed; a large thin piece of anything as metal, glass, ice *etc*; a piece of paper; a sail; the rope fastened to the lower corner of a sail. – *n* **'sheeting** any material from which sheets are made. – *ns* **'sheet-anchor** a large anchor for use in emergencies; **'sheet-'lightning** lightning which appears in great sheets or flashes.

sheikh [shāk] *n* an Arab chief.

'shekel *n* (*hist*) a Jewish weight and coin; (*pl coll*) money.

shelf *n* a board fixed on a wall, for laying things on; a flat layer of rock, a ledge; a sandbank: – *pl* **shelves** [shelvz]. – *v* **shelve** to put up shelves in; to put aside (a problem *etc*) *usu* for later consideration; (of land) to slope gently.

shell *n* a hard outer covering (of a shellfish, egg, nut *etc*); a husk or pod (*eg* of peas); a metal case filled with explosive fired from a gun; any framework, as of a building not yet completed, or burnt out. *Only the shell of the warehouse was left.* – *v* to take the shell from (a nut, egg *etc*); to fire shells at. – *n* **'shellfish** a water creature covered with a shell (as oyster, limpet, mussel).

'shelter *n* a building or something else which acts as a protection from harm, rain, wind *etc*; the state of being protected from any of these. – *v* to give protection to; to put in a place of shelter or protection; to go to, stay in, a place of shelter. – **take shelter** to go to a place of shelter.

shelve *see* **shelf**.

shepherd ['shepərd] *n* one who looks after sheep: – *fem* **'shepherdess**. – *v* to watch over carefully, to guide. – *n* **shepherd's pie** a dish of minced meat covered with mashed potatoes.

'sherbet *n* (powder for making) a fizzy drink.

'sheriff *n* the chief representative of the king *etc* in a county whose duties include keeping the peace; (in Scotland) the chief judge of county.

'sherry *n* a strong kind of wine, often drunk before a meal.

shied *see* **shy**.

shield [shēld] *n* anything that protects from harm *etc*; (*hist*) a broad piece of metal *etc* carried as part of a soldier's armour as a defence against weapons; a shield-shaped trophy won in a competition *etc*; a shield-shaped plaque bearing a coat-of-arms. – *v* to protect from harm, to defend, shelter.

shift *v* to move (something), change the position of, transfer: *shift the furniture*: *shift the blame*; to change position or direction. *The wind shifted*; to get rid of. – *n* a change: *shift of emphasis*; a change of position, transfer; a group of workers on duty at the same time: *day shift*: *night shift*; a specified period of work or duty; a kind of loose-fitting dress. – *adjs* **'shiftless** having no set plan or purpose, lazy; **'shifty** not to be trusted, looking dishonest. – **shift for oneself** to manage to get on by one's own efforts.

'shilling *n* before 1971, the name of the silver-coloured coin worth $\frac{1}{20}$ of £1 (now the 5 pence piece).

'shillyshally *v* to hesitate in making up one's mind, to waver: – *pt* **'shillyshallied**.

'shimmer *v* to shine with a quivering or unsteady light. – Also *n*.

shin *n* the front part of the leg below the knee. – **shin up** to climb.

'shindy *n* (*coll*) a noise, uproar.

shine *v* to (cause to) give out or reflect light; to be bright; to polish (shoes *etc*); to be very good at. *He shines at arithmetic*: – *pt, pp* **shone** [shon]. *n* brightness; an act of polishing. – *adjs* **'shining** very bright and clear; to be admired, distinguished: *a shining example*; **'shiny** glossy, polished.

shingle ['shingl] *n* coarse gravel (made up of rounded stones) on the shores of rivers or of the sea. – *npl* **'shingles** a type of infectious disease causing a painful rash.

'shinty *n* in Scotland, a kind of ball game, something like hockey.

shiny *see* **shine**.

ship *n* any large vessel for journeys across water. – *v* to take on to a ship; to send by ship; to go by ship: – *pt* **shipped**. – *ns* **'shipment** an act of putting on board ship; a load of goods sent by ship; **'shipping**. – *ns* **ship chandler** one who deals in ship's stores; **'shipmate** a fellow-sailor. – *adj* **'shipshape** in good order, neat, trim. – *n* **'shipwreck** the sinking or destruction of a ship (*esp* by accident); a wrecked ship; ruin. – *adj* **'shipwrecked** involved in a shipwreck. – *ns* **'shipwright** one who is employed to build or repair ships; **'shipyard** the yard in which ships are built or repaired.

'shire *n* a county.

shirk *v* to avoid or evade (doing one's duty *etc*). – *n* **'shirker**.

shirt *n* a kind of garment worn by men on the upper part of the body, *usu* having a collar, sleeves and buttons down the front; a similar garment for a woman.

'shiver *v* to tremble (as with cold or fear); to break into small pieces, shatter. – *n* the act of shivering; a small broken piece: *shivers of glass*.

shoal *n* a great number, *esp* of fishes, together in one place; a shallow place, a sandbank.

shock *n* a sudden blow, coming with great force; a feeling of fright, horror, dismay *etc*; a state of weakness or illness that may follow such feelings; the effect on the body of an electric current passing through it; an earthquake; a bushy mass (of hair). – *v* to give a shock to; to upset or horrify. – *adj* **'shocking** causing horror or dismay; disgusting. – *n* **'shock-absorber** a device (in an aircraft, car *etc*) for lessening the impact or force of bumps.

shod *adj* wearing shoes. – *v see* **shoe**.

'shoddy *adj* of poor material or quality: *shoddy goods*; mean: *a shoddy trick*.

shoe [shoo] *n* a stiff outer covering for the foot, not reaching above the ankle;

à rim of iron nailed to the hoof of a horse. – *v* to put shoes on (a horse): – *pt, pp* **shod** [shod]. – *ns* '**shoehorn** a curved piece of horn, metal *etc* used for making one's shoe slip easily over one's heel; '**shoelace**, '**shoestring** a kind of cord or string used for fastening a shoe; '**shoemaker** one who makes and mends shoes. – **on a shoestring** with very little money.

shone *see* **shine**.

shoo! *interj* used to scare away birds, animals *etc*. – *v* to drive or scare away.

shook *see* **shake**.

shoot *v* to send a bullet from a gun, or an arrow from a bow; to hit or kill with an arrow, bullet *etc*; to send, let fly swiftly and with force; to kick for a goal; to score (a goal); (of plants) to put forth new buds *etc*; to photograph or film; to move very swiftly or suddenly; to slide (a bolt): – *pt, pp* **shot**. – *n* a new sprout *etc* on a plant; an expedition to shoot game; land where game is shot. – *ns* '**shooting-brake** an estate car; '**shooting-'star** a meteor.

shop *n* a place where goods are sold; a workshop or a place where any industry is carried on. – *v* to visit shops and buy goods: – *pt* **shopped**. – *n* '**shopper**. – *ns* '**shopkeeper** one who keeps a shop of his own; '**shoplifter** one who steals goods from a shop; **shop steward** in a factory *etc*, a worker elected by the other workers as their representative. – **talk shop** (*coll*) to talk about one's work when one is off duty.

shore [shōr] *n* the land bordering on a sea or lake. – *v* to prop (up), support: *shore up the wall*: *shore up a failing organization*.

shorn *see* **shear**.

short *adj* not long: *a short piece of string*; not tall: *a short man*; brief, not lasting long: *a short talk*; not enough, less than it should be; (of a person or his manner) rude, sharp, abrupt; (of pastry) crisp and crumbling easily. – *adv* suddenly, abruptly. *He stopped short*; not as far as intended. *The shot fell short*. – *n* a short film; a short-circuit; (*pl*) short trousers. – *v* to short-circuit. – *n* '**shortage** a lack. – *v* '**shorten** to make less in length. – *adv* '**shortly** soon; curtly, abruptly; briefly. – *ns* '**shortbread** a kind of thick biscuit made of butter and flour *etc*; '**short-'circuit** the missing out, *usu* accidentally, of a major part of an intended electric circuit, sometimes causing blowing of fuses. – *v* (of an electrical appliance) to develop or un-

dergo a short-circuit; to bypass (a difficulty *etc*). – *ns* '**shortcoming** a fault, a defect; **short cut** a short way of going somewhere or doing something: '**shorthand** a method of swift writing using strokes and dots to show sounds. – *adj* '**short-'handed** having fewer workers than usual. – *n* **short list** a list of candidates for a job who have been selected from the total number of those applying for it. – *adjs* '**short'lived** living or lasting only a short time; '**short-'sighted** seeing clearly only things which are near; taking no account of what may happen in the future; '**short-'tempered** easily made angry; '**short-'term** intended to last only a short time. – **give short shrift to** to waste little time or consideration on; **in short** in a few words; **short of** not having enough: *short of money*; less than, not as much or as far as: *£3 short of the price*: *5 miles short of London*; without going as far as. *He did not know how to get the money, short of stealing it.*

shot *n* something which is shot or fired; small lead bullets, used in cartridges; a single act of shooting; the sound of a gun being fired; the distance covered by a bullet, ball, arrow *etc*; a marksman; a throw, stroke, turn *etc* in a game or competition; an attempt (at doing something, at guessing *etc*); a photograph; a scene in a motion picture. – *adj* (of silk *etc*) showing showing colours; streaked or mixed with (a colour *etc*). – *v see* **shoot**. – *n* '**shotgun** a light type of gun which fires shot. – **a shot in the dark** a guess.

should [shood] *v* the form of the verb **shall** used to express a condition. *I should go if I had time*; used to mean 'ought to'. *You should know that already.*

shoulder ['shōldər] *n* the part of the body between the neck and the upper arm; the upper part of the foreleg of an animal; anything resembling a shoulder in shape: *the shoulder of the hill.* – *v* to carry on the shoulder(s); to bear the full weight of (a burden *etc*); to push with the shoulder. – *n* '**shoulderblade** the broad flat bone of the shoulder.

shout *n* a loud cry or call; a loud burst (of laughter *etc*). – Also *v*.

shove [shuv] *v* to push with force, thrust, push aside. – Also *n*.

shovel ['shuvl] *n* a kind of spade-like tool used for lifting or shifting coal, gravel *etc*. – *v* to lift or move with a shovel.

show [shō] *v* to allow, or cause, to be seen. *Show her your new dress*; to be able to be seen. *Your underskirt is showing*; to exhibit, display (an art collection *etc*); to point out (the way *etc*); to direct, guide. *Show her to a seat*; to make clear, demonstrate. *That shows that I was right*: – *pt* **showed**, *pp* **shown**. – *n* the act of showing; display; an exhibition; a performance, an entertainment. – *adj* **'showy** bright, gaudy; (too) obvious, striking. – *ns* **show business** the branch of the theatre concerned with variety entertainments; **'showroom** a room where goods are laid out for people to see. – **show off** to show or display (something); to try to impress others with one's talents, possessions *etc*; **show up** to (cause to) stand out clearly; to expose, to make the faults of (someone, something) obvious.

shower ['showər] *n* a short fall of rain; a large quantity: *a shower of questions*; a showerbath; the apparatus which sprays water for this; the place where this apparatus is kept; (*US*) a party at which gifts are given *eg* to someone about to be married. – *v* to pour (something) down on; to bathe under a shower. – *adj* **'showery** raining from time to time. – *n* **'showerbath** a bath in which water is sprayed from above. – *adj* **'showerproof** (of material, a coat *etc*) able to withstand light rain.

shown *see* **show**.

shrank *see* **shrink**.

'shrapnel *n* a shell containing bullets *etc* which scatter with explosion; splinters or fragments of the shell, metal, a bomb *etc*.

shred *n* a long, narrow piece, cut or torn off; a scrap, a very small amount: *not a shred of evidence*. – *v* to cut or tear into shreds: – *pt* **'shredded**.

shrew [shroo] *n* a small mouse-like type of animal with a long nose; a noisy, quarrelsome or scolding woman. – *adj* **'shrewish** quarrelsome, ill-tempered.

shrewd [shrood] *adj* clever, sometimes also cunning: *shrewd commonsense*: *a shrewd businessman*.

shriek [shrēk] *v* to utter (with) a shrill scream or laugh. – Also *n*.

shrill *adj* (of a sound or voice) high in tone, piercing. – *adv* **'shrilly**.

shrimp *n* a small, long-tailed kind of eatable shellfish; (*coll*) a small person.

shrine *n* a holy or sacred place.

shrink *v* to (cause to) become smaller; to draw back in fear and disgust (from): – *pt* **shrank**, *pp* **shrunk**. – *n* **'shrinkage** the amount by which a thing grows smaller. – *adj* **'shrunken** shrunk.

'shrivel *v* to dry up, wrinkle, wither: – *pt* **'shrivelled**.

shroud *n* the cloth round a dead body; anything which covers: *a shroud of mist*; (*pl*) the rope from the mast-head to a ship's sides. – *v* to cover (up) as with a shroud.

shrub *n* a small bush or woody plant. – *n* **'shrubbery** a place where shrubs grow: – *pl* **'shrubberies**.

shrug *v* to show doubt, lack of interest *etc* by drawing up the shoulders: – *pt* **shrugged**. – Also *n*. – **shrug off** to dismiss or to treat as being unimportant: *shrug off a problem*.

shrunk, shrunken *see* **shrink**.

'shudder *v* to tremble from fear, cold, disgust. – Also *n*.

'shuffle *v* to mix, rearrange (*eg* playing cards); to move by dragging or sliding the feet along the ground without lifting them; to move (the feet) in this way. – Also *n*.

shun *v* to avoid, keep clear of. *She shuns her old friends*: – *pt* **shunned**.

shunt *v* to move (railway trains, engines *etc*) on to a side track.

shut *v* to move (a door, window, lid *etc*) so that it covers an opening; to close, lock (a building *etc*). *We shut the shop at 12.30*; to become closed. *The door shut with a bang*; to confine, put (something or someone) in something to prevent from going free. *Shut the dog in his kennel*: – *pres p* **'shutting**, *pt* **shut**. – *n* **'shutter** a cover for a window or opening (as in a camera). – **shut down** to close (a factory *etc*); **shut up** to close completely; (*coll*) to (cause to) stop speaking or making other noise.

'shuttle *n* the part of a weaving loom which carries the cross thread from side to side. – *adj* (of a bus or train service *etc*) going to and fro between two places. – *n* **'shuttlecock** a rounded cork stuck with feathers, used in the game of badminton.

shy *adj* (of a wild animal) easily frightened, timid; lacking confidence in the presence of others, *esp* strangers; not wanting to attract attention. – *v* to jump or turn suddenly aside in fear; to throw, toss: – *pt* **shied**. – *n* a try, an attempt. – *n* **'shyness**. – *adv* **'shyly**. – **fight shy of** to avoid, keep away from.

'sibilant *adj, n* (of) a hissing sound.

'sibyl *n* (*myth*) a woman able to tell the future, a prophetess.

sick *adj* wanting to vomit; vomiting; not well, ill; (with **of**) tired of. – *v* **'sicken** to make or become sick. – *adjs* **'sickening** causing sickness, disgust, weariness; **'sickly** unhealthy; causing sickness; feeble. – *n* **'sickness** illness. – *ns* **sick bed, sick room** a bed, room, in which there is an ill person; **sick leave** time taken off duty because of illness.

'sickle *n* a hooked knife for cutting or reaping grain, hay *etc*.

side *n* an edge, border or boundary line; a surface of something, *esp* one that is not the top, bottom, front or back; either surface of a piece of paper, cloth *etc*; the right or left part of the body (*esp* between the hip and armpit); a division or part: *the north side of the town*; an aspect, point of view: *all sides of the problem*; a slope (of a hill); a team or party which is opposing another. – *adj* on or towards the side: *side door*; indirect, additional but less important: *side issue*. – *v* (with **with**) to support (one person, group *etc* against another). – *n* **'siding** a short line of rails on which trucks *etc* are shunted off the main line. – *ns* **'sideboard** a piece of furniture in a dining room *etc* for holding dishes *etc*; **'sidecar** a small car for a passenger, attached to a motorcycle; **side effect** an additional (often bad) effect (*esp* of a medicine, drug *etc*); **'sideline** an extra bit of business, outside one's regular job or activity. – *adj, adv* **'sidelong** from or to the side: *a sidelong glance*. – *n* **'sideshow** a less important show (that is part of a larger one). – *v* **'sidestep** to avoid by stepping to one side; **'sidetrack** to turn (a person) away from what he was going to do or say. – *n* **'sidewalk** (*US*) a pavement, footpath. – *adv* **'sideways** with the side foremost; towards the side. – **take sides** to choose to support (a party, person) against another.

'sidle *v* to go or move sideways; to move in a stealthy way.

siege [sēj] *n* an attempt to capture a town, fort *etc* by keeping it surrounded by an armed force; a constant attempt to gain control of. – **lay siege to** to besiege.

si'erra *n* a range of mountains with jagged peaks.

si'esta *n* a short sleep or rest, *esp* one taken in the afternoon.

sieve [siv] *n* a container with a mesh or very small holes used to separate liquids from solids, fine, small pieces from large, coarse pieces *etc*. – *v* to put through a sieve.

sift *v* to separate by passing through a sieve; to consider and examine closely: *sifting all the evidence*.

sigh [sī] *v* to take a long, deep-sounding breath, showing tiredness, sadness, longing *etc*. – Also *n*.

sight [sīt] *n* the act or power of seeing; a view, a glimpse. *He caught sight of her*; (often *pl*) something worth seeing: *the sights of London*; something or someone seen that is unusual, ridiculous, shocking *etc*. *She's quite a sight in that hat*; (on a gun) a guide to the eye in taking aim. – *v* to get a view of, see suddenly; to look at through the sight of a gun. – *ns* **'sight-reading** playing or singing from music that one has not seen previously; **'sightseeing** visiting the chief buildings, monuments *etc* of a place.

sign [sīn] *n* a mark with a special meaning, a symbol: + *is the sign of addition*; a movement (such as a nod, wave of the hand) to show one's meaning; (a board with) an advertisement or notice giving information (*eg* the name of a shopkeeper); something which shows what is happening or what is going to happen: *signs of irritation: a sign of good weather*. – *v* to write one's name (on a document, cheque *etc*); to make a sign or gesture to; to show (one's meaning) by a sign or gesture. – *ns* **'signboard** a board with a notice; **'signpost** a post with a sign, *esp* one showing the direction and distances of certain places. – **sign on** to enter one's name on a list for work, the army *etc*.

'signal *n* a sign (as a gesture, light, sound) giving a command, warning or other message; something used for this purpose: *railway signals*; the wave, sound received or sent out by a radio set *etc*: – *pt* **'signalled**. – *v* to make signals (to); to send (information) by signal. – *adj* remarkable. – *n* **'signalman** one who works railway signals, or who sends signals.

signature ['signəchər] *n* a signed name; an act of signing; the flats or sharps at the beginning of a piece of music which show its key, or the sign showing its time. – *n* **'signatory** one who has signed an agreement *etc*: – *pl* **'signatories**. – *n* **signature tune** a tune used to identify a particular performer, radio or television series *etc* played at the beginning and/or end of the programme.

'signet *n* a small seal, *esp* one bearing one's initials *etc* and set into a ring (**signet ring**).

'signify *v* to mean, to be a sign of; to show, make known by a gesture *etc*. *He signified his disapproval by a shake of the head*; to have meaning or importance: –

pt '**signified**. – *n* **sig'nificance** meaning; importance. – *adj* **sig'nificant** meaning much; important: *no significant change*.

'**silage** *n* green crops kept as cattle-food.

'**silence** *n* absence or lack of sound or speech; a time of quietness. – *v* to cause to be silent. – *n* '**silencer** a device (on a car engine, gun *etc*) for making noise less. – *adj* '**silent** free from noise; not speaking.

silhouette [silŏo'et] *n* an outline drawing (of a person) *esp* in profile, and *usu* filled in with black; a dark shape or outline (of someone, something) seen against the light.

'**silica** *n* a white or colourless substance, of which flint, sandstone, quartz *etc* are mostly made up.

silk *n* very fine, soft fibres, spun by silkworms; thread or cloth made from it. – *adj* made of silk; like silk, soft, smooth. – *adjs* '**silken** made of silk; like silk; '**silky** like silk. – *n* '**silkworm** the caterpillar of certain moths which spins silk.

sill *n* a ledge of wood, stone *etc* such as that below a window or a door.

'**silly** *adj* foolish, not sensible.

'**silo** *n* a tower-like building for storing grain; a pit or airtight chamber for holding silage.

silt *n* sand or mud left behind by flowing water. – **silt up** to (cause to) become blocked by mud.

'**silver** *n* an element, a type of white metal, able to take on a high polish; money made of silver or of a metal alloy used instead of it; objects (*esp* cutlery) made of, or plated with, silver. – *adj* made of, or looking like, silver. – *v* to cover with silver; to become like silver. – *adj* '**silvery** like silver; (of sound) ringing and musical. – *ns* '**silverfish** a kind of wingless, silvery insect, sometimes found in houses; **silver foil**, **silver paper** kinds of wrapping materials made of metal, having a silvery appearance; '**silversmith** one who makes or sells articles of silver; **silver wedding** *etc* a 25th anniversary of wedding *etc*.

'**simian** *adj* ape-like.

'**similar** *adj* (almost) alike or like. – *n* **simi'larity**: – *pl* **simi'larities**. – *adv* '**similarly** in the same, or a similar, way; likewise, also.

simile ['siməli] *n* a form of expression using 'like' or 'as', in which one thing is likened to another that is well-known for a particular quality (*eg* 'as black as night', 'to swim like a fish').

'**simmer** *v* to cook gently just below or just at boiling-point.

'**simper** *v* to smile in a silly manner; to say with a simper. – *n* a silly smile.

'**simple** *adj* easy, not difficult, or not complicated; plain, not fancy: *a simple hairstyle*; ordinary: *simple, everyday objects*; of humble rank: *a simple peasant*; mere, nothing but: *the simple truth*; too trusting, easily cheated; foolish, half-witted. – *ns* '**simpleton** a foolish person; **sim'plicity** the state of being simple; **simplifi'cation** an act of making simpler; a simple form. – *v* '**simplify** to make simpler: – *pt* '**simplified**. – *adv* '**simply** in a simple manner; merely. *I do it simply for the pay*; absolutely: *simply beautiful*.

'**simulate** *v* to pretend, make a pretence of: *simulated illness*; to have an appearance of, look like. – *adj* '**simulated** pretended; having the appearance of: *simulated leather*. – *n* **simu'lation**.

simultaneous [siməl'tāniəs] *adj* happening, or done, at the same time. – *adv* **simul'taneously**.

sin *n* a wicked act, *esp* one which breaks the laws of one's religion; wrongdoing; (*coll*) a shame, pity. – *v* to commit a sin, do wrong: – *pt* **sinned**. – *adj* '**sinful** wicked. – *n* '**sinner**. – *n* **original sin** the supposed sinful nature of all human beings since the time of Adam's sin.

since *adv* (often with **ever**) from that time onwards. *I have avoided him* (*ever*) *since*; at a later time. *We have since become friends*; ago: *long since*; from the time of: *since his arrival*. – *conj* after the time when. *I have been at home since I returned from Italy*; because. *Since you are going, I will go too*.

sin'cere *adj* honest in word and deed, meaning what one says or does; true: *a sincere friend*; truly felt: *a sincere desire*. – *n* **sincerity** [sin'serəti].

sinecure ['sinikūr] *n* a job in which one receives money but has little or no work to do.

sinew ['sinū] *n* a tough cord or band that joins a muscle to a bone; (*pl*) equipment and resources necessary for (something): *sinews of war*. – *adj* '**sinewy** having (strong) sinews; strong, tough.

sing *v* to make musical sounds with one's voice; to utter (words, a song *etc*) by doing this: – *pt* **sang**, *pp* **sung**. – *n* '**singer**. – *n* '**sing-song** a gathering of people singing informally together; an up-and-down tone of voice. – Also *adj*.

singe [sinj] *v* to burn slightly on the

surface, scorch. – Also *n.*

single ['siŋgl] *adj* one only; not double; not married; for one person: *a single bed*; between two people: *single combat*; for one direction of a journey: *a single ticket.* – *n* '**singleness** the state of being single. – *adv* '**singly** one by one, separately. – *adjs* '**single-'handed** working *etc* by oneself; '**single-'minded** having one aim only. – **single out** to pick out, treat differently in some way.

singlet ['siŋglit] *n* a vest, an undershirt, worn as underwear or as sportswear by runners *etc.*

singular ['siŋgülər] *adj* (in grammar, the opposite of **plural**) showing one person, thing *etc*; exceptional: *singular success*; unusual, strange: *a singular sight.* – *adv* '**singularly** strangely, exceptionally.

'**sinister** *adj* suggesting evil to; evil-looking.

sink *v* to (cause to) go down below the surface of the water *etc*; to go down or become less. *His hopes sank*; (of a very ill person) to become weaker; to lower oneself (into): *to sink into a chair*; to make by digging (a well *etc*); to push (one's teeth *etc*) deep into (something); to invest (money *etc*) into a business: – *pt* **sank**, *pp* **sunk**. – *n* a kind of basin in a kitchen, bathroom *etc*, with a water supply connected to it and a drain for carrying off dirty water *etc*. – *n* '**sinker** a weight fixed to a fishing line *etc*. – *adjs* **sunk** on a lower level than the surroundings; sunken; (*coll*) defeated, done for; '**sunken** that has been sunk; (of cheeks *etc*) hollow.

'**sinuous** *adj* bending in and out, winding.

'**sinus** *n* a hollow or air cavity, *esp* an air cavity in the head connected with the nose: – *pl* '**sinuses**.

sip *v* to drink in very small quantities: – *pt* **sipped**. – Also *n.*

'**siphon** *n* a bent tube for drawing off liquids from one container into another; a glass bottle, for soda water *etc*, containing such a tube. – *v* to draw (off) through a siphon; (with **off**) to take (part of something) away gradually. *He siphoned off some of the club's funds.*

sir *n* a polite form of address used to a man; **Sir** the title of a knight or baronet.

'**sire** *n* a male parent (*esp* a horse); (*hist*) a title used in speaking to a king. – *v* (of an animal) to be the male parent of.

'**siren** *n* a kind of instrument that gives out a loud hooting noise as a warning or signal; (*myth*) a sea nymph whose singing enchanted sailors and tempted them into danger; an attractive but dangerous woman.

'**sirloin** *n* the upper part of the loin of beef.

'**sisal** *n* a fibre from a kind of West Indian plant, used for making ropes.

'**sister** *n* a female born of the same parents as oneself; a senior nurse, often in charge of a hospital ward or department; a member of a religious group or community of women (*eg* a nun). – *adj* closely related; alike *eg* in design: *a sister ship.* – *adj* '**sisterly** like a sister. – *ns* '**sisterhood** the state of being a sister; a group of women formed for purposes of religion, good works *etc*; '**sister-in-law** the sister of one's husband or of one's wife; the wife of one's brother or of one's brother-in-law.

sit *v* to rest on the buttocks, to be seated; (of birds) to perch; to rest on eggs in order to hatch them; to be an official member: *to sit in parliament*: *to sit on a committee*; (of a court, parliament *etc*) to meet officially; to pose (for) a photographer, painter *etc*; to take (an examination *etc*): – *pres p* '**sitting**, *pt, pp* **sat.** – *ns* '**sitter** one who poses for a portrait *etc*; a babysitter; a bird sitting on eggs; '**sitting** the state or time of sitting. – *adj* seated; for sitting in or on; (of a member of parliament, tenant *etc*) actually in office or in possession. – *ns* '**sit-in** an occupation of a building *etc* by protestors; '**sitting-room** a room chiefly for sitting in. – **sit tight** to be unwilling to move; **sit up** to sit with one's back straight; to remain up instead of going to bed.

site *n* a place where a building, town *etc* is, was or is to be put up or placed. – *v* to select a place for (a building *etc*).

'**situated** *adj* placed. – *n* situ'**ation** the place where anything stands; a job, employment; a state of affairs, circumstances: *in an awkward situation.*

six *n* the number 6. – *adj* 6 in number. – *adj* **sixth** the last of six (things *etc*). – *n* one of six equal parts.

'**sixpence** *n* a silver-coloured coin worth $\frac{1}{40}$ of £1. – *adj* '**sixpenny** costing sixpence.

'**six'teen** *n* the number 16. – *adj* 16 in number. – *adj* '**six'teenth** the last of sixteen (things *etc*). – *n* one of sixteen equal parts.

'**sixty** *n* the number 60. – *adj* 60 in number. – *adj* '**sixtieth** the last of sixty (things *etc*). – *n* one of sixty equal parts.

size *n* space taken up by anything; measurements, dimensions (of someone or something); largeness; one of a number of classes into which shoes and clothes are grouped according to size. *He takes size 8 in shoes*; a weak kind of glue. – *adj* **'siz(e)able** fairly large. – **size up** to form an opinion or estimation of a person, situation *etc.*

'sizzle *v* to make a hissing sound; to fry or scorch.

skate *n* a steel blade attached to a boot for gliding on ice; *see* also **rollerskate**; a type of large flatfish. – *v* to move on skates.

skein [skān] *n* a coil of thread or yarn, loosely tied in a knot.

skeleton ['skelitn] *n* the bony framework of an animal or person, without the flesh; any framework or outline. – *adj* (of *eg* staff, crew *etc*) reduced to a very small or minimum number. *Over Christmas only a skeleton staff was working.* – *adj* **'skeletal** of, like a skeleton. – *n* **skeleton key** a key from which the inner part has been cut away so that it can open many different locks.

sketch *n* a rough plan or painting or drawing; a short or rough account; a short play, dramatic scene *etc*: – *pl* **'sketches**. – *v* to draw, describe a plan roughly; to give the chief points of; to draw in pencil or ink. – *adj* **'sketchy** roughly done; not thorough, incomplete. *My knowledge of that period of history is rather sketchy.*

skew [skū] *adj, adv* off the straight, slanting. – *v* to set or be set at a slant.

skewer ['skūər] *n* a long pin of wood or metal for holding meat together while roasting *etc.* – *v* to fasten, fix, with a skewer or with something sharp.

ski [skē] *n* one of a pair of long narrow strips of wood *etc* that can be attached to boots for gliding over snow: – *pl* **skis**. – *v* to travel on, use, skis: – *pres p* **'skiing**, *pt* **skied** [skēd].

skid *n* a slide sideways. *The car went into a skid*; a wedge *etc* put under a wheel to check it on a steep place; (*pl*) log(s), plank(s) *etc* on which things can be moved by sliding. – *v* (of wheels) to slide along without turning; to slip sideways.

skiff *n* a small light boat.

skill *n* cleverness at doing a thing, either from practice or as a natural gift. – *adjs* **'skilful** having or showing skill; **skilled** having skill, *esp* through training; (of a job) requiring skill.

'skillet *n* a small metal pan with a long handle for frying food.

skim *v* to remove floating matter (*eg* cream, scum *etc*) from the surface of (something); to move lightly and quickly over (a surface); to read quickly, missing parts: – *pt* **skimmed**. – *n* **'skim-'milk** milk from which the cream has been skimmed.

skimp *v* to give (someone) hardly enough; to do (a job) imperfectly; to spend too little money (on). *She skimped on clothes.* – *adj* **'skimpy** too small; (of clothes) too short or tight.

skin *n* the natural outer covering of an animal or person; a thin outer layer, as on a fruit; a (thin) film or layer that forms on a liquid. – *v* to strip the skin from: – *pt* **skinned**. – *adj* **'skinny** very thin. – *adj* **'skin-'deep** as deep as the skin only, on the surface, – *n* **'skinflint** a very mean person. – **by the skin of one's teeth** very narrowly.

skip *v* to go along with a rhythmic step and hop; to jump over a turning rope; to leap, *esp* lightly or joyfully; to leave out (parts of a book, a meal *etc*): – *pt* **skipped**. – *n* an act of skipping; the captain of a side at bowls *etc.* – *n* **skipping rope** a rope used in skipping.

'skipper *n* the captain of a ship, aeroplane or team.

'skirmish *n* a fight between small parties of soldiers; a short sharp contest or disagreement: – *pl* **'skirmishes**. – Also *v*.

skirt *n* a garment, worn by women, that hangs from the waist; the lower part of a dress; (*pl*) the outer edge or border. – *v* to pass along, or lie along, the edge of. – *n* **'skirting (board)** the narrow board next to the floor round the walls of a room.

skit *n* a piece of writing, short play *etc* that makes fun of a person or event *etc.*

'skittish *adj* too frisky or lively.

'skittle *n* a bottle-shaped wooden (*usu*) object, a ninepin; (*pl*) a game in which skittles are knocked over by a ball.

skive *v* (*coll*) to avoid doing a duty.

skulk *v* to wait about, stay hidden (often for a bad purpose); to move in a stealthy or sneaking way.

skull *n* the bony case which encloses the brain; the head. – *n* **'skullcap** a cap which fits closely to the head. – **skull and crossbones** the sign on a pirate's flag.

skunk *n* a kind of small American animal which defends itself by squirting out an evil-smelling liquid; a contemptible person.

skȳ *n* (often in *pl* **skies**) the upper

atmosphere, the heavens; the weather or climate. – *ns* '**skylark** the common lark which sings while hovering far overhead; '**skylarking** mischievous behaviour; '**skylight** a window in a roof or ceiling; '**skyline** the horizon; '**skyscraper** a high building of very many storeys.

slab *n* a thick slice, or thick flat piece of anything: *a slab of stone*: *a slab of cake*.

slack *adj* not firmly stretched; not firmly in position; not strict; lazy and careless; not busy: *the slack season in hotels.* – *n* the loose part of a rope; small coal and coal-dust; (*pl*) trousers. – *v* to do less work than one should, to be lazy; to slacken. – *v* '**slacken** to make or become looser; to make or become less active, less busy or less fast *etc*.

slag *n* waste material left from metal-smelting.

slain *see* **slay**.

slake *v* to quench, satisfy (thirst, longing *etc*); to put out (fire); to mix (lime) with water.

'**slalom** *n* a downhill, zigzag ski run among posts or trees; an obstacle race in canoes.

slam *v* to shut (a door, lid *etc*) with a bang or loud noise; to put down with a loud noise: – *pt* **slammed**. – *n* the act of slamming; (also **grand slam**) a winning of every trick in cards or every contest in a competition *etc*.

'**slander** *n* untrue statement(s) made in speech, not in writing, with the purpose of doing harm to a person's reputation. – *v* to speak slander against (someone). – *adj* '**slanderous**.

slang *n* popular words and phrases (often in use only for a short time) that are used in informal, everyday speech or writing, but not in formal speech or writing; the special language of a particular group: *Cockney slang.* – *v* to scold, abuse.

slant *v* to slope; to place, lie, move diagonally or in a sloping position or way; to give or present (facts or information) in a special way, *esp* in a distorted way that suits one's own purpose. – *n* a slope; a diagonal direction; a way of considering or thinking about something, point of view.

slap *n* a blow with the palm of the hand or anything flat. – *v* to give a slap to: – *pt* **slapped**. – *adjs* '**slapdash** hasty, careless; '**slapstick** (of comedy) boisterous, funny in a very obvious way. – Also *n*.

slash *v* to make long cuts in; to strike at violently. – *n* a long cut; a sweeping blow: – *pl* '**slashes**.

slat *n* a thin strip of wood, metal or other material. – *adj* '**slatted** having slats.

slate *n* an easily split rock of dull blue-grey, used for roofing or (formerly) commonly for writing upon. – *adj* made of slate; slate-coloured. – *v* to cover with slate; to say harsh things to or about: *to slate a play*.

'**slattern** *n* a woman of untidy or dirty appearance or habits.

slaughter ['slötər] *n* the killing of animals, *esp* for food; cruel killing, *esp* of great numbers of people. – *v* to kill for food; to kill brutally. – *n* '**slaughterhouse** a place where animals are killed in order to be sold for food.

slave *n* (*hist*) one forced to work for a master to whom he belongs; one who serves another in a devoted way; one who works very hard; one who is addicted (to): *a slave to fashion.* – *v* to work like a slave. – *n* **slavery** ['slāvəri] the state of being a slave; the system of owning slaves. – *adj* '**slavish** slavelike; (thinking or acting) exactly according to rules or instructions.

slaver ['slavər] *n* saliva running from the mouth. – *v* to let the saliva run out of the mouth.

slay *v* to kill: – *pt* **slew**, *pp* **slain**.

sledge *n* a vehicle with runners, made for sliding upon snow (also **sled**). – *v* to ride on a sledge. – *n* '**sledgehammer** a kind of large, heavy hammer.

sleek *adj* smooth, glossy; well-fed and well-cared for; (of a woman *etc*) elegant, well-groomed.

sleep *v* to rest with one's eyes closed and in a state of natural unconsciousness: – *pt* **slept** [slept]. – *n* '**sleeper** one who sleeps; a beam of wood or metal *etc* supporting railway lines; a sleeping car or sleeping berth on a railway train. – *adjs* '**sleepless** unable to sleep, without sleep; '**sleepy** drowsy, wanting to sleep; looking, seeming like this. – *ns* **sleeping bag** a kind of large warm bag for sleeping in, used by campers *etc*; **sleeping car** a railway coach with beds or berths; '**sleepwalker** one who walks *etc* while asleep. – **go to sleep** to pass into the state of being asleep; (of the limbs) to become numb or to tingle; **put to sleep** to cause to go to sleep or to cause to become unconscious; to put (an animal) to death painlessly, *usu* by an injection of a drug.

sleet *n* rain mixed with snow or hail.

sleeve *n* the part of a garment which covers the arm; a cover for a gramophone record; something (*esp* in machinery) that covers as a sleeve does. – *adj* '**sleeveless** without sleeves.

sleigh [slā] *n* a sledge, sometimes a large horse-drawn one.

sleight [slīt]: *n* '**sleight-of-'hand** skill and quickness of hand movement in performing card tricks *etc*.

'**slender** *adj* thin or narrow; slim; small in amount: *by a slender margin*.

sleuth [slōōth] *n* one who tracks down criminals, a detective.

slew [slōō] *v see* slay; to (cause to) swing round: – *pt* **slewed**.

slice *n* a thin, broad piece (of something); a broad-bladed utensil for serving fish *etc*. – *v* to cut into slices; to cut through; to cut (off from *etc*); to hit (a ball) in such a way that it curves away to the right.

slick *adj* smart, clever, often in a sly way; sleek, smooth. – *n* a thin layer of spilt oil.

slide *v* to (cause to) move smoothly over a surface; to slip; to pass quietly or secretly: – *pt* **slid** [slid]. – *n* an act of sliding; a smooth, slippery slope or track; a chute; a groove or rail on which a thing slides; a fastening for the hair; a picture for showing on a screen; a piece of glass on which to place objects to be examined under a microscope. – *ns* '**slide-rule** an instrument used for calculating, made up of one ruler sliding against another; **sliding scale** a scale of wages, charges *etc* which can be changed as conditions change.

slight [slīt] *adj* of little amount or importance: *a slight breeze*: *a slight quarrel*; (of a person) small, slender. – *v* to treat as unimportant, to insult by ignoring. – Also *n*.

slim *adj* slender, thin; small, slight: *a slim chance*. – *v* to make slender; to use means (such as eating less) to become slender: – *pt* **slimmed**.

slime *n* thin, slippery mud, or other matter that is soft, sticky and half liquid. – *adj* '**slimy** covered with slime; like slime; oily, greasy.

sling *n* a bandage hanging from the neck or shoulders to support an injured arm; a strap with a string attached to each end, for flinging a stone; a net of ropes, chains *etc* for hoisting, carrying and lowering heavy objects. – *v* to throw with a sling; to move or swing by means of a sling; (*coll*) to throw: – *pt* **slung**.

slink *v*, to sneak away, move stealthily: – *pt* **slunk**.

slip *v* to slide accidentally and lose one's footing or balance. *She slipped on the* ice; to fall out of place, or out of one's control. *The plate slipped from my grasp*; to (cause to) move quickly and easily; to (cause to) move quietly, quickly and secretly; to escape from: *to slip one's mind*: – *pt* **slipped**. – *n* act of slipping; an error, a slight mistake; a cutting from a plant; a strip or narrow piece of anything (*eg* paper); a slim, slight person: *a slip of a girl*; a smooth slope on which a ship is built (also '**slipway**); a type of undergarment worn under a dress, a petticoat; a cover for a pillow; in cricket, a fielding position. – *n* '**slipper** a loose indoor shoe. – *adj* '**slippery** so smooth as to cause slipping; not trustworthy. – *n* '**slipknot** a knot made with a loop so that it can slip. – *adj* '**slipshod** untidy, careless. – *ns* '**slipstream** the stream of air driven back by an aircraft propeller *etc*; **slipway** *see* slip (*n*) above. – **slip up** to make a mistake (*n* '**slip-up**).

slit *v* to make a long narrow cut in; to cut into strips: – *pres p* '**slitting**, *pt* **slit**. – *n* a long narrow cut or opening.

slither ['slidhər] *v* to slide or slip about (*eg* on mud); to move with a gliding motion. – *adj* '**slithery** slippery.

'**sliver** *n* a thin strip or slice.

'**slobber** *v* to let saliva dribble from the mouth, slaver.

sloe *n* the small black fruit of a type of shrub called '**blackthorn**.

slog *v* to work or plod on steadily, *esp* against difficulty: – *pt* **slogged**. – Also *n*.

'**slogan** *n* an easily remembered and frequently repeated phrase which is used in advertising *etc*.

sloop *n* a type of one-masted sailing vessel.

slop *v* to (cause to) flow over or spill; to splash: – *pt* **slopped**. – *n* spilt liquid; (*pl*) dirty water; (*pl*) thin, tasteless food. – *adj* '**sloppy** wet, muddy; careless, untidy; silly, sentimental.

slope *n* a position or direction that is neither level nor upright, a slant; a surface with one end higher than the other (*eg* a hillside). – *v* to (cause to) be in a slanting, sloping position.

slosh *v* to splash; (*coll*) to hit.

slot *n* a small, narrow opening (*esp* one to receive coins); a position. – *v* to make a slot in; (sometimes with **into**) to find a position or place for: – *pt* '**slotted**. – *n* **slot machine** a machine (often containing small articles for sale) worked by putting a coin in a slot.

sloth *n* laziness; a kind of slow-moving animal that lives in trees in S. America.

– adj 'slothful lazy.
slouch n a hunched-up body position. –
v to walk with shoulders rounded and
head hanging.
slough¹ [slow] n a bog or marsh.
slough² [sluf] n the cast-off skin of a
snake – v to cast off (eg a skin); (of skin
etc) to come (off).
'**slovenly** ['sluvnli] adj untidy, careless,
dirty.
slow [slō] adj not fast; not hasty or
hurrying; (of a clock etc) behind in
time; not quick in learning, dull. – v
(often with **down**) to make or become
slower. – adv '**slowly**. – n '**slowcoach**
one who is slow of movement. – adj
'**slow-'motion** much slower than normal movement; (of a film) slower than
actual motion. – Also n and adv. – n
'**slow-worm** a kind of snake-like, legless lizard.
sludge n soft, slimy mud.
slug n a kind of snail-like animal with no
shell; a small piece of metal used as a
bullet; a heavy blow. – n '**sluggard** one
who is slow and lazy in his habits. – adj
'**sluggish** moving slowly.
sluice [slōōs] n a sliding gate for controlling a flow of water in an artificial
channel (also '**sluicegate**); the channel
or the stream which flows through it. –
v to clean out with a strong flow of
water.
slum n an overcrowded part of a town
where the houses are dirty and unhealthy; such a house.
'**slumber** v to sleep. – n sleep.
'**slump** v to fall or sink suddenly and
heavily; to lose value suddenly. – n a
sudden fall in values, prices etc.
slung see **sling**.
slunk see **slink**.
slur v to pronounce indistinctly; to
damage (a reputation etc), speak evil
of: – pt **slurred**. – n a blot or stain (on
one's reputation); a criticism, insult.
slush n watery mud; melting snow;
something very sentimental; sentimen-
tality. – adj '**slushy** covered with, or
like, slush; sentimental.
slut n a dirty, untidy woman. – adj
'**sluttish**.
slȳ adj cunning; wily; deceitful. – adv
'**slyly**. – n '**slyness**. – **on the sly**
secretly.
smack v to strike smartly, slap; to have a
trace or suggestion (of). This smacks of
treason. – n an act of smacking; the
sound made by smacking; a boisterous
kiss; a taste, flavour; a trace, a suggestion; a small type of fishing vessel. –
adv with sudden violence. He ran

smack into the door.
small [smöl] adj little, not big or much;
not important: a small matter; not
having a large or successful business: a
small businessman; (of voice) soft. – n
the most slender or narrow part: the
small of the back. – adv into small
pieces: to cut up small. – ns pl '**small-
arms** (weapons, esp pistols, rifles etc)
that can be carried by a man; **small
hours** the hours just after midnight. –
adj '**small-'minded** having narrow
opinions, ungenerous. – ns '**smallpox**
a serious kind of infectious illness,
causing a rash of large pimples
(**pocks**); **small talk** (polite) conversation about nothing very important.
smart adj clever and quick in thought or
action; well-dressed; brisk; sharp, stinging. – n sharp, stinging pain. – v (of
the body, or part of it) to feel a sharp,
stinging pain; to feel annoyed, resentful etc after being insulted etc.
smash v to (cause to) break in pieces,
shatter; to strike with force. He smashed
the ball with his racket; to crash (into
etc). The car smashed into the wall. – n
an act of smashing; a crash or collision
(of vehicles); the ruin of a business etc :
– pl '**smashes**.
'**smattering** n a very slight knowledge (of
a subject).
smear v to spread (something sticky or
oily); to spread, smudge (a surface)
with (something sticky etc); to become
smeared; to slander, insult (a person or
reputation). – Also n.
smell n the sense, or power, of being
aware of things through one's nose; an
act of using this sense or the nose; that
which is noticed by it. – v to notice by
using one's sense of smell. I smell gas;
to use one's sense of smell on. Smell this
fish; to give off a smell. This room
smells: – pt **smelled; smelt** [smelt]. –
adj '**smelly** having a bad smell. – n
'**smelling-salts** strong-smelling chemicals in a bottle, used to revive fainting
persons. – **smell out** to find out by
prying or inquiring closely.
smelt n a type of fish of the salmon kind.
– v to melt (ore) to separate the
metal from other material; see also v
smell.
smile v to show pleasure by drawing up
the corners of the lips; (sometimes with
on) to be favourable to. Fortune smiled
on him. – n an act of smiling.
smirch v to stain, soil. – n a stain.
smirk v to smile in a self-satisfied or
foolish manner. – Also n.
smite v to strike. hit hard: – pt **smote**,

pp **smitten** ['smitn]. – **smitten with** affected by; strongly attracted by.

smith *n* a worker in metals; a blacksmith. – *n* **'smithy** the workshop of a smith.

smithereens [smithə'rēnz] *npl* fragments.

smitten *see* **smite**.

smock *n* a loose shirt-like garment (sometimes worn over other clothes as a protection).

smog *n* smoky fog.

smoke *n* the cloud-like gases and particles of soot given off by anything burning; an act of smoking (a cigarette *etc*). – *v* to give off smoke; to draw in and puff out the smoke of tobacco from a cigarette, pipe *etc*; to dry, cure, preserve (ham, fish *etc*) by applying smoke; to darken (*eg* glass) by applying smoke. – *adj* **'smokeless** having no smoke; burning without smoke. – *n* **'smoker** one who smokes; a railway compartment in which smoking is allowed. – *adj* **'smoky** giving out smoke; full of smoke; like smoke. – *n* **'smokescreen** anything meant to confuse or mislead. *His bookshop was a smokescreen for his drug trading.*

smooth [smoōdh] *adj* not rough; having an even surface; without lumps: *a smooth sauce*; hairless; without breaks, stops or jolts: *smooth movement: smooth journey*; (too) agreeable in manner, often with the intention of deceiving. – *v* to make smooth; to calm, soothe; to free from difficulty.

smote *see* **smite**.

smother ['smudhər] *v* to kill by keeping air from, *esp* by means of a thick covering over the nose and mouth; to die by this means; to cover up, conceal (feelings *etc*); to put down, suppress (a rebellion *etc*).

smoulder ['smōldər] *v* to burn slowly without bursting into flame; to exist in a hidden state; to show otherwise hidden emotion, *eg* anger, hate. *His eyes smouldered with hate.*

smudge *n* a smear. – *v* to make dirty with spots or smears; to smear.

smug *adj* well-satisfied, too obviously pleased with oneself.

'smuggle *v* to take (goods) into, or out of, a country without paying the taxes fixed by law; to send or take secretly. – *n* **'smuggler** one who smuggles.

smut *n* a spot of dirt or soot; vulgar or indecent talk *etc*. – *adj* **'smutty** dirty, grimy; (of talk *etc*) indecent, vulgar.

snack *n* a light, hasty meal.

snag *n* a difficulty, an obstacle. *A great many snags had to be overcome.* – *v* to catch or tear on something sharp.

snail *n* a kind of soft-bodied, small, crawling animal with a shell; a person who is very slow.

snake *n* any of a group of legless reptiles with long bodies which moves along the ground with a winding movement; anything snake-like in form or movement; a cunning, deceitful person.

snap *v* to make a sudden bite; (with **up**) to eat up, or grab, eagerly; to break, or shut suddenly with a sharp noise; to cause (the fingers) to make a sharp noise; to speak sharply; to take a photograph of: – *pt* **snapped**. – *n* an act of snapping; the noise made by snapping; a sudden spell (*eg* of cold weather); a simple type of card game; a photograph. – *adj* **'snappy** irritable, inclined to speak sharply. – *ns* **'snapdragon** a type of garden plant whose flower, when pinched, opens and shuts like a mouth; **'snapshot** a quickly taken photograph.

snare *n* a noose or loop of string or wire *etc* that draws tight when pulled, for catching an animal; a trap; a hidden danger or temptation. – *v* to catch in or with a snare.

snarl *v* to growl, showing the teeth; to speak in a furious, spiteful tone; to (cause to) become tangled. *This piece of rope is snarled up.* – *n* a growl or furious noise; a tangle or knot; a muddled or confused state or condition.

snatch *v* to seize or grab suddenly; to take quickly when one has time: *to snatch an hour's sleep.* – *n* an attempt to seize; a small piece or quantity: *a snatch of music*: – *pl* **'snatches**.

sneak *v* to creep or move in a stealthy, secretive way; to tell tales, tell on others. – *n* a person who tells tales; a deceitful, underhand person. – *adj* **'sneaky**.

sneer *v* to show contempt by a scornful expression, words *etc*. – Also *n*.

sneeze *v* to make a sudden, unintentional and violent blowing noise through the nose. – Also *n*.

'snicker *v* to snigger.

sniff *v* to draw in air through the nose with a slight noise, sometimes because one has a cold *etc*, sometimes to show disapproval; to smell (a scent *etc*); (with **at**) to treat with scorn or suspicion. – Also *n*.

'snigger *v* to laugh in a quiet, sly manner. – Also *n*.

snip *v* to cut off sharply, *esp* with a single cut of scissors *etc*: – *pt* **snipped**. – *n* a cut with scissors; a small piece snipped off; (*coll*) a bargain. *The dress was a snip at the price.* – *n* '**snippet** a little piece, *esp* of information or gossip.

snipe *n* a type of bird with a long straight beak, found in marshy places. – *v* (with **at**) to shoot at from a place of hiding; (with **at**) to attack with a series of critical remarks. – *n* '**sniper**.

'**snivel** *v* to have a running nose (*eg* because of a cold); to whine or complain tearfully: – *pt* '**snivelled**. – Also *n*.

snob *n* a person who admires people of high rank or social class, and looks down on those in a lower class *etc* than himself. – *adj* '**snobbish**. – *ns* '**snobbery**; '**snobbishness**.

snood *n* (*old*) a kind of net worn by women at the back of the head to keep the hair in place.

'**snooker** *n* a type of game like billiards, using twenty-two coloured balls.

snoop *v* to spy or pry in a sneaking secretive way. – Also *n*.

snooze *v* to sleep lightly, doze. – Also *n*.

snore *v* to make a snorting noise in one's sleep as one breathes in. – Also *n*.

'**snorkel** *n* a tube or tubes with ends above the water, through which air is brought into a submarine; a similar device to enable an underwater swimmer to breathe.

snort *v* to force air noisily through the nostrils as horses *etc* do; to make such a noise to express disapproval, anger, laughter *etc*. – Also *n*.

snot *n* mucus of the nose.

snout *n* the sticking-out nose and mouth part of an animal, *eg* of a pig.

snow [snō] *n* frozen water vapour which falls in light white flakes. – *v* to fall down in, or like, flakes of snow. – *adj* '**snowy** full of snow; covered with snow; white, pure. – *n* '**snowball** a ball made of snow pressed hard together. – *v* to throw snowballs; to grow increasingly quickly. *Unemployment has snowballed recently.* – *ns* **snow blindness** dimness of sight caused by the brightness of light reflected from the snow. '**snowdrift** a bank of snow blown together by the wind; '**snowdrop** a kind of small white flower growing from a bulb in early spring; '**snowflake** a flake of snow; '**snowline** the height up a mountain above which there is always snow; '**snowman** a figure shaped like a human being, made of snow; '**snowplough** a large kind of vehicle for clearing snow from the roads *etc*; '**snow-shoe** a long broad frame with a mesh, one of a pair for walking on top of snow.

snub *v* to treat or speak to in an abrupt, scornful way, insult: – *pt* **snubbed**. – *n* an act of snubbing. – *adj* (of the nose) short and turned up at the end.

snuff *v* to put out or trim the wick of (a candle). – *n* powdered tobacco for drawing up into the nose. – *n* '**snuff-box** a box for snuff.

'**snuffle** *v* to make a sniffing noise or talk through the nose (*esp* as the result of a cold). – Also *n*.

snug *adj* lying close and warm; cosy, comfortable; closely fitting; neat and trim. – *v* '**snuggle** to curl up comfortably; to draw close to for warmth, affection *etc*.

so *adv* as shown. *Holding his hand a few inches above the floor, he said 'It is so high'*; to such an extent, to a great extent. *It was so heavy that we left it behind. I am so happy*; in this or that way. *Point your toe so*; correct. *Is that so?*; (used in contradicting) indeed. *It's not true. Yes, it is so.* – *conj* therefore. *You don't need it, so don't buy it.* – *n* '**so-and-so** (*coll*) this or that person or thing. – *adjs* '**so-'called** called (*usu* wrongly) by such a name: *a so-called musician*; '**so-'so** not particularly good. – **so as to** in order to. *Leave early so as to be in time*; **so far** up to this or that point; **so forth** more of the same sort of thing: *pots, pans and so forth*; **so much for** that is the end of. *So much for that idea!*; **so that** with the purpose that. *Wash this dress so that you may wear it tomorrow*; with the result that. *The letter arrived torn so that he was unable to read it*; **so what?** What difference does it make? Does it matter?

soak *v* to (let) stand in a liquid until wet through; to drench (with); (with **up**) to suck up, absorb. – Also *adv*: *soaking wet*. – *n* a wetting, drenching.

soap *n* a mixture containing oils or fats and other substances, used in washing. – *v* to use soap on. – *adj* '**soapy** like soap; covered with, or full of soap. – *n* '**soap-box** a small box for holding soap; a makeshift platform for standing on when speaking to a crowd out of doors. – *npl* '**soapsuds** soapy water worked into a froth.

soar *v* to fly high into the air; (of prices) to rise high and quickly.

sob *v* to weep noisily: – *pt* **sobbed**. – Also *n*.

'**sober** *adj* not drunk; having a serious mind; of formal style; not brightly coloured. – *v* (sometimes with **up**) to make or become sober. – *adv* '**soberly**. – *ns* '**soberness, so'briety** the state of being sober.

'**soccer** *n* the game played under the rules of the Football Association, with eleven players a side.

sociable ['sōshəbl] *adj* fond of the company of others, friendly. – *ns* **socia'bility,** '**sociableness**.

social *see* **society**.

so'ciety *n* mankind considered as a whole; a community of people; a group of people joined together for a purpose, an association or club; the class of people who are wealthy, fashionable or of high rank; company, companionship. *I enjoy his society.* – *adj* **social** ['sōshəl] of society; of the way of life or organization of people in a community: *social history*; living in communities. *Ants and wasps are social insects*; of companionship: *a social gathering*; of rank or level in society: *social class.* – *ns* '**socialism** the belief that a country's wealth (its industries *etc*) should belong to the people as a whole, not to private owners; a system in which the state runs the country's wealth; '**socialist; sociology** [sōsi'oləji] the science which studies human society. – *ns* **social security** the system (paid for by the community in general) of providing insurance against old age, illness, unemployment *etc*; **social work** work which deals with the care of the people in a community, *esp* of the poor or underprivileged *etc*; **social worker**.

sock *n* a short stocking.

'**socket** *n* a hollow into which something is fitted: *an electric socket*.

sod *n* a piece of earth with grass growing on it, a turf.

'**sōda** *n* the name of several substances formed from sodium, *esp* one in the form of crystals (**sodium carbonate**) used for washing, or one in a powdery form (**sodium bicarbonate**) used in baking; soda-water. – *n* '**sodium** a metallic element from which many substances are formed, including common salt (**sodium chloride**). – *n* '**soda-water** water through which gas has been passed, making it fizzy.

'**sodden** *adj* soaked through and through.

sodium *see* **soda**.

'**sōfa** *n* a kind of long, stuffed seat with back and arms.

soft *adj* easily put out of shape when pressed; not hard or not firm; not loud; (of colours) not bright or glaring; not strict enough; lacking strength, cour-

age, determination; lacking common sense, weak in the mind; (of drinks) not alcoholic; (of water) containing little calcium *etc*. – *adv* gently, quietly. – *v* **soften** ['sofn] to make or grow soft. – *adj* '**soft-'hearted** (too) kind and generous. – *ns* '**software** (in computers) programs *etc* as opposed to the machines; '**softwood** the wood of a cone-bearing tree (as fir, larch).

'**soggy** *adj* soaked; soft and wet.

soil *n* the upper layer of the earth in which plants grow; loose earth; dirt. – *v* make dirty.

sojourn ['sojərn] *v* to stay for a time. – Also *n*.

solace ['soləs] *n* something which makes pain or sorrow easier to bear, comfort. – *v* to comfort.

'**sōlar** *adj* of the sun; influenced by the sun. – *n* **solar system** the sun with the planets (including earth) going round it.

sold *see* **sell**.

'**sōlder** *n* melted metal used for joining metal surfaces. – *v* to join (with solder).

soldier ['sōljər] *n* a man in military service, *esp* one who is not an officer.

sole *n* the underside of the foot or of a boot or shoe; a small type of flat fish. – *adj* only: *the sole survivor*; belonging to one person or group only: *a sole right.* – *v* to put a sole on (a shoe). – *adv* '**solely** only, alone.

solemn ['soləm] *adj* serious, earnest; (of an occasion *etc*) celebrated with special, *usu* religious, ceremonies. – *n* **solemnity** [sə'lemnəti]. – *v* '**solemnize** to carry out (a wedding *etc*) with religious ceremonies.

'**sol-'fa** *n* (in music) a system of syllables (do, ray, me *etc*) to be sung to the notes of a scale.

so'licit *v* to ask earnestly for (something): *solicit advice*; to ask (a person for something). – *n* **so'licitor** a lawyer who advises people about legal matters. – *adj* **so'licitous** anxious; considerate, careful. – *n* **so'licitude** care or anxiety (about a matter or about a person).

'**solid** *adj* fixed in shape, not in the form of gas or liquid; of three dimensions, having length, breadth and height; not hollow; hard, firm or strongly made; made or formed completely of one substance: *solid silver*; reliable, sound: *a solid businessman*; (*coll*) without a break: *three solid hours' work.* – *n* a substance that is solid; a figure that has three dimensions. – *n* **soli'darity** unity of arms, interests *etc.* – *v* **so'lidifȳ** to make or become firm or solid: – *pt* **so'lidified**. – *n* **so'lidity** [sə'lidəti] the state of being solid.

soliloquy [sə'liləkwi] *n* (a) speech to oneself, *esp* on the stage: – *pl* **so'liloquies**. – *v* **so'liloquize** to speak to oneself, *esp* on the stage.

'**solitary** *adj* lone, alone or lonely; single. *Not a solitary crumb remained.*

'**solitude** *n* the state of being alone; lack of company.

'**sōlo** *n* a musical piece for one singer or player: – *pl* '**solos**. – *adj* performed by one person alone: *a solo aeroplane flight.* – *n* '**soloist** one who plays or sings a solo.

solstice ['solstis] *n* the time of longest daylight (**summer solstice** about 21 June) or longest dark (**winter solstice** about 21 December).

'**solūble** *adj* able to be dissolved or made liquid; (of difficulties, problems *etc*) able to be solved. – *n* **solu'bility**.

solution [sə'lōōshən] *n* the act of dissolving; a liquid with something dissolved in it; the act of solving a problem *etc*; an answer to a problem, puzzle *etc*.

solve *v* to clear up or explain (a mystery); to discover the answer or solution to. – *n* '**solvency** the state of being able to pay all debts. – *adj* '**solvent** able to pay all debts. – *n* anything that dissolves another substance.

sombre ['sombər] *adj* gloomy, dark, dismal.

som'brero *n* a kind of broad-brimmed hat: – *pl* **som'breros**.

some [sum] *adj* several: *some people in the garden*; a few: *some oranges, but not many*; a little: *some bread, but not much*; certain. *Some people are rich.* – *pron* a number or part out of a quantity. *It's very good – please try some!*; certain people. *Some will be jealous.* – *prons* '**somebody**, '**someone** an unknown or unnamed person: *somebody I'd never seen before*; a person of importance. *He really is somebody now.* – *adv* '**somehow** in some way or other. – *pron* '**something** a thing not known or not stated; a thing of importance; a slight amount, degree. *He has something of his father's looks.* – *advs* '**sometime** at a time not known or stated definitely; '**sometimes** at times, now and then; '**somewhat** rather: *somewhat boring*; '**somewhere** in some place.

somersault ['sumərsolt] *n* a forward or backward turning leap or roll in which the heels go over the head. – Also *v*.

som'nambūlist *n* a sleepwalker.

'**somnolence** *n* sleepiness. – *adj* '**somnolent** sleepy; causing sleepiness.

son [sun] *n* a male child. – *n* '**son-in-law** one's daughter's husband.

so'nata *n* a piece of music with three or more movements, *usu* for one instrument.

song *n* singing; something (intended to be) sung. – *ns* '**songbird** a bird that sings; '**songster** a singer: – *fem* '**songstress**. – **bought for a song** bought very cheaply.

'**sonic** *adj* of sound waves. – *n* **sonic boom** an explosive sound that can be heard when an aircraft travels faster than the speed of sound.

'**sonnet** *n* a type of poem in fourteen lines.

'**sonorous** *adj* giving a clear, loud sound.

soon *adv* in a short time from now or from the time mentioned. *He will come soon*; early: *too soon to tell*; (with **as**) as readily, as willingly. *I would as soon stand as sit.* – *adv* '**sooner** more willingly, rather. *I would sooner stand than sit.* – **sooner or later** at some time in the future.

soot *n* the black powder left by smoke. – *adj* '**sooty** like, or covered with, soot.

soothe [sōōdh] *v* to calm or comfort (a person, feelings *etc*); to help or ease (a pain *etc*). – *adj* '**soothing**.

sop *n* bread dipped in soup *etc*; something (*eg* a bribe) given to keep a person quiet. – *v* to soak (up). – *adj* '**sopping** wet through.

so'phisticated *adj* (of a person) full of experience, accustomed to an elegant, cultured way of life; (of ways of thought, or machinery *etc*) highly developed, complicated, elaborate.

sopo'rific *adj* causing sleep. – *n* something which causes sleep.

so'prano *n* (a woman or boy) with) a singing voice of high pitch: – *pl* **so'pranos**.

'**sorcerer** *n* one who works magic spells; a wizard: – *fem* '**sorceress**. – *n* '**sorcery** magic, witchcraft.

'**sordid** *adj* dirty, filthy; mean, selfish; contemptible.

sore *adj* painful. – *n* a painful, inflamed spot on the skin. – *adv* '**sorely** very greatly: *sorely in need.* – *n* '**soreness**.

'**sorrel** *n* a type of plant with sour-tasting leaves.

sorrow ['sorō] *n* sadness (caused by a loss, disappointment *etc*). – *v* to be sad. – *adj* '**sorrowful**.

'**sorry** *adj* feeling regret about something one has done. *I'm sorry I mentioned it*;

feeling sympathy or pity (for): *sorry for you*; miserable: *in a sorry state*.

sort *n* a kind of (person or thing): *the sort of sweets I like*. – *v* to separate things, putting each in its place. *They sort letters at the post office*. – **a sort of** used of something which is like something else, but not exactly. *He wore a sort of crown*; **of a sort, of sorts** of a (*usu* poor) kind: *a party of sorts*; **out of sorts** not feeling very well.

sortie ['sörti] *n* a sudden attack made by the defenders of a place on those who are trying to capture it.

SOS ['esō'es] *n* a code signal calling for help; any call for help.

sot *n* a drunkard. – *adj* '**sottish** foolish; stupid with drink.

sotto voce ['sotō'vōchi] *adv* in a low voice, so as not to be overheard.

soufflé ['sōōflā] *n* a kind of light cooked dish, made of whisked whites of eggs *etc*.

sough [sow] *v* (of the wind) to make a sighing sound. – Also *n*.

sought *see* **seek**.

soul [sōl] *n* the spirit, the part of a person which is not the body; a person: *a dear old soul*; a perfect example (of): *the soul of kindness*. – *adjs* '**soulful** full of feeling; '**soulless** (of a task) dull, very boring.

sound *n* anything that can be heard, a noise; a distance from which something may be heard: *within the sound of Bow Bells*; a narrow passage of water, *esp* one connecting two seas. – *v* to strike one as being. *That sounds awful*; (with **like**) to resemble in sound. *That sounds like Henry's voice*; to cause to make a noise. *He sounded his hooter*; to examine by listening carefully to: *to sound the patient's chest*; to measure (the depths of water); to try to find out a person's opinions. *I'll sound him out tomorrow*. – *adj* healthy, strong; (of sleep) deep; thorough: *a sound beating*; reliable: *sound opinions*. – *adv* deeply: *sound asleep*. – *n* '**sound-barrier** the point at which an aircraft's speed is near to the speed of sound. – *adj* '**sound-proof** built or made so that sound cannot pass in or out. – *n* '**sound-track** the strip on a film where the speech and music is recorded.

soup [sōōp] *n* a liquid food made from meat, vegetables *etc*.

'**sour** *adj* having an acid or bitter taste, often as a stage in going bad: *sour milk*; bad-tempered. – *v* to make sour.

source [sörs] *n* the place where something has its beginning or is found; a

spring, *esp* one from which a river flows.

souse *v* to soak (*eg* herrings) in salted water *etc*.

south *n* one of the four chief directions, that to one's left as one faces the setting sun. – Also *adj, adv*. – *adjs* **southerly** ['sudhərli] towards the south; (of wind) from the south; '**southern** of, from or in the south. – *n* '**southerner** a person living in a southern region or country. – *n* '**south-'east, (-'west)** the point of the compass midway between south and east or south and west. – Also *adjs*. – *adv* **southward** ['sowthwərd] towards the south. – *ns* **South Pole** the southern end of the imaginary axis on which the earth turns; **sou**"**wester** a kind of waterproof hat.

souvenir [sōōvə'nēr] *n* something (bought or given) which reminds one of a person, place or occasion.

sovereign ['sovrin] *n* a king or queen; (*old*) a British gold coin worth £1. – *adj* supreme, highest: *our sovereign lord*; having its own government: *sovereign state*. – *n* '**sovereignty** highest power.

sow[1] [sow] *n* a female pig.

sow[2] [sō] *v* to scatter (seeds so that they may grow); to cover (an area) with seeds: – *pt* **sowed**, *pp* **sown, sowed**. – *n* '**sower**.

'**soya bean** *n* a kind of bean, rich in protein, used as a substitute for meat *etc* (also **soy bean**). – *n* **soy(a) sauce** a sauce made from soya beans used in Chinese *etc* cooking.

spa *n* a place where people go to drink or bathe in the water from a natural spring.

space *n* a gap or an empty place; the distance between objects; an uncovered part (as on a sheet of paper); length of time: *in the space of a day*; the empty region in which all stars, planets *etc* are situated. – *v* to put things apart from each other, leaving room between them. – *adj* **spacious** ['spāshəs] having plenty of room. – *n* '**spaciousness**. – *ns* '**spacecraft** a machine for travelling in space; '**spaceman** a traveller in space; '**spaceship** a manned spacecraft.

spade *n* a tool with a broad blade for digging in the earth; one of the four suits of playing cards. – **call a spade a spade** to say plainly and clearly what one means.

spaghetti [spə'geti] *n* an Italian food in the form of what paste made into long sticks which soften when boiled.

spake *v* (*old*) spoke.

span *n* the distance between the tips of a man's finger and thumb when the hand is spread out (about 23 centimetres, 9 inches); the full time anything lasts; an arch of a bridge. – *v* to stretch across. *The bridge spans the river*: – *pt* **spanned**.

spangle ['spaŋgl] *n* a thin sparkling piece of metal used as an ornament. – *v* to sprinkle with spangles *etc*.

spaniel ['spanyəl] *n* a breed of dog with large, hanging ears.

spank *v* to strike with the flat of the hand. – *n* a slap with the hand, *esp* on the buttocks. – *n* **'spanking**. – *adj* fast: ·*a spanking pace*.

'spanner *n* a tool used to tighten or loosen nuts, screws *etc*.

spar *n* a long piece of wood or metal used as a ship's mast or its crosspiece. – *v* to fight with the fists; to indulge in an argument. – *pt* **sparred**.

spare *v* to do without. *I can't spare you today*; to afford, set aside. *I can't spare the time to do it*; to treat with mercy, hold oneself back from killing, injuring *etc*; to avoid causing (trouble *etc*) to (a person). – *adj* extra, not yet in use: *a spare tyre*; thin, small: *spare but strong*. – *n* another of the same kind (*eg* a tyre, part of a machine) kept for or available for emergencies. – *adj* **'sparing** careful, economical. *Be sparing in your use of pencils*. – **to spare** over and above what is needed.

spark *n* a small red-hot part thrown off from something that is burning; a trace: *a spark of humanity*; a lively person. – *v* to make sparks. – *n* **'sparking-plug, 'spark-plug** a device in a car engine that produces a spark to set on fire explosive gases.

'sparkle *n* a little spark; brightness or liveliness; bubbles, as in wine. – *v* to shine in a glittering way; to be lively or witty; to bubble. – *adj* **'sparkling** glittering; witty; (of drinks) bubbling, fizzy.

sparrow ['sparō] *n* a type of small dull-coloured bird. – *n* **'sparrowhawk** a type of short-winged hawk.

sparse *adj* thinly scattered; not much, not enough.

'spartan *adj* (of conditions, life *etc*) hard, without luxury.

spasm ['spazəm] *n* a sudden jerk of the muscles which one cannot prevent; a strong, short burst (*eg* of anger, work). – *adj* **spas'modic** occurring in spasms; coming *etc* now and again, not regularly. – *adv* **spas'modically**.

'spastic *adj*, *n* (of) one suffering from

brain damage which has resulted in extreme muscle spasm and paralysis.

spat *see* **spit**.

spate *n* flood. *The river is in spate*; a sudden rush. *A spate of new books*.

spatial ['spāshəl] *adj* of or relating to space.

spats *npl* short gaiters reaching just above the ankle.

'spatter *v* to splash (*eg* with mud).

'spatula *n* a kind of tool or utensil with a broad, blunt blade.

spawn *n* a mass of eggs of fish, frogs *etc*. – *v* (of fishes, frogs *etc*) to lay eggs; to cause, produce in large quantities.

speak *v* to say words, talk; to hold a conversation (with); to make a speech; to be able to talk (a certain language): – *pt* **spoke**, *pp* **'spoken**. – **speak one's mind** to give one's opinion boldly; **speak up** to speak more loudly or clearly; to give one's opinion boldly.

spear *n* a long weapon, with an iron or steel point; a long, pointed shoot or leaf (*esp* of grass). – *v* to pierce with a spear or something similar.

special ['speshəl] *adj* not ordinary, exceptional: *a special occasion*: *a special friend*; put on *etc* for a particular purpose: *a special train*; belonging to one person or thing and not to others: *his special skills*: *a special tool for drilling holes*. – *ns* **'specialist** one who makes a very deep study of one branch of a subject or field. *Dr Brown is a heart specialist*; **speciality** [speshi'aləti] something for which one is well-known. *Cream cakes are their speciality*. – *v* **'specialize** to work in, or study, a particular job, subject *etc*. – *n* **speciali'zation**. – *adj* **'specialized** (of knowledge) obtained by specializing. – *n* **'specialty** a branch of work in which one specializes. *There are many specialties in medicine*.

species ['spēshēz] *n* a group of plants or animals which are alike in most ways; a kind (of anything): – *pl* **'species; specie** ['spēshē] gold and silver coins.

spe'cific *adj* giving all the details clearly; particular, exactly stated: *a specific purpose*. – *adv* **spe'cifically**. – *n* **specifi'cation** the act of specifying or the thing specified; a full description of details (*eg* in a plan, contract). – *v* **'specify** to set down or say clearly (what is wanted); to make particular mention of: – *pt* **'specified**.

'specimen *n* something used as a sample of a group or kind of anything, *esp* for study or for putting in a collection.

specious ['spēshəs] *adj* looking or seeming good but really not so good.

speck *n* a small spot; a tiny piece (*eg* of dust). – *n* '**speckle** a spot on a different-coloured background. – *adj* '**speckled** dotted with speckles.

'**spectacle** *n* a sight, *esp* one which is striking or wonderful; (*pl*) glasses which a person wears to help his eyesight. – *adj* **spec'tacular** making a great show or display; impressive.

spec'tātor *n* one who watches (an event *eg* a football match).

spectre ['spektər] *n* a ghost. – *adj* '**spectral** ghostly.

'**spectrum** *n* the band of colours as seen in a rainbow, sometimes formed when light passes through water or glass; the range or extent of anything: – *pls* '**spectra**, '**spectrums**.

'**speculate** *v* to guess; to wonder (about); to buy goods, shares *etc* in order to sell them again at a profit. – *n* **specu'lation**. – *adj* '**speculative** speculating.

sped *see* **speed**.

speech *n* the power of making sounds which have meaning for other people; a way of speaking. *His speech is always clear*; a (formal) talk given to an audience: – *pl* '**speeches**. – *adj* '**speechless** so surprised *etc* that one cannot speak. – *n* **speech day** the day at the end of a school year when speeches are made and prizes given out.

speed *n* quickness of, or rate of, movement or action. – *v* to (cause to) move along quickly, to hurry: – *pt* **sped** [sped]; to drive very fast in a motor car *etc* (*esp* faster than is allowed by law): – *pt* '**speeded**. – *n* '**speeding** driving at an (illegally) high speed. – *adj* '**speedy** going quickly. – *ns* **speed limit** the greatest speed permitted on a particular road; **spee'dometer** an instrument that shows how fast one is travelling; '**speedway** a motor-cycle racing track.

'**speedwell** *n* a type of small plant with blue flowers.

spell *n* words which, when spoken, are supposed to have magic power; magic or other powerful influence; a (short) space of time; a turn (at work, rest, play). – *v* to give or write correctly the letters which make up a word; to mean, imply. *This defeat spells disaster for us all*: – *pt* **spelled**, **spelt** [spelt]. – *n* '**spelling** the ability to spell words; the study of spelling words correctly. – *adj* '**spellbound** charmed, held by a spell. – **spell out** to say (something) very frankly or clearly.

spelt *see* **spell**.

spend *v* to use (money) for buying; to use (energy *etc*); to pass (time). *I spent a week there*; to use up energy, force. *The storm spent itself and the sun shone*: – *pt* **spent**. – *adj* **spent** exhausted; having lost force or power: *a spent bullet*. – *n* '**spendthrift** one who spends money freely and carelessly.

sperm *n* the fluid in a male that fertilizes the female egg. – *n* '**sperm-whale** a kind of whale from the head of which **spermaceti** [spərmə'seti] a waxy substance is obtained.

spew [spū] *v* to vomit.

sphagnum ['sfagnəm] *n* a kind of moss.

sphere *n* a ball or similar perfectly round object; a position or level in society. *He moves in the highest spheres*; range (of influence or action). – *adj* **spherical** ['sferikəl] having the shape of a sphere.

Sphinx *n* (*myth*) a monster with the head of a woman and the body of a lioness; the large stone model of the Sphinx in Egypt; **sphinx** a person whose real thoughts one cannot guess.

spice *n* any substance used for flavouring *eg* pepper, nutmeg; anything that adds liveliness, interest. – *v* to flavour with spice. – *adj* '**spicy** full of spices; lively and sometimes slightly indecent: *a spicy tale*. – *n* '**spiciness**.

'**spick-and-'span** *adj* neat, clean and tidy.

'**spider** *n* a kind of small, insect-like creature with eight legs, that spins a web. – *adj* '**spidery** like a spider; (of handwriting) having fine, sprawling strokes.

spiel [shpēl] *n* (*coll*) a (long or often repeated) story or speech.

spike *n* a pointed piece or rod (of wood, metal *etc*); a type of large nail; an ear of corn; a head of flowers. – *v* to pierce with a spike; to make useless. – *adjs* **spiked** having spikes (*esp* of shoes for running); '**spiky** having spikes or a sharp point.

spill *v* to (allow liquid to) run out or overflow: – *pt* **spilt**, **spilled** [spilt]. – *n* a fall; a thin strip of wood or twisted paper for lighting a candle, a pipe *etc*. – *n* '**spillage** an act of spilling or what is spilt. – **spill the beans** (*coll*) to give away a secret, *esp* unintentionally.

spin *v* to draw out (cotton, wool, silk *etc*) and twist into threads; (to cause) to whirl round quickly; to travel quickly, *esp* on wheels; to produce a fine thread as a spider does: – *pres p* '**spinning**, *pt* **spun**. – *n* a whirling motion; a ride (*esp* on wheels). – *ns* '**spinner; spinne'ret**

in a spider *etc*, the organ for producing thread. – *ns* **'spin'drier** a machine for taking water out of clothes by whirling them round; **spinning wheel** a machine for spinning thread, consisting of a wheel which drives spindles. – **spin a yarn** to tell a long story; **spin out** to make to last a long or longer time.

spinach ['spinij] *n* a type of plant whose leaves are eaten as a vegetable.

spinal *see* **spine**.

'spindle *n* the pin from which the thread is twisted in spinning wool or cotton; a pin on which anything turns round (*eg* that in the centre of the turntable of a record-player). – *adj* **'spindly** long and thin.

'spindrift *n* the spray blown from the tops of waves.

spine *n* the line of linked bones running down the back in animals and humans, the backbone; a ridge; a stiff, pointed spike which is part of an animal's body (*eg* a porcupine); a thorn. – *adjs* **'spineless** having no spine; weak; **'spiny** full of or covered with spines. – *n* **spinal cord** a cord of nerve cells in the spine.

spinet [spi'net] *n* a kind of small harpsichord.

'spinney *n* a small clump of trees: – *pl* **'spinneys**.

'spinster *n* a woman who is not married.

spiral *adj* coiled round like a spring; winding round and round, getting further and further away from the centre. – *n* anything with this shape; a movement of this kind; an increase *etc* which gets ever more rapid. – *v* to move in a spiral; to increase *etc* ever more rapidly: – *pt* **'spiralled**.

'spire *n* a tall, sharp-pointed tower (*esp* on the roof of a church).

'spirit *n* the soul; a being without a body, a ghost: *an evil spirit*; liveliness, boldness. *He acted with spirit*; a feeling or attitude: *a spirit of kindness*; the intended meaning: *the spirit of the laws*; a distilled liquid, *esp* alcohol; (*pl*) strong alcoholic drinks in general (*eg* whisky); (*pl*) state of mind, mood: *in high spirits*. – *v* (*esp* with **away**) to remove, as if by magic. – *adjs* **'spirited** lively; **'spiritūal** having to do with the soul or with ghosts. – *n* (also **Negro spiritual**) an emotional, religious song of a kind developed by the Negro slaves of America. – *ns* **'spiritualism** the belief that living people can communicate with the souls of dead people; **'spiritualist** one who holds this belief.

spit *n* the liquid which forms in a person's mouth (also **'spittle**). – *n* a metal bar on which meat is roasted; a long piece of land running into the sea. – *v* to throw liquid out from the mouth; to rain slightly: – *pres p* **'spitting**, *pt* **spat**; to pierce with something sharp: – *pt* **'spitted**. – *n* **spit'toon** a kind of dish into which people may spit.

spite *n* the wish to hurt (*esp* feelings). – *v* to annoy out of spite. – *adj* **'spiteful**. – **in spite of** taking no notice of. *He left in spite of his father's command*; although something has happened or is a fact. *The ground was dry in spite of all the rain that had fallen*.

spittle *see* **spit**.

splash *v* to spatter with water, mud *etc*; to move or fall with a splash or splashes. – *n* the sound made by, or the scattering of liquid caused by, something hitting water *etc*; a mark made by splashing (*eg* on one's clothes); a bright patch: *a splash of colour*: – *pl* **'splashes**. – **make a splash** to attract a lot of attention.

splay *v* to turn out at an angle. – *adj* **'splay-'footed** with flat feet turned outward.

spleen *n* a spongy, blood-filled organ inside the body, near the stomach; bad temper. – *adj* **splenetic** [splə'netik] irritable.

'splendid *adj* magnificent; brilliant; (*coll*) very good. – *n* **'splendour**.

splice *v* to join (*esp* two ends of a rope by twining the threads together). – *n* a joint so made.

splint *n* a piece of wood *etc* tied to a broken limb to keep it in a fixed position. – *n* **'splinter** a sharp, thin, broken piece of wood, glass *etc*. – *v* to split into splinters. – *n* **splinter group** a group which breaks away from a larger one.

split *v* to cut or break lengthways; to crack or break; to divide into pieces or into groups *etc*: – *pres p* **'splitting**, *pt* **split**. – *n* a crack, break or division; (*pl*) (with **the**) the trick of going down on the floor with one leg stretched forward and the other back. – *adj* **'splitting** (of a headache) very bad. – **a split second** a fraction of a second; **split one's sides** to laugh very heartily.

'splutter *v* to make spitting noises; to speak hastily and unclearly. – Also *n*.

spoil *v* to make bad or useless; to damage or ruin; to give in to the wishes of (a child *etc*) and so possibly make his character, behaviour *etc* worse; (of food *etc*) to become bad or useless: – *pt* **spoilt, spoiled**; to rob, plunder: – *pt* **spoiled**. – *n* (often *pl*) plunder. – *n* **spōli'ation** plundering. – *n* **'spoilsport** one who spoils, or won't join in, others' fun. – **spoiling for** eager for (*esp* a fight).

spoke *n* one of the ribs or bars from the centre to the rim of a wheel. – *v see* **speak**.

spoken *see* **speak**.

'spokesman *n* one who speaks on behalf of others.

spoliation *see* **spoil**.

sponge [spunj] *n* a kind of sea animal; its soft, elastic skeleton which can soak up water and is used for washing *etc*; a manmade object like this used for washing *etc*; a kind of light cake or pudding. – *v* to wipe with a sponge; to live off money *etc* given by others. – *n* **'sponger** one who lives at others' expense. – *adj* **'spongy** soft like a sponge. – **throw in the sponge** to give up a fight or struggle.

'sponsor *n* a person who makes himself responsible for introducing something, a promoter; one who promises to pay a certain sum of money to a charity *etc* if another person completes a set task (*eg* a walk, swim *etc*); a business firm which pays for a radio or television programme *etc* and advertises its products during it. – *v* to act as a sponsor to. – *n* **'sponsorship** the act of sponsoring.

spontaneous [spɔn'tāniəs] *adj* done readily, not thought about beforehand; natural, not forced. – *n* **spontaneity** [spontə'nāəti].

spoof *n* a trick played as a joke, a hoax. – Also *v, adj*.

spook *n* a ghost. – *adj* **'spooky**.

spool *n* a reel for thread, film *etc*.

spoon *n* hollow-shaped piece of metal *etc* fixed to a handle and used for lifting food to the mouth. – *v* to lift with a spoon. – *v* **'spoon'feed** to teach (a person) in a way that does not make him think for himself.

'spoonerism *n* a mistake in speaking in which the first sounds of words change position, as in *every crook and nanny* (*every nook and cranny*).

spoor *n* the footmarks or trail left by an animal.

spo'radic *adj* happening here and there, or now and again. – *adv* **spo'radically**.

spore *n* the seed of certain plants (*eg* ferns, fungi).

'sporran *n* kind of purse worn hanging in front of a kilt.

sport *n* games such as football, cricket, fishing, hunting *etc* in general; any one game of this type; a good-natured, obliging person. – *v* to have fun, play; to wear. *He was sporting a pink tie.* – *adj* **'sporting** of, or liking, sport; believing in fair play, good-natured. – *ns* **sporting chance** a reasonably good chance; **sports car** a small, fast car with only two seats; **'sportsman** one who enjoys sports; one who shows a spirit of fairness in sports. – *adj* **'sportsmanlike**.

spot *n* a small mark or stain (of mud, paint *etc*); a round mark as part of a pattern on material *etc*; a pimple; a place: *the spot where Nelson fell.* – *v* to mark with spots; to catch sight of: – *pt* **'spotted**. – *adjs* **'spotless** very clean; **'spotted, 'spotty** covered with spots. – *n* **'spotlight** a light that is shone on an actor on the stage. – *v* to show up clearly; to draw attention to. – **in a spot** in trouble; **on the spot** in the place where a person or thing is most needed; right away, immediately; in an embarrassing or difficult position.

spouse *n* a husband or wife.

spout *n* the part of a kettle, teapot *etc* through which the liquid it contains is poured out; a strong jet of liquid. – *v* to pour or spurt out. *Water spouted from the hole in the tank.*

sprain *n* a painful twisting (*eg* of an ankle). – Also *v*.

sprang *see* **spring**.

sprat *n* a type of small fish similar to a herring.

sprawl *v* to sit, lie or fall with the limbs spread out widely or carelessly; (of a town *etc*) to spread out in an untidy, irregular way.

spray *n* a fine mist of liquid like that made by a waterfall; a device with many small holes (as on a watering-can or shower) or other instrument for producing spray; a liquid for spraying; a twig or shoot spreading out in branches or flowers. – *v* to cover with a mist or fine jets of liquid.

spread [spred] *v* to put or go more widely or thinly over an area. *He spread the butter on the slice of bread*; to cover. *He spread the bread with jam*; to open out (*eg* one's arms, a map); to go, scatter, or distribute over a wide area, over a length of time, amongst many people *etc*: – *pt* **spread**. – *n* the act of spreading; the extent or range (of something); a food which is spread on bread: *sandwich spread*; (*coll*) a (large) meal laid out on a table. – *adj* **'spread-**

'**eagled** with limbs spread out.

spree *n* a careless, merry spell of some activity: *a spending spree.*

sprig *n* a small twig or shoot.

sprightly ['spritli] *adj* lively, gay. – *n* '**sprightliness**.

spring *v* to jump, leap; to move swiftly (*usu* upwards); (with **back**) to return suddenly to an earlier shape or position when released (like the string of a bow *etc*); to set off (a trap *etc*); to give, reveal unexpectedly. *He sprang the news on me*; to come from. *His bravery springs from his love of adventure*: – *pt* **sprang**, *pp* **sprung**. – *n* a leap; a coil of wire, such as that used in a mattress; the ability to stretch and spring back; bounce, energy; a small stream flowing out from the ground; the season which follows winter when plants begin to grow again. – *adj* '**springy** able to spring back into its former shape, position *etc*, elastic. – *ns* '**springboard** a springy board from which swimmers may dive; '**springbok** a type of deer found in South Africa; '**spring-cleaning** a thorough cleaning of a house, *esp* in the spring. – **spring a leak** to begin to leak; **spring up** to appear suddenly.

'**sprinkle** *v* to scatter or cover in small drops or pieces. – *ns* '**sprinkler** something which sprinkles water; '**sprinkling** a few.

sprint *v* to run at full speed. – *n* a short running race. – *n* '**sprinter**.

sprite *n* (*myth*) a fairy or elf.

'**sprocket** *n* one of a set of teeth on the rim of a wheel.

sprout *v* to begin to grow; to put out new shoots. – *n* a young bud; (*pl*) Brussels sprouts.

spruce [sprōōs] *adj* neat, smart. – *n* a kind of fir-tree.

sprung *see* **spring**.

sprȳ *adj* lively, active.

spume *n* froth, foam.

spun *see* **spin**.

spunk *n* pluck.

spur *n* a sharp point worn by a horse-rider on his heel and used to urge on his horse; a claw-like point at the back of a bird's (*esp* a cock's) leg; anything that urges a person on; a small line of mountains running off from a larger range. – *v* to use spurs on (a horse); to urge on: – *pt* **spurred**. – **on the spur of the moment** without thinking beforehand.

'**spūrious** *adj* not genuine, false.

spurn *v* to cast aside, reject with scorn. *He spurned my offer of help.*

spurt *v* to pour out in a sudden stream. – *n* a sudden stream pouring or squirting out; a sudden increase of effort.

sputnik ['spŏŏtnik] *n* a kind of small, manmade earth satellite.

'**sputter** *v* to make a noise as of spitting and throw out moisture in drops.

'**spūtum** *n* mucus and spittle from the nose, throat *etc*.

spȳ *n* a person who secretly collects (and reports) information about another person, country, firm *etc*: – *pl* **spies**. – *v* to catch sight of; (with **on**) to watch secretly: – *pt* **spied**. – *n* '**spyglass** a small telescope.

squabble ['skwobl] *v* to quarrel noisily. – Also *n*.

squad [skwod] *n* a group of soldiers, workmen *etc* doing a particular job; a group of people. – *n* '**squadron** a division of a regiment, section of a fleet or group of aeroplanes. – *n* **squadron leader** in the air force, an officer below a wing commander.

squalid ['skwolid] *adj* very dirty, filthy; contemptible. – *n* '**squalor**.

squall [skwöl] *n* a sudden violent storm, gust of shower; a squeal or scream. – *v* to cry out loudly. – *adj* '**squally**.

squander ['skwondər] *v* to waste (one's money, goods, strength *etc*).

square *n* a figure with four equal sides and four right angles shaped thus: □; an open space enclosed by buildings in a town *etc*; the answer when a number is multiplied by itself (*eg* the square of 3 is 9). – *adj* shaped like a square; (in games) equal in scores; (of two or more people) not owing one another anything; straight, level. – *v* to make like a square; to straighten (the shoulders); to multiply a number by itself; to (make to) fit or agree. *That doesn't square with what you said earlier*; (with **up**) to settle (a debt). – *adv* in a straight or level position; directly; exactly: *hit square on the nose*. – *ns* **square deal** fair treatment; **square foot, square metre** *etc* an area equal to that of a square each side of which is one foot, one metre *etc* long; **square meal** a large, satisfying meal; **square root** the number which, multiplied by itself, gives a certain other number (*eg* 4 is the square root of 16).

squash [skwosh] *v* to crush flat or to a pulp; to put down, defeat (rebellion *etc*). – *n* a crushing or crowding; a mass (*usu* of people) crowded together; a drink made from the juice of crushed fruit; a game with rackets and a rubber ball played in a walled court (also

squash rackets).

squat [skwot] v to sit down on the heels; to settle without permission on land or in property which one does not pay rent for: – pt '**squatted**. – adj short and thick. – n '**squatter** one who squats in a building, on land etc.

squaw n a North American Indian woman or wife.

squawk v to give a harsh cry. – Also n.

squeak v to give a short, high-pitched sound. – Also n. – adj '**squeaky**.

squeal v to give a loud, shrill cry; (coll) to inform on. – Also n.

'**squeamish** adj easily sickened or shocked; feeling sick.

squeeze v to press together; to grasp tightly; to force out (liquid or juice from) by pressing; to force a way. He squeezed through the hole in the wall. – n a squeezing or pressing; a few drops got by squeezing: a squeeze of lemon juice; a crowd of people crushed together.

squelch n a sound made eg by walking through marshy ground. – Also v.

squib n a type of small firework.

squid n a type of sea animal of the cuttlefish kind.

'**squiggle** n a curly or wavy mark. – Also v. – adj '**squiggly**.

squint v to screw up the eyes in looking at something; to have the eyes looking in different directions. – n a fault in eyesight which causes squinting; (coll) a quick, close glance.

'**squire** n a country gentleman, esp one who owns a lot of the land in a certain district; (hist) a knight's servant.

squirm v to wriggle, twist the body, esp in pain or embarrassment.

'**squirrel** n a type of small gnawing animal (usu either reddish-brown or grey) with a bushy tail.

squirt v to shoot out, or wet with, a narrow jet of liquid. – Also n.

stab v to wound or pierce with a pointed weapon; to poke (at): – pt **stabbed**. – n the act of stabbing; a wound made by stabbing; a sharp feeling (of pain etc). – **have a stab at** to make an attempt at.

'**stable** n a building for keeping horses. – v to put or keep (horses) in a stable. – adj firm, steady. – n **stability** [stə'bilati] steadiness. – v '**stabilize** to make steady.

stac'cato adj (of speech, sounds) sharp and separate, like the sound of tapping; (in music) with each note sounded separately and clearly.

stack n a large pile (of straw, hay, wood etc). – v to pile in a stack.

'**stādium** n a large sports-ground or race-course with seats for spectators.

staff n a stick or pole carried in the hand; the five lines and four spaces on which music is written or printed (also **stave**); workers employed in a business, school etc; a group of army officers who assist a commanding officer. – v to supply (a school etc) with staff.

stag n a male deer. – n **stag party** a party for men only.

stage n a platform esp for performing or acting on; (with **the**) the theatre, or the job of working as an actor. He chose the stage as a career; period, step in development (of something): the first stage of the plan; a landing place (eg for boats); a part of a journey; a stopping place on a journey. – v to prepare and put on a performance of (a play etc); to arrange (an event, eg an exhibition). – ns '**stage-coach** (hist) a coach running every day with passengers; '**stage-fright** an actor's fear when he acts in public esp for the first time; **stage whisper** a loud whisper. – **on the stage** in(to) the theatre-world.

'**stagger** v to walk unsteadily, totter; to astonish; to arrange (people's hours of work etc) so that they do not begin or end together. – adjs '**staggered**; '**staggering** astonishing.

'**stagnant** adj (of water) standing still, not flowing and therefore not pure. – v **stag'nate** (of water) to remain still and so become impure; to remain for a long time in the same (dull) circumstances and so become bored, inactive etc. – n **stag'nation**.

staid adj set in one's ways, sedate.

stain v to give a different colour to (wood etc); to mark or make dirty by accident. – n a liquid which dyes or colours something; a mark which is not easily removed; something shameful in one's character or reputation. – ns **stained glass** glass with colour fixed into its surface; **stainless steel** a mixture of steel and chromium which does not rust.

stair n one or all of a number of steps one after the other; (pl) a series or flight of steps. – n '**staircase** a stretch of stairs with rails on one or both sides.

stake n a strong stick pointed at one end; the money that one puts down as a bet; (hist) the post to which people were tied to be burned. – v to mark the limits or boundaries (of a field etc) with stakes; to bet (money); to risk. – **at stake** to be won or lost; in great danger. His life is at stake; **have a**

stake in to be concerned in (because one has something to gain or lose); **stake a claim** to establish one's ownership or right (to something).

'**stalactite** *n* an icicle-shaped spike of limestone hanging from the roof of a cave, formed by the dripping of water containing lime. – *n* '**stalagmite** a similar spike of limestone, like a stalactite, rising from the floor of a cave.

stale *adj* (of food *etc*) no longer fresh; no longer interesting because heard, done *etc* too often before; not able to do one's best (because of overworking, boredom *etc*).

'**stalemate** *n* (in chess) a position in which a player cannot move without putting his king in danger; in a quarrel or argument, a position in which neither side can win.

stalk [stök] *n* the stem of a plant or of a leaf or flower. – *v* to walk stiffly or proudly; (in hunting) to go quietly up to animals (*eg* deer) in order to shoot at close range. – *n* '**stalker**.

stall [stöl] *n* (a division for one animal in) a stable, cowshed *etc*; a table *etc* on which things are laid out for sale; an open-fronted shop; a seat in a church (*esp* for choir or clergy); (*usu pl*) theatre seat(s) on the ground floor. – *v* (of a car engine *etc*) to come to a halt without the driver intending it to do so; (of an aircraft) to lose flying speed and so fall out of control for a time; (*coll*) to avoid action or decision for the time being.

'**stallion** *n* a male horse, *esp* one kept for breeding purposes.

stalwart ['stölwərt] *adj* brave, stout-hearted. – Also *n*.

'**stamen** *n* one of the thread-like spikes in the middle of a flower which bear the pollen.

'**stamina** *n* strength, power to keep going.

'**stammer** *v* to have difficulty in saying the first letter of words in speaking; to stumble over words. – Also *n*.

stamp *v* to bring the foot down firmly (and noisily) on the ground; to stick a (postage) stamp on; to mark with a design, words *etc* using ink and a flat surface on which the design *etc* is moulded or cut; to fix or mark deeply: *stamped in his mind.* – *n* the act of stamping; a design *etc* made by stamping; the object with which stamping is done; kind, sort: *a man of a different stamp*; see also **postage stamp**. – **stamp out** to put out (a fire) by stamping; to crush (*eg* a rebellion).

stam'pede *n* a wild rush of frightened animals; a sudden, wild rush of people: *a stampede to the sale.* – Also *v*.

stance *n* one's manner of standing.

stanch [stänch] or **staunch** [stönch] *v* to stop from flowing (*esp* blood from a wound).

stanchion ['stänshən] *n* an upright iron bar used as a support (*eg* in windows, ships).

stand *v* to be on one's feet (not lying or sitting down); to rise to one's feet; (of an object) to (cause to) be in a particular place. *The wardrobe stood by the door. He stood the case in the corner*; to bear. *I cannot stand this heat*; to treat (someone) to. *I will stand you tea*; to remain. *This law still stands*; to be a candidate (for). *He stood for parliament*; to be short (for). *PO stands for Post Office*: – *pt* **stood**. – *n* something on which anything is placed; an object made to hold, or for hanging, things: *a hat-stand*; lines of raised seats from which people may watch games *etc*; an effort made to support, defend, resist *etc*: *a stand against violence*; (*US*) a witness box in a law court. – *n* '**standing** one's social position or reputation. – *adj* on one's feet; placed on end; not moving; lasting, permanent: *a standing joke.* – *adj* **stand-'offish** unfriendly. – *ns* '**standpoint** the position from which one looks at (*eg* a question, problem), point of view; '**standstill** a complete stop. – **stand by** to be ready or available to be used or help in an emergency *etc* (*n* '**standby**); **stand down** to withdraw (from a contest) or resign (from a job); **stand fast** to refuse to give in; **stand in (for)** to take another's place, job *etc* for a time (*n* '**stand-in**); **stand out** to stick out, to be noticeable; **stand to reason** to be likely or reasonable; **stand up for** to defend strongly; **stand up to** to bear bravely; to face or oppose bravely.

'**standard** *n* a level against which things may be judged; a level of excellence aimed at. *She has very high moral standards*; a large flag, badge *etc* on a pole. – *adj* normal, usual. *£1 is the standard charge*; ordinary, without extras: *the standard model of this car.* – *v* '**standardize** to make all of one kind, size *etc*. – *n* **standardi'zation**. – *n* **standard lamp** a kind of tall lamp which stands on the floor of a room *etc*. – **standard of living** a level of material comfort considered necessary by a particular group of society *etc*.

stank *see* **stink**.

'**stanza** *n* a group of lines making up a part of a poem, a verse.

'**staple** *n* a U-shaped iron nail; a piece of wire driven through sheets of paper and folded to fasten them together; the thing, material *etc* which forms the largest part (of a country's output, a person's diet *etc*); a fibre of wool, cotton *etc*. – *v* to fasten with a staple. – *adj* chief, main.

star *n* any of the bodies in the sky appearing as points of light; the fixed bodies which are really distant suns, not the planets; an object, shape or figure with a number of pointed rays (often five); a leading actor or actress or other well-known performer. – *adj* for or of a star (in a film *etc*). – *v* to act the chief part (in a play or film); (of a play *etc*) to have as its star: – *pt* **starred**. – *adj* '**starry** full of stars; shining like stars. – *ns* '**stardom** the state of being a leading performer; '**starfish** a type of small sea creature with five points or arms. – **Stars and Stripes** the flag of the United States of America.

starboard ['stärbərd] *n* the right side of a ship, as one looks towards the bow (or front). –Also *adj*.

starch *n* a white carbohydrate (found in flour, potatoes, bread, biscuits *etc*); a form of this used for stiffening clothes: – *pl* '**starches**. – *adj* '**starchy** (of food) containing starch; stiff and unfriendly.

stare *v* to look with a fixed gaze. – Also *n*.

stark *adj* barren, bare; harsh, severe; sheer: *stark idiocy*. – *adv* completely: *stark naked*.

'**starling** *n* a type of common bird with dark, glossy feathers.

starry *see* **star**.

start *v* to begin (an action). *He started to walk home*; to get (a machine *etc*) working. *He started the car*; to jump or jerk (*eg* in surprise). – *n* the act of starting (*eg* on a task, journey); a sudden movement of the body; a sudden shock. *You gave me a start*; in a race *etc* the advantage of beginning before, or farther forward than, others, or the amount of this. *The youngest runner got a start of five metres*.

'**startle** *v* to give a shock or fright to. – *adjs* '**startled**; '**startling**.

starve *v* to die for want of food; to suffer greatly from hunger; to deprive (of something needed or wanted badly). *I'm starved of company here*. – *n* **star-**'**vation**.

state *n* the condition (of something): *the bad state of the roads*; the people of a country under a government; (*US*) an area and its people with its own laws forming part of the whole country; a government and its officials; great show, pomp. *The king drove by in state*. – *adj* of the government; national and ceremonial: *state occasions*; (*US*) of a certain state of America. *The state capital of Texas is Austin*. – *v* to tell, say or write (*esp* clearly and fully). – *adj* '**stately** noble-looking; dignified. – *n* '**stateliness**. – *n* '**statement** that which is said or written. – *ns* '**state-room** a large cabin in a ship; '**statesman** one skilled in government. – *adj* '**statesmanlike**.

'**static** *adj* not moving. – *n* atmospheric disturbances causing poor reception of radio or television programmes; electricity on the surface of objects which will not conduct it *eg* hair, nylons *etc* (also **static electricity**).

'**station** *n* a place with a ticket office, waiting rooms *etc* where trains, buses or coaches stop to pick up or set down passengers; a place which is the centre for work or duty of any kind: *fire station*: *police station*; one's rank or position: *a humble station*. – *v* to assign to a position or place; to take up a position. *He stationed himself at the corner of the road*. – *adj* '**stationary** standing still, not moving.

'**stationery** *n* writing paper, envelopes, pens *etc*. – *n* '**stationer** one who sells these.

sta'**tistics** *npl* figures and facts set out in order: *statistics of road accidents for last year*; the study of these. *Statistics is not an easy subject*. – *adj* **sta**'**tistical**. – *n* **statis**'**tician** one who produces or studies statistics.

statue ['statū] *n* a likeness of a person or animal carved in stone, metal *etc*. – *n* **statu**'**ette** a small statue. – *adj* **statuesque** [statū'esk] like a statue in dignity *etc*.

'**stature** *n* height; importance, reputation.

'**status** *n* position, rank (of a person) in the eyes of others. – *ns* **status quo** the state of affairs now existing, or existing before a certain time or event; **status symbol** a possession which is thought to show the high status of the owner (*eg* a powerful car).

'**statute** *n* a written law of a country. – *adj* '**statutory** according to law.

staunch *adj* firm, loyal; trustworthy. – *v* see **stanch**.

stave *n* (in music) the staff; one of the strips of wood making the side of a cask or tub. – *v* (with **in**) to crush in, make a hole in; (with **off**) to keep away, delay: – *pt* **staved, stove.**

stay *v* to continue to be: *stay calm: stay here*; to live (for a time). *I stayed with my brother when I went to London*; (*old*) to stop. – *n* time spent in a place; a strong rope running from the side of a ship to the mast-head; (*pl, old*) corsets. – **stay put** to remain in the same place.

St 'Bernard *n* a breed of large dog.

stead [sted] *n* place. *I shall go in your stead.* – **stand one in good stead** to turn out to be helpful to one. *His knowledge of German stood him in good stead.*

steadfast ['stedfäst] *adj* steady, fixed; faithful and true.

steady ['stedi] *adj* firm, not moving or changing; not easily upset or put off from doing something; even, regular, unchanging: *moving at a steady pace.* – *v* to make or become steady: – *pt* **'steadied.** – *n* **'steadiness.**

steak [stāk] *n* a *usu* thick slice of meat *etc* for cooking.

steal *v* to take (what does not belong to one) without permission; to move quietly; to take quickly. *He stole a look at her*: – *pt* **stole,** *pp* **'stolen.**

stealth [stelth] *n* a secret way of doing, acting *etc.* – *adj* **'stealthy.** – *adv* **'stealthily.**

steam *n* vapour from hot liquid, *esp* from boiling water; power produced by steam: *in the days of steam.* – *v* to give off steam; to cook by steam; to open, loosen, by putting into steam: *to steam open an envelope*; to move, travel by steam. – *adj* **'steamy.** – *n* **'steamer** a ship driven by steam. – *ns* **'steamboat** a steamer; **'steam-engine** an engine (*esp* a railway engine) worked by steam; **'steamroller** a steam-driven engine with large and very heavy wheels, used for flattening the surfaces of roads; **'steamship** a steamer. – **steam up** (of glass) to become covered with condensed steam in the form of small drops of water.

steed *n* (*old*) a horse.

steel *n* a very hard mixture of iron and carbon; a bar of steel on which knives may be sharpened; (*hist*) a piece of steel against which a flint is struck to make sparks. – *adj* **'steely** hard, cold, strong *etc* like steel. – **of steel** hard, like steel: *a grip of steel*; **steel oneself** to get up courage (to).

steep *adj* (of a slope, hill *etc*) rising nearly straight up; (*coll*, of a price) too great. – *v* to soak (in a liquid); to fill with knowledge and experience (of a subject). *He is steeped in French literature.*

'steeple *n* a tower of a church *etc* rising to a point, a spire. – *ns* **'steeplechase** a race run across open country, over hedges *etc*; a race over a course on which obstacles (*eg* walls) have been made; **'steeplejack** one who climbs steeples or other high buildings to make repairs.

steer *n* a young ox raised for its beef. – *v* to control the course of (a car, ship, discussion *etc*); to follow (a course). – *ns* **'steerage** (*old*) the part of a ship set aside for the passengers who pay the lowest fares; **'steering** the parts of a ship, motor-car *etc* which have to do with steering. – *n* **'steering-wheel** the wheel in a car used by the driver to steer it. – **steer clear of** to keep away from.

'stellar *adj* of the stars.

stem *n* the part of a plant from which the leaves and flowers grow; the thin support of a wine-glass. – *v* to stop (the flow *etc* of). *He tried to stem the flow of people*; to start, spring (from). *Hate stems from envy*: – *pt* **stemmed.**

stench *n* a strong unpleasant smell.

'stencil *n* a sheet of metal, cardboard *etc* with a pattern cut out; the drawing or design made by rubbing ink or brushing paint *etc* over a cut-out pattern; a piece of waxed paper on which words are cut with a typewriter, and which is then used to make copies. – *v* to make a design or copy in one of these ways: – *pt* **'stencilled.**

ste'nography (*US*) *n* shorthand. – *n* **ste'nographer** (*US*) a shorthand typist.

stentorian [sten'tōriən] *adj* (of the voice) very loud.

step *n* one movement of the leg in walking, running *etc*; the distance covered by this; a particular movement of the feet, as in dancing; the sound made by the foot in walking *etc*; one of the parts of a stair or ladder on which one stands; a move in a plan, career *etc*. *The first step is to find out where we are*; a way of walking: *a proud step*; (*pl*) a flight of stairs; (*pl*) a step-ladder. – *v* to take a step; to walk: – *pt* **stepped.** – *ns* **'step-ladder** a ladder with a support on which it rests; **'stepping-stone** a stone rising above water or mud, used to cross on; anything that helps one to advance. – **in step** (of two or more people walking) with the same foot going forward at the same time; acting *etc* in agreement (with); **out of step** not in step (with); **step up** to increase (*eg* production); **take steps** to begin to do something for a certain purpose. *I shall take steps to have the guilty person punished.*

step- *prefix* showing a relationship between people which results from a second marriage, as in '**step-father**, '**stepmother**, '**stepson**, '**stepdaughter**.

steppe [step] *n* a dry, grassy treeless plain in SE Europe and Asia.

stereo ['sterio] *adj* short for **stereophonic**. – *n* stereophonic equipment.

stereo- [sterio] *prefix* having to do with three dimensions.

stereophonic [sterio'fonik] *adj* (of sound, a recording *etc*) giving a life-like effect, with different instruments, voices *etc* coming from different directions.

stereotype ['steriotip] *n* a metal plate having on its surface moulded letters *etc* for printing; something fixed and unchanging; a person of a well-known type. – *adj* '**stereotyped** fixed, not changing. *He has stereotyped ideas.*

'**sterile** *adj* unable to have children, produce fruit, ideas *etc*; free from germs. – *n* **sterility** [stə'riləti] the state of being sterile. – *v* '**sterilize** to make unable to have children, bear young *etc*; to kill germs by boiling or other means. – *n* **sterili'zation** the act of sterilizing.

'**sterling** *n* a name for British money *esp* when used in international trading: *one pound sterling*. – *adj* (of silver) of a certain standard of purity; worthy, good. *He has many sterling qualities.*

stern *adj* angry or displeased in look, manner, or voice; severe, strict, harsh: *a stern prison sentence*. – *n* the back part of a ship. – *n* '**sternness** the state of being stern.

'**stertorous** *adj* making a snoring noise.

'**stethoscope** *n* an instrument by means of which a doctor listens to a person's heartbeats, breathing *etc*.

stevedore ['stēvədör] *n* one who loads and unloads ships.

stew [stū] *v* to cook by boiling slowly. – *n* a dish of stewed food, *esp* one containing meat and vegetables; (*coll*) a state of worry.

steward ['stūərd] *n* a passengers' attendant on a ship or aeroplane; one who shows people to their seats at a meeting *etc*; an official at a race meeting *etc*; one who manages an estate or farm for someone else. – *n* '**stewardess** a female steward, *esp* one who waits on passen-

gers in an aeroplane (also **air hostess**).

stick *n* a long thin piece of wood; a branch or twig from a tree; a piece of wood shaped for a special purpose: *hockey-stick: drumstick*; a long piece (*eg* of rhubarb). – *v* to push or thrust (something). *Stick the knife in your belt*; to fix with glue *etc. I'll stick the pieces back together*; to be or become caught, fixed or held back. *The car is stuck in the ditch*; to hold fast to, keep to (*eg* a decision): – *pt* **stuck**. – *adj* '**sticky** clinging closely (like glue, treacle *etc*); covered with something sticky; difficult: *a sticky problem*. – *n* '**stickiness**. – *ns* '**sticking-plaster** a kind of tape with a sticky surface, used for putting on cuts; '**stick-in-the-mud** a person who is against new ideas, change *etc*. – **stick up for** to speak in defence of.

'**stickleback** *n* a type of small river-fish with prickles on its back.

'**stickler** *n* one who attaches great importance to a particular (often small) matter: *a stickler for punctuality*.

stiff *adj* not easily bent or moved; (of a mixture, dough *etc*) thick, not easily stirred; cold and distant in one's manner; hard, difficult: *a stiff examination*; severe: *a stiff penalty*; strong: *a stiff drink*. – *v* '**stiffen** to make or become stiff. – *adj* '**stiff-'necked** proud, obstinate.

'**stifle** *v* to suffocate; to put out (flames); to keep back (tears, a yawn *etc*). – *adj* '**stifling** very hot and stuffy.

'**stigma** *n* a mark of disgrace: – *pl* **stig'mata**; in a flower, the top of the pistil: – *pl* '**stigmas**. – *v* '**stigmatize** to mark, describe as something bad: *stigmatized for life*.

stile *n* a step or set of steps for climbing over a wall or fence.

sti'letto *n* a dagger, or a type of instrument, with a narrow blade: – *pl* **sti'lettos**. – *n* **stiletto heel** a high, thin heel on a shoe.

still *adj* not moving; calm, without wind; quiet; (of drinks) not fizzy. – *v* to make calm or quiet. – *adv* up to the present time or the time spoken of. *He was still there*; even so, nevertheless. *It's difficult but we must still try*; even: *still more people*. – *n* an apparatus for distilling spirits (*eg* whisky). – *n* '**stillness** the state of being still. – *adj* '**stillborn** (of a child) dead at birth. – *ns* **still life** a picture of something that is not living (as a bowl of fruit *etc*); '**stillroom** a pantry or room where drinks, food *etc* are kept.

'**stilted** *adj* stiff, not natural.

stilts *npl* long poles with footrests on which a person may walk clear of the ground; tall poles (*eg* to support a house built above water).

'stimūlant *n* something which makes a part of the body more active or which makes one feel livelier. – *v* **'stimulate** to make more active; to encourage. – *n* **'stimulus** something that brings on a reaction in a living thing; something that rouses (a person *etc*) to action or greater effort: – *pl* **stimuli** ['stimūlē].

sting *n* the part of some animals and plants (as the wasp, the nettle) which can prick the skin and cause pain or irritation; the act of piercing with a sting; the wound, swelling or pain caused by a sting. – *v* to pierce with a sting or cause pain like that of a sting; to be painful, to smart. *The smoke made his eyes sting*; to hurt the feelings of. *She was stung by his words*: – *pt* **stung**.

stingy ['stinji] *adj* mean, not generous.

stink *n* a bad smell. – *v* to give out a bad smell: – *pt* **stank**, *pp* **stunk**.

stint *v* to allow (someone) very little. *He doesn't stint himself*. – *n* limit. *He praised him without stint*; a fixed amount of work: *my daily stint*.

'stipend *n* pay (*esp* of a clergyman).

'stipūlate *v* to state as a condition (of doing something). – *n* **stipu'lation** something stipulated, a condition.

stir *v* to set (liquid) in motion, *esp* with a spoon *etc* moved circularly; to move slightly. *He stirred in his sleep*; to arouse (a person, a feeling *etc*): – *pt* **stirred**. – *n* disturbance, fuss. – *adj* **'stirring** exciting. – **stir up** to rouse, cause (*eg* trouble).

'stirrup *n* a metal loop hung from a horse's saddle as a support for the rider's foot.

stitch *n* the loop made in a thread, wool *etc* by a needle in sewing or knitting; a sharp, sudden pain in one's side: – *pl* **'stitches**. – *v* to put stitches in, to sew.

stoat *n* a type of small fierce animal similar to a weasel, sometimes called an ermine when in its white winter fur.

stock *n* family, race: *of ancient stock*; goods in a shop, warehouse *etc*; the capital of a business company divided into shares; the animals of a farm (also **'livestock**); liquid (used for soup) obtained by boiling meat, bones *etc*; a type of scented garden flower; the handle of a whip, rifle *etc*; (*pl, hist*) a wooden frame, with holes for the ankles and wrists, in which criminals *etc* were fastened as a punishment; (*pl*) the wooden framework upon which a ship is supported when being built. – *v* to keep a supply of (for sale); to supply (a farm with animals *etc*). – *adj* usual, known by everyone: *a stock joke*; usually stocked (by a shop *etc*). – *ns* **'stock-broker** a person who buys and sell shares in business companies on behalf of others; **stock exchange** a place where stocks and shares are bought and sold; an association of people who do this; **'stock-in-'trade** the necessary equipment *etc* for a particular trade *etc*; a person's usual ways of speaking, acting *etc*. *Sarcasm is part of his stock-in-trade*; **stock market** the stock exchange; dealings in stocks and shares; **'stockpile** a store, a reserve supply. – *v* to build up a store. – *adj* **'stock-'still** perfectly still. – *n* **'stocktaking** a regular check of the goods in a shop or warehouse. – **take stock of** to form an opinion or estimation about (a situation *etc*).

stoc'kade *n* a fence of strong posts set up round an area or building for defence.

'stocking *n* a close fitting covering in a knitted fabric (wool, nylon *etc*) for the leg and foot.

'stocky *adj* short and stout. – *n* **'stockiness**.

'stodgy *adj* (of food) heavy, not easily digested; (of a person, book *etc*) dull. – *n* **'stodginess**.

'stōic *n* one who bears pain, hardship *etc* without showing any sign of feeling it. – *adj* **'stoical**. – *n* **'stoicism** the bearing of pain *etc* patiently.

stoke *v* to put coal, wood, or other fuel on (a fire). – *n* **'stoker** one who looks after a furnace.

stole *n* a length of silk, linen or fur worn over the shoulders. – *v see* **steal**.

stolen *see* **steal**.

'stolid *adj* (of a person *etc*) dull; not easily excited. – *n* **sto'lidity**.

stomach ['stumək] *n* the bag-like part of the body into which the food passes when swallowed; desire or courage (for something). *He had no stomach for the fight*. – *v* to put up with, bear. *I can't stomach her rudeness*.

stone *n* the material of which rocks are composed; a (small) loose piece of this; a piece of this shaped for a certain purpose: *tombstone*; a precious stone (*eg* a diamond); the hard shell round the seed of some fruits (*eg* peach, cherry); a measure of weight (14 lb, 6·35 kilogrammes); a piece of hard material that forms in the kidney, bladder *etc*, causing pain. – *v* to throw stones at; to take the stones out of fruit. – *adj* made of stone. – *adj* **'stony** like stone; covered with stones; hard, cold in manner: *a stony stare.* – *adjs* **'stone-'cold** very cold; **'stone-'dead, 'stone-'deaf** completely dead, deaf. – *ns* **'stoneware** a kind of pottery made out of coarse clay; **'stonework** that which is built of stone *esp* the stone parts of a building. – **a stone's throw** a very short distance; **leave no stone unturned** to do everything possible.

stood *see* **stand**.

stooge [stōoj] *n* a person who is used by another to do a (*usu* humble or unpleasant) job.

stool *n* a seat without a back.

stoop *v* to bend the body forward and downward; to be low or wicked enough to do a certain thing. *I wouldn't stoop to stealing.* – *n* the act of stooping; a forward bend of the body.

stop *v* to bring to a halt: *stop the car*; to prevent from doing: *stop him from working*; to put an end to: *stop this nonsense*; to come to an end. *The rain has stopped*; (with **up**) to block (a hole *etc*): – *pt* **stopped**. – *n* the state of being stopped; a place where something stops; a full stop; a knob on an organ which brings certain pipes into use. – *ns* **'stoppage** something which blocks up (*eg* a tube or a passage in the body); a halt (*eg* in work in a factory); **'stopper** something that stops up an opening (*esp* in the neck of a bottle, jar *etc*). – *ns* **'stopcock** a tap for controlling the flow of liquid through a pipe; **'stopgap** something which is used in an emergency until something better is found; **stop press** a space in a newspaper for news put in at the last minute: **'stopwatch** a watch with a hand that can be stopped and started, used in timing races.

store *n* a supply (*eg* of goods) from which things are taken when needed; a place where goods are kept; a shop; a collected amount or number. – *v* to put aside for future use. – *n* **'storage** the act of storing; the state of being stored. *Our furniture is in storage.* – *ns* **'storehouse, 'storeroom** a building or room where goods are stored. – **in store for** awaiting. *There is trouble in store for you*; **set (great) store by** to value highly.

'storey ['stōri] *n* all that part of a building on the same floor: – *pl* **'storeys**.

stork *n* a type of wading bird with a long bill, neck and legs.

storm *n* a sudden burst of bad weather (*esp* with heavy rain, lightning, thun-

der, high wind); a violent outbreak (*eg* of anger). – *v* to be in a fury; to rain, blow *etc* violently; to attack (a stronghold *etc*) violently. – *adj* **'stormy**.

story ['stōri] *n* an account of an event or events, real or imaginary: – *pl* **'stories**.

stout *adj* fat; brave. *They put up a stout resistance*; strong: *a stout stick.* – *n* a strong, dark-coloured kind of beer. – *n* **'stoutness**. – *adj* **'stout-'hearted** having a brave heart.

stove *n* an apparatus using coal, gas or electricity *etc*, used for heating, cooking *etc*. – *v see* **stave**.

stow [stō] *v* to pack or put away; to fill, pack. – *n* **'stowaway** one who hides himself in a ship so that he may travel without paying a fare.

'straddle *v* to stand or walk with legs apart; to sit with one leg on each side of (*eg* a chair or horse).

'straggle *v* to wander from the line of a march *etc*; to lag behind; to grow or spread beyond the intended limits. *His long beard straggled over his chest.* – *n* **'straggler** one who straggles. – *adj* **'straggly** spread out untidily.

straight [strāt] *adj* not bent or curved: *a straight line*; direct, frank, honest: *a straight answer*; in the proper position or order. *Your tie isn't straight*; (of a hanging picture *etc*) placed level with ceiling or floor; without anything added: *a straight vodka*; expressionless. *He kept a straight face.* – *adv* by the shortest way, directly: *straight across the desert*; at once, without delay. *I came straight here after work*; fairly, frankly. *He's not playing straight with you.* – *n* (with **the**) the straight part of a racecourse *etc.* – *v* **'straighten** to make straight. – *n* **'straightness** the state of being straight. – *n* **straight fight** a contest between two people only. – *adj* **straight'forward** without any difficulties; honest, frank. – **straight away**, (*old*) **'straight'way** immediately.

strain *v* to hurt (a muscle or other part of the body) by overworking or misusing it; to work or to use to the fullest. *He strained his ears to hear the whisper*; to make a great effort. *He strained to reach the rope*; to stretch too far, to the point of breaking (a person's patience *etc*); to separate liquid from a mixture of liquids and solids by passing it through a sieve. – *n* the act of straining; a hurt to a muscle *etc* caused by straining it; (the effect of) too much work, worry *etc*: *suffering from strain*; too great a demand: *a strain on my patience*; manner. *He grumbled on in the same strain for* *hours*; a streak: *a strain of selfishness*; a tune; a kind, breed: *a strain of fowls.* – *adj* **strained** not natural, done with effort: *a strained conversation*; unfriendly: *strained relations between them.* – *n* **'strainer** a sieve.

strait *n* a narrow strip of sea between two pieces of land; (*pl*) difficulties, hardships: *in sore straits.* – *adj* **'straitened** poor and needy. – *n* **'straitjacket** a jacket with long sleeves tied behind to prevent a violent or insane person from using his arms. – *adj* **'strait'laced** strict in attitude and behaviour.

strand *n* a length of something soft and fine (*eg* hair, thread); (*old*) the shore of a sea or lake. – *adj* **'stranded** (of a ship) run aground on the shore; left helpless without money or friends.

strange [strānj] *adj* unusual, odd: *a strange look on his face*; not known, seen, heard *etc* before, unfamiliar: *the method was strange to me*; not accustomed (to); foreign: *a strange country.* – *adv* **'strangely.** – *ns* **'strangeness; 'stranger** a person who is unknown to one; a visitor. – **a stranger to** a person who is quite unfamiliar with. *He is no stranger to misfortune.*

strangle ['straŋgl] *v* to kill by gripping or squeezing the throat tightly; to keep in, prevent oneself from giving (*eg* a scream, a sigh); to stop the growth of. – *n* **strangū'lation.** – *n* **'stranglehold** a tight control over something which prevents it from escaping, growing *etc.*

strap *n* a narrow strip of leather, cloth *etc* used to hold things in place or together *etc.* – *v* to bind or fasten with a strap *etc*; to beat with a strap: – *pt* **strapped.** – *adj* **'strapping** tall and strong.

stratagem ['stratəjəm] *n* a cunning act, meant to deceive and outwit an enemy.

strategy ['stratəji] *n* the art of guiding, forming or carrying out a plan: – *pl* **'strategies.** – *adj* **stra'tēgic** of strategy; done according to a strategy: *a strategic retreat*; giving an advantage: *a strategic position.* – *n* **strategist** ['stratəjist] one who plans military operations.

'stratosphere *n* the layer of the earth's atmosphere between 10 and 60 kilometres above the earth.

'stratum *n* a layer of rock or soil; a level of society. – *pl* **'strata.** – *v* **'stratifȳ** to form layers or levels: – *pt* **'stratified.** – *n* **stratifi'cation.**

'stratus *n* low, spread-out clouds.

straw *n* the stalk on which corn grows; a quantity or bundle of corn stalks; a paper or plastic tube for sucking

up a drink.

'strawberry *n* a type of small, juicy, red fruit or the low creeping plant which bears it.

stray *v* to wander; to lose one's way, become separated (from companions *etc*). – *adj* wandering, lost; happening *etc* here and there: *a stray example.* – *n* a wandering animal which has been abandoned or lost.

streak *n* a line or stripe different in colour from that which surrounds it; a smear of dirt, polish *etc*; a flash (*eg* of lightning); a trace of some quality in one's character: *a streak of selfishness.* – *v* to mark with streaks; (*coll*) to move very fast. – *adjs* **streaked; 'streaky** marked with streaks. – *n* **'streakiness.** – *n* **streaky bacon** bacon with streaks of fat and lean.

stream *n* a flow (of water, air, light *etc*); a small river, a brook; any steady flow of people or things: *a stream of traffic.* – *v* to flow or pour out. – *ns* **'streamer** a long strip *usu* of paper, used for decorating rooms *etc* (*esp* at Christmas); a narrow flag blowing in the wind; **'streamlet** a small stream. – *v* **'streamline** to shape (a vehicle *etc*) so that it may cut through the air or water as easily as possible; to make more efficient. *We've streamlined our methods since last year.*

street *n* a road lined with houses *etc.* – **streets ahead of** much better. *etc* than.

strength, strengthen *see* **strong.**

'strenuous *adj* making or needing great effort: *strenuous resistance*: *a strenuous game.* – *n* **'strenuousness.**

stress *n* force, pressure, pull *etc* of one thing on another; physical or nervous pressure or strain; emphasis, importance; extra weight laid on a part of a word (as in *butter*); physical or nervous strain: *the stress of modern life*: – *pl* **'stresses.** – *v* to put stress, pressure, emphasis or strain on.

stretch *v* to draw out to greater length, or too far, or from one point to another: *to stretch elastic*: *to stretch a rope from post to post*; to be able to be drawn out to a greater length or width. *That material stretches*; to (cause to) lie or spread (out); to (cause to) exert (oneself). *The work stretched him to the full*; to hold (out); to make (something, *eg* words, the law) appear to mean more than it does. – *n* the act of stretching; the state of being stretched; a length in distance or time: *a stretch of bad road*: – *pl* **'stretches.** – *n* **'stretcher** a light folding bed with handles for carrying the sick or wounded. – **at a stretch** continuously: *three hours at a stretch.*

strew [stroo] *v* to scatter: *papers strewn over the floor*; to cover, sprinkle (with). *The floor was strewn with papers*: – *pt* **strewed**, *pp* **strewn, strewed**.

'stricken *adj* wounded; deeply affected (*eg* by illness); struck.

strict *adj* (of a person) insisting on exact obedience to rules; exact: *the strict meaning of a word*; allowing no exception: *strict orders*; severe. – *ns* **'strictness; 'stricture** criticism, blame.

stride *v* to walk with long steps; to take a long step; to walk over, along *etc*: – *pt* **strode**, *pp* **stridden** ['stridn]. – *n* a long step; the distance covered by a step; a step forward.

'strident *adj* (of a sound) harsh, grating. – *n* **'stridency**.

strife *n* quarrelling; fighting.

strike *v* to hit with force. *The bullet struck his helmet*; to give, deliver (a blow); to knock: *to strike one's head on the beam*; to attack. *The enemy struck at dawn*; to light (a match); to make (a musical note) sound; (of a clock) to sound (*eg* at ten o'clock with ten chimes); (often with **off** or **out**) to cross out, cancel; to hit or discover suddenly: *strike oil*; to take a course. *He struck out across the fields*; to stop working (in support of a claim for more pay *etc*); to give (someone) the impression of being. *Did he strike you as lazy?*; to affect, impress. *I am struck by her beauty*; to make (an agreement *etc*): – *pt*, *pp* **struck**. – *adj* **'striking** noticeable: *a striking resemblance*; impressive. – **strike camp** to take down tents; **strike home** (of a blow) to hit the point aimed at; (of a remark) to have the intended effect; **strike up** to begin to play or sing (a tune); to begin (a friendship, conversation *etc*).

string *n* a long narrow cord for binding, tying *etc* made of threads twisted together; a piece of wire, gut *etc* in a violin *etc*; (*pl*) the stringed instruments played by a bow in an orchestra; a line of objects threaded together: *a string of pearls*; a number of things coming one after another: *a string of curses*. – *v* to put on a string; to stretch out in a line: – *pt*, *pp* **strung**. – *adj* **stringed** having strings. – *adj* **'stringy** like string.

stringent ['strinjənt] *adj* binding strongly, strictly enforced: *stringent rules*. – *n* **'stringency** strictness.

strip *v* to pull (off) (in strips); to remove (*eg* leaves, fruit) from; to remove the clothes from; to deprive: *stripped of his*

disguise; to make bare or empty: *strip the room*: – *pt* **stripped**. – *n* a long narrow piece (*eg* of paper). – *n* **'stripcar'toon** a line of drawings which tell a story (often an amusing one).

stripe *n* a band of colour *etc* different from the background on which it lies; a blow with a whip or rod. – *v* to make stripes on. – *adj* **'stripy**.

'stripling *n* a growing youth.

strive *v* to try hard; (*old*) to fight: – *pt* **strove**, *pp* **striven** ['strivn].

strode *see* **stride**.

stroke *n* the act of striking; a blow (as with a sword, whip); something unexpected: *a stroke of good luck*; one movement (as of a pen, an oar); one chime of a clock; (in swimming) one complete movement of the arms and legs; a particular style of swimming: *breast stroke*; a way of striking the ball (*eg* in tennis, cricket); a single effort or action: *at a stroke*; an achievement; a sudden attack of illness causing paralysis or loss of feeling in the body. – *v* to rub gently *esp* as a sign of affection.

stroll *v* to walk slowly in a relaxed way. – Also *n*.

strong *adj* not easily worn away: *strong cloth*; not easily defeated *etc*; powerful in attack, not easily resisted: *a strong wind*; (of persons, animals) having great muscular strength, resistance to illness *etc*; (of a person or one's character) forceful, commanding respect or obedience; (of smells, colours *etc*) striking, very noticeable; (of a feeling) intense: *a strong dislike*; in number. *Their army was 2,000 strong*. – *n* **strength** the state of being strong; an available number or force (of soldiers, volunteers *etc*). – *v* **'strengthen** to make, or become strong or stronger. – *adv* **'strongly**. – *ns* **'strongbox** a box for storing valuable objects or money; **'stronghold** a place built to withstand attack, a fortress; **'strongroom** a room for storing valuable objects or money. – **on the strength of** encouraged by or counting on.

strop *n* a strip of leather on which a razor is sharpened. – *v* to sharpen a razor: – *pt* **stropped**.

strove *see* **strive**.

struck *see* **strike**.

'structure *n* a building; a framework; the way the parts of anything are arranged: *the structure of a flower*: *the structure of a story*. – *adj* **'structural**.

'struggle *v* to try hard (to do something); to twist and fight to escape. *He struggled but they were too strong for him*; to fight (with or against someone); to move with difficulty. *He struggled through the mud.* – *n* a great effort; a fight.

strum *v* to play (on a guitar or piano) in a relaxed way: – *pt* **strummed**. – Also *n*.

strung *see* **string**.

strut *v* to walk in a proud manner: – *pt* **'strutted**. – *n* a proud way of walking; a bar *etc* which supports something.

strychnine ['strikněn] *n* a bitter, poisonous drug.

stub *n* a small stump (as of a pencil, cigarette). – *v* to put out, (*eg* a cigarette) by pressure against something; to knock (one's toe) painfully against something: – *pt* **stubbed**. – *adj* **'stubby** short, thick and strong.

'stubble *n* the short ends of the stalks of corn left in the ground after it is cut; a short growth of beard.

'stubborn *adj* unwilling to give way, obstinate; (of resistance, an attempt *etc*) strong, determined; difficult to manage or deal with. – *n* **'stubbornness**.

stubby *see* **stub**.

stucco ['stukō] *n* a kind of plaster (used for covering walls, moulding ornaments *etc*); work done in stucco: – *pl* **'stuccos**.

stuck *see* **stick**.

stud *n* a nail with a large head; a knob on a surface (often for ornament); a button with two heads for fastening a collar; a collection of horses kept for breeding, or for racing or hunting. – *v* to cover or fit with studs; to sprinkle, or be sprinkled over, thickly (with). *The meadow is studded with flowers.*

'student *n* one who studies, *esp* at college, university *etc*.

'studio *n* the workshop of an artist or photographer; a building or place in which cinema films are made; a room from which television or radio programmes are broadcast: – *pl* **'studios**.

'studious *adj* studying carefully and much; careful: *his studious avoidance of quarrels.* – *n* **'studiousness**.

'study *v* to gain knowledge of (a subject) by reading, experiment *etc*; to look carefully at; to consider carefully (*eg* a problem): – *pt* **'studied**. – *n* the gaining of knowledge of a subject: *the study of history*; a room where one reads and writes; a piece of music which is meant to develop the skill of the player; a work of art done as an exercise, or to try out ideas for a later work: – *pl* **'studies**. – *adj* **'studied** done on purpose, intentional: *a studied insult*; too careful, not natural: *a studied smile.*

stuff *n* the material of which anything is made; cloth, fabric; substance or material of any kind (used *esp* if the name of it is not known). *What is that stuff all over the wall?* – *v* to pack full; to fill the skin of (a dead animal) to preserve it, in such a way that it looks as it did when alive; (of a turkey *etc*) to fill with stuffing before cooking. – *n* **'stuffing** anything (*eg* feathers, scraps of material) used to stuff a cushion, chair *etc*; breadcrumbs, onions *etc* packed inside a fowl or other meat and cooked with it. – *adj* **'stuffy** (of a room *etc*) full of stale air, badly ventilated; (*coll*) dull, having old-fashioned ideas. – *n* **'stuffiness**.

'stultify *v* to dull the mind, make stupid: – *pt* **'stultified**. – *adj* **'stultifying**.

'stumble *v* to trip in walking; to walk as if blind, unsteadily; to make mistakes or hesitate in speaking; (with **on**) to find by chance. – *n* the act of stumbling. – *n* **stumbling block** a difficulty in the way of a plan or of progress.

stump *n* the part (of something, such as a tree, leg, tooth) left after the main part has been cut, worn *etc* away; (in cricket) one of the three wooden stakes which make up a wicket. – *v* (in cricket) to put out (a batsman) by touching the stumps with the ball; to puzzle completely; to walk stiffly or heavily. – *adj* **'stumpy** short and thick.

stun *v* to knock senseless (by a blow *etc*); to surprise or shock very greatly. *He was stunned by the news of her death*: – *pt* **stunned**.

stung *see* **sting**.

stunk *see* **stink**.

stunt *n* a daring trick; something done to attract attention: *a publicity stunt.* – *v* to stop the growth of. – *adj* **'stunted** small and badly shaped.

stupefy ['stūpifī] *v* to make stupid, deaden the feelings of; to astonish: – *pt* **'stupefied**. – *n* **stupe'faction**.

stu'pendous *adj* wonderful, amazing (*eg* because of size and power).

'stupid *adj* foolish: *a stupid thing to do*; dull, slow at learning; stupefied (*eg* from lack of sleep). – *ns* **stu'pidity**; **'stupor** the state of being only partly conscious.

'sturdy *adj* strong, well built; healthy. – *n* **'sturdiness**.

sturgeon ['stōrjən] *n* a type of large fish from which caviare is taken.

'stutter *v* to utter one's words in a halting, jerky way, to stammer. – *n* a stammer.

sty(e) [stɪ] *n* an inflamed swelling on the eyelid: – *pls* **sties, styes**; *see* also **pigsty**.

style *n* manner of acting, writing, speaking, painting *etc*; fashion: *in the style of the late 19th century*; an air of elegance. *He has a certain style*; the middle part of the pistil of a flower. – *v* to call, name. *He styled himself 'Lord John'.* – *adj* **'stylish** smart, elegant, fashionable. – **in style** with no expense or effort spared.

'stylus *n* a needle for a record-player: – *pl* **'styluses**.

suave [swäv] *adj* (of a person or his manner) polite and pleasant (*esp* on the surface).

sub- *prefix* under, below; less than; less in rank or importance.

'subaltern *n* an officer in the army under the rank of captain.

'subcom'mittee *n* a committee with powers given to it by a larger one.

subconscious ['sub'konshəs] *adj, n* (of) the workings of the mind of which a person is not himself aware.

'subdi'vide *v* to divide into smaller parts. – *n* **'subdi'vision** a part made by subdividing.

subdue [səb'dū] *v* to conquer (an enemy *etc*); to keep under control (*eg* a desire one has); to make less bright (as a colour, a light); to make quieter. *He seemed subdued after the fight.*

'subject *adj* under the power of another: *a subject nation*; (with **to**) liable to suffer from (*eg* colds, acne); (with **to**) depending on. *This plan is subject to your approval.* – *n* one under the power of another: *the king's subjects*; a member of a nation: *a British subject*; something or someone spoken or written about, studied *etc*; in a sentence or clause, the word(s) standing for the person or thing which does the action shown by the verb (as in 'The *cat* sat on the mat'). – *v* **sub'ject** (often with **to**) to force to submit (to). – *n* **sub'jection** the act of subjecting or the state of being subjected. – *adj* **sub'jective** (of an attitude *etc*) arising only from one's own personal feelings, thoughts *etc*, not impartial.

'subjūgate *v* to bring under one's power; to make obedient.

sublieutenant [sublef'tenənt] *n* an officer in the navy below the rank of lieutenant.

su'blime *adj* very noble, great or grand. – *n* **sublimity** [sə'bliməti].

submarine [submə'rēn] *n* a ship which can travel under water. – *adj* under the surface of the sea.

sub'merge *v* to cover with water; to sink. – *ns* **sub'mergence**; **sub'mersion**.

sub'mit *v* to give in, yield; to place (a matter) before someone so that he can give his opinion: – *pt* **sub'mitted**. – *n* **sub'mission** an act of submitting; readiness to yield, meekness; something (as an idea, statement *etc*) offered for consideration. – *adj* **sub'missive** meek, yielding easily.

su'bordinate *adj* (often with **to**) lower in rank, power, importance *etc* (than). – *n* a person who is subordinate. – *v* (with **to**) to consider as of less importance than. – *n* **subordi'nation** state of being subordinate; act of subordinating.

su'born *v* to persuade (a person) *esp* by bribery to do something illegal.

subpoena [sə'pēnə] *n* an order for a person to appear in court. – Also *v*.

sub'scribe *v* to make a contribution, *esp* of money towards (a charity *etc*); to promise to take and pay for a number of issues (of a magazine *etc*); (with **to**) to agree with (an idea, statement *etc*). – *n* **subscription** [səb'skripshən] an act of subscribing; money subscribed.

'subsequent *adj* following, coming after.

sub'servient *adj* weak-willed, ready to do as one is told. – *n* **sub'servience**.

sub'side *v* to settle down, sink lower, in the earth; (of flood water, noise *etc*) to get less and less. – *n* **subsidence** ['subsidəns] (of ground, a building *etc*) a falling or sinking down.

'subsidy *n* money paid by a government *etc* to help an industry *etc*: – *pl* **'subsidies**. – *adj* **sub'sidiary** acting as a help; of less importance; (of a company or firm) controlled by another company (also *n*). – *v* **'subsidize** to give money as a help.

sub'sist *v* to exist; (with **on**) to live on (a kind of food *etc*). – *n* **sub'sistence** state of existing; means of living, of survival; (state of having) the bare necessities for survival.

'subsoil *n* the layer of the earth just below the surface soil.

'substance *n* a material or a material object that can be seen and felt. *Glue is a sticky substance*; general meaning (of a talk, essay *etc*); thickness, solidity; wealth, property: *a man of substance*. – *adj* **sub'stantial** solid, strong; large: *a substantial building*; able to be seen and felt; in the main, but not in detail: *substantial agreement*. – *adv* **sub'stantially** for the most part: *substantially the same*. – *v* **sub'stantiate** to give proof of, or evidence for. – *n* **'substantive** (in grammar) a noun.

'**substitute** *v* (with **for**) to put in place or instead of. – *n* a person or thing acting or used instead of another. – *n* **sub·sti'tution**.

'**sub'stratum** *n* a layer lying underneath; a foundation: – *pl* '**sub'strata**.

subterfuge ['subtərfūj] *n* a cunning trick to get out of a difficulty *etc*.

subterranean [subtə'rāniən] *adj* found under the ground.

'**subtitle** *n* a second additional title (of a book *etc*); on a film, a translation of foreign speech, appearing at the bottom of the screen.

subtle ['sutl] *adj* difficult to describe or explain: *a subtle difference*; cunning: *by a subtle means*. – *n* **subtlety** ['sutlti] the state of being subtle; something subtle: – *pl* '**subtleties**. – *adv* '**subtly**.

sub'tract *v* to take away (a part from); to take away (one number from another). – *n* **sub'traction**.

'**suburb** *n* an area of houses *etc* on the outskirts of a town. – *adj* **su'burban** of suburbs. – *n* **su'burbia** suburbs.

sub'versive *adj* likely to overthrow, destroy (government, discipline *etc*).

'**subway** *n* an underground way for pedestrians *etc*; an underground railway.

succeed [sək'sēd] *v* (with **in**) to manage to do what one has been trying to do; to get on well; to take the place of, follow. *He was succeeded as chairman by his son*; (often with **to**) to follow in order (to the throne *etc*). – *n* **suc'cess** [sək'ses] the doing of what one has been trying to do; a person who succeeds; a thing that turns out well: – *pl* **suc'cesses**. – *adj* **suc'cessful** having achieved what one aimed at; having achieved wealth, importance *etc*; turning out as one had planned. – *n* **suc'cession** the act of following after; the right of becoming the next holder (of a throne *etc*); a number of things coming one after the other: *a succession of victories*. – *adj* **suc'cessive** following one after the other. – *n* **suc'cessor** one who comes after, follows in a post *etc*. – **in succession** one after another.

succinct [sək'siŋkt] *adj* in a few words, brief, concise.

succour ['sukər] *v* to help in time of distress. – *n* help.

'**succulent** *adj* juicy; (of a plant) having thick, juicy leaves or stems.

succumb [sə'kum] *v* to yield (to). *He succumbed to temptation*.

such *adj* of a particular kind previously mentioned. *Such things are difficult to find*; similar: *doctors, nurses, and such people*; so great. *His excitement was such that he shouted out loud*; used for emphasis. *It's such a terrible job!* – *pron* thing(s), people *etc*, of a kind already mentioned. *Such as these are not to be trusted*. – *adj, pron* '**such-and-such** any given (person or thing): *such-and-such a book*. – **as such** by itself. *The music is unpleasant as such, but it suits my purpose*; **such as** of the same kind as: *birds such as ducks and swans*.

suck *v* to draw into the mouth; to draw milk from with the mouth; to hold in the mouth and lick hard (*eg* a sweet); (often with **up, in**) to draw in, absorb. – *n* a sucking action; the act of sucking. – *n* '**sucker** a side shoot rising from the root of a plant; an organ on an animal by which it sticks to objects; a pad (of rubber *etc*) which can stick to a surface; (*coll*) someone easily fooled. – *v* '**suckle** (of a woman or female animal) to give milk from the breast or teat. – *n* '**suckling** a baby or young animal which still sucks its mother's milk.

'**suction** *n* the act of sucking; the act or process of reducing the air pressure, and so producing a vacuum, on part of the surface of a substance (*eg* on a liquid so that it is drawn up into a tube *etc*) or between surfaces (*eg* a rubber pad and a wall so that they stick together).

'**sudden** *adj* happening all at once *etc* without being expected: *a sudden attack*. – *adv* '**suddenly**. – *n* '**suddenness**.

suds *npl* frothy, soapy water.

sue [sōō] *v* to start a law case against.

suede [swād] *n* a kind of leather with a soft, dull surface. – Also *adj*.

suet ['sōoit] *n* a kind of hard animal fat.

'**suffer** *v* to feel pain or punishment; to bear, endure; (*old*) to allow; to go through, undergo (a change *etc*). – *n* '**suffering**. – **on sufferance** allowed or tolerated but not really wanted. *He's here on sufferance*.

suf'fice *v* to be enough, or good enough. – *adj* **sufficient** [sə'fishənt] enough.

'**suffix** *n* a small part added to the end of a word to make another word, as *-ness* to ·*good* to make *goodness*, *-ly* to *quick* to make *quickly etc*: – *pl* '**suffixes**.

'**suffocate** *v* to kill by preventing the breathing of; to die from lack of air; to (cause to) feel unable to breathe freely. – *n* **suffo'cation**.

'**suffrage** *n* a vote; the right to vote.

suffuse [sə'fūz] *v* to spread over. *A blush suffused her face*. – *n* **suf'fusion**.

sugar ['shōogər] *n* a sweet substance got

mostly from sugar-cane and sugar-beet. – v to mix or sprinkle with sugar. – adj 'sugary tasting of, or like, sugar; too sweet. – ns 'sugar-beet a type of vegetable whose root yields sugar; 'sugar-cane a type of tall grass from whose juice sugar is obtained.

suggest [sə'jest] v to put forward, pro-pose (an idea etc); to put into the mind, to hint. – n sug'gestion an act of suggesting; an idea put forward; a slight trace: a suggestion of anger in her voice. – adjs sug'gestible easily influ-enced by suggestions; sug'gestive that suggests something particular, esp something improper. He made sugges-tive remarks to her; (with of) giving the idea of: suggestive of mental illness.

suicide ['sooisid] n the taking of one's own life; one who kills himself. – adj sui'cidal of suicide; likely to cause one's death or ruin: suicidal action.

suit [soot] n a set of clothes to be worn together; a case in a law court; a request for permission to court a lady; one of the four divisions (spades, hearts, diamonds, clubs) of playing cards. – v to be convenient or suitable for, to please. The climate suits me; to look well on. The dress suits you; (with to) to make fitting or suitable for. He suited his words to the occasion. – adj 'suitable fitting the purpose; just what is wanted, convenient. – ns suita'bility; 'suitor one who tries to gain the love of a woman. – n 'suitcase a travelling case for carrying clothes etc. – follow suit to do just as someone else has done.

suite [swēt] n a number of things in a set, as rooms, furniture, pieces of music etc; the body of attendants who go with an important person.

sulk v to keep silent because one is displeased. – adj 'sulky. – the sulks a fit of sulking.

'sullen adj angry and silent, sulky. – n 'sullenness.

'sully v to make less pure, to dirty: – pt 'sullied.

'sulphur n an element, a yellow sub-stance found in the ground which gives off a choking smell when burnt, used in matches, gunpowder etc. – n sul-phuric acid [sul'fūrik] a powerful acid much used in industry.

'sultan n the king or ruler in some Eastern countries. – n sul'tana a sul-tan's wife; a kind of raisin.

'sultry adj (of weather) very hot and close; passionate.

sum n the amount or total made by two or more things added together; a quan-tity of money; a question or problem in arithmetic; the general meaning (of something said or written). – n sum total the sum of several smaller sums; the main point, total effect. – sum up to give the main points of (a discussion, evidence in a trial etc (n 'summing-'up).

'summary n a shortened form (of a story, statement etc) giving only the main points. – adj short; quick; done with-out wasting time or words. – adv sum'marily. – v 'summarize to state briefly, make a summary of.

'summer n the warmest season of the year. – Also adj. – n 'summerhouse a small house for sitting in, in a garden.

'summit n the highest point (of a hill etc). – n summit conference a confer-ence between heads of governments.

'summon v to order (a person) to come to oneself, to a court of law etc; (with up) to gather up (one's courage, strength etc). – n 'summons an order to appear in court: – pl 'summonses.

sump n the part of a motor-engine which contains the oil; a small pit into which water drains and out of which it can be pumped.

'sumptuous adj costly, splendid.

sun n the round body in the sky which gives light and heat to the earth and to the other planets revolving round it; sunshine. – v (with oneself) to sit, lie in the sunshine, sunbathe: – pt sun-ned. – adj 'sunny full of sunshine; cheerful: a sunny nature. – v 'sunbathe to lie or sit in the sun to acquire a suntan. – ns 'sunbeam a ray of light from the sun; 'sunburn a burning or redness of the skin caused by too much exposure to the sun. – adjs 'sunburned, 'sunburnt affected by sunburn. – ns 'sundial an instrument for telling the time from the shadow of a rod or plate on its surface cast by the sun; 'sunflower a large type of yellow flower with petals like rays of the sun; 'sunlight the light from the sun. – adj 'sunlit lighted up by the sun. – ns 'sunrise the (time of the) rising of the sun in the morning; 'sunset the (time of the) setting of the sun in the evening; 'sunshine bright sunlight; cheerful-ness; 'sunstroke a serious type of illness caused by being out in very hot sunshine for too long; 'suntan a browning of the skin caused by expos-ure to the sun, often acquired deliber-ately by sitting or lying in the sun.

sundae ['sundā] n a type of sweet food

made up of ice cream served with fruit, syrup *etc.*

'Sunday *n* the first day of the week, in the Christian religion set aside for worship.

'sundry *adj* several, various: *sundry articles for sale.* – *npl* **'sundries** odds and ends.

sung *see* **sing**.

sunk, sunken *see* **sink**.

sup *v* to eat or drink in small mouthfuls: *sup one's soup*; (*old*) to eat one's evening meal: – *pt* **supped**.

super ['sōōpər] *adj* (*coll*) extremely good.

super- [sōōpər] *prefix* above, beyond, very, too.

superannuate [sōōpə'ranūāt] *v* to cause (a person) to retire from a job because of old age, *usu* with a pension. – *n* **superannu'ation** such a pension.

superb [sōō'pərb] *adj* magnificent, very fine, excellent: *a superb view.*

supercilious [sōōpər'siliəs] *adj* looking down on others, haughty.

superficial [sōōpər'fishəl] *adj* (of a wound *etc*) affecting the surface of the skin only, not deep; not thorough or detailed: *a superficial interest*; apparent at first glance, not actual: *a superficial likeness*; (of a person) not capable of deep thoughts or feelings. – *n* **superfici'ality**.

superfluous [sōō'pərflōōəs] *adj* beyond what is enough or necessary. – *n* **super'fluity**.

superhuman ['sōōpər'hūmən] *adj* divine; greater than would be expected of an ordinary person: *superhuman effort*.

superimpose ['sōōpərim'pōz] *v* to lay or place (one thing on another thing).

superintend [sōōpərin'tend] *v* to be in charge or control, manage. – *n* **superin'tendent** one who is in charge of an institution, building *etc*; a police officer above a chief inspector.

superior [sōō'pēriər] *adj* higher in place, rank or excellence; better or greater than others in some way: *superior forces*: *superior goods*; having an air of being better than others. – *n* a person who is better than, or higher in rank than, others. – *n* **superi'ority**.

superlative [sōō'pərlətiv] *adj* better than, or going beyond, all others: *superlative skill*; (in grammar) an adjective or adverb of the highest degree of comparison, as *kindest, worst, most quickly*.

'supermarket *n* a kind of large self-service store selling food *etc.*

supernatural [sōōpər'nachərəl] *adj* not happening in the ordinary course of nature, miraculous.

supersede [sōōpər'sēd] *v* to take the place of. *He superseded him as headmaster*; to replace (something with something else).

supersonic ['sōōpər'sonik] *adj* faster than the speed of sound: *a supersonic aeroplane.*

superstition [sōōpər'stishən] *n* belief in magic and in things which cannot be explained by reason; an example of such belief: *the superstition that one should not walk under ladders.* – *adj* **super'stitious** having superstitions.

supervise ['sōōpərviz] *v* to be in charge of some work and see that it is properly done. – *ns* **supervision** [sōōpər'vizhən] the act of supervising; control, inspection; **supervisor** ['sōōpərvizər].

supine ['sōōpin] *adj* lying on the back; not showing any interest or energy.

'supper *n* a meal taken in the evening.

sup'plant *v* to take the place of somebody (sometimes by cunning means) or of something. *The baby supplanted the dog in her affections.*

'supple *adj* bending or moving easily; (of an object) bending easily without breaking. – *n* **'suppleness**. – *adv* **supply** ['supli].

supplement ['supləmənt] *n* something added *esp* to supply a need or lack; a special part added to the ordinary part of a newspaper or magazine. – *v* **supple'ment** to make or be an addition to. *Her earnings supplemented his income.* – *adj* **supple'mentary** added to supply a need; additional.

'suppliant *adj* asking earnestly and humbly. – *n* one who asks in this way. – *n* **suppli'cation** a humble, earnest request.

sup'plȳ *v* to provide (what is wanted or needed); to provide (someone) with (something): – *pt* **sup'plied**. – *n* an act of supplying; something supplied; a stock or store; (*pl*) **sup'plies** a stock of necessary things, as food, equipment, money. – *adj* **sup'ply** (of a teacher *etc*) filling another's place or position for a time.

supply² *see* **supple**.

support [sə'pört] *v* to hold up, take part of the weight of; to help or encourage; to supply with a means of living: *to support a family*; to bear, put up with. *I can't support lies.* – *n* an act of supporting; something that supports. – *n* **sup'porter** one who supports (*esp* a football club *etc*).

suppose [sə'pōz] *v* to take as true,

313

assume (often for the sake of argument or discussion). *Let us suppose that we have £100 to spend*; to think, believe, think probable. *I suppose you know*; used in the form of a command to give a polite order. *Suppose you go now.* – *adj* **sup'posed** believed (often mistakenly or with too little evidence) to be so: *his supposed kindness.* – *adv* **supposedly** [sə'pōzidli] according to what is supposed. – **sup'posing (that)** if, in the event that. *Supposing it rains.* – *n* **suppo'sition** the act of supposing; something supposed. – **be supposed to** to be required or expected to (do).

sup'press *v* to crush, put down (a rebellion *etc*); to keep back (a yawn, a piece of news *etc*). – *n* **sup'pression** the act of suppressing.

'**suppūrate** *v* (of a wound *etc*) to be full of, or discharge, pus.

supra- [sōōprə] *prefix* above.

supreme [soo'prēm] *adj* highest, most powerful: *supreme ruler*; greatest: *supreme courage.* – *n* **supremacy** [soo'preməsi] the state of being supreme; highest power or authority.

'**surcharge** *n* an extra charge or tax.

sure [shoor] *adj* having no doubt. *I'm sure that I can be there*; certain (to do, happen *etc*). *He is sure to go*; reliable, dependable: *a sure method.* – Also *adv.* – *adv* '**surely** certainly, without doubt; sometimes expressing a little doubt. *Surely you will not go?*; without hesitation, mistake, failure *etc*. – *n* **surety** ['shōōrəti] a person who promises that another person will do something (as appear in court *etc*); a pledge or guarantee: – *pl* '**sureties**. – *adj* '**sure-'footed** unlikely to slip or stumble. – **be sure** see to it that. *Be sure that he does it*; **make sure** to act so that, or to check that, something is sure; **sure of oneself** confident; **to be sure!** certainly!; undoubtedly. *To be sure, you are correct!*

surf *n* the foam made by the breaking of waves. – *n* '**surfing** the sport of riding on a surfboard. – *n* '**surfboard** a long, narrow board on which a person can ride over the surf.

'**surface** *n* the outside or top part of anything (as of the earth, of a road *etc*). – *v* to come up to the surface of (water *etc*); to put a (smooth) surface on. – *adj* on the surface; travelling on the surface of land or water: *surface mail.*

surfeit ['sɔrfit] *n* too much of anything.

surge [sɔrj] *v* to move (forward) like waves; to rise suddenly or excessively. – *n* the rising or swelling of a large

wave; a movement like this; a sudden rise or increase (of pain *etc*).

surgeon ['sɔrjən] *n* a doctor who treats injuries and diseases by operations in which the body sometimes has to be cut (to remove a diseased part *etc*). – *n* **surgery** ['sɔrjəri] the act, or art, of treating diseases, injuries, by operation; a doctor's or dentist's consulting room: – *pl* '**surgeries**. – *adj* '**surgical**.

'**surly** *adj* gruff, rude, ill-mannered. – *n* '**surliness**.

surmise [sər'mīz] *v* to suppose, to guess. – *n* '**surmise**.

sur'mount *v* to overcome (a difficulty *etc*); to be on the top of, to climb, or get, over. – *adj* **sur'mountable**.

'**surname** *n* a person's last name, his family name.

sur'pass *v* to go beyond, to be more or better than. *His work surpassed my expectations..*

surplice ['sɔrpləs] *n* a loose white gown worn by clergymen *etc*.

'**surplus** *n* the amount left over after what is needed has been used up. – Also *adj*.

surprise [sər'prīz] *n* the feeling or emotion caused by an unexpected or sudden happening; an unexpected happening *etc*. – *v* to cause a person to feel surprise; to come upon (a person, an enemy *etc*) suddenly and without warning. – **take by surprise** to come upon (or capture) without warning.

sur'render *v* to give up, give in, yield. *He surrendered to the enemy*; to hand over. *He surrendered the note to the teacher.* – Also *n*.

surrep'titious *adj* done in a secret, underhand way.

sur'round *v* to come, or be, all round (someone or something); to enclose, put round. – *n* a border. – *npl* **sur-'roundings** the country lying around (a place); the people and places with which one has to do in one's daily life.

'**surtax** *n* an extra tax *esp* on income.

surveillance [sər'vāləns] *n* a close watch or constant guard.

survey [sər'vā] *v* to look over; to inspect, examine; to make careful measurements of (a piece of land *etc*): – *pt* sur'veyed. – *n* 'survey a general view; a detailed examination or inspection; a piece of writing *etc* giving results of this; a careful measuring of land *etc*; a map made with the measurements obtained: – *pl* '**surveys**. – *n* **sur'veyor** one who makes surveys of land, buildings *etc*.

sur'vive *v* to remain alive, to continue to exist (after an event *etc*); to live longer

than. *He survived his wife.* – *ns*
sur'vival the state of surviving; anything (as a custom, relic *etc*) that remains from earlier times; **sur'vivor** one who remains alive: *the only survivor of the crash.*

susceptible [sə'septəbl] *adj* (with **to**) liable to be affected by: *susceptible to colds*; (of a person or his feelings) easily affected. – *n* **suscepti'bility.**

sus'pect *v* to be inclined to think (a person *etc*) guilty. *I suspect her of the crime*; to distrust, have doubts about. *I suspected his air of frankness*; to guess. *I suspect that we're wrong.* – *n* **'suspect** a person *etc* thought to be guilty of a crime *etc.* – *adj* arousing doubt, suspected. – *n* **suspicion** [səs'pishən] the act of suspecting; a feeling of doubt or mistrust; an opinion, a guess. – *adj* **sus'picious** suspecting, or inclined to suspect or distrust; arousing, causing suspicion.

sus'pend *v* to hang; to keep from falling or sinking: *particles suspended in a liquid*; to stop for a time or postpone: *to suspend business*; to take away a job, privilege *etc* from, *esp* for a time. *They suspended the student from classes.* – *ns* **sus'pender** an elastic strap to keep up socks or stockings; (*US, pl*) braces; **sus'pense** a state of being undecided; a state of uncertainty or worry; **sus'pension** the act of suspending; the state of being suspended; the state of a solid which is mixed with a liquid or gas and does not sink or dissolve in it. – *n* **suspension bridge** a bridge which is suspended from cables hanging from towers.

suspicion *see* **suspect.**

sus'tain *v* to hold up, support; to bear (an attack *etc*) without giving way; to suffer (an injury *etc*); to give strength to. *This food will sustain you*; to keep up, keep going: *sustain a conversation.* – *n* **'sustenance** food, nourishment.

swab [swob] *n* a mop for cleaning a ship's deck; a piece of cottonwool used for various medical purposes, as cleaning parts of the body. – *v* to clean with a swab: – *pt* **swabbed.**

swaddle ['swodl] *v* to wrap up (a young baby) tightly. – *npl* **swaddling clothes** (*old*) strips of cloth used to wrap up a young baby.

'swagger *v* to walk proudly, swinging the arms and body; to boast. – Also *n.*

swain *n* (*old*) a young man.

swallow ['swolō] *v* to make (food or drink) pass over the throat into the stomach; (with **up**) to cause to disap-

pear; to receive (an insult *etc*) without objecting or rejecting; to keep back (tears, a laugh *etc*). – *n* an act of swallowing; a type of bird with pointed wings and a forked tail.

swamp [swomp] *n* wet, marshy ground. – *v* to cause (a boat) to fill with water; to overwhelm: *swamped with work.*

swan [swon] *n* a large, stately type of water bird, *usu* white, with a long neck. – *n* **swan song** the last work of a musician, writer *etc.*

swank *v* (*coll*) to show off: – Also *n.* – *adj* **'swanky.**

swap, swop [swop] *v* to give one thing in exchange for another. *They swapped stamps:* – *pt* **swapped.**

sward [swörd] *n* (in poetry *etc*) a patch of green turf.

swarm [swörm] *n* a large number of insects flying or moving together, *eg* bees; a dense moving crowd. – *v* (of bees) to gather together in great numbers; to move in crowds; to be crowded with. *The ruins swarmed with tourists*; (with **up**) to climb up (a wall *etc*).

swarthy ['swördhi] *adj* dark-skinned.

swashbuckling ['swoshbukliŋ] *adj* bold, swaggering: *a swashbuckling pirate.*

swat [swot] *v* to crush (a fly *etc*): – *pt* **'swatted.** – *n* an instrument for doing this.

swath [swoth], **swathe** [swādh] *n* a line of corn or grass cut by a scythe; a strip.

swathe [swādh] *v* to wrap round with clothes or bandages. – *n see* **swath.**

sway *v* to move, swing, in a rocking manner; to (cause to) bend in one direction or to one side; to influence. *He swayed the audience.* – *n* the act of swaying; a swaying movement; rule, power: *to hold sway over.*

swear [swār] *v* to promise or declare solemnly; to vow; to curse, using the name of God or other sacred things without respect; to make (someone) take an oath: *to swear a person to secrecy*: – *pt* **swore** [swör], *pp* **sworn.** – *adj* **sworn** holding steadily to one's attitude *etc*: *sworn friends: sworn enemies.* – *n* **swear word** a word used in swearing or cursing. – **swear by** to rely on, have complete faith in.

sweat [swet] *n* the moisture from the skin, perspiration. – *v* to give out sweat; (*coll*) to work hard. – *n* **'sweater** a jersey, a pullover. – *adj* **'sweaty** wet, or stained with, sweat. – *n* **sweated labour** hard work for which very little pay is given.

swede *n* a kind of large yellow turnip.

sweep *v* to clean (a floor *etc*) with a brush or broom; (often with **up**) to gather up or remove (dust *etc*) by sweeping; to carry (away, along, off) with a long brushing movement; to travel over quickly, to move with speed (and force). *This disease is sweeping the country*; to move quickly in a proud manner (*eg* from a room); (with **of**) to clear (something) of: *to sweep the sea of enemy mines*; to curve widely or stretch far: – *pt* **swept** [swept]. – *n* an act of sweeping; a sweeping movement; a curve or a stretch; a chimney sweeper; a sweepstake. – *adj* **'sweeping** that sweeps; (of a victory *etc*) great, overwhelming; (of a statement *etc*) too general, allowing no exceptions, rash. – *n* **'sweepstake** a system of gambling on a race *etc*, in which those who take part stake money which goes to the holder of the winning ticket *etc*.

sweet *adj* having the taste of sugar, not salty, sour or bitter; pleasing to the taste; pleasant to hear or smell; kindly, agreeable, charming. – *n* a small piece of sweet substance, as of chocolate, toffee, candy *etc*; something sweet served towards the end of a meal, a pudding. – *v* **'sweeten** to make or become sweet or sweeter. – *n* **'sweetener**. – *n* **'sweetness**. – *ns* **'sweetheart** a boyfriend or girlfriend; a darling; **'sweetmeat** (*old*) a sweet, candy *etc*; **sweet pea** a type of sweet-smelling climbing flower grown in gardens; **sweet tooth** a liking for sweet-tasting things; **sweet william** a sweet-smelling type of garden flower.

swell *v* to grow or make larger, greater, louder *etc*; (of the sea) to rise into waves: – *pp* **'swollen**. – *n* an act of swelling; an increase in size *etc*; large, heaving waves; a gradual rise in the height of the ground. – *adj* (*coll*) fine, splendid. – *n* a dandy. – *n* **'swelling** a swollen part of the body, a lump.

'swelter *v* to be too hot. – *adj* **'sweltering** very hot.

swept *see* **sweep**.

swerve *v* to turn quickly to one side. – Also *n*.

swift *adj* moving quickly; rapid, quick. – *n* a type of bird rather like the swallow. – *n* **'swiftness**.

swig *n* a mouthful of liquid, a large drink. – *v* to gulp down: – *pt* **swigged**.

swill *v* to wash out; (*coll*) to drink a great deal. – *n* (partly) liquid food given to pigs; (*coll*) a big drink.

swim *v* a move on or in water, using arms, legs, fins, tails *etc*; to cross by swimming: *to swim a river*; to float, not sink; to move with a gliding motion; to be dizzy; to be covered (with liquid): *meat swimming in grease*: – *pres p* **'swimming**, *pt* **swam**, *pp* **swum**. – *n* an act of swimming, or a motion like it. – *n* **'swimmer** one who swims. – *adv* **'swimmingly** smoothly, easily, successfully. – *ns* **swimming bath**, **swimming pool**, an area of water, *usu* a large kind of tank, designed for swimming, diving in *etc*.

'swindle *v* to cheat (someone); to get (money *etc* from someone) by cheating. – *n* a fraud, a deception. – *n* **'swindler**.

swine *n* (*old*) a pig: – *pl* **swine**. – *n* **'swineherd** (*old*) a person who looks after pigs.

swing *v* to move to and fro, to sway; to move backwards and forwards on a swinging seat; to (cause to) turn or whirl round; to walk quickly, moving the arms to and fro: – *pt* **swung**. – *n* an act of swinging; a swinging movement; a seat for swinging, hung on ropes *etc* from a support. – *n* **swing bridge** a kind of bridge that swings open to let ships pass. – **in full swing** going on busily.

swingeing ['swinjin] *adj* very great: *swingeing cuts in taxation*.

swingle *see* **flail**.

swipe *v* to strike with a sweeping blow. – Also *n*.

swirl *v* to sweep along with a whirling motion. – Also *n*.

swish *v* to strike *etc* (something) with a whistling or rustling sound; to move making such a noise. *She swished out of the room in her long dress*. – Also *n*.

switch *n* a small lever or handle *eg* for turning an electric current on and off; an act of switching; a change: *a switch of support*; a thin stick: – *pl* **'switches**. – *v* to strike with a switch; to turn (off or on an electric current *etc*) by means of a switch; to (cause to) change or turn. *The men switched jobs. She hastily switched the conversation*. – *ns* **'switchback** a road or railway with steep ups and downs or sharp turns; **'switchboard** a board with equipment for making telephone connections.

'swivel *n* a type of joint between two parts of an object that enables one part to turn or pivot without the other. – *v* to turn on, or as if on, a swivel: – *pt* **'swivelled**.

swollen *see* **swell**.

swoon *v* (*old*) to faint. – Also *n*.

swoop *v* to come down with a sweep (as a hawk does on its prey). – *n* a sudden downward rush. – **at one fell swoop** all at one time, at a stroke.

swop *see* **swap**.

sword [sörd] *n* a type of weapon with a long blade for cutting or piercing. – *n* **'swordfish** a large type of fish with a long pointed upper jaw like a sword.

swore, sworn *see* **swear**.

'sycamore *n* a name given to several different types of trees, the maple, plane, and a kind of fig tree.

'sycophant *n* a person who flatters (someone) in order to gain some advantage for himself. – *adj* **syco'phantic**.

'syllable *n* a word or part of a word uttered by only one effort of the voice. (*Cheese* has one syllable, *but-ter* two, *mar-gar-ine* three). – *adj* **syl'labic**.

'syllabus *n* a programme or list *eg* of lectures, classes *etc*: – *pls* **'syllabuses, 'syllabi**.

sylph *n* (*myth*) a type of fairy supposed to inhabit the air; a slender, graceful woman.

'symbol *n* a thing that stands for or represents another, as the cross, which stands for Christianity; a sign used as a short way of stating something, as the signs + meaning plus, O meaning oxygen. – *adjs* **sym'bolic, sym'bolical** of, or using, symbols; standing as a symbol of. – *n* **'symbolism** the use of symbols to express ideas *esp* in art and literature. – *v* **'symbolize** to be a symbol of.

'symmetry *n* the state in which two parts, on either side of a dividing line, are equal in size, shape and position. *The extension spoiled the symmetry of the building.* – *adj* **sym'metrical** having symmetry, not lopsided in appearance.

'sympathy *n* a feeling of pity or sorrow for a person in trouble; the state of being in agreement with, or of being able to understand, the feelings, attitudes *etc* of others. – *adj* **sympa'thetic** feeling, showing sympathy: (with **to** or **towards**) inclined to be in favour of; *sympathetic to the scheme.* – *v* **'sympathize** (sometimes with **with**) to express or feel sympathy.

'symphony *n* a long piece of music for an orchestra of many different instruments: – *pl* **'symphonies**.

symposium [sim'pōziəm] *n* a meeting or conference for the discussion of some subject; a collection of essays dealing with a single subject.

'symptom *n* something that indicates the existence of something, a sign (*esp* of a disease). *A rash is one symptom of measles.* – *adj* **sympto'matic**.

syn- *prefix* with, together.

synagogue ['sinəgog] *n* a Jewish place of worship.

synchronize ['siŋkrəniz] *v* to happen at the same time; to (cause to) agree in time: *synchronize watches.*

syncopate ['siŋkəpāt] *v* to change the beat in music by putting the accent on beats not usually accented. – *n* **synco'pation**.

'syndicate *n* a number of persons who join together to manage some piece of business.

'synod *n* a meeting of clergymen.

'synonym *n* a word which has the same (or nearly the same) meaning as another as 'ass' and 'donkey'; 'brave' and 'courageous', 'to hide' and 'to conceal'. – *adj* **sy'nonymous** (sometimes with **with**) having the same meaning.

sy'nopsis *n* a short summary of the main points of a book, speech *etc*: – *pl* **sy'nopsēs**.

'syntax *n* (rules for) the correct putting together of words into sentences. – *adjs* **syn'tactic, syn'tactical**.

'synthesis *n* the act of making a whole by putting together its separate parts, *esp* the making of a substance by combining chemical elements. – *v* **'synthesize** to make (*eg* a drug) by synthesis. – *adj* **syn'thetic** made artificially and looking like, but not the same as, the natural product: *synthetic rubber*: *synthetic leather*; not natural, pretended: *synthetic charm.*

syringe [si'rinj] *n* a tube with a rubber bulb or piston for sucking up, and squirting out, liquid; an instrument of this kind with a needle, used by doctors for injecting drugs *etc*. – *v* to wash out, clean, with a syringe.

'syrup *n* water, or the juice of fruits, boiled with sugar and made thick and sticky; a purified form of treacle.

'system *n* an arrangement of many parts which work together: *a railway system*: *the solar system*; a way of organizing: *a system of government*: *a system of education*; a regular way of doing something, a plan, a method; the body, or parts of the body, thought of as working as a whole. *His system won't stand the treatment*: *the digestive system.* – *adj* **syste'matic** following a system; methodical.

T

tab *n* a small tag or flap by which anything is gripped.

'tabard *n* a short sleeveless tunic-like garment.

'tabby *n* a striped cat, *esp* female: – *pl* **'tabbies**. – *n* **'tabby-cat**.

'tabernacle *n* a place of worship.

'table *n* a piece of furniture with a flat top and standing on legs; food, supply of food on a table; a statement of facts or figures set out in columns: *timetable*: *multiplication tables*. – *v* to make into a list or table; to put forward for discussion. – *ns* **'tablecloth** a cloth for covering a table; **'tableland** a raised stretch of land with a level surface; **table linen** tablecloths, napkins *etc*; **'tablespoon** a large size of spoon; **table tennis** a type of game played on a table with small bats and a light ball.

tableau ['tablō] *n* a striking group or scene: – *pl* **tableaux** ['tablōz].

'tablet *n* a small flat plate, slab or surface on which to write, cut inscriptions, paint, *etc*; a small flat cake or piece`(of soap, chocolate *etc*); a pill.

'tabloid *n* a small-sized newspaper, *esp* one that gives news in shortened and often simplified form and often contains many pictures. – Also *adj*.

ta'boo *n, adj* (something) forbidden for religious reasons or not approved by social custom. *Certain slang words are considered taboo*.

'tabor *n* a small kind of drum.

'tabulate *v* to set out (information *etc*) in columns or rows. – *adj* **'tabular**.

'tacit *adj* understood but not spoken aloud, silent: *tacit agreement*. – *adj* **'taciturn** not inclined to talk. – *n* taci'turnity.

tack *n* a kind of short sharp nail with a ·broad head; a sideways movement of a sailing ship so that it may sail against the wind; a direction, a course; in sewing, a large stitch to be taken out later. – *v* to fasten with tacks; to sew with tacks; (of sailing ships) to move from side to side across the face of the wind.

'tackle *n* the ropes, rigging, *etc* of a ship; equipment, tools, gear: *fishing tackle*; ropes and pulleys for raising heavy weights; an act of tackling. – *v* to seize, come to grips with or try to deal with; (in football, hockey *etc*) to try to stop, or take the ball from, another player.

'tacky *adj* sticky.

tact *n* care and skill in dealing with people so as to avoid hurting and offending. – *adjs* **'tactful; 'tactless**.

'tactics *n* a way of acting in order to gain success or advantage; the art of arranging troops or warships successfully during a battle. – *adj* **'tactical** of tactics, of clever and successful planning. – *n* **tac'tician** one who plans and acts cleverly.

'tadpole *n* a young frog or toad in its first stage of life.

'taffeta *n* a kind of thin, glossy cloth made of silk *etc*.

tag *n* a metal point at the end of a shoelace; a label: *a price tag*; any saying or quotation that is often repeated: *a Latin tag*; a kind of chasing game played by children (also **tig**). – *v* to put a tag or tags on. – **tag on to, tag after** to follow (a person) closely and continually. *His little brother tags after him*.

tail *n* the part of an animal, bird or fish which sticks out behind the rest of its body; anything like a tail in position or shape: *tail of an aeroplane*; (*pl*) the side of a coin that does not bear the head; (*pl*) a tail-coat. – *v* (*coll*) to follow closely. *The detective tailed him for three days*; to remove the tails from (gooseberries *etc*). – *n* **'tail-coat** a type of coat with a divided tail, part of a man's evening dress; **'tail-'end** the very end (of a procession *etc*); **'tail-light** the light at the back of a motor-car, cycle, *etc*; **'tail-spin** (in aeroplanes) a steep, spinning, downward dive. – **tail off** to become less, fewer or worse. *The number of spectators tailed off*; **turn tail** to run away.

'tailor *n* one who cuts out and makes suits, overcoats *etc*. – *v* to make and fit (outer clothes); to make to fit the circumstances, adapt: *tailor your expenditure to your earnings*.

taint *v* to spoil by touching or bringing into contact with something bad or rotten; to corrupt. – *n* a trace of decay or of evil.

take *v* to lay hold of, grasp; to choose. *Take a card!*; to accept, agree to have (a seat, a biscuit, a rest, responsibility *etc*); to have room for. *The car takes eight passengers*; to eat, swallow (food, drink); to get or have regularly. *He takes sugar*; to capture (a fort *etc*); to subtract. *Take 3 from 6*; to lead, carry, drive: *to take pigs to market*; to use, make use of. *Take care!*; to require. *It takes courage*; to travel by (a train *etc*); to feel (pride, pleasure *etc*) (in); to photograph. *He took three shots of the village*; to understand (a statement *etc* in a certain way); (of an inoculation *etc*) to be effective; (of a plant) to root; to become popular, to please: – *pt* **took**, *pp* **'taken**. – *adj* **'taking** pleasing, attractive. – *n* an act of taking; (*pl*) money received from things sold. – **take account of** to consider, to remember; **take advantage of** to make use of (an opportunity); to treat or use (a person) unfairly; **take after** to be like in appearance or ways; **take care of** to look after; **take down** to write, note, down; **take for** to believe (mistakenly) to be. *I took him for his brother*; **take heed** to pay careful attention; **take ill** to become ill; **take in** to include; to receive; to understand. *I didn't take in what you said*; to make something smaller: *take in a dress*; to cheat, deceive. *You took me in with your impersonation*; **take leave of** to say goodbye; to depart from; **take (someone's) life** to kill (someone); **taken with** attracted to; **take off** to remove (clothes *etc*); to imitate unkindly; (of an aircraft) to leave the ground (*n* **'take-off**); **take on** to undertake (work *etc*); to accept (as an opponent). *He will take you on at tennis*; **take over** to take control of (*eg* a business) (*n* **'takeover**); **take part (in)** to share, help (in); **take pity on** to show pity for; **take place** to happen; **take to** to turn to (flight *etc*) in an emergency. *He took to his heels and ran away*; to be attracted by; to begin to do or use regularly. *He took to rising early*; **take to heart** to be deeply affected or upset by; **take up** to lift, raise; to occupy (space, time *etc*); to begin to learn, show interest in. *He has taken up chess.*

talc *n* a soft type of mineral, soapy to the touch. – *n* **talcum powder** a fine kind of powder, used for rubbing on to the body, made from talc.

tale *n* story; an untrue story, a lie.

'talent *n* a special ability or skill: *a talent for drawing*; (*hist*) a measure of weight or the value of this weight of gold or silver. – *adj* **'talented** skilled, gifted.

talisman ['talizmən] *n* an object supposed to have magic powers, a charm.

talk [tök] *v* to speak; to gossip; to give information. – *n* conversation; gossip; the subject of conversation; a discus-

sion or lecture. – *adj* **'talkative** inclined to chatter. – *n* **'talking-'to** a scolding. – **talk over** to discuss; to persuade; **talk round** to discuss (something) without coming to the main point; to persuade; **talk shop** *see* **shop.**

tall [töl] *adj* high or higher than usual or normal; *a tall person*: *a tall building*; hard to believe: *a tall story.* – *n* **'tallness.** – *ns* **'tallboy** a tall kind of chest of drawers; **tall order** (an instruction to do) something unreasonably difficult.

tallow ['talō] *n* the fat of animals, melted down to make soap, candles *etc*.

'tally *n* an account; a ticket, label; (*old*) a stick with notches cut in it for keeping an account or score: – *pl* **'tallies.** – *v* to agree (with). *His story tallies with yours*: – *pt* **'tallied.**

'tally-'ho! *interj* a cry used by huntsmen.

'talon *n* the claw of a bird of prey.

tambourine [tambə'rēn] *n* a kind of small one-sided drum with tinkling metal discs set into the sides.

tame *adj* (of animals) not wild, used to living with human beings; dull, not exciting. – *v* to make tame; to subdue, make humble.

'tamper *v* (with **with**) to meddle with so as to damage, alter *etc*. *He tampered with the machine.*

'tampon *n* a piece of cotton-wool *etc* inserted in a wound *etc* to stop bleeding or absorb blood.

tan *v* to make an animal's skin into leather by treating it with tannin; to make or become brown *esp* by exposure to the sun: – *pt* **tanned.** – *n* a yellowish-brown colour; suntan. – *ns* **'tanner** one whose work is tanning; **'tannery** a place where leather is made; **'tannin** any of several substances got from plants, used in tanning, dyeing *etc*; one of these substances present in tea.

'tandem *n* a long bicycle with two seats and two sets of pedals one behind the other. – *adv* one behind the other.

tang *n* a strong taste, flavour or smell: *the tang of the sea.*

tangent ['tanjənt] *n* a straight line which touches a circle or curve but does not cut into it. – **go off at a tangent** to go off suddenly in another direction or on a different line of thought.

tangerine [tanjə'rēn] *n* a small type of orange.

tangible ['tanjəbl] *adj* able to be felt by touching; real, definite: *tangible profits.*

tangle ['taŋgl] *v* to mix, twist together in

knots; to make or become difficult or confusing. – Also *n*.

tango ['taŋgō] *n* a type of dance, *orig* from S. America: – *pl* '**tangos**.

tank *n* a large container for water, petrol, gas *etc*; a heavy steel-covered vehicle armed with guns and moving on caterpillar wheels. – *n* '**tanker** a ship or large lorry for carrying oil; an aircraft carrying fuel.

'**tankard** *n* a large drinking mug of metal, glass *etc*.

tannin *see* **tan**.

'**tantalize** *v* to annoy, to torment, by offering something and keeping it out of reach. – *adj* '**tantalizing**.

'**tantamount: tantamount to** coming to the same thing as, equivalent to: *tantamount to stealing*.

'**tantrum** *n* a fit of rage or bad temper.

tap *n* a light touch or knock; any of several devices (*esp* one with a handle and a valve that can be opened and shut) for controlling the flow of liquid, gas *etc*. – *v* to knock or strike lightly; to draw on, start using (a source, supply *etc*); to attach a listening device secretly to (telephone wires): – *pt* **tapped**. – *n* '**tap-dance** a dance done with special shoes that make a tapping sound. – **on tap** ready, available, for use.

tape *n* a narrow band or strip of strong cloth used for tying *etc*; a piece of string stretched above the finishing line on a racetrack; a narrow strip of paper, plastic, metal *etc* used for measuring, sound recording, filming *etc*. – *v* to fasten with tape; to record (sound) on tape. – *ns* '**tape-measure** a strong tape marked off in centimetres *etc* for measuring; '**tape-recorder** a kind of instrument for recording sound on magnetic tape; '**tapeworm** a type of long worm sometimes found in the intestines of humans and animals. – **have (someone** or **something) taped** to have a thorough understanding of the characteristics, worth *etc* (of a person or thing). *They've had him taped from the start*.

'**tāper** *n* a long, thin kind of candle; a long waxed wick used for lighting lamps *etc*, a spill. – *v* to make or become thinner at one end. – *adj* '**tapering**.

tapestry ['tapəstri] *n* a cloth with designs or figures woven into it (hung on walls as a decoration or used to cover furniture): – *pl* '**tapestries**.

tapi'ōca *n* a kind of food got from the root of the cassava plant and used for making puddings.

'**tāpir** *n* a kind of wild animal something like a large pig.

tar *n* any of several kinds of thick, black, sticky liquid, got from wood or coal, used in roadmaking *etc*; (*coll*) a sailor. – *v* to smear with tar: – *pt* **tarred**. – *adj* '**tarry** like, or covered with, tar. – **tarred with the same brush** having the same faults (as someone else).

ta'rantula *n* a type of large, poisonous spider.

'**tardy** *adj* slow; late. – *n* '**tardiness**.

tare *n* the weight of a box, truck *etc* when empty; (in the Bible) a weed found growing among corn.

target ['tärgit] *n* a mark to fire or aim at, in shooting, archery, darts *etc*; something (*eg* a result) that is aimed at: *a target of £3,000*; a person at whom unfriendly remarks *etc* are aimed. *He is always the target of her criticism*.

'**tariff** *n* a list of prices; a list of the taxes to be paid on goods brought into a country.

'**tarma'cadam** *n* a mixture of small stones and tar used to make road surfaces *etc*. – *n* '**tarmac** the surface of a road or airport runway made of tarmacadam; '**Tarmac** ® (*US*) tarmacadam.

'**tarnish** *v* (of metals) to (cause to) become dull or discoloured; to spoil (one's reputation *etc*).

tar'paulin *n* (a sheet of) strong cloth made waterproof (with tar).

'**tarry** *v* to stay behind, linger; to be slow or late. – *adj see* **tar**.

tart *n* a small pie containing fruit, jam, vegetables *etc*. – *adj* (of taste) sharp, sour.

'**tartan** *n* woollen (or other) cloth woven with a pattern of squares of different colours, originally used by clans of the Scottish Highlands; any one of these patterns: *the Cameron tartan*. – Also *adj*.

'**tartar** *n* a substance that gathers on the teeth; a difficult, demanding and irritable person; a substance that forms inside wine casks. – **cream of tartar** a white powder obtained from the tartar from wine casks, used in baking.

task *n* a set piece of work to be done. – *ns* **task force** a group of people gathered together with the purpose of performing a special or specific task; '**taskmaster** one who sets and supervises tasks: *a hard taskmaster*. – **take to task** to scold, find fault with.

'**tassel** *n* a hanging bunch of threads, used as an ornament on a hat *etc*; anything like this, *esp* a hanging cluster of flowers such as a catkin.

tāste v to try by eating or drinking a little; to eat or drink a little of; to recognize (a flavour). *I can taste the lemon in this pudding*; to have a particular flavour: *to taste of garlic*; to experience: *to taste success*. – n the act or sense of tasting; a flavour; a small quantity (of food or drink); a liking: *a taste for music*; the ability to judge what is suitable (in behaviour, dress *etc*) or what is fine, beautiful *etc*. – adjs **'tasteful** showing good taste and judgement; **'tasteless** without flavour; not tasteful; **'tasty** having a good flavour.

'tatters npl torn, ragged pieces. – adj **'tattered** ragged.

'tattle n gossip. – Also v.

tat'too n a design marked on the skin by tattooing; a drumming or drumbeat; a military outdoor display at night with music *etc*. – v to prick coloured designs into the skin. – adj **tat'tooed** marked with tattoos.

taught *see* **teach**.

taunt v to tease or jeer at unkindly. – Also n.

taut adj pulled tight; tense, in a state of strain. – v **'tauten** to make or become tight.

tau'tology n a form of repetition in which the same thing is said in different ways, as in 'He *hit* and *struck* me'.

'tavern n a public house, an inn.

'tawdry adj cheap-looking and gaudy.

'tawny adj yellowish-brown.

tax n a charge made by the government on incomes, certain types of goods *etc*, to help pay for the running of the state; a strain, a burden: *a severe tax on his patience*: – pl **'taxes**. – v to make (persons) pay a tax; to put a strain on. *She will tax her strength*; (with **with**) to accuse of. *I taxed him with laziness*. – n **tax'ation** the act or system of taxing; taxes. – n **'taxpayer** one who pays taxes.

'taxi n a motor-car which may be hired, with a driver: – pl **'taxis**. – v to travel in a taxi; (of aeroplanes) to run along the ground: – pp **'taxiing**, pt **'taxied**.

'taxidermy n the art of preparing and stuffing the skins of animals to make them lifelike. – n **'taxidermist** a person who does this work.

tea n a type of plant grown in India, China *etc* or its dried and prepared leaves; a drink made by adding boiling water to these; any drink looking, or made, like tea: *beef tea*: *herbal tea*; an afternoon meal at which tea is drunk. – ns **'teacake** a kind of light, flat bun; **tea chest** a tall box of thin wood in which tea is packed for export, often used as a packing case for other goods; **'teacup** a cup of medium size from which to drink tea; **'teapot** a pot with a spout, for making and pouring tea; **'teaspoon** a small spoon.

teach v to give (someone) skill or knowledge. *Miss Brown teaches my daughter*; to give knowledge of, or training in (a subject or an art). *He teaches French*; to be a teacher. *She decided to teach*: – pt **taught** [töt]. – ns **'teacher** one whose job is to give knowledge or skill; **'teaching** the work of a teacher; guidance, instruction; (often *pl*) beliefs, rules of conduct *etc* that are preached or taught.

teak n a type of tree from the East Indies; its very hard wood; a type of African tree.

teal n a small water bird of the duck kind.

team n a group of people working together; a side in a game: *a football team*; two or more animals working together: *a team of oxen*. – n **team spirit** willingness to work loyally as a team or as a member of a team. – **team (up) with** to join together with, join forces with.

tear[1] n a drop of liquid coming from the eye; (*pl*) grief. – adj **'tearful** inclined to weep; causing tears. – n **tear gas** a type of gas which causes the eyes to stream with tears, used against rioters *etc*. – **in tears** weeping.

tear[2] [tār] v to pull with force (apart, away, down *etc*); to make a hole or split in (material *etc eg* by pulling it away from something it is attached to); to hurt deeply. *The story tears my heart*; (*coll*) to rush. *He tore off down the road*: – pt **tore**, pp **torn**. – n a hole, or split, made by tearing.

tease [tēz] v to annoy, irritate on purpose. *He's teasing the cat*; to pretend playfully to upset or annoy. *I'm only teasing*; to untangle (sheep's wool *etc*) with a comb; sort out (a problem or puzzle). – n one who teases. – n **'teaser** a problem, a puzzle.

teasel ['tēzl] n a type of prickly plant.

teat n the part of an animal through which milk passes to its young; a rubber object shaped like this attached to a baby's feeding bottle.

technical ['teknikəl] adj of, belonging to, a particular art or skill, *esp* of a mechanical or industrial kind: *a technical term*: *a technical expert*; according to strict laws or rules: *a technical defeat*. – n **techni'cality** a technical detail or point; the state of being technical: – pl techni'calities. – adv 'technically in a technical way; in technique; according to strict legal or technical rules, strictly speaking. – ns tech'nician one who has trained skill in the practical side of an art; technique [tek'nēk] the way in which a (skilled) process etc is carried out, a method; tech'nology (the study of) science applied to practical (esp industrial) purposes; technical means and skills of a particular civilization, period etc. – adj techno'logical. – n tech'nologist.

'teddy(bear) n a stuffed toy bear.

'tēdious adj long and tiresome. – n 'tedium the quality of being tedious.

tee n the square of level ground from which a golf-ball is driven; the peg or sand heap on which the ball is placed for driving. – v to place (a ball) on a tee.

teem v to be very plentiful; (with with) to be full of; to rain heavily.

teens npl the years of one's age from thirteen to nineteen. – adj 'teenage suitable for, or typical of, those in the teens. – n 'teenager a person in the teens.

teeth see tooth.

teethe [tēdh] v (of a baby) to grow the first teeth.

tee'tōtal adj never taking an alcoholic drink. – n tee'totaller.

tele- [teli] prefix at a distance.

'telegram n a message sent by telegraph.

'telegraph n an instrument or system for sending messages to a distance esp using wires and electricity. – v to send (a message) by telegraph. – adj tele-'graphic of a telegraph; short, brief, concise.

'telemessage n a message sent by telex or telephone (replacing telegram).

te'lepathy n the communication of ideas etc from one person to another without the use of sight, hearing or the other bodily senses. – adj tele'pathic.

'telephone n an instrument for speaking to a person at a distance, using an electric current which travels along a wire, or using radio waves. – v to send (a message) by telephone. – n te'lephonist one whose job is operating a telephone switchboard.

'tele'phōto adj of a lens used for obtaining large images of distant objects.

'teleprinter n a telegraph system in which messages are sent out at one place, and received and printed at another, by machines resembling typewriters; one of these machines.

'telescope n a kind of tube fitted with lenses or magnifying glasses which makes distant objects seem larger and nearer. – v to push or be pushed together so that one thing slides inside another; to fit, close or slide in such a way; to force together, compress.

'television n the sending of pictures from a distance, and the reproduction of them on a screen; (also television set) an apparatus for receiving these pictures. – v 'televise to send a picture (of) by television. They televised the football match.

telex ['teleks] n a Post Office service involving the sending of messages by means of teleprinters; a message sent in this way.

tell v to say or express in words. He is telling the truth; to give the facts of (a story); to inform, give information. He told me when the train left; to order, command. Tell her to go away!; to make out, to distinguish. Can you tell one twin from the other?; to give away a secret; to be effective, produce results. Good training will tell in the end: – pt tōld. – n 'teller one who tells; a bank clerk who receives and pays out money; one who counts votes at an election. – adj 'telling having a great or marked effect: a telling remark. – all told altogether, counting all; tell off (coll) to scold; tell on to have an effect on; to give information about (a person); tell tales to give away information not intended to be given about the misdeeds of others (n, adj 'tell-tale).

te'merity n rashness, boldness.

'temper n one's usual state of mind. He is of an even temper; a passing mood: in a good temper; a tendency to get angry easily; (a mood of) anger; the amount of hardness in metal, glass etc. – v to bring metal (or other material) to the right degree of hardness by heating and cooling; to make less severe. – lose one's temper to show anger.

'temperament n one's nature as it affects the way one feels, acts etc, disposition. – adj tempera'mental of temperament; excitable, emotional.

'temperate adj moderate, well-controlled in temper, eating or drinking habits etc; (of climate) neither very hot nor very cold. – ns 'temperance the state of being temperate; the habit of not drinking much (or any) alcohol; 'temperature amount, degree of heat or cold: a body heat higher than normal. The little boy has a temperature.

'tempest n a storm, with great wind. – adj tem'pestūous very stormy, like a tempest; (of a person etc) passionate, violently emotional.

'**template** *n* a thin plate cut in a certain shape, for use as a pattern for drawing round.

'**temple** *n* a building in which people worship; a church; either of the flat parts of the head on each side of the forehead.

'**tempo** *n* the speed at which music is played; the speed or rate of any activity: *the tempo of life*.

'**temporal** *adj* of, belonging to this world or this life only, not eternal or of the soul or spirit; belonging to time.

'**temporary** *adj* lasting, used *etc* only for a time, not permanent. – *v* '**temporize** to avoid taking a definite decision or action (in order to give oneself more time).

tempt *v* to try to persuade or to entice, *esp* to evil; to attract; to cause to be inclined (to). *I am tempted to end the quarrel.* – *n* **temp'tation** the act of tempting; the state or feeling of being tempted; that which tempts. – *adj* '**tempting** attractive.

ten *n* the number 10. – *adj* 10 in number. – *adj* **tenth** the last of ten (things). – *n* one of ten equal parts.

'**tenable** *adj* (of a position, a theory *etc*) able to be held or defended.

tenacious [tə'nāshəs] *adj* keeping a firm hold or grip; obstinate, persistent, determined. – *n* **tenacity** [tə'nasəti].

'**tenant** *n* one who pays rent to another for the use of a house, building, land *etc*. – *n* '**tenancy** the holding of a house, farm *etc* by a tenant; the period of this holding. – *adj* '**tenanted** occupied, lived in.

tend *v* to be likely or inclined (to do something). *These flowers tend to wilt*; (with **towards**) to move, lean, slope in a certain direction; to take care of, look after. – *n* '**tendency** a leaning or inclination (towards): *a tendency to alcoholism*: – *pl* '**tendencies**.

'**tender** *adj* soft, not hard or tough; easily hurt or damaged; hurting when touched; very young: *of tender years*; loving, gentle. – *v* to offer (a resignation *etc*) formally; to make a tender (for a job). – *n* an offer, *esp* to take on work, supply goods *etc* for a fixed price; a small boat that carries stores for a large one; a truck for coal and water attached to a steam railway engine. – *adj* '**tender-'hearted** inclined to be kind and sympathetic. – **legal tender** coins or notes which must be accepted when offered in payment.

'**tendon** *n* a tough cord joining a muscle to a bone or other part.

'**tendril** *n* a thin curling part of some kinds of climbing plants (as the pea) which attaches itself to a support; a curling strand of hair.

'**tenet** *n* a belief, opinion.

'**tennis** *n* a type of game for two or four players using rackets to hit a ball to each other over a net on the ground or floor. – *n* **tennis court** a place made level and prepared for tennis.

'**tenon** *n* a projecting bit at the end of a piece of wood made to fit a **mortise**.

'**tenor** *n* (a man with) a singing voice of the highest normal pitch for an adult male; a musical part for such a voice; the general course: *the even tenor of country life*; the general meaning (of a speech *etc*).

tense *n* the form of a verb that shows time of action, as in '*I was*' (**past tense**), '*I am*' (**present tense**), *I shall be* (**future tense**). – *adj* tightly stretched; nervous, strained: *tense with excitement*. – *n* '**tension** the act of stretching; the state of being stretched; strain, anxiety.

tent *n* a movable shelter made of canvas or other material, supported by poles, and secured by ropes and pegs to the ground.

'**tentacle** *n* a long thin flexible part of an animal used to feel, grasp *etc* (*eg* the arm of an octopus).

'**tentative** *adj* experimental, not fully worked out or developed: *a tentative offer*; uncertain, hesitating: *a tentative smile*.

'**tenterhooks: on tenterhooks** uncertain and very anxious about what will happen.

tenth *see* **ten**.

'**tenūous** *adj* slender, weak: *a tenuous connection*.

'**tenure** *n* the holding of property, or of a post or employment; the terms or conditions, or the period, of this.

'**tepid** *adj* (only) slightly warm.

tercen'tēnary *n* the 300th anniversary of an event *etc*.

term *n* a length of time: *a term of imprisonment*; a division of a school or university year: *the autumn term*; a word or expression: *medical terms*; (*pl*) the rules or conditions of an agreement or a bargain; (*pl*) fixed charges; (*pl*) footing, relationship, relations, between people. *He is on good terms with his neighbours*. – *v* to name, to call. – **come to terms, make terms** to reach an agreement or understanding: **in terms of** from the point of view of: *in* terms of numbers.

'**termagant** n a noisy, bad-tempered woman.

'**terminal** adj of, or growing at, the end: a terminal bud; occurring just before death: a terminal disease. – n an end; a point of connection in an electric circuit; a terminus; a building containing the arrival and departure areas at an airport; a place in a town centre connected by a bus service to a nearby airport.

'**terminate** v to bring, or come, to an end or limit. He terminated the discussion. – n termi'nation an act of ending; an end.

termi'nology n the special words or expressions used in a particular art, science etc.

'**terminus** n the end; one of the end places or points on a railway, bus route etc: – pls termini ['tɔrminē], 'terminuses.

'**termite** n a pale-coloured wood-eating kind of insect, like an ant.

tern n a type of sea bird like a small gull.

terrace ['terəs] n a raised level bank of earth like a big step; any raised flat place; a connected row of houses. – v to form into a terrace or terraces.

'**terra'cotta** n a brownish-red mixture of clay and sand used for small statues, pottery etc.

'**terra 'firma** n land as opposed to water.

ter'rain n a stretch of country (esp considered with reference to its physical features or as a battle field). The terrain is a bit rocky.

ter'restrial adj of, or living on, the earth.

'**terrible** adj causing great fear: a terrible sight; causing great hardship or distress: a terrible disaster; (coll) very bad: a terrible singer.

'**terrier** n a name given to many breeds of small dog.

'**terrify** v to frighten greatly: – pt 'terrified. – adj ter'rific causing terror, dreadful; (coll) huge, amazing; (coll) attractive, enjoyable etc: a terrific party.

'**territory** n a stretch of land, a region; the land under the control of a ruler or state; an area in which a salesman etc works; a field of activity or interest. – adj terri'torial of, belonging to a territory. – n territorial waters seas close to, and considered to belong to, a country.

'**terror** n very great fear; anything which causes great fear. – ns 'terrorism the activity or methods of terrorists; 'terrorist one who tries to frighten people into doing what he wants. – Also adj. –

v 'terrorize to frighten very greatly.

terse adj (of a speech etc) using few words; (of a person) speaking in such a way, curt. – n 'terseness.

test n a set of questions or exercises, a short examination; something done to find out whether a thing is good, reliable etc. We carried out tests on the new car; a means of finding the presence of: test for radioactivity; a happening that shows up a good or bad quality: a test of one's courage. – v to try, to carry out tests on. – ns test match in cricket etc, one of a series of matches between two countries; test pilot one who tests new aircraft; test tube a glass tube closed at one end used in chemical tests.

'**testament** n a written statement esp of what one desires to be done with one's personal property after death, a will. – n tes'tātor the person who writes a will: – fem tes'tātrix. – Old Testament, New Testament the two main divisions of the Bible.

'**testicle** n one of two glands in the male body in which sperm is produced.

'**testif̄y** v to give evidence esp in a law court; to make a (solemn) declaration of; (with to) to show, give evidence of. His recent action testifies to his inadequacy: – pt 'testified. – ns testi'mōnial (written) statement telling what one knows about a person's character, abilities etc; a gift given to show respect or thanks for services given; 'testimony the statement made by one who testifies; evidence.

testy adj easily made angry, irritable.

'**tetanus** n a type of serious disease which causes the muscles of the jaw and other parts to become stiff, caused by an infected wound etc.

tête-à-tête ['tātä'tāt] n a private talk between two people.

tether ['tedhər] n a rope or chain for tying an animal, allowing it to feed within a certain area only. – v to tie with a tether; to limit the freedom of.

text n the main part of a book, the written or printed words of the author, not the pictures, notes etc; a printed or written version of a speech, play etc; a passage from the Bible about which a sermon is preached; anything used as the subject of a speech, essay etc. – adj 'textual of, in, a text. – n 'textbook a book used for instruction, giving the main facts about a subject.

'**textile** adj of weaving; woven. – n cloth or fabric formed by weaving.

'**texture** n the quality of cloth resulting

from the way it has been woven: *loose texture*; the quality of a substance which is noticeable through touch or taste: *a rough texture: lumpy texture.*

than [dhan] *conj, prep* used in comparisons: *easier than I thought: better than usual.*

thane *n* (*hist*) a noble who held land from the king or a higher noble.

thank *v* to express appreciation, gratitude to (someone) for a favour, service, gift *etc.* – *npl* **thanks** expression of gratitude. – *adjs* '**thankful** grateful; relieved and glad; '**thankless** (of a task *etc*) neither worthwhile nor appreciated. – *n* '**thanksgiving** the act of giving thanks; a church service giving thanks to God; **Thanks'giving** (*US*) a day (the last Thursday of November) set apart for this. – **thanks to** with the help of. *We arrived on time, thanks to our friends*; owing to. *We were late, thanks to our car breaking down*; **thank you, thank you very much, thanks** polite expressions used to thank someone for something.

that [dhat] *adj, pron* used to point out a thing, person *etc* (opposite of **this**): *that woman over there. Don't say that* (*pl* **those** [dhōz]). Also *relative pron. Those are the clothes that he wore. Those are the people that we saw yesterday.* – *adv* to such an extent or degree. *I didn't know you'd be that late.* – *conj* used in reporting speech. *I said that I knew*; or to connect clauses. *It's good to know that you are well.*

thatch *n* straw, rushes *etc* used to make the roof of a house. – *v* to cover with thatch.

thaw *v* (of ice, snow *etc*) to melt; to cause to melt; (of frozen foods) to (cause to) cease to be frozen; to become friendly. – *n* the (time of) melting of ice and snow by heat; the change in the weather that causes this.

the [dhə, dhi] *adj* used to refer to particular person(s), thing(s) *etc*: *the boy in the park: the jacket I'm wearing*; or to refer to all or any of a general class or type. *The horse is of great use to man.* The form [dhə] is used before words beginning with a consonant, *eg* boy, or consonant sound, *eg* eucalyptus; [dhi] is used before words beginning with a vowel, *eg* ant, or vowel sound, *eg* honour.

theatre, (*US*) **theater** ['thēətər] *n* a place where public performances (of plays, *etc*) are seen; a room in a hospital for surgical operations; the profession of actors. – *adj* **the'atrical** of theatres

or acting; behaving as if in a play, over-dramatic.

thee [dhē] *pron* (*old*) you (*sing*) as the object of a sentence.

theft *see* **thief**.

their [dhār] *adj* belonging to them: *their car.* – *pron* **theirs**. *The red house is theirs.*

them [dhem] *pron* persons or things already spoken about (as object of a verb). *We've seen them*; those: *one of them over in the corner.* – *pron* **them'selves** used reflexively. *They hurt themselves*; used for emphasis. *They'll have to do it by themselves.*

theme *n* the subject of a discussion, essay *etc*; in music, a main melody which may often be repeated. – *n* **theme song, theme tune** a tune that is repeated often in a play, film, television series *etc* and is connected with a certain character, subject *etc.*

then [dhen] *adv* at that time; after that. *And then where did you go?* – *conj* in that case, therefore. *If you're ill, then why are you not in bed?*

thence [dhens] *adv* (*old*) from that time or place.

theodolite [thi'odəlīt] *n* a type of instrument for measuring angles, used in surveying land.

theology [thi'oləji] *n* the science of the study of God, and of man's duty to Him. – *n* **theo'lōgian** one who makes a study of theology. – *adj* **theological** [thiə'lojikəl].

'**thēorem** *n* (in mathematics) something (to be) proved by reasoning, shown step by step.

'**thēory** *n* an explanation which one thinks is correct but has not been proved or tested; the main ideas (*esp* as opposed to practice or performance) in an art, science *etc*: – *pl* '**theories**. – *adj* **theo'retic(al)** of theory, not actual experience or practice. – *adv* **theo'retically** in theory. – *v* '**theorize** to form theories.

'**therapy** *n* treatment of disease, disorder *etc.* – *adj* **therapeutic** [therə'pūtik] of therapy; healing, curing. – *n* '**therapist** one who gives therapeutic treatment: *a speech therapist.*

there [dhār] *adv* at, in or to that place. *What did you do there? There he is in the corner.* – *pron* used (with some form of the verb to be) as a subject of a sentence or clause when the real subject follows the verb. *There is no-one at home.* – *advs* **therea'bouts** approximately in that place or of that number, time *etc*; **there'after** after that; **there'by** by that means; **'therefore** for this or that reason; **thereu'pon** because of this or that; immediately.

therm *n* a unit of heat used in the measurement of gas. – *adj* **'thermal** of heat; of hot springs.

thermometer [thər'momitər] *n* an instrument for measuring temperature of various kinds.

'Thermos (flask) ® *n* a kind of vacuum flask.

'thermostat *n* a device for automatically controlling temperature (*eg* of a room).

the'saurus *n* a book giving information (as a dictionary, encyclopaedia *etc*) *esp* one listing words and their synonyms.

these *see* **this**.

'thesis *n* a long piece of written work (often done for a university degree) discussing a particular subject in detail; a statement of a point of view: – *pl* **'theses**.

they [dhā] *pron* some persons, animals or things already spoken about (used only as the subject of a verb). *They followed the others*.

thick *adj* not thin; having a large, or a certain, distance between opposite sides: *a thick slice*: *two inches thick*; (of a mixture *etc*) containing solid matter, semi-solid, stiff: *a thick soup*; dense, difficult to see through or to pass through: *thick fog*: *thick woods*; (of speech) not clear; (*coll*) stupid; (*coll*) very friendly. – *n* the thickest, most crowded or active part: *in the thick of the fight*. – *v* **'thicken** to make or become thick or thicker: *to thicken a sauce*. – *ns* **'thicket** a group of close-set trees and bushes; **'thickness** the quality of being thick; the distance between opposite sides; a layer. – *adjs* **'thick'set** closely set or planted; having a thick sturdy body; **'thick-'skinned** not sensitive or easily hurt.

thief [thēf] *n* one who steals: – *pl* **thieves**. – *v* **thieve** [thēv] to steal. – *n* **'thieving** the act or activity of thieving. – *adj* **'thievish** inclined to thieve; of a thief. – *n* **theft** [theft] (an act of) stealing.

thigh [thī] *n* the thick, fleshy part of the leg between the knee and the hip.

'thimble *n* a kind of metal *etc* cap to protect the finger and push the needle in sewing.

thin *adj* having little distance between opposite sides: *thin paper*: *thin slice*; slim, not fat; not dense or crowded: *a thin population*; poor in quality: *a thin wine*; (of a mixture *etc*) not thick or stiff, not containing solid matter: *a thin*

soup. – *v* to make or become thin or thinner: – *pt* **thinned**. – *n* **'thinness**. – *adj* **'thin-'skinned** sensitive, easily hurt.

thine [dhīn] *adj* (*old*) belonging to you (used before words beginning with a vowel or a vowel sound): *thine enemies*. – *pron*. *My heart is thine*.

thing *n* an object that is not living; (*coll*) a person: *a nice old thing*; (*pl*) belongings; any individual object, fact, quality, idea *etc* that one may think of or refer to. *Several things must be taken into consideration*.

think *v* to work things out, to reason; to form ideas in the mind; to believe, judge or consider. *I think that we should go*. *I think her stupid*; (with **of**) to intend. *He is thinking of leaving*: – *pt* **thought** [thöt]. – *n* **think better of** to change one's mind about; **think highly, much, well of** to have a good opinion of; **think nothing of** to have a poor opinion of; not to regard as difficult; **think out** to work out in the mind.

third *adj* the last of three (things). – *n* one of three equal parts. – *adj* **'third-'rate** of very poor quality.

thirst *n* the dry feeling in the mouth caused by lack of drink; an eager desire (for anything): *thirst for power*. – *v* to feel thirsty; (with **for**) to desire eagerly. – *adj* **'thirsty** having thirst; (of earth) parched, dry; eager (for).

'thir'teen *n* the number 13. – *adj* thirteen in number. – *adj* **'thir'teenth** the last of thirteen (things). – *n* one of thirteen equal parts.

'thirty *n* the number 30. – *adj* thirty in number. – *adj* **'thirtieth** the last of thirty (things). – *n* one of thirty equal parts.

this [dhis] *adj*, *pron* used to point out a thing, person *etc*, *esp* one nearby or close in time (opposite of **that**): *this book in my hand*. *Take this instead*; to such an extent or degree: *this early*: – *pl* **these** [dhēz].

thistle ['thisl] *n* a prickly type of plant with purple flowers. – *n* **'thistledown** the feathery bristles of the seeds of the thistle.

thither ['dhidhər] *adv* to that place.

tho' [dhō] short for **though**.

thong *n* a piece or strap of leather to fasten anything; the lash of a whip.

thorax ['thōraks] *n* the chest in the human or animal body; the middle section of an insect's body.

thorn *n* a sharp, woody prickly part sticking out from the stem of a plant; a bush or shrub with thorns, *esp* the hawthorn. – *adj* '**thorny** full of thorns; prickly; difficult, causing arguments: *a thorny problem.* – **thorn in the flesh** a cause of constant irritation.

thorough ['thurə] *adj* complete, absolute: *a thorough muddle*; (of a person *etc*) very careful, attending to every detail. – *adv* '**thoroughly**. – *ns* '**thoroughbred** an animal of pure breed; '**thoroughfare** a public street; a passage or way through or the right to use it: *no thoroughfare.* – *adj* '**thoroughgoing** thorough, complete.

those *see* **that**.

thou [dhow] *pron* (*old*) you as the subject of a sentence.

though [dhō] *conj* although. *Though he disliked it, he ate it all.* – *adv* (*coll*) however. *I wish I'd never said it, though.*

thought [thōt] *n* (the act of) thinking; that which one thinks, an idea; an opinion; consideration: *after much thought.* – *v see* **think**. – *adjs* '**thoughtful** full of thought; thinking of others, considerate; '**thoughtless** showing lack of thought; inconsiderate.

thousand ['thowzənd] *n* the number 1,000. – *adj* a thousand in number. – *adj* '**thousandth** the last of a thousand (things). – *n* one of a thousand equal parts.

thrall [thrôl]: **in thrall** enchanted or fascinated.

thrash *v* to beat or flog soundly; to move or toss violently (about); (with **out**) to discuss (a problem *etc*) thoroughly; to thresh (grain). – *n* '**thrashing** a flogging, a beating.

thread [thred] *n* a very thin line or cord of any substance (*eg* of cotton, wool, silk), *esp* one twisted and drawn out; the ridge which goes in a spiral round a screw; (in a story *etc*) a connected series of details in correct order. – *v* to put a thread through a needle, a bead *etc*; to make (one's way) in a narrow space. – *adj* '**threadbare** (of clothes) worn thin. – *n* '**threadworm** a kind of tiny, thread-like worm which lives in the intestines of humans.

threat [thret] *n* a warning that one intends to hurt or to punish; a warning of something bad that may come: *a threat of war*; something likely to cause harm: *a threat to our plans.* – *v* '**threaten** to make a threat. *He threatened to kill himself*; to suggest the approach of something unpleasant; to be a danger to.

three *n* the number 3. – *adj* 3 in number. – *See* also **third**.

thresh *v* to beat out (grain) from straw (also **thrash**).

threshold ['thresh-ōld] *n* a piece of wood or stone under the door of a building; a doorway; an entry or beginning: *on the threshold of a new era.*

threw *see* **throw**.

thrice *adv* three times.

thrift *n* careful management of money or goods, in order that one may save. – *adj* '**thrifty** careful about spending.

thrill *n* an excited feeling; quivering, vibration. – *v* to (cause to) feel excitement. – *n* '**thriller** an exciting story (*usu* about crime and detection). – *adj* '**thrilling** very exciting.

thrive *v* to grow strong and healthy; to get on well, be successful.

thro' [thrōō] short for **through**.

throat *n* the back part of the mouth where the openings to the stomach, windpipe and nose are; the front part of the neck.

throb *v* (of pulse *etc*) to beat *esp* more strongly than normal; to beat or vibrate rhythmically and regularly: – *pt* **throbbed**.

throes *npl* great suffering or struggle. – **in the throes of** in the middle of (a struggle, doing a task *etc*).

throm'bōsis *n* the forming of a clot in a blood vessel.

throne *n* the seat of a king or bishop; the king *etc* or his power.

throng *n* a crowd. – *v* to move in a crowd; to crowd, fill (a place).

'**throttle** *n* (in engines) the part through which steam or petrol can be turned on or off. – *v* to choke by gripping the throat.

through [thrōō] *prep* into from one direction and out of in the other: *through the tunnel*; from end to end, side to side *etc* of: *all through the performance*; by way of: *related through his grandmother*; as a result of: *through his mother's influence*; (*US*) from . . . to (inclusive). *Monday through Friday is five days.* – *adv* into and out, from beginning to end *etc*: *straight through*: *all the way through.* – *adj* without break or change: *a through train to London*; (*coll*) finished. *Are you through with the newspaper?*; (of a telephone call) connected. *I couldn't get through this morning.* – *adv* '**through-and-**'**through** completely, entirely: *a gentleman through-and-through.* – *prep* **through-**'**out** in all parts of: *throughout the country*; from start to finish of: *throughout the journey.* – Also *adv.*

throw [thrō] *v* to send through the air

with force; (of a horse *etc*) to cause (a person) to fall to the ground; to shape (pottery) on a wheel; to give (a party): – *pt* **threw** [thrōo], *pp* **thrown**. – *n* the act of throwing; the distance a thing is thrown: *within a stone's throw of the house*.

thru [thrōo] *(US)* short form of **through**.

thrush *n* a type of singing bird with a speckled breast; a type of disease causing white spots in the mouth: – *pl* '**thrushes**.

thrust *v* to push with force; to make a sudden push forward with a pointed weapon; (with **on, upon**) to force (something, oneself) upon: – *pt, pp* **thrust**. – *n* a stab; a pushing force.

thud *n* a dull, hollow sound like that made by a heavy body falling. – *v* to move or fall with such a sounds: – *pt* '**thudded**.

thug *n* a violent, brutal person.

thumb [thum] *n* the short, thick finger of the hand. – *v* to turn over or dirty (the pages of a book) with the thumb or fingers. – *n* '**thumbscrew** (*hist*) an instrument of torture which worked by squashing the thumbs. – **under someone's thumb** under one's control.

thump *n* a heavy blow. – *v* to beat heavily; to move or fall with a dull, heavy noise.

'**thunder** *n* the deep rumbling sound heard after a flash of lightning; any loud, rumbling noise. – *v* to produce the sound of, or a sound like, thunder; to shout out angrily. – *adjs* '**thunderous** like thunder; very angry; '**thundery** (of weather) sultry, bringing thunder. – *ns* '**thunderbolt** a flash of lightning followed by thunder; a very great and sudden surprise; '**thunderclap** a sudden roar of thunder. – *adj* '**thunderstruck** overcome by surprise.

Thursday ['thŏrzdi] *n* the fifth day of the week.

thus [dhus] *adv* in this or that manner. *He always talks thus*; to this degree or extent: *thus far*; because of this, therefore. *Thus, we must go on*.

thwart [thwört] *v* to hinder (a person) from carrying out a plan, intention *etc*; to prevent (an attempt *etc*). – *n* a cross seat for rowers in a boat.

thy (dhī) *adj* (*old*) belonging to you: *thy wife and children*.

thyme [tim] *n* a kind of small sweet-smelling herb used for seasoning food.

'**thyroid gland** *n* a large gland in the neck which influences the rate at which energy is used by the body.

ti'ara *n* a jewelled ornament for the head like a crown.

'**tibia** *n* the bone of the shin, the larger of the two bones between knee and ankle.

tic *n* a twitching motion of certain muscles, *esp* of the face.

tick *n* a light mark (√) used to mark as correct, to mark off in a list *etc*; a tiny animal which bites dogs, sheep *etc*; the cloth cover of a mattress, pillow *etc*; a small quick noise, made regularly by a clock, watch *etc*; (*coll*) a moment. – *v* to mark with a tick; (of a clock *etc*) to produce regular ticks. – *n* '**ticking** the noise made by a clock *etc*; the type of material from which mattress covers *etc* are made. – *n* **ticker tape** paper tape used in a kind of automatic machine that prints the latest news of share prices *etc*.

'**ticket** *n* a marked card or paper giving the owner a right to do something (*eg* travel by train *etc*, enter a theatre *etc*); a card or label stating the price *etc* of something.

'**tickle** *v* to excite the surface nerves of a part of the body by touching lightly and so cause to laugh; to please or amuse. – *adjs* '**ticklish** tickly; not easy to deal with: *a ticklish problem*; '**tickly** sensitive to tickling.

tide *n* the rise and fall of the sea which happens regularly twice each day; time, season: *Christmastide*. – *adj* '**tidal**. – *ns* **tidal wave** an enormous wave in the sea often caused by an earthquake *etc*; **tide over** to help to get over a difficulty for a time.

'**tidings** *npl* news.

'**tidy** *adj* in good order, neat; (*coll*) fairly big: *a tidy sum of money*. – *v* to make neat: – *pt* '**tidied**. – *n* '**tidiness**.

tie *v* to fasten with a cord, string *etc*; to knot or put a bow in (string, shoelaces *etc*); to join, unite; to limit, restrict: *tied to a tight schedule*; to score the same number of points (in a game *etc*), to draw: – *pt* **tied**. – *n* a band of fabric worn round the neck, tied with a knot or bow; something that connects: *ties of friendship*; something that restricts or limits; an equal score in a competition *etc*; a game or match to be played.

tier [tēr] *n* a row of seats *etc*, *usu* with others above or below it.

tiff *n* a slight quarrel.

tig *see* **tag**.

'**tiger** *n* a large, fierce, animal of the cat family with tawny coat striped with black: – *fem* '**tigress**. – *n* **tiger lily** a kind of lily with large spotted flowers.

tight [tīt] *adj* packed closely; firmly stretched, not loose; fitting (too) closely; (of money *etc*) hard to obtain; (*coll*) drunk. – *v* 'tighten to make or become tight or tighter. – *npl* tights a close-fitting garment covering the legs and body as far as the waist. – *n* 'tightrope a tightly stretched rope on which acrobats perform. – a tight corner an awkward situation.

tile *n* a piece of baked clay used in covering floors, roofs *etc*. – *v* to cover with tiles.

till *n* in a shop, a container or drawer for money. – *v* to prepare, cultivate (land); to plough. – *prep, conj see* until. – *n* 'tillage the act of tilling; tilled land.

'tiller *n* the handle of a boat's rudder.

tilt *v* to fall into, or place in, a sloping position; (*hist*) to joust; (*hist*) (with at) to attack on horseback, using a lance. – *n* a slant; a thrust, a jab. – at full tilt with full speed and force.

'timber *n* wood for building *etc*; trees suitable for this; a wooden beam in a house or ship.

timbre [tambr] *n* the quality of a (musical) sound or voice.

time *n* the hour of the day; the period at which something happens; (often *pl*) a particular period: *in modern times*; opportunity, interval of leisure: *no time to listen*; a suitable or right moment. *Now is the time to ask*; one of a number of occasions. *He won four times*; (*pl*) used to mean 'multiplied by': *two times four*; the rhythm or the rate of performance of a piece of music. – *adj* of time; arranged to go off *etc*, at a particular time: *a time bomb*. – *v* to measure the minutes, seconds *etc* taken by (work, someone racing *etc*); to choose the time for (well, badly *etc*): *to time one's entrance well*. – *adjs* 'timeless not belonging *etc* to any particular time; never ending: *timeless beauty*; 'timely coming at the right moment: *a timely reminder*. – *adj* 'time-honoured (of a custom *etc*) respected because it has lasted a long time. – *ns* 'timepiece (*old*) a clock or watch; 'timetable a list showing times of classes, arrivals or departures of trains *etc*. – at times occasionally; do time (*slang*) to serve a prison sentence; in time early enough; on time, up to time punctual; the time being the present time.

'timid *adjs* easily frightened; shy. – *n* ti'midity.

'timorous *adj* very timid.

'timpani, 'tympani *npl* kettledrums. – *n* 'timpanist, 'tympanist one who

plays these.

tin *n* an element, a silvery-white kind of metal; a box or can made of 'tinplate, thin iron covered with tin or other metal. – *v* to cover with tin; to pack (food *etc*) in tins: – *pt* tinned. – *adj* 'tinny like tin; (of sound) thin, high-pitched. – *n* 'tinfoil a very thin sheet of tin or other metal, used for wrapping.

'tincture *n* a slight tinge (of colour); a characteristic quality; a medicine mixed in alcohol.

'tinder *n* dry material easily set alight by a spark.

tine *n* a spike of a fork or of a deer's antler.

tinge [tinj] *v* to tint, colour slightly; (with with) to add a slight amount of something to. – *n* a slight amount (of colour, or other quality): *a tinge of blue*: *a tinge of sadness*.

tingle ['tingl] *v* to feel a sharp, thrilling or prickling sensation: *to tingle with excitement*: *to tingle with pain*. – Also *n*.

'tinker *n* a mender of kettles, pans *etc*. – *v* to work clumsily or unskilfully; to meddle (with).

'tinkle *v* to (cause to) make a light, ringing sound, to clink or jingle. – Also *n*.

'tinsel *n* a sparkling, glittering substance used for decoration.

tint *n* a variety or shade of a colour. – *v* to give a slight colour to.

'tiny *adj* very small.

tip *n* the top or point of anything *usu* of something thin or tapering; a piece of useful information, a hint; a small gift of money (to a waiter *etc*); a dump for rubbish; a tap or light stroke. – *v* to (cause to) slant; (with over) to (cause to) overturn; (with out, into) to empty out, into; (also with off) to give a hint to; to give a small gift of money; to put a tip on; to strike lightly: – *pt* tipped. – *n* 'tipster one who gives hints about racing.

'tipple *v* (*coll*) to take alcoholic drink in small quantities and often. – *n* an alcoholic drink. – *n* 'tippler.

'tipsy *adj* rather drunk.

'tiptoe *v* to walk on one's toes, often in order to go very quietly. – on tiptoe(s) (standing, walking *etc*) on one's toes.

ti'rade *n* a long, bitter, scolding speech.

'tire *v* to make, or become, weary or without patience or interest to go on. – *n* (*US*) a tyre. – *adjs* 'tired weary; (with of) bored with; 'tireless never becoming weary; never resting; 'tiresome making weary; long and dull; annoying: *a tiresome child*; 'tiring causing tiredness or weariness: *a tiring journey.*

'**tiro** *n* a beginner.

tissue ['tishōō] *n* substance of which the organs of the body are made: *muscle tissue*; a mass, network (of lies, nonsense *etc*); a piece of soft absorbent paper, *esp* a paper handkerchief; finely woven cloth. – *n* **tissue paper** a kind of thin, soft paper.

tit *n* any of several types of small birds: *blue tit*: *great tit*; a teat. – **tit for tat** blow for blow, repayment of injury with injury.

ti'tānium *n* an element, a light, strong type of metal used in aircraft.

'**titbit** *n* a tasty little piece of food *etc*.

tithe [tidh] *n* (*hist*) a tax paid to the church, a tenth part of one's income, produce *etc*.

'**titivate** *v* to make smarter, improve the appearance of. *She is always titivating* (*herself*).

'**title** *n* the name of a book, poem *etc*; a word in front of a name to show rank, honour or office held (as *Sir, Lord, Major etc*) or used in addressing any person formally (as *Mr, Mrs etc*); right, claim (to money, an estate *etc*). – *adjs* '**titled** having a title which shows noble rank; **titular** ['titūlər] having the title without the duties of an office *etc*. – *ns* **title deed** a document that proves a right to ownership (of a house *etc*); **title page** the page of a book on which are the title, author's name *etc*; **title rôle** the part in a play which is the same as the title *eg Hamlet.*

'**titter** *v* to giggle. – Also *n.*

'**tittle** *n* a very small part.

'**tittletattle** *n* a gossip, chatter.

titular *see* title.

to [tōō] *prep* showing the place or direction aimed for. *Let's go to the cinema*: *moving to the west*; showing the indirect object in a phrase, sentence *etc*. *Give it to me*; used before a verb to indicate the infinite. *To be great is to be misunderstood*; showing that one thing *etc* belongs with another in some way: *the key to the door*; compared with. *This is nothing to what happened before*; about, concerning. *What did he say to that?*; showing a ratio, proportion *etc*. *The odds are six to one against*; showing the purpose or result of an action. *Tear it to pieces.* – *adv* (almost) closed. *Pull the door to.* – **to and fro** backwards and forwards.

toad *n* a type of reptile like a large frog. – *v* '**toady** to give way to a person's wishes, or flatter him, to gain his favour. – *n* one who does this. – *n* '**toadstool** any of several kinds of mushroom-like fungi, often poisonous.

toast *v* to make bread brown by means of the direct heat of fire, gas flame, or electricity; to take a drink and wish success or health to (a person); to warm (one's feet *etc*) at a fire. – *n* bread toasted; the person to whom a toast is drunk; an act of drinking a toast; the call to drink a toast. – *n* '**toaster** an electric machine for toasting bread. – *ns* '**toastmaster** the announcer of toasts at a public dinner; '**toastrack** a stand with partitions for slices of toast.

to'bacco *n* a type of plant whose dried leaves are used for smoking. – *n* **to'bacconist** one who sells tobacco, cigarettes *etc*.

to'boggan *n* a kind of long, light sledge. – *v* to go in a toboggan.

to'day *adv, n* (on) this day; (at) the present time.

'**toddle** *v* to walk unsteadily, with short steps. – *n* '**toddler** a young child just able to walk.

to-do [tə'dōō] *n* a bustle, commotion.

toe *n* one of the five finger-like end parts of the foot; the front part of an animal's foot; the front part of a shoe, golf club *etc*. – **on one's toes** alert, ready for action; **toe the line** to do as one is told.

'**toffee** *n* a kind of sweet made of sugar and butter.

'**tōga** *n* (*hist*) the loose outer garment worn by a citizen of ancient Rome.

together [tə'gedhər] *adv* with each other, in place or time: *to stay together*: *to happen together*; in or into union or connection: *to nail planks together*; by joint action. *Together we won.*

togs *npl* (*coll*) clothes.

toil *v* to work hard and long; to walk, move *etc* with effort. – *n* hard work. – *n* '**toiler**.

'**toilet** *n* the act of washing oneself, doing one's hair *etc*; (a room containing) a receptacle for waste matter from the body, *usu* equipped with a water-supply for flushing this away.

'**tōken** *n* a mark or sign: *a token of my friendship*; a piece of metal or plastic, or a card *etc*, with an official marking, for use in place of money: *a bus token*: *a book token*. – *adj* acting as a symbol of one's opinion, intentions *etc*: *a token strike.*

told *see* tell.

tolerable ['tolərəbl] *adj* able to be borne or endured; fairly good: *a tolerable pianist*. – *n* '**tolerance** putting up with and being fair to people whose ways and opinions are different from one's own; an ability to resist the effects of (hardship, a drug *etc*). – *adj* 'tolerant. – *v* 'tolerate to bear, endure; to put up with; to allow. – *n* tole'ration.

tōll *v* to sound (a large bell) slowly, as for a funeral; (of a bell) to be sounded thus. – *n* a tax charged for crossing a bridge *etc*; loss, damage. – **take toll** to cause damage or loss.

'tomahawk *n* (*hist*) a light kind of axe once used as a weapon and tool by the N. American Indians.

tomato [tə'mätō, (*US*) tə'mātō] *n* a type of fleshy, juicy fruit, *usu* red, used in salads, sauces *etc*: – *pl* to'matoes.

tomb [tōōm] *n* a grave; a vault or chamber in which a dead body is placed. – *n* 'tombstone a stone placed over a grave in memory of the dead person.

tom'bōla *n* a kind of lottery.

'tomboy *n* a girl who prefers boy's activities *etc* to those of girls.

'tomcat *n* a male cat.

tome *n* a large heavy (*usu* learned) book.

tom'foolery *n* silly behaviour.

tomorrow [tə'morō] *adv, n* (on) the day after today; (in) the future. *The children of tomorrow will learn from our mistakes.*

'tom'tit *n* a kind of small bird.

'tomtom *n* a kind of Indian drum *usu* beaten with the hands.

ton [tun] *n* a measure of weight equal to 2240 pounds, about 1016 kilogrammes, a unit (100 cubic feet) of space in a ship. – *n* 'tonnage the space available in a ship, measured in tons. – **metric ton** (also **tonne**) 1000 kilogrammes.

tone *n* sound; the quality of sound: *a harsh tone*; (in music) one of the larger intervals in a scale (as between C and D); the quality of the voice as it varies in pitch, loudness *etc*, expressing the mood of the speaker: *a gentle tone*; a shade of colour; bodily firmness or strength. – *v* (sometimes with **in**) to blend, fit in well; (with **down**) to make or become softer, less harsh *etc*; (with **up**) to give strength to (muscles *etc*). – *n* **tonic** ['tonik] something (*eg* a medicine) which gives one strength and energy; (in music) the keynote of a scale. – *adj* of tones or sounds; of a tonic.

tongs *npl* an instrument for lifting and grasping coals, sugar lumps *etc*.

tongue [tuŋ] *n* the fleshy organ inside the mouth, used in tasting, speaking, and swallowing; anything resembling this, as a leather flap in a shoe or a long, thin strip of land; the tongue of an animal served as food; a language: *his mother tongue.* – *adj* 'tongue-tied not able to speak freely. – *n* 'tongue-twister a phrase, sentence *etc* not easy to say quickly, *eg* She sells sea shells.

tonic *see* tone.

tonight [tə'nīt] *adv, n* (on) the night of the present day.

tonnage, tonne *see* ton.

'tonsil *n* one of a pair of soft, fleshy lumps at the back of the throat. – *n* tonsil'litis reddening and painfulness of the tonsils.

tonsure ['tonshər] *n* the shaving of the top of the head of priests and monks; the part of the head so shaved.

too *adv* to a greater extent, in a greater quantity *etc* than is wanted or thought suitable. *He's too fat. It's too cold for swimming. There are too many people in the room*; (with a negative) very, particularly: *not feeling too well* (*ie* not feeling very well); also, as well. *I'm feeling quite cold, too.*

took *see* take.

tool *n* an instrument for doing work, *esp* by hand.

toot *n* the sound of a horn. – Also *v*.

tooth *n* any of the hard, bony objects projecting from the gums, arranged in two rows in the mouth, used for biting and chewing; anything resembling a tooth; the points of a saw, cogwheel, comb *etc*: – *pl* teeth. – *adj* 'toothsome pleasant to the taste. – *ns* 'toothache pain in a tooth; 'toothpaste, 'tooth-powder a kind of paste, powder, used for cleaning the teeth; 'toothpick a small sharp instrument for picking out anything (*eg* meat) from between the teeth. – **tooth and nail** with all one's strength and fury.

top *n* the highest part of anything; the upper surface; the highest place or rank; a lid; a circus tent; a kind of spinning toy. – *adj* highest, chief. – *v* to cover on the top; to rise above; to do better than; to reach the top of; to take off the top of: – *pt* topped. – *adj* 'topmost highest, uppermost. – *ns* 'topboot a tall boot with a light-coloured band round the top; 'topcoat an overcoat; top dog (*coll*) a winner or leader; top hat a man's tall silk hat. – *adjs* 'top-'heavy having the upper part too heavy for the lower; 'top'notch of the highest quality; 'top-'secret (of information *etc*) very secret.

'tōpaz *n* a type of precious stone, of various colours.

'tōper *n* one who takes much strong

alcoholic drink.

'**topi**, '**topee** *n* a helmet-like hat used in hot countries as a protection against the sun.

'**tōpiary** *n* the art of trimming bushes, hedges *etc* into decorative shapes, *eg* animals.

'**topic** *n* a subject spoken or written about. – *adj* '**topical** of present interest, concerned with present events; of a topic.

to'**pography** *n* (the description of) the features of the land in a certain region. – *adj* **topo'graphical**.

'**topple** *v* to (cause to) be unsteady and fall.

'**topsy'turvy** *adj, adv* (turned) upside down.

torch *n* a small hand-held light with a switch and electric battery; (*old*) a flaming piece of wood or coarse rope carried as a light: – *pl* '**torches**.

tore *see* **tear**.

toreador ['toriǝdör] *n* a bullfighter *esp* one mounted on horseback.

tor'ment *v* to treat cruelly and cause great suffering to; to worry greatly; to tease. – *n* '**torment** great pain, suffering, worry; a cause of these. – *n* **tor'mentor**.

torn *see* **tear**.

tor'nādo *n* a violent whirling wind that causes great damage: – *pl* **tor'nadoes**.

tor'pēdo *n* a large cigar-shaped type of missile fired by ships, planes *etc*: – *pl* **tor'pedoes**. – *v* to hit or sink (a ship) with a torpedo: – *pt* **tor'pedoed**.

'**torpid** *adj* slow, dull, stupid. – *ns* **tor'pidity**, '**torpor** dullness.

'**torrent** *n* a rushing stream; a heavy downpour of rain; a violent flow (of words *etc*): *a torrent of abuse*. – *adj* **torrential** [tǝ'renshǝl] like a torrent.

'**torrid** *adj* parched by heat; very hot.

'**torso** *n* the body, without head or limbs.

tortoise ['törtǝs] *n* a four-footed, slow-moving kind of reptile, covered with a hard shell. – *n* '**tortoiseshell** the shell of a kind of sea turtle, used in making ornamental articles. – *adj* made of this shell; of the colour of this shell, mottled brown, yellow and black: *a tortoiseshell cat*.

'**tortūous** *adj* winding, roundabout, not straightforward.

'**torture** *v* to treat a person cruelly or painfully, as a punishment or to force him to confess something; to cause to suffer. – *n* the act, or activity, of torturing; great suffering.

Tory ['töri] *n, adj* (a member) of the Conservative Party.

toss *v* to throw up in the air; to throw up (a coin) to see which side is uppermost when it falls; to turn oneself restlessly from side to side; (of a ship) to be thrown about by rough water. – Also *n*. – **toss up** to toss a coin.

tot *n* a little child; a small amount of alcoholic drink, *usu* spirits. – **tot up** to add up.

'**tōtal** *adj* whole: *total number*; complete. *The car was a total wreck.* – *n* the entire amount; the sum of amounts added together. – *v* to add up; to amount to: – *pt* '**totalled**. – *adv* '**totally** completely. – *adj* **totali'tarian** of government by a single party that allows no rivals. – *n* '**totalizator** (for short, **tote**) a machine to work out the amount of money to be paid to those who bet on winning horses.

tote *see* **total**.

'**tōtem** *n* among N. American Indians *etc*, an (image of an) animal or plant used as the badge or sign of a tribe. – *n* **totem pole** a pole on which totems are carved and painted.

'**totter** *v* to shake as if about to fall; to stagger.

toucan ['tōōkǝn] *n* a type of S. American bird with a very big beak.

touch [tuch] *v* to feel (with the hand); to come or be in contact (with). *A leaf touched his cheek*; to move, affect the feelings of. *The story touched those who heard it*; to mark slightly with colour. *The sky was touched with gold*; to reach the standard of. *I can't touch him at chess*; to have anything to do with. *I wouldn't touch a job like that*; to eat or drink. *He won't touch alcohol*; to concern (a person); (*coll*) to persuade (someone) to lend one money. *I touched him for £1.* – *n* the act of touching; the physical sense of touch. *The blind man felt his way by touch*; a small quantity or degree: *a touch of salt*; (of an artist, pianist *etc*) skill or style; (in football) the ground beyond the edges of the pitch marked off by '**touchlines**. – *prep* '**touching** about, concerning. – *adj* causing emotion, moving. – *adj* '**touchy** easily offended. – *n* '**touchiness**. – *adj* '**touch-and-'go** very uncertain. *It's touch-and-go whether we'll get it done on time.* – *n* '**touchstone** a test or standard of measurement of quality *etc*. – **in (out of) touch with** in (not in) communication or contact with; **touch down** (of an aircraft) to land (*n* '**touchdown**); **touch off** to cause to happen: *touch off a riot*; **touch on** to mention briefly;

tough / **trade**

touch up to improve (a drawing or photograph *etc*) by making details clearer *etc*.

tough [tuf] *adj* strong, not easily broken; (of meat *etc*) hard to chew; (of persons) strong, able to stand hardship or strain; difficult to cope with or overcome: *tough opposition*. – *v* 'toughen to (cause to) become tough.

toupee ['tōōpā] *n* a small wig or piece of false hair worn to cover a bald spot.

tour [tōōr] *n* a journey in which one visits various places; a pleasure trip. – *v* to make a tour (of). – *ns* 'tourism the activities of tourists and of those who cater for their needs and pleasure; 'tourist a person who travels for pleasure, and visits places of interest to him.

tournament ['tōōrnəmənt] *n* a competition (in chess, tennis *etc*) involving many contests and players; (*hist*) a meeting at which knights fought together on horseback.

tourniquet ['tōōrnikā] *n* a bandage tied tightly round a limb to prevent great loss of blood from a wound.

tousled ['towzld] *adj* (*esp* of hair) untidy, tangled.

tout *v* to go about looking for support, votes, buyers *etc*. – *n* one who does this; one who gives information useful to people who bet on horse races.

tow [tō] *v* to pull (*eg* a ship, a barge, a motor-car) with a rope (attached to another ship, a horse or another vehicle). – *n* the act of towing; the rope used for towing; the coarse part of flax or hemp. – *adj* 'tow-'headed with light-coloured hair; having tousled hair. – *n* 'towpath a path alongside a canal used by horses which tow barges. – in tow under protection or guidance; on tow being towed.

towards, toward [tə'wôrd(z)] *prep* (moving, keeping) in the direction of (a place, person *etc*). *He walked towards his house*; to (a person, thing *etc*): *his attitude towards his son*; as a help, contribution to. *He gave £1 towards the price of her present*; near, about (a time *etc*): *towards four o'clock*.

towel ['towəl] *n* a cloth or piece of absorbent paper for drying or wiping (*eg* the skin after washing). – *v* to rub with a towel: – *pt* 'towelled. – *n* 'towelling a kind of (cotton) cloth often used for making towels.

tower ['towər] *n* a high narrow building, or a high narrow part of another building (*eg* of a castle). – *v* to rise high (over, above). – *adj* 'towering rising high; violent: *a towering rage*.

town [town] *n* a place, larger than a village, in which there is a large collection of buildings, including houses, shops *etc*. – *ns* town crier (mainly *hist*) one whose job it is to make public announcements in a town; town hall the building where the official business of a town is done; town planning planning of the future development of a town.

toxin *n* a naturally occurring poison (produced by animals, plants, bacteria *etc*). – *adj* 'toxic poisonous; caused by poison.

toy *n* an object made for a child to play with; an object for amusement only. – toy with to play or trifle with.

trace *n* a mark or sign left behind; a footprint; a small amount; a line drawn by an instrument recording a change (*eg* in temperature); (*pl*) the straps by which a horse pulls a cart *etc* along. – *v* to follow the tracks of, or the course of; to copy (a drawing *etc*) on thin, transparent paper placed over it. – *adj* 'traceable able to to be traced (to). – *ns* tracery ['trāsəri] the decorated stonework holding the glass in some church windows; 'tracing a traced copy.

track *n* a mark left; (*pl*) footprints; a path or rough road; a racecourse (for runners, cyclists *etc*); a railway line; an endless band on which wheels of a tank *etc* travel. – *v* to follow by the marks, footprints *etc* left by (*eg* an animal). – *n* 'tracksuit a warm suit worn while jogging *etc*, before and after an athletic performance *etc*. – keep or lose track of to keep or fail to keep aware of the whereabouts or progress of; make tracks (for) to set off (towards); track down to pursue or search for (someone or something) until caught or found.

tract *n* a stretch of land; a short pamphlet, *esp* on a religious subject; a system made up of connected parts of the body: *the digestive tract*.

tractable *adj* easily made to do what is wanted.

traction *n* the act of pulling or dragging; the state of being pulled. – *n* traction engine a road steam-engine.

tractor *n* a motor vehicle for pulling loads, ploughs *etc*.

trade *n* the buying and selling of goods; one's occupation, craft, job. *He is a carpenter by trade*. – *v* to buy and sell; to have business dealings (with); to deal (in); to exchange, swap. – *n* 'trader one who buys and sells. – *ns* 'trademark a registered mark or name put on goods to show that they are

333

made by a certain company (and forbidden to be used by others); **'trades-man** a shopkeeper; a workman in a skilled trade; **trade union** a group of workers of the same trade who join together to bargain with employers for fair wages *etc*; **trade unionist** a member of a trade union; **'tradewind** a wind which blows towards the equator (from the north-east and south-east). – **trade in** to give as part-payment for something else (*eg* an old car for a new one); **trade on** to take (*usu* unfair) advantage of. *He traded on the fact that the manager was his cousin.*

tra'dition *n* the handing-down of customs, beliefs, stories *etc* from generation to generation; a custom, belief *etc* handed down in this way. – *adj* **tra'ditional**.

'traffic *n* the motor-cars, buses, cycles, boats *etc* which use roads, waterways *etc*; trade; dishonest dealings (as in drugs). – *v* to trade; to deal (in): – *pt* **'trafficked**. – *npl* **traffic lights** lights of changing colours for controlling traffic at road junctions or street crossings.

tragedy ['trajədi] *n* a very sad event or one with very unfortunate results; a play about unhappy events and with a sad ending: – *pl* **'tragedies**. – *adj* **'tragic** of tragedy; very sad.

trail *v* to draw along, in or through: *trailing his foot through the water*; to hang down (from) or be dragged loosely behind; to hunt (animals) by following footprints *etc*; to walk wearily; (of a plant) to grow over (such as the ground, a wall). – *n* a track (of an animal); a pathway through a wild region; something left stretching behind one: *a trail of dust.* – *n* **'trailer** a vehicle pulled behind a motor-car; in a cinema, a short film advertising a longer film to be shown at a later date.

train *n* a railway engine with carriages or trucks; the part of a dress which hangs down behind the wearer; the attendants who follow an important person; a line (of thought, events *etc*); a line of animals carrying persons or baggage. – *v* to prepare oneself by practice, exercise *etc* (as for a sporting event, a job or profession); to educate: *a child trained in good habits*; to exercise (animals or people) in preparation for a race *etc*; to tame and teach (an animal); (with **on** or **at**) to aim, point (a gun, telescope *etc*) at; to make (a tree or plant) grow (in a certain direction). – *ns* **trai'nee** a person who is being trained; **'trainer**

one who trains people or animals for a sport, or race, circus performance *etc*; **'training** preparation for a sport; experience or learning of the practical side of a job. – *n* **'trainbearer** one who carries the train of a person's dress, robe *etc*.

trait *n* a point that stands out in a person's character. *Patience is one of his good traits.*

'traitor *n* one who goes over to the enemy's side, or gives away secrets to the enemy; one who betrays when he has been trusted. – *adj* **'traitorous**.

tra'jectory *n* the curved path of something (*eg* a bullet) moving through the air or through space.

tram *n* a long car running on rails and driven *usu* by electric power for carrying passengers along streets (also **'tramcar**). – *ns* **'tramline** a rail of tramway; (*pl*) in tennis or badminton, the parallel lines marked at the sides of the court; **'tramway** a system of tracks on which trams run.

'trammel *n* (often *pl*) anything which hinders movement. – *v* to hinder: – *pt* **'trammelled**.

tramp *v* to walk with heavy footsteps; to walk along, over *etc*. *He tramped the streets in search of a job.* – *n* a person with no fixed home and no job, who lives *usu* by begging; a journey made on foot; the sound of marching feet; a small cargo-boat with no fixed route.

'trample *v* to tread under foot, stamp on; (*usu* with **on**) to treat roughly or unfeelingly; to tread heavily.

trampoline ['trampəlēn] *n* a bed-like framework holding a sheet of elastic material for bouncing on, used by gymnasts *etc*.

trance *n* a sleeplike or half-conscious state.

'tranquil *adj* quiet, peaceful. – *n* **tran'quillity**. – *v* **'tranquillize** to make calm. – *n* **'tranquillizer** a drug to calm the nerves or cause sleep.

trans- [trans, tranz] *prefix* across, through.

transact [tran'sakt] *v* to do (a piece of business). – *n* **tran'saction** a piece of business, a deal.

transatlantic [tranzət'lantik] *adj* crossing the Atlantic Ocean: *transatlantic yacht race*; across or over the Atlantic: *transatlantic friends.*

transcend [tran'send] *v* to be, or rise, above. *He transcended the difficulty*; to be, or do, better than.

trans'cribe *v* to copy from one book *etc* into another or from one form of writing (*eg* shorthand) into another (*eg* ordinary writing); to adapt (a piece of music) for a particular instrument, group of instruments *etc*. – *n* **trans'cription** [trans'kripshən] the act of transcribing: a written copy.

'**transept** *n* the part of a church which lies across the main part.

trans'fer *v* to remove to another place; to hand over to another person: – *pt* **trans'ferred**. – *n* '**transfer** the act of transferring; a design or picture which can be transferred from one surface to another. – *adj* **trans'ferable** able to be transferred. – *n* '**transference**.

transfigure [trans'figər] *v* to change (greatly and for the better) the form or appearance of. – *n* **transfigu'ration**.

trans'fix *v* to make unable to move, act *etc* (*eg* because of surprise): *transfixed by the sight*; to pierce through (as with a sword).

trans'form *v* to (cause to) change in shape or appearance *etc*. – *ns* **transfor'mation**; **trans'former** an apparatus for changing electrical energy from one voltage to another.

transfuse [trans'fūz] *v* to pass (liquid) from one thing to another; to transfer (blood of one person) to the body of another. – *n* **trans'fusion** the act of transfusing *esp* the act of passing blood from one person into the veins of another for medical purposes.

transgress [trans'gres] *v* to break a rule, law *etc*. – *ns* **trans'gression** the act of breaking a rule, law *etc*; **trans'gressor** one who breaks a rule, law *etc*.

transient ['tranziənt] *adj* not lasting, passing. – *n* '**transience**.

transistor [tran'sistər] *n* a small device, made up of a crystal enclosed in plastic or metal, which controls the flow of an electrical current; a portable radio set using these.

transit ['transit] *n* the carrying or movement of goods, passengers *etc* from place to place; the passing of a planet between the sun and the earth. – *n* **tran'sition** [tran'zishən] a change from one form, place, appearance *etc* to another. – *adjs* **tran'sitional**; '**transitory** lasting only for a short time.

'**transitive** *adj* in grammar, of a verb, having an object (as the verb '*hit*' in 'He *hit* the ball').

translate [trans'lāt] *v* to turn (something said or written) into another language: *to translate from French into English*. – *ns* **trans'lation** the act of translating; something trans-

lated; **trans'lator** one who translates.

translucent [trans'lōōsnt] *adj* allowing light to pass through, but not transparent. – *n* **trans'lucence**.

transmit [tranz'mit] *v* to pass on (*eg* a message, news, heat); (of a television or radio station) to send out signals which are received as programmes: – *pt* **trans'mitted**. – *ns* **trans'mission** the act of transmitting; a radio or television broadcast; **trans'mitter** an instrument for transmitting (*esp* radio signals).

'**transom** *n* a beam across a window or the top of a door.

trans'parent *adj* able to be seen through; easily seen to be true or false: *a transparent excuse*. – *n* **trans'parency** the state of being transparent; a photograph printed on transparent material and viewed by means of light shining through it: – *pl* **trans'parencies**.

trans'pire *v* (of secrets) to become known; to happen. *He told me what had transpired*; to pass out (moisture *etc*) through pores of the skin or through the surface of leaves.

trans'plant *v* to lift and plant (a growing plant) in another place; to remove (skin) and graft it on another part of the same body; to remove (an organ, *eg* a kidney) and graft it in another person or animal. – *n* '**transplant** the act of transplanting; a transplanted organ, plant *etc*. – *n* **transplan'tation**.

transport [trans'pört] *v* to carry from one place to another; to overcome with strong feeling: *transported with delight*; (*hist*) to send (a prisoner) to a prison in a different country. – *n* '**transport** the act of transporting; any means of carrying persons or goods: *rail transport*: *air transport*; strong feeling: *transports of joy*. – *n* **transpor'tation** the act of transporting; means of transport; (*hist*) punishment of prisoners by sending them to a prison in a different country.

transpose [trans'pōz] *v* to cause (two things) to change places; to change (a piece of music) from one key to another. – *n* **transpo'sition**.

transverse ['tranzvörs] *adj* lying, placed *etc* across: *transverse beams in the roof*.

trap *n* a device for, or means of, catching animals *etc*; a plan or trick for taking a person by surprise; a bend in a pipe which is kept full of water, for preventing the escape of air or gas; a carriage with two wheels. – *v* to catch in a trap, or in such a way that escape is not possible: – *pt* **trapped**. – *n* '**trapper** one who makes a living by catching animals, *usu* for their skins and fur. – *n* **'trap'door** a door in a floor or ceiling.

tra'peze *n* a swing used in performing gymnastic exercises or feats (as in a circus).

tra'pēzium *n* a figure with four sides, two of which are parallel.

'trappings *npl* clothes or ornaments suitable for a particular person or occasion; ornaments put on horses.

trash *n* something of little worth, rubbish. – *adj* **'trashy**. – *n* **'trash-can** (*US*) a container for household rubbish, a dustbin.

trauma ['trömə] *n* injury (*eg* a wound) to the body; a very violent or distressing experience which has a lasting effect on a person; a condition (of a person) caused in this way. – *adj* **trau'matic**.

'travail *n* (*old*) hard work. – Also *v*.

'travel *v* to go on a journey; to move; to go along, across; to visit foreign countries: – *pt* **'travelled**. – *n* the act of travelling. – *n* **'traveller** one who travels; a travelling representative of a business firm who tries to obtain orders for his firm's products.

tra'verse *v* to go across, pass through. – *n* **'traverse** something that crosses or lies across; a going across a rock face *etc*; a zigzag track of a ship.

travesty ['travəsti] *n* a poor or ridiculous imitation (of something): *a travesty of justice*: – *pl* **'travesties**.

trawl *v* to fish by dragging a trawl along the bottom of the sea. – *n* a wide-mouthed, bag-shaped net. – *n* **'trawler** a boat used for trawling.

tray *n* a flat piece of wood, metal *etc* with a low edge, on which dishes *etc* may be carried.

treachery ['trechəri] *n* the act of betraying those who have trusted one. – *adj* **'treacherous** betraying, or likely to betray; dangerous: *a treacherous path over the marsh*. – *adv* **'treacherously**.

'treacle *n* a thick, dark syrup produced from sugar when it is being refined.

tread [tred] *v* to walk on or along; (with **on**) to put one's foot on; to crush, trample under foot: – *pt* **trod**, *pp* **'trodden**. – *n* a step; one's way of walking; the part of a tyre which touches the ground. – *n* **'treadle** the part of a machine which is worked by the foot. – *n* **'treadmill** (*hist*) a mill turned by the weight of persons who were made to walk on steps fixed round a big wheel; any tiring, routine work. – **tread on someone's toes** to offend or upset a person; **tread water** to keep oneself afloat in an upright position by

moving the arms and legs.

treason ['trēzn] *n* disloyalty to one's own country or its government (*eg* by giving away its secrets to an enemy, trying to overthrow it) (also **high treason**). – *adj* **'treasonable** consisting of, or involving, treason.

treasure ['trezhər] *n* a store of money, gold, precious stones *etc*; anything of great value or highly prized. – *v* to value greatly; to keep carefully because one values greatly. *She treasures the mirror her mother left her*. – *ns* **'treasurer** one who has charge of the money (*eg* of a club); **'Treasury, 'treasury** the part of a government which has charge of the country's money: – *pl* **'treasuries**. – *n* **'treasure-trove** treasure or money found hidden, the owner of which is unknown.

treat *v* to deal with, handle, use, act towards (in a certain manner). *I was treated very well in prison*; to try to cure a person (of a disease); to try to cure (a disease); to write or speak about; to buy (someone a meal, drink *etc*); to deal (with), try to arrange (a peace treaty *etc* with). – *n* something special (*eg* an outing) that gives much pleasure. *They went to the pantomime as a treat*. – *n* **'treatment** the act of treating (*eg* a disease); remedies or medicine: *a new treatment for cancer*; the way in which any thing or person is dealt with: *rough treatment*.

treatise ['trētiz] *n* a long, detailed essay *etc* on some subject.

'treaty *n* an agreement made between countries: – *pl* **'treaties**.

'treble *adj* threefold, three times the normal: *wood of treble thickness*; high in pitch: *treble note*. – *v* to (cause to) become three times as great. – *n* the highest part in singing; one (*esp* a child) who sings the treble part of a song.

tree *n* the largest kind of plant with a thick, firm wooden stem and branches; anything like a tree in shape.

trek *n* a long or wearisome journey; (*old*) a journey, *esp* by wagon. – *v* to make a long hard journey; (*old*) to make a journey by wagon: – *pt* **trekked**.

'trellis *n* a network of strips, *usu* of wood, used for holding up growing plants *etc*: – *pl* **'trellises**.

'tremble *v* to shake (*eg* with cold, fear, weakness); to feel fear (for another person's safety *etc*). – *n* the act of trembling; a fit of trembling.

tre'mendous *adj* very great or strong; (*coll*) very good, excellent. – *adv* tre'**mendously** (*coll*) very.

'**tremor** *n* a shaking or quivering.

'**tremūlous** *adj* shaking; showing fear: *a tremulous voice*.

trench *n* a long narrow ditch dug in the ground (*eg* by soldiers as a protection against enemy fire): – *pl* '**trenches**. – *v* to dig a trench in. – *n* '**trenchcoat** a kind of waterproof overcoat with a belt.

'**trenchant** *adj* going deep, hurting: *a trenchant remark*; (of a policy *etc*) effective, vigorous.

'**trencher** *n* (*old*) a wooden plate. – *n* '**trencherman** a person able to eat large meals: *a good trencherman*.

trend *n* a general direction: *the trend of events*. – *adj* '**trendy** (*coll*) fashionable.

trepi'dation *n* fear, nervousness.

'**trespass** *v* to go illegally (on another's land *etc*); (with **on**) to take or demand too much of. *She trespasses on my time*; to sin. – *n* the act of trespassing: – *pl* '**trespasses**. – *n* '**trespasser**.

tress *n* a (long) lock of hair; (*pl*) '**tresses** hair, *usu* long.

trestle ['tresl] *n* a wooden support with legs, used for holding up a table, platform *etc*.

trews [trōōz] *npl* tartan trousers.

tri- *prefix* three.

trial *see* **try**.

triangle ['triaŋgl] *n* a figure with three sides and three angles: △; a triangular metal musical instrument, played by striking with a small rod. – *adj* **tri'angūlar** having the shape of a triangle.

tribe *n* a race or family who are all descended from the same ancestor; a group of families, *esp* of a primitive or wandering people ruled by a chief. – *adj* '**tribal**. – *n* '**tribesman** a man belonging to a tribe.

tribū'lation *n* great hardship or sorrow.

tri'būnal *n* a group of persons appointed to give judgement, *esp* on an appeal (*eg* against a high rent); a court of justice.

'**tribune** *n* (*hist*) a high official elected by the common people in ancient Rome.

'**tribūtary** *n* a stream that flows into a river or other stream; one who gives money as a tribute: – *pl* '**tributaries**. – Also *adj*.

'**tribute** *n* an expression, in word or deed, of praise, thanks *etc*: *a warm tribute to his courage*; money paid regularly by one nation or ruler to another in return for protection or peace.

trice: in a trice in a very short time.

trick *n* a cunning or skilful action (to puzzle, deceive, amuse *etc*): *a conjuring trick*: *a dirty trick*; in card games, the

cards picked up by the winner when each player has played a card. – *adj* meant to deceive: *trick photography*. – *v* to cheat by some quick or cunning action. – *ns* '**trickery** cheating; '**trickster** one who deceives by tricks. – *adj* '**tricky** not easy to do.

'**trickle** *v* to flow in small amounts; to come, go *etc* slowly and in small numbers. *People began to trickle into the hall*. – Also *n*.

tricolour, (*US*) **tricolor** ['trikələr] *n* the flag of France, which is made up of three upright stripes (red, white, blue).

'**tricycle** *n* a kind of cycle with three wheels.

'**trident** *n* a three-pronged spear.

tried *see* **try**.

tri'ennial *adj* lasting for three years; happening every third year.

tries *see* **try**.

'**trifle** *n* anything of little value; a small amount; a pudding of whipped cream, sponge-cake, wine *etc*. – *v* (with **with**) to act towards without sufficient respect. *I am in no mood to be trifled with*; to amuse oneself in an idle way (with). *He trifled with her affections*; to behave in a light, thoughtless manner. – *adj* '**trifling** very small in value or quantity.

'**trigger** *n* a small lever on a gun which, when pulled with the finger, causes the bullet to be fired. – *v* (*usu* with **off**) to start, be the cause of, an important event, chain of events *etc*.

trigonometry [trigə'nomətri] *n* the branch of mathematics which has to do chiefly with the relationship between the sides and angles of triangles. – *adj* **trigono'metric(al)**.

trill *v* to sing, play or utter in a quivering or bird-like way. – *n* a trilled sound; in music, a rapid repeating of two notes several times.

'**trillion** *n* a million million millions; (*US*, now often in Britain) a million millions.

'**trilogy** *n* a group of three related plays, novels *etc* by the same author, meant to be seen or read as a whole.

trim *v* to clip the edges or ends of (*eg* a hedge, the hair); to arrange (sails, cargo) so that a boat is ready for sailing; to decorate (*eg* a hat): – *pt* **trimmed**. – *n* the act of trimming; dress: *in hunting trim*. – *adj* tidy, in good order, neat. – *n* '**trimming** a fancy part added (*eg* to a dress, cake) as a decoration; a bit cut off while trimming (cloth, paper *etc*). – **in good trim** in good order; fit.

'**Trinity** *n* in Christian belief, the three

Persons (Father, Son and Holy Ghost) who together make one God.

'**trinket** *n* a small ornament (*esp* one of little value).

trio ['trēō] *n* (a piece of music for) three performers; three people or things: – *pl* '**trios**.

trip *v* (often with **up**) to (cause to) stumble or fall; to move with short, light steps; (with **up**) to (cause to) make a mistake: – *pt* **tripped**. – *n* a voyage or journey for pleasure or business; a light short step. – *n* '**tripper** one who goes on a short pleasure trip, *usu* a day trip.

tri'partite *adj* in, or having, three parts; (of an agreement *etc*) reached by, and binding, three countries.

tripe *n* part of the stomach of the cow or sheep used as food; (*coll*) rubbish, nonsense.

'**triple** *adj* made up of three; three times as large (as something else, as usual *etc*). – *v* to make or become three times as large. – *n* '**triplet** one of three children or animals born of the same mother at one time; three rhyming lines in a poem; (in music) a group of three notes played in the time of two.

'**triplicate: in triplicate** in, or in the form of, three copies.

'**tripod** *n* a three-legged stand (*esp* for a camera).

trite *adj* (of a remark, saying *etc*) used so often that it has little force or meaning.

'**triumph** *n* a great success or victory; a state of celebration, great joy, pride *etc* after a success: *ride in triumph through the streets.* – *v* to win a victory; to rejoice openly because of a victory (*esp* over the person one has defeated). – *adjs* **tri'umphal** of triumph; used *etc* in celebrating a triumph; **tri'umphant** victorious; showing joy because of, or celebrating, triumph.

trivia *npl* unimportant matters or details. – *adj* '**trivial** of very little importance. – *ns* **trivi'ality** something unimportant; trivialness: – *pl* **trivi'alities**; '**trivialness** the state of being trivial.

trod, trodden *see* **tread**.

troll *n* (*myth*) a creature, giant or dwarf, who lives in a cave *etc*.

'**trolley** *n* a small cart (*eg* as used by porters at railway stations); in a supermarket, a large basket on wheels; a table on wheels, *usu* with two or more surfaces one above the other, used for serving tea *etc*: – *pl* '**trolleys**. – *n* '**trolley-bus** a bus which gets its power from overhead wires.

'**trollop** *n* a careless, untidy woman.

trom'bone *n* a type of brass wind instrument with a sliding tube which changes the notes.

troop *n* a crowd or collection of people or animals; (*pl*) soldiers; a unit in cavalry *etc*. – *v* to gather in numbers; to go in a group. *They all trooped out.* – *n* '**trooper** a horse-soldier. – *n* '**troopship** a ship for carrying soldiers. – **troop the colour(s)** to carry a regiment's flag past the lined-up soldiers of the regiment.

'**trophy** *n* something taken from an enemy and kept in memory of the victory; a prize such as a silver cup won in a sports competition *etc*: – *pl* '**trophies**.

'**tropic** *n* either of two imaginary circles running round the earth at about 23 degrees north (*Tropic of Cancer*) or south (*Tropic of Capricorn*) of the equator; (*pl*) the hot regions near or between these circles. – *adj* '**tropic(al)** of the tropics; growing in hot countries; very hot.

trot *v* (of a horse) to run with short, high steps; (of a person) to run slowly with short steps; to make (a horse) trot: – *pt* '**trotted**. – *n* the pace of a horse or person when trotting. – *npl* '**trotters** the feet of pigs or sheep, *esp* when used as food.

troubadour ['trōōbədōr] *n* (*hist*) a wandering singer, *esp* in France.

trouble ['trubl] *v* to cause worry, uneasiness, sorrow *etc* to; to cause inconvenience to; to make an effort, bother (to). *I didn't trouble to ring him.* – *n* worry, uneasiness; difficulty; disturbance; something which causes worry, difficulty *etc*; a disease; care and effort put into doing something. – *adj* '**troublesome** causing difficulty or inconvenience. – *n* '**troubleshooter** one whose job is to solve difficulties (*eg* in a firm's business activities).

trough [trof] *n* a long, open container for holding animals' food, water *etc*; an area of low atmospheric pressure; a dip between two sea waves.

trounce *v* to punish or beat severely; to defeat heavily.

troupe [trōōp] *n* a company (of actors, dancers *etc*).

trousers ['trowzərz] *npl* an outer garment for the lower part of the body which covers each leg separately. – *adj* '**trouser** of a pair of trousers: *trouser leg*.

trousseau ['trōōsō] *n* a bride's outfit for her wedding: – *pls* '**trousseaux**, '**trousseaus**.

trout *n* a type of river fish, used as food.

trowel ['trowǝl] *n* a small spade used in gardening; a similar tool with a flat blade, used for spreading mortar *etc.*

troy weight *n* a system of weights for weighing gold, gems *etc.*

truant ['trooǝnt] *n* someone who stays away from school *etc* without permission. - Also *adj.* - *n* **'truancy.** - **play truant** to stay away from school, work *etc* without permission *etc.*

truce [trooss] *n* a rest from fighting or quarrelling agreed to by both sides.

truck *n* a wagon for carrying goods (*esp* on a railway); a strong lorry for carrying heavy loads. - **have no truck with** to refuse to have dealings with (*eg* a person).

'truculent *adj* fierce and threatening, aggressive. - *n* **'truculence.**

trudge *v* to walk with heavy steps, as if tired.

true [troo] *adj* (of a story, book *etc*) telling of something which really happened; correct, not invented or wrong. *It's true that the earth is round*; accurate: *a true idea of its appearance*; faithful: *a true friend*; real, properly so called. *The spider is not a true insect*; rightful: *the true heir to the title*; in the correct or intended position. - *adv* **'truly.** - *ns* **'truism** a statement which is so clearly true that it is not worth making; **truth** the state of being true; a true statement; the facts. - *adj* **'truthful** (of a person) *usu* telling the truth, not lying; (of a statement *etc*) true. - *adv* **'truthfully.** - *n* **'truthfulness.**

'truffle *n* (often *pl*) a type of round fungus found underground and much valued as a flavouring for food.

trug *n* a shallow basket used in gardening.

trump *n* in some card games, (any card of) a suit having a higher value than cards of other suits. - *v* to play a card which is a trump. - *n* **trump card** a card which is a trump; something kept in reserve as a means of winning a contest, argument *etc.* - **trump up** to make up, invent (*eg* a story, evidence against a person); **turn up trumps** to play one's part nobly when things are difficult.

'trumpery *n* something showy but worthless: - *pl* **'trumperies.**

'trumpet *n* a brass musical instrument with a clear, high-pitched tone; the cry of an elephant. - *v* to announce (*eg* news) so that all may hear; to blow a trumpet; (*esp* of an elephant) to make a noise like a trumpet.

trun'cated *adj* cut off at the top or end; shortened: *a truncated version of the play.*

truncheon ['trunchǝn] *n* a short heavy staff or baton such as that used by policemen.

'trundle *v* to wheel or roll along. *He trundled his wheelbarrow down the path.*

trunk *n* the main stem of a tree; the body (not counting the head, arms, or legs) of a person or animal; the long nose of an elephant; a large box or chest for clothes *etc*; (*pl*) short pants worn by boys and men, *esp* for swimming. - *ns* **'trunk-call** a telephone call to a distant place; **trunk road** a main road.

truss *n* a bundle (*eg* of hay, straw); a system of beams to support a bridge *etc*; a kind of supporting bandage: - *pl* **'trusses.** - *v* to bind, tie tightly (up); (*usu* with **up**) to prepare (a bird ready for cooking) by tying up the legs and wings.

trust *n* belief in the power, reality, truth or goodness (of a thing or person): *have trust in our leaders*; something (*eg* a task) given one in the belief that one will do it faithfully; charge, keeping. *The child was put in my trust*; an arrangement by which something (*eg* money) is given to a person for use in a particular way; a number of business firms working closely together. - *v* to have faith or confidence (in); to give (a person something) in the belief that he will use it well *etc. I can't trust your sister with my tennis racket*; to feel confident (that). *I trust that you can find your way here.* - *n* **trus'tee** one who keeps something in trust for another. - *adjs* **'trustful, 'trusting** ready to trust, not suspicious; **'trustworthy, 'trusty** able to be depended on. - **take on trust** to believe without checking or testing.

truth, truthful *see* **true.**

try *v* to attempt, make an effort (to do something); to test by using: *try this new soap*; to test severely, strain. *You're trying my patience*; to attempt to use, open *etc. I tried the door but it was locked*; to judge (a prisoner) in a court of law: - *pt* **tried.** - *n* an effort, attempt; one of the ways of scoring in Rugby football: - *pl* **tries.** - *n* **trial** ['trial] the act of testing or trying (*eg* something new, one's patience *etc*); a test; the judging (of a prisoner) in a court of law; suffering. - Also *adj.* - *adj* **'trying** hard to bear; testing. - **on trial** being tried (*esp* in a court of law); for the purpose of trying out: *goods sent on trial*; being tested. *I'm on trial with this* *firm*; **trial and error** the trying of various methods or choices until the right one is found; **try on** to put on (clothing) to see if it fits *etc*; **try out** to test by using.

tryst *n* (*old*) an arrangement to meet someone at a certain place.

tsar, tzar, czar [zär] *n* the title of the former emperors of Russia: – *fem* **tsarina, tzarina, czarina** [zä'rēnə].

tsetse ['tsetsi] *n* a kind of African biting fly which causes dangerous diseases to men and animals (also **tsetse fly**).

tub *n* a round wooden container used for washing *etc*; a bath; a round container (*esp* for ice cream).

'tūba *n* a large brass musical instrument giving a low note.

'tubby *adj* fat and round.

tube *n* a hollow, cylinder-shaped object through which liquid may pass; an organ of this kind in humans, animals *etc*; a container from which something may be squeezed (*eg* toothpaste); an underground railway system; a cathode-ray tube. – *n* **'tubing** a length or lengths of tube. – *adj* **'tūbūlar** shaped like a tube.

'tūber *n* a swelling on the underground stem of a plant (*eg* a potato).

tū'bercū'lōsis *n* an infectious disease, *usu* affecting the lungs.

tuck *n* a fold stitched in a piece of cloth; (*coll*) sweets, cakes *etc*. – *v* to gather (cloth) together into a fold; to fold or push (into or under a place); (with **in** or **up**) to push bedclothes closely round (a person in bed). – *n* **tuck shop** a shop (*esp* in a school) where sweets, cakes *etc* are sold. – **tuck in** (*coll*) to eat with enjoyment or greedily.

Tuesday ['tūzdi] *n* the third day of the week.

tuft *n* a bunch or clump of grass, hair *etc*.

tug *v* to pull hard; to pull along: – *pt* **tugged**. – *n* a strong pull; a tugboat. – *ns* **'tugboat** a small but powerful ship used for towing larger ones; **'tug-of-'war** a contest in which two sides, holding the ends of a strong rope, pull against each other.

tū'ition *n* teaching; private coaching or teaching.

'tūlip *n* a type of flower with cup-shaped flowers grown from a bulb.

tūlle *n* a kind of cloth made of thin silk or rayon net.

'tumble *v* to (cause to) fall or come down suddenly and violently; to roll, toss (about); to do acrobatic tricks; to throw into disorder. – *n* a fall; a confused state. – *n* **'tumbler** a large

drinking glass; an acrobat. – *adj* **'tumbledown** falling to pieces. – **tumble to** to understand suddenly.

'tumbrel, 'tumbril *n* (*hist*) a two-wheeled cart of the kind used to take victims to the guillotine during the French Revolution.

'tummy *n* (*coll*) stomach.

tumour ['tūmər] *n* an abnormal growth on or in the body.

'tūmult *n* a great noise (made by a crowd); excitement, agitation: *the tumult within him.* – *adj* **tu'multūous**.

'tūmūlus *n* a man-made mound of earth, *esp* over a tomb.

tun *n* a large cask, *esp* for wine.

tuna ['tōōnə] *n* a type of large sea fish, used as food (also **'tunny**).

'tundra *n* a level treeless plain in Arctic regions.

tune *n* notes put together in a certain order, a melody; the music of a song. – *v* to put (a musical instrument) in tune; to adjust a radio set to a particular station; (sometimes with **up**) to improve the working of an engine. – *adj* **'tuneful** having a pleasant or easily heard tune; like a tune. – *adv* **'tunefully**. – *n* **tuning fork** a steel fork which, when struck, gives a note of a certain pitch. – **change one's tune** to change one's opinions, attitudes *etc*; **in tune** (of a musical instrument) having each note adjusted to agree with the others or with the notes of other instruments *etc*; (of a person's voice) agreeing with the notes of other voices or instruments; (of a person) in agreement (with); **to the tune of** to the sum of.

'tungsten *n* an element, a grey metal.

'tūnic *n* a soldier's or policeman's jacket; (*hist*) a loose garment reaching to the knees, worn in ancient Greece and Rome; any similar modern garment: *gym-tunic.*

'tunnel *n* an underground passage (*eg* for a railway train), *esp* one cut through a hill or under a river *etc*. – *v* to make a tunnel; (of an animal) to burrow: – *pt* **'tunnelled**.

tunny *see* **tuna**.

'turban *n* a long piece of cloth wound round the head, worn *esp* by Mohammedans; a kind of hat resembling this.

'turbid *adj* (of liquid *etc*) muddy, clouded.

'turbine *n* a kind of engine, *usu* with curved blades, turned by the action of water, steam, hot air *etc*.

turbo- *prefix* used of engines in which a turbine is used or of aeroplanes having such engines.

'**turbot** *n* a type of large flat sea fish, used as food.

'**turbulent** *adj* (of times, conditions *etc*) disturbed, in a restless state; (of persons) likely to cause a disturbance or riot. – *n* '**turbulence** the state of being turbulent; in the atmosphere, irregular movement of air currents, *esp* when affecting the flight of aircraft.

tu'reen *n* a large dish for holding soup at table.

turf *n* grass and the soil below it; (with **the**) (the world of) horseracing. – *v* to cover with turf. – **turf out** (*coll*) to throw out.

'**turgid** *adj* swollen; (of language) sounding grand but meaning little, pompous.

'**turkey** *n* a type of large farmyard bird, used as food: – *pl* '**turkeys**.

Turkish bath *n* a type of hot air or steam bath in which a person is made to sweat heavily, is massaged and then slowly cooled.

'**turmoil** *n* state of wild, confused movement or disorder. *His mind was in a turmoil.*

turn *v* to (make to) go round: *wheels turning*; to face or go in the opposite direction. *He turned and walked away*; to change direction. *The road turns sharply to the left*; to direct (*eg* attention); (with **on**) to move, swing *etc* (on something as a centre). *The door turns on its hinges*; (of milk) to go sour; to (cause to) become. *His hair turned white*; (of leaves) to change colour; to shape in a lathe; to pass (the age of). *She must have turned 40.* – *n* the act of turning; a point where one may change direction *eg* where a road joins another. *Take the first turn on the left. His career took a new turn*; a bend (*eg* in a road); a chance or duty (to do something shared by several people): *your turn to wash the car*; an act (*eg* in a circus); a short stroll: *a turn along the beach*; a fit of dizziness, shock *etc*; requirement. *This will serve our turn.* – *n* '**turning** the act of turning; a point where a road *etc* joins another; the act of shaping in a lathe. – *ns* '**turncoat** one who betrays his party, his principles *etc*; '**turning-point** the point at which a turn or an important change takes place; '**turnover** rate of change or replacement (*eg* of workers in a firm *etc*); the total amount of sales made by a firm during a certain time; '**turnpike** (*hist*) a gate across a road which opened when the user paid a toll; (*US*) a road on which a toll is paid; '**turnstile** a gate which turns, allowing only one person

to pass at a time; '**turntable** a revolving platform for turning a railway engine round; the revolving part of a record-player on which the record rests. – **by turns**, in turn, one after another in a regular order; **do someone a good (**or **bad) turn** to act helpfully (or unhelpfully) towards someone; **to a turn** exactly, perfectly: *lamb cooked to a turn*; **turn against** to become hostile to; **turn down** say no to, refuse (*eg* an offer, a request); to reduce, make less (heat, volume of sound *etc*); **turn in** to go to bed; to hand over to those in authority; **turn off** to stop the flow of (a tap); to switch off the power for (a television *etc*); **turn on** to set running (*eg* water from a tap); to switch on power for (a television *etc*); to depend (on). *Everything turns on the weather*; to become angry with (someone) unexpectedly; **turn one's head** to fill with pride or conceit; **turn out** to make to leave, drive out; to make, produce; to empty: *turn out the attic*; (of a crowd) to come out, gather for a special purpose (*n* '**turnout**). *A large crowd turned out for the Queen's visit*; to switch off (a light); to prove (to be). *He turned out to be right*; **turn to** to set to work; to go to for help *etc*; **turn up** to appear, arrive; to be found; to increase (*eg* heat, volume of sound *etc*).

'**turnip** *n* a type of plant with a large round root used as a vegetable.

'**turpentine** *n* an oil got from certain trees and used for mixing paints, cleaning paint brushes *etc*.

'**turpitude** *n* wickedness.

turquoise ['tɜrkwoiz] *n* a type of greenish-blue precious stone.

'**turret** *n* a small tower on a castle or other building; a tower on which guns are mounted, *esp* on a warship. – *adj* '**turreted** having turrets.

'**turtle** *n* a kind of large tortoise which lives in water. – *ns* '**turtledove** a type of dove noted for its sweet, soft song; '**turtleneck** (a garment with) a high, round neck; **turtle soup** a soup made from the flesh of a type of turtle. – **turn turtle** (of a boat *etc*) to turn upside down, capsize.

tusk *n* a large tooth (one of a pair) sticking out from the mouth of certain animals (*eg* the elephant, the walrus).

'**tussle** *n* a struggle. – Also *v.*

'**tussock** *n* a tuft of grass.

tutelage ['tjutilij] *n* the state of being protected (by a guardian). – *adj* '**tutelary** protecting.

'**tutor** *n* a teacher of students (*eg* in a

college, a university *etc*); a teacher employed privately to teach one or a few pupils at a time. – *v* to teach. – *adj* **tutorial** [tū'tōriəl] of a tutor. – *n* a meeting for study or discussion between a tutor and his student(s).

tutu ['tōōtōō] *n* a ballet dancer's short, stiff, spreading skirt.

twaddle ['twodl] *n* nonsense.

twain *n* (*old*) two. – **in twain** in two, apart.

twang *n* a tone of voice in which the words seem to come through the nose; a sound like that of a tightly-stretched string being plucked. – *v* to (cause to) make such a sound.

tweak *v* to pull with a sudden jerk, twitch. – Also *n*.

tweed *n* a kind of woollen cloth with a rough surface; (*pl*) clothes, or a suit, made of this cloth. – Also *adj*.

'tweezers *npl* small pincers (for pulling out hairs, holding small things *etc*).

twelve *n* the number 12. – *adj* 12 in number. – *adj* **twelfth** the last of twelve (things *etc*). – *n* one of twelve equal parts.

'twenty *n* the number 20. – *adj* 20 in number. – *adj* **'twentieth** the last of twenty (things *etc*). – *n* one of twenty equal parts.

twice *adv* two times.

'twiddle *v* to play with, twirl idly. – **twiddle one's thumbs** to turn the thumbs around one another; to have nothing to do.

twig *n* a small branch of a tree.

twilight ['twīlīt] *n* the faint light between sunset and night, or before sunrise; the state or time just before or *esp* after the greatest power (of something): *the twilight of the dictator's power*.

twill *n* a kind of strong cloth with a ridged appearance.

twin *n* one of two children or animals born of the same mother at the same birth; one of two things exactly the same. – *adj* born at the same birth; very like another; made up of two parts or things which are alike. – *n* **twin bed** one of two matching single beds. – *adj* **'twin-'screw** (of an aeroplane) having two separate propellers. – *n* **'twinset** a matching cardigan and jumper.

twine *n* a strong kind of string made of twisted threads. – *v* to wind or twist together; to wind (about or around something).

twinge [twinj] *n* a sudden, sharp pain.

'twinkle *v* (of a star *etc*) to shine with light which seems to vary in brightness;

(of eyes) to shine with amusement *etc*. – *ns* **'twinkle**, **'twinkling** the act or state of twinkling. – **in a twinkling** in an instant.

twirl *v* to turn or spin round quickly and lightly; to turn (something) round and round with the fingers. – Also *n*.

twist *v* to wind (as two threads) together; to wind (round or about something); to make (*eg* a rope) into a coil; to bend out of shape. *The great heat twisted the metal bars*; to bend or wrench painfully (*eg* one's ankle); to make (*eg* facts) appear to have a meaning which is really false. – *n* the act of twisting; a painful wrench; something twisted: *a twist of tissue paper*. – *n* **'twister** (*coll*) a dishonest and unreliable person.

twitch *v* to pull with a sudden light jerk; to jerk slightly and suddenly. *A muscle in his face twitched.* – Also *n*.

'twitter *n* high, rapidly repeated sounds, as made by small birds; slight nervous excitement. – *v* (of a bird) to make a series of high quivering notes, chirp continuously; (of a person) to talk continuously (in a bird-like voice).

two [tōō] *n* the number 2. – *adj* 2 in number. – *adjs* **'two-'faced** deceitful, insincere; **'twofold** double. – *see also* **twice**.

ty̱'coon *n* a business man of great wealth and power.

tympani, tympanist *see* **timpani**.

type *n* kind: *a new type of farming*; an example which has all the usual characteristics of its, his *etc* kind; a small block (*usu* of metal) on which is a raised letter or sign, used for printing; a set of these; printed lettering. – *v* to write on a typewriter; to use a typewriter; to identify or classify as a particular type: *to type blood.* – *n* **'typist** one whose work is to use a typewriter and *usu* to do other secretarial or clerical tasks. – *v* **'typecast** to give (an actor) the part of a character very like himself, or a part of a kind which he has successfully played before. – *n* **'typewriter** a machine with keys which, when struck, cause letters to be printed on a sheet of paper.

'ty̱phoid *adj, n* (of) an infectious disease caused by germs in infected food or drinking water.

ty̱'phoon *n* a violent storm of wind and rain in Eastern seas.

'ty̱phus *n* a dangerous fever carried by lice.

'typical *adj* having or showing the usual characteristics: *a typical Englishman. It's typical of him to put the blame on* others. – adv 'typically.

'typify v to be a good example of. He typifies the Englishman abroad. – pt 'typified.

'tyrant n a ruler who governs cruelly and unjustly. – adjs tyrannical [ti'ranikəl], 'tyrannous like a tyrant,

cruel. – v 'tyrannize to act as a tyrant; to rule (over) harshly. – n 'tyranny the rule of a tyrant.

'tyre, (US) 'tire n a thick rubber cover round a motor or cycle wheel.

tyro see tiro.

tzar see tsar.

U

ū'biquitous adj being everywhere at once; found everywhere. – n u'biquity.

'udder n the bag-like part of a cow, goat etc with teats which supply milk for their young or for man.

'ugly adj unpleasant to look at or hear; threatening, dangerous: an ugly situation. – n 'ugliness.

ukelele [ūkə'lāli] n a type of small, stringed musical instrument played like a banjo.

'ulcer n an open sore on the inside or the outside of the body. – adj 'ulcerated having an ulcer or ulcers.

ul'tērior adj beyond what is admitted or seen: an ulterior motive.

'ultimate adj last, final. – adv 'ultimately finally, in the end.

ulti'mātum n a final demand sent by one person, nation etc to another, with a threat to break off discussion, declare war etc if the demand is not met.

ultra- prefix very: ultra-careful; beyond: ultramicroscopic.

ultramarine [ultrəmə'rēn] adj, n (of) a deep blue colour.

ultra'sonic adj beyond the range of human hearing.

ultra'violet adj (of light) having rays of slightly shorter wavelength than visible light, which cause objects they strike to glow with various colours and cause tanning of the skin.

'umber n a mineral substance used to produce a brown paint.

um'bilical adj of the navel.

'umbrage n a feeling of offence or hurt. He took umbrage at my words.

um'brella n an object made up of a folding covered framework on a stick which protects against rain.

'umpire n (in cricket, tennis etc) a person who sees that the game is played according to the rules and decides doubtful points; a judge who is asked to settle a dispute. – v to act as an umpire.

un- prefix not: unequal; (with verbs)

used to show the reversal of an action: unfasten.

un'able adj lacking enough strength, power, skill etc.

unac'countable adj not able to be explained. – adv unac'countably.

una'dulterated adj pure, not mixed with anything else.

ū'nanimous adj all of the same opinion. We were unanimous; agreed to by all: a unanimous decision. – n una'nimity.

unap'proachable adj unfriendly and stiff in manner.

unas'sūming adj modest.

una'ware adj not knowing, ignorant (of): unaware of the danger. – adv una'wares without warning; without meaning to, unintentionally.

un'balanced adj mad; lacking balance: an unbalanced view.

unbeliever [unbi'lēvər] n one who does not follow a certain religion.

un'bend v to behave in a natural way without pride or stiffness. – adj un'bending severe.

un'bounded adj not limited, very great: unbounded enthusiasm.

un'bridled adj not kept under control: unbridled fury.

un'burden: unburden oneself to tell one's secrets or problems freely (to another).

uncalled [un'köld]: uncalled for quite unnecessary. His remarks were uncalled for.

un'canny adj strange, mysterious.

un'cared: uncared for not looked after properly.

un'certain adj not certain, doubtful; not definitely known; changeable: uncertain weather.

un'charted adj not shown on a map or chart; little known.

'uncle n the brother of one's father or mother; the husband of one's father's or mother's sister.

un'clean adj dirty, impure.

un'coil v to unwind.

un'common *adj* not common, strange. – *adv* **un'commonly** very: *uncommonly well.*

uncompromising [un'komprəmiziŋ] *adj* not willing to give in or make concessions to others.

unconscionable [un'konshənəbl] *adj* more than is reasonable: *unconscionable demands.*

unconscious [un'konshəs] *adj* senseless, stunned (*eg* by an accident); not aware (of); not recognized by the person concerned: *an unconscious prejudice against women.* – *n* the deepest level of the mind.

uncouth [un'kōōth] *adj* clumsy, awkward; rude.

un'daunted *adj* fearless; not discouraged.

unde'niable *adj* not able to be denied, clearly true.

'under *prep* directly below or beneath: *under the stone*; less than: *bought for under £1*; for, within the authority or command of: *under General Montgomery*; going through, suffering: *under attack*; having, using: *under a false name*; in accordance with: *under our agreement.* – *adv* in or to a lower position, condition *etc*; beneath the surface of the water. – **under age** younger than the legal age of independence or freedom; **under way** in motion, started.

under- *prefix* below, beneath; lower (in position or rank); too little.

undercarriage ['undərkarij] *n* the wheels of an aeroplane and their supports.

underclothes ['undərklōdhz] *npl* clothes worn next to the skin under other clothes.

undercover ['undər'kuvər] *adj* acting or done in secret: *an undercover agent (ie a spy).*

'undercurrent *n* a flow or movement under the surface; a half-hidden feeling, tendency *etc*: *an undercurrent of despair beneath his confident words.*

under'cut *v* to sell at a lower price than (someone else).

underde'veloped *adj* not fully grown; (of a country) lacking modern agricultural and industrial systems, and with a low standard of living.

'underdog *n* the weaker side, or the loser in any conflict or fight.

underdone [undər'dun] *adj* (of food) not quite cooked.

under'estimate *v* to estimate at less than the real worth, value *etc*.

under'foot *adv* under the feet.

under'go *v* to suffer or endure; to receive (*eg* as medical treatment): – *pt* **under'went**, *pp* **under'gone**.

under'graduate *n* a university student who has not yet passed his final examinations.

under'ground *adj* below the surface of the ground; secret. – *n* **'underground** a railway which runs in a tunnel beneath the surface of the ground.

undergrowth ['undərgrōth] *n* shrubs or low plants growing amongst trees.

'underhand *adj* sly, deceitful. – Also *adv.*

under'lie *v* to be the hidden cause or source of. – *adj* **under'lying**.

under'line *v* to draw a line under; to stress the importance of, emphasize.

'underling *n* a person of lower rank.

under'mine *v* to do damage to, weaken gradually (health, authority *etc*).

under'neath *adv*, *prep* in a lower position (than), beneath. *Have you searched underneath (the table)?: a jacket underneath his overcoat.*

'underpass *n* a road passing under another one.

under'pay *v* to pay too little.

underprivileged [undər'privilijd] *adj* not having normal living standards or rights.

under'rate *v* to think too little of, underestimate. *He underrates his ability.*

undersigned [undər'sind] *n* (with **the**) the person or persons whose names are written at the end of a letter or statement.

'underskirt *n* a thin skirt worn under another skirt.

under'stand *v* to see the meaning of (something); to appreciate the reasons for. *I don't understand his behaviour*; to have a thorough knowledge of: *understand children: understand finance*; to have the impression that. *I understood that you had gone home*; to take for granted as part of an agreement: – *pt* **under'stood**. – *adj* **under'standable**. – *n* **under'standing** the act or power of seeing the full meaning of (something); an agreement; condition: *on the understanding that we both pay half the price*; appreciation of another's feelings, difficulties *etc*. – *adj* able to understand another's feelings, sympathetic.

under'statement *n* a statement which does not give the whole truth, making less of certain details than is actually the case.

'understudy *n* an actor who learns the part of another actor so that he may take his place if necessary. – Also v.

under'take v to promise (to do something); to take upon oneself (a task, duty etc). *I undertook the task alone.* – *ns* **'undertaker** one whose job is to organize funerals; **'undertaking** something which is being attempted or done; a promise; the business of an undertaker.

'undertone n a soft voice; a partly hidden meaning, feeling etc: *an undertone of discontent.*

undertow ['undərtō] n a current below the surface of the water which moves in a direction opposite to the surface movement.

undervalue [undər'valū] v to value (something) below the real worth.

underwear ['undərwār] n underclothes.

underworld ['undərwörld] n the criminal world or level of society; (*myth*) the place where spirits go after death.

underwriter ['undəritər] n one who insures ships. – v **under'write** to accept for insurance; to accept responsibility or liability for.

undo [un'dōō] v to unfasten (a coat, parcel etc); to wipe out the effect of, reverse. *You will undo all the good he did;* (*hist*) to ruin (*esp* one's reputation). *Alas, I am undone:* – *pt* **un'did**, *pp* **un'done**. – n **un'doing** ruin. *His boldness will be his undoing.*

undoubted [un'dowtid] adj not to be doubted. – adv **un'doubtedly** without doubt, certainly.

un'dress v to take the clothes off.

undue [un'dū] adj too much, more than is necessary: *undue expense.* – adv **un'duly**: *unduly worried.*

'undulate v to move as waves do; to have a rolling, wavelike appearance. *The countryside undulated gently.* – adj **'undulating.** – n **undu'lation.**

unearth [un'ŏrth] v to bring or dig out from the earth, or from a place of hiding. – adj **un'earthly** strange, as if not of this world; (*coll*) absurd, *esp* absurdly early: *at this unearthly hour.*

uneasy [un'ēzi] adj anxious, worried. – n **un'easiness.**

unem'ployed adj without a job; not in use. – *npl* (with **the**) unemployed people as a group. – n **unem'ployment** the state of being unemployed; the total number of unemployed people in a country.

un'equal adj not equal; unfair: *an unequal distribution of profits;* lacking enough strength, skill etc for (a task): *unequal to the job.* – adj **un'equalled** without an equal, unique.

unequivocal [uni'kwivəkəl] adj clear, not ambiguous: *unequivocal orders.*

un'erring adj always right, never making a mistake: *unerring judgement.*

un'even adj not smooth or level; not all of the same quality etc. *This work is very uneven.*

unex'pected adj not expected, sudden.

un'failing adj never failing, never likely to fail: *unfailing accuracy.*

un'fair adj not just.

un'faithful adj not true to one's marriage vows; failing to keep one's promises.

unfasten [un'fäsn] v to loosen, undo (*eg* a buttoned coat).

un'feeling adj harsh, hard-hearted.

un'fit adj not suitable; not good enough, or not in a suitable state (to, for): *water unfit for drinking: unfit to travel;* not as vigorous (physically or mentally) as one could be. – v to make unfit or unsuitable: – *pt* **un'fitted.**

un'flagging adj not tiring or losing strength.

un'flinching adj brave, not put off by pain, opposition etc.

un'fold v to spread out; to give details of (as a story, plan); (of details of a plot etc) to become known.

unfor'gettable adj of such a kind as never to be forgotten.

unfortunate [un'förchənət] adj unlucky; regrettable: *an unfortunate manner in dealing with people.*

un'founded adj not based on facts or reality, untrue.

un'furl v to unfold (*eg* a flag).

un'gainly adj clumsy, awkward.

ungracious [un'grāshəs] adj rude, not polite.

un'grateful adj not showing thanks for kindness.

unguarded [un'gärdid] adj without protection; careless: *an unguarded remark.*

unguent ['ungwənt] n ointment.

un'happy adj miserable, sad; unfortunate. – adv **un'happily.** – n **un'happiness.**

unhealthy [un'helthi] adj not well, ill; harmful to health: *an unhealthy climate;* showing that one is not well: *an unhealthy complexion.*

unhinge [un'hinj] v to send (a person) mad.

un'horse v to throw from a horse.

ūni- prefix one, a single.

'ūnicorn n (*myth*) an animal with one straight horn on its forehead.

'ūniform adj the same in all parts, at all times etc, never varying. – n the form of clothes worn by soldiers, sailors, chil-

dren at a certain school *etc*. – *n*
uni'formity sameness.

'**unify** *v* to make into one: – *pt* '**unified**. –
n **unifi'cation**.

uninter'rupted *adj* not interrupted;
continuing without a break or stoppage; (of a view) not blocked by
anything.

'**union** *n* the act of joining together; the
state of being joined together; marriage; countries or states joined together; a trade union. – *n* **Union Jack**
the flag of the United Kingdom.

unique [yōo'nēk] *adj* without a like or
equal: *a unique sense of timing*.

unisex ['ūniseks] *adj* in a style that can
be worn, used *etc* by both males and
females.

'**unison** *n* identity, exact sameness, of
musical pitch; singing or playing (a
musical passage) at the same pitch;
agreement, accord. – **in unison** all
together.

'**unit** *n* a single thing, person or group,
esp when considered as part of a larger
whole: *storage unit*: *army unit*; a fixed
amount, length *etc* used as a standard
by which other amounts *etc* are measured (*eg* metres, litres, centimetres
etc); the smallest whole number *ie* the
number one. – *adj* '**unitary** existing as
a unit, not divided; using or based on
units. – *n* '**unity** the state of being in
complete agreement; the state of being
one or a whole; the number one.

ū'nite *v* to join together; to become one;
to act together. – *adj* **u'nited**.

'**universe** *n* all created things, including
the earth and all heavenly bodies;
mankind. – *adj* **uni'versal** of the
universe; of, affecting, including all,
sometimes all mankind. *The drought
was universal*. – *adv* **uni'versally**.

ūni'versity *n* a place of learning where a
wide range of subjects are taught to a
high level, and which gives degrees to
those of its students who pass its
examinations: – *pl* **uni'versities**.

un'kempt *adj* untidy.

un'kind *adj* not kind; harsh, cruel.

un'leash *v* to set free (a dog *etc*); to let
loose (*eg* one's anger).

un'less *conj* if . . . not. *Unless he's here
soon, I'm going* (*ie* if he's not here soon).
Unless you come, I'm not going (*ie* if you
don't come as well).

un'like *adj* different, not similar. – *prep*
different from; not characteristic of. *It
was unlike her to run away*.

un'likely *adj* not probable. *It's unlikely
that it will rain today*; probably not
true: *an unlikely tale*.

un'load *v* to take the load from; to
remove the charge from a gun.

un'looked-for *adj* not expected: *un-
looked-for happiness*.

un'loose *v* to set free; to make loose.

un'lucky *adj* not lucky or fortunate;
unsuccessful. – *adv* **un'luckily**.

un'manly *adj* weak, cowardly.

un'mask *v* to take a mask or covering off;
to show the true character of; to bring
to light (a plot *etc*).

un'matched *adj* without an equal.

un'mentionable *adj* not fit to be spoken
of, scandalous, indecent: *unmentionable
deeds*.

unmis'tākable *adj* very clear; impossible to confuse with any other: *Jack's
unmistakable shock of orange hair*.

un'mitigated *adj* complete, absolute: *an
unmitigated disgrace*.

unmoved [un'mōovd] *adj* not affected:
unmoved by her sobbing; firm.

unnecessary [un'nesəsəri] *adj* not
necessary; avoidable.

unobtrusive [unəb'trōosiv] *adj* not
obvious or conspicuous; modest.

un'pack *v* to open (a piece of luggage)
and remove the contents (*eg* clothes).

un'palatable *adj* not pleasing to the
taste; not pleasant to have to face up to:
the unpalatable facts.

un'paralleled *adj* having no equal: *an
earthquake of unparalleled severity*.

un'pick *v* to take out (*eg* stitches) from
by picking.

unpre'meditated *adj* done without having been planned: *unpremeditated
murder*.

unprepossessing [unprēpə'zesiŋ] *adj*
not attractive.

unpre'tentious *adj* modest, not showy
or affected.

un'principled *adj* without (moral) principles.

un'ravel *v* to unwind or take the knots
out of; to solve (a problem or mystery):
– *pt* **un'ravelled**.

unre'mitting *adj* never stopping, unending: *unremitting rain*.

unre'quited *adj* (*esp* of love) not given in
return.

un'rest *n* a state of trouble or discontent,
esp among a group of people: *political
unrest*.

un'rivalled *adj* without an equal.

unruly [un'rōoli] *adj* badly behaved; not
obeying laws or rules. – *n* **un'ruliness**.

unsavoury [un'sāvəri] *adj* very unpleasant, causing a feeling of disgust.

unscathed [un'skādhd] *adj* not harmed.

unscrew [un'skrōo] *v* to loosen
(something screwed in).

unseasonable [un'sēzənəbl] *adj* (of weather) not suitable to the time of year; not well-timed.

un'seat *v* to remove from a seat *esp* from a political seat. *He was unseated at the last election*; to throw from the saddle (of a horse).

un'seen *adj* not seen. – *n* a passage from a foreign language to be translated without previous preparation.

un'settle *v* to disturb, upset. – *adj* **un'settled** disturbed; (of weather) changeable; (of a bill *etc*) unpaid.

unsightly [un'sītli] *adj* ugly.

unso'phisticated *adj* simple; lacking experience of the world.

un'sound *adj* (of reasoning *etc*) not correct; (of one's mind) not sane; (of fruit *etc*) rotten.

un'speakable *adj* incapable of being expressed in words, *esp* too bad to describe: *unspeakable rudeness.*

un'studied *adj* natural, not forced: *unstudied charm.*

unsus'pecting *adj* not aware of coming danger.

un'thinkable *adj* very unlikely; too bad to be thought of.

un'til, till *prep* up to (the time of). *Wait until* (till) *Saturday*: *until* (till) *he died.* – Also *conj. Keep walking until* (till) *you come to the church.*

un'timely *adj* happening before the proper time: *untimely arrival*; not suitable to the occasion: *untimely remark.*

unto ['untoo] *prep* (*old*) equal in meaning to **to** in most senses; however, **unto** cannot indicate the infinitive.

un'told *adj* not told; too great to be counted or measured: *untold riches.*

untoward [untə'wörd] *adj* unlucky, unfortunate; inconvenient.

untrue [un'troo] *adj* not true, false; not faithful. – *n* **un'truth** a lie. – *adj* **un'truthful.**

unusual [un'ūzhooəl] *adj* not usual; rare, remarkable.

un'varnished *adj* not varnished; plain, straightforward: *the unvarnished truth.*

unveil [un'vāl] *v* to remove a veil from; to remove a cover from (*esp* a statue, memorial *etc*); to bring to light (*eg* an evil plot).

un'well *adj* not in good health.

unwieldy [un'wēldi] *adj* not easily moved or handled. – *n* **un'wieldiness.**

un'witting *adj* unintended: *an unwitting insult*; unaware. – *adv* **un'wittingly.**

un'wonted *adj* unaccustomed, not usual: *unwonted cheerfulness.*

unworthy [un'wördhi] *adj* not worthy; low, worthless, despicable; (with **of**) not deserving (*eg* of attention); less good than one would expect. *That drawing is unworthy of you.*

up *adv* towards or in a higher position: *came up the hill*; completely, so as to finish. *Drink up your tea*; to a larger size *etc*: *blow up a balloon*; as far as a given place. *He came up to me and shook hands*; towards a more important city *etc*, not necessarily from the south: *going up to London from Manchester.* – *superl* **'uppermost.** – *prep* towards or in the higher part of: *climbed up the ladder*; along: *walking up the street.* – *adj* ascending, going *etc* up. *Use the up escalator*; ahead (in score): *2 goals up*; better off, richer: *£2 up on the deal*; risen. *The sun is up*; (of a given length of time) ended. *Your time is up*; (*coll*) wrong. *What's up with her today?*: – *comp* **'upper,** *superls* **'uppermost, 'upmost.** – *n* **'upper** (often *pl*) the part(s) of a shoe *etc* above the sole. – *n* **'uppercut** a punch which swings up from below. – *adj* **'up-to-'date** modern, in touch with recent ideas *etc*. – **the upper hand** control, dominance; **up and about** awake, out of bed (*esp* after an illness); **ups and downs** times of good and bad luck, business *etc*; **up to** until: *up to the present*; capable of (doing). *Are you up to the job?*; a duty belonging to (someone). *It's up to you to do it*; doing, *esp* something cunning *etc*: *up to his tricks again.*

up'braid *v* to scold.

'upbringing *n* the rearing of or the training given to, or received by, a child.

'up-'country *adv, adj* inland.

up'grade *v* to raise to a more important position; to improve the quality of.

up'heaval *n* a violent shaking (*eg* an earthquake); a great disturbance or change.

'up'hill *adj* going upwards; difficult: *an uphill struggle.* – *adv* upwards.

up'hold *v* to support (*eg* a person, an action); to maintain, keep going (*eg* a tradition): – *pt* **up'held.** – *n* **up'holder.**

up'holster *v* to fit chairs, sofas *etc* with springs, stuffing, covers *etc*. – *ns* **up-'holsterer** one who upholsters furniture; **up'holstery** covers, cushions *etc*.

'upkeep *n* the act of keeping (*eg* a house or car) in a good state of repair; the cost of this.

'upland *n* high ground; (*pl*) a hilly or mountainous region. – Also *adj.*

upmost, upper, uppermost *see* **up.**

u'pon *prep* on the top of: *upon the table*;

at, after the time of: *upon completion of the task.*

upright ['uprīt] *adj* standing up, vertical; just and honest. – *n* an upright post, piano *etc.*

uprising ['uprizing] *n* the act of rising against a government *etc*; a revolt.

'uproar *n* a noisy disturbance. – *adj* **up'roarious** very noisy.

up'root *v* to tear up by the roots; to cause (*eg* a family) to leave home and go to live in another place. *The Browns were uprooted again when Mr Brown changed his job.*

up'set *v* to make unhappy, angry *etc*; to overturn; to be overturned; to disturb, put out of order (*eg* one's digestion); to ruin (plans *etc*): – *pt* **up'set**, *pres p* **up'setting**. – *adj* distressed, unhappy *etc*; ill. – *n* **'upset** an act of upsetting; state of being upset; distress; the cause of this.

'upshot *n* a result or end of a matter. *The upshot of all this was that they went home.*

'upside-'down *adj, adv* with the top part underneath; in confusion.

upstage ['up'stāj] *adv* away from the footlights on a theatre stage. – *adj* (*coll*) haughty, proud.

'up'stairs *adv* in or to the upper storey(s) of a house *etc.* – Also *n, adj.*

up'standing *adj* honest, respectable; strong and healthy; standing up. *Be upstanding and drink the king's health.*

'upstart *n* one who has recently risen quickly from a humble to a high position, *esp* one who claims to be more important than he is.

up'stream *adv* higher up a river or stream, towards the source.

'uptake: quick on the uptake quick to understand.

ū'rānium *n* an element, a radioactive metal.

'urban *adj* of, consisting of or living in a town or city (opposite of **rural**).

ur'bane *adj* polite in a smooth way. – *n* **urbanity** [ər'banəti] state of being urbane; (*pl*) **ur'banities** urbane actions.

'urchin *n* a small boy, *esp* a dirty, ragged one.

urge [ərj] *v* to drive (on); to try to persuade. *He urged me to go home*; to advise, advocate earnestly. *He urged caution.* – *n* a strong desire or impulse. – *adj* **'urgent** requiring immediate attention or action; eagerly calling for immediate action. – *n* **'urgency.**

urine ['ūrin] *n* the waste liquid passed out of the bodies of animals and humans from the bladder. – *adj* **'urinary.** – *v*

'urinate to pass urine from the bladder.

urn *n* a vase for the ashes of the dead; a large metal vessel, with a tap, used for making and pouring out tea *etc.*

us *pron* the word used by a speaker or writer in mentioning himself or herself together with other people (as the object in a sentence). *They beat us. Show it to us.*

use [ūz] *v* to put to some purpose. *Use a knife to open it*; to bring into action. *Use your common sense*; (often with **up**) to spend, exhaust (*eg* one's patience, energy); to treat. *He used his wife cruelly.* – *n* use [ūs] the act of using; value or suitability for a (or any) purpose: *no use to anybody*; state of being used. *It's in use at the moment*; custom. – *n* **usage** ['ūzij] act or manner of using; the established way of using (a word *etc*); custom, habit; treatment: *rough usage.* – *adjs* **used** [ūzd] employed, put to a purpose; not new: *used cars*; **useful** ['ūsfool] serving a purpose; helpful. – *adv* **'usefully.** – *n* **'usefulness.** – *adj* **'useless** having no use or effect. – *n* **'uselessness.** – **no use** useless; **used to** [ūst] accustomed to. *We're not used to poverty*; (used together with another verb) was or were in the habit of (doing something). *We used to go there every year.*

'usher *n* one who shows people to their seats in a theatre *etc*: – *fem* **ushe'rette.** – *v* to lead (in, into, to).

usual ['ūzhōoəl] *adj* done, happening *etc* most often: *the usual way of doing things*; customary: *with his usual cheerfulness*; ordinary. – *adv* **'usually** on most occasions.

usurp [ū'zərp] *v* to take possession of (*eg* a throne) by force or without the right to do so. – *n* **u'surper.**

usury ['ūzhəori] *n* the lending of money in return for a (*usu* very) high rate of interest on the loan. – *n* **'usurer** a moneylender who demands a very high rate of interest.

ū'tensil *n* an instrument, vessel *etc* commonly used, *esp* in the home (*eg* a ladle, knife, pan).

'ūterus *n* the womb.

ū'tility *n* usefulness; a useful public service (*eg* the supplying of water, gas *etc*): – *pl* **u'tilities.**

'ūtilize *v* to make use of. – *n* **utili'zation.**

'utmōst *adj* greatest possible: *the utmost care*; furthest. – **do one's utmost** to make the greatest possible effort.

'utter *v* to give out, produce with the

voice (words, a scream *etc*). – *adj* complete, total: *utter darkness*. – *adv* '**utterly**.

'**ūvūla** *n* the small piece of flesh which hangs down from the palate right at the back of the mouth.

V

'**vācant** *adj* empty; not occupied; (of a look, expression *etc*) showing no interest or intelligence. – *n* '**vacancy** a post, job or place that has not been filled: – *pl* '**vacancies**. – *v* **va'cate** to leave empty, to cease to occupy. – *n* **va'cation** the act of vacating; a holiday.

vaccine ['vaksēn] *n* a substance made from the germs that cause a disease, given to people and animals to try to prevent them taking that disease. – *v* **vaccinate** ['vaksināt] to protect against a disease by giving a vaccine to, *eg* by injecting it into the skin. – *n* **vacci'nation**.

'**vacillate** *v* to move from one opinion to another, to waver.

'**vacūous** *adj* empty, stupid.

vacuum ['vakūm] *n* a space from which (almost) all air has been removed. – *ns* **vacuum cleaner** a machine which cleans carpets *etc* by sucking up the dust; **vacuum flask** a container which has double walls with a vacuum between them, for keeping liquids *etc* hot or cold.

'**vagabond** *n* one who has no settled home, a wanderer; a rascal, a rogue.

'**vāgary** *n* (often *pl* '**vagaries**) strange, unexpected behaviour: *the vagaries of human nature*.

va'gīna *n* a part of the female body involved in reproduction of young.

'**vāgrant** *adj* wandering, unsettled. – *n* a wanderer or tramp, with no settled home. – *n* '**vagrancy** the state of being a tramp.

vague [vāg] *adj* not clear; not definite: *a vague idea*: *a vague accusation*: *a vague shape*; not practical or efficient, forgetful: *a vague old lady*.

vain *adj* conceited; useless: *vain efforts*; empty, meaningless: *vain promises*. – *n* **vanity** ['vanɔti] conceit; worthlessness; something vain and worthless. – **in vain** without success.

vainglory [vān'glöri] *n* boastfulness. – *adj* **vain'glorious** boastful.

'**valance** *n* a hanging frill round the edge of a bed.

vale *n* a valley.

valediction [vali'dikshɔn] *n* a farewell. – *adj* **vale'dictory** saying farewell.

'**vālency** *n* (in chemistry) the combining power of an atom or group. In water, H_2O, oxygen shows valency two.

'**valentine** *n* a greetings card sent on St Valentine's Day (14 February) or a sweetheart chosen then.

'**valet** *n* a manservant.

valetudinarian [valitūdi'nāriɔn] *adj*, *n* (of) one who is over-anxious about health.

'**valiant** *adj* brave.

'**valid** *adj* sound, acceptable. *He has a valid reason for not going*; that can be lawfully used, legally in force: *a valid passport*. – *n* **va'lidity**.

'**valley** *n* low land between hills, often having a river flowing through it: – *pl* '**valleys**.

valour ['valɔr] *n* courage, bravery. – *adj* '**valorous**.

value ['valū] *n* worth; price; purchasing power (of a coin *etc*); importance; usefulness; (in algebra) a number or quantity put as equal to an expression. *In this case the value of x is 8.* – *v* to put a price on; to think highly of. – *adj* '**valuable** of great value. – *npl* '**valuables** articles of worth. – *n* **valu'ation** the act of valuing; an estimated price or value. – *adj* '**valueless** worthless. – *ns* '**valuer**, '**valuator** one trained to estimate the value of property.

valve *n* a device (*eg* that in a tyre) for allowing air, steam or liquid to flow in one direction only; a small flap with a similar effect, controlling the flow of blood in the body; a part of a radio or television set which looks like a light bulb and is used to control the flow of electricity.

vamp *n* the upper part of a boot or shoe; a woman who sets out to attract men. – *v* to patch; to play quickly made-up music on the piano; to try to attract men.

'**vampire** *n* a dead person supposed to rise at night and suck the blood of sleeping people. – *n* **vampire bat** any of several types of bats, including a S. American type that sucks blood.

van *n* a covered or closed-in vehicle or wagon for carrying goods by road or rail; short for **vanguard**.

'vandal *n* a person who pointlessly destroys or damages public buildings *etc*. – *n* **'vandalism** the activity of a vandal. – *v* **'vandalize** to damage by vandalism.

vane *n* a weathercock; the blade of a windmill, propeller *etc*.

vanguard ['vangärd] *n* the part of an army going in front of the main body; the leading group in a movement *etc*.

va'nilla *n* a sweet-scented flavouring substance obtained from the pods of a type of orchid.

'vanish *v* to go out of sight; to fade away to nothing.

vanity *see* **vain**.

'vanquish *v* to defeat.

'vantage point *n* a position giving one an advantage or a clear view.

'vapid *adj* dull, uninteresting.

vapour ['vāpər] *n* the air-like or gas-like state of a substance that is usually liquid or solid: *water vapour*; mist or smoke in the air. – *v* **'vaporize** to (cause to) change into vapour. – *n* **'vaporizer** an apparatus for sending out liquid in a very fine spray.

variable, variance, variation *see* **vary**.

'varicose *adj* (of a vein *usu* of the leg) swollen, enlarged.

variegated ['vārigātid] *adj* marked with different colours, varied in colour.

va'riety *n* the quality of being of many kinds, of being different; a mixed collection: *a variety of books*; a sort, kind: *a variety of potato*; mixed theatrical entertainment including dances, songs, comic acts *etc*: – *pl* **va'rieties**. – *adj* **various** ['vāriəs] of different kinds; several. *After various attempts we gave up*.

'varlet *n* (*old*) a rascal.

'varnish *n* a sticky liquid which gives a glossy surface to paper, wood *etc*. – *v* to cover with varnish; to cover up (faults).

'vāry *v* to make, be, or become different; to make changes in (a routine *etc*); to differ, disagree: – *pt* **'varied**. – *adj* **'variable** changeable; that may be varied. – *n* something that varies *eg* in value. – *ns* **'variance** a state of differing or disagreement; **'variant** a different form or version. – Also *adj*. – *n* **vari'ation** a varying, a change; the extent of a difference or change. *In the desert there are great variations of temperature*; (in music *etc*) a repetition, in a

slightly different form, of a main theme. – **at variance** in disagreement.

vase [väz] *n* a jar of pottery, glass *etc*, used as an ornament or for holding cut flowers.

Vaseline ® ['vasəlēn] *n* a type of ointment made from petroleum.

'vassal *n* (*hist*) one who held land from an overlord in return for certain services.

vast *adj* of very great size or amount. – *n* **'vastness**.

vat *n* a large tub or tank, used *esp* in fermenting liquors and dyeing.

vaudeville ['vōdəvil] *n* an entertainment with dances and songs, *usu* comic.

vault *n* an arched roof; an underground room, a cellar. – *v* to leap, *esp* supporting one's weight on one's hands, or on a pole.

vaunt *v* to boast.

veal *n* the flesh of a calf, used as food.

veer *v* to change direction; to change course; to change mood, opinions *etc*.

vegetable ['vejitəbl] *n* a plant, *esp* one grown for food. – *adj* of plants; made from or consisting of plants: *vegetable dye*: *vegetable matter*. – *ns* **vege'tarian** one who eats no meat but lives wholly on vegetable food, and (*usu*) milk, eggs *etc*; **vege'tation** plants in general; the plants of a place or region. – *v* **'vegetate** to grow as a plant does; to lead a dull, aimless life. *She sits at home and vegetates*.

vehement ['vēəmənt] *adj* emphatic and forceful in expressing one's opinions *etc*. – *n* **'vehemence**.

vehicle ['vēəkl] *n* a means of transport *esp* one with wheels, used on land: *motor vehicle*; a means (as television, newspapers *etc*) of carrying information *etc*. – *adj* **vehicular** [vi'hikūlər].

veil [vāl] *n* a piece of cloth or netting worn to shade or hide the face; anything that hides or covers up. – *v* to cover with a veil; to hide. – **take the veil** to become a nun.

vein [vān] *n* one of the tubes which carry the blood back to the heart; a small rib of a leaf; a thin layer of mineral in a rock; a streak in wood, stone *etc*; a mood or personal characteristic: *a vein of cheerfulness*. – *adj* **veined** marked with veins.

veldt [velt] *n* (in S. Africa) open grass-country, with few or no trees.

'vellum *n* a fine parchment used for bookbinding *etc*, made from the skins of calves, kids or lambs; paper *etc* made in imitation of this.

ve'locity *n* rate or speed of movement; swiftness.

velour(s) [və'lōōr] *n* a type of material with a soft, velvet-like surface.

'velvet *n* a type of cloth made from silk *etc*, with a thick, soft surface; velveteen. – *adj* made of velvet; like velvet. – *n* velve'teen a fabric looking like velvet, but made of cotton. – *adj* 'velvety soft, like velvet.

'venal *adj* willing to be bribed; (of an act) unworthy, done for a bribe.

vend *v* to sell. – *n* 'vendor one who sells (also 'vender). – *n* vending machine a slot machine.

ven'detta *n* a bitter, long-lasting quarrel or feud.

ve'neer *v* to cover a piece of wood with another thin piece of finer quality; to (try to) give a good appearance to what is really bad. – *n* a thin layer (of fine wood) forming a surface; a false outward show hiding some bad quality *etc*: *a veneer of good manners.*

venerable ['venərəbl] *adj* worthy of respect because of age, exceptional goodness *etc*. – *v* 'venerate to respect or honour greatly. – *n* vene'ration the act of venerating; great respect.

venereal disease [və'nēriəl] *n* a type of disease which can be passed on through sexual intercourse.

Venetian blind [və'nēshən] *n* a blind for windows, formed of thin movable strips of metal, plastic *etc* hung on tapes.

vengeance ['venjəns] *n* punishment given, harm done in return for wrong or injury, revenge. – *adj* 'vengeful seeking revenge. – **with a vengeance** with unexpected force or enthusiasm.

'venial *adj* (of a sin *etc*) not very bad, pardonable.

'venison *n* the flesh of the deer, used as food.

'venom *n* poison; spite. – *adj* 'venomous poisonous; spiteful.

vent *n* a small opening; a hole to allow air, smoke *etc* to pass through; an outlet; a slit at the bottom of the back of a coat *etc*. – *v* to pour out, express (one's rage or other strong feeling) in some way. – **give vent to** to vent.

'ventilate *v* to allow fresh air to pass through (a room *etc*); to talk about, discuss. – *ns* venti'lation; 'ventilator a kind of grating or other device for bringing in fresh air.

'ventricle *n* a small cavity, *esp* in the brain or heart.

ven'triloquist *n* one who can speak without any obvious movement of the lips, making his voice appear to come from a puppet *etc*. – *n* ven'triloquism.

'venture *n* a piece of business or other undertaking which involves some risk. – *v* to risk; to dare; to do or say something at the risk of causing annoyance *etc*. *I ventured to remark that I didn't like her dress.* – *adjs* 'venturous; 'venturesome.

venue ['venū] *n* the scene of an event, *eg* a sports contest, a conference.

veracious [və'rāshəs] *adj* truthful. – *n* veracity [və'rasəti] truthfulness.

ve'randa(h) *n* a kind of terrace with a roof supported by pillars, extending along the side of a house.

verb *n* the word that tells what a person or thing does or experiences. I *ran.* He *had no* idea. She *was hit.* – *adj* 'verbal of verbs; of words; spoken, not written: *a verbal report.* – *adv* 'verbally in spoken words. – *adv* ver'bātim in the exact words, word for word. *He told me what she said, verbatim.* – *adj* ver'bose using more words than necessary. – *n* verbosity [vər'bosəti] the fault of being verbose, or of speaking too much.

'verdant *adj* green with grass or leaves. – *n* 'verdure green vegetation.

'verdict *n* the decision given by a judge at the end of a trial; a person's opinion on a matter.

verdigris ['vərdigrēs] *n* the greenish rust of copper, brass, or bronze.

verge [vərj] *n* a border, *esp* the grassy border along the edge of a road; edge, brink: *on the verge of a mental breakdown.* – *v* (with **on**) to be on the borderline of, close to. *It verges on the indecent.* – *n* 'verger a church caretaker, or church official.

'verifȳ *v* to prove, show to be true, to confirm: – *pt* 'verified. – *adj* 'verifiable able to be verified. – *n* verifi'cation.

'verily *adv* (*old*) in truth.

verisi'militude *n* likeness to life; appearance of truth.

'verity *n* truth. – *adj* 'veritable true; real, genuine.

vermicelli [vərmi'cheli] *n* a type of food like spaghetti but in much thinner pieces.

ver'milion *adj, n* (of) a bright red colour.

'vermin *n* animals, insects *etc* that are considered pests, *eg* rats, mice, fleas, lice *etc*. – *adj* 'verminous full of vermin.

vermouth ['vərməth] *n* a kind of drink containing white wine flavoured with wormwood.

ver'nacular *n* the ordinary spoken language of a country or district. – Also *adj*.

'vernal *adj* of the season of spring.

verruca [və'rōōkə] *n* a wart, used *esp* of one on the foot.

'versatile *adj* able to turn easily from one subject or task to another; (of a material, a tool or other object) useful in many different ways. – *n* **versa'tility**.

verse *n* a number of lines of poetry grouped according to a plan; poetry as opposed to prose; a short division of a chapter of the Bible; a line of poetry. – *n* **'version** an account from one point of view; a form: *another version of the same game*; a translation. – **versed in** knowing much about, skilled or experienced in.

'versus *prep* against (often shortened to **v**).

'vertebra *n* one of the bones of the spine: – *pl* **vertebrae** ['vɔrtibrē]. – *n* **'vertebrate** an animal having a backbone.

'vertex *n* the top or summit; the point of a cone, pyramid or angle: – *pl* **vertices** ['vɔrtisēz]. – *adj* **'vertical** standing upright; straight up and down.

'vertigo *n* giddiness, dizziness.

verve *n* lively spirit, enthusiasm.

'very *adv* to a great extent or degree: *very beautiful; very quickly; exactly. He has done the very same job for 30 years.* – *adj* same, identical. *The very people who claimed to support him voted against him*; ideal, exactly what is wanted: *the very man for the job*; actual: *in the very act of stealing*; mere: *the very thought of blood*.

'vespers *npl* a church service in the evening.

'vessel *n* a ship; a container, *usu* for a liquid; a tube conducting fluids in the body: *blood vessels*.

vest *n* an undergarment for the top half of the body; (*esp US*) a waistcoat.

'vestibule *n* an entrance hall; a lobby.

vestige ['vestij] *n* a trace, evidence (of something existing, being present *etc*): *no vestige of life*. – *adj* **ves'tigial** surviving only as a trace or indication that something once existed: *vestigial wings*.

'vestment *n* a ceremonial garment, *esp* part of the dress worn by clergymen during a service.

'vestry *n* a room in a church in which vestments are kept.

vet *n* short for **veterinary surgeon**. – *v* to examine or check (and pass as correct): – *pt* **'vetted**.

vetch *n* a type of plant of the pea family.

veteran ['vetərən] *adj* old, experienced. – *n* one who has given long service; an old soldier; (*US*) anyone who has served in the armed forces.

veterinary [vetə'rinəri] *adj* having to do with the curing of diseases of animals. – *ns* **veterinary surgeon**, (*US*) **veteri'narian** a doctor for animals.

'vēto *n* the power or right to forbid; an act of forbidding: – *pl* **'vetoes**. – *v* to forbid: – *pres p* **'vetoing**, *pt* **'vetoed**.

vex *v* to annoy; to cause trouble to. – *n* **vex'ation** the state of being vexed; something that vexes. – *adj* **vex'atious** causing annoyance or trouble.

'via *prep* by way of: *to Oxford via London*: *into films via small parts in the theatre*.

'viable *adj* capable of living or surviving; able to be managed, practicable. *Is this a viable proposition?*

'viaduct *n* a long bridge for carrying a railway or road over a valley, river *etc*.

'viands *npl* (*old*) food.

vi'brate *v* to (cause to) shake, tremble or quiver; to (cause to) swing to and fro in a regular (and *usu* rapid) movement; (of sound) to resound, ring. – *adj* **'vibrant** full of energy; thrilling. – *n* **vi'bration** the act of vibrating; the state of being vibrated; a rapid to-and-fro movement. – *adj* **'vibratory** of vibration.

'vicar *n* a clergyman in charge of a parish in the Church of England. – *n* **'vicarage** the house of a vicar.

vi'cārious *adj* filling the place of another person; done or suffered on behalf of another person; not experienced personally but imagined through the experience of others: *vicarious pleasure*. – *adv* **vi'cariously**.

vice *n* a bad habit, a serious (moral) fault; wickedness, immorality; a kind of tool with two jaws for gripping objects firmly. – *a j* **vicious** ['vishəs] wicked; spiteful. – *n* **vicious circle** a bad situation whose results cause it to get worse.

vice- *prefix* second in rank to, having authority to act in place of, as in **'vice-'admiral, 'vice-'chairman, 'vice-'president.**

viceroy ['visroi] *n* one who governs a large kingdom in the name of his king.

vice versa ['visi'vərsə] *adv* the other way round. *I needed his help and vice versa*(*ie* he needed mine).

vi'cinity *n* nearness; neighbourhood.

vicious *see* **vice**.

vi'cissitude *n* a change from one state to

another; (*pl*) changes of luck.

victim *n* a person who is killed or harmed, intentionally or by accident: *the victim of a vicious attack*: *a victim of the financial situation*; an animal for sacrifice. – *v* **'victimize** to treat unjustly or with unnecessary harshness; to make a victim of.

'victor *n* a winner (of a contest *etc*). – *adj* **victorious** [vik'tōriəs] successful in a battle or other contest. – *n* **victory** ['viktəri] success in any battle, struggle or contest: – *pl* **'victories**.

victuals ['vitlz] *npl* food.

video ['vidiō] *adj, n* (having to do with) the recording or broadcasting of television pictures and sound: – *pl* **'videos**. – *v* to record (a film, television broadcast *etc*) on videotape: – *pres p* **'videoing**, *pt* **'videoed**. – *n* **'videotape** magnetic tape for carrying pictures and sound.

vie *v* (*usu* with **with**) to try to do better than: – *pres p* **'vȳing**, *pt* **vied**.

view [vū] *n* a sight; a range or field of sight: *a good view*; a scene; an opinion. – *v* to look at; to watch (television); to consider. – *n* **'viewpoint** a place from which a scene is viewed; one's way of looking at a matter (also **point of view**). – **in view** in sight; in one's mind as an aim; **in view of** taking into consideration; **on view** on show; ready for inspecting; **with a view to** with the purpose or intention of.

vigil ['vijil] *n* a time of watching or of keeping awake at night (sometimes before a religious festival). – *n* **'vigilance** watchfulness, alertness. – *adj* **'vigilant**. – *n* **vigilante** [viji'lanti] a member of a group taking upon itself the task of keeping order in an unsettled or disorderly community.

vignette [vi'nyet] *n* a little design or portrait; a short description or character sketch.

vigour ['vigər] *n* strength of body or mind, energy. – *n* **'vigorous** strong, healthy; forceful: *a vigorous attack*.

'Viking *n* (*hist*) a Norse invader of W. Europe.

vile *adj* wicked; very bad; disgusting. – *v* **'vilify** to say wicked things about: – *pt* **'vilified**.

'villa *n* a house, *usu* detached; a house in the country *etc* used for holidays.

'village *n* a collection of houses, not big enough to be called a town. – *n* **'villager** one who lives in a village.

villain ['vilən] *n* a wicked person, a scoundrel; a rascal. – *adj* **'villainous** wicked. – *n* **'villainy** wickedness: – *pl*

'villainies.

villein ['vilān] *n* (*hist*) a serf.

'vindicate *v* to clear from blame; to justify.

vin'dictive *adj* revengeful; spiteful.

vine *n* a type of climbing plant that bears grapes; any climbing or trailing plant. – *ns* **vinery** ['vinəri] a hot-house for growing vines; **vineyard** ['vinyärd] a place planted with grape vines.

vinegar ['vinigər] *n* a sour-tasting kind of liquid made from wine, beer *etc*, used as seasoning, for pickling *etc*.

'vintage *n* the gathering of ripe grapes; the grapes gathered; wine of a particular year, *esp* when of very high quality; the time or period of origin or manufacture. *What vintage is your car?* – *adj* of a vintage; (of wine) of a particular year and *usu* of very high quality; (of a play *etc*) of high quality and characteristic of the author *etc*. – *n* **vintage car** one of a very early type, still able to run.

'vintner *n* a wineseller.

vi'ōla *n* a kind of large violin. – *n* **'viola** any member of the family of plants which include violets and pansies.

'violate *v* to break (a law, a treaty *etc*); to do harm to, *esp* to rape; to treat with disrespect; to disturb, interrupt. – *ns* **vio'lation**; **'violator**.

'violent *adj* acting or done with great force: *a violent storm*: *a violent blow*; caused by violence: *a violent death*; uncontrollable: *a violent temper*. – *n* **'violence** great roughness and force.

'violet *n* a kind of small bluish-purple flower.

vio'lin *n* a type of musical instrument with four strings, played with a bow. – *n* **vio'linist** one who plays the violin.

violoncello [viələn'chelō] *see* **cello**.

'viper *n see* **adder**; a vicious or treacherous person.

vi'rago *n* a noisy, bad-tempered woman: – *pl* **vi'ragos**.

'virgin *n* one, *esp* a woman, who has had no sexual intercourse. – *adj* of a virgin; pure, untouched. – *adj* **'virginal** of, like, a virgin. – **the Virgin Mary** the mother of Jesus.

'virginal *n* (often *pl*) an early type of musical instrument, with a keyboard. – *adj see* **virgin**.

'virile *adj* manly; strong, vigorous. – *n* **virility** [və'riləti] manhood; manliness; strength, vigour.

virtue ['vərtū] *n* goodness of character and behaviour; a good quality *eg* honesty, generosity *etc*; a good point. *One virtue of plastic crockery is that it doesn't break.* – *adj* **'virtual** in effect, though not in strict fact. *Because of the weakness of the king she was the virtual ruler.* – *adv* '**virtually**: *virtually in complete charge.* – *adj* '**virtuous** good, just, honest. – **by virtue of** because of.

virtu'**ōso** *n* a highly skilled performance on a musical instrument or in another art: – *pl* virtu'**osos**. – *n* **virtuosity** [vərtū'osəti].

'**virūlent** *adj* full of poison; bitter, spiteful; (of a disease) dangerous. – *n* '**virulence**.

'**virus** *n* any of several kinds of germs that are smaller than any bacteria, and cause certain diseases, as mumps, chickenpox *etc*.

visa ['vēzə] *n* the mark put on one's passport by the authorities of a country, to show that one may travel in that country.

visage ['vizij] *n* the face.

vis-à-vis ['vēzä'vē] *prep* in relation to, compared with: *his hopes vis-à-vis his abilities.*

viscera ['visərə] *npl* the inner parts of the body.

viscid ['visid] *adj* viscous.

viscount ['vīkownt] *n* a title of nobility next below an earl: – *fem* '**viscountess**.

'**viscous** (of a liquid) sticky, not flowing easily. – *n* **vis'cosity**.

visible ['vizəbl] *adj* able to be seen. – *n* **visi'bility** the clearness with which objects may be seen; the extent or range of vision as affected by fog, rain *etc*.

vision ['vizhən] *n* the act or power of seeing; something seen in the imagination; a strange, supernatural sight; the ability to foresee likely future events. – *adj* '**visionary** seen in imagination only, not real. – *n* a person who forms plans which are difficult or impossible to carry out.

visit ['vizit] *v* to go to see; to call on; to stay with as a guest. – *n* a call at a person's house or at a place of interest *etc*; a short stay. – *ns* **visi'tation** a visit of an important official, or of a supernatural being; a great misfortune, seen as a punishment from God; '**visitor** one who makes a visit.

visor ['vīzər] *n* a part of a helmet covering the face; a movable shade on a car's windscreen; the peak of a cap for shading the eyes.

'**vista** *n* a view, *esp* one seen through or along an avenue of trees, or other long, narrow opening.

visual ['vizhōōəl] *adj* of, concerned with, or received through, sight: *visual aids.* – *v* '**visualize** to form a clear picture of in the mind.

'**vital** *adj* of the greatest importance: *vital information*; necessary to life; of life; vigorous, energetic: *a vital personality.* – *n* **vi'tality** life; liveliness, strength; ability to go on living. – *v* '**vitalize** to give life or vigour to. – *npl* '**vitals** (*old*) parts of the body necessary for life.

'**vitamins** *npl* any of a group of substances necessary for health, different ones occurring in different natural foods.

vitiate ['vishiāt] *v* to spoil or damage.

vitreous ['vitriəs] *adj* of, or like, glass. – *v* '**vitrifȳ** to make or become, glasslike: – *pt* '**vitrified**.

'**vitriol** *n* sulphuric acid. – *adj* **vitri'olic** biting, scathing: *vitriolic criticism.*

vituperate [vi'tūpərāt] *v* to be rude to, abuse. – *n* **vitupe'ration**. – *adj* **vi'tuperative** abusive, very rude.

vivacious [vi'vāshəs] *adj* lively, sprightly. – *n* **vivacity** [vi'vasəti] liveliness of behaviour.

'**viva** *n* an oral examination (short for **viva voce** ['vivə'vōsi]).

vi'vārium *n* a tank or other enclosure for keeping living creatures.

'**vivid** *adj* life-like; brilliant, striking.

vivi'section *n* the carrying out of experiments on living animals.

'**vixen** *n* a female fox; an ill-tempered woman.

viz *adv* namely. *Three games are played in this school, viz football, hockey and cricket.*

vizier [vi'zēr] *n* (mainly *hist*) a minister of state in some Eastern countries.

vo'cabūlary *n* the stock or range of words used by a person or a group *etc*; the words of a language; a list of words in alphabetical order, with their meanings.

'**vōcal** *adj* of the voice; expressing one's opinions *etc* loudly and fully. – *n* '**vocalist** a singer.

vo'cation *n* an occupation or profession, *esp* one to which one feels called (by God) to dedicate oneself. *Nursing is a vocation*; a strong inclination or desire to follow a particular course of action or work.

vociferous [və'sifərəs] *adj* loud in speech, noisy.

'**vodka** *n* an alcoholic spirit made from grain or from potatoes.

vogue [vōg] *n* the fashion of the moment; popularity. – **in vogue** in fashion.

voice *n* the sound produced from the mouth in speech or song; ability to sing; (the right to express) an opinion. – *v* to express (an opinion *etc*).

void *adj* empty, vacant; not valid. – *n* an empty space. – **void of** lacking completely.

'volatile *adj* (of a liquid) quickly turning into vapour; (of a person) changeable in mood or behaviour.

vol'cāno *n* a mountain, *usu* cone-shaped, with an opening through which molten rock, ashes *etc* are, or have been, periodically thrown up from inside the earth: – *pl* **vol'canoes.** – *adj* **volcanic** [vol'kanik] of volcanoes; caused or produced by heat within the earth.

vole *n* any of several kinds of small rodents, including the water rat.

vo'lition *n* an act of will or of choosing. *He did it of his own volition.*

'volley *n* a number of shots fired or missiles thrown at the same time; an outburst (of words); (in tennis) a return of a ball before it reaches the ground: – *pl* **'volleys.** – *v* to shoot or throw in a volley; to return (a ball) before it reaches the ground.

vōlt *n* the unit used in measuring the force of electricity. – *n* **'voltage** electrical force measured in volts.

'volūble *adj* (speaking) with a great flow of words. – *n* **volu'bility.**

'volume *n* a book, often one of a series; the amount of space taken up by anything; amount: *the volume of trade*; loudness or fullness (of sound). – *adj* **voluminous** [və'lōōminəs] bulky, of great volume.

'voluntary *adj* done, or acting, by choice, not under compulsion; (working) without payment. – *n* a piece of organ music of the organist's choice played at a church service.

volun'teer *n* one who offers to perform some task, service *etc* of his own accord. – *v* to offer to do something of one's own accord; to give (information, an opinion *etc*) unasked.

voluptuous [və'lupchōōəs] *adj* full of, or too fond of, the pleasures of life.

'vomit *v* to throw up the contents of the stomach through the mouth. – *n* the substance thrown up by vomiting.

voracious [və'rāshəs] *adj* very greedy, difficult to satisfy: *a voracious appetite*: *a voracious reader.* – *n* **voracity** [və'rasəti].

'vortex *n* a whirlpool; a whirlwind: – *pl* **vortices** ['vörtisēz] or **'vortexes.**

'vōtary *n* one who has made a vow to do some good service; a devoted worshipper or admirer: – *pl* **'votaries.**

vote *v* to give one's support to (a particular candidate, a proposal *etc*) by putting a mark on a paper, or by raising one's hand *etc*; to decide by voting. – *n* a formal expression of a wish or opinion by voting; the right to vote. – *n* **'voter** one who votes.

vouch *v* (with **for**) to say that one is sure of or can guarantee. *I can vouch for his courage.* – *n* **'voucher** a paper which says that money or goods will be given for it. – *v* **vouch'safe** to give or grant (a reply, privilege *etc*).

vow [vow] *n* a solemn promise or declaration *esp* one made to God. – *v* to make a vow; to threaten (revenge *etc*).

vowel ['vowəl] *n* any of many simple sounds made by the voice that do not require the use of tongue, teeth or lips; the letters a, e, i, o and u (or various combinations of them), which represent those sounds.

'voyage *n* a journey, *esp* one by sea. – *v* to make a journey.

'vulgar *adj* coarse, ill-mannered; indecent; of the common people. – *n* **vul'garity.** – *n* **vulgar fraction** a fraction not written as a decimal, *eg* a half written ¹/₂, not 0·5.

'vulnerable *adj* exposed to, in danger of, attack; liable to be hurt in body or feelings.

'vulture *n* a large type of bird that lives chiefly on the flesh of dead animals.

W

wad [wod] *n* a mass or lump of loose material (as wool, cloth, paper) pressed together; a bunch of banknotes. – *n* **'wadding** soft material (*eg* cotton wool) used for packing, padding *etc.*

waddle ['wodl] *v* to walk with short, unsteady steps, moving from side to side as a duck does. – Also *n.*

wade *v* to walk through water, mud *etc*; to get through (work, a book *etc*) with difficulty. – *n* **'wader** a type of long-legged bird that wades in search of food; (*pl*) high waterproof boots (as worn by anglers) for wading.

wadi ['wodi] *n* in North Africa, the rocky bed of a river, dry except in the rainy season.

'wāfer *n* a very thin, light type of biscuit,

as that eaten with ice cream; a very thin slice of anything.

waffle ['wofl] *n* (*esp US*) a kind of light, crisp cake made from butter, cooked in a **'waffle-iron**; pointless, long-drawn-out talk. – *v* to talk long and meaninglessly.

waft [woft] *v* to carry or drift lightly through the air or over water.

wag *v* to move from side to side or up and down: – *pt* **wagged**. – *n* an act of wagging; a person who is always joking. – *adj* **'waggish** always joking.

wage [wāj] *v* to carry on (a war *etc*). – *n* (often *pl*) payment for work. – *n* **'wager** a bet. – *v* to bet.

'waggle *v* to move from side to side in an unsteady manner. – Also *n*.

'wag(g)on *n* a strong four-wheeled vehicle for carrying loads; an open railway carriage for goods; .(*US*) a trolley for carrying food.

'wagtail *n* a small black and white type of bird with a long tail which wags up and down.

waif *n* an uncared-for or homeless child or other person or animal. – **waifs and strays** people, animals, without a home.

wail *v* to cry or moan (for sorrow). – Also *n*.

wain *n* (*old*) a wagon.

'wainscot *n* the wooden lining or panelling sometimes found round (the lower part of) the walls of a room.

waist *n* the narrow part of one's body, between ribs and hips. – *n* **waistcoat** ['wāskōt] a short, sleeveless jacket (worn by men under the outer jacket).

wait *v* to put off or delay action (until a certain event occurs); (with **for**) to remain in expectation or readiness for (a person or thing), to await; to act as a waiter. – *n* a delay; (*pl*) singers of Christmas carols. – *ns* **'waiter, 'waitress** a man, a woman, whose job it is to serve people at table. – *ns* **waiting list** a list of people needing, and waiting for, something; **waiting room** a room in which to wait (at a station *etc*). – **wait (up)on** to serve (someone) at table; to act as a servant to.

waive *v* to give up (a claim or right).

wake *v* (often with **up**) (to cause) to stop sleeping: – *pt* **woke, waked**, *pp* **'woken, 'wakened**. – *n* a night of watching beside a dead body; a feast or holiday; a streak of foamy water left in the track of a ship. – *adj* **'wakeful** not sleeping, unable to sleep. – *v* **'waken** to wake, arouse or be aroused. – *adj* **'waking** (of, belonging to the state of)

being or becoming awake. – **in the wake of** immediately behind or after.

walk [wök] *v* to cause to move along on foot; to travel along (the streets *etc*) on foot. – *n* an act of walking; a manner of walking; a distance (to be) walked over; a place for walking: *a covered walk*. – *ns* **'walkie-'talkie** a wireless set for sending and receiving messages, carried on the body; **walking stick** a stick used for support when walking; **'walk-over** an easy victory. – **walk of life** one's rank or occupation; **walk the plank** (*hist*) to be put to death by pirates by being made to walk off the end of a plank sticking out over a ship's side.

wall [wöl] *n* something built of stone, brick *etc* used to separate, or to enclose; the side of a building. – *v* (with **in, up, off** *etc*) to enclose or separate with a wall. – *ns* **'wallflower** a kind of sweet-smelling spring flower; a person who is continually without a partner at a dance *etc*; **'wallpaper** paper used in house decorating for covering walls.

wallaby ['woləbi] *n* a small kind of kangaroo: – *pl* **'wallabies**.

wallet ['wolit] *n* a small flat case of a soft material (as leather *etc*) for holding bank notes, personal documents *etc*.

wallop ['woləp] *v* (*coll*) to beat, to hit. – Also *n*.

wallow ['wolō] *v* to roll about with enjoyment (in water, mud *etc*).

walnut ['wölnut] *n* a type of tree whose wood is used for making furniture; its nut.

walrus ['wölrəs] *n* a large type of sea animal, like a seal, with two long tusks: – *pl* **'walruses**.

waltz ['wölts] *n* a kind of dance with a whirling motion performed by couples; music (with three beats to each bar) for this. – *v* to dance a waltz.

wan [won] *adj* pale and sickly-looking.

wand [wond] *n* a long slender rod as used by a conjuror, or, in stories *etc*, by fairies, magicians *etc*.

wander ['wondər] *v* to go from place to place, to roam with no definite purpose; to go astray; to be disordered in one's mind because of illness *etc*. – *n* **'wanderer**. – *n* **'wanderlust** a keen desire for travel.

wane *v* to become smaller (opposite of **wax**); to lose power, importance *etc*. – **on the wane** becoming less.

wangle ['waŋgl] *v* to get, manage, achieve, through craftiness, skilful planning *etc*.

want [wont] *v* to wish for; to need; to

lack. – *n* poverty; scarcity; need; lack.
– *adjs* **'wanted** looked for, *esp* by the
police; **'wanting** absent, missing;
without; not good enough; feeble-
minded; (with **in**) lacking.

wanton ['wontən] *adj* (of a destructive
act, of cruelty *etc*) thoughtless, pointless, without motive.

war [wör] *n* an armed struggle, *esp*
between nations. – *v* (with **against**) to
fight in a war, make war against: – *pres p*
'warring. – *n* **'warrior** a fighting
man, a great fighter. – *ns* **'war-cry** a
phrase or word shouted aloud in battle,
for encouragement; **'warfare** the
carrying on of war, armed struggle;
'warhead the part of a missile containing the explosive. – *adj* **'warlike** fond
of war; threatening war. – *n* **'warship** a
ship equipped for war, with guns *etc*. –
on the warpath in a fighting or angry
mood.

warble ['wörbl] *v* to sing like a bird, to
trill. – *n* **'warbler** any of several types
of singing birds.

ward [wörd] *v* (with **off**) to keep off,
defend oneself against (a blow *etc*). – *n*
in a hospital *etc* a room containing a
number of beds; one of the parts into
which a town is divided for voting; a
person who is in the care of a guardian.
– *ns* **'warden** one who guards a game
reserve *etc*; a person in charge of a
hostel or college; **'warder** a prison
guard: – *fem* **'wardress**; **'wardrobe** a
cupboard for clothes; a person's supply
of clothes; **'wardroom** a room for
officers on a warship.

ware *n* manufactured material (often
pottery); now *usu* used as part of a
word: *earthenware*: *glassware*: *iron-
ware etc*; (*pl*) goods for sale. – *n*
'warehouse a building where goods
are stored.

warm [wörm] *adj* fairly hot; (of clothes)
keeping the wearer warm; (of a person
or his behaviour *etc*) earnest, sincere,
friendly, loving. – *v* to make or become
warm. – *n* **warmth**. – *adjs* **'warm-
'blooded** having a blood temperature
higher than that of the surrounding
atmosphere; **'warm-'hearted** kind,
generous.

warn [wörn] *v* to tell (a person) beforehand about possible danger, misfortune *etc*. *I warned him about the icy
roads*; to give (cautionary) advice to. *I
warned him not to be late*. – *n* **'warning**
something (*eg* a person's words, a
notice *etc*) that warns.

warp [wörp] *v* to (cause to) become
twisted out of shape; to cause to think,

reason *etc* wrongly. *His previous experiences had warped his judgement*. – *n* the
threads stretched lengthwise on a loom,
to be crossed by the **weft**.

warrant ['worənt] *n* something which
gives a person the authority or right to
do a certain thing; a certificate *etc*
granting such authority: *a search warrant*. – *v* to justify, be a good enough
reason for. *Such a crime does not warrant
such punishment*. – *adj* **'warranted**
guaranteed. – **I warrant you, I'll
warrant** you may be sure, I assure
you.

warren ['worən] *n* a place full of rabbit
burrows.

wart [wört] *n* a small hard growth on the
skin. – *n* **'wart-hog** a kind of wild pig
found in Africa.

'wāry *adj* cautious, on one's guard. – *adv*
'warily. – *n* **'wariness**.

was *see* **be**.

wash [wosh] *v* to clean with water, soap
etc; to clean oneself with water *etc*; (of
water) to flow over or against; to sweep
(away, along *etc*) by force of water. – *n*
a washing; a streak of foamy water left
behind by a moving boat; a liquid with
which anything is washed; a thin coat
of paint *etc*: – *pl* **'washes**. – *ns* **'washer**
a person or thing that washes; a flat ring
of metal, rubber *etc* for keeping nuts or
joints tight; **'washing** the act of cleaning by water; clothes (to be) washed. –
ns **'washerwoman** a woman who is
paid to wash clothes; **washhand
basin** a kind of basin (with taps and a
plug) in which to wash one's hands and
face; **washing machine** a machine
(*usu* driven by electricity) for washing
clothes. – **wash one's hands of** to
have nothing further to do with; **wash
up** to wash dishes *etc*.

wasp [wosp] *n* a stinging, winged type of
insect, with a slender, yellow and black
striped body.

wassail ['wosl] *v* (*old*) to hold a merry
drinking meeting. – Also *n*.

wāste *adj* thrown away, rejected as
useless or worthless: *waste paper*: *waste
materials*; (of ground or land) uncultivated, or barren and desolate. – *v* to use
or spend (money, time, energy,
materials) extravagantly, or with too
little result or profit; to (cause to) decay
or wear away gradually. – *n* extravagant
use, squandering; rubbish, waste material; uncultivated land; an unbroken
expanse, a stretch (of water, snow *etc*).
– *n* **'wastage** amount wasted; loss
through decay or (wasteful) use. – *adj*
'wasteful involving or causing waste,

extravagant. – n 'waster, 'wastrel an idle, good-for-nothing person. – ns wastepaper basket a basket for (paper) rubbish; 'wastepipe a pipe for carrying away dirty water or semi-liquid waste matter.

watch [woch] v to look at, observe, closely; (often with over) to look after, to mind; (old) to keep awake. – n the act of keeping guard; one who keeps, or those who keep, guard; a sailor's period of duty on deck (usu four hours); a kind of small clock for the pocket or wrist: – pl 'watches. – adj 'watchful alert, cautious. – ns 'watchman a man who guards a building etc, esp at night; 'watchword a motto or slogan.

water ['wötər] n a clear liquid without taste or smell when pure, which falls as rain; any collection of it, as an ocean, sea, lake, river etc; saliva, urine or other bodily fluids. – v to supply with water; to dilute or mix with water; (of the mouth) to fill with saliva; (of the eyes) to fill with tears. – adj 'watery full of, or like, water; tasteless, dull. – ns water biscuit a crisp kind of biscuit, a cracker; water butt a large barrel for rain water; 'water-closet (usu WC) a toilet, a lavatory; 'water-colour a paint used by mixing with water, not with oil; a painting done with this paint; 'watercress a small type of plant found beside streams, used for salads etc; 'waterfall a place where a river falls from a height, usu over a ledge of rock; 'waterhen a dark-coloured type of bird which lives about ponds or rivers; 'waterlily a type of plant growing in ponds etc with flat floating leaves and large flowers. – adj 'waterlogged filled with water; saturated with, or soaked with, water. – ns 'water-main a large underground pipe carrying a public water supply; 'watermark a faint design showing the maker's name, crest etc in a sheet of writing paper; 'watermelon a type of large, very juicy, fruit; 'watermill a mill driven by water; water polo a type of game played by swimmers (seven on each side) with a floating ball. – adj 'waterproof not allowing water to pass through. – n an outer garment made of waterproof material. – ns water rat a kind of vole; 'watershed a ridge or line separating the valleys of two rivers. – adj 'watertight so closely fitted or made that water cannot leak through. – ns 'waterway a channel along which ships can sail; 'waterwheel a wheel moved by water. – npl 'waterworks

the place where the water of a town is made pure and stored.

watt [wot] n a unit of electric power. – n 'wattage electric power measured in watts.

wattle ['wotl] n twigs and branches interwoven, used for fences etc; an Australian type of tree; a fleshy part hanging from the neck of a turkey.

wave n a moving ridge on the surface of the water; anything resembling this, as a ridge or curve in the hair; a vibration travelling through the air or through space conveying light, sound etc; a gesture made with the hand; a rush of anything (as of despair, enthusiasm, crime etc). – v to make a sign with the hand; to (cause to) move to and fro, or flutter; to (cause to) curl or curve. – adj 'wavy having waves. – n 'wavelength the distance from one (high, low etc) point on a wave or vibration to the next similar point.

'wäver v to be unsteady or uncertain, to falter.

wax n the sticky, fatty substance of which bees make their cells; any substance like it, as that in the ear; a quickly hardening substance used for sealing letters etc. – adj made of wax. – v to rub with wax; to grow, increase (opposite of wane). – adjs 'waxen made of, or like, wax; pale; 'waxy of, or like, wax. – npl 'waxworks a place where wax models of well-known people are shown.

way n an opening, a passage: the way out; road, path; room to go forward or to pass: to block the way; direction. He went that way; route. Do you know the way?; distance: a long way; condition: in a bad way; means, method. Find a way of doing this; manner: in a clumsy way; one's own wishes or choice. He gets his own way. – -ways (used with another word) in the direction of: lengthways: sideways. – n 'wayfarer a traveller, usu on foot. – v way'lay to wait for and stop (a person). – n 'wayside the edge of a road or path. – Also adj. – adj 'wayward wilful, following one's own way. – by the way incidentally, in passing; by way of travelling through; as if, with the purpose of. He did it by way of helping me; in the way blocking one's progress; make one's way to go (to).

WC see water-closet.

we pron the word used by a speaker or writer in mentioning himself or herself together with other people (as the subject of a verb). We chased them *away from the fire.*

weak *adj* not strong, feeble; lacking determination, easily persuaded; easily overcome: *weak opposition.* – *v* **'weaken** to make or become weak. – *n* **'weakling** a person or animal lacking strength. – *adj* **'weakly** lacking strength, sickly. – *n* **'weakness** lack of strength; a fault; a special fondness (for): *a weakness for chocolate.* – *adj* **'weak'kneed** lacking determination.

weal *n* a raised mark on the skin caused by a blow from a whip *etc*.

wealth [welth] *n* riches; a large quantity: *a wealth of information.* – *adj* **'wealthy** rich.

wean *v* to make (a child or other young animal) used to food other than the mother's milk; (with **from**) to cause (a person) gradually to give up (a bad habit *etc*).

weapon ['wepən] *n* an instrument used for fighting, as a sword, gun *etc*; any means of attack.

wear [wār] *v* to be dressed in, to have on the body; to arrange (one's hair *etc*) in a particular way; to have (a beard, moustache) on the face; to have, to show. *She was wearing a triumphant expression*; to damage, to make gradually less, by use, by rubbing *etc*; to be damaged, become less, in this way; to last: *to wear well*: – *pt* **wore**, *pp* **worn**. – *n* use by wearing: *for my own wear*; damage by use; ability to last; clothes *etc*: *school wear*. – *adj* **'wearable** fit to be worn. – *n* **'wearer**. – *adj* **'wearing** tiring, exhausting; worn, damaged by use; tired. – **wear and tear** damage by ordinary use; **wear off** to pass away gradually; **wear on** to become later. *The afternoon wore on*; **wear out** to make or become unfit for further use; to exhaust (*adj* **'worn-'out**).

'weary *adj* tired, having used up one's strength or patience; tiring, boring. – *v* to make or become tired, bored or impatient: – *pt* **'wearied**. – *adj* **'wearisome** causing tiredness, boredom or impatience. – **weary of** tired of, bored with.

weasel ['wēzl] *n* a type of small wild animal with a long and slender body, that lives on mice, birds *etc*.

weather ['wedhər] *n* the state of the atmosphere (heat, coldness, cloudiness *etc*). – *v* to (cause to) dry, wear away, become discoloured *etc*, through exposure to the air; to come safely through (a storm, difficulty *etc*). – *adj* **'weather-beaten** showing signs of having been out in all weathers. – *ns* **'weathercock,**

'weathervane a flat piece of metal (often in the shape of a cock) that swings round with, and shows the direction of, the wind.

weave *v* to pass threads over and under each other on a loom *etc* to form cloth; to plait cane, willow-sticks *etc*; to put together (a story, plan *etc*); to move in and out between objects, or to move from side to side. *He wove his way through the traffic*: – *pt* **wove**, *pp* **'woven**. – *n* **'weaver** one who weaves.

web *n* the net made by a spider, a cobweb; the skin between the toes of ducks, swans, frogs *etc*; something woven. – *adj* **webbed** (of feet) having the toes joined by a web. – *n* **'webbing** a type of strong, woven tape of nylon *etc*, used for belts *etc*. – *adjs* **'web-'footed**, **-'toed** having webbed feet or toes.

wed *v* to marry: – *pt* **'wedded**. – *n* **'wedding** marriage; a marriage ceremony. – *n* **'wedlock** the state of being married.

we'd [wēd] short for **we would, we should** or **we had**.

wedge [wej] *n* a piece of wood, metal *etc* thick at one end but sloping to a thin edge at the other used in splitting wood, stone *etc*, forcing two surfaces apart, or for fixing firmly (doors *etc*); anything shaped like a wedge. – *v* to fix, or to become fixed, with or as if with a wedge; to push or squeeze (in). *He wedged himself in amongst the crowd.*

Wednesday ['wenzdi] *n* the fourth day of the week.

wee *adj* (mainly *Scots*) small, tiny.

weed *n* any useless, troublesome plant; a weak, worthless person; (*pl*) a widow's mourning clothes. – *v* to clear (a garden *etc*) of weeds. – *adj* **'weedy** full of weeds; like a weed; (of a man) very thin and weak, unmanly.

week *n* the space of seven days, *esp* from Sunday to Saturday; the working days of the week, not (Saturday and) Sunday. – *adj* **'weekly** happening, or done, once a week. – *adv* once a week. – *n* a newspaper, magazine *etc* coming out once a week. – *ns* **'weekday** any day except (Saturday and) Sunday; **'week'end** the time from Saturday to Monday.

weep *v* to shed tears; to ooze or drip: *a weeping wound.* – *adj* **'weeping** (of the willow tree *etc*) having drooping branches.

'weevil *n* any of several types of small beetles that destroy grain, flour *etc*.

weft *see* **warp**.

weigh [wā] *v* to find out how heavy a thing is (by putting it on a scale *etc*); to have a certain heaviness. *It weighs 1 kilogramme*; to raise (a ship's anchor); (of burdens, cares *etc*) to press down, be heavy or troublesome; to consider (a matter, a point) carefully; to be of importance. – *n* **weight** the amount that anything weighs; a piece of metal weighing a certain amount (*eg* a 100 gramme weight *etc*); something heavy, a load or burden; importance. – *v* to make heavy by adding or attaching a weight. – *adj* **'weightless**. – *n* **'weightlessness** absence of the pull of gravity. – *adj* **'weighty** heavy; important – *n* **'weighbridge** a large scale for weighing vehicles. – **weigh in** to test one's weight before a boxing match; **weigh out** to measure out a quantity by weighing it on a scale.

weir [wēr] *n* a dam across a stream.

weird [wērd] *adj* mysterious, supernatural; odd, strange.

welcome ['welkəm] *v* to receive with kindness or pleasure; to accept or undergo gladly. *I welcome the challenge.* – *n* a welcoming, a kindly reception. – *adj* received with gladness; causing gladness. – **welcome!** *interj* used to express a greeting to a guest; **welcome (to)** permitted (to do or take something). *You are welcome to help yourself*; **you're welcome!** polite expression used in reply to an expression of thanks.

weld *v* to join (pieces of metal *etc*) by pressure, with or without heating; to join closely. – *n* a joint made by welding. – *n* **'welder**.

'welfare *n* comfort, good health, freedom from want. – *n* **welfare state** country with health service, insurance against unemployment, pensions for those who cannot work *etc*.

well *n* a spring of water; a shaft (*usu* circular) made in the earth so as to obtain water, oil *etc*; any similar enclosed space, as that round which a staircase winds. – *v* (often with **up**) to rise up and gush. – *adj* in good health. – *adv* in a good or correct manner: *to speak well*; thoroughly. *He was well beaten*; successfully: *to do well*; conveniently. *That will fit in well with my plans*: – *comp* **better**, *superl* **best**. – *interj* expressing surprise, or used in explaining, narrating *etc*. – *adj* **'well-ad'vised** wise. – *n* **'well-'being** welfare; contentment. – *adjs* **'well-'bred**, **'well-'mannered** having good manners; **'well-dis'posed** (with **to**,

towards) inclined to favour; **'well-in'formed** having or showing knowledge; **'well-'known** familiar; celebrated, famous; **'well-'meaning** having good intentions; **'well-'meant** rightly, kindly intended; **'well-'off** rich; **'well-to-'do** rich; **'well-'read** having read many good books. – *n* **'well-wisher** one who wishes a person success. – **as well (as)** in addition (to); **it is well (as well, just as well)** it is a good thing, fortunate.

we'll [wēl] short for **we shall** or **will**.

'wellingtons *npl* high rubber boots covering the lower part of the legs.

'welsh 'rarebit *n* a dish made of cheese melted on toast.

welt *n* a firm edging or band (as on a garment, at the wrist, waist *etc*); a weal.

'welter *v* to roll about or wallow. – *n* a state of great disorder; a confused mass: *a welter of information about holiday travel.*

wench *n* (*old*) a young woman, a girl: – *pl* **'wenches**.

wend: wend one's way to make one's way (slowly).

went *see* **go**.

wept *see* **weep**.

were *see* **be**.

we're [wēr] short for **we are**.

werewolf ['wērwoolf] *n* (*myth*) a person supposed to be able to change himself for a time into a wolf.

west *n* one of the four chief directions, that in which the sun sets. – Also *adj*, *adv*. – *adjs* **'westerly** lying or moving towards the west; (of wind) from the west; **'western** in, of, belonging to, the west. – *n* a film or story about the life of the early settlers in the western United States (the **Wild West**). – *n* **'westerner** a person belonging to the west. – *adjs* **'westernmost** most westerly; **'westward** towards the west. – Also *adv* (often **'westwards**).

wet *adj* containing, soaked with, covered with, water or other liquid; rainy: *a wet day*. – *n* water; rain. – *v* to make wet: – *pt* **wet**, **'wetted**.

whack *n* a loud slap or blow. – Also *v*.

whale *n* a very large kind of mammal (not fish) living in the sea. – *v* to catch whales. – *n* **'whaler** a person or ship engaged in catching whales. – *ns* **'whalebone** a light bendable substance obtained from the upper jaw of certain whales; **whale oil** oil obtained from the blubber of a whale.

wharf [wörf] *n* a landing stage for loading and unloading ships: – *pls*

wharfs, wharves. – n **wharfinger** ['wörfinjər] one who looks after a wharf.

what [wot] adj, pron used to indicate something about which a question is being asked. *What street is this? What are you doing?* – adj any . . . that. *Give me what books you have.* – conj anything that. *I'll take what you can give me.* – adj, adv, pron used for emphasis in exclamations. *What clothes she wears! What bad taste she has! You did what!* – pron, adj **what**'ever anything (that). *Show me whatever you have*; no matter what: *whatever happens.* – adj **what**so'ever at all: *nothing whatsoever to do with me.* – **what about?** used in asking whether the listener would like (to do) something. *What about a glass of milk?*; **what if?** what will or would happen if . . .? *What if he comes back?*; **what with . . . and** because of. *What with having no exercise and being overweight, he had a heart attack.*

wheat n a grain from which the flour used for making bread *etc* is made. – adj **'wheaten** made of wheat; wholemeal. – n **'wheatear** a type of small bird, visiting Britain in summer.

'wheedle v to beg, to coax, using flattery *etc.*

'wheel n a circular frame or disc turning on an axle, used for transporting things *etc*; a steering-wheel (of a car *etc*). – v to move or push on wheels; to turn like a wheel or in a wide curve; to turn (round) suddenly. *She wheeled round in surprise.* – ns **'wheelbarrow** a handcart with one wheel in front, two handles and legs behind; **'wheelchair** a chair on wheels for an invalid; **'wheelhouse** the shelter in which a ship's steering-wheel is placed; **'wheelwright** one who makes wheels and carriages.

wheeze v to breathe with a whistling or croaking sound and with difficulty.

whelk n a type of small shellfish, used as food.

whelp n a young lion; a puppy. – v (of lions, dogs *etc*) to give birth to young ones.

when adv at what time? *When did you arrive?* – adv, conj (at, during) the time at which. *I know when you left. I fell when I was coming in.* – relative pron at which: *at the time when I saw him.* – conj seeing that, since. *Why walk when you have a car?* – adv **whence** (old) from what place? *Whence did you appear?* – conj (to the place) from which. *He's gone back (to the country) whence he came.* – adv, conj **whence'forth** (old) whence. – adv, conj **when'ever** at any given time. *Come and see me whenever you're ready*; at every time. *I go whenever I get the chance.*

where [wār] adv, conj to or in what place (?). *Where are you going? Do you know where we are?* – relative pron, conj (in the place) in which, (to the place) to which. *Sit in the seat where you were put! Go where he tells you to go. It's still where it was.* – adv, conj **wherea'bouts** near or in what place? *Whereabouts is it? I don't know whereabouts it is.* – n **'whereabouts** the place where a person or thing is. *I don't know his whereabouts.* – conj **where'as** when in fact. *He thought I was lying, whereas I was telling the truth*; but, on the other hand. *He's tall, whereas I'm short.* – adv, conj **'wherefore** (old) for which reason (?). – conj **whereu'pon** at or after which time, event *etc.* – adv **wher'ever** at what place? *Wherever did you go?* – conj to any place: *wherever you may go.* – n **'wherewithal** ['wārwidhöl] the means of doing something; money.

'wherry n a type of shallow, light boat: – pl **'wherries.**

whet v to sharpen (a knife *etc*) by rubbing; to make (one's desire, appetite *etc*) keener: – pt **'whetted.** – n **'whetstone** a stone on which knives *etc* may be sharpened.

whether ['wedhər] conj if. *I don't know whether it's possible (or not).*

which adj, pron used (often in questions) to refer to a particular person or thing from a group. *Which (colour) do you like best?*; the one that. *Show me which (dress) you would like.* – Also relative pron. *This church, which will soon be pulled down, is very old: the chair which you are sitting on.* – adj, pron **which'ever** any (one), no matter which. *I'll take whichever (book) you don't want: whichever way I turned.* – **which is which** which is one and which is the other. *Mary and Susan are twins and I can't tell which is which.*

whiff n a sudden puff (of scent, smoke, gas *etc*).

while, whilst conjs during the time that: *while I'm at the office*; although. *While I sympathize, I can't really help.* – n **while** a space of time. – v (with **away**) to pass (time) without boredom. *He whiled away the time by reading.*

whim n a sudden thought, fancy, or desire. – adj **whimsical** ['wimzikəl] full of whims, fanciful; humorous. – n **'whimsy** a whim: – pl **'whimsies.**

'**whimper** v to cry with a low, whining voice. – Also n.

whin n gorse.

whine v to utter a high-pitched, complaining cry; to complain unnecessarily. – Also n.

'**whinny** v (of horses) to neigh: – pl '**whinnies**. – Also n.

whip n a lash, with a handle, for punishing or urging on (horses etc); in parliament, a member of a party whose duty it is to see that his party-members are there to give their vote when needed. – v to hit, punish, drive, with a lash; to beat (eggs, cream etc) into a froth; to snatch (away, off, out, up etc): to whip out a revolver; to move fast, like a whip: – pt **whipped**. – n '**whipping** a beating with a whip. – ns '**whip-'hand** the advantage in a fight, argument etc; '**whippersnapper** a small, unimportant, impertinent person.

'**whippet** n a breed of racing dog, like a small greyhound.

whir(r) n a sound of fast, continuous whirling. – v to move, whirl, with a buzzing noise: – pt **whirred**.

whirl v to turn round quickly; to carry (off, away etc) quickly. – n a fast round-and-round movement; great excitement, confusion. Everyone was in a whirl over the wedding arrangements. – ns '**whirlpool** a place in a river, sea etc where the current moves in a circle; '**whirlwind** a very violent current of wind with a whirling motion.

whisk v to move, carry, sweep, quickly and lightly; to beat or whip (a mixture). – n a quick sweeping movement; a type of kitchen utensil for beating mixtures; a small bunch of twigs, bristles etc used to dust, brush etc.

'**whisker** n (usu pl) hair on the sides of a man's face; a long bristle on the upper lip of a cat etc.

'**whisky**, (Irish and US) '**whiskey** n a kind of alcoholic spirit made from grain.

'**whisper** v to speak very softly, using the breath only, not the voice; to make a soft, rustling sound. – Also n.

whist n a type of card game for four players.

whistle ['wisl] v to make a high-pitched sound by forcing breath through the lips or teeth; to make such a sound with an instrument; to move with such a sound, as a bullet or arrow does. – n the sound made by whistling; any instrument for whistling.

whit n a tiny bit: not a whit better.

white adj of the colour of pure snow; pale or light-coloured: white skin: white wine; of a pale-coloured complexion. – n something white; a person with a pale-coloured complexion of European race; the part of an egg surrounding the yolk. – v '**whiten** to make or become white or whiter. – ns '**whiteness**; '**whiting** a white powder made by grinding down chalk; a small type of fish related to the cod. – ns **white ant** a termite; '**whitebait** the young of herring or sprats; **white elephant** something useless and unwanted, esp something costly and troublesome to maintain. – adj '**white'hot** having reached a degree of heat at which metals etc glow with a white light (hotter than **red-hot**). – ns **white paper** a statement (printed on white paper) issued by the government for the information of parliament; '**whitewash** a mixture of whiting, or lime, and water, for whitening walls etc. – v to put whitewash on; to (try to) cover up the faults of, give a good appearance to.

whither ['widhər] adv, conj (old) to what place(?).

whitlow ['witlō] n an infected swelling beside the finger or toenail.

'**Whitsun, Whit** adjs of, or of the week beginning with, the seventh Sunday after Easter.

'**whittle** v to pare or cut (wood etc) with a knife; (with **away** or **down**) to make gradually less. She whittled away his savings.

whiz(z) v to move with a hissing sound, as an arrow does; to move very fast: – pt **whizzed**.

who [hoo] pron used (often in questions) to refer to a person or people unknown or unnamed (only as the subject of a verb). Who is that woman in the green hat?; (coll) used as the object in a sentence. Who did you choose? Who did you give it to? – relative pron. I knew the woman who died. Do you know who those people are? – prons **who'ever** any person or people; **whom** (often in questions) used to refer to a person or people unknown or unnamed (only as the object in a sentence). Whom did you see? To whom shall I speak? – conj. Do you know to whom I gave it? – relative pron: the person whom I liked best.

whole [hōl] adj complete; consisting of all, with nothing or no one missing; not broken; in good health. – n the entire thing. – adv '**wholly** entirely, altogether. – adj '**whole'hearted** enthusiastic, generous. – n '**wholemeal**

flour made from the entire wheat grain. – Also *adj*. – *n* '**wholesale** the sale of goods in large quantities to a shop *etc* from which they can be bought in small quantities by ordinary buyers. – *adj* buying, selling, bought, sold, through wholesale; on a large scale: *wholesale killing*. – *adj* '**wholesome** giving health, healthy. – **on the whole** when everything is taken into account.

who'll [hōōl] short for **who will, who shall**.

whom *see* **who**.

whoop *n* a loud cry, rising in pitch. – Also *v*. – *n* **whooping-cough** ['hōōpiŋkof] an infectious type of disease in which violent bouts of coughing are followed by a whoop as the breath is drawn in.

whortleberry ['wɔrtlbəri] *n* bilberry.

whose [hōōz] *adj, pron* belonging to whom, which person(?). *Whose (jacket) is this? – relative pron. Show me the boy whose father is a policeman. – conj. Do you know whose pen this is?*

whȳ *adv, pron* for which (reason). *Why are you not finished? Tell me (the reason) why you came here?* – **the whys and wherefores** (all) the reasons, details.

wick *n* the twisted threads (of cotton *etc*) in a candle or lamp which draw up the oil or grease to the flame.

wicked ['wikid] *adj* evil, sinful; mischievous, spiteful. – *n* '**wickedness**.

'**wicker** *adj* (of a chair *etc*) made of woven willow twigs *etc*.

'**wicket** *n* a small gate or door, *esp* in or beside a larger one; (in cricket) the set of three stumps, or one of these, at which the ball is bowled; the ground between the bowler and the batsman.

wide *adj* broad, not narrow; stretching far; measuring a certain amount from side to side: *5 centimetres wide*. – *adv* off the target. *The shots went wide*; (often with **apart**) far apart: *to hold one's arms wide*. – *adv* '**widely** over a wide area; among many: *widely believed*; far apart. – *v* '**widen** to make or become wide or wider. – *ns* '**wideness; width** [width] measurement across, from side to side; large extent. – *adjs* '**wide-a'wake** fully awake; alert; '**wide-'eyed** with eyes wide-open (in surprise *etc*); '**wide-'open** opened to the full extent; '**widespread** spread over a large area or among many: *a widespread belief*. – **wide of the mark** off the target, inaccurate.

widow ['widō] *n* a woman whose husband is dead. – *n* '**widower** a man whose wife is dead.

width *see* **wide**.

wield [wēld] *v* to swing or handle (a cricket bat, sword *etc*); to use (power, authority *etc*).

wife *n* a married woman; the woman to whom one is married; (*old*) a woman: – *pl* **wives**.

wig *n* an artificial covering of hair for the head.

'**wiggle** *v* to (cause to) move from side to side with jerky or twisting movements. – Also *n*. – *adj* '**wiggly**.

'**wigwam** *n* a conical tent of skins, as formerly made by N. American Indians.

wild *adj* (of animals) not tamed; (of plants) not cultivated in a garden *etc*; uncivilized; unruly, uncontrolled, violent; (of weather) stormy; frantic, mad: *wild with anxiety*; (of a remark, a guess *etc*) rash, inaccurate. – *n* (*usu pl*) an uncultivated or uncivilized region. – *ns* **wild boar** a wild type of pig; '**wildcat** a wild type of European cat. – *adj* (of a workers' strike) not supported or permitted by trade union officials. – *ns* '**wildfire** lightning without thunder; '**wildfowl** wild birds, *esp* those shot as game. – **like wildfire** very quickly; **wild-goose chase** a troublesome and useless errand.

'**wilderness** *n* a wild, uncultivated, or desolate region.

wile *n* a crafty trick. – *adj* '**wily**.

will *n* the power to choose or decide; desire: *against my will*; determination: *the will to win*; feeling towards someone: *goodwill: illwill*; a written statement about what is to be done with one's property after one's death. – *v* to (try to) influence someone by exercising one's will. *He willed her to win*; to hand down (property *etc*) by will: – *pt* **willed**; also used to form future tenses of other verbs when the subject is **he, she, it, you** or **they**. *You will see me there*; (*coll*) often used for the same purpose when the subject is **I** or **we**. *I will tell you later*; used for emphasis, or to express a promise, when the subject is **I** or **we**. *I will do it if possible*: – *pt* **would** [wood]. (*See* also **shall, would**). – *adjs* '**wilful** fond of having one's own way; intentional: *wilful damage*; '**willing** ready to do what is asked; eager. – **at will** as or when one chooses; **with a will** eagerly.

'**will-o'-the-'wisp** *n* a pale light sometimes seen by night over marshy places.

willow ['wilō] *n* a type of tree with long slender branches, or its wood (used in cricket bats). – *adj* '**willowy** slender, graceful: *a willowy figure.*

'**willy'nilly** *adv* whether one wishes or not.

wilt *v* (of flowers) to droop; to lose strength. *He wilts in hot weather.*

wily *see* **wile**.

win *v* to gain by contest (a victory *etc*), by luck (money in gambling *etc*), by effort (the love of someone *etc*); to come first in a contest, to be victorious; (often with **over**) to gain the support or friendship of. *He finally won over his mother-in-law:* – *pt* **won** [wun]. – *n* an act of winning; a victory. – *adj* '**winning** victorious, successful; charming, attractive: *a winning smile.* – *npl* '**winnings** money *etc* that has been won.

wince *v* to shrink or start back in pain *etc*, to flinch. *Her playing of the violin made him wince.*

wincey'ette *n* a type of brushed cotton cloth.

winch *n* a handle or crank for turning a wheel; a machine for lifting things up, worked by winding a rope round a revolving cylinder: – *pl* '**winches**. – **winch up** lift up with a winch.

wind[1] *n* air in motion, a current of air; breath; air carrying a scent (of game *etc*); air or gas in the stomach or intestines; the wind instruments in an orchestra. – *v* to put out of breath. – *adj* '**windy** (of weather) with a strong wind blowing; (of a place) exposed to strong winds. – *ns* '**windfall** a fruit blown from a tree; an unexpected gain or advantage, *eg* a sum of money; **wind instrument** any of many kinds of musical instruments sounded by wind, *esp* by the breath; '**windjammer** a type of sailing ship; '**windmill** a type of mill whose machinery is driven by sails which are moved by the wind, used for pumping water, grinding grain *etc*; '**windpipe** the tube leading from the mouth to the lungs; '**windscreen** a pane of glass in front of the driver of a motor-car *etc*; '**windshield** (*US*) a windscreen. – *adj* '**windswept** exposed to strong winds and showing the effects of it: *windswept hair.* – *n, adj, adv* '**windward** (in) the direction from which the wind blows. – **get the wind up** (*coll*) to become afraid; **get wind of** (*coll*) to hear about in an indirect way.

wind[2] *v* to turn, twist or coil; (sometimes with **up**) to screw up the spring of (a watch, clockwork toy *etc*); to wrap closely: – *pt* **wound**. – *n* '**winder** a knob, key *etc* for winding a clock *etc*. – *adj* '**winding** curving, twisting. – **wind one's way** to make one's way *esp*

by turning and twisting; **wind up** to bring or come to an end. *He wound up the meeting;* **wound up** tense, agitated.

'**windlass** *n* a machine for lifting up or hauling, a winch.

window ['windō] *n* an opening in the wall of a building *etc* (protected by glass) to let in light and air (or, in a shop, to display goods).

wine *n* an alcoholic drink made from the fermented juice of grapes or other fruit; a rich dark red colour. – *n* '**winepress** a machine in which the juice is squeezed out of grapes.

wing *n* one of the arm-like limbs of a bird, bat, or insect by means of which it flies; one of the two projections resembling these on the sides of an aeroplane; anything else resembling a wing, as a part of a house built out to the side; the side of a stage, where actors *etc* wait; (in football *etc*) a player at the edge of the field. – *v* to wound in the wing. *He's winged the grouse;* to soar. – *adj* **winged** having wings; swift. – *n* **wing commander** a high-ranking officer in the air force. – **(up)on the wing** flying, in motion; **under someone's wing** under the protection or care of someone.

wink *v* to open and close an eye quickly; to give a hint by winking; (of lights *etc*) to flicker, twinkle. – *n* an act of winking; a hint given by winking. – **forty winks** a short sleep.

'**winkle** *n* a type of shellfish, the periwinkle, used as food. – **winkle out** to force out gradually. *He winkled the information out of his son.*

winnow ['winō] *v* to separate the chaff from the grain by wind.

winsome ['winsəm] *adj* charming.

'**winter** *n* the cold season of the year. – *adj* of, belonging to, or suitable for winter. – *v* to pass the winter. *They wintered in the South of France;* to keep, feed (sheep *etc*) during the winter. – *adj* '**wintry** like winter, cold, stormy; cheerless, unfriendly: *a wintry smile:* – *ns pl* **winter quarters** a place to stay during the winter (*esp* for soldiers); **winter sports** sports on snow or ice (skiing, tobogganing *etc*).

wipe *v* to clean or dry by rubbing; (with **away, out, off, up**) to clear away. – *n* the act of cleaning by rubbing. – *n* '**wiper** one of a pair of moving arm-like parts which wipe the windscreen of a car.

'**wire** *n* a thread-like length of metal; the metal thread used in communication by telephone *etc*; (*coll*) a telegram. – *adj* made of wire. – *v* to bind or fasten with wire; (*coll*) to send a telegram; to supply (a building *etc*) with wires for carrying an electric current. – *adj* 'wireless (of communication by telephone, telegraph *etc*) by radio waves. – *n* an apparatus for sending or receiving messages or broadcasts by radio waves, a radio set. – *adj* 'wiry made of, or like wire; (of a person) thin but strong. – *n* 'wire-'netting network (used for henruns *etc*) made of wire.

wireless *see* wire.

wise [wiz] *adj* full of learning or knowledge; able to use knowledge well, judging rightly; sensible. – -wise (used with another word) in the manner or way of: *crabwise*; of, with reference or regard to: *careerwise*. – *n* wisdom ['wizdəm] the quality of being wise. – *npl* wisdom teeth four large back teeth which do not appear in a person until after childhood. – *n* wiseacre ['wizākər] (*old*) one who mistakenly thinks he is very wise.

wish *v* to feel or express a desire or want. *I wish he'd go*; (*usu* with for) to long for, desire, want: *she wished for riches*; to hope for on behalf of (someone): *to wish someone luck*. – *n* desire, longing; a thing desired or wanted. *Her great wish was to go abroad*; an expression of desire. *She made a wish*; (*pl*) expression of hope for another's happiness, good fortune *etc*. *She sends you her good wishes*: – *pl* 'wishes. – *n* 'wishbone a forked bone in the breast of fowls. – *adj* 'wishful wishing, eager. – *n* wishful thinking basing one's belief on (false) hopes rather than known facts. – wish someone well to feel goodwill towards someone.

wishywashy ['wishiwoshi] *adj* (of liquids) thin and weak; (of a person) feeble, not energetic or lively; lacking colour.

wisp *n* a small tuft or strand: *a wisp of hair*. – *adj* 'wispy.

'wistful *adj* thoughtful and rather sad, as if longing for something. *The child cast a wistful glance at the toys in the window*. – *adv* 'wistfully.

wit *n* (often *pl*) understanding, intelligence, common sense; the ability to express ideas cleverly, neatly, and funnily; a person who can do this. – -witted (used with another adjective) having wits (of a certain kind): *slow-witted*: *quick-witted*. – *adv* 'wittingly knowingly. – *adj* 'witty clever and amusing. – *n* 'witticism a witty remark. – at one's wits' end unable to

solve one's difficulties, desperate; keep one's wits about one to keep alert; to wit namely, that is to say.

witch *n* a woman supposed to have magic power obtained through evil spirits; an ugly old woman: – *pl* 'witches. – *ns* 'witchcraft magic performed by a witch; witch doctor in African tribes, one believed to have magical powers to cure illnesses *etc*; 'witch-'hazel a type of N. American shrub; a healing lotion made from its bark and leaves.

with [widh] *prep* in the company of. *I was walking with my father*; by means of. *Cut it with a knife*; in the same direction as: *drifting with the current*; against: *fighting with his brother*; on the same side as; having: *a man with a limp*; in the keeping of. *Leave your bag with me*.

withdraw [widh'drö] *v* to go back or away; to take away, remove (troops, money from the bank *etc*); to take back (an insult *etc*): – *pt* withdrew [widh'drōō], *pp* with'drawn. – *n* with'drawal an act of withdrawing. – *adj* with'drawn (of a place) lonely, isolated; (of a person) unwilling to communicate with others, unsociable.

wither ['widhər] *v* to (cause to) fade, dry up or decay; to cause to feel very unimportant, embarrassed *etc*. *She withered him with a look*. – *adj* 'withering drying up, dying; (of a remark, glance *etc*) scornful, sarcastic. – *npl* 'withers the ridge between the shoulder bones of a horse.

withhold [widh'hōld] *v* to keep back, refuse to give: – *pt* with'held.

within [wi'dhin] *prep* inside (the limits of): *within the hour*: *within the law*. – *adv* on the inside.

without [wi'dhout] *prep* in the absence of. *They went without you*; not having: *without a penny*; outside (the limits of): *without the terms of the agreement*. – *adv* (*old*) on the outside; out-of-doors.

withstand [widh'stand] *v* to oppose or resist successfully.

'witness *n* one who sees or has direct knowledge of a thing; one who gives evidence, *esp* in a law court; (something that provides) proof or evidence: – *pl* 'witnesses. – *v* to see, be present at; to sign one's name to show one's belief in the genuineness of (someone else's signature); to give or be evidence, to bear witness. – *n* witness box the stand from which a witness in a law court gives evidence. – bear witness to give or be evidence of: *to bear witness to his honesty*.

'**wizard** *n* a man who is supposed to have the power of magic. – *n* '**wizardry** magic.

wizened ['wiznd] *adj* dried up, shrivelled: *a wizened old man.*

woad *n* a blue dye; the plant from which it is obtained.

'**wobble** *v* to rock unsteadily from side to side. – Also *n.* – *adj* '**wobbly**.

woe *n* grief, misery; a cause of sorrow, a trouble. – *adj* '**woeful** sorrowful; pitiful. – *adj* **woebegone** ['wōbigon] dismal, sad-looking.

wolf [wōolf] *n* a type of wild animal of the dog kind that hunts in packs: – *pl* **wolves**. – *v* to eat greedily. *The starving child wolfed down the meat.* – *adj* '**wolfish** of, or like, a wolf. – *n* '**wolfhound** a large breed of dog formerly used in hunting wolves. – **cry wolf** to give a false alarm; **keep the wolf from the door** to keep away hunger or want.

wolverine ['wŏolvərēn] *n* a type of wild animal of the weasel family.

woman ['wŏomən] *n* an adult human female; human females in general; a domestic help: – *pl* **women** ['wimin]. – *n* '**womanhood** the state of being a woman. – *adj* '**womanish** (of a man) not manly. – *n* '**woman'kind, 'women'kind, 'womenfolk** women generally. – *adj* '**womanly** of, like, suitable for, a woman.

womb [wōom] *n* the part of a female mammal's body in which the young develop and stay till birth.

'**wombat** *n* a type of small, beaver-like, Australian animal, with a pouch.

won *see* **win**.

wonder ['wundər] *n* the state of mind produced by something unexpected or extraordinary, surprise, awe; something strange, amazing or miraculous. – *v* to be curious, or in doubt. *I wonder what will happen. I wonder whether to go;* to feel surprise or amazement (at, that). – *adjs* '**wonderful,** (*old*) '**wondrous** arousing wonder, strange, marvellous. – *ns* '**wonderland** a land of wonderful things, a fairy-like place; '**wonderment** (*old*) amazement.

wŏnt *adj* (*old*) accustomed (to do something). – *n* habit.

won't [wōnt] short for **will not**.

woo *v* to try to win the love of (someone), *esp* with the intention of marrying; to try to gain (*eg* success): – *pt* **wooed**. – *n* '**wooer**.

wood *n* (sometimes *pl*) a group of growing trees; the hard part of a tree, *esp* when cut or sawn for use in building

etc, or for fuel. – *adjs* '**wooded** covered with trees; '**wooden** made of, or like, wood; dull, stiff, not lively; '**woody** like wood; wooded. – *ns* '**woodbine** the honeysuckle; '**woodchuck** same as **marmot;** '**woodcock** a type of game bird related to the snipe; '**woodcut** a picture engraved on wood or a print made from it; '**woodcutter** a man who fells trees, cuts up wood *etc;* '**woodland** land covered with trees; '**woodlouse** a type of insect with a jointed shell found under stones *etc* (*pl* '**woodlice**); '**woodpecker** a bird that pecks holes in the barks of trees with its beak, in search of insects; '**woodwind** wind instruments, made of wood (or sometimes of metal, as silver) *eg* flute, clarinet; '**woodwork** the making of wooden articles, carpentry; the wooden parts of a house, room *etc;* '**woodworm** the larva of a certain beetle that bores holes in wood and destroys it.

wool *n* the soft hair of sheep and other animals; yarn or cloth made of wool; any light fluffy or fleecy material resembling wool. – *n, adj* '**woollen** (a garment *etc*) made of wool. – *adj* '**woolly** made of, or like, wool; vague, hazy. – *n* a knitted garment: – *pl* '**woollies**. – *n* '**woolgathering** daydreaming.

word [wɜrd] *n* a written or spoken sign showing a thing or an idea; (*pl*) speech, talk: *gentle words;* news: *word of his death;* a promise: *to break one's word.* – *v* to choose words for. *He worded his refusal carefully.* – *n* '**wording** choice, or arrangement, of words. – *adj* '**wordy** using too many words. – **have words** (*coll*) to quarrel; **in a word** in short, to sum up; **take someone at his word** to treat what someone says as true; **take someone's word for something** to trust that what someone says is true; **word for word** in the exact words.

work [wɜrk] *n* a physical or mental effort or exertion made to achieve or make something *etc;* a job, employment: *out of work;* a task. *I've got work to do;* anything made or done; something, as a book, a painting, a musical composition *etc,* produced by art; the manner of working, workmanship: *poor work;* (*pl*) a factory *etc;* (*pl*) the mechanism (of a watch *etc*); (*pl*) deeds: *good works.* – *v* to be engaged in physical or mental work; to be employed; to (cause machinery *etc* to) run or operate smoothly and efficiently;

(of a plan *etc*) to be successful; to get or put into a position or stated condition slowly and gradually. *The screw worked loose*; to organize, manage, control: – *pt* **worked** (*old* **wrought**). – *adj* **'workable** able to be done, practical. – *n* **'worker** one who works *esp* in a manual job. – *adj* **'workaday** ordinary, unexciting. – *ns* **working class** the social class including manual workers; **working day, working hours** a day, the hours, that one spends at work, on duty *etc*; **'workman** one who works with his hands. – *adj* **'workmanlike** done with skill. – *ns* **'workmanship** the skill of a workman; the manner of making (something); **'workshop** a room or building where manufacturing, manual work *etc* is done. – **work out** to solve; to discover as a result of deep thought; (of a situation *etc*) to turn out all right in the end; **work up** to arouse, excite. *He worked himself up into a fury.*

world [wŭrld] *n* the earth and all things on it; mankind; any planet or star; the universe; a state of existence: *the next world*; a particular area of life or activity: *the insect world*: *the world of entertainment*; a great deal: *a world of good*. – *adj* **'worldly** belonging to, or concerned with, material things such as money, possessions *etc*, not the soul or spirit. – *adj* **'world'wide** stretching all over the world. – Also *adv*.

worm [wŭrm] *n* an earthworm or any similar small creeping animal without a backbone; (*coll*) a low, contemptible person; anything spiral-shaped, *eg* the thread of a screw; (*pl*) the condition of having worms of some kind in the intestines (in humans *usu* threadworms). – *v* to move like a worm, or gradually and stealthily (in or into); (*usu* with **out**) to obtain, draw out (information) bit by bit.

wormwood ['wŭrmwŏod] *n* a type of plant with a bitter taste.

worn, worn-out *see* **wear**.

worry ['wuri] *v* to shake or tear (something) with the teeth as a dog does; to annoy; to (cause to) be troubled and anxious. – *n* uneasiness, anxiety, or a cause of this: – *pl* **'worries**.

worse [wŭrs] *adj* bad or evil to a greater degree; more ill. – *adv* badly to a greater degree, in a more severe or evil way. *It's raining worse than ever.* – *v* **'worsen** to (cause to) become worse. – **worse off** in a worse position, less wealthy *etc*.

worship ['wŭrship] *n* a religious ceremony or service; deep reverence or adoration; a title of honour (used in addressing mayors of cities *etc*). – *v* to pay honour to (God, *esp* at a church service); to adore or admire deeply: – *pt* **'worshipped**. – *adj* **'worshipful** full of reverence; worthy of honour.

worst [wŭrst] *adj* bad or evil to the greatest degree. – *adv* badly to the greatest degree, defeat: – *pt* **'worsted**. – **at worst** under the least favourable circumstances; **if the worst comes to the worst** if the worst possible circumstances occur.

worsted ['wŭrstid] *n* (a strong cloth made of) a type of fine woollen yarn. – *v* *see* **worst**.

worth [wŭrth] *n* value; price; importance; excellence of character *etc*. – *adj* equal in value to; deserving of: *worth considering*. – *adjs* **'worthless** of no merit or value; **worthy** ['wŭrdhi] (sometimes with **of**) deserving, suitable; of good character. – *n* a highly respected person *esp* a local person: – *pl* **'worthies**. – *adj* **worth-while** ['wŭrth'wil] deserving time and effort. – **worth one's while** worth the trouble spent.

would [wŏod] the form of the verb **will** used to express a condition. *He would go if he could*; used for emphasis. *I tell you I would do it if possible*; (*old*) expressing a wish. *I would (that) he were gone.*

would-be ['wŏodbē] *adj* trying to be or pretending to be: *a would-be actor: a would-be aristocrat.*

wound [wŏond] *n* any cut or injury caused by force, as by a weapon, in an accident *etc*; a hurt to one's feelings. – *v* to make a wound in; to hurt the feelings of. – *adj* **'wounded** having a wound, injured, hurt.

wrack [rak] *n* seaweed cast up on the shore.

wraith [rāth] *n* an apparition, *esp* of a living person; a ghost.

wrangle ['raŋgl] *v* to quarrel noisily. – Also *n*.

wrap [rap] *v* to fold or roll (something round something); (often with **up**) to cover by folding or winding something round: – *pt* **wrapped**. – *n* a covering such as a cloak or shawl. – *n* **'wrapper** a loose paper book cover, or other (paper) cover, as that round a sweet *etc*.

wrath [roth] *n* violent anger. – *adj* **'wrathful** very angry.

wreak [rēk] *v* to carry out (*eg* vengeance); to cause (havoc *etc*); to give way to, act as prompted by (one's anger *etc*).

wreath [rēth] *n* a ring or garland of flowers or leaves; a curling wisp or drift of smoke, mist *etc*. – *v* **wreathe** [rēdh] to twine about or encircle.

wreck [rek] *n* destruction, *esp* of a ship by the sea; the remains of anything destroyed *esp* a ship; a person whose health or nerves *etc* are in bad condition. – *v* to destroy. – *n* **'wreckage** the remains of something wrecked.

wren [ren] *n* a very small type of bird.

wrench [rench] *v* to pull with a twisting motion, or violently; to sprain (one's ankle *etc*). – *n* a violent twist; a type of tool for gripping and turning nuts, bolts *etc*; sadness caused by parting from someone or something: – *pl* **'wrenches**.

wrest [rest] *v* to twist or take by force.

wrestle ['resl] *v* to struggle with someone, trying to bring him down; (with **with**) to think deeply about (and try to solve) (a problem *etc*). – *ns* **'wrestler** one who wrestles as a sport; **'wrestling** the sport in which two people struggle to throw each other to the ground.

wretch [rech] *n* a miserable, pitiable person; a worthless or contemptible person: – *pl* **'wretches**. – *adj* **wretched** ['rechid] very miserable; worthless, very bad. – *n* **'wretchedness**.

wriggle ['rigl] *v* to twist to and fro; to move by doing this, as a worm does; to escape (out of a difficulty *etc*).

-wright [rit] (used with another word) a maker: *shipwright*: *playwright*.

wring [ring] *v* to twist or squeeze (*esp* water out of wet clothes *etc*); to clasp and unclasp (one's hands) in grief, anxiety *etc*; to cause pain to. *The story wrung everybody's heart*; to force (something from a person *eg* a promise): – *pt* **wrung**. – *n* **'wringer** a machine for forcing water from wet clothes.

wrinkle ['ringkl] *n* a small crease or fold on the skin or other surface. – *v* to make or become wrinkled. – *adj* **'wrinkly**.

wrist [rist] *n* the joint by which the hand is joined to the arm.

writ [rit] *n* a formal document which orders one to do something (as appear in a law court).

write [rit] *v* to form letters with a pen, pencil *etc*; to put into writing: *to write one's name*; to compose (a poem, a book *etc*); to send a letter (to): – *pt* **wrote**, *pp* **written** ['ritn]. – *ns* **writer** ['ritər] one who writes, *esp* an author; **'writing** putting (something) down in letters; (often *pl*) something composed and written. – **write down** to record in writing; **write off** to cancel, or to regard as lost for ever (*n* **'write-off**); **write up** to make a written record of.

writhe [ridh] *v* to twist or roll about in pain *etc*.

wrong [rong] *adj* not correct; not right or just; evil; not what is intended. *He took the wrong umbrella*; unsuitable: *the wrong weather for camping*; mistaken. *You are wrong if you think that.* – *n* whatever is not right or just; an injury done to another. – *v* to do wrong to, to harm. – *adj* **'wrongful** not lawful or just. – *adv* **'wrongly**. – *n* **'wrong'doer** one who does wrong. – *n* **'wrong-'doing**. – **go wrong** to fail to work properly; to fail to reach a successful conclusion; to make a mistake or mistakes; **in the wrong** guilty of injustice or error.

wrote *see* **write**.

wrought [röt] *adj* (*old*) made, manufactured. – *v see* **work**. – *n* **'wrought-'iron** a form of iron, able to be hammered, rather than cast, into shape. – *adj* **'wrought-'up** agitated, anxious.

wrung *see* **wring**.

wry [ri] *adj* twisted or turned to one side: *a wry neck*; slightly mocking or bitter: *a wry remark*. – *adv* **'wryly**.

X

X-rays ['eks'rāz] *npl* rays that can pass through many substances impossible for light to pass through, and produce, on photographic film, a shadow picture (called an X-ray) of the object through which they have passed. – *v* **'X-ray** to photograph by X-rays.

xenophobia [zenə'fōbiə] *n* hatred of foreigners or strangers. – *adj* **xeno-**

'phobic.

Xerox ® ['zēroks] *n* a type of photographic process used for copying documents; a copy made in this way. – Also *adj*. – *v* to copy by Xerox.

xylophone ['ziləfōn] *n* a musical instrument made up of a series of wooden plates graded in size, which the player strikes with hammers.

Y

yacht [yot] *n* a sailing or motor-driven vessel for racing, cruising *etc*. – *ns* 'yachting sailing a yacht; 'yachtsman.

yak *n* a long-haired type of ox, found in Tibet.

yam *n* any of several types of potato-like tropical plants, used as food.

yank *v* (*coll*) to tug or pull with a violent jerk. – Also *n*.

yap *v* to bark sharply: – *pt* **yapped**.

yard *n* a measure of length (0·9144 of a metre, or 3 feet); a long beam on a mast for spreading sails (of which each half is called a '**yard-arm**); an enclosed space *esp* one near a building or one used for special work: *railway yard: shipbuilding yard*; (*US*) a garden. – *n* 'yardstick a stick a yard long, for measuring; any standard of measurement.

yarn *n* wool, cotton, *etc* spun into thread; one of the threads of a rope; a story, a tale, *esp* a long, improbable one. – *v* to tell stories.

yarrow ['yarō] *n* a strong-smelling type of plant with flat clusters of white flowers.

'**yashmak** *n* the veil worn by Moslem women, covering the face below the eyes.

yawl *n* a ship's small rowing boat; a small fishing boat or type of sailing boat.

yawn *v* unintentionally to take a deep breath *usu* with wide-open mouth, from boredom, sleepiness *etc*; (of a hole *etc*) to be wide open, to gape. – Also *n*.

ye *pron* (*old*) you.

yea [yā] *adv* (*old*) yes.

year *n* the time taken by the earth to go once round the sun, about 365 days; the period 1 January to 31 December, or a period of twelve months starting at any point; (*pl*) age: *wise for his years*. – *n* 'yearling an animal a year old. – *adj* 'yearly happening every year, once a year, or in one year. – Also *adv*.

yearn [yėrn] *v* to long (for, to do something *etc*); to feel pity or tenderness (for). – *n* 'yearning an eager longing.

yeast *n* a substance which causes fermentation, used in brewing beer, and to make the dough rise in bread-baking *etc*.

yell *v* to utter a loud, shrill cry, to scream. – Also *n*.

yellow ['yelō] *adj*, *n* (of) the colour of gold, the yolk of an egg, or butter. – *v* to become yellow, *usu* with age. – *n* 'yellowhammer a type of bird of the finch kind, yellow in colour.

yelp *v* a sharp bark or cry. – Also *n*.

yen *n* the standard unit of Japanese currency; (*coll*) a strong desire, longing. *He has a yen to go back home.*

yeoman ['yōmən] *n* (*hist*) a farmer with his own land. – *n* 'yeomanry (*hist*) farmers; (*hist*) a troop of cavalrymen serving voluntarily in the British army. – **Yeomen of the Guard** the company acting as bodyguard to the British king or queen on certain occasions.

yes *interj* expressing agreement or consent. – *n* an expression of agreement or consent; a vote in favour.

yesterday ['yestərdi] *adv*, *n* (on) the day before today; (in) the past.

yet *adv* by now, by this time. *Have you heard yet?*; still, before the matter is finished. *He may win yet*. – *conj* but, nevertheless. *I am defeated, yet I shall not surrender*. – **yet another** and another one still; **yet more** a still greater number or quantity.

Yeti *see* **Abominable Snowman**.

yew [yōō] *n* a type of tree with dark green leaves and red berries or its wood.

yield [yēld] *v* to give in, surrender, give up; to give way to pressure or persuasion; to produce (a crop, results *etc*). – *n* amount produced. – *adj* 'yielding giving way easily.

'**yodel** *v* to sing changing frequently from an ordinary to a very high-pitched voice and back again: – *pt* 'yodelled.

'**yoga** *n* a Hindu system of philosophy and meditation, often involving special physical exercises.

yog(h)(o)urt ['yogərt] *n* a semi-liquid type of food made from fermented milk.

yoke *n* a wooden frame joining oxen when pulling a plough, cart, *etc*; a pair (of oxen, horses); something that joins together; a frame placed across the shoulders for carrying pails *etc*; slavery; domination; a part of a garment fitting over the neck and shoulders; a part of a skirt fitting closely over the hips. – *v* to put a yoke on; to join together.

'**yokel** *n* a country man or boy, used insultingly.

yolk [yōk] *n* the yellow part of an egg.

'**yonder** *adv* in that place (at a distance

but within sight). – Also *adj.*

yore [yör]: **of yore** formerly, in times past.

you [yōō] *pron* the person(s) spoken or written to, used as the *sing* or *pl* subject or object of a verb.

you'd [yōōd] short for **you would, should, had.**

you'll [yōōl] short for **you will, shall.**

young [yuŋ] *adj* in early life; in the early part of growth. – *n* the offspring of animals; (with **the**) young people. – *n* **'youngster** a young person.

your [yōōr] *adj* belonging to you: *your father.* – *pron* **yours.** *This seat is yours.* – *pron* **your'self** used reflexively. *Don't worry yourself*; used for emphasis. *You yourself can't go, but your representative can*: – *pl* **your'selves.** – **Yours, Yours faithfully, Yours sincerely, Yours truly** expressions used before one's signature at the end of a letter.

you're [yōōər] short for **you are.**

youth [yōōth] *n* the state of being young; the early part of life; a young man; young people in general. – *adj* **'youthful** young; fresh and vigorous. – *n* **youth hostel** a hostel where hikers *etc* may spend the night.

you've [yōōv] short for **you have.**

'Yo-Yo ® *n* a type of toy consisting of a reel which spins up and down on a string.

Yule [yōōl] *n* the season or feast of Christmas. – *n* **'Yuletide** Christmas time.

Z

'zāny *adj* (*coll*) crazy, clown-like.

zeal *n* enthusiasm; keenness, determination. – *n* **zealot** ['zelət] one who is very keen, an enthusiast. – *adj* **'zealous** full of zeal.

'zēbra *n* a type of striped African animal of the horse family. – *n* **zebra crossing** a street crossing, painted in stripes, for pedestrians.

'zenith *n* the point of the heavens which is exactly overhead; the highest point (of achievement *etc*).

'zephyr *n* a soft, gentle breeze.

'zēro *n* nothing or the sign for it (0); the point (marked 0) from which a scale (*eg* on a thermometer) begins. – *n* **zero hour** the exact time fixed for some action, operation *etc.*

zest *n* relish, keen enjoyment; orange or lemon peel. – *adj* **'zestful.**

'zigzag *adj* (of a line, road *etc*) having sharp bends or angles. – Also *adv.* – *v* to move in a zigzag manner or course: – *pt* **'zigzagged.**

zinc *n* an element, a bluish-white kind of metal.

'zinnia *n* a type of tropical American plant of the thistle family.

zip *n* a zip fastener; a whizzing sound, like that of a flying bullet; (*coll*) energy, vigour. – *v* to fasten with a zip fastener; to whizz: – *pt* **zipped.** – *n* **zip fastener** a device for fastening (garments *etc*) in which two rows of metal or nylon teeth are caused to fit into each other when a sliding tab is pulled between them.

zither ['zidhər] *n* a type of flat, stringed musical instrument, played with the fingers.

'zōdiac *n* an imaginary strip of the heavens, divided into twelve equal parts called the **signs of the zodiac**, each named after a particular group of stars.

zone *n* any of the five great bands into which the earth's surface is divided according to temperature: *temperate zone*; an area, region, section of a country, town *etc, esp* one marked off for a particular purpose: *a no-parking zone: a smokeless zone.* – *v* to divide into zones.

zoo *n* a zoological garden. – *adj* **zoo'logical** of animals; of a zoo. – *n* **zo'ologist** one who studies animal life. – *n* **zoology** [zōō'oləji] the science of animal life. – *n* **zoological garden** a place where wild animals are kept and shown.

zoom *v* to move with a loud, low buzzing noise; to make such a noise; (of an aircraft) to climb sharply at high speed for a short time; (of prices *etc*) to increase sharply; (of a special kind of camera lens (**zoom lens**)) to make a distant object appear gradually nearer without the camera being moved.

Appendices

Computing

access To gain control of a computer system or to retrieve data from a storage device (e.g. main memory) or peripheral unit (e.g. magnetic disk drive).

access time The time taken to retrieve data or information from a storage device. Access times can vary according to the type of storage device used, e.g. access time from a magnetic disk is shorter than from magnetic tape.

acoustic coupler A device which converts electrical pulses from a key-operated machine to sound (acoustic waves) for transmission and reception along telephone lines to and from a computer, permitting computers to be connected with a terminal by a modem and telephone handset.

address As information is entered into a computer, each place in which the information is stored has an address. That address alters as information is moved around. An address is itself a number.

ALGOL Algorithmic Orientated Language. A high level computer programming language used especially for scientific and mathematical applications.

analogue computer A type of computer in which varying electrical currents or voltages, etc. are used to represent other quantities (e.g. forces, speeds) proportionally in working out problems.

applications software A computer program or set of programs designed to carry out specific tasks (e.g. a business application, a game, word processing).

archive (1) To archive is the process of storing data files on a computer in a retrievable form (e.g. hard or floppy disk). (2) Archives are files stored on hard or floppy disk, usually data files rather than software.

ASCII American Standard Code for Information Interchange. An international standard computer code in which eight binary bits are combined to represent letters, numbers and symbols on a computer keyboard. Most VDUs and printers use this code.

assembler A computer program which converts a symbolic language program automatically into a machine language program which can then be directly executed by the computer.

assembly language A programming language in which each statement corresponds to a machine language instruction. It is usually given some form of mnemonic (e.g. BASIC, COBOL).

audio response A spoken reply from a computer, using a pre-defined limited vocabulary.

backing storage Storage media, such as magnetic disks, apart from the computer's main memory. Data and programs held in backing storage have to be transferred into the core store before use.

back-up copy A copy made of the working disk so that, in the event of accident to the working disk, all data is not lost completely.

BASIC Beginner's All-purpose Symbolic Instruction Code. A high level programming language designed for use in a number of various forms for microcomputers.

batch processing The method of processing data by computer which groups together a collection of transactions and processes them as a single unit (a batch) rather than as individual items.

baud rate A measure of the number of bits per second travelling from one part of a computer system to another, or between computers.

binary A method of counting using only two alternative values: 1 or 0, on or off.

bit An acronym for *binary digit*. The smallest unit of information used in a computer, having one of two values, 1 or 0. The CPU of a computer is often described according to the number of bits that it can process or access at one time (e.g. a 32 bit CPU).

bootstrap A method of inputting data prior to the loading of a computer program in order that the program can be loaded.

buffer (1) Memory space in a printer which stores the characters for printing. A printer with a buffer memory can perform more complex printing functions than one that will only print characters as they are fed from the computer. (2) An area where data can be temporarily stored whilst being transferred from one unit to another.

bug An error or defect in a computer system or computer program.

byte An acronym for *by eight*. The most common unit of computer storage, a byte (a group of eight bits) is equivalent to one character, symbol or two numerical digits. One byte contains enough information to represent one ASCII character.

cathode ray tube/terminal (CRT) A screen similar to a television screen which displays text from a computer. As keys are struck by the operator, letters or symbols appear on the screen.

central processing unit (CPU) The part of the computer system which co-ordinates the whole system, where all parts of the computer system are linked together and where the calculations and manipulation of data take place.

chip A single integrated circuit formed on the surface of a piece of silicon etched with tiny electronic circuits. It is between 1 and 5 cm in length and can have between 6 and 40 external connections.

COBOL Common Business Orientated Language. A high level computer programming language designed for use in business applications and the manipulation of business data, using terms which are related to ordinary English words.

code A machine language representation of a character.

cold start A complete restart of a computer following major failure or breakdown.

computer output microfilm (COM) Sometimes called computer output microfiche. Instead of producing paper output, COM systems reduce the same information to microfilm (or microfiche).

compatibility The ability of two devices, whether hardware or software, to work in conjunction, e.g. if a magnetic disk used on one computer can be read by another computer, the two computers are said to be compatible.

corruption The unintended alteration or mutilation of computer data during processing, storage or transmission.

CP/M Control Program for Microprocessors. A widely used disk operating system for microcomputers.

crash When computer hardware or software malfunctions, or when a program which is running cannot be completed or re-started, a computer system is said to have crashed.

cursor A marker on a VDU indicating the point at which text should be entered. Appearances can vary, some cursors are boxes, triangles or underlines, and some flash on and off.

data Numbers or characters which provide the building blocks for information. Data is normally deemed to be input into a computer in order that information can be output.

database An organised collection of files of information that has been systematically recorded. The files can be interconnected and form the base of an organisation's data processing system, with specific reference to information retrieval.

data processing Clerical, arithmetical and logical operations on data. In the context of information technology, data processing implies the use of a computer in its operations.

debug To test a computer program or routine and to isolate and correct errors to get rid of bugs or faults.

default The value of a variable which is used by a computer system, unless it is specifically altered by the keyboard to use another value.

density The amount of storage space on a magnetic disk.

direct access The ability to access data in a storage and retrieval system directly without having to scan any part of the storage file first. Each record's storage location is completely unconnected with any other record storage.

disk A flat circular medium used for magnetic backing storage of information and programs. A disk is divided into recording tracks and sub-divided into sectors.

disk capacity The amount of storage space on a disk.

disk drive An electro-mechanical device which houses a magnetic disk effecting necessary movement and writing to or reading from the disk.

disk operating system (DOS) Software that manages the storage and retrieval of information on disk and controls the operation of all activities relating to the use of magnetic disks in a computer system.

dot matrix printer A printer capable of producing work at high speed which uses a series of electrically hammered moving pins to create characters made up of a pattern of dots. Printed output material is not considered to be of letter quality.

double density disk A magnetic disk with twice the storage capacity of a standard disk of the same dimension.

down In computing terms, a system is said to be down when it is not operating.

download The transference of data or programs from one computer to another, e.g. from a mainframe to a microcomputer.

downtime A period when computer equipment is not operating because of malfunction, maintenance, etc.

dump The transfer of data from one computer storage area to another or, more usually, to output.

dumping The copying of contents of a storage area onto another medium usually for the purpose of security or checking.

external storage Any storage medium which is portable (e.g. magnetic disks).

facsimile transmission (fax) A system which can transmit over a telecommunications link a complete copy of the form and content of a document.

field A section of a computer record designated for the storage of specific information. A fixed field has a defined, unvarying length, whereas a variable field can be assigned different length values.

fifth generation computer The coming generation of computers with greatly increased processing power which facilitates the running of user-friendly artificial intelligence software.

file An organised and structured collection of information recorded as a unit with an identifying name.

fixed head Read/write heads in a CPU or disk drive which are kept stationary.

fixed head disk A disk memory with one read/write head for track on the disk.

floppy disk A thin disk made of a flexible material with one or both sides coated to accept magnetic recording, usually either 5¼ inches or 8 inches in diameter. Also known as a **magnetic disk**.

flowchart A graphical representation showing the sequence of events and choices which need to be made in the solution of a problem, using symbolic shapes and usually, although not exclusively, relating to a computer program.

flowcharting A method of representing a series of events with lines which represent inter-connection and symbols which represent events or processes. Systems flowcharts represent the relationship between events in a data processing system. Program flowcharts show the logical components of a computer program.

foreground A facility of some computers whereby high priority tasks can be carried out whilst those of low priority are also being carried out in the background.

format (1) To format is to arrange data or text according to specific instructions. (2) An arrangement of data, which may refer to the layout of a printed document, the order of instructions in a program or the arrangement of data in a computer file.

formula A term used in spreadsheet software. If several columns of figures have to be totalled, or a percentage of each calculated, a formula can be set up to do this and then run.

FORTRAN Formula Translator. A high level computer programming language used specifically for scientific, technical or mathematical applications.

fourth generation computers The majority of contemporary computers.

hard copy Permanent output from a computer and usually synonymous with print on paper.

hard disk A magnetic disk hermetically sealed to prevent contamination by dust and moisture offering large storage capacity and used for the bulk storage of computer data.

hard sectoring The marking of sector boundaries on a magnetic disk by the punching of holes in the disk. All available space can be used for data storage.

hardware The magnetic, electrical, mechanical and electronic components which make up a computer.

hash Data which is nonsense.

head A device which reads and records or erases information on a computer storage medium.

hexidecimal code A data code which uses the base 16 as compared with base 2 for binary code and base 10 for decimal code.

high level language A computer programming language which allows a user to employ instructions close to his/her own familiar language rather than machine code. The higher the level of the language, the nearer the language is to English language.

high resolution The fineness of detail distinguishable in an image and often referred to the screen of a VDU.

icon An image on the screen of an advanced microcomputer resembling a familiar office object (e.g. document, tray) and representing a work area in the computer. The work area is accessed by moving the cursor to the icon and then pressing a key to call up that work area.

image printer Using optical technology, a printer which will compose an image of a complete page from digital input, the final copy being produced as print on paper.

immediate access store A storage area in a computer into which information can be written and from which it can be instantly read no matter where it is in the store.

incompatibility If a program capable of running on one computer cannot be run on another computer, the software is said to be incompatible.

input The putting in of information to a computer by an operator from a keyboard and therefore being information received by a computer.

input device `A piece of equipment which allows data and instructions to be entered into a computer's memory (e.g. keyboard, terminal, light pen, MICR, OCR).

integrated In reference to computer packages, sometimes called a suite, the linking together of a database, spreadsheet, word processing and graphics which can interact actively.

integrated circuit See **chip**.

intelligent terminal A terminal which has some processing or computing capabilities independent from the computer it is connected to.

interface The connecting link between two parts of a computer system, e.g. the cable that runs between a word processing terminal and its disk drive.

internal storage The internal **read only memory** of a computer where programs and data are stored.

joystick A device in the form of a unit with a small stick which moves the cursor on a VDU.

laser disk A form of video used to access information held on a disk rather than on a tape. The disk is read by decoding patterns produced by a laser light reflected off the disk's surface.

laser printer A printer using a laser light source to write on paper which is then passed through an ink powder. Ink is attracted to the area on the paper which has been written on and excess powder is removed. The ink is then fixed by chemical treatment or heat.

liquid crystal display (LCD) Liquid crystals can be switched from an opaque to a transparent state when interposed between a light source and an observer. LCD is often used on calculators.

load To enter information or a program into a computer from a storage device.

log on/off To initiate or terminate on-line interaction with a computer.

loop A series of instructions within a computer program which are performed continuously until a condition which has been pre-determined is met, when the computer will exit from the loop and carry on with the next instruction in the original program.

low level language A computer language which is very close to the computer's own machine code. Each low level language instruction has its own direct machine code equivalent.

machine code A binary code used in machine language for a machine's basic instructions which are directly acceptable to the CPU of a computer system.

machine language A language used by a computer for internal communications with its related parts and the language in which a computer performs arithmetic and editing functions.

macro code An instructional code capable of generating several machine instructions. Also known as macro.

magnetic card A piece of cardboard or plastic with a magnetisable surface on which data can be recorded.

magnetic disk See **floppy disk**.

mainframe The CPU of a large computer installation with many terminals attached and distinguishing the computer from a minicomputer or microcomputer.

megabyte 1048576 bytes, frequently referred to as one million bytes and used to measure storage capacity of a computer or CPU.

memory A device in the CPU of a computer which can store information for extraction by the computer when required. Memory is measured in **bytes**.

microcomputer A category for the smallest computers which uses a microprocessor as its processing element, having sufficient peripherals and memory to link with the outside world and store information.

microprocessor Sometimes a synonym for microcomputer but more correctly the central processor in which all elements of a control unit are contained on a single chip.

minicomputer A medium-sized computer, smaller than mainframe but larger than micro, with either general or specialised usage including process control, often used by a medium sized company to keep records, payroll, stock, etc.

modem An acronym for *modulator/demodulator*. A device for converting a digital signal from a computer into an analogue signal which can then be transmitted along a standard telephone line.

mouse A device which can be rolled across the surface of a graphics table. When a button on the mouse is depressed, the computer will address the item in the mouse position. Commonly used with **icons**.

MS DOS A commercial name for a **disk operating system**.

network A computer system where a number of components at a physical distance from each other can be interconnected by telecommunications channels.

off-line A terminal or other computer component not connected to or controlled by a CPU.

on-line A terminal or other component directly connected to the CPU in a computer system and which will interact directly with the central processor.

operating system A collection of programs contained in a computer used to control the sequencing of processing of other programs from the operation of various input and output devices.

optical character recognition (OCR) A technique in which information in the form of characters, numbers or symbols is read by an optical scanning device, or optical character reader, which converts the information into computer readable form.

PASCAL Program Appliqué à la Sélection et la Compilation Automatique de la Littérature. A large multi-disciplinary database compiled by the French Centre Nationale de la Recherche Scientifique. Sometimes referred to as a high level language used for general programming work.

peripheral Any unit of a computer (e.g. disk drive, joystick, light pen, card reader, magnetic tape unit, printer) which connects in different ways to the central processor and memory and which forms input and output devices.

program A set of instructions which a computer carries out in sequence enabling the computer to operate and carry out specific tasks.

programming language The language in which coded instructions are written for a computer.

random access memory (RAM) Memory into which information can be written and from which it may read in a random access fashion. The size of a computer's random access memory is a measure of the computer's power.

read The copying of information from a storage medium, or the electronic retrieval of information.

read only A term used in reference to memory and magnetic disks. If a disk has been write protected, its contents can be read but nothing can be written to it. This facility provides a safeguard against the accidental erasure of data, information and programs stored on a disk.

read only memory (ROM) A store of memory from which information can only be read or copied. Usually it is a permanent store holding software which is permanently or firmly in place. Sometimes referred to as firmware.

real time A computer system is said to be operating in real time if the system operates synchronously, responding to a request from a terminal and the processing of information which is fed in takes place straightaway.

retrieval The way in which a computer searches for particular files or parts of files in response to a request from a user and loads those files to the cursor or screen.

sequential access The storage and retrieval of records and information which has been recorded in sequence (e.g. on magnetic tape). Information to be accessed is searched for in an order of start to finish, until the required text is encountered. Also known as serial access.

sequential storage The storage of records in an order where the next available space after the storage of the previous record is used.

serial The travelling of electrical patterns of bits down a wire to a computer, one after the other. Often referred to as serial bit stream.

serial interface An interface in which access time involves a waiting time where serial bit transmission is used.

serial storage Storage on a magnetic device in which words appear in sequence often inferring that access time will include a waiting time.

shared facility A computer system in which several pieces of equipment use the same facility (e.g. a disk drive, a printer). Also known as shared resource.

shared logic   A computer system consisting of work stations made up of keyboards and VDUs which are connected to a CPU, usually with a hard disk. The terminals operate under central control.

soft copy   Computer output on a medium which cannot be read by an observer e.g. floppy disk or computer output as displayed on the screen of a VDU.

software   A generic term for programs, operating systems, packages and compilers which are used to direct the operations of a computer or other hardware and which can be run on computer hardware, consisting of patterns of binary information.

speech generation   The production of human speech by a computer using a limited vocabulary where often the computer can read back the information given to it.

split screen   The displaying of more than one image on the screen of a VDU. Areas of the screen are referred to as 'windows'.

spreadsheet   An application program which provides a matrix into which data can be entered and manipulated and intended for use in forecasting and financial planning.

storage   Another word for memory in a computer system, or the medium on which information can be stored.

system   An organised set of computer components which interact to allow the processing of data.

systems analysis   The task of analysing computer systems and determining how a computer system can be made more efficient (normally used for business applications).

systems analyst   A person trained in the investigation, analysis and design of computer systems (often for business applications) who can provide solutions to the most effective way of processing data.

systems software   Software used to run the operating system of a computer. Also known as operating software.

tape   An input or output storage device for a computer. There are two kinds of tape: paper and magnetic.

terminal   A peripheral device consisting of a keyboard and screen, linked to a computer used to input data and receive output from the computer, or for sending and receiving data over a communications channel.

time sharing   A computer system that allows many terminals or users to concurrently share a central computer, each user having the impression that he or she has the sole use of the computer.

touch screen   A terminal with a screen which is sensitive to the touch of the user. Positions touched usually using a finger or a light pen are recorded by the computer as a signal allowing data to be input or a command to be followed.

variable   (See **variable block** under Word Processing p 390).

visual display unit (VDU)   A cathode ray tube on which the output of a computer can be displayed.

Winchester disk   A form of backing storage for a computer consisting of a magnetic disk in an hermetically sealed container which is very powerful. Sometimes referred to as a rigid or **hard disk**.

window   A feature of some advanced microcomputer systems in which the VDU screen is split into sections, called 'windows', enabling the operation of different sections of the memory to be seen at the same time.

working disk   A back-up copy of a disk is made and stored in a safe place and the original disk becomes the working disk, i.e. the disk which is being worked on at the present time. If for any reason the working disk is damaged, the back-up disk can be used to make another working copy.

Word processing

alphanumeric   Describing any combination of letters of the alphabet and Arabic numerals which can be processed by a computer.

background   A facility of some computers whereby low priority tasks can be performed whilst those of high priority are also being performed in the foreground.

bi-directional printing   The printing of lines both right to left and left to right, eliminating the need for a return to the beginning of the line.

block   In computing, a group of records or information units handled as a single unit and stored in adjacent locations on magnetic tape or disk. In many magnetic storage devices only complete blocks can be accessed or transferred.

boilerplate   A passage of text used repeatedly in various contexts which can be inserted in different files.

centring   Locating a heading or other words of text equidistant between the left and right margins.

central processing unit (CPU)   The part of a computer system which co-ordinates the whole system, where all parts of the system are linked together and where the calculations and manipulation of data takes place.

character A generic expression for a letter of the alphabet, a number, a symbol or a punctuation mark printed or displayed on a screen.

character set The collection of numbers, letters, symbols and graphics that can be generated by a particular system.

command key A special key or set of keys on a keyboard which has been defined to carry out certain tasks (e.g. underscoring, saving data).

communicating word processors Word processors connected via a network to allow very rapid office-to-office and/or business-to-business communication of text.

communications A peripheral piece of hardware enabling a word processor to communicate with other equipment.

conditional page break A facility on most word processors that once the page length has been determined for a file, the word processor can be programmed to insert its own page break.

control key A key on a computer keyboard which when depressed with a variety of other keys gives additional facilities for the manipulation of files.

cpi Characters per inch. The number of characters to every horizontal inch of typing, usually 10, 12 or 15. Also known as **pitch**.

create The term given to the setting up of a new file in computing or word processing.

cursor A marker on a VDU indicating the point at which text should be entered.

cut and paste Marking the text to be repositioned (cut) and moving it to a new location (paste). A labour-saving feature when large blocks of text have to be moved.

daisy wheel The name given to a print where the type head is circular and the characters are attached round it on the ends of stalks.

daisy wheel printer A printer having a wheel which rotates at speed until the required character is brought before a hammer. The character is then struck by the hammer against the ribbon. Daisy wheels are interchangeable to facilitate different typefaces and produce letter-quality printout.

dictionary A library; a file of text with special applications (e.g. a spelling dictionary).

discretionary hyphen A hyphen inserted between syllables of a word which runs on from one line of text to the next and which is automatically deleted when the line length is changed.

display format The total number of characters visible on screen, expressed either as the total number or as the number of lines and characters in each line.

distributed logic   Computer systems where logic or intelligence are distributed in the system rather than located centrally e.g. some word processing systems link intelligent terminals which may make shared use of other resources such as storage, printer.

document   A medium and the data recorded on it. Most commonly refers to print on paper.

document based system   A word processing program where each file is produced as a whole document and not divided on screen into pages.

document merge   A facility of most word processors to join together two separate documents making one final document. If more than two documents are integrated, the process is referred to as document assembly.

dual pitch printer   A printer which has the facility to switch from one type size to another by the movement of a switch.

edit   The process of removing or inserting information by an operator when a record is passed through a computer.

erase   To delete or obliterate a file or an item of data.

error detection   A facility of communications which ensures that text has not been corrupted during transmission.

flag   Information which can be added to computer data in order to characterise the data or to provide information about it. Sometimes called a marker, point or a tag.

footer   A page number, catchword or other short piece of text printed at the bottom of each page, below the last line of text.

format   The layout or arrangement of the text on screen or on paper.

free-form text database   A facility of some word processing programmes whereby files can be organised in a specified manner and then any word or combination of words can be located, the items identified being scrolled in a window on screen.

function key   One or more keys on a keyboard which allow a user to issue a series of commands with one key depression, provided that the keys have been allocated special functions.

global search   A feature which activates the cursor to find every occurrence of a pre-determined character, word or phrase in a file.

global search and replace   An editing function in word processing where the cursor will search for each occurrence of a particular character, word or phrase and replace it with another pre-determined character, word or phrase.

glossary   Any set of frequently used passages of text (**boilerplates**).

header   A page number, catchword or other short piece of text printed at the top of each page, above the first line of text.

help menu A facility which enables a WP operator to find information on available commands and their syntax without leaving the program in use and without having to refer to the manual.

impact printing A means of printing where the characters are formed on the paper by means of a hammer striking the ribbon (e.g. dot matrix printers, line printers).

insert The addition of a word, phrase or paragraph to any text that has already been produced.

insert mode Any text that is typed at a keyboard which is added to the version already appearing on the visual display unit.

justified text Text which has an even right margin equal to the left margin and where the right hand margin appears vertically straight.

justify To adjust the positions of words on a page, distributing additional space in lines so that the right margin forms a straight vertical and parallel edge to the left margin.

letter quality The term usually refers to output from a printer where the printing is indistinguishable from that typed on a good electric typewriter.

letter quality printer Any printer that can produce print of the same quality as a good electric typewriter.

line feed A facility of most printers to automatically move the paper up through the printing mechanism one line at a time.

line graphics A facility which enables some word processors to draw boxes or other horizontal or vertical lines round a passage of text.

list processing A facility which enables word processors to automatically merge predetermined lists of data (e.g. names and addresses) in a standard passage of text, creating a new document.

logic-seeking Describing a printer which automatically skips over blank spaces in the text and so prints faster.

mail merge The process of combining a document file and a mailing list in word processing for the production of a standard letter.

mark (block) A function which enables an operator to cut and paste passages of text by inserting special code markers at the beginning and end of a passage.

matrix printer A printer in which each character is made up of a series of dots produced by a print head pushing a pattern of wires against a ribbon and onto the paper which also moves across the paper.

menu A list of possible options or facilities presented to the user from data or word processing software on a computer.

merge The combining of information from two or more sources (e.g.

address lists or mailing lists with document files or form letters).

mnemonics In word processing, a code of a few characters which initiates commands (e.g. erasing a file, moving a block, re-formatting a page).

mode Any operating function on a word processor.

multi-access Describing a system which enables several operators to use it simultaneously.

non-impact printing Printers which do not require physical impact for printing characters on paper (e.g. ink jet printing and electrostatic printing).

numeric Describing a field or character only able to contain or indicate a numeral.

numeric keypad A keyboard containing only numerals.

output Information transmitted by a computer or its storage devices to a screen or printer. It may be in the form of print on paper, punched cards or paper tape.

output device A device capable of receiving information from a central processor or peripheral unit which translates computer information into another medium (e.g. a VDU, printer).

overwrite The writing of data into a computer's memory where data previously held in a location is replaced with the new data.

page The amount of text which can be displayed on screen, or a passage of text divided from another by a page break.

pagebased system A feature of some word processing programs where each file is produced in pages making up a whole document. The hard copy output is the same as it appears on the screen of a VDU.

page break An internal command which informs the printer to start a new page.

page control A feature which allows a WP operator to address the length of the typing page to suit the display of text, or omit pages of typed text which will still be numbered chronologically within the document, for the later insertion of diagrams or drawings.

page feed A facility of most printers to roll up the paper one page at a time through the printing mechanism.

pagination (1) The numbering of pages in a document. (2) A word processing function used to create and number pages.

pitch The number of characters per horizontal inch of typing (e.g. 10, 12 or 15). Also known as **cpi**.

printer An output device from a computer which produces hard copy (text on paper) concerned with speed, quality and price.

print out The reproduction of text (printed paper output) on paper which a computer produces via a printer.

print pause A command facility which stops the printer for paper change, ribbon change, paper jam, etc. automatically.

prompt A computer initiated message to the operator used to indicate that particular information is required before the program can proceed any further.

protocol A set of standards which govern a format of communications to be exchanged between two devices in a communications system.

queue The processing of jobs or items (e.g. data awaiting action, execution or transmission). If terminals in a multi-user system send a file for printing simultaneously, the files will be queued and printed in rotation.

recall Transferring stored text to enable it to be edited or printed.

records management A facility of some word processors which allows for the sorting, editing, storage, etc. of data which may not be related to text.

reformat A feature whereby after the insertion, modification or deletion of text in a file, the format of the file can automatically be readjusted to give a good finished copy within the pre-set margins or line length.

repagination Automatic alteration of page numbering and size—a feature which is normally used after the editing of text, particularly in document-based systems.

required hyphen A hyphen in a compound word or expression which is not automatically deleted when the length of a line is altered.

reverse printer A printer capable of printing right to left, and left to right. Also known as a bi-directional printer.

ruler line A line across the top or bottom of a VDU screen which indicates the margin positions and the tabulation which has been set.

run The execution of a computer program, suite of programs or routine.

save A term used to refer to the storing of data on storage media (e.g. on magnetic disks).

scan The examination of material e.g. a word processing document, a page of a document or the conversion of data into machine readable form.

scroll The movement of text up and down or across a VDU so that the user can view the whole of a document or, on systems that display only half pages, the whole of a page.

search An examination of information in computer file to find the occurrence of a character, word or phrase.

search and replace A facility in which every occurrence of a specified character, word or phrase is replaced with a pre-defined character, word or phrase. Also known as global exchange or global search and replace.

shared logic A computer system consisting of work stations made up of keyboards and VDUs which are connected to a CPU, usually with a hard disk. The terminals operate under central control.

sort The arrangement of items of information into a meaningful order, often into alphabetical, numerical or chronological order.

spelling check In word processing, a program which uses a standard or specialised dictionary which can be added to by the user. When the program is run, the text is checked for spelling errors which the user can correct.

stand-alone A piece of equipment which can operate independently of any other equipment e.g. a work station which can operate on its own without being connected with a CPU is a stand-alone system. Often a category for word processors which are self contained and require no additional equipment.

standard paragraphs Text that is frequently used, stored and available for insertion into assembled documents.

standard text A facility which enables the operator to store and recall rapidly and easily words and phrases and often paragraphs that are used frequently.

stationery In word processing, single-sheet stationery describes the standard A4 format, fed into a printer sheet by sheet. Continuous stationery consists of a long strip of paper perforated at the end of each sheet and, at the sides with sprocket holes, allowing it to be fed into a printer by a tractor feed.

status line The line at the top or bottom of the screen which gives details of the work being performed (e.g. file name, page, line and column numbers, line spacing).

stop code (switch code) A special character identifying the location in the text at which data can be later inserted automatically.

strikeover A facility to type one character over another character, so that both characters (letters, numbers, symbols or a combination of these) appear in one type space.

string A group of items which are arranged in sequence according to a set of pre-defined rules (e.g. a set of consecutive characters in a computer memory).

string search A facility sometimes referred to as the find facility; when a string of characters is typed to the search, the file will be searched for where that string appears. Also known as search facility.

text editing The editing of text, which may be carried out on any form of computer from a mainframe with appropriate software to a dedicated word processor.

text editor Software which manipulates the text of computer programs themselves.

text processing Computer editing and subsequent production of text. Often used as a synonym for word processing, although text processing more commonly refers to the handling of very large quantities of text.

thermal printer A method of printing using paper coated with a dye that darkens at predetermined temperatures to produce a copy of an image.

tractor feed A piece of equipment which attaches to a printer using continuous stationery: two belts of circular studs catch the sprocket holes in the stationery to feed it through.

unconditional page break A feature of word processing programs where the operator works through a document checking page breaks and putting in unconditional page breaks where necessary.

underscore The underlining facility on word processing software.

variable block A piece of information that can be substituted for another piece of information if requested by the user. Often referred to as a variable.

visual display unit (VDU) A cathode ray tube, which looks similar to a television screen and which displays text from a computer.

word count facility Found on some document-based word processing systems, the number of words typed at any one time appears on the screen.

word processing The electronic storage, editing and manipulating of text using an electronic keyboard, computer and printer where text is stored on a magnetic medium except for final output which is in the form of print on paper.

word processor (WP) An electronic device used for the storage, editing and manipulation of text and consisting of a keyboard, an internal memory or storage, external storage, logic and printer. There are three main types: stand-alone, shared logic and distributed logic.

wordwrap A term referring to the way in which a partially typed word is automatically moved to a new line if the length of the word proves too long to fit into the existing line. Also known as wraparound.

write protect The covering of the exposed part of a floppy disk where information can be written to or read from, by a tag so that information can no longer be written on to the disk, but the reading of information from the disk is not interfered with.

write protect tag   A tag used to prevent data being written onto a magnetic disk.

Foreign words and phrases

à bas   Down, down with! *(Fr)*
ab initio   From the beginning *(L)*
à compte   On account; in part payment *(Fr)*
ad finem   To the end *(L)*
ad gustem   According to taste *(L)*
ad hoc   For this special purpose *(L)*
ad infinitum   Without any apparent end *(L)*
ad interim   In the meanwhile *(L)*
ad libitum   At pleasure; as much as/in any way that one desires *(L)*
ad nauseam   To a sickening degree *(L)*
ad rem   To the point; to the purpose *(L)*
ad verbum   Word for word; literally *(L)*
affair d'amour/affaire de cœur   A love affair *(Fr)*
aficionado   An ardent follower, fan *(Sp)*
à fond   To the bottom; thoroughly *(Fr)*
agent provocateur   One paid to associate with a person, party or group, with the purpose of leading them to commit acts which will make them liable to punishment *(Fr)*
à la carte   According to the menu, each dish priced separately *(Fr)*
alter idem   Another precisely similar *(L)*
amor vincit omnia   Love conquers all things *(L)*
ante meridiem   Before noon *(L)*
à point   To the point; exactly right; opportunely *(Fr)*
apologia   A defence; justification *(L)*
au fait   Expert, knowledgeable about something *(Fr)*
au gratin   With breadcrumbs *(Fr)*
au pis aller   At the worst *(Fr)*
autre temps, autre mœurs   Other times, other manners *(Fr)*
avant-garde   Very modern; ahead of (artistic) fashion *(Fr)*
bête noir   What one hates most *(Fr)*
bona fide   In good faith; genuine *(L)*
bona vacantia   Unclaimed goods *(L)*
bonhomie   Easy good nature *(Fr)*

carpe diem Enjoy the present day; seize the opportunity *(L)*

carte blanche Freedom of action; (literally) a blank paper *(Fr)*

cause célèbre A very famous trial *(Fr)*

caveat emptor Let the buyer beware; at the buyer's risk *(L)*

ceteris paribus Other things being equal *(L)*

chacun à son goût Each to his own taste *(Fr)*

cherchez la femme Look for the woman; there's a woman at the bottom of it *(Fr)*

cogito ergo sum I think, therefore I am *(L)*

comme il faut As it should be *(Fr)*

compos mentis Of sound mind *(L)*

cordon bleu Blue ribbon; a cook of the highest excellence *(Fr)*

corpus delicti The body, substance or foundation of the offence *(L)*

cosi fan tutte That is what all women do; women are all like that *(It)*

coup de main A sudden enterprise or effort *(Fr)*

crème de la crème The very best *(Fr)*

cri de cœur A cry from the heart *(Fr)*

cui bono? For whose benefit is it?; who gains by it? *(L)*

de bonne grâce With good grace; willingly *(Fr)*

de haut en bas From top to bottom; contemptuously *(Fr)*

déjà vu A feeling of having previously experienced something as it happens *(Fr)*

Deo gratias Thanks to God *(L)*

de rigueur Absolutely necessary because of etiquette, fashion, etc. *(Fr)*

Dieu et mon droit God and my right *(Fr)*

dolce far niente Sweet doing-nothing; sweet idleness *(It)*

double entendre A word or phrase with two meanings, one straightforward and one subtle or indecent *(Fr)*

dramatis personae The characters of a drama or play *(L)*

dulce et decorum est (pro patria mori) It is sweet and glorious (to die for one's country) *(L)*

dum spiro, spero While I breathe, I hope *(L)*

ecce homo Behold the man *(L)* (The words of Pontius Pilate)

embarras de richesses Too much of a good thing *(Fr)*

enfant terrible A child whose sayings embarrass his elders; a person who embarrasses his colleagues in a similar way *(Fr)*

en masse In a body; all together *(Fr)*

en passant In passing; by the way *(Fr)*

entente cordiale A friendly agreement or relationship between states *(Fr)*

errare est humanum To err is human *(L)*

esprit de corps   Regard for the honour of the body to which one belongs *(Fr)*

et ego in Arcadia   I too have lived in Arcadia; I too had that experience *(L)*

et tu, Brute!   You too, Brutus? *(L)* (Caesar's alleged exclamation when he saw Brutus amongst his assassins)

eureka!   I have found (it)! *(Gr)* (Archimedes' alleged exclamation when he thought of a way to determine the purity of the gold in the King of Syracuse's crown)

ex cathedra   From the episcopal or papal throne or professional chair; with high authority *(L)*

exempli gratia   By way of example *(L)*

ex libris   From the books of/library of *(L)*

fait accompli   An accomplished fact; a thing already done *(Fr)*

faux pas   A mistake; social blunder *(Fr)*

festina lente   Hasten gently; hurry slowly *(L)*

furor loquendi/scribendi   A rage for speaking/writing *(L)*

genius loci   The guardian spirit of the place *(L)*

gloria in excelsis   Glory to God in the highest *(L)*

grande dame   A lady of aristocratic manner and forceful personality *(Fr)*

hasta mañana   Until tomorrow *(Sp)*

hic sepultus   Here (is) buried *(L)*

hoi polloi   The masses; the rabble; the vulgar *(Gr)*

honi soit qui mal y pense   Shame to him who thinks evil; the shame be his who thinks ill of it *(L)*

ibidem (ibid.)   In the same place, thing or case *(L)*

idée fixe   A fixed idea; an obsession *(Fr)*

in extremis   At the point of death or in desperate circumstances *(L)*

in flagrante delicto   In the very act; (literally) while the crime is blazing *(L)*

infra dignitatem (infra dig)   Beneath one's dignity *(L)*

in re   In the matter of *(L)*

in statu quo   In the former state *(L)*

inter alia   Amongst other things *(L)*

inter nos   Between ourselves *(L)*

in toto   Entirely *(L)*

in vino veritas   In wine is truth; wine brings out the truth *(L)*

ipso facto   By that very fact; thereby *(L)*

joie de vivre   Joy of living *(Fr)*

Kirche, Küche, Kinder   Church, kitchen, children *(Ger)*

laissez faire   A general principle of non-interference *(Fr)*

le beau monde   The fashionable world *(Fr)*

magnum bonum   A great good *(L)*

magnum opus   A great work; someone's greatest achievement *(L)*

maître d'hôtel   A house-steward, major-domo, a manager or head-waiter of an hotel *(Fr)*

mala fide   With bad faith; treacherously *(L)*

mal à propos   Ill-timed *(Fr)*

mea culpa   By my own fault *(L)*

memento mori   Remember death; a reminder of death *(L)*

mens sana in corpore sano   A sound mind in a sound body *(L)*

mirabile dictu   Wonderful to tell *(L)*

modus operandi   Manner of operation; way of going about a job *(L)*

morituri te salutamus   We who are about to die salute you *(L)* (The greeting given by the gladiators to the emperor)

mot juste   The word which exactly fits the context *(L)*

nemine contradicente (nem con)   Without opposition, with no-one speaking to the contrary *(L)*

nemo me impune lacessit   No-one provokes me with impunity *(L)* (the motto of Scotland)

nihil ad rem   Nothing to the point *(L)*

nil desperandum   Never despair *(L)*

noli me tangere   Don't touch me *(L)* (the words of Jesus quoted from John's Gospel, but now often used as a general warning against interference)

nom de guerre   A pseudonym; (literally) a war name *(Fr)*

non sequitur   A remark or action unconnected with what has gone before; a conclusion that does not follow logically from the premises *(L)*

nota bene (NB)   Mark well; take good note *(L)*

nouveau riche   One who has only lately acquired wealth; an upstart *(Fr)*

obiter dictum   A thing said by the way; a cursory remark *(L)*

onus probandi   The burden of proving *(L)*

O tempora! O mores!   Oh the times! Oh the manners/customs!; What times! What conduct! *(L)*

pari passu   With equal pace; together *(L)*

per ardua ad astra   By steep and difficult ways to the stars; the way to the stars is not easy *(L)*

per diem   By the day *(L)*

persona non grata   An unacceptable person *(L)*

pièce de résistance   The best or most important item; the substantial course at dinner *(Fr)*

pied-à-terre A dwelling kept for temporary, secondary or occasional use, usually in a city *(Fr)*

pis aller Makeshift; the worst or last shift *(Fr)*

plus ça change, plus c'est la même chose The more that it changes the more it is the same thing, i.e. no superficial or apparent change alters its essential nature *(Fr)*

post meridiem After noon *(L)*

prima facie At first sight *(L)*

pur sang Of pure blood; total *(Fr)*

qui s'excuse s'accuse He who excuses himself accuses himself; whoever makes too many or unnecessary excuses lays himself open to suspicion *(Fr)*

quod erat demonstrandum (the thing) which was to be proved or demonstrated *(L)*

raison d'être The reason for the existence of something *(Fr)*

rara avis A rare person or thing; (literally) a rare bird *(L)*

res judicata A case or law suit already decided *(L)*

rien ne va plus (Literally) nothing goes any more—used by croupiers to indicate that no more bets may be placed *(Fr)*

sang froid Coolness of behaviour; calmness; (literally) cold blood *(Fr)*

sans souci Without care or worry *(Fr)*

savoir faire Knowledge of what to do and how to do it *(Fr)*

semper idem Always the same *(L)*

se non è vero, è ben trovato If it is not true, it is cleverly invented *(It)*

solvitur ambulando It is solved in walking, i.e. the problem is solved by actually doing it, by practical experiment *(L)*

sub judice Under (legal) consideration *(L)*

suum cuique Let each have his own *(L)*

taedium vitae Weariness of life *(L)*

tant mieux/pis So much the better/worse *(Fr)*

tempus fugit Time flies *(L)*

terra incognita An unknown country *(L)*

tour de force A feat of strength or skill *(Fr)*

tout court Quite brief(ly), without preface; simply or brusquely *(Fr)*

ultima ratio regum The last argument of kings—the cannon, war *(L)*

urbi et orbi To the city (Rome) and the world; to everyone *(L)*

uti possidetis The principle of letting e.g. belligerents keep what they have acquired; (literally) as you possess *(L)*

vade mecum A handbook or pocket-companion; (literally) go with me *(L)*

veni, vidi, vici I came, I saw, I conquered *(L)* (The words of Julius Caesar)

ventre à terre   Flat out; at full speed; (literally) belly to the ground *(Fr)*

verbatim (et literatim)   Word for word (and letter for letter) *(L)*

videlicet (viz)   To wit, namely *(L)*

vigilante   An unofficial peacekeeper or protector of a group; member of a vigilance committee *(Sp)*

vivat rex/regina   Long live the king/queen *(L)*

vox populi, vox Dei   The voice of the people is the voice of God *(L)*

ABBREVIATIONS IN COMMON USE

(1) *It is now usual to spell abbreviations, especially of scientific terms and names of international organisations, without stops. In the list below, the stops are generally omitted, but it should be understood that in most cases neither method of writing (with or without stops) is wrong.*

(2) *Abbreviaitons for the names of societies and associations are given, but abbreviations for the designations of those belonging to any particular organisations—as Associate, Fellow, Associate Fellow, Member, or Associate Member—are not specifically included.*

A   Associate ... see note (2) above; amateur; Academician; argon; ampere; angstrom; atomic (in **A-bomb**); denoting the first, or a high, class (as in **A-road**); advanced (in **A-level**); Austria (IVR)

Å   Ångström

a   are (metric measure); accepted; acre; active; afternoon; *annus* year; *ante* before

ā, āā   in prescriptions, *ana* (Gr), i.e. of each a like quantity

AA   Automobile Association; Alcoholics Anonymous; anti-aircraft

AAA   Amateur Athletic Association; American Automobile Association

AAM   air-to-air missile

AAQMG   Assistant Adjutant and Quartermaster General

AAS   *Academiae Americanae Socius* Fellow of the American Academy

AB   able-bodied seaman; *Artium Baccalaureus* Bachelor of Arts

ABA   Amateur Boxing Association

Abb.   Abbess; Abbot; Abbey

abbr., abbrev.   abbreviated; abbreviation

ABC   Associated British Cinemas; American Broadcasting Corporation; Australian Broadcasting Corporation

abd   abdicated; abridged

ABFM   American Board of Foreign Missions

ab init   *ab initio* from the beginning

abl   ablative

ABM   anti-ballistic missile

Abp   Archbishop

abr   abridged; abridgment

ABS   Associate of the Building Societies Institute; Association of Broadcasting Staff

abs, absol.   absolute(ly)

abs re   *absente reo* the accused being absent

ABTA   Association of British Travel Agents

AC   aircraft(s)man; Aero Club; Alpine Club; *ante Christum* before Christ; (or **ac**) alternating current (*elect.*); Companion of the Order of Australia

Ac   actinium

A/C, a/c   account

ACA   Associate of the Institute of Chartered Accountants

ACAS Advisory, Conciliation and Arbitration Service

acc (or **acct, a/c**) account; accountant; (or **accus**) accusative; according

ACGB Arts Council of Great Britain

ACP African, Caribbean and Pacific

ACT Australian Capital Territory

act. active; acting

ACTT Association of Cinematographic Television and Allied Technicians

ACU Association of Commonwealth Universities

ACW aircraft(s)woman

AD *anno Domini* in the year of the Lord; Dame of the Order of Australia

ad (or **advt**) advertisement; after date; *ante diem* before the day

ADC aide-de-camp; (or **AD and C**) advise duration and charge

ad fin *ad finem* at, towards, or to, the end

ad inf *ad infinitum* to infinity

ad init *ad initium* at or to the beginning

ad int *ad interim* in the meantime

adj adjective; adjourned; adjustment

Adjt Adjutant

Adjt-Gen Adjutant-General

ad lib *ad libitum* at pleasure

ad loc *ad locum* at the place

Adm Admiral

admin administration

ADP automatic data processing

adv advent; adverb; *adversus* against; advocate; advisory

ad val *ad valorem* according to value

advt advertisement

ae, aet *aetatis* of his age, aged (so many years)

AEA Atomic Energy Authority (UK)

AEB Associated Examining Board

AEC Atomic Energy Commission (US)

AEI Associated Electrical Industries

AERE Atomic Energy Research Establishment

AEU Amalgamated Engineering Union

AF Associate Fellow . . . see note (2) above; Admiral of the Fleet; audio frequency

AFA Amateur Football Association

AFC Air Force Cross

AFG Afghanistan (IVR)

AFL-CIO American Federation of Labor and Congress of Industrial Organizations

AFM Air Force Medal

AG Adjutant-General; (or **A-G**) Attorney-General; *Aktiengesellschaft* (Ger) joint stock company

Ag *argentum* silver

AGM, agm annual general meeting

AGR advanced gas-cooled reactor

agr, agric agriculture

Agt Agent

AH *anno Hegirae* in the year of Hegira—i.e. from the flight of Mohammed (AD 622, 13 Sept)

Ah ampere hour

AHA Area Health Authority

AHS *anno humanae salutis* in the year of human salvation

AI artificial insemination

AIBD Association of International Bond Dealers

AID artificial insemination by donor; Agency for International Development (US)

AIDS acquired immune deficiency syndrome

AIH artificial insemination by husband

AK Knight of the Order of Australia

AL Albania (IVR)

Al aluminium

Al(a) Alabama

Alas Alaska

Alba Alberta

Alcan Aluminium Company of Canada

Ald Alderman

alg algebra

alt alternate; altitude; alto

Alta Alberta

AM Associate Member . . . see note (2) above; *Artium Magister* Master of Arts; (or **am**) *ante meridiem* before noon; *Anno Mundi* in the year of the world; *Ave Maria* Hail Mary; amplitude modulation; Member of the Order of Australia

Am americium

Am, Amer America; American

AMC American Motors Corporation

AMDG *ad majorem Dei gloriam* to the greater glory of God

AMMA Assistant Masters' and Mistresses' Association

ammo ammunition
amp ampere
amt amount; air mail transfer
amu atomic mass unit
an. *anno* in the year; anonymous; *ante* before
anal analysis; analogy
anat anatomy
anc ancient(ly)
ANC African National Congress
Ang *Anglice* in English
anme *anonyme* (Fr) limited liability
anon anonymous
ans answer
antiq antiquities; antiquarian
Anzac (a soldier serving with the) Australian-New Zealand Army Corps
Anzus (the alliance between) Australia, New Zealand and the United States
AO Army Order; Officer of the Order of Australia
AOB any other business
AOCB any other competent business
AOC-in-C Air Officer Commanding-in-Chief
AOF Ancient Order of Foresters
aor aorist
AP Associated Press
APEX Association of Professional, Executive, Clerical and Computer Staff
apo apogee
Apoc Apocalypse; Apocrypha(l)
app appendix; apparent(ly); apprentice
appro approval; approbation
approx approximate(ly)
APR annual percentage rate
Apr April
APRC *anno post Romam conditam* in the year after the founding of Rome (753 BC)
AQ achievement quotient
aq *aqua* water
Ar argon
Ar, Arab Arabic
ar *anno regni* in the year of the reign
ar, arr arrive(s); arrival
ARA Associate of the Royal Academy
ARAMCO Arabian-American Oil Company
ARC Agricultural Research Council

arccos inverse cosine
arch archaic; architecture
archaeol archaeology; archaeological
Archd Archdeacon; Archduke
archit architecture
arcsin inverse sine
arctan inverse tangent
arg *argentum* silver
arith arithmetic(al)
Ariz Arizona
Ark Arkansas
ARP Air Raid Precautions
ARR *anno regni regis* or *reginae* in the year of the king's or the queen's reign
arr arranged; arrive(s); arrival
art article; artificial; (or **arty**) artillery
AS Anglo-Saxon; *anno salutis* in the year of salvation; Assistant Secretary
As arsenic
ASA Amateur Swimming Association; American Standards Association
asap as soon as possible
ASC American Society of Cinematographers
Asda Associated Dairies
Asdic an acronym from Allied (or Anti-) Submarine Detection and Investigation Committee, used for a particular device for locating submerged objects
ASE Amalgamated Society of Engineers; Association for Science Education
ASEAN Association of South-East Asian Nations
ASF Associate of the Institute of Shipping and Forwarding Agents
ASH Action on Smoking and Health
ASLEF Associated Society of Locomotive Engineers and Firemen
ASM air-to-surface missile
ASP accelerated surface post
Ass, Assoc Association
Asst Assistant
AST Atlantic Standard Time
ASTMS Association of Scientific, Technical and Managerial Staffs
astr, astron astronomy
astrol astrology
AT Alternative Technology
ATA Air Transport Auxiliary
ATC Air Training Corps; air traffic control; automatic train control

ATM automated teller machine
atm atmosphere
at no, at numb atomic number
Att Attic (Greek); Attorney
Att-Gen Attorney-General
attrib attribute(d); attributive(ly)
Atty Attorney
ATV Associated Television
at wt atomic weight
AU (or **ÅU**) Ångström unit (now usu. Ångström; abbrev. Å); astronomical unit
Au *aurum* gold
AUC *anno urbis conditae* or *ab urbe condita* in the year from the building of the city—Rome (753 BC)
AUEW Amalgamated Union of Engineering Workers
Aufl *Auflage* (Ger) edition
Aug August
AUS Australia, including Papua New Guinea (IVR)
AUT Association of University Teachers
aut, auto automatic
Auth Ver, AV Authorised Version
AV audio-visual
av *annos vixit* lived (so many) years
av (or **ave**) avenue; average
AVM Air Vice-Marshal
avoir, avdp avoirdupois
AWOL absent, or absence, without official leave
AWRE Atomic Weapons Research Establishment
ax axiom
az azimuth

B Baron; British; Bachelor; boron; bel; black (on lead pencils); Belgium (IVR)
2B, 3B same as **BB, BBB** (on lead pencils)
b born; book; bowled; breadth
BA *Baccalaureus Artium* Bachelor of Arts; British America; British Association (for the Advancement of Science); British Academy; Buenos Aires; British Airways; Booksellers' Association (of Great Britain and Ireland)
Ba barium
BAA British Airports Authority
BABS beam, or blind, approach beacon system

BAC British Aircraft Corporation
Bach Bachelor
BACIE British Association for Commercial and Industrial Education
BACS Bankers' Automated Clearing Service
BAFTA British Academy of Film and Television Arts
BAgr(ic) Bachelor of Agriculture
BAI *Baccalaureus in Arte Ingeniaria* Bachelor of Engineering
bal balance
BALPA British Airline Pilots' Association
B and B bed and breakfast
B and FBS British and Foreign Bible Society
BAOR British Army of the Rhine
Bap, Bapt Baptist
bap, bapt baptised
Bar Barrister
bar baritone
BArch Bachelor of Architecture
Bart Baronet
Bart's St Bartholomew's Hospital, London
BASF *Badische Anilin und Soda-Fabrik* (German chemical company)
BAT British-American Tobacco Company
bat, batt battalion; battery
BB Boys' Brigade; double, or very, black (on lead pencils)
bb books
BBB triple black, blacker than **BB** (on lead pencils)
BBBC British Boxing Board of Control
BBC British Broadcasting Corporation (orig. Company)
BBFC British Board of Film Censors
BC before Christ; Board of Control; British Columbia; Battery Commander
BCAL British Caledonian (Airways)
BCC British Council of Churches
bcg bacillus of Calmette and Guérin, an attenuated strain of the tubercle bacillus, used for inoculation
BCh *Baccalaureus Chirurgiae* Bachelor of Surgery
BCL Bachelor of Civil Law
BCom(m) Bachelor of Commerce
BCS British Computer Society

BD   Bachelor of Divinity
bd   bound
BDA   British Dental Association
Bde   Brigade
BDH   British Drug Houses
BDI   *Bundesverband der Deutschen Industrie* (Ger) Federation of German Industry
BDS   Bachelor of Dental Surgery
bds   boards
BE   Bachelor of Engineering; Board of Education
Be   beryllium
B/E, be   bill of exchange
BEAB   British Electrical Approvals Board
BEAMA   British Electrical and Allied Manufacturers' Association
BEd   Bachelor of Education
Beds   Bedfordshire
BEF   British Expeditionary Force
bef   before
Belg   Belgian; Belgium; Belgic
BEM   British Empire Medal
Benelux   a name for Belgium, the Netherlands and Luxembourg
BEng   Bachelor of Engineering
Berks   Berkshire
B ès L   *Bachelier ès Lettres* (Fr) Bachelor of Letters
B ès S   *Bachelier ès Sciences* (Fr) Bachelor of Sciences
bet.   between
BeV   billion electron-volt(s) (in USA, where billion means 1000 million, same as **GeV**)
bf   brought forward
BFPO   British Forces Post Office
BG   Bulgaria (IVR)
bhp   brake horse-power
BHS   British Home Stores
Bi   bismuth
Bib   Bible
Bibl   Biblical
bibl   bibliotheca (=a library, book-collection, or catalogue)
biblio, bibliog   bibliography
BICC   British Insulated Callender's Cables
BIFU   Banking Insurance and Finance Union
BIM   British Institute of Management
biog   biography
biol   biology

BIPM   *Bureau International des Poids et Mesures* (Fr) International Bureau of Weights and Measures
BIR   British Institute of Radiology
BIS   Bank for International Settlements
bis   bissextile (=having a day added, as a leap year)
bk   book; bank; bark
bkg   banking
bkt   basket
BL   Bachelor of Law; Bachelor of Letters; British Legion; British Leyland; British Library
bl   barrel; bale; (or **B/L**) bill of lading
BLAISE   British Library Automated Information Service
bldg   building
BLESMA   British Limbless Ex-Servicemen's Association
BLit(t)   *Baccalaureus Lit(t)erarum* Bachelor of Literature or Letters
BLLD   British Library Lending Division
BLMC   British Leyland Motor Corporation
BLRD   British Library Reference Division
Blvd   Boulevard
BM   Bachelor of Medicine; British Museum; Brigade Major
BMA   British Medical Association
BMEWS   ballistic missile early warning system
BMJ   British Medical Journal
BML   British Museum Library
BMus   Bachelor of Music
BMW   *Bayerische Motoren Werke* (Ger) Bavarian motor works
Bn   Baron
bn   battalion
BNEC   British National Export Council
BNFL   British Nuclear Fuels Limited
BNOC   British National Oil Corporation
bo   branch office; buyer's option; (or **BO**) body odour
BOA   British Optical Association
BOC   British Oxygen Company
BOCM   British Oil and Cake Mills
Bol   Bolivia
bor   borough

BOSS Bureau of State Security (South Africa)

bot botany; bought; bottle

BOTB British Overseas Trade Board

Boul Boulevard

BP British Pharmacopoeia; British Petroleum; Baden-Powell; be prepared

Bp Bishop

bp boiling-point; bills of parcels; bills payable; (or **b pl**) birthplace; *bonum publicum* the public good

BPC British Printing Corporation; British Pharmaceutical Codex

BPharm Bachelor of Pharmacy

BPhil *Baccalaureus Philosophiae* Bachelor of Philosophy

BQ *bene quiescat* may he (or she) rest well

BR British Rail; Brazil (IVR)

Br bromine

Br Brother

br bank rate; branch; brig; brown; bridge

Braz Brazil; Brazilian

BRCS British Red Cross Society

BRD *Bundesrepublik Deutschland* (Ger) German Federal Republic

b rec bills receivable

Bret Breton

Brig Brigadier

Brig-Gen Brigadier-General

Brit Britain; Britannia; British; Briton

Bro Brother

Bros Brothers

BRS British Road Services

BS Bachelor of Science or of Surgery; Blessed Sacrament; balance sheet; (or **bs**) bill of sale; British Shipbuilders

BSA Building Societies Association; Birmingham Small Arms

BSAC British Sub Aqua Club

BSC British Steel Corporation; British Sugar Corporation

BSc Bachelor of Science

BSI British Standards Institution; Building Societies Institute

BSM British School of Motoring

BS(S) British Standards (Specification)

BST British Summer Time; British Standard Time

Bt Baronet

BT British Telecom

BTA British Tourist Authority

BTEC Business and Technical Education Council

Btu British thermal unit

bu. bushel(s)

Bucks Buckinghamshire

Bulg Bulgaria; Bulgarian

BUNAC British Universities North America Club

BUPA British United Provident Association

bus., bush. bushel(s)

BV *Beata Virgo* Blessed Virgin; *bene vale* farewell

BVM The Blessed Virgin Mary

BVM(&)S Bachelor of Veterinary Medicine and Surgery

C carbon; Conservative

°C degree(s) Celsius, centigrade

c centi-; *caput* chapter; cent; centime; *circa* about; caught

¢ cent(s)

© copyright

CA Chartered Accountant (Scotland); County Alderman

Ca calcium

ca *circa* about; cases

CAA Civil Aviation Authority

CAB Civil Aeronautics Board (USA); Citizens Advice Bureau

cad cash against documents

CAI computer-aided instruction

CAL computer-assisted learning

cal calorie

Cal, Calif California

Cam, Camb Cambridge

Cambs Cambridgeshire

CAMRA Campaign for Real Ale

CAN customs assigned number

Can Canada; Canadian; Canon; Canto

C and A Clemens and August (clothing stores)

C and G City and Guilds (of London Institute)

C & W country and western music

Cant Canterbury; Canticles

Cantab *Cantabrigiensis* of Cambridge

Cantuar *Cantuaria* Canterbury; *Cantuariensis* of Canterbury

CAP Common Agricultural Policy

cap capital; *caput* chapter; *capitulum* head, chapter; *capiat* let him (or her) take

caps capitals (in printing)

Capt Captain

CAR Central African Republic

Car. *Carolus* Charles

car. carat

CARD Campaign Against Racial Discrimination

Card. Cardinal

Cards Cardiganshire

CARE Co-operative for American Relief to Everywhere

Caricom Caribbean Community and Common Market

CASE Confederation for the Advancement of State Education

CAT College of Advanced Technology; computer-aided typesetting

cat. catechism; catalogue

Cath. Catholic

cath. cathedral

CB Companion of the Order of the Bath; confined (or confinement) to barracks; Citizens' Band (radio); cash book

CBC Canadian Broadcasting Corporation

CBE Commander of the Order of the British Empire

CBI Confederation of British Industry

CBM Californian Business Machines

CBS Confraternity of the Blessed Sacrament; Columbia Broadcasting System

CC County Council; Cricket Club; closed circuit (transmission); Companion of the Order of Canada; Chamber of Commerce

cc cubic-centimetre(s); *capita* chapters; carbon copy

CCA current cost accounting

CCCP see **USSR**

CCF Combined Cadet Force

CCPR Central Council of Physical Recreation

CCS Corporation of Certified Secretaries

CD *Corps Diplomatique* (Fr) Diplomatic Corps; Civil Defence; contagious disease(s)

Cd cadmium

c/d carried down

CDN Canada (IVR)

Cdr Commander

CDSO Companion of the Distinguished Service Order

CDV Civil Defence Volunteers

CE Civil Engineer; Council of Europe

Ce cerium

CEDO Centre for Education Development Overseas (formerly **CREDO**)

CEGB Central Electricity Generating Board

CEI Council of Engineering Institutions

cel celebrated

Celt. Celtic

cen central; century

CEng Chartered Engineer

cent *centum* a hundred; century; central

CENTO Central Treaty Organisation

CERN *Conseil Européen pour la Recherche Nucléaire* (Fr) European Organisation for Nuclear Research

cert certainty; (or **certif**) certificate; certificated; certify

CET Central European Time

cet par *ceteris paribus* other things being equal

CF Chaplain to the Forces

Cf californium

cf calf (book-binding)

cf *confer* compare

cf (and) i cost, freight, and insurance

CFAFr Communauté Financière Africaine franc

CFPFr Communauté Française du Pacific franc

cg centigram(me)(s)

cg centre of gravity

CG(L)I City and Guilds (of London) Institute

CGPM *Conférence Générale des Poids et Mesures* (Fr) General Conference of Weights and Measures

CGS (or **cgs**) centimetre-gramme-second (unit or system); Chief of the General Staff

CGT capital gains tax; *Confédération Générale du Travail* (Fr) General Confederation of Labour

CH Companion of Honour; *Confederatio Helvetica* Switzerland (also IVR)

Ch Chief; China; Church; Champion

ch central heating; chaldron; chapter; child

Chamb. Chamberlain
Chanc. Chancellor; Chancery
Chap. Chaplain; Chapter
CHAPS Clearing House Automated Payments System
Chas Charles
ChB *Chirurgiae Baccalaureus* Bachelor of Surgery
chem chemistry; chemical
Ch Hist Church History
Chin. China; Chinese
ChJ Chief-Justice
ChM *Chirurgiae Magister* Master of Surgery
choc chocolate
Chr Christ; Christian
chron chronicle; chronology; chronological
CI Channel Islands
CIA Central Intelligence Agency (USA)
Cia *Compagnia* (It) Company
CID Criminal Investigation Department; Council of Industrial Design
CIE *Córas Iompair Éireann* (Ir) Transport Organisation of Ireland
Cie *Compagnie* (Fr) Company
cif cost, insurance, freight
CIGS Chief of Imperial General Staff (now **CGS**)
CII Chartered Insurance Institute
CIM Commission on Industry and Manpower
C-in-C Commander-in-Chief
CIPFA Chartered Institute of Public Finance and Accountancy
CIPM *Comité International des Poids et Mesures* (Fr) International Committee of Weights and Measures
CIR Commission on Industrial Relations
cir, circ *circa, circiter, circum* about
circs circumstances
CIS Chartered Institute of Secretaries
CIT Chartered Institute of Transport
cit citation; citizen
civ civil; civilian
CJ Chief-Justice
Cl chlorine
cl centilitre(s); *cum laude* with praise; class; clause
class classical; classification
CLitt Companion of Literature

CLR computer language recorder
CLT computer language translator
CM Certificated Master: Corresponding Member; Common Metre; *Chirurgiae Magister* Master of Surgery; Member of the Order of Canada
Cm curium
cm centimetre(s)
CMG Companion of the Order of St Michael and St George
CMI computer-managed instruction
Cmnd Command Paper
CMRST Committee on Manpower Resources for Science and Technology
CMS Church Missionary Society
CNAA Council for National Academic Awards
CND Campaign for Nuclear Disarmament
CNR Canadian National Railway
CNS central nervous system
CO conscientious objector; Colonial Office (before Aug. 1966); Commonwealth Office (from Aug. 1966; see also **FCO**); Commanding Officer; Criminal Office; Crown Office
Co cobalt; Company; County
c/o care of
coad coadjutor
Cod. Codex
COD, cod cash (or collect) on delivery
co-ed co-educational
C of A Certificate of Airworthiness
C of E Church of England; Council of Europe
C of I Church of Ireland
C of S Church of Scotland; Chief of Staff
cog cognate
cog centre of gravity
COGB Certified Official Government Business
COHSE Confederation of Health Service Employees
COI Central Office of Information
COL computer-oriented language
Col Colonel; Colorado
col column
coll college; colleague; collector; colloquial
collat collateral(ly)
colloq colloquial(ly)

Colo Colorado
COM computer output microfilm
Com Commander; Commodore; Committee; Commissioner; Commonwealth; Communist
com common; comedy: commerce; committee; commune
Comdr Commander
Comdt Commandant
COMECON Council for Mutual Economic Aid, or Assistance (Communist Nations)
comm commentary; commander; communication
Commissr Commissioner
commn commission
Commy Commissary; Communist
comp comparative; compositor; compare; compound; compounded
compar comparative; comparison
COMSAT Communications Satellite (USA)
Com Ver Common Version
Con Consul
con *contra* against; *conju(n)x* consort; conclusion; conversation; convenience
conc concentrated; concentration
Cong Congress; Congregation(al)
conj conjunction; conjunctive
Conn Connecticut
conn connection; connected; connotation
cons consonant
Consols Consolidated Funds
cont, contd continued
contr contracted; contraction
contr bon mor *contra bonos mores* contrary to good manners or morals
conv conventional
co-op co-operative
Cop, Copt Coptic
Cor Corinthians; Coroner
Cor Mem Corresponding Member
corol, coroll corollary
Corp Corporation; Corporal
corr corrupted; corruption; correspond
Cor Sec Corresponding Secretary
CoS Chief of Staff
cos cosine
CP Clerk of the Peace; Common Pleas; carriage paid; College of Preceptors; Communist Party; Cape Province (S. Africa)

cp candle-power; compare
CPA Chartered Patent Agent
CPAC Consumer Protection Advisory Committee
CPAG Child Poverty Action Group
CPC Clerk of the Privy Council
CPI, cpi consumer price index; characters per inch
Cpl Corporal
cpp current purchasing power
CPR Canadian Pacific Railway
CPS *Custos Privati Sigilli* Keeper of the Privy Seal; (or **cps**) characters per second
CPSA Civil and Public Services Association
CPU central processing unit
CR *Carolus rex* King Charles; *civis romanus* a Roman citizen; *Custos Rotulorum* Keeper of the Rolls
Cr chromium
cr credit; creditor; crown
CRAC Careers Research and Advisory Centre
CRE Commission for Racial Equality
cres, cresc crescendo; crescent
CRMP Corps of Royal Military Police
CRO cathode-ray oscillograph; Commonwealth Relations Office (until 1966); Criminal Records Office
CRT cathode-ray tube
CS Court of Session; Clerk to the Signet; Civil Service; Christian Science; Chemical Society; orthobenzylidene malononitrile, an irritant 'gas' synthesised (1928) by *C*orson and *S*toughton; Czechoslovakia (IVR)
Cs caesium
c/s cycles per second (hertz)
CSE Certificate of Secondary Education
CSEU Confederation of Shipbuilding and Engineering Unions
CSIRO Commonwealth Scientific and Industrial Research Organisation
CSO community service order
CSP Council for Scientific Policy; Chartered Society of Physiotherapists
CST Central Standard Time
CSU Civil Service Union
CSV community service volunteer
CSYS Certificate of Sixth Year Studies
C/T credit transfer

Ct Connecticut
ct cent; carat
CTC Cyclists' Touring Club
CTOL conventional take-off and landing
CTT capital transfer tax
Cu *cuprum* copper
cu, cub cubic
CUP Cambridge University Press
cur, curt current (this month)
cusec cubic feet per second
CV, cv *curriculum vitae* (see Dict), or *cursus vitae* course, progress, of life
cva cerebrovascular accident
CVO Commander of the (Royal) Victorian Order
CWO, cwo cash with order
cwr continuous welded rail
CWS Co-operative Wholesale Society
cwt hundred-weight(s)—**c** (*centum* a hundred), **wt** (weight)

D deuterium; Federal Republic of Germany (IVR)
3-D three-dimensional
d day; diameter; *dele* delete; dead; died; deserted; degree; *denarius* or *denarii* a penny or pence (before 1971): duke
DA District Attorney; Diploma of Art
D(A)AG Deputy (Assistant) Adjutant-General
Dan Daniel; Danish
D and C dilatation and curettage (an operation which cleans out a body-cavity, esp. the womb)
DATEC data and telecommunications
dau daughter
dB decibel
DBE Dame Commander of the Order of the British Empire
DC *da capo* (It) return to the beginning (*mus*); District of Columbia; (or **dc**) direct current (*elect*): District Commissioner
DCL Doctor of Civil Law; Distillers Company Limited
DCM Distinguished Conduct Medal
DCMG Dame Commander of the Order of St Michael and St George
DCS Deputy Clerk of Session
DCVO Dame Commander of the (Royal) Victorian Order

DD *Divinitatis Doctor* Doctor of Divinity
dd, D/D days after date; day's date; direct debit
DDD *dat, dicat, dedicat* gives, devotes, and dedicates; *dono dedit dedicavit* gave and dedicated as a gift
DDR *Deutsche Demokratische Republik* (Ger) German Democratic Republic (also IVR)
DDS Doctor of Dental Surgery
DDT dichlorodiphenyltrichloroethane, an insecticide
DE Department of Employment
DEA Department of Economic Affairs
Dec December
dec deceased
dec, decl declaration; declension
DEd Doctor of Education
def definition; (or **deft**) defendant
deg degree(s)
Del Delaware
del delegate; (or **delt**) *delineavit* drew it
demon, demons demonstrative
DEng Doctor of Engineering
dent dental; dentist; dentistry
DEP Department of Employment and Productivity
Dep, Dept, dep, dept department; deputy
dep deposed; depart(s); departure
der, deriv derivation; derived
derv diesel engine fuel oil (from *d*iesel engined *r*oad *v*ehicle)
DES Department of Education and Science
DesRCA Designer of the Royal College of Art
DEW distant early warning
DF Defender of the Faith; Dean of the Faculty
DFC Distinguished Flying Cross
DFM Distinguished Flying Medal
dft defendant; draft
DG *Dei gratia* by the grace of God
dg decigram(me)(s)
dh *das heisst* (Ger) that is to say
DHSS Department of Health and Social Services (formerly Security)
dial dialect
diam diameter
DIC Diploma of the Imperial College

dict   dictator; dictionary
diff   different; difference
DIG   Disabled Income Group
DIH   Diploma in Industrial Health
dil   dilute
DIN   *Deutsche Industrie Normen* (Ger) German Industrial Standards
DIng   *Doctor Ingeniariae* Doctor of Engineering
Dip   Diploma, as eg **Dip Ed,** Diploma in Education, **Dip Tech,** Diploma in Technology
Dir   Director
dis   discontinued
disc   discount; discoverer
diss   dissertation
dist   distance; distinguish; district; distilled
div   divide; division; divine; divorced; dividend
DIY   do-it-yourself
DJ   disc-jockey
DK   Denmark (IVR)
DL   Deputy Lieutenant
dl   decilitre(s)
DLit(t)   *Doctor litterarum* or *litteraturae* Doctor of Letters or Literature
DM   Deutsche Mark (Federal German currency)
dm   decimetre(s)
DMus   Doctor of Music
DMZ   demilitarised zone
DNA   deoxyribonucleic acids
DNB   Dictionary of National Biography
do   *ditto* (It) the same (aforesaid)
DOA   dead on arrival
dob   date of birth
DOC   District Officer Commanding
DOE   Department of the Environment
DOG   Directory of Opportunities for Graduates
DOM   *Deo optimo maximo* to God, best and greatest; *Dominus Omnium Magister* God the master of all; dirty old man
Dom   *Dominus* Lord; Dominion
dom   domestic
DOMS   Diploma in Ophthalmic Medicine and Surgery
Dor   Doric
doz   dozen
DP   Displaced Person; data processing; duly performed (the work of the class)
DPH   Diploma in Public Health

DPh, DPhil   *Doctor Philosophiae* Doctor of Philosophy
DPM   Diploma in Psychological Medicine
dpm   disintegrations per minute
DPP   Director of Public Prosecutions
dpt   department
Dr   Doctor; debtor; drummer; driver; drachma (Greek currency)
dr   dead reckoning; dram; drawer
DS   *dal segno* (It) from the sign (*mus*); disseminated sclerosis
ds, D/S   days after sight
DSC   Distinguished Service Cross
DSc   *Doctor Scientiae* Doctor of Science
DSM   Distinguished Service Medal
DSO   Distinguished Service Order
dsp   *decessit sine prole* died without issue
DT   data transmission; (or **dt, DT's, dt's**) delirium tremens
DTh   *Doctor Theologiae* Doctor of Theology
DTI   Department of Trade and Industry
DV   *Deo volente* God willing
dvp   *decessit vita patris* died in father's lifetime
dwt   pennyweight—**d** (*denarius* a penny), **wt** (weight)
dyn   dyne; dynamo; dynamometer

E   East; English; Spain (IVR)
E   energy
E and OE   errors and omissions excepted
eaon   except as otherwise noted
EAPS   European Association of Professional Secretaries
Ebor   *Eboracum* York; *Eboracensis* of York
EBU   European Broadcasting Union
EC   East Central; Established Church; European Community; Electricity Council
EC $ East Caribbean dollar
ECE   Economic Commission for Europe
ECG   electrocardiogram (-graph)
ECG(D)   Export Credits Guarantee (Department)
ECO   English Chamber Orchestra
ECSC   European Coal and Steel Community

ECT   electroconvulsive therapy
ECTU   European Confederation of Trade Unions
ECU   English Church Union; European currency unit
Ed   Editor
ed, edit   edited; edition
EdB   Bachelor of Education
EDC   European Defence Community
EDF   European Development Fund
Edin   Edinburgh
edit   edited; edition
EDP   electronic data processing
EDS   English Dialect Society
EE   errors excepted
EEC   European Economic Community
EEG   electroencephalogram (-graph)
EET   Eastern European Time
EETS   Early English Text Society
EFL   English as a foreign language
EFT   electronic funds transfer
EFTA   European Free Trade Association
EFTPOS   electronic funds transfer at point of sale
eg, eg, ex gr   *exempli gratia* for example
EGU   English Golf Union
EI   East Indies
EIS   Educational Institute of Scotland
El Al   Israeli airline (lit. 'towards the sky')
elec, elect   electric; electricity
ELT   English language teaching
EMA   European Monetary Agreement
EMF   European Monetary Fund
emf   electromotive force
EMI   EMI Limited (formerly Electrical and Musical Industries Limited)
Emp   Emperor, Empress
EMS   European Monetary System
emu   electromagnetic unit
enc(s)   enclosure(s)
ENE   east-north-east
ENEA   European Nuclear Energy Agency
Eng   England; English
eng   engineer; engraver; engraving
Ens   Ensign
ENSA   Entertainments National Services Association
ENT   Ear, Nose and Throat
Env Ext   Envoy Extraordinary
EOC   Equal Opportunities Commission
eod   every other day

EP   extended play (record): electroplated
Ep   Epistle
EPA   European Productivity Agency
EPIC   Exchange Price Information Service
EPNS   electroplated nickel silver; English Place-Name Society
EPU   European Payments Union
ER   *Elisabeth Regina* Elizabeth, Queen
ER(I)   *Edwardus Rex (Imperator)* Edward, King (and Emperor)
ERNIE   *e*lectronic *r*andom *n*umber *i*ndicator *e*quipment (computer)
ESA   European Space Agency
Esc   escudo (Portuguese currency)
ESE   east-south-east
ESL   English as a second language
ESN   educationally subnormal
ESP   extra-sensory perception
esp, espec   especially
Esq, Esqr   Esquire
ESRC   Economic and Social Research Council
ESRO   European Space Research Organisation
ESSO   Standard Oil
EST   Eastern Standard Time; electric shock treatment
est   established; estimated
ESU   English-Speaking Union
ET   Arab Republic of Egypt (IVR)
ETA   estimated time of arrival
et al   *et alii, aliae,* or *alia* and others; *et alibi* and elsewhere
etc, &c   *et ceteri* or *cetera* and the others, and so forth
ETD   estimated time of departure
et seq or **sq** (sing), *et sequens* **et sqq** (pl) *et sequentes* or *sequentia* and the following
ETU   Electrical Trades Union
ety, etym   etymology; etymological
EU   Evangelical Union
Eu   europium
Euratom   *Eu*ropean *Atom*ic Energy Community
eV   electron-volt
ex   examined; example: exception; executive; export
Exc   Excellency
exc   except; exception
ex div   *extra dividendum* without dividend
ex gr   *exempli gratia* for the sake of example
ex lib   *ex libris* from the books (of)—as on bookplates

ex officio   by virtue of his office (Lat)

exp   export; exponential

exr   executor

exrx   executrix

ext   extension; externally; extinct; extra; extract

F   Fellow . . . see note (2); Fahrenheit; fluorine; France (IVR)

F   force

f   following; farthing; feminine; fathom; foot; forte; folio

f   frequency

FA   Football Association; Faculty of Actuaries

Fa   Florida

fam   familiar; family

FAO   Food and Agriculture Organisation

FAS   Fellow of the Society of Arts; Fellow of the Antiquarian Society

fas   free alongside ship

FBA   Fellow of the British Academy

FBI   Federal Bureau of Investigation

FCA   Fellow of the Institute of Chartered Accountants

FCO   Foreign and Commonwealth Office (**FO** and **CO** combined in 1968)

fcp, fcap   foolscap

FD   *Fidei Defensor* Defender of the Faith

Fe   *ferrum* iron

Feb   February

fec   *fecit* did it, or made it (sing.)

fem   feminine

FET   field-effect transistor

feud   feudal

ff   *fecerunt* did it, or made it (pl); folios; following (pl)

ff   fortissimo

FH   fire hydrant

FIAT   *Fabbrica Italiana Automobile Torino* (It) Italian Motor Works in Turin

Fid Def   *Fidei Defensor* Defender of the Faith

FIDO   Fog Investigation and Dispersal Operation; Film Industry Defence Organisation

fi fa   *fieri facias* that you cause to be made (a writ of execution)

FIFA   *Fédération Internationale de Football Association* (Fr) International Association Football Federation

FIFO   first in, first out

fig   figure; figurative(ly)

FIS   Family Income Supplement

fl   *floruit* flourished; florin

Flor, Fla   Florida

fl oz   fluid ounce(s)

FM   frequency modulation; Field-Marshal

Fm   fermium

fm   fathom

FO   Foreign Office (see **FCO**); Field Officer; Flying Officer

fo, fol   folio

fob   free on board

FOC   father of the chapel

foc   free of charge

FOE   Friends of Europe; Friends of the Earth

for   free on rail

FP   fireplug; former pupil; Free Presbyterian

fp   forte-piano; freezing-point

FPA   Family Planning Association

FPS   foot-pound-second

Fr   francium; franc; Father; France; French; Friar; Friday

fr   fragment; franc; frequently

frat   fraternise; fraternity

FRCP   Fellow of the Royal College of Physicians (**Edin,** of Edinburgh; **Lond,** of London; **Irel,** of Ireland)

FRCPS Glas   Fellow of the Royal College of Physicians and Surgeons of Glasgow

FRCS   Fellow of the Royal College of Surgeons (**Ed,** of Edinburgh; **Eng,** of England; **Irel,** of Ireland)

F(R)FPSG   (formerly) Fellow of the (Royal) Faculty of Physicans and Surgeons of Glasgow (now **FRCPS Glas**)

FRG   Federal Republic of Germany

FRPS   Fellow of the Royal Photographic Society

FRS   Fellow of the Royal Society (**E,** of Edinburgh)

FSF   Fellow of the Institute of Shipping and Forwarding Agents

FT   Financial Times

ft   foot, feet; fort

fth, fthm   fathom

fur   furlong(s)

fut   future

fz   sforzando (*mus*)

G Gauss; giga-

G constant of gravitation, the factor linking force with mass and distance

g gram(me)

g acceleration of gravity

GA General Assembly

Ga gallium; Georgia

Gael Gaelic

gal, gall gallon(s)

G and S Gilbert and Sullivan

GATT General Agreement on Tariffs and Trade

gaz gazette; gazetteer

GB Great Britain (also IVR)

GBE (Knight or Dame) Grand Cross of the British Empire

gbh grievous bodily harm

GBS George Bernard Shaw

GC George Cross

GCA ground control(led) approach system or control apparatus

GCB (Knight) Grand Cross of the Bath

GCE General Certificate of Education

GCH (Knight) Grand Cross of Hanover

GCHQ Government Communications Headquarters

GCM General Court-Martial; (or **gcm**) greatest common measure

GCMG (Knight) Grand Cross of the Order of St Michael and St George

GCVO (Knight or Dame) Grand Cross of the (Royal) Victorian Order

Gd gadolinium

GDI gross domestic income

gdns gardens

GDP gross domestic product

GDR German Democratic Republic

Ge germanium

GEC General Electric Company

Gen Genesis; (or **Genl**) General

gen gender; genitive; genus; general

gent gentleman

Geo Georgia; George

geog geography

geol geology

geom geometry

Ger German

GeV giga-electron-volt (the equivalent of a thousand million electron-volts, same value in Europe as **BeV** in USA)

GHQ General Headquarters

GI government (or general) issue (US Army); hence, common soldier

Gib Gibraltar

GIGO garbage in, garbage out

Gk Greek

GKN Guest, Keen and Nettlefold

Gl glucinum (now beryllium)

Glam Glamorganshire

GLC Greater London Council

Gld guilder (Dutch currency)

GLORIA Geological Long Range Asdic

Glos Gloucestershire

GM George Medal; (or **G-M**) Geiger-Müller counter; General Motors

gm gram(me)

GMBATU General, Municipal, Boilermakers and Allied Trades Union

GmbH *Gesellschaft mit beschränkter Haftung* (Ger) limited liability company

GMC General Medical Council

GMT Greenwich Mean Time

GMWU General and Municipal Workers Union (now **GMBATU**)

GNP gross national product

GOC General Officer Commanding

Gov Governor; (or **Govt**) Government

GP General Practitioner; Gallup poll; *Gloria Patri* glory to the Father

GPO General Post Office

GR Greece (IVR)

Gr Greek

gr grain; grammar; grouse; gunner

gram grammar

GR(I) *Georgius Rex (Imperator)* George, King (and Emperor)

GS General Staff; General Service; Geological Society; Grammar School

GSM gram(me)s per square metre

GSO General Staff Officer

GSP Good Service Pension

GT *gran turismo* used of a fast motor-car built for touring in style

GUM *Gosudarstvenni Universalni Magazin* (Russ) State Universal Store

GUS Great Universal Stores

H hydrogen; Henry; hydrant; hospital; hard (on lead pencils); Hungary (IVR)

2H same as **HH** (on lead pencils)

h hour

h height

HA Heavy Artillery

Ha hahnium

ha hectare; *hoc anno* this year

HAC Honourable Artillery Company; high-alumina cement

h and c hot and cold (water laid on)

Hants Hampshire (*Hantshaving,* orig. name of county)

HB hard black (on lead pencils)

hbar hectobar

HBM His (or Her) Britannic Majesty

HC Heralds' College; House of Commons; Holy Communion

HCF (or **Hon CF**) Honorary Chaplain to the Forces; (or **hcf**) highest common factor

HCM His (or Her) Catholic Majesty

HE His Excellency; His Eminence; high explosive; horizontal equivalent

He helium

Heb, Hebr Hebrew; Hebrews

HEH His (or Her) Exalted Highness

her heraldry; *heres* heir

Herts Hertfordshire

HF high frequency

Hf hafnium

hf half; **hf-bd** half-bound; **hf-cf** half-calf; **hf-mor** half-morocco

HG His (or Her) Grace

Hg *hydrargyrum* mercury

HGV heavy goods vehicle

HH His (or Her) Highness; very hard (on lead pencils)

HIDB Highlands and Islands Development Board

Hi-Fi, hi-fi high fidelity

HIH His (or Her) Imperial Highness

HIM His (or Her) Imperial Majesty

HIS *hic iacet sepultus* here lies buried

hist historian; history; historical

HJ(S) *hic jacet (sepultus)* here lies (buried)

HK House of Keys (Isle of Man); Hong Kong (also IVR)

hl hectolitre(s)

HM His (or Her) Majesty

HMA Headmasters' Association

HMAS His (or Her) Majesty's Australian Ship

HMC His (or Her) Majesty's Customs; Headmasters' Conference

HMCS His (or Her) Majesty's Canadian Ship

HMG His (or Her) Majesty's Government

HMI His (or Her) Majesty's Inspector, Inspectorate

HML His (or Her) Majesty's Lieutenant

HMP *hoc monumentum posuit* erected this monument

HMS His (or Her) Majesty's Ship or Service

HMSO His (or Her) Majesty's Stationery Office

HMV His Master's Voice (gramophone company)

HNC Higher National Certificate

HND Higher National Diploma

Ho holmium

ho house

Hon Honourable; Honorary

Hons Honours

Hon Sec Honorary Secretary

hor horizon; horology

hort, hortic horticulture; horticultural

HP hire-purchase; High Priest; half-pay; (or **hp**) horse-power

HQ headquarters

HR House of Representatives; Home Rule

Hr Herr

hr hour

HRE Holy Roman Emperor or Empire

HRH His (or Her) Royal Highness

HRIP *hic requiescit in pace* here rests in peace

HS *hic situs* here is laid

HSE Health and Safety Executive; *hic sepultus* (or *situs*) *est* here is buried (or laid)

HSH His (or Her) Serene Highness

HSS *Historiae Societatis Socius* Fellow of the Historical Society

HT high tension

HTV Harlech Television

Hunts Huntingdonshire

HWM high water mark

Hz Hertz (cycles per second)

I iodine; Island, Isle; Italy (IVR)

I electric current

IA Institute of Actuaries

Ia Iowa

IAAF International Amateur Athletic Federation

IAAS Incorporated Association of Architects and Surveyors

IAEA International Atomic Energy Agency

IAM Institute of Advanced Motorists

IAS Indian Administrative Service

IATA International Air Transport Association

IB Institute of Bankers

IBA Independent Broadcasting Authority

ib, ibid *ibidem* in the same place

IBM International Business Machines (computer manufacturers)

IBRD International Bank for Reconstruction and Development (World Bank)

IC integrated circuit

i/c in charge

ICA Institute of Contemporary Arts; Institute of Chartered Accountants

ICAO International Civil Aviation Organisation

ICBM intercontinental ballistic missile

ICE Institution of Civil Engineers; internal combustion engine

ICFC Industrial and Commercial Finance Corporation

IChemE Institution of Chemical Engineers

ICI Imperial Chemical Industries

ICJ International Court of Justice

ICL International Computers Limited

ICMA Institute of Cost and Management Accountants

ICRC International Committee of the Red Cross

ICS Indian Civil Service (in Republic of India, **IAS**)

ID Intelligence Department; identification; infectious diseases

Id Idaho

id *idem* the same

IDA International Development Association

IDD International direct dialling

IDN *in Dei nomine* in the name of God

IDV International Distillers and Vintners

i.e., ie *id est* that is

IEC International Electrotechnical Commission

IEE Institution of Electrical Engineers

IF intermediate frequency; insufficient funds

IFC International Finance Corporation

IHC, IHS for the Greek capitals **IHC** (**H**, capital eta (= **E**) and **C**, a form of sigma (= **S**)), first two and last letters of *Iesous* Jesus, often misread as *Jesus Hominum Salvator* Jesus Saviour of Men

ihp indicated horse-power

IL Institute of Linguists; Israel (IVR)

ILC irreversible letter of credit

ILEA Inner London Education Authority

Ill Illinois

ill illustration; illustrated

ILN Illustrated London News

ILO International Labour Organisation or (its secretariat) International Labour Office

ILP Independent Labour Party

IMechE Institution of Mechanical Engineers

IMF International Monetary Fund

imit imitative

IMM Institution of Mining and Metallurgy

Imp Imperial; *Imperator* Emperor

imp (or **imperf**) imperfect; (or **imper**) imperative; *imprimatur* let it be printed; (or **impers**) impersonal

IMunE Institution of Municipal Engineers

In indium

in inch(es)

inc including; incorporated

incl including; included

IND same as **IDN**; India (IVR)

Ind Indiana; Independent

ind, indic indicative

indecl indeclinable

indef indefinite

indiv individual

Ind Ter Indian Territory

inf *infra* below; infantry; infinitive

infra dig *infra dignitatem* beneath one's dignity

init *initio* in the beginning

in lim *in limine* on the threshold, at the outset

in loc *in loco* in its place

in loc cit *in loco citato* in the place cited

in pr *in principio* in the beginning

INRI *Jesus Nazarenus Rex Judaeorum* Jesus of Nazareth King of the Jews

Inst Institute

inst instant—the present month; institute

InstP Institute of Physics

instn institution

int interest; interior; interpreter; international; integral

Intelsat International Telecommunications Satellite Consortium
interj interjection
Interpol International Criminal Police Commission
interrog interrogation; interrogative(ly)
in trans *in transitu* in transit
intrans intransitive
intro, introd introduction
inv *invenit* designed it; invented; invoice
IOB Institute of Building
IOC International Olympic Committee
IoJ Institute of Journalists
IOM Isle of Man
IOU I owe you
IOW Isle of Wight
IPA Institute of Practitioners in Advertising; International Publishers' Association; International Phonetic Alphabet
IPC International Publishing Corporation
IPCS Institution of Professional Civil Servants
IQ Intelligence Quotient
iq *idem quod* the same as
IQPS Institute of Qualified Private Secretaries
IQS Institute of Quantity Surveyors
IR Iran (IVR)
Ir iridium; Irish
IRC International Red Cross
IRA Irish Republican Army
IRB Irish Republican Brotherhood
IRBM intermediate range ballistic missile
Irel. Ireland
IRL Ireland (IVR)
IRQ Iraq (IVR)
ISBN International Standard Book Number
ISCh Incorporated Society of Chiropodists
ISD international subscriber dialling
ISF Institute of Forwarding and Shipping Agents
Is(l) island
ISO Imperial Service Order; International Organisation for Standardisation
ISS International Social Service
ISSN International Standard Serial Number

ISTC Iron and Steel Trades Confederation
IT Information Technology
It Italian; Italian vermouth
ITA Independent Television Authority (now **IBA**)
ita initial teaching alphabet
ital italic; Italian
ITN Independent Television News
ITO International Trade Organisation
ITT International Telephone and Telegraph Corporation
ITU International Telecommunications Union
ITV Independent Television
IU international unit
IU(C)D intra-uterine (contraceptive) device
IUPAC International Union of Pure and Applied Chemistry
IUPAP International Union of Pure and Applied Physics
IVR International Vehicle Registration
IW Isle of Wight

J joule; Japan (IVR)
J Judge; Justice
JAL Japan Air Lines
Jan January
Jas James
JC *Juris Consultus* Jurisconsult; Jesus Christ; Justice Clerk
JCD *Juris Civilis Doctor* Doctor of Civil Law
JCR junior common room
JFK John Fitzgerald Kennedy
JHS same as **IHC**
JMB Joint Matriculation Board
Josh Joshua
JP Justice of the Peace
Jr, Jun, Junr Junior
JUD *Juris Utriusque Doctor* Doctor both of Canon and of Civil Law
Jul July
Jun June; Junior
junc junction
jurisp jurisprudence

K Kelvin (thermometer scale); kelvin; *kalium* potassium; kilobyte
k kilo-
Kan Kansas

KB   Knight of the Bath; Knight Bachelor; King's Bench
KBE   Knight Commander of the Order of the British Empire
KC   King's Counsel; King's College; Kennel Club
KCB   Knight Commander of the Bath
KCMG   Knight Commander of the Order of St Michael and St George
KCVO   Knight Commander of the (Royal) Victorian Order
Ken   Kentucky
KG   Knight of the Order of the Garter
kg   kilogram(me)(s)
KGB   *Komitet Gosudarstvennoi Bezopasnosti* (Russ) Committee of State Security
KGCB   Knight of the Grand Cross of the Bath
kilo   kilogram(me); kilometre
kk   *kaiserlich-königlich* (Ger) Imperial-Royal
KKK   Ku Klux Klan
KL   Kuala Lumpur
KLH   Knight of the Legion of Honour
KLM   *Koninklijke Luchtvaart Maatschappij* (Du) Royal Dutch Airlines
KM   Knight of Malta
km   kilometre(s)
kn   knot (nautical, etc, measure)
KO, ko   knock out; kick off
K of L   Knight of Labour
kpg, kph   kilometres per gallon, hour
Kr   krypton
kr   kreutzer; krone
Ks   Kansas
KT   Knight of the Thistle
Kt   Knight Bachelor
kV   kilovolt
kW   kilowatt
kWh   kilowatt-hour
Ky   Kentucky

L   Lake; Latin; Liberal; lumen; learner (driver); *libra* pound; Luxembourg (IVR)
L   symbol for inductance; luminance
l   litre (the abbreviation, though the accepted one, is undesirable as liable to be misread); latitude; league; left; long; (or **lb**) *libra* pound
l   length
LA   Law Agent; Literate in Arts; Los Angeles; Library Association

La   lanthanum; Louisiana
Lab   Labour
lab   laboratory
LAC   Licentiate of the Apothecaries' Company
LAMDA   London Academy of Music and Dramatic Art
Lancs   Lancashire
lang   language
LAR   Libya (IVR)
LASER   *l*ight *a*mplification by *s*timulated *e*mission of *r*adiation
Lat   Latin
lat   latitude
lb   *libra* pound (in weight)
lb, lbw   leg before wicket
LBC   London Broadcasting Company
lc   lower-case (in printing); *loco citato* in the place cited; left centre; letter of credit
LCCI   London Chamber of Commerce and Industry
LCD   liquid crystal display
LCh, LChir   *Licentiatus Chirurgiae* Licentiate in Surgery
LCJ   Lord Chief-Justice
LCM, lcm   least common multiple
Ld   Lord
Ldp, Lp   Lordship
LDS   Licentiate in Dental Surgery
LDV   Local Defence Volunteers (later Home Guard)
LEA   Local Education Authority
LEAP   Life Education for the Autistic Person
lect   lecture
LED   light emitting diode
leg   legal; legate; legislature
Leics   Leicestershire
LEPRA   Leprosy Relief Assocation
lex   lexicon
LF   low frequency
LGU   Ladies Golf Union
lh   left hand
LHD   *Litterarum Humaniorum Doctor* Doctor of Humane Letters
LI   Long Island; Light Infantry
Li   lithium
Lib   Liberal
lib   *liber* book
lib cat   library catalogue
Lieut   Lieutenant
LIFO   last in, first out
LILO   last in, last out
Lincs   Lincolnshire

liq liquid
lit literal(ly); literature
lith, litho, lithog lithograph; lithography
Lit Hum *litterae humaniores* humane letters, the humanities
Lit(t)D *Litterarum Doctor* Doctor of Letters
LJ Lord Justice
LLB *Legum Baccalaureus* Bachelor of Laws
LLCM Licentiate of the London College of Music
LLD *Legum Doctor* Doctor of Laws
LLM *Legum Magister* Master of Laws
LM long metre
lm lumen
ln natural logarithm
LNG liquefied natural gas
LOB Location of Offices Bureau
loc cit *loco citato* at the place quoted
L of C line of communication
log logarithm
lon, long longitude
Lond London
Lonrho *London Rhodesian* (industrial conglomerate)
loq *loquitur* speaks
LP long-playing (record); Lord Provost; low pressure; Labour Party
LPG liquefied petroleum gas
LPO London Philharmonic Orchestra
Lr lawrencium; lira (Italian currency)
LRAM Licentiate of the Royal Academy of Music
LRCP Licentiate of the Royal College of Physicians (**Edin,** of Edinburgh; **Lond,** of London; **Irel,** of Ireland)
LRCS Licentiate of the Royal College of Surgeons (**Ed,** of Edinburgh; **Eng,** of England; **Irel,** of Ireland)
LSA Licentiate of the Society of Apothecaries
LSD lysergic acid diethylamide (a hallucinatory drug)
L.S.D. *librae, solidi, denarii* pounds, shillings, pence
LSE London School of Economics
LSO London Symphony Orchestra
LT low tension
Lt Lieutenant
LTA Lawn Tennis Association
Lt-Col Lieutenant-Colonel
Ltd limited liability

Lt-Gen Lieutenant-General
LTh Licentiate in Theology
Lu lutetium
LV luncheon voucher
LVO Lieutenant of the Royal Victorian Order
LWM low water mark
LWT London Weekend Television

M Member . . . see note (2); mega-
M, m *mille* a thousand
M *Monsieur* (Fr) Mr (pl **MM**)
m milli-; metre; mile; married; masculine; *meridiem* noon
m mass
3M Minnesota Mining and Manufacturing Company
MA *Magister Artium* Master of Arts
mach machinery
MAFF Ministry of Agriculture, Fisheries and Food
mag magazine; magnetic
Maj Major
MAL Malaysia (IVR)
Man, Manit Manitoba
Man Dir Managing Director
M & B ® a trademark of May & Baker Ltd (used eg. for sulphonamides prepared by this firm and, esp. formerly, others)
M & S Marks & Spencer
Mar March
marg margin; marginal; margarine
Marq Marquis
mas, masc masculine
MASER *m*icrowave *a*mplification by *s*timulated *e*mission of *r*adiation
Mass Massachusetts
math, maths mathematics
Matt Matthew
max maximum
mb millibar
MB *Medicinae Baccalaureus* Bachelor of Medicine; mark of the Beast
MBE Member of the Order of the British Empire
MC Member of Congress; Master of Ceremonies; Military Cross
MCC Marylebone Cricket Club; Member of the County Council
MCh *Magister Chirurgiae* Master of Surgery

MCP male chauvinist pig
Mc/s megacycles per second (megahertz)
MD *Medicinae Doctor* Doctor of Medicine; mentally deficient; Managing Director
Md mendelevium; Maryland
Mdlle, Mlle *Mademoiselle* (Fr) Miss
Mdm Madam
MDS Master of Dental Surgery
ME Methodist Episcopal; Mining or Mechanical Engineer, Most Excellent; Middle English
Me Maine
mech mechanic; mechanical
MEd Master of Education
med medical; medicine; mediaeval; *medius, -a, -um* middle
Mem Member
mem memorandum; *memento* remember
memo memorandum
MEP Member of the European Parliament
Messrs *Messieurs* (Fr) Sirs, Gentlemen; used as pl of **Mr**
met, meteor meteorology
metal, metall metallurgy
meth(s) methylated spirits
MeV mega-electron-volt(s)
MEX Mexico (IVR)
Mex Mexico; Mexican
MEZ *Mitteleuropäische Zeit* (Ger) Central European Time
mf mezzo-forte
mfd manufactured
MFH Master of Foxhounds
mfrs manufacturers
MG machine-gun; Morris Garage
Mg magnesium
mg milligram(me)(s)
Mgr Monseigneur, Monsignor
MHG Middle High German
MHR Member of the House of Representatives
MHz megahertz
MI Military Intelligence; **MI5** Security Services, **MI6** Secret Intelligence Service (initials based on wartime Military Intelligence departments)
Mi Mississippi
Mich Michigan
MICR magnetic ink character recognition
MIDAS Missile Defence Alarm System

Middx Middlesex
mil, milit. military
Min Ministry
min mineralogy; minimum; minute
Minn Minnesota
MIRV Multiple Independently Targeted Re-entry Vehicle (type of missile)
misc miscellaneous; miscellany
Miss Mississippi
MIT Massachusetts Institute of Technology
MJ megajoule(s)
MJI Member of the Institute of Journalists
MK (on cars) mark
Mkk markka (Finnish currency)
MKS metre-kilogram-second unit, or system
MKSA metre-kilogram-second-ampere unit, or system
ml millilitre(s)
MLA Member of Legislative Assembly; Modern Language Association
MLC Member of Legislative Council; Meat and Livestock Commission
MLitt *Magister Litterarum* Master of Letters or Literature
Mlle *Mademoiselle* (Fr) Miss;—pl **Mlles** *Mesdemoiselles.*
MLR minimum lending rate
MM (Their) Majesties;·Martyrs; Military Medal
MM. *Messieurs* (Fr) Gentlemen, Sirs
mm millimetre(s)
Mme *Madame* (Fr) Mrs;—pl **Mmes** *Mesdames*
MN Merchant Navy
Mn manganese
MO Medical Officer
Mo molybdenum; Missouri
mo month
MOD Ministry of Defence
mod modern; moderate
mod con modern convenience
MOH Medical Officer of Health
mol mole (unit)
mol wt molecular weight
Mon Monmouthshire; Monday
Monsig Monsignor
Mont Montana; Montgomeryshire
mos months
MOS(T) metal oxide silicon (transistors)
MOT Ministry of Transport

MP Member of Parliament; Military Police; Metropolitan Police; Municipal Police (US); mounted police

mp mezzo-piano; melting-point

MPDS Market Price Display Service

mpg, mph miles per gallon, hour

MPharm Master of Pharmacy

MPS Member of the Pharmaceutical Society; Member of the Philological Society

MR Master of the Rolls

Mr Mister; Master

MRA Moral Rearmament

MRC Medical Research Council

MRCA multirole combat aircraft

MRG Minority Rights Group

Mrs Mistress (fem of **Mr,** Mister)·

MS manuscript; Master of Surgery; *Memoriae Sacrum* Sacred to the Memory; milestone; multiple sclerosis

Ms see Dictionary

ms millisecond(s); (or **M/S**) months (after)

MSC Manpower Services Commission

MSc Master of Science

MSF medium standard frequency

msl mean sea-level

MSS manuscripts

MST mountain standard time

MSW Medical Social Worker

MT Mechanical Transport; mean time

Mt, mt mount

MTh Master of Theology

mth month

Mts, mts mountains

mus music; museum

MusB(ac) Bachelor of Music

MusD(oc) Doctor of Music

MusM Master of Music

mv merchant vessel; motor vessel; muzzle velocity

MVO Member of the Royal Victorian Order

MW medium wave

Mx Middlesex

myth mythology; mythological

N nitrogen; newton; North, Northern; Norway (IVR)

n name; noun; *natus* born; neuter; noon; nano-

Na *natrium* sodium

NAAFI Navy, Army, and Air-Force Institute(s) (providing canteens for the armed forces)

NABM National Association of British Manufacturers

NACRO National Association for the Care and Resettlement of Offenders

NALGO National and Local Government Officers' Association

N and Q Notes and Queries

NASA National Aeronautics and Space Administration (USA)

Nat National

nat *natus* born

nat hist natural history

NATO North Atlantic Treaty Organisation

nat ord natural order

Nat Phil natural philosophy

Nat Sci Natural Science(s)

NATSOPA National Society of Operative Printers, Graphical and Media Personnel

NATTKE National Association of Television, Theatrical, and Kinematographic Employees

Nat West NatWest, National Westminster Bank

naut nautical

nav naval; navigation

NAVAR combined navigation and radar system

Nazi *Nazionale Sozialisten* (Ger) German National Socialist Party

NB New Brunswick; North Britain; North British; North bag (in postal sorting); (or **nb**) *nota bene* note well, or take notice

Nb niobium

NBC National Broadcasting Company (USA)

NBL National Book League

NBS National Bureau of Standards (USA)

NC New Church; numerical control; North Carolina

NCB National Coal Board (now British Coal)

NCCL National Council for Civil Liberties

NCO non-commissioned officer

NCR National Cash Register Company; no carbon required

ncv no commercial value

Nd neodymium
ND, NDak North Dakota
nd no date, not dated
NDPS National Data Processing Service
NE north-east; New England
Ne neon
NEB New English Bible; National Enterprise Board
Neb, Nebr Nebraska
NEC National Executive Committee; National Exhibition Centre
NED New English Dictionary (now **OED**)
NEDC National Economic Development Council (Neddy)
NEDO National Economic Development Office
neg negative
NEI *non est inventus* has not been found
nem con *nemine contradicente* no one contradicting
nem diss *nemine dissentiente* no one dissenting
NERC Natural Environment Research Council
Neth Netherlands
neut neuter
Nev Nevada
New M New Mexico
N/F no funds
NF Norman French; Northern French; National Front; Newfoundland (also **Nfd**)
NFER National Foundation for Educational Research
NFS National Fire Service
NFT National Film Theatre
NFU National Farmers' Union
NFWI National Federation of Women's Institutes
NGA National Graphical Association
NH New Hampshire
NHBRC National House-Builders' Registration Council (or Certificate)
NHI National Health Insurance
NHS National Health Service
NI Northern Ireland; national insurance
Ni nickel
NIRC National Industrial Relations Court
NJ New Jersey
NKVD *Narodny Komitet Vnutrennikh Del* (Russ) People's Committee of Internal Affairs

NL Netherlands (IVR)
NLRB National Labor Relations Board (USA)
NM, N Mex New Mexico
n mile international nautical mile
NNE north-north-east
NNW north-north-west
NO New Orleans; natural order
no (or **No**) *numero* (in) number; not out
nom, nomin nominative
non-coll non-collegiate
non-com non-commissioned
Noncon Nonconformist
non obst *non obstante* notwithstanding
non pros *non prosequitur* does not prosecute
non seq *non sequitur* it does not follow
non-U not upper class
NOP National Opinion Poll
nop not otherwise provided
Northants Northamptonshire
Northd Northumberland
Nos, nos numbers
Notts Nottinghamshire
Nov November
NP Notary Public; New Providence; (or **np**) new paragraph
np no place (of publication)
NPFA National Playing Fields Association
NPG National Portrait Gallery
NPL National Physical Laboratory
npl noun plural
nr near
NRA National Rifle Association
NRDC National Research Development Corporation
NS New Style; Nova Scotia
ns nanosecond(s); not specified; nouns
NSB National Savings Bank
n sing noun singular
NSPCC National Society for Prevention of Cruelty to Children
NSRA National Small-Bore Rifle Association
NSW New South Wales
NT New Testament; Northern Territory; National Trust
NTDA National Trade Development Association
ntp normal temperature and pressure
NTS National Trust for Scotland
NU name unknown

NUGMW   National Union of General and Municipal Workers
NUI   National University of Ireland
NUJ   National Union of Journalists
NUM   National Union of Mineworkers
NUPE   National Union of Public Employees
NUR   National Union of Railwaymen
NUS   National Union of Students; National Union of Seamen
NUT   National Union of Teachers
NV   New Version
NV(A)LA   National Viewers' and Listeners' Association
nvd   no value declared
NW   north-west
NWT   North-west Territory (Canada)
NY   New York (city or state)
NYC   New York City
NYO   National Youth Orchestra
NZ   New Zealand (also IVR)

O   oxygen; Ohio
o/a   on account of
O&C   Oxford and Cambridge (Schools Examination Board)
O & M   organisation and method
OAP   Old Age Pension or Pensioner
OAPEC   Organisation of Arab Petroleum-Exporting Countries
OAS   on active service; Organisation of American States
OAU   Organisation of African Unity
ob   *obiit* died
obdt   obedient
OBE   Officer of the Order of the British Empire
obj   object; objective
obl   oblique; oblong
obs   obsolete; observation
o/c   overcharge
OC   Officer Commanding; Officer of the Order of Canada
OCF   Officiating Chaplain to the Forces
OCR   optical character recognition or reader
Oct   October
oct   octavo
OCTU   Officer Cadet Training Unit
OD   Ordnance Datum or Data
O/D   overdrawn

OE   Old English
OECD   Organisation for Economic Co-operation and Development
OED   Oxford English Dictionary
OF   Old French; Oddfellow
off.   official; officinal
OFT   Office of Fair Trading
OHMS   On His (or Her) Majesty's Service
OK   see Dictionary
Okla   Oklahoma
OM   Order of Merit; Old Measurement
OMR   optical mark recognition
ono   or near(est) offer
Ont   Ontario
Op   Opera; Opus
op   out of print; opposite; operation
op cit   *opere citato* in the work cited
OPEC   Organisation of Petroleum-Exporting Countries
opp   opposed; opposite
Ops   Operations; Operations Officer; Operations room
OR   other ranks; operations research
Or, Ore, Oreg   Oregon
ord   ordained; order; ordinary; ordnance
orig   origin; original(ly)
OS   Old Style; Ordinary Seaman; outsize; Ordnance Survey
O/S   outstanding
osp   *obiit sine prole* died without issue
OT   Old Testament; occupational therapy
OTC   Officers' Training Corps
OU   Open University
OUP   Oxford University Press
Oxbridge   *Ox*ford and Cam*bridge*.
Oxf   Oxford
OXFAM   *Ox*ford Committee for *Fam*ine Relief
Oxon   *Oxonia* Oxford; *Oxoniensis* of Oxford; Oxfordshire
oz   ounce(s) (15th cent. It *ōz*, abbreviation of *onza*)

P   phosphorus; parking; President; Prince; pedal; Portugal (IVR)
P   power
p   new penny; new pence; piano; pico-; page; participle
P&P   postage and packing
PA   Press Association; Publishers

Association; personal assistant; Public
Address (system)

Pa protactinium; pascal

Pa, Penn Pennsylvania

pa past

p.a. (or **pa**) per annum; participial
adjective

PABX private automatic branch
exchange

Pal Palestine

pam pamphlet

Pan Panama

Pan Am Pan-American (World Airways
Incorporated)

P and O Peninsular and Oriental
(Steamship Navigation Co)

pa p past participle

par paragraph; parallel; parish

pass passive

pa t past tense

Pat Off Patent Office

PAYE Pay As You Earn (Income
Tax)

PB Pharmacopoeia Britannica;
Plymouth Brethren

Pb *plumbum* lead

PBX private branch exchange

PC Police Constable; Privy Councillor;
Patres Conscripti Conscript Fathers

pc postcard; per cent

pce piece

PCS Principal Clerk of Session

Pd palladium

pd paid

PDI pre-delivery inspection

PDR People's Democratic Republic

PDSA People's Dispensary for Sick
Animals

PE Protestant Episcopal; physical
education

p/e price-earnings ratio

PEC photoelectric cell

ped pedal

PEI Prince Edward Island

PEN Poets, Playwrights, Editors,
Essayists, and Novelists

Pen Peninsula

Penn, Pa Pennsylvania

PEP Political and Economic Planning;
personal equity plan

per period; person

per an per annum

per cent see Dictionary

perf perfect

per pro *per procurationem* by the agency
(of)

Pers Persian

pers person; personal

Pes peseta (Spanish currency)

PF Procurator Fiscal; Patriotic Front

Pf pfennig (German currency)

pf piano-forte

PG paying guest

Pg Portugal; Portuguese

PGA Professional Golfers' Association

phar, pharm pharmaceutical;
pharmacopoeia; pharmacy

PhB *Philosophiae Baccalaureus* Bachelor of
Philosophy

PhD *Philosophiae Doctor* Doctor of
Philosophy

Phil Philadelphia; philology;
philological; philosophy; philosophical

phon, phonet phonetics

phonog phonography

phot photography

phr phrase

phys physiology; physics; physician

PIA Pakistan International Airlines

PIB Prices and Incomes Board

pinx *pinxit* painted it

PL Poet Laureate; Public Library

pl plural

PLA Port of London Authority

PLC, plc Public Limited Company

PLO Palestine Liberation Organisation

PLP Parliamentary Labour Party

PLR public lending right

plu, plur plural

plup pluperfect

PM Past Master; (or **pm**) *post meridiem*
after noon; Postmaster; (or **pm**) *post
mortem* after death; Prime Minister;
Provost-Marshal

Pm promethium

pm premium

PMG Postmaster-General;
Paymaster-General

PMO Principal Medical Officer

Pmr Paymaster

PMRAFNS Princess Mary's Royal Air
Force Nursing Service

pn promissory note

PNdB perceived noise decibel

PO Post Office; Petty Officer; Pilot
Officer

Po polonium

po postal order; pole

pod   pay on delivery
Pol Econ   Political Economy
pop   population; popular
POP   Post Office preferred
pos, posit   positive
POUNC   Post Office Users' National Council
POW   prisoner of war
PP   parish priest; present pupil; past President
pp   pages; *per procurationem* by proxy (also *per pro* for and on behalf of); pianissimo; past participle
ppc   picture post-card
PPE   Philosophy, Politics and Economics
PPI   Plan Position Indicator; printed postage impression
PPS   *post postscriptum* a later additional postscript; Parliamentary Private Secretary
PQ   Province of Quebec
PR   prize ring; Puerto Rico; proportional representation; *Populus Romanus* the Roman people; public relations
Pr   Prince; priest; Provençal
pr   pair; per; present; price
PRA   pre-recorded address; President of the Royal Academy
Preb   Prebend; Prebendary
pref   preface
prep   preparation; preparatory; preposition
Pres   President
pres p   present participle
pret   preterite
Prin   Principal
PRN   *pro re nata* for special occasion arising
PRO   Public Relations Officer; Public Record Office
pro   professional; prostitute; probationary
prob   probably
Prof   Professor
pron   pronoun
PROP   Preservation of the Rights of Prisoners
prop   proper(ly); proposition; property
Prot   Protestant
pro tem   *pro tempore* for the time being
Prov   Proverbs; Provincial; Provost

RAC   Royal Automobile Club; Royal Armoured Corps; Royal Agricultural College
Rad   Radical
rad   radian; *radix* root
RADA   Royal Academy of Dramatic Art
RADC   Royal Army Dental Corps
RAE   Royal Aircraft Establishment
RAEC   Royal Army Educational Corps
RAeS   Royal Aeronautical Society
RAF   Royal Air Force
RAM   Royal Academy of Music; random access memory
ram   relative atomic mass
RAMC   Royal Army Medical Corps
RAN   Royal Australian Navy
R and A   Royal and Ancient (Golf Club) St Andrews
R and B   rhythm and blues (type of popular music)
R and D   research and development
RAOC   Royal Army Ordnance Corps
RAPC   Royal Army Pay Corps
RAS   Royal Astronomical Society; Royal Asiatic Society
RAVC   Royal Army Veterinary Corps
RBA   Royal Society of British Artists
RBS   Royal Society of British Sculptors
RC   Roman Catholic; Red Cross; Royal College of Art
RCA   Royal Canadian Academy; Radio Corporation of America
RCAF   Royal Canadian Air Force
RCM   Royal College of Music; Regimental Court-Martial
RCMP   Royal Canadian Mounted Police
RCN   Royal Canadian Navy
RCOG   Royal College of Obstetricians and Gynaecologists
RCP   Royal College of Physicians
RCS   Royal College of Surgeons; Royal Corps of Signals; Royal College of Science
RCT   Royal Corps of Transport
RCVS   Royal College of Veterinary Surgeons
RD   Rural Dean; Naval Reserve Decoration; (or **R/D**) refer to drawer
Rd   Road; rand (S African currency)
RDC   Rural District Council

RDI Designer for Industry of the Royal Society of Arts

RDS Royal Dublin Society

RE Royal Engineers; Royal Society of Etchers and Engravers; Royal Exchange

re with reference/regard to

Réau Réaumur's thermometric scale

rec *recipe* take; record; receipt

recd received

REconS Royal Economic Society

ref referee; reference

Ref Ch Reformed Church

reg, regd registered

Reg Prof Regius Professor

regt regiment

rel relating; relation; relative

rel d relative density

REME Royal Electrical and Mechanical Engineers

rep representative; republic; report; reporter

rept receipt; report

retd retired; returned

Rev revise(d); revision; (or **Revd**) Reverend

rev revolution

Rev Ver Revised Version

RF *République française* (Fr) French Republic; radio frequency

RFC Rugby Football Club

RFU Rugby Football Union

RGG Royal Grenadier Guards

RGN Registered General Nurse

RGS Royal Geographical Society

Rgt Regiment

RH Royal Highness

rh right hand

RHA Royal Horse Artillery; Royal Hibernian Academy; Road Haulage Association; Regional Health Authority

rhet rhetoric; rhetorical

RHF Royal Highland Fusiliers

RHG Royal Horse Guards

RHistS Royal Historical Society

RHM Rank Hovis McDougall

RHS Royal Humane Society; Royal Horticultural Society; Royal Historical Society; Royal Highland Show

RI Royal Institute of Painters in Water Colours; Rhode Island; religious instruction; Indonesia (IVR)

RIA Royal Irish Academy

RIAM Royal Irish Academy of Music

RIBA Royal Institute of British Architects

RIC Royal Irish Constabulary; Royal Institute of Chemistry

RICS Royal Institution of Chartered Surveyors

RIGB Royal Institution of Great Britain

RIP *requiescat in pace* may he (or she) rest in peace

RIPHH Royal Institute of Public Health and Hygiene

RJET remote job entry terminal

RL Lebanon (IVR); Rugby League

RLO returned letter office

RLS Robert Louis Stevenson

Rly, rly railway

RM Royal Mail; Royal Marines

RMA Royal Military Academy, Sandhurst; Royal Marine Artillery

RMetS Royal Meteorological Society

RMO Resident Medical Officer

RMP (Corps of) Royal Military Police

RMS Royal Mail Steamer; Royal Microscopical Society

RN Royal Navy

Rn radon

RNAS Royal Naval Air Service(s)

RNIB Royal National Institute for the Blind

RNLI Royal National Lifeboat Institution

RNR Royal Naval Reserve

RNVR Royal Naval Volunteer Reserve

RNZAF Royal New Zealand Air Force

RNZN Royal New Zealand Navy

ro *recto* on the right-hand page

ROC Royal Observer Corps

ROI Royal Institute of Oil Painters

ROM read only memory

Rom Romans

rom roman (in printing)

Ro-Ro roll-on-roll-off

RoSPA see **RSPA**

RP Reformed Presbyterian; Regius Professor; Received Pronunciation; Royal Society of Portrait Painters

RPA radiation protection adviser

RPI retail price index

RPM retail price maintenance

rpm, rps revolutions per minute, second

RPO Royal Philharmonic Orchestra

RPS Royal Photographic Society

RR Right Reverend

RRE   Radar Research Establishment
RRP   recommended retail price
RS   Royal Society
RSA   Royal Society of Antiquaries; Royal Society of Arts; Royal Scottish Academy or Academician; Republic of South Africa
RSC   Royal Shakespeare Company
RSE   Royal Society of Edinburgh
RSFSR   Russian Soviet Federated Socialist Republic
RSG   Regional Seats of Government
RSL   Royal Society of Literature
RSM   Regimental Sergeant-Major; Royal Society of Medicine; Royal School of Music
RSO   railway sub-office; railway sorting office; rural sub-office; radiological safety officer; Resident Surgical Officer
RSPA, RoSPA   Royal Society for the Prevention of Accidents
RSPB   Royal Society for the Protection of Birds
RSPCA   Royal Society for the Prevention of Cruelty to Animals
RSS   (or **SRS**) *Regiae Societatis Socius* Fellow of the Royal Society; Royal Statistical Society
RSV   Revised Standard Version
RSVP   *répondez s'il vous plaît* (Fr) reply, if you please
RT   radiotelephone, -phony
RTE   *Radio Telefís Éireann* (Ir) Irish Television
Rt Hon   Right Honourable
RTO   Railway Transportation (or Traffic) Officer
RTPI   Royal Town Planning Institute
Rt Rev   Right Reverend
RTZ   Rio Tinto Zinc Corporation Limited
RU   Rugby Union
Ru   ruthenium
RUC   Royal Ulster Constabulary
R-unit   Röntgen unit—unit of measurement of X-ray radiation
RV   Revised Version
RWS   Royal Society of Painters in Water Colours
Ry, ry   railway
RYA   Royal Yachting Association
RYS   Royal Yacht Squadron
RZS   Royal Zoological Society (**E,** of Edinburgh)

S   sulphur; square; stokes; siemens; South; Sabbath; Saint; society; sun; Sweden (IVR)
s   second(s)
$ dollar
SA   South Africa; South America; South Australia; Salvation Army; sex-appeal; *Société anonyme* (Fr) limited liability company; Society of Arts; Society of Antiquaries (**Scot,** of Scotland)
sa   *secundum artem* according to art; *sine anno* without date
sae   stamped addressed envelope
Salop   Shropshire
SALT   Strategic Arms Limitation Talks
SAM   surface-to-air missile
SARAH   Search and Rescue and Homing
SAS   *Societatis Antiquariorum Socius* Fellow of the Society of Antiquaries; Scandinavian Airlines System; Special Air Service
Sask   Saskatchewan
Sat   Saturday
S.A.T.B.   soprano, alto, tenor, bass
SAYE   save as you earn
Sb   *stibium* antimony
SBN   Standard Book Number
SC   *senatus consultum* a decree of the Roman senate; Special Constable; Supreme Court; Staff College; Staff Corps; South Carolina
Sc   scandium
sc   *scilicet* namely; *sculpsit* (he) sculptured (this); (or **s. caps, sm. caps**) small capitals (in printing)
s/c   self-contained
ScB   *Scientiae Baccalaureus* Bachelor of Science
ScD   *Scientiae Doctor* Doctor of Science
SCE   Scottish Certificate of Education
SCF   Save the Children Fund
Sch   schilling (Austrian currency); school
sci fa   *scire facias* that you cause to know
sci-fi   science fiction
scil, sciz,   *scilicet* namely (cf **viz**)
SCL   Student of Civil Law
SCM   Student Christian Movement; State Certified Midwife
Scot   Scotland; Scottish
ScotBIC   Scottish Business in the Community
SCR   senior common room

Script Scripture

SCUBA self-contained underwater breathing apparatus

sculp, sculpt *sculpsit* (he) sculptured (this); sculpture; sculptor

SD, S Dak South Dakota

sd *sine die* without a day (fixed)

SDA Scottish Development Agency

SDC single data converter

SDLP Social and Democratic Labour Party

SDP social, domestic and pleasure; Social Democratic Party

SDR special drawing rights

SE south-east; Society of Engineers

Se selenium

SEAC South-East Asia Command

SEATO South-East Asia Treaty Organisation

Sec, Secy Secretary

sec secant; *secundum* in accordance with; second; section

sec leg *secundum legem* according to law

sec reg *secundum regulam* according to rule

sect section

SED Scottish Education Department

Sem seminary; Semitic

SEN State Enrolled Nurse

Sen Senator; senior

Sep, Sept September; Septuagint

seq *sequens* following (pl **seqq,** *sequentes* or *sequentia*)

SERC Science and Education Research Council

Serg, Sergt Sergeant

Sess Session

SF science fiction; Sinn Fein; signal frequency; Finland (IVR)

SFA Scottish Football Association; Sweet Fanny Adams (= nothing at all)

SFr Swiss franc

sfz sforzando

SG Solicitor-General

sg specific gravity

SGHWR steam-generating heavy water reactor

SGP Singapore (IVR)

SHAEF Supreme Headquarters of the Allied Expeditionary Force

SHAPE Supreme Headquarters Allied Powers Europe

shv *sub hoc verbo* or *sub hac voce* under this word

SI Système International (d'Unités)

Si silicon

sic so written

sig signature

sin sine

sing singular

SIPRI Stockholm International Peace Research Institute

SIS Secret Intelligence Service

SJ Society of Jesus

SL Solicitor at Law; Sergeant-at-Law; (or **S Lat**) South latitude

SLADE Society of Lithographic Artists, Designers, Engravers and Process Workers

sld sailed

slp *sine legitima prole* without lawful issue

SM Short Metre; Sergeant-Major

Sm samarium

Smith. Inst. Smithsonian Institution

SMLondSoc *Societatis Medicae Londiniensis Socius* Member of the London Medical Society

SMM *Sancta Mater Maria* Holy Mother Mary

SMMT Society of Motor Manufacturers and Traders

SMO Senior Medical Officer

SMP School Mathematics Project

smp *sine mascula prole* without male issue

Sn *stannum* tin

sn *secundum naturam* according to nature

SNCF *Société Nationale des Chemins de Fer français* (Fr) French national railways

SNO Scottish National Orchestra

SNP Scottish National Party

SO Staff Officer; Signal Officer; standing order; special order

so seller's option

Soc Society

SOGAT Society of Graphical and Allied Trades

Sol, Solr Solicitor

sol solution

Sol-Gen Solicitor-General

sop soprano

SOS see Dictionary

Sp Spanish

sp *sine prole* without issue; spelling; species (pl **spp.**)

SPCK Society for Promoting Christian Knowledge

SPG Special Patrol Group

sp gr   specific gravity (now relative density)

SPQR   *Senatus Populusque Romanus* the Senate and People of Rome

SPR   Society for Psychical Research

sps   *sine prole superstite* without surviving issue

spt   seaport

SPUC   Society for the Protection of the Unborn Child

sp vol   specific volume

sq   (or **Sq**) square; *sequens* following (in pl **sqq,** *sequentes* or *sequentia*)

sqn   squadron

SR   Southern Region

Sr   senior; Sir; Señor; strontium

sr   steradian

SRC   Science Research Council; Student Representative Council

SRCh   State Registered Chiropodist

SRI   *Sacrum Romanum Imperium* Holy Roman Empire

SRN   State Registered Nurse

SRS   (or **RSS**) *Societatis Regiae Socius* Fellow of the Royal Society

SRU   Scottish Rugby Union

SS   Saints; *Schutzstaffel* (Ger) Hitler's bodyguard

ss   steamship; screw steamer

SSAFA   Soldiers', Sailors' and Airmen's Families Association

SSC   Solicitor before the Supreme Court (Scotland); *Societas Sanctae Crucis* Society of the Holy Cross

SSD   *Sanctissimus Dominus* Most Holy Lord (the Pope)

SSE   south-south-east

SSM   surface-to-surface missile

SSN   Standard Serial Number

SSRC   Social Science Research Council

SST   supersonic transport

SSW   south-south-west

St   Saint; Strait; Street

st   stone (weight)

Staffs   Staffordshire

STD   subscriber trunk dialling

std   standard

Ste   *Sainte* (Fr) fem of Saint

ster, stereo   stereophonic; stereotype

ster, stg   sterling

stet   let it stand

STOL   short take-off and landing

STP   *Sanctae Theologiae Professor* Professor of Theology

stp   standard temperature and pressure

str   steamer

str   strong

STS   Scottish Text Society

STUC   Scottish Trades Union Congress

STV   Scottish Television; Single Transferable Vote

SU   strontium unit—unit of measurement of strontium radiation; Scripture Union; Soviet Union (also IVR)

sub   subject

subj   subject; subjunctive

subst   substitute; substantive

suf, suff   suffix

sup   superfine; superior; (or **superl**) superlative; supreme; *supra* above; supine; supplement

superl   superlative

supp, suppl   supplement

Supr   Supreme

Supt   Superintendent

Surg   surgeon; surgery

sv   *sub voce* under that heading; *sub verbo* under the word

SW   south-west; small women('s); short wave

SWALK   sealed with a loving kiss

SWAPO   South West Africa People's Organisation

SWG   standard wire gauge

syn   synonym

T   tritium

t   tonne (cf **l,** litre)

t   time

TA   Territorial Army

tal qual   *talis qualis* just as they come, average quality

tan   tangent

TASS   *Telegrafnoye Agentsvo Sovietskovo Soyuza* (Russ) telegraph agency of the Soviet Union; Technical, Administrative and Supervisory Section (of **AUEW**)

Tb   terbium

TB   tuberculosis

Tc   technetium

TCCB   Test and County Cricket Board

TCD   Trinity College Dublin; Twentieth Century Dictionary

TCL   Trinity College of Music, London

TCP   trichlorophenylmethyliodosalicyl (a proprietary germicide)

TD Territorial Decoration; *Teachta Dála* (Ir) member of the Dail
Te tellurium
tech. technical; technology
TEFL teaching English as a foreign language
tel telephone
tel, teleg telegram; telegraph
temp temporal; *tempore* in the time of; temperature; temporary
Ten, Tenn Tennessee
ten tenor
Ter, Terr Territory; terrace
term termination
TES Times Educational Supplement
TESL teaching English as a second language
Test Testament
Teut Teutonic
Tex Texas
Text Rec *textus receptus* the revised text
TF Territorial Force
tf till forbidden
TFR Territorial Force Reserve
TGWU Transport and General Workers' Union
Th thorium; Thursday
ThD Doctor of Theology
theat theatrical
theol theology; theologian
THES Times Higher Educational Supplement
THF Trust Houses Forte
ThL Theological Licentiate
Tho, Thos Thomas
TI Tube Investments
Ti titanium
tid *ter in die* thrice a day
TIF *Transports Internationaux par Chemin de Fer* (Fr) International Rail Transport
TIR *Transports Internationaux Routiers* (Fr) International Road Transport
TIROS Television and Infrared Observation Satellite
Tl thallium
TLS Times Literary Supplement
TM transcendental meditation
Tm thulium
TN trade name
TNT trinitrotoluene (explosive)
TO turn over; Telegraph-office; Transport Officer
Toc H Talbot House
TPI Town Planning Institute

tpr teleprinter
TR Turkey (IVR)
tr transpose; transactions; translator; trustee; transfer
trans transitive; translated; translation; transpose
TRH Their Royal Highnesses
trig trigonometry
Trin Trinity
TSB Trustee Savings Bank
TSO town sub-office
TT teetotal; Tourist Trophy; tuberculin tested
Tu, Tues, Tue Tuesday
TUC Trades Union Congress
TV television
TVA Tennessee Valley Authority
TVP texturised vegetable protein
TWA Trans-World Airlines
TWI Training within Industry
typ, typo typographer; typography

U uranium; Unionist; upper-class; Uruguay (IVR)
UAE United Arab Emirates
UAR United Arab Republic
UC, uc upper case (capital letters)
UCAR Union of Central African Republics
UCATT Union of Construction, Allied Trades and Technicians
UCCA Universities Central Council on Admissions
UCL University College London
UDA Ulster Defence Association
UDC Urban District Council; Universal Decimal Classification
UDI Unilateral Declaration of Independence
UDR Ulster Defence Regiment
UDT United Dominions Trust
UEFA Union of European Football Associations
UF United Free Church (of Scotland)
UFO unidentified flying object
UGC University Grants Committee
UHF ultra high frequency
UJD *Utriusque Juris Doctor* Doctor of both Laws (Canon and Civil)
UK United Kingdom
UKAEA United Kingdom Atomic Energy Authority
ULCC ultra large crude carriers

ult, ulto   *ultimo* in the last (month); ultimate(ly)

UMIST   University of Manchester Institute of Science and Technology

UN   United Nations

UNA   United Nations Association

UNCTAD, Unctad   United Nations Commission for Trade and Development

UNEP   United Nations Environment Programme

UNESCO   United Nations Educational, Scientific and Cultural Organisation

UNICEF   United Nations International Children's Emergency Fund—now United Nations Children's Fund

UNIDO   United Nations Industrial Development Organisation

Unit   Unitarian

Univ   University; Universalist

UNO   United Nations Organisation

UNRRA   United Nations Relief and Rehabilitation Administration

UP   United Presbyterian; United Press

UPU   Universal Postal Union

UPW   Union of Post Office Workers

Uru   Uruguay

US   United States; United Service(s); Under-secretary

us   *ut supra* as above

US(A)   United States (of America) (also IVR); United States Army

USAF   United States Air Force

USCL   United Society for Christian Literature

USDAW   Union of Shop, Distributive and Allied Workers

USIS   United States Information Service

USN   United States Navy

USPG   United Society for the Propagation of the Gospel

USS   United States Ship or Steamer

USSR   (also **CCCP** (Russ)) Union of Soviet Socialist Republics

usu   usually

USW   ultrasonic waves; ultrashort waves

usw   *und so weiter* (Ger) and so forth

UT   Universal Time

Ut   Utah

ut dict   *ut dictum* as said

ut sup   *ut supra* as above

UU   Ulster Unionist

uv   ultraviolet

UVF   Ulster Volunteer Force

UWIST   University of Wales Institute of Science and Technology

V   vanadium; volt

V   symbol for electric potential difference

v   velocity; *versus* against; *vide* see; verb; verse; volume

VA   Royal Order of Victoria and Albert; Vicar Apostolic; volt-ampere(s)

Va   Virginia

vac   vacuum; vacation

VAD   Voluntary Aid Detachment

val   value

V and A   Victoria and Albert Museum

var   variant; variety; variable

var lect   *varia lectio* variant reading

VAT   Value-added Tax

Vat   Vatican

vb   verb

VC   Victoria Cross; Vice-Chancellor; Vice-Consul

VCR   video cassette recorder

VD   Venereal Disease(s); Volunteer (Officers') Decoration

vd   various dates; vapour density

VDC   Volunteer Defence Corps

VDQS   *Vins délimités de qualité supérieure* (Fr) wines of superior quality from approved vineyards

VDU   visual display unit

VE   Victory in Europe (1945)

veg   vegetable(s)

Ven   Venerable

VERA   versatile reactor assembly; vision electronic recording apparatus

verb sap   *verbum sapienti,* or **verb sat,** *verbum sat(is)* a word to the wise is enough

Vet, Veter   Veterinary

Vet Surg   Veterinary Surgeon

VF   voice frequency; video frequency

VG   Vicar-General; (or **vg**) very good

vg   *verbi gratia* for example

VHF   very high frequency

vi   verb intransitive

via   by way of

Vic   Vicar; Vicarage

Vict   Victoria; Victoria University

vid   *vide* see

vil(l)   village

VIP   Very Important Person

VIR   *Victoria Imperatrix Regina* (see **VRI**)

Vis, Visc Viscount

viz *videlicet* namely (z = mediaeval Latin symbol of contraction)

VJ Victory over Japan (1945)

vl *varia lectio* variant reading (pl **vvll**)

VLCC very large crude carrier

VLF very low frequency

VN voucher number

vo *verso* on the left-hand page

voc vocative

vocab vocabulary

vol volunteer; volume

VP Vice-President

VR *Victoria Regina* Queen Victoria

VRD Volunteer Reserve Decoration

VRI *Victoria Regina et Imperatrix* Victoria, Queen and Empress

VRQ verbal reasoning quotient

VS Veterinary Surgeon; *volti subito* turn quickly

VSO Voluntary Service Overseas

VSOP very special old pale

Vt Vermont

v t verb transitive

V.TO(L) vertical take-off (and landing)

VTR video tape recorder

Vul, Vulg Vulgate

vul, vulg vulgar

vvll see **vl**

VW *Volkswagen* (Ger) people's car

vy various years

W *wolframium* tungsten; watt; West; Welsh; women('s)

w weak; with

WA West Africa; Western Australia

WAAC Women's Army Auxiliary Corps (now **WRAC**)

WAAF Women's Auxiliary Air Force (earlier and later **WRAF**)

Wash Washington

WASP White Anglo-Saxon Protestant

Wb weber

WBA West Bromwich Albion Football Club; World Boxing Association of America

WBC World Boxing Council

WC water-closet; Western Central; Wesleyan Chapel

WCC World Council of Churches

W/Cdr Wing-Commander

WCT World Championship Tennis

W/E week ending

WEA Workers' Educational Association

Wed Wednesday

wef with effect from

WEU Western European Union

wf wrong fount (in printing)

WFTU World Federation of Trade Unions

wg wire gauge

WHO World Health Organisation

WI West Indies; Women's Institute

Wilts Wiltshire

Wis Wisconsin

wk week

WLF Women's Liberal Federation

Wm William

WMO World Meteorological Organisation

WNP Welsh Nationalist Party

WNW west-north-west

WO War Office (1964 absorbed in Ministry of Defence); Warrant Officer; walk-over

Worcs Worcestershire

Wp, Wpfl Worshipful

WP Warsaw Pact; word processing

wp weather permitting; word processing

wpb wastepaper basket

wpm words per minute

WR Western Region

WRAC Women's Royal Army Corps

WRAF Women's Royal Air Force

WRI Women's Rural Institute

WRNS Women's Royal Naval Service

WRVS Women's Royal Voluntary Service (previously **WVS**)

WS Writer to the Signet

WSW west-south-west

wt weight

W Va West Virginia

WVS Women's Voluntary Service (now **WRVS**)

WWF World Wildlife Fund

Wy, Wyo Wyoming

X, Xt Christ. (X = Greek *Ch*)

x *ex* (Latin without), as in **x d,** ex dividend

Xe xenon

Xm, Xmas Christmas

Xn, Xtian Christian

Y   yttrium; yen (Japanese currency)
y   year; yard
Yb   ytterbium
yd   yard
ye   the (the **y** not being a **y** but representing the old letter thorn, þ)
Yeo   Yeomanry
YHA   Youth Hostels Association
YMCA   Young Men's Christian Association
Yn   yen (Japanese currency)
Yorks   Yorkshire
yr   your; younger; year

yt   that (*y* as in **ye** above)
YTV   Yorkshire Television
YU   Yugoslavia (IVR)
YWCA   Young Women's Christian Association

ZA   South Africa (IVR)
zB   *zum Beispiel* (Ger) for example
Zn   zinc
ZPG   zero population growth
Zr   zirconium
ZST   Zone Standard Time

Roman numerals

I	=	1	L	=	50
II	=	2	LI	=	51
III	=	3	LII, etc.	=	52, etc.
IV	=	4	LX	=	60
V	=	5	LXI	=	61
VI	=	6	LXII, etc.	=	62, etc.
VII	=	7	LXX	=	70
VIII	=	8	LXXI	=	71
IX	=	9	LXXII, etc.	=	72, etc.
X	=	10	LXXX	=	80
XI	=	11	LXXXI	=	81
XII	=	12	LXXXII, etc.	=	82, etc.
XIII	=	13	XC	=	90
XIV	=	14	XCI	=	91
XV	=	15	XCII, etc.	=	92, etc.
XVI	=	16			
XVII	=	17	C	=	100
XVIII	=	18	CC	=	200
XIX	=	19	CCC	=	300
XX	=	20	CD	=	400
XXI	=	21	D	=	500
XXII, etc.	=	22, etc.	DC	=	600
XXX	=	30	DCC	=	700
XXXI	=	31	DCCC	=	800
XXXII, etc.	=	32, etc.	CM	=	900
XL	=	40			
XLI	=	41	M	=	1000
XLII, etc.	=	42, etc.	MM	=	2000

Greek alphabet

A	α	alpha	=a	N	ν	nū	=n
B	β	bēta	=b	Ξ	ξ	xī	=x (ks)
Γ	γ	gamma	=g	O	o	omīcron	=o
Δ	δ	delta	=d	Π	π	pī	=p
E	ϵ	epsīlon	=e	P	ϱ	rhō	=r
Z	ζ	zēta	=z	Σ	$\varsigma\sigma$	sigma	=s
H	η	ēta	=ē	T	τ	tau	=t
Θ	$\theta \vartheta$	thēta	=th (th)	Υ	υ	ūpsīlon	=u (yōō, oŏ, ü)
I	ι	iōta	=i				(often transcribed y)
K	$\varkappa$	kappa	=k	Φ	ϕ	phī	=ph (f)
Λ	λ	lambda	=l	X	χ	chī	=kh (hh)
							(often transcribed ch, as in Latin)
M	μ	mū	=m	Ψ	ψ	psī	=ps
				Ω	ω	ōmega	=ō

The Greek alphabet, apart from its use as the official script in Greek-speaking areas, is of worldwide importance as a source of symbols used in all branches of science and mathematics. The equivalents in our alphabet given above are intended as a guide to transliteration and as an indication of the anglicised pronunciation of ancient Greek. We have not attempted to describe modern Greek pronunciation.

Mathematical symbols

+	plus		⊂	is a subset of
−	minus		∃	there exists
±	plus or minus		∀	for all values of
×	multiply by		*	denotes an operation
÷	divide by		⇔	is equivalent to; if and only if
=	is equal to		⇒	implies
≡	is identically equal to		{} Ø	empty set
≈ ≑	is approximately equal to		{x, y}	the set whose members are x and y
≠	is not equal to		E	universal set
>	is greater than		N	the set of natural numbers
≫	is much greater than		W	the set of whole numbers
≯	is not greater than		Z	the set of integers
<	is less than		Q	the set of rational numbers
≪	is much less than		R	the set of real numbers
≮	is not less than		C	the set of complex numbers
≥	is greater than or equal to		→	maps to
≤	is less than or equal to		∴	therefore
∩	intersection		∵	because
∪	union		∠	angle
∈	is member of set		∥	parallel
			⊥	perpendicular

Chambers Commerce Series

The up-to-date series for school and college students, embracing the full range of business and vocational subjects.

Business Studies
Mark Juby

A comprehensive introduction to all aspects of business activity. The book covers the GCSE National Criteria in Business Studies, plus key areas of GCSE Commerce and Understanding Industrial Society courses. *Business Studies* is also geared to BTEC, LCCI, O/Standard Grade, RSA and SCOTVEC Courses.

Bookkeeping and Accounting
Harold Randall and David Beckwith

A comprehensive introduction, showing how financial records are made, maintained and used in business. The book is of especial value to students on AAT, BTEC, GCSE, LCCI, PEI, RSA and SCOTVEC syllabuses.

Typing
June Rowley

An introduction to basic typing theory and practice, ideal for a wide variety of secretarial and vocational courses including BTEC, CPVE, GCSE, LCCI, PEI, RSA and SCOTVEC.

Word Processing
Barbara Shaw

Covers everything from text editing to repagination and mail merge – all the practical word processing skills. Ideal for BTEC, LCCI, PEI, RSA and SCOTVEC courses.

Business Calculations
David Browning

A step-by-step guide to mathematics in business practice, from simple arithmetic to elementary statistics. Geared to courses of many varieties – CPVE, BTEC, LCCI, RSA and SCOTVEC; GCSE and O/Standard Grade Mathematics, professional training.

Business Law
Janice Elliot Montague

A practical introduction to the law, how it works and influences business procedures. *Business Law* covers relevant components of a host of syllabuses – ATT, ALS, BTEC, ICA, ICAS, ICMA, ILE, IOB, IPS, LCCI, SCCA, SCOTVEC.

The Business of Government
J. Denis Derbyshire

A straightforward introduction to British government, how it works in practice and how it influences business procedures. Covers key elements of Politics and Public Administration syllabuses, including BTEC, GCSE, RSA, O/Standard Grade, Modern Studies, SCOTVEC; an ideal reference text for A Level and Higher Grade courses.

Keyboarding
Derek Stananought

A book of exercises and advice on the skills needed in the age of new technology and the electronic office. Includes training material in basic keyboarding, proofreading, speed development, practical application of typing techniques. Ideal for secretarial and vocational courses – BTEC, CPVE, LCCI, PEI, RSA, SCOTVEC.

Secretarial Duties
Penny Anson

A complete guide to all the practical aspects of a
professional secretary's work. Covers the syllabuses of
the important courses, including BTEC, CPVE, LCCI,
PEI, RSA, SCOTVEC.

Office Procedures
Ruth Martindale

A straightforward explanation of the work involved in
running a modern office. Well illustrated, up-to-date,
takes full account of the latest technology and procedures.
Covers the syllabus requirements of BTEC, LCCI,
Pitman, RSA, SCOTVEC.

Chambers Commercial Reference Series

Straightforward guides to all the essential terms used in
the business world. Ideal for students on a wide range
of introductory business and vocational courses.
Written in clear, simple English.

Bookkeeping and Accounting Terms
Anthony Nielsen

Business Terms
John Simpson

Office Practice Terms
Josephine Hewitt

Office Technology Terms
Elizabeth King

Computer Terms
Sandra Carter

Business Law Terms
Stephen Foster

Printing and Publishing Terms
Martin H. Manser

Chambers
Office
Oracle

The ideal office reference book for
managers and secretaries everywhere.
The *Oracle* gives expert and helpful
advice on all aspects of office work –
composing letters, conducting
meetings, organising conferences,
choosing equipment, planning travel;
postal services, telecommunications,
banking, advertising are covered;
there are glossaries of business,
computing, medical, legal and
financial terms *plus a full*
English dictionary.